Principles of Marketing

Principles of Marketing

Seventh Edition

PHILIP KOTLER
Northwestern University

GARY ARMSTRONG
University of North Carolina

 Prentice Hall, Englewood Cliffs, New Jersey 07632

Library of Congress Cataloging-in-Publication Data

Kotler, Philip.
  Principles of marketing / Philip Kotler, Gary Armstrong. — 7th
ed.
    p. cm.
  Includes bibliographical references and index.
  ISBN 0-13-190208-3
  1. Marketing. I. Armstrong, Gary. II. Title.
HF5415.K6314 1996
658.8—dc20   95-32226
                                                        CIP

Acquisitions Editor: David Borkowsky
Senior Project Manager: Alana Zdinak
Production management, composition, and prepress: GTS Graphics, Inc.
Assistant Editor: Melissa Steffens
Development Editor: Mark Palmer
Interior Design: Rosemarie Votta
Cover Design: Rosemarie Votta
Design Director: Patricia Wosczyk
Photo research: Meyers Photo-Art
Ad research: Deborah Kopka
Manufacturing Buyer: Vincent Scelta
Director of Production/Manufacturing: Joanne Jay
Editorial Assistant: Theresa Festa

Cover Art: Sharmen Liao, Inc.

 ©1996 by Prentice Hall, Inc.
A Simon and Schuster Company
Englewood Cliffs, NJ 07632

10 9 8 7 6 5 4 3 2 1
ISBN 0-13-190208-3

Prentice-Hall International (UK) Limited, *London*
Prentice-Hall of Australia Pty. Limited, *Sydney*
Prentice-Hall Canada Inc., *Toronto*
Prentice-Hall Hispanoamericana, S. A., *Mexico*
Prentice-Hall of India Private Limited, *New Delhi*
Prentice-Hall of Japan, Inc., *Tokyo*
Simon & Schuster Asia Pte. Ltd., *Singapore*
Editoria Prentice-Hall do Brazil, Ltda., *Rio de Janeiro*

About the Authors

As a team, Philip Kotler and Gary Armstrong provide a blend of skills uniquely suited to writing an introductory marketing text. Professor Kotler is one of the world's leading authorities on marketing. Professor Armstrong is an award-winning teacher of undergraduate business students. Together they make the complex world of marketing practical, approachable, and enjoyable.

Philip Kotler is S. C. Johnson & Son Distinguished Professor of International Marketing at the Kellogg Graduate School of Management, Northwestern University. He received his master's degree at the University of Chicago and his Ph.D. at M.I.T., both in economics. Dr. Kotler is author of *Marketing Management: Analysis, Planning, Implementation, and Control* (Prentice Hall), now in its eighth edition and the most widely used marketing textbook in graduate schools of business. He has authored several other successful books and he has written over 90 articles for leading journals. He is the only three-time winner of the coveted Alpha Kappa Psi award for the best annual article in the *Journal of Marketing*. Dr. Kotler's numerous major honors include the Paul D. Converse Award given by the American Marketing Association to honor "outstanding contributions to science in marketing" and the Stuart Henderson Britt Award as Marketer of the Year. In 1985, he was named the first recipient of two major awards: the Distinguished Marketing Educator of the Year Award given by the American Marketing Association and the Philip Kotler Award for Excellence in Health Care Marketing presented by the Academy for Health Care Services Marketing. In 1989, he received the Charles Coolidge Parlin Award, which each year honors an outstanding leader in the field of marketing. Dr. Kotler has served as chairman of the College on Marketing of the Institute of Management Sciences (TIMS) and a director of the American Marketing Association. He has consulted with many major U.S. and foreign companies on marketing strategy.

Gary Armstrong is Professor and Chair of Marketing in the Kenan-Flagler Business School at the University of North Carolina at Chapel Hill. He holds undergraduate and master's degrees in business from Wayne State University in Detroit, and he received his Ph.D. in marketing from Northwestern University. Dr. Armstrong has contributed numerous articles to leading business journals. As a consultant and researcher, he has worked with many companies on marketing research, sales management, and marketing strategy. But Professor Armstrong's first love is teaching. He has been very active in the teaching and administration of North Carolina's undergraduate business program. His recent administrative posts include Associate Director of the Undergraduate Business Program, Director of the Business Honors Program, and others. He works closely with business student groups and has received several campuswide and Business School teaching awards. He is the only repeat recipient of the school's highly regarded Award for Excellence in Undergraduate Teaching, which he won for the third time in 1993.

Contents

PART VI: EXTENDING MARKETING

Preface

Marketing is the business function that identifies customer needs and wants, determines which target markets the organization can serve best, and designs appropriate products, services, and programs to serve these markets. However, marketing is much more than just an isolated business function—it is a philosophy that guides the entire organization. The goal of marketing is to create customer satisfaction profitably by building value-laden relationships with important customers. The marketing department cannot accomplish this goal by itself. It must team up closely with other departments in the company and partner with other organizations throughout its entire value-delivery system to provide superior value to customers. Thus, marketing calls upon everyone in the organization to "think customer" and to do all they can to help create and deliver superior customer value and satisfaction. As Professor Stephen Burnett of Northwestern puts it, "In a truly great marketing organization, you can't tell who's in the marketing department. Everyone in the organization has to make decisions based on the impact on the consumer."

Many people see marketing only as advertising or selling. But real marketing does not involve the art of selling what you make so much as knowing *what* to make! Organizations gain market leadership by understanding consumer needs and finding solutions that delight customers through superior value, quality, and service. If customer value and satisfaction are absent, no amount of advertising or selling can compensate.

Marketing is all around us, and we all need to know something about it. Marketing is used not only by manufacturing companies, wholesalers, and retailers, but by all kinds of individuals and organizations. Lawyers, accountants, and doctors use marketing to manage demand for their services. So do hospitals, museums, and performing arts groups. No politician can get the needed votes, and no resort the needed tourists, without developing and carrying out marketing plans. *Principles of Marketing* is designed to help students learn about and apply the basic concepts and practices of modern marketing as they are used in a wide variety of settings: in product and service firms, consumer and business markets, profit and nonprofit organizations, domestic and global companies, and small and large businesses.

People throughout these organizations need to know how to define and segment a market and how to position themselves strongly by developing need-satisfying products and services for chosen target segments. They must know how to price their offerings to make them attractive and affordable and how to choose and manage intermediaries to make their products available to customers. And they need to know how to advertise and promote products so customers will know about and want them. Clearly, marketers need a broad range of skills in order to sense, serve, and satisfy consumer needs.

Students also need to know marketing in their roles as consumers and citizens. Someone is always trying to sell us something, so we need to recognize the methods they use. And when students enter the job market, they must do "marketing research" to find the best opportunities and the best ways to "market themselves" to prospective employers. Many will start their careers with marketing jobs in sales forces, in retailing, in advertising, in research, or in one of a dozen other marketing areas.

APPROACH AND OBJECTIVES

Principles of Marketing takes a *practical, managerial* approach to marketing. It provides a rich depth of practical examples and applications, showing the major decisions that marketing managers face in their efforts to balance the organization's objectives and resources against needs and opportunities in the marketplace. Each chapter opens with a major example describing an actual company situation. Boxed Marketing Highlights, short examples, color illustrations, video cases, company cases, and color illustrations highlight high-interest ideas, stories, and marketing strategies.

Principles of Marketing tells the stories that reveal the drama of modern marketing; Home Depot's zeal for taking care of customers; Ritz-Carlton's penchant for taking care of those who take care of customers; Levi-Strauss & Co.'s startling success in finding new ways to grow, both in the United States and abroad; Church & Dwight's climb to become "king of the (mole)hill" with Arm & Hammer baking soda products; how Dow Plastics achieved leadership in its business-to-business markets by selling "customer success"; Motorola's quest for customer-driven, "six-sigma" quality; P&G's struggle to bring sanity back to food prices; Black & Decker's new-product success through listening to the customer; how Coca-Cola abandoned Madison Avenue and "went Hollywood" to create its breakthrough, always cool, Always Coca-Cola advertising campaign; how Revlon sells not just products, but hopes and dreams; how Disney gives consumers an America that still works the way it's supposed to; Gerber's difficult social responsibility decisions following a product tampering scare. These and dozens of other examples and illustrations throughout each chapter reinforce key concepts and bring marketing to life.

Thus, *Principles of Marketing* gives the marketing student a comprehensive and innovative, managerial and practical introduction to marketing. Its style and extensive use of examples and illustrations make the book straightforward, easy-to-read, and enjoyable.

CHANGES IN THE SEVENTH EDITION

The seventh edition of *Principles of Marketing* offers important improvements in organization, content, and style. The revisions emphasize a number of major new marketing themes, including:

◆ *Delivering superior customer value, satisfaction, and quality*—market-centered strategy and "taking care of the customer."

◆ *Relationship marketing*—*keeping* customers and capturing *customer lifetime value* by building value-laden customer relationships.

◆ *Total marketing quality*—the importance of customer-driven, total quality as a means of delivering total customer satisfaction.

◆ *Value-delivery systems*—cross-functional teamwork within companies and cross-company, supply-chain partnerships to create effective customer value-delivery systems.

◆ *Global marketing*—chapter-by-chapter integrated coverage, plus a full chapter focusing on international marketing considerations.

◆ *Marketing ethics, environmentalism, and social responsibility*—chapter-by-chapter integrated coverage, plus a full chapter on marketing ethics and social responsibility.

A carefully revised Chapter 1 introduces and integrates the above topics to set the stage at the beginning of the course. An innovative Chapter 18 on building customer relationships through value, satisfaction, and quality returns the student to these important concepts as a means of tying marketing together at the end of the course. In between, each chapter reflects the current marketing emphasis on delivering customer value and satisfaction and on building customer relationships.

Other major additions to the seventh edition include:

◆ *Marketing communications*—major and important new material in Chapter 15 on the *new marketing communications environment, direct marketing,* and *integrated marketing communications.*

◆ *Sales management*—in Chapter 17, new sections on *sales force strategy and structure, team selling,* and *relationship marketing.*

◆ *Marketing logistics*—completely revised coverage of physical distribution to include important new issues in *integrated marketing logistics* and *supply-chain management.* Also, a new section on *hybrid channels.*

◆ *Product and brand strategy*—significant new material on brand quality and brand strategy, including *co-branding, multibranding,* and *packaging and the environment.*

◆ *Marketing management and competitive strategies*—Chapter 19 combines with Chapter 18 to provide the most complete coverage of competitive marketing strategy of any introductory marketing text. New material has been added, including a section on customer value disciplines. These chapters help students to integrate what they've learned about marketing strategy and tactics around the key concept of gaining competitive advantage through the delivery of customer value, satisfaction, and quality.

The seventh edition contains many other important changes. This edition has fewer chapters; the two chapters on consumer behavior have been combined to create a single, more streamlined Chapter 5. The text has an exciting new integrated design. Many new chapter-opening examples and Marketing Highlight exhibits illustrate important new concepts with actual business applications. Dozens of new examples have been added within the running text. All tables, figures, examples, and references throughout the text have been thoroughly updated. The seventh edition of *Principles of Marketing* contains dozens of new photos and advertisements that illustrate key points and make the text more effective and appealing. All the real-life company cases in the seventh edition are new or revised, and the text comes with an exciting new collection of company video cases. These company and video cases, and the quality videos that accompany them, help to bring the real world directly into the classroom.

LEARNING AIDS

Many aids are provided within this book to help students learn about marketing. The main ones are:

◆ *Chapter-opening objectives.* Each chapter begins with learning objectives that preview the flow of concepts in the chapter.

◆ *Chapter-ending summaries of objectives.* At the end of each chapter, summaries are provided for each chapter objective to reinforce main points and concepts.

◆ *Chapter-opening examples.* Each chapter starts with a dramatic marketing story that introduces the chapter material and arouses student interest.

◆ *Full-color figures, photographs, advertisements, and illustrations.* Throughout each chapter, key concepts and applications are illustrated with strong, full-color visual materials.

◆ *Marketing highlights.* Additional examples and important information are highlighted in Marketing Highlight exhibits throughout the text.

♦ *Review questions and exercises.* Each chapter contains a set of discussion questions covering the main chapter points and "applying the concepts" exercises that build individual and group process and leadership skills.

♦ *Key terms.* Key terms are highlighted within the text, defined in page margins, and listed at the end of each chapter with page references.

♦ *Company cases.* Company cases for class or written discussion are provided at the end of each chapter, with integrative comprehensive cases following each major part of the text. These cases challenge students to apply marketing principles to real companies in real situations.

♦ *Video cases.* Nine written video cases are provided at key points in the text, supported by exciting new and original videos developed especially for the seventh edition of *Principles of Marketing*. The videos and cases help to bring key marketing concepts and issues to life in the classroom.

♦ *Appendixes.* Two appendixes, "Marketing Arithmetic" and "Careers in Marketing," provide additional, practical information for students.

♦ *Glossary.* At the end of the book, an extensive glossary provides quick reference to the key terms found in the book.

♦ *Indexes.* Subject, company, and author indexes reference all information and examples in the book.

SUPPLEMENTS

A successful marketing course requires more than a well-written book. Today's classroom requires a dedicated teacher and a fully-integrated teaching system. *Principles of Marketing* is supported by an extensively revised and expanded system of supplemental learning and teaching aids:

FOR THE INSTRUCTOR

♦ *ON LOCATION! Custom Case Videos for Marketing.* Broadcast journalism and marketing education meet to create a series of custom produced case videos that have all the fast-paced and engaging qualities of TV and focus on the successful marketing activities of nine dynamic companies. Take your students on a field trip to New York City where MTV Networks targets Generation X, or to Alaska, where Mountain Travel, Inc. capitalizes on the adventure travel market. Each video is approximately six to eight minutes in length and is tied directly to the issue-oriented end-of-part video case studies in *Principles of Marketing*.

♦ *Instructor's Resource Manual (ISBN# 0-13-436817-7).* This comprehensive guide includes a chapter summary for a quick overview, a list of key teaching objectives, and answers to all end-of-chapter discussion and case questions. A highly detailed lecture outline cuts preparation time by thoroughly integrating the video material, cases, and transparencies. In addition, the manual includes a comprehensive video guide that summarizes each video and provides answers to the video case discussion questions.

♦ *Instructor's Electronic Resource Manual.* This manual is available electronically on 3.5" disks (IBM version only).

♦ *Test Item File.* The test item file contains over 2,000 multiple-choice, true/false, and essay questions.

♦ *3.5" IBM Test Manager.* This powerful computerized testing package, available for DOS-based computers, allows instructors to create their own personalized exams using questions from the Test Item File. It offers full mouse support, complete questions editing, random test generation, graphics, and printing capabilities. Toll-free technical support is offered to all users, and the Test Manager is free upon adoption.

- *Color Transparencies.* Two hundred full-color transparencies highlight key concepts for presentation. Each transparency is accompanied by a full page of teaching notes that include relevant key terms and discussion points from the chapters as well as additional material from supplementary sources.

- *Electronic Transparencies.* All acetates and lecture notes are available on Powerpoint 4.0. The disk is designed to allow you to present the transparency to your class electronically and also may be used as part of a Presentation Manager lecture.

- *Presentation Manager for Marketing.* An application of the popular Authorware software program, Presentation Manager allows you to easily prearrange your multimedia classroom lecture by accessing any of our available media materials on laserdisk, VHS tape, CD-ROM, and 3.5" disk. Choose the order of the materials you would like to present in class from a list that appears on-screen, and Presentation Manager for Marketing will do the rest.

- *New York Times/Prentice Hall "Themes of the Times" Program for Marketing.* Prentice Hall and *The New York Times,* one of the world's top news publications, join to expand your students' knowledge beyond the walls of the classroom. Upon adoption, professors and students receive a specialized "mini-newspaper" containing a broad spectrum of carefully chosen articles that focus on events and issues in the world of marketing as well as on some of the news-making marketing professionals of the 1990s. To ensure complete timeliness, this supplement is updated twice a year.

FOR THE STUDENT

- *Learning Guide.* The Learning Guide includes chapter overviews, objectives, key terms and definitions, and detailed outlines for note-taking and review. A special applications section, "Applying Terms and Concepts," is designed to illustrate and apply topics in marketing. Each case in the section either is a synopsis of a recent article in marketing or has been drawn from the author's experiences in the field. To reinforce students' understanding of the chapter material, the guide includes a section of multiple-choice and true/false questions. Additional sections include a marketing research paper, a project outline, and a special careers appendix.

- *Career Paths in Marketing.* Prentice Hall, in conjunction with Convergence Multimedia, is proud to be the exclusive educational distributor of "Career Paths in Marketing." Winner of the New Media Invision gold medal, this interactive CD-ROM includes over 250 short video clips that highlight marketing professionals, provide information on successful applicant profiles, and outline entry requirements. Special modules focus on interview skills, resumes, networking, and negotiation. Students can ask career questions to successful marketing managers featured in the Kotler text and videocases! This CD-ROM is available at a special discount rate when ordered with *Principles of Marketing.*

ACKNOWLEDGMENTS

No book is the work only of its authors. We owe much to the pioneers of marketing who first identified its major issues and developed its concepts and techniques. Our thanks also go to our colleagues at the J. L. Kellogg Graduate School of Management, Northwestern University, and at the Kenan-Flagler Business School, University of North Carolina at Chapel Hill, for ideas and suggestions. We owe special thanks to Lew Brown and Martha McEnally, both of the University of North Carolina, Greensboro, for their valuable work in preparing high-quality company cases and video cases, respectively. We thank Lewis Hershey for his work in preparing the *Instructor's Resource Manual, Test Item File,* and *Color Transparencies Package.* We want to acknowledge Rick Starr, who prepared chapter objective summaries, discussion questions, and exercises. Thanks also go to Tom Paczkowski for the *Student Learning Guide.* Finally, we thank Mark Palmer for his help in so many phases of the text's development, and Betsey Christian for her able editing assistance.

Many reviewers at other colleges provided valuable comments and suggestions. We are indebted to the following colleagues:

Martin St. John	Westmoreland County Community College
Preyas Desai	Purdue University
Carl Obermiller	Seattle University
Richard Leventhal	Metropolitan State College–Denver
Allen L. Appell	San Francisco State University
John Stovall	University of Illinois–Chicago
Jeff Streiter	SUNY Brockport
H. Lee Meadow	Northern Illinois University
Alan T. Shao	University of North Carolina–Charlotte
David M. Nemi	Niagara County Community College
Sherilyn Zeigler	University of Hawaii
J. Ford Laumer, Jr.	Auburn University
Donna Tillman	California State Polytechnic University

We also owe a great deal to the people at Prentice Hall who helped develop this book. Marketing editor David Borkowsky supplied many good ideas and substantial support and encouragement (sometimes even prodding). We also owe much thanks to Alana Zdinak and Heather Stratton who helped shepherd the project smoothly through production. Additional thanks go to Deborah Kopka and Joan Meyers-Murie.

Finally, we owe many thanks to our families—Kathy, KC, and Mandy Armstrong, and Nancy, Amy, Melissa, and Jessica Kotler—for their constant support and encouragement. To them, we dedicate this book.

Philip Kotler
Gary Armstrong

Principles
of Marketing

Marketing in a Changing World

CREATING CUSTOMER VALUE AND SATISFACTION

Home Depot, the giant do-it-yourself home improvement chain, is an outstanding marketing company. The reason: Home Depot is more than just customer-driven—it's customer-*obsessed*. In the words of co-founder and chief executive, Bernie Marcus, "All of our people understand what the Holy Grail is. It's not the bottom line. It's an almost blind, passionate commitment to taking care of customers."

At first glance, a cavernous Home Depot store doesn't look like much. With its cement floors and drafty warehouse-like interior, the store offers all the atmosphere of an airplane hangar. But the chances are good that you'll find exactly what you're looking for, priced to make it a real value. Home Depot carries a huge assortment of more than 35,000 items—anything and everything related to home improvement. And its prices run 20 to 30 percent below those of local hardware stores.

Home Depot provides more than the right products at the right prices, however. Perhaps the best part of shopping at Home Depot is the high quality of its customer service. Bernie Marcus and his partner, Arthur Blank, founded Home Depot with the simple mission of helping customers solve their home improvement problems. Their goal: "To take ham-handed homeowners who lack the confidence to do more than screw in a light bulb and transform them into Mr. and Ms. Fixits." Accomplishing this mission takes more than simply peddling the store's products and taking the customers' money. It means building lasting relationships with customers by helping them to solve their home improvement problems.

Bernie and Arthur understand the importance of customer satisfaction. They calculate that a satisfied customer is worth more than $25,000 in customer lifetime value ($38 per store visit, times 30 visits per year, times about 22 years of patronage). Customer satisfaction, in turn, results from interactions with well-trained, highly motivated employees who consistently provide good value and high-quality service. "The most important part of our formula," says Arthur, "is the quality of caring that takes place in our stores between the employee and the customer." Thus, at Home Depot, taking care of customers begins with taking care of employees.

Home Depot attracts the best salespeople by paying above average salaries; then it trains them thoroughly. All employees take regular "product knowledge" classes to gain hands-on experience with problems customers will face. When it comes to creating customer value and satisfaction, Home Depot treats its employees as partners. All full-time employees receive at least 7 percent of their annual salary in company stock. As a result, Home Depot employees take ownership in the business of serving customers. Each employee wears a bright orange apron that says, "Hello, I'm ———, a Home Depot stockholder. Let me help you."

To further motivate employees, Bernie and Arthur have become energetic crusaders in the cause of customer service. For example, four Sundays a year at 6:30 AM, the two don their own orange aprons and air *Breakfast with Bernie and Arthur*—a good old-fashioned revival broadcast live over closed-circuit TV to the company's 70,000 employees nationwide. According to one account, "Bernie regularly rouses his disciples with the following: 'Where do you go if you want a job?' They yell back: 'Sears . . . Lowe's . . . Builders Square.' 'Where do you go if you want a *career*?' 'HOME DEPOT!' they roar. At times, when the excitement becomes feverish, Marcus has been known to grab a resisting Blank, plant a noisy kiss on his cheek, and exclaim, 'Arthur, I love you!'"

Home Depot avoids the high-pressure sales techniques used by some retailers. Instead, it encourages salespeople to build long-term relationships with customers—to spend whatever time it takes, visit after visit, to solve customer problems. Home Depot pays employees a straight salary so that they can spend as much time as necessary with customers without worrying about making the sale. Bernie Marcus declares, "The day I'm dead with an apple in my mouth is the day we'll pay commissions." In fact, rather than pushing customers to *overspend,* employees are trained to help customers spend *less* than they expected. "I love it when shoppers tell me they were prepared to spend $150 and our people showed them how to do the job for four or five bucks," says Bernie.

Taking care of customers has made Home Depot one of today's most successful retailers. Founded in 1978, in less than 20 years it has grown explosively to become the nation's largest do-it-yourself chain. Home Depot sales have grown more than 35 percent each of the last ten years, and the company has delivered a ten-year average annual return of 45.5 percent. In fact, a current problem in some stores is too many customers—some outlets are generating an astounding $600 of sales per square foot (compared with Wal-Mart at $250 and Kmart at $150). This has created problems with clogged aisles, stockouts, too few salespeople, and long checkout lines. Although many retailers would welcome this kind of problem, it bothers Bernie and Arthur greatly, and they've quickly taken corrective action. Continued success, they know, depends on the passionate pursuit of customer satisfaction. Bernie will tell you, "Every customer has to be treated like your mother, your father, your sister, or your brother." And you certainly wouldn't want to keep your mother waiting in line.[1]

Many factors contribute to making a business successful: great strategy, dedicated employees, good information systems, excellent implementation. However, today's successful companies at all levels have one thing in common—they are strongly customer focused and heavily committed to marketing. These companies share an absolute dedication to understanding and satisfying the needs of customers in well-defined target markets. They motivate everyone in the organization to produce superior value for their customers, leading to high levels of customer satisfaction. As Bernie Marcus of Home Depot asserts, "All of our people understand what the Holy Grail is. It's not the bottom line. It's an almost blind, passionate commitment to taking care of customers."[2]

Marketing, more than any other business function, deals with customers. Creating customer value and satisfaction are at the very heart of modern marketing thinking and practice. Although we will explore more detailed definitions of marketing later in this chapter, perhaps the simplest definition is this one: Marketing is the delivery of customer satisfaction at a profit. The goal of marketing is to attract new customers by promising superior value, and to keep current customers by delivering satisfaction.

Wal-Mart has become the world's largest retailer by delivering on its promise "We sell for less—always." Federal Express dominates the U.S. small-package freight industry by consistently making good on its promise of fast, reliable small package delivery. Ritz-Carlton promises—and delivers—truly "memorable experiences" for its hotel guests. And Coca-Cola, long the world's leading soft drink, delivers on the simple but enduring promise, "Always Coca-Cola"—always thirst-quenching, always good with food, always cool, always a part of your life. These and other highly successful companies know that if they take care of their customers, market share and profits will follow.

Some people think that only large business organizations operating in highly developed economies use marketing, but sound marketing is critical to the success of every organization—whether large or small, for-profit or nonprofit, domestic or global. Large for-profit firms such as Coca-Cola, McDonald's, Sony, IBM, General Electric, Federal Express, Wal-Mart, and Marriott use marketing. But so do nonprofit organizations such as colleges, hospitals, museums, symphonies, and even churches. Moreover, marketing is practiced not only in the United States but also in the rest of the world. Most countries in North and South America, Western Europe, and the Far East have well-developed marketing systems. Even in Eastern Europe and the former Soviet republics, where marketing has long had a bad name, dramatic political and social changes have created new opportunities for marketing. Business and government leaders in most of these nations are eager to learn everything they can about modern marketing practices.

You already know a lot about marketing—it's all around you. You see the results of marketing in the abundance of products that line the store shelves in your nearby shopping mall. You see marketing in the advertisements that fill your TV screen, magazines, and mailbox. At home, at school, where you work, where you play—you are exposed to marketing in almost everything you do. Yet, there is much more to marketing than meets the consumer's casual eye. Behind it all is a massive network of people and activities competing for your attention and purchasing dollars.

The remaining pages of this book will give you a more complete and formal introduction to the basic concepts and practices of today's marketing. In this chapter, we begin by defining marketing and its core concepts, describing the major philosophies of marketing thinking and practice, and discussing some of the major new challenges that marketers now face.

WHAT IS MARKETING?

What does the term *marketing* mean? Many people think of marketing only as selling and advertising. And no wonder—every day we are bombarded with television commercials, newspaper ads, direct mail, and sales calls. Someone is always trying to sell us something. It seems that we cannot escape death, taxes, or selling.

Therefore, you may be surprised to learn that selling and advertising are only the tip of the marketing iceberg. Although they are important, they are only two of many marketing functions, and often not the most important ones. Today, marketing must be understood not in the old sense of making a sale—"telling and selling"—but in the new sense of *satisfying customer needs*. If the marketer does a good job of understanding consumer needs; develops products that provide superior value; and prices, distributes, and promotes them effectively, these products will sell very easily.

Everyone knows something about "hot" products. When Sony designed its first Walkman, when Nintendo first offered its improved video game console, and when Ford introduced its Taurus model, these manufacturers were swamped with orders. They had designed the "right" products: not "me-too" products, but ones offering new benefits. Peter Drucker, a leading management thinker, has put it this way: "The aim of marketing is to make selling superfluous. The aim is to know and understand the customer so well that the product or service fits . . . and sells itself."[3]

Thus, selling and advertising are only part of a larger "marketing mix"—a set of marketing tools that work together to affect the marketplace. We define **marketing** as a social and managerial process by which individuals and groups obtain what they need and want through creating and exchanging products and value with others. To explain this definition, we examine the following important terms: *needs, wants, and demands; products; value, satisfaction, and quality; exchange, transactions, and relationships;* and *markets.* Figure 1-1 shows that these core marketing concepts are linked, with each concept building on the one before it.

Marketing
A social and managerial process by which individuals and groups obtain what they need and want through creating and exchanging products and value with others.

FIGURE 1-1 *Core marketing concepts*

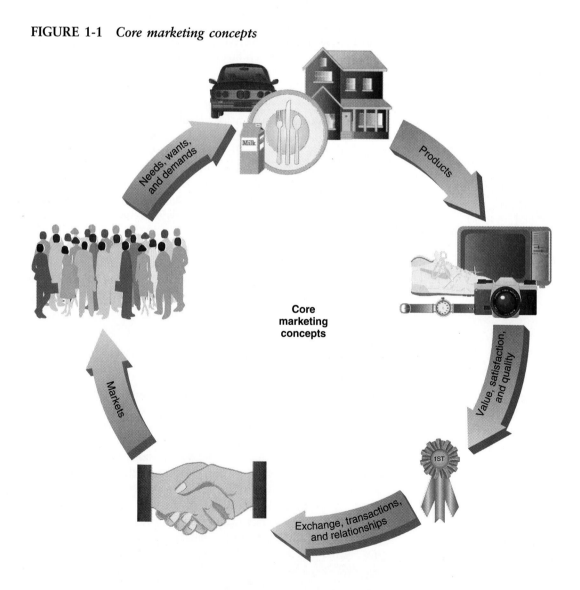

Core
marketing
concepts

Needs, wants, and demands

Products

Value, satisfaction, and quality

Exchange, transactions, and relationships

Markets

UNDERSTANDING CONSUMER NEEDS AND WANTS

No one knows better than Mom, right? But does she know how much underwear you own? Jockey International does. Or the number of ice cubes you put in a glass? Coca-Cola knows that one. Or how about which pretzels you usually eat first, the broken ones or the whole ones? Try asking Frito-Lay. Big companies know the whats, wheres, hows, and whens of their consumers' needs, wants, and demands. They figure out all sorts of things about us that we don't even know ourselves. To marketers, this isn't trivial pursuit—knowing all about customer needs is the cornerstone of effective marketing. Most companies research us in detail and amass mountains of facts.

Coke knows that we put 3.2 ice cubes in a glass, see 69 of its commercials every year, and prefer cans to pop out of vending machines at a temperature of 35 degrees. One million of us drink Coke with breakfast every day. Each new day brings piles of fresh research reports detailing our buying habits and preferences. Did you know that 38 percent of Americans would rather have a tooth pulled than take their car to a dealership for repairs? We each spend $20 a year on flowers; Arkansas has the lowest consumption of peanut butter in the United States; 51 percent of all males put their left pants leg on first, whereas 65 percent of women start with the right leg; and if you send a husband and a wife to the store separately to buy beer, there is a 90 per-cent chance they will return with different brands.

Nothing about our behavior is sacred. Procter & Gamble once conducted a study to find out whether most of us fold or crumple our toilet paper; another study showed that 68 percent of consumers prefer their toilet paper to unwind over the spool rather than under. Abbott Laboratories figured out that one in four of us has "problem" dandruff, and Kimberly Clark, which makes Kleenex, has calculated that the average person blows his or her nose 256 times a year.

It's not that Americans are all that easy to figure out. A few years ago, Campbell Soup gave up trying to learn our opinions about the ideal-sized meatball after a series of tests showed that we prefer one so big it wouldn't fit in the can.

Hoover hooked up timers and other equipment to vacuum cleaners in people's homes and learned that we spend about 35 minutes each week vacuuming, sucking up about 8 pounds of dust each year and using 6 bags to do so. Banks know that we write about 24 checks a month, and pharmaceutical companies know that all of us together take 52 million as-pirins and 30 million sleeping pills a year. In fact, almost everything we swallow is closely monitored by someone. Each year, we consume 156 hamburgers, 95 hot dogs, 283 eggs, 5 pounds of yogurt, 9 pounds of cereal, 2 pounds of peanut butter, and 46 quarts of popcorn. We spend 90 minutes a day preparing our food and 40 minutes a day munching it. And as a nation, we down $650 million of antacid a year to help digest the food we eat.

Of all businesses, however, the prize for research thoroughness may go to toothpaste makers. Among other things, they know that our favorite toothbrush color is blue and that only 37 percent of us are using one that's more than six months old. About 47 percent of us put water on our brush before we apply the paste, 15 percent put water on after the paste, 24 percent do both, and 14 percent don't wet the brush at all.

Thus, most big marketing companies have answers to all the what, where, when, and how questions about their consumer demand. Seemingly trivial facts add up quickly and provide important input for designing marketing strategies. But to influence demand, marketers need the answer to one more question: Beyond knowing the whats and wherefores of demand, they need to know the *whys*—what *causes* us to want the things we buy? That's a much harder question to answer.

Sources: John Koten, "You Aren't Para-noid If You Feel Someone Eyes You Constantly," *Wall Street Journal,* March 29, 1985, pp. 1, 22; and "Offbeat Market-ing," *Sales & Marketing Management,* January 1990, p. 35.

NEEDS, WANTS, AND DEMANDS

Needs
States of felt deprivation.

The most basic concept underlying marketing is that of human needs. **Human needs** are states of felt deprivation. Humans have many complex needs. These include basic *physical* needs for food, clothing, warmth, and safety; *social* needs for belonging and affection; and *individual* needs for knowledge and self-expression. These needs are not invented by marketers; they are a basic part of the human makeup. When a need is not satisfied, a person will try either to reduce the need or look for an object that will satisfy it. People in less-developed societies may try to reduce their desires and satisfy them with what is available. People in industrial societies may try to find or develop objects that will satisfy their needs.

Wants
The form taken by human needs as they are shaped by culture and individual personality.

Wants are the form taken by human needs as they are shaped by culture and individual personality. A hungry person in the United States may want a ham-burger, French fries, and a Coke. A hungry person in Bali may want mangoes, suckling pig, and beans. Wants are described in terms of objects that will satisfy needs. As a society evolves, the wants of its members expand. As people are exposed to more objects that arouse their interest and desire, producers try to provide more want-satisfying products and services.

People have almost unlimited wants but limited resources. Thus, they want to choose products that provide the most value and satisfaction for their money. When backed by buying power, wants become **demands.** Consumers view products as bundles of benefits and choose products that give them the best bundle for their money. Thus, a Honda Civic means basic transportation, low price, and fuel economy. A Mercedes means comfort, luxury, and status. Given their wants and resources, people demand products with the benefits that add up to the most satisfaction.

Outstanding marketing companies go to great lengths to learn about and understand their customers' needs, wants, and demands. They conduct consumer research, focus groups, and customer clinics. They analyze customer complaint, inquiry, warranty, and service data. They train salespeople to be on the lookout for unfulfilled customer needs. They observe customers using their own and competing products, and interview them in depth about their likes and dislikes.[4] Understanding customer needs, wants, and demands in detail provides important input for designing marketing strategies (see Marketing Highlight 1-1).

In these outstanding companies, people at all levels—including top management—stay close to customers in an ongoing effort to understand their needs and wants. For example, top executives from Wal-Mart spend two days each week visiting stores and mingling with customers. At Disney World, at least once in his or her career, every manager spends a day touring the park in a Mickey, Minnie, Goofy, or other character costume. Moreover, all Disney World managers spend a week each year on the front line—taking tickets, selling popcorn, or loading and unloading rides. At Motorola, in addition to surveying customers about their quality needs, analyzing customer complaints, and studying customer service records, top executives routinely visit customers at their offices to gain better insights into their needs. And at Marriott, International, Inc. to stay in touch with customers, chairman of the board and president Bill Marriott personally reads some 10 percent of the 8,000 letters and 2 percent of the 750,000 guest comment cards submitted by customers each year.

PRODUCTS

People satisfy their needs and wants with products. A **product** is anything that can be offered to a market to satisfy a need or want. Usually, the word *product* suggests a physical object, such as a car, a television set, or a bar of soap. However, the concept of *product* is not limited to physical objects—anything capable of satisfying a need can be called a product. The importance of physical goods lies not so much in owning them as in the benefits they provide. We

Demands
Human wants that are backed by buying power.

Product
Anything that can be offered to a market for attention, acquisition, use, or consumption that might satisfy a want or need. It includes physical objects, services, persons, places, organizations, and ideas.

Outstanding marketing companies like Marriott stay close to customers. Chairman Bill Marriott personally reads guest comment cards and letters, then talks to customers through ads like this one.

Products do not have to be physical objects. In this ad, the "product" is tennis. "Imagine six hours of classes, one after another, interrupted only by a couple of fish sticks . . . Introduce your kids to tennis."

don't buy food to look at, but because it satisfies our hunger. We don't buy a microwave to admire, but because it cooks our food.

Marketers often use the expressions *goods* and *services* to distinguish between physical products and intangible ones. Moreover, consumers obtain benefits through other vehicles, such as *persons, places, organizations, activities,* and *ideas.* Consumers decide which entertainers to watch on television, which places to visit on vacation, which organizations to support through contributions, and which ideas to adopt. Thus, the term *product* covers physical goods, services, and a variety of other vehicles that can satisfy consumers' needs and wants. If at times the term *product* does not seem to fit, we could substitute other terms such as *satisfier, resource,* or *offer.*

Many sellers make the mistake of paying more attention to the physical products they offer than to the benefits produced by these products. They see themselves as selling a product rather than providing a solution to a need. A manufacturer of drill bits may think that the customer needs a drill bit, but what the customer *really* needs is a hole. These sellers may suffer from "marketing myopia."[5] They are so taken with their products that they focus only on existing wants and lose sight of underlying customer needs. They forget that a physical product is only a tool to solve a consumer problem. These sellers have trouble if a new product comes along that serves the need better or less expensively. The customer with the same *need* will *want* the new product.

VALUE, SATISFACTION, AND QUALITY

Consumers usually face a broad array of products and services that might satisfy a given need. How do they choose among these many products and services? Consumers make buying choices based on their perceptions of the value that various products and services deliver.

Customer value is the difference between the values the customer gains from owning and using a product and the costs of obtaining the product. For example, Federal Express customers gain a number of benefits. The most obvious are fast and reliable package delivery. However, when using Federal Express, customers

Customer value
The difference between the values the customer gains from owning and using a product and the costs of obtaining the product.

also may receive some status and image values. Using Federal Express usually makes both the package sender and the receiver feel more important. When deciding whether to send a package via Federal Express, customers will weigh these and other values against the money, effort, and psychic costs of using the service. Moreover, they will compare the value of using Federal Express against the value of using other shippers—UPS, Airborne, the U.S. Postal Service—and select the one that gives them the greatest delivered value.

Customers often do not judge product values and costs accurately or objectively. They act on *perceived* value. For example, does Federal Express really provide faster, more reliable delivery? If so, is this better service worth the higher prices FedEx charges? The Postal Service argues that its express service is comparable, and its prices are much lower. However, judging by market share, most consumers perceive otherwise. Federal Express dominates with more than a 45 percent share of the U.S. express-delivery market, compared with the Postal Service's 8 percent.[6] The Postal Service's challenge is to change these customer value perceptions.

Customer satisfaction
The extent to which a product's perceived performance matches a buyer's expectations. If the product's performance falls short of expectations, the buyer is dissatisfied. If performance matches or exceeds expectations, the buyer is satisfied or delighted.

Customer satisfaction depends on a product's perceived performance in delivering value relative to a buyer's expectations. If the product's performance falls short of the customer's expectations, the buyer is dissatisfied. If performance matches expectations, the buyer is satisfied. If performance exceeds expectations, the buyer is delighted. Outstanding marketing companies go out of their way to keep their customers satisfied. Satisfied customers make repeat purchases, and they tell others about their good experiences with the product. The key is to match customer expectations with company performance. Smart companies aim to *delight* customers by promising only what they can deliver, then delivering *more* than they promise.

Customer satisfaction is closely linked to quality. In recent years, many companies have adopted **total quality management** (TQM) programs, designed to constantly improve the quality of their products, services, and marketing processes. Quality has a direct impact on product performance, and hence on customer satisfaction.

Total quality management (TQM)
Programs designed to constantly improve the quality of products, services, and marketing processes.

In the narrowest sense, quality can be defined as "freedom from defects." But most customer-centered companies go beyond this narrow definition of quality. Instead, they define quality in terms of customer satisfaction. For example, the vice president of quality at Motorola, a company that pioneered total quality efforts in the United States, says that "Quality has to do something for the customer. . . . Our definition of a defect is 'if the customer doesn't like it, it's a defect.'"[7] Similarly, the American Society for Quality Control defines *quality* as the totality of features and characteristics of a product or service that bear on its ability to *satisfy customer needs*. These customer-focused definitions suggest that a company has achieved total quality only when its products or services meet or exceed customer expectations. Thus, the fundamental aim of today's *total quality* movement has become *total customer satisfaction*. Quality begins with customer needs and ends with customer satisfaction.

EXCHANGE, TRANSACTIONS, AND RELATIONSHIPS

Marketing occurs when people decide to satisfy needs and wants through exchange. **Exchange** is the act of obtaining a desired object from someone by offering something in return. Exchange is only one of many ways people can obtain a desired object. For example, hungry people can find food by hunting, fishing, or gathering fruit. They could beg for food or take food from someone else. Or they could offer money, another good, or a service in return for food.

Exchange
The act of obtaining a desired object from someone by offering something in return.

Transaction
A trade between two parties that involves at least two things of value, agreed-upon conditions, a time of agreement, and a place of agreement.

Relationship marketing
The process of creating, maintaining, and enhancing strong, value-laden relationships with customers and other stakeholders.

Market
The set of all actual and potential buyers of a product or service.

As a means of satisfying needs, exchange has much in its favor. People do not have to prey on others or depend on donations. Nor must they possess the skills to produce every necessity for themselves. They can concentrate on making things they are good at making and trade them for needed items made by others. Thus, exchange allows a society to produce much more than it would with any alternative system.

Exchange is the core concept of marketing. For an exchange to take place, several conditions must be satisfied. Of course, at least two parties must participate, and each must have something of value to the other. Each party also must want to deal with the other party and each must be free to accept or reject the other's offer. Finally, each party must be able to communicate and deliver.

These conditions simply make exchange *possible*. Whether exchange actually *takes place* depends on the parties' coming to an agreement. If they agree, we must conclude that the act of exchange has left both of them better off, or at least not worse off. After all, each was free to reject or accept the offer. In this sense, exchange creates value just as production creates value. It gives people more consumption possibilities.

Whereas exchange is the core concept of marketing, a transaction is marketing's unit of measurement. A **transaction** consists of a trade of values between two parties. In a transaction, we must be able to say that one party gives X to another party and gets Y in return. For example, you pay Sears $350 for a television set. This is a classic *monetary transaction,* but not all transactions involve money. In a *barter transaction,* you might trade your old refrigerator in return for a neighbor's secondhand television set.

Relationship marketing: To get to know them better, Ford invites customers to brainstorming sessions. "We talk about cars, sure. But we often talk about NON-CAR THINGS: computers, the environment, and quality in very general terms."

In the broadest sense, the marketer tries to bring about a response to some offer. The response may be more than simply "buying" or "trading" goods and services. A political candidate, for instance, wants a response called "votes," a church wants "membership," and a social-action group wants "idea acceptance." Marketing consists of actions taken to obtain a desired response from a target audience toward some product, service, idea, or other object.

Transaction marketing is part of the larger idea of **relationship marketing.** Beyond creating short-term transactions, marketers need to build long-term relationships with valued customers, distributors, dealers, and suppliers. They must build strong economic and social ties by promising and consistently delivering high-quality products, good service, and fair prices. Increasingly, marketing is shifting from trying to maximize the profit on each individual transaction to maximizing mutually beneficial relationships with consumers and other parties. The operating assumption is: Build good relationships and profitable transactions will follow.

MARKETS

The concept of exchange leads to the concept of a market. A **market** is the set of actual and potential buyers of a product. These buyers share a particular need or want that can be satisfied through exchange. Thus, the

size of a market depends on the number of people who exhibit the need, have resources to engage in exchange, and are willing to offer these resources in exchange for what they want.

Originally the term *market* stood for the place where buyers and sellers gathered to exchange their goods, such as a village square. Economists use the term *market* to refer to a collection of buyers and sellers who transact in a particular product class, as in the housing market or the grain market. Marketers, however, see the sellers as constituting an industry and the buyers as constituting a market. The relationship between the *industry* and the *market* is shown in Figure 1-2. Sellers and the buyers are connected by four flows. The sellers send products, services, and communications to the market; in return, they receive money and information. The inner loop shows an exchange of money for goods; the outer loop shows an exchange of information.

FIGURE 1-2 *A simple marketing system*

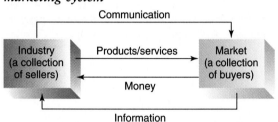

Modern economies operate on the principle of division of labor, where each person specializes in producing something, receives payment, and buys needed things with this money. Thus, modern economies abound in markets. Producers go to resource markets (raw-material markets, labor markets, money markets), buy resources, turn them into goods and services, and sell them to middlemen, who sell them to consumers. The consumers sell their labor, for which they receive income to pay for the goods and services they buy. The government is another market that plays several roles. It buys goods from resource, producer, and middlemen markets; it pays them; it taxes these markets (including consumer markets); and it returns needed public services. Thus, each nation's economy and the whole world economy consist of complex interacting sets of markets that are linked through exchange processes.

Businesspeople use the term *markets* to cover various groupings of customers. They talk about *need markets* (such as the health-seekers); *product markets* (such as the consumer-electronics market); *demographic markets* (such as teens or the baby boomers); and *geographic markets* (such as the Southeasten United States or Western Europe). Or they extend the concept to cover noncustomer groupings as well, such as *financial markets, labor markets,* and *donor markets.*

MARKETING

The concept of markets finally brings us full circle to the concept of marketing. Marketing means managing markets to bring about exchanges for the purpose of satisfying human needs and wants. Thus, we return to our definition of marketing as a process by which individuals and groups obtain what they need and want by creating and exchanging products and value with others.

FIGURE 1-3 *Main actors and forces in a modern marketing system*

Exchange processes involve work. Sellers must search for buyers, identify their needs, design good products and services, set prices for them, promote them, and store and deliver them. Activities such as product development, research, communication, distribution, pricing, and service are core marketing activities.

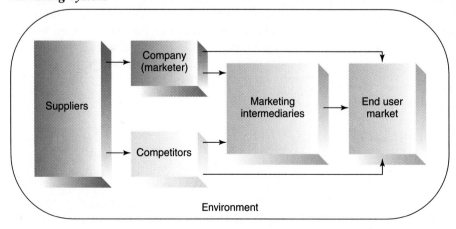

Although we normally think of marketing as being carried on by sellers, buyers also carry on marketing activities. Consumers do "marketing" when they search for the goods they need at prices they can afford. Company purchasing agents do "marketing" when they track down sellers and bargain for good terms.

Figure 1-3 shows the main elements in a modern marketing system. In the usual situation, marketing involves serving a market of end users in the face of competitors. The company and the competitors send their respective products and messages directly to consumers or through marketing intermediaries (middlemen) to the end users. All of the actors in the system are affected by major environmental forces (demographic, economic, physical, technological, political/legal, social/cultural).

Each party in the system adds value for the next level. Thus, a company's success depends not only on its own actions, but also on how well the entire value chain serves the needs of final consumers. Wal-Mart cannot fulfill its promise of low prices unless its suppliers provide merchandise at low costs. And Ford cannot deliver high quality to car buyers unless its dealers provide outstanding service.

MARKETING MANAGEMENT

Marketing management
The analysis, planning, implementation, and control of programs designed to create, build, and maintain beneficial exchanges with target buyers for the purpose of achieving organizational objectives.

We define **marketing management** as the analysis, planning, implementation, and control of programs designed to create, build, and maintain beneficial exchanges with target buyers for the purpose of achieving organizational objectives. Thus, marketing management involves managing demand, which in turn involves managing customer relationships.

DEMAND MANAGEMENT

Most people think of marketing management as finding enough customers for the company's current output, but this is too limited a view. The organization has a desired level of demand for its products. At any point in time, there may be no demand, adequate demand, irregular demand, or too much demand, and marketing management must find ways to deal with these different demand states. Marketing management is concerned not only with finding and increasing demand, but also with changing or even reducing it.

Demarketing
Marketing to reduce demand temporarily or permanently—the aim is not to destroy demand, but only to reduce or shift it.

For example, Golden Gate Bridge sometimes carries an unsafe level of traffic, and Yosemite National Park is badly overcrowded in the summertime. And power companies sometimes have trouble meeting demand during peak usage periods. In these and other cases of excess demand, the needed marketing task, called **demarketing,** is to reduce demand temporarily or permanently. The aim of demarketing is not to destroy demand, but only to reduce or shift it.[8] Thus, marketing management seeks to affect the level, timing, and nature of demand in a way that helps the organization achieve its objectives. Simply put, marketing management is *demand management.*

BUILDING PROFITABLE CUSTOMER RELATIONSHIPS

Managing demand means managing customers. A company's demand comes from two groups: new customers and repeat customers. Traditional marketing theory and practice have focused on attracting new customers and making the sale. Today, however, the emphasis is shifting. Beyond designing strategies to *attract* new customers and create *transactions* with them, companies now are going all out to *retain* current customers and build lasting customer *relationships.*

Why the new emphasis on keeping customers? In the past, companies facing an expanding economy and rapidly growing markets could practice the "leaky-bucket" approach to marketing. Growing markets meant a plentiful supply of new customers. Companies could keep filling the marketing bucket with new customers without worrying about losing old customers through the holes in the bottom of the bucket. However, companies today are facing some new marketing realities. Changing demographics, a slow-growth economy, more sophisticated competitors, and overcapacity in many industries—all of these factors mean that there are fewer new customers to go around. Many companies now are fighting for shares of flat or fading markets. Thus, the costs of attracting new customers are rising. In fact, it costs five times as much to attract a new customer as it does to keep a current customer satisfied.[9]

Companies are also realizing that losing a customer means more than losing a single sale—it means losing the entire stream of purchases that the customer would make over a lifetime of patronage. For example, the *customer lifetime value* of a Taco Bell customer exceeds $12,000.[10] For General Motors or Ford, the customer lifetime value of a customer might well exceed $340,000. Thus, working to retain customers makes good economic sense. A company can lose money on a specific transaction, but still benefit greatly from a long-term relationship.

Attracting new customers remains an important marketing management task. However, the focus today is shifting toward retaining current customers and building profitable, long-term relationships with them. The key to customer retention is superior customer value and satisfaction. With this in mind, many companies are going to extremes to keep their customers satisfied. (See Marketing Highlight 1-2.)

MARKETING MANAGEMENT PHILOSOPHIES

We describe marketing management as carrying out tasks to achieve desired exchanges with target markets. What *philosophy* should guide these marketing efforts? What weight should be given to the interests of the organization, customers, and society? Very often these interests conflict.

There are five alternative concepts under which organizations conduct their marketing activities: the *production, product, selling, marketing,* and *societal marketing* concepts.

THE PRODUCTION CONCEPT

Production concept
The philosophy that consumers will favor products that are available and highly affordable and that management should therefore focus on improving production and distribution efficiency.

The **production concept** holds that consumers will favor products that are available and highly affordable. Therefore, management should focus on improving production and distribution efficiency. This concept is one of the oldest philosophies that guides sellers.

The production concept is still a useful philosophy in two types of situations. The first occurs when the demand for a product exceeds the supply. Here, management should look for ways to increase production. The second situation occurs when the product's cost is too high and improved productivity is needed to bring it down. For example, Henry Ford's whole philosophy was to perfect the production of the Model T so that its cost could be reduced and more people could afford it. He joked about offering people a car of any color as long as it was black.

For many years, Texas Instruments (TI) followed a philosophy of increased production and lower costs in order to bring down prices. It won a major share of the American hand-held calculator market using this approach. However, companies operating under a production philosophy run a major risk of focusing too

CUSTOMER RELATIONSHIPS: KEEPING CUSTOMERS SATISFIED

Some companies go to extremes to coddle their customers. Consider the following examples:

◆ An L. L. Bean customer says he lost all his fishing equipment—and nearly his life—when a raft he bought from the company leaked and forced him to swim to shore. He recovered the raft and sent it to the company along with a letter asking for a new raft and $700 to cover the fishing equipment he says he lost. He gets both.

◆ A woman visits a Nordstrom department store to buy a gift for a friend. She's in a hurry and leaves the store immediately after making her purchase. The Nordstrom salesclerk gift-wraps the item at no charge and later drops it off at the customer's home.

◆ An American Express cardholder fails to pay more than $5,000 of his September bill. He explains that during the summer he'd purchased expensive rugs in Turkey. When he got home, appraisals showed that the rugs were worth half of what he'd paid. Rather than asking suspicious questions or demanding payment, the American Express representative notes the dispute, asks for a letter summarizing the appraisers' estimates, and offers to help solve the problem. And until the conflict is resolved, American Express doesn't ask for payment.

◆ Under the sultry summer sun, a Southwest Airlines flight attendant pulls shut the door and the Boeing 737 pushes away. Meanwhile, a ticket holder, sweat streaming from her face, races down the jetway, only to find that she's arrived too late. However, the Southwest pilot spies the anguished passenger and returns to the gate to pick her up. Says Southwest's executive vice president for customers, "It broke every rule in the book, but we congratulated the pilot on a job well done."

◆ A frustrated homeowner faces a difficult and potentially costly home plumbing repair. He visits the nearby Home Depot store, prowls the aisles, and picks up an armful of parts and supplies—$67 worth in all—that he thinks he'll need to do the job. However, before he gets to the checkout counter, a Home Depot salesperson heads him off. After some coaxing, the salesperson finally convinces the do-it-yourselfer that there's a simpler solution to his repair problem. The cost: $5.99 and a lot less trouble.

From a dollars-and-cents point of view, these examples sound like a crazy way to do business. How can you make money by giving away your products, providing free extra services, talking your customers into paying less, or letting customers get away without paying their bills on time? Yet studies show that going to such extremes to keep customers happy—though costly—goes hand in hand with good financial performance. Satisfied customers come back again and again. Thus, in today's highly competitive marketplace, companies can well afford to lose money on one transaction if it helps to cement a profitable long-term customer relationship.

Keeping customers satisfied involves more than simply opening a complaint department, smiling a lot, and being nice. Companies that do the best job of taking care of customers set high customer service standards and often make seemingly outlandish efforts to achieve them. At these companies, exceptional value and service are more than a set of policies or actions—they are a company-wide attitude, an important part of the overall company culture. Concern for the consumer becomes a matter of pride for everyone in the company. American Express loves to tell stories about how its people have rescued customers from disasters ranging from civil wars to earthquakes, no matter what the cost. The company gives cash rewards of up to $1,000 to "Great Performers," such as Barbara Weber, who moved mountains of State Department and Treasury Department bureaucracy to refund $980 in stolen traveler's checks to a customer stranded in Cuba. Four Seasons Hotels, long known for its outstanding service, tells its employees the story of Ron Dyment, a doorman in Toronto who forgot to load a departing guest's briefcase in his taxi. The doorman called the guest, a lawyer in Washington, DC, and learned that he desperately needed the briefcase for a meeting the following morning. Without first asking for approval from management, Dyment hopped on a plane and returned the briefcase. The company named Dyment Employee of the Year. Similarly, the Nordstrom department store chain thrives on stories about its service heroics, such as employees dropping off orders at customers' homes or warming up cars while customers spend a little more time shopping. There's even a story about a customer who got a refund on a tire—Nordstrom doesn't carry tires, but it prides itself on a no-questions-asked return policy!

There's no simple formula for taking care of customers, but neither is it a mystery. According to the president of L. L. Bean, "A lot of people have fancy things to say about customer service . . . but it's just a day-in, day-out, ongoing, never-ending, unremitting, persevering, compassionate type of activity." For the companies that do it well, it's also very rewarding.

Sources: Bill Kelley, "Five Companies That Do It Right—and Make It Pay," *Sales & Marketing Management,* April 1988, pp. 57–64; Richard S. Teitelbaum, "Keeping Promises," *Fortune,* special issue on "The Tough New Consumer," Autumn/Winter 1993, pp. 32–33; and Patricia Sellers, "Companies That Serve You Best," *Fortune,* May 31, 1993, pp. 74–88.

narrowly on their own operations. For example, when TI used this strategy in the digital watch market, it failed. Although TI's watches were priced low, customers did not find them very attractive. In its drive to bring down prices, TI lost sight of something else that its customers wanted—namely, affordable, *attractive* digital watches.

THE PRODUCT CONCEPT

Product concept
The idea that consumers will favor products that offer the most quality, performance, and features and that the organization should therefore devote its energy to making continuous product improvements. A detailed version of the new-product idea stated in meaningful consumer terms.

Another major concept guiding sellers, the **product concept,** holds that consumers will favor products that offer the most quality, performance, and innovative features. Thus, an organization should devote energy to making continuous product improvements. Some manufacturers believe that if they can build a better mousetrap, the world will beat a path to their door.[11] But they are often rudely shocked. Buyers may well be looking for a better solution to a mouse problem, but not necessarily for a better mousetrap. The solution might be a chemical spray, an exterminating service, or something that works better than a mousetrap. Furthermore, a better mousetrap will not sell unless the manufacturer designs, packages, and prices it attractively; places it in convenient distribution channels; brings it to the attention of people who need it; and convinces buyers that it is a better product.

The product concept also can lead to "marketing myopia." For instance, railroad management once thought that users wanted *trains* rather than *transportation* and overlooked the growing challenge of airlines, buses, trucks, and automobiles. Many colleges have assumed that high school graduates want a liberal arts education and have thus overlooked the increasing challenge of vocational schools.

THE SELLING CONCEPT

Selling concept
The idea that consumers will not buy enough of the organization's products unless the organization undertakes a large-scale selling and promotion effort.

Many organizations follow the **selling concept,** which holds that consumers will not buy enough of the organization's products unless it undertakes a large-scale selling and promotion effort. The concept is typically practiced with *unsought goods*—those that buyers do not normally think of buying, such as encyclopedias or insurance. These industries must be good at tracking down prospects and selling them on product benefits. The selling concept also is practiced in the nonprofit area. A political party, for example, will vigorously sell its candidate to voters as a fantastic person for the job. The candidate works in voting precincts from dawn to dusk—shaking hands, kissing babies, meeting donors, and making speeches. Much money is spent on radio and television advertising, posters, and mailings. The candidate's flaws are hidden from the public because the aim is to get the sale, not to worry about consumer satisfaction afterward.

Most firms practice the selling concept when they have overcapacity. Their aim is to sell what they make rather than make what the market wants. Thus, marketing based on hard selling carries high risks. It focuses on creating sales transactions rather than on building long-term, profitable relationships with customers. It assumes that customers who are coaxed into buying the product will like it. Or, if they don't like it, they will possibly forget their disappointment and buy it again later. These are usually poor assumptions to make about buyers. Most studies show that dissatisfied customers do not buy again. Worse yet, while the average satisfied customer tells three others about good experiences, the average dissatisfied customer tells ten others his or her bad experiences.[12]

THE MARKETING CONCEPT

Marketing concept
The marketing management philosophy that holds that achieving organizational goals depends on determining the needs and wants of target markets and delivering the desired satisfactions more effectively and efficiently than competitors do.

The **marketing concept** holds that achieving organizational goals depends on determining the needs and wants of target markets and delivering the desired satisfactions more effectively and efficiently than competitors do. The marketing concept has been stated in colorful ways such as "We make it happen for you" (Marriott); "To fly, to serve" (British Airways); and "We're not satisfied until you are" (GE). JCPenney's motto also summarizes the marketing concept: "To do all in our power to pack the customer's dollar full of value, quality, and satisfaction."

The selling concept and the marketing concept are sometimes confused. Figure 1-4 compares the two concepts. The selling concept takes an *inside-out* perspective. It starts with the factory, focuses on the company's existing products, and calls for heavy selling and promotion to obtain profitable sales. It focuses heavily on customer conquest—getting short-terms sales with little concern about who buys or why. In contrast, the marketing concept takes an *outside-in* perspective. It starts with a well-defined market, focuses on customer needs, coordinates all the marketing activities affecting customers, and makes profits by creating long-term customer relationships based on customer value and satisfaction. Under the marketing concept, companies produce what consumers want, thereby satisfying consumers and making profits.[13]

FIGURE 1-4 *The selling and marketing concepts contrasted*

Many successful and well-known companies have adopted the marketing concept. Procter & Gamble, Disney, Wal-Mart, Marriott, Nordstrom, and McDonald's follow it faithfully (see Marketing Highlight 1-3). L. L. Bean, the highly successful catalog retailer of clothing and outdoor sporting equipment, was founded on the marketing concept. In 1912, in his first circulars, L. L. Bean included the following notice: "I do not consider a sale complete until goods are worn out and the customer still is satisfied. We will thank anyone to return goods that are not perfectly satisfactory . . . Above all things we wish to avoid having a dissatisfied customer."

Today, L. L. Bean dedicates itself to giving "perfect satisfaction in every way." To inspire its employees to practice the marketing concept, L. L. Bean displays posters around its offices that proclaim the following:

> What is a customer? A customer is the most important person ever in this company—in person or by mail. A customer is not dependent on us, we are dependent on him. A customer is not an interruption of our work, he is the purpose of it. We are not doing a favor by serving him, he is doing us a favor by giving us the opportunity to do so. A customer is not someone to argue or match wits with—nobody ever won an argument with a customer. A customer is a person who brings us his wants—it is our job to handle them profitably to him and to ourselves.

In contrast, many companies claim to practice the marketing concept, but do not. They have the *forms* of marketing, such as a marketing vice-president, product managers, marketing plans, and marketing research, but this does not mean that they are *market-focused* and *customer-driven* companies. The question is whether they are finely tuned to changing customer needs and competitor strategies. Formerly great companies—General Motors, IBM, Sears, Zenith—all lost substantial market share because they failed to adjust their marketing strategies to the changing marketplace.

Several years of hard work are needed to turn a sales-oriented company into a marketing-oriented company. The goal is to build customer satisfaction into the very fabric of the firm. Customer satisfaction is no longer a fad. As one marketing analyst notes: "It's becoming a way of life in corporate America . . . as embedded into corporate cultures as information technology and strategic planning."[14]

McDonald's Applies the Marketing Concept

McDonald's Corporation, the fast-food hamburger retailer, is a master marketer. With 14,000 outlets in 73 countries and more than $23 billion in annual systemwide sales, McDonald's doubles the sales of its nearest rival, Burger King, and triples those of third-place Wendy's. Nineteen million customers pass through the famous golden arches each day, and an astounding 96 percent of all Americans eat at McDonald's each year. McDonald's now serves 145 hamburgers per second. Credit for this performance belongs to a strong marketing orientation: McDonald's knows how to serve people and adapt to changing consumer wants.

items, and opened new outlets in high-traffic areas.

Kroc's marketing philosophy is captured in McDonald's motto of "Q.S.C. & V.," which stands for quality, service, cleanliness, and value. Customers enter a spotlessly clean restaurant, walk up to a friendly counterperson, quickly receive a good-tasting meal, and eat it there or take it out. There are no jukeboxes or telephones to create a teenage hangout. Nor are there any cigarette machines or newspaper racks—McDonald's is a family affair, appealing strongly to children.

McDonald's has mastered the art of serving consumers, and it carefully teaches the basics to its employ-

service to local tastes and customs. It serves corn soup and teriaki burgers in Japan, pasta salads in Rome, and wine and live piano music with its McNuggets in Paris. When McDonald's opened its first restaurant in Moscow, it quickly won the hearts of Russian consumers. However, the company had to overcome some monstrous hurdles in order to meet its high standards for consumer satisfaction in this new market. It had to educate suppliers, employees, and even consumers about the time-tested, McDonald's way of doing things. Technical experts with special strains of disease-resistant seed were brought in from Canada to teach Russian farmers how to grow russet

McDonald's delivers "quality, service, cleanliness, and value" to customers around the world, here in the world's largest McDonald's in Beijing.

Before McDonald's appeared, Americans could get hamburgers in restaurants or diners. But consumers often encountered poor-quality hamburgers, slow and unfriendly service, unattractive decor, unclean conditions, and a noisy atmosphere. In 1955, Ray Kroc, a 52-year-old salesman of milkshake-mixing machines, became excited about a string of seven restaurants owned by Richard and Maurice McDonald. Kroc liked their fast-food restaurant concept and bought the chain for $2.7 million. He decided to expand the chain by selling franchises, and the number of restaurants grew rapidly. As times changed, so did McDonald's. It expanded its sit-down sections, improved the decor, launched a breakfast menu, added new food

ees and franchisees. All franchisees take training courses at McDonald's "Hamburger University" in Elk Grove Village, Illinois. They emerge with a degree in "Hamburgerology" and a minor in French fries. McDonald's monitors product and service quality through continuous customer surveys and puts great energy into improving hamburger production methods in order to simplify operations, bring down costs, speed up service, and bring greater value to customers. Beyond these efforts, each McDonald's restaurant works to become a part of its neighborhood through community involvement and service projects.

In its 2,700 restaurants outside of the United States, McDonald's carefully customizes its menu and

Burbank potatoes for French fries, and the company built its own pasteurizing plant to ensure a plentiful supply of fresh milk. It trained Russian managers at Hamburger University and subjected each of 630 new employees (most of whom didn't know a Chicken McNugget from an Egg McMuffin) to 16 to 20 hours of training on such essentials as cooking meat patties, assembling Filet-O-Fish sandwiches, and giving service with a smile. McDonald's even had to train consumers—most Muscovites had never seen a fast-food restaurant. Customers waiting in line were shown videos telling them everything from how to order and pay at the counter to how to handle a Big Mac. And in its usual way, McDonald's began immediately to build community involvement. On opening day, it held a kick-off party for 700 Muscovite orphans, and it donated all opening-day proceeds to the Moscow Children's Fund. As a result, the new Moscow restaurant got off to a very successful start. About 50,000 customers swarmed through the restaurant during its first day of business.

Riding on its success in Moscow, McDonald's continues to pursue opportunities to serve new customers around the globe. It recently opened its largest restaurant anywhere, in Beijing, China. The 28,000-square-foot restaurant has 29 cash registers and seats 700 people. Through this huge Beijing outlet, Mc-

Donald's expects to treat more than ten thousand customers each day to its special brand of customer care.

Thus, McDonald's focus on consumers has made it the world's largest food-service organization. It now captures about 20 percent of America's fast-food business and is rapidly expanding its worldwide presence. McDonald's has been the nation's most profitable retailer over the past ten years. The company's huge success has been reflected in the increased value of its stock over the years: 250 shares of McDonald's stock purchased for less than $6,000 in 1965 would be worth well over a million dollars today!

Sources: Gail McKnight, "Here Comes Bolshoi Mac," *USA Today Weekend,* January 26–28, 1990, pp. 4–5; Rosemarie Boyle, "McDonald's Gives Soviets Something Worth Waiting For," *Advertising Age,* March 19, 1990, p. 61; "Food Draws Raves, Prices Don't at Beijing McDonald's Opening," *Durham Herald-Sun,* April 12, 1992, p. B12; Marcia Berss, "Empty Tables," *Forbes,* December 6, 1993, pp. 232–233; and Jeanne Whalen, "McDonald's Shaking Marketing Agencies," *Advertising Age,* September 19, 1994, p. 4; and Andrew E. Serwer, "McDonald's Conquers the World," *Fortune,* October 17, 1994, pp. 103–16.

Societal marketing concept
The idea that the organization should determine the needs, wants, and interests of target markets and deliver the desired satisfactions more effectively and efficiently than competitors in a way that maintains or improves the consumer's and society's well-being.

However, the marketing concept does not mean that a company should try to give *all* consumers *everything* they want. Marketers must balance creating more value for customers against making profits for the company. The purpose of marketing is not to *maximize* customer satisfaction. As one marketing expert notes, "The shortest definition of marketing I know is 'meeting needs profitably.' The purpose of marketing is to generate customer value [at a profit]. The truth is [that the relationship with a customer] will break up if value evaporates. You've got to continue to generate more value for the consumer but not give away the house. It's a very delicate balance."[15]

The Societal Marketing Concept

The **societal marketing concept** holds that the organization should determine the needs, wants, and interests of target markets. It should then deliver superior value to customers in a way that maintains or improves the consumer's *and the society's* well-being. The societal marketing concept is the newest of the five marketing management philosophies.

The societal marketing concept questions whether the pure marketing concept is adequate in an age of environmental problems, resource shortages, rapid population growth, worldwide economic problems, and neglected social services.

FIGURE 1-5 *Three considerations underlying the societal marketing concept*

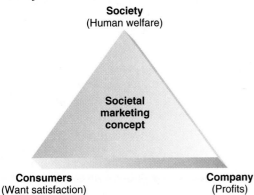

It asks if the firm that senses, serves, and satisfies individual wants is always doing what's best for consumers and society in the long run. According to the societal marketing concept, the pure marketing concept overlooks possible conflicts between consumer *short-run wants* and consumer *long-run welfare*.

Consider the Coca-Cola Company. Most people see it as a highly responsible corporation producing fine soft drinks that satisfy consumer tastes. Yet some consumer and environmental groups have voiced concerns that Coke has little nutritional value, can harm people's teeth, contains caffeine, and adds to the litter problem with disposable bottles and cans.

Such concerns and conflicts led to the societal marketing concept. As Figure 1-5 shows, the societal marketing concept

Our Credo

We believe our first responsibility is to the doctors, nurses and patients,
to mothers and fathers and all others who use our products and services.
In meeting their needs everything we do must be of high quality.
We must constantly strive to reduce our costs
in order to maintain reasonable prices.
Customers' orders must be serviced promptly and accurately.
Our suppliers and distributors must have an opportunity
to make a fair profit.

We are responsible to our employees,
the men and women who work with us throughout the world.
Everyone must be considered as an individual.
We must respect their dignity and recognize their merit.
They must have a sense of security in their jobs.
Compensation must be fair and adequate,
and working conditions clean, orderly and safe.
We must be mindful of ways to help our employees fulfill
their family responsibilities.
Employees must feel free to make suggestions and complaints.
There must be equal opportunity for employment, development
and advancement for those qualified.
We must provide competent management,
and their actions must be just and ethical.

We are responsible to the communities in which we live and work
and to the world community as well.
We must be good citizens — support good works and charities
and bear our fair share of taxes.
We must encourage civic improvements and better health and education.
We must maintain in good order
the property we are privileged to use,
protecting the environment and natural resources.

Our final responsibility is to our stockholders.
Business must make a sound profit.
We must experiment with new ideas.
Research must be carried on, innovative programs developed
and mistakes paid for.
New equipment must be purchased, new facilities provided
and new products launched.
Reserves must be created to provide for adverse times.
When we operate according to these principles,
the stockholders should realize a fair return.

Johnson & Johnson

Johnson & Johnson's concern for society is summarized in its credo and in the company's actions over the years. Says one J&J executive, "It's just plain good business."

calls upon marketers to balance three considerations in setting their marketing policies: company profits, consumer wants, and society's interests. Originally, most companies based their marketing decisions largely on short-run company profit. Eventually, they began to recognize the long-run importance of satisfying consumer wants, and the marketing concept emerged. Now many companies are beginning to think of society's interests when making their marketing decisions.

One such company is Johnson & Johnson, rated recently in a *Fortune* magazine poll as America's most admired company for community and environmental responsibility. J&J's concern for societal interests is summarized in a company document called "Our Credo," which stresses honesty, integrity, and putting people before profits. Under this credo, Johnson & Johnson would rather take a big loss than ship a bad batch of one of its products. And the company supports many community and employee programs that benefit its consumers and workers, and the environment. J&J's chief executive puts it this way: "If we keep trying to do what's right, at the end of the day we believe the marketplace will reward us."[16]

The company backs these words with actions. Consider the tragic tampering case in which eight people died from swallowing cyanide-laced capsules of Tylenol, a Johnson & Johnson brand. Although J&J believed that the pills had been altered in only a few stores, not in the factory, it quickly recalled all of its product. The recall cost the company $240 million in earnings. In the long run, however, the company's swift recall of Tylenol strengthened consumer confidence and loyalty, and Tylenol remains the nation's leading brand of pain reliever. In this and other cases, J&J management has found that doing what's right benefits both consumers and the company. Says the chief executive: "The Credo should not be viewed as some kind of social welfare program . . . it's just plain good business."[17] Thus, over the years, Johnson & Johnson's dedication to consumers and community service has made it one of America's most admired companies, *and* one of the most profitable.

MARKETING CHALLENGES INTO THE NEXT CENTURY

Marketing operates within a dynamic global environment. Every decade calls upon marketing managers to think freshly about their marketing objectives and practices. Rapid changes can quickly make yesterday's winning strategies out of date. As management thought-leader Peter Drucker once observed, a company's winning formula for the last decade will probably be its undoing in the next decade.

What are the marketing challenges as we head into the twenty-first century? Today's companies are wrestling with changing customer values and orientations; economic stagnation; environmental decline; increased global competition; and a host of other economic, political, and social problems. However, these problems also provide marketing opportunities. We now look more deeply into several key trends and forces that are changing the marketing landscape and challenging marketing strategy: growth of nonprofit marketing, rapid globalization, the changing world economy, and the call for more socially responsible actions.

GROWTH OF NONPROFIT MARKETING

In the past, marketing has been most widely applied in the business sector. In recent years, however, marketing also has become a major component in the strategies of many nonprofit organizations, such as colleges, hospitals, museums, symphonies, and even churches. Consider the following examples:

> As hospital costs and room rates soar, many hospitals face underutilization, especially in their maternity and pediatrics sections. Many have taken steps toward marketing. A Philadelphia hospital, competing for maternity patients, offered a steak and champagne dinner with candlelight for new parents. St. Mary's Medical Center in Evanston, Indiana, uses innovative billboards to promote its emergency care service. Other hospitals, in an effort to attract physicians, have installed services such as saunas, chauffeurs, and private tennis courts.[18]
>
> Before even opening its doors, one new church hired a research firm to find out what its customers would want. The research showed that "unchurched"—people with no current church connection—found church boring and church services irrelevant to their everyday lives. They complained churches were always hitting them up for money. So the church added contemporary music and skits, loosened its dress codes, and presented sermons on topics such as money management and parenting. Its direct mail piece read: "Given up on the church? We don't blame you. Lots of people have. They're fed up with boring sermons, ritual that doesn't mean anything . . . music that nobody likes . . . [and] preachers who seem to be more interested in your wallet than you . . . . Church can be different. Give us a shot." The results have been impressive. Since opening its doors a little more than a year ago, the church has attracted nearly 400 members, 80 percent of whom were not previously attending church.[19]

Similarly, many private colleges, facing declining enrollments and rising costs, are using marketing to compete for students and funds. They are defining target markets, improving their communication and promotion, and responding better to student needs and wants. Many of America's 300,000 churches, having trouble keeping members and attracting financial support, are conducting marketing research to gain a better understanding of member needs, and are redesigning their "service offerings" accordingly. Many performing arts groups—even the Lyric Opera Company of Chicago, which has seasonal sellouts—face huge operating deficits that they must cover by more aggressive donor marketing. Finally, many longstanding nonprofit organizations—the YMCA, the Salvation Army, the Girl Scouts—have lost members and are now modernizing their missions and "products" to attract more members and donors.[20]

Even government agencies have shown an increased interest in marketing. For example, the U.S. Army has a marketing plan to attract recruits, and various government agencies are now designing *social marketing campaigns* to encourage energy conservation and concern for the environment, or to discourage smoking, excessive drinking, and drug use. The once-stodgy U.S. Postal Service has developed innovative marketing plans. For example, in one nationwide campaign, the postal service worked to gain support for the U.S. Olympic team:

> An official Olympic sponsor, the postal service launched a promotion designed to shower Olympic athletes with cards and to raise money for the team. It sponsored Olympic Spirit Week at 28,000 post offices around the nation, where it invited customers to sign a piece of the "world's largest postcard," a 348 foot by 523 foot giant that said "America Salutes Team USA." Customers who

TAKING ADVANTAGE OF GLOBAL OPPORTUNITIES

Many U.S. companies are moving aggressively to take advantage of global marketing opportunities. Here are just three examples.

Although Coca-Cola Classic captures 20 percent of the U.S. soft-drink market, the U.S. cola market has shrunk from 64 percent of all soft-drink sales in 1984 to only 59 percent now. To

example, in the first six months of 1994 alone, the company opened plants or re-entered markets in seven countries, including Russia, Poland, India, South Africa, and Vietnam.

Coca-Cola is revving up every aspect of its global marketing—cutting-edge advertising, new packaging, product sampling, and event sponsorships. It has treated the entire world to its innovative "Always Coca-Cola" advertising campaign, featuring everything from star-gazing polar bears to punk rockers. The company successfully resurrected the classic contour Coke bottle—the world's best-known package. Coke also revived another classic marketing practice—consumer sampling. This summer, it gave away thousands of gallons of free Coke to German consumers. As a result of these and other actions, Coke's third-quarter worldwide sales grew at an eye-popping rate of 12 percent, more than twice the growth rate of domestic sales.

Toys 'Я' Us
Toys 'Я' Us spent several years slogging through the swamps of Japanese bureaucracy before it was

Companies like Coca-Cola are moving aggressively to take advantage of global growth opportunities.

Coca-Cola
Coca-Cola has recently watched the domestic cola market go flat.

counter slow growth at home, Coca-Cola has expanded its international operations at a furious pace. For

---

donated a dollar received two regular-size copies of the card. They were encouraged to send one copy to an Olympic athlete and keep the other as a souvenir. The postal service planned to spend about $100 million on Olympic sponsorship but expected a net profit of about $50 million through increased sales of postal products.[21]

The continued growth of nonprofit and public sector marketing presents new and exciting challenges for marketing managers.

RAPID GLOBALIZATION

The world economy has undergone radical change during the past two decades. Geographical and cultural distances have shrunk with the advent of jet planes, fax machines, global computer and telephone hookups, world television satellite broadcasts, and other technical advances. This has allowed companies to greatly expand their geographical market coverage, purchasing, and manufacturing. The result is a vastly more complex marketing environment, for both companies and consumers.

Today, almost every company, large or small, is touched in some way by global competition—from the neighborhood florist that buys its flowers from Mexican nurseries, to the small New York clothing retailer that sources its merchandise in Asia, to the U.S. electronics manufacturer competing in its home markets with giant Japanese rivals, to the large American consumer goods producer introducing new products into emerging markets abroad.

allowed to open the very first large U.S. discount store in Japan, the world's No. 2 toy market behind the United States. The entry of this foreign giant has Japanese toymakers and retailers edgy. The typical small Japanese toy store stocks only 1,000 to 2,000 items, whereas Toys 'Я' Us stores carry as many as 15,000. And the discounter will likely offer toys at prices 10 percent to 15 percent below those of competitors.

The opening of the first Japanese store was "astonishing," attracting more than 60,000 visitors in the first three days. After just two years, Toys 'Я' Us now has 16 Japanese stores, each drawing huge crowds and grabbing a 4 percent share of the market. Within two more years, it plans to have 35 stores and a 10 percent market share. The U.S. retailer appears to be benefiting from profound social change in Japan. According to one source, "Japan's absentee, workaholic salaryman father is increasingly becoming a relic, and his successor is taking life easier, spending more time with his family. Japanese families now spend more time together. . . . On Sunday they . . . go

out to lunch and then browse at a big store like Toys 'Я' Us. . . . Toys 'Я' Us has made shopping a form of leisure in Japan."

If the company succeeds in Japan as well as it has in Europe, Japanese retailers will have their hands full. Toys 'Я' Us began with just five European stores in 1985 but now has 76 and more opening. European sales, now about $800 million, are growing at triple the rate of total company sales.

MTV

After ten years of relentless growth in America, Music Television's (MTV) home market has become saturated. However, the U.S. music video network is exploding abroad. For example, it's a monster hit in Europe. Set up in 1990, MTV Europe now reaches 27 countries and 59 million homes, almost a million more than U.S. MTV.

The network is aggressively pan-European—its programming and advertising are the same throughout Europe, and they are all in English. It has almost single-handedly created a Euro-language of simplified English. MTV meets the common concerns of

teens worldwide, broadcasting news and socially conscious programing such as features on the plight of European immigrants and notes on global warming. MTV Europe has convinced advertisers that a true "Euroconsumer" exists. It delivers advertising from companies such as Levi Strauss, Procter & Gamble, Apple Computer, and Pepsi-Cola to a huge international audience. The company also operates MTV Asia, MTV Latino, and MTV Japan. In all, MTV reaches more than 240 million homes in 63 territories around the world.

Sources: Quote from Gale Eisenstodt, "Bull in the Japan Shop," *Forbes,* January 31, 1994, pp. 41–42. Also see Patricia Kranz, "Roll Over, Lenin: The Cola Wars Hit Russia," *Business Week,* May 16, 1994, p. 6; Claudia Penteado, "Pepsi Challenges Coke in Brazil," *Advertising Age,* January 16, 1995, p. 12.; Maria Mallory, "Behemoth on a Tear," *Business Week,* October 3, 1994; Kevin Cote, "Toys 'Я' Us Grows in Europe," *Advertising Age,* April 27, 1992, p. 1–16; "MTV: Rock On," *The Economist,* August 3, 1991, p. 66; and Shawn Tully, "Teens: The Most Global Market of All," *Fortune,* May 16, 1994, pp. 90–97.

American firms have been challenged at home by the skillful marketing of European and Asian multinationals. Companies like Toyota, Siemens, Nestlé, Sony, and Samsung often have outperformed their U.S. competitors in American markets. Similarly, U.S. companies in a wide range of industries have found new opportunities abroad. General Motors, Exxon, IBM, General Electric, Du Pont, Motorola, Coca-Cola, and dozens of other American companies have developed truly global operations, making and selling their products worldwide. Marketing Highlight 1-4 provides just a few of countless examples of U.S. companies taking advantage of international marketing opportunities.

Today, companies are not only trying to sell more of their locally produced goods in international markets, they also are buying more components and supplies abroad. For example, Bill Blass, one of America's top fashion designers, may choose cloth woven from Australian wool with printed designs from Italy. He will design a dress and fax the drawing to a Hong Kong agent who will place the order with a mainland China factory. Finished dresses will be airfreighted to New York, where they will be redistributed to department and specialty stores around the country.

Many domestically purchased goods and services are "hybrids," with design, materials purchases, manufacturing, and marketing taking place in several countries. Americans who decide to "buy American" might reasonably decide to avoid Hondas and purchase Dodge Colts. Imagine their surprise when they learn that the Colt actually was made in Japan, whereas the Honda was primarily assembled in the United States from American-made parts.

Thus, managers in countries around the world are asking: Just what is global marketing? How does it differ from domestic marketing? How do global competitors and forces affect our business? To what extent should we "go global"? Many companies are forming strategic alliances with foreign companies, even competitors, who serve as suppliers or marketing partners. The past few years have produced some surprising alliances between competitors such as Ford and Mazda, General Electric and Matsushita, and AT&T and Olivetti. Winning companies in the next century may well be those that have built the best global networks.[22]

THE CHANGING WORLD ECONOMY

A large part of the world has grown poorer during the past few decades. A sluggish world economy has resulted in more difficult times for both consumers and marketers. Around the world, people's needs are greater than ever, but in many areas, people lack the means to pay for needed goods. Markets, after all, consist of people with needs *and* purchasing power. In many cases, the latter is currently lacking. In the United States, although wages have risen, real buying power has declined, especially for the less-skilled members of the work force. Many U.S. households have managed to maintain their buying power only because both spouses work. However, many workers have lost their jobs as manufacturers have "downsized" to cut costs.

Current economic conditions create both problems and opportunities for marketers. Some companies are facing declining demand and see few opportunities for growth. Others, however, are developing new solutions to changing consumer problems. Many are finding ways to offer consumers "more for less." Wal-Mart rose to market leadership on two principles, emblazoned on every Wal-Mart store: "Satisfaction Guaranteed" and "We Sell for Less—Always." Consumers enter a Wal-Mart store, are welcomed by a friendly greeter, and find a huge assortment of good-quality merchandise at everyday low prices. The same principle explains the explosive growth of factory outlet malls and discount chains—these days, customers want value. This even applies to luxury products: Toyota introduced its successful Lexus luxury automobile with the headline "Perhaps the First Time in History that Trading a $72,000 Car for a $36,000 Car Could Be Considered Trading Up."

THE CALL FOR MORE ETHICS AND SOCIAL RESPONSIBILITY

A third factor in today's marketing environment is the increased call for companies to take responsibility for the social and environmental impact of their actions. Corporate ethics has become a hot topic in almost every business arena, from the corporate boardroom to the business school classroom. And few companies can ignore the renewed and very demanding environmental movement.

The ethics and environmental movements will place even stricter demands on companies in the future. Consider recent environmental developments. After the fall of communism the West was shocked to find out about the massive environmental negligence of the former Eastern Bloc governments. In many Eastern European countries, the air is fouled, the water is polluted, and the soil is poisoned by chemical dumping. In June 1992, representatives from more than one hundred countries attended the Earth Summit in Rio de Janeiro to consider how to handle such problems as the destruction of rain forests, global warming, endangered species, and other environmental threats. Clearly, in the future, companies will be held to an increasingly higher standard of environmental responsibility in their marketing and manufacturing activities.

Today's forward-thinking companies are responding strongly to the ethics and environmental movements. Here, ITT states "All of our companies share a common goal: To improve the quality of life. Because it's not just how you make a living that's important, it's how you live."

THE NEW MARKETING LANDSCAPE

The past decade taught business firms everywhere a humbling lesson. Domestic companies learned that they can no longer ignore global markets and competitors. Successful firms in mature industries learned that they cannot overlook emerging markets, technologies, and management approaches. Companies of every sort learned that they cannot remain inwardly focused, ignoring the needs of customers and their environment.

The most powerful U.S. companies of the 1970s included General Motors, Sears, and RCA. But all three of these giant companies failed at marketing, and today, all three are struggling. Each failed to understand its changing marketplace, its customers, and the need to provide value. Today, General Motors is still trying to figure out why so many consumers around the world switched to Japanese and European cars. Mighty Sears has lost its way, losing share both to fashionable department and specialty stores on the one hand, and to discount mass merchandisers on the other. RCA, inventor of so many new products, never quite mastered the art of marketing and now puts its name on products largely imported from Asia.

As we move into the next century, companies will have to become customer oriented and market driven in all that they do. It's not enough to be product or technology driven—too many companies still design their products without customer input, only to find them rejected in the marketplace. It's not enough to be good at winning new customers—too many companies forget about customers after the sale, only to lose their future business. Not surprisingly, we are now seeing a flood of books with titles such as *The Customer Driven Company, Keep the Customer, Customers for Life, Total Customer Service: The Ultimate Weapon,* and *The Only Thing that Matters: Bringing the Customer into the Center of Your Business.*[23] These books emphasize that the key to success on the rapidly changing marketing landscape will be a strong focus on the marketplace and a total marketing commitment to providing value to customers.

Summary

Although many factors contribute to business success, today's successful companies share a strong customer focus and a heavy commitment to marketing. *Marketing* is a social and managerial process by which individuals and groups obtain what they need and want through creating and exchanging products and value with others. Underlying marketing is the fundamental concept of human *need*, which is a state of felt deprivation. A basic need is shaped by culture and personality into a human *want*. This want, when backed by buying power, becomes a *demand*.

Marketers address these demands by creating appropriate *products* and services. These products satisfy needs and wants by offering customer *value*, the customer's perception of the difference between the benefits of owning and using the product and what it costs to obtain it. If the product offers good value, it will create customer *satisfaction*. The complex idea of quality is closely tied to satisfaction. *Quality* means not only freedom from defects, but also that the product offers the satisfaction which the customer seeks.

Marketing occurs when people decide to satisfy needs and wants through a process of *exchange*. When values are actually traded between two parties, a *transaction* occurs. If a series of transactions occurs between the same parties, a long-term *relationship* develops. Developing such a relationship with customers through strong social and economic ties has become an important goal for many marketers.

Marketing management is the process by which marketers achieve their organizational objectives. The core of this process is managing the level, timing, and composition of *demand* by retaining current customers and attracting new ones. This is accomplished by developing marketing programs for the target market through a process of analysis, planning, implementation, and control. When properly done, this will result in long-term *profitable customer relationships*.

Marketing management can be guided by five different philosophies. The *production concept* is based on the idea that low cost is of the highest importance, and the task of management is to concentrate on production volume and efficiency to bring down costs and prices. The *product concept* holds that consumers favor quality products, and that if products are good enough little promotional effort will be required. The *selling concept* assumes that heavy selling and promotional efforts are needed to stimulate adequate demand for the product. The *marketing concept* holds that a company gains competitive advantage by understanding the needs and wants of a clearly defined target market, and using this understanding to do a superior job of delivering satisfaction to these customers. The *societal marketing concept* expands on the marketing concept by stressing that a company should seek to generate customer goodwill, but must also enhance long-term societal well-being.

Marketing operates within a dynamic global environment, and is facing new challenges as we approach the turn of the century. The success of the marketing concept is now widely understood, spurring *growth in nonprofit marketing* as these organizations begin using the tools and techniques of marketing management. The environment is changing as well, with almost every company being affected by *rapid globalization*. The *changing world economy*, which has been sluggish for a long period of time, has resulted in more difficult times for both consumers and marketers. These challenges are intensified by a demand that marketers conduct all of their business with an emphasis on *more ethics* and *social responsibility*. Taken together, these changes define *a new marketing landscape*. Companies that succeed in this environment will have a strong focus on the changing marketplace and a total commitment to using the tools of marketing to provide real value to customers.

Key Terms

Customer value	Demarketing	Marketing
Customer satisfaction	Exchange	Marketing concept
Demands	Market	Marketing management

Needs	Relationship marketing	Total quality management
Product	Selling concept	Transaction
Product concept	Societal marketing concept	Wants
Production concept		

Discussing the Issues

1. Discuss why *you* should study marketing.

2. Historian Arnold Toynbee and economist John Kenneth Galbraith have argued that the desires stimulated by marketing efforts are not genuine: "A man who is hungry need never be told of his need for food." Decide whether this is a valid criticism of marketing. Explain why or why not.

3. Many people dislike or fear certain products and would not "demand" them at any price. Can you suggest ways that a health-care marketer might manage the *negative* demand for such products as colon cancer screenings?

4. Changes in the world's political structure and balance of power are leading to smaller U.S. military budgets. Before these changes were made, defense contractors followed the product concept and focused on high technology. Based on your analysis, do you think that military suppliers now need to change to the marketing concept? Identify who their customers are.

5. Identify the single biggest difference between the marketing concept and the production, product, and selling concepts. Discuss which concepts are easiest to apply in the short run. Predict which concept you believe can offer the best long-term success.

6. According to economist Milton Friedman, "Few trends could so thoroughly undermine the very foundations of our free society as the acceptance by corporate officials of a social responsibility other than to make as much money for their stockholders as possible." Do you agree or disagree with Friedman's statement? What are some drawbacks of the societal marketing concept?

Applying the Concepts

1. Go to McDonald's and order a sandwich. Note the questions you are asked, and observe how special orders are handled. Next, go to Wendy's, Burger King, or a local pizza restaurant and order a sandwich or a pizza. Note the questions you are asked here, and observe whether special orders are handled the same way as they are at McDonald's.
   ◆ Did you observe any significant differences in how orders are handled?
   ◆ Consider the differences you saw. Do you think the restaurants have different marketing management philosophies? Which is closest to the marketing concept? Is one closer to the selling or production concept?
   ◆ What are the advantages of closely following the marketing concept? Are there any disadvantages?

2. Take a trip to your local mall. Find the directory sign. List five major categories of stores, such as department stores, shoe, book, and women's clothing shops, and restaurants. List the competing stores in each category, and take a walk past them and quickly observe their merchandise and style. Take a look at the public spaces of the mall, and note how they are decorated. Watch the shoppers in the mall.
   ◆ Are the competing stores really unique, or could one pretty much substitute for another?
   ◆ Did the shoppers efficiently buy items from a shopping list, as in a grocery store, or were they taking a different approach?
   ◆ Four basic goals for the marketing system have been suggested: maximizing consumption, consumer satisfaction, choice, or quality of life. Discuss whether you think the mall serves some of these goals better than others.

References

1. Quotes in this Home Depot tale are from Patricia Sellers, "Companies That Serve You Best," *Fortune*, May 31, 1993, pp. 74–88. Also see Shirley A. Lazo, "Speaking of Dividends," *Barron's*, June 7, 1993, p. 59; Leslie Bayor, "Blank Fills Out the Niche for Home Depot Growth," *Advertising Age*, February 1, 1993, p. S5; and Graham Button, "The Man Who Almost Walked Out on Ross Perot," *Forbes*, November 22, 1993, pp. 68–76.

2. Patricia Sellers, "Companies That Serve You Best," p. 88.

3. Peter F. Drucker, *Management: Tasks, Responsibilities, Practices* (New York: Harper & Row, 1973), pp. 64–65.

4. See P. Ranganath Nayak, Albert C. Chen, and James F. Reider, "Listening to Customers," *Prism*, Arthur D. Little, Inc., Second Quarter, 1993, pp. 43–57.

5. See Theodore Levitt's classic article, "Marketing Myopia," *Harvard Business Review*, July–August 1960, pp. 45–56.

6. See "Pass the Parcel," *The Economist*, March 21, 1992, pp. 73–74; "ATW Awards 20 Years of Excellence in Cargo Service: Federal Express," *Air Transport World*, February 1994, pp. 48–52; and Michel Syrett, "Questions of Quality," *Asian Business*, March 1994, pp. 34–37.

7. Lois Therrien, "Motorola and NEC: Going for Glory," *Business Week*, special issue on quality, 1991, pp. 60–61.

8. For more discussion on demand states, see Philip Kotler, *Marketing Management: Analysis, Planning, Implementation, and Control* (Englewood Cliffs, NJ: Prentice Hall, 1994), pp. 14–15.

9. See Joan C. Szabo, "Service=Survival," *Nation's Business*, March 1989, pp. 16–24; and Kevin J. Clancy and Robert S. Shulman, "Breaking the Mold," *Sales & Marketing Management*, January 1994, pp. 82–84.

10. Patricia Sellers, "Companies That Serve You Best," pp. 74–88.

11. Ralph Waldo Emerson offered this advice: "If a man . . . makes a better mousetrap . . . the world will beat a path to his door." Several companies, however, have built better mousetraps and failed. One was a laser mousetrap costing $1,500. Contrary to popular assumptions, people do not automatically learn about new products, believe product claims, or willingly pay higher prices.

12. Barry Farber and Joyce Wycoff, "Customer Service: Evolution and Revolution," *Sales & Marketing Management*, May 1991, p. 47.

13. See Don E. Schultz, "Traditional Marketers Have Become Obsolete," *Marketing News*, June 6, 1994, p. 11.

14. Howard Schlossberg, "Customer Satisfaction: Not a Fad, but a Way of Life," *Marketing News*, June 10, 1991, p. 18. Also see Bernard J. Jaworski and Ajay K. Kohli, "Market Orientation: Antecedents and Consequences," *Journal of Marketing*, July 1993, pp. 53–70.

15. Thomas E. Caruso, "Kotler: Future Marketers Will Focus on Customer Data Base to Compete Globally," *Marketing News*, June 8, 1992, pp. 21–22.

16. See "Leaders of the Most Admired," *Fortune*, January 29, 1990, pp. 40–54.

17. Ibid., p. 54.

18. For other examples, and for a good review of nonprofit marketing, see Philip Kotler and Alan R. Andreasen, *Strategic Marketing for Nonprofit Organizations* (Englewood Cliffs, NJ: Prentice Hall, 1991).

19. See Cyndee Miller, "Churches Turn to Research for Help in Saving New Souls," *Marketing News*, April 11, 1994, pp. 1, 2.

20. For more examples, see Philip Kotler and Karen Fox, *Strategic Marketing for Educational Institutions* (Englewood Cliffs, NJ: Prentice Hall, 1985); Bradley G. Morrison and Julie Gordon Dalgleish, *Waiting in the Wings: A Larger Audience for the Arts and How to Develop It* (New York: ACA Books, 1987); and Norman Shawchuck, Philip Kotler, Bruce Wren, and Gustave Rath, *Marketing for Congregations: Choosing to Serve People More Effectively* (Nashville, TN: Abingdon Press, 1993); and Cyndee Miller, "Churches Turn to Research for Help in Saving New Souls," *Marketing News*, April 11, 1994, pp. 1, 2.

21. Christy Fisher, "Postal Service Plans First-Class Promotion," *Advertising Age*, April 6, 1992, p. 26. Also see Cyndee Miller, "U.S. Postal Service Discovers the Merits of Marketing," *Marketing News*, February 1, 1993, pp. 9, 18.

22. For more on strategic alliances, see Jordan D. Lewis, *Partnerships for Profit: Structuring and Managing Strategic Alliances* (New York: The Free Press, 1990); Peter Lorange and Johan Roos, *Strategic Alliances: Formation, Implementation, and Evolution* (Cambridge, MA: Blackwell Publishers, 1992); and Frederick E. Webster, Jr., "The Changing Role of Marketing in the Corporation," *Journal of Marketing*, October 1992, pp. 1–17.

23. Richard C. Whitely, *The Customer Driven Company* (Reading, MA: Addison-Wesley, 1991); Robert L. Desanick, *Keep the Customer* (Boston: Houghton Mifflin Co., 1990); Charles Sewell, *Customers for Life: How to Turn the One-Time Buyer into a Lifetime Customer* (New York: Pocket Books, 1990); William H. Davidow and Bro Uttal, *Total Customer Service: The Ultimate Weapon* (New York: Harper & Row, 1989); and Karl Albrecht, *The Only Thing that Matters: Bringing the Customer into the Center of Your Business* (New York: Harper Business, 1992).

Company Case 1

DOORGUARD: TRYING TO MAKE A DENT IN THE MARKET

"Hey, Steven!"

Steven Harris looked up to see Todd Smith striding across the student parking lot at the University of South Carolina.

"Hello, Todd!" Steven responded as he finished locking his car door.

"Wow! Is this your car?" asked Todd, admiring the new red Mustang convertible.

"You've got it. That's one reason my summer was so good. This was the third year that I've worked with my brother's yard maintenance service in Myrtle Beach. Not only did I have a good time, but with the money I saved from the three summers I was able to buy this car."

"I'm impressed. I notice you parked way out here away from any other cars."

"You bet. It didn't make much difference with my old Chevy, but I sure don't want thoughtless people denting the sides of my new car. People really dented the sides of my old car, especially in these student parking lots with their narrow spaces."

"You know," added Todd, "there ought to be a law against banging doors into other people's cars. Or someone should come up with some way to protect car doors. Those rubber strips that manufacturers put on never seem to be in the right place."

"I agree," replied Steven, "or maybe cars should have a device that automatically dents the other car in return. Maybe that would make people more careful!"

Steven and Todd both laughed at the thought of such a device and began to dream up other wild ideas to solve the problem as they walked toward the registrar's office.

Over the next several days, Steven found himself thinking more and more about the problem of preventing side-panel damage. He had always been a tinkerer, and he had fairly well-developed mechanical instincts. With the job outlook for college graduates in the doldrums, an entrepreneurial venture began to look attractive.

Steven remembered one of his professors discussing the success of the people who had launched AutoShades, the cardboard panels used behind auto windshields to keep cars cool. AutoShades' inventors had succeeded because their product really worked. Further, because they could print on the panels, companies could use the product as a sales-promotion tool. Steven believed that if he could design a device to protect car doors that also served an advertising function, he too

could be successful. He began to think more seriously about developing such a product.

THE PRODUCT

Steven mentioned his project to a friend, a recent graduate with a degree in mechanical engineering. The engineer suggested a panel, perhaps made of rubber, that would attach to the outside of the car door. The panel would have to be lightweight, impact resistant, and waterproof.

After talking to numerous suppliers of resilient materials and visiting several trade shows, Steven found a unique foam that showed promise. Manufactured by a local firm, MiniCell 200 (M200) was lightweight, impact absorbent, and relatively thin (½ inch). The driver could roll it up for easy storage. M200 also had several drawbacks, however. It was expensive, could not be exposed to sunlight, and tore easily.

Steven thought he could resolve the problems by finding a fabric cover for the foam. He experimented with a material that had a sunlight blocker and high tear resistance, and came in a variety of colors. However, the material did not readily accept screen printing, an attribute that Steven believed to be necessary for the project's success. Steven discussed this problem with the manufacturer. Several weeks later, the manufacturer had developed a new way to treat the material so that it accepted printing.

Having worked his way through the cover-material issue, Steven began experimenting with methods for attaching the panel to a car. He knew ease of use would be critical to his product's success, as it had been for AutoShades. Steven finally decided to use magnets, which could be easily attached to the foam, making the product easy to use.

Steven also spent an entire afternoon selecting a name for the product. He evaluated several names, such as DoorGuard, DDent, DentGuard, AbsorbaDoor, and DoorMate. On pure instinct, he chose DoorGuard.

Steven now had a name, but he realized that he still did not have a complete product. If he used only the magnets to attach the product to a door, what would prevent someone from stealing the panels? After trying several unsuccessful theft-prevention ideas, Steven settled on a cable that attached to the foam panel. After attaching the DoorGuard panel to the door, the user would toss the other end of the cable inside the car, then close and lock the door. Anyone who tried to steal the device would tear the panel, making it useless.

Steven believed he had now developed the perfect product. It absorbed impact from other car doors, resisted theft and water damage, stored easily in the trunk or back seat, and accepted screen printing. Exhibit 1-1 illustrates a DoorGuard panel in use.

EXHIBIT 1-1   *Illustration of DoorGuard in Use*

Steven next turned his attention to producing the new product. He knew that he did not have the time, experience, and money to make the product himself. As a result, he approached organizations like Jobs for the Handicapped and Goodwill Industries that might assemble products inexpensively. He eventually found an organization that could do everything needed to assemble and print one set of two panels.

Almost as an afterthought, Steven considered price. Based on a total cost of $14.74 per complete set of two panels, Steven used a 100 percent markup on cost (and a little psychological pricing) to arrive at a suggested retail price of $29.95 per set (See Exhibit 1-2). Now that he had designed, named, and priced the product, Steven considered what market he would attack.

EXHIBIT 1-2   *DoorGuard Cost/Price*

Cost per panel		
M200 ½" 1′ × 4′ Panel	$ 2.90	
Cover Material 1½ sq. yds.	1.12	
Magnets 3′	.90	
Cable 3′	.45	
Misc. (screen print, packaging)	.50	
Assembly	1.50	
Total Cost per Panel	7.37	
Cost per set of two panels	$14.74	
Retail price per set*	$29.95	

*100 percent markup on cost

THE MARKET

Steven knew that he should research the market potential, but believed that he had little basis for developing a reasonable estimate of DoorGuard's sales potential. Us-

ing secondary sources, he found that there were 122.8 million cars in use in the United States. Nearly 80 percent of these cars were at least three years old; 50 percent were at least six years old. Because there were no products comparable to DoorGuard on the market, Steven wasn't certain what portion of the car owners would purchase the new product. AutoShades appeared to be about the only close comparison, but there was a huge cost difference: AutoShades cost from $1.49 to $6.00, whereas DoorGuard would cost nearly $30.00. Many companies gave away sun shades as advertising specialties; few companies would do the same with DoorGuard.

Still, Steven believed that DoorGuard targeted a wide-open market. He knew that last year's new car sales in the United States totaled 9,853,000. Few new-car buyers purchased factory-installed body-protection packages. Steven felt that a person paying $15,000 or more for a car would pay a reasonable price to protect it. This helped to explain the success of AutoShades. Sales had started slowly for the initial sun shade—a piece of plain cardboard. But once the creators added graphics and messages to their products, AutoShades' sales heated up. Sales exceeded $20 million one year.

Steven dreamed about such spectacular sales results for DoorGuard. If he could capture just 5 percent of the new-car market, he would be selling nearly 500,000 sets. And sales to only 5 percent of the owners of the 122,800,000 cars on the road would generate sales of more than 6,100,000 DoorGuard sets. With such heady potential in mind, Steven began to think through the details of introducing DoorGuard.

THE MARKETING APPROACH

Steven considered three different approaches for distributing the product. First, Steven thought that he might interest a national retail chain, such as Sears or Kmart, in carrying the product—both had large auto-supply departments. When he considered catalog sales, two catalog companies came to mind as potential distributors—Sharper Image and Brookstone. These catalogs reached people who could afford to purchase DoorGuard. Finally, Steven considered selling direct to large companies such as R. J. Reynolds or Anheuser-Busch who could offer the product as an advertising specialty or premium item. Steven wondered which of these distribution avenues would be best, or if he should consider others.

When Steven returned from class late one Thursday afternoon, he felt tired but excited. With the pressures and costs of his senior year, Steven's time and resources were scarce. Despite all of his development work, DoorGuard was still just an idea. He realized that he had no concrete notion about how to proceed. He knew that DoorGuard could be a great product but now realized how complicated it would be to take the idea to the market. He pulled out his yellow legal pad and started a new list of things he needed to do on the project. He glanced out the window at his new car, parked in the far corner of the parking lot. Steven smiled to himself. "Still no dents," he thought, "and I'm going to keep it that way."

QUESTIONS

1. What consumer needs and wants does DoorGuard satisfy?

2. Which of the marketing management philosophies discussed in the text is Steven Harris following?

3. If, as the text indicates, a market is "the set of actual and potential buyers of a product," what market does Steven wish to serve with Door-Guard?

4. What problems does Steven face? Has he forgotten to consider anything?

5. What recommendations would you make to Steven Harris? How can he adopt the marketing concept? What items should he put on his marketing "to-do" list?

Source: Adapted from "DoorMate: A New Product Venture" by Thomas H. Stevenson, University of North Carolina at Charlotte. Used with permission of the North American Case Research Association and Professor Stevenson.

Strategic Planning and the Marketing Process

Invented in 1850 by Levi Strauss, a Bavarian immigrant who sold canvas pants to California gold seekers, blue jeans have long been an institution in American life. And Levi Strauss & Co. has long dominated the jeans industry. From the 1950s through the 1970s, as the baby boom caused an explosion in the number of young people, selling jeans was easy. Levi Strauss concentrated on simply trying to make enough jeans to satisfy a seemingly insatiable market. However, by the early 1980s, the baby boomers were aging and their tastes were changing with their waistlines—they bought fewer jeans and wore them longer. Meanwhile, the 18- to 24-year-old segment, the group traditionally most likely to buy jeans, was shrinking. Thus, Levi Strauss found itself fighting for a share in a fading jeans market.

At first, despite the declining market, Levi Strauss & Co. stuck closely to its basic jeans business. It sought growth by substantially increasing its advertising and selling through national retailers like Sears and JC Penney. When these tactics failed, Levi Strauss tried diversification into faster-growing fashion and specialty apparel businesses. It hastily had added more than 75 new lines, including high fashions, sportswear, and athletic wear. By 1984, Levi Strauss had diversified into a muddled array of businesses ranging from its true blue jeans to men's hats, skiwear, running suits, and even women's polyester pants and denim maternity wear. The results were disastrous: Profits plunged by 79 percent in just one year.

In 1985, in an effort to turn around an ailing Levi Strauss & Co., new management implemented a bold new strategic plan. It sold most of the ill-fated fashion and specialty apparel businesses and took the company back to what it had always done best—making and selling jeans. For starters, Levi rejuvenated its flagship product, the basic button-fly, shrink-to-fit 501 jeans. It invested $38 million in the now-classic "501 blues" advertising campaign, a series of hip, documentary-style "reality ads." Never before had a company spent so much on a single item of clothing. At the time, many analysts questioned this strategy. As one put it, "That's just too much to spend on one lousy pair of jeans." However, the 501 blues campaign spoke

OBJECTIVES

When you finish this chapter, you should be able to accomplish the following:

1. Explain strategic planning, and discuss how it relates to the **company mission, objectives,** and **goals**.

2. Identify and define methods for **designing the business portfolio, developing growth strategies,** and **planning functional strategies**.

3. Outline **the marketing process,** explaining the concepts of **target consumers,** using **marketing strategies for competitive advantage,** and **developing the marketing mix**.

4. List the elements involved in **managing the marketing effort,** including **marketing analysis,** the key elements of **the marketing plan,** and the primary tasks of **marketing implementation and control**.

for all of the company's products. It reminded consumers of Levi Strauss's strong tradition and refocused the company on its basic, blue jeans heritage. During the next four years, the campaign would more than double the sales of 501s.

Building on this solid-blue base, Levi Strauss began to add new products. For example, it successfully added prewashed, stone washed, and brightly colored jeans to its basic line. In late 1986, Levi Strauss introduced Dockers, casual and comfortable cotton pants targeted toward the aging male baby boomers. A natural extension of the jeans business, the new line had even broader appeal than anticipated. Not only did adults buy Dockers, so did their children. It seems that every American adolescent boy needed at least one pair of casual cotton pants dressy enough to wear when meeting his girlfriend's parents. In the decade since its introduction, the Dockers line has become a one-billion-dollar-a-year success. Levi Strauss has continued to develop new products for the aging boomers, such as loose-fitting jeans for men who've outgrown the company's slimmer-cut 501s.

In addition to introducing new products, Levi Strauss & Co. also stepped up its efforts to develop new markets. In 1991, for example, it developed a jeans advertising campaign designed especially for women and launched an innovative three-year, $12 million "Jeans for Women" advertising campaign featuring renderings of the female form in blue jeans by female artists. It also aired a national Spanish-language TV advertising campaign aimed at increasing its appeal to the young, fast-growing, and brand-loyal Hispanic market.

But Levi Strauss's most dramatic turnaround has been in its international markets. Levi Strauss now has become the only truly global U.S. apparel maker. Its strategy is to "think globally, act locally." It operates a closely coordinated worldwide marketing, manufacturing, and distribution system. Twice each year, Levi Strauss brings together managers from around the world to share product and advertising ideas and to search for those that have global appeal. For example, the Dockers line originated in Argentina, but has now become a worldwide bestseller. However, within its global strategy, Levi Strauss encourages local units to tailor products and programs to their home markets. For example, in Brazil, it developed the Feminina line of curvaceously cut jeans that provide the ultratight fit that Brazilian women favor.

In most markets abroad, Levi Strauss & Co. boldly plays up its deep American roots. For example, James Dean is a central figure in almost all Levi's advertising in Japan. Indonesian ads show Levi-clad teenagers driving around Dubuque, Iowa, in 1960s convertibles. And almost all foreign ads feature English-language music. However, whereas Americans usually think of their Levi's as basic knockaround wear, most European and Asian consumers view them as upscale fashion statements. The prices match the snob appeal—a pair of Levi's 501 jeans selling for $30 in the United States goes for about $63 in Tokyo and $88 in Paris.

Levi Strauss's aggressive and innovative global marketing efforts have produced stunning results. As the domestic market continues to shrink, foreign sales have accounted for most of Levi Strauss's growth. In 1994, overseas markets yielded 34 percent of the company's total sales and 46 percent of its profit before corporate expenses and interest. Perhaps more impressive, its foreign business is growing at five times the growth rate of its domestic business. Levi Strauss continues to look for new international market opportunities. For example, the first Rumanian shop to officially sell Levi's jeans recently opened to large crowds, and Levi Strauss is now selling to jeans-starved consumers in India, Eastern Europe, and Russia.

Dramatic strategic and marketing planning actions have transformed Levi Strauss into a vigorous and profitable company, one better matched to its changing market opportunities. By building a strong base in its core jeans business, coupled with well-planned product and market development, Levi Strauss has found ways to grow profitably despite the decline in the domestic jeans market. As one company observer suggests, Levi Strauss has learned that "with the right mix of persistence and smarts, [planning new products and] cracking new markets can seem as effortless as breaking in a new pair of Levi's stone-washed jeans."[1]

All companies must look ahead and develop long-term strategies to meet the changing conditions in their industries. Each company must find the game plan that makes the most sense given its specific situation, opportunities, objectives, and resources. The hard task of selecting an overall company strategy for long-run survival and growth is called *strategic planning*.

Marketing plays an important role in strategic planning. It provides information and other inputs to help prepare the strategic plan. In turn, strategic planning defines marketing's role in the organization. Guided by the strategic plan, marketing works with other departments in the organization to achieve overall strategic objectives.

In this chapter, we look first at the organization's overall strategic planning. Next, we discuss marketing's role in the organization as it is defined by the overall strategic plan. Finally, we explain the marketing management process—the process that marketers undertake to carry out their role in the organization.

STRATEGIC PLANNING

Many companies operate without formal plans. In new companies, managers are sometimes so busy they have no time for planning. In small companies, managers sometimes think that only large corporations need formal planning. In mature companies, many managers argue that they have done well without formal planning, and that therefore it cannot be too important. They may resist taking the time to prepare a written plan. They may argue that the marketplace changes too quickly for a plan to be useful—that it would end up collecting dust.

Yet formal planning can yield many benefits for all types of companies, large and small, new and mature. It encourages management to think ahead systematically. It forces the company to sharpen its objectives and policies, leads to better coordination of company efforts, and provides clearer performance standards for control. The argument that planning is less useful in a fast-changing environment makes little sense. In fact, the opposite is true: Sound planning helps the company to anticipate and respond quickly to environmental changes, and to better prepare for sudden developments.

Companies usually prepare annual plans, long-range plans, and strategic plans. The *annual plan* is a short-term marketing plan that describes the current marketing situation, company objectives, the marketing strategy for the year, the action program, budgets, and controls. The *long-range plan* describes the major factors and forces affecting the organization during the next several years. It includes the long-term objectives, the major marketing strategies that will be used to attain them, and the resources required. This long-range plan is reviewed and updated each year so that the company always has a current long-range plan.

Whereas the company's annual and long-range plans deal with current businesses and how to keep them going, the strategic plan involves adapting the firm to take advantage of opportunities in its constantly changing environment. We define **strategic planning** as the process of developing and maintaining a strategic fit between the organization's goals and capabilities and its changing marketing opportunities.

Strategic planning sets the stage for the rest of the planning in the firm. It relies on defining a clear company mission, setting supporting company objectives,

Strategic planning
The process of developing and maintaining a strategic fit between the organization's goals and capabilities and its changing marketing opportunities. It relies on developing a clear company mission, supporting objectives, a sound business portfolio, and coordinated functional strategies.

designing a sound business portfolio, and coordinating functional strategies (see Figure 2-1). At the corporate level, the company first defines its overall purpose and mission. This mission then is turned into detailed supporting objectives that guide the whole company. Next, headquarters decides what portfolio of businesses and products is best for the company and how much support to give each one. In turn, each business and product unit must develop detailed marketing and other departmental plans that support the companywide plan. Thus, marketing planning occurs at the business-unit, product, and market levels. It supports company strategic planning with more detailed planning for specific marketing opportunities.[2]

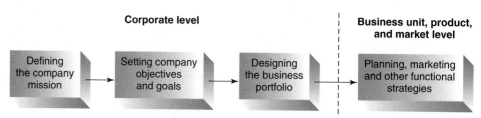

FIGURE 2-1   *Steps in strategic planning*

DEFINING THE COMPANY MISSION

An organization exists to accomplish something. At first, it has a clear purpose or mission, but over time its mission may become unclear as the organization grows and adds new products and markets. Or the mission may remain clear, but some managers may no longer be committed to it. Or the mission may remain clear but may no longer be the best choice given new conditions in the environment.

When management senses that the organization is drifting, it must renew its search for purpose. It is time to ask: What is our business? Who is the customer? What do consumers value? What will our business be? What should our business be? These simple-sounding questions are among the most difficult the company will ever have to answer. Successful companies continuously raise these questions and answer them carefully and completely.

Many organizations develop formal mission statements that answer these questions. A **mission statement** is a statement of the organization's purpose—what it wants to accomplish in the larger environment. A clear mission statement acts as an "invisible hand" that guides people in the organization so that they can work independently and yet collectively toward overall organizational goals.

Traditionally, companies have defined their businesses in product terms ("We manufacture furniture"), or in technological terms ("We are a chemical-processing firm"). But mission statements should be *market oriented*. Market definitions of a business are better than product or technological definitions. Products and technologies eventually become outdated, but basic market needs may last forever. A market-oriented mission statement defines the business in terms of satisfying basic customer needs. Thus, AT&T is in the communications business, not the telephone business. Citibank Visa defines its business not as issuing credit cards, but as allowing customers to exchange value—to exchange assets such as cash on deposit or equity in a home for virtually anything, anywhere in the world. And 3M does more than just make adhesives, scientific equipment, and health-care products. It solves people's problems by putting innovation to work for them. Table 2-1 provides several other examples of product-oriented versus market-oriented business definitions.

Mission statement
A statement of the organization's purpose—what it wants to accomplish in the larger environment.

TABLE 2-1 *Market-Oriented Business Definitions*

COMPANY	PRODUCT-ORIENTED DEFINITION	MARKET-ORIENTED DEFINITION
Revlon	We make cosmetics	We sell lifestyle and self-expression; success and status; memories, hopes and dreams
Disney	We run theme parks	We provide fantasies and entertainment—a place where America still works the way it's supposed to
Wal-Mart	We run discount stores	We offer products and services that deliver value to middle-Americans
Xerox	We make copying, fax, and other office machines	We make businesses more productive by helping them scan, store, retrieve, revise, distribute, print, and publish documents
O. M. Scott	We sell grass seed and fertilizer	We deliver green, healthy-looking yards
Home Depot	We sell tools and home repair/improvement items	We provide advice and solutions that transform ham-handed homeowners into Mr. and Ms. Fixits

Management should avoid making its mission too narrow or too broad. A pencil manufacturer that says it is in the communication equipment business is stating its mission too broadly. Missions should be *realistic*—Singapore Airlines would be deluding itself if it adopted the mission to become the world's largest airline. Missions should also be *specific*. Many mission statements are written for public relations purposes and lack specific, workable guidelines. The statement "We want to become the leading company in this industry by producing the highest-quality products with the best service at the lowest prices" sounds good, but it is full of generalities and contradictions. It will not help the company make tough decisions. Missions should fit the *market environment*. The Girl Scouts of America would not recruit successfully in today's environment with their former mission: "to prepare young girls for motherhood and wifely duties."

The organization should base its mission on its *distinctive competencies*. McDonald's could probably enter the solar energy business, but that would not take advantage of its core competence—providing low-cost food and fast service to large groups of customers. Finally, mission statements should be *motivating*. A company's mission should not be stated as making more sales or profits—profits are only a reward for undertaking a useful activity. A company's employees need to feel that their work is significant and that it contributes to people's lives. Contrast the missions of IBM and Microsoft, the huge computer software company. When IBM sales were $50 billion, president John Akers said that IBM's goal was to become a $100 billion company by the end of the century. Meanwhile, Microsoft's long-term goal has been IAYF—"information at your fingertips"—to put information at the fingertips of every person. Microsoft's mission is much more motivating than IBM's.

Missions are best when guided by a *vision,* an almost "impossible dream." Sony's president, Akio Morita, wanted everyone to have access to "personal portable sound," and his company created the Walkman. Fred Smith wanted to deliver mail anywhere in the United States before 10:30 AM the next day, and he created Federal Express. Thomas Monaghan wanted to deliver hot pizza to any home within 30 minutes, and he created Domino's Pizza. Sam Walton wanted to bring modern discount principles to small-town Americans, and he created Wal-Mart.

Company mission: 3M states its mission not as making office products, but as creating innovations that "make your work—make your life—simpler, more efficient, more productive."

The company's mission statement should provide a vision and direction for the company for the next ten to twenty years. Companies do not revise their missions every few years in response to each new turn in the environment. Still, a company must redefine its mission if that mission has lost credibility or no longer defines an optimal course for the company.[3]

SETTING COMPANY OBJECTIVES AND GOALS

The company's mission needs to be turned into detailed supporting objectives for each level of management. Each manager should have objectives and be responsible for reaching them. For example, International Minerals and Chemical Corporation is in many businesses, including the fertilizer business. The fertilizer division does not say that its mission is to produce fertilizer. Instead, it says that its mission is to "increase agricultural productivity." This mission leads to a hierarchy of objectives, including business objectives and marketing objectives. The mission of increasing agricultural productivity leads to the company's business objective of researching new fertilizers that promise higher yields. But research is expensive and requires improved profits to plow back into research programs. So improving profits becomes another major business objective. Profits can be improved by increasing sales or reducing costs. Sales can be increased by improving the company's share of the U.S. market, by entering new foreign markets, or both. These goals then become the company's current marketing objectives.

Marketing strategies must be developed to support these marketing objectives. To increase its U.S. market share, the company may increase its product's availability and promotion. To enter new foreign markets, the company may cut prices and target large farms abroad. These are its broad marketing strategies. Each broad marketing strategy must then be defined in greater detail. For example, increasing the product's promotion may require more salespeople and more advertising; if so, both requirements will have to be spelled out. In this way, the firm's mission is translated into a set of objectives for the current period. The objectives should be as specific as possible. The objective to "increase our market share" is not as useful as the objective to "increase our market share to 15 percent by the end of the second year."

Business portfolio
The collection of businesses and products that make up the company.

DESIGNING THE BUSINESS PORTFOLIO

Guided by the company's mission statement and objectives, management now must plan its **business portfolio**—the collection of businesses and products that make up the company. The best business portfolio is the one that best fits the company's strengths and weaknesses to opportunities in the environment. The company must (1) analyze its *current* business portfolio and decide which businesses should receive more, less, or no investment, and (2) develop growth strategies for adding *new* products or businesses to the portfolio.

ANALYZING THE CURRENT BUSINESS PORTFOLIO

Portfolio analysis
A tool by which management identifies and evaluates the various businesses that make up the company.

Strategic business unit (SBU)
A unit of the company that has a separate mission and objectives and that can be planned independently from other company businesses. An SBU can be a company division, a product line within a division, or sometimes a single product or brand.

Growth-share matrix
A portfolio-planning method that evaluates a company's strategic business units in terms of their market growth rate and relative market share. SBUs are classified as stars, cash cows, question marks, or dogs.

Stars
High-growth, high-share businesses or products that often require heavy investment to finance their rapid growth.

Many companies operate several businesses. However, they often fail to define them carefully. The major activity in strategic planning is business **portfolio analysis,** whereby management evaluates the businesses making up the company. The company will want to put strong resources into its more profitable businesses and phase down or drop its weaker ones. For example, in recent years, Dial Corp has strengthened its portfolio by selling off its less attractive businesses: bus line (Greyhound), knitting supplies, meatpacking, and computer leasing businesses. At the same time, it invested more heavily in its consumer products (Dial soap, Armour Star meats, Purex laundry products, and others) and services (Premier Cruise Lines, Dobbs airport services).

Management's first step is to identify the key businesses making up the company. These can be called the strategic business units. A **strategic business unit (SBU)** is a unit of the company that has a separate mission and objectives and that can be planned independently from other company businesses. An SBU can be a company division, a product line within a division, or sometimes a single product or brand.

The next step in business portfolio analysis calls for management to assess the attractiveness of its various SBUs and decide how much support each deserves. In some companies, this is done informally. Management looks at the company's collection of businesses or products and uses judgment to decide how much each SBU should contribute and receive. Other companies use formal portfolio-planning methods.

The purpose of strategic planning is to find ways in which the company can best use its strengths to take advantage of attractive opportunities in the environment. So most standard portfolio-analysis methods evaluate SBUs on two important dimensions—the attractiveness of the SBU's market or industry and the strength of the SBU's position in that market or industry. The best known portfolio-planning methods were developed by the Boston Consulting Group, a leading management consulting firm, and by General Electric.

FIGURE 2-2   *The BCG growth-share matrix*

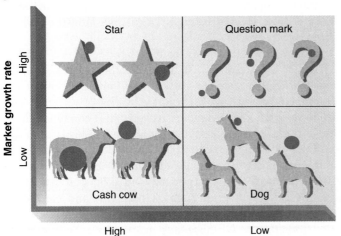

The Boston Consulting Group Approach
Using the Boston Consulting Group (BCG) approach, a company classifies all its SBUs according to the **growth-share matrix** shown in Figure 2-2. On the vertical axis, *market growth rate* provides a measure of market attractiveness. On the horizontal axis, *relative market share* serves as a measure of company strength in the market. By dividing the growth-share matrix as indicated, four types of SBUs can be distinguished:

◆ **Stars.** Stars are high-growth, high-share businesses or products. They often need heavy investment to finance their rapid growth. Eventually their growth will slow down, and they will turn into cash cows.

Cash cows
Low-growth, high-share businesses or products; established and successful units that generate cash the company uses to pay its bills and support other business units that need investment.

Question marks
Low-share business units in high-growth markets that require a lot of cash in order to hold their share or become stars.

Dogs
Low-growth, low-share businesses and products that may generate enough cash to maintain themselves but do not promise to be large sources of cash.

- ◆ **Cash cows.** Cash cows are low-growth, high-share businesses or products. These established and successful SBUs need less investment to hold their market share. Thus, they produce a lot of cash that the company uses to pay its bills and to support other SBUs that need investment.

- ◆ **Question marks.** Question marks are low-share business units in high-growth markets. They require a lot of cash to hold their share, let alone increase it. Management has to think hard about which question marks it should try to build into stars and which should be phased out.

- ◆ **Dogs.** Dogs are low-growth, low-share businesses and products. They may generate enough cash to maintain themselves, but do not promise to be large sources of cash.

The ten circles in the growth-share matrix represent a company's ten current SBUs. The company has two stars, two cash cows, three question marks, and three dogs. The areas of the circles are proportional to the SBU's dollar sales. This company is in fair shape, although not in good shape. It wants to invest in the more promising question marks to make them stars, and to maintain the stars so that they will become cash cows as their markets mature. Fortunately, it has two good-sized cash cows whose income helps finance the company's question marks, stars, and dogs. The company should take some decisive action concerning its dogs and its question marks. The picture would be worse if the company had no stars, if it had too many dogs, or if it had only one weak cash cow.

Once it has classified its SBUs, the company must determine what role each will play in the future. One of four strategies can be pursued for each SBU. The company can invest more in the business unit in order to *build* its share. Or it can invest just enough to *hold* the SBU's share at the current level. It can *harvest* the SBU, milking its short-term cash flow regardless of the long-term effect. Finally, the company can *divest* the SBU by selling it or phasing it out and using the resources elsewhere.

As time passes, SBUs change their positions in the growth-share matrix. Each SBU has a life cycle. Many SBUs start out as question marks and move into the star category if they succeed. They later become cash cows as market growth falls, then finally die off or turn into dogs toward the end of their life cycle. The company needs to add new products and units continuously so that some of them will become stars and, eventually, cash cows that will help finance other SBUs.

The General Electric Approach

General Electric introduced a comprehensive portfolio planning tool called a *strategic business-planning grid* (see Figure 2-3). Like the BCG approach, it uses a matrix with two dimensions—one representing industry attractiveness (the vertical axis) and one representing company strength in the industry (the horizontal axis). The best businesses are those located in highly attractive industries where the company has high business strength.

The GE approach considers many factors besides market growth rate as part of industry attractiveness. It uses an industry attractiveness index made up of market size, market growth rate, industry profit margin, amount of competition, seasonality and cyclicality of demand, and industry cost structure. Each of these factors is rated and combined in an index of industry attractiveness. For our purposes, an industry's attractiveness will be described as high, medium, or low. As an example, Kraft has identified numerous highly attractive industries—natural foods, specialty frozen foods, physical fitness products, and others. It has withdrawn from less attractive industries such as bulk oils and cardboard packaging.

For *business strength,* the GE approach again uses an index rather than a simple measure of relative market share. The business strength index

FIGURE 2-3 *General Electric's strategic business-planning grid*

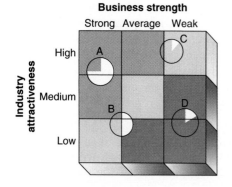

includes factors such as the company's relative market share, price competitiveness, product quality, customer and market knowledge, sales effectiveness, and geographic advantages. These factors are rated and combined in an index of business strength, which can be described as strong, average, or weak. Thus, Kraft has substantial business strength in food and related industries, but is relatively weak in the home appliances industry.

The grid is divided into three zones. The green cells at the upper left include the strong SBUs in which the company should invest and grow. The yellow diagonal cells contain SBUs that are medium in overall attractiveness. The company should maintain its level of investment in these SBUs. The three red cells at the lower right indicate SBUs that are low in overall attractiveness. The company should give serious thought to harvesting or divesting these SBUs.

The circles represent four company SBUs; the areas of the circles are proportional to the relative sizes of the industries in which these SBUs compete. The pie slices within the circles represent each SBU's market share. Thus, circle A represents a company SBU with a 75 percent market share in a good-sized, highly attractive industry in which the company has strong business strength. Circle B represents an SBU that has a 50 percent market share, but the industry is not very attractive. Circles C and D represent two other company SBUs in industries where the company has small market shares and not much business strength. Altogether, the company should build A, maintain B, and make some hard decisions on what to do with C and D.

Management also would plot the projected positions of the SBUs with and without changes in strategies. By comparing current and projected business grids, management can identify the major strategic issues and opportunities it faces.

Problems with Matrix Approaches

The BCG, GE, and other formal methods revolutionized strategic planning. However, such approaches have limitations. They can be difficult, time-consuming, and costly to implement. Management may find it difficult to define SBUs and measure market share and growth. In addition, these approaches focus on classifying *current* businesses but provide little advice for *future* planning. Management must still rely on its own judgment to set the business objectives for each SBU, to determine what resources each will be given, and to figure out which new businesses should be added.

Formal planning approaches also can lead the company to place too much emphasis on market-share growth or growth through entry into attractive new markets. Using these approaches, many companies plunged into unrelated and new high-growth businesses that they did not know how to manage—with very bad results. At the same time, these companies often were too quick to abandon, sell, or milk to death their healthy mature businesses. As a result, many companies that diversified too broadly in the past now are narrowing their focus and getting back to the basics of serving one or a few industries that they know best.

Despite these and other problems, and although many companies have dropped formal matrix methods in favor of more customized approaches that are better suited to their situations, most companies remain firmly committed to strategic planning. Roughly 75 percent of the Fortune 500 companies practice some form of portfolio planning.[4]

Such analysis is no cure-all for finding the best strategy. But it can help management to understand the company's overall situation, to see how each business or product contributes, to assign resources to its businesses, and to orient the company for future success. When used properly, strategic planning is just one important aspect of overall strategic management, a way of thinking about how to manage a business.[5]

DEVELOPING GROWTH STRATEGIES

Beyond evaluating current businesses, designing the business portfolio involves finding businesses and products the company should consider in the future. One useful device for identifying growth opportunities is the **product/market expansion grid**,[6] shown in Figure 2-4. We apply it here to Levi Strauss & Co.

First, Levi Strauss management might consider whether the company's major brands can achieve deeper **market penetration**—making more sales to present customers without changing products in any way. For example, to increase its jeans sales, Levi Strauss might cut prices, increase advertising, get its products into more stores, or obtain better store displays and point-of-purchase merchandising from its retailers. Basically, Levi Strauss management would like to increase usage by current customers and attract customers of other clothing brands to Levi's.

Second, Levi Strauss management might consider possibilities for **market development**—identifying and developing new markets for its current products. For instance, managers could review new *demographic markets*—children, senior consumers, women, ethnic groups—to see if any new groups could be encouraged to buy Levi Strauss products for the first time or to buy more of them. For example, Levi Strauss recently launched new advertising campaigns to boost its jeans sales in female and Hispanic markets. Managers also could review new *geographical markets*. During the past few years, Levi Strauss has substantially increased its marketing efforts and sales to Western Europe, Asia, and Latin America. It now is targeting newly opened markets in Eastern Europe, Russia, India, and China.

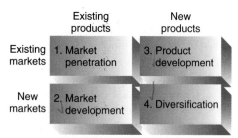

	Existing products	New products
Existing markets	1. Market penetration	3. Product development
New markets	2. Market development	4. Diversification

FIGURE 2-4 *Market opportunity identification through the product/ market expansion grid*

Market penetration: Clorox increased market penetration by suggesting new household uses for its bleach.

Third, management could consider **product development**—offering modified or new products to current markets. Current Levi Strauss products could be offered in new styles, sizes, and colors. Or Levi Strauss could offer new lines and launch new brands of casual clothing to appeal to different users or to obtain more business from current customers. This occurred when Levi Strauss introduced its Dockers line, which now accounts for more than $1 billion in annual sales.

Fourth, Levi Strauss might consider **diversification**. It could start up or buy businesses outside of its current products and markets. For example, the company could move into industries such as men's fashions, recreational and exercise apparel, or other related businesses. Some companies try to identify the most attractive emerging industries. They feel that half the secret of success is to enter attractive industries instead of trying to be efficient in unattractive ones. However, a company that diversifies too broadly into unfamiliar products or industries can lose its market focus. For example, as discussed in the chapter opening example, prior to 1984 Levi Strauss diversified hastily into a jumbled array of businesses, including skiwear, men's suits and hats, and other specialty apparel. In 1985, however, new management sold these unrelated businesses, refocused the company on its core business of denim jeans, and designed a solid growth strategy featuring closely related new products

How To Keep Your Pet From Living Like An Animal.

When Pet Odors Become A Pet Peeve, Here's How To Get Rid Of Them With Clorox® Bleach.

Travel gets pets so excited, the poor things just can't contain themselves. So it's a good idea to wipe down pet carriers inside and out with the Clorox Bleach Cleaning Solution* at final destinations.

Doggy beds can create some doggone irritating household odors. But it's easy to take care of. Just throw Rover's pillow cover and blanket in the wash with a little Clorox Bleach, then dry. Hey, it'll smell better than it has in a dog's age. Follow directions on bottle.

Most dogs are just drooling to get their mouths on another toy. Which is fine. But after a while, all those toys can start to make even the tidiest home smell like, well, doghreath. Eliminate bothersome odors by giving your dog's toys a one-minute soak in the Clorox Bleach Cleaning Solution* once a week.

Everyone knows how easily smells here spread all over the house. Fortunately, getting rid of litter box odors is as easy as washing your cat's empty litter box with the Clorox Bleach Cleaning Solution.*

You'll be happy to know that using Clorox Bleach is always an environmentally sound choice. That's because after its work is done, Clorox Bleach breaks down to little more than salt and water.

*Clorox Bleach Cleaning Solution
• Mix 3/4 cup Regular Clorox Bleach with one gallon of water.
• Rinse items first with water. Then apply Clorox Bleach Cleaning Solution and let stand for 5 minutes. Rinse well and let dry.

Limited space? Try our handy quart size bottle.

The Simple Solution For A Healthy Home.

and bolder efforts to develop international markets. These actions resulted in a dramatic turnaround in the company's sales and profits.

PLANNING FUNCTIONAL STRATEGIES

Product/market expansion grid
A portfolio-planning tool for identifying company growth opportunities through market penetration, market development, product development, or diversification.

Market penetration
A strategy for company growth by increasing sales of current products to current market segments without changing the product in any way.

Market development
A strategy for company growth by identifying and developing new market segments for current company products.

Product development
A strategy for company growth by offering modified or new products to current market segments. Developing the product concept into a physical product in order to assure that the product idea can be turned into a workable product.

Diversification
A strategy for company growth by starting up or acquiring businesses outside the company's current products and markets.

The company's strategic plan establishes what kinds of businesses the company will be in and its objectives for each. Then, within each business unit more detailed planning must take place. The major functional departments in each unit—marketing, finance, accounting, purchasing, manufacturing, human resources, and others—must work together to accomplish strategic objectives.

Each functional department deals with different publics to obtain inputs the business needs—inputs like cash, labor, raw materials, research ideas, and manufacturing processes. For example, marketing brings in revenues by negotiating exchanges with consumers. Finance arranges exchanges with lenders and stockholders to obtain cash. Thus, the marketing and finance departments must work together to obtain needed funds. Similarly, the human resources department supplies labor, and the purchasing department obtains materials needed for operations and manufacturing.

Marketing's Role in Strategic Planning

There is much overlap between overall company strategy and marketing strategy. Marketing looks at consumer needs and the company's ability to satisfy them; these same factors guide the company mission and objectives. Most company strategy planning deals with marketing variables—market share, market development, growth—and it is sometimes hard to separate strategic planning from marketing planning. In fact, some companies refer to their strategic planning as "strategic marketing planning."

Marketing plays a key role in the company's strategic planning in several ways. First, marketing provides a guiding *philosophy*—the marketing concept—which suggests company strategy should revolve around serving the needs of important consumer groups. Second, marketing provides *inputs* to strategic planners by helping to identify attractive market opportunities and by assessing the firm's potential to take advantage of them. Finally, within individual business units, marketing designs *strategies* for reaching the unit's objectives.

Within each business unit, marketing management must determine the best way to help achieve strategic objectives. Some marketing managers will find that their objective is not necessarily to build sales. Rather, it may be to hold existing sales with a smaller marketing budget, or it actually may be to reduce demand. Thus, marketing management must manage demand to the level decided on by the strategic planning prepared at headquarters. Marketing helps to assess each business unit's potential, but once the unit's objective is set, marketing's task is to carry it out profitably.

Marketing and the Other Business Functions

Confusion persists about marketing's importance in the firm. In some firms, it is just another function—all functions count in the company and none takes leadership. At the other extreme, some marketers claim that marketing is the *major* function of the firm. They quote management consultant Peter Drucker, who says "The aim of the business is to create customers." They say it is marketing's job to define the company's mission, products, and markets and to direct the other functions in the task of serving customers.

More enlightened marketers prefer to put the *customer* at the center of the company. These marketers argue that the firm cannot succeed without customers, so the crucial task is to attract and hold them. Customers are attracted by promises and held through satisfaction, and marketing defines the promise and ensures its delivery. However, because actual consumer satisfaction is affected by the performance of other departments, *all* functions should work together to deliver superior customer value and satisfaction. Marketing plays an integrative role to help ensure that all departments work together toward consumer satisfaction.

Conflict between Departments

Each business function has a different view of which publics and activities are most important. Manufacturing focuses on suppliers and production; finance is concerned with stockholders and sound investment; marketing emphasizes consumers and products, pricing, promotion, and distribution. Ideally, all the different functions should work in harmony to produce value for consumers. But in practice, departmental relations are full of conflicts and misunderstandings. The marketing department takes the consumer's point of view. But when marketing tries to develop customer satisfaction, it often causes other departments to do a poorer job *in their terms*. Marketing department actions can increase purchasing costs, disrupt production schedules, increase inventories, and create budget headaches. Thus, the other departments may resist bending their efforts to the will of the marketing department.

Yet marketers must get all departments to "think consumer" and to put the consumer at the center of company activity. Customer satisfaction requires a total company effort to deliver superior value to target customers.

> Creating value for buyers is much more than a "marketing function"; rather, [it's] analogous to a symphony orchestra in which the contribution of each subgroup is tailored and integrated by a conductor—with a synergistic effect. A seller must draw upon and integrate effectively . . . its entire human and other capital resources. . . . [Creating superior value for buyers] is the proper focus of the entire business and not merely of a single department in it.[7]

The Du Pont "Adopt a Customer" program recognizes the importance of having people in all of its functions who are "close to the customer." Through this program, Du Pont encourages people on the manufacturing line at many of its plants to develop and maintain a direct relationship with the customer. The manufacturing representatives meet with the assigned customer once a year and interact regularly by phone to learn about the company's needs and problems. Then, they represent the customer on the factory floor. If quality or delivery problems arise, the manufacturing representative is more likely to see the adopted customer's point of view and to make decisions that will keep this customer happy.[8]

Thus, marketing management can best gain support for its goal of consumer satisfaction by working to understand the company's other departments. Marketing managers must work closely with managers of other functions to develop a system of functional plans under which the different departments can work together to accomplish the company's overall strategic objectives.

THE MARKETING PROCESS

Marketing process
The process of (1) analyzing marketing opportunities; (2) selecting target markets; (3) developing the marketing mix; and (4) managing the marketing effort.

The strategic plan defines the company's overall mission and objectives. Within each business unit, marketing plays a role in helping to accomplish the overall strategic objectives. Marketing's role and activities in the organization are shown in Figure 2-5, which summarizes the entire **marketing process** and the forces influencing company marketing strategy.

Target consumers stand in the center. The company identifies the total market, divides it into smaller segments, selects the most promising segments, and

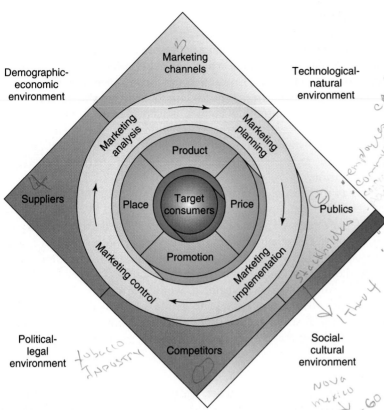

FIGURE 2-5 *Factors influencing company marketing strategy*

focuses on serving and satisfying these segments. It designs a marketing mix made up of factors under its control—product, price, place, and promotion. To find the best marketing mix and put it into action, the company engages in marketing analysis, planning, implementation, and control. Through these activities, the company watches and adapts to the marketing environment. We will now look briefly at each element in the marketing process. In later chapters, we will discuss each element in more depth.

TARGET CONSUMERS

To succeed in today's competitive marketplace, companies must be customer centered, winning customers from competitors by delivering greater value. But before it can satisfy consumers, a company must first understand their needs and wants. Thus, sound marketing requires a careful analysis of consumers. Companies know that they cannot satisfy all consumers in a given market—at least not all consumers in the same way. There are too many different kinds of consumers with too many different kinds of needs. And some companies are in a better position to serve certain segments of the market. Thus, each company must divide up the total market, choose the best segments, and design strategies for profitably serving chosen segments better than its competitors do. This process involves four steps: *demand measurement and forecasting, market segmentation, market targeting,* and *market positioning.*

Demand Measurement and Forecasting

Suppose a company is looking at possible markets for a potential new product. First, the company needs to make a careful estimate of the current and future size of the market and its various segments. To estimate current market size, the company would identify all competing products, estimate the current sales of these products, and determine whether the market is large enough to profitably support another product.

Equally important is future market growth. Companies want to enter markets that show strong growth prospects. Growth potential may depend on the growth rate of certain age, income, and nationality groups that use the product. Growth also may be related to larger developments in the environment, such as economic conditions, the crime rate, and lifestyle changes. For example, the future market for quality children's toys and clothing is strongly related to current birth rates, trends in consumer affluence, and projected family lifestyles. Forecasting the effect of these environmental forces is difficult, but it must be done in order to make decisions about the market. The company's marketing information specialists probably will use complex techniques to measure and forecast demand.

Market Segmentation

Suppose the demand forecast looks good. The company must now decide how to enter the market. The market consists of many types of customers, products, and needs, and the marketer has to determine which segments offer the best opportunity for achieving company objectives. Consumers can be grouped in various ways based on geographic factors (countries, regions, cities); demographic factors (sex, age, income, education); psychographic factors (social classes, lifestyles); and behavioral factors (purchase occasions, benefits sought, usage rates). The process of dividing a market into distinct groups of buyers with different needs, characteristics, or behavior who might require separate products or marketing mixes is called **market segmentation.**

Market segmentation
Dividing a market into distinct groups of buyers with different needs, characteristics, or behavior who might require separate products or marketing mixes.

Market segment
A group of consumers who respond in a similar way to a given set of marketing stimuli.

Every market has market segments, but not all ways of segmenting a market are equally useful. For example, Tylenol would gain little by distinguishing between male and female users of pain relievers if both respond the same way to marketing efforts. A **market segment** consists of consumers who respond in a similar way to a given set of marketing efforts. In the car market, for example, consumers who choose the biggest, most comfortable car regardless of price make up one market segment. Another market segment would be customers who care mainly about price and operating economy. It would be difficult to make one model of car that was the first choice of every consumer. Companies are wise to focus their efforts on meeting the distinct needs of one or more market segments.

Market Targeting

After a company has defined market segments, it can enter one or many segments of a given market. **Market targeting** involves evaluating each market segment's attractiveness and selecting one or more segments to enter. A company should target segments in which it can generate the greatest customer value and sustain it over time. A company with limited resources might decide to serve only one or a few special segments. This strategy limits sales, but can be very profitable. Or a company might choose to serve several related segments—perhaps those with different kinds of customers but with the same basic wants. Or a large company might decide to offer a complete range of products to serve all market segments.

Market targeting
The process of evaluating each market segment's attractiveness and selecting one or more segments to enter.

Most companies enter a new market by serving a single segment, and if this proves successful, they add segments. Large companies eventually seek full market coverage. They want to be the "General Motors" of their industry. GM says that it makes a car for every "person, purse, and personality." The leading company normally has different products designed to meet the special needs of each segment.

Market Positioning

After a company has decided which market segments to enter, it must decide what "positions" it wants to occupy in those segments. A product's *position* is the place the product occupies relative to competitors in consumers' minds. If a product is perceived to be exactly like another product on the market, consumers would have no reason to buy it.

Market positioning
Arranging for a product to occupy a clear, distinctive, and desirable place relative to competing products in the minds of target consumers. Formulating competitive positioning for a product and a detailed marketing mix.

Market positioning is arranging for a product to occupy a clear, distinctive, and desirable place in the minds of target consumers relative to competing products. Thus, marketers plan positions that distinguish their products from competing brands and give them the greatest strategic advantage in their target markets. For example, Chrysler compares its cars to those of various competitors and concludes "Advantage: Chrysler." At Ford "quality is job one," and Mazda "just feels right." Jaguar is positioned as "a blending of art and machine," whereas Saab is

Market positioning: Red Roof Inns positions on value—it doesn't "add frills that only add to your bill." In contrast, Four Seasons Hotels positions on luxury. For those who can afford it, Four Seasons offers endless amenities— such as a seamstress, a valet, and a "tireless individual who collects your shoes each night and returns them at dawn, polished to perfection."

"the most intelligent car ever built." Mercedes is "engineered like no other car in the world," the Lincoln Town Car is "what a luxury car should be," and the luxurious Bentley is "the closest a car can come to having wings." Such deceptively simple statements form the backbone of a product's marketing strategy.

In positioning its product, the company first identifies possible competitive advantages on which to build the position. To gain competitive advantage, the company must offer greater value to chosen target segments, either by charging lower prices than competitors do or by offering more benefits to justify higher prices. But if the company positions the product as *offering* greater value, it must then *deliver* that greater value. Thus, effective positioning begins with actually *differentiating* the company's marketing offer so that it gives consumers more value than they are offered by the competition. Once the company has chosen a desired position, it must take strong steps to deliver and communicate that position to target consumers. The company's entire marketing program should support the chosen positioning strategy.

MARKETING STRATEGIES FOR COMPETITIVE ADVANTAGE

To be successful, the company must do a better job than its competitors of satisfying target consumers. Thus, marketing strategies must be geared to the needs of consumers and also to the strategies of competitors. Based on its size and industry position, the company must decide how it will position itself relative to competitors in order to gain the strongest possible competitive advantage.

Designing competitive marketing strategies begins with thorough competitor analysis. The company constantly compares the value and customer satisfaction delivered by its products, prices, channels, and promotion with that of its close competitors. In this way it can discern areas of potential advantage and disadvantage. The company must formally or informally monitor the competitive environment to answer these and other important questions: Who are our competitors? What are their objectives and strategies? What are their strengths and weaknesses? And how will they react to different competitive strategies we might use?

The competitive marketing strategy a company adopts depends on its industry position. A firm that dominates a market can adopt one or more of several *market-leader* strategies. Well-known leaders include Coca-Cola (soft drinks), McDonald's (fast food), Caterpillar (large construction equipment), Kodak (photographic film), Wal-Mart (retailing), and Boeing (aircraft). *Market challengers* are runner-up companies that aggressively attack competitors to get more market share. For example, Pepsi challenges Coke and Compaq challenges IBM. The challenger might attack the market leader, other firms its own size, or smaller local and regional competitors. Some runner-up firms will choose to follow rather than challenge the market leader. Firms using *market-follower* strategies seek stable market shares and profits by following competitors' product offers, prices, and marketing programs. Smaller firms in a market, or even larger firms that lack established positions, often adopt *market-nicher* strategies. They specialize in serving market niches that major competitors overlook or ignore (see Marketing Highlight 2-1). "Nichers" avoid direct confrontations with the majors by specializing along market, customer, product, or marketing-mix lines. Through smart niching, low-share firms in an industry can be as profitable as their larger competitors. We will discuss competitive marketing strategies more fully in Chapter 20.

DEVELOPING THE MARKETING MIX

Marketing mix
The set of controllable tactical marketing tools—product, price, place, and promotion—that the firm blends to produce the response it wants in the target market.

Once the company has decided on its overall competitive marketing strategy, it is ready to begin planning the details of the marketing mix. The marketing mix is one of the major concepts in modern marketing. We define **marketing mix** as the set of controllable tactical marketing tools that the firm blends to produce the response it wants in the target market. The marketing mix consists of everything the firm can do to influence the demand for its product. The many possibilities can be collected into four groups of variables known as the "four Ps": *product, price, place,* and *promotion.*[9] Figure 2-6 shows the particular marketing tools under each P.

Product means the "goods-and-service" combination the company offers to the target market. Thus, a Ford Taurus "product" consists of nuts and bolts, spark plugs, pistons, headlights, and thousands of other parts. Ford offers several Taurus styles and dozens of optional features. The car comes fully serviced and with a comprehensive warranty that is as much a part of the product as the tailpipe.

Price is the amount of money customers have to pay to obtain the product. Ford calculates suggested retail prices that its dealers might charge for each Tau-

FIGURE 2-6 *The four Ps of the marketing mix*

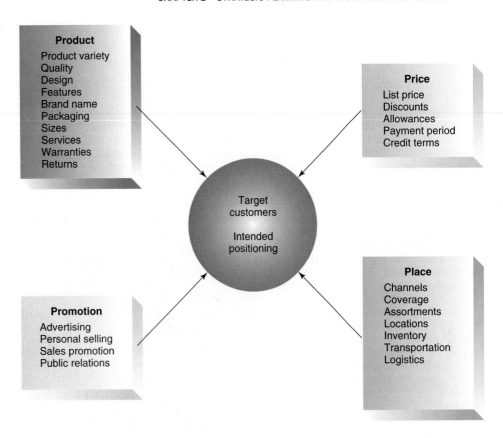

rus. But Ford dealers rarely charge the full sticker price. Instead, they negotiate the price with each customer, offering discounts, trade-in allowances, and credit terms to adjust for the current competitive situation and to bring the price into line with the buyer's perception of the car's value.

Place includes company activities that make the product available to target consumers. Ford maintains a large body of independently owned dealerships that sell the company's many different models. Ford selects its dealers carefully and supports them strongly. The dealers keep an inventory of Ford automobiles, demonstrate them to potential buyers, negotiate prices, close sales, and service the cars after the sale.

Promotion means activities that communicate the merits of the product and persuade target customers to buy it. Ford spends more than $600 million each year on advertising to tell consumers about the company and its products. Dealership salespeople assist potential buyers and persuade them that Ford is the best car for them. Ford and its dealers offer special promotions—sales, cash rebates, low financing rates—as added purchase incentives.

An effective marketing program blends all of the marketing mix elements into a coordinated program designed to achieve the company's marketing objectives by delivering value to consumers. The marketing mix constitutes the company's tactical tool kit for establishing strong positioning in target markets. However, note that the four *P*s represent the sellers' view of the marketing tools available for influencing buyers. From a consumer viewpoint, each marketing tool is designed to deliver a customer benefit. One marketing expert[10] suggests that companies should view the four *P*s in terms of the customer's four *C*s:

VERNOR'S THRIVES IN THE SHADOWS OF THE GIANTS

You've probably never heard of *Vernor's Ginger Ale.* And if you tried it, you might not even think it tastes like ginger ale. Vernor's is "aged in oak," the company boasts, and "deliciously different." The caramel-colored soft drink is sweeter and smoother than other ginger ales you've tasted. But to many people in Detroit who grew up with Vernor's, there's nothing quite like it. They drink it cold and hot; morning, noon, and night; summer and winter; from the bottle and at the soda fountain counter. They like the way the bubbles tickle their noses. And they'll say you haven't lived until you've tasted a Vernor's ice-cream float. To many, Vernor's even has some minor medicinal qualities—they use warm Vernor's to settle a child's upset stomach or to soothe a sore throat. To most Detroit adults, the familiar green and yellow packaging brings back many pleasant childhood memories.

The soft-drink industry is headed by two giants—Coca-Cola leads with a 41 percent market share and Pepsi challenges strongly with about 31 percent. Coke and Pepsi are the main combatants in the "soft-drink wars." They wage constant and pitched battles for retail shelf space. Their weapons include a steady stream of new products, heavy price discounts, an army of distributor salespeople, and huge advertising and promotion budgets.

A few "second-tier" brands—such as Dr Pepper, 7-Up, and Royal Crown—capture a combined 20 percent or so of the market. They challenge Coke and Pepsi in the smaller cola and noncola segments. When Coke and Pepsi battle for shelf space, these second-tier brands often get squeezed. Coke and Pepsi set the ground rules, and if the smaller brands don't follow along, they risk being pushed out or gobbled up.

At the same time, a group of specialty producers who concentrate on small but loyal market segments fights for what's left of the market. Although large in number, each of these small firms holds a tiny market share—usually less than one percent. Vernor's falls into this "all others" group, along with A&W root beer, Shasta sodas, Squirt, Faygo, Soho Natural Soda, Yoo-Hoo, Dr Brown's Cream Soda, A.J. Canfield's Diet Chocolate Fudge Soda, and a dozen

Through smart market niching, Vernors prospers in the shadows of the soft-drink giants

others. While Dr Pepper and 7-Up merely get squeezed in the soft-drink wars, these small fry risk being crushed.

When you compare Vernor's to Coca-Cola, for example, you wonder how Vernor's survives. Coca-Cola spends almost $400 million a year advertising its soft drinks; Vernor's spends less than $1 million. Coke offers a long list of brands and brand versions—Coke Classic, Coke II, Cherry Coke, Diet Coke, Caffeine-Free Coke, Diet Cherry Coke, Caffeine-Free Diet Coke, Sprite, Tab, Mellow Yellow, Minute Maid soda, and others; Vernor's sells only two versions—original and diet. Coke's large distributor salesforce sways retailers with huge discounts and promotion allowances; Vernor's has only a small marketing budget and carries little clout with retailers. When you are lucky enough to find Vernor's at your local supermarket, it's usually tucked away on the bottom shelf with other specialty beverages. Even in Detroit, the company's stronghold, stores usually give Vernor's only a few shelf facings, compared with 50 or 100 facings for the many Coca-Cola brands.

Yet Vernor's does more than survive—it thrives! How? Instead of going head-to-head with the bigger companies in the major soft-drink segments, Vernor's "niches" in the market. It concentrates on serving the special needs of loyal Vernor's drinkers. Vernor's knows that it could never seriously challenge Coca-Cola for a large share of the soft-drink market. But it also knows that Coca-Cola could never create another Vernor's ginger ale—at least not in the minds of Vernor's drinkers. As long as Vernor's keeps these special customers happy, it can capture a small but profitable share of the market. And "small" in this market is nothing to sneeze at—a one percent market share equals $470 million in retail sales! Thus, through smart market niching, Vernor's prospers in the shadows of the soft-drink giants.

Sources: See Betsy Bauer, "Giants Loom Larger Over Pint-Sized Soft-Drink Firms," *USA Today,* May 27, 1986, p. 5B; Walecia Konrad, "The Cola Kings are Feeling a Bit Jumpy," *Business Week,* July 13, 1992, p. 112–113; and Elizabeth Lesly, "A&W's Summer Plans: Hitting the Warpath," *Business Week,* April 12, 1993, pp. 53–54; and Chad Rubel, "Dr. Pepper–7Up Join Pepsi, Coke in Soda Wars," *Marketing News,* April 10, 1995, p. 8.

Four Ps   *Four Cs*
Product   Customer needs and wants
Price   Cost to the customer
Place   Convenience
Promotion   Communication

Thus, winning companies will be those that can meet customer needs economically and conveniently and with effective communication.

MANAGING THE MARKETING EFFORT

The company wants to design and put into action the marketing mix that will best achieve its objectives in its target markets. This involves four marketing management functions—*analysis, planning, implementation,* and *control.* Figure 2-7 shows the relationship between these marketing activities. The company first develops overall strategic plans. These company-wide strategic plans are then translated into marketing and other plans for each division, product, and brand.

FIGURE 2-7 *The relationship between analysis, planning, implementation, and control*

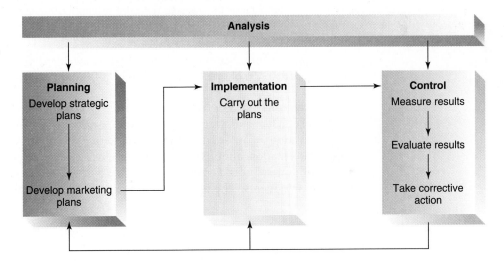

Through implementation, the company turns the strategic and marketing plans into actions that will achieve the company's strategic objectives. Marketing plans are implemented by people in the marketing organization who work with others both inside and outside the company. Control consists of measuring and evaluating the results of marketing plans and activities and taking corrective action to make sure objectives are being reached. Marketing analysis provides information and evaluations needed for all of the other marketing activities.

MARKETING ANALYSIS

Managing the marketing function begins with a complete analysis of the company's situation. The company must analyze its markets and marketing environment to find attractive opportunities and to avoid environmental threats. It must analyze company strengths and weaknesses, as well as current and possible marketing actions, to determine which opportunities it can best pursue. Marketing analysis feeds information and other inputs to each of the other marketing management functions. Marketing analysis is discussed more fully in Chapter 4.

MARKETING PLANNING

Through strategic planning, the company decides what it wants to do with each business unit. Marketing planning involves deciding on marketing strategies that will help the company attain its overall strategic objectives. A detailed marketing plan is needed for each business, product, or brand. What does a marketing plan look like? Our discussion focuses on product or brand plans. A product or brand plan should contain the following sections: *executive summary, current marketing situation, threats and opportunities, objectives and issues, marketing strategies, action programs, budgets,* and *controls* (see Table 2-2).

Executive Summary

Executive summary
The opening section of the marketing plan that presents a short summary of the main goals and recommendations to be presented in the plan.

The marketing plan should open with a short **executive summary** of the main goals and recommendations to be presented in the plan. Here is a short example:

> The 1996 Marketing Plan outlines an approach to attaining a significant increase in company sales and profits over the preceding year. The sales target is $200 million, a planned 20 percent sales gain. We think this increase is attainable because of the improved economic, competitive, and distribution picture. The target operating margin is $25 million, a 25 percent increase over last year. To achieve these goals, the sales promotion budget will be $4.8 million, or 2 percent of projected sales. The advertising budget will be $7.2 million, or 3 percent of projected sales. . . . [More details follow.]

The executive summary helps top management to find the plan's major points quickly. A table of contents should follow the executive summary.

Current Marketing Situation

The first major section of the plan describes the target market and the company's position in it. In the current marketing situation section, the planner provides information about the market, product performance, competition, and distribution. It includes a *market description* that defines the market, including major market segments. The planner shows market size, in total and by segment, for the past

TABLE 2-2 *Contents of a Marketing Plan*

SECTION	PURPOSE
Executive summary	Presents a brief overview of the proposed plan for quick management review.
Current marketing situation	Presents relevant background data on the market, product, competition, and distribution.
Threats and opportunity analysis	Identifies the main threats and opportunities that might impact the product.
Objectives and issues	Defines the company's objectives for the product in the areas of sales, market share, and profit, and the issues that will affect these objectives.
Marketing strategy	Presents the broad marketing approach that will be used to achieve the plan's objectives.
Action programs	Specifies *what* will be done, *who* will do it, *when* it will be done, and *how much* it will cost.
Budgets	A projected profit and loss statement that forecasts the expected financial outcomes from the plan.
Controls	Indicates how the progress of the plan will be monitored.

Marketers must continually plan their analysis, implementation, and control activities.

several years, and then reviews customer needs and factors in the marketing environment that may affect customer purchasing. Next, the *product review* shows sales, prices, and gross margins of the major products in the product line. A section on *competition* identifies major competitors and discusses each of their strategies for product quality, pricing, distribution, and promotion. It also shows the market shares held by the company and each competitor. Finally, a section on *distribution* describes recent sales trends and developments in the major distribution channels.

Threats and Opportunities

This section requires the manager to look ahead for major threats and opportunities that the product might face. Its purpose is to make the manager anticipate important developments that can have an impact on the firm. Managers should list as many threats and opportunities as they can imagine. Suppose Ralston-Purina's pet food division comes up with the following list:

- A large competitor has just announced that it will introduce a new premium pet food line, backed by a huge advertising and sales promotion blitz.

- Industry analysts predict that supermarket chain buyers will face more than 10,000 new grocery product introductions next year. The buyers are expected to accept only 38 percent of these new products and give each one only five months to prove itself.

- Because of improving economic conditions, pet ownership is expected to increase in almost all segments of the U.S. population.

- The company's researchers have found a way to make a new pet food that is low in fat and calories, yet highly nutritious and tasty. This product will appeal strongly to many of today's pet food buyers, who are almost as concerned about their pets' health as they are about their own.

- Pet ownership and concern about proper pet care are increasing rapidly in foreign markets, especially in developing nations.

The first two items are *threats*. Not all threats call for the same attention or concern—Purina managers should assess the likelihood of each threat and the potential damage each could cause. The manager should then focus on the most probable and harmful threats and prepare plans in advance to meet them.

The last three items in the list are marketing opportunities—attractive arenas for marketing action in which Purina could enjoy a competitive advantage. Purina managers should assess each opportunity according to its potential attractiveness and the company's probability of success. Companies can rarely find ideal opportunities that exactly fit their objectives and resources. The development of opportunities involves risks. When evaluating opportunities, managers must decide whether the expected returns justify these risks.

Objectives and Issues

Having studied the product's threats and opportunities, the manager can now set objectives and consider issues that will affect them. The objectives should be stated as goals the company would like to attain during the plan's term. For example, the manager might want to achieve a 15 percent market share, a 20 percent pretax profit on sales, and a 25 percent pretax profit on investment. Suppose the current market share is only 10 percent. This poses a key issue: How can market share be increased? The manager should consider the major issues involved in trying to increase market share.

Marketing Strategies

Marketing strategy
The marketing logic by which the business unit hopes to achieve its marketing objectives.

In this section of the marketing plan, the manager outlines the broad marketing strategy or "game plan" for attaining the objectives. **Marketing strategy** is the marketing logic by which the business unit hopes to achieve its marketing objectives. It consists of specific strategies for target markets, positioning, the marketing mix, and marketing expenditure levels. Marketing strategy should detail the market segments on which the company will focus. These segments differ in their needs and wants, responses to marketing, and profitability. The company would be smart to put its effort and energy into those market segments it can best serve from a competitive point of view, and then develop a marketing strategy for each targeted segment.

The manager should also outline specific strategies for such marketing mix elements as new products, field sales, advertising, sales promotion, prices, and distribution. The manager should explain how each strategy responds to the threats, opportunities, and critical issues spelled out earlier in the plan.

Action Programs

Marketing strategies should be turned into specific action programs that answer the following questions: *What* will be done? *When* will it be done? *Who* is responsible for doing it? And *how much* will it cost? For example, the manager may want to increase sales promotion as a key strategy for winning market share. A sales promotion action plan should be drawn up to outline special offers and their dates, trade shows entered, new point-of-purchase displays, and other promotions. The action plan shows when activities will be started, reviewed, and completed.

Budgets

Action plans allow the manager to make a supporting *marketing budget* that is essentially a projected profit-and-loss statement. For revenues, it shows the forecasted number of units that would be sold and the average net price. On the expense side, it shows the cost of production, physical distribution, and marketing. The difference is the projected profit. Higher management will review the budget and either approve or modify it. Once approved, the budget is the basis for materials buying, production scheduling, personnel planning, and marketing operations. Budgeting can be very difficult, and budgeting methods range from simple "rules of thumb" to complex computer models.[11]

Controls

The last section of the plan outlines the controls that will be used to monitor progress. Typically, goals and budgets are spelled out for each month or quarter. This practice allows higher management to review the results each period and to spot businesses or products that are not meeting their goals. The managers of these businesses and products have to explain these problems and the corrective actions they will take.

MARKETING IMPLEMENTATION

Planning good strategies is only a start toward successful marketing. A brilliant marketing strategy counts for little if the company fails to implement it properly. **Marketing implementation** is the process that turns marketing strategies and *plans* into marketing *actions* in order to accomplish strategic marketing objectives. Implementation involves day-to-day, month-to-month activities that effectively put the marketing plan to work. Whereas marketing planning addresses the *what* and *why* of marketing activities, implementation addresses the *who, where, when,* and *how.*

> **Marketing implementation**
> The process that turns marketing strategies and plans into marketing actions in order to accomplish strategic marketing objectives.

Many managers think that "doing things right" (implementation) is as important as, or even more important than, "doing the right things" (strategy). The fact is that both are critical to success. However, companies can gain competitive advantages through effective implementation. One firm can have essentially the same strategy as another, yet win in the marketplace through faster or better execution. Still, implementation is difficult—it is often easier to think up good marketing strategies than it is to carry them out.

People at all levels of the marketing system must work together to implement marketing plans and strategies. At Procter & Gamble, for example, marketing implementation requires day-to-day decisions and actions by thousands of people both inside and outside the organization. Marketing managers make decisions about target segments, branding, packaging, pricing, promoting, and distributing. They work with people elsewhere in the company to get support for their products and programs. They talk with engineering about product design, with manufacturing about production and inventory levels, and with finance about funding and cash flows. They also work with outside people, such as advertising agencies to plan ad campaigns and the media to obtain publicity support. The salesforce urges retailers to advertise P&G products, provide ample shelf space, and use company displays.

Successful implementation depends on several key elements. First, it requires an *action program* that pulls all of the people and activities together. The action program shows what must be done, who will do it, and how decisions and actions will be coordinated to reach the company's marketing objectives. Second, the company's formal *organization structure* plays an important role in implementing marketing strategy. In their study of successful companies, Peters and Waterman found that these firms tended to have simple, flexible structures that allowed them to adapt quickly to changing conditions.[12] Their structures also tended to be more informal—Hewlett-Packard's MBWA (management by walking around), 3M's "clubs" to create small-group interaction. However, the structures used by these companies may not be right for other types of firms, and many of the study's excellent companies have had to change their structures as their strategies and situations changed. For example, the same informal structure that made Hewlett-Packard so successful caused problems later. The company has since moved toward a more formal structure (see Marketing Highlight 2-2).

HEWLETT-PACKARD'S STRUCTURE EVOLVES

In 1939, two engineers, Bill Hewlett and David Packard, started Hewlett-Packard in a Palo Alto garage to build test equipment. At the start, Bill and Dave did everything themselves, from designing and building their equipment to marketing it. As the firm grew out of the garage and began to offer more types of test equipment, Hewlett and Packard could no longer make all the necessary operating

decisions themselves. They hired functional managers to run various company activities. These managers were relatively autonomous, but they were still closely tied to the owners.

By the mid-1970s, Hewlett-Packard's 42 divisions employed more than 30,000 people. The company's structure evolved to support its heavy emphasis on innovation and autonomy. Each division operated as

an independent unit and was responsible for its own strategic planning, product development, marketing programs, and implementation.

In 1982, in their book *In Search of Excellence,* Peters and Waterman cited H-P's structure as a major reason for the company's continued excellence. They praised H-P's unrestrictive structure and high degree of informal communication (its MBWA

Hewlett-Packard began in this garage in 1939. It now operates globally through a sophisticated complex of facilities and communications networks. Its structure and culture have changed with growth.

The company's *decision and reward systems*—operating procedures that guide planning, budgeting, compensation, and other activities—also affect implementation. For example, if a company compensates managers for short-run results, they will have little incentive to work toward long-run objectives. Effective implementation also requires careful *human resources* planning. At all levels, the company must fill its structure and systems with people who have the needed skills, motivation, and personal characteristics. In recent years, more and more companies have recognized that long-run human resources planning can give the company a strong competitive advantage.

Finally, to be successfully implemented, the firm's marketing strategies must fit with its company culture. *Company culture* is a system of values and beliefs shared by people in an organization—the company's collective identity and meaning. Marketing strategies that do not fit the company's culture will be difficult to implement. For example, a decision by Procter & Gamble to increase sales by reducing product quality and charging low prices would not work well. It would be resisted by P&G people at all levels who identify strongly with the company's

style—management by wandering around) that fostered autonomy by decentralizing decision-making responsibility and authority. The approach became known as the "H-P Way," a structure that encouraged innovation by abolishing rigid chains of command and putting managers and employees on a first-name basis.

But by the mid-1980s, although still profitable, Hewlett-Packard had begun to encounter problems in the fast-changing personal computer and minicomputer markets. In a new climate that required its fiercely autonomous divisions to work together in product development and marketing, H-P's famed innovative culture—with its heavy emphasis on autonomy and entrepreneurship—became a hindrance. Thus, Hewlett-Packard moved to bring its structure and culture in line with its changing situation. It established a system of committees to foster communication within and across its many divisions and to coordinate product development, marketing, and other activities.

The new structure seemed to work well—for a while. However, the move toward centralization soon got out of hand. The committees kept multiplying, and soon every decision was made by committee. By the late 1980s, the "H-P Way" was completely bogged down by unwieldy bureaucracy. Entering the 1990s, H-P had no fewer than 38 in-house committees

that made decisions on everything from technical specifications for new products to the best cities for staging product launches. Instead of enhancing communication, this suffocating structure pushed up costs and increased H-P's decision-making and market-reaction time. For example, in one case, it took almost 100 people over seven weeks just to come up with a name for the company's New Wave Computing software.

In the fast-paced workstation and personal computer markets, H-P's sluggish decision making put it at a serious disadvantage against such nimble competitors as Compaq Computer Corporation and Sun Microsystems. When one of H-P's most important projects, a series of high-speed work stations, slipped a year behind schedule as a result of seemingly endless committee meetings, top management finally took action. It removed the project's 200 engineers from the formal management structure so that they could continue work on the project free of the usual committee red tape. The workstation crisis convinced H-P management that it must make similar changes throughout the company. In fact, Bill Hewlett and Dave Packard themselves stepped in to help break the bureaucracy and restore a measure of decentralization. The result was a sweeping reorganization that wiped out H-P's committee structure and

flattened the organization. A typical top executive who once dealt with 38 committees now deals with only three. Global, crossfunctional teams now run individual H-P businesses. Despite the company's huge size—98,400 employees worldwide and $25 billion in annual sales—its small, nimble, autonomous units can react quickly to the market.

Thus, in less than a decade, Hewlett-Packard's structure has evolved from the highly decentralized and informal "H-P Way" to a highly centralized committee system and back again to a point in between. H-P is not likely to find a single best structure that will satisfy all of its future needs. Rather, it must continue adapting its structure to suit the requirements of its ever-changing environment.

Sources: See Thomas J. Peters and Robert H. Waterman, *In Search of Excellence: Lessons from America's Best-Run Companies* (New York: Harper & Row, 1982); Donald F. Harvey, *Business Policy and Strategic Management* (Columbus, OH: Charles E. Merrill, 1982), pp. 269–270; "Who's Excellent Now?" *Business Week,* November 5, 1984, pp. 76–78; Barbara Buell, Robert D. Hof, and Gary McWilliams, "Hewlett-Packard Rethinks Itself," *Business Week,* April 1, 1991, pp. 76–79; and Alan Deutschman, "How H-P Continues to Grow and Grow," *Fortune,* May 2, 1994, pp. 90–100.

reputation for quality. Because company culture is so hard to change, companies usually design strategies that fit their current cultures, rather than trying to change their styles and cultures to fit new strategies.

In summary, successful marketing implementation depends on how well the company blends the five elements—action programs, organization structure, decision and reward systems, human resources, and company culture—into a cohesive program that supports its strategies.

MARKETING DEPARTMENT ORGANIZATION

The company must design a marketing department that can carry out marketing analysis, planning, implementation, and control. If the company is very small, one person might do all of the marketing work—research, selling, advertising, customer service, and other activities. As the company expands, a marketing department organization emerges to plan and carry out marketing activities. In large

RETHINKING BRAND MANAGEMENT

Brand management has become a fixture in most consumer packaged goods companies. Brand managers plan long-term brand strategy and watch over their brand's profits. Working closely with advertising agencies, they create national advertising campaigns to build market share and long-term consumer brand loyalty. The brand management system made sense in its earlier days, when the food companies were all-powerful, consumers were brand loyal, and national media could reach mass markets effectively. Recently, however, many companies have begun to question whether this system fits well with today's radically different marketing realities.

Two major environmental forces are causing companies to rethink brand management. First, consumers, markets, and marketing strategies have changed dramatically. Today's consumers face an ever-growing set of acceptable brands and are exposed to never-ending price promotions. As a result, they are becoming less brand loyal. Also, whereas brand managers have traditionally focused on long-term, national brand-building strategies targeting mass audiences, today's marketplace realities demand shorter-term, sales-building strategies designed for local markets.

A second major force affecting brand management is the growing

Rethinking the role of the product manager: Campbell set up "brand sales managers."

power of retailers. Larger, more powerful, and better-informed retailers are now demanding more trade promotions in exchange for scarce shelf space. The increase in trade promotion spending leaves fewer dollars for national advertising, the brand manager's primary marketing tool. Retailers also want more customized "multibrand" promotions that span many of the producer's brands and help retailers to compete better. Such promotions are beyond the scope of any single brand manager and must be designed at higher levels of the company.

These and other changes have significantly changed the way companies market their products, causing marketers to rethink the brand management system that has served them so well for many years. Although it is unlikely that brand managers will soon be extinct, many companies are now groping for alternative ways to manage their brands.

One alternative is to change the nature of the brand manager's job. For example, some companies are asking their brand managers to spend more time in the field working with salespeople, learning what is happening in stores and getting closer to the customer. Campbell Soup created "brand sales managers," combination product managers and salespeople charged with handling brands in the field, working with the trade, and

companies, this department contains many specialists. Thus, General Mills has product managers, salespeople and sales managers, market researchers, advertising experts, and other specialists.

Modern marketing departments can be arranged in several ways. The most common form of marketing organization is the *functional organization* in which different marketing activities are headed by a functional specialist—a sales manager, advertising manager, marketing research manager, customer service manager, new-product manager. A company that sells across the country or internationally often uses a *geographic organization* in which its sales and marketing people are assigned to specific countries, regions, and districts. Geographic organization allows salespeople to settle into a territory, get to know their customers, and work with a minimum of travel time and cost.

Companies with many, very different products or brands often create a *product management organization*. Using this approach, a product manager develops and implements a complete strategy and marketing program for a specific product or brand. Product management first appeared in the Procter & Gamble Company in 1929. A new company soap, Camay, was not doing well, and a young P&G executive was assigned to give his exclusive attention to developing and promoting this product. He was successful, and the company soon added other prod-

designing more localized brand strategies.

As another alternative, Procter & Gamble, Colgate-Palmolive, Kraft-General Foods, RJR-Nabisco, and other companies have adopted *category management* systems. Under this system, brand managers report to a category manager who has total responsibility for an entire product line. For example, at Procter & Gamble, the brand manager for Dawn liquid dishwashing detergent reports to a manager who is responsible for Dawn, Ivory, Joy, and all other liquid detergents. The liquids manager, in turn, reports to a manager who is responsible for all of P&G's packaged soaps and detergents, including dishwashing detergents, and liquid and dry laundry detergents.

Category management offers many advantages. First, rather than focusing on specific brands, category managers shape the company's entire category offering. This results in a more complete and coordinated category offer. Perhaps the most important benefit of category management is that it links up better with new retailer "category buying" systems, in which retailers have begun making their individual buyers responsible for

working with all suppliers of a specific product category.

Some companies are combining category management with another concept: *brand teams* or *category teams*. For example, instead of having several cookie brand managers, Nabisco has three cookie category management teams—one each for adult rich cookies, nutritional cookies, and children's cookies. Headed by a category manager, each category team includes several marketing people—brand managers, a sales planning manager, and a marketing information specialist—who handle brand strategy, advertising, and sales promotion. Each team also includes specialists from finance, research and development, manufacturing, engineering, and distribution. Thus, category managers act as small businesspeople, with complete responsibility for an entire category and with a full complement of people to help them plan and implement category marketing strategies.

Thus, although brand managers are far from extinct, their jobs are changing. Such changes are much needed. The brand management system is product driven, not customer driven. Brand managers focus

on pushing their brands out to anyone and everyone, and they often concentrate so heavily on a single brand that they lose sight of the marketplace. Even category management focuses on products, for example, "cookies" as opposed to "Oreos." But today, more than ever, companies must start not with brands, but with the needs of the consumers and retailers that these brands serve. Colgate recently took a step in this direction. It moved from *brand management* (Colgate brand toothpaste) to *category management* (all Colgate-Palmolive toothpaste brands) to a new stage, *customer need management* (customers' oral health needs). This last stage finally gets the organization to focus on customer needs.

Sources: See Robert Dewar and Don Schultz, "The Product Manager: An Idea Whose Time Has Gone," *Marketing Communications,* May 1989, pp. 28–35; "Death of the Brand Manager," *The Economist,* April 9, 1994, pp. 67–68; and George S. Low and Ronald A. Fullerton, "Brands, Brand Management, and the Brand Manager System: A Critical-Historical Evaluation," *Journal of Marketing Research,* May 1994, pp. 173–190.

uct managers.[13] Since then, many firms, especially in the food, soap, toiletries, and chemical industries, have set up product management organizations. Today, the product management system is firmly entrenched. However, recent dramatic changes in the marketing environment have caused many companies to rethink the role of the product manager (see Marketing Highlight 2-3).

For companies that sell one product line to many different types of markets that have different needs and preferences, a *market management organization* might be best. Many companies are organized along market lines. A market management organization is similar to the product management organization. Market managers are responsible for developing long-range and annual plans for the sales and profits in their markets. This system's main advantage is that the company is organized around the needs of specific customer segments.

Large companies that produce many different products flowing into many different geographic and customer markets use some *combination* of the functional, geographic, product, and market organization forms. This assures that each function, product, and market receives its share of management attention. However, it can also add costly layers of management and reduce organizational flexibility. Still, the benefits of organizational specialization usually outweigh the drawbacks.[14]

MARKETING CONTROL

Marketing control
The process of measuring and evaluating the results of marketing strategies and plans, and taking corrective action to ensure that marketing objectives are attained.

Because many surprises occur during the implementation of marketing plans, the marketing department must practice constant marketing control. **Marketing control** involves evaluating the results of marketing strategies and plans and taking corrective action to ensure that objectives are attained. It involves the four steps shown in Figure 2-8. Management first sets specific marketing goals. It then measures its performance in the marketplace and evaluates the causes of any differences between expected and actual performance. Finally, management takes corrective action to close the gaps between its goals and its performance. This may require changing the action programs or even changing the goals.

FIGURE 2-8 *The control process*

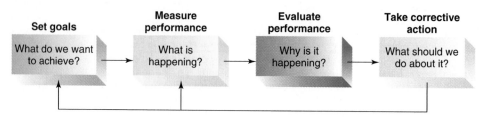

Operating control involves checking ongoing performance against the annual plan and taking corrective action when necessary. Its purpose is to ensure that the company achieves the sales, profits, and other goals set out in its annual plan. It also involves determining the profitability of different products, territories, markets, and channels. *Strategic control* involves looking at whether the company's basic strategies are well matched to its opportunities. Marketing strategies and programs can quickly become outdated, and each company should periodically reassess its overall approach to the marketplace. A major tool for such strategic control is a **marketing audit**. The marketing audit is a comprehensive, systematic, independent, and periodic examination of a company's environment, objectives, strategies, and activities to determine problem areas and opportunities. The audit provides good input for a plan of action to improve the company's marketing performance.[15]

Marketing audit
A comprehensive, systematic, independent, and periodic examination of a company's environment, objectives, strategies, and activities to determine problem areas and opportunities and to recommend a plan of action to improve the company's marketing performance.

The marketing audit covers *all* major marketing areas of a business, not just a few trouble spots. It is normally conducted by an objective and experienced outside party who is independent of the marketing department. Table 2-3 shows the kinds of questions the marketing auditor might ask. The findings may come as a surprise—and sometimes as a shock—to management. Management then decides which actions make sense and how and when to implement them.

THE MARKETING ENVIRONMENT

Managing the marketing function would be hard enough if the marketer had to deal only with the controllable marketing-mix variables. But the company operates in a complex marketing environment, consisting of uncontrollable forces to which the company must adapt. The environment produces both threats and opportunities. The company must carefully analyze its environment so that it can avoid the threats and take advantage of the opportunities.

The company's marketing environment includes forces close to the company that affect its ability to serve its consumers, such as other company departments, channel members, suppliers, competitors, and publics. It also includes broader demographic and economic forces, political and legal forces, technological and ecological forces, and social and cultural forces. The company must consider all of these forces when developing and positioning its offer to the target market. The marketing environment is discussed more fully in Chapter 3.

TABLE 2-3 *Marketing Audit Questions*

MARKETING ENVIRONMENT AUDIT
The Macroenvironment

1. *Demographic.* What major demographic trends pose threats and opportunities for this company?
2. *Economic.* What developments in income, prices, savings, and credit will impact the company?
3. *Natural.* What is the outlook for costs and availability of natural resources and energy? Is the company environmentally responsible?
4. *Technology.* What technological changes are occurring? What is the company's position on technology?
5. *Political.* What current and proposed laws will affect company strategy?
6. *Cultural.* What is the public's attitude toward business and the company's products? What changes in consumer lifestyles might have an impact?

The Task Environment

1. *Markets.* What is happening to market size, growth, geographic distribution, and profits? What are the major market segments?
2. *Customers.* How do customers rate the company on product quality, service, and price? How do they make their buying decisions?
3. *Competitors.* Who are the major competitors? What are their strategies, market shares, and strengths and weaknesses?
4. *Channels.* What main channels does the company use to distribute products to customers? How are they performing?
5. *Suppliers.* What trends are affecting suppliers? What is the outlook for the availability of key production resources?
6. *Publics.* What key publics provide problems or opportunities? How should the company deal with these publics?

MARKETING STRATEGY AUDIT

1. *Business mission.* Is the mission clearly defined and market oriented?
2. *Marketing objectives.* Has the company set clear objectives to guide marketing planning and performance? Do these objectives fit with company opportunities and resources?
3. *Marketing strategy.* Does the company have a sound marketing strategy for achieving its objectives?
4. *Budgets.* Has the company budgeted sufficient resources to segments, products, territories, and marketing mix elements?

MARKETING ORGANIZATION AUDIT

1. *Formal structure.* Does the chief marketing officer have adequate authority over activities affecting customer satisfaction? Are marketing activities optimally structured along functional, product, market, and territory lines?
2. *Functional efficiency.* Do marketing and sales communicate effectively? Is the marketing staff well trained, supervised, motivated, and evaluated?
3. *Interface efficiency.* Does the marketing staff work well with manufacturing, R&D, purchasing, human resources, and other nonmarketing areas?

MARKETING SYSTEMS AUDIT

1. *Marketing information system.* Is the marketing intelligence system providing accurate and timely information about marketplace developments? Are company decision makers using marketing research effectively?

TABLE 2-3 *continued*

2. *Marketing planning system.* Does the company prepare annual, long-term, and strategic plans? Are they used?

3. *Marketing control system.* Are annual plan objectives being achieved? Does management periodically analyze the sales and profitability of products, markets, territories, and channels?

4. *New-product development.* Is the company well organized to gather, generate, and screen new-product ideas? Does it carry out adequate product and market testing? Has the company succeeded with new products?

MARKETING PRODUCTIVITY AUDIT

1. *Profitability Analysis.* How profitable are the company's different products, markets, territories, and channels? Should the company enter, expand, or withdraw from any business segments? What would be the consequences?

2. *Cost-effectiveness analysis.* Do any marketing activities have excessive costs? How can costs be reduced?

MARKETING FUNCTION AUDIT

1. *Products.* Has the company developed sound product-line objectives? Should some products be phased out? Should some new products be added? Would some products benefit from quality, style, or feature changes?

2. *Price.* What are the company's pricing objectives, policies, strategies, and procedures? Are the company's prices in line with customers' perceived value? Are price promotions used properly?

3. *Distribution.* What are the distribution objectives and strategies? Does the company have adequate market coverage and service? Should existing channels be changed or new ones added?

4. *Advertising, sales promotion, and publicity.* What are the company's promotion objectives? How is the budget determined? Is it sufficient? Are advertising messages and media well developed and received? Does the company have well-developed sales promotion and public relations programs?

5. *Salesforce.* What are the company's salesforce objectives? Is the salesforce large enough? Is it properly organized? Is it well trained, supervised, and motivated? How is the salesforce rated relative to those of competitors?

Summary

Strategic planning is the process of developing a formal strategy for long-run survival and growth. Typically the process involves *defining the company mission* and *setting objectives and goals* down in strategic plans, long-range plans, and annual plans. Not all companies use formal planning, and many others use their planning poorly. When done well, however, formal planning offers several benefits. It encourages management to think ahead systematically, leads to sharper objectives and policies, fosters better coordination of efforts, and provides clearer performance standards.

A key part of the planning process is *developing a business portfolio* which is consistent with the company mission. Specific analytic techniques can be used, such as the *Boston Consulting Group growth-share matrix* and the *General Electric strategic business grid*. These techniques illustrate different aspects of each business in the portfolio, and can help in making decisions about how much support should be given to different businesses. Such matrix approaches do have drawbacks, however. They are often difficult to use, and focus only on current businesses, giving little advice for future planning. *Developing growth strategies* can be aided by the *product/market expansion grid*, which suggests four possible avenues for growth: market penetration, market development, product development, and diversification.

Another important aspect of the planning process is developing *functional strategies* and plans. Once strategic objectives have been defined, each business unit must prepare a set of functional plans that coordinates the activities of the marketing, finance, manufacturing, and other departments. Each of these departments has a different view about which objectives and activities are most important. The marketing department emphasizes the consumer's point of view, but must also work effectively with managers of other functions to develop plans which will best accomplish the firm's overall objectives.

The *marketing process* matches consumer needs with company capabilities and goals. Consumers are at the center of the marketing process. The company must analyze the market, divide it into logical groups through the process of *market segmentation*, and select the segments it can best serve. These are the company's *target consumers*.

The company then designs a *marketing mix* to differentiate its product, creating a *competitive advantage* through an effective *market positioning*.

There are many steps to managing the marketing effort. Each business must prepare *marketing plans* for its products, brands, and markets. The main parts of a marketing plan are the *executive summary, current marketing situation, threats and opportunities, objectives and issues, marketing strategies, action programs,* and *budgets and controls*.

Marketing plans, however clever they may be, are effective only if they are properly implemented. This requires that the marketing strategies be translated into an effective *action plan*, which defines crucial tasks, assigns them to specific people, and establishes a timetable. Good human resources planning is essential to maintaining effective implementation. The *marketing department organization* structure also effects the way plans are implemented.

Finally, marketing organizations monitor and fine-tune their plans through a process of *marketing control*. Operating control assures that the annual profit and volume goals will be met, and that short-term plans are appropriate. Strategic control makes certain that the longer-term aspects of the plan, including objectives, strategies, and systems, continue to fit with the current and anticipated marketing environment. Conducting periodic *marketing audits* offers a way to formalize these aspects of marketing control.

Key Terms

Business portfolio	Market segment	Mission statement
Cash cows	Market segmentation	Portfolio analysis
Diversification	Market targeting	Product development
Dogs	Marketing audit	Product/market expansion grid
Executive summary	Marketing control	Question marks
Growth-share matrix	Marketing implementation	Stars
Market development	Marketing process	Strategic business unit (SBU)
Market penetration	Marketing mix	Strategic planning
Market positioning	Marketing strategy	

Discussing the Issues

1. Name some of the benefits of a "rolling" five-year plan—that is, why should managers take time to write a five-year plan that will be changed every year?

2. In a series of job interviews, you ask three recruiters to describe the missions of their companies. One says, "To make profits." Another says, "To create customers." The third says, "To fight world hunger." Analyze and discuss what these mission statements tell you about each of the companies.

3. An electronics manufacturer obtains the semiconductors it uses in production from a company-owned subsidiary that also sells to other manufacturers. The subsidiary is smaller and less profitable than are competing producers, and its growth rate has been below the industry average during the past five years. Define which cell of the BCG growth-share matrix this strategic business unit would fall into. What should the parent company do with this SBU?

4. As companies become more customer and marketing oriented, many departments find that they must change their traditional way of doing things. List several examples of ways that a company's finance, accounting, and engineering departments can help the company become more marketing oriented.

5. The General Electric strategic business-planning grid provides a broad overview that can be very helpful in strategic decision making. Identify the types of decisions for which this grid would be helpful. Are there other types of strategic decisions where it is not useful?

6. Blockbuster Video is the market leader in home video rentals. It offers two-night rentals, large attractive stores, and a wide variety at moderately high prices. Discuss how you would use market challenger, market follower, and market nicher strategies to compete with Blockbuster.

Applying the Concepts

1. Sit down with an AM-FM radio and pencil and paper. Make a simple chart with four columns titled: *Frequency, Call Letters* (optional but helpful), *Format,* and *Notes.* Tune across the AM and FM bands from beginning to end, and make brief notes for each station with adequate reception. In the *Format* column, note the type of programming, such as student-run, public, classic rock, hip-hop, religious, and so forth. Under the *Notes* column, write down any station slogans you hear (such as "Your Concert Connection"), events that the station is sponsoring, and the types of advertising you hear.

   - Total the number of stations you received, and add up how many stations share each format. How many different market segments do these stations appear to target?

   - Are any of these stations positioned in an unusually clear and distinctive way? How?

   - Do advertisers choose different types of stations for different types of products? Does their market segmentation make sense? Give examples.

2. Think about the shopping area near your campus. Assume that you wish to start a business here, and are looking for a promising opportunity for a restaurant, a clothing store, or a music store.

   - Is there an opportunity to open a distinctive and promising business? Describe your target market, and how you would serve it differently than current businesses do.

   - What sort of marketing mix would you use for your business?

References

1. See "Levi's: The Jeans Giant Slipped as the Market Shifted," *Business Week,* November 5, 1984, pp. 79–80; Miriam Rozen, "The 501 Blues," *Madison Avenue,* November 1984, pp. 22–26; Marc Beauchamp, "Tight Fit," *Forbes,* August 11, 1986; Joshua Hyatt, "Levi Strauss Learns a Fitting Lesson," *Inc.,* August 1985, p. 17; Maria Shao, "For Levi's, A Flattering Fit Overseas," *Business Week,* November 5, 1990, pp. 76–77; "A Comfortable Fit," *The Economist,* June 22, 1991, pp. 67–68; Nina Monk, "The Levi Straddle," *Forbes,* January 17, 1994, pp. 44–45; and Alice Z. Cuneo, "Levi Strauss Sizes the Retail Scene," *Advertising Age,* January 23, 1995, p. 4.

2. For a more detailed discussion of corporate and business-level strategic planning as they apply to marketing, see Philip Kotler, *Marketing Management: Analysis, Planning, Implementation, and Control,* 8th ed. (Englewood Cliffs, NJ: Prentice Hall, 1994), Chapters 3 and 4.

3. For more on mission statements, see David A. Aaker, *Strategic Market Management,* 2nd ed. (New York: Wiley, 1988), Chap. 3; Laura Nash, "Mission Statements—Mirrors and Windows," *Harvard Business Review,* March–April 1988, pp. 155–156; Fred R. David, "How Companies Define Their Mission Statements," *Long Range Planning,* Vol. 22, No. 1, 1989, pp. 90–97; and David L. Calfee, "Get Your Mission Statement Working!" *Management Review,* January 1993, pp. 54–57.

4. Richard G. Hamermesh, "Making Planning Strategic," *Harvard Business Review,* July–August 1986, pp. 115–120. Also see Henry Mintzberg, "The Rise and Fall of Strategic Planning," *Harvard Business Review,* January–February 1994, pp. 107–114.

5. See Daniel H. Gray, "Uses and Misuses of Strategic Planning," *Harvard Business Review,* January–February 1986, pp. 89–96; and Roger A. Kerin, Vijay Mahajan, and P. Rajan Varadarajan, *Contemporary Perspectives on Strategic Planning* (Boston: Allyn & Bacon, 1990).

6. H. Igor Ansoff, "Strategies for Diversification," *Harvard Business Review,* September–October 1957, pp. 113–124.

7. John C. Narver and Stanley F. Slater, "The Effect of a Market Orientation on Business Profitability," *Journal of Marketing,* October 1990, pp. 20–35.

8. See Brian Dumaine, "Creating a New Company Culture," *Fortune,* January 15, 1990, p. 128.

9. The four *P* classification was first suggested by E. Jerome McCarthy, *Basic Marketing: A Managerial Approach* (Homewood, IL: Irwin, 1960). For more discussion of this classification scheme, see Walter van Waterschoot and Christophe Van den Bulte, "The 4P Classification of the Marketing Mix Revisited," *Journal of Marketing,* October 1992, pp. 83–93.

10. Robert Lauterborn, "New Marketing Litany: Four P's Passé; C-Words Take Over," *Advertising Age,* October 1, 1990, p. 26.

11. For an interesting discussion of marketing budgeting methods and processes, see Nigel F. Piercy, "The Marketing Budgeting Process: Marketing Management Implications," *Journal of Marketing,* October 1987, pp. 45–59.

12. See Thomas J. Peters and Robert H. Waterman, *In Search of Excellence: Lessons from America's Best-Run Companies* (New York: Harper & Row, 1982). For an excellent summary of the study's findings on structure, see Aaker, *Strategic Market Management,* pp. 154–157.

13. Joseph Winski, "One Brand, One Manager," *Advertising Age,* August 20, 1987, p. 86.

14. For more complete discussions of marketing organization approaches and issues, see Robert W. Ruekert, Orville C. Walker, Jr., and Kenneth J. Roering, "The Organization of Marketing Activities: A Contingency Theory of Structure and Performance," *Journal of Marketing,* Winter 1985, pp. 13–25; and Ravi S. Achrol, "Evolution of the Marketing Organization: New Forms for Turbulent Environments," *Journal of Marketing,* October 1991, pp. 77–93.

15. For details, see Kotler, *Marketing Management: Analysis, Planning, Implementation, and Control,* 8th ed., Chap. 27.

Company Case 2

TRAP-EASE AMERICA: THE BIG CHEESE OF MOUSETRAPS

One April morning, Martha House, president of Trap-Ease America, entered her office in Costa Mesa, California. She paused for a moment to contemplate the Ralph Waldo Emerson quote which she had framed and hung near her desk.

If a man [can] . . . make a better mousetrap than his neighbor . . . the world will make a beaten path to his door.

Perhaps, she mused, Emerson knew something that she didn't. She *had* the better mousetrap—Trap-Ease—but the world didn't seem all that excited about it.

Martha had just returned from the National Hardware Show in Chicago. Standing in the trade show display booth for long hours and answering the same questions hundreds of times had been tiring. Yet, this show had excited her. Each year, National Hardware Show officials held a contest to select the best new product introduced at the show. Of the more than 300 new products introduced at that year's show, her mousetrap had won first place. Such notoriety was not new for the Trap-Ease mousetrap. *People* magazine had written about the mousetrap in an article, and numerous talk shows and trade publications had featured it. Despite all of this attention, however, the expected demand for the trap had not materialized. Martha hoped that this award might stimulate increased interest and sales.

A group of investors who had obtained worldwide rights to market the innovative mousetrap had formed Trap-Ease America in January. In return for marketing rights, the group agreed to pay the inventor and patent holder, a retired rancher, a royalty fee for each trap sold. The group then hired Martha to serve as president and to develop and manage the Trap-Ease America organization.

The Trap-Ease, a simple yet clever device, is manufactured by a plastics firm under contract with Trap-Ease America. It consists of a square, plastic tube measuring about 6 inches long and 1½ inches square. The tube bends in the middle at a 30-degree angle, so that when the front part of the tube rests on a flat surface, the other end is elevated. The elevated ends holds a removable cap into which the user places bait (cheese, dog food, or some other tidbit). A hinged door is attached to the front end of the tube. When the trap is "open," this door rests on two narrow "stilts" attached to the two bottom corners of the door.

The trap works with simple efficiency. A mouse, smelling the bait, enters the tube through the open end. As it walks up the angled bottom toward the bait, its weight makes the elevated end of the trap drop downward. This elevates the open end, allowing the hinged door to swing closed, trapping the mouse. Small teeth on the ends of the stilts catch in a groove on the bottom of the trap, locking the door closed. The mouse can be disposed of live, or it can be left alone for a few hours to suffocate in the trap.

Martha felt the trap had many advantages for the consumer when compared with traditional spring-loaded traps or poisons. Consumers can use it safely and easily with no risk of catching their fingers while loading it. It poses no injury or poisoning threat to children or pets. Furthermore, with Trap-Ease, consumers can avoid the unpleasant "mess" they encounter with the violent spring-loaded traps—it creates no "clean-up" problem. Finally, the consumer can reuse the trap or simply throw it away.

Martha's early research suggested that women are the best target market for the Trap-Ease. Men, it seems, are more willing to buy and use the traditional, spring-loaded trap. The targeted women, however, do not like the traditional trap. They often stay at home and take care of their children. Thus, they want a means of dealing with the mouse problem that avoids the unpleasantness and risks that the standard trap creates in the home.

To reach this target market, Martha decided to distribute Trap-Ease through national grocery, hardware, and drug chains such as Safeway, Kmart, Hechingers, and CB Drug. She sold the trap directly to these large retailers, avoiding any wholesalers or other middlemen.

The traps sold in packages of two, with a suggested retail price of $2.49. Although this price made the Trap-Ease about five to ten times more expensive than smaller, standard traps, consumers appeared to offer little initial price resistance. The manufacturing cost for the Trap-Ease, including freight and packaging costs, was about 31 cents per unit. The company paid an additional 8.2 cents per unit in royalty fees. Martha priced the traps to retailers at 99 cents per unit and estimated that, after sales and volume discounts, Trap-Ease would realize net revenues from retailers of 75 cents per unit.

To promote the product, Martha had budgeted approximately $60,000 for the first year. She planned to use $50,000 of this amount for travel costs to visit trade shows and to make sales calls on retailers. She would use the remaining $10,000 for advertising. So far, however, because the mousetrap had generated so much publicity, she had not felt that she needed to do much advertising. Still, she had placed advertising in *Good Housekeeping* and in other "home and shelter" magazines. Martha was the company's only "salesperson," but she intended to hire more salespeople soon.

Martha had initially forecasted Trap-Ease's first-year sales at five million units. Through April, however, the company had sold only several hundred thousand units. Martha wondered if most new products got off to such a slow start, or if she was doing something wrong. She had detected some problems, although none seemed overly serious. For one, there had not been enough repeat buying. For another, she had noted that many of the retailers on whom she called kept their sample mousetraps on their desks as conversation pieces—she wanted the traps to be used and demonstrated. Martha wondered if consumers were also buying the traps as novelties rather than as solutions to their mouse problems.

Martha knew that the investor group believed that Trap-Ease America had a "once-in-a-lifetime chance" with its innovative mousetrap. She sensed the group's impatience. She had budgeted approximately $250,000 in administrative and fixed costs for the first year (not including marketing costs). To keep the investors happy, the company needed to sell enough traps to cover those costs and make a reasonable profit.

In these first few months, Martha had learned that marketing a new product is not an easy task. For example, one national retailer had placed a large order with instructions that the order was to be delivered to the loading dock at one of its warehouses between 1:00 and 3:00 PM on a specified day. When the truck delivering the order had arrived late, the retailer had refused to accept the shipment. The retailer had told Martha it would be a year before she got another chance. Perhaps, Martha thought, she should send the retailer and other customers a copy of Emerson's famous quote.

QUESTIONS

1. Martha and the Trap-Ease America Investors feel they face a "once-in-a-lifetime" opportunity. What information do they need to evaluate this opportunity? How do you think the group would write its mission statement? How would *you* write it?

2. Has Martha identified the best target market for Trap-Ease? What other market segments might the firm target?

3. How has the company positioned the Trap-Ease relative to the chosen target market? Could it position the product in other ways?

4. Describe the current marketing mix for Trap-Ease. Do you see any problems with this mix?

5. Who is Trap-Ease America's competition?

6. How would you change Trap-Ease's marketing strategy? What kinds of control procedures would you establish for this strategy?

The Marketing Environment

3

Houston Effler & Partners Inc., the white-hot Boston-based advertising agency, earns its fees by helping clients like Converse and Sun Apparel communicate effectively with their changing and sometimes hard-to-understand customers. As head of the youth marketing department at Houston Effler, 25-year-old Jane Rinzler (shown opposite) is one of the first card-carrying Generation Xers to be hired to explain her post-boomer generation to puzzled clients. "Just explain to me," one blurted recently, "why they pierce their eyebrows."

As part of her job, Rinzler prowls nightclubs, conducts focus groups, schmoozes with mainstream GenXers in malls and hip-hoppers on swank Newbury Street, and generally takes the pulse of her nearly 40 million fellow Americans in their 20s. Then, she puts on a business suit and feeds her intelligence reports to her bosses and to Houston Effler clients hoping to tap into this lucrative new demographic market.

On a recent afternoon, Rinzler briefed a group of executives from Converse. The agency's largest account, the footwear company markets heavily to GenXers and teens. Rinzler talked about Converse All-Stars, reporting what she has heard on the streets of Los Angeles, New York, Dallas, and Seattle about the 77-year-old sneakers. Bottom line? She announced that the shoes' longevity is well appreciated among the Generation Xers, former latchkey kids who grew up surrounded by divorce, economic instability, and disappearing jobs. "Stay true to the fact you have a classic," she advises the group. "Anything that's trusted will do well with these kids."

Rinzler likes to think of herself as a translator. "The needs and wants of this generation are so different," she says, "and . . . some people are confounded by it." Houston Effler's CEO, Doug Houston, himself a classic baby boomer, considers the GenXers a breed apart. To illustrate both his point and the influence of Rinzler, he slides two recent magazine ads across his desk. Both are for jeans made by Sun Apparel. One of the ads, in color, is aimed primarily at teenagers. It is splashy and direct. The other, in black and white, is targeted at Generation X. Subdued and subtle, it is more image than message. "Two

OBJECTIVES

When you finish this chapter, you should be able to accomplish the following:

1. List and discuss the importance of the elements of the **company's microenvironment**, including the **company, marketing intermediaries, customers, competitors,** and **publics.**

2. Explain the broad concept of the **company's macroenvironment.**

3. Outline the key changes occurring in important elements of the company's macroenvironment, including shifts in the **demographic, economic, technological, political, cultural,** and **natural environments.**

years ago, we wouldn't have known enough to separate the two groups," Houston says.

As another example, Rinzler shows a magazine ad for Converse's Jack Purcell sneakers. The black and white ad shows a young, casually dressed twentysomething woman wearing Jack Purcells without socks while leafing through what appears to be a Victoria's Secret catalog. "Oh yeah," the woman is shown to be thinking, "I stand around the gazebo in my underwear all the time." That's *it*, except for a logo in the lower corner. Not only is the sell as soft as silk, but the ad makes low-key fun of a favorite Generation X target: advertising itself.

The GenXers are a skeptical bunch who can see through the hype and glitz. Rinzler comments, "It works because it doesn't put the product in your face. It shows a lifestyle that twentysomethings can see themselves part of. The woman isn't Cindy Crawford. And mocking advertising works because twentysomethings are tired of being manipulated. But you have to do it subtly."

Rinzler is intense, dresses out at the Gap and Banana Republic (the other women in the agency favor the Ann Taylor look), has an indefatigably chirpy voice, and is never far from a Diet Coke or her Coach appointment book. But not everyone in his or her 20s lives on Diet Coke and shops the Gap. So Rinzler might do Newbury Street with someone like 21-year-old Tony Bertone, who describes himself as "kind of like a consultant for a computer company." Rinzler sees Bertone as a fashion trendsetter, the kind of guy who wears what mainstreamers like herself will be donning somewhere down the road. She'll spend a few hours with him, talking a little and listening a lot: He's one of *her* translators. She'll also pay him $200 courtesy of Converse and likely lay some footwear on him.

"The lounge look is coming back, you know what I'm saying?" Bertone announced on a recent morning as he and Rinzler eased their way through Allston Beat, a cutting-edge clothing store on Newbury. "Like bowling shirts and three-button polos."

"That was last year, don't you think?" Rinzler commented politely. She was wearing a navy blue jersey, white jeans and, fittingly, white Jack Purcells. Her cellular phone was tucked into her brown suede backpack. She was carrying a legal-size pad on which she occasionally made notes on what, according to Bertone, is particularly out front these days. The list included the Internet, OK Soda commercials, and videos by Nine Inch Nails.

"The scumbag look!" Bertone countered. "The Indiana trailer trash look! Thin people! Thin mustaches! Tailored pants! Black shoes! People really looking greasy! . . . Everyone looks trashy. Trashy is fresh. You know what I'm saying?" Rinzler nodded and wrote eagerly on her pad. GenXers might understand all of this, but it would be gibberish to most of the boomer generation. For this reason, the lounge look, bowling shirts, and the Internet would all turn up on her list of currently hot items when she later made her presentation to Converse.

Houston Effler's success depends on its ability to help clients like Converse navigate the complex and changing marketing environment, helping them to understand better the forces that impact their customers. Changing demographics—the aging of the baby boomers, the rise of GenXers, and others—constitute one of today's most important environmental forces. For the better part of their lives, the Generation Xers weren't even considered a target market, let alone a generation. Now, however, they're being *discovered*. For this reason, Rinzler may be the first of a new breed that will work its way into corporate America. It doesn't hurt Houston Effler to be able to tell prospective clients that it claims firsthand knowledge of the generation that often bamboozles most over-30s.[1]

A company's **marketing environment** consists of the actors and forces outside marketing that affect marketing management's ability to develop and maintain successful relationships with its target customers. The marketing environment offers both opportunities and threats. Successful companies know the vital impor-

Marketing environment
The actors and forces outside marketing that affect marketing management's ability to develop and maintain successful transactions with its target customers.

tance of constantly watching and adapting to the changing environment. Too many other companies, unfortunately, fail to think of change as opportunity. They ignore or resist critical changes until it is almost too late. Their strategies, structures, systems, and culture grow increasingly out of date. Corporations as mighty as General Motors, IBM, and Sears have faced crises because they ignored environmental changes for too long.

A company's marketers take the major responsibility of identifying significant changes in the environment. More than any other group in the company, marketers must be the trend trackers and opportunity seekers. Although every manager in an organization needs to observe the outside environment, marketers have two special aptitudes. They have disciplined methods—marketing intelligence and marketing research—for collecting information about the marketing environment. They also normally spend more time in the customer and competitor environment. By conducting systematic environmental scanning, marketers are able to revise and adapt marketing strategies to meet new challenges and opportunities in the marketplace.

The marketing environment is made up of a *microenvironment* and a *macroenvironment*. The **microenvironment** consists of the forces close to the company that affect its ability to serve its customers—the company, suppliers, marketing channel firms, customer markets, competitors, and publics. The **macroenvironment** consists of the larger societal forces that affect the whole microenvironment—demographic, economic, natural, technological, political, and cultural forces. We look first at the company's microenvironment.

Microenvironment
The forces close to the company that affect its ability to serve its customers—the company, market channel firms, customer markets, competitors, and publics.

Macroenvironment
The larger societal forces that affect the whole microenvironment—demographic, economic, natural, technological, political, and cultural forces.

THE COMPANY'S MICROENVIRONMENT

Marketing management's job is to attract and build relationships with customers by creating customer value and satisfaction. However, marketing managers cannot accomplish this task alone. Their success will depend on other actors in the company's microenvironment—other company departments, suppliers, marketing intermediaries, customers, competitors, and various publics.

THE COMPANY

In designing marketing plans, marketing management takes other company groups into account—groups such as top management, finance, research and development (R&D), purchasing, manufacturing, and accounting. All these interrelated groups form the internal environment (see Figure 3-1). Top management sets the company's mission, objectives, broad strategies, and policies. Marketing managers must make decisions within the plans made by top management, and marketing plans must be approved by top management before they can be implemented.

Marketing managers also must work closely with other company departments. Finance is concerned with finding and using funds to carry out the marketing plan. The R&D department focuses on the problems of designing safe and attractive products. Purchasing worries about getting supplies and materials, whereas manufacturing is responsible for producing the desired quality and quantity of products. Accounting has to measure revenues and costs to help marketing know how well it is achieving its objectives. Together, all of these departments have an impact on the marketing department's plans and actions. Under the marketing

FIGURE 3-1 *The company's internal environment*

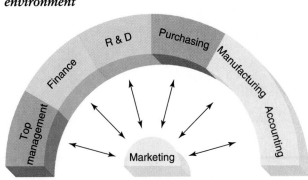

concept, all of these functions must "think consumer," and they should work in harmony to provide superior customer value and satisfaction.

SUPPLIERS

Suppliers are an important link in the company's overall customer "value delivery system." They provide the resources needed by the company to produce its goods and services. Supplier developments can seriously affect marketing. Marketing managers must watch supply availability—supply shortages or delays, labor strikes, and other events can cost sales in the short run and damage customer satisfaction in the long run. Marketing managers also monitor the price trends of their key inputs. Rising supply costs may force price increases that can harm the company's sales volume.

Marketing intermediaries
Firms that help the company to promote, sell, and distribute its goods to final buyers; they include middlemen, physical distribution firms, marketing-service agencies, and financial intermediaries.

Financial intermediaries: Firms like Credit Suisse offer a wide range of international financial services, from Atlanta and Abu Dhabi to Barcelona and Beijing.

MARKETING INTERMEDIARIES

Marketing intermediaries help the company to promote, sell, and distribute its goods to final buyers. They include *resellers, physical distribution firms, marketing services agencies,* and *financial intermediaries. Resellers* are distribution channel firms that help the company find customers or make sales to them. These include wholesalers and retailers who buy and resell merchandise. Selecting and working with resellers is not easy. No longer do manufacturers have many small, independent resellers from which to choose. They now face large and growing reseller organizations. These organizations frequently have enough power to dictate terms or even shut the manufacturer out of large markets.

Physical distribution firms help the company to stock and move goods from their points of origin to their destinations. Working with warehouse and transportation firms, a company must determine the best ways to store and ship goods, balancing such factors as cost, delivery, speed, and safety. *Marketing services agencies* are the marketing research firms, advertising agencies, media firms, and marketing consulting firms that help the company target and promote its products to the right markets. When the company decides to use one of these agencies, it must choose carefully because these firms vary in creativity, quality, service, and price. *Financial intermediaries* include banks, credit companies, insurance companies, and other businesses that help finance transactions or insure against the risks associated with the buying and selling of goods. Most firms and customers depend on financial intermediaries to finance their transactions.

Like suppliers, marketing intermediaries form an important component of the company's overall value delivery system. In its quest to create satisfying customer relationships, the company must do more than just optimize its own performance. It must partner effectively with suppliers and marketing intermediaries to optimize the performance of the entire system.

Saint Bernard

Incredibly Swiss.

Statue in the Forbidden City, Beijing

Incredibly International.

Reliability, loyalty and mutual trust are essential prerequisites for successful banking. That's why Credit Suisse attaches so much importance to personal service. Wherever you are, we can offer you all the advantages of a modern universal bank. Together with our partner organization, CS First Boston Inc., we have firmly established ourselves as one of the world's foremost international financial services groups. As a global provider of Swiss quality, Credit Suisse is second to none.

We do more to keep you ▲ at the top.

CREDIT SUISSE
CS

Zurich (Head Office) · Abu Dhabi · Atlanta · Beijing · Bogotá · Buenos Aires · Cairo · Calgary · Caracas · Chicago · Frankfurt · Gibraltar · Guernsey · Hong Kong · Houston · Johannesburg · London · Los Angeles · Luxembourg · Madrid · Manama (Bahrain) · Melbourne · Mexico City · Miami · Monte Carlo · Montevideo · Montreal · Munich · Nassau (Bahamas) · New York · Nuremberg · Osaka · Paris · Rio de Janeiro · San Francisco · São Paulo · Singapore · Stuttgart · Taipeh · Tehran · Tokyo · Toronto · Vancouver

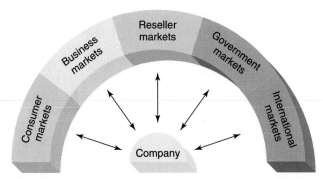

FIGURE 3-2 *Types of customer markets*

CUSTOMERS

The company needs to study its customer markets closely. Figure 3-2 shows five types of customer markets. *Consumer markets* consist of individuals and households that buy goods and services for personal consumption. *Business markets* buy goods and services for further processing or for use in their production process, whereas *reseller markets* buy goods and services to resell at a profit. *Government markets* are made up of government agencies that buy goods and services in order to produce public services or transfer the goods and services to others who need them. Finally, *international markets* consist of these buyers in other countries, including consumers, producers, resellers, and governments. Each market type has special characteristics that call for careful study by the seller.

COMPETITORS

The marketing concept states that to be successful, a company must provide greater customer value and satisfaction than its competitors. Thus, marketers must do more than simply adapt to the needs of target consumers. They also must gain strategic advantage by positioning their offerings strongly against competitors' offerings in the minds of consumers.

No single competitive marketing strategy is best for all companies. Each firm should consider its own size and industry position compared to those of its competitors. Large firms with dominant positions in an industry can use certain strategies that smaller firms cannot afford. But being large is not enough. There are winning strategies for large firms, but there are also losing ones. And small firms can develop strategies that give them better rates of return than large firms enjoy.

PUBLICS

Public
Any group that has an actual or potential interest in or impact on an organization's ability to achieve its objectives.

FIGURE 3-3 *Types of publics*

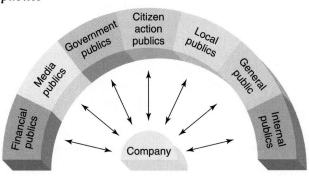

The company's marketing environment also includes various publics. A **public** is any group that has an actual or potential interest in or impact on an organization's ability to achieve its objectives. Figure 3-3 shows seven types of publics.

◆ *Financial publics.* Financial publics influence the company's ability to obtain funds. Banks, investment houses, and stockholders are the major financial publics.

◆ *Media publics.* Media publics are those that carry news, features, and editorial opinion. They include newspapers, magazines, and radio and television stations.

◆ *Government publics.* Management must take government developments into account. Marketers must often consult the company's lawyers on issues of product safety, truth-in-advertising, and other matters.

◆ *Citizen-action publics.* A company's marketing decisions may be questioned by consumer organizations, environmental groups, minority groups, and others. Its public relations department can help it stay in touch with consumer and citizen groups.

Companies market to internal publics as well as to customers: WalMart includes employees as models in its advertising, making them feel good about working for the company.

◆ *Local publics.* Every company has local publics, such as neighborhood residents and community organizations. Large companies usually appoint a community-relations officer to deal with the community, attend meetings, answer questions, and contribute to worthwhile causes.

◆ *General public.* A company needs to be concerned about the general public's attitude toward its products and activities. The public's image of the company affects its buying.

◆ *Internal publics.* A company's internal publics include its workers, managers, volunteers, and the board of directors. Large companies use newsletters and other means to inform and motivate their internal publics. When employees feel good about their company, this positive attitude spills over to external publics.

A company can prepare marketing plans for these major publics as well as for its customer markets. Suppose the company wants a specific response from a particular public, such as goodwill, favorable word of mouth, or donations of time or money. The company would have to design an offer to this public that is attractive enough to produce the desired response.

THE COMPANY'S MACROENVIRONMENT

The company and all of the other actors operate in a larger macroenvironment of forces that shape opportunities and pose threats to the company. Figure 3-4 shows the six major forces in the company's macroenvironment. In the remaining sections of this chapter, we examine these forces and show how they affect marketing plans.

Demography
The study of human populations in terms of size, density, location, age, sex, race, occupation, and other statistics.

FIGURE 3-4 *Major forces in the company's macroenvironment*

DEMOGRAPHIC ENVIRONMENT

Demography is the study of human populations in terms of size, density, location, age, gender, race, occupation, and other statistics. The demographic environment is of major interest to marketers because it involves people, and people make up markets.

The world population is growing at an explosive rate. It now totals more than 5.4 billion and will reach 6.2 billion by the year 2000.[2] This population explosion has been of major concern to governments and various groups throughout the world for two reasons. First, the earth's finite resources can support only so many people, particularly at the living standards to which many countries aspire. The concern is that unchecked population growth and consumption may eventually result in insufficient food supply, depletion

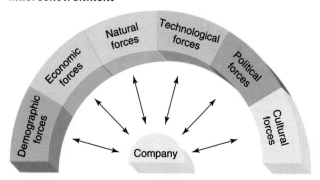

of key minerals, overcrowding, pollution, and an overall deterioration in the quality of life.

The second cause for concern is that the greatest population growth occurs in countries and communities that can least afford it. The less-developed regions of the world currently account for 76 percent of the world population and are growing at 2 percent per year. In contrast, the population in the more-developed regions is growing at only 0.6 percent per year. Less-developed countries often find it difficult to feed, clothe, and educate their growing populations. Moreover, the poorer families in these countries often have the most children, and this reinforces the cycle of poverty.

The explosive world population growth has major implications for business. A growing population means growing human needs to satisfy. Depending on purchasing power, it may also mean growing market opportunities. Thus, marketers keep close track of demographic trends and developments in their markets, both at home and abroad. They track changing age and family structures, geographic population shifts, educational characteristics, and population diversity. Here, we discuss the most important demographic trends in the United States.

Changing Age Structure of the U.S. Population

The U.S. population stood at more than 260 million in 1994 and may reach 300 million by the year 2020. The single most important demographic trend in the United States is the changing age structure of the population. The U.S. population is getting *older* for two reasons. First, there is a long-term slowdown in the birthrate, so there are fewer young people to pull the population's average age down. Second, life expectancy is increasing, so there are more older people to pull the average age up.

Baby boom
The major increase in the annual birthrate following World War II and lasting until the early 1960s. The "baby boomers," now moving into middle age, are a prime target for marketers.

During the **baby boom** that followed World War II and lasted until the early 1960s, the annual birthrate reached an all-time high. The baby boom created a huge "bulge" in the U.S. age distribution—the 75 million baby boomers now account for almost one-third of the nation's population. And as the baby-boom generation ages, the nation's average age climbs with it. Because of its sheer size, many major demographic and socioeconomic changes in the United States are tied to the baby-boom generation (see Marketing Highlight 3-1).

The baby boom was followed by a "birth dearth," and by the mid-1970s the birthrate had fallen sharply. This decrease was caused by smaller family sizes resulting from Americans' desire to improve their personal living standards, from the increasing desire of women to work outside the home, and from improved birth control. Although family sizes are expected to remain smaller, the birthrate has climbed again as the baby-boom generation moves through the childbearing years and creates a second but smaller "baby boomlet." However, following this boomlet, the birthrate will again decline as we move into the twenty-first century.[3]

To serve the large and growing "kid market," many retailers are opening separate children's chains. For example, Toys 'Я' Us opened Kids 'Я' Us.

THE BRANDS YOU WANT   AT PRICES YOU'LL LOVE

TABLE 3-1 *Percent Distribution of the U.S. Population by Age*

AGE GROUP	1995	2000	2005	2010	2030	2040	2050
Under 5	7.6	7.4	6.9	6.6	6.4	6.4	6.4
5 to 13	12.8	13.1	13.1	12.5	11.7	11.5	11.6
14 to 17	5.3	5.6	5.7	5.9	5.3	5.3	5.2
18 to 24	10.8	9.5	9.5	9.8	9.1	9.2	9.0
25 to 34	17.3	15.5	13.6	12.7	12.4	12.4	12.5
35 to 44	15.1	16.2	16.3	14.8	12.9	12.9	12.2
45 to 64	18.6	19.9	22.2	24.9	22.1	22.1	22.5
65 & older	12.5	12.8	12.7	12.7	20.2	20.2	20.6

Source: U.S. Census Bureau, Current Population Reports, as reported in Melissa Campanelli, "Selling to Seniors: A Waiting Game," *Sales & Marketing Management,* June 1994, p. 69.

Table 3-1 shows the changing age distribution of the U.S. population through 2050. The differing growth rates for various age groups will strongly affect marketers' targeting strategies. For example, the baby boomlet has created a large and growing "kid market." Children under 17 years of age influence an estimated $295 billion worth of purchases each year. After years of "bust," markets for children's toys and games, clothes, furniture, and food are enjoying a "boom." For instance, Sony and other electronics firms are now offering products designed for children. Many retailers are opening separate children's clothing chains, such as GapKids and Kids 'Я' Us. Such markets will continue to grow through the remainder of the century before again decreasing as the baby boomers move out of their childbearing years.[4]

At the other end of the spectrum, the 65-and-over group now makes up fewer than 13 percent of all Americans. By 2030, however, it will make up more than 20 percent of the population—there will be about as many people 65 and older as there are people 18 and younger. As this group grows, so will the demand for retirement communities, quieter forms of recreation, single-portion food packaging, life-care and health-care services, and leisure travel.[5]

Folgers and other brands are targeting smaller households with single-serve portions.

Freshly brewed coffee for ten.

For one.

Folgers Coffee Singles
THE ULTIMATE ONE CUP COFFEE MACHINE.

The Changing American Family

The American ideal of the two-children, two-car suburban family has lately been losing some of its luster. People are marrying later and having fewer children. Despite the recent "baby boomlet," the number of married couples with children will continue to decline through the end of the century. In fact, couples with no children under 18 now make up almost half of all families.[6]

Also, the number of working women has increased greatly. Currently, in the United States, 58 percent of all women 16 and older are working or looking for a job. It is expected that 65 percent of women will be in the labor force by 2005.[7] Marketers of tires, automobiles, insurance, travel, and financial services are increasingly directing their advertising to working women. As a result of the shift in the traditional roles and values of husbands and wives, with husbands assuming more domestic functions such as shopping and child care, more food and household appliance marketers are targeting husbands.

Finally, the number of nonfamily households is increasing. Many young adults leave home and move into apartments. Other adults choose to remain single. Still others are divorced or widowed people living alone. By the year 2000, 47 percent of all households will be nonfamily or single-parent households—the fastest-growing categories of households. These groups have their own special needs. For example, they need smaller apartments; inexpensive and smaller appliances, furniture, and furnishings; and food that is packaged in smaller sizes.

Geographic Shifts in Population

Americans are a mobile people with about 18 percent, or 43 million people, moving each year. Among the major trends are the following:[8]

◆ *Movement to the Sunbelt states.* During the 1980s, the populations in the West and South grew. In contrast, many of the Midwest and Northeast states lost population. These shifts are continuing through the 1990s (see Figure 3-5). These population shifts interest marketers because people in different regions buy differently. For example, the movement to the Sunbelt states will lessen the demand for warm clothing and home heating equipment and increase the demand for air conditioning.

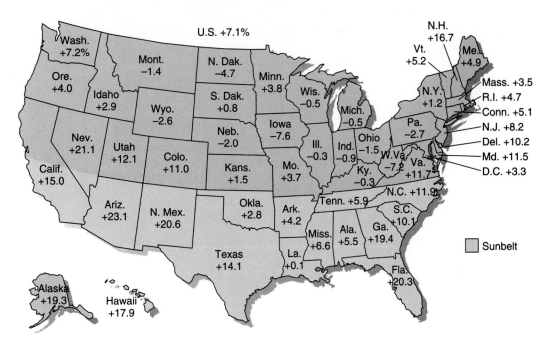

FIGURE 3-5 *Projected population growth rates: 1990 to 2000*
Source: U.S. Department of Commerce, Bureau of Census.

◆ *Movement from rural to urban and suburban areas.* For more than a century, Americans have been moving from rural to metropolitan areas. The metropolitan areas show a faster pace of living, more commuting, higher incomes, and greater variety of goods and services than can be found in the small towns and rural areas that dot the United States.

◆ *Movement from the city to the suburbs.* In the 1950s, Americans made a massive exit from the cities to the suburbs. Big cities became surrounded by even bigger suburbs. Today, the migration to the suburbs continues, and the suburbs are spilling over into rural areas. The U.S. Census Bureau calls sprawling urban areas *MSAs* (Metropolitan Statistical Areas). Companies use MSAs in researching the best geographical segments for their products and in deciding where to buy advertising time. MSA research shows, for example, that people in Seattle buy more toothbrushes per capita than any other U.S. city, people in Salt Lake City eat more candy bars, folks from New Orleans use more ketchup, and those in Miami drink more prune juice.[9]

THE BABY BOOMERS AND THE GENERATION XERS

Demographics involve people, and people make up markets. Thus, marketers track demographic trends and groups carefully. Two of today's most important demographic groups are the so-called *baby boomers* and the *generation Xers*.

The Baby Boomers

The postwar baby boom, which began in 1946 and ran through 1964, produced 75 million babies. Since then, the baby boomers have become one of the biggest forces shaping the marketing environment. The boomers have presented a moving target, creating new markets as they grew through infancy to preadolescent, teenage, young-adult, and now middle-age years.

The baby boomers account for a third of the population but make up 40 percent of the work force and earn over half of all personal income. Today, the aging boomers are moving to the suburbs, settling into home ownership, and raising families. They are also reaching their peak earning and spending years. Thus, they constitute a lucrative market for housing, furniture and appliances, children's products, low-calorie foods and beverages, physical fitness products, high-priced cars, convenience products, and financial services.

Baby boomers cut across all walks of life. But marketers typically have paid the most attention to the

Converse targets Generation Xers with this black and white ad for Jack Purcell sneakers. The ad is "soft sell," and makes fun of a favorite GenXer target— advertising itself.

small upper crust of the boomer generation—its more educated, mobile, and wealthy segments. These segments have gone by many names. In

the 1980s, they were called "yuppies" (young urban professionals); "bumpies" (black upwardly mobile professionals); "yummies" (young upwardly mobile mommies), and "DINKs" (dual-income, no-kids couples). In the 1990s, however, yuppies and DINKs have given way to a new breed, with names such as DEWKs (dual earners with kids); MOBYs (mother older, baby younger); WOOFs (well-off older folks); or just plain GRUMPIES (just what the name suggests).

The older boomers are now in their fifties; the youngest are in their thirties. Thus, the boomers are evolving from the "youthquake generation" to the "backache generation." They're slowing up, having children, and settling down. They're experiencing the pangs of midlife and rethinking the purpose and value of their work, responsibilities, and relationships. The maturing boomers are approaching life with a new stability and reasonableness in the way they live, think, eat, and spend. The boomers have shifted their focus from the outside world to the inside world. Community and family values have become more important, and staying home with the family has become their favorite way to spend an evening. The upscale boomers still exert their affluence, but they indulge

A Better-Educated and More White-Collar Population

The U.S. population is becoming better educated. The rising number of educated people will increase the demand for quality products, books, magazines, and travel. It suggests a decline in television viewing because college-educated consumers watch less TV than does the population at large. The work force also is becoming more white collar. Between 1950 and 1985, the proportion of white-collar workers rose from 41 percent to 54 percent, that of blue-collar workers declined from 47 percent to 33 percent, and that of service workers increased from 12 percent to 14 percent. These trends have continued through the 1990s.[10]

Increasing Ethnic and Racial Diversity

The United States has often been called a "melting pot" in which diverse groups from many nations and cultures have melted into a single, more homogeneous whole. But there are increasing signs that such melting did not occur. Rather, the United States seems to have become more of a "salad bowl" in which various groups have mixed together but have maintained their diversity by retaining and valuing important ethnic and cultural differences.

themselves in more subtle and sensible ways.

The Generation Xers

Some marketers think that focusing on the boomers has caused companies to overlook other important segments, especially younger consumers. As noted in the chapter-opening example, focus has shifted in recent years to a new group, those born between 1965 and 1976. Author Douglas Coupland calls them "Generation X," because they lie in the shadow of the boomers and lack obvious distinguishing characteristics. Others call them baby busters, or twentysomethings, or Yiffies—young, individualistic, freedom-minded, few.

Unlike the boomers, the Xers do not share dramatic and wrenching experiences, such as the Vietnam War and Watergate, that might have unified their subculture and lifestyle. However, they do share a different set of influences. Increasing divorce rates and higher employment for mothers have made them the first generation of latchkey kids. Whereas the boomers created a sexual revolution, the Xers have lived in the age of AIDS. Having grown up during times of recession and corporate downsizing, they have developed a pessimistic economic outlook. This outlook is aggravated by problems in finding good jobs—the management ranks already are well stocked with boomers who won't retire for another 20 years or more.

As a result, the Xers are a more skeptical bunch, cynical of frivolous marketing pitches that promise easy success. They know better. The Xers buy lots of products, such as sweaters, boots, cosmetics, electronics, cars, fast food, beer, computers, and mountain bikes. However, their cynicism makes them more savvy shoppers. Because they often did much of the family shopping while growing up, they are experienced shoppers. Their financial pressures make them value conscious, and they like lower prices and a more functional look. The Generation Xers respond to honesty in advertising, as exemplified by Nike ads that focus on fitness and a healthy lifestyle instead of hyping shoes. They like irreverence and sass and ads that mock the traditional advertising approach.

Generation Xers share new cultural concerns. They care about the environment and respond favorably to companies such as The Body Shop and Ben & Jerry's, which have proven records of environmentally and socially responsible actions. Although they seek success, the Xers are less materialistic. They want better quality of life and are more interested in job satisfaction than in sacrificing personal happiness and growth for promotion. They prize experience, not acquisition.

The Generation Xers will have a big impact on the work place and marketplace of the future. There are now 40 million of them poised to displace the lifestyles, culture, and materialistic values of the baby boomers. By the year 2010, they will have overtaken the baby boomers as a primary market for almost every product category.

Sources: Howard Schlossberg, "Aging Baby Boomers Give Marketers a Lot of Changes to Consider," *Advertising Age,* April 12, 1993, p. 10; Campbell Gibson, "The Four Baby Booms," *American Demographics,* November 1993, pp. 36–40; Cyndee Miller, "Xers Know They're a Target Market, and They Hate That," *Marketing News,* December 6, 1993, pp. 2, 15; Jeff Giles, "Generalizations X," *Newsweek,* June 6, 1994, pp. 62–69; Nathan Cobb, "Agent X," *The Boston Globe,* September 28, 1994, pp. 35, 40; and Nicholas Zill and John Robinson, "The Generation X Difference," *American Demographics,* April 1995, pp. 24–39.

The U.S. population is 84 percent white, with blacks making up another 12 percent. The Hispanic population has grown rapidly and now stands at over 22 million people, almost 9 percent of the U.S. population. The U.S. Asian population also has grown rapidly in recent years and now totals more than 7 million people.[11] Many marketers of food, clothing, furniture, and other products have targeted specially designed products and promotions to one or more of these groups.

ECONOMIC ENVIRONMENT

Economic environment
Factors that affect consumer buying power and spending patterns.

Markets require buying power as well as people. The **economic environment** consists of factors that affect consumer purchasing power and spending patterns. Nations vary greatly in the their levels and distribution of income. Some countries have *subsistence economies*—they consume most of their own agricultural and industrial output. These countries offer few market opportunities. At the other extreme are *industrial economies,* which constitute rich markets for many different kinds of goods. Marketers must pay close attention to major trends and

Dale color a tu vida con Levi's **517** COLLECTION BOOT CUT

To match the growing ethnic diversity of the U.S. market, companies are creating more and more products for specific ethnic markets. Here Levi Strauss targets the fast-growing Hispanic market.

consumer spending patterns, both across and within their world markets. Following are some of the major economic trends in the United States.

Changes in Income

In the early 1980s, the U.S. economy entered its longest peacetime boom. During the "roaring eighties," American consumers fell into a consumption frenzy, fueled by income growth, federal tax reductions, rapid increases in housing values, and a boom in borrowing. They bought and bought, seemingly without caution, amassing record levels of debt. "It was fashionable to describe yourself as 'born to shop.' When the going gets tough, it was said, the tough go shopping. In the 1980s, many Americans became literally addicted to personal consumption."[12]

However, the free spending and high expectations were dashed by the recession in the early 1990s. Once again, consumers have sobered up, pulled back, and adjusted to leaner times. *Value marketing* has become the watchword for many marketers during this economic downturn. Rather than offering high quality at a high price, or lesser quality at very low prices, marketers are looking for ways to offer today's more financially cautious buyers greater value—just the right combination of product quality and good service at a fair price.

The baby-boom generation is moving into its prime wage-earning years, and the number of small families headed by dual-career couples continues to increase. Thus, many consumers will continue to demand quality products and better service, and they will be able to pay for them. They will spend more on time-saving products and services, travel and entertainment, physical fitness products, cultural activities, and continuing education.

However, the 1990s is also the decade of the "squeezed consumer." Along with rising incomes in some segments have come increased financial burdens—repaying debts acquired during the spending splurges of the 1980s, facing declining home values and increased taxes, and saving ahead for college tuition payments and retirement. These financially squeezed consumers continue to spend more slowly and carefully than in the previous decade. And they seek greater value in the products and services they buy.

Marketers should pay attention to *income distribution* as well as average income. Income distribution in the United States is still very skewed. At the top are *upper-class* consumers, whose spending patterns are not affected by current economic events and who are a major market for luxury goods. There is a comfortable *middle class* that is somewhat careful about its spending but can still afford the good life some of the time. The *working class* must stick close to the basics of food, clothing, and shelter and must try hard to save. Finally, the *underclass* (persons on welfare and many retirees) must count their pennies when making even the most basic purchases.

Changing Consumer Spending Patterns

Engel's laws
Differences noted over a century ago by Ernst Engel in how people shift their spending across food, housing, transportation, health care, and other goods and services categories as family income rises.

Table 3-2 shows the proportion of total expenditures made by U.S. households at different income levels for major categories of goods and services. Food, housing, and transportation use up most household income. However, consumers at different income levels have different spending patterns. Some of these differences were noted over a century ago by Ernst Engel, who studied how people shifted their spending as their income rose. He found that as family income rises, the percentage spent on food declines, the percentage spent on housing remains constant (except for such utilities as gas, electricity, and public services, which decrease), and both the percentage spent on other categories and that devoted to savings increase. **Engel's laws** generally have been supported by later studies.

TABLE 3-2 *Consumer Spending at Different Income Levels*

	INCOME LEVEL		
Expenditure	$10,000–15,000	$20,000–30,000	$50,000 and Over
Food	17.7%	15.8%	12.6%
Housing	24.8	23.0	24.9
Utilities	8.6	7.1	4.7
Clothing	5.4	5.8	5.8
Transportation	17.4	19.1	17.6
Health Care	7.8	5.5	3.7
Entertainment	3.7	4.7	6.1
Tobacco	1.5	1.2	0.5
Contributions	2.2	2.9	4.3
Insurance and Pensions	4.5	8.2	13.2
Other	6.3	6.7	6.6

Source: Consumer Expenditure Survey, U.S. Department of Labor, Bureau of Labor Statistics, Bulletin 2383, August 1991, pp. 15–17.

Changes in major economic variables such as income, cost of living, interest rates, and savings and borrowing patterns have a large impact on the marketplace. Companies watch these variables by using economic forecasting. Businesses do not have to be wiped out by an economic downturn or caught short in a boom. With adequate warning, they can take advantage of changes in the economic environment.

Natural environment
Natural resources that are needed as inputs by marketers or that are affected by marketing activities.

NATURAL ENVIRONMENT

The **natural environment** involves the natural resources that are needed as inputs by marketers or that are affected by marketing activities. Environmental concerns have grown steadily during the past two decades. Some trend analysts have labeled

Many companies are responding to consumer demands for more environmentally responsible products. Here, Chrysler notes "we are years ahead of government guidelines."

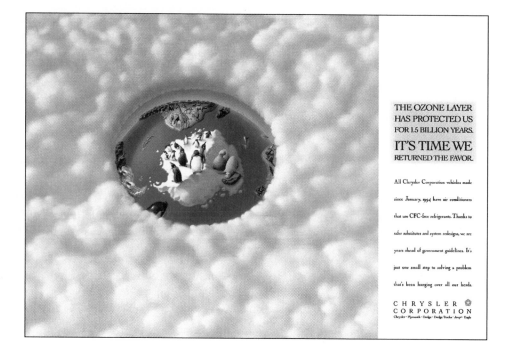

THE OZONE LAYER HAS PROTECTED US FOR 1.5 BILLION YEARS. **IT'S TIME WE** RETURNED THE FAVOR.

All Chrysler Corporation vehicles made since January, 1994 have air conditioners that use CFC-free refrigerants. Thanks to safer substitutes and system redesigns, we are years ahead of government guidelines. It's just one small step to solving a problem that's been hanging over all our heads.

C H R Y S L E R
C O R P O R A T I O N
Chrysler · Plymouth · Dodge · Dodge Trucks · Jeep · Eagle

the 1990s as the "Earth Decade," claiming that the natural environment is the major worldwide issue facing business and the public. In many cities around the world, air and water pollution have reached dangerous levels. World concern continues to mount about the depletion of the earth's ozone layer and the resulting "greenhouse effect," a dangerous warming of the earth. And many environmentalists fear that we soon will be buried in our own trash. Marketers should be aware of four trends in the natural environment.

Shortages of Raw Materials

Air and water may seem to be infinite resources, but some groups see long-run dangers. They warn of the potential dangers that propellants used in aerosol cans pose to the ozone layer. Water shortage is already a big problem in some parts of the United States and the world. Renewable resources, such as forests and food, also have to be used wisely. Companies in the forestry business are required to reforest timberlands in order to protect the soil and to ensure enough wood supplies to meet future demand. Food supply can be a major problem because more and more of the world's limited farmable land is being developed for urban areas.

Nonrenewable resources, such as oil, coal, and various minerals, pose a serious problem. Firms making products that require these increasingly scarce resources face large cost increases, even if the materials do remain available. They may not find it easy to pass these costs on to the consumer. However, firms engaged in research and development and in exploration can help by developing new sources and materials.

Increased Cost of Energy

One nonrenewable resource, oil, has created the most serious problem for future economic growth. The major industrial economies of the world depend heavily on oil, and until economical energy substitutes can be developed, oil will continue to dominate the world political and economic picture. Large increases in the price of oil during the 1970s, and dramatic events like the 1991 Persian Gulf War that affect oil availability, have spurred the search for alternative forms of energy. Coal is again popular; and many companies are searching for practical ways to harness solar, nuclear, wind, and other forms of energy. In fact, hundreds of firms already are offering products that use solar energy for heating homes and other uses.

Increased Pollution

Industry almost always will damage the quality of the natural environment. Consider the disposal of chemical and nuclear wastes; the dangerous mercury levels in the ocean; the quantity of chemical pollutants in the soil and food supply; and the littering of the environment with nonbiodegradable bottles, plastics, and other packaging materials.

In contrast, public concern creates a marketing opportunity for alert companies. Such concern creates a large market for pollution control solutions such as scrubbers, recycling centers, and landfill systems. It leads to a search for new ways to produce and package goods that do not cause environmental damage. Concern for the natural environment has spawned the so-called *green movement*. Increasing numbers of consumers have begun doing more business with ecologically responsible companies and avoiding those whose actions harm the environment. They buy "environmentally friendly" products, even if these products cost more. Many companies are responding to such consumer demands with ecologically safer products, recyclable or biodegradable packaging, better pollution controls, and more energy-efficient operations.[13]

Government Intervention in Natural Resource Management

The governments of different countries vary in their concern and efforts to promote a clean environment. For example, the German government vigorously pursues environmental quality, partly because of the strong public green movement and partly because of the ecological devastation in former East Germany. In contrast, many poor nations do little about pollution, largely because they lack the needed funds or political will. It is in the interests of richer nations to subsidize poorer ones to control pollution, but today even the richer nations lack the vast funds and political accord required to mount a worldwide environmental effort. The major hope is that companies around the world accept more social responsibility, and that less expensive devices can be found to control and reduce pollution.

In the United States, the Environmental Protection Agency (EPA) was created in 1970 to set and enforce pollution standards and to conduct research on the causes and effects of pollution. In the future, companies doing business in the United States can expect strong controls from government and pressure groups. Instead of opposing regulation, marketers should help develop solutions to the material and energy problems facing the world.

TECHNOLOGICAL ENVIRONMENT

Technological environment
Forces that create new technologies, creating new product and market opportunities.

The **technological environment** is perhaps the most dramatic force now shaping our destiny. Technology has released such wonders as antibiotics, organ transplants, and notebook computers. It also has released such horrors as the nuclear missiles, nerve gas, and the machine gun. It has released such mixed blessings as the automobile, television, and credit cards. Our attitude toward technology depends on whether we are more impressed with its wonders or its blunders.

Every new technology replaces an older technology. Transistors hurt the vacuum-tube industry, xerography hurt the carbon-paper business, the auto hurt the railroads, and compact discs hurt phonograph records. When old industries fought or ignored new technologies, their businesses declined.

Different countries vary in their concern for the environment. For example, partly because of ecological devastation like that shown here in former East Germany, the German government now vigorously pursues environmental quality.

New technologies create new markets and opportunities. The marketer should watch the following trends in technology.

Fast Pace of Technological Change

Many of today's common products were not available even a hundred years ago. Abraham Lincoln did not know about automobiles, airplanes, phonographs, radios, or the electric light. Woodrow Wilson did not know about television, aerosol cans, home freezers, automatic dishwashers, room air conditioners, antibiotics, or computers. Franklin Delano Roosevelt did not know about xerography, synthetic detergents, tape recorders, birth control pills, or earth satellites. And John F. Kennedy did not know about personal computers, compact disc players, digital watches, VCRs, or fax machines. Companies that do not keep up with technological change soon will find their products outdated. And they will miss new product and market opportunities.

Scientists today are working on a wide range of new technologies that will revolutionize our products and their manufacturing processes. Exciting work is being done in biotechnology, miniature electronics, robotics, and materials science. Scientists today are working on the following promising new products and services:

Practical solar energy	Tiny but powerful supercomputers	Effective superconductors
Cancer cures		Electric cars
Chemical control of mental health	Household robots that do cooking and cleaning	Electronic anesthetic for pain killing
Car navigation systems		
Commercial space shuttle	Nonfattening, tasty, nutritious foods	Voice- and gesture-controlled computers

Scientists also speculate on fantasy products, such as flying cars, three-dimensional televisions, space colonies, and human clones. The challenge in each case is not only technical but also commercial—to make *practical, affordable* versions of these products.

High R&D Budgets

The United States leads the world in research and development spending. In 1993, R&D spending exceeded $160 billion, although it has been dropping slightly in recent years. The federal government supplied almost half of total R&D funds.[14] Government research can be a rich source of new product and service ideas. Many companies also spend heavily on their own R&D. For example, companies such as General Motors, IBM, and AT&T spend billions on R&D each year. Today's research usually is carried out by research teams rather than by lone inventors like Thomas Edison, Samuel Morse, or Alexander Graham Bell. Managing company scientists is a major challenge. They may resent too much cost control and are sometimes more interested in solving scientific problems than in creating marketable products. Companies are adding marketing people to R&D teams to try to obtain a stronger marketing orientation.

Concentration on Minor Improvements

As a result of the high cost of developing and introducing new technologies, many companies are making minor product improvements instead of gambling on major innovations. Even basic research companies like Du Pont, Bell Laboratories, and Pfizer are being cautious. Most companies are content to put their money into copying competitors' products, making minor feature and style improvements, or offering simple extensions of current brands. Thus, much research is defensive rather than offensive.

Increased Regulation

As products become more complex, the public needs to know that they are safe. Thus, government agencies investigate and ban potentially unsafe products. In the United States, the Federal Food and Drug Administration has set up complex regulations for testing new drugs. The Consumer Product Safety Commission sets safety standards for consumer products and penalizes companies that fail to meet them. Such regulations have resulted in much higher research costs and in longer times between new-product ideas and their introductions. Marketers should be aware of these regulations when seeking and developing new products.

As this Siemens ad suggests, research and development has changed considerably over the years. Lone inventors have been replaced by research teams employed by large companies or other organizations.

SIEMENS

1895. That was then.

Working in a small laboratory, Wilhelm Roentgen made the world's first x-ray images. Working with him, Siemens patented and manufactured the world's first x-ray tubes.

1993. This is now.

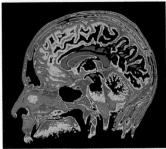

This modern magnetic resonance image lets doctors see into the human body more clearly than ever before. It is a product of years of Siemens investment in research and development. Happily, you don't have to be a scientist to appreciate the results. Doctors, hospitals and clinics throughout America are giving their patients better care because of Siemens advances in many forms of diagnostic imaging, including ultrasound, magnetic resonance, nuclear imaging and computed tomography. And that's the kind of result we can all feel good about.
Siemens. Precision Thinking.

Marketers need to understand the changing technological environment and the ways that new technologies can serve human needs. They need to work closely with R&D people to encourage more market-oriented research. They also must be alert to the possible negative aspects of any innovation that might harm users or arouse opposition.

POLITICAL ENVIRONMENT

Political environment
Laws, government agencies, and pressure groups that influence and limit various organizations and individuals in a given society.

Marketing decisions are strongly affected by developments in the political environment. The **political environment** consists of laws, government agencies, and pressure groups that influence and limit various organizations and individuals in a given society.

Legislation Regulating Business

Even the most liberal advocates of free-market economies agree that the system works best with at least some regulation. Well-conceived regulation can encourage competition and ensure fair markets for goods and services. Thus, governments develop *public policy* to guide commerce—sets of laws and regulations that limit business for the good of society as a whole. Almost every marketing activity is subject to a wide range of laws and regulations.

INCREASING LEGISLATION. Legislation affecting business around the world has increased steadily over the years. The United States has many laws on its books covering such issues as competition, fair trade practices, environmental protection, product safety, truth in advertising, packaging and labeling, pricing, and other important areas (see Table 3-3). The European Commission has been active in establishing a new framework of laws covering competitive behavior, product standards, product liability, and commercial transactions for the twelve member nations of the European Community. Several countries have gone farther than the United States in passing strong consumerism legislation. For example, Norway bans several forms of sales promotion—trading stamps, contests, premiums—as being inappropriate or unfair ways of promoting products. Thailand requires food processors selling national brands to market low-price brands also, so that low-income consumers can find economy brands on the shelves. In India, food companies must obtain special approval to launch brands that duplicate those already existing on the market, such as additional cola drinks or new brands of rice.

Understanding the public policy implications of a particular marketing activity is not a simple matter. For example, in the United States, there are many laws created at the national, state, and local levels, and these regulations often overlap. Aspirins sold in Dallas are governed both by federal labeling laws and by Texas state advertising laws. Moreover, regulations are constantly changing—what was allowed last year may now be prohibited, and what was prohibited may now be allowed. For example, with the demise of the Soviet bloc, ex-Soviet nations are rapidly passing laws to both regulate and promote an open market economy. Marketers must work hard to keep up with changes in regulations and their interpretations.

Business legislation has been enacted for a number of reasons. The first is to *protect companies* from each other. Although business executives may praise competition, they sometimes try to neutralize it when it threatens them. So laws are passed to define and prevent unfair competition. In the United States, such laws are enforced by the Federal Trade Commission and the Antitrust Division of the Attorney General's office.

The second purpose of government regulation is to *protect consumers* from unfair business practices. Some firms, if left alone, would make shoddy products, tell lies in their advertising, and deceive consumers through their packaging and pricing. Unfair business practices have been defined and are enforced by various agencies.

The third purpose of government regulation is to *protect the interests of society* against unrestrained business behavior. Profitable business activity does not always create a better quality of life. Regulation arises to ensure that firms take responsibility for the social costs of their production or products.

CHANGING GOVERNMENT AGENCY ENFORCEMENT.   International marketers will encounter dozens, or even hundreds, of agencies set up to enforce trade policies and regulations. In the United States, Congress has established federal regulatory agencies such as the Federal Trade Commission, the Food and Drug Administration, the Interstate Commerce Commission, the Federal Communications Commission, the Federal Power Commission, the Civil Aeronautics Board, the Consumer Products Safety Commission, the Environmental Protection Agency, and the Office of Consumer Affairs. Because such government agencies have some discretion in enforcing the laws, they can have a major impact on a company's marketing performance. At times, the staffs of these agencies have appeared to be overly eager and unpredictable. Some of the agencies sometimes have been dominated by lawyers and economists who lacked a practical sense of how business and marketing works. In recent years, the Federal Trade Commission has added staff marketing experts who can better understand complex business issues.

New laws and their enforcement will continue or increase. Business executives must watch these developments when planning their products and marketing programs. Marketers need to know about the major laws protecting competition, consumers, and society. They need to understand these laws at the local, state, national, and international levels.[15]

INCREASED EMPHASIS ON ETHICS AND SOCIALLY RESPONSIBLE ACTIONS.   Written regulations cannot possibly cover all potential marketing abuses, and existing laws are often difficult to enforce. However, beyond written laws and regulations, business is also governed by social codes and rules of professional ethics. Enlightened companies encourage their managers to look beyond what the regulatory system allows and to simply "do the right thing." These socially responsible firms actively seek out ways to protect the long-run interests of their consumers and the environment.

The recent rash of business scandals and increased concerns about the environment have created fresh interest in the issues of ethics and social responsibility. Almost every aspect of marketing involves such issues. Unfortunately, because these issues usually involve conflicting interests, well-meaning people can disagree honestly about the right course of action in a particular situation. Thus, many industrial and professional trade associations have suggested codes of ethics, and many companies now are developing policies and guidelines to deal with complex social responsibility issues.

Throughout the text, we present Marketing Highlight exhibits that summarize the main public policy and social responsibility issues surrounding major marketing decisions. These exhibits discuss the legal issues that marketers should understand and the common ethical and societal concerns that marketers face. In Chapter 23, we discuss a broad range of societal marketing issues in greater depth.

Cultural environment
Institutions and other forces that affect society's basic values, perceptions, preferences, and behaviors.

CULTURAL ENVIRONMENT

The **cultural environment** is made up of institutions and other forces that affect a society's basic values, perceptions, preferences, and behaviors. People grow up in a particular society that shapes their basic beliefs and values. They absorb a world

TABLE 3-3 *Milestone U.S. Legislation Affecting Marketing*

Sherman Antitrust Act (1890)

Prohibits (a) "monopolies or attempts to monopolize"; and (b) "contracts, combinations, or conspiracies in restraint of trade" in interstate and foreign commerce.

Federal Food and Drug Act (1906)

Forbids the manufacture, sale, or transport of adulterated or fraudulently labeled foods and drugs in interstate commerce. Supplanted by the Food, Drug, and Cosmetic Act, 1938; amended by Food Additives Amendment in 1958 and the Kefauver-Harris Amendment in 1962. The 1962 amendment deals with pretesting of drugs for safety and effectiveness and labeling of drugs by generic name.

Meat Inspection Act (1906)

Provides for the enforcement of sanitary regulations in meat-packaging establishments and for federal inspection of all companies selling meats in interstate commerce.

Federal Trade Commission Act (1914)

Establishes the commission, a body of specialists with broad powers to investigate and to issue cease-and-desist orders to enforce Section 5, which declares that "unfair methods of competition in commerce are unlawful."

Clayton Act (1914)

Supplements the Sherman Act by prohibiting certain specific practices (certain types of price discrimination, tying clauses and exclusive dealing, intercorporate stockholdings, and interlocking directorates) "where the effect . . . may be to substantially lessen competition or tend to create a monopoly in any line of commerce." Provides that violating corporate officials can be held individually responsible; exempts labor and agricultural organizations from its provisions.

Robinson-Patman Act (1936)

Amends the Clayton Act. Adds the phrase "to injure, destroy, or prevent competition." Defines price discrimination as unlawful (subject to certain defenses) and provides the FTC with the right to establish limits on quantity discounts, to forbid brokerage allowances except to independent brokers, and to prohibit promotional allowances or the furnishing of services or facilities except where made available to all "on proportionately equal terms."

Miller-Tydings Act (1937)

Amends the Sherman Act to exempt interstate fair-trade (price fixing) agreements from antitrust prosecution. (The McGuire Act, 1952, reinstates the legality of the nonsigner clause.)

Wheeler-Lea Act (1938)

Prohibits unfair and deceptive acts and practices regardless of whether competition is injured; places advertising of foods and drugs under FTC jurisdiction.

Lanham Trademark Act (1946)

Requires that trademarks must be distinctive and makes it illegal to make any false representation of goods or services entering interstate commerce.

Antimerger Act (1950)

Amends Section 7 of the Clayton Act by broadening the power to prevent intercorporate acquisitions where the acquisition may have a substantially adverse effect on competition.

Automobile Information Disclosure Act (1958)

Prohibits car dealers from inflating the factory price of new cars.

National Traffic and Safety Act (1958)

Provides for the creation of compulsory safety standards for automobiles and tires.

TABLE 3-3   *continued*

Fair Packaging and Labeling Act (1966)

Provides for the regulation of the packaging and labeling of consumer goods. Requires manufacturers to state what the package contains, who made it, and how much it contains. Permits industries' voluntary adoption of uniform packaging standards.

Child Protection Act (1966)

Bans sale of hazardous toys and articles. Amended in 1969 to include articles that pose electrical, mechanical, or thermal hazards.

Federal Cigarette Labeling and Advertising Act (1967)

Requires that cigarette packages contain the following statement: "Warning: The Surgeon General Has Determined That Cigarette Smoking Is Dangerous to Your Health."

Truth-in-Lending Act (1968)

Requires lenders to state the true costs of a credit transaction, outlaws the use of actual or threatened violence in collecting loans, and restricts the amount of garnishments. Established a National Commission on Consumer Finance.

National Environmental Policy Act (1969)

Establishes a national policy on the environment and provides for the establishment of the Council on Environmental Quality. The Environmental Protection Agency was established by Reorganization Plan No. 3 of 1970.

Fair Credit Reporting Act (1970)

Ensures that a consumer's credit report will contain only accurate, relevant, and recent information and will be confidential unless requested for an appropriate reason by a proper party.

Consumer Product Safety Act (1972)

Establishes the Consumer Product Safety Commission and authorizes it to set safety standards for consumer products as well as exact penalties for failure to uphold the standards.

Consumer Goods Pricing Act (1975)

Prohibits the use of price maintenance agreements among manufacturers and resellers in interstate commerce.

Magnuson-Moss Warranty/FTC Improvement Act (1975)

Authorizes the FTC to determine rules concerning consumer warranties and provides for consumer access to means of redress, such as the "class action" suit. Also expands FTC regulatory powers over unfair or deceptive acts or practices.

Equal Credit Opportunity Act (1975)

Prohibits discrimination in a credit transaction because of sex, marital status, race, national origin, religion, age, or receipt of public assistance.

Fair Debt Collection Practice Act (1978)

Makes it illegal to abuse any person and make false statements or use unfair methods when collecting a debt.

FTC Improvement Act (1980)

Provides the House of Representatives and Senate jointly with veto power over FTC Trade Regulation Rules. Enacted to limit FTC's powers to regulate "unfairness" issues.

Toy Safety Act (1984)

Gives the government the power to recall dangerous toys quickly when they are found.

Nutrition Labeling and Education Act (1990)

Requires that food product labels provide detailed nutritional information.

view that defines their relationships with others. The following cultural characteristics can affect marketing decision making.

Persistence of Cultural Values

People in a given society hold many beliefs and values. Their core beliefs and values have a high degree of persistence. For example, most Americans believe in working, getting married, giving to charity, and being honest. These beliefs shape more specific attitudes and behaviors found in everyday life. *Core* beliefs and values are passed on from parents to children and are reinforced by schools, churches, business, and government.

Secondary beliefs and values are more open to change. Believing in marriage is a core belief; believing that people should get married early in life is a secondary belief. Marketers have some chance of changing secondary values, but little chance

POPCORN'S TEN CULTURAL TRENDS

Futurist Faith Popcorn runs Brain-Reserve, a marketing consulting firm that monitors cultural trends and advises companies such as AT&T, Citibank, Black & Decker, Hoffman-La Roche, Nissan, Rubbermaid, and many others on how these trends will affect their marketing and other business decisions. Using its trend predictions, BrainReserve offers several services: BrainJam generates new product ideas for clients, and BrandRenewal attempts to breathe new life into fading brands. Future-Focus develops marketing strategies and concepts that create long-term competitive advantage. Another service, TrendBank, is a database containing culture monitoring and consumer interview information. Popcorn and her associates have identified ten major cultural trends affecting U.S. consumers:

1. *Cashing out:* the urge to change one's life to a slower but more rewarding pace. An executive suddenly quits his or her career, escapes the hassles of big city life, and turns up in Vermont or Montana running a small newspaper, managing a bed-and-breakfast establishment, or starting a band. People cash out because they don't think the stress is worth it. They nostalgically try to return to small-town values, seeking clean air,

safe schools, and plain-speaking neighbors.

2. *Cocooning:* the impulse to stay inside when the outside gets too tough and scary. More people are turning their homes

Marketers follow cultural trends, such as "cocooning," in order to spot new marketing opportunities or threats.

into nests: redecorating their houses, becoming "couch potatoes," watching TV movies, ordering from catalogs, and using answering machines to filter out the outside world. In reaction to increases in crime and other social problems, cocooners are burrowing in and building bunkers. Self-preservation is

the underlying theme. Another breed is Wandering Cocoons, people who eat in their cars and communicate through their car phones. Socialized Cocooners form a small group of friends who frequently get together for conversation or for "salooning."

3. *Down-aging:* the tendency to act and feel younger than one's age. Today's sex symbols include Cher (over 45), Paul Newman (over 65), and Elizabeth Taylor (over 60). Older people spend more on youthful clothes, hair coloring, and facial plastic surgery. They engage in more playful behavior and act in ways previously thought not to be appropriate for their age group. They buy adult toys, attend adult camps, and sign up for adventure vacations.

4. *Egonomics:* the desire to develop individuality in order to be seen and treated as different from others. This is not an ego trip, but simply the wish to individualize oneself through possessions and experiences. People increasingly subscribe to narrow-interest magazines; join small groups with narrow missions; and buy customized clothing, cars, and cosmetics. Egonom-

of changing core values. For example, family-planning marketers could argue more effectively that people should get married later than that they should not get married at all.

Shifts in Secondary Cultural Values

Although core values are fairly persistent, cultural swings do take place. Consider the impact of popular music groups, movie personalities, and other celebrities on young people's hair styling, clothing, and sexual norms. Marketers want to predict cultural shifts in order to spot new opportunities or threats. Several firms offer "futures" forecasts in this connection. For example, the Yankelovich marketing research firm tracks 41 U.S. cultural values, such as "anti-bigness," "mysticism," "living for today," "away from possessions," and "sensuousness." The firm describes the percentage of the population who share the attitude as well as the

ics gives marketers an opportunity to succeed by offering customized goods, services, and experiences.

5. *Fantasy Adventure*: the need to find emotional escapes to offset one's daily routines. People might seek vacations, eat exotic foods, go to Disneyland and other fantasy parks, or redecorate their homes with a Sante Fe look. For marketers, this is an opportunity to create new fantasy products and services, or to add fantasy touches to their current products and services.

6. *99 Lives:* the desperate state of people who must juggle many roles and responsibilities. An example is the "Super-Mom" who must handle a full-time career while also managing her home and children. People today feel time-poor. They attempt to relieve time pressures by using fax machines and car phones, eating at fast food restaurants, and through other means. Marketers can meet this need by creating *cluster marketing* enterprises—all-in-one service stops, such as Video Town Launderette which, in addition to its laundry facilities, includes a tanning room, an exercise bike, copying and fax

machines, and 6,000 video titles for rent.

7. *S.O.S. (Save Our Society):* the drive on the part of a growing number of people to make society more socially responsible with respect to education, ethics, and the environment. People join groups to promote more social responsibility on the part of companies and other citizens. The best response for marketers is to urge their own companies to practice more socially responsible marketing.

8. *Small indulgences:* the need on the part of stressed-out consumers for occasional emotional fixes. A consumer might not be able to afford a two-week trip to Europe, but might spend a weekend in New Orleans instead. He or she might eat healthily all week, then splurge with a pint of superpremium Haagen-Dazs ice cream over the weekend. Marketers should be aware of the ways in which consumers feel deprived and look for opportunities to offer small indulgences that provide an emotional lift.

9. *Staying Alive:* the drive to live longer and better lives. People now know that their lifestyles can kill them—eating the

wrong foods, smoking, breathing bad air, abusing drugs. They are increasingly taking responsibility for their own health and choosing better foods, exercising more regularly, and relaxing more often. Marketers can meet these needs by designing healthier products and services for consumers.

10. *The vigilante consumer:* Vigilante consumers are those who will no longer tolerate shoddy products and poor service. They want companies to be more aware and responsive. They want auto companies to take back "lemons" and fully refund their money. They subscribe to the *National Boycott News* and *Consumer Reports,* join MADD (Mothers Against Drunk Driving), buy "green products," and look for lists of good companies and bad companies. Marketers must serve as the consciences of their companies to bring these consumers better, more responsible products and services.

Source: This summary is drawn from various pages of Faith Popcorn, *The Popcorn Report* (New York: Harper Business, 1992).

percentage who go against the trend. For instance, the percentage of people who value physical fitness and well-being has risen steadily over the years. Such information helps marketers cater to trends with appropriate products and communication appeals. (See Marketing Highlight 3-2 for a summary of today's cultural trends.)

The major cultural values of a society are expressed in people's views of themselves and others, as well as in their views of organizations, society, nature, and the universe.

PEOPLE'S VIEWS OF THEMSELVES. People vary in their emphasis on serving themselves versus serving others. Some people seek personal pleasure, wanting fun, change, and escape. Others seek self-realization through religion, recreation, or the avid pursuit of careers or other life goals. People use products, brands, and services as a means of self-expression, and they buy products and services that match their views of themselves.

In the 1980s, personal ambition and materialism increased dramatically, with significant marketing implications. In a "me-society," people buy their "dream cars" and take their "dream vacations." They spend more time in outdoor health activities (jogging, tennis), in thought, and on arts and crafts. The leisure industry (camping, boating, arts and crafts, and sports) faces good growth prospects in a society where people seek self-fulfillment.

PEOPLE'S VIEWS OF OTHERS. More recently, observers have noted a shift from a "me-society" to a "we-society" in which more people want to be with and serve others. Flashy spending and self-indulgence appear to be on the way out, whereas saving, family concerns, and helping others are on the rise. This suggests a bright future for "social support" products and services that improve direct communication between people, such as health clubs, family vacations, and games. It also suggests a growing market for "social substitutes"—things like VCRs and computers that allow people who are alone to feel that they are not.

PEOPLE'S VIEWS OF ORGANIZATIONS. People vary in their attitudes toward corporations, government agencies, trade unions, universities, and other organizations. By and large, people are willing to work for major organizations, and they expect them, in turn, to carry out society's work. In recent years, there has been a decline in organizational loyalty and a growing skepticism among Americans regarding business and political organizations and institutions. People are giving a little less to their organizations and are trusting them less. For example, in a recent survey of U.S. heads of households, 75 percent agreed that most big companies are out for themselves.[16]

This trend suggests that organizations need to find new ways to win consumer confidence. They need to review their advertising communications to make sure their messages are honest. Also, they need to review their various activities to make sure that they are coming across as "good corporate citizens." More companies are linking themselves to worthwhile causes, measuring their images with important publics, and using public relations to build more positive images (see Marketing Highlight 3-3).

PEOPLE'S VIEWS OF SOCIETY. People vary in their attitudes toward their society, from patriots who defend it, to reformers who want to change it, to malcontents who want to leave it. People's orientation to their society influences their consumption patterns, levels of savings, and attitudes toward the marketplace.

The 1980s and 1990s have seen an increase in consumer patriotism. Many U.S. companies have responded with "made in America" themes and flag-waving promotions. For example, Black & Decker recently has added a flag-like symbol to its tools. And for the past several years, the American textile industry has blitzed

Residence Inn is now located in 42 states.

Please excuse the flag waving, but we now have over 160 locations across the country. Designed for extended stays, our rooms are 50% larger, have full kitchens and in most rooms, a fireplace. To reserve your room at $65-105 a night, call 800-331-3131. And get the 42 star treatment.

Many companies have responded to an increase in consumer patriotism with "flag-waving" ads and programs.

consumers with its "Crafted with Pride in the USA" advertising campaign, insisting that "made in the USA" matters. In 1991, many companies used patriotic appeals and promotions to express their support of American troops in the Persian Gulf War and to ride the wave of national pride and patriotism that followed.[17]

PEOPLE'S VIEWS OF NATURE. People vary in their attitudes toward the natural world. Some feel ruled by it, others feel in harmony with it, and still others seek to master it. A long-term trend has been people's growing mastery over nature through technology and the belief that nature is bountiful. More recently, however, people have recognized that nature is finite and fragile—that it can be destroyed or spoiled by human activities.

Love of nature is leading to more camping, hiking, boating, fishing, and other outdoor activities. Business has responded by offering more hiking gear, camping equipment, better insect repellents, and other products for nature enthusiasts. Tour operators are offering more tours to wilderness areas. Food producers have found growing markets for "natural" products like natural cereal, natural ice cream, and health foods. Marketing communicators are using appealing natural backgrounds in advertising their products.

PEOPLE'S VIEWS OF THE UNIVERSE. Finally, people vary in their beliefs about the origin of the universe and their place in it. Although most Americans practice religion, religious conviction and practice have been dropping off gradually through the years. As people lose their religious orientation, they seek goods and experiences with more immediate satisfactions. During the 1980s, people increasingly measured success in terms of career achievement, wealth, and worldly possessions. Some futurists, however, have noted an emerging renewal of interest in religion, perhaps as a part of a broader search for a new inner purpose. In the 1990s, people are moving away from materialism and dog-eat-dog ambition to seek more permanent values and a more certain grasp of right and wrong. As one trend tracker suggests: "The Nineties will see a marked change in the way society defines success, with achievements such as a happy family life and service to one's community replacing money as the measure of one's worth."[18] She continues, "The Nineties will be a far less cynical decade than the Eighties. Yes, we will still care what things cost. But we will seek to value only those things—family, community, earth, faith—that will endure."[19]

Environmental management perspective
A management perspective in which the firm takes aggressive actions to affect the publics and forces in its marketing environment rather than simply watching and reacting to it.

RESPONDING TO THE MARKETING ENVIRONMENT

Many companies view the marketing environment as an "uncontrollable" element to which they must adapt. They passively accept the marketing environment and do not try to change it. They analyze the environmental forces and design strategies that will help the company avoid the threats and take advantage of the opportunities the environment provides.

Other companies take an **environmental management perspective.**[20] Rather than simply watching and reacting, these firms take aggressive actions to affect the

CAUSE-RELATED MARKETING: DOING WELL BY DOING GOOD

These days, every product seems to be tied to some cause. Buy Hellmann's mayonnaise or Skippy peanut butter and help "Keep America Beautiful." Drink Tang and earn money for Mothers Against Drunk Driving. Or, if you want to help the Leukemia Society of America, buy Helping Hand trash bags or toilet paper. Pay for these purchases with the right charge card and you can support a local cultural arts group or help fight cancer or heart disease.

Cause-related marketing has become one of the hottest forms of corporate giving. It lets companies "do well by doing good" by linking purchases of the company's products or services with fund raising for worthwhile causes or charitable organizations. Cause-related marketing has grown rapidly since the early 1980s, when American Express offered to donate 1 cent to the restoration of the Statue of Liberty for each use of its charge card. American Express ended up having to contribute $1.7 million, but the cause-related campaign produced a 28 percent increase in card usage.

Companies now sponsor dozens of cause-related marketing campaigns each year. Many are backed by large budgets and a full complement of marketing activities. Here are recent examples:

Johnson & Johnson teamed with the Children's Hospital Medical Center and the National Safety Council to sponsor a five-year cause-related marketing campaign to reduce preventable children's injuries, the leading killer of children. Some 43 other nonprofit groups including the American Red Cross, National Parent Teachers Association, and the Boy and Girl Scouts of America helped to promote the campaign. The campaign offered consumers a free Safe Kids safety kit for children in exchange for proofs of purchase. Consumers could also buy a Child's Safety Video for $9.95. The video featured a game show format that made learning about safety entertaining as well as educational. To promote the campaign, J&J distributed almost 50 million advertising inserts in daily newspapers and developed a special information kit for retailers containing posters, floor

displays, and other in-store promotion materials. Safe Kids Safety Tip Sheets and emergency phone stickers were also available as free consumer handouts.

Procter & Gamble has sponsored many cause-related marketing campaigns. For example, during the past many years, P&G has mailed out billions of coupons on behalf of the Special Olympics for retarded children, helping make the event a household name. P&G supports its Special Olympics efforts with national advertising and public relations, and its salespeople work with local volunteers to encourage retailers to build point-of-purchase displays. In another recent cause-related marketing effort, Procter & Gamble has set up the Jif Children's Education Fund. For every pound of Jif peanut butter sold during the three-month promotion, P&G donates 10 cents to the fund, which will be distributed to parent-teacher groups at registered elementary schools in America. The program is designed to raise more than $4 million for U.S. elementary education.

Through focus group studies, Levi Strauss learned that young

publics and forces in their marketing environment. Such companies hire lobbyists to influence legislation affecting their industries and stage media events to gain favorable press coverage. They run "advertorials" (ads expressing editorial points of view) to shape public opinion. They press lawsuits and file complaints with regulators to keep competitors in line, and they form contractual agreements to better control their distribution channels.

However, other companies find positive ways to overcome seemingly uncontrollable environmental constraints. For example, Citicorp, the U.S. banking giant, had been trying for years to start full-service banking in Maryland. It had only credit card and small service operations in the state. Under Maryland law, out-of-state banks could provide only certain services and were barred from advertising, setting up branches, and other types of marketing. In March 1985, Citicorp offered to build a major credit card center in Maryland that would create 1,000 white-collar jobs, and it also offered the state $1 million in cash for the property where it would locate. By imaginatively designing a proposal to benefit Maryland, Citicorp became the first out-of-state bank to provide full banking services there.[21]

Marketing management cannot always affect environmental forces. In many cases, it must settle for simply watching and reacting to the environment. For example, a company would have little success trying to influence geographic population shifts, the economic environment, or major cultural values. But whenever possible, smart marketing managers will take a *proactive* rather than *reactive* approach to the marketing environment.

parents were greatly frustrated in their efforts to get their preschoolers dressed in the morning rush to work and daycare. The company also learned that only 40 percent of the parents knew of its Little Levi's line of clothing for young children. So Levi paid the Bank Street College of Education to create a booklet for preschoolers called "Let's Get Dressed!" The activity booklet uses fun games and puzzles to teach kids how to dress themselves. A companion booklet provides tips for parents on how to take the hassle out of dressing their children. Retailers offered the booklets as a gift with purchases of Little Levi's clothing and supported the campaign with instore promotions and local ads. Readers were given an address from which they could order the booklets for 50 cents. The campaign also received substantial publicity coverage on TV talk shows and in national women's magazines. Sales of Little Levi's have tripled since the case-related marketing campaign began.

Cause-related marketing has stirred some controversy. Critics are concerned that cause-related marketing might eventually undercut traditional "no-strings" corporate giving, as more and more companies grow to expect marketing benefits from their contributions. Critics also worry that cause-related marketing will cause a shift in corporate charitable support toward more visible, popular, and low-risk charities—those with more certain and substantial marketing appeal. For example, MasterCard's Choose to Make a Difference campaign raises money for six charities, each selected in part because of its popularity in a consumer poll. Finally, critics worry that cause-related marketing is more a strategy for selling than a strategy for giving, that "cause-related" marketing is really "cause-exploitative" marketing. Thus, companies using cause-related marketing might find themselves walking a fine line between increased sales and an improved image, and charges of exploitation.

However, if handled well, cause-related marketing can greatly benefit both the company and the charitable organization. The company gains an effective marketing tool while building a more positive public image. The charitable organization gains greater visibility and important new sources of funding. This additional funding can be substantial. In total, such campaigns now contribute some $100 million annually to the coffers of charitable organizations, and surveys show that these cause-related contributions usually add to, rather than undercut, direct company contributions. Thus, when cause marketing works, everyone wins.

Sources: See Cyndee Miller, "Drug Company Begins Its Own Children's Crusade," *Marketing News,* June 6, 1988, pp. 1, 2; "School Kids Snack for Cash," *Advertising Age,* February 2, 1990, p. 36; Melanie Rigney and Julie Steenhuysen, "Conscience Raising," *Advertising Age,* August 26, 1991, p. 19; Nancy Arnott, "Marketing with a Passion," *Sales & Marketing Management,* January 1994, pp. 64–71; Geoffrey Smith, "Are Good Causes Good Marketing?" *Business Week,* March 21, 1994, pp. 64–65; and Craig Smith, "The New Corporate Philanthropy," *Harvard Business Review,* May–June 1994, pp. 105–116.

Summary

All companies operate within a *marketing environment.* This environment consists of all the actors and forces that affect the company's ability to transact effectively with its target market. This environment can be divided into the *microenvironment* and *macroenvironment.*

The *microenvironment* consists of five components. The first is the company's *internal environment,* its departmental and managerial structure, which affects the decision making of marketing management. The second component is *marketing intermediaries,* the marketing channel firms that cooperate to create value. The third component is the group of *customers* that the company can sell to, including consumers, producers, resellers, the government, and international markets. The fourth component consists of the company's *competitors* which attempt to lure away the company's customers. The final component of the microenvironment is the group of *publics* that have an interest in or impact on an organization's ability to achieve its marketing objectives. These constituencies include financial, media, government, citizen action, local, general, and internal publics.

A company is also affected by the broader *macroenvironment,* which is composed of the major forces that pose opportunities and create threats for the company. The *demographic environment* presents marketers with the challenges of changing age and family structures, geographic population shifts, a population that is becoming better-educated and more white-collar, and increasing ethnic and racial diversity. The *economic environment* shows changing patterns of real income and shifts in consumer spending patterns. The *natural environment* has pending shortages of certain raw materials, growing energy costs, higher pollution levels, more government intervention in natural resource management, and higher levels of citizen concern and activism about these issues. The *technological environment* reveals rapid technological change, unlimited opportunities for innovation, a need for high research and development expenditures, emphasis on minor improvements rather than major discoveries, and growing regulation of technological change. The political environment shows struggles in opposing directions: increasing business regulation and strong government agency enforcement, but louder calls for these trends to stop. In addition, there is growth in public interest groups. Finally, the cultural environment shows long-term trends towards a "we-society," less organizational loyalty, increasing patriotism and conservatism, greater appreciation for nature, and a search for more meaningful and enduring values.

Key Terms

Baby boom
Cultural environment
Demography
Economic environment
Engel's laws

Environmental management perspective
Macroenvironment
Marketing environment
Marketing intermediaries

Microenvironment
Natural environment
Political environment
Public
Technological environment

Discussing the Issues

1. In the 1930s President Franklin Roosevelt used his cigarette holder as a personal "trademark." Would a president be seen smoking today? Discuss how the cultural environment has changed. How might a cigarette manufacturer market its products differently to meet this new environment?

2. What environmental trends will affect the success of Walt Disney Company throughout the 1990s? If you were in charge of marketing at Disney, what plans would you make to deal with these trends?

3. Immigration is an important component of U.S. population growth. Currently, there is one legal immigrant for every six or seven people born in the United States, twice the ratio of 20 years ago. How will this trend affect marketing over the next five years? over the next 50 years?

4. Americans are becoming more concerned about the natural environment. Explain how this trend would affect a company that markets plastic sandwich bags. List and explain some effective responses to this trend.

5. A major alcoholic beverage marketer is planning to introduce an "adult soft drink"—a socially acceptable substitute for stronger drinks that would be cheaper and lower in alcohol than wine coolers. What cultural and other factors might affect the success of this product?

6. Some marketing goals, such as improved quality, require strong support from an internal public—a company's own employees. But surveys show that employees increasingly distrust management, and company loyalty is eroding. How can a company market internally to help meet its goals? Identify some alternative approaches.

Applying the Concepts

1. Changes in the marketing environment mean that marketers must meet new consumer needs that may be quite different—even directly opposite—from those in the past. Ben & Jerry's became successful by making great-tasting ice cream with a huge butterfat content. They now offer lowfat frozen yogurt to appeal to soft-in-the-middle baby boomers. You can track changes in the marketing environment by looking at how companies modify their products.

   ◆ Make a list of the products you encounter in one day that claim to be "low" or "high" in some ingredient, such as low-tar cigarettes, or high-fiber cereal.

◆ Take your list, and write down similar products that seem to offer the opposite characteristics.

◆ In each case, which product do you think came first? Do you think that this is an effective response to a changing marketing environment?

2. The political environment can have a direct impact on marketers and their plans. In 1993, the inauguration of Bill Clinton as President of the United States signaled that the political environment was likely to change significantly through the mid-1990s.

◆ Name three industries that will probably have their marketing plans and strategies affected by the political changes in Washington.

◆ For each of the industries that you named, list three potential strategies to help adapt to the coming changes in the political environment.

◆ Although environmental changes appear likely, are they *certain*? How should companies plan for unsettled conditions?

References

1. Adapted from portions of Nathan Cobb, "Agent X," *The Boston Globe*, September 28, 1994, pp. 35, 40.

2. Much of the global statistical data in this chapter are drawn from the *World Almanac and Book of Facts*, 1993.

3. See Thomas Exter, "And Baby Makes 20 Million," *American Demographics*, July 1991, p. 55; Joseph Spiers, "The Baby Boomlet Is for Real," *Fortune*, February 10, 1992, pp. 101–104; Joe Schwartz, "Is the Baby Boomlet Ending?" *American Demographics*, May 1992, p. 9; and Christopher Farrell, "The Baby Boomlet May Kick in a Little Growth," *Business Week*, January 10, 1994, p. 66.

4. See Christopher Power, "Getting 'Em While They're Young," *Business Week*, September 9, 1991, pp. 94–95; James U. McNeal, "Growing Up in the Market," *American Demographics*, October 1992, pp. 46–50; Horst Stipp, "New Ways to Reach Children," *American Demographics*, August 1993, pp. 50–56; and Laura Zinn, "Teens: Here Comes the Biggest Wave Yet," *Business Week*, April 11, 1994, pp. 76–86.

5. See Diane Crispell and William H. Frey, "American Maturity," *American Demographics*, March 1993, pp. 31–42; Charles F. Longino, "Myths of an Aging America," *American Demographics*, August 1994, pp. 36–43; and Melissa Campanelli, "Selling to Seniors: A Waiting Game," *Sales & Marketing Management*, June 1994, p. 69.

6. These and other statistics in this section are from "The Future of Households," *American Demographics*, December 1993, pp. 27–39; and Melissa Campanelli, "It's All in the Family," *Sales & Marketing Management*, April 1994, p. 53.

7. Judith Waldrop, "What Do Working Women Want?" *American Demographics*, September 1994, pp. 36–38.

8. See Joe Schwartz, "On the Road Again," *American Demographics*, April 1987, pp. 39–42; "Americans Keep Going West—And South," *Business Week*, May 16, 1988, p. 30; and Judith Waldrop and Thomas Exter, "The Legacy of the 1980s," *American Demographics*, March 1991, pp. 33–38.

9. See Thomas Moore, "Different Folks, Different Strokes," *Fortune*, September 16, 1985, pp. 65–68; and Sharon O'Malley, "The Rural Rebound," *American Demographics*, May 1994, pp. 24–29.

10. See Fabian Linden, "In the Rearview Mirror," *American Demographics*, April 1984, pp. 4–5. For more reading, see Bryant Robey and Cheryl Russell, "A Portrait of the American Worker," *American Demographics*, March 1984, pp. 17–21.

11. See *American Diversity*, American Demographic Desk Reference Series, No. 1, July 1991; Brian Bremner, "A Spicier Stew in the Melting Pot," *Business Week*, December 21, 1992, pp. 29–30; Cyndee Miller, "Researcher Says U.S. Is More of a Bowl than a Melting Pot," *Marketing News*, May 10, 1993, p. 6; and Peter Francese, "America at Mid-Decade," *American Demographics*, February 1995, pp. 23–30.

12. James W. Hughes, "Understanding the Squeezed Consumer," *American Demographics*, July 1991, pp. 44–50. Also see Patricia Sellers, "Winning Over the New Consumer," *Fortune*, July 29, 1991, pp. 113–125; and Brian O'Reilly, "Preparing for Leaner Times," *Fortune*, January 27, 1992, pp. 40–47.

13. For more discussion, see the "Environmentalism" section in Chapter 23. Also see Jacquelyn Ottman, "Environmentalism Will Be *the* Trend of the '90s," *Marketing News*, December 7, 1992, p. 13; Carl Frankel, "Blueprint for Green Marketing," *American Demographics*, April 1992, pp. 34–38; Robert Rehak, "Green Marketing Awash in Third Wave," *Advertising Age*, November 22, 1993, p. 22; and Peter Stisser, "A Deeper Shade of Green," *American Demographics*, March 1994. pp. 24–29.

14. John Carey, "Could America Afford the Transistor Today?" *Business Week*, March 7, 1994, pp. 80–84.

15. For a summary of U.S. legal developments in marketing, see Louis W. Stern and Thomas L. Eovaldi, *Legal Aspects of Marketing Strategy: Antitrust and Consumer Protection Issues* (Englewood Cliffs, NJ: Prentice Hall, 1984); and Robert J. Posch, Jr., *The Complete Guide to Marketing and the Law* (Englewood Cliffs, NJ: Prentice Hall, 1988).

16. Adrienne Ward Fawcett, "Lifestyle Study," *Advertising Age*, April 18, 1994, pp. 12–13.

17. See Kenneth Dreyfack, "Draping Old Glory Around Just About Everything," *Business Week*, October 27, 1986, pp. 66–67; Pat Sloan, "Ads Go All-American," *Advertising Age*, July 28, 1986, pp. 3, 52; "Retailers Rallying 'Round the Flag," *Advertising Age*, February 11, 1991, p. 4; and Gary Levin, "BASH, BASH, BASH: U.S. Marketers Turn Red, White, and Blue Against Japan," *Advertising Age*, February 3, 1992, pp. 1, 44.

18. Anne B. Fisher, "A Brewing Revolt Against the Rich," *Fortune*, December 17, 1990, pp. 89–94.

19. Anne B. Fisher, "What Consumers Want in the 1990s," *Fortune*, January 21, 1990, p. 112. Also see Joseph M. Winski, "Who We Are, How We Live, What We Think," *Advertising Age*, January 20, 1992, pp. 16–18; and John Huey, "Finding New Heros for a New Era," *Fortune*, January 25, 1993, pp. 62–69.

20. See Carl P. Zeithaml and Valerie A. Zeithaml, "Environmental Management: Revising the Marketing Perspective," *Journal of Marketing*, Spring 1984, pp. 46–53.

21. Philip Kotler, "Megamarketing," *Harvard Business Review*, March–April 1986, p. 117.

Company Case 3

JCPENNEY: DOING IT RIGHT

TODAY'S IMAGE

Stodgy. Unfortunately, that's the word that came to mind for many shoppers when they thought about JCPenney department stores. "When I was growing up, our family would never have thought of darkening Penney's door," Peggy Olney notes as she examines a linen jacket in Penney's Dallas store. "We thought their stuff was cheap." Now, however, the 27-year-old mother of two adds that "I've discovered that Penney offers good quality products at reasonable prices. Our family shops here regularly, and I've even been using Penney's catalog." Such turnarounds are more common these days for the nation's fourth largest retailer. With projected 1994 sales of over $20 billion, and with sales growing at a compound annual rate of 7.6 percent, JCPenney is doing things right in the often turbulent U.S. department store industry.

PENNEY'S HISTORY

James Cash Penney founded the chain in 1902 in Kemmerer, Wyoming. Penney used a reputation for value to become the dominant ready-to-wear clothes merchant in small town America. Following World War II, however, the U.S. population began to shift from cities to the suburbs, and from small towns to metropolitan areas. The chain responded by opening stores in the large shopping malls that blossomed in the 1950s and 1960s. It broadened its merchandise to include more durable goods to help the new suburbanites furnish their homes.

This strategy worked well into the 1970s. However, in the early 1980s, Penney's sales flattened and its profit margins shrank. Penney's managers found that shoppers were buying only 38 percent of their home furnishings and less than 20 percent of their paint and hardware in regional malls. On the other hand, these same consumers purchased 72 percent of all women's apparel and 68 percent of all men's clothing in these malls.

A TURNAROUND

In 1983, William R. Howell took over as chairperson of Penney's Board of Directors. He realized that traditional retailing strategies would no longer work. Penney's core customers, lower- and middle-income families, watched the same television shows and read the same magazines as the higher-income, urbanite families. Although these core customers still wanted to be practical, they also wanted to be in style.

Howell launched a multi-year repositioning strategy. First, Penney dropped its major appliances, paint, hardware, lawn and garden, and automotive departments and closed most of its restaurants. Next, the company started a $1.5 billion store-modernization program. Finally, in 1988, Penney abandoned home electronics, hard sporting goods, and photography products. Altogether, Penney dropped or discontinued products and services that accounted for $1.5 billion in annual sales.

The new JCPenney focused only on selling men's, women's, and children's apparel and "soft" home furnishings. With these changes, Penney moved from a general merchandiser of commodity goods to a chain that offered fashionable, quality merchandise. Its stores targeted the 50 percent of American families with annual incomes of $30–70,000 that accounted for 60 percent of both disposable income and department-store expenditures. All these changes paid off in 1989 as Penney's net income soared to a record $822 million on sales of $16.1 billion.

Then, the bottom dropped out. In its push into fashion merchandise, Penney had expanded its selection of higher-priced lines. In 1990, Iraq invaded Kuwait, and the U.S. economy plunged into recession. These events made consumers more cautious about their futures and more conservative in their spending. The changes also hammered Penney's earnings. Profits plunged 42 percent in 1990 to $577 million, and they fell again to $528 million in 1991.

Penney's managers decided it was time to return to the chain's focus on moderately priced merchandise. First, they made nationwide, permanent price cuts of 10 percent or more on many items. But beyond just lowering prices, they decided to *increase* quality. Penney expanded its quality inspection team from 20 people in 1990 to over 200 by 1993. These inspectors worked with Penney's suppliers to audit their factories, rank them for quality, and compare their products' quality with that of other retailers' products.

Then, Penney improved its communications technology. It installed a Direct Broadcast system in 1,100 stores that allowed its buyers to see merchandise by video and place orders via computer. This system cut the time for store buying decisions from two weeks to a few days and improved the buyers' ability to shape merchandise mixes to serve particular markets. Penney also adjusted its merchandise mix in 170 stores to serve the Hispanic and African-American shoppers in their specific market areas. Finally, Penney operated a toll-free, 24-hour, 7-day-a-week customer phone service. Response time for 90 percent of the calls was 30 seconds, and Penney delivered 90 percent of all orders within two working days.

Even with all this done, Penney's managers realized that they would need to do more to keep the chain from looking like other retailers who would adopt value-pricing strategies. Penney needed a competitive advantage.

DEVELOPING A COMPETITIVE ADVANTAGE

In the 1980s, William Howell visited suppliers of well-known, upscale fashion merchandise, such as Liz Claiborne, in an effort to convince them to let Penney carry their lines. However, many of these suppliers still viewed Penney as dowdy and downscale, and they refused. So, Howell decided that Penney would have to build a fashion image for some of its own private-label brands. It needed to develop and position these brands as national labels that could compete with brands such as Claiborne, the Gap, and Hart Schaffner & Marx. As a result, Penney developed labels like Worthington, Hunt Club, St. John's Bay, Jacqueline Ferrar, and Stafford and targeted specific customer groups, such as professional women. It also hired designers and managers for each

brand and challenged the managers to develop a unique identity to go with each brand. The brands were not to be just look-alikes of other national brands.

Penney's thoroughly test marketed each new product. Using the Direct Broadcast system, it beamed product pictures and specifications to 16 stores in different regions, where groups of selected customers gave their reactions. Once Penney approved a product, the company's inspectors made sure the manufacturers made the product to specifications.

Penney now had a competitive advantage—top-quality national brands available at reasonable prices. To get the word out, it hired a major Dallas advertising firm, Temerlin McClain, to develop a $100 million campaign. The agency developed ads that featured individual clothing items and stressed their quality. New television ads took shoppers inside Penney's stores so they could see the quality for themselves. Spots showed famous labels, such as Nike and Dockers, along side Penney's brands. Close-ups showed labels with "pure silk" or "100% cotton" to emphasize the quality. The ads also showed lots of "sale" signs and emphasized value. Penney backed up these ads by developing in-store displays that placed Penney's brands side-by-side with outside brands. Shoppers noticed that the look and quality of Penney's and outside brands were similar, but Penney's brands sold for about 20 percent less.

The branding, advertising, and value-pricing strategies worked. Overall, 1992's sales improved to $18 billion, up 11 percent over 1992. The Worthington brand alone racked up a 25 percent sales increase in 1992, with sales topping $300 million.

In 1993, Penney began testing its first-ever television ads for its catalog, hoping to take advantage of Sears's decision to drop out of the catalog business. Although the catalog didn't offer hard items, such as hardware and appliances, Penney hoped it could capture some of Sears's catalog shoppers who were interested in apparel and home furnishings.

WHAT NEXT?

With all this success, it might be easy for Penney's managers to take it easy. After all, in its 1993 department store industry analysis, *Chain Store Age Executive* magazine noted that JCPenney was leading the department store comeback. However, Penney still sees plenty of room for improvement. Each of its 1,246 stores averaged only a little more than $12 million in sales for the 1993 fiscal year. The stores also had only $137 in sales per square foot of store space (a traditional way of measuring retail store productivity). In contrast, the nine leading department store chains (including Penney) had $21 million in average store sales and $167 in sales per square foot. If it is to keep pace with the industry's projected 6 percent annual growth rate, Penney must find methods to improve sales and to grow.

One method is entering international markets. Penney already is ahead of many competitors in international expansion. Penney's thrust began in 1991 when a group of managers urged the company to create an international division. As a result, Penney has moved into foreign markets like Portugal, Japan, and Mexico. Mexico represents Penney's biggest effort—and its biggest gamble. Penney's executives decided to enter Mexico when they found that Mexicans traveling north to shop accounted for 60 percent of sales in its 22 stores near the U.S./Mexican border. Penney also believes that passage of the North American Free-Trade Agreement (NAFTA) will improve the environment for retailing in Mexico. By late 1996, it intends to have seven stores in Mexico averaging 165,000 square feet in size, comparable to its largest U.S. stores.

But other chains, such as Wal-Mart and Kmart, also see the opportunities in Mexico and are moving swiftly to develop the Mexican market. The question is, can JCPenney stay ahead of competition and lead the way in developing international markets as it has led retailing's turnaround in the United States? And can it do this while continuing to improve its U.S. operations?

QUESTIONS

1. Which actors in JCPenney's microenvironment have been important in shaping its marketing strategies?

2. Which forces in the macroenvironment have shaped the evolution of JCPenney's marketing strategies?

3. What microenvironmental and macroenvironmental factors should JCPenney consider as it enters foreign markets?

4. What recommendations would you make to help JCPenney improve sales in its U.S. stores?

Sources: Howard Schlossberg, "Retailers Reassessing Themselves to Stay in Touch with Consumers," *Marketing News,* March 29, 1993, pp. 8–9; Wendy Zellner, "Penney's Rediscovers Its Calling," *Business Week,* April 5, 1993, pp. 51–52; Zina Moukheiber, "Our Competitive Advantage," *Forbes,* April 12, 1993, pp. 59–62; Julie N. Forsyth, "Department Store Industry Restructures for the '90s," *Chain Store Age Executive,* August 1993, pp. 25A–30A; "JCPenney Targets Middle America," *Discount Merchandiser,* August 1993, pp. 106–107; Elaine Underwood, "JCPenney Pitches Ethnics," *Brandweek,* September 13, 1993, p. 10; Bob Ortega, "Penney Pushes Abroad In Unusually Big Way As It Pursues Growth," *Wall Street Journal,* February 1, 1994, p. A1.

Video Case 1

PATAGONIA: AIMING FOR NO GROWTH

Patagonia's bright blues, reds, and purples are often spotted on adventurers shooting white-water rapids, climbing mountainsides, whizzing down ski slopes, and occasionally just lying around—anywhere in the world. Patagonia is a study in contrasts—it is a very successful company even though it tries to *discourage* consumption.

Yvon Chouinard, a young Californian, founded Patagonia in 1957 to sell his handmade mountain-climbing equipment. Sales grew slowly until 1972, when he decided to include clothing—rugby shirts and canvas shorts—in his small outdoor-equipment catalog. To move these products, he offered a money-back guarantee, which was feasible only because he sold high-quality, high-priced, and durable products. As sales grew, Chouinard began to design and introduce newer, innovative fabrics, making products such as foamback raingear, pile and bunting outerwear, and polypropylene underwear. Patagonia's strategy has been to compete on innovation rather than costs. The company is known not for low prices but for developing new materials and designs.

The heady eighties were the perfect growth period for Patagonia. Consumers were brand- and not price-conscious—they wanted quality. They had discovered adventure travel and were engaging in outdoor activities in record numbers. Style, individualism, and image were "in." Magazine articles celebrated Chouinard's idea of work—spending six to eight months a year hiking, fishing, climbing, and surfing to "test" his new designs and develop new product ideas. As a "fun hog," he was devoted to any nonmotorized outdoor activity. And as "Patagonia's outside man," he was able to gauge the functionality, comfort, and usefulness of outdoor gear he sold.

Patagonia's concern for the environment contributes significantly to its image. For example, as early as 1972, Chouinard abandoned production of traditional mountain-climbing pitons in favor of chocks that could be inserted into cracks in a rock face, leaving no holes or other damage. Other climbers willingly followed Chouinard's lead by switching to the more environmentally responsible chocks. In 1985, Patagonia began giving away 10 percent of its pretax profits—

usually in small amounts of from $1,000 to $3,000—to less well-known environmental groups. Today, it donates one percent of sales or 10 percent of pretax profit, whichever is greater. To date, the company has given away more than $3.5 million, along with free goods that organizations can sell or auction off to raise funds.

In 1991, recession struck, sales stalled, and inventory piled up, eventually causing Patagonia to sell goods below cost. An *INC.* magazine article entitled "Lost in Patagonia" concluded that the firm would not survive. The article claimed that Patagonia lacked "real business managers" who walk the shop floor daily and pay close attention to costs. However, a quick glance around any trail shop will tell you that Patagonia survived. How? First, it maintained close contact with its market through its Guide Line service, which customers can call for help when planning outdoor activities anywhere in the world. Also, each Patagonia catalog features a "Capture a Patagoniac" appeal, soliciting pictures of customers engaging in outdoor activities (and wearing Patagonia clothing, of course). The company uses these pictures in its catalogs, carefully identifying every Patagoniac. Buy from Patagonia, send in your pictures, and *you* might be featured in the next catalog.

Patagonia has also established a no growth policy by dropping 30 percent of its clothing lines and reducing the number of styles it offers (it sells only two styles of ski pants, for example). It no longer buys mailing lists, has reduced the size of catalogs, and limits the number of catalogs it produces to two a year. The company has even reduced its advertising spending, and it sells only to dealers who get preseason orders in first. Patagonia focuses on making multifunctional clothing, such as jackets for skiing, hiking and kayaking. And it is faithful to a basic Patagonia design premise—uncluttered function. Under this premise, it develops totally functional designs that eliminate all unnecessary features, use the least material possible, and last as long as possible.

Patagonia has also adopted an environmental audit to determine the impact of all goods and supplies it uses. This has led them to change dyes and packaging, eliminate the use of formaldehyde, use organic cotton, and work with suppliers to recycle waste by-products. A major accomplishment was the introduction of PCR Synchilla—a fleecelike fabric made with recycled plastic soda bottles. In 1994, production of its pricey PCR Synchilla sweaters, coats, and gloves consumed eight million recycled two-liter bottles.

Through these actions, Patagonia has unleashed a debate about the social responsibilities and obligations of business. Chouinard hopes to decrease consumption in developed countries so that the Earth's inhabitants will not overly tax the planet's resources. But critics contend that his actions will have little effect on consumption levels. Some point out that the key to reducing consumption lies in reducing sales, not the number of styles available in a product category. Other critics contend that consumers turned off by Patagonia's high prices and lack of styles will simply buy a variety of ski pants elsewhere, leaving consumption levels unaffected. Still others claim that Chouinard confuses environmental impact with environmental damage—that use of the Earth's resources should be evaluated on the basis of the tremendous benefits that result. Finally, some people really don't want to reduce their standard of living, and they don't want Chouinard coercing them into doing so. This last argument may be the most telling one—Chouinard may find that changing cultural patterns is no easy task.

QUESTIONS

1. How does Patagonia exemplify the marketing concept? The societal marketing concept?

2. What type of marketing strategy has Patagonia pursued?

3. How has Patagonia responded to the forces in the macroenvironment?

4. Are the critics right? Or will Patagonia's actions help reduce consumption?

Sources: "Can Slower Growth Save the World?" *Business and Society Review*,, Spring 1993, pp. 10–20; Fleming Meeks, "The Man Is the Message," *Forbes,* April 17, 1989, pp. 148–152; Edward O. Welles, "Lost in Patagonia," *INC.*, August 1992, pp. 44–57; and numerous company-supplied materials. The author gratefully thanks Ms. Lu Setnicka for her assistance with this case.

MasterCard:
Charging the Competition

Fred Snook, owner of Fred's Bicycle Shop, finished adding the column of figures and looked up. "With the accessories, the total comes to $438.57, Mr. White. How would you like to pay for this?"

Lew White glanced over at his daughter Lauren, who was supporting a new Cannondale mountain bike. In August, Lauren would be entering the University of Michigan. Lauren figured that she would need a bike to get around the huge campus. She had asked her dad to buy the bike as a graduation present.

"Well, Fred, I guess I'll just put it on one of these credit cards," Lew replied as he pulled out his tri-fold wallet and opened it to display six different credit cards. "Which ones do you take?" he asked.

"I can take any major credit card you have, Mr. White. It doesn't make any difference to me," Fred responded.

Lew shuffled through his stack of cards. "Let's see. If I use American Express, I avoid any interest charges, but the company will expect me to pay in 30 days. That will be hard with Lauren's first tuition payment due soon. I could use my U.S. Air Visa card and earn some more free air miles, but I have lots of frequent flier miles already. Or, I could use the MasterCard that's associated with my old fraternity. That way, I'd be making a contribution to the new scholarship fund. I could use my new General Motors card and earn credit toward the purchase of a new car. I certainly couldn't afford a new car any other way during the next four years! Or, I could use my Citibank MasterCard so that the bank will extend the warranty on Lauren's bike."

"Dad!"

"Okay, okay. It's just getting so complicated just to decide which credit card to use."

The Credit Card Industry

It hasn't always been this way. The credit card industry began in 1951 when Franklin National Bank of Long Island issued its customers a card with their account number on it. Customers could use this card to charge purchases at merchants who also banked at Franklin National. The bank charged the merchant a fee for processing the transaction. By 1959, approximately 150 banks offered credit cards, but they required the customer to pay off the balances in a month or two. Then they began to extend the repayment time period if the customer paid a monthly finance charge.

In the mid-1960s, banks began to form voluntary alliances so that they could offer cards with a common label. BankAmericard started the trend, becoming Visa in 1977. Master Charge evolved into MasterCard in 1979. Visa and MasterCard were thus *nonprofit associations* made up of member banks. Each association had a board of directors to set policies to guide member banks' issuance of its cards. The associations also had staffs to run their operations and to help market their cards to banks and merchants. Many individual banks were members of both Visa and MasterCard. The banks themselves decided which cards to issue.

What Happens When You "Charge It"

When a customer presents a MasterCard credit card to pay for a purchase, the merchant first obtains approval from the merchant's bank. The merchant's bank uses MasterCard's computer network, which links it to the bank that issued the consumer's credit card, to get approval. Upon approval, the customer receives the merchandise and signs a charge slip. The merchant then presents this slip to its bank. That bank subtracts an average 1.9 percent discount fee and pays the merchant the balance. So, on a $100 purchase, the bank pays the merchant $98.10.

The merchant's bank then submits the charge to MasterCard, which submits the charge to the bank that issued the card. The card-issuing bank subtracts an average interchange fee of 1.3 percent of the original amount and pays the rest to MasterCard. MasterCard then pays the merchant's bank. On the $100 charge, the merchant's bank receives $98.70, $.60 more than it paid the merchant. Both the merchant's bank and the card-issuing bank pay small fees to MasterCard. The card-issuing bank then bills the customer for the original amount, and the customer either pays the bill right away or over time with interest.

MAKING MONEY

Until the mid-1980s, banks pretty much had their way in the credit card industry. Visa, MasterCard, and American Express, which had entered the business in 1958, dominated the industry. It was hard for banks not to make money on their credit cards.

The banks made money three ways. First, they charged credit card customers annual fees. Then, they charged the customer interest on the unpaid balance each month, usually at a rate of 18 percent per year or higher. Finally, they charged the merchants who accepted their cards "discount" fees on each purchase. With a system like this, bank credit cards produced gross margins in the 50 percent range and became banks' most profitable businesses.

While they were making all this money, the banks focused on getting their cards accepted at more establishments. Most stores that took either Visa *or* Master-Card seemed to accept the other card as well. Fewer stores accepted American Express because it charged a higher discount fee (3.5 percent on average versus about 2 percent for Visa and MasterCard). American Express users had to pay their accounts in full each month and thus paid no interest on outstanding balances.

Gasoline companies, such as Texaco, British Petroleum, and Exxon, issued the only other widely accepted credit cards. Although some of these cards had tie-in programs with hotels, motels, or other travel-related services, most merchants did not accept them for normal consumer purchases.

At the other end of the scale were the retail charge cards issued by individual stores (often called *proprietary cards*) that customers could use only at that particular store. Retailers such as Sears, Macy's, Belk Stores, JCPenney, and Nordstrom's issued their own cards.

NEW COMPETITION ENTERS

In the mid-1980s, however, competition jumped into the credit card arena from an unexpected source. Nonbanks examined the industry and saw the attractive profits. The opportunities were too good to pass up. In 1986, armed with the competitive advantage of a list of 70 million credit cardholders, Sears launched the Discover card. Although other banks had needed to spend from $25 to $80 to get each new cardholder, Sears had an acquisition cost of $6! Sears attracted cardholders by charging no annual fee and offering customers a rebate of up to 1 percent of every dollar charged. Although a $1,000 balance produced only a $2.50 rebate, customers seemed to appreciate even that modest amount. By 1990, Sears had 34 million Discover cards in circulation, a 6 percent market share. More importantly, Discover produced $80 million in earnings for Sears at a time when the company needed the profits badly.

Suddenly, the credit card business became a battle for market share. The banks found three ways to fight back. First, they began buying customers by purchasing the credit card portfolios of savings and loans and other troubled financial institutions. Second, they differentiated their cards by adding services. For example, American Express introduced its Buyer's Assurance plan in 1986, which extended manufacturers' warranties by up to a year on goods purchased using American Express cards. Visa responded in 1988 with its Visa Gold card, which offered enhanced services for a higher annual fee. Finally, in some cases, the banks even lowered prices. Some banks began to offer no-fee Visa cards and MasterCards. Others offered "affinity" cards. Banks issued these cards in association with sports teams, service organizations, environmental groups, and universities. When a cardholder with an affinity card used it, the bank made a small contribution to the affiliated organization, thus lowering its gross margin.

These counterattacks, however, did not deter another nonbank entrant, AT&T. Like Sears, AT&T looked at the credit card industry and saw substantial profit potential. AT&T had the advantge of access to the credit histories of its 70 million long-distance customers. It could easily pre-qualify these customers, lowering its exposure to bad credit risks.

AT&T introduced its Universal card by offering it to customers at no fee *for life* and at an interest rate of prime plus 8.9 percent. In addition, the Universal card carried 90-day purchase insurance against loss, warranties doubled up to a year, $100,000 travel accident insurance, rental car insurance, and 10 percent off on AT&T long-distance calls billed to the card. AT&T also offered instant credit on disputed charges and said it would represent the customer in those disputes.

AT&T set up a customer service system using its phone network. Service representatives used custom computer workstations that gave them immediate access to customer information. Just days after the launch, 15,000 customers an hour were calling AT&T's offices.

Whereas Sears's Discover Card had been a wake-up call for the banks, AT&T's Universal card caused them to sound "battle stations." With American Express adding services and AT&T cutting price and adding services, the banks saw a full frontal assault on their prized profit generator.

MATURITY AND RECESSION

The average U.S. adult had three of the approximately 260 million general purpose credit cards in circulation. Three out of four people had at least one card, and many people were canceling one or more cards that they had. The credit card market appeared saturated.

Further, after years of astounding growth in charge volume, Americans were charging less. In 1990, dollar charge volume grew only 20 percent, slow growth by previous industry standards. In 1991, charges grew only 15 percent, and in 1992, only 5.9 percent. Moreover, the amount of credit card debt outstanding, a source of interest income, remained virtually flat in 1992 at $247 billion.

Despite all the price cutting, however, the average credit card interest rate remained at 17.5 percent, down only slightly in the last year, although rates ranged from 7 percent to 21 percent. The cost of delinquencies and fraud accounted for 4.5 percent of outstanding balances, up 50 percent in the last two years. Of course, the recession of the early 1990s contributed to the slowdown in the industry's growth. Consumers were slower to use their credit cards, and their concerns about the future made them more prone to pay off or reduce their balances.

Visa and MasterCard felt these changes on their income statements. Combined profits for the two organizations declined 27 percent from $3.32 billion to $2.4 billion, and after-tax return on assets declined from 2.3 percent to 1.5 percent. The percentage of cardholders carrying a no-fee card doubled to 41 percent in the last two years.

MASTERCARD FIGHTS BACK

MasterCard and its member banks, however, were not going to take all this lying down. Working with General Electric, MasterCard developed a "co-branded" credit card. Co-branded cards featured both the name of the company sponsoring the card and the name of the associated credit card organization. In late 1992, GE Capital Corporation announced the GE Rewards MasterCard that featured both the GE and MasterCard logos. Although the GE card charged an annual $25 fee, it gave the customer $10 for every $500 charged. In addition, it offered $10 vouchers each quarter from two dozen well-known companies such as, Hertz, Sprint, Macy's, Kmart, or Toys 'Я' Us, which also joined as partners in the card.

Then, just a week later, General Motors announced its new GM MasterCard. The GM card required no annual fee and carried an adjustable rate of 10.4 percent above prime. The card allowed customers to earn a 5 percent rebate on their charges, up to an annual total of $500, toward the purchase of a GM car or truck (excluding the Saturn). Customers could also accumulate the rebates over seven years, meaning they could earn up to a $3,500 rebate, not counting additional dealer discounts. Further, GM, like GE, also had partners such as Avis, Marriott, and MCI. Customers earned a 5 percent rebate with no cap on purchases from these partners. GM said that it would mail packets describing its new card to 30 million households and spend $60 million advertising the card. Analysts predicted that GM would issue 3.5 million cards within two years.

VISA PONDERS

MasterCard has moved aggressively into co-branding. It sees co-branding as a way to catch up with Visa, which dominates the worldwide general-purpose credit card business with a 50.9 percent share as compared to MasterCard's 29.5 percent. MasterCard already has 26 percent of its 90 million U.S. cards as either affinity or co-branded cards, compared to 10 percent for the industry as a whole. MasterCard sees many more opportunities to build volume by converting department store or gasoline credit cards to co-branded MasterCards.

Co-branding seems to offer benefits for everyone involved. When merchants join a co-branding program, they gain the opportunity to offer a payment option tied to a nationally recognized payment system. Because the store's name remains on the card, the store builds loyalty. The sponsoring bank earns the transaction fees, adds value to its services, and may gain profitable customers cost-efficiently. The bank can cross-sell other products or services. MasterCard can claim more transactions, and both it and the member bank gain marketing information on a new set of cardholders. Also, the customer gets rebates or other benefits, such as a discount on a new car.

MasterCard actively pursues co-branding opportunities as a part of its market segmentation program. Because it believes that the trend is toward the conversion of proprietary cards, such as store-based credit cards, into national cards, MasterCard has divided the proprietary card market into three segments: telephone, retail, and gasoline company cards. The retail segment includes department stores, specialty stores, and regional chain stores that now issue proprietary cards.

Despite co-branding appeal, however, Visa has moved cautiously into that area. Although Visa has specific policies and leaves the co-branding decision up to member banks, it has no market segmentation program like MasterCard's. Visa questions the wisdom of making co-branding a separate marketing program.

MasterCard and Visa are pursuing different strategic paths on this latest front in the credit card wars. Whether Visa will be more aggressive on co-branding is not clear, but MasterCard has sent clear signals that it wants to be more than just number two.

QUESTIONS

1. Do credit cards contribute to accomplishing the goals of the marketing system? Why or why not?
2. What forces in the macroenvironment have shaped the credit card industry's growth and development?
3. What competitive marketing strategies have Visa, MasterCard, American Express, and the nonbank entrants like AT&T followed?
4. How have the various competitors in the credit card industry used the marketing management process outlined in the text?
5. Using the product/market expansion grid, identify marketing opportunities that MasterCard should pursue. What other marketing recommendations would you make to MasterCard?

Sources: Bill Saporito, "Who's Winning the Credit Card War," *Fortune*, July 2, 1990, pp. 66–71; "Credit Cards: Plastic Profits Go Pop," *The Economist*, September 12, 1992, p. 92; Gary Levin, "Co-Branding Trend Takes Credit Cards," *Advertising Age*, November 11, 1991, p. 69; Wanda Cantrell, "The Party's Over for Bank Cards," *Bank Management*, June 1992, pp. 44–48; Mark Arend, "Card Associations Weigh Co-Branding Merits," *ABA Banking Journal*, September 1992, pp. 84–86; Adam Bryant, "Raising the Stakes in a War of Plastic," *New York Times*, September 13, 1992, section 3, p. 13; Adam Bryant, "G.M.'s Bold Move into Credit Cards," *New York Times*, September 10, 1992, section D, p. 5.

Marketing Research and Information Systems

4

W hen Duncan Black and Alonzo Decker opened their first machine shop in 1910, portable power tools had yet to be invented. The typical industrial electric drill was a cumbersome, 50-pound unit—two people were required to operate it, with a third controlling the power source. Black and Decker saw the need for a smaller, easier-to-use tool and designed a revolutionary new model—one with a smaller motor, a pistol grip, and a trigger switch. The rest is history. The original Black & Decker portable drill now resides in the Smithsonian Institution's National Museum of American History, and Black & Decker is now a leading marketer of portable power tools.

Black & Decker owes much of its success to its relentless efforts to learn all it can about customers. In 1991, market research revealed a growing but underserved power tool segment—serious do-it-yourselfers (SDIYers)—those who take on large, complex home improvement projects by themselves. Some 22 million strong, these serious handymen need more than the run-of-the-mill, entry-level tools used by occasional do-it-yourselfers, but less than the expensive, high-quality tools used by professionals. Black & Decker set out to develop a mid-range line, Quantum, that would bridge the gap between entry level and professional tools.

The Quantum quest began with exhaustive consumer research to find out exactly what these serious do-it-yourselfers wanted in their power tools. Black & Decker first enlisted the services of 50 typical SDIYers—male homeowners, aged 25 to 54, who own more than six power tools, and who undertake one or more major home improvement projects every year. For more than four months, these 50 people were subjected to intense scrutiny, serving like mice in a cage as a kind of living laboratory. According to *Fortune* magazine: "They were questioned about the tools they use and why they had picked particular brands. B&D executives hung out with them in their homes and around their workshops. They watched how the 50 used their tools and asked why they liked or disliked certain ones, how the tools felt in their hands, and even how they cleaned up their workspace when they finished. The B&D

OBJECTIVES

When you finish this chapter, you should be able to accomplish the following:

1. Explain the concept of the **marketing information system**, emphasizing ways of **assessing information needs**, the sources used for **developing information**, and ways of **distributing information**.

2. Outline the **marketing research process**, including **defining the problem and research objectives** and developing the **research plan**.

3. Discuss the key issues of **planning primary data collection, implementing the research plan**, and interpreting and reporting the findings.

people tagged along on shopping trips too, monitoring what the SDIYers bought and how much they spent. On occasion executives even took an industrial psychologist with them on home visits, hoping this would tell even more about what the customer wanted." Black & Decker followed up this initial market research by interviewing hundreds of tool customers who had mailed in warranty cards, asking similar questions about tool preferences and buying behavior.

Once it understood their needs and preferences, Black & Decker set out to create a line of tools that would give the SDIYers what they wanted. It created a "fusion team"—85 Black & Decker employees from around the world, including marketers, engineers, designers, finance people, and others. Poring over the research findings, Team Quantum addressed consumers' concerns one by one. SDIYers wanted safer tools—new Quantum saws featured an auto braking system that stopped the saw blade within just two seconds of turning off the saw. Customers wanted cordless tools that held their power long enough to complete long jobs—the team created a more powerful drill with a battery pack that recharged in only an hour instead of 24 hours. The handymen wanted tools that required less clean-up after the day's work was done. So the new Quantum circular saws and sanders came equipped with a bag attachment that sucked up sawdust and eliminated clean-up. Finally, although confident about their own abilities, the SDIYers sometimes wanted access to expert advice on their tools and projects. To satisfy this requirement, Black & Decker set up *Powersource: The Information Network for Serious Do-It-Yourselfers*. This innovative program provided a toll-free hotline staffed by experienced advisers ready to answer home repair questions from 7 A.M. to 10 P.M., seven days a week. *Powersource* also offered customers an assortment of detailed plans for building furniture and other home improvement projects, and a subscription to *Shop Talk,* a newsletter containing workshop tips and project guides.

Black & Decker relied on additional consumer research to guide other important decisions. Quantum tools were colored a deep green because consumers associated this color with quality and reliability. Even the Quantum name was based on research—consumers could pronounce it easily, and they felt that the name suggested a product that was a step above others.

The new Quantum line, introduced in mid-1993 as "Serious Tools for Serious Projects," became an immediate success. Sales were brisk, and the line won a number of retailing awards, including the highly regarded Retailers' Choice Award from *Do-It-Yourself Retailing* magazine. And based on the new tool line, and on its strong commitment to customer service, Black & Decker earned Vendor of the Year Awards from Wal-Mart, Builders Square, Channel Home Centers, and a number of other retailers.

Despite this early success, Black & Decker continued to listen to its customers. Within a few months of the Quantum introduction, the company held a three-day phone-a-thon to gather the thoughts of 2,500 customers concerning their new Quantum tools. As *Fortune* reports: "Nearly 200 employees—assembly-line workers, marketing executives, and everyone in between—flew from around the world to company headquarters in Towson, Maryland, where the cafeteria had been set up with phone banks, computers, and, in the words of Quantum program manager Clifford Hall, 'lots of pizza.' Says he: 'We want everyone associated with Quantum to hear what the consumer has to say.'" All of this marketing research appears to be paying off handsomely. According to one industry analyst, "Black & Decker has become very good at taking market share away from rival companies. They just know their customer."[1]

In order to produce superior value and satisfaction for customers, companies need information at almost every turn. As the Black & Decker story highlights, good products and marketing programs begin with a thorough understanding of consumer needs and wants. Companies also need an abundance of information on competitors, resellers, and other actors and forces in the marketplace. Increasingly, marketers are viewing information not just as an input for making better decisions, but also as an important strategic asset and marketing tool.[2]

During the past century, most companies were small and knew their customers firsthand. Managers picked up marketing information by being around people, observing them, and asking questions. During this century, however, many factors have increased the need for more and better information. As companies become national or international in scope, they need more information on larger, more distant markets. As incomes increase and buyers become more selective, sellers need better information about how buyers respond to different products and appeals. As sellers use more complex marketing approaches and face more competition, they need information on the effectiveness of their marketing tools. Finally, in today's more rapidly changing environments, managers need more up-to-date information to make timely decisions.

The supply of information also has increased greatly. John Neisbitt suggests that the United States is undergoing a "megashift" from an industrial to an information-based economy.[3] He found that more than 65 percent of the U.S. work force now is employed in producing or processing information, compared to only 17 percent in 1950. Using improved computer systems and other technologies, companies now can provide information in great quantities. In fact, today's managers sometimes receive too much information. For example, one study found that with all the companies offering data, and with all the information now available through supermarket scanners, a packaged-goods brand manager is bombarded with one million to one *billion* new numbers each week.[4] As Neisbitt points out: "Running out of information is not a problem, but drowning in it is."[5]

Yet marketers frequently complain that they lack enough information of the *right* kind or have too much of the *wrong* kind. Or marketing information is so widely spread throughout the company that it takes great effort to locate even simple facts. Often, important information arrives too late to be useful, or on-time information is not accurate. So marketing managers need more and better information. Companies have greater capacity to provide managers with information, but often have not made good use of it. Many companies are now studying their managers' information needs and designing information systems to meet those needs.

THE MARKETING INFORMATION SYSTEM

Marketing information system (MIS)
People, equipment, and procedures to gather, sort, analyze, evaluate, and distribute needed, timely, and accurate information to marketing decision makers.

A **marketing information system (MIS)** consists of people, equipment, and procedures to gather, sort, analyze, evaluate, and distribute needed, timely, and accurate information to marketing decision makers. Figure 4-1 shows that the MIS begins and ends with marketing managers. First, it interacts with these managers to *assess information needs*. Next, it *develops needed information* from internal company records, marketing intelligence activities, and marketing research. *Information analysis* processes the information to make it more useful. Finally, the MIS *distributes information* to managers in the right form at the right time to help them make better marketing decisions.

ASSESSING INFORMATION NEEDS

A good marketing information system balances the information managers would *like* to have against what they really *need* and what is *feasible* to offer. The company begins by interviewing managers to find out what information they would

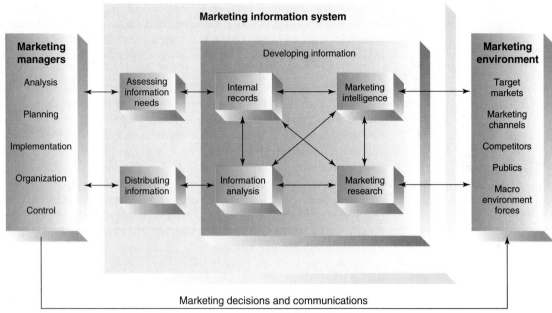

Marketing decisions and communications

FIGURE 4-1 *The marketing information system*

like (see Table 4-1 for a useful set of questions). But managers do not always need all the information they ask for, and they may not ask for all they really need. Moreover, the MIS cannot always supply all the information managers request.

Some managers will ask for whatever information they can get without thinking carefully about what they really need. Too much information can be as harmful as too little. Other managers may omit things they ought to know, or may not know to ask for some types of information they should have. For example, managers might need to know that a competitor plans to introduce a new product during the coming year. Because they do not know about the new product, they do not think to ask about it. The MIS must watch the marketing environment in order to provide decision makers with information they should have to make key marketing decisions.

Sometimes the company cannot provide the needed information, either because it is not available or because of MIS limitations. For example, a brand manager might want to know how competitors will change their advertising budgets next year and how these changes will affect industry market shares. The information on planned budgets probably is not available. Even if it is, the company's MIS may not be advanced enough to forecast resulting changes in market shares.

TABLE 4-1 *Questions for Assessing Marketing Information Needs*

1. What types of decisions do you make regularly?
2. What types of information do you need in order to make these decisions?
3. What types of useful information do you get regularly?
4. What types of information would you like to get that you are not getting now?
5. What types of information do you get now that you don't really need?
6. What information would you want daily? weekly? monthly? yearly?
7. What topics would you like to be kept informed about?
8. What databases would be useful to you?
9. What types of information analysis programs would you like to have?
10. What would be the four most helpful improvements that could be made in the present information system?

Finally, the costs of obtaining, processing, storing, and delivering information can mount quickly. The company must decide whether the benefits of having an item of information are worth the costs of providing it, and both value and cost are often hard to assess. By itself, information has no worth; its value comes from its *use*. In many cases, additional information will do little to change or improve a manager's decision, or the costs of the information may exceed the returns from the improved decision. Marketers should not assume that additional information will always be worth obtaining. Rather, they should weigh carefully the costs of additional information against the benefits resulting from it.

DEVELOPING INFORMATION

The information needed by marketing managers can be obtained from *internal company records, marketing intelligence,* and *marketing research.* The information analysis system then processes this information to make it more useful for managers.

Internal Records

Internal records information
Information gathered from sources within the company to evaluate marketing performance and to detect marketing problems and opportunities.

Most marketing managers use internal records and reports regularly, especially for making day-to-day planning, implementation, and control decisions. **Internal records information** consists of information gathered from sources within the company to evaluate marketing performance and to identify marketing problems and opportunities. The accounting department prepares financial statements and keeps detailed records of sales, costs, and cash flows. Manufacturing reports on production schedules, shipments, and inventories. The salesforce reports on reseller reactions and competitor activities. The marketing department maintains a database of customer demographics, psychographics, and buying behavior. The customer service department provides information on customer satisfaction or service problems. Research studies done for one department may provide useful information for several others. Managers can use information gathered from these and other sources within the company to evaluate performance, detect problems, and create new marketing opportunities.

Here are examples of how companies use internal records information in making better marketing decisions:[6]

Spiegel: Tucked away inside the bowels of many a computerized billing system are megabytes of data about what customers order. . . . Spiegel, the big direct-mail marketer, mined its database and hit gold [in the form of] *E Style,* a catalog aimed at black women. To create it, Spiegel [advertised] its regular wish book in *Ebony* and *Essence* magazines to create a mailing list. Then, using its database, Spiegel kept track of these customers' purchasing patterns, using what they bought as a guide to putting together a catalogue with specific appeal to African American women. *E Style,* for instance, offers lots of hats because Spiegel's database shows that black women buy them. . . . *E Style* sales are running 50 percent above the company's original projections.

Frito-Lay: Frito-Lay uses its sophisticated internal information system to analyze daily sales performance. Each day, Frito-Lay's salespeople report their day's efforts via hand-held computers to Frito-Lay headquarters in Dallas. Twenty-four hours later, Frito-Lay's marketing managers have a complete report analyzing the previous day's sales of Fritos, Doritos, and other brands. The system helps marketing managers make better decisions and makes the salespeople more effective. It greatly reduces the number of hours spent filling out reports, giving salespeople extra time for selling. Frito-Lay's sales are going up 10 percent to 12 percent a year without the addition of a single salesperson.

Internal records usually can be accessed more quickly and cheaply than other information sources, but they also present some problems. Because internal information was collected for other purposes, it may be incomplete or in the wrong form for making marketing decisions. For example, sales and cost data used by the accounting department for preparing financial statements must be adapted for use in evaluating product, salesforce, or channel performance. In addition, a large company produces great amounts of information, and keeping track of it all is difficult. The marketing information system must gather, organize, process, and index this mountain of information so that managers can find it easily and quickly.

INTELLIGENCE GATHERING: SNOOPING ON COMPETITORS

Competitive intelligence gathering has grown dramatically as more and more companies need to know what their competitors are doing. Such well-known companies as Ford, Motorola, Westinghouse, General Electric, Gillette, Avon, Del Monte, Kraft, Marriott, and JCPenney are known to be busy snooping on their competitors.

Techniques that companies use to collect their own marketing intelligence fall into four major groups.

Getting Information from Recruits and Competitors' Employees

Companies can obtain intelligence through job interviews or from conversations with competitors' employees. According to *Fortune*:

> When they interview students for jobs, some companies pay special attention

to those who have worked for competitors, even temporarily. Job seekers are eager to impress and often have not been warned about divulging what is proprietary. They sometimes volunteer valuable information.

Companies send engineers to conferences and trade shows to question competitors' technical people. Often conversations start innocently—just a few fellow technicians discussing processes and problems . . . [yet competitors'] engineers and scientists often brag about surmounting technical challenges, in the process divulging sensitive information.

Companies sometimes advertise and hold interviews for jobs that don't exist in order to entice competitors' employees to spill the beans . . . Often applicants have toiled in obscurity or feel that their careers have

stalled. They're dying to impress somebody.

Getting Information from People Who Do Business with Competitors

Key customers can keep the company informed about competitors and their products:

> For example, a while back Gillette told a large Canadian account the date on which it planned to begin selling its new Good News disposable razor in the United States. The Canadian distributor promptly called Bic and told it about the impending product launch. Bic put on a crash program and was able to start selling its razor shortly after Gillette did.

Intelligence can also be gathered by infiltrating customers' business operations:

> Companies may provide their engineers free of charge to customers . . . The close, cooperative relationship that the engineers on loan cultivate with the customers' design staff often enables them to learn what new products competitors are pitching.

Getting Information from Published Materials and Public Documents

Keeping track of seemingly meaningless published information can provide competitor intelligence. For instance, the types of people sought in help-wanted ads can indicate something about a competitor's new strategies and products. Government agencies are another good source. For example:

> Although it is often illegal for a company to photograph a competitor's

Four other car companies have already bought one. Whatever do you suppose they want them for?

Porsche 968: The next evolution.

Collecting intelligence: Porsche notes that "it's not unusual for car companies to check out each other's creations . . . A new Porsche gets an inordinate amount of attention."

Marketing Intelligence

Marketing intelligence
Everyday information about developments in the marketing environment that helps managers prepare and adjust marketing plans.

Marketing intelligence is everyday information about developments in the marketing environment. The marketing intelligence system determines what intelligence is needed, collects it by searching the environment, and delivers it to marketing managers.

Marketing intelligence can be gathered from many sources. Much intelligence can be collected from the company's own personnel—executives, engineers and scientists, purchasing agents, and the salesforce. But company people are often busy and fail to pass on important information. The company must "sell" its people on their importance as intelligence gatherers, train them to spot new developments, and urge them to report intelligence back to the company.

plant from the air, there are legitimate ways to get the photos . . . Aerial photos often are on file with the U.S. Geological Survey or Environmental Protection Agency. These are public documents, available for a nominal fee.

Zoning and tax assessment offices often have tax information on local factories and even blueprints of the facilities, showing square footage and types of machinery. This information is all publicly available.

Getting Information by Observing Competitors or Analyzing Physical Evidence

Companies can get to know competitors better by buying their products or examining other physical evidence. An increasingly important form of competitive intelligence is benchmarking, taking apart competitors' products and imitating or improving on their best features. Popular since the early 1980s, benchmarking has helped Xerox turn around its copying business and Ford develop the successful Taurus.

When Ford decided to build a better car back in the early Eighties, it compiled a list of some 400 features its customers said were the most important, then set about finding the car with the best of each. Then it tried to match or top the best of the competition. The result: the hot-selling Taurus. Updating the Taurus in 1992, Ford benchmarked all over again.

By 1993, thanks in large part to such benchmarking efforts, the Taurus had overtaken the Honda Accord as America's best-selling passenger car.

Beyond looking at competitors' products, companies can examine

many other types of physical evidence:

In the absence of better information on market share and the volume of product competitors are shipping, companies have measured the rust on rails of railroad sidings to their competitors' plants or have counted the tractor-trailers leaving loading bays.

Some companies even rifle their competitors' garbage:

Once it has left the competitors' premises, refuse is legally considered abandoned property. While some companies now shred the paper coming out of their design labs, they often neglect to do this for almost-as-revealing refuse from the marketing or public relations departments.

In a recent example of garbage snatching, Avon admitted that it had hired private detectives to paw through the dumpster of rival Mary Kay Cosmetics. Although an outraged Mary Kay sued to get its garbage back, Avon claimed that it had done nothing illegal. The dumpster had been located in a public parking lot, and Avon had videotapes to prove it.

The growing use of marketing intelligence, with companies pushing to outsmart and outdo one another, raises a number of ethical issues. Although most of the above techniques are legal, and some are considered to be shrewdly competitive, many involve questionable ethics. In a recent survey, senior executives rated the ethics of various marketing intelligence practices. Many practices were rated as "clearly unethical," such as planting spies in competitors' facilities, bribing competitors' employees, and conducting phony job interviews.

Others—such as reverse engineering, surveying competitors' customers, and reviewing competitors' patent applications, job advertisements, and financial statements—were perceived as "clearly ethical." More of a problem, however, are practices rated in the middle, such as obtaining intelligence information by searching competitors' trash, hiring away competitors' key executives or other employees, or posing as a potential customer or supplier.

Companies should take advantage of publicly available information, but they should avoid practices that might be considered illegal or unethical. With all the legitimate intelligence sources now available, a company does not have to break the law or accepted codes of ethics to get good intelligence.

Sources: Excerpts from Steven Flax, "How to Snoop on Your Competitors," *Fortune,* May 14, 1984, pp. 29–33; Brian Dumaine, "Corporate Spies Snoop to Conquer," *Fortune,* November 7, 1988, pp. 68–76; and Jeremy Main, "How to Steal the Best Ideas Around," *Fortune,* October 19, 1992, pp. 102–106. Copyright © 1984, 1988, and 1992, Time Inc. All rights reserved. Also see Wendy Zellner and Bruce Hager, "Dumpster Raids? That's Not Very Ladylike, Avon," *Business Week,* April 1, 1991, p. 32; Benjamin Gilda, George Gordon, and Ephraim Sudit, "Identifying Gaps and Blind Spots in Competitive Intelligence," *Long Range Planning,* December 1993, pp. 107–113; and Shaker A. Zahra, "Unethical Practices in Competitive Analysis: Patterns, Causes and Effects," *Journal of Business Ethics,* 13, 1994, pp. 53–62.

The company also must get suppliers, resellers, and customers to pass along important intelligence. Information on competitors can be obtained from what they say about themselves in annual reports, speeches and press releases, and advertisements. The company also can learn about competitors from what others say about them in business publications and at trade shows. Or the company can watch what competitors do—buying and analyzing competitors' products, monitoring their sales, and checking for new patents (see Marketing Highlight 4-1).

Companies also buy intelligence information from outside suppliers. Nielsen Marketing Research sells data on brand shares, retail prices, and percentages of stores stocking different brands. Information Resources, Inc., sells supermarket scanner purchase data from a panel of 67,000 households nationally, with measures of trial and repeat purchasing, brand loyalty, and buyer demographics.

For a fee, companies can subscribe to any of more than 3,000 online databases or information search services. For example, the *Adtrack* online database tracks all the advertisements of a quarter page or larger from 150 major consumer and business publications. Companies can use these data to assess their own and competitors' advertising strategies and styles, shares of advertising space, media usage, and ad budgets. The *Donnelly Demographics* database provides demographic data from the U.S. census plus Donnelly's own demographic projections by state, city, or zip code. Companies can use it to measure markets and develop segmentation strategies. The *Electronic Yellow Pages,* which contains listings from nearly all the nation's 4,800 phone books, is the largest directory of American companies available. A firm such as Burger King might use this database to count McDonald's restaurants in different geographic locations. Online databases are available in most parts of the world. For example, the *Eurobases* and *Euroscope* databases provide a wealth of information on commercial, legal, and cultural aspects of European affairs.[7]

A readily available online database exists to fill almost any marketing information need. General database services such as CompuServe, Dialog, and Nexis put an incredible wealth of information at the fingertips of marketing decision makers. A company doing business in Germany can check out CompuServe's German Company Library of financial and product information on over 48,000 German-owned firms. A U.S. auto parts manufacturer can punch up Dun & Bradstreet Financial Profiles and Company Reports to develop biographical sketches of key General Motors, Ford, and Chrysler executives. Just about any information a marketer might need—demographic data, today's Associated Press news wire reports, a list of active U.S. trademarks in the United States—is available from online databases.[8]

Some companies set up a department to collect and circulate marketing intelligence. The staff scans major publications, summarizes important news, and sends bulletins to marketing managers. The department members develop a file of intelligence information and help managers evaluate new information. These services greatly improve the quality of information available to marketing managers.[9]

Marketing Research

Marketing research
The function that links the consumer, customer, and public to the marketer through information—information used to identify and define marketing opportunities and problems; to generate, refine, and evaluate marketing actions; to monitor marketing performance; and to improve understanding of the marketing process.

Managers cannot always wait for information to arrive in bits and pieces from the marketing intelligence system. They often require formal studies of specific situations. For example, Toshiba wants to know how many and what kinds of people or companies will buy its new superfast laptop computer. Or Barat College in Lake Forest, Illinois needs to know what percentage of its target market has heard of Barat, how they heard, what they know, and how they feel about Barat. In such situations, the marketing intelligence system will not provide the detailed information needed. Managers will need marketing research.

We define **marketing research** as the function that links the marketer to consumers and the public through information. It is used to identify and define marketing opportunities and problems; to generate, refine, and evaluate marketing actions; to monitor marketing performance; and to improve understanding of the marketing process.[10] Every marketer needs research. Marketing researchers engage in a wide variety of activities, ranging from market potential and market share studies, to assessments of customer satisfaction and purchase behavior, to studies of pricing, product, distribution, and promotion activities.

A company can conduct marketing research in its own research department or have some or all of it done outside. Whether a company uses outside firms depends on its own research skills and resources. Although most large companies have their own marketing research departments, they often use outside firms to do special research tasks or special studies. A company with no research department has to buy the services of research firms.

Information Analysis

Information gathered by the company's marketing intelligence and marketing research systems often requires more analysis, and sometimes managers may need more help to apply the information to their marketing problems and decisions. This help may include advanced statistical analysis to learn more about both the relationships within a set of data and their statistical reliability. Such analysis allows managers to go beyond means and standard deviations in the data and to answer questions such as the following:

◆ What are the major variables affecting my sales and how important is each one?

◆ What are the best variables for segmenting my market, and how many segments exist?

◆ What are the best predictors of which consumers are likely to buy my brand versus my competitor's brand?

◆ If I raised my price 10 percent and increased my advertising expenditures 20 percent, what would happen to sales?

Information analysis might also involve a collection of mathematical models that will help marketers make better decisions. Each model represents some real system, process, or outcome. These models can help answer the questions of *what if* and *which is best*. During the past 20 years, marketing scientists have developed numerous models to help marketing managers make better marketing-mix decisions, design sales territories and sales-call plans, select sites for retail outlets, develop optimal advertising mixes, and forecast new-product sales.[11]

DISTRIBUTING INFORMATION

Marketing information has no value until managers use it to make better marketing decisions. The information gathered through marketing intelligence and marketing research must be distributed to the right marketing managers at the right time. Most companies have centralized marketing information systems that provide managers with regular performance reports, intelligence updates, and reports on the results of studies. Managers need these routine reports for making regular planning, implementation, and control decisions. But marketing managers also may need nonroutine information for special situations and on-the-spot decisions. For example, a sales manager having trouble with a large customer may want a summary of the account's sales and profitability over the past year. Or a retail store manager who has run out of a best-selling product may want to know the current inventory levels in the chain's other stores. In companies with only centralized information systems, these managers must request the information from the MIS staff and wait. Often, the information arrives too late to be useful.

Developments in information technology have caused a revolution in information distribution. With recent advances in computers, software, and telecommunication, most companies are decentralizing their marketing information systems. In many companies, marketing managers have direct access to the information network through personal computers and other means. From any location, they can obtain information from internal records or outside information services, analyze the information using statistical packages and models, prepare reports on a word processor or desk-top publishing system, and communicate with others in the network through electronic communications.

Such systems offer exciting prospects. They allow the managers to get the information they need directly and quickly and to tailor it to their own needs. As more managers develop the skills needed to use such systems, and as improvements in the technology make them more economical, more and more marketing companies will use decentralized marketing information systems.

THE MARKETING RESEARCH PROCESS

The marketing research process (see Figure 4-2) consists of four steps: *defining the problem and research objectives, developing the research plan, implementing the research plan,* and *interpreting and reporting the findings.*

FIGURE 4-2 *The marketing research process*

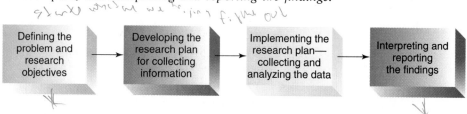

DEFINING THE PROBLEM AND RESEARCH OBJECTIVES

The marketing manager and the researcher must work closely together to define the problem carefully, and they must agree on the research objectives. The manager best understands the decision for which information is needed; the researcher best understands marketing research and how to obtain the information.

Managers must know enough about marketing research to help in the planning and in the interpretation of research results. If they know little about marketing research, they may obtain the wrong information, accept wrong conclusions, or ask for information that costs too much. Experienced marketing researchers who understand the manager's problem also should be involved at this stage. The researcher must be able to help the manager define the problem and suggest ways that research can help the manager make better decisions.

Defining the problem and research objectives is often the hardest step in the research process. The manager may know that something is wrong, without knowing the specific causes. For example, managers of a large discount retail store chain hastily decided that falling sales were caused by poor advertising, and they ordered research to test the company's advertising. When this research showed that current advertising was reaching the right people with the right message, the managers were puzzled. It turned out that the real problem was that the chain was not delivering the prices, products, and service promised in the advertising. Careful problem definition would have avoided the cost and delay of doing advertising research. In the classic New Coke case, the Coca-Cola Company defined its research problem too narrowly, with disastrous results (see Marketing Highlight 4-2).

THE RISE AND FALL OF NEW COKE: WHAT'S THE PROBLEM?

In 1985, the Coca-Cola Company made a classic marketing blunder. After 99 successful years, it set aside its long-standing rule—"don't mess with Mother Coke"—and dropped its original formula Coke! In its place came *New* Coke with a sweeter, smoother taste.

At first, amid the introductory flurry of advertising and publicity, New Coke sold well. But sales soon went flat, as a stunned public reacted. Coke began receiving sacks of mail and more than 1,500 phone calls each day from angry consumers. A group called "Old Cola Drinkers" staged protests, handed out T-shirts, and threatened a class-action suit unless Coca-Cola brought back the old formula. Most marketing experts predicted that New Coke would be the "Edsel of the Eighties." After only three months, the Coca-Cola Company brought old Coke back. Now called "Coke Classic," it sold side-by-side with New Coke on supermarket shelves. The company said that New Coke would remain its "flagship" brand, but consumers had a different idea. By the end of 1985, Classic was outselling New Coke in supermarkets by two to one.

Quick reaction saved the company from potential disaster. It stepped up efforts for Coke Classic and slotted New Coke into a supporting role. Coke Classic again became the company's main brand—and the country's leading soft drink. New Coke became the company's "attack brand"—its Pepsi stopper—and ads boldly compared New Coke's taste with Pepsi's. Still, New Coke managed only a 2 percent market share. In the spring of 1990, the company repackaged New Coke and relaunched it as a brand extension with a new name—Coke II. In 1992, after two years of test marketing in Spokane, Washington, Coca-Cola expanded Coke II distribution to several major U.S. cities. New ads proclaimed "Real Cola Taste Plus the Sweetness of Pepsi." However, with a minuscule market share of .3 percent, Coke II appeared destined to do little more than pester rival Pepsi.

Why was New Coke introduced in the first place? What went wrong? Many analysts blame the blunder on poor marketing research.

In the early 1980s, although Coke was still the leading soft drink, it was slowly losing market share to Pepsi. For years, Pepsi had successfully mounted the "Pepsi Challenge," a series of televised taste tests showing that consumers preferred the sweeter taste of Pepsi. By early 1985, although Coke led in the overall market, Pepsi led in share of supermarket sales by 2 percent. (That doesn't sound like much, but 2 percent of the huge soft-drink market amounts to $960 million in retail sales!) Coca-Cola had to do something to stop the loss of its market share, and the solu-

When Coca-Cola introduced New Coke, consumers reacted angrily—they staged protests, handed out T-shirts, and threatened class action suits to get the old formula back.

tion appeared to be a change in Coke's taste.

Coca-Cola began the largest new product research project in the company's history. It spent more than two years and $4 million on research before settling on a new formula. It conducted some 200,000 taste tests—30,000 on the final formula alone. In blind tests, 60 percent of consumers chose the new Coke over the old, and 52 percent chose it over Pepsi. Research showed that New Coke would be a winner and the company introduced it with confidence. So what happened?

Looking back, we can see that Coke defined its marketing research problem too narrowly. The research looked only at taste; it did not explore consumers' feelings about dropping

the old Coke and replacing it with a new version. It took no account of the *intangibles*—Coke's name, history, packaging, cultural heritage, and image. However, to many people, Coke stands alongside baseball, hot dogs, and apple pie as an American institution; it represents the very fabric of America. Coke's symbolic meaning turned out to be more important to many consumers than its taste. Research addressing a broader set of issues would have detected these strong emotions.

Coke's managers also may have used poor judgment in interpreting the research and planning strategies around it. For example, they took the finding that 60 percent of consumers preferred New Coke's taste to mean that the new product would win in the marketplace, as when a political candidate wins with 60 percent of the vote. But it also meant that 40 percent still liked the original formula. By dropping the old Coke, the company trampled the taste buds of the large core of loyal Coke drinkers who didn't want a change. The company might have been wiser to leave the old Coke alone and introduce New Coke as a brand extension, as it later did successfully with Cherry Coke.

The Coca-Cola Company has one of the largest, best managed, and most advanced marketing research operations in America. Good marketing research has kept the company atop the rough-and-tumble soft-drink market for decades. But marketing research is far from an exact science. Consumers are full of surprises, and figuring them out can be awfully tough. If Coca-Cola can make a large marketing research mistake, any company can.

Sources: See "Coke 'Family' Sales Fly as New Coke Stumbles," *Advertising Age,* January 17, 1986, p. 1; Jack Honomichl, "Missing Ingredients in 'New' Coke's Research," *Advertising Age,* July 22, 1985, p. 1; Patricia Winters, "Coke II Enters Markets without Splashy Fanfare," *Advertising Age,* August 24, 1992, p. 2; Adam Shell, "Coca-Cola Keeps Fizz in Brand Name," *Public Relations Journal,* January 1994, p. VI; and Leah Richard, "Remembering New Coke," *Advertising Age,* April 17, 1995, p. 6.

Exploratory research
Marketing research to gather preliminary information that will help to better define problems and suggest hypotheses.

Descriptive research
Marketing research to better describe marketing problems, situations, or markets, such as the market potential for a product or the demographics and attitudes of consumers.

Causal research
Marketing research to test hypotheses about cause-and-effect relationships.

After the problem has been defined carefully, the manager and researcher must set the research objectives. A marketing research project might have one of three types of objectives. The objective of **exploratory research** is to gather preliminary information that will help define the problem and suggest hypotheses. The objective of **descriptive research** is to describe things such as the market potential for a product or the demographics and attitudes of consumers who buy the product. The objective of **causal research** is to test hypotheses about cause-and-effect relationships. For example, would a 10 percent decrease in tuition at a private college result in an enrollment increase sufficient to offset the reduced tuition? Managers often start with exploratory research and later follow with descriptive or causal research.

The statement of the problem and research objectives guides the entire research process. The manager and researcher should put the statement in writing to be certain that they agree on the purpose and expected results of the research.

DEVELOPING THE RESEARCH PLAN

The second step of the marketing research process calls for determining the information needed, developing a plan for gathering it efficiently, and presenting the plan to marketing management. The plan outlines sources of existing data and spells out the specific research approaches, contact methods, sampling plans, and instruments that researchers will use to gather new data.

Determining Specific Information Needs

Research objectives must be translated into specific information needs. For example, suppose Campbell decides to conduct research on how consumers would react to the company replacing its familiar red and white can with new bowl-shaped plastic containers that it has used successfully for a number of its other products. The containers would cost more, but would allow consumers to heat the soup in a microwave oven and eat it without using dishes. This research might call for the following specific information:

- The demographic, economic, and lifestyle characteristics of current soup users. (Busy working couples might find the convenience of the new packaging worth the price; families with children might want to pay less and wash the pan and bowls.)

- Consumer-usage patterns for soup: how much soup they eat, where, and when. (The new packaging might be ideal for adults eating lunch on the go, but less convenient for parents feeding lunch to several children.)

- The number of microwave ovens in consumer and commercial markets. (The number of microwaves in homes and business lunchrooms will limit the demand for the new containers.)

- Retailer reactions to the new packaging. (Failure to get retailer support could hurt sales of the new package.)

- Consumer attitudes toward the new packaging. (The red and white Campbell can has become an American institution—will consumers accept the new packaging?)

- Forecasts of sales of both new and current packages. (Will the new packaging increase Campbell's profits?)

Campbell managers will need these and many other types of information to decide whether to introduce the new packaging.

Secondary data
Information that already exists somewhere, having been collected for another purpose.

Gathering Secondary Information

To meet the manager's information needs, the researcher can gather secondary data, primary data, or both. **Secondary data** consist of information that already

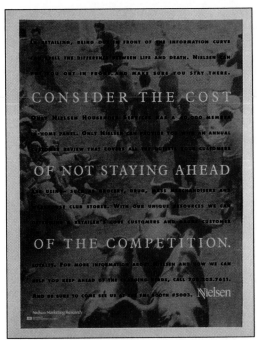

Secondary data sources: Here Nielsen Marketing Research suggests that information from its 40,000-member in-house consumer panel will give retailers a competitive edge by helping them to define their core customers and to gauge customer loyalty.

Primary data
Information collected for the specific purpose at hand.

Observational research
The gathering of primary data by observing relevant people, actions, and situations.

exists somewhere, having been collected for another purpose. **Primary data** consist of information collected for the specific purpose at hand.

Researchers usually start by gathering secondary data. Table 4-2 shows the many secondary data sources, including *internal* and *external* sources.[12] Secondary data usually can be obtained more quickly and at a lower cost than primary data. For example, a visit to the library might provide all the information Campbell needs on microwave oven usage, at almost no cost. A study to collect primary information might take weeks or months and cost thousands of dollars. Also, secondary sources sometimes can provide data an individual company cannot collect on its own—information that either is not directly available or would be too expensive to collect. For example, it would be too expensive for Campbell to conduct a continuing retail store audit to find out about the market shares, prices, and displays of competitors' brands. But it can buy the Nielsen Scantrack service, which provides this information from 3,000 scanner-equipped supermarkets in 50 U.S. markets.

Secondary data can also present problems. The needed information may not exist—researchers can rarely obtain all the data they need from secondary sources. For example, Campbell will not find existing information about consumer reactions to new packaging that it has not yet placed on the market. Even when data can be found, they might not be very usable. The researcher must evaluate secondary information carefully to make certain it is *relevant* (fits research project needs), *accurate* (reliably collected and reported), *current* (up-to-date enough for current decisions), and *impartial* (objectively collected and reported).

Secondary data provide a good starting point for research and often help to define problems and research objectives. In most cases, however, the company must also collect primary data.

Planning Primary Data Collection

Good decisions require good data. Just as researchers must carefully evaluate the quality of secondary information, they also must take great care when collecting primary data to assure that it will be relevant, accurate, current, and unbiased information. Table 4-3 shows that designing a plan for primary data collection calls for a number of decisions on *research approaches, contact methods, sampling plan,* and *research instruments.*

RESEARCH APPROACHES. **Observational research** is the gathering of primary data by observing relevant people, actions, and situations. For example:

◆ A videogame manufacturer learns more about how kids buy and use its games by videotaping them as they play at home and watching them shop in malls.

◆ A bank evaluates possible new branch locations by checking traffic patterns, neighborhood conditions, and the locations of competing branches.

◆ A maker of personal care products pretests its ads by showing them to people and measuring eye movements, pulse rates, and other physical reactions.

◆ A department store chain sends observers who pose as customers into its stores to check on store conditions and customer service.

◆ A museum checks the popularity of various exhibits by noting the amount of floor wear around them.

TABLE 4-2 *Sources of Secondary Data*

Internal sources

Internal sources include company profit and loss statements, balance sheets, sales figures, sales call reports, invoices, inventory records, and prior research reports.

Government publications

Statistical Abstract of the U.S., updated annually, provides summary data on demographic, economic, social, and other aspects of the American economy and society.

U.S. Industrial Outlook provides projections of industrial activity by industry and includes data on production, sales, shipments, employment, etc.

Marketing Information Guide provides a monthly annotated bibliography of marketing information.

Other government publications include the *Annual Survey of Manufacturers; Business Statistics; Census of Manufacturers; Census of Population; Census of Retail Trade, Wholesale Trade,* and *Selected Service Industries; Federal Reserve Bulletin;* and *Survey of Current Business.*

Periodicals and books

Standard & Poor's Industry Surveys provide updated statistics and analyses of industries.

Moody's Manuals provide financial data and names of executives in major companies.

Marketing journals include the *Journal of Marketing, Journal of Marketing Research,* and *Journal of Consumer Research.*

Useful trade magazines include *Advertising Age, Chain Store Age, Progressive Grocer, Sales & Marketing Management,* and *Stores.*

Useful general business magazines include *Business Week, Fortune, Forbes,* and *Harvard Business Review.*

Commercial Data

Here are just a few of the dozens of commercial research houses selling data to subscribers:

Nielsen Marketing Research (a division of D&B Marketing Information Services) provides supermarket scanner data on sales, market share, and retail prices (ScanTrack), data on household purchasing (Scantrack National Electronic Household Panel), data on television audiences (Nielsen National Television Index), and others.

Information Resources, Inc. provides supermarket scanner data for tracking grocery product movement (InfoScan) and single-source data collection (BehaviorScan).

The Arbitron Company provides local market radio audience and advertising expenditure information, along with a wealth of other media and ad spending data.

MMRI (Simmons Market Research Bureau) provides annual reports covering television markets, sporting goods, and proprietary drugs, giving lifestyle and geodemographic data by sex, income, age, and brand preferences (selective markets and media reaching them).

International Data

Here are only a few of the many sources providing international information:

United Nations publications include the *Statistical Yearbook,* a comprehensive source of international data for socio-economic indicators; *Demographic Yearbook,* a collection of demographics data and vital statistics for 220 countries; and the *International Trade Statistics Yearbook,* which provides information on foreign trade for specific countries and commodities.

Europa Yearbook provides surveys on history, politics, population, economy, and natural resources for most countries of the world, along with information on major international organizations.

Other sources include *Political Risk Yearbook, Country Studies, OECD Economic Surveys, Economic Survey of Europe, Asian Economic Handbook,* and *International Financial Statistics.*

TABLE 4-3   *Planning Primary Data Collection*

RESEARCH APPROACHES	CONTACT METHODS	SAMPLING PLAN	RESEARCH INSTRUMENTS
Observation	Mail	Sampling unit	Questionnaire
Survey	Telephone	Sample size	Mechanical instruments
Experiment	Personal	Sampling procedure	

Single-source data systems
Electronic monitoring systems that link consumers' exposure to television advertising and promotion (measured using television meters) with what they buy in stores (measured using store checkout scanners).

Survey research
The gathering of primary data by asking people questions about their knowledge, attitudes, preferences, and buying behavior.

Several companies sell information collected through *mechanical* observation. For example, Nielsen Media Research attaches *people meters* to television sets in selected homes to record who watches which programs. It then provides summaries of the size and demographic makeup of audiences for different television programs. The television networks use these ratings to judge program popularity and to set charges for advertising time. Advertisers use the ratings when selecting programs for their commercials. *Checkout scanners* in retail stores record consumer purchases in detail. Consumer products companies and retailers use scanner information to assess and improve product sales and store performance. Some marketing research firms now offer **single-source data systems** that electronically monitor both consumers' purchases and consumers' exposure to various marketing activities in an effort to better evaluate the link between the two (see Marketing Highlight 4-3).

Observational research can be used to obtain information that people are unwilling or unable to provide. In some cases, observation may be the only way to obtain the needed information. In contrast, some things simply cannot be observed, such as feelings, attitudes and motives, or private behavior. Long-term or infrequent behavior is also difficult to observe. Because of these limitations, researchers often use observation along with other data collection methods.

Survey research is the approach best suited for gathering *descriptive* information. A company that wants to know about people's knowledge, attitudes, preferences, or buying behavior often can find out by asking individuals directly.

Mechanical observation: Nielsen Media Research attaches people meters to televisions in selected homes to record program viewership.

SINGLE-SOURCE DATA SYSTEMS: A POWERFUL WAY TO MEASURE MARKETING IMPACT

Information Resources, Inc., knows all there is to know about the members of its panel households—what they eat for lunch; what they put in their coffee; and what they use to wash their hair, quench their thirsts, or make up their faces. The research company electronically monitors the television programs these people watch and tracks the brands they buy, the coupons they use, where they shop, and what newspapers and magazines they read. These households are a part of IRI's BehaviorScan service, a *single-source data system* that links consumers' exposure to television advertising, sales promotion, and other marketing efforts with their store purchases. BehaviorScan and other single-source data systems have revolutionized the way consumer products companies measure the impact of their marketing activities.

The basics of single-source research are straightforward, and the IRI BehaviorScan system provides a good example. IRI maintains a panel of 60,000 households in 27 markets. The company meters each home's television set to track who watches what and when, and it quizzes family members to find out what they read. It carefully records important facts about each household, such as family income, age of children, lifestyle, and product and store buying history.

IRI also employs a panel of retail stores in each of its markets. For a fee, these stores agree to carry the new products that IRI wishes to test and they allow IRI to control such factors as shelf location, stocking, point-of-purchase displays, and pricing for these products.

Each BehaviorScan household receives an identification number. When household members shop for groceries in IRI panel stores, they give their identification number to the store checkout clerk. All the information about the family's purchases—brands bought, package sizes, prices paid—is recorded by the store's electronic scanner and immediately entered by computer into the family's purchase file. The system also records any other in-store factors that might affect purchase decisions, such as special competitor price promotions or shelf displays.

Thus, IRI builds a complete record of each household's demographic and psychographic makeup, purchasing behavior, media habits, and the conditions surrounding purchase. But IRI takes the process a step farther. Through cable television, IRI controls the advertisements being sent to each household. It can beam different ads and promotions to different panel households and then use the purchasing information obtained from scanners to assess which ads had more or less impact and how various promotions affected different kinds of consumers. In short, from a single source, companies can obtain information that links their marketing efforts directly with consumer buying behavior.

BehaviorScan and other single-source systems have their drawbacks, and some researchers are skeptical. One hitch is that such systems produce truckloads of data, more than most companies can handle. Another problem is cost: Single-source data can cost marketers hundreds of thousands of dollars a year per brand. Also, because such systems are set up in only a few market areas, usually small cities, the marketer often finds it difficult to generalize from the measures and results. Finally, although single-source systems provide important information for assessing the impact of promotion and advertising, they shed little light on the effects of other key marketing actions.

Despite these drawbacks, more and more companies are relying on single-source data systems to test new products and new marketing strategies. When properly used, such systems can provide marketers with fast and detailed information about how their products are selling, who is buying them, and what factors affect purchase.

Sources: See Joanne Lipman, "Single-Source Ad Research Heralds Detailed Look at Household Habits," *Wall Street Journal,* February 16, 1988, p. 39; Joe Schwartz, "Back to the Source," *American Demographics,* January 1989, pp. 22–26; Magid H. Abraham and Leonard M. Lodish, "Getting the Most Out of Advertising and Promotion," *Harvard Business Review,* May–June 1990, pp. 50–60; and Howard Schlossberg, "IRI, Nielsen Slug It Out in 'Scanning Wars,'" *Marketing News,* September 2, 1991, pp. 1, 47.

Survey research is the most widely used method for primary data collection, and it is often the only method used in a research study. More than 72 million Americans are interviewed each year in surveys.[13] The major advantage of survey research is its flexibility. It can be used to obtain many different kinds of information in many different situations. Depending on the survey design, it also may provide information more quickly and at lower cost than observational or experimental research.

However, survey research also presents some problems. Sometimes people are unable to answer survey questions because they cannot remember or have never thought about what they do and why. Or people may be unwilling to respond to unknown interviewers or about things they consider private. Respondents may answer survey questions even when they do not know the answer in order to appear smarter or more informed. Or they may try to help the interviewer by giving pleasing answers. Finally, busy people may not take the time, or they might resent the intrusion into their privacy.

Whereas observation is best suited for exploratory research and surveys for descriptive research, **experimental research** is best suited for gathering *causal* information. Experiments involve selecting matched groups of subjects, giving them different treatments, controlling unrelated factors, and checking for differences in group responses. Thus, experimental research tries to explain cause-and-effect relationships. Observation and surveys may be used to collect information in experimental research.

Before adding a new sandwich to the menu, researchers at McDonald's might use experiments to answer questions such as the following:

◆ How much will the new sandwich increase McDonald's sales?
◆ How will the new sandwich affect the sales of other menu items?
◆ Which advertising approach would have the greatest effect on sales of the sandwich?
◆ How would different prices affect the sales of the product?
◆ Should the new item be targeted toward adults, children, or both?

To test the effects of two different prices, McDonald's could set up the following simple experiment. It could introduce the new sandwich at one price in its restaurants in one city and at another price in restaurants in another city. If the cities are similar, and if all other marketing efforts for the sandwich are the same, then differences in sales in the two cities could be related to the price charged. More complex experiments could be designed to include other variables and other locations.

CONTACT METHODS. Information can be collected by mail, telephone, or personal interview. Table 4-4 shows the strengths and weaknesses of each of these contact methods.

Mail questionnaires can be used to collect large amounts of information at a low cost per respondent. Respondents may give more honest answers to more personal questions on a mail questionnaire than to an unknown interviewer in person or over the phone. Also, no interviewer is involved to bias the respondent's answers. However, mail questionnaires are not very flexible—all respondents answer the same questions in a fixed order, and the researcher cannot adapt the questionnaire based on earlier answers. Mail surveys usually take longer to complete, and the response rate—the number of people returning completed questionnaires—is often very low. Finally, the researcher often has little control over the mail questionnaire sample. Even with a good mailing list, it is hard to control *who* at the mailing address fills out the questionnaire.

Experimental research
The gathering of primary data by selecting matched groups of subjects, giving them different treatments, controlling related factors, and checking for differences in group responses.

TABLE 4-4   *Strengths and Weaknesses of the Three Contact Methods*

	MAIL	TELEPHONE	PERSONAL
1. Flexibility	Poor	Good	Excellent
2. Quantity of data that can be collected	Good	Fair	Excellent
3. Control of interviewer effects	Excellent	Fair	Poor
4. Control of sample	Fair	Excellent	Fair
5. Speed of data collection	Poor	Excellent	Good
6. Response rate	Poor	Good	Good
7. Cost	Good	Fair	Poor

Source: Adapted with permission of Macmillan Publishing Company from *Marketing Research: Measurement and Method*, 6th ed., by Donald S. Tull and Del I. Hawkins. Copyright © 1993 by Macmillan Publishing Company.

Telephone interviewing is the best method for gathering information quickly, and it provides greater flexibility than mail questionnaires. Interviewers can explain difficult questions, and they can skip some questions or probe on others depending on the answers they receive. Response rates tend to be higher than with mail questionnaires, and telephone interviewing also allows greater sample control. Interviewers can ask to speak to respondents with the desired characteristics, or even by name.

However, with telephone interviewing, the cost per respondent is higher than with mail questionnaires. Also, people may not want to discuss personal questions with an interviewer. Using an interviewer also introduces interviewer bias—the way interviewers talk, how they ask questions, and other differences may affect respondents' answers. Finally, different interviewers may interpret and record responses differently, and under time pressures some interviewers might even cheat by recording answers without asking questions.

Personal interviewing takes two forms—individual and group interviewing. *Individual interviewing* involves talking with people in their homes or offices, on the street, or in shopping malls. Such interviewing is flexible. Trained interviewers can hold a respondent's attention for a long time and can explain difficult questions. They can guide interviews, explore issues, and probe as the situation requires. They can show subjects actual products, advertisements, or packages and observe reactions and behavior. In most cases, personal interviews can be conducted fairly quickly. However, individual personal interviews may cost three to four times as much as telephone interviews.

Group interviewing consists of inviting six to ten people to gather for a few hours with a trained moderator to talk about a product, service, or organization. The participants normally are paid a small sum for attending. The meeting is held in a pleasant place and refreshments are served to foster an informal setting. The moderator encourages free and easy discussion, hoping that group interactions will bring out actual feelings and thoughts. At the same time, the moderator "focuses" the discussion—hence the name **focus-group interviewing.** The comments are recorded through written notes or on videotapes that are studied later.

Today, modern communications technology is changing the way that focus groups are conducted:

> In the old days, advertisers and agencies flew their staff to Atlanta or Little Rock to watch focus groups from behind one-way mirrors. The staff usually spent more time in hotels and taxis than they did doing research. Today, they are staying home. Video-conferencing links, television monitors, remote-control cameras, and digital transmission are boosting the amount of focus group research done over long-distance lines. . . . Clients are linked directly with [distant] focus group facilities. . . . [In a typical video-conferencing system], two cameras focused on the group are controlled by clients who hold a remote keypad. Executives in a far-off boardroom can zoom in on faces and pan the focus group at will. . . . A two-way sound system connects remote viewers to the backroom, focus group room, and directly to the monitor's earpiece. [Recently], while testing new product names in one focus group, the [client's] creative director . . . had an idea and contacted the moderator, who tested the new name on the spot.[14]

Focus-group interviewing has become one of the major marketing research tools for gaining insight into consumer thoughts and feelings. However, focus-group studies usually employ small sample sizes to keep time and costs down, and it may be hard to generalize from the results. Because interviewers have more freedom in personal interviews, the problem of interviewer bias is greater.

Which contact method is best depends on what information the researcher wants, as well as the number and types of respondents to be contacted. Advances in computers and communications have had a large impact on methods of obtain-

Focus-group interviewing
Personal interviewing that consists of inviting six to ten people to gather for a few hours with a trained interviewer to talk about a product, service, or organization. The interviewer "focuses" the group discussion on important issues.

Marketing researchers observe a focus group session.

Sample
A segment of the population selected for marketing research to represent the population as a whole.

Computer-assisted telephone interviewing: The interviewer reads questions from the screen and types the respondent's answers directly into the computer, reducing errors and saving time.

ing information. For example, most research firms now do Computer Assisted Telephone Interviewing (CATI). Professional interviewers call respondents around the country, often using phone numbers drawn at random. When the respondent answers, the interviewer reads a set of questions from a video screen and types the respondent's answers directly into the computer. Other research firms set up terminals in shopping centers—respondents sit down at a terminal, read questions from a screen, and type their own answers into the computer. Some researchers are even using Completely Automated Telephone Surveys (CATS), which employ voice response technology to conduct interviews. The recorded voice of an interviewer asks the questions, and respondents answer by pressing numbers on their pushbutton phones.[15]

SAMPLING PLANS.   Marketing researchers usually draw conclusions about large groups of consumers by studying a small sample of the total consumer population. A **sample** is a segment of the population selected to represent the population as a whole. Ideally, the sample should be representative so that the researcher can make accurate estimates of the thoughts and behaviors of the larger population.

Designing the sample requires three decisions. First, *who* is to be surveyed (what *sampling unit*)? The answer to this question is not always obvious. For example, to study the decision-making process for a family automobile purchase, should the researcher interview the husband, wife, other family members, dealership salespeople, or all of these? The researcher must determine what information is needed and who is most likely to have it.

Second, *how many* people should be surveyed (what *sample size*)? Large samples give more reliable results than small samples. However, it is not necessary to sample the entire target market or even a large portion to get reliable results. If well chosen, samples of less than 1 percent of a population can often give good reliability.

Third, *how* should the people in the sample be *chosen* (what *sampling procedure*)? Table 4-5 describes different kinds of samples. Using *probability samples,* each population member has a known chance of being included in the sample, and researchers can calculate confidence limits for sampling error. But when probability sampling costs too much or takes too much time, marketing researchers often take *nonprobability samples,* even though their sampling error cannot be measured. These varied ways of drawing samples have different costs and time limitations, as well as different accuracy and statistical properties. Which method is best depends on the needs of the research project.

TABLE 4-5 *Types of Samples*

PROBABILITY SAMPLE	
Simple random sample	Every member of the population has a known and equal chance of selection.
Stratified random sample	The population is divided into mutually exclusive groups (such as age groups), and random samples are drawn from each group.
	The population is divided into mutually exclusive groups (such as blocks), and the researcher draws a sample of the groups to interview.
NONPROBABILITY SAMPLE	
Convenience sample	The researcher selects the easiest population members from which to obtain information.
Judgment sample	The researcher uses his or her judgment to select population members who are good prospects for accurate information.
	The researcher finds and interviews a prescribed number of people in each of several categories.

RESEARCH INSTRUMENTS.   In collecting primary data, marketing researchers have a choice of two main research instruments—the *questionnaire* and *mechanical devices.* The *questionnaire,* by far the most common instrument, is very flexible—there are many ways to ask questions. Questionnaires must be developed carefully and tested before they can be used on a large scale. A carelessly prepared questionnaire usually contains several errors (see Table 4-6).

In preparing a questionnaire, the marketing researcher must first decide what questions to ask. Questionnaires frequently leave out questions that should be answered and include questions that cannot be answered, will not be answered, or need not be answered. Each question should be checked to see that it contributes to the research objectives.

The *form* of each question is also important. *Closed-end questions* include all the possible answers, and subjects make choices among them. Part A of Table 4-7 shows the most common forms of closed-end questions as they might appear in a survey of Delta Airlines customers. *Open-end questions* allow respondents to answer in their own words. The most common forms are shown in Part B of Table 4-7. Open-end questions often reveal more than closed-end questions because

TABLE 4-6 *A "Questionable Questionnaire"*

Suppose that a summer camp director had prepared the following questionnaire to use in interviewing the parents of prospective campers. How would you assess each question?

1. What is your income to the nearest hundred dollars?

    People don't usually know their income to the nearest hundred dollars nor do they want to reveal their income that closely. Moreover, a researcher should never open a questionnaire with such a personal question.

2. Are you a strong or a weak supporter of overnight summer camping for your children?

    What do "strong" and "weak" mean?

3. Do your children behave themselves well at a summer camp?

    Yes ( )   No ( )

    "Behave" is a relative term. Furthermore, are "yes" and "no" the best response options for this question? Besides, will people want to answer this? Why ask the question in the first place?

4. How many camps mailed literature to you last April? this April?

    Who can remember this?

5. What are the most salient and determinant attributes in your evaluation of summer camps?

    What are "salient" and "determinant" attributes? Don't use big words on me!

6. Do you think it is right to deprive your child of the opportunity to grow into a mature person through the experience of summer camping?

    A loaded question. Given the bias, how can any parent answer "yes"?

respondents are not limited in their answers. Open-end questions are especially useful in exploratory research, when the researcher is trying to find out *what* people think but not measuring *how many* people think in a certain way. Closed-end questions, on the other hand, provide answers that are easier to interpret and tabulate.

Researchers should also use care in the *wording* and *ordering* of questions. They should use simple, direct, unbiased wording. Questions should be arranged in a logical order. The first question should create interest if possible, and difficult or personal questions should be asked last so that respondents do not become defensive.

Although questionnaires are the most common research instrument, *mechanical instruments* also are used. We discussed two mechanical instruments—people meters and supermarket scanners—earlier in the chapter. Another group of mechanical devices measures subjects' physical responses. For example, a galvanometer measures the strength of interest or emotions aroused by a subject's

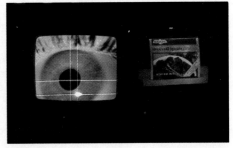

Mechanical research instruments: Eye cameras determine where eyes land and how long they linger on a given item.

TABLE 4-7 *Types of Questions*

A. CLOSED-END QUESTIONS

Name	Description	Example
Dichotomous	A question offering two answer choices.	"In arranging this trip, did you personally phone Delta?" Yes ☐　　No ☐
Multiple choice	A question offering three or more answer choices.	"With whom are you traveling on this flight?" No one ☐　　Children only ☐ Spouse ☐　　Business associates/friends/relatives ☐ Spouse and children ☐　　An organized tour group ☐
Likert scale	A statement with which the respondent shows the amount of agreement or disagreement.	"Small airlines generally give better service than large ones." Strongly disagree　Disagree　Neither agree nor disagree　Agree　Strongly agree 1 ☐　　2 ☐　　3 ☐　　4 ☐　　5 ☐
Semantic differential	A scale is inscribed between two bipolar words, and the respondent selects the point that represents the direction and intensity of his or her feelings.	*Delta Airlines* Large ___X__ : ___ : ___ : ___ : ___ : ___ : Small Experienced ___ : ___ : ___ : ___ : __X__ : ___ : Inexperienced Modern ___ : ___ : ___ : __X__ : ___ : ___ : Old-fashioned
Importance scale	A scale that rates the importance of some attribute from "not at all important" to "extremely important."	"Airline food service to me is" Extremely Important　Very Important　Somewhat Important　Not very Important　Not at all Important 1 ____　　2 ____　　3 ____　　4 ____　　5 ____
Rating scale	A scale that rates some attribute from "poor" to "excellent."	"Delta's food service is" Excellent　Very good　Good　Fair　Poor 1 ____　　2 ____　　3 ____　　4 ____　　5 ____
Intention-to-buy scale	A scale that describes the respondent's intentions to buy.	"If in-flight telephone service were available on a long flight, I would" Definitely buy　Probably buy　Not certain　Probably not buy　Definitely not buy 1 ____　　2 ____　　3 ____　　4 ____　　5 ____

B. OPEN-END QUESTIONS

Name	Description	Example
Completely unstructured	A question that respondents can answer in an almost unlimited number of ways.	"What is your opinion of Delta Airlines?"
Word association	Words are presented, one at a time, and respondents mention the first word that comes to mind.	"What is the first word that comes to mind when you hear the following?" Airline _____ Delta _____ Travel _____
Sentence completion	Incomplete sentences are presented, one at a time, and respondents complete the sentence.	"When I choose an airline, the most important consideration in my decision is _____"
Story completion	An incomplete story is presented, and respondents are asked to complete it.	"I flew Delta a few days ago. I noticed that the exterior and interior of the plane had very bright colors. This aroused in me the following thoughts and feelings." *Now complete the story.*
Picture completion	A picture of two characters is presented, with one making a statement. Respondents are asked to identify with the other and fill in the empty balloon.	 Fill in the empty balloon.
Thematic Apperception Tests (TAT)	A picture is presented, and respondents are asked to make up a story about what they think is happening or may happen in the picture.	 Make up a story about what you see.

exposure to different stimuli, such as an ad or picture. The galvanometer detects the minute degree of sweating that accompanies emotional arousal. The tachistoscope flashes an ad to a subject at an exposure range from less than one-hundredth of a second to several seconds. After each exposure, respondents describe everything they recall. Eye cameras are used to study respondents' eye movements to determine at what points their eyes focus first and how long they linger on a given item.[16]

Presenting the Research Plan

At this stage, the marketing researcher should summarize the plan in a *written proposal*. A written proposal is especially important when the research project is large and complex or when an outside firm carries it out. The proposal should cover the management problems addressed and the research objectives, the information to be obtained, the sources of secondary information or methods for collecting primary data, and the way the results will help management decision making. The proposal also should include research costs. A written research plan or proposal assures that the marketing manager and researchers have considered all the important aspects of the research, and that they agree on why and how the research will be done.

IMPLEMENTING THE RESEARCH PLAN

The researcher next puts the marketing research plan into action. This involves collecting, processing, and analyzing the information. Data collection can be carried out by the company's marketing research staff or by outside firms. The company keeps more control over the collection process and data quality by using its own staff. However, outside firms that specialize in data collection often can do the job more quickly and at lower cost.

The data collection phase of the marketing research process is generally the most expensive and the most subject to error. The researcher should watch fieldwork closely to make sure that the plan is implemented correctly and to guard against problems with contacting respondents, with respondents who refuse to cooperate or who give biased or dishonest answers, and with interviewers who make mistakes or take shortcuts.

Researchers must process and analyze the collected data to isolate important information and findings. They need to check data from questionnaires for accuracy and completeness and code it for computer analysis. The researchers then tabulate the results and compute averages and other statistical measures.

INTERPRETING AND REPORTING THE FINDINGS

The researcher must now interpret the findings, draw conclusions, and report them to management. The researcher should not try to overwhelm managers with numbers and fancy statistical techniques. Rather, the researcher should present important findings that are useful in the major decisions faced by management.

Interpretation should not be left only to the researchers, however. They are often experts in research design and statistics, but the marketing manager knows more about the problem and the decisions that must be made. In many cases, findings can be interpreted in different ways, and discussions between researchers and managers will help point to the best interpretations. The manager will also want to check that the research project was carried out properly and that all the necessary analysis was completed. Or, after seeing the findings, the manager may have additional questions that can be answered through further sifting of the data.

Finally, the manager is the one who ultimately must decide what action the research suggests. The researchers may even make the data directly available to marketing managers so that they can perform new analyses and test new relationships on their own.

Interpretation is an important phase of the marketing process. The best research is meaningless if the manager blindly accepts wrong interpretations from the researcher. Similarly, managers may have biased interpretations—they tend to accept research results that show what they expected and to reject those that they did not expect or hope for. Thus, managers and researchers must work together closely when interpreting research results, and both must share responsibility for the research process and resulting decisions.[17]

OTHER MARKETING RESEARCH CONSIDERATIONS

This section discusses marketing research in two special contexts: marketing research by small businesses and nonprofit organizations, and international marketing research. Finally, we look at public policy and ethics issues in marketing research.

Marketing Research in Small Businesses and Nonprofit Organizations

Managers of small businesses and nonprofit organizations often think that marketing research can be done only by experts in large companies with big research budgets. But many of the marketing research techniques discussed in this chapter also can be used by smaller organizations in a less formal manner and at little or no expense.

Managers of small businesses and nonprofit organizations can obtain good marketing information simply by *observing* things around them. For example, retailers can evaluate new locations by observing vehicle and pedestrian traffic. They can visit competing stores to check on facilities and prices. They can evaluate their customer mix by recording how many and what kinds of customers shop in the store at different times. Competitor advertising can be monitored by collecting advertisements from local media.

Managers can conduct informal *surveys* using small convenience samples. The director of an art museum can learn what patrons think about new exhibits by conducting informal "focus groups"—inviting small groups to lunch and having discussions on topics of interest. Retail salespeople can talk with customers visiting the store; hospital officials can interview patients. Restaurant managers might make random phone calls during slack hours to interview consumers about where they eat out and what they think of various restaurants in the area.

Managers also can conduct their own simple *experiments*. For example, by changing the themes in regular fund-raising mailings and watching the results, a nonprofit manager can find out much about which marketing strategies work best. By varying newspaper advertisements, a store manager can learn the effects of things such as ad size and position, price coupons, and media used.

Small organizations can obtain most of the secondary data available to large businesses. In addition, many associations, local media, chambers of commerce, and government agencies provide special help to small organizations. The U.S. Small Business Administration offers dozens of free publications that give advice on topics ranging from planning advertising to ordering business signs. Local newspapers often provide information on local shoppers and their buying patterns.

In summary, secondary data collection, observation, surveys, and experiments can all be used effectively by small organizations with small budgets. Although these informal research methods are less complex and less costly, they still must be conducted carefully. Managers must think carefully about the objectives of the research, formulate questions in advance, recognize the biases introduced by smaller samples and less skilled researchers, and conduct the research systematically.

International Marketing Research

International marketing researchers follow the same steps as domestic researchers, from defining the research problem and developing a research plan to interpreting and reporting the results. However, these researchers often face more and different problems. Whereas domestic researchers deal with fairly homogeneous markets within a single country, international researchers deal with differing markets in many different countries. These markets often vary greatly in their levels of economic development, cultures and customs, and buying patterns.

In many foreign markets, the international researcher has a difficult time finding good *secondary data*. Whereas U.S. marketing researchers can obtain reliable secondary data from any of dozens of domestic research services, many countries have almost no research services at all. Even the largest international research services operate in only a relative handful of countries. For example, Nielsen Marketing Research, a division of Dun & Bradstreet Information Services and the world's largest marketing research company, has offices in only 35 countries outside the United States.[18] Thus, even when secondary information is available, it usually must be obtained from many different sources on a country-by-country basis, making the information difficult to combine or compare.

Because of the scarcity of good secondary data, international researchers often must collect their own primary data. Here, again, researchers face problems not found domestically. For example, they may find it difficult simply to develop good samples. U.S. researchers can use current telephone directories, census tract data, and any of several sources of socioeconomic data to construct samples. However, such information is largely lacking in many countries.

Once the sample is drawn, the U.S. researcher usually can reach most respondents easily by telephone, by mail, or in person. Reaching respondents is often not

Customs in some countries prohibit people from talking with strangers—a researcher simply may not be allowed to speak with people about brand attitudes or buying behavior.

so easy in other parts of the world. Researchers in Mexico cannot rely on telephone and mail data collection—most data collection is door to door and concentrated in three or four of the largest cities. And most surveys in Mexico bypass the large segment of the population where native tribes speak languages other than Spanish. In some countries, few people have phones—there are only four phones per thousand people in Egypt, six per thousand in Turkey, and thirty-two per thousand in Argentina. In other countries, the postal system is notoriously unreliable. In Brazil, for instance, an estimated 30 percent of the mail is never delivered. In many developing countries, poor roads and transportation systems make certain areas hard to reach, making personal interviews difficult and expensive.[19]

Differences in cultures from country to country cause additional problems for international researchers. Language is the most obvious culprit. For example, questionnaires must be prepared in one language and then translated into the languages of each country researched. Responses then must be translated back into the original language for analysis and interpretation. This adds to research costs and increases the risks of error.

Translating a questionnaire from one language to another is anything but easy. Many idioms, phrases, and statements mean different things in different cultures. For example, a Danish executive noted: "Check this out by having a different translator put back into English what you've translated from English. You'll get the shock of your life. I remember [an example in which] 'out of sight, out of mind' had become 'invisible things are insane.' "[20]

Buying roles and consumer decision processes vary greatly from country to country, further complicating international marketing research. Consumers in different countries also vary in their attitudes toward marketing research. People in one country may be very willing to respond; in other countries, nonresponse can be a major problem. For example, customs in some Islamic countries prohibit people from talking with strangers—a researcher simply may not be allowed to speak by phone with women about brand attitudes or buying behavior. In certain cultures, research questions often are considered too personal. For example, in many Latin American countries, people may feel embarrassed to talk with researchers about their choices of shampoo, deodorant, or other personal care products. Even when respondents are *willing* to respond, they may not be *able* to because of high functional illiteracy rates. And middle-class people in developing countries often make false claims in order to appear well-off. For example, in a study of tea consumption in India, over 70 percent of middle-income respondents claimed that they used one of several national brands. However, the researchers had good reason to doubt these results—more than 60 percent of the tea sold in India is unbranded generic tea.

Despite these problems, the recent growth of international marketing has resulted in a rapid increase in the use of international marketing research. Global companies have little choice but to conduct such research. Although the costs and problems associated with international research may be high, the costs of not doing it—in terms of missed opportunities and mistakes—might be even higher. Once recognized, many of the problems associated with international marketing research can be overcome or avoided.

Public Policy and Ethics in Marketing Research

When properly used, marketing research benefits both the sponsoring company and its customers. It helps the company to make better marketing decisions, which in turn results in products and services that better meet the needs of consumers. However, when misused, marketing research also can abuse and annoy consumers. Marketing Highlight 4-4 summarizes the major public policy and ethics issues surrounding marketing research.

PUBLIC POLICY AND ETHICS IN MARKETING RESEARCH

Most marketing research benefits both the sponsoring company and its consumers. Through marketing research, companies learn more about consumers' needs, resulting in more satisfying products and services. However, the misuse of marketing research can also harm or annoy consumers. Two major public policy and ethics issues in marketing research are intrusions on consumer privacy and the misuse of research findings.

Intrusions on Consumer Privacy

Most consumers feel positively about marketing research and believe that it serves a useful purpose. Some actually enjoy being interviewed and giving their opinions. However, others strongly resent or even mistrust marketing research. A few consumers fear that researchers might use sophisticated techniques to probe our deepest feelings, and then use this knowledge to manipulate our buying. Others may have been taken in by previous "research surveys" that actually turned out to be attempts to sell them something. Still other consumers confuse legitimate marketing research studies with telemarketing or database development efforts and say "no" before the interviewer can even begin. Most, however, simply resent the intrusion. They dislike mail or telephone surveys that are too long or too personal, or that interrupt them at inconvenient times.

Increasing consumer resentment has become a major problem for the research industry. This resentment has led to lower survey response rates in recent years—one study found that 38 percent of Americans now refuse to be interviewed in an average survey, up dramatically from a decade ago. The research industry is considering several options for responding to this problem. One is to expand its "Your Opinion Counts" program to educate consumers about the benefits of marketing research and to distinguish it from telephone selling and database building. Another option is to provide a toll-free number that people can call to verify that a survey is legitimate. The industry also has considered adopting

broad standards, perhaps based on Europe's International Code of Marketing and Social Research Practice. This code outlines researchers' responsibilities to respondents and to the general public. For example, it says that researchers should make their names and addresses available to participants, and it bans companies from representing activities like database compilation or sales and promotional pitches as research.

Misuse of Research Findings

Research studies can be powerful persuasion tools—companies often use study results as claims in their advertising and promotion. Today, however, many research studies appear to be little more than vehicles for pitching the sponsor's products. In fact, in some cases, the research surveys appear to have been designed just to produce the intended effect. Few advertisers openly rig their research designs or blatantly misrepresent the findings—most abuses tend to be subtle "stretches." Consider the following examples:

> A study by Chrysler contends that Americans overwhelmingly prefer Chrysler to Toyota after test driving both. However, the study included just 100 people in each of two tests. More importantly, none of the people surveyed owned a foreign car, so they appear to be favorably predisposed to U.S. cars.

> Levi Strauss reports that when it asked college students which clothes would be most popular this year, 90 percent said Levi's 501 jeans. However, Levi's were the only jeans on the list.

> A Black Flag survey asks: "A roach disk . . . poisons a roach slowly. The dying roach returns to the nest and after it dies is eaten by other roaches. In turn these roaches become poisoned and die. How effective do you think this type of product would be in killing roaches?" Not surprisingly, 79 percent said effective.

> A poll sponsored by the disposable diaper industry asked: "It is estimated that disposable diapers account for less than 2 percent of the trash in

today's landfills. In contrast, beverage containers, third-class mail, and yard waste are estimated to account for about 21 percent of the trash in landfills. Given this, in your opinion, would it be fair to ban disposable diapers?" Again, not surprisingly, 84 percent said no.

Thus, subtle manipulations of the study's sample, or the choice or wording of questions, can greatly affect the conclusions reached.

In others cases, so-called independent research studies actually are paid for by companies with an interest in the outcome. Small changes in study assumptions or in how results are interpreted can subtly affect the direction of the results. For example, at least four widely quoted studies compare the environmental effects of using disposable diapers to those of using cloth diapers. The two studies sponsored by the cloth-diaper industry conclude that cloth diapers are more environmentally friendly. Not surprisingly, the other two studies, sponsored by the paper-diaper industry, conclude just the opposite. Yet both appear to be correct *given* the underlying assumptions used.

Recognizing that surveys can be abused, several associations—including the American Marketing Association and the Council of American Survey Research Organizations—have developed codes of research ethics and standards of conduct. In the end, however, unethical or inappropriate actions cannot simply be regulated away. Each company must accept responsibility for policing the conduct and reporting of its own marketing research to protect consumers' best interests and its own.

Sources: Excerpts from Cynthia Crossen, "Studies Galore Support Products and Positions, but Are They Reliable?" *Wall Street Journal,* November 14, 1991, pp. A1, A9. Also see Betsy Spethmann, "Cautious Consumers Have Surveyers Wary," *Advertising Age,* June 10, 1991, p. 34; "MRA Study Shows Refusal Rates Are Highest at Start of Process," *Marketing News,* August 16, 1993, p. A15.

Summary

Marketing research and marketing information systems are crucial to the success of modern companies. They provide the information that links marketers with their customers, and provides the background needed to make effective decisions on a wide range of issues. A well-designed *marketing information system* begins and ends with the user. Its purpose is to provide marketers with the right type and the right amount of needed information.

This process begins with *assessing information needs* by interviewing marketing managers and surveying their decision environment to determine what information is desired, needed, and feasible to offer. The managers running the marketing information system next *develop information* and assist marketers in using it more effectively. *Internal records* such as sales reports, product costs, inventories and account information can be inexpensive to obtain and very valuable. This information must usually be summarized and adapted to provide meaningful input for marketing decisions, however.

The *marketing intelligence system* also provides executives with up-to-date information about developments in the external marketing environment. This intelligence may come from sources with a relationship to the company such as employees, customers, suppliers, or resellers. Intelligence may also come from more public sources such as competitor actions, published reports, advertising, or other activities in the environment.

Marketing research is a four-step process of collecting information that is relevant to a specific marketing problem facing the company. First the manager and researcher *define the problem* and *set the research objectives,* which may be *exploratory, descriptive,* or *causal.* Next they develop a *research plan* for collecting data from primary and secondary sources. *Primary data collection* is more involved and requires selecting a *research approach,* choosing a *contact method,* designing a *sampling plan,* and developing a *research instrument.* The third step is *implementing the market research plan* by collecting, processing, and analyzing the information. The fourth and final step is *interpreting and reporting the findings.* These findings are then distributed to the right managers at the right times to help them make informed marketing decisions.

Key Terms

Causal research
Descriptive research
Experimental research
Exploratory research
Focus-group interviewing
Internal records information

Marketing information system (MIS)
Marketing intelligence
Marketing research
Observational research
Primary data

Sample
Secondary data
Single-source data systems
Survey research

Discussing the Issues

1. You are a research supplier, designing and conducting studies for a variety of companies. Explain the *most* important thing you can do to ensure that your clients will get their money's worth from your services.

2. Companies often test new products in plain white packages with no brand name or other marketing information. Discuss what this "blind" testing really measures. Are there any issues in applying these results to the "real" world?

3. Companies often face quickly changing environments. Analyze whether market research information can "go stale." What issues does a manager face in using these research results?

4. Name what type of research would be appropriate in the following situations, and explain why:
   a. Kellogg wants to investigate the impact of young children on their parents' decisions to buy breakfast foods.

b. Your college bookstore wants to get some insights into how students feel about the store's merchandise, prices, and service.

c. McDonald's is considering where to locate a new outlet in a fast-growing suburb.

d. Gillette wants to determine whether a new line of deodorant for children will be profitable.

5. Focus-group interviewing is both a widely used and widely criticized research technique in marketing. List the advantages and disadvantages of focus groups. Suggest some kinds of questions that are suitable for exploration by using focus groups.

6. The IRI data system (Marketing Highlight 4-3) gets its information from panels of volunteers who subscribe to cable television and live in small cities. Assess whether these people are typical. Discuss whether you think this makes a difference in how a marketer should interpret IRI data.

Applying the Concepts

1. "Blind" taste tests often have surprising results. Demonstrate this by conducting a product test in your classroom.

    ◆ Purchase three comparable brands of soda such as Coca-Cola, Pepsi, and a regional favorite or store brand. Also buy three small paper cups for each student. Remove *all* identification from the bottles including labels and caps, and use paper to cover any differences in bottle design. Label the brands with neutral terms such as Brand G, Brand H, and Brand I. Pour a small sample of each into labeled cups and distribute them.

    ◆ Ask questions and tabulate the answers: (a) What brand do you normally prefer? (b) Which sample do you prefer? (c) What brand do you think each sample is?

    ◆ Write students' preferences on the board, then reveal which brand was which sample. Are the results what you had expected? Why or why not?

2. Run a small focus group in class to learn about the pros and cons of this technique.

    ◆ Pick one class member as a moderator, and select six to eight other volunteers. Try to include at least one strong personality and one shy member. Set them up in a circle at the front of class.

    ◆ Discuss a modestly controversial issue that is of current interest to the class. Avoid issues that are very controversial or emotional. Run the group for 10 to 15 minutes.

    ◆ Discuss the focus group "results" with the class. Were the conclusions fair or biased? What did class members find useful about the technique, and what problems did they see?

References

1. Quotes from Susan Caminiti, "A Star Is Born," *Fortune*, special issue on "The Tough New Consumer," Autumn/Winter 1993, pp. 44–47. Also see Terry Lefton, "B&D Retools with Quantum," *Brandweek*, July 5, 1993, p. 4; and Black & Decker's 1993 Annual Report, p. 9.

2. Rashi Glazer, "Marketing in an Information-Intensive Environment: Strategic Implications of Knowledge as an Asset," *Journal of Marketing*, October 1991, pp. 1–19.

3. John Neisbitt, *Megatrends: Ten New Directions Transforming Our Lives* (New York: Warner Books, 1984).

4. "Harnessing the Data Explosion," *Sales & Marketing Management*, January 1987, p. 31; and Joseph M. Winski, "Gentle Rain Turns Into Torrent," *Advertising Age*, June 3, 1991, p. 34.

5. Neisbitt, *Megatrends*, p. 16.

6. See Jeffrey Rotfeder and Jim Bartimo, "How Software Is Making Food Sales a Piece of Cake," *Business Week*, July 2, 1990, pp. 54–55; and Terence P. Paré, "How to Find Out What They Want," *Fortune*, special issue on "The Tough New Consumer," Autumn/Winter 1993, pp. 39–41.

7. See Katherine S. Chaing, "How to Find Online Information," *American Demographics*, September 1993, pp. 52–55; and Diana Bentley, "Switched On About the EC," *International Management*, January/February 1993, p. 74–76.

8. See Christel Beard and Betsy Wiesendanger, "The Marketer's Guide to Online Databases," *Sales & Marketing Management*, January 1993, pp. 36–41.

9. For more on collecting competitive intelligence, see Gary B. Roush, "A Program for Sharing Corporate Intelligence," *Journal of Business Strategy*, January–February 1991, pp. 4–7; Sunil Babbar and Arun Rai, "Competitive Intelligence for International Business," *Long Range Planning*, June 1993, pp. 103–113; Benjamin Gilda, George Gordon, and Ephraim Sudit, "Identifying Gaps and Blind Spots in Competitive Intelligence," *Long Range Planning*, December 1993, pp. 107–113; and Shaker A. Zahra, "Unethical Practices in Competitive Analysis: Patterns, Causes and Effects," *Journal of Business Ethics*, 13, 1994, pp. 53–62.

10. This definition is based on one adopted by the American Marketing Association in 1987.

11. For more on statistical analysis, consult a standard text, such as Donald S. Tull and Del I. Hawkins, *Marketing Research* (New York: Macmillan, 1993). For a review of marketing models, see Gary L. Lilien, Philip Kotler, and Sridhar Moorthy, *Marketing Models* (Englewood Cliffs: Prentice Hall, 1992).

12. For more information on secondary sources of business and marketing data, see Gilbert A. Churchill, Jr., *Marketing Research: Methodological Foundations*, 5th ed. (Chicago: The Dryden Press, 1991), pp. 287–303; *The Best 100 Sources of Marketing Information*, a supplement to *American Demographics*, 1989; "1993 Directory of International Marketing Research Firms," *Marketing News*, March 1, 1993; and Jack Honomichl, "The Honomichl 50: The 1994 Honomichl Business Report on the Marketing Research Industry," a special section in *Marketing News*, June 6, 1994.

13. Mark Landler, "The 'Bloodbath' in Market Research," *Business Week*, February 11, 1991, pp. 72–74.

14. Rebecca Piirto Heather, "Future Focus Groups," *American Demographics*, January 1994, p. 6. Also see Norton Paley, "Getting in Focus," *Sales & Marketing Management*, March 1995, pp. 92–94; and Leslie M. Harris, "Technology, Techniques Drive Focus Group Trends," *Marketing News*, February 27, 1995, p. 8.

15. Diane Crispell, "People Talk, Computers Listen," *American Demographics*, October 1989, p. 8; and Peter J. DePaulo and Rick Weitzer, "Interactive Phones Technology Delivers Survey Data Quickly," *Marketing News*, June 6, 1994, pp. 33–34.

16. For more on mechanical measures, see Michael J. McCarthy, "Mind Probe," *Wall Street Journal*, March 22, 1991, p. B3.

17. For a discussion of the importance of the relationship between market researchers and research users, see Christine Moorman, Gerald Zaltman, and Rohit Deshpande, "Relationships Between Providers and Users of Market Research: The Dynamics of Trust Within and Between Organizations," *Journal of Marketing Research*, August 1992, pp. 314–328; Christine Moorman, Rohit Deshpande, and Gerald Zaltman, "Factors Affecting Trust in Market Research Relationships," *Journal of Marketing*, January 1993, pp. 81–101; and Arlene Farber Sirkin, "Maximizing the Client–Researcher Partnership," *Marketing News*, September 13, 1994, p. 38.

18. Jack Honomichl, "Top 50 U.S. Marketing/Ad/Opinion Research Firms Profiled," *Marketing News*, June 6, 1994, p. H2.

19. Many of the examples in this section, along with others, are found in Subhash C. Jain, *International Marketing Management*, 3rd ed. (Boston: PWS-Kent Publishing Company, 1990), pp. 334–339. Also see Vern Terpstra and Ravi Sarathy, *International Marketing* (Chicago: The Dryden Press, 1991), pp. 208–213; and Jack Honomichl, "Research Cultures Are Different in Mexico, Canada," *Marketing News*, May 5, 1993, pp. 12–13.

20. Jain, *International Marketing Management*, p. 338.

Company Case 4

ACT I: FEELING OUT THE APPLIANCE CONTROLS MARKET

Wallace C. Leyshon, president and CEO of Appliance Control Technology (ACT), looked up from the copy of *Appliance Manufacturer Magazine* he was reading as Gregory Pearl, ACT's director of marketing, entered his office.

Leyshon had recently founded ACT after leaving his position as business director of Motorola's electronic control appliance division. The Motorola division had achieved $30 million in sales and employed almost 600 people worldwide. But Leyshon felt that Motorola was pursuing conventional industry strategies such as manufacturing its products in foreign countries (offshore).

Leyshon believed that the industry was ready for an unconventional strategy, and he had left Motorola to begin his own business. ACT would focus on designing, manufacturing, and selling touch-sensitive digital control panels for home appliances such as microwave ovens, ranges, and washing machines. These panels allow consumers to control appliances at the touch of a finger to set cooking time or to select the "cook" or "defrost" cycles on a microwave oven, for example. These controls replace the buttons and dials found on many appliances.

The home appliance industry is mature—shipments by U.S. manufacturers grew only 5 percent annually from 1986 to 1990. Furthermore, the Association of Home Appliance Manufacturers estimates that the number of home appliances per U.S. household rose from 3.3 in 1960 to 4.1 in 1970, to 5.4 in 1982, and to 6.1 in 1987. Industry analysts question whether this level of penetration can increase further.

However, despite slow growth in the appliance industry as a whole, Leyshon's research predicts that sales of digital control panels for appliances could grow at a whopping 22 percent a year during the early 1990s. Only about 20 percent of American-made appliances now include digital controls. However, one industry analyst notes that, with the success of microwave ovens and videocassette recorders, consumers have become increasingly comfortable with digital touch-sensitive controls. Leyshon believes that increased consumer familiarity has opened the way for manufacturers to include digital control panels in other types of home appliances that users currently control with dials and buttons (electromechanical controls). With a digital control, for example, a standard electric range could offer users the wide range of special cooking programs that microwave ovens now provide.

After starting ACT, Leyshon landed a significant contract with a major microwave oven manufacturer. With this customer's business to support ACT, Leyshon realized he needed to conduct marketing research to help him develop a marketing strategy to attack the appliance controls market. Although there were only a limited number of digital controls suppliers and five major

manufacturers in the industry, Leyshon could find very little readily available marketing research on the appliance controls industry, especially on digital controls.

"How's your morning going, Wallace?" Gregory Pearl asked as he entered Leyshon's office.

"Fine, Gregory. I was just looking through this magazine to see if I could find anything to help us in our marketing research. Notice this graph, for instance. It appears that appliance shipments are turning down again. (See Exhibit 4-1.) What have you got for me?"

"Well, during our last discussion, we outlined the market research process we want to follow" (see Exhibit 4-2). "Based on that outline, I've tried to write some research goals, develop a list of specific questions for our proposed telephone interviews, and figure out just whom we should call" (see Exhibit 4-3 on page 138). "In fact, I've even drafted a preliminary version of the questionnaire" (see Exhibit 4-4 on page 139).

Leyshon was pleased with his marketing director's progress. "Okay, let's take a look at what you've done. Then we can decide where we go from here."

EXHIBIT 4-2 *Steps in ACT marketing research process*

1. Identify and articulate the problem.
2. Identify research goals.
3. Determine the information needed to achieve the research goals.
4. Determine research design.
5. Decide on research sample (i.e., whom to call).
6. Determine content of the individual questions.
7. Construct a questionnaire.
8. Test the questionnaire.
9. Adjust the questionnaire based on the test results.
10. Conduct the interviews.
11. Write up the results of each interview.
12. Write a report.

EXHIBIT 4-1 *Shipments of major home appliances in units (excluding microwaves).*

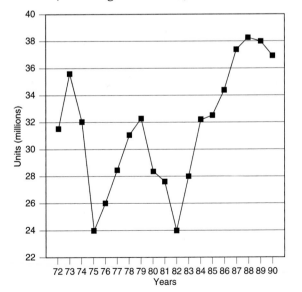

Sources: Association of Home Appliance Manufacturers and U.S. Department of Commerce.

QUESTIONS

1. Based on information in the case and in exhibits 4-3 and 4-4, just what *is* Leyshon trying to learn through marketing research? What additional trends and information might he want to monitor as a part of his ongoing marketing information system?

2. What sources of marketing intelligence can ACT use to gather information on the industry and its competition?

Source: Appliance Control Technology cooperated in the development of this case.

3. Based on the marketing research process discussed in the text, what is ACT's marketing research objective, and what problem is the company addressing? Evaluate ACT's marketing research process (Exhibit 4-2).

4. What sources of secondary data might ACT use?

5. What decisions has ACT made about its research approach, contact method, and sampling plan?

6. Evaluate ACT's proposed questionnaire (Exhibit 4-4). Does it address the issues raised in Exhibit 4-3? What changes would you recommend?

EXHIBIT 4-3 *ACT marketing research design issues*

I. Survey goals
   A. Gain insight into best strategy for approaching the electronic controls market.
      1. Types of appliances
      2. Features
      3. Cost issues
      4. Tactical selling techniques
   B. Determine how ACT can best serve original equipment manufacturers (OEMs).
      1. Research and development
      2. Partnering
      3. Product-development cycle

II. Specific questions to be addressed
   A. What problems do equipment manufacturers and retailers face in making and selling home appliances? How can ACT help solve those problems?
   B. Who are the decision makers in the electronics buying process? Who has the power between the retailer and the equipment manufacturer?
   C. Are there any unidentified issues from ACT's, the manufacturers', or the retailers' perspectives?
   D. How rapidly will manufacturers adopt electronic controls for their appliances, by category of appliances?
   E. How sensitive are manufacturers to the price of electronic controls versus standard electromechanical controls?
   F. What are manufacturers' impressions of suppliers' strengths and weaknesses?
   G. What features and issues other than price drive the use of electronic controls?
   H. How can manufacturers use electronic controls to add value to mid-level appliances?
   I. How can a supplier be a better partner to manufacturers?
   J. What can a supplier do to help speed up manufacturers' product-development efforts?

III. Who should be interviewed?
   A. Manufacturers
      1. Functional areas
         a. Purchasing
         b. Marketing
         c. Engineering
      2. Specific companies
         a. Whirlpool
         b. Frigidaire
         c. General Electric
         d. Maytag
         e. Raytheon
   B. Retailers
      1. Functional areas
         a. Buyers
         b. Store-level management
         c. Floor sales personnel
      2. Specific companies
         a. Sears
         b. Montgomery Ward
         c. Highland
         d. Wal-Mart
   C. Other
      1. Association of Home

EXHIBIT 4-4   *Version 1—ACT marketing research questionnaire*

Introduction

ACT is conducting a survey of decision makers and industry experts in the electronic appliance controls industry. We would appreciate your help in answering our questions. Your responses will be reported anonymously, if they are reported at all. Your responses will be used to help ACT determine how to serve the appliance industry better.

Questions

1. A. What are your opinions on the level of electronic controls usage, expressed in percentages, in the following appliance categories for 1991 and 1996?

    B. What are your opinions on the average cost per electronic control by appliance category in 1991 and 1996?

Category	Percent of units using electronic controls in:		Average cost per control unit in:	
	1991	1996	1991	1996
Dishwashers	_____	_____	_____	_____
Dryers, electric	_____	_____	_____	_____
Dryers, gas	_____	_____	_____	_____
Microwaves	_____	_____	_____	_____
Ranges, electric	_____	_____	_____	_____
Ranges, gas	_____	_____	_____	_____
Refrigerators	_____	_____	_____	_____
Washers	_____	_____	_____	_____
Room air conditioners	_____	_____	_____	_____

2. For each of the following categories, what price must a supplier charge for an electronic control unit such that a manufacturer would be indifferent as to using electronic or electromechanical controls, taking into account the differences in functions and features?

Category	Price per electronic unit
Dishwashers	_____
Dryers, electric	_____
Dryers, gas	_____
Microwaves	_____
Ranges, electric	_____
Ranges, gas	_____
Refrigerators	_____
Washers	_____
Room air conditioners	_____

3. What features, functions, and attributes do electronic controls need to have if they are to be used more often in appliances?

4. What impact will the upcoming Department of Energy regulations have on the appliance industry?

5. What can an electronic controls company do to be a better supplier?

Consumer Markets and Consumer Buyer Behavior

5

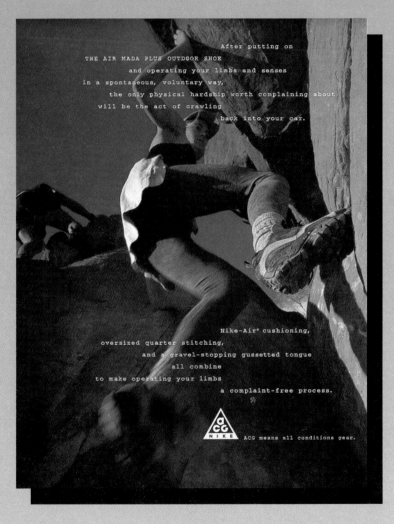

In the early 1980s, Nike won the opening battle in what many now call the "great sneaker wars." Based on the power of its running shoes, which were designed for fitness but used mostly for fun, Nike unseated Adidas and sprinted into the lead in the $6 billion U.S. athletic shoe market. But fashion is fickle, and Nike's lead was short-lived. In 1986, upstart Reebok caught Nike from behind with its new, soft leather aerobics shoe. It turned sweaty sneakers into fashion statements and zoomed to the front. By 1987, Reebok had captured over 30 percent of the market, while Nike's share had slumped to 18 percent.

In 1988, however, Nike retaliated. It targeted the reemerging "performance" market with the hard-hitting $20 million "Just Do It" advertising campaign featuring sports stars. The company also introduced dozens of new products aimed at narrow segments in the rapidly fragmenting athletic shoe market. By 1990, Nike was selling footwear for almost every conceivable sport: hiking, walking, cycling—even cheerleading and windsurfing. The numbers attest to the rejuvenated Nike: Its current market share is 32 percent and growing, and Reebok's share has fallen to less than 22 percent. In the basketball shoe segment, Nike owns a 50 percent share, compared with only 15 percent for Reebok.

Because sneakers can be a major means of self-expression, people's choices are usually shaped by a rich mix of influences. Thus, understanding consumer behavior in this seesaw market can be extremely difficult; trying to predict behavior can be even tougher. The shoe companies introduce scores of new styles and colors every year, chasing fads that often fade at blinding speed. One day salespeople will sell all they can get of a new style; the next day they can't discount it enough.

Mistakes can be costly. For example, consider Reebok's disastrous 1993 introduction of its Shaq Attaq model. Endorsed by basketball rookie sensation Shaquille O'Neal, the Shaq Attaq arrived in stores with a loud thud. The new sneakers were white with light blue trim, and they cost about $130. Unfortunately, black shoes were the hot look that year, and few customers wanted to pay more than $100. The Shaq Attaq

OBJECTIVES

When you finish this chapter, you should be able to accomplish the following:

1. Name the elements of the stimulus-response **model of consumer behavior.**

2. Outline the major **characteristics affecting consumer behavior,** and list some of the specific **cultural, social, personal,** and **psychological factors** that influence consumers.

3. Identify and define the **consumer buying roles** of **initiator, influencer, decider, buyer,** and **user.**

4. Illustrate different types of **buying decision behavior,** including **complex, dissonance-reducing, habitual,** and **variety-seeking buying behavior.**

5. Explain the **buyer decision process** and discuss **need recognition, information search, evaluation of alternatives,** the **purchase decision** and **postpurchase behavior.**

6. Express the basics of the **buyer decision process for new products** and identify **stages in the adoption process, individual differences in innovativeness** and the **influence of product characteristics on the rate of adoption.**

launch turned out to be a comedy of errors. In the first half of 1993, Reebok's sales of basketball shoes fell 20 percent.

The fickle youth market is the biggest battleground in the sneaker wars, and the inner city is at the center of that. Consumers between 15 and 22 years old buy 30 percent of all sneakers and influence an additional 10 percent through word of mouth. Many trends start in the nation's inner cities and spread to suburbia and the rest of middle America. Urban kids represent authenticity to kids in the suburbs, so trends that catch on in the inner city often spread quickly to the rest of the country. It isn't surprising, then, that sneaker makers openly court inner-city shoe store owners and kids. Nike and the other shoe manufacturers often give free sneakers to trend-setting teens whom the masses copy. Reebok even rebuilds inner-city playgrounds and repaves basketball courts to woo this constituency. And companies often launch new sneakers first in the inner city to see how they catch on before going national.

These days, shoes are the first and foremost fashion statement. Gone are the days when sneakers were mostly cheap, functional, and drab, when the choices were white or black canvas, low top or high top, with maybe a variation or two for avid runners. Now, sneakers are a status symbol, a subculture. Sneaker prices start at around $50 a pair and run to more than $180. You can get good sneakers for less, but nobody who is anybody would be caught dead in them.

Sneaker crazes are often hard to explain. For example, the early-1990s fad of wearing sneakers with the laces untied apparently began because proud owners wanted to keep their shoes looking factory fresh. Pretty soon, everyone was doing it, and that was just the beginning. Next, some wearers untied the lace on one shoe only; then, they removed the laces completely. Soon after that, wearers switched back to tying their shoes, but with laces from a different shoe. Then, many were wearing sneakers that didn't match—say, a white Chuck Taylor Converse on one foot and a Black Cons Converse on the other—but brands couldn't be mixed. In some neighborhoods, teenage girls have reported that the first thing they look at when a boy asks them out is his choice of sneakers. Teenage romances have been thwarted by brand differences.

Now, tastes in sneakers appear to have changed once again, with Generation Xers leading the way. Losing favor are high-tech shoes that pump up, fasten with Velcro, blink, or glow in the dark. Today's sneaker buyers appear to be heading back to the basics, looking for, of all things, authenticity and sensibility in their sneakers statements. Notes one analyst: "Turn off your LED heel lights. And for heaven's sakes, stop inflating that silly pump! Generation Xers and hip boomers alike are downscaling with down-to-earth antique sneaks—Pro Keds, Converse One Stars and Dr. Js, Adidas Gazelles, and Puma Swedes. 'We're all teched-out,' explains [one industry insider. Says another,] 'Things are so complicated now. People are naturally looking back.'"

Like previous fashion swings, this return-to-the-classics craze has trickled up, not down—it comes from the streets. Today's Xers prefer the "athe-leisure" look befitting their more laid-back lifestyles. They don't work out in their sneakers, they wear them to work, then to trance dance at all-night raves. Some are turning away from sneakers altogether, instead opting for hiking boots and other rugged footwear from fast-growing outdoor shoe makers like Timberland Company.

Nike's oldest competitor, Converse, is taking full advantage of recent trends. It's featuring its once-again fashionable Converse All Star. First introduced in 1917, this venerable veteran of the sneaker wars has sold an estimated 520 million pairs over the past 75 years. Converse is also bringing back models from its 1970s catalogs, including the One Star, its Pro Leather model (worn by 1970s basketball great Julius Irving), and the Jack Purcell (originally a badminton shoe, later popular with tennis players of the 1960s).

Thus, today, the sneaker wars continue to rage, and Nike is watching its flanks for new trends and new competitors. Sneaker fashions come and go rapidly, reflecting the ever-changing lives and lifestyles of the consumers who buy the shoes. Nike knows that winning the sneaker wars, or even just surviving, requires a keen understanding of consumer behavior.[1]

The Nike example shows that many different factors affect consumer buying behavior. Buying behavior is never simple, yet understanding it is the essential task of marketing management.

Consumer buying behavior
The buying behavior of final consumers—individuals and households who buy goods and services for personal consumption.

Consumer market
All the individuals and households who buy or acquire goods and services for personal consumption.

This chapter explores the dynamics of consumer behavior and the consumer market. **Consumer buying behavior** refers to the buying behavior of final consumers—individuals and households who buy goods and services for personal consumption. All of these final consumers combined make up the **consumer market.** The American consumer market consists of about 254 million people who consume many trillions of dollars worth of goods and services each year, making it one of the most attractive consumer markets in the world. The world consumer market consists of more than five *billion* people. At present growth rates, the world population will exceed seven billion people by 2010.[2]

Consumers around the world vary tremendously in age, income, education level, and tastes. They also buy an incredible variety of goods and services. How these diverse consumers make their choices among various products embraces a fascinating array of factors.

MODEL OF CONSUMER BEHAVIOR

Consumers make many buying decisions every day. Most large companies research consumer buying decisions in great detail to answer questions about what consumers buy, where they buy, how and how much they buy, when they buy, and why they buy. Marketers can study consumer purchases to find answers to questions about what they buy, where, and how much. But learning about the *whys* of consumer buying behavior is not so easy—the answers are often locked deep within the consumer's head.

The central question for marketers is: How do consumers respond to various marketing efforts the company might use? The company that really understands how consumers will respond to different product features, prices, and advertising appeals has a great advantage over its competitors. The starting point is the stimulus-response model of buyer behavior shown in Figure 5-1. This figure shows that marketing and other stimuli enter the consumer's "black box" and produce certain responses. Marketers must figure out what is in the buyer's black box.[3]

Marketing stimuli consist of the four *P*s: product, price, place, and promotion. Other stimuli include major forces and events in the buyer's environment: economic, technological, political, and cultural. All these inputs enter the buyer's

FIGURE 5-1 *Model of buyer behavior*

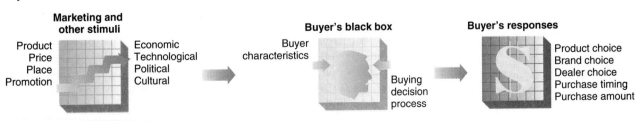

Marketing and other stimuli		Buyer's black box	Buyer's responses
Product	Economic	Buyer	Product choice
Price	Technological	characteristics	Brand choice
Place	Political	Buying	Dealer choice
Promotion	Cultural	decision	Purchase timing
		process	Purchase amount

black box, where they are turned into a set of observable buyer responses: product choice, brand choice, dealer choice, purchase timing, and purchase amount.

The marketer wants to understand how the stimuli are changed into responses inside the consumer's black box, which has two parts. First, the buyer's characteristics influence how he or she perceives and reacts to the stimuli. Second, the buyer's decision process itself affects the buyer's behavior. This chapter looks first at buyer characteristics as they affect buying behavior, and then discusses the buyer decision process.

CHARACTERISTICS AFFECTING CONSUMER BEHAVIOR

Consumer purchases are influenced strongly by cultural, social, personal, and psychological characteristics, shown in Figure 5-2. For the most part, marketers cannot control such factors, but they must take them into account. We illustrate these characteristics for the case of a hypothetical consumer named Jennifer Flores. Jennifer is a married college graduate who works as a brand manager in a leading consumer packaged-goods company. She wants to find a new leisure-time activity that will provide some contrast to her working day. This need has led her to consider buying a camera and taking up photography. Many characteristics in her background will affect the way she evaluates cameras and chooses a brand.

FIGURE 5-2 *Factors influencing consumer behavior*

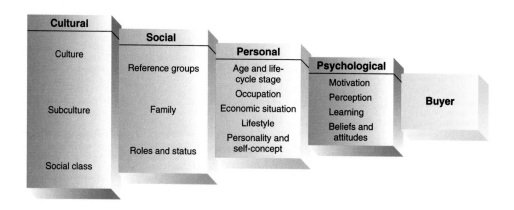

CULTURAL FACTORS

Cultural factors exert the broadest and deepest influence on consumer behavior. The marketer needs to understand the role played by the buyer's *culture, subculture,* and *social class.*

Culture

Culture
The set of basic values, perceptions, wants, and behaviors learned by a member of society from family and other important institutions.

Culture is the most basic cause of a person's wants and behavior. Human behavior is largely learned. Growing up in a society, a child learns basic values, perceptions, wants, and behaviors from the family and other important institutions. A child in the United States normally learns or is exposed to the following values: achievement and success, activity and involvement, efficiency and practicality, progress, material comfort, individualism, freedom, humanitarianism, youthfulness, and fitness and health.

Every group or society has a culture, and cultural influences on buying behavior may vary greatly from country to country. Failure to adjust to these differences can result in ineffective marketing or embarrassing mistakes. For example, business representatives of a U.S. community trying to market itself in Taiwan found this out the hard way. Seeking more foreign trade, they arrived in Taiwan bearing gifts of green baseball caps. It turned out that the trip was scheduled a month before Taiwan elections, and that green was the color of the political opposition party. Worse yet, the visitors learned after the fact that according to Taiwan culture, a man wears green to signify that his wife has been unfaithful. The head of the community delegation later noted: "I don't know whatever happened to those green hats, but the trip gave us an understanding of the extreme differences in our cultures."[4] International marketers must understand the culture in each international market and adapt their marketing strategies accordingly.

Jennifer Flores's cultural background will affect her camera buying decision. Jennifer's desire to own a camera may result from her being raised in a modern society that has developed camera technology and a whole set of consumer learnings and values. Jennifer knows what cameras are. She knows how to read instructions, and her society has accepted the idea of women photographers.

Marketers are always trying to spot *cultural shifts* in order to discover new products that might be wanted. For example, the cultural shift toward greater concern about health and fitness has created a huge industry for exercise equipment and clothing, lower-fat and more natural foods, and health and fitness services. The shift toward informality has resulted in more demand for casual clothing and simpler home furnishings. And the increased desire for leisure time has resulted in more demand for convenience products and services, such as microwave ovens and fast food. It also has created a huge catalog-shopping industry. More than 6,500 catalog companies—ranging from giant retailers like JCPenney and Spiegel to specialty retailers like Land's End, Sharper Image, and Royal Silk—bombard American households with 13.5 billion catalogs each year.[5]

Subculture

Subculture
A group of people with shared value systems based on common life experiences and situations.

Each culture contains smaller **subcultures**, or groups of people with shared value systems based on common life experiences and situations. Subcultures include nationalities, religions, racial groups, and geographic regions. Many subcultures make up important market segments, and marketers often design products and marketing programs tailored to their needs. Here are examples of three such important subculture groups.[6]

HISPANIC CONSUMERS. The U.S. Hispanic market—Americans of Cuban, Mexican, Central American, South American, and Puerto Rican descent—consists of 25.5 million consumers who buy more than $206 billion of goods and services each year. Expected to number almost 40 million by the year 2010, Hispanics are easy to reach through the growing selection of Spanish-language broadcast and print media that cater to them. Hispanics have long been a target for marketers of food, beverages, and household care products. But as the segment's buying power increases, Hispanics are now emerging as an attractive market for pricier products such as computers, financial services, photography equipment, large appliances, life insurance, and automobiles. Hispanic consumers tend to buy more branded, higher-quality products—generics don't sell well to Hispanics. Perhaps more important, Hispanics are very brand loyal, and they favor companies who show special interest in them. Because of the segment's strong brand loyalty, companies that get the first foothold have an important head start in this fast-growing market. Targeting Hispanics may also provide an additional benefit. With the

McDonald's targets important subcultures, such as blacks and mature consumers.

passage of the North American Free Trade Agreement (NAFTA)—which reduces trade barriers between the United States, Mexico, and Canada—U.S. and Mexican companies are seeking new opportunities to market "pan-American" brands. Companies on both sides of the border see the U.S. Hispanic population as a bridge for spanning U.S. and Latin American markets.

BLACK CONSUMERS. If the U.S. population of 31 million black Americans, with a total purchasing power of $218 billion annually, were a separate nation, their buying power would rank twelfth in the free world. The black population in the United States is growing in affluence and sophistication. Blacks spend relatively more than whites on clothing, personal care, home furnishings, and fragrances; and relatively less on food, transportation, and recreation. Although more price conscious, blacks are also strongly motivated by quality and selection. They place more importance than other groups on brand names, are more brand loyal, do less "shopping around," and shop more at neighborhood stores. In recent years, many large companies—Sears, McDonald's, Procter & Gamble, Coca-Cola—have stepped up their efforts to tap this lucrative market. They employ black-owned advertising agencies and place ads in black consumer magazines. Some companies develop special products, packaging, and appeals for the black consumer market. During the past few years, JCPenney has revamped about 170 stores to target African-Americans, changing its merchandise and store layout, and using black models in its ads.

MATURE CONSUMERS. As the U.S. population ages, "mature" consumers—those 65 and older—are becoming a very attractive market. Now 32 million strong, the seniors market will grow to over 40 million consumers by the year 2000. Seniors are better off financially, spending about $200 billion each year, and they average twice the disposable income of consumers in the under-35 group. Too often stereo-typed as feeble-minded geezers glued to their rocking chairs, seniors have long been the target of the makers of laxatives, tonics, and denture products. But many marketers know that most seniors are not sick, feeble, deaf, or confused. Most are healthy and active, and they have many of the same needs and wants as younger consumers. Because seniors have more time and money, they are an ideal market for exotic travel, restaurants, high-tech home entertainment products, leisure goods and services, designer furniture and fashions, financial services, and life- and health-care services. Their desire to look as young as they feel makes seniors good candidates for specially designed cosmetics and personal care products, health foods, home physical fitness products, and other items that combat aging. As the seniors segment grows in size and buying power, and as the stereotypes of seniors as doddering, creaky, impoverished shut-ins fade, more and more marketers are developing special strategies for this important market. For example, Sears' 40,000-member "Mature Club" offers older consumers 25 percent discounts on everything from eyeglasses to lawnmowers. Southwestern Bell publishes the "Silver Pages," crammed full of ads offering discounts and coupons to 20 million seniors in 90 markets. To appeal more to mature consumers, McDonald's employs older folks as hosts and hostesses in its restaurants and casts them in its ads. And GrandTravel of Chevy Chase, Maryland, sponsors barge trips through Holland, safaris to Kenya, and other exotic vacations for grandparents and their grandchildren.

Jennifer Flores's buying behavior will be influenced by her subculture identification. These factors will affect her food preferences, clothing choices, recreation activities, and career goals. Subcultures attach different meanings to picture taking, and this could affect both Jennifer's interest in cameras and the brand she buys.

Social Class

Social classes
Relatively permanent and ordered divisions in a society whose members share similar values, interests, and behaviors.

Almost every society has some form of social class structure. **Social classes** are society's relatively permanent and ordered divisions whose members share similar values, interests, and behaviors. Social scientists have identified the seven American social classes (see Table 5-1).

Social class is not determined by a single factor, such as income, but is measured as a combination of occupation, income, education, wealth, and other variables. In some social systems, members of different classes are reared for certain roles and cannot change their social positions. In the United States, however, the lines between social classes are not fixed and rigid; people can move to a higher social class or drop into a lower one. Marketers are interested in social class because people within a given social class tend to exhibit similar buying behavior.

Social classes show distinct product and brand preferences in areas such as clothing, home furnishings, leisure activity, and automobiles. Jennifer Flores's social class may affect her camera decision. If she comes from a higher social class background, her family probably owned an expensive camera and she may have dabbled in photography.

SOCIAL FACTORS

A consumer's behavior also is influenced by social factors, such as the consumer's *small groups, family,* and *social roles and status.*

Group
Two or more people who interact to accomplish individual or mutual goals.

Groups

A person's behavior is influenced by many small **groups**. Groups that have a direct influence and to which a person belongs are called *membership groups*. Some are

TABLE 5-1 *Characteristics of Seven Major American Social Classes*

UPPER UPPERS (LESS THAN 1 PERCENT)

Upper uppers are the social elite who live on inherited wealth and have well-known family backgrounds. They give large sums to charity, run debutante balls, own more than one home, and send their children to the finest schools. They are a market for jewelry, antiques, homes, and vacations. They often buy and dress conservatively rather than showing off their wealth. While small in number, upper uppers serve as a reference group for others.

LOWER UPPERS (ABOUT 2 PERCENT)

Lower uppers have earned high income or wealth through exceptional ability in the professions or business. They usually begin in the middle class. They tend to be active in social and civic affairs and buy for themselves and their children the symbols of status, such as expensive homes, schools, swimming pools, and automobiles. They include the new rich who consume conspicuously to impress those below them. They want to be accepted in the upper-upper stratum, a status more likely to be achieved by their children than by themselves.

UPPER MIDDLES (12 PERCENT)

Upper middles possess neither family status nor unusual wealth. They are primarily concerned with "career." They have attained positions as professionals, independent businesspersons, and corporate managers. They believe in education and want their children to develop professional or administrative skills. They are joiners and highly civic-minded. They are the quality market for good homes, clothes, furniture, and appliances.

MIDDLE CLASS (32 PERCENT)

The middle class is made up of average-pay white- and blue-collar workers who live on "the better side of town" and try to "do the proper things." To keep up with the trends, they often buy products that are popular. Most are concerned with fashion, seeking the better brand names. Better living means owning a nice home in a nice neighborhood with good schools. They believe in spending more money on worthwhile experiences for their children and aiming them toward a college education.

WORKING CLASS (38 PERCENT)

The working class consists of those who lead a "working class lifestyle," whatever their income, school background, or job. They depend heavily on relatives for economic and emotional support, for advice on purchases, and for assistance in times of trouble. The working class maintains sharper sex role divisions and stereotyping.

UPPER LOWERS (9 PERCENT)

Upper lowers are working (are not on welfare), although their living standard is just above poverty. They perform unskilled work for very poor pay although they strive toward a higher class. Often, upper lowers lack education. Although they fall near the poverty line financially, they manage to "present a picture of self-discipline" and "maintain some effort at cleanliness."

LOWER LOWERS (7 PERCENT)

Lower lowers are on welfare, visibly poverty stricken, and usually out of work or have "the dirtiest jobs." Often they are not interested in finding a job and are permanently dependent on public aid or charity for income. Their homes, clothes, and possessions are "dirty," "raggedy," and "broken-down."

Source: See Richard P. Coleman, "The Continuing Significance of Social Class to Marketing," *Journal of Consumer Research,* December 1983, pp. 265–280, © Journal of Consumer Research, Inc., 1983.

primary groups with whom there is regular but informal interaction—such as family, friends, neighbors, and co-workers. Some are *secondary groups,* which are more formal and have less regular interaction. These include organizations like religious groups, professional associations, and trade unions.

Reference groups serve as direct (face-to-face) or indirect points of comparison or reference in forming a person's attitudes or behavior. People often are influenced by reference groups to which they do not belong. For example, an *aspirational group* is one to which the individual wishes to belong, as when a teenage basketball player hopes to play someday for the Chicago Bulls. He identifies with this group, although there is no face-to-face contact between him and the team. Marketers try to identify the reference groups of their target markets. Reference groups expose a person to new behaviors and lifestyles, influence the person's attitudes and self-concept, and create pressures to conform that may affect the person's product and brand choices.

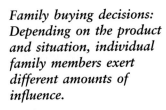

Opinion leaders
People within a reference group who, because of special skills, knowledge, personality, or other characteristics, exert influence on others.

Manufacturers of products and brands subject to strong group influence must figure out how to reach the opinion leaders in the relevant reference groups. **Opinion leaders** are people within a reference group who, because of special skills, knowledge, personality, or other characteristics, exert influence on others. Opinion leaders are found at all levels of society, and one person may be an opinion leader in certain product areas and an opinion follower in others. Marketers try to identify opinion leaders for their products and direct marketing efforts toward them. Chrysler used opinion leaders to launch its LH-series cars—the Concorde, Dodge Intrepid, and Eagle Vision. It lent cars on weekends to 6,000 community and business leaders in 25 cities. In surveys, 98 percent of the test-drivers said that they would recommend the models to friends. And it appears that they did— Chrysler sold out production the first year.[7]

The importance of group influence varies across products and brands. It tends to be strongest when the product is visible to others whom the buyer respects. Purchases of products that are bought and used privately are not much affected by group influences because neither the product nor the brand will be noticed by others. If Jennifer Flores buys a camera, both the product and the brand will be visible to others she respects, and her decision to buy the camera and her brand choice may be influenced strongly by some of her groups, such as friends who belong to a photography club.

Family

Family members can strongly influence buyer behavior. The family is the most important consumer buying organization in society, and it has been researched extensively. Marketers are interested in the roles and influence of the husband, wife, and children on the purchase of different products and services.

Family buying decisions: Depending on the product and situation, individual family members exert different amounts of influence.

Husband-wife involvement varies widely by product category and by stage in the buying process. Buying roles change with evolving consumer lifestyles. In the United States, the wife traditionally has been the main purchasing agent for the family, especially in the areas of food, household products, and clothing. But with 70 percent of women holding jobs outside the home and the willingness of husbands to do more of the family's purchasing, all this is changing. For example, women now buy about 45 percent of all cars and men account for about 40 percent of food-shopping dollars.[8] Such roles vary widely in different countries and social classes. As always, marketers must research specific patterns in their target markets.

In the case of expensive products and services, husbands and wives more often make joint decisions. Jennifer Flores's husband may play an *influencer role* in her camera-buying decision. He may have an opinion about her buying a camera and about the kind of camera to buy. At the same time, she will be the primary decider, purchaser, and user.[9]

Roles and Status

A person belongs to many groups—family, clubs, organizations. The person's position in each group can be defined in terms of both role and status. With her parents, Jennifer Flores plays the role of daughter; in her family, she plays the role of wife; in her company, she plays the role of brand manager. A *role* consists of the activities people are expected to perform according to the persons around them. Each of Jennifer's roles will influence some of her buying behavior.

Each role carries a *status* reflecting the general esteem given to it by society. People often choose products that show their status in society. For example, the role of brand manager has more status in our society than the role of daughter. As a brand manager, Jennifer will buy the kind of clothing that reflects her role and status.

PERSONAL FACTORS

A buyer's decisions also are influenced by personal characteristics such as the buyer's *age and life-cycle stage, occupation, economic situation, lifestyle,* and *personality and self-concept.*

Age and Life-Cycle Stage

People change the goods and services they buy over their lifetimes. Tastes in food, clothes, furniture, and recreation are often age related. Buying is also shaped by the stage of the *family life cycle*—the stages through which families might pass as they mature over time. Table 5-2 lists the stages of the family life cycle. Marketers often define their target markets in terms of life-cycle stage and develop appropriate products and marketing plans for each stage. Traditional family life-cycle stages include young singles and married couples with children. Today, however, marketers are increasingly catering to a growing number of alternative, nontraditional stages such as unmarried couples, couples marrying later in life, childless couples, single parents, extended parents (those with young adult children returning home), and others.

TABLE 5-2   *Family Life-Cycle Stages*

YOUNG	MIDDLE-AGED	OLDER
Single	Single	Older married
Married without children	Married without children	Older unmarried
Married with children	Married with children	
Divorced with children	Married without dependent children	
	Divorced without children	
	Divorced with children	
	Divorced without dependent children	

Sources: Adapted from Patrick E. Murphy and William A. Staples, "A Modernized Family Life Cycle," *Journal of Consumer Research,* June 1979, p. 16; © Journal of Consumer Research, Inc., 1979. Also see Leon G. Schiffman and Leslie Lazar Kanuk, *Consumer Behavior* (Englewood Cliffs, NJ: Prentice Hall, 1994), pp. 361–370.

Occupation

A person's occupation affects the goods and services bought. Blue-collar workers tend to buy more work clothes, whereas white-collar workers buy more suits and ties. Marketers try to identify the occupational groups that have an above-average interest in their products and services. A company can even specialize in making products needed by a given occupational group. Thus, computer software companies will design different products for brand managers, accountants, engineers, lawyers, and doctors.

Economic Situation

A person's economic situation will affect product choice. Jennifer Flores can consider buying an expensive Nikon if she has enough spendable income, savings, or borrowing power. Marketers of income-sensitive goods watch trends in personal income, savings, and interest rates. If economic indicators point to a recession, marketers can take steps to redesign, reposition, and reprice their products closely.

Lifestyle

Lifestyle
A person's pattern of living as expressed in his or her activities, interests, and opinions.

Psychographics
The technique of measuring lifestyles and developing lifestyle classifications; it involves measuring the major AIO dimensions (activities, interests, opinions).

People coming from the same subculture, social class, and occupation may have quite different lifestyles. **Lifestyle** is a person's pattern of living as expressed in his or her **psychographics**. It involves measuring consumers' major *AIO dimensions*—*activities* (work, hobbies, shopping, sports, social events), *interests* (food, fashion, family, recreation), and *opinions* (about themselves, social issues, business, products). Lifestyle captures something more than the person's social class or personality; it profiles a person's whole pattern of acting and interacting in the world.

Several research firms have developed lifestyle classifications. The most widely used is the SRI *Values and Lifestyles (VALS)* typology. VALS2 classifies people according to how they spend their time and money. It divides consumers into eight groups based on two major dimensions: self-orientation and resources (see Figure 5-3). *Self-orientation* groups include *principle-oriented* consumers who buy based upon their views of the world; *status-oriented* buyers who base their pur-

FIGURE 5-3 *VALS2 Lifestyle Classifications*

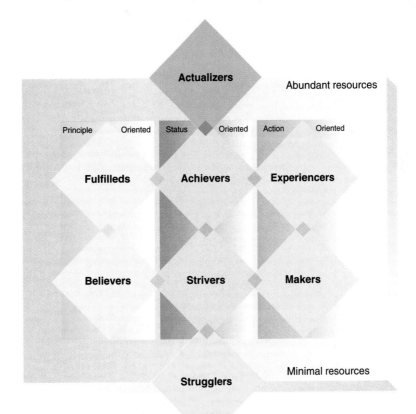

Source: Reprinted with permission of SRI International, Menlo Park, CA. VALS2 is a registered trademark of SRI International.

Lifestyles: Lee Relaxed Riders fit the lifestyle of the modern woman on the go. "Nobody fits your body . . . or the way you live . . . better than Lee."

Dig in the garden. Wash the car. Go to a movie.
Walk the dog. Burp the kid.

Lee Relaxed Rider® jeans are designed to fit the natural curves of a woman's body. But most importantly, they're designed to fit the natural curves of a woman's life. Dress them up. Or dress them down. When you're ready to go. Or when it's time to relax. Nobody fits your body...or the way you live...better than Lee.

R E L A X E D · R I D E R S

Lee

The brand that fits.

chases on the actions and opinions of others; and *action-oriented* buyers who are driven by their desire for activity, variety, and risk taking. Consumers within each orientation are further classified into those with *abundant resources* and those with *minimal resources.* Consumers with either very high or very low levels of resources are classified without regard to their self-orientations (actualizers, strugglers). The eight VALS2 groups are:[10]

◆ *Actualizers*—People with the highest incomes and so many resources that they can indulge in any or all self-orientations. Image is important to them, not for status, but as an extension of their taste, independence, and character. They have wide-ranging interests, are open to change, and tend to buy "the finer things in life."

◆ *Fulfilleds*—Mature, responsible, well-educated professionals. Their leisure activities center on their homes, but they are well-informed and open to new ideas. They have high incomes, but are practical, value-oriented consumers.

◆ *Believers*—Conservative, predictable consumers with more modest incomes who favor American products and established brands. Their lives are centered on family, church, community, and nation.

◆ *Achievers*—Successful, work-oriented, politically conservative people who get their satisfaction from their jobs and families. They respect authority and the status quo, and favor established products and services that show off their success.

◆ *Strivers*—People with values similar to those of achievers, but fewer economic, social, and psychological resources. Style is extremely important to them as they strive to emulate consumers in other, more resourceful groups.

◆ *Experiencers*—Avid consumers who spend heavily on clothes, fast food, music, and other youthful favorites. The youngest of all groups, they have a lot of energy, which they pour into physical exercise and social activities. They especially like new things.

◆ *Makers*—People who like to affect their environment in practical ways. They value self-sufficiency and focus on the familiar—family, work, and physical recreation. As consumers, they are unimpressed by material possessions other than those with a practical purpose.

◆ *Strugglers*—People with the lowest incomes and too few resources to be included in any consumer orientation. With their limited means, they tend to be brand-loyal consumers.

Iron City beer, a well-known brand in Pittsburgh, used VALS2 to update its image and improve sales. Iron City was losing sales—its aging core users were drinking less beer, and younger men weren't buying the brand. According to VALS research, experiencers drink the most beer, followed by strivers. To assess Iron City's image problems, the company interviewed men in these categories. It gave the men stacks of pictures of different kinds of people and asked them to identify first Iron City brand users and then people most like themselves. The men pictured Iron City drinkers as blue-collar steelworkers stopping off at the local bar. However, they saw themselves as more modern, hard working, and fun loving. They strongly rejected the outmoded, heavy-industry image of Pittsburgh. Based on this research, Iron City created ads linking its beer to the new self-image of target consumers. The ads mingled images of the old Pittsburgh with those of the new, dynamic city and scenes of young experiencers and strivers having fun and working hard. Within just one month of the start of the campaign, Iron City sales shot up by 26 percent.[11]

These lifestyle classifications are by no means universal—they can vary significantly from country to country. For example, McCann-Erickson London found the following British lifestyles: Avant Guardians (interested in change); Pontificators (traditionalists, very British); Chameleons (follow the crowd); and Sleepwalkers (contented underachievers). Backer Spielvogel Bates Worldwide found five global lifestyles that they believe span country borders and cultural systems: strivers (young, active people seeking instant gratification); achievers (more successful, affluent people who value status and quality); the pressured (people bogged down by life's daily problems); adapters (older consumers who live comfortably and are content with their lives); and traditionals (people who represent the old values and culture, who resist change, and who are loyal to tried and true products).[12]

When used carefully, the lifestyle concept can help the marketer understand changing consumer values and how they affect buying behavior. Jennifer Flores, for example, can choose to live the role of a capable homemaker, a career woman, or a free spirit—or all three. She plays several roles, and the way she blends them expresses her lifestyle. If she becomes a professional photographer, this would change her lifestyle, in turn changing what and how she buys.

Personality and Self-Concept

Personality
A person's distinguishing psychological characteristics that lead to relatively consistent and lasting responses to his or her own environment.

Each person's distinct personality influences his or her buying behavior. **Personality** refers to the unique psychological characteristics that lead to relatively consistent and lasting responses to one's own environment. Personality is usually described in terms of traits such as self-confidence, dominance, sociability, autonomy, defensiveness, adaptability, and aggressiveness. Personality can be useful in analyzing consumer behavior for certain product or brand choices. For example, coffee makers have discovered that heavy coffee drinkers tend to be high on sociability. Thus, Maxwell House ads show people relaxing and socializing over a cup of steaming coffee.

Many marketers use a concept related to personality—a person's *self-concept* (also called *self-image*). The basic self-concept premise is that people's possessions contribute to and reflect their identities; that is, "we are what we have." Thus, in order to understand consumer behavior, the marketer must first understand the relationship between consumer self-concept and possessions. For example, the founder and chief executive of Barnes & Noble, the nation's number-one bookseller, notes that people buy books to support their self-images:

> People have the mistaken notion that the thing you do with books is read them. Wrong.... People buy books for what the purchase says about them—their taste, their cultivation, their trendiness. Their aim ... is to connect themselves, or those to whom they give the books as gifts, with all the other refined owners of Edgar Allen Poe collections or sensitive owners of Virginia Woolf collections. ... [The result is that] you can sell books as consumer products, with seductive displays, flashy posters, an emphasis on the glamour of the book, and the fashionableness of the bestseller and the trendy author.[13]

Jennifer Flores may see herself as outgoing, creative, and active. Therefore, she will favor a camera that projects the same qualities. If the Nikon is promoted as a camera for outgoing, creative, and active people, then its brand image will match her self-image.

PSYCHOLOGICAL FACTORS

A person's buying choices are further influenced by four major psychological factors: *motivation, perception, learning,* and *beliefs and attitudes.*

Motivation

We know that Jennifer Flores became interested in buying a camera. Why? What is she *really* seeking? What *needs* is she trying to satisfy?

A person has many needs at any given time. Some are *biological,* arising from states of tension such as hunger, thirst, or discomfort. Others are *psychological,* arising from the need for recognition, esteem, or belonging. Most of these needs will not be strong enough to motivate the person to act at a given point in time. A need becomes a *motive* when it is aroused to a sufficient level of intensity. A **motive** (or *drive*) is a need that is sufficiently pressing to direct the person to seek satisfaction. Psychologists have developed theories of human motivation. Two of the most popular—the theories of Sigmund Freud and Abraham Maslow—have quite different meanings for consumer analysis and marketing.

Motive (drive)
A need that is sufficiently pressing to direct the person to seek satisfaction of the need.

FREUD'S THEORY OF MOTIVATION.   Freud assumes that people are largely unconscious about the real psychological forces shaping their behavior. He sees the person as growing up and repressing many urges. These urges are never eliminated or under perfect control; they emerge in dreams, in slips of the tongue, in neurotic and obsessive behavior, or ultimately in psychoses.

Thus, Freud suggests that a person does not fully understand his or her motivation. If Jennifer Flores wants to purchase an expensive camera, she may describe her motive as wanting a hobby or career. At a deeper level, she may be purchasing the camera to impress others with her creative talent. At a still deeper level, she may be buying the camera to feel young and independent again.

Motivation researchers collect in-depth information from small samples of consumers to uncover the deeper motives for their product choices. They use nondirective depth interviews and various "projective techniques" to throw the ego off guard—techniques such as word association, sentence completion, picture interpretation, and role playing. Motivation researchers have reached some interesting and sometimes odd conclusions about what may be in the buyer's mind regarding certain purchases. For example, one classic study concluded that consumers resist prunes because they are wrinkled looking and remind people of sickness and old age. Despite its sometimes unusual conclusions, motivation research remains a useful tool for marketers seeking a deeper understanding of consumer behavior (see Marketing Highlight 5-1).[14]

"TOUCHY-FEELY" RESEARCH INTO CONSUMER MOTIVATIONS

The term *motivation research* refers to qualitative research designed to probe consumers' hidden, subconscious motivations. Because consumers often don't know or can't describe just why they act as they do, motivation researchers use a variety of nondirective and projective techniques to uncover underlying emotions and attitudes toward brands and buying situations. The techniques range from sentence completion, word association, and inkblot or cartoon interpretation tests, to having consumers describe typical brand users or form daydreams and fantasies about brands or buying situations. Some of these techniques verge on the bizarre. One writer offers the following tongue-in-cheek summary of a motivation research session:

Good morning, ladies and gentlemen. We've called you here today for a little consumer research. Now, lie down on the couch, toss your inhibitions out the window, and let's try a little free association. First, think about brands as if they were your *friends*. Imagine you could talk to your TV dinner. What would he say? And what would you say to him? . . . Now, think of your shampoo as an animal. Go on, don't be shy. Would it be a panda or a lion? A snake or a wooly worm? For our final exercise, let's all sit up and pull out our magic markers. Draw a picture of a typical cake-mix user. Would she wear an apron or a negligee? A business suit or a can-can dress?

Such projective techniques seem pretty goofy. But more and more, marketers are turning to these touchy-feely approaches to probe consumer psyches and develop better marketing strategies.

Many advertising agencies employ teams of psychologists, anthropologists, and other social scientists to carry out motivation research. One agency routinely conducts one-on-one, therapy-like interviews to delve into the inner workings of consumers. Another agency asks consumers to describe their favorite brands as animals or cars (say, Cadillacs versus Chevrolets) in order to assess the prestige associated with

various brands. Still another agency has consumers draw figures of typical brand users:

In one instance, the agency asked 50 interviewees to sketch likely buyers of two different brands of cake mixes. Consistently, the group portrayed Pillsbury customers as apron-clad, grandmotherly types, while they pictured Duncan Hines purchasers as svelte, contemporary women.

In a similar study, American Express had people sketch likely users of its gold card versus its green card. Respondents depicted gold card holders as active, broad-shouldered men;

Motivation research: When asked to sketch figures of typical cake-mix users, subjects portrayed Pillsbury customers as grandmotherly types and Duncan Hines buyers as svelte and contemporary.

green card holders were perceived as "couch potatoes" lounging in front of television sets. Based on these results, the company positioned its gold card as a symbol of responsibility for people capable of controlling their lives and finances.

Some motivation research studies employ more basic techniques, such as simply mingling with or watching consumers to find out what makes them tick. Saatchi & Saatchi (an advertising agency) hired an anthropologist to spend time in Texas sidling up to Wrangler blue jeans wearers at rodeos and barbecues. His findings showed what the jeans company suspected: Wrangler buyers identify with cowboys. The company responded by running ads with plenty of Western touches.

In an effort to understanding the teenage consumer market better, BSB Worldwide (another ad agency) videotaped teenagers' rooms in 25 countries. It found surprising similarities across countries and cultures:

From the steamy playgrounds of Los Angeles to the stately boulevards of Singapore, kids show amazing similarities in taste, language, and attitude. . . . From the gear and posters on display, it's hard to tell whether the rooms are in Los Angeles, Mexico City, or Tokyo. Basketballs sit alongside soccer balls. Closets overflow with staples from an international, unisex uniform: baggy Levi's or Diesel jeans, NBA jackets, and rugged shoes from Timberland or Doc Martens.

Similarly, researchers at Sega of America's ad agency have learned a lot about videogame buying behavior by hanging around with 150 kids in their bedrooms and by shopping with them in malls. Above all else, they learned, do everything fast. As a result, in Sega's most recent 15-second commercials, some images fly by so quickly that adults cannot recall seeing them, even after repeated showings. The kids, weaned on MTV, recollect them keenly.

Some marketers dismiss such motivation research as mumbo-jumbo. And these approaches do present some problems: The samples are small, and researcher interpretations of results are often highly subjective, sometimes leading to rather exotic explanations of otherwise ordinary buying behavior. However, others believe strongly that these approaches can provide interesting nuggets of insight into the relationships between consumers and the brands they buy. To marketers who use them, motivation research techniques provide a flexible and varied means of gaining insights into deeply held and often mysterious motivations behind consumer buying behavior.

Sources: Excerpts from Annetta Miller and Dody Tsiantar, "Psyching Out Consumers," *Newsweek,* February 27, 1989, pp. 46–47; and Shawn Tully, "Teens: The Most Global Market of All," *Fortune,* May 6, 1994, pp. 90–97. Also see Rebecca Piirto, "Words that Sell," *American Demographics,* January 1992, p. 6; and "They Understand Your Kids," *Fortune,* Special Issue, Autumn/Winter 1993, pp. 29–30.

FIGURE 5-4 *Maslow's hierarchy of needs*
Source: Adapted from Motivation and Personality, 2nd ed., by Abraham H. Maslow. Copyright © 1970 by Abraham H. Maslow. Reprinted by permission of Harper & Row, Publishers, Inc.

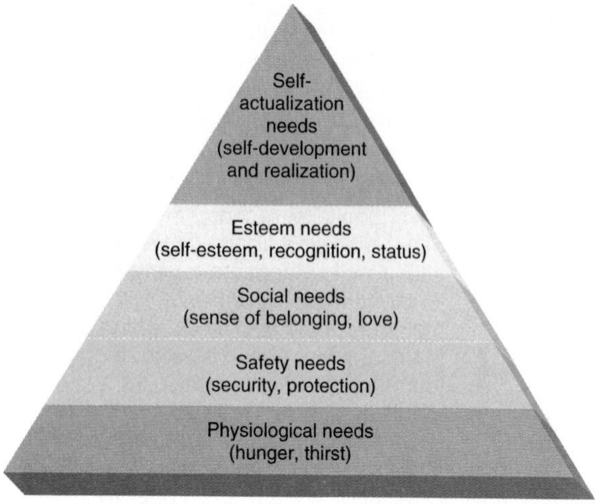

MASLOW'S THEORY OF MOTIVATION. Abraham Maslow sought to explain why people are driven by particular needs at particular times.[15] Why does one person spend much time and energy on personal safety and another on gaining the esteem of others? Maslow's answer is that human needs are arranged in a hierarchy, from the most pressing to the least pressing. Maslow's hierarchy of needs is shown in Figure 5-4. In order of importance, they are *physiological* needs, *safety* needs, *social* needs, *esteem* needs, and *self-actualization* needs. A person tries to satisfy the most important need first. When that need is satisfied, it will stop being a motivator and the person will then try to satisfy the next most important need. For example, starving people (physiological needs) will not take an interest in the latest happenings in the art world (self-actualization needs), nor in how they are seen or esteemed by others (social or esteem needs), nor even in whether they are breathing clean air (safety needs). But as each important need is satisfied, the next most important need will come into play.

What light does Maslow's theory throw on Jennifer Flores's interest in buying a camera? We can guess that Jennifer has satisfied her physiological, safety, and social needs; they do not motivate her interest in cameras. Her camera interest might come from a strong need for more esteem from others. Or it might come from a need for self-actualization—she might want to be a creative person and express herself through photography.

Perception

A motivated person is ready to act. How the person acts is influenced by his or her perception of the situation. Two people with the same motivation and in the same situation may act quite differently because they perceive the situation differently. Jennifer Flores might consider a fast-talking camera salesperson loud and phony. Another camera buyer might consider the same salesperson intelligent and helpful.

Perception
The process by which people select, organize, and interpret information to form a meaningful picture of the world.

Why do people perceive the same situation differently? All of us learn by the flow of information through our five senses: sight, hearing, smell, touch, and taste. However, each of us receives, organizes, and interprets this sensory information in an individual way. **Perception** is the process by which people select, organize, and interpret information to form a meaningful picture of the world.

People can form different perceptions of the same stimulus because of three perceptual processes: selective attention, selective distortion, and selective retention. People are exposed to a great amount of stimuli every day. For example, the average person may be exposed to more than 1,500 ads in a single day. It is impossible for a person to pay attention to all these stimuli. *Selective attention*—the tendency for people to screen out most of the information to which they are exposed—means that marketers have to work especially hard to attract the consumer's attention. Their message will be lost on most people who are not in the market for the product. Moreover, even people who are in the market may not notice the message unless it stands out from the surrounding sea of other ads.

Even noted stimuli do not always come across in the intended way. Each person fits incoming information into an existing mind-set. *Selective distortion* describes the tendency of people to interpret information in a way that will support what they already believe. Jennifer Flores may hear the salesperson mention some good and bad points about a competing camera brand. Because she already has a strong leaning toward Nikon, she is likely to distort those points in order to conclude that Nikon is the better camera. Selective distortion means that marketers must try to understand the mind-sets of consumers and how these will affect interpretations of advertising and sales information.

People also will forget much that they learn. They tend to retain information that supports their attitudes and beliefs. Because of *selective retention*, Jennifer is likely to remember good points made about the Nikon and to forget good points made about competing cameras.

Because of selective exposure, distortion, and retention, marketers have to work hard to get their messages through. This fact explains why marketers use so much drama and repetition in sending messages to their market. Interestingly, although most marketers worry about whether their offers will be perceived at all, some consumers are worried that they will be affected by marketing messages without even knowing it (see Marketing Highlight 5-2).

Learning

Learning
Changes in an individual's behavior arising from experience.

When people act, they learn. **Learning** describes changes in an individual's behavior arising from experience. Learning theorists say that most human behavior is learned. Learning occurs through the interplay of *drives, stimuli, cues, responses,* and *reinforcement.*

We saw that Jennifer Flores has a drive for self-actualization. A *drive* is a strong internal stimulus that calls for action. Her drive becomes a motive when it is directed toward a particular *stimulus object,* in this case a camera. Jennifer's response to the idea of buying a camera is conditioned by the surrounding cues. *Cues* are minor stimuli that determine when, where, and how the person responds. Seeing cameras in a shop window, hearing of a special sale price, and receiving her husband's support are all cues that can influence Jennifer's *response* to her interest in buying a camera.

Suppose Jennifer buys the Nikon. If the experience is rewarding, she will probably use the camera more and more. Her response to cameras will be *reinforced.* Then the next time she shops for a camera, binoculars, or some similar product, the probability is greater that she will buy a Nikon product.

The practical significance of learning theory for marketers is that they can build up demand for a product by associating it with strong drives, using motivating cues, and providing positive reinforcement.

Beliefs and Attitudes

Belief
A descriptive thought that a person holds about something.

Through doing and learning, people acquire beliefs and attitudes. These, in turn, influence their buying behavior. A **belief** is a descriptive thought that a person has about something. Jennifer Flores may believe that a Nikon camera takes great pictures, stands up well under hard use, and costs $550. These beliefs may be based on real knowledge, opinion, or faith, and may or may not carry an emotional charge. For example, Jennifer Flores's belief that a Nikon camera is heavy may or may not matter to her decision.

Marketers are interested in the beliefs that people formulate about specific products and services, because these beliefs make up product and brand images that affect buying behavior. If some of the beliefs are wrong and prevent purchase, the marketer will want to launch a campaign to correct them.

Attitude
A person's consistently favorable or unfavorable evaluations, feelings, and tendencies toward an object or idea.

People have attitudes regarding religion, politics, clothes, music, food, and almost everything else. An **attitude** describes a person's relatively consistent evaluations, feelings, and tendencies toward an object or idea. Attitudes put people into a frame of mind of liking or disliking things, of moving toward or away from them. Thus, Jennifer Flores may hold such attitudes as "Buy the best," "The Japanese make the best products in the world," and "Creativity and self-expression are among the most important things in life." If so, the Nikon camera would fit well into Jennifer's existing attitudes.

SUBLIMINAL PERCEPTION—CAN CONSUMERS BE AFFECTED WITHOUT KNOWING IT?

In 1957, a researcher announced that he had flashed the phrases "Eat popcorn" and "Drink Coca-Cola" on a screen in a New Jersey movie theater every five seconds for 1/300th of a second. He reported that although the audience did not consciously recognize these messages, viewers absorbed them subconsciously and bought 58 percent more popcorn and 18 percent more Coke. Suddenly advertising agencies and consumer-protection groups became intensely interested in *subliminal perception.* People voiced fears of being brainwashed, and California and Canada declared the practice illegal. Although the researcher later

Q. CAN YOU FIND THE HIDDEN PLEASURE IN REFRESHING SEAGRAM'S GIN?

A. If you think this is just a bubble, look again.

Seagram's Extra Dry Gin

Seagram's pokes fun at subliminal advertising.

admitted to making up the data, and scientists failed to replicate the original results in other studies, the issue did not die. In 1974, Wilson Bryan Key claimed in his book *Subliminal Seduction* that consumers were still being manipulated by advertisers in print ads and television commercials.

Subliminal perception has since been studied by many psychologists and consumer researchers. None of these experts have been able to show that subliminal messages have any effect on consumer behavior. It appears that subliminal advertising simply doesn't have the power attributed to it by its critics. Most advertisers scoff at the notion of an industry conspiracy to manipulate consumers through "invisible" messages. As one advertising agency executive put it, "We have enough trouble persuading

consumers using a series of up-front thirty-second ads—how could we do it in 1/300th of a second?"

Although advertisers may avoid outright subliminal advertising, some critics claim that television advertising employs techniques approaching the subliminal. With more and more viewers reaching for their remote controls to avoid ads by switching channels or fast-forwarding through VCR tapes, advertisers are using new tricks to grab viewer attention and to affect consumers in ways they may not be aware of. Many ad agencies employ psychologists and neurophysiologists to help develop subtle psychological advertising strategies.

For example, some advertisers purposely try to confuse viewers, throw them off balance, or even make them uncomfortable:

> [They use] film footage that wouldn't pass muster with a junior-high film club. You have to stare at the screen just to figure out what's going on—and that, of course, is the idea. Take the ads for Wang computers. In these hazy, washed-out spots, people walk partially in and out of the camera frame talking in computer jargon. But the confusion grabs attention. . . . Even people who don't understand a word are riveted to the screen.

Other advertisers use the rapid-fire technique. Images flash by so quickly you can barely register them. Pontiac used such "machine-gun editing" in recent ads—the longest shot flashed

by in one and one-half seconds, the shortest in one-quarter of a second. The ads scored high in viewer recall.

Some advertisers go after our ears as well as our eyes, taking advantage of the powerful effects some sounds have on human brain waves:

> Advertisers are using sounds to take advantage of the automatic systems built into the brain that force you to stop what you're doing and refocus on the screen. . . . You can't ignore these sounds. That's why commercials are starting off with noises ranging from a baby crying (Advil) to a car horn (Hertz) to a factory whistle (Almond Joy). In seeking the right sound . . . advertisers can be downright merciless. . . . Ads for Nuprin pain reliever kick off by assaulting viewers with the whine of a dentist's drill . . . to help the viewer recall the type of pain we've all experienced. Hey, thanks.

A few experts are concerned that new high-tech advertising might even hypnotize consumers, whether knowingly or not. They suggest that several techniques—rapid scene changes, pulsating music and sounds, repetitive phrases, and flashing logos—might actually start to put some viewers under.

Some critics think that such subtle, hard-to-resist psychological techniques are unfair to consumers—that advertisers can use these techniques to bypass consumers' defenses and affect them without their being aware of it. The advertisers who use these techniques, however, view them as innovative, creative approaches to advertising.

Sources: Excerpts from David H. Freedman, "Why You Watch Commercials—Whether You Mean to or Not," *TV Guide,* February 20, 1988, pp. 4–7. Also see Wilson Bryan Key, *The Age of Manipulation: The Con in Confidence, The Sin in Sincere* (New York: Holt, 1989); Timothy E. Moore, "Subliminal Advertising: What You See Is What You Get," *Journal of Marketing,* Spring 1982, pp. 38–47; Michael J. McCarthy, "Mind Probe," *Wall Street Journal,* March 22, 1991, p. B3; and Martha Rogers and Kirk H. Smith, "Public Perceptions of Subliminal Advertising," *Journal of Advertising Research,* March/April 1993, pp. 10–17.

Attitudes are hard to change, but it can be done. Honda's classic "You meet the nicest people on a Honda" campaign changed people's attitudes about who rides motorcycles.

Attitudes are difficult to change. A person's attitudes fit into a pattern, and to change one attitude may require difficult adjustments in many others. Thus, a company should usually try to fit its products into existing attitudes rather than attempt to change attitudes. Of course, there are exceptions in which the great cost of trying to change attitudes may pay off. For example, in the late 1950s, Honda entered the U.S. motorcycle market facing a major decision. It could either sell its motorcycles to the small but already established motorcycle market or try to increase the size of this market by attracting new types of consumers. Increasing the size of the market would be more difficult and expensive because many people had negative attitudes toward motorcycles. They associated motorcycles with black leather jackets, switchblades, and outlaws. Despite these adverse attitudes, Honda took the second course of action. It launched a major campaign to position motorcycles as good clean fun. Its theme "You meet the nicest people on a Honda" worked well, and many people adopted a new attitude toward motorcycles. Going into the 1990s, however, Honda faced a similar problem. With the aging of the baby boomers, the market had once again shifted toward only hard-core motorcycling enthusiasts. So Honda again set out to change consumer attitudes. It unveiled a new "Come Ride With Us" campaign to reestablish the wholesomeness of motorcycling and to position it as fun and exciting for everyone.[16]

We can now appreciate the many forces acting on consumer behavior. The consumer's choice results from the complex interplay of cultural, social, personal, and psychological factors. Although many of these factors cannot be influenced by the marketer, they can be useful in identifying interested buyers and in shaping products and appeals to serve consumer needs better.

Now that we have looked at the influences that affect buyers, we are ready to look at how consumers make buying decisions—at consumer buying roles, types of buying decision behavior, and the buyer decision process.

CONSUMER BUYING ROLES

The marketer needs to know what people are involved in the buying decision and what role each person plays. For many products, it is fairly easy to identify the decision maker. For example, men normally choose their own shaving equipment and women choose their own clothes. However, consider the purchase of a family car. The suggestion to buy a new car might come from the oldest child. A friend might advise the family on what kind of car to buy. The husband might choose the make; the wife might select the style and options. The husband and wife might then make the final decision jointly, and the wife might use the car more than her husband.

People might play any of several roles in a buying decision:

◆ *Initiator:* the person who first suggests or thinks of the idea of buying a particular product or service

◆ *Influencer:* a person whose views or advice influences the buying decision

◆ *Decider:* the person who ultimately makes a buying decision or any part of it—whether to buy, what to buy, how to buy, or where to buy

◆ *Buyer:* the person who makes an actual purchase

◆ *User:* the person who consumes or uses a product or service

Knowing the main buying participants and the roles they play helps the marketer fine-tune the marketing program. If Chevrolet finds that husbands make buying decisions for the family minivan, it will direct most of its advertising for these models toward husbands. But Chevy ads will include wives, children, and others who might initiate or influence the buying decision. In addition, Chevrolet will design its minivans with features that meet the needs of all buying decision participants.

TYPES OF BUYING DECISION BEHAVIOR

Complex buying behavior
Consumer buying behavior in situations characterized by high consumer involvement in a purchase and significant perceived differences among brands.

Buying behavior differs greatly for a tube of toothpaste, a tennis racket, an expensive camera, and a new car. More complex decisions usually involve more buying participants and more buyer deliberation. Figure 5-5 shows types of consumer buying behavior based on the degree of buyer involvement and the degree of differences among brands.[17]

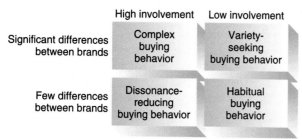

FIGURE 5-5 *Four Types of Buying Behavior*
Source: Adapted from Henry Assael, *Consumer Behavior and Marketing Action* (Boston: Kent Publishing Company, 1987), p. 87. Copyright © 1987 by Wadsworth, Inc. Printed by permission of Kent Publishing Company, a division of Wadsworth, Inc.

COMPLEX BUYING BEHAVIOR

Consumers undertake **complex buying behavior** when they are highly involved in a purchase and perceive significant differences among brands. Consumers may be highly involved when the product is expensive, risky, purchased infrequently, and highly self-expressive. Typically, the consumer has much to learn about the product category. For example, a personal computer buyer may not know what attributes to consider. Many product features carry no real meaning: a "Pentium chip," "super VGA resolution," or "8 megs of RAM."

This buyer will pass through a learning process, first developing beliefs about the product, then attitudes, and then making a thoughtful purchase choice. Marketers of high-involvement products must understand the information-gathering and evaluation behavior of high-involvement consumers. They need to help buyers learn about product-class attributes and their relative importance, and about what the company's brand offers on the important attributes. Marketers need to differentiate their brand's features, perhaps by describing the brand's benefits using print media with long copy. They must motivate store salespeople and the buyer's acquaintances to influence the final brand choice.

Dissonance-reducing buying behavior
Consumer buying behavior in situations characterized by high involvement but few perceived differences among brands.

DISSONANCE-REDUCING BUYING BEHAVIOR

Dissonance-reducing buying behavior occurs when consumers are highly involved with an expensive, infrequent, or risky purchase, but see little difference among brands. For example, consumers buying carpeting may face a high-involvement decision because carpeting is expensive and self-expressive. Yet buyers may consider most carpet brands in a given price range to be the same. In this case, because perceived brand differences are not large, buyers may shop around to learn what is available, but buy relatively quickly. They may respond primarily to a good price or to purchase convenience.

After the purchase, consumers might experience *postpurchase dissonance* (after-sale discomfort) when they notice certain disadvantages of the purchased carpet brand or hear favorable things about brands not purchased. To counter such dissonance, the marketer's after-sale communications should provide evidence and support to help consumers feel good about their brand choices.

Habitual Buying Behavior

Habitual buying behavior
Consumer buying behavior in situations characterized by low consumer involvement and few significant perceived brand differences.

Habitual buying behavior occurs under conditions of low consumer involvement and little significant brand difference. For example, take salt. Consumers have little involvement in this product category—they simply go to the store and reach for a brand. If they keep reaching for the same brand, it is out of habit rather than strong brand loyalty. Consumers appear to have low involvement with most low-cost, frequently purchased products.

In such cases, consumer behavior does not pass through the usual belief-attitude-behavior sequence. Consumers do not search extensively for information about the brands, evaluate brand characteristics, and make weighty decisions about which brands to buy. Instead, they passively receive information as they watch television or read magazines. Ad repetition creates *brand familiarity* rather than *brand conviction*. Consumers do not form strong attitudes toward a brand; they select the brand because it is familiar. Because they are not highly involved with the product, consumers may not evaluate the choice even after purchase. Thus, the buying process involves brand beliefs formed by passive learning, followed by purchase behavior, which may or may not be followed by evaluation.

Marketers can convert low-involvement products into higher-involvement ones by linking them to involving situations. Here Nestlé creates involvement with soap-opera-like ads featuring the romantic relationship between two neighbors, Tony and Sharon.

Because buyers are not highly committed to any brands, marketers of low-involvement products with few brand differences often use price and sales promotions to stimulate product trial. In advertising for a low-involvement product, ad copy should stress only a few key points. Visual symbols and imagery are important because they can be remembered easily and associated with the brand. Ad campaigns should include high repetition of short-duration messages. Television is usually more effective than print media because it is a low-involvement medium suitable for passive learning. Advertising planning should be based on classical conditioning theory, in which buyers learn to identify a certain product by a symbol repeatedly attached to it.

Marketers can try to convert low-involvement products into higher-involvement ones by linking them to some involving issue. Procter & Gamble does this when it links Crest toothpaste to avoiding cavities. Or the product can be linked to some involving personal situation. Nestlé did this in a recent series of ads for Taster's Choice coffee, each consisting of a new soap-opera-like episode featuring the evolving romantic relationship between two neighbors. At best, these strategies can raise consumer involvement from a low to a moderate level. However, they are not likely to propel the consumer into highly involved buying behavior.

VARIETY-SEEKING BUYING BEHAVIOR

Variety-seeking buying behavior
Consumer buying behavior in situations characterized by low consumer involvement but significant perceived brand differences.

Consumers undertake **variety-seeking buying behavior** in situations characterized by low consumer involvement, but significant perceived brand differences. In such cases, consumers often do a lot of brand switching. For example, when buying cookies, a consumer may hold some beliefs, choose a cookie brand without much evaluation, then evaluate that brand during consumption. But the next time, the consumer might pick another brand out of boredom or simply to try something different. Brand switching occurs for the sake of variety rather than because of dissatisfaction.

In such product categories, the marketing strategy may differ for the market leader and minor brands. The market leader will try to encourage habitual buying behavior by dominating shelf space, keeping shelves fully stocked, and running frequent reminder advertising. Challenger firms will encourage variety seeking by offering lower prices, special deals, coupons, free samples, and advertising that presents reasons for trying something new.

THE BUYER DECISION PROCESS

We are now ready to examine the stages buyers pass through to reach a buying decision. Figure 5-6 shows the consumer as passing through five stages: *need recognition, information search, evaluation of alternatives, purchase decision,* and *postpurchase behavior.* Clearly, the buying process starts long before actual purchase and continues long after. Marketers need to focus on the entire buying process rather than on just the purchase decision.

FIGURE 5-6 *Buyer decision process*

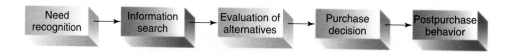

The figure implies that consumers pass through all five stages with every purchase. But in more routine purchases, consumers often skip or reverse some of these stages. A woman buying her regular brand of toothpaste would recognize the need and go right to the purchase decision, skipping information search and evaluation. However, we use the model in Figure 5-6 because it shows all the considerations that arise when a consumer faces a new and complex purchase situation.

To illustrate this model, we will again follow Jennifer Flores and try to understand how she became interested in buying an expensive camera, and the stages she went through to make the final choice.

NEED RECOGNITION

Need recognition
The first stage of the buyer decision process in which the consumer recognizes a problem or need.

The buying process starts with **need recognition**—with the buyer recognizing a problem or need. The buyer senses a difference between his or her *actual* state and some *desired* state. The need can be triggered by *internal stimuli* when one of the person's normal needs—hunger, thirst, sex—rises to a level high enough to become a drive. A need can also be triggered by *external stimuli*. Jennifer Flores

Let's say you have a kid.

Let's say your kid's always getting messages on your answering machine.

Let's say you've got to sit through all his messages to hear your own.

Let's say he's popular.

Let's say he's real popular.

With The Message Center from Pacific Bell, your phone messages are for your ears only. And your kid's messages—thank goodness—are for his ears only.

You see, unlike an answering machine, The Message Center is a service that comes to you through your phone itself. So instead of broadcasting your messages through a speaker, it delivers them quietly and discreetly, just like a regular phone call.

But the privacy of The Message Center doesn't stop there. Your Message Center Mailbox can be unlocked only by the secret password that you've chosen. No one else knows it—not even Pacific Bell—and you can change it as often as you wish.

For the ultimate in privacy, you can add optional Extension Mailboxes for every member of your household. That way, you'll get your messages, they'll get their messages, and no one has to get anyone else's messages.

By the way, you don't have to give up any of The Message Center's security when you're away from home. You can pick up your messages from practically any touchtone phone anywhere in the world with the same level of privacy.

But even if it weren't so private, The Message Center would still be the most sophisticated way to get your messages. It requires no machine, it answers even when you're on another call, it gives the time and date of every message, and it offers timesaving options like Group Messaging.

To find out more, call Pacific Bell at 1-800-273-7000 and ask about The Message Center.

Or, if you're busy, have your kid call.

The Message Center
PACIFIC ✱ BELL.
1-800-273-7000

©1993 Pacific Bell Information Services.
A Pacific Telesis company.

Need recognition can be triggered by advertising. This Pacific Bell ad alerts parents to the need for The Message Service: "Let's say your kid's always getting messages on your answering machine . . . Let's say he's real popular."

passes a bakery and the sight of freshly baked bread stimulates her hunger; she admires a neighbor's new car; or she watches a television commercial for a Caribbean vacation. At this stage, the marketer should research consumers to find out what kinds of needs or problems arise, what brought them about, and how they led the consumer to this particular product.

Jennifer Flores might answer that she felt the need for a new hobby when her busy season at work slowed down, and she thought of cameras after talking to a friend about photography. By gathering such information, the marketer can identify the factors that most often trigger interest in the product and can develop marketing programs that involve these factors.

INFORMATION SEARCH

An aroused consumer may or may not search for more information. If the consumer's drive is strong and a satisfying product is near at hand, the consumer is likely to buy it then. If not, the consumer may store the need in memory or undertake an **information search** related to the need.

At one level, the consumer may simply enter *heightened attention*. Here Jennifer Flores becomes more receptive to information about cameras. She pays attention to camera ads, cameras used by friends, and camera conversations. Or Jennifer may go into *active information search*, in which she looks for reading material, phones friends, and gathers information in other ways. The amount of searching she does will

Information search
The stage of the buyer decision process in which the consumer is aroused to search for more information; the consumer may simply have heightened attention or may go into active information search.

depend on the strength of her drive, the amount of information she starts with, the ease of obtaining more information, the value she places on additional information, and the satisfaction she gets from searching.

The consumer can obtain information from any of several sources. These include:

- *Personal sources:* family, friends, neighbors, acquaintances
- *Commercial sources:* advertising, salespeople, dealers, packaging, displays
- *Public sources:* mass media, consumer-rating organizations
- *Experiential sources:* handling, examining, using the product

The relative influence of these information sources varies with the product and the buyer. Generally, the consumer receives the most information about a product from commercial sources—those controlled by the marketer. The most effective sources, however, tend to be personal. Personal sources appear to be even more important in influencing the purchase of services.[18] Commercial sources normally *inform* the buyer, but personal sources *legitimize* or *evaluate* products for the buyer. For example, doctors normally learn of new drugs from commercial sources, but turn to other doctors for evaluative information.

As more information is obtained, the consumer's awareness and knowledge of the available brands and features increases. In her information search, Jennifer Flores learned about the many camera brands available. The information also helped her drop certain brands from consideration. A company must design its marketing mix to make prospects aware of and knowledgeable about its brand. It should carefully identify consumers' sources of information and the importance of each source. Consumers should be asked how they first heard about the brand, what information they received, and what importance they placed on different information sources.

EVALUATION OF ALTERNATIVES

Alternative evaluation
The stage of the buyer decision process in which the consumer uses information to evaluate alternative brands in the choice set.

We have seen how the consumer uses information to arrive at a set of final brand choices. How does the consumer choose among the alternative brands? The marketer needs to know about **alternative evaluation**—that is, how the consumer processes information to arrive at brand choices. Unfortunately, consumers do not use a simple and single evaluation process in all buying situations. Instead, several evaluation processes are at work.

Certain basic concepts help explain consumer evaluation processes. First, we assume that each consumer sees a product as a bundle of *product attributes*. For cameras, product attributes might include picture quality, ease of use, camera size, price, and other features. Consumers will vary as to which of these attributes they consider relevant, and they will pay the most attention to those attributes connected with their needs.

Second, the consumer will attach different *degrees of importance* to different attributes according to his or her unique needs and wants. Third, the consumer is likely to develop a set of *brand beliefs* about where each brand stands on each attribute. The set of beliefs held about a particular brand is known as the **brand image.** Based on his or her experience and the effects of selective perception, distortion, and retention, the consumer's beliefs may differ from true attributes.

Brand image
The set of beliefs consumers hold about a particular brand.

Fourth, the consumer's expected *total product satisfaction* will vary with levels of different attributes. For example, Jennifer Flores may expect her satisfaction from a camera to increase with better picture quality; to peak with a medium-weight camera as opposed to a very light or very heavy one; and to be higher for a 35-mm camera than for a 110-mm camera. If we combine the attribute levels that give her the highest perceived satisfaction, they make up Jennifer's ideal camera. The camera would also be her preferred camera if it were available and affordable.

Fifth, the consumer arrives at attitudes toward the different brands through some *evaluation procedure*. Consumers have been found to use one or more of several evaluation procedures, depending on the consumer and the buying decision.

We will illustrate these concepts with Jennifer Flores' camera-buying situation. Suppose Jennifer has narrowed her choices to four cameras. And suppose that she is primarily interested in four attributes—picture quality, ease of use, camera size, and price. Jennifer has formed beliefs about how each brand rates on each attribute. The marketer wishes to predict which camera Jennifer will buy.

Clearly, if one camera rated best on all the attributes, we could predict that Jennifer would choose it. But the brands vary in appeal. Some buyers will base their buying decision on only one attribute, and their choices are easy to predict. If Jennifer wants picture quality above everything, she will buy the camera that she thinks has the best picture quality. But most buyers consider several attributes, each with different importance. If we knew the importance weights that Jennifer assigns to each of the four attributes, we could predict her camera choice more reliably.

How consumers go about evaluating purchase alternatives depends on the individual consumer and the specific buying situation. In some cases, consumers use careful calculations and logical thinking. At other times, the same consumers do little or no evaluating; instead they buy on impulse and rely on intuition. Sometimes consumers make buying decisions on their own; sometimes they turn to friends, consumer guides, or salespeople for buying advice.

Marketers should study buyers to find out how they actually evaluate brand alternatives. If they know what evaluative processes go on, marketers can take steps to influence the buyer's decision. Suppose Jennifer is inclined to buy a Nikon camera because she rates it high on picture quality and ease of use. What strategies might another camera maker, say Minolta, use to influence people like Jennifer? There are several. Minolta could modify its camera so that it delivers better pictures or other features that consumers like Jennifer want. It could try to change buyers' beliefs about how its camera rates on key attributes, especially if consumers currently underestimate the camera's qualities. It could try to change buyers' beliefs about Nikon and other competitors. Finally, it could try to change the list of attributes that buyers consider, or the importance attached to these attributes. For example, it might advertise that all good cameras have about equal picture quality, and that its lighter-weight, lower-priced camera is a better buy for people like Jennifer.

PURCHASE DECISION

Purchase decision
The stage of the buyer decision process in which the consumer actually buys the product.

In the evaluation stage, the consumer ranks brands and forms purchase intentions. Generally, the consumer's **purchase decision** will be to buy the most preferred brand, but two factors can come between the purchase *intention* and the purchase *decision*. The first factor is the *attitudes of others*. If Jennifer Flores's husband feels strongly that Jennifer should buy the lowest-priced camera, then the chances of Jennifer buying a more expensive camera will be reduced.

The second factor is *unexpected situational factors*. The consumer may form a purchase intention based on factors such as expected income, expected price, and expected product benefits. However, unexpected events may change the purchase intention. Jennifer Flores may lose her job, some other purchase may become more urgent, or a friend may report being disappointed in her preferred camera. Or a close competitor may drop its price. Thus, preferences and even purchase intentions do not always result in actual purchase choice.

POSTPURCHASE BEHAVIOR

Postpurchase behavior
The stage of the buyer decision process in which consumers take further action after purchase based their satisfaction or dissatisfaction.

The marketer's job does not end when the product is bought. After purchasing the product, the consumer will be satisfied or dissatisfied and will engage in **postpurchase behavior** of interest to the marketer. What determines whether the buyer is satisfied or dissatisfied with a purchase? The answer lies in the relationship between the *consumer's expectations* and the product's *perceived performance*. If the product falls short of expectations, the consumer is disappointed; if it meets expectations, the consumer is satisfied; if it exceeds expectations, the consumer is delighted.

Consumers base their expectations on information they receive from sellers, friends, and other sources. If the seller exaggerates the product's performance, consumer expectations will not be met, and dissatisfaction will result. The larger the gap between expectations and performance, the greater the consumer's dissatisfaction. This suggests that sellers should make product claims that faithfully represent the product's performance so that buyers are satisfied.

Some sellers might even understate performance levels to boost consumer satisfaction with the product. For example, Boeing sells aircraft worth tens of millions of dollars each, and consumer satisfaction is important for repeat purchases and the company's reputation. Boeing's salespeople tend to be conservative when they estimate their product's potential benefits. They almost always underestimate fuel efficiency—they promise a 5 percent savings that turns out to be 8 percent. Customers are delighted with better-than-expected performance; they buy again and tell other potential customers that Boeing lives up to its promises.

Cognitive dissonance
Buyer discomfort caused by postpurchase conflict.

Almost all major purchases result in **cognitive dissonance,** or discomfort caused by postpurchase conflict. After the purchase, consumers are satisfied with the benefits of the chosen brand and are glad to avoid the drawbacks of the brands not bought. However, every purchase involves compromise. Consumers feel uneasy about acquiring the drawbacks of the chosen brand and about losing the benefits of the brands not purchased. Thus, consumers feel at least some postpurchase dissonance for every purchase.[19]

Why is it so important to satisfy the customer? Such satisfaction is important because a company's sales come from two basic groups—*new customers* and *retained customers*. It usually costs more to attract new customers than to retain current ones, and the best way to retain current customers is to keep them satisfied. Satisfied customers buy a product again, talk favorably to others about the product, pay less attention to competing brands and advertising, and buy other products from the company. Many marketers go beyond merely *meeting* the expectations of customers—they aim to *delight* the customer. A delighted customer is even more likely to purchase again and to talk favorably about the product and company.

A dissatisfied consumer responds differently. Whereas, on average, a satisfied customer tells 3 people about a good product experience, a dissatisfied customer gripes to 11 people. In fact, one study showed that 13 percent of the people who had a problem with an organization complained about the company to more than 20 people.[20] Clearly, bad word of mouth travels farther and faster than good word of mouth and can quickly damage consumer attitudes about a company and its products.

Therefore, a company would be wise to measure customer satisfaction regularly. It cannot simply rely on dissatisfied customers to volunteer their complaints when they are dissatisfied. Some 96 percent of unhappy customers never tell the company about their problem. Companies should set up systems that *encourage* customers to complain (see Marketing Highlight 5-3). In this way, the company can learn how well it is doing and how it can improve. The 3M Company claims that over two-thirds of its new-product ideas come from listening to customer complaints. But listening is not enough—the company also must respond constructively to the complaints it receives.

Beyond seeking out and responding to complaints, marketers can take additional steps to reduce consumer postpurchase dissatisfaction and to help customers feel good about their purchases. For example, Toyota writes or phones new car owners with congratulations on having selected a fine car. It places ads showing satisfied owners talking about their new cars ("I love what you do for me, Toyota!"). Toyota also obtains customer suggestions for improvements and lists the location of available services.

THE BUYER DECISION PROCESS FOR NEW PRODUCTS

We have looked at the stages buyers go through in trying to satisfy a need. Buyers may pass quickly or slowly through these stages, and some of the stages may even be reversed. Much depends on the nature of the buyer, the product, and the buying situation.

We now look at how buyers approach the purchase of new products. A **new product** is a good, service, or idea that is perceived by some potential customers as new. It may have been around for a while, but our interest is in how consumers learn about products for the first time and make decisions on whether to adopt them. We define the **adoption process** as "the mental process through which an individual passes from first learning about an innovation to final adoption,"[21] and *adoption* as the decision by an individual to become a regular user of the product.

New product
A good, service, or idea that is perceived by some potential customers as new.

Adoption process
The mental process through which an individual passes from first hearing about an innovation to final adoption.

STAGES IN THE ADOPTION PROCESS

Consumers go through five stages in the process of adopting a new product:

◆ *Awareness.* The consumer becomes aware of the new product, but lacks information about it.

◆ *Interest.* The consumer seeks information about the new product.

◆ *Evaluation.* The consumer considers whether trying the new product makes sense.

◆ *Trial.* The consumer tries the new product on a small scale to improve his or her estimate of its value.

◆ *Adoption.* The consumer decides to make full and regular use of the new product.

This model suggests that the new-product marketer should think about how to help consumers move through these stages. A manufacturer of large-screen televisions may discover that many consumers in the interest stage do not move to the trial stage because of uncertainty and the large investment. If these same consumers would be willing to use a large-screen television on a trial basis for a small fee, the manufacturer should consider offering a trial-use plan with an option to buy.

FIGURE 5-7 *Adopter categorization on the basis of relative time of adoption of innovations*
Source: Redrawn from Everett M. Rogers, *Diffusion of Innovations*, 3rd ed. (New York: 1983), p. 247. Adapted with permission of Macmillan Publishing Company, Inc. Copyright © 1962, 1971, 1983 by the Free Press.

INDIVIDUAL DIFFERENCES IN INNOVATIVENESS

People differ greatly in their readiness to try new products. In each product area, there are "consumption pioneers" and early adopters. Other individuals adopt new products much later. People can be classified into the adopter categories shown in Figure 5-7. After a slow start, an increasing number of people adopt the new product. The number of adopters reaches a peak and then drops off as fewer nonadopters remain. Innovators are defined as the first 2½ percent of the buyers to adopt a new idea (those beyond two standard deviations from mean adoption time); the early adopters are the next 13½ percent (between one and two standard deviations); and so forth.

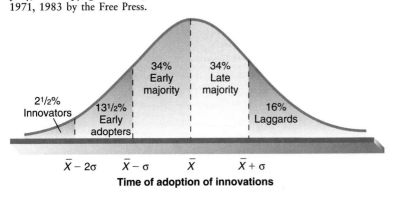

Time of adoption of innovations

POSTPURCHASE SATISFACTION: TURNING COMPANY CRITICS INTO LOYAL CUSTOMERS

What should companies do with dissatisfied customers? Everything they can! Unhappy customers not only stop buying but also can quickly damage the company's image. Studies show that customers tell four times as many other people about bad experiences

over, customers whose complaints have been satisfactorily resolved tell an average of five other people about the good treatment they received. Thus, enlightened companies don't try to hide from dissatisfied customers. To the contrary, they go out of their way to *encourage* customers to

lems and diffuse customer anger. They arm customer service representatives with liberal return and refund policies and other damage-control tools. Some companies go to extremes to see things the customer's way and to reward complaining, seemingly without regard for profit impact. For example, Hechinger, the large hardware and garden products retailer, accepts returns of items even when customers have obviously abused them. In other cases, it sends a dozen roses to purchasers who are particularly upset. Specialty retailer Neiman Marcus is equally gracious with complainers. "We're not just looking for today's sale. We want a long-term relationship with our customers," says Gwen Baum, the chain's director of customer satisfaction. "If that means taking back a piece of Baccarat crystal that isn't from one of our stores, we'll do it." This generosity appears to help profits more than harm them—both Hechinger and Neiman Marcus enjoy earnings well above industry averages. Such actions create tremendous buyer loyalty and goodwill, and for most retailers, customers who return items that they bought elsewhere or have already used account for less than 5 percent of all returns.

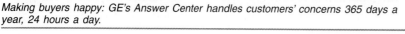

Making buyers happy: GE's Answer Center handles customers' concerns 365 days a year, 24 hours a day.

as they do about good ones. In contrast, dealing effectively with gripes can actually boost customer loyalty and the company's image. According to one study, 95 percent of consumers who register complaints will again do business with the company if their complaint is resolved quickly. More-

complain, then bend over backwards to make disgruntled buyers happy again.

The first opportunity to handle gripes often comes at the point of purchase. Many retailers and other service firms teach their customer-contact people how to resolve prob-

Many companies have also set up toll-free 800-number systems to

---

The five adopter groups have differing values. *Innovators* are venturesome—they try new ideas at some risk. *Early adopters* are guided by respect—they are opinion leaders in their communities and adopt new ideas early but carefully. The *early majority* are deliberate—although they rarely are leaders, they adopt new ideas before the average person. The *late majority* are skeptical—they adopt an innovation only after a majority of people have tried it. Finally, *laggards* are tradition-bound—they are suspicious of changes and adopt the innovation only when it has become something of a tradition itself.

This adopter classification suggests that an innovating firm should research the characteristics of innovators and early adopters and should direct marketing efforts to them. In general, innovators tend to be relatively younger, better educated, and higher in income than later adopters and nonadopters. They are more receptive to unfamiliar things, rely more on their own values and judgment, and are more willing to take risks. They are less brand loyal and more likely to take advantage of special promotions such as discounts, coupons, and samples.

coax out and deal with consumer problems. Today, more than two-thirds all U.S. manufacturers offer 800 numbers to handle complaints, inquiries, and orders. For example, Coca-Cola set up its 1-800-GET-COKE lines in late 1983 after studies showed that only 1 unhappy person in 50 bothers to complain. "The other 49 simply switch brands," explains the company's director of consumer affairs, "so it just makes good sense to seek them out."

Procter & Gamble puts an 800 number on every consumer product it sells in the United States. P&G now receives about 800,000 mail and phone contacts about its products each year—mostly complaints, requests for information, and testimonials. The 800-number system serves as an early warning signal for product and customer problems. So far, the system has resulted in hundreds of actions and improvements ranging from tracking down batches of defective packages to putting high-altitude baking instructions on Duncan Hines brownies packages.

Every weekday, Pillsbury handles more than 2,000 people who call its 800 number with complaints, compliments, and questions. On the day before Thanksgiving, the busiest day, Pillsbury's customer service reps, mostly women with college degrees and training in nutrition and home economics, assist 3,000 callers with their holiday dinners. For callers who speak little or no English, Pillsbury can dial an AT&T number that hooks up interpreters for any of 140 languages in a three-way call with the customer and company.

General Electric's Answer Center may be the most extensive 800-number system in the nation. It handles over 3 million calls a year, 5 percent of them complaints. At the heart of the system is a giant database that provides the center's service reps with instant access to over 1 million answers concerning 8,500 models in 120 product lines. The center receives some unusual calls, as when a submarine off the Connecticut coast requested help fixing a motor, or when technicians on a James Bond film couldn't get their underwater lights working. Still, according to GE, its people resolve 90 percent of complaints or inquiries on the first call, and complainers often become even more loyal customers. Although the company spends an average of $3.50 per call, it reaps two to three times that much in new sales and warranty savings.

The best way to keep customers happy is to provide good products and services in the first place. Short of that, however, a company must develop a good system for ferreting out and handling consumer problems. Such a system can be much more than a necessary evil—customer happiness usually shows up on the company's bottom line. One recent study found that dollars invested in complaint-handling and inquiry systems yield an average return of between 100 and 200 percent. Maryanne Rasmussen, vice-president of worldwide quality at American Express, offers this formula: "Better complaint handling equals higher customer satisfaction equals higher brand loyalty equals higher performance."

Sources: Quotes from Patricia Sellers, "How to Handle Consumer Gripes," *Fortune,* October 24, 1988, pp. 88–100. Also see Joyce Wycoff, "Customer Service: Evolution and Revolution," *Sales & Marketing Management,* May 1991, pp. 44–51; Frank Rose, "Now Quality Means Service Too," *Fortune,* April 22, 1991, pp. 97–108; Roland T. Rust, Bala Subramanian, and Mark Wells, "Making Complaints a Management Tool," *Marketing Management,* Fall 1992, pp. 41–45; Carl Quintanilla and Richard Gibson, " 'Do Call Us': More Companies Install 1-800 Phone Lines," *Wall Street Journal,* April 20, 1994, pp. B1, B4; and "Calming Upset Customers," *Sales & Marketing Management,* April 1994, p. 55.

INFLUENCE OF PRODUCT CHARACTERISTICS ON RATE OF ADOPTION

The characteristics of the new product affect its rate of adoption. Some products catch on almost overnight (Frisbees), whereas others take a long time to gain acceptance (personal computers). Five characteristics are especially important in influencing an innovation's rate of adoption. For example, consider the characteristics of large-screen televisions in relation to the rate of adoption:

◆ *Relative advantage:* the degree to which the innovation appears superior to existing products. The greater the perceived relative advantage of using a large-screen TV—say, in picture quality and ease of viewing—the sooner such TVs will be adopted.

◆ *Compatibility:* the degree to which the innovation fits the values and experiences of potential consumers. Large-screen TVs, for example, are highly compatible with the lifestyles found in upper-middle-class homes.

◆ *Complexity:* the degree to which the innovation is difficult to understand or use. Large-screen TVs are not very complex and will therefore take less time to penetrate U.S. homes than more complex innovations.

◆ *Divisibility:* the degree to which the innovation may be tried on a limited basis. Large-screen TVs are expensive. To the extent that people can lease them with an option to buy, their rate of adoption will increase.

◆ *Communicability:* the degree to which the results of using the innovation can be observed or described to others. Because large-screen TVs lend themselves to demonstration and description, their use will spread faster among consumers.

Other characteristics influence the rate of adoption, such as initial and ongoing costs, risk and uncertainty, and social approval. The new-product marketer has to research all these factors when developing the new product and its marketing program.

CONSUMER BEHAVIOR ACROSS INTERNATIONAL BORDERS

Understanding consumer behavior is difficult enough for companies marketing within the borders of a single country. For companies operating in many countries, however, understanding and serving the needs of consumers can be daunting. Although consumers in different countries may have some things in common, their values, attitudes, and behaviors often vary greatly. International marketers must understand such differences and adjust their products and marketing programs accordingly.

Sometimes the differences are obvious. For example, in the United States, where most people eat cereal regularly for breakfast, Kellogg focuses its marketing on persuading consumers to select a Kellogg brand rather than a competitor's brand. In France, however, where most people prefer croissants and coffee or no breakfast at all, Kellogg advertising simply attempts to convince people that they should eat cereal for breakfast. Its packaging includes step-by-step instructions on how to prepare cereal.

Often, differences across international markets are more subtle. They may result from physical differences in consumers and their environments. For example, Remington makes smaller electric shavers to fit the smaller hands of Japanese consumers; and battery-powered shavers for the British market, where few bathrooms have electrical outlets. Other differences result from varying customs. Consider the following examples:

◆ Shaking your head from side to side means "no" in most countries but "yes" in Bulgaria and Sri Lanka.

◆ In South America, Southern Europe, and many Arab countries, touching another person is a sign of warmth and friendship. In the Orient, it is considered an invasion of privacy.

◆ In Norway or Malaysia, it's rude to leave something on your plate when eating; in Egypt, it's rude *not* to leave something on your plate.

◆ A door-to-door salesperson might find it tough going in Italy, where it is improper for a man to call on a woman if she is home alone.[22]

Failing to understand such differences in customs and behaviors from one country to another can spell disaster for a marketer's international products and programs.

Marketers must decide on the degree to which they will adapt their products and marketing programs to meet the unique cultures and needs of consumers in various markets. On the one hand, they want to standardize their offerings in order to simplify operations and take advantage of cost economies. On the other hand, adapting marketing efforts within each country results in products and programs that better satisfy the needs of local consumers. The question of whether to adapt or standardize the marketing mix across international markets has created a lively debate in recent years (see Marketing Highlight 5-4).

CONSUMER-BEHAVIOR DIFFERENCES ACROSS BORDERS: GLOBAL STANDARDIZATION OR ADAPTATION?

MARKETING HIGHLIGHT 5 - 4

The marketing concept holds that marketing programs will be more effective if tailored to the unique needs of each targeted customer group. If this concept applies within a country, it should apply even more in international markets where demographic, economic, political, and cultural conditions vary widely. Consumers in different countries have varied needs and wants, spending power, product preferences, and shopping patterns. Because most marketers believe that these differences are hard to change, they adapt their products, prices, distribution channels, and promotion approaches to fit consumer desires in each country.

However, some global marketers are bothered by what they see as too much adaptation. For example, Gillette sells over eight hundred products in more than two hundred countries. It now finds itself in a situation where it uses different brand names and formulations for the same products in different countries. For example, Gillette's Silkience shampoo is called Soyance in France, Sientel in Italy, and Silience in Germany; it uses the same formula in some cases but varies it in others. It also varies the product's advertising messages because each Gillette country manager proposes several changes that he or she thinks will increase local sales. These and similar adaptations for its hundreds of other products raise Gillette's costs and dilute its global brand power.

As a result, many companies have imposed more standardization on their products and marketing efforts. They have created so-called world brands that are marketed in much the same way worldwide.

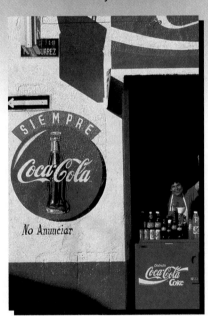

Coca-Cola sells highly standardized products worldwide, but even Coke adapts its product and packaging somewhat to local tastes and conditions.

Whereas traditional marketers cater to differences between specific markets with highly adapted products, marketers who standardize globally sell more or less the same product the same way to all consumers.

These marketers believe that advances in communication, transportation, and travel are turning the world into a common marketplace. They claim that people around the world want basically the same products and lifestyles. Everyone wants things that make life easier and that increase both free time and buying power. Despite what consumers say they want, all consumers want good products at lower prices.

Thus, proponents of global standardization claim that international marketers should adapt products and marketing programs only when local wants cannot be changed or avoided. Standardization results in lower production, distribution, marketing, and management costs, and thus lets the company offer consumers higher quality and more reliable products at lower prices. They would advise an auto company to make a world car, a shampoo company to make a world shampoo, and a farm-equipment company to make a world tractor. And, in fact, some companies have successfully marketed global products—for example, Coca-Cola, McDonald's hamburgers, A. T. Cross pens and pencils, Black & Decker tools, and Sony Walkmans. Yet, even in these cases, companies make some adaptations. Coca-Cola is less sweet or less carbonated in certain countries; McDonald's uses chili sauce instead of ketchup on its hamburgers in Mexico; and Cross pens and pencils have different advertising messages in some countries.

Moreover, the assertion that global standardization will lead to lower costs and prices, causing more goods to be snapped up by price-sensitive consumers, is debatable. Mattel Toys had sold its Barbie Doll successfully in dozens of countries without modification, but in Japan, it did not sell well. Takara, Mattel's Japanese licensee, surveyed eighth-grade Japanese girls and their parents and found that they thought the doll's breasts were too big and that its legs were too long. Mattel, however, was reluctant to modify the doll because this would require additional production, packaging, and advertising costs. Finally, Takara won out and Mattel made a special Japanese Barbie. Within two years, Takara had sold over two million of the modified dolls. Clearly, incremental revenues far exceeded the incremental costs.

Rather than assuming that their products can be introduced without change in other countries, companies should review possible adaptations in product features, brand name, packaging, advertising themes, prices, and other elements and determine which would add more revenues than costs. One study showed that companies made adaptations in one or more of these areas in 80 percent of their foreign-directed products.

So which approach is best—global standardization or adaptation? Clearly, standardization is not an all-or-nothing proposition, but rather a matter of degree. Companies are justified in looking for more standardization to help keep down costs and prices and build greater global brand power. But they must remember that although standardization saves money, competitors are always ready to offer more of what consumers in each country want, and that they might pay dearly for replacing long-run marketing thinking with short-run financial thinking. Some international marketers suggest that companies should "think globally but act locally." The corporate level gives strategic direction; local units focus on the individual consumer differences. Global marketing, yes; global standardization, not necessarily.

Sources: See Theodore Levitt, "The Globalization of Markets," *Harvard Business Review,* May–June 1983, pp. 92–102; Kamran Kashani, "Beware the Pitfalls of Global Marketing," *Harvard Business Review,* September–October 1989, pp. 91–98; Saeed Saminee and Kendall Roth, "The Influence of Global Marketing Standardization on Performance," *Journal of Marketing,* April 1992, pp. 1–17; David M. Szymanski, Sundar G. Bharadwaj, and Rajan Varadarajan, "Standardization versus Adaptation of International Marketing Strategy: An Empirical Investigation," *Journal of Marketing,* October 1993, pp. 1–17; and Ashish Banerjee, "Global Campaigns Don't Work; Multinationals Do," *Advertising Age,* April 18, 1994, p. 23.

Summary

This chapter proposes a basic *model of consumer behavior.* In this model, marketing and other stimuli affect a consumer who has certain personal characteristics and a particular buyer decision process. The consumer responds with certain observable buyer responses, including product choice, brand choice, dealer choice, purchase timing, and purchase amount.

Marketers must understand how consumer buyer behavior is affected by a buyer's particular characteristics and personal decision process. Buyer characteristics include four major components: *cultural, social, personal, and psychological factors. Culture* is the most basic determinant of a person's wants and behavior. It includes the basic values, perceptions, preferences and behaviors that a person learns from family and other institutions. *Social factors* also influence a buyer's behavior. Product and brand choices are strongly affected by a person's *reference groups,* including family, friends, and social and professional organizations. *Personal factors* such as *age and life-cycle stage, occupation, economic situation, lifestyle* and *personality* also influence buying decisions. Finally, consumer behavior is also influenced by four major *psychological factors—motivation, perception, learning,* and *beliefs and attitudes.*

Some buying decisions involve only one decision maker, but in other decisions several consumers may participate by playing different *buying roles.* These possible roles include *initiator, influencer, decider, buyer* and *user.* In some cases each of these roles is played by a different person, but in other decisions the same person may take on several distinct roles.

There are four different types of buying decision behavior. The type of decision behavior employed is affected by the complexity of the buying situation, the number of participants, and the amount of buying effort required, the level of buyer involvement, and the degree of difference among brands. Consumers may engage in complex, dissonance-reducing, habitual, or variety-seeking buying behavior. Marketers can be more effective when they understand the type of buying behavior their consumers are most likely to employ.

Before making a purchase, consumers go through a decision process consisting of *need recognition, information search, evaluation of alternatives,* the *purchase decision,* and *postpurchase behavior.* The marketer's job is to understand the buyer's behavior at each stage and the influences that are operating. This allows the marketer to develop significant and effective marketing programs for the target market.

The buyer decision process for new products adds additional complexity, with consumers passing through the stages of *awareness, interest, evaluation, trial,* and finally *adoption.* Consumers respond to new products at different rates depending upon individual differences in innova-

tiveness, whether they are *innovators, early adopters, early majority, late majority,* or *laggards.* Finally, the characteristics of the new product itself—*relative advantage, compatibility, complexity, divisibility,* and *communicability*—will affect the rate of adoption.

Consumer behavior is complex and difficult to understand even in a familiar country. Marketers who must deal with *consumer behavior across international borders* face an additional challenge. Consumers in different countries may vary dramatically in values, attitudes, and behaviors. These differences often require significant changes in products and marketing programs to achieve success in international markets.

Key Terms

Adoption process
Alternative evaluation
Attitude
Belief
Brand image
Cognitive dissonance
Complex buying behavior
Consumer buying behavior
Consumer market
Culture

Dissonance-reducing buying behavior
Groups
Habitual buying behavior
Information search
Learning
Lifestyle
Motive (or drive)
Need recognition
New product

Opinion leaders
Perception
Personality
Postpurchase behavior
Psychographics
Purchase decision
Social classes
Subculture
Variety-seeking buying behavior

Discussing the Issues

1. List several factors which you could add to the model shown in Figure 5-1 to make it a more complete description of consumer behavior.

2. In designing the advertising for a soft drink, which would you find more helpful: information about consumer demographics or consumer lifestyles? Give examples of how you would use each type of information.

3. Think about a very good or very bad experience you have had with a product. Discuss how this shaped your beliefs about this product. How long will these beliefs last?

4. Consumers play many different roles in the buying process: initiator, influencer, decider, buyer, and user. Name who plays

each of these roles when a mother is buying Mighty Morphin Power Rangers breakfast cereal, L'Eggs pantyhose, Purina Dog Chow, and a new VCR.

5. Decide why the postpurchase behavior stage is included in the model of the buying process. Explain what relevance this stage has for marketers.

6. For many Americans, changing to a healthier lifestyle would be an innovation. This might require changes in diet, exercise, smoking, and drinking. Discuss this innovation in terms of its relative advantage, compatibility, complexity, divisibility, and communicability. Is a healthy lifestyle likely to be adopted quickly by most Americans?

Applying the Concepts

1. Different types of products can fulfill different functional and psychological needs.
   ◆ List five public or private luxury products that are very interesting or important to you. Some possibilities might include cars, clothing, sports equipment, or cosmetics. List five other necessities that you use which have little interest to you, such as pencils, laundry detergent, or gasoline.
   ◆ Make a list of words that describe how you feel about each of the products you listed. Are there differences between the types of words you used for luxuries and necessities? What does this tell you about the different psychological needs these products fulfill?

2. Examining our own purchases can reveal ways in which buying decisions really occur.
   ◆ Describe the five stages of your own buyer decision process for a major purchase such as a camera, stereo, or car.
   ◆ Next, describe your decision process for a minor purchase such as a candy bar or a soda.
   ◆ Are the decision processes the same for major and minor purchases? Which steps differ, and why do they change?

References

1. Portions adapted from Joseph Pereira, "The Well-Heeled: Pricey Sneakers Worn in Inner City Help Set Nation's Fashion Trend," *Wall Street Journal,* December 1, 1988, pp. 1, 6. Excerpts from Geoffrey Smith, "Can Reebok Regain Its Balance?" *Business Week,* December 20, 1993, pp. 108–109; and Elizabeth Snead, "For Complex Times, Simple Footwear," *USA Today,* February 7, 1994, pp. D1, D2. Also see Dori Jones Yang and Michael Oneal, "Can Nike Just Do It?" *Business Week,* April 18, 1994, pp. 86–90; and Geoffrey Smith, "Sneakers That Jump Into the Past," *Business Week,* March 13, 1995, p. 71.

2. See Philip Cateora, *International Marketing,* 8th ed. (Homewood, IL.: Irwin, 1993), pp. 74–75.

3. Several models of the consumer buying process have been developed by marketing scholars. The most prominent models are those of John A. Howard and Jagdish N. Sheth, *The Theory of Buyer Behavior* (New York: John Wiley, 1969); Francesco M. Nicosia, *Consumer Decision Processes* (Englewood Cliffs, NJ: Prentice Hall, 1966); James F. Engel, Roger D. Blackwell, and Paul W. Miniard, *Consumer Behavior,* 5th ed. (New York: Holt, Rinehart & Winston, 1986); and James R. Bettman, *An Information Processing Theory of Consumer Choice* (Reading, MA: Addison-Wesley, 1979). For a summary, see Leon G. Schiffman and Leslie Lazar Kanuk, *Consumer Behavior,* 5th ed. (Englewood Cliffs, NJ: Prentice Hall, 1994), pp. 644–656.

4. For this and other examples of the effects of culture in international marketing, see Philip R. Cateora, *International Marketing,* Chapter 4.

5. See Kenneth Labich, "Class in America," *Fortune,* February 4, 1994, pp. 114–126, here p. 120.

6. For more on marketing to Hispanics, blacks, and mature consumers, see Christy Fisher, "Hispanic Media See Siesta Ending," *Advertising Age,* January 24, 1994, pp. S1, S6; Leah Rickard, "Minorities Show Brand Loyalty," *Advertising Age,* May 9, 1994, p. 29; Thomas G. Exter, "The Largest Minority," *American Demographics,* February 1993, p. 59; "Marketing to Hispanics," special report in *Advertising Age,* January 13, 1995, pp. 29–38; Eugene Morris, "The Difference in Black and White," *American Demographics,* January 1993, pp. 44–49; Raymond Serafin and Riccardo A. Davis, "Detroit Moves to Woo Blacks," *Advertising Age,* April 11, 1994, p. 10; Melissa Campanelli, "The Senior Market: Rewriting the Demographics and Definitions," *Sales & Marketing Management,* February 1991, pp. 63–70; Tibbett L. Speer, "Older Consumers Follow Different Rules," *American Demographics,* February 1993, pp. 21–22; and Cyndee Miller, "Image of Seniors Improves in Ads," *Marketing News,* December 6, 1993, p. 8.

7. Patricia Sellers, "The Best Way to Reach Your Buyers," *Fortune,* special issue on "The Tough New Consumer," Autumn/Winter, 1993, pp. 14–17.

8. Debra Goldman, "Spotlight Men," *Adweek,* August 13, 1990, pp. M1–M6; Dennis Rodkin, "A Manly Sport: Building Loyalty," *Advertising Age,* April 15, 1991, pp. S1, S12; Nancy Ten Kate, "Who Buys the Pants in the Family?" *American Demographics,* January 1992, p. 12; and Laura Zinn, "Real Men Buy Paper Towels, Too," *Business Week,* November 9, 1992, pp. 75–76.

9. For more on family decision making, see Schiffman and Kanuk, *Consumer Behavior,* Chap. 12; Michael B. Menasco and David J. Curry, "Utility and Choice: An Empirical Study of Husband/Wife Decision Making," *Journal of Consumer Research,* June 1989, pp. 87–97; Kim P. Corfman, "Perceptions of Relative Influence: Formation and Measurement," *Journal of Marketing Research,* May 1991, pp. 125–136; "The Family as a Consumer," special issue of *Psychology and Marketing,* March/April 1993; and Robert Boutilier, "Fam-

ily's Strings," *American Demographics,* August 1993, pp. 44–47.

10. See Martha Farnsworth Riche, "Psychographics for the 1990s," *American Demographics,* July 1989, pp. 25–31.

11. This and other examples of companies using VALS2 can be found in Rebecca Piirto, "Measuring Minds in the 1990s," *American Demographics,* December 1990, pp. 35–39; and Piirto, "VALS the Second Time," *American Demographics,* July 1991, p. 6.

12. See "Ad Agency Finds Five Global Segments," *Marketing News,* January 8, 1990, pp. 9, 17.

13. Myron Magnet, "Let's Go For Growth," *Fortune,* March 7, 1994, p. 70.

14. See Annetta Miller and Dody Tsiantar, "Psyching Out Consumers," *Newsweek,* February 27, 1989, pp. 46–47; and Rebecca Piirto, "Words that Sell," *American Demographics,* January 1992, p. 6.

15. Abraham H. Maslow, *Motivation and Personality,* 2nd ed. (New York: Harper & Row, 1970), pp. 80–106. Also see Rudy Schrocer, "Maslow's Hierarchy of Needs as a Framework for Identifying Emotional Triggers," *Marketing Review,* February 1991, pp. 26, 28.

16. See "Honda Hopes to Win New Riders by Emphasizing 'Fun' of Cycles," *Marketing News,* August 28, 1989, p. 6.

17. See Henry Assael, *Consumer Behavior and Marketing Action* (Boston: Kent Publishing, 1987), Chap. 4. An earlier classification of three types of consumer buying behavior—routine response behavior, limited problem solving, and extensive problem solving—can be found in John A. Howard and Jagdish Sheth, *The Theory of Consumer Behavior* (New York: John Wiley, 1969), pp. 27–28. Also see John A. Howard, *Consumer Behavior in Marketing Strategy* (Englewood Cliffs, NJ: Prentice Hall, 1989).

18. Keith B. Murray, "A Test of Services Marketing Theory: Consumer Information Acquisition Theory," *Journal of Marketing,* January 1991, pp. 10–25.

19. See Leon Festinger, *A Theory of Cognitive Dissonance* (Stanford, CA: Stanford University Press, 1957); and Leon G. Schiffman and Leslie Lazar Kanuk, *Consumer Behavior* (Englewood Cliffs, NJ: Prentice Hall, 1994), pp. 274–275.

20. See Karl Albrect and Ron Zemke, *Service America!* (Homewood, IL: Dow-Jones Irwin, 1985), pp. 6–7; and Frank Rose, "Now Quality Means Service Too," *Fortune,* April 22, 1991, pp. 97–108.

21. The following discussion draws heavily from Everett M. Rogers, *Diffusion of Innovations,* 3rd ed. (New York: Free Press, 1983). Also see Hubert Gatignon and Thomas S. Robertson, "A Propositional Inventory for New Diffusion Research," *Journal of Consumer Research,* March 1985, pp. 849–867.

22. For these and other examples, see William J. Stanton, Michael J. Etzel, and Bruce J. Walker, *Fundamentals of Marketing* (New York: McGraw-Hill, Inc., 1991), p. 536.

Company Case 5

SHISEIDO: RETHINKING THE FUTURE

"We need to rethink what a human being is," observes Seigo Matsouka, a consultant and conference leader, as he begins a four-day conference for 20 Shiseido division managers. Shiseido (She-she-doe) is Japan's largest cosmetics company. Yet its managers and the managers at many other Japanese companies worry that Japan's traditional hierarchical business structure and its emphasis on consensus-based decision making will not serve their companies well in the future. Although Japanese companies have done well at improving existing products, they have not done as well at developing new products and markets. Thus, they need to stimulate their managers to think creatively, something that these companies have not previously expected from their managers.

Why are successful Japanese companies suddenly so concerned? Consider Noriko Shida, a 21-year-old student who is shopping at an upscale retail store in a chic Tokyo shopping district. As Noriko examines a tube of Shiseido's expensive lipstick, she turns up her nose at the price. "I find good colors at places like this," she sniffs. "Then I go and buy the same product at a discount store." Welcome to the new Japan. Even in a country known for its loyal, demanding customers, Japanese managers are learning that consumers have minds of their own. Changing consumer behavior will require new marketing approaches.

Shiseido, which chose its name from the Chinese classics, was the first firm to introduce Western-style toothpaste to Japan in *1888!* It also opened Japan's first soda fountain in 1902. However, Shiseido developed its competitive advantage in the 1920s. In this period of high inflation, Shiseido worked out a unique arrangement with retailers. The retailers agreed to sell *only* Shiseido's cosmetics in exchange for a commitment that Shiseido would buy back any unsold cosmetics. With this understanding, Shiseido became both manufacturer and wholesaler and developed a network of 25,000 Japanese retailers that sold its products exclusively. These shops represent about one-half of all cosmetics and pharmaceutical shops in Japan. The system allowed Shiseido to control distribution and develop a pricy image. Shiseido rode this distribution channel and its high prices to annual sales of over 500 billion yen (about $4.8 billion) by 1990.

In April 1991, partly in response to U.S. government pressure, Japan lifted its retail price controls on cosmetics, drugs, and other small products priced under about $10. In other product-markets, such deregulation had increased distribution costs and allowed foreign companies to challenge Japanese firms in their home market. However, Shiseido had already learned to contend with foreign competition. Clinique Laboratories from the United States had earlier gained a 7 percent share of the Japanese market by selling through leading department stores that traditional Japanese cosmetics firms avoided. Shiseido had countered this threat by developing "CL Shops," or cosmetic counseling centers, where employees provided more detailed advice to customers in fashionably redesigned retail settings.

Deregulation had also caused dramatic price cuts and had fostered the rise of discount stores in other product markets. In cosmetics, entrepreneurs like Yukio Higuchi responded quickly by founding discount chains like Kawachiya Shuhan Company. Before Shiseido cut off his supply, Higuchi drew crowds of shoppers by selling Shiseido products at a 30 percent discount. Higuchi persisted, arguing that the belief "that quality only comes at a high price is weakening." Further, he noted, "cosmetics will have to become cheaper as consumers become wiser." Most Japanese observers agree. They note that consumers want competition, and they want discount stores. Even supermarkets are getting ready to introduce cheap, private-label cosmetics.

Such changes represent a major shift that has left the previously well-protected Japanese consumer-product companies and retailers badly shaken. Shiseido is responding to these changes on two fronts. First, it is cutting costs and refocusing on lower-priced cosmetics. It has opened a highly automated factory that uses robots to carry out almost all the steps in making cosmetics. The plant produces as many cosmetics as one of Shiseido's other factories, but with one-third the employees.

Second, Shiseido is looking for more growth overseas. Already, it operates 21 subsidiaries and six factories in 30 countries. By 1996, it wants to increase international sales by 50 percent to 100 billion yen. If it is to reach this goal, Shiseido must do well in the United States. In early 1994, the company shifted its U.S. marketing strategy, focusing more on skin-care products and on splashy new print ads. It relocated more than 700 of its U.S. sales counters to urban areas with more growth potential. It also renovated the sales counters to provide a "new image," with more eyecatching displays that hailed Shiseido's advanced skin-care program. Shiseido will also launch a new brand to attract men and two new fragrances for women.

Shiseido's refocusing seems to be on target with changes in the U.S. market. Industry observers note that executives from packaged-goods companies have taken over most cosmetic company marketing programs. They are discarding the sexy models in glamorous locales in favor of scientific-sounding claims and coupons. One ad claims, "In just one week, fine dry lines and wrinkles are reduced by over 38 percent." Another ad offers $1 coupons and a money-back guarantee. Revlon has even attacked Clinique directly by producing an ad that proclaims "Clinique mascara can cost twice as much as ALMAY mascara."

Industry executives suggest that these marketing changes reflect increasing consumer savvy. "A consumer in the '90s is as smart a consumer as you can get," one notes. "She's reading labels, she understands how ingredients work, she wants products that truly perform." Another executive adds that some of the industry's changes are in response to consumers who are more value-conscious. "In the '90s, even people with very high incomes are very price-conscious."

It appears that Tokyo's Noriko Shida may not be much different from shoppers in Los Angeles or New York City. But can Japanese cosmetics manufacturers like Shiseido repeat Japanese successes in the U.S. car and consumer electronics markets? Some analysts argue that Americans see Japanese products as technically advanced and reliable but short on soul. The Japanese have a high-tech rather than a high-chic image, one that is good for stereos but not for perfumes. Japanese managers often sneer at image-driven selling, believing that their products perform better than those of their rivals. Thus, Japanese cosmetics companies spend almost 4 percent of their sales on R&D, about double the amount American companies spend.

But some observers argue that cosmetics is an image-driven market in which companies have a hard time convincing consumers of product differences. They wonder if the American or Japanese companies can succeed with scientific claims, coupons, or fancy sales counters. Can they transform whimsical beauty products into natural, high-tech, essential products?

The aging of the baby-boom generation has already thrust the U.S. cosmetics market into turmoil. Do these older consumers still want the same cosmetics that 20-year-old models promote? Can cosmetics companies succeed by stressing skin care? Do women want cosmetics companies telling them that if they don't use these products, they will wake up with bunches of wrinkles? And will women continue to buy their cosmetics in department and specialty stores, or will they join the trend toward buying cosmetics in mass-merchandise stores?

As Shiseido's executives struggle with these questions and try to understand consumers, Seigo Matsouka repeats, "So, what does it mean to be human?"

QUESTIONS

1. How do consumers' cultural, social, personal, and psychological characteristics affect their cosmetics shopping behavior, and how do these factors affect the way cosmetics executives see consumers? How are these factors changing?

2. Who is involved in a consumer's decision to purchase cosmetics, and what role does each participant play?

3. What types of buying decision behavior are involved in purchasing cosmetics?

4. Describe the buying decision process for cosmetics.

5. What marketing recommendations would you make to Shiseido as it seeks to increase its sales in the U.S. market?

Sources: "The Softer Samurai," *The Economist,* May 12, 1990, p. 73; "Facing Up," *The Economist,* July 13, 1991, pp. 71–72; Louise do Rosario, "Make Up and Mend," *Far Eastern Economic Review,* December 19, 1991, pp. 70–71; Emily Thornton, "Japan's Struggle To Be Creative," *Fortune,* April 19, 1993, pp. 129–134; "Fragrance Helps You Live Longer," *The Economist,* October 23, 1993, p. 86; Jennifer Cody, "Shiseido Strives for a Whole New Look," *Wall Street Journal,* May 27, 1994, p. B5; Suein L. Hwang, "Makeup Ads Downplay Glamour for Value," *Wall Street Journal,* June 20, 1994, p. B6; Paulette Thomas, "Peddling Youth Gets Some New Wrinkles," *Wall Street Journal,* October, 24, 1994, p. B1.

Business Markets and
Business Buyer Behavior

6

Gulfstream Aerospace Corporation sells business jets with price tags as high as $27 million. Identifying potential buyers isn't a problem—worldwide, only about 4,200 customers, including 40 governments, have the wherewithal to own and operate multimillion dollar business aircraft. Customers include Disney, American Express, Coca-Cola, General Motors, IBM, and many others, including King Fahd of Saudi Arabia. Gulfstream's more difficult problems involve reaching key decision makers for jet purchases, understanding their complex motivations and decision processes, analyzing what factors will be important in their decisions, and designing marketing approaches.

Gulfstream recognizes the importance of *rational* motives and *objective* factors in buyers' decisions. Customers justify the expense of a corporate jet on utilitarian grounds, such as security, flexibility, responsiveness to customers, and efficient time use. A company buying a jet will evaluate Gulfstream aircraft on quality and performance, prices, operating costs, and service. At times, these "objective factors" may appear to be the only things that drive the buying decision. But having a superior product isn't enough to land the sale: Gulfstream also must consider the more subtle *human factors* that affect the choice of a jet.

The purchase process may be initiated by the chief executive officer (CEO), a board member wishing to increase efficiency or security, the company's chief pilot, or through Gulfstream efforts like advertising or a sales visit. The CEO will be central in deciding whether to buy the jet, but he or she will be heavily influenced by the company's pilot, financial officer, and members of top management. The involvement of so many people in the purchase decision creates a group dynamic that Gulfstream must factor into its sales planning. Who makes up the buying group? How will the parties interact? Who will dominate and who submit? What priorities do the individuals have?

Each party in the buying process has subtle roles and needs. For example, the salesperson who tries to impress both the CEO with depreciation schedules and the chief pilot with

OBJECTIVES

When you finish this chapter, you should be able to accomplish the following:

1. List the **characteristics of business markets,** explaining **market structure and demand,** the **nature of the buying unit,** and the **decision process.**

2. Outline the **model of business buyer behavior.**

3. Discuss **business buyer behavior, types of buying situations, participants in the business buying process,** and **major influences on business buyers.**

4. Identify and define the steps of the **business buying process.**

5. Contrast the differences among **business markets, institutional markets,** and **government markets.**

minimum runway statistics will almost certainly not sell a plane if he or she overlooks the psychological and emotional components of the buying decision. The chief pilot, as an equipment expert, often has veto power over purchase decisions and may be able to stop the purchase of a certain brand of jet by simply expressing a negative opinion about, say, the plane's bad weather capabilities. In this sense, the pilot not only influences the decision but also serves as an information "gatekeeper" by advising management on the equipment to select. The users of the jet—middle and upper management of the buying company, important customers, and others—may have at least an indirect role in choosing the equipment. Although the corporate legal staff will handle the purchase agreement and the purchasing department will acquire the jet, these parties may have little to say about whether or how the plane will be obtained and which type will be selected.

According to one salesperson, in dealing with the CEO, the biggest factor is not the plane's hefty pricetag, but its image. You need all the numbers for support, but if you can't find the kid inside the CEO and excite him or her with the raw beauty of the new plane, you'll never sell the equipment. If you sell the excitement, you sell the jet.

Some buying influences may come as a big surprise. Gulfstream may never really know who is behind the purchase of a plane. Although many people inside the customer company can be influential, the most important influence may turn out to be the CEO's wife. As one salesperson notes: "Wives are behind the CEO's decisions on a lot of things, not just airplanes. . . . A crucial moment in a deal comes when the CEO's wife takes off her shoes and starts decorating the plane."

In some ways, selling corporate jets to business buyers is like selling cars and kitchen appliances to families. Gulfstream asks the same questions as consumer marketers: Who are the buyers and what are their needs? How do buyers make their buying decisions and what factors influence these decisions? What marketing program will be most effective? But the answers to these questions are usually different for the business buyer. Thus, Gulfstream faces many of the same challenges as consumer marketers—and some additional ones.[1]

Business market
All the organizations that buy goods and services to use in the production of other products and services or for the purpose of reselling or renting them to others at a profit.

Business buying process
The decision-making process by which business buyers establish the need for purchased products and services and identify, evaluate, and choose among alternative brands and suppliers.

In one way or another, most large companies sell to other organizations. Many companies, such as Du Pont, Xerox, Boeing, Motorola, and countless other firms, sell *most* of their products to other businesses. Even large consumer-products companies, which make products used by final consumers, must first sell their products to other businesses. For example, General Mills makes many familiar consumer products—Cheerios, Betty Crocker cake mixes, Gold Medal flour, and others. But to sell these products to consumers, General Mills must first sell them to the wholesalers and retailers that serve the consumer market. General Mills also sells products such as specialty chemicals directly to other businesses.

The **business market** consists of all the organizations that buy goods and services to use in the production of other products and services that are sold, rented, or supplied to others. It also includes retailing and wholesaling firms that acquire goods for the purpose of reselling or renting them to others at a profit. The **business buying process** is the decision-making process by which business buyers establish the need for purchased products and services, and identify, evaluate, and choose among alternative brands and suppliers.[2] Companies that sell to other business organizations must do their best to understand business markets and business buyer behavior.

BUSINESS MARKETS

The business market is *huge:* In the United States alone, it consists of over 13 million organizations that buy trillions of dollars worth of goods and services each year. In fact, business markets involve far more dollars and items than do consumer markets. For example, think about the large number of business transactions involved in the production and sale of a single set of Goodyear Tires. Various suppliers sell Goodyear the rubber, steel, equipment, and other goods that it needs to produce the tires. Goodyear then sells the finished tires to retailers, who in turn sell them to consumers. Thus, many sets of *business* purchases were made for only one set of *consumer* purchases. In addition, Goodyear sells tires as original equipment to manufacturers who install them on new vehicles, and as replacement tires to companies that maintain their own fleets of company cars, trucks, buses, or other vehicles.

CHARACTERISTICS OF BUSINESS MARKETS

In some ways, business markets are similar to consumer markets. Both involve people who assume buying roles and make purchase decisions to satisfy needs. However, business markets differ in many ways from consumer markets.[3] The main differences, shown in Table 6-1 and discussed below, are in *market structure and demand,* the *nature of the buying unit,* and the *types of decisions and the decision process* involved.

TABLE 6-1 *Characteristics of Business Markets*

MARKETING STRUCTURE AND DEMAND

- ◆ Business markets contain *fewer but larger buyers.*
- ◆ Business customers are more *geographically concentrated.*
- ◆ Business buyer demand is *derived* from final consumer demand.
- ◆ Demand in many business markets is *more inelastic*—not affected as much in the short run by price changes.
- ◆ Demand in business market *fluctuates more,* and more quickly.

NATURE OF THE BUYING UNIT

- ◆ Business purchases involve *more buyers.*
- ◆ Business buying involves a *more professional purchasing effort.*

TYPES OF DECISIONS AND THE DECISION PROCESS

- ◆ Business buyers usually face more *complex buying decisions.*
- ◆ The business buying process is *more formalized.*
- ◆ In business buying, buyers and sellers work more closely together and build close long-run *relationships.*

OTHER CHARACTERISTICS

- ◆ Business buyers often *buy directly* from producers, rather than through retailers or wholesalers.
- ◆ Business buyers often practice *reciprocity,* buying from suppliers who also buy from them.
- ◆ Business buyers more often *lease* equipment rather than buying it outright.

Market Structure and Demand

The business marketer normally deals with *far fewer but far larger buyers* than the consumer marketer does. For example, when Goodyear sells replacement tires to final consumers, its potential market includes the owners of the millions of cars currently in use in the United States. But Goodyear's fate in the business market

INTEL: YOU CAN'T SEE IT, BUT YOU'RE GOING TO LOVE IT

I n mid-1991, Intel launched its "Intel Inside" advertising campaign to sell personal computer buyers on the virtues of Intel microprocessors, the tiny chips that serve as the brains of microcomputers. So what, you say? Lots of companies run big consumer ad campaigns. However, although such a campaign might be business as usual for companies like Coca-Cola, Nike, or IBM that market products directly to final consumers, it was anything but usual for Intel.

Computer buyers can't buy a microprocessor chip directly—in fact, most will never even see one. Demand for microprocessors is *derived demand*—it comes from demand for products that *contain* microprocessors. Consumers simply buy the computer and take whatever brand of chip the computer manufacturer chooses to include. Traditionally, chip companies like Intel market only to the manufacturers who buy chips directly. In contrast, the innovative "Intel Inside" campaign appeals directly to computer buyers—Intel's customers' customers. If Intel can create brand preference among buyers for *its* chips, this in turn will make Intel chips more attractive to computer manufacturers.

Intel invented the first microprocessor in 1971 and for more than 20 years has held a near-monopoly, dominating the chip market for desktop computers. Its sales and profits have soared accordingly. In the decade since IBM introduced its first PCs based on Intel's 8088 microprocessor, Intel sales have jumped ninefold to almost $9 billion, and its earnings have grown even faster. Its popular i286, i386, i486, and Pentium chips power 75 percent of all PCs sold today.

However, a rush of imitators— Advanced Micro Devices (AMD), Cyrix, and others—have cracked Intel's monopoly, flooding the market with new and improved clones of Intel chips. The onslaught of clones quickly escalated into a price war for Intel's earlier-generation chips, denting

Intel launched its highly successful "Intel Inside" logo advertising campaign to convince computer buyers that it really does matter what chip comes inside their computers.

Derived demand
Business demand that ultimately comes from (derives from) the demand for consumer goods.

depends on getting orders from one of only a few large auto makers. Even in large business markets, a few buyers normally account for most of the purchasing.

Business markets are also more *geographically concentrated.* More than half the nation's business buyers are concentrated in eight states: California, New York, Ohio, Illinois, Michigan, Texas, Pennsylvania, and New Jersey. Further, business demand is **derived demand**—it ultimately derives from the demand for consumer goods. General Motors buys steel because consumers buy cars. If consumer demand for cars drops, so will the demand for steel and all the other products used to make cars. Therefore, business marketers sometimes promote their products directly to final consumers to increase business demand (see Marketing Highlight 6-1).

Many business markets have *inelastic demand;* that is, total demand for many business products is not affected much by price changes, especially in the short run. A drop in the price of leather will not cause shoe manufacturers to buy much more leather unless it results in lower shoe prices that, in turn, will increase consumer demand for shoes.

Finally, business markets have more *fluctuating demand.* The demand for many business goods and services tends to change more—and more quickly—than the demand for consumer goods and services does. A small percentage increase in consumer demand can cause large increases in business demand. Sometimes a rise

Intel's bottom line. And although Intel has the next-generation Pentium processor market to itself for now, the cloners will soon offer these higher-level chips as well. Perhaps more ominous, three large and skillful competitors—IBM, Apple, and Motorola—joined forces to create the PowerPC chip, an ultrafast but inexpensive chip based on a different technology.

Intel has responded fiercely to the growing competition, slashing prices, spending heavily to develop new chips, and advertising to differentiate its products. In 1994, Intel invested a whopping $1 billion in R&D and $2.4 billion in capital spending to get new products to the market more quickly. Its Pentium microprocessor is a veritable one-chip mainframe. The Pentium processor contains 3.3 million transistors and will process 100 million instructions per second (MIPS), as compared to only one-half million transistors and five MIPS for the old i386 chip. Intel plans to create a new chip family every two years. By the year 2000, it will offer a chip with an astounding 100 million transistors and 2 *billion* instructions per second—that's roughly equal to today's supercomputers.

Still, the clone makers are likely to continue nipping at Intel's heels, and advertising provides another means by which Intel can differentiate its "originals" from competitors' imitations. The "Intel Inside" program consists of two major efforts. First, in its brand-awareness ads, Intel attempts to convince microcomputer buyers that Intel microprocessors really are better. The first ad of the series contained the headline "How to spot the very best PC" nestled in a bed of colorful "Intel Inside" logos. The ad copy advised:

> Intel is the world's leader in microprocessor design and development. In fact, Intel introduced the very first microprocessor. So with the Intel Inside logo, you know you've got unquestioned compatibility and unparalleled quality. And you'll know you're getting the very best in PC technology.

As a second major element of the "Intel Inside" program, Intel subsidizes ads by PC manufacturers that include the "Intel Inside" logo. So far, more than 100 companies have featured the logo in their ads, including IBM, NCR, Dell, Zenith Data Systems, and AST. Participating manufacturers claim that the campaign has increased their advertising effectiveness. "The 'Intel Inside' program has been a good program for us," says the advertising manager of a large computer manufacturing firm. "It has helped add some credibility and enhancements to our messages." In the first two years of the campaign, more than $250 million worth of "Intel Inside" logo advertising appeared, with computer manufacturers picking up an estimated $150 million of the bill.

It remains to be seen whether the "Intel Inside" program can continue to convince buyers to care about what chips come in their computers. But as long as microprocessors remain anonymous little lumps hidden inside a user's computer, Intel remains at the mercy of the clone makers and other competitors. In contrast, if Intel can convince buyers that its chips are superior, it will achieve a strong advantage in its dealings with computer makers.

Sources: Quote from Kate Bertrand, "Advertising a Chip You'll Never See," *Business Marketing*, February 1992, p. 19. Also see Richard Brandt, "Intel: What a Tease—and What a Strategy," *Business Week*, February 22, 1993, p. 40; Nancy Arnott, "Inside Intel's Marketing Coup," *Sales & Marketing Management*, February 1994, pp. 78-81; and Robert D. Hof, "Intel: Far Beyond the Pentium," *Business Week,* February 20, 1995, pp. 88–90. Intel Inside, i286, i386, i486, and Pentium are trademarks or registered trademarks of Intel Corporation.

of only 10 percent in consumer demand can cause as much as a 200 percent rise in business demand during the next period.

Nature of the Buying Unit

Compared with consumer purchases, a business purchase usually involves *more buyers* and a *more professional purchasing effort*. Often, business buying is done by trained purchasing agents who spend their working lives learning how to buy better. The more complex the purchase, the more likely that several people will participate in the decision-making process. Buying committees made up of technical experts and top management are common in the buying of major goods. Therefore, business marketers must have well-trained salespeople to deal with well-trained buyers.

Types of Decisions and the Decision Process

Business buyers usually face *more complex* buying decisions than do consumer buyers. Purchases often involve large sums of money, complex technical and economic considerations, and interactions among many people at many levels of the buyer's organization. Because the purchases are more complex, business buyers may take longer to make their decisions. For example, the purchase of a large computer system might take many months or more than a year to complete and could involve millions of dollars, thousands of technical details, and dozens of people ranging from top management to lower-level users.

The business buying process tends to be *more formalized* than the consumer buying process. Large business purchases usually call for detailed product specifications, written purchase orders, careful supplier searches, and formal approval. The buying firm might even prepare policy manuals that detail the purchase process.

Finally, in the business buying process, buyer and seller are often much *more dependent* on each other. Consumer marketers are usually at a distance from their customers. In contrast, business marketers may roll up their sleeves and work closely with their customers during all stages of the buying process—from helping customers define problems, to finding solutions, to supporting after-sale operation. They often customize their offerings to individual customer needs. In the short run, sales go to suppliers who meet buyers' immediate product and service needs. However, business marketers also must build close *long-run* relationships with customers. In the long run, business marketers keep a customer's sales by meeting current needs *and* by working with customers to help them succeed with their own customers (see Marketing Highlight 6-2).[4]

Other Characteristics of Business Markets

Business buyers often engage in *direct purchasing*. They buy directly from producers rather than through middlemen, especially for items that are technically complex or expensive. For example, Ryder buys thousands of trucks each year in all shapes and sizes. It rents some of these trucks to move-it-yourself customers (the familiar yellow Ryder trucks), leases some to other companies for their truck fleets, and uses the rest in its own freight-hauling businesses. When Ryder buys GMC trucks, it purchases them directly from General Motors rather than from independent GM truck dealers. Similarly, American Airlines buys airplanes directly from Boeing, Kroger buys package goods directly from Procter & Gamble, and the United States government buys personal computers directly from IBM.

Business buyers often practice *reciprocity*, selecting suppliers who also buy from them. For example, a paper company might buy needed chemicals from a chemical company that in turn buys the company's paper. The Federal Trade Commission and the Justice Department's antitrust division forbid reciprocity if it shuts out competition in an unfair manner. A buyer still can choose a supplier that it also sells something to, but the buyer should be able to show that it is getting competitive prices, quality, and service from that supplier.[5]

Finally, business buyers increasingly are *leasing* equipment instead of buying it outright. American companies lease over $108 billion of equipment each year—everything from printing presses to power plants, helicopters to hay balers, and office copiers to offshore drilling rigs. The lessee can gain a number of advantages, such as having more available capital, getting the seller's latest products, receiving better servicing, and gaining some tax advantages. The lessor often ends up with a larger net income and the chance to sell to customers who might not have been able to afford outright purchase.

A MODEL OF BUSINESS BUYER BEHAVIOR

At the most basic level, marketers want to know how business buyers will respond to various marketing stimuli. Figure 6-1 shows a model of business buyer behavior. In this model, marketing and other stimuli affect the buying organization and produce certain buyer responses. As with consumer buying, the marketing stimuli for business buying consist of the four *P*s: product, price, place, and promotion. Other stimuli include major forces in the environment: economic, technological,

BUSINESS MARKETERS SELL CUSTOMER SUCCESS

In the late 1980s, the Dow chemical company realigned its dozen or so widely varied plastics businesses into a single business unit called Dow Plastics. One of the first things Dow had to do was to decide how to position its new division competitively. Initial research with Dow's and competitors' customers showed that Dow

service, or lack thereof, that they received from all three suppliers. "Vendors peddled resins as a commodity," says the head of Dow Plastics' research and advertising agency. "They competed on price and delivered on time, but gave no service."

These findings led to a positioning strategy that went far beyond

but customer success. Says the agency executive, "Whether they're using Dow's plastics to make bags for Safeway or for complex aerospace applications, we have to help them succeed in their markets." This new thinking was summed up in the positioning statement: "We don't succeed unless you do."

The new positioning helped Dow Plastics to become a truly customer-oriented company. It got Dow out of selling plastics and into selling customer success. The slogan and underlying philosophy created a unifying identity for the business—one based on building relationships with customers and helping them to succeed with their own businesses. Customer problems became more than just engineering challenges. Dow's customers sell to somebody else, so the company now faced new challenges of marketing to and helping satisfy customers' customers.

As a result of its new customer-relationship orientation, Dow Plastics has now become a leader in the plastics industry. The customer-success philosophy permeates everything the business does. Whenever company people encounter a new product or market, the first question they always ask is, "How does this fit with 'We don't succeed unless you do.'?"

Source: Portions adapted from Nancy Arnott, "Getting the Picture: The Grand Design—We Don't Succeed Unless You Do," *Sales & Marketing Management,* June 1994, pp. 74–76.

Dow Plastics tells customers, "We don't succeed unless you do." Building deeper customer relationships helped Dow move from number three to become a leader in its market.

Plastics rated a distant third in customer preference behind industry leaders Du Pont and GE Plastics. The research also revealed, however, that customers were unhappy with the

simply selling good products and delivering them on time. Dow Plastics set out to build deeper relationships with customers. The company was selling not just products and services,

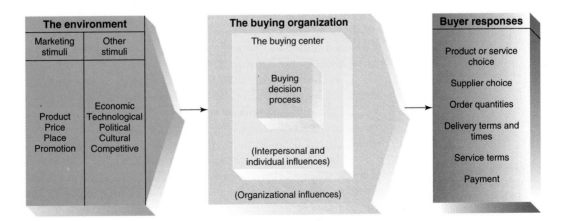

FIGURE 6-1 *A model of business buyer behavior*

political, cultural, and competitive. These stimuli enter the organization and are turned into buyer responses: product or service choice; supplier choice; order quantities; and delivery, service, and payment terms. In order to design good marketing-mix strategies, the marketer must understand what happens within the organization to turn stimuli into purchase responses.

Within the organization, buying activity consists of two major parts: the buying center, made up of all the people involved in the buying decision, and the buying decision process. The model shows that the buying center and the buying decision process are influenced by internal organizational, interpersonal, and individual factors as well as by external environmental factors.

BUSINESS BUYER BEHAVIOR

The model in Figure 6-1 suggests four questions about business buyer behavior: What buying decisions do business buyers make? Who participates in the buying process? What are the major influences on buyers? How do business buyers make their buying decisions?

MAJOR TYPES OF BUYING SITUATIONS

There are three major types of buying situations.[6] At one extreme is the *straight rebuy*, which is a fairly routine decision. At the other extreme is the *new task*, which may call for thorough research. In the middle is the *modified rebuy*, which requires some research.

Straight rebuy
A business buying situation in which the buyer routinely reorders something without any modifications.

In a **straight rebuy,** the buyer reorders something without any modifications. It is usually handled on a routine basis by the purchasing department. Based on past buying satisfaction, the buyer simply chooses from the various suppliers on its list. "In" suppliers try to maintain product and service quality. They often propose automatic reordering systems so that the purchasing agent will save reordering time. The "out" suppliers try to offer something new or exploit dissatisfaction so that the buyer will consider them. They try to get their foot in the door with a small order and then enlarge their purchase share over time.

Modified rebuy
A business buying situation in which the buyer wants to modify product specifications, prices, terms, or suppliers.

In a **modified rebuy,** the buyer wants to modify product specifications, prices, terms, or suppliers. The modified rebuy usually involves more decision participants than the straight rebuy. The "in" suppliers may become nervous and feel pressured to put their best foot forward to protect an account. "Out" suppliers may see the modified rebuy situation as an opportunity to make a better offer and gain new business.

New task
A business buying situation in which the buyer purchases a product or service for the first time.

A company buying a product or service for the first time faces a **new-task** situation. In such cases, the greater the cost or risk, the larger the number of decision participants and the greater their efforts to collect information will be. The new-task situation is the marketer's greatest opportunity and challenge. The marketer not only tries to reach as many key buying influences as possible, but also provides help and information.

The buyer makes the fewest decisions in the straight rebuy and the most in the new-task decision. In the new-task situation, the buyer must decide on product specifications, suppliers, price limits, payment terms, order quantities, delivery times, and service terms. The order of these decisions varies with each situation, and different decision participants influence each choice.

Systems buying
Buying a packaged solution to a problem and without all the separate decisions involved.

Many business buyers prefer to buy a packaged solution to a problem from a single seller. Called **systems buying,** this practice began with government buying of major weapons and communication systems. Instead of buying and putting all the components together, the government asked for bids from suppliers who would supply the components *and* assemble the package or system.

Sellers increasingly have recognized that buyers like this method and have adopted systems selling as a marketing tool.[7] Systems selling is a two-step process. First, the supplier sells a group of interlocking products. For example, the supplier sells not only glue, but also applicators and dryers. Second, the supplier sells a system of production, inventory control, distribution, and other services to meet the buyer's need for a smooth-running operation.

Systems selling is a key business marketing strategy for winning and holding accounts. The contract often goes to the firm that provides the most complete system meeting the customer's needs. For example, the Indonesian government requested bids to build a cement factory near Jakarta. An American firm's proposal included choosing the site, designing the cement factory, hiring the construction crews, assembling the materials and equipment, and turning the finished factory over to the Indonesian government. A Japanese firm's proposal included all of these services, plus hiring and training workers to run the factory, exporting the cement through their trading companies, and using the cement to build some needed roads and new office buildings in Jakarta. Although the Japanese firm's proposal cost more, it won the contract. Clearly the Japanese viewed the problem not as one of just building a cement factory (the narrow view of systems selling) but of running it in a way that would contribute to the country's economy. They took the broadest view of the customer's needs. This is true systems selling.

PARTICIPANTS IN THE BUSINESS BUYING PROCESS

Who does the buying of the trillions of dollars worth of goods and services needed by business organizations? The decision-making unit of a buying organization is called its **buying center,** defined as all the individuals and units that participate in the business decision-making process.[8]

The buying center includes all members of the organization who play any of five roles in the purchase decision process.[9]

Buying center
All the individuals and units that participate in the business buying-decision process.

Users
Members of the organization who will use the product or service; users often initiate the buying proposal and help define product specifications.

Influencers
People in an organization's buying center who affect the buying decision; they often help define specifications and also provide information for evaluating alternatives.

Buyer
The person who makes an actual purchase.

Deciders
People in the organization's buying center who have formal or informal power to select or approve the final suppliers.

Gatekeepers
People in the organization's buying center who control the flow of information to others.

- ◆ **Users** are members of the organization who will use the product or service. In many cases, users initiate the buying proposal and help define product specifications.
- ◆ **Influencers** affect the buying decision. They often help define specifications and also provide information for evaluating alternatives. Technical personnel are particularly important influencers.
- ◆ **Buyers** have formal authority to select the supplier and arrange terms of purchase. Buyers may help shape product specifications, but they play their major role in selecting vendors and in negotiating. In more complex purchases, buyers might include high-level officers participating in the negotiations.
- ◆ **Deciders** have formal or informal power to select or approve the final suppliers. In routine buying, the buyers are often the deciders, or at least the approvers.
- ◆ **Gatekeepers** control the flow of information to others. For example, purchasing agents often have authority to prevent salespersons from seeing users or deciders. Other gatekeepers include technical personnel and even personal secretaries.

The buying center is not a fixed and formally identified unit within the buying organization. It is a set of buying roles assumed by different people for different purchases. Within the organization, the size and makeup of the buying center will vary for different products and for different buying situations. For some

This ad recognizes the secretary as a key buying influence.

routine purchases, one person—say a purchasing agent—may assume all the buying center roles and serve as the only person involved in the buying decision. For more complex purchases, the buying center may include 20 or 30 people from different levels and departments in the organization. One study of business buying showed that the typical business equipment purchase involved seven people from three management levels representing four different departments.[10]

The buying center concept presents a major marketing challenge. The business marketer must learn who participates in the decision, each participant's relative influence, and what evaluation criteria each decision participant uses. For example, Baxter International, the large healthcare products and services company, sells disposable surgical gowns to hospitals. It tries to identify the hospital personnel involved in this buying decision. They are the vice-president of purchasing, the operating room administrator, and the surgeons. Each participant plays a different role. The vice-president of purchasing analyzes whether the hospital should buy disposable gowns or reusable gowns. If analysis favors disposable gowns, then the operating room administrator compares competing products and prices and makes a choice. This administrator considers the gown's absorbency, antiseptic quality, design, and cost, and normally buys the brand that meets requirements at the lowest cost. Finally, surgeons affect the decision later by reporting their satisfaction or dissatisfaction with the brand.

The buying center usually includes some obvious participants who are involved formally in the buying decision. For example, the decision to buy a corporate jet will probably involve the company's CEO, chief pilot, a purchasing agent, some legal staff, a member of top management, and others formally charged with the buying decision. It may also involve less obvious, informal participants,

Industrial buyers respond to more than just economic factors. In this ad, the words stress performance but the illustration suggests a smooth, comfortable ride.

some of whom may actually make or strongly affect the buying decision. Sometimes, even the people in the buying center are not aware of all the buying participants. As the Gulfstream example showed, the decision about which corporate jet to buy may actually be made by a corporate board member who has an interest in flying and who knows a lot about airplanes. This board member may work behind the scenes to sway the decision. Many business buying decisions result from the complex interactions of ever-changing buying center participants.

MAJOR INFLUENCES ON BUSINESS BUYERS

Business buyers are subject to many influences when they make their buying decisions. Some marketers assume that the major influences are economic. They think buyers will favor the supplier who offers the lowest price, or the best product, or the most service. They concentrate on offering strong economic benefits to buyers. However, business buyers actually respond to both economic and personal factors. Far from being cold, calculating, and impersonal, business buyers are human and social as well. They react to both reason and emotion.

When suppliers' offers are very similar, business buyers have little basis for strictly rational choice. Because they can meet organizational goals with any supplier, buyers can allow personal factors to play a larger role in their decisions. However, when competing products differ greatly, business buyers are more accountable for their choice and tend to pay more attention to economic factors.

Figure 6-2 lists various groups of influences on business buyers—environmental, organizational, interpersonal, and individual.[11]

Environmental Factors

Business buyers are influenced heavily by factors in the current and expected *economic environment,* such as the level of primary demand, the economic outlook, and the cost of money. As economic uncertainty rises, business buyers cut back on new investments and attempt to reduce their inventories.

An increasingly important environmental factor is shortages in key materials. Many companies now are more willing to buy and hold larger inventories of

INTERNATIONAL MARKETING MANNERS: WHEN IN ROME, DO AS THE ROMANS DO

Picture this: Consolidated Amalgamation, Inc., thinks it's time that the rest of the world enjoyed the same fine products it has offered American consumers for two generations. It dispatches vice-president Harry E. Slicksmile to Europe to explore the territory. Mr. Slicksmile stops first in London, where he makes short work of some bankers—he rings them up on the phone. He handles Parisians with similar ease: After securing a table at La Tour d'Argent, he greets his luncheon guest, the director of an industrial engineering firm, with the words, "Just call me Harry, Jacques."

Wrong. Six months later, Consolidated Amalgamation has nothing to show for the trip but a pile of bills. In Europe, they weren't wild about Harry.

This hypothetical case has been exaggerated for emphasis. Americans are seldom such dolts. But experts say success in international business has a lot to do with knowing the territory and its people. By learning English and extending themselves in other ways, the world's business leaders have met Americans more than halfway. In contrast, Americans too often do little except assume that others will march to their music. "We

He'd *not* be pleased," explains an expert on French business practices. "It's considered poor taste," he continues. "Even after months of business dealings, I'd wait for him or her to make the invitation [to use first names] . . . You are always right, in Europe, to say 'Mister.' "

Harry's flashy presentation would likely have been a flop with the Germans, who dislike overstatement and ostentatiousness. According to one German expert, however, German businessmen have become accustomed to dealing with Americans. Although differences in body language and customs remain, the past 20 years have softened them. "I hugged an American woman at a business meeting last night," he said. "That would be normal in France, but [older] Germans still have difficulty [with the custom]." He says that calling secretaries by their first names would still be considered rude: "They have a right to be called by the surname. You'd certainly ask—and get—permission first."

When Harry Slicksmile grabbed his new Japanese acquaintance by the arm, the executive probably considered him disrespectful and presumptuous. Harry made matters worse by tossing his business card. Japanese people revere the business card as an extension of self and as an indicator of rank. They do not *hand* it to people, they *present* it—with both hands. In addition, the Japanese are sticklers about rank. Unlike Americans, they don't heap praise on subordinates in a room; they will praise only the highest-ranking official present.

Hapless Harry's last gaffe was assuming that Italians are like Hollywood's stereotypes of them. The flair for design and style that has characterized Italian culture for centuries is embodied in the businesspeople of Milan and Rome. They dress beautifully and admire flair, but they blanch at garishness or impropriety in others' attire.

In order to compete successfully in global markets, or even to deal effectively with international firms in their home markets, American companies must help their managers to

In order to succeed in global markets, American companies must help their managers to understand the needs, customs and cultures of international business buyers.

In Germany, Mr. Slicksmile is a powerhouse. Whisking through a lavish, state-of-the-art marketing presentation, complete with flip charts and audiovisuals, he shows 'em that this Georgia boy *knows* how to make a buck. Heading on to Milan, Harry strikes up a conversation with the Japanese businessman sitting next to him on the plane. He flips his card onto the guy's tray and, when the two say good-bye, shakes hands warmly and clasps the man's right arm. Later, for his appointment with the owner of an Italian packaging-design firm, our hero wears his comfy corduroy sport coat, khaki pants, and Topsiders. Everybody knows Italians are zany and laid back, right?

want things to be 'American' when we travel. Fast. Convenient. Easy. So we become 'ugly Americans' by demanding that others change," says one American world trade expert. "I think more business would be done if we tried harder."

Poor Harry tried, all right, but in all the wrong ways. The English do not, as a rule, make deals over the phone as much as Americans do. It's not so much a "cultural" difference as a difference in approach. A proper Frenchman neither likes instant familiarity—questions about family, church, or alma mater—nor refers to strangers by their first names. "That poor fellow, Jacques, probably wouldn't show anything, but he'd recoil.

understand the needs, customs, and cultures of international business buyers. Here are additional examples of a few rules of social and business etiquette that American managers should understand when doing business abroad.

◆ **France** Dress conservatively, except in the south where more casual clothes are worn. Do not refer to people by their first names—the French are formal with strangers.

◆ **Germany** Be especially punctual. An American businessman invited to someone's home should present flowers, preferably unwrapped, to the hostess. During introductions, greet women first and wait until, or if, they extend their hands before extending yours.

◆ **Italy** Whether you dress conservatively or go native in a Giorgio Armani suit, keep in mind that Italian businesspeople are style conscious. Make appointments well in advance. Prepare for and be patient with Italian bureaucracies.

◆ **United Kingdom** Toasts are often given at formal dinners. If the host honors you with a toast, be prepared to reciprocate. Business entertaining is done more often at lunch than at dinner.

◆ **Saudi Arabia** Although men will kiss each other in greeting, they will never kiss a woman in public. An American woman should wait for a man to extend his hand before offering hers. If a Saudi offers refreshment, accept—it is an insult to decline it.

◆ **Japan** Don't imitate Japanese bowing customs unless you understand them thoroughly—who bows to whom, how many times, and when. It's a complicated ritual. Presenting business cards is another ritual. Carry many cards, present them with both hands so your name can be easily read, and hand them to others in order of descending rank. Expect Japanese business executives to take time making decisions and to work through all of the details before making a commitment.

Sources: Adapted from Susan Harte, "When in Rome, You Should Learn to Do What the Romans Do," *The Atlanta Journal-Constitution,* January 22, 1990, pp. D1, D6. Also see Lufthansa's *Business Travel Guide/Europe;* and Sergey Frank, "Global Negotiating," *Sales & Marketing Management,* May 1992, pp. 64–69.

scarce materials to ensure adequate supply. Business buyers also are affected by technological, political, and competitive developments in the environment. Culture and customs can strongly influence business buyer reactions to the marketer's behavior and strategies, especially in the international marketing environment (see Marketing Highlight 6-3). The business marketer must watch these factors, determine how they will affect the buyer, and try to turn these challenges into opportunities.

Organizational Factors

Each buying organization has its own objectives, policies, procedures, structure, and systems, which must be understood by the business marketer. Questions such as these arise: How many people are involved in the buying decision? Who are

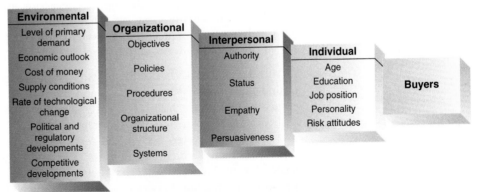

FIGURE 6-2   *Major influences on business buying behavior*

they? What are their evaluative criteria? What are the company's policies and limits on its buyers? In addition, the business marketer should be aware of the following organizational trends in the purchasing area.

UPGRADED PURCHASING.   Purchasing departments have often occupied a low position in the management hierarchy, even though they often manage more than half of the company's costs. However, many companies recently have upgraded their purchasing departments. Several large corporations have elevated the heads of purchasing to the position of vice-president. Some companies have combined several functions—such as purchasing, inventory control, production scheduling, and traffic—into a high-level function called *strategic materials management*. Purchasing departments in many multinational companies have responsibility for purchasing materials and service around the world. Many companies are offering higher compensation in order to attract top talent in the purchasing area. This means that business marketers also must upgrade their salespeople to match the quality of today's business buyers.

CENTRALIZED PURCHASING.   In companies consisting of many divisions with differing needs, much of the purchasing is carried out at the division level. Recently, however, some large companies have tried to recentralize purchasing. Headquarters identifies materials purchased by several divisions and buys them centrally. Centralized purchasing gives the company more purchasing clout, which can produce substantial savings. For the business marketer, this development means dealing with fewer, higher-level buyers. Instead of using regional salesforces to sell to a large buyer's separate plants, the seller may use a *national account salesforce* to service the buyer. For example, at Xerox, over 250 national account managers each handle one to five large national accounts with many scattered locations. The national account managers coordinate the efforts of an entire Xerox team—specialists, analysts, salespeople for individual products—to sell and service important national customers. National account selling is challenging and demands both a high-level salesforce and sophisticated marketing effort.

LONG-TERM CONTRACTS.   Business buyers are increasingly seeking long-term contracts with suppliers. For example, General Motors wants to buy from a small number of suppliers who are willing to locate close to GM's plants and produce high-quality components. Many business marketers also offer *electronic data interchange (EDI)* systems to their customers. When using such systems, the seller links customers' computers to its own, allowing customers to order needed items instantly by entering orders directly into the computer. The orders are transmitted automatically to the supplier. Many hospitals order directly from Baxter using order-taking terminals in their stockrooms.

PURCHASING PERFORMANCE EVALUATION.   Some companies are setting up incentive systems to reward purchasing managers for especially good purchasing performance, in much the same way that salespeople receive bonuses for especially good selling performance. These systems should lead purchasing managers to increase their pressure on sellers for the best terms.

JUST-IN-TIME PRODUCTION SYSTEMS.   Over the past several years, businesses around the world have adopted several innovative manufacturing concepts, such as *just-in-time production (JIT)*, early supplier involvement, value analysis, total quality management, and flexible manufacturing. These practices greatly affect how business marketers sell to and service their customers. For example, just-in-time means that production materials arrive at the customer's factory exactly when needed for production, rather than being stored by the customer until used. It calls for close coordination between the production schedules of supplier and customer so that neither has to carry much inventory.

Business marketers need to be aware of the problems and opportunities that JIT creates. First, buyers can achieve maximum cost savings from JIT only if they receive consistently high-quality goods. Thus, business marketers need to work closely with customers and meet their high quality standards. Second, because JIT involves frequent delivery, many business marketers have set up locations closer to their large JIT customers. For example, Kasle Steel set up a mill within Buick City to serve the General Motors plant there. Also, single sourcing is increasing rapidly under JIT—customers often award long-term contracts to only one or a few trusted suppliers. Thus, whereas General Motors still uses more than 3,500 suppliers, Toyota, which has totally adopted JIT, uses fewer than 250 suppliers. Therefore, JIT means that a business marketer may have to make large commitments to major customers. Finally, JIT requires that the buyer and seller work closely together to speed up the order-delivery process and to reduce costs. Thus, many marketers have set up computerized electronic data interchange systems that link them to their JIT customers.[12]

Interpersonal Factors

The buying center usually includes many participants who influence each other. The business marketer often finds it difficult to determine what kinds of *interpersonal factors* and group dynamics enter into the buying process. As one writer notes: "Managers do not wear tags that say 'decision maker' or 'unimportant person.' The powerful are often invisible, at least to vendor representatives."[13] Nor does the buying center participant with the highest rank always have the most influence. Participants may have influence in the buying decision because they control rewards and punishments, are well liked, have special expertise, or have a special relationship with other important participants. Interpersonal factors are often very subtle. Whenever possible, business marketers must try to understand these factors and design strategies that take them into account.

Individual Factors

Each participant in the business buying decision process brings in personal motives, perceptions, and preferences. These individual factors are affected by personal characteristics such as age, income, education, professional identification, personality, and attitudes toward risk. Also, buyers have different buying styles. Some may be technical types who make in-depth analyses of competitive proposals before choosing a supplier. Other buyers may be intuitive negotiators who are adept at pitting the sellers against one another for the best deal.

THE BUSINESS BUYING PROCESS

Table 6-2 lists the eight stages of the business buying process.[14] Buyers who face a new-task buying situation usually go through all stages of the buying process. Buyers making modified or straight rebuys may skip some of the stages. We will examine these steps for the typical new-task buying situation.

Problem Recognition

Problem recognition
The first stage of the business buying process in which someone in the company recognizes a problem or need that can be met by acquiring a good or a service.

The buying process begins when someone in the company recognizes a problem or need that can be met by acquiring a specific good or service. **Problem recognition** can result from internal or external stimuli. Internally, the company may decide to launch a new product that requires new production equipment and materials. Or a machine may break down and need new parts. Perhaps a purchasing manager is unhappy with a current supplier's product quality, service, or prices. Externally, the buyer may get some new ideas at a trade show, see an ad, or receive a call from a salesperson who offers a better product or a lower price. In fact, in

TABLE 6-2   *Major Stages of the Business Buying Process in Relation to Major Buying Situations*

STAGES OF THE BUYING PROCESS	BUYING SITUATIONS		
	New Task	Modified Rebuy	Straight Rebuy
1. Problem recognition	Yes	Maybe	No
2. General need description	Yes	Maybe	No
3. Product specification	Yes	Yes	Yes
4. Supplier search	Yes	Maybe	No
5. Proposal solicitation	Yes	Maybe	No
6. Supplier selection	Yes	Maybe	No
7. Order-routine specification	Yes	Maybe	No
8. Performance review	Yes	Yes	Yes

Source: Adapted from Patrick J. Robinson, Charles W. Faris, and Yoram Wind, *Industrial Buying and Creative Marketing* (Boston: Allyn & Bacon, 1967), p. 14.

As this Cigna ad shows, business marketers often use advertising to alert customers to potential problems, then show how their products provide solutions.

their advertising, business marketers often alert customers to potential problems, and then show how their products provide solutions.

General Need Description

Having recognized a need, the buyer next prepares a **general need description** that describes the characteristics and quantity of the needed item. For standard items, this process presents few problems. For complex items, however, the buyer may have to work with others—engineers, users, consultants—to define the item. The team may want to rank the importance of reliability, durability, price, and other attributes desired in the item. In this phase, the alert business marketer can help the buyers define their needs and provide information about the value of different product characteristics.

Product Specification

The buying organization next develops the item's technical **product specifications**, often with the help of a value analysis engineering team. **Value analysis** is an approach to cost reduction in which components are studied carefully to determine if they can be redesigned, standardized, or made by less costly methods of production. The team decides on the best product characteristics and specifies them accordingly. Sellers, too, can use value analysis as a tool to help secure a new account. By showing buyers a better way to make an object, outside sellers can turn straight rebuy situations into new-task situations that give them a chance to obtain new business.

Supplier Search

The buyer now conducts a **supplier search** to find the best vendors. The buyer can compile a small list of qualified suppliers by reviewing trade directories,

General need description
The stage in the business buying process in which the company describes the general characteristics and quantity of a needed item.

Product specification
The stage of the business buying process in which the buying organization decides on and specifies the best technical product characteristics for a needed item.

Value analysis
An approach to cost reduction in which components are studied carefully to determine if they can be redesigned, standardized, or made by less costly methods of production.

Supplier search
The stage of the business buying process in which the buyer tries to find the best vendors.

Proposal solicitation
The stage of the business buying process in which the buyer invites qualified suppliers to submit proposals.

Supplier selection
The stage of the business buying process in which the buyer reviews proposals and selects a supplier or suppliers.

doing a computer search, or phoning other companies for recommendations. The newer the buying task, and the more complex and costly the item, the greater the amount of time the buyer will spend searching for suppliers. The supplier's task is to get listed in major directories and build a good reputation in the marketplace. Salespeople should watch for companies in the process of searching for suppliers and make certain that their firm is considered.

Proposal Solicitation

In the **proposal solicitation** stage of the business buying process, the buyer invites qualified suppliers to submit proposals. In response, some suppliers will send only a catalog or a salesperson. However, when the item is complex or expensive, the buyer will usually require detailed written proposals or formal presentations from each potential supplier.

Business marketers must be skilled in researching, writing, and presenting proposals in response to buyer proposal solicitations. Proposals should be marketing documents, not just technical documents. Presentations should inspire confidence and should make the marketer's company stand out from the competition.

Supplier Selection

The members of the buying center now review the proposals and select a supplier or suppliers. During **supplier selection**, the buying center often will draw up a list of the desired supplier attributes and their relative importance. In one survey, purchasing executives listed the following attributes as most important in influencing the relationship between supplier and customer: quality products and services, on-time delivery, ethical corporate behavior, honest communication, and competitive prices.[15] Other important factors include repair and servicing capabilities, technical aid and advice, geographic location, performance history, and reputation. The members of the buying center will rate suppliers against these attributes and identify the best suppliers. They often use a supplier evaluation form similar to the one shown in Table 6-3. The supplier in this example rates excellent on quality, service, responsiveness, and reputation, but only fair on price and delivery. The buyer will now have to decide how important the two weaknesses are and compare these ratings to those of other possible suppliers. The ratings could be redone using importance weightings for the seven attributes.

The importance of various supplier attributes depends on the type of purchase situation the buyer faces.[16] One study of 220 purchasing managers showed that economic criteria were most important in situations involving routine purchases of standard products. Performance criteria became more important in purchases of nonstandard, more complex products. The supplier's ability to adapt to the buyer's changing needs was important for almost all types of purchases.

TABLE 6-3 *An Example of Supplier Analysis*

SUPPLIER ATTRIBUTE	RATING				
	Very poor (1)	Poor (2)	Fair (3)	Good (4)	Excellent (5)
Price competitiveness			X		
Product quality, reliability					X
Service and repair capabilities					X
On-time delivery			X		
Quality of sales representatives				X	
Overall responsiveness to customer needs					X
Overall reputation					X
Average score = 4.29					

Buyers may attempt to negotiate with preferred suppliers for better prices and terms before making the final selections. In the end, they may select a single supplier or a few suppliers. Many buyers prefer multiple sources of supplies to avoid being totally dependent on one supplier and to allow comparisons of prices and performance of several suppliers over time.

Order-Routine Specification

Order-routine specification
The stage of the business buying process in which the buyer writes the final order with the chosen supplier(s), listing the technical specifications, quantity needed, expected time of delivery, return policies, and warranties.

The buyer now prepares an **order-routine specification.** It includes the final order with the chosen supplier or suppliers and lists items such as technical specifications, quantity needed, expected time of delivery, return policies, and warranties. In the case of maintenance, repair, and operating items, buyers may use *blanket contracts* rather than periodic purchase orders. A blanket contract creates a long-term relationship in which the supplier promises to resupply the buyer as needed at agreed prices for a set time period. The seller holds the stock and the buyer's computer automatically prints out an order to the seller when stock is needed. A blanket order eliminates the expensive process of renegotiating a purchase each time stock is required. It also allows buyers to write more, but smaller purchase orders, resulting in lower inventory levels and carrying costs.

Blanket contracting leads to more single-source buying and to buying more items from that source. This practice locks the supplier in tighter with the buyer and makes it difficult for other suppliers to break in unless the buyer becomes dissatisfied with prices or service.

Performance Review

Performance review
The stage of the business buying process in which the buyer rates its satisfaction with suppliers, deciding whether to continue, modify, or drop them.

In this stage, the buyer reviews supplier performance. The buyer may contact users and ask them to rate their satisfaction. The **performance review** may lead the buyer to continue, modify, or drop the arrangement. The seller's job is to monitor the same factors used by the buyer to make sure that the seller is giving the expected satisfaction.

We have described the stages that typically would occur in a new-task buying situation. The eight-stage model provides a simple view of the business buying decision process. The actual process is usually much more complex. In the modified rebuy or straight rebuy situation, some of these stages would be compressed or bypassed. Each organization buys in its own way, and each buying situation has unique requirements. Different buying center participants may be involved at different stages of the process. Although certain buying-process steps usually do occur, buyers do not always follow them in the same order, and they may add other steps. Often, buyers will repeat certain stages of the process.

INSTITUTIONAL AND GOVERNMENT MARKETS

So far, our discussion of organizational buying has focused largely on the buying behavior of business buyers. Much of this discussion also applies to the buying practices of institutional and government organizations. However, these two non-business markets have additional characteristics and needs. Thus, in this final section, we will address the special features of institutional and government markets.

INSTITUTIONAL MARKETS

Institutional market
Schools, hospitals, nursing homes, prisons, and other institutions that provide goods and services to people in their care.

The **institutional market** consists of schools, hospitals, nursing homes, prisons, and other institutions that provide goods and services to people in their care. Institutions differ from one another in their sponsors and in their objectives. For exam-

Government market
Governmental units—federal, state, and local—that purchase or rent goods and services for carrying out the main functions of government.

The government market offers many opportunities for companies. Here Southern Bell markets its services to local and county governments.

ple, Humana hospitals are operated for profit, whereas a nonprofit Sisters of Charity Hospital provides health care to the poor and a government-run hospital might provide special services to veterans.

Many institutional markets are characterized by low budgets and captive patrons. For example, hospital patients have little choice but to eat whatever food the hospital supplies. A hospital purchasing agent has to decide on the quality of food to buy for patients. Because the food is provided as a part of a total service package, the buying objective is not profit. Nor is strict cost minimization the goal—patients receiving poor-quality food will complain to others and damage the hospital's reputation. Thus, the hospital purchasing agent must search for institutional food vendors whose quality meets or exceeds a certain minimum standard and whose prices are low.

Many marketers set up separate divisions to meet the special characteristics and needs of institutional buyers. For example, Heinz produces, packages, and prices its ketchup and other products differently to better serve the requirements of hospitals, colleges, and other institutional markets.

Don Bryant, Southern Bell

"Our customer needs to improve public service.

Whether you're managing a local or county-wide government, the best communications system for the job is our central office-based ESSX® service. It provides cost-effective, centralized communications that can tie all your departments, agencies and locations into one consistent network. And it meets your specific needs. For example, you can cut back on ESSX service in winter when outdoor activity drops and pools and parks are closed. For time-of-day shifts, you can use fewer lines to schools and city hall at night, while providing more lines to fire and police departments. And power failure protection is a standard feature. Since our people are in the telecommunications business 24 hours a day, your people don't have to be. ESSX service gives you and the taxpayer more for every dollar. And it not only helps you get more done, it helps you get more out of the technology you already have in place."
For more information, call 1 800 522-BELL.

Southern Bell's The One To Turn To.

Southern Bell

A *BELL*SOUTH COMPANY

GOVERNMENT MARKETS

The **government market** offers large opportunities for many companies. In the United States alone, federal, state, and local governments contain more than 82,000 buying units. And various levels of government in countries around the world offer vast selling opportunities. Government buying and business buying are similar in many ways. But there are also differences that must be understood by companies that wish to sell products and services to governments. To succeed in the government market, sellers must locate key decision makers, identify the factors that affect buyer behavior, and understand the buying decision process.

U.S. federal government buying units operate in both the civilian and military sectors. Various government departments, administrations, agencies, boards, commissions, executive offices, and other units carry out federal civilian buying. At the same time, the *General Services Administration* helps to centralize the buying of commonly used items in the civilian section (for example, office furniture and equipment, vehicles, fuels) and in standardizing buying procedures for the other agencies. Federal military buying is carried out by the Defense

Department, largely through the *Defense Logistics Agency* and the Army, Navy, and Air Force. In an effort to reduce costly duplication, the Defense Logistics Agency buys and distributes supplies used by all military services. It operates six supply centers, which specialize in construction, electronics, fuel, personnel support, business products, and general supplies. State and local buying agencies include school districts, highway departments, hospitals, housing agencies, and many others. Each has its own buying process that sellers must master.

Major Influences on Government Buyers

Like consumer and business buyers, government buyers are affected by environmental, organizational, interpersonal, and individual factors. One unique thing about government buying is that it is carefully watched by outside publics, ranging from Congress to a variety of private groups interested in how the government spends taxpayers' money. Because their spending decisions are subject to public review, government organizations are buried in paperwork. Elaborate forms must be filled out and signed before purchases are approved. The level of bureaucracy is high and marketers must cut through this red tape.

Noneconomic criteria also play a growing role in government buying. Government buyers are asked to favor depressed business firms and areas; small business firms; minority-owned firms; and business firms that avoid race, sex, or age discrimination. Sellers need to keep these factors in mind when deciding to seek government business.

Government organizations typically require suppliers to submit bids, and they normally award contracts to the lowest bidders. In some cases, however, government buyers make allowances for superior quality or for a firm's reputation for completing contracts on time. Governments also will buy on a negotiated-contract basis for complex projects that involve major R&D costs and risks, or when there is little effective competition. Governments tend to favor domestic suppliers over foreign suppliers, which is a major complaint of international businesses. Each country tends to favor its own nationals, even when nondomestic firms make superior offers. The European Economic Commission is trying to reduce such biases.

Government Buyer Decision Process

Government buying practices often seem complex and frustrating to suppliers, who have voiced many complaints about government purchasing procedures. These include too much paperwork and bureaucracy, needless regulations, emphasis on low bid prices, decision-making delays, frequent shifts in buying personnel, and too many policy changes. Yet, despite such obstacles, selling to the government often can be mastered in a short time. The government is generally helpful in providing information about its buying needs and procedures. Government is often as eager to attract new suppliers as the suppliers are to find customers.

For example, the Small Business Administration prints a booklet entitled *U.S. Government Purchasing, Specifications, and Sales Directory,* which lists thousands of items most frequently purchased by the government and the specific agencies most frequently buying them. The Government Printing Office issues the *Commerce Business Daily,* which lists major current and planned purchases and recent contract awards, both of which can provide leads to subcontracting markets. The Commerce Department publishes *Business America,* which provides interpretations of government policies and programs and gives concise information on potential worldwide trade opportunities. In several major cities, the General Services Administration operates *Business Service Centers* with staffs to provide a complete education on the way government agencies buy, the steps that suppliers should follow, and the procurement opportunities available. Various trade magazines and associations provide information on how to reach schools, hospitals, highway departments, and other government agencies.

Many companies that sell to the government have not been marketing oriented for a number of reasons. Total government spending is determined by elected officials rather than by any marketing effort to develop this market. Government buying has emphasized price, making suppliers invest their effort in technology to bring costs down. When the product's characteristics are specified carefully, product differentiation is not a marketing factor. Nor do advertising or personal selling matter much in winning bids on an open-bid basis.

More companies, such as Rockwell International, Eastman Kodak, and Goodyear, are now setting up separate marketing departments for government marketing efforts. These companies want to coordinate bids and prepare them more scientifically, to propose projects to meet government needs rather than just respond to government requests, to gather competitive intelligence, and to prepare stronger communications to describe the company's competence.[17]

Summary

The *business market* is vast. In many ways it is similar to the consumer market, but the business *market structure* generally has fewer and larger buyers who are more geographically concentrated. Business *market demand* also differs from the consumer market, and tends to be *derived*, largely *inelastic*, and more *fluctuating*. Within these markets, business buyers face more complex purchasing decisions. To handle this complexity, businesses often use more buyers who are better trained and more professional than the typical consumer buyer.

Business buyers make decisions that vary with the three types of buying situations: *straight rebuys, modified rebuys,* and *new tasks*. These tasks are handled by the *buying center,* the decision-making unit of a buying organization, which can consist of many persons playing many roles. As with the consumer marketplace, there are many *environmental, individual,* and *interpersonal factors* that affect business buyers, as well as *organizational factors* that are unique to businesses.

The business buying process can be quite involved, with eight basic stages: *problem recognition, general need description, product specification, supplier search, proposal solicitation, supplier selection, order-routine specification,* and *performance review.* As business buyers grow more sophisticated, marketers must continue to respond in appropriate ways.

The institutional market is very large, consisting of schools, hospitals, prisons, and other institutions that provide goods and services to people in their care. These markets generally have low budgets and captive patrons who can deal only with that particular institution. The government market is also vast and quite diverse. Specialized government buyers purchase products and services for defense, education, public welfare, and other public needs, usually through an open-bidding or negotiated-contract process. A high level of oversight by Congress and other watchdog groups tends to make government purchase decisions slow and deliberate, with many levels of approval needed.

Key Terms

Business market

Business buying process

Buyers

Buying center

Deciders

Derived demand

Gatekeepers

General need description

Government market

Influencers

Institutional market

Modified rebuy

New task

Order-routine specification

Performance review

Problem recognition

Product specification

Proposal solicitation

Straight rebuy

Supplier search

Supplier selection

Systems buying

Users

Value analysis

Discussing the Issues

1. Apple Computer paid top prices for millions of computer memory chips during an industry-wide shortage. Soon afterward, demand for memory dropped, and the chips became cheap and plentiful—leaving Apple with millions of dollars in losses. Suggest how a long-term contract might have helped in this situation.

2. Identify which of the major types of buying situations are represented by the following: (a) Chrysler's purchase of computers that go in cars and adjust engine performance to changing driving conditions, (b) Volkswagen's purchase of spark plugs for its line of vans, and (c) Honda's purchase of light bulbs for a new Acura model.

3. Explain how a marketer of office equipment could identify the buying center for a law firm's purchase of dictation equipment for each of its partners.

4. Discuss the major environmental factors that would affect the purchase of radar speed detectors by statewide and local police forces.

5. NutraSweet and other companies have advertised products to the general public that consumers aren't able to buy. Determine how this strategy might help a company sell products to resellers.

6. Assume you are selling a fleet of cars to be used by a company's sales force. The salespeople need larger cars, which are more profitable for you, but the fleet buyer wants to buy smaller cars. List who might be in the buying center. Outline how you could meet the varying needs of these participants.

Applying the Concepts

1. Many companies that were formerly vertically integrated, producing their own raw materials or parts, are now using outside suppliers to produce them instead. The extreme examples of this practice, such as Dell Computer, own no production facilities and have suppliers make everything to order. This type of company has been nicknamed a "virtual corporation."
   - Determine whether you think that buyers and suppliers are likely to be closer or more adversarial in this type of corporate structure.
   - Name the advantages and disadvantages of this sort of supplier relationship for (a) the buyer and (b) the supplier.

2. American corporations are working to improve quality, and many are using techniques such as Continuous Quality Improvement [CQI]. A major element of CQI is *feedback:* when defects are discovered, the cause of the problem is tracked down and changes are made to prevent problems in the future.
   - List some of the ways using CQI might affect the relationship and information flow between buyers and suppliers.
   - Using CQI also means that purchasing agents become responsible for quality as well as costs. How does this change the role of the purchasing department within the firm?

References

1. Portions adapted from Thomas V. Bonoma, "Major Sales: Who Really Does the Buying," *Harvard Business Review,* May–June 1982. Copyright © 1982 by the President and Fellows of Harvard College; all rights reserved. Quote from John Huey, "The Ab-solute Best Way to Fly," *Fortune,* May 30, 1994, pp. 121–128. Also see William C Symonds and David Greising, "A Dogfight Over 950 Customers," *Business Week,* February 6, 1995, p. 66.

2. This definition is adapted from Frederick E. Webster, Jr., and Yoram Wind, *Organizational Buying Behavior* (Englewood Cliffs, NJ: Prentice Hall, 1972), p. 2.

3. For discussions of similarities and differences in consumer and business marketing, see Edward F. Fern and James R. Brown, "The Industrial/Consumer Marketing Dichotomy: A Case of Insufficient Justification," *Journal of Marketing,* Fall 1984, pp. 68–77; and Ron J. Kornakovich, "Consumer Methods Work for Business Marketing: Yes; No," *Marketing News,* November 21, 1988, pp. 4, 13–14.

4. See James C. Anderson and James A. Narus, "Value–Based Segmentation, Targeting, and Relationship-Building in Business Markets," ISBM Report #12–1989, The Institute for the Study of Business Markets, Pennsylvania State University, University Park, PA, 1989; Lawrence A. Crosby, Kenneth R. Evans, and Deborah Cowles, "Relationship Quality and Services Selling: An Interpersonal Influence Perspective," *Journal of Marketing,* July 1990, pp. 68–81; Barry J. Farber and Joyce Wycoff, "Relationships: Six Steps to Success," *Sales & Marketing Management,* April 1992, pp. 50–58; and Minda Zetlin, "It's All the Same to Me," *Sales & Marketing Management,* February 1994, pp. 71–75.

5. See Louis W. Stern and Thomas L. Eovaldi, *Legal Aspects of Marketing Strategy* (Englewood Cliffs, NJ: Prentice Hall, 1984), pp. 330–331; and Robert J. Posch, Jr., *The Complete Guide to Marketing and the Law* (Englewood Cliffs, NJ: Prentice Hall, 1988), pp. 339–340.

6. Patrick J. Robinson, Charles W. Faris, and Yoram Wind, *Industrial Buying Behavior and Creative Marketing* (Boston: Allyn & Bacon, 1967). Also see Erin Anderson, Weyien Chu, and Barton Weitz, "Industrial Purchasing: An Empirical Exploration of the Buyclass Framework," *Journal of Marketing,* July 1987, pp. 71–86.

7. For more on systems selling, see Robert R. Reeder, Edward G. Brierty, and Betty H. Reeder, *Industrial Marketing: Analysis, Planning, and Control* (Englewood Cliffs, NJ: Prentice Hall, 1991), pp. 264–267.

8. Webster and Wind, *Organizational Buying Behavior,* p. 6. For more reading on buying centers, see Bonoma, "Major Sales: Who Really Does the Buying"; and Donald W. Jackson, Jr., Janet E. Keith, and Richard K. Burdick, "Purchasing Agents' Perceptions of Industrial Buying Center Influence: A Situational Approach," *Journal of Marketing,* Fall 1984, pp. 75–83.

9. Webster and Wind, *Organizational Buying Behavior,* pp. 78–80.

10. Wesley J. Johnson and Thomas V. Bonoma, "Purchase Process for Capital Equipment and Services," *Industrial Marketing Management,* Vol. 10, 1981, pp. 258–259. Also see Philip L. Dawes, Grahame R. Dowling, and Paul G. Patterson, "Factors Affecting the Structure of Buying Centers for the Purchase of Professional Advisory Services," *International Journal of Research in Marketing,* August 1992, pp. 269–279; and Robert D. McWilliams, Earl Naumann, and Stan Scott, "Determining Buying Center Size" *Industrial Marketing Management,* February 1992, pp. 43–49.

11. Webster and Wind, *Organizational Buying Behavior,* pp. 33–37.

12. See Gary L. Frazier, Robert E. Spekman, and Charles R. O'Neal, "Just-In-Time Exchange Relationships in Industrial Markets," *Journal of Marketing,* October 1988, pp. 52–57; Ernest Raia, "JIT in the '90s: Zeroing in on Leadtimes," *Purchasing,* September 26, 1991, pp. 54–57; and Sang-Lin Han, David T. Wilson, and Shirish P. Dant, "Buyer-Supplier Relationships Today," *Industrial Marketing Management,* November 1993, pp. 331–338.

13. Bonoma, "Major Sales," p. 114. Also see Ajay Kohli, "Determinants of Influence in Organizational Buying: A Contingency Approach," *Journal of Marketing,* July 1989, pp. 50–65.

14. Robinson, Faris, and Wind, *Industrial Buying Behavior,* p. 14.

15. See "What Buyers Really Want," *Sales & Marketing Management,* October 1989, p. 30.

16. Donald R. Lehmann and John O'Shaughnessy, "Decision Criteria Used in Buying Different Categories of Products," *Journal of Purchasing and Materials Management,* Spring 1982, pp. 9–14.

17. For more on U.S. government buying, see Warren H. Suss, "How to Sell to Uncle Sam," *Harvard Business Review,* November–December 1984, pp. 136–144; Don Hill, "Who Says Uncle Sam's a Tough Sell?" *Sales & Marketing Management,* July 1988, pp. 56–60; John C. Franke, "Marketing to the Government: Contracts There for Those Who Know Where to Look," *Marketing News,* October 9, 1989, pp. 1, 7; and Mark L. Goldstein, "Customer No. 1: Federal Government Has Voracious Appetite," *Advertising Age,* June 11, 1990, pp. M13–M14.

Company Case 6

ACT II: CONTROLLING AN INDUSTRIAL MARKET

Gregory Pearl, director of marketing for Appliance Control Technology (ACT), listened as Wallace Leyshon, ACT's president and CEO, conducted another meeting with a reporter from a national business magazine. ACT designs, manufactures, and markets touch-sensitive digital controls for home appliances such as microwave ovens, ranges, and washing machines. These controls allow users to direct the operations of appliances without using the traditional buttons and dials.

"My vision is that someday soon the consumer

who owns a midpriced washer and dryer will be able to touch a digital keypad once and the washer or dryer will do everything else. All the consumer will have to do is touch the keypad to tell the unit what types of clothes are inside. For example, once the user tells the washer that the load contains delicate fabrics, it will automatically determine the size of the load, add water at the right temperature, and dispense the correct amount of detergent at the right time. As for the dryer, once the consumer indicates the types of clothes, it will dry the clothes at the correct temperature and cylinder speed, sense the moisture content, and shut off automatically when the clothes are dry. That would save consumers a lot of time and worry, and it would save a lot of energy. Now consumers have to push lots of buttons and turn dials (electromechanical controls), and they have to be experts at knowing the right things to do to wash all kinds of clothes. In fact, significant progress has already been made in this direction in Europe."

"That sounds exciting," the reporter responded, "but is there a *market* for these electronic controls?"

"As you know," Leyshon continued, "the home appliance market is mature—the value of U.S. manufacturers' shipments totaled a little over $18 billion in 1990 and total units sold grew at an average rate of only 5.6 percent per year from 1980 to 1990. The growth rate is only 4.3 percent over that same period if you exclude microwave ovens. But the good news is that only an estimated 20 percent of home appliances offer the consumer touch-sensitive electronic controls, and most of these are high-end appliances. I think we can produce digital controls cheaply enough so that manufacturers can offer them in midrange appliances. There's huge growth potential in the electronic controls market. And there are actually only five customers: General Electric, Whirlpool, Frigidaire, Maytag, and Raytheon. We know our customers. Furthermore, I think final consumers are ready for touch-sensitive controls on electric ranges and other appliances because they've gotten used to using such controls on microwave ovens."

"What's your marketing strategy to get these manufacturers to adopt electronic controls for their appliances?" asked the reporter.

"Gregory and I are continuously reviewing our marketing strategy. In fact, he has just completed some marketing research that we hope will help us make some additional marketing decisions."

"As you are aware," Leyshon continued, "a key part of our strategy is to manufacture our control units in the United States. Manufacturers are very sensitive about the prices of components in their appliances. Conventional wisdom in the controls industry is that you must manufacture in foreign countries, offshore, to keep your costs down. I just don't think this conventional strategy is necessary. Sure, you might save a little money

on wages, but direct labor is only a small percentage of the product's cost. When you go offshore, you add the shipping costs, import-export fees and charges, and additional management personnel. When you look at the whole package, you don't save much money at all, and you make things much more complex. If I build my products in the United States, my research and development, engineering, and production staffs are just a few steps from each other. If a problem develops, we can solve it quickly. That's hard to do over the phone with an engineer who may be thousands of miles away."

The reporter interrupted. "You also mentioned that manufacturers are price sensitive and that they use electronic controls only on their more expensive appliances. How are you going to be price competitive with the standard electromechanical controls?"

Brian Althoff, ACT's vice-president of operations, who had joined the meeting, took up where Leyshon left off. "Another key part of our strategy is standardization. Many control manufacturers design and build controls specifically for one appliance manufacturer, or even for one particular product that the manufacturer offers. This practice causes two problems. First, it increases costs because of all the different controls that are required. Second, it increases development time because the control maker has to design specific controls for each new product or product change. ACT's strategy will be to develop standard controls that a manufacturer can use across model lines. The touchpad will look different, and the products will have different features. But the control unit, microprocessor, components, and circuit boards will be basically the same for all units. We will use software to change the features and functions from unit to unit. This way we can make more controls of the same type, lowering our costs and passing the savings on to the customer."

The reporter was impressed. "That sounds good, but have you done it?"

"Yes," Leyshon answered enthusiastically. "For example, take our contract with a major company to supply controls for its microwave ovens. The company was using 12 different controls. We replaced those with just two controls, one for domestic models and one for export models. We priced our controls significantly lower than the competitive control it replaced. And we think the savings are even greater when you realize that the company and ACT can carry lower inventories because we don't have all these different models. Also, product-development lead times will be shorter."

"What do you mean by product-development lead times?" asked the reporter.

Gregory Pearl explained. "Remember that ACT sells to appliance manufacturers. These manufacturers either sell their own brand of appliances, such as Whirlpool, or they serve as original equipment manufacturers (OEMs) to retailers, such as Sears, selling them private-label brands like Kenmore. If Sears, for example, decides that it wants to offer a new buyer, it will give the OEM's marketing staff suggestions for the new product. The OEM's marketing staff will develop ideas for product features and give those ideas to the engineering staff so that it can develop a preliminary design and give the specifications for the new dryer to its purchasing department. The purchasing department will then send the specifications to suppliers, including control suppliers, who will submit bids to the OEM to supply the parts at certain prices. A series of negotiations then takes place between the suppliers and the OEM on prices and features. By the time all this has happened, it may have been a long time since Sears said it wanted a new dryer.

"If the appliance requires a new control, the maker must design it before it can know how to build and price the control. Or, the control maker may realize that Sear's or the OEM's ideas are outdated, because new technology or competitive products have made them obsolete," Pearl concluded.

"The process is too complicated and too slow," Leyshon interjected. "There's a good chance that by the time Sears's ideas have gone through all these groups, there may have been many communication problems."

"We want to change all this. We think that Sears's product-development staff, the appliance manufacturer's product-development staff, and ACT should all sit down together at the start of the process and jointly develop specifications to meet price and performance objectives. We will all have the same information and the process should go much faster with fewer changes along the way."

"Haven't I read that this is the way the Japanese carry out product development?" the reporter asked.

"That's exactly right, and the Koreans, too," Leyshon agreed. "And we'd better start doing it this way also if we are going to have a chance in what is rapidly becoming a global market."

"Who is your competition?"

"We have two groups of competitors: the electromechanical control makers and the electronic equipment makers. The electromechanical group is trying to convert to the new technology, but it will be a difficult process for them. They'll have to make their own products obsolete, and that's hard for companies to do.

"I'm more concerned about the firms now making electronic controls. We have some competition there, but they are following traditional industry strategies."

The reporter paused briefly, then asked, "You mentioned the size of the home appliance industry, but how big is the controls market?"

"We estimate that the controls market in the United States and Europe is about $2 billion a year with the market equally split between the two," Pearl an-

swered. "In fact, the European market may be a little larger. Electronic controls account for a little less than 50 percent of the market."

"This all sounds very interesting," the reporter remarked as he arose from his chair. "I'd like to look over the material you gave me and set up another appointment for next week. I believe our editor will be very interested in what you are trying to accomplish and may want to make this a feature story. I want to make sure I've understood all you've told me so I can accurately capture your story in the article. Thanks for your time. I'll let you three get back to work."

After the reporter had left, Leyshon, Althoff, and Pearl returned to the conference table.

"Well, what do you think?" asked Pearl.

Leyshon reflected for a moment before responding. "Well, I guess some publicity won't hurt us. If they decide to do the article, I just hope they'll do a good job.

"While I've got you here, tell me what you've concluded from the market research project."

Pearl had been conducting telephone interviews with manufacturers, retailers, and others in the home appliance industry over the last two months to gain insight into industry practices. He had used an open-ended questionnaire (see Company Case 4) as a script for the interviews, and had recorded the information from each interview. He had prepared a set of exhibits summarizing the results.

"First, we interviewed 67 people from manufacturers, such as engineers, marketers, and purchasing agents. We also talked to 20 respondents from retailers, such as buyers, and 15 others with industry knowledge. We were interested in determining the respondents' best estimates of the percentage of appliances using electronic controls by type of appliance for 1991 and their projections for 1996. This exhibit summarizes their estimates (see Exhibit 6-1). I have also summarized the

EXHIBIT 6-1   *Estimated electronic controls penetration rates: 1991 and 1996*

	1991 (%)	1996 (%)	5-Year Change Multiple
Dishwashers	5	10	2.0 times
Dryers, electric	5	15	3.0 times
Dryers, gas	5	15	3.0 times
Microwaves	90	90	1.0 times
Ranges, electric	20	50	2.5 times
Ranges, gas	15	40	2.7 times
Refrigerators	2	5–50	2.5–25.0 times
Washers	5	15	3.0 times
Room air conditioners	10	25	2.5 times

Source: Appliance Control Technology.

respondents' key comments on these pages (see Exhibit 6-2). Finally, I've developed two tables on market shares and price points that may help us (Exhibits 6-3 and 6-4).

Let me give you two a few minutes to familiarize yourselves with these exhibits. Then we can discuss them and begin shaping our strategy."

EXHIBIT 6-2   *ACT market survey results—selected comments made by survey respondents, grouped by functional area*

I. Manufacturers: Engineers
- Suppliers need to tell the story of the electronic system better.
- I feel electronic controls costs are equal to those of electromechanical, or even cheaper if the entire control system is considered.
- An important trend in supplier development . . . is to become involved up front with the manufacturer.
- The issue in electronic controls is not the technology, but the supplier; that is, the technology is reliable.

II. Manufacturers: Marketing
- Two to three years in development is too long for any electronics program.
- Why aren't electronic controls in white goods (stoves, washers, dryers, and so on) as reliable as those in microwave ovens?
- Manufacturers perceive that electronic controls costs are not in line with the benefits provided. There needs to be more parity between cost/benefit.
- If electronic controls were at cost parity, they would quickly replace electromechanical controls.

III. Manufacturers: Purchasing
- Electronics needs to offer some type of feature to encourage customers to pay a premium.
- Consumers need to be convinced of the reliability.
- Suppliers need to be proactive and innovative.

IV. Trade Groups, Including Publishers and Editors
- Electronic controls are the wave of the future.
- Cost is probably the major issue holding back electronics at this time.
- Energy efficiency is now a big problem.

V. Retailers
- Price is a major issue.
- Consumers are frightened by the complexity of electronics. For electronics to gain greater acceptance, they need to be simpler.
- If possible, electronics should get down to just one button. Just load the machine, press the button, and let it run.

Source: Internal research, Appliance Control Technology.

EXHIBIT 6-3   *Market shares for major appliances (%)—1990*

	ELECTROLUX	GENERAL ELECTRIC	MAYTAG	RAYTHEON	WHIRLPOOL	OTHER
Dishwashers	19	35	11	N/A	34	1
Dryers, electric	8	19	15	4	52	2
Dryers, gas	9	13	15	3	55	4
Freezers	32	N/A	22	6	36	4
Ranges, electric	19	47	11	6	15	2
Ranges, gas	20	34	21	20	N/A	5
Refrigerators	19	36	7	9	27	2
Washers	9	15	17	4	52	3

Source: Appliance Magazine.

EXHIBIT 6-4   *Home appliance industry: key brand names by price point*

	MANUFACTURER				
Price Point	**Electrolux**	**General Electric**	**Maytag**	**Raytheon**	**Whirlpool**
Premium-priced	Frigidaire	Monarch	Jenn-Air Maytag	Amana	KitchenAid Bauknecht
Midpriced	Frigidaire Westinghouse	General Electric	Maytag Magic Chef	Caloric Speed Queen	Kenmore Whirlpool
Lower priced	Westinghouse Kelvinator	RCA Hotpoint	Admiral Norge	Caloric	Roper Estate
——	Gibson		Signature		

Source: Merrill Lynch.

QUESTIONS

1. Outline ACT's current marketing strategy. What decisions does ACT need to make?

2. What is the nature of demand in the home appliance industry? What factors shape that demand?

3. What is the nature of the buying decision process in the home appliance industry? How is ACT trying to change that process?

4. Who is involved in the buying center in a manufacturer's decisions concerning appliance controls?

5. What environmental and organizational factors should ACT consider in developing its strategy for dealing with buying centers?

6. What recommendations would you make to help ACT develop its marketing strategy?

Source: Based in part on Tom Richman, "Made in the U.S.A.," in *Anatomy of a Start-Up,* Boston: Goldhirsh Group, Inc., 1991, pp. 241–252. Used with permission. Appliance Control Technology also contributed information for this case.

Video Case 2

THE M/A/R/C GROUP: TALKING TO CUSTOMERS

The M/A/R/C Group is one of the 10 largest marketing intelligence firms in North America. The M/A/R/C Group's primary philosophy of business is building collaborative partnerships with every client. The M/A/R/C Group chooses to be judged based on the success of their customers and clients. This partnership is fostered through a work team approach, meaning that each client has a team of researchers, a senior partner, an account executive, an analyst, a project manager, and staff experts.

Scott Bailey, a senior vice president at M/A/R/C, describes M/A/R/C's approach as follows: "Talking to customers—that is the real service that we offer our clients. Many marketing managers are too far removed from their market. At M/A/R/C we develop custom-designed research to talk to the client's actual or potential customers—we are the link between the client company and its market.

"There are three ways that we contact customers: telephone, mail, and field suppliers. Through our banks of telephone interviewers, we can select representative and probability samples of users, nonusers, and potential users of the product or brand—using random-digit dialing. With computer assisted interviewing, telephone operators can easily switch from one questionnaire to another as research needs change. If clients prefer, we send mail surveys. They are less expensive but take longer to complete. To talk to consumers in person or to show them products, we can use our field suppliers, who can either do mall intercept surveys or telephone households to identify participants willing to come to a central facility for an interview or test.

"Our research techniques and tools are not the critically distinguishing characteristic of our firm. Instead, it's the customization of each client's research and the all-important contact with our client's customers. We can do a lot of sophisticated computer analyses and graphing. And we have well-known models, such as ASSESSOR for forecasting sales and MACRO EXPLORER for identifying target audiences and developing marketing strategies. But what really matters is the customer contact and the quality of the information collected. Did we contact the right consumers? Did we ask them the right questions?

"Suppose a midsized food processing firm has developed a nonfat chocolate dessert product but can't decide if they should market it as a thicker-textured pudding-type product or a lighter, fluffier mousse-type product. To help them determine which product version to market, we could use field work—either mall-intercept surveys or interviews in central facilities. Although mall surveys will get results more quickly, mall samples may not be representative. During the day, it might be all housewives. Besides, different socioeconomic groups patronize different shopping centers. Using telephone solicitation to recruit participants for a central-facility interview produces a more representative sample. However, it takes longer and costs more.

"Once the client knows which product version consumers prefer—let's say the mousse product—it could develop several different product concepts. One concept might play off the more cosmopolitan image of mousse as opposed to pudding. Another might emphasize weight control and focus on the light aspect, such as fewer calories. A third concept might be that mousse is perfect when you just want a little dessert—after lunch, perhaps. To determine the most marketable concept, we can describe the concepts over the telepone or mail a written description to consumers. If consumers must see the product, we could use field operators in a mall or central facility.

"Once the company selects a concept, we could use a HUT (Home Use Test) to predict sales or market share. For these tests, we would recruit respondents through a field operation (mall or telephone) and give them samples of the product to use at home. About a week later, through telephone callback interviews, we would find out how they liked the product and the likelihood of their purchasing it and then use these responses to predict the product's market share. At the same time, we would ask detailed questions about pricing or about where consumers shop for such products to help marketing managers with pricing and distribution decisions.

"After the product is introduced, we can track its success by telephoning randomly selected households to determine if consumers are familiar with nonfat dessert products, which ones they use, and why. If the client requires even more information, we can identify users of the product to determine their satisfaction with it.

"For any marketing problem, we can custom design research that provides the right information so that our clients will make the right marketing decisions. That's why we're here."

QUESTIONS

1. Suppose you were responsible for marketing the new nonfat chocolate dessert. What are the pros and cons of the mall intercept or central facility tests to determine which product version to introduce? Which would you use?

2. What are the pros and cons of the different kinds of concept tests? Which would you use?

3. Why would a firm need both a concept test and a HUT?

4. What are the differences in the two types of surveys described in the next-to-last paragraph? Why would identifying users cost more?

Sources: M/A/R/C company reports and personal interviews with Scott Bailey of M/A/R/C.

Video Case 3

DHL WORLDWIDE EXPRESS

Michael Douglas as Thomas Sanders in the 1994 movie, *Disclosure*: "Maybe you should send some of the problem disc drives to us to check out."

Malaysian Production Manager: "Sure, I'll send them right away—DHL. You should get them tomorrow."

Although DHL may not be a common household name, it is so well known as an international air express carrier that many businesses—even ones made up for the movies—think in terms of "sending it DHL." DHL began as a small San Francisco firm founded by three entrepreneurs—Adrian *D*alsey, Larry *H*illblom and Robert *L*ynn—to shuttle bills of lading between Hawaii and California. Today, DHL Worldwide Express has become a major international carrier serving businesses around the globe. DHL now has 35,000 employees worldwide, serving 224 countries with 9,700 courier vehicles and 137 aircraft, and connecting 19 major hubs and 1,900 service stations. Ironically, DHL is not as well known in its home country as it is in the rest of the world.

DHL uses a worldwide hub-and-spoke system. Packages, letters, and other documents are collected locally and sent to the nearest service center. From there they are sent to a hub, where they are sorted according to destination and transported to service centers in each country. There they are re-sorted and begin the last leg of their journey to a local destination.

The Brussels hub is a prime example of the system. Each night starting at 10:30 P.M., more than 120,000 documents and packages begin arriving at the hub. As the items are unloaded, workers throw them onto $15 million worth of sorting machines, resembling a crazy amusement-park ride. Dozens of conveyor belts whisk the parcels away. As many as 400 people sort packages and put them on other belts, hurrying to get them loaded on trucks and airplanes by 3:00 A.M.

In another room, more than 50 people frantically read paperwork in dozens of languages so that all the parcels can clear customs. Without them, delivery of packages would be delayed. In-house translators and customs clearance services are among DHL's distinguishing characteristics. Another is that DHL hires its own people to deliver documents and packages abroad, in contrast to most other carriers, which hire local agencies. As a result, customers can be certain that their packages will never leave DHL's hands until they reach their locations.

DHL operates a global information network that enables it to track each item throughout its journey. The backbone of this system is DHLNET—a high-speed data network developed jointly by DHL and IBM. DHL employees enter shipment information when packages enter the system. Each package's airway bill has a unique barcoded number that is scanned into DHL's information network at each stage of its journey. The system provides DHL management with information on routing, delivery times, and volumes. Also, it allows many DHL customers, who are linked to the DHL network through the Electronic Data Interchange (EDI) service, to track their own packages directly. DHL also created a system called EasyShip, which lets customers prepare their own shipping documents and maintain databases of customer addresses in-house. DHL will install an EasyShip computer free of charge in the customer's office or provide software that can be used on the customer's computer system.

In addition to its traditional services, such as overnight mail for documents and parcels, same-day service between locations in the United States and to some foreign countries, and international air freight, DHL has become a provider of logistics services. As corporations downsize and attempt to reduce costs, they have begun to reduce their investment in inventories and ware-houses by outsourcing logistics functions. An example is DHL's experience with Japan's Kubota. DHL ware-houses spare parts for Kubota computers. When customers call the Kubota service number, they actually reach DHL, which immediately ships needed parts through the DHL system. Another example is Bendon, Ltd., a New Zealand manufacturer of women's lingerie. In the past, it took 10 days for Bendon to ship goods to Australia. However, through its alliance with DHL, Bendon can now accept orders until 1:00 P.M. for next-morning delivery in Australia. By using DHL's information system, Bendon knows that all its shipments have cleared customs, and it receives delivery reports on all shipments. As a result, Bendon can invoice customers more quickly, improving its cash flow and reducing inventories.

Since the passage of NAFTA, Mexico has become one of the most important non-U.S. markets for air express services. DHL entered Mexico in 1978 and is presently the major carrier there, expediting shipments to 400 Mexican cities. It has in-house customs brokers to provide clearance of goods and to collect all shipping documents for the customer. But competition in Mexico is heating up as hundreds of courier services vie for business there. UPS is making a major push, and the Mexican Postal Service has created Estafeta, Aeroflash, and Mexpost to provide international and domestic services. Some Mexican businesses, unsatisfied with the delivery times and higher prices of private companies, now rely on the Mexican Postal Service. In response, DHL has tried lowering prices by creating special discount tariffs, and it now offers same-day delivery in certain parts of the country.

QUESTIONS

1. What are the major characteristics of DHL's service? Why would each of these be important to a customer?

2. For buyers of DHL's services, what type of buying situation is each of the following?
   a. delivery of letters
   b. use of the EasyShip computer
   c. use of DHL to warehouse and deliver the buyer's product.

3. What sort of environmental influences affect a buyer's decision to use DHL?

Sources: Brian Coleman, "Courier Firms Regroup as Faxes and Factories Alter Delivery Industry," *Wall Street Journal Europe,* May 6, 1993, reprint; Dora Delgado, "Is My Package There Yet?" *Business Mexico,* April 1994, pp. 10–11; John Marcom, "Battle of Zaventem," *Forbes,* April 29, 1991, p. 58; and numerous company-supplied documents. The author gratefully thanks Dean Christon of DHL for his help with this case.

MOTOROLA: JEEPERS, CREEPERS, WHERE'D YOU GET THOSE BEEPERS?

Dr. Niccolette Williamson leaned forward in her seat in University Medical Center's auditorium and studied the overhead being projected on the screen. Dr. Williamson, an ophthalmologist who specialized in cataract surgery, was interested in learning the latest developments in the use of lasers to remove the clouded lens from a patient's eye. Just as the presenter made an important point, Dr. Williamson felt the Motorola Bravo pager on her belt vibrate. Glancing at the display, she recognized her office number and realized that there must be an emergency. She had asked her assistant not to disturb her during this presentation otherwise.

As she stood and picked her way down the row to the aisle, Williamson leaned over and asked a friend to take notes for her, telling him that she had to call her office to check on a patient. Walking up the aisle, she wondered to herself, "How did we ever make it without pagers, and how will we ever get anything done with pagers!"

A few minutes later, Dr. Williamson's daughter Mary prepared to recite her lines from a scene in a play based on John Steinbeck's book, *The Grapes of Wrath*, which the Jefferson High Drama Club was rehearsing. Just as she was about to speak, she heard a beeper emit a tone. The drama instructor looked up from his notes in disgust at this interruption and saw four members of the cast looking at their beepers to see whose beeper signaled. Mary glanced at the display on her neon green Motorola Bravo Express beeper and read, "942-7574 007." She didn't recognize the number, but the "007" was her mother's code.

Mary sheepishly apologized to the drama instructor for having forgotten to put the beeper in the vibrate mode. She asked to be excused to call her mother, suggesting that it must be important.

"Okay, okay. We'll take a short break while Mary makes her call. But you folks have to stop bringing these beepers to practice. We're never going to be ready if our practices keep getting interrupted by all your phone calls. If Shakespeare had encountered this problem, we would have fewer plays."

Mary called her mother, who informed her that she had an emergency operation and that she would be very late getting home.

"You'll have to pick up your brother after soccer practice. Tell your dad that I'll be late. You'll need to help with supper also. Sorry to bother you. Apologize to Mr. Miles for the interruption, but it surely is good to be able to find you at times like this."

BACKGROUND

When Motorola Chairman Robert W. Galvin's father founded the Schaumburg, Illinois, company in 1928, neither he nor those working with him could have foreseen communication technology's rapid advance. Originally, the company manufactured and marketed car radios, taking its name from a combination of the words *motor* and *Victrola* (an early brand name for radios).

During the following years, Motorola entered the television, automotive electronics, semiconductor, pager, and cellular telephone businesses. Intense competition from Japanese electronics firms, however, forced Motorola from the television and even car radio markets. Then, in the mid-1980s, Japanese firms flooded the U.S.

market with higher-quality pagers and cellular telephones, smashing Motorola's virtual monopoly of those two product markets.

Motorola, however, did not roll over and play dead. It learned from the very Japanese companies that were beating it in the marketplace. Under Galvin's leadership, the company dramatically improved product quality, reduced costs through improved manufacturing processes, and fought for market share. It supported these efforts by funneling billions into employee training, capital improvements, and research and development. Further, the company built on its strengths in marketing and software development, areas where its Japanese rivals were not as strong.

Motorola's efforts paid off. It reclaimed a leadership role in both U.S. and international semiconductor markets. The company also developed an especially strong position in the booming cellular phone market. The company separated its cellular phone business from its communications division, which made two-way radios and pagers, and cut development time for new phones in half. In 1989, Motorola introduced the MicroTac cellular phone. The phone was small enough to fit in a coat pocket and flipped open for use. Workers and robots assembled the MicroTac's 400 parts in 2 hours, down from the 40 hours required to assemble a similar phone in 1985. Motorola hoped that MicroTac and its other cellular phones would allow it to capture a significant portion of the estimated 10.5 million new cellular users who would sign up for cellular service between 1990 and 1995.

Also in 1989, Motorola scooped the competition by introducing the first wristwatch pager, a Dick-Tracy-like device developed in cooperation with Timex, which sold for $300. This was quite an achievement for the only remaining American producer of pagers as of 1985. Motorola realized that it had been taking too long to build pagers and that its products had erratic quality. As it did with cellular phones, Motorola revised the entire pager business process, from ordering to delivery. The company adopted the goal of delivering high-quality pagers that it customized to meet the customers' needs, but that also took advantage of economies of scale. Now, 20 minutes after a salesperson enters an order, the automated assembly line that includes 27 robots begins to produce the order. Motorola's efforts resulted in the wristwatch pager and the Bravo and Bravo Express pagers.

How Pagers Work

Motorola does not sell its pagers directly to end users. It sells to companies that the federal government licenses to serve as radio common carriers (RCCs). These firms have radio towers that serve designated geographic areas.

The RCCs sell their pagers in one of three ways. First, they may sell directly to business or nonbusiness end customers by establishing one or more offices in the geographic areas they serve. Customers come into these offices to buy or rent paging units. When they sign up for the service, the company provides each customer with a unique telephone number for his or her pager. The customer pays a monthly fee for use of the pager and usually a small monthly maintenance fee. Second, the RCC may sell through retailers. The company will package a pager and instructions and provide it to a retailer, such as Best Stores, Kmart, or electronics stores. Customers then purchase the pager at the retail store. The package contains usage instructions and an 800 telephone number for the customer to call to initiate service and billing. Third, some RCCs have authorized resellers who sell and initiate service for the customer. Customers may not even be aware of which RCC provides service for their units.

After customers obtain their pagers, they tell the pager's telephone number to people that they want to be able to call the pager. When someone dials the pager's telephone number from any touchtone telephone, the telephone system routes the call to the RCC's radio tower. The caller hears a beep tone and pushes the buttons on the telephone to enter the telephone number that the person with the pager should call. The caller can also enter additional numbers that serve as a code to identify the caller or to communicate other information. Equipment at the tower converts all this information to a radio signal that only the pager with that particular telephone number can receive. If that pager owner has the pager turned on and is in the RCC's service area, he or she will receive the message.

The pager owner will hear one to three beeps, indicating an incoming message, and will see the telephone number and other codes appear on the pager's LCD display. Some pagers offer the option of having the pager vibrate instead of emitting a beep tone. Other pagers can receive and display written messages. These systems require a special terminal to enter the message. Other pagers actually receive the caller's spoken message and broadcast it to the pager wearer. Pagers can store messages for later viewing and can "stamp" them with the time and date received.

Bravo Starts a Trend

Motorola launched the Bravo model in 1987. This pager was no larger than a box of kitchen matches, and each pager worked on a unique combination of an access code and radio frequency. The Bravo's smaller size made it more appealing to users.

When Motorola introduced the Bravo, as for its other pagers, it expected that the target markets would be construction workers and doctors and other medical personnel. These business customers are often in remote locations away from a telephone or must respond to emergencies. Motorola also knew that there would be one unwanted business customer, the illegal drug dealer. Media reports had shown that many drug dealers were using pagers to keep in contact with suppliers or customers. As a result, some school systems banned pagers from their schools. Some sources estimated that, despite the popular culture's association of pagers with drug dealing, only one percent of customers used pagers in this manner.

However, Motorola didn't anticipate nonbusiness customers' interest in pagers. The new pagers attracted nonbusiness customers for several reasons. First, Motorola and the other manufacturers had steadily reduced the pager's size. The user could easily conceal the pager, which could fit in the palm of a hand. It was no longer a bulky box hanging on one's belt; in fact, pagers weighed as little as 4 ounces. Further, the pager could vibrate to inform the customer of a call as opposed to making a loud beep that disturbed others. Second, with increased production volume, manufacturers could reduce prices. Pagers ranged in price from $60 to $120, down from $400 just ten years ago. Third, besides the reduced purchase price, monthly service ranged from $9 to $15 for a basic package that included up to 300 calls per month.

With the lower prices, smaller sizes, and improved features, consumers began to find all sorts of uses for the pager, which they usually called the beeper. Adults realized that they did not have to be doctors or construction workers to afford or need a beeper. Adults with elderly parents, for example, may want a beeper to allow them to stay in contact. Or, they may just need to be available to family, friends, the baby sitter, or childcare centers or schools.

However, teenagers surprised Motorola and the other pager manufacturers by becoming the "hot" market segment. Teenagers who liked to hang out at the local mall for long hours discovered that personal beepers allowed them to keep in touch with friends. Wealthy teenagers realized that they could use the beepers to screen their calls and keep their monthly cellular phone bills under control. Popular teenagers perceived that the beeper allowed their friends to find them no matter where they were. Others noted that their friends could call them directly using the beeper, without having to go through their parents as they would when using the home telephone. Further, although many teenagers bought their own pagers, parents often bought them for their kids so they could find them at mealtime. This allowed kids not to have to tell their parents where they were going to be all the time, because the parents could beep them. Many teenagers could not resist this combination of freedom and access.

No one knows the size of the teenage market, but one major dealer estimated that teenagers accounted for 20 percent of its sales. Industry sources estimated that the total U.S. pager market grew 11 percent, to 4.1 million units in 1992. Another source estimated that the *retail* market (sales to nonbusiness customers) grew 50 percent to 600,000 units in 1992 and that it would reach 3.2 million retail units annually by 1996.

Telocator Network of America, the paging industry's trade association, estimated that Motorola controlled 85 percent of the $500 million annual pager market. Considering rental and leasing fees and monthly service charges, Telocator estimated the pager market to account for $2 billion in annual sales with 12 million pagers in use. Some observers predicted that by the year 2000 there will be 50 million pagers nationwide with most of the growth coming from personal use.

Pager manufacturers and other firms have been quick to react to this trend. In 1991, Motorola introduced the Bravo Express, the first colored pagers. Teenagers found the clear and neon green models so popular that Motorola introduced neon shades of pink, yellow, and blue in 1992. Swatch produced a $250 watch with limited pager features, calling it the Piepser (German for beeper). A blue jeans manufacturer introduced jeans with beeper pockets. One firm tied the pager to satellite technology to allow a person to beep anyone who was near any city in the United States, Canada, and Mexico. Some parents have found this service helpful for keeping in touch with out-of-town college students.

Despite the practical uses for pagers, however, no one could deny the product's image and status features. Having a beeper on one's belt has suddenly become the "in" thing in many high schools, especially in the Northeast. Some observers report that many teenagers continue to wear their beepers although the service agency had stopped service for them because of nonpayment. Other observers report an increase in the theft of garage door openers because they look like pagers when worn! The colored pagers even allow teenagers to make fashion statements.

BACK AT PLAY PRACTICE

Mary Williamson returned to the rehearsal and apologized again to Mr. Miles. Following practice, she realized that she and her friend Susan had been planning to get together early that evening to study for a biology test. Mary thought that she should call Susan to postpone the session until later because of her change in plans. However, Mary didn't know where Susan was and would have to hope that she was at home.

"Guess I'd better encourage Susan to get a beeper," she thought.

QUESTIONS

1. Motorola and other firms are interested in catering to the teenagers who want to use pagers. How would you conduct market research to learn more about this market?

2. How do teenagers' cultural, social, personal, and psychological characteristics affect their consumer behavior with respect to pagers?

3. How will pagers' product characteristics affect their rate of adoption? Would you predict a fast or slow rate of adoption for pagers in the teenage market?

4. Pagers represent a product originally targeted for organizational or business markets that has made the transition to the consumer market. What factors caused this transition? How are the marketing mixes for pagers different between organizational and consumer markets?

5. If an RCC's salesperson knows that local school systems have banned pagers or suspects that a potential teenage customer may be involved in drugs, should the salesperson sell or rent a pager to teenagers?

6. What marketing recommendations would you make to Motorola to help it address the teenage market?

Sources: William J. Hampton, "What Is Motorola Making at This Factory? History," *Business Week*, December 5, 1988, pp. 168D–H; Lois Therrien, "The Rival Japan Respects," *Business Week*, November 13, 1989, pp. 108–118; Jagannath Dubashi, "The Bandit Standoff," *Financial World*, September 17, 1991, pp. 48–50; Jonathan Rabinovitz, "Teen-Agers' Beepers: Communications as Fashion," *New York Times*, March 18, 1991, p. 1A; Cathy Singer, "Now Hear This: The Beeper Has Become a Status Symbol," *New York Times*, June 28, 1992, p. 1LI; William M. Bulkeley, "More and More Teens Can't Live Without Beepers on Their Belts," *Wall Street Journal*, December 7, 1992, p. B5. Motorola also contributed information for this case.

Measuring and Forecasting Demand

7

Qantas, Australia's international airline, has experienced a demand bonanza. Its market area in the Pacific Basin contains some of the fastest-growing economies in the world—including Japan; Australia; and the four newly industrialized countries of Hong Kong, Singapore, South Korea, and Taiwan. Thus, the area's growth rate for air travel far exceeds world averages. Industry forecasts suggest that Pacific Basin air travel will capture a 40 percent share of all international air passenger traffic by the year 2000.

Such explosive growth presents a huge opportunity for Qantas and the other airlines serving the Pacific Basin. However, it also presents some serious headaches. To take *advantage* of the growing demand, Qantas must first *forecast* it accurately and prepare to *meet* it. Air-travel demand has many dimensions. Qantas must forecast how many and what kinds of people will be traveling, where they will want to go, and when. It must project total demand as well as demand in each specific market it intends to serve. And Qantas must estimate what share of this total demand it can capture under alternative marketing strategies and in various competitive circumstances. Moreover, it must forecast demand not just for next year, but also for the next two years, five years, and even further into the future.

Forecasting air-travel demand is no easy task. A host of factors affect how often people will travel and where they will go. In order to make accurate demand forecasts, Qantas must first anticipate changes in the host of factors that influence demand—worldwide and country-by-country economic conditions, demographic characteristics, population growth, political developments, technological advances, competitive activity, and others. Qantas has little control over many of these factors.

Demand can shift quickly and dramatically. For example, relative economic growth and political stability in Japan, Australia, and the other Pacific Basin countries have caused a virtual explosion of demand for air travel there. Ever-increasing numbers of tourists from around the world are visiting these areas. In Australia, for instance, foreign tourism will almost triple during the decade of the 1990s. Also, people from the

OBJECTIVES

When you finish this chapter, you should be able to accomplish the following:

1. Name the different ways of **defining the market.**

2. Discuss **measuring current market demand,** and contrast the differences between the **market-buildup method** and the **market-factor index method.**

3. List and explain several ways of **forecasting future demand,** including a **survey of buyers' intentions, composites of sales force opinions** or **expert opinions, test marketing, time-series analysis, leading indicators,** and **statistical demand analysis.**

Pacific Basin countries are themselves traveling more. For example, almost 12 million Japanese took holidays abroad last year, a 10 percent increase over the previous year. Forecasting demand in the face of such drastic shifts can be difficult.

To make things even more complicated, Qantas must forecast more than just demand. It must also anticipate the many factors that can affect its ability to meet that demand. For example, what airport facilities will be available and how will this affect Qantas? Will there be enough skilled labor to staff and maintain its aircraft? In the Pacific Basin, as demand has skyrocketed, the support system has not. A shortage of runways and airport terminal space already limits the number of flights Qantas can schedule. As a result, Qantas may decide to purchase fewer but larger planes. Fewer planes would require fewer crews, and larger planes can hold more passengers at one time, which can make flights more profitable.

Qantas bases many important decisions on its forecasts. Perhaps the most important decision involves aircraft purchases. To meet burgeoning demand, Qantas knows that it will need more planes. But how many more planes? At about $135 million for each new Boeing 747-400, ordering even a few too many planes can be very costly. On the other hand, if Qantas buys too few planes, it has few short-run solutions. It usually takes about two years to get delivery of a new plane. If Qantas overestimates demand by even a few percentage points, it will be burdened with costly overcapacity. If it underestimates demand, it could miss out on profit opportunities and disappoint customers who prefer to fly Qantas, resulting in long-term losses of sales and goodwill.

Ultimately, for Qantas, the forecasting problem is more than a matter of temporary gains or losses of customer satisfaction and sales—it's a matter of survival. Thus, Qantas has a lot flying on the accuracy of its forecasts.[1]

When a company finds an attractive market, it must estimate that market's current size and future potential carefully. The company can lose a lot of profit by overestimating or underestimating the market. This chapter presents the principles and tools for measuring and forecasting market demand. The next chapter will look at the more qualitative aspects of markets, and at how companies segment their markets and select the most attractive segments.

Demand can be measured and forecasted on many levels. Figure 7-1 shows 75 different types of demand measurement! For example, Motorola, the telecommunications and electronics products giant, might measure demand for five different *product levels:* for a specific model of pager (product item); for its entire line of pagers (product line); for all pagers made by Motorola and its competitors (product category); for its total sales from pagers, cellular phones, computer chips, and other products (company sales); or for the combined sales of Motorola, Intel, NEC, Panasonic, and all other competitors (industry sales). Motorola might also measure demand for a specific customer, territory, region, or country; or for an entire worldwide market. Finally, Motorola might prepare short-range, medium-range, and long-range forecasts for its various product and geographic markets.

Each demand measure serves a specific purpose. Motorola might forecast short-run demand for pagers in United States as a basis for ordering raw materials, planning production, and borrowing cash. Or it might forecast long-run Asian demand for cellular phones as a basis for designing an international market expansion strategy.

FIGURE 7-1 *Seventy-five types of demand measurement (5×5×3)*

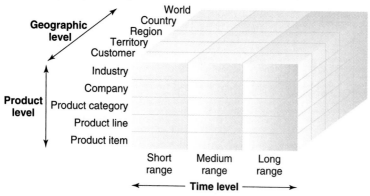

DEFINING THE MARKET

Market demand measurement calls for a clear understanding of the market involved. The term *market* has acquired many meanings over the years. In its original meaning, a market is a physical place where buyers and sellers gather to exchange goods and services. Medieval towns had market squares where sellers brought their goods and buyers shopped for goods. In today's cities, buying and selling occur in shopping areas rather than markets. To an economist, a market describes all the buyers and sellers who transact over some good or service. Thus, the soft-drink market consists of sellers such as Coca-Cola and PepsiCo, and of all the consumers who buy soft drinks.

To a marketer, a **market** is the set of all actual and potential buyers of a product or service. A market is the set of buyers, and an **industry** is the set of sellers. The size of a market hinges on the number of buyers who might exist for a particular market offer. Potential buyers for a product or service have four characteristics: *interest, income, access,* and *qualifications*.

Consider the consumer market for Honda motorcycles. To assess its market, Honda first must estimate the number of consumers who have a potential interest in owning a motorcycle. To do this, the company might contact a random sample of consumers and ask the following question: "Do you have an interest in buying and owning a motorcycle?" If one person out of ten says yes, Honda might assume that 10 percent of the total number of consumers would constitute the potential market for motorcycles.

However, consumer interest alone is not enough to define the motorcycle market. Potential consumers must have enough income to afford the product. They must be able to answer yes to the question: "Can you afford to buy a motorcycle?" The higher the price, the lower the number of people who can answer yes to this question. Thus, market size depends on both interest and income.

Other barriers further reduce motorcycle market size. For example, if Honda does not distribute its products in certain less developed countries, potential consumers in those countries are not available as customers. Or in some markets, sales might be restricted to certain groups. For example, some states or countries might ban the sale of motorcycles to anyone under 18 years of age. In these areas, younger consumers would not qualify as Honda motorcycle customers. Thus, Honda's potential market consists of the set of consumers who have interest, income, access, and qualifications for motorcycles.

To develop effective targeting strategies, and to manage their marketing efforts effectively, companies must be good at both measuring *current* market demand and forecasting *future* demand. Overly optimistic estimates of current or future demand can result in costly overcapacity or excess inventories. Underestimating demand can mean missed sales and profit opportunities.

Market
The set of all actual and potential buyers of a product or service.

Industry
A group of firms that offer a product or class of products that are close substitutes for each other. The set of all sellers of a product or service.

MEASURING CURRENT MARKET DEMAND

We now turn to some practical methods for estimating current market demand. Marketers will want to estimate three different aspects of current market demand—*total market demand, area market demand,* and *actual sales and market shares.*

ESTIMATING TOTAL MARKET DEMAND

The **total market demand** for a product or service is the total volume that would be bought by a defined consumer group in a defined geographic area in a defined

Total market demand
The total volume of a product or service that would be bought by a defined consumer group in a defined geographic area in a defined time period in a defined marketing environment under a defined level and mix of industry marketing effort.

FIGURE 7-2 *Market demand*

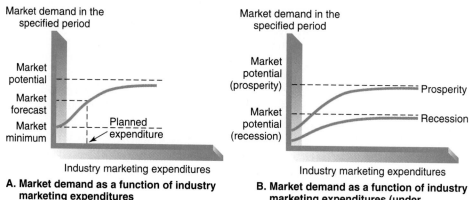

A. Market demand as a function of industry marketing expenditures

B. Market demand as a function of industry marketing expenditures (under prosperity vs. recession)

Market potential
The upper limit of market demand.

Primary demand
The level of total demand for all brands of a given product or service—for example, the total demand for motorcycles.

Selective demand
The demand for a given brand of a product or service.

Operating in a nonexpandable cookie market, Nabisco concentrates on increasing selective demand for its Oreo brand.

POMPADOREO

time period in a defined marketing environment under a defined level and mix of industry marketing effort.

Total market demand is not a fixed number, but a function of the stated conditions. For example, next year's total market demand for ice cream in the United States will depend on how much the makers of Sealtest, Breyers, Häagen-Dazs, Ben & Jerry's, and other brands spend on marketing. It will also depend on many environmental factors, ranging from the level of consumer health concerns to the weather in key market areas. The demand for the premium ice cream brands will be affected by economic conditions.

Part A of Figure 7-2 shows the relationship between total market demand and various market conditions. The horizontal axis shows different possible levels of industry marketing expenditures in a given time period. The vertical axis shows the resulting demand level. The curve shows the estimated level of market demand at varying levels of industry marketing effort. Some minimum level of sales would take place without any marketing expenditures. Greater marketing expenditures would yield higher levels of demand, first at an increasing rate, and then at a decreasing rate. Marketing efforts above a certain level would not cause much more demand. This upper limit of market demand is called **market potential**. The industry market forecast shows the expected level of market demand corresponding to the planned level of industry marketing effort in the given environment.[2]

The distance between the market minimum and the market potential shows the overall sensitivity of demand to marketing efforts. Some markets, such as the market for compact disc players, are *expandable*—their size is strongly affected by the level of industry marketing expenditures. In Figure 7-2A, in an expandable market, the distance between the market minimum and market potential would be fairly large. In a *nonexpandable* market, such as the market for opera, market demand is not much affected by the level of marketing expenditures; the distance between the market minimum and marketing potential would be fairly small.

Companies selling in mature, nonexpandable markets often take **primary demand**—total demand for all brands of a given product or service—as given. They concentrate their marketing resources on building **selective demand**—demand for *their* brand of the product or service. For example, in the United States, where it faces a mature and largely nonexpandable total soft drink market, Coca-Cola directs most of its marketing energies toward building consumer preference for Coke, Diet Coke, Sprite, and its other brands. However, in countries such as China or Russia, which are characterized by huge but largely untapped market potential, Coca-Cola attempts to build the primary demand for soft drinks, as well as preference for its own brands.

Different marketing environments produce different market demand curves. For example, the market for new cars is stronger during prosperity than during recession. Figure 7-2B shows the relationship of market demand to the environment. A given level of marketing expenditure always results in more demand during prosperity than it does during a recession. The main point is that marketers should carefully define the situation for which they are estimating market demand.

Companies have developed various practical methods for estimating total market demand. We will illustrate two here. Suppose Warner Communications Company wants to estimate the total annual sales of recorded compact discs. A common way to estimate total market demand is as follows:

$$Q = n \times q \times p$$

where

Q = total market demand

n = number of buyers in the market

q = quantity purchased by an average buyer per year

p = price of an average unit

Thus, if there are 100 million buyers of compact discs each year, the average buyer buys six discs a year, and the average price is \$14, then the total market demand for discs is \$8.4 billion (= 100,000,000 × 6 × \$14).

A variation of this approach is the *chain ratio method*. This method involves multiplying a base number by a chain of adjusting percentages. For example, suppose Thompson Consumer Electronics (TCE) wants to estimate the market potential for its new RCA Digital Satellite System. This system uses a small 18-inch wide home satellite dish mounted on a rooftop, windowsill, or porch railing to receive digital television signals relayed from two high power satellites in space. System prices start at \$700 for the satellite dish, decoder box, and remote control. Customers can subscribe to more than 150 channels, all with crystal-clear digital quality pictures and CD-quality sound. Initially, TCE will target households in small towns and rural areas where cable TV is limited or lacking. TCE can make a U.S. demand estimate for the RCA Digital Satellite System using a chain of calculations like the following:

Estimating total market demand for a new product like RCA's Digital Satellite System presents a difficult challenge.

Total number of U.S. households

× The percentage of U.S. households located in small towns and rural areas not served well by cable television

× The percentage of these small town and rural households with moderate or heavy television usage

× The percentage of moderate or heavy usage households with enough discretionary income to buy RCA's home satellite dish

This simple chain of calculations would provide only a rough estimate of potential demand. However, more detailed chains involving additional segments and other qualifying factors would yield more accurate and refined estimates.[3]

ESTIMATING AREA MARKET DEMAND

Companies face the problem of selecting the best sales territories and allocating their marketing budget optimally among these territories. Therefore, they need to estimate the market potential of different cities, states, and countries (see Marketing Highlight 7-1). Two major methods are available: the *market-buildup method*, which is used primarily by business goods firms, and the *market-factor index method*, which is used primarily by consumer goods firms.

Market-Buildup Method

Market-buildup method
A forecasting method that calls for identifying all the potential buyers in each market and estimating their potential purchases.

The **market-buildup method** calls for identifying all the potential buyers in each market and estimating their potential purchases. Suppose a manufacturer of mining instruments developed an instrument that can be used in the field to test the actual proportion of gold content in gold-bearing ores. By using it, miners would not waste their time digging deposits of ore containing too little gold to be commercially profitable. The manufacturer wants to price the instrument at $1,000. It sees each mine as buying one or more instruments, depending on the mine's size. The company wants to determine the market potential for this instrument in each mining state. It would hire a salesperson to cover each state that has a market potential of over $300,000. The company wants to start by finding the market potential in Colorado.

To estimate the market potential in Colorado, the manufacturer can consult the Standard Industrial Classification (SIC) developed by the U.S. Bureau of the Census. The SIC is the government's coding system that classifies industries, for purposes of data collection and reporting, according to the product produced or operation performed. Each major industrial group is assigned a two-digit code—metal mining bears the code number 10. Within metal mining are further breakdowns into three-digit SIC numbers (the gold and silver ores category has the code number 104). Finally, gold and silver ores are subdivided into further SIC groups, with four-digit code numbers (lode gold is 1042, and placer gold is 1043). Our manufacturer is interested in gold mines that mine both lode deposits (those mined from underground) and placer deposits (those mined by dredging or washing).

Next, the manufacturer can turn to the Census of Mining to determine the number of gold-mining operations in each state, their locations within the state, and the number of employees, annual sales, and net worth. Using the data on Colorado, the company prepares the market potential estimate shown in Table 7-1. Column 1 classifies mines into three groups based on the number of employees. Column 2 shows the number of mines in each group. Column 3 shows the potential number of instruments that mines in each size class might buy. Column 4

TABLE 7-1 *Market-Buildup Method Using SIC: Instrument Market Potential in Colorado*

SIC	(1) Number of employees	(2) Number of mines	(3) Potential Number of instruments per size class	(4) Unit market potential (2 × 3)	(5) Dollar market potential (at $1,000 each)
1042 (lode deposits)	Under 10	80	1	80	
	10 to 50	50	2	100	
	Over 50	20	4	80	
		150		260	$260,000
1043 (placer deposits)	Under 10	40	1	40	
	10 to 50	20	2	40	
	Over 50	10	3	30	
		70		110	110,000
					$370,000

KFC FINDS MORE POTENTIAL IN ASIA THAN IN THE UNITED STATES

Kentucky Fried Chicken's success in Asia dramatizes the case for becoming a global firm. Had PepsiCo's KFC Corporation remained only a domestic U.S. business, its overall fortunes would have fallen. In 1991, for example, its U.S. sales fell 5 percent as health-minded American consumers reduced their intake of fried foods and as other fast-food competitors moved up.

Not so in Asia. KFC, not McDonald's, is the fast-food leader in China, South Korea, Malaysia, Thailand, and Indonesia, and it is second only to McDonald's in Japan and Singapore. KFC's 1,470 outlets average $1.2 million per store, about 60 percent more than its average U.S. stores. In Tiananmen Square, KFC operates its busiest outlet, a 701-seat restaurant serving 2.5 million customers a year. No wonder KFC plans to double its number of Asian outlets during the next five years.

Why is KFC so successful in Asia? First, many of the large Asian cities have a growing concentration of young middle-class urban workers with rising incomes. Fast-food outlets represent a step up from buying food at hawkers' stalls, and Asians are willing to pay more for the quality, comfort, and prestige of sitting in a trendy, air-conditioned, well-decorated, American-style restaurant. Second, Asian women have been entering the labor force in large numbers, leaving them with less time for cooking meals at home. Third,

chicken is more familiar to the Asian palate than pizza, and more available than beef. Further, chicken faces none of the religious strictures that beef faces in India or that pork faces in Muslim countries.

KFC is growing faster in Asia than in the United States.

KFC serves its standard chicken, mashed potatoes, and cole slaw throughout Asia but has offered a few adaptations, such as Hot Wings (a spicier chicken) in Thailand, and fried fish and chicken curry in Japan.

Through its rapid expansion into Asia, and into many other parts of the world, KFC now reaps more than one-half of its sales from outside the United States. Clearly, companies must increasingly view the world as their market. They must identify those areas that promise the greatest potential sales and profit growth, whether in their neighborhood, state, nation, or the world beyond.

Source: See Andrew Tanzer, "Hot Wings Take Off," *Forbes,* January 18, 1993, p. 74; and Greg Ferrell, "The World on a String," *Brandweek,* October 11, 1993, pp. 26–30.

shows the unit market potential (column 2 times column 3). Finally, column 5 shows the dollar market potential, given that each instrument sells for $1,000. Colorado has a market potential of $370,000. Therefore, the mining instrument manufacturer should hire one salesperson for Colorado. In the same way, companies in other industries can use the market-buildup method to estimate market potential in specific market areas.

Market-Factor Index Method

Consumer goods companies also have to estimate area market potentials. Consider the following example: A manufacturer of men's dress shirts wishes to evaluate its sales performance relative to market potential in several major market areas, starting with Indianapolis. It estimates total national potential for dress shirts at about $2 billion per year. The company's current nationwide sales are

$140 million, about a 7 percent share of the total potential market. Its sales in the Indianapolis metropolitan area are $1,100,000. It wants to know whether its share of the Indianapolis market is higher or lower than its national 7 percent market share. To find this out, the company first needs to calculate market potential in the Indianapolis area.

Market-factor index method A forecasting method that identifies market factors that correlate with market potential and combines them into a weighted index.

A common method for calculating area market potential is the **market-factor index method,** which identifies market factors that correlate with market potential and combines them into a weighted index. An excellent example of this method is called the *buying power index,* which is published each year by *Sales & Marketing Management* magazine in its *Survey of Buying Power.*[4] This survey estimates the buying power, or "ability to buy," for each region, state, and metropolitan area of the nation. Table 7-2 shows sample tables from this survey. The

TABLE 7-2 *Sample Tables from Sales & Marketing Management's Survey of Buying Power*

S&MM ESTIMATES: 12/31/92	POPULATION							
METRO AREA County City	**Total Pop. (Thousands)**	**% of U.S.**	**Median Age of Pop.**	**% of Population by Age Group**				**Households (Thousands)**
				18–24 Years	**25–34 Years**	**35–49 Years**	**50 & Over**	
INDIANAPOLIS	**1,452.3**	**.5596**	**33.3**	**9.3**	**17.0**	**22.7**	**24.4**	**558.7**
Boone	39.1	.0150	35.4	6.8	14.9	24.5	26.2	14.3
Hamilton	127.0	.0490	33.6	6.9	16.1	27.1	20.7	45.6
Hancock	48.6	.0187	35.3	7.9	13.8	25.9	24.7	17.1
Hendricks	81.2	.0313	34.2	8.0	15.3	25.6	23.1	27.9
Johnson	96.6	.0372	33.6	9.5	15.4	24.4	23.4	34.6
Madison	131.9	.0509	35.9	9.6	14.1	22.6	28.8	50.3
•Anderson	60.9	.0235	35.3	11.0	14.2	19.9	30.6	24.9
Marion	827.6	.3188	32.6	10.0	18.6	21.2	24.4	333.2
•Indianapolis	760.7	.2931	32.5	10.1	18.5	21.1	24.2	305.4
Morgan	58.8	.0227	33.9	8.7	14.8	23.9	24.5	20.5
Shelby	41.5	.0160	34.0	8.4	15.4	22.2	26.3	15.2
SUBURBAN TOTAL	630.7	.2430	34.3	8.2	15.5	24.8	24.2	228.4

S&MM ESTIMATES: 12/31/92	RETAIL SALES BY STORE GROUP					
METRO AREA County City	**Total Retail Sales ($000)**	**Food ($000)**	**Eating & Drinking Places ($000)**	**General Mdse. ($000)**	**Furniture/ Furnish. Appliance ($000)**	**Automotive ($000)**	**Drug ($000)**
INDIANAPOLIS	**13,710,089**	**1,877,649**	**1,514,931**	**1,805,793**	**774,565**	**3,381,980**	**494,470**
Boone	249,699	37,276	27,593	13,981	44,955	39,230	12,434
Hamilton	925,550	156,658	107,901	94,495	52,009	222,923	33,831
Hancock	240,751	41,507	23,609	16,764	5,881	79,096	11,701
Hendricks	454,296	111,458	45,397	62,603	12,860	94,041	11,482
Johnson	820,421	87,504	78,325	213,525	35,232	194,708	24,473
Madison	998,254	163,919	105,904	135,820	42,849	270,339	48,233
•Anderson	703,096	120,754	81,947	92,417	33,884	177,290	32,772
Marion	9,458,444	1,149,343	1,066,979	1,216,403	559,249	2,354,765	328,378
•Indianapolis	9,078,224	1,065,874	1,007,601	1,193,042	545,347	2,287,304	315,786
Morgan	332,523	68,057	38,408	18,306	10,898	82,311	12,879
Shelby	230,151	61,927	20,815	33,896	10,632	44,567	11,059
SUBURBAN TOTAL	3,928,769	691,021	425,383	520,334	195,334	917,386	145,912

TABLE 7-2 *Continued*

S&MM ESTIMATES: 12/31/92

METRO AREA County City	Total EBI ($000)	Median Hsld. EBI	% of Hslds. by EBI Group: (A) $10,000–$19,999 (B) $20,000–$34,999 (C) $35,000–$49,999 (D) $50,000 & Over				Buying Power Index
			A	B	C	D	
INDIANAPOLIS	24,950,845	37,565	14.3	22.7	20.2	33.5	.6089
Boone	772,234	43,366	11.8	19.6	19.6	41.5	.0159
Hamilton	2,839,730	52,150	7.9	17.3	17.8	52.7	.0572
Hancock	817,957	43,097	12.0	20.3	22.1	40.0	.0169
Hendricks	1,462,208	47,950	9.5	18.0	20.6	47.2	.0304
Johnson	1,781,629	44,587	11.0	20.1	20.4	42.8	.0406
Madison	1,712,431	28,870	19.8	25.2	18.9	21.6	.0452
•Anderson	754,015	24,587	22.0	25.5	16.5	16.7	.0239
Marion	14,037,509	35,171	15.3	24.0	20.4	29.9	.3686
•Indianapolis	12,784,164	35,020	15.4	23.8	20.2	29.9	.3429
Morgan	887,902	39,371	13.9	22.1	22.7	34.1	.0199
Shelby	639,245	37,258	14.6	23.8	22.6	31.0	.0142
SUBURBAN TOTAL	11,412,666	42,657	12.0	20.9	20.7	40.1	.2421

Source: Sales & Marketing Management, August 30, 1994, pp. C50–C53.

buying power index is based on three factors: the area's share of the nation's *population, effective buying income,* and *retail sales.* The buying power index (BPI) for a specific area is given by

BPI = .2 × percentage of national population in the area

+ .5 × the percentage of effective buying income in the area

+ .3 × percentage of national retail sales in the area

Using this index, the shirt manufacturer looks up the Indianapolis metropolitan area and finds that this market has .5561 percent of the nation's population, .5847 percent of the nation's effective buying income, and .6332 percent of the nation's retail sales. Thus, buying power index for Indianapolis is:

BPI = (.2 × .5561) + (.5 × .5847) + (.3 × .6332) = .5935

That is, Indianapolis should account for .5935 percent of the nation's total potential demand for dress shirts. Because the total national potential is $2 billion each year, total potential in Indianapolis equals $2 billion × .005935 = $11,870,000. Thus, the company's sales in Indianapolis of $1,100,000 amount to a $1,100,000 ÷ $11,870,000 = 9.3 percent share of area market potential. Comparing this with its 7 percent national share, the company appears to be doing better in Indianapolis than in other parts of the country.

The weights used in the buying power index are somewhat arbitrary. They apply mainly to consumer goods that are neither low-priced staples nor high-priced luxury goods. Other weights can be used. Also, the manufacturer would want to adjust the market potential for additional factors, such as level of competition in the market, local promotion costs, seasonal changes in demand, and unique local market characteristics.

A NEW TOOL FOR REFINING MARKET DEMAND ESTIMATES AND CHOOSING THE BEST MARKET TARGETS

Several business information services have arisen to help marketing planners link U.S. Census data with lifestyle patterns to better refine their estimates of market potential down to ZIP code levels, neighborhoods, and even blocks. Among the leading services are PRIZM (by Claritas) and ClusterPLUS (by Donnelley Marketing Information Services). These "geodemographic" data services can help marketing planners find the best ZIP code areas in which to concentrate their marketing efforts.

Using a host of demographic and socioeconomic factors drawn from the U.S. Census data, the PRIZM system has classified every one of the over 500,000 U.S. neighborhood markets into one of 62 clusters.

> You're 35 years old. The price tag on your suits shows that you're a success. You drive a Volvo. You know your way around the olive-oil section of the store, buy fresh-ground coffee, and go on scuba-diving trips. You're living out your own, individual version of the good life in the suburbs. You're unique—not some demographic cliche. Wrong. You're a prime example of [PRIZM's] "Kids & Cul-de-Sacs" .... If you consume, you can't hide from Zip Code seer Claritas.

The "kids & cul-de-sacs" cluster points to a new migration to the suburbs. Other PRIZM clusters include "blue blood estates," "money and brains," "young literati," "shotguns and pickups," "tobacco roads," "American dreams," and "grey power." The clusters were formed by manipulating characteristics such as education, income, occupation, family life cycle, housing, ethnicity, and urbanization. For example, "blue blood estates"

neighborhoods are suburban areas populated mostly by active, college-educated, successful managers and professionals. They include some of America's wealthiest neighborhoods, areas characterized by low household density, highly homogeneous residents, a heavy family orientation, and mostly single-unit housing. In contrast, the "shotguns and pickups" clusters include the hundreds of small villages and four-corners towns that dot America's rural areas. "American dreams" reflects new waves of American immigrants; "young literati" taps Generation X. Each of the other clusters has a unique combination of characteristics.

Companies can combine these geodemographic PRIZM clusters with other data on product and service usage, media usage, and lifestyles to get a better picture of specific market areas. For example, the "shotguns and pickups" cluster is populated by lower-middle-class, blue-collar consumers who use chain saws and snuff and buy more canning jars, dried soups, and powdered soft drinks. The "Hispanic mix" cluster prefers high-quality dresses, nonfilter cigarettes, and lip gloss. People in this cluster are highly brand conscious, quality conscious, and brand loyal. They have a strong family and home orientation. Such information provides a powerful tool for refining demand estimates, selecting target markets, and shaping promotion messages.

One large packaged-goods company used Donnelley's Cluster-PLUS system in combination with Nielsen television ratings and data from Simmons Market Research Bureau to more effectively market an ingredient used in baking cakes and cookies. The company first identified

the geodemographic clusters most likely to contain consumers who regularly bake from scratch. According to Simmons data, the top-ranking cluster is "Low-Mobility Rural Families"—39 percent of this group bake heavily from scratch, far greater than the 17 percent national average. Merging the ten highest-ranking clusters, the company identified the best prospects as older, rural, and blue-collar consumers in the South and Midwest.

Next, using Nielsen ratings, the company examined the television viewing habits of the ten best clusters. It turns out that the from-scratch bakers watch many highly rated programs, but some less popular programs are also popular with this group. The packaged-goods company improved its efficiency by running ads only on programs reaching large concentrations of from-scratch bakers, regardless of the size of the total audience. Thus, the ClusterPLUS-Simmons-Nielsen connection resulted in a basic shift in the company's television advertising, from a mass-media, "shotgun" approach to a more highly targeted one.

Sources: Quote from Christina Del Valle, "They Know Where You Live—And How You Buy," *Business Week,* February 7, 1994, p. 89. Also see Michael J. Weiss, *The Clustering of America* (New York: Harper & Row, 1988); Martha Farnsworth Riche, "New Frontiers for Geodemographics," *American Demographics,* June 1990, p. 20; Leon G. Schiffman and Leslie Lazar Kanuk, *Consumer Behavior,* 4th ed. (Englewood Cliffs, NJ: Prentice Hall, 1991), Chap. 13; and Susan Mitchell, "Birds of a Feather," *American Demographics,* February 1995, p. 40.

Many companies compute additional area demand measures. Marketers now can refine state-by-state and city-by-city measures down to census tracts or ZIP codes. Census tracts are small areas about the size of a neighborhood, and ZIP code areas (designated by the U.S. Post Office) are larger areas, often the size of small towns. Information on population size, family income, and other characteristics is available for each type of unit. Marketers can use this data to estimate demand in neighborhoods or other smaller geographic units within large cities.

Marketing Highlight 7-2 describes some marketing firms that provide ZIP code or census information useful for refining market demand estimates and for improving customer targeting.

ESTIMATING ACTUAL SALES AND MARKET SHARES

Besides estimating total and area demand, a company will want to know the actual industry sales in its market. Thus, it must identify its competitors and estimate their sales.

Industry's trade associations often collect and publish total industry sales, although not individual company sales. In this way, each company can evaluate its performance against the industry as a whole. Suppose the company's sales are increasing at a rate of 5 percent a year and industry sales are increasing at 10 percent. This company actually is losing its relative standing in the industry.

Another way to estimate sales is to buy reports from marketing research firms that audit total sales and brand sales. For example, Nielsen, IRI, and other marketing research firms use scanner data to audit the retail sales of various product categories in supermarkets and drug stores, and they sell this information to interested companies. A company can obtain data on total product category sales as well as brand sales. It can compare its performance with that of the total industry or any particular competitor to see whether it is gaining or losing in its relative standing.[5]

FORECASTING FUTURE DEMAND

Forecasting
The art of estimating future demand by anticipating what buyers are likely to do under a given set of conditions.

Having looked at ways to estimate current market demand, we now examine ways to forecast future demand. **Forecasting** is the art of estimating future demand by anticipating what buyers are likely to do under a given set of future conditions. Very few products or services lend themselves to easy forecasting. Those that do generally involve a product with steady sales, or sales growth, in a stable competitive situation. But most markets do not have stable total and company demand, so good forecasting becomes a key factor in company success. Poor forecasting can lead to overly large inventories, costly price markdowns, or lost sales due to items being out of stock. The more unstable the demand, the more the company needs accurate forecasts and elaborate forecasting procedures.

Companies commonly use a three-stage procedure to arrive at a sales forecast. First they make an *environmental forecast,* followed by an *industry forecast,* followed by a *company sales forecast.* The environmental forecast calls for projecting inflation, unemployment, interest rates, consumer spending and saving, business investment, government expenditures, net exports, and other environmental events important to the company. The result is a forecast of gross domestic product, which is used along with other indicators to forecast industry sales. Then the company prepares its sales forecast by assuming that it will win a certain share of industry sales.

Companies use several specific techniques to forecast their sales. Table 7-3 lists many of these techniques.[6] All forecasts are built on one of three information bases: what people say, what people do, or what people have done. The first basis—*what people say*—involves surveying the opinions of buyers or those close to them, such as salespeople or outside experts. It

TABLE 7-3 *Common Sales Forecasting Techniques*

BASED ON:	METHODS
What people say	Surveys of buyers' intentions
	Composite sales force opinions
	Expert opinion
What people do	Test markets
What people have done	Time-series analysis
	Leading indicators
	Statistical demand analysis

Forecasting is the art of estimating future demand, generally no easy task. When Burger King licensed action figures from the hit Disney movie, The Lion King, *demand was triple the forecasted amount. At the same time, McDonald's featured Happy Meal toys from* The Flintstones *movie, a failure at the box office.*

includes three methods: surveys of buyer intentions, composites of salesforce opinions, and expert opinion. Building a forecast on *what people do* involves putting the product into a test market to assess buyer response. The final basis—*what people have done*—involves analyzing records of past buying behavior or using time-series analysis or statistical demand analysis.

SURVEY OF BUYERS' INTENTIONS

One way to forecast what buyers will do is to ask them directly. This suggests that the forecaster should survey buyers. Surveys are especially valuable if the buyers have clearly formed intentions, will carry them out, and can describe them to interviewers. However, this is sometimes not the case, and marketers must be careful when using consumer survey data to make forecasts (see Marketing Highlight 7-3).

Several research organizations conduct periodic surveys of consumer buying intentions. These organizations ask questions like the following:

Do you intend to buy an automobile within the next six months?

0	.1	.2	.3	.4	.5	.6	.7	.8	.9	1.0
No chance		Slight chance		Fair chance		Good chance		Strong chance		For certain

This is called a *purchase probability scale*. In addition, the various surveys ask about the consumer's present and future personal finances, and his or her expectations about the economy. The various bits of information are combined into a *consumer sentiment measure* (Survey Research Center of the University of Michigan) or a *consumer confidence measure* (Sindlinger and Company). Consumer durable goods companies subscribe to these indexes to help them anticipate major shifts in consumer buying intentions so that they can adjust their production and marketing plans accordingly.

For *business buying,* various agencies carry out intention surveys about plant, equipment, and materials purchases. The two best-known surveys are conducted by the U.S. Department of Commerce and McGraw-Hill. Most of the estimates have been within 10 percent of the actual outcomes.

SnackWell's: The Inexact Science of Forecasting Demand

Was it making the best of a poor forecast, or was it a ploy that was planned all along? That's what most marketers want to know about Nabisco's Snack-Well's Devil's Food Cookie Cakes, but probably never will.

In August 1992, Nabisco launched its SnackWell's line, made up of six cookie and crackers products. Aimed at the health-conscious consumer, each item was fat-free or made with reduced fat. The most popular, by far, turned out to be the Devil's Food Cookie Cakes. They were so popular, in fact, that six months after hitting store shelves, they were out of stock. However, that didn't stop the demand for them.

Ravenous consumers followed SnackWell's delivery trucks and harassed drivers who wouldn't sell them cookies by the case. After being stopped and verbally assaulted by disappointed shoppers, smart retailers hid their supplies of Devil's Food Cookie Cakes behind courtesy booths. They would dole out the 50-calorie cookies only to those who asked. People in Florida formed "cookie pools" for the boxes of 12, which sell for about $2.20. Whenever a member chanced upon the cookies, she would buy the store's entire supply and distribute it to her fellow cookie monsters.

Nabisco quickly launched its "cookie man" advertising campaign to explain why it couldn't meet customer demand and to persuade customers to try another product in the line—one that was still on store shelves. Each "cookie man" commercial told a different story about a SnackWell's employee set upon by persistent women who wanted the SnackWell's cookies. For example, one commercial featured a SnackWell's delivery man ambushed by three women eager to buy SnackWell's Creme Sandwich cookies. Much to the driver's dismay, the truck broke down. He ended up sharing the cookies, exclaiming, "Cookie man, you'd better bake some more."

In early 1993, Nabisco also ran a full-page advertisement in *USA Today* apologizing for the dearth of Devil's Food. As an alternative, it suggested that consumers try the newest SnackWell's introductions, Creme Sandwich Cookies or Cracked Pepper Crackers. Nabisco also conducted in-store sampling and a national coupon campaign. Three months later, it used the same strategy—sorry we can't give you what you want but try this new item—to launch its Chocolate Sandwich Cookie, which is now the brand's top selling product. Since the SnackWell's brand was launched, the number of products in the line has almost doubled. In 1993, retail sales of the brand surpassed $220 million.

While such sales success sounds too good to be born out of faulty market research, the company insists this is the case. Before Nabisco launched its new product line, it conducted extensive research, including focus groups and customer surveys. Based on the numbers gathered, the company claims it had no reason to forecast that Devil's Food cookies would stand out from the other five products. It wasn't until six months after the Devil's Food launch that the demand started to outstrip the supply. At that point, Nabisco found itself scrambling to build extra capacity to produce the popular cookie.

So, was one of 1993's most brilliant marketing strategies part of a devious master plan? Probably not. It now appears to be no more than a brilliant recovery from initially faulty forecasts. It seems that Nabisco is slow to learn from experience. In 1912, it launched three items but failed to accurately forecast the tremendous popularity of one of them. That year, the company couldn't keep its new Oreo Cookies on the shelves.

Source: Adapted from Weld F. Royal, "SnackWell's: Yes, We Have No Cookie Cakes," *Sales & Marketing Management,* September 1994, p. 80.

Composite of Salesforce Opinions

When buyer interviewing is impractical, the company may base its sales forecasts on information provided by the salesforce. The company typically asks its salespeople to estimate sales by product for their individual territories. It then adds up the individual estimates to arrive at an overall sales forecast.

Few companies use their salesforce's estimates without some adjustments. Salespeople are biased observers. They may be naturally pessimistic or optimistic, or they may go to one extreme or another because of recent sales setbacks or successes. Furthermore, they are often unaware of larger economic developments and they do not always know how their company's marketing plans will affect future sales in their territories. They may understate demand so that the company will set a low sales quota. They may not have the time to prepare careful estimates or may not consider it worthwhile.

Assuming these biases can be countered, a number of benefits can be gained by involving the salesforce in forecasting. Salespeople may have better insights into developing trends than any other group. After participating in the forecasting process, the salespeople may have greater confidence in their quotas and more incentive to achieve them. Also, such "grassroots" forecasting provides estimates broken down by product, territory, customer, and salesperson.[7]

EXPERT OPINION

In 1945, then-IBM chairman Thomas Watson forecast a worldwide market for about five computers.

Companies can also obtain forecasts by turning to experts. Experts include dealers, distributors, suppliers, marketing consultants, and trade associations. Thus, auto companies survey their dealers periodically for their forecasts of short-term demand. Dealer estimates, however, are subject to the same strengths and weaknesses as salesforce estimates.

Many companies buy economic and industry forecasts from well-known firms such as Data Resources, Wharton Econometric, and Chase Econometric. These forecasting specialists are in a better position than the company to prepare economic forecasts because they have more data available and more forecasting expertise.

Occasionally companies will invite a special group of experts to prepare a forecast. The experts may be asked to exchange views and come up with a group estimate (group discussion method). Or they may be asked to supply their estimates individually, with the company analyst combining them into a single estimate. Finally, they may supply individual estimates and assumptions that are reviewed by a company analyst, revised, and followed by further rounds of estimation (called the Delphi method).

Experts can provide good insights upon which to base forecasts, but they can also be wrong. For example, in 1943, IBM Chairman Thomas J. Watson predicted "I think there's a world market for about five computers." And in 1946, Daryl F. Zanuck, head of 20th Century Fox, made this pronouncement: "TV won't be able to hold on to any market it captures after the first six months. People will soon get tired of staring at a plywood box every night."[8] Where possible, the company should back up experts' opinions with estimates obtained using other methods.

TEST MARKETING

Where buyers do not plan their purchases carefully or where experts are not available or reliable, the company may want to conduct a direct test market. A direct test market is especially useful in forecasting new-product sales or established-product sales in a new distribution channel or territory. Test marketing is discussed in Chapter 11.

TIME-SERIES ANALYSIS

Time-series analysis
Breaking down past sales into its trend, cycle, season, and erratic components, then recombining these components to produce a sales forecast.

Many firms base their forecasts on past sales. They assume that the causes of past sales can be uncovered through statistical analysis. Then, analysts can use the causal relations to predict future sales. **Time-series analysis** consists of breaking down the original sales into four components—trend, cycle, season, and erratic components—then recombining these components to produce the sales forecast.

Trend is the long-term, underlying pattern of growth or decline in sales resulting from basic changes in population, capital formation, and technology. It is found by fitting a straight or curved line through past sales. *Cycle* captures the medium-term, wavelike movement of sales resulting from changes in general economic and competitive activity. The cyclical component can be useful for medium-range forecasting. Cyclical swings, however, are difficult to predict because they do not occur on a regular basis. *Season* refers to a consistent pattern of sales movements within the year. The term *season* describes any recurrent hourly, weekly, monthly, or quarterly sales pattern. The seasonal component may be related to weather, holidays, and trade customs. The seasonal pattern provides a norm for forecasting short-range sales. Finally, *erratic events* include fads, strikes, snow storms, earthquakes, riots, fires, and other disturbances. These components, by definition, are unpredictable and should be removed from past data to see the more normal behavior of sales.

Suppose an insurance company sold 12,000 new life insurance policies this year and wants to predict next year's December sales. The long-term trend shows a 5 percent sales growth rate per year. This information alone suggests sales next year of 12,600 (= 12,000 × 1.05). However, a business recession is expected next year and probably will result in total sales achieving only 90 percent of the expected trend-adjusted sales. Sales next year will more likely be 12,600 × .90 = 11,340. If sales were the same each month, monthly sales would be 11,340 ÷ 12 = 945. However, December is an above-average month for insurance policy sales, with a seasonal index standing at 1.30. Therefore December sales may be as high as 945 × 1.3 = 1,228.5. The company expects no erratic events, such as strikes or new insurance regulations. Thus, it estimates new policy sales next December at 1,228.5 policies.

LEADING INDICATORS

Leading indicators
Time series that change in the same direction but in advance of company sales.

Many companies try to forecast their sales by finding one or more **leading indicators**—other time series that change in the same direction but in advance of company sales. For example, a plumbing supply company might find that its sales lag behind the housing starts index by about four months. The housing starts index would then be a useful leading indicator. The National Bureau of Economic Research has identified 12 of the best leading indicators, and their values are published monthly in the *Survey of Current Business.*

STATISTICAL DEMAND ANALYSIS

Statistical demand analysis
A set of statistical procedures used to discover the most important real factors affecting sales and their relative influence; the most commonly analyzed factors are prices, income, population, and promotion.

Time-series analysis treats past and future sales as a function of time, rather than as a function of any real demand factors. But many real factors affect the sales of any product. **Statistical demand analysis** is a set of statistical procedures used to discover the most important real factors affecting sales and their relative influence. The factors most commonly analyzed are prices, income, population, and promotion.

Statistical demand analysis consists of expressing sales (Q) as a dependent variable and trying to explain sales as a function of a number of independent demand variables $X_1, X_2, \ldots, X_n$. That is:

$$Q = f(X_1, X_2, \ldots, X_n)$$

Using a technique called *multiple-regression analysis,* various equation forms can be statistically fitted to the data in the search for the best predicting factors and equation.[9]

For example, a soft-drink company found that the per capita sales of soft drinks by state was well explained by[10]

$$Q = -145.5 + 6.46X_1 - 2.37X_2$$

where

X_1 = mean annual temperature of the state (Fahrenheit)

X_2 = annual per capita income in the state (in hundreds)

For example, New Jersey had a mean annual temperature of 54 degrees and an annual per capita income of 24 (in hundreds). Using the equation, we would predict per capita soft-drink consumption in New Jersey to be

$$Q = -145.5 + 6.46(54) - 2.37(24) = 146.6$$

Actual per capita consumption was 143. If the equation predicted this well for other states, it would serve as a useful forecasting tool. Marketing management would predict next year's mean temperature and per capita income for each state and use the equation to predict next year's sales.

Statistical demand analysis can be very complex, and the marketer must take care in designing, conducting, and interpreting such analysis. Yet constantly improving computer technology has made statistical demand analysis an increasingly popular approach to forecasting.

Summary

To carry out their responsibilities, marketing managers need measures of current and future market size. We *define the market* as the set of actual and potential consumers of a product or service. A market is the group of buyers, and an industry is a group of sellers that serve it. The consumers in the market have varying levels of *interest, income, access,* and *qualifications* for a particular product.

One key task for marketers is *measuring current market demand,* which can be viewed in terms of *total market demand* or *area market demand.* Total market demand is not a fixed number, but a function of the marketing environment including the level and mix of industry marketing effort. Marketers can estimate total market demand using the chain ratio method. This method involves multiplying a base number representing every potential customer by a series of percentages. These percentages adjust the base number downward to develop an estimate of the approximate number of truly qualified potential customers.

Area market demand is a way of estimating the demand within a particular city, state, or country. Two major methods are used for estimating area market demand, the *market-buildup method* and the *market-factor index method.* The market-buildup method calls for identifying how many potential buyers there are in each market and estimating the size of their potential purchases. The market-factor index method is an alternate method which identifies market factors that correlate with market potential, and then combines them into a weighted index, such as the buying power index.

Companies also want to know the *actual industry sales* in its market as a way of judging their own relative success and the strength of their competitors. Estimating actual industry sales requires identifying competitors and using some method to estimate the sales of each. Finally, companies estimate the market shares of competitors to judge their relative performance.

Making effective market decisions also requires that companies be able to *forecast future demand.* There are several methods for forecasting based on what people say. A survey of buyers' intentions simply asks buyers what they plan to do. A composite of salesforce opinions relies on the fact that salespersons, though often biased, are close to their customers, and have good insights into what future orders may be. A similar method is developing a consensus of expert opinion.

Other methods of forecasting future demand are examining what people do by *test marketing,* or by studying what they have done in the past. The key methods for forecasting based on past behavior are *time-series analysis,* studying *leading indicators,* and *statistical demand analysis.* In all cases, the best forecasting method to use depends on the purpose of the forecast, the type of product, and the availability and reliability of data.

Key Terms

Forecasting

Industry

Leading indicators

Market

Market-buildup method

Market-factor index method

Market potential

Primary demand

Selective demand

Statistical demand analysis

Time-series analysis

Total market demand

Discussing the Issues

1. In market measurement and forecasting, decide which is the more serious problem: *overestimating* demand, or *underestimating* it?

2. Retailers depend upon the Christmas season for up to 40 percent of the total year's sales. Many analysts forecast the strength of the Christmas retailing season by projecting from the sales level on a *single day,* the Friday after Thanksgiving. Explain the issues in using such a forecast. Is it more difficult to forecast such highly seasonal demand?

3. Many long-term trends occur because of changes in technology or the environment. What effect have automobile catalytic converters had on the market for leaded and unleaded gasoline? Suggest a way that higher gasoline prices have affected spark plug manufacturers. Were these changes predictable?

4. Hess's, a chain of department stores, is looking for desirable locations for new stores. Decide which aspect of market demand Hess's would be interested in measuring, and what measuring methods they would use, in choosing where to locate new stores. What census tract or zip-code information would be relevant?

5. As marketing manager for Cat's Pride cat litter, you have seen sales jump 50 percent in the last year after years of relatively stable sales. Explain how you will forecast sales for the coming year.

6. List some leading indicators that might help you predict sales of diapers, cars, or hamburgers. Can you describe a general procedure for finding leading indicators of product sales?

Applying the Concepts

1. Look at your school's schedule of classes for the coming semester. Examine the course offerings in your major area and try to predict which courses will have low, medium, and high demand. What factors do you think affect demand for courses? If a new course were offered, list what information you would want to know in order to predict the level of demand for it.

2. People often make their own judgments about the potential for new products. You may hear someone say a new product will "never sell," or, perhaps, that it will "sell like hotcakes." Try to recall some recent new product or service that you saw and made an informal prediction about. What was the product? What attracted your attention enough to get you to comment on the product's future? What was your forecast? Were you correct?

References

1. Hamish McDonald, "Caught on the Hop," *Far Eastern Economic Review,* February 18, 1988, pp. 72–73; "Qantas Embarks on Major Fleet Expansion Plan," *Aviation Week & Space Technology,* June 20, 1988, pp. 39, 42–43; Michael Westlake, "Stand-By Room Only," *Far Eastern Economic Review,* June 2, 1988,

pp. 72–75; Paul Proctor, "Pacific Rim Carriers Struggle to Cope with Impending Traffic Boom," *Aviation Week & Space Technology*, November 20, 1989, pp. 110–111; Ian Jarrett, "Kangaroo Runs Into Turbulence," *Asian Business*, August 1993, p. 62. Additional information supplied by Qantas Airways, Ltd., April, 1993; and Geoffrey Lee Martin, "Qantas Mixes Old, New in Pride-Filled Campaign," *Advertising Age*, August 22, 1994, p. 40.

2. For further discussion, see Gary L. Lilien, Philip Kotler, and K. Sridhar Moorthy, *Marketing Models* (Englewood Cliffs, NJ: Prentice-Hall, 1992).

3. For more on forecasting total market demand, see F. William Barnett, "Four Steps to Forecast Total Market Demand," *Harvard Business Review*, July–August 1988, pp. 28–34; and "Forecasting the Potential for New Industrial Products," *Industrial Marketing Management*, no. 4, 1989, pp. 307–312.

4. For more on using this survey, see "A User's Guide to the Survey of Buying Power," *Sales & Marketing Management*, August 30, 1993, pp. A4–A19.

5. For a more comprehensive discussion of measuring market demand, see Philip Kotler, *Marketing Management: Analysis, Planning, Implementation, and Control,* 8th ed. (Englewood Cliffs, NJ: Prentice Hall, 1994), Chapter 10.

6. For a listing and analysis of these and other forecasting techniques, see David M. Georgoff and Robert G. Murdick, "Manager's Guide to Forecasting," *Harvard Business Review*, January–February 1986, pp. 110–120; and Donald S. Tull and Del I. Hawkins, *Marketing Research: Measurement and Method*, 6th ed. (New York: Macmillan, 1990), Chapter 21. For a listing of common forecasting problems, see John B. Mahaffie, "Why Forecasts Fail," *American Demographics*, March 1995, pp. 34–40.

7. For more on the salesforce composite method, see Tull and Hawkins, *Marketing Research: Measurement and Method,* pp. 705–706.

8. See "Sometimes Expert Opinion Isn't All It Should Be," *Go,* September–October 1985, p. 2.

9. See Tull and Hawkins, *Marketing Research: Measurement and Method,* pp. 686–691.

10. See "The Du Pont Company," in *Marketing Research: Text and Cases,* 3rd ed., Harper W. Boyd, Jr., Ralph Westfall, and Stanley Stasch, eds. (Homewood, IL: Irwin, 1977), pp. 498–500.

Company Case 7

MATTEL: FORECASTING CHILD'S PLAY

The Mattel toy designer held everyone's interest as he prepared to push the green launch button. The assembled Hot Wheels brand managers and Mattel top executives marveled as a tiny plastic car, called Top Speed, leaped off the launcher, zipped through a plastic accelerator tube, and whizzed around the race track's curves and loops. The managers were impressed, especially given that Mattel's designers had developed the new car models at Mattel's toy-design center in El Segundo, California, in only five months. However, they knew that many challenges remained. They wondered if the new toy would be the market hit they needed or whether it would turn out to be just another of the nightmares that were all too common in the toy industry.

NIGHTMARES

It's every parent's nightmare. Suddenly the kids start asking for something called Mighty Morphin Power Rangers for Christmas. First, they have to explain to their parents what a Mighty Morphin is, while giving them that "don't-grown-ups-know-anything" look. Then the parents start looking for the toys casually on shopping trips. No luck. Then, Mom takes a day off from work to do some serious looking. Still, no luck. Over the weekend, Dad sneaks off to a major mall in another city while mom calls out-of-town relatives to ask them to look. Again, they come up empty handed. It's panic time! Christmas is only two weeks away and all the kids are talking about is Mighty Morphin Power Rangers. How can mom and dad explain that Santa has run out of Power Rangers?

It's also every toy retailer's nightmare. Buyers travel to New York City every February for the annual Toy Fair, a trade show where toy manufacturers present their products. About 25,000 retail toy buyers attend the show to place orders for the following Christmas season. As they wander down the aisles, they see the usual assortment of brand extensions for the perennial favorites like Barbie, G.I. Joe, and Hot Wheels. However, they also see 5,000–6,000 new toys each year, 80 percent of which won't be around next year. The trick is to pick those that will be big hits.

So, a buyer places a small order for something new called Mighty Morphin Power Rangers. The manufacturer, Bandai America, claims that the toys will be popular after the September start of a television show about the Rangers. Later in the year, the toys begin to sell, even before the television show debuts. The buyer's not sure what to make of it and decides to wait until two weeks into the show to see how the new product moves. The delay proves costly. By the time the buyer places a new order in early October, every other retailer has seen the same trend and has also reordered. Bandai is able to ship only 600,000 Power Rangers despite orders for 12 *million!* During the next two months, angry parents flood the buyer's store wanting to know how they will explain to their children that Santa ran out of Power Rangers.

This process is no picnic for toy manufacturers either. The annual Toy Show is a make-or-break event—the Super Bowl of toys. Sometime well before the February show, manufacturers have to decide which toys to present, which toys will be popular *two* Christmases away. Then they have to hope that they can manufacture enough toys between February and late summer to meet demand. To make matters worse, the major retailers like Toys 'R' Us and Wal-Mart have moved to a just-in-time philosophy to replenish inventory. Instead of placing one big order for toys, they place small orders initially, then reorder based on demand. They want to replace toys on their shelves just as they sell out. This strategy improves cash flow and avoids storerooms full of dud toys. But the just-in-time plan has a significant disadvantage for both retailers and manufacturers. If a surprise hit appears, neither can gear up fast enough to respond.

THE TOY INDUSTRY

The toy industry is risky. If companies bet right, they make a lot of money. If not, they lose a lot of money. Toys are also big business. The Toy Manufacturers' Association estimated that the U.S. toy market produced sales of $17.5 billion in 1993, up 1.6 percent over 1992, which was up 12 percent from 1991. The European market is almost as big as the U.S. market at $16.7 billion. U.S. manufacturers invent, engineer, and market about two-thirds of all the toys in the world.

Analysts attribute toy industry growth to three factors. First, although birth rates in developed countries are declining, parents tend to buy more toys and more expensive toys for their children. Second, the increased number of divorced or separated parents often means the children have many adult relatives to give them toys. Also, many women are waiting later to have children, meaning they and their families may have higher disposable incomes.

MATTEL'S TOP SPEED

Mattel is one of the key players in the toy industry. With annual sales of $2.7 billion, it owns the 35-year-old Barbie and 25-year-old Hot Wheels brands. Barbie alone accounted for 35 percent of Mattel's sales. Barbie's success, however, has created problems. In 1994, Mattel needed to lessen its dependence on the Barbie line. It also wanted to reverse a string of recent failures in its boys' division, including the Masters of the Universe and Demolition Man action figures.

As a result, Mattel prepared to launch its Top Speed brand, the first Hot Wheels made from lightweight plastic rather than die-cast metal. The lighter-weight cars could zip around faster. The translucent plastic also allowed Mattel to give the 2½ inch cars iridescent body colors it believed would appeal to 7-to-10-year-old boys.

Further, Top Speed cars, unlike traditional Hot-Wheels' models, did not resemble real cars. They had a futuristic design, more like Indianapolis-style racing cars. The cars featured detailed engines; a floating front axle to improve performance on the track; stylish, molded mag wheels; and a front-mounted launching hook. Special rubber bands contained in a launcher powered the lightweight cars, allowing them to be hurled along tracks and through clear plastic tubes at amazing speeds. Mattel planned to offer Top Speed cars in six different models, each with its own exciting name: Cryo Pump, Road Vac, Corkscrew, Shock Rod, Sting Shot, and Back Burner.

Mattel planned to package the cars in pairs, including a tube and launcher, with each pair selling for about $5 at retail. This price compared favorably with a $2 per car retail price for traditional Hot Wheels' models. Kids could also buy special tracks to run the cars on, priced in the $25–30 range. Or they could make their own obstacle courses or drag race with their friends.

As they prepared to launch the new product, Top Speed's brand managers knew how easy it is to underestimate or overestimate toy demand, and they did not relish explaining the resulting nightmare to top management. To decide how many Top Speed cars to produce, they had to forecast how young boys would react to the new toy. They knew that forecasting would not be child's play.

QUESTIONS

1. How should Mattel and other toy manufacturers go about deciding which toys to produce and forecasting what the demand for those toys would be?

2. If you were a toy retailer, how would you forecast the demand for toys in your stores?

3. How would Mattel's forecasting approaches change if it wanted to offer its toys in foreign markets?

Sources: Allyson L. Stewart, "Rules of the Toy Game Different for Europe's Kids," *Marketing News,* October 25, 1993, p. 6; Joseph Pereira, "Toy Industry Find It's Harder and Harder to Pick the Winners," *Wall Street Journal,* December 21, 1993, p. A1; Eric Schine, "Mattel's Wild Race to Market," *Business Week,* February 21, 1994, pp. 62–63; David Miller, "NAFTA Paves Way for All Latin America," *Discount Store News,* May 16, 1994, p. 84; Cyndee Miller, "Finding Next Big Toy Is Not Child's Play," *Marketing News,* May 23, 1994, p. 2.

Market Segmentation, Targeting, and Positioning for Competitive Advantage

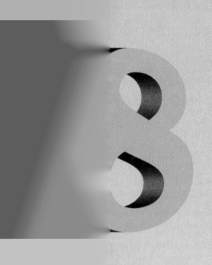

Procter & Gamble makes eleven brands of laundry detergent (Tide, Cheer, Bold, Gain, Era, Dash, Oxydol, Solo, Dreft, Ivory Snow, and Ariel). It also sells eight brands of hand soap (Zest, Coast, Ivory, Safeguard, Camay, Oil of Olay, Kirk's, and Lava); six shampoos (Prell, Head & Shoulders, Ivory, Pert, Pantene, and Vidal Sassoon); four brands each of liquid dishwashing detergents (Joy, Ivory, Dawn, and Liquid Cascade), toothpaste (Crest, Gleam, Complete, and Denquel), and coffee (Folger's, High Point, Butternut, and Maryland Club); three brands each of floor cleaner (Spic & Span, Top Job, and Mr. Clean) and toilet tissue (Charmin, Banner, and Summit); and two brands each of deodorant (Secret and Sure), cooking oil (Crisco and Puritan), fabric softener (Downy and Bounce), and disposable diapers (Pampers and Luvs). Moreover, many of the brands are offered in several sizes and formulations (for example, you can buy large or small packages of powdered or liquid Tide in any of three forms—regular, unscented, or with bleach).

These P&G brands compete with one another on the same supermarket shelves. But why would P&G introduce several brands in one category instead of concentrating its resources on a single leading brand? The answer lies in the fact that different people want different *mixes of benefits* from the products they buy. Take laundry detergents as an example. People use laundry detergents to get their clothes clean. But they also want other things from their detergents—such as economy, bleaching power, fabric softening, fresh smell, strength or mildness, and lots of suds. We all want *some* of every one of these benefits from our detergent, but we may have different *priorities* for each benefit. To some people, cleaning and bleaching power are most important; to others, fabric softening matters most; still others want a mild, fresh-scented detergent. Thus, there are groups—or segments—of laundry detergent buyers, and each segment seeks a special combination of benefits.

Procter & Gamble has identified at least eleven important laundry detergent segments, along with numerous subsegments, and has developed a different brand designed to meet

OBJECTIVES

When you finish this chapter, you should be able to accomplish the following:

1. Explain **market segmentation,** and identify several possible **bases for segmenting consumer markets, business markets,** and **international markets.**

2. List and distinguish among the **requirements for effective segmentation: measurability, accessibility, substantiality,** and **actionability.**

3. Outline the process of **evaluating market segments,** and suggest some methods for **selecting market segments.**

4. Illustrate the concept of **positioning for competitive advantage** by offering specific examples.

5. Discuss **choosing and implementing a positioning strategy,** and contrast positionings based on **product, service, personnel,** and **image differentiation.**

the special needs of each. The eleven P&G brands are positioned for different segments as follows:

- *Tide* is "so powerful, it cleans down to the fiber." It's the all-purpose family detergent for extra-tough laundry jobs. "Tide's in, dirt's out." *Tide with Bleach* is "so powerful, it whitens down to the fiber."

- *Cheer* with Color Guard gives "outstanding cleaning *and* color protection. So your family's clothes look clean, bright, and more like new." Cheer is also specially formulated for use in hot, warm, or cold water—it's "all tempera-Cheer." *Cheer Free* is "dermatologist tested . . . contains no irritating perfume or dye."

- *Bold* is the detergent with fabric softener. It "cleans, softens, and controls static." Bold liquid adds "the fresh fabric softener scent."

- *Gain*, originally P&G's "enzyme" detergent, was repositioned as the detergent that gives you clean, fresh-smelling clothes—it "freshens like sunshine."

- *Era* has "built-in stain removers." It "gets tough stains out and does a great job on your whole wash too."

- *Dash* is P&G's value entry. It "attacks tough dirt," but "Dash does it for a great low price."

- *Oxydol* contains bleach. It "makes your white clothes really white and your colored clothes really bright. So don't reach for the bleach—grab a box of Ox!"

- *Solo* contains detergent and fabric softener in liquid form. It's targeted heavily toward the Northeast, a strong liquid detergent market.

- *Dreft* is also formulated for baby's diapers and clothes. It contains borax, "nature's natural sweetener" for "a clean you can trust."

- *Ivory Snow* is "Ninety-nine and forty-four one hundredths percent pure." It's the "mild, gentle soap for diapers and baby clothes."

- *Ariel* is a tough cleaner targeted to the Hispanic market. It's also the No. 1 brand in Mexico and P&G's major brand in Europe.

By segmenting the market and having several detergent brands, P&G has an attractive offering for consumers in all important preference groups. All its brands combined capture more than a 53 percent share of the $3.2 billion U.S. laundry detergent market—much more than any single brand could obtain by itself.

MARKETS

Organizations that sell to consumer and business markets recognize that they cannot appeal to all buyers in those markets, or at least not to all buyers in the same way. Buyers are too numerous, too widely scattered, and too varied in their needs and buying practices. And different companies vary widely in their abilities to serve different segments of the market. Rather than trying to compete in an entire market, sometimes against superior competitors, each company must identify the parts of the market that it can serve best.

Sellers have not always practiced this philosophy. Their thinking has passed through three stages:

- *Mass marketing.* In mass marketing, the seller mass produces, mass distributes, and mass promotes one product to all buyers. At one time, Coca-Cola produced only one drink for the whole market, hoping it would appeal to everyone. The argument for mass marketing is that it should lead to the lowest costs and prices and create the largest potential market.

◆ *Product-variety marketing.* Here, the seller produces two or more products that have different features, styles, quality, sizes, and so on. Later, Coca-Cola produced several soft drinks packaged in different sizes and containers. They were designed to offer variety to buyers rather than to appeal to different market segments. The argument for product-variety marketing is that consumers have different tastes that change over time. Consumers seek variety and change.

◆ *Target marketing.* Here, the seller identifies market segments, selects one or more of them, and develops products and marketing mixes tailored to each. For example, Coca-Cola now produces soft drinks for the sugared-cola segment (Coca-Cola Classic and Cherry Coke), the diet segment (Diet Coke and Tab), the no-caffeine segment (Caffeine Free Coke), and the noncola segment (Minute Maid sodas).

Today's companies are moving away from mass marketing and product-variety marketing and toward target marketing. Target marketing can better help sellers find their marketing opportunities. Sellers can develop the right product for each target market and adjust their prices, distribution channels, and advertising to reach the target market efficiently. Instead of scattering their marketing efforts (the "shotgun" approach), they can focus on the buyers who have greater purchase interest (the "rifle" approach).

As a result of the increasing fragmentation of American mass markets into hundreds of micromarkets, each with different needs and lifestyles, target marketing is increasingly taking the form of **micromarketing**. Using micromarketing, companies tailor their marketing programs to the needs and wants of narrowly defined geographic, demographic, psychographic, or behavior segments. The ultimate form of target marketing is *customized marketing* in which the company adapts its product and marketing program to the needs of a specific customer or buying organization (see Marketing Highlight 8-1).

Figure 8-1 shows the three major steps in target marketing. The first is **market segmentation**—dividing a market into distinct groups of buyers with different needs, characteristics, or behavior who might require separate products or marketing mixes. The company identifies different ways to segment the market and develops profiles of the resulting market segments. The second step is **market targeting**—evaluating each market segment's attractiveness and selecting one or more of the market segments to enter. The third step is **market positioning**—setting the competitive positioning for the product and creating a detailed marketing mix.

Micromarketing
A form of target marketing in which companies tailor their marketing programs to the needs and wants of narrowly defined geographic, demographic, psychographic, or behavioral segments.

Market segmentation
Dividing a market into distinct groups of buyers with different needs, characteristics, or behavior who might require separate products or marketing mixes.

Market targeting
The process of evaluating each market segment's attractiveness and selecting one or more segments to enter.

Market positioning
Arranging for a product to occupy a clear, distinctive, and desirable place relative to competing products in the minds of target consumers. Formulating competitive positioning for a product and a detailed marketing mix.

FIGURE 8-1 *Steps in market segmentation, targeting, and positioning*

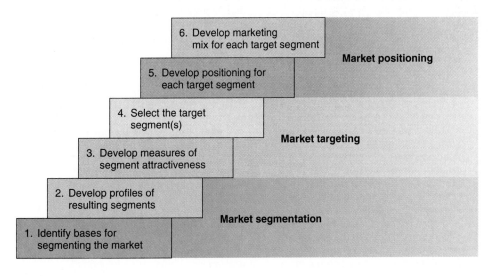

MICROMARKETING: A NEW MARKETING ERA?

For most of this century, major consumer-products companies have held fast to mass marketing principles, marketing the same set of products in about the same way to all consumers. But recently, many have tried a new approach—*micromarketing*. Instead of using standardized marketing, they are tailoring their products and programs to suit the tastes of specific geographic, demographic, psychographic, and behavioral segments.

Several factors have fueled the move toward micromarketing. First, the American mass market has slowly broken down into a profusion of smaller micromarkets—the baby boomer segment here, the Generation Xers there; here the Hispanic market, there the black market; here working women, there single parents; here the Sun Belt, there the Rust Belt. Today, marketers find it very hard to create a single product or program that appeals to all of these diverse groups. Second, improved information and marketing research technologies have also spurred micromarketing. For example, retail store scanners now allow instant tracking of product sales from store to store, helping companies pinpoint exactly which specific segments are buying what. Third, scanners give retailers mountains of market information, and this information gives them more power over manufacturers. Retailers generally prefer localized promotions targeted toward the characteristics of consumers in their own cities and neighborhoods. Thus, to keep retailers happy, and to get precious retail shelf space for their products, manufacturers must now do more micromarketing.

One of the most common forms of micromarketing is *regionalization*—tailoring brands and promotions to suit individual geographic regions, cities, and even neighborhoods or specific stores. Campbell Soup, a pioneer in regionalization, has created many successful regional brands. For example, it sells spicy Ranchero beans, Brunswick stew, and spicy hot chili in the Southwest, Cajun gumbo soup in the South, and red bean soup in Hispanic areas. Beyond regionalization, companies are also targeting specific demographic, psychographic, and behavioral micromarkets. For example, for its Crest toothpaste, Procter & Gamble uses six separate advertising campaigns targeting different age and ethnic segments including kids, blacks, and Hispanics. To reach these and other micromarkets, Procter & Gamble uses highly focused media, such as cable television, direct mail, event sponsorships, electronic point-of-purchase media, and advertising display boards in locations such as doctors' and dentists' waiting rooms or elementary and high school cafeterias.

In the extreme, micromarketing becomes *mass customization*—serving large numbers of customers, but giving each exactly what he or she wants. Marketers now are experimenting with new systems for providing customized products and services ranging from hotel stays and furniture to clothing and bicycles. For example, Ritz-Carlton makes a computerized record of individual guest preferences available to all of its 28 hotels. If a guest asked for a foam pillow the last time she stayed at the Ritz in Montreal, there will be one ready for her months or even years later when she checks into the Ritz in Atlanta.

Software Sportswear, of Greenwich, Connecticut, makes customized swimsuits using a video monitor and special computer software. A computer, linked to a camera, calculates customer's measurements and prints out a custom-fitted pattern for a bathing suit. The video screen shows the bedazzled and delighted buyer how the new suit will look from the front, side, and rear. The buyer chooses the fabric from about 150 samples, the custom-made design is sent to the producer's tailors, and the suit is stitched up in about a week.

Another example is a Japanese bicycle manufacturer that uses flexible manufacturing to turn out large numbers of bikes specially fitted to the needs of individual buyers. Customers visit their local bike shop where the shopkeeper measures them on a special frame and faxes the specifications to the factory. At the factory, the measurements are punched into a computer, which creates blueprints in three minutes that would take a draftsman 60 times that long. The computer then guides robots and workers through the production process. The factory is ready to produce any of 11,231,862 variations on 18 bicycle models in 199 color patterns and about as many sizes as there are people. The price is steep—between $545 and $3,200—but within two weeks the buyer is riding a custom-made, one-of-a-kind machine.

Business-to-business marketers are also finding new ways to customize their offerings. For example, Motorola salespeople now use a hand-held computer to custom design pagers following customer wishes. The design data are transmitted to the Motorola factory and production starts within 17 minutes. The customized pagers are ready for shipment within two hours.

Although micromarketing offers much promise, it also presents some problems. Trying to serve dozens or even hundreds of diverse micromarkets is vastly more complex than mass marketing. And offering many different products and promotion programs results in higher manufacturing and marketing costs. Thus, some marketers view micromarketing as just a fad—they think companies will quickly find that the extra sales gained will not cover the additional costs. But others think that micromarketing will revolutionize the way consumer products are marketed. Gone are the days, they say, when a company can effectively market one product to masses of consumers using a single promotion program. To these marketers, micromarketing signals the start of a whole new marketing era.

Sources: See Shawn McKenna, *The Complete Guide to Regional Marketing* (Homewood, IL: Business One Irwin, 1992); B. Joseph Pine, *Mass Customization* (Boston: Harvard Business School Press, 1993); and Roberta Maynard, "Tailoring Products for a Niche of One," *Nation's Business,* November 1993, p. 42; B. Joseph Pine II, Don Peppers, and Martha Rogers, "Do You Want to Keep Your Customers Forever?" *Harvard Business Review,* March–April 1995, pp. 103–114.

MARKET SEGMENTATION

Markets consist of buyers, and buyers differ in one or more ways. They may differ in their wants, resources, locations, buying attitudes, and buying practices. Because buyers have unique needs and wants, each buyer is potentially a separate market. Ideally, then, a seller might design a separate marketing program for each buyer. For example, Boeing manufactures airplanes for only a few buyers and customizes its products and marketing program to satisfy each specific customer.

However, most sellers face larger numbers of smaller buyers and do not find complete segmentation worthwhile. Instead, they look for broad *classes* of buyers who differ in their product needs or buying responses. For example, General Motors has found that high- and low-income groups differ in their car-buying needs and wants. It also knows that young consumers' needs and wants differ from those of older consumers. Thus, GM has designed specific models for different income and age groups. In fact, it sells models for segments with varied *combinations* of age and income. For instance, GM designed its Buick Park Avenue for older, higher-income consumers. Age and income are only two of many bases that companies use for segmenting their markets.

BASES FOR SEGMENTING CONSUMER MARKETS

There is no single way to segment a market. A marketer has to try different segmentation variables, alone and in combination, to find the best way to view the market structure. Table 8-1 outlines the major variables that might be used in segmenting consumer markets. Here we look at the major *geographic, demographic, psychographic,* and *behavioral variables.*

Geographic Segmentation

Geographic segmentation
Dividing a market into different geographical units such as nations, states, regions, counties, cities, or neighborhoods.

Geographic segmentation calls for dividing the market into different geographical units such as nations, regions, states, counties, cities, or neighborhoods. A company may decide to operate in one or a few geographical areas, or to operate in all areas but pay attention to geographical differences in needs and wants. For example, Campbell sells Cajun gumbo soup in Louisiana and Mississippi, and makes its nacho cheese soup spicier in Texas and California.

S. C. Johnson & Son practices geographic segmentation for its arsenal of Raid bug killers by emphasizing the right products in the right geographic areas at the right times. When its dominant share of the household insecticide market

Geographic segmentation: Fleeing the fiercely competitve major cities, Hampton Inn is setting up smaller units in small-town America. This Hampton Inn has 54 rooms instead of the usual 135.

TABLE 8-1   *Major Segmentation Variables for Consumer Markets*

VARIABLE	TYPICAL BREAKDOWNS
Geographic	
Region	Pacific, Mountain, West North Central, West South Central, East North Central, East South Central, South Atlantic, Middle Atlantic, New England
County size	A, B, C, D
City size	Under 5,000; 5,000–20,000; 20,000–50,000; 50,000–100,000; 100,000–250,000; 250,000–500,000; 500,000–1,000,000; 1,000,000–4,000,000; 4,000,000 and over
Density	Urban, suburban, rural
Climate	Northern, Southern
Demographic	
Age	Under 6, 6–11, 12–19, 20–34, 35–49, 50–64, 65+
Gender	Male, female
Family size	1–2, 3–4, 5+
Family life cycle	Young, single; young, married, no children; young, married, youngest child under 6; young married, youngest child 6 or over; older, married, with children; older, married, no children under 18; older, single; other
Income	Under $10,000; $10,000–$15,000; $15,000–$20,000; $20,000–$30,000; $30,000–$50,000; $50,000–$75,000; $75,000 and over
Occupation	Professional and technical; managers, officials, and proprietors; clerical, sales; craftsmen, foremen; operatives; farmers; retired; students; homemakers; unemployed
Education	Grade school or less; some high school; high school graduate; some college; college graduate
Religion	Catholic, Protestant, Jewish, other
Race	White, black, Asian, Hispanic
Nationality	American, British, French, German, Scandinavian, Italian, Latin American, Middle Eastern, Japanese
Psychographic	
Social class	Lower lowers, upper lowers, working class, middle class, upper middles, lower uppers, upper uppers
Lifestyle	Achievers, believers, strivers
Personality	Compulsive, gregarious, authoritarian, ambitious
Behavioral	
Purchase occasion	Regular occasion, special occasion
Benefits sought	Quality, service, economy
User status	Nonuser, ex-user, potential user, first-time user, regular user
Usage rate	Light user, medium user, heavy user
Loyalty status	None, medium, strong, absolute
Readiness state	Unaware, aware, informed, interested, desirous, intending to buy
Attitude toward product	Enthusiastic, positive, indifferent, negative, hostile

leveled off just above 40 percent, "Johnson figured out where and when different bugs were about to start biting, stinging, and otherwise making people's lives miserable. The company promoted cockroach zappers in roach capitals such as Houston and New York and flea sprays in flea-bitten cities like Tampa and Birmingham. Since the program began last year, Raid has increased its market share in 16 of 18 regions and its overall piece of the $450-million-a-year U.S. insecticide market by five percentage points."[1]

Many companies today are "regionalizing" their marketing programs—localizing their products, advertising, promotion, and sales efforts to fit the needs of individual regions, cities, and even neighborhoods. For example, P&G sells Ariel laundry detergent primarily in Los Angeles, San Diego, San Francisco, Miami, and south Texas, areas with larger concentrations of Hispanic consumers.[2] Others are seeking to cultivate as yet untapped territory. For example, many large companies are fleeing the fiercely competitive major cities and suburbs to set up shop in small-town America. McDonald's recently began opening a chain of smaller-format Golden Arches Cafes in towns too small for its standard-sized restaurants. Hampton Inns is pursuing a similar strategy. For example, Townsend, Tennessee, with a population of only 329, is small even by small-town standards. But looks can be deceiving. Situated on a heavily traveled and picturesque route between Knoxville and the Smoky Mountains, the village serves both business and vacation travelers. Hampton Inns, the 290-motel chain, opened a unit in Townsend and plans to open 100 more in small towns by 1996. It costs less to operate in these towns, and the company builds smaller units to match lower volume. The Townsend Hampton Inn, for example, has 54 rooms instead of the usual 135.[3]

Demographic segmentation
Dividing the market into groups based on demographic variables such as age, sex, family size, family life cycle, income, occupation, education, religion, race, and nationality.

Demographic Segmentation

Demographic segmentation consists of dividing the market into groups based on variables such as age, gender, family size, family life cycle, income, occupation, education, religion, race, and nationality. Demographic factors are the most popular bases for segmenting customer groups. One reason is that consumer needs,

THE BEST FRIENDS
A LITTLE CUT EVER HAD.

PICKUP

EQUAL WORK,
EQUAL PLAY.

Demographic segmentation: Johnson & Johnson targets children with Band-Aid Sesame Street Bandages; Big Bird and Cookie Monster "help turn little people's tears into great big smiles." Toyota is marketing to women who "aren't only working hard, they're playing hard."

wants, and usage rates often vary closely with demographic variables. Another is that demographic variables are easier to measure than most other types of variables. Even when market segments are first defined using other bases, such as personality or behavior, their demographic characteristics must be known in order to assess the size of the target market and to reach it efficiently.

Age and life-cycle segmentation
Dividing a market into different age and life-cycle groups.

AGE AND LIFE-CYCLE STAGE.   Consumer needs and wants change with age. Some companies use **age and life-cycle segmentation,** offering different products or using different marketing approaches for different age and life-cycle groups. For example, many companies now use different products and appeals to target teens, Generation Xers (twenty-somethings), baby boomers, or mature consumers. For example, Mazda targets its 929 model at baby boomers, using conservative advertising cues—women in pearls, classical music—and themes of luxury and safety. In contrast, Mazda aims its MX-3 at Generation Xers, using bright colors, loud music, and the pitch that it had taken the "plain old apple pie car and replaced it with a jalapeno."[4] McDonald's targets children, teens, adults, and seniors with different ads and media. Its ads directed at teens feature dance-beat music, adventure, and fast-paced cutting from scene to scene; ads to seniors are softer and more sentimental.

However, marketers must be careful to guard against stereotypes when using age and life-cycle segmentation. Although you might find some 70-year-olds in wheelchairs, you will find others on tennis courts. Similarly, whereas some 40-year-old couples are sending their children off to college, others are just beginning new families. Thus, age is often a poor predictor of a person's life cycle, health, work or family status, needs, and buying power.

Gender segmentation
Dividing a market into different groups based on sex.

GENDER.   **Gender segmentation** has long been used in clothing, cosmetics, and magazines. Recently, other marketers have noticed opportunities for gender segmentation. For example, although early deodorants were used by both sexes, many producers are now featuring unisex brands. Procter & Gamble was among the first with Secret, a brand specially formulated for a woman's chemistry, packaged and advertised to reinforce the female image.

The automobile industry also uses gender segmentation extensively. Women buy nearly half of all new cars sold in the United States and influence 80 percent of all new-car purchasing decisions. Thus, women have become a valued target market for the auto companies. "Selling to women should be no different than selling to men," notes one analyst. "But there are subtleties that make a difference."[5] Women have different frames, less upper-body strength, and greater safety concerns. To address these issues, automakers are designing cars with hoods and trunks that are easier to open, seats that are easier to adjust, and seat belts that fit women better. They've also increased their safety focus, emphasizing features such as air bags and remote door locks.

In advertising, more and more car manufacturers are targeting women directly. In contrast to the car advertising of past decades, these ads portray women as competent and knowledgeable consumers who are interested in what a car is all about, not just the color. For example, in one Pontiac ad, a savvy young woman brings her brother to a dealership to help her pick a color for her new car. In another, "a woman daydreams about a romantic ride with an attractive male, wending along a coastal highway that brings them to an elegant restaurant. She's driving."[6]

Income segmentation
Dividing a market into different income groups.

INCOME.   **Income segmentation** has long been used by the marketers of products and services such as automobiles, boats, clothing, cosmetics, and travel. Many companies target affluent consumers with luxury goods and convenience services. Stores like Neiman-Marcus pitch everything from expensive jewelry, fine fashions, and exotic furs to glazed Australian apricots priced at $20 a pound.

However, not all companies that use income segmentation target the affluent. About 40 percent of U.S. households have incomes of $25,000 or less. Despite their lower spending power, the nation's 40 million lower-income households offer an attractive market to many marketers. Many companies, such as Family Dollar stores, profitably target lower-income consumers. When Family Dollar real estate experts scout locations for new stores, they look for lower-middle-class neighborhoods where people wear less expensive shoes and drive old cars that drip a lot of oil. The income of a typical Family Dollar customer rarely exceeds $17,000 a year, and the average customer spends only about $6 per trip to the store. Yet the store's low-income strategy has made it one of the most profitable discount chains in the country. Chase Manhattan Bank is even opening up accounts for and issuing credit cards to homeless war veterans who live in New York. Some 350 vets have opened accounts with a combined balance of more than $2 million (largely because of lump-sum benefits they receive for injuries).[7]

MULTIVARIATE DEMOGRAPHIC SEGMENTATION.   Most companies will segment a market by combining two or more demographic variables. Consider the market for deodorant soaps. The top-selling deodorant soap brands are used by many different kinds of consumers, but two demographic variables—gender and age—coupled with geographic region, are the most useful in distinguishing the users of one brand from those of another.[8]

Men and women differ in their deodorant soap preferences. Top men's brands include Dial, Safeguard, and Irish Spring—these brands account for over 30 percent of the total men's soap market. Women, in contrast, prefer Dial, Zest, and Coast, which account for 23 percent of the total women's soap market. The leading deodorant soaps also appeal differently to different age segments. For example, Dial appeals more to men aged 45 to 68 than to younger men; women aged 35 to 44, however, are more likely than the average woman to use Dial. Coast appeals much more to younger men and women than to older people—men and women aged 18 to 24 are about a third more likely than the average to use Coast. Finally, deodorant soap preferences differ by region of the country. Although men in all geographic regions use deodorant soap, New Englanders use more Dial, southerners favor Safeguard, and westerners prefer Irish Spring. Thus, no single demographic variable captures all of the differences among the needs and preferences of deodorant soap buyers. To better define important market segments, soap marketers must use multivariate demographic segmentation.

Psychographic Segmentation

Psychographic segmentation divides buyers into different groups based on social class, lifestyle, or personality characteristics. People in the same demographic group can have very different psychographic make-ups.

SOCIAL CLASS.   In Chapter 5, we described American social classes and showed that social class has a strong effect on preferences in cars, clothes, home furnishings, leisure activities, reading habits, and retailers. Many companies design products or services for specific social classes, building in features that appeal to these classes.

LIFESTYLE.   As discussed in Chapter 5, people's interest in various goods is affected by their lifestyles, and the goods they buy express those lifestyles. Marketers are increasingly segmenting their markets by consumer lifestyles. For example, Duck Head apparel tar-

Psychographic segmentation Dividing a market into different groups based on social class, lifestyle, or personality characteristics.

Lifestyle segmentation: Duck Head targets a casual student lifestyle, claiming, "You can't get them old until you get them new."

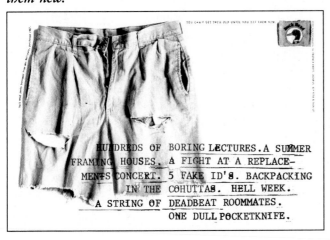

HUNDREDS OF BORING LECTURES. A SUMMER FRAMING HOUSES. A FIGHT AT A REPLACEMENTS CONCERT. 5 FAKE ID's. BACKPACKING IN THE COHUTTAS. HELL WEEK. A STRING OF DEADBEAT ROOMMATES. ONE DULL POCKETKNIFE.

gets a casual student lifestyle, claiming "You can't get them old until you get them new." *Redbook* magazine targets a lifestyle segment it calls "*Redbook* Jugglers," defined as 25- to 44-year-old women who must juggle husband, family, home, and job. According to a recent *Redbook* ad, "She's a product of the 'me generation,' the thirty-something woman who balances home, family, and career—more than any generation before her, she refuses to put her own pleasures aside. She's old enough to know what she wants. And young enough to go after it." According to *Redbook*, this consumer makes an ideal target for marketers of health food and fitness products. She wears out more exercise shoes, swallows more vitamins, drinks more diet soda, and works out more often than do other consumer groups.

PERSONALITY.   Marketers also have used personality variables to segment markets, giving their products personalities that correspond to consumer personalities. Successful market segmentation strategies based on personality have been used for products such as cosmetics, cigarettes, insurance, and liquor.[9]

Honda's marketing campaign for its motor scooters provides a good example of personality segmentation. Honda *appears* to target its Spree, Elite, and Aero motor scooters at hip and trendy 14- to 22-year-olds. But it *actually* designs ads for a much broader personality group. One ad, for example, shows a delighted child bouncing up and down on his bed while the announcer says, "You've been trying to get there all your life." The ad reminds viewers of the euphoric feelings they got when they broke away from authority and did things their parents told them not to do. It suggests that they can feel that way again by riding a Honda scooter. So even though Honda seems to be targeting young consumers, the ads appeal to trendsetters and independent personalities in all age groups. In fact, over half of Honda's scooter sales are to young professionals and older buyers—15 percent are purchased by the over-50 group. Honda is appealing to the rebellious, independent kid in all of us.[10]

Behavioral Segmentation

Behavioral segmentation divides buyers into groups based on their knowledge, attitudes, uses, or responses to a product. Many marketers believe that behavior variables are the best starting point for building market segments.

OCCASIONS.   Buyers can be grouped according to occasions when they get the idea to buy, actually make their purchase, or use the purchased item. **Occasion segmentation** can help firms build up product usage. For example, orange juice

---

Behavioral segmentation
Dividing a market into groups based on consumer knowledge, attitude, use, or response to a product.

Occasion segmentation
Dividing the market into groups according to occasions when buyers get the idea to buy, actually make their purchase, or use the purchased item.

Occasion segmentation: Kodak has developed special versions of its single-use camera for about any picture-taking occasion, from underwater photography to taking baby pictures.

most often is consumed at breakfast, but orange growers have promoted drinking orange juice as a cool and refreshing drink at other times of the day. In contrast, Coca-Cola's "Coke in the Morning" advertising campaign attempts to increase Coke consumption by promoting the beverage as an early morning pick-me-up. Some holidays, such as Mother's Day and Father's Day, were originally promoted partly to increase the sale of candy, flowers, cards, and other gifts. The Curtis Candy Company promoted the "trick-or-treat" custom at Halloween to encourage every home to have candy ready for eager little callers knocking at the door.

Kodak uses occasion segmentation in designing and marketing its single-use cameras. The customer simply snaps off the roll of pictures and returns the film, camera and all, to be processed. By mixing lenses, film speeds, and accessories, Kodak has developed special versions of the camera for about any picture-taking occasion, from underwater photography to taking baby pictures:

> Standing on the edge of the Grand Canyon? [Single-use cameras] can take panoramic, wide-angle shots. Snorkeling? Focus on that flounder with a [different single-use camera]. Sports fans are another target: Kodak now markets a telephoto version with ultrafast . . . film for the stadium set. . . . Planners are looking at a model equipped with a short focal-length lens and fast film requiring less light . . . they figure parents would like . . . to take snapshots of their babies without the disturbing flash. . . . In one Japanese catalog aimed at young women, Kodak sells a package of five pastel-colored cameras . . . including a version with a fish-eye lens to create a rosy, romantic glow.[11]

Benefit segmentation
Dividing the market into groups according to the different benefits that consumers seek from the product.

BENEFITS SOUGHT.   A powerful form of segmentation is to group buyers according to the different *benefits* that they seek from the product. **Benefit segmentation** requires finding the major benefits people look for in the product class, the kinds of people who look for each benefit, and the major brands that deliver each benefit. One of the best examples of benefit segmentation was conducted in the toothpaste market (see Table 8-2). Research found four benefit segments: economic, medicinal, cosmetic, and taste. Each benefit group had special demographic, behavioral, and psychographic characteristics. For example, the people seeking to prevent decay tended to have large families, were heavy toothpaste users, and were conservative. Each segment also favored certain brands. Most current brands appeal to one of these segments. For example, Crest toothpaste stresses protection and appeals to the family segment, whereas Aim looks and tastes good and appeals to children.

Companies can use benefit segmentation to clarify the benefit segment to which they are appealing, its characteristics, and the major competing brands. They also can search for new benefits and launch brands that deliver them.

TABLE 8-2   *Benefit Segmentation of the Toothpaste Market*

BENEFIT SEGMENTS	DEMOGRAPHICS	BEHAVIOR	PSYCHOGRAPHICS	FAVORED BRANDS
Economy (low price)	Men	Heavy users	High autonomy, value oriented	Brands on sale
Medicinal (decay prevention)	Large families	Heavy users	Hypochondriacal, conservative	Crest
Cosmetic (bright teeth)	Teens, young adults	Smokers	High sociability, active	Aqua-Fresh, Ultra Brite
Taste (good tasting)	Children	Spearmint lovers	High self-involvement, hedonistic	Colgate, Aim

Source: Adapted from Russell J. Haley, "Benefit Segmentation: A Decision-Oriented Research Tool," *Journal of Marketing,* July 1968, pp. 30–35. Also see Haley, "Benefit Segmentation: Backwards and Forwards," *Journal of Advertising Research,* February–March 1984, pp. 19–25; and Haley, "Benefit Segmentation—20 Years Later," *Journal of Consumer Marketing,* Vol. 1, 1984, pp. 5–14.

USER STATUS. Markets can be segmented into groups of nonusers, ex-users, potential users, first-time users, and regular users of a product. Potential users and regular users may require different kinds of marketing appeals. For example, one study found that blood donors are low in self-esteem, low risk takers, and more highly concerned about their health; nondonors tend to be the opposite on all three dimensions. This suggests that social agencies should use different marketing approaches for keeping current donors and attracting new ones. A company's market position will also influence its focus. Market share leaders will focus on attracting potential users, whereas smaller firms will focus on attracting current users away from the market leader.

USAGE RATE. Markets also can be segmented into light-, medium-, and heavy-user groups. Heavy users are often a small percentage of the market, but account for a high percentage of total buying. Figure 8-2 shows usage rates for some popular consumer products. Product users were divided into two halves, a light-user half and a heavy-user half, according to their buying rates for the specific products. Using beer as an example, the figure shows that 41 percent of the households studied buy beer. However, the heavy-user half accounted for 87 percent of the beer consumed—almost seven times as much as the light-user half. Clearly, a beer company would prefer to attract one heavy user to its brand rather than several light users. Thus, most beer companies target the heavy beer drinker, using appeals such as Schaefer's "one beer to have when you're having more than one."

LOYALTY STATUS. A market can also be segmented by consumer loyalty. Consumers can be loyal to brands (Tide), stores (Wal-Mart), and companies (Ford). Buyers can be divided into groups according to their degree of loyalty. Some consumers are completely loyal—they buy one brand all the time. Others are somewhat loyal—they are loyal to two or three brands of a given product or favor one brand while sometimes buying others. Still other buyers show no loyalty to any

FIGURE 8-2 *Heavy and light users of common consumer products*
Source: See Victor J. Cook and William A. Mindak, "A Search for Constants: The 'Heavy User' Revisited!" *Journal of Consumer Marketing,* Vol. 1, No. 4 (Spring 1984), p. 80.

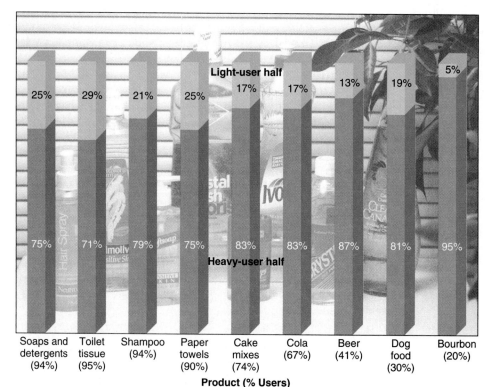

brand. They either want something different each time they buy or they buy whatever's on sale.

A company can learn a lot by analyzing loyalty patterns in its market. It should start by studying its own loyal customers. Colgate finds that its loyal buyers are more middle class, have larger families, and are more health conscious. These characteristics pinpoint the target market for Colgate. By studying its less loyal buyers, the company can detect which brands are most competitive with its own. If many Colgate buyers also buy Crest, Colgate can attempt to improve its positioning against Crest, possibly by using direct-comparison advertising. By looking at customers who are shifting away from its brand, the company can learn about its marketing weaknesses. As for nonloyals, the company may attract them by putting its brand on sale.

Companies need to be careful when using brand loyalty in their segmentation strategies. What appear to be brand-loyal purchase patterns might reflect little more than *habit, indifference,* a *low price,* or *unavailability* of other brands. Thus, frequent or regular purchasing may not be the same as brand loyalty—marketers must examine the motivations behind observed purchase patterns.

SEGMENTING BUSINESS MARKETS

Consumer and business marketers use many of the same variables to segment their markets. Business buyers can be segmented geographically or by benefits sought, user status, usage rate, and loyalty status. Yet, business marketers also use some additional variables. As Table 8-3 shows, these include business customer *demographics* (industry, company size); *operating characteristics; purchasing approaches; situational factors;* and *personal characteristics.*[12]

The table lists major questions that business marketers should ask in determining which customers they want to serve. By going after segments instead of the whole market, companies have a much better chance to deliver value to consumers and to receive maximum rewards for close attention to consumer needs. Thus, Goodyear and other tire companies should decide which *industries* they want to serve. Manufacturers buying tires vary in their needs. Makers of luxury and high-performance cars want higher-grade tires than makers of economy models. And the tires needed by aircraft manufacturers must meet much higher safety standards than tires needed by farm tractor manufacturers.

Within the chosen industry, a company can further segment by *customer size* or *geographic location.* The company might set up separate systems for dealing with larger or multiple-location customers. For example, Steelcase, a major producer of office furniture, first segments customers into ten industries, including banking, insurance, and electronics. Next, company salespeople work with independent Steelcase dealers to handle smaller, local, or regional Steelcase customers in each segment. But many national, multiple-location customers, such as Exxon or IBM, have special needs that may reach beyond the scope of individual dealers. So Steelcase uses national accounts managers to help its dealer networks handle its national accounts.

Within a given target industry and customer size, the company can segment by *purchase approaches and criteria.* For example, government, university, and industrial laboratories typically differ in their purchase criteria for scientific instruments. Government labs need low prices (because they have difficulty in getting funds to buy instruments) and service contracts (because they can easily get money to maintain instruments). University labs want equipment that needs little regular service because they don't have service people on their payrolls. Industrial labs need highly reliable equipment because they cannot afford downtime.

Table 8-3 focuses on business buyer *characteristics*. However, as in consumer segmentation, many marketers believe that *buying behavior* and *benefits* provide the best basis for segmenting business markets. For example, a recent study of the customers of Signode Corporation's industrial packaging division revealed four segments, each seeking a different mix of price and service benefits:

♦ *Programmed buyers.* These buyers view Signode's products as not very important to their operations. They buy the products as a routine purchase, usually pay full price, and accept below-average service. Clearly, this is a highly profitable segment for Signode.

♦ *Relationship buyers.* These buyers regard Signode's packaging products as moderately important and are knowledgeable about competitors' offerings. They prefer to buy from Signode as long as its price is reasonably competitive. They receive a small discount and a modest amount of service. This segment is Signode's second most profitable.

♦ *Transaction buyers.* These buyers see Signode's products as very important to their operations. They are price and service sensitive. They receive about a 10 percent discount and above-average service. They are knowledgeable about competitors' offerings and are ready to switch for a better price, even if it means losing some service.

♦ *Bargain hunters.* These buyers see Signode's products as very important and demand the deepest discount and the highest service. They know the alternative suppliers, bargain hard, and are ready to switch at the slightest dissatisfaction. Signode needs these buyers for volume purposes, but they are not very profitable.[13]

This segmentation scheme has helped Signode to do a better job of designing marketing strategies that take into account each segment's unique reactions to varying levels of price and service.[14]

SEGMENTING INTERNATIONAL MARKETS

Few companies have either the resources or the will to operate in all, or even most, of the countries that dot the globe. Although some large companies, such as Coca-Cola or Sony, sell products in more than 150 countries, most international firms focus on a smaller set. Operating in many countries presents new challenges. The different countries of the world, even those that are close together, can vary dramatically in their economic, cultural, and political makeup. Thus, just as they do within their domestic markets, international firms need to group their world markets into segments with distinct buying needs and behaviors.

Companies can segment international markets using one or a combination of several variables. They can segment by *geographic location,* grouping countries by regions such as Western Europe, the Pacific Rim, the Middle East, or Africa. In fact, countries in many regions already have organized geographically into market groups or "free trade zones," such as the European Union, the European Free Trade Association, and the North American Free Trade Association. These associations reduce trade barriers between member countries, creating larger and more homogeneous markets.

Geographic segmentation assumes that nations close to one another will have many common traits and behaviors. Although this is often the case, there are many exceptions. For example, although the United States and Canada have much in common, both differ culturally and economically from neighboring Mexico. Even within a region, consumers can differ widely. For example, many U.S. marketers think that all Central and South American countries are the same, including their 400 million inhabitants. However, the Dominican Republic is no more like Brazil than Italy is like Sweden. Many Latin Americans don't speak Spanish, including

TABLE 8-3   *Major Segmentation Variables for Business Markets*

DEMOGRAPHICS

Industry: Which industries that buy this product should we focus on?

Company size: What size companies should we focus on?

Location: What geographical areas should we focus on?

OPERATING VARIABLES

Technology: What customer technologies should we focus on?

User/nonuser status: Should we focus on heavy, medium, or light users or nonusers?

Customer capabilities: Should we focus on customers needing many services or few services?

PURCHASING APPROACHES

Purchasing function organization: Should we focus on companies with highly centralized or decentralized purchasing organizations?

Power structure: Should we focus on companies that are engineering dominated, financially dominated, or marketing dominated?

Nature of existing relationships: Should we focus on companies with which we already have strong relationships or simply go after the most desirable companies?

General purchase policies: Should we focus on companies that prefer leasing? Service contracts? Systems purchases? Sealed bidding?

Purchasing criteria: Should we focus on companies that are seeking quality? Service? Price?

SITUATIONAL FACTORS

Urgency: Should we focus on companies that need quick delivery or service?

Specific application: Should we focus on certain applications of our product rather than all applications?

Size of order: Should we focus on large or small orders?

PERSONAL CHARACTERISTICS

Buyer-seller similarity: Should we focus on companies whose people and values are similar to ours?

Attitudes toward risk: Should we focus on risk-taking or risk-avoiding customers?

Loyalty: Should we focus on companies that show high loyalty to their suppliers?

Source: Adapted from Thomas V. Bonoma and Benson P. Shapiro, *Segmenting the Industrial Market* (Lexington, MA: Lexington Books, 1983). Also see John Berrigan and Carl Finkbeiner, *Segmentation Marketing: New Methods for Capturing Business* (New York: Harper-Business, 1992).

140 million Portuguese-speaking Brazilians and the millions in other countries who speak a variety of Indian dialects.[15]

World markets can be segmented on the basis of *economic factors.* For example, countries might be grouped by population income levels or by their overall level of economic development. Some countries, such as the so-called Group of Seven—the United States, Britain, France, Germany, Japan, Canada, and Italy—have established, highly industrialized economies. Other countries have newly industrialized or developing economies (Singapore, Taiwan, Korea, Brazil, Mexico). Still others are less developed (China, India). A company's economic structure shapes its population's product and service needs and, therefore, the marketing opportunities it offers.

Countries can be segmented by *political and legal factors* such as the type and stability of government, receptivity to foreign firms, monetary regulations, and the amount of bureaucracy. Such factors can play a crucial role in a company's choice of which countries to enter and how. *Cultural factors* also can be used, grouping markets according to common languages, religions, values and attitudes, customs, and behavioral patterns.

Segmenting international markets on the basis of geographic, economic, political, cultural, and other factors assumes that segments should consist of clusters of countries. However, many companies use a different approach, called **intermarket segmentation**. Using this approach, they form segments of consumers who have similar needs and buying behavior even though they are located in different countries. For example, Mercedes-Benz targets the world's well-to-do, regardless of their country. And Pepsi uses ads filled with kids, sports, and rock music to target the world's teenagers. It recently introduced sugar-free Pepsi Max in 16 countries, including Britain, Australia, and Japan, with a single set of ads aimed at teens who like to live on the wild side.[16]

Similarly, an agricultural chemicals manufacturer might focus on small farmers in a variety of developing countries:

> These [small farmers], whether from Pakistan or Indonesia or Kenya or Mexico, appear to represent common needs and behavior patterns. Most of them till the land using bullock carts and have very little cash to buy agricultural inputs. They lack the education . . . to appreciate fully the value of using fertilizer and depend on government help for such things as seeds, pesticides, and fertilizer. They acquire farming needs from local suppliers and count on word-of-mouth to learn and accept new things and ideas. Thus, even though these farmers are in different countries continents apart, and even though they speak different languages and have different cultural backgrounds, they may represent a homogeneous market segment.[17]

Intermarket segmentation
Forming segments of consumers who have similar needs and buying behavior even though they are located in different countries.

REQUIREMENTS FOR EFFECTIVE SEGMENTATION

Clearly, there are many ways to segment a market, but not all segmentations are effective. For example, buyers of table salt could be divided into blond and brunette customers. But hair color obviously does not affect the purchase of salt. Furthermore, if all salt buyers bought the same amount of salt each month, believed all salt is the same, and wanted to pay the same price, the company would not benefit from segmenting this market.

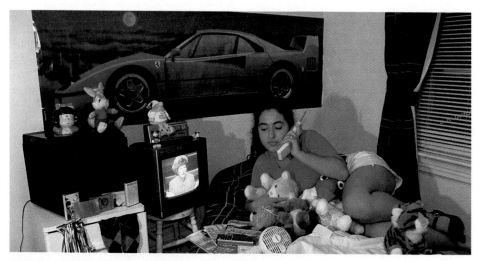

Intermarket separation: Teens show surprising similarity no matter where in the world they live. For instance, this young woman could live almost anywhere. Thus, many companies target teenagers with worldwide marketing campaigns.

To be useful, market segments must have the following characteristics:

♦ *Measurability.* The size, purchasing power, and profiles of the segments can be measured. Certain segmentation variables are difficult to measure. For example, there are 24 million left-handed people in the United States—almost equaling the entire population of Canada. Yet few products are targeted toward this left-handed segment. The major problem may be that the segment is hard to identify and measure. There are no data on the demographics of lefties, and the Census Bureau does not keep track of left-handedness in its surveys. Private data companies keep reams of statistics on other demographic segments, but not on left-handers.[18]

♦ *Accessibility.* The market segments can be effectively reached and served. Suppose a perfume company finds that heavy users of its brand are single women who stay out late and socialize a lot. Unless this group lives or shops at certain places and is exposed to certain media, its members will be difficult to reach.

♦ *Substantiality.* The market segments are large or profitable enough to serve. A segment should be the largest possible homogeneous group worth pursuing with a tailored marketing program. It would not pay, for example, for an automobile manufacturer to develop cars for persons whose height is less than four feet.

♦ *Actionability.* Effective programs can be designed for attracting and serving the segments. For example, although one small airline identified seven market segments, its staff was too small to develop separate marketing programs for each segment.

MARKET TARGETING

Marketing segmentation reveals the firm's market-segment opportunities. The firm now has to evaluate the various segments and decide how many and which ones to target. We now look at how companies evaluate and select target segments.

EVALUATING MARKET SEGMENTS

In evaluating different market segments, a firm must look at three factors: segment size and growth, segment structural attractiveness, and company objectives and resources.

Segment Size and Growth
The company must first collect and analyze data on current segment sales, growth rates, and expected profitability for various segments. It will be interested in segments that have the right size and growth characteristics. But "right size and growth" is a relative matter. Some companies will want to target segments with large current sales, a high growth rate, and a high profit margin. However, the largest, fastest-growing segments are not always the most attractive ones for every company. Smaller companies may find that they lack the skills and resources needed to serve the larger segments, or that these segments are too competitive. Such companies may select segments that are smaller and less attractive, in an absolute sense, but that are potentially more profitable for them.

Segment Structural Attractiveness
A segment might have desirable size and growth and still not offer attractive profits. The company must examine several major structural factors that affect long-run segment attractiveness.[19] For example, a segment is less attractive if it already contains many strong and aggressive *competitors.* The existence of many actual

or potential *substitute products* may limit prices and the profits that can be earned in a segment. The relative *power of buyers* also affects segment attractiveness. If the buyers in a segment possess strong bargaining power relative to sellers, they will try to force prices down, demand more quality or services, and set competitors against one another, all at the expense of seller profitability. Finally, a segment may be less attractive if it contains *powerful suppliers* who can control prices or reduce the quality or quantity of ordered goods and services. Suppliers tend to be powerful when they are large and concentrated, when few substitutes exist, or when the supplied product is an important input.

Company Objectives and Resources

Even if a segment has the right size and growth and is structurally attractive, the company must consider its own objectives and resources in relation to that segment. Some attractive segments could be dismissed quickly because they do not mesh with the company's long-run objectives. Although such segments might be tempting in themselves, they might divert the company's attention and energies away from its main goals. Or they might be a poor choice from an environmental, political, or social-responsibility viewpoint. For example, in recent years, several companies and industries have been criticized for unfairly targeting vulnerable segments—children, the aged, low-income minorities, and others—with questionable products or tactics (see Marketing Highlight 8-2).

If a segment fits the company's objectives, the company then must decide whether it possesses the skills and resources needed to succeed in that segment. If the company lacks the strengths needed to compete successfully in a segment and cannot readily obtain them, it should not enter the segment. Even if the company possesses the *required* strengths, it needs to employ skills and resources *superior* to those of the competition in order to really win in a market segment. The company should enter segments only where it can offer superior value and gain advantages over competitors.

Target market
A set of buyers sharing common needs or characteristics that the company decides to serve.

Undifferentiated marketing
A market-coverage strategy in which a firm decides to ignore market segment differences and go after the whole market with one offer.

FIGURE 8-3 *Three alternative market-coverage strategies*

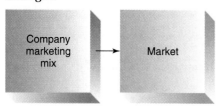

A. Undifferentiated marketing

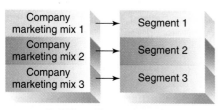

B. Differentiated marketing

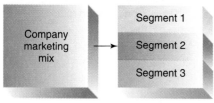

C. Concentrated marketing

SELECTING MARKET SEGMENTS

After evaluating different segments, the company must now decide which and how many segments to serve. This is the problem of *target-market selection*. A **target market** consists of a set of buyers who share common needs or characteristics that the company decides to serve. Figure 8-3 shows that the firm can adopt one of three market-coverage strategies: *undifferentiated marketing*, *differentiated marketing*, and *concentrated marketing*.

Undifferentiated Marketing

Using an **undifferentiated marketing** strategy, a firm might decide to ignore market segment differences and go after the whole market with one offer. The offer will focus on what is *common* in the needs of consumers rather than on what is *different*. The company designs a product and a marketing program that appeal to the largest number of buyers. It relies on mass distribution and mass advertising, and it aims to give the product a superior image in people's minds. An example of undifferentiated marketing is the Hershey Company's marketing some years ago of only one chocolate candy bar for everyone.

Undifferentiated marketing provides cost economies. The narrow product line keeps down production, inventory, and transportation costs. The undifferentiated advertising program keeps down advertising

SOCIALLY RESPONSIBLE MARKET TARGETING

Market segmentation and targeting form the core of modern marketing strategy. Smart targeting helps companies to be more efficient and effective by focusing on the segments that they can satisfy best. Targeting also benefits consumers—companies reach specific groups of consumers with offers carefully tailored to satisfy their needs. However, market targeting sometimes generates controversy and concern. Issues usually involve the targeting of vulnerable or disadvantaged consumers with controversial or potentially harmful products.

For example, over the years, the cereal industry has been heavily criticized for its marketing efforts directed toward children. Critics worry that sophisticated advertising, in which high-powered appeals are presented through the mouths of lovable animated characters, will overwhelm children's defenses. They claim that toys and other premiums offered with cereals will distract children and make them want a particular cereal for the wrong reasons. All of this, critics fear, will entice children to gobble too much sugared cereal or to eat poorly balanced breakfasts. The marketers of toys and other children's products have been similarly battered, often with good justification. Some critics have even called for a complete ban on advertising to children. Children cannot understand the selling intent of the advertiser, critics reason, so any advertising targeted toward children is inherently unfair. To encourage responsible advertising to children, the Children's Advertising Review Unit, the advertising industry's self-regulatory agency, has published extensive children's advertising guidelines that recognize the special needs of child audiences.

Cigarette, beer, and fast-food marketers also have generated much controversy in recent years by their attempts to target inner-city minority consumers. For example, McDonald's and other chains have drawn criticism for pitching their high-fat, salt-laden fare to low-income, inner-city residents who are much more likely than suburbanites to be heavy consumers. R. J. Reynolds took heavy flak in 1990 when it announced plans to market Uptown, a menthol cigarette targeted toward low-income blacks. It quickly dropped the brand in the face of a loud public outcry and heavy pressure from black leaders. G. Heileman Brewing made a similar mistake

Most attempts to target minorities and other special segments benefit targeted customers. For example, Maybelline developed Shades of You cosmetics to meet the special needs of black women.

with PowerMaster, a potent malt liquor targeted toward the black community. Although the brand seemed to make sense initially, it was ill-fated from the start:

> Sales of ordinary beer (3.5 percent alcohol) have slowly been going pfffft for years now, while sales of some higher-proof beers have risen 25 to 30 percent annually. So the decision by G. Heileman Brewing to extend its Colt 45 malt liquor line with Power-Master, a new high-test malt (5.9 percent alcohol), wasn't [at first glance] dumb. But malt liquor is consumed primarily by blacks. And targeting blacks with anything less wholesome than farina has become risky. . . . Heileman nonetheless rushed in where a smarter company might reasonably have hesitated. . . . PowerMaster became "a magnet of controversy from the moment it raised its alcohol-enhanced head. Federal officials, industry leaders, black activists, and media types weighed in with protests that Power-Master . . . was an example of a bad product, bad marketing, and, essentially, a bad idea." . . . [Only] weeks after its planned debut, [PowerMaster] was just a malty memory.

Even some industry insiders objected to the Heileman's targeting tactics. For example, when the PowerMaster controversy erupted, the president of Anheuser-Busch wrote to Heileman's chairman, suggesting that the planned product might indicate "that we put profits before the consideration of the communities we serve."

Not all attempts to target children, minorities, or other special segments draw such criticism. In fact, most provide benefits to targeted consumers. For example, Colgate-Palmolive's Colgate Junior toothpaste has special features designed to get children to brush longer and more often—it's less foamy, has a milder taste, and contains sparkles, and it exits the tube in a star-shaped column. Golden Ribbon Playthings has developed a highly acclaimed and very successful black character doll named "Huggy Bean" targeted toward minority consumers. Huggy comes with books and toys that connect her with her African heritage. Many cosmetics companies have responded to the special needs of minority segments by adding products specifically designed for black, Hispanic, or Asian women. For example, Maybelline introduced a highly successful line called Shades of You targeted to black women, and other companies have followed with their own lines of multicultural products.

Thus, in market targeting, the issue is not really *who* is targeted but rather *how* and for *what*. Controversies arise when marketers attempt to profit at the expense of targeted segments—when they unfairly target vulnerable segments or target them with questionable products or tactics. Socially responsible marketing calls for segmentation and targeting that serve not just the interests of the company, but also the interests of those targeted.

Sources: Excerpts from "PowerMaster," *Fortune,* January 13, 1992, p. 82. Also see "Selling Sin to Blacks," *Fortune,* October 21, 1991, p. 100; Dorothy J. Gaiter, "Black-Owned Firms Are Catching an Afrocentric Wave," *Wall Street Journal,* January 8, 1992, p. B2; Cyndee Miller, "Cosmetics Firms Finally Discover the Ethnic Market," *Marketing News,* August 30, 1993, p. 2; and Michael Wilke, "Toy Companies Take Up Diversity Banner," *Advertising Age,* February 27, 1995, pp. 1, 8.

costs. The absence of segment marketing research and planning lowers the costs of marketing research and product management.

Most modern marketers, however, have strong doubts about this strategy. Difficulties arise in developing a product or brand that will satisfy all consumers. Firms using undifferentiated marketing typically develop an offer aimed at the largest segments in the market. When several firms do this, heavy competition develops in the largest segments, and less satisfaction results in the smaller ones. The final result is that the larger segments may be less profitable because they attract heavy competition. Recognition of this problem has led firms to be more interested in smaller market segments.

Differentiated Marketing

Differentiated marketing
A market-coverage strategy in which a firm decides to target several market segments and designs separate offers for each.

Using a **differentiated marketing** strategy, a firm decides to target several market segments and designs separate offers for each. General Motors tries to produce a car for every "purse, purpose, and personality." Nike offers athletic shoes for a dozen or more different sports, from running, fencing, and aerobics to bicycling and baseball. And Wal-Mart appeals to the needs of different shopper segments with Wal-Mart discount stores, Wal-Mart Supercenters, and Sam's Warehouse stores. By offering product and marketing variations, these companies hope for higher sales and a stronger position within each market segment. They hope that a stronger position in several segments will strengthen consumers' overall identification of the company with the product category. They also hope for more loyal purchasing, because the firm's offer better matches each segment's desires.

Differentiated marketing typically creates more total sales than does undifferentiated marketing, and a growing number of firms have adopted this strategy. Procter & Gamble gets a higher total market share with eleven brands of laundry detergent than it could with only one. But differentiated marketing also increases the costs of doing business. Modifying a product to meet different market-segment needs usually involves extra research and development, engineering, or special tooling costs. A firm usually finds it more expensive to produce, say, ten units of ten different products than one hundred units of one product. Developing separate marketing plans for the separate segments requires extra marketing research, forecasting, sales analysis, promotion planning, and channel management. And trying to reach different market segments with different advertising increases promotion costs. Thus, the company must weigh increased sales against increased costs when deciding on a differentiated marketing strategy.

Concentrated Marketing

Concentrated marketing
A market-coverage strategy in which a firm goes after a large share of one or a few submarkets.

A third market-coverage strategy, **concentrated marketing,** is especially appealing when company resources are limited. Instead of going after a small share of a large market, the firm goes after a large share of one or a few submarkets. For example, Oshkosh Truck is the world's largest producer of airport rescue trucks and front-loading concrete mixers. Recycled Paper Products concentrates on the market for alternative greeting cards. And Soho Natural Sodas concentrates on a narrow segment of the soft-drink market. Concentrated marketing provides an excellent way for small new businesses to get a foothold against larger, more resourceful competitors.

Through concentrated marketing, the firm achieves a strong market position in the segments (or niches) it serves because of its greater knowledge of the segments' needs and the special reputation it acquires (see Marketing Highlight 8-3). It also enjoys many operating economies because of specialization in production, distribution, and promotion. If the segment is well chosen, the firm can earn a high rate of return on its investment.

MARKET NICHING: KING OF THE (MOLE)HILL

Ask almost anyone you know to name a brand of baking soda and they'll answer without hesitating: Arm & Hammer. In fact, they'll find it hard to name any other brand. Arm & Hammer baking soda, in its familiar little yellow box, has dominated the U.S. market for more than 115 years. But ask that same person to name the company that *makes* Arm & Hammer baking soda and they'll probably draw a blank. The company is Church & Dwight. And although you won't find the firm listed among the Fortune 500, Church & Dwight is a giant in its baking soda niche. Founded in 1846, Church & Dwight is the world's leading producer of sodium bicarbonate—good ol' NaHCO$_3$.

Until the late 1960s, Church & Dwight was pretty much a one-product company, marketing sodium bicarbonate to consumers as Arm & Hammer baking soda, or selling it in bulk to other companies for a variety of uses, from cake mixes to fire extinguishers. During the past two decades, however, as the consumer market for pure baking soda has matured, Church & Dwight has expanded its niche dramatically by finding ever more uses for its versatile white powder. In 1970, the company began its push into new consumer markets with a line of laundry products that capitalized both on the powerful Arm & Hammer brand name and on consumer concerns about the environment. It introduced phosphate-free—but sodium-bicarbonate-rich—Arm & Hammer detergent, which has since become the company's best-selling product, accounting for about a third of total sales. During the 1980s, Church & Dwight followed with a number of well-known consumer products, ranging from baking soda toothpaste to carpet deodorizers and air fresheners.

Although baking soda-based consumer products make up the bulk of Church & Dwight's current sales, the usefulness of sodium bicarbonate extends well beyond household cooking and cleaning. Church & Dwight also does a brisk and growing industrial business, which now contributes about 25 percent of annual sales. Business applications range from baking soda as a leavening agent in

bakery products to use in oil-well drilling muds. It's even used in animal nutrition products. For example, Church & Dwight markets an Arm & Hammer product called Megalac, a high-energy feed supplement that helps dairy cows neutralize digestive acids and supplements the sodium bicarbonate produced naturally, resulting in better feed efficiency and increased milk production.

Business markets may provide some of Church & Dwight's best opportunities for growth. As the world looks for new, more environmentally friendly solutions to nagging problems, the company has responded with a smorgasbord of new uses and products. For example, it recently introduced Armex, a blasting material

Well-focused Church & Dwight has built a commanding position by concentrating on small, highly specialized niches.

made of baking soda and other ingredients. Armex has many advantages over current silicon-based sandblasting media, which can contribute to silicosis, a lung disease. Armex not only eliminates health and environmental hazards, it also has a more delicate touch—the sharp edges of its baking soda crystals wear down faster, stripping paint and grime without damaging underlying surfaces. Armex was originally developed to help strip tar and paint from the inside of the Statue of Liberty. Among the company's other new products is Armakleen, an industrial cleanser for printed circuit boards. It provides an environmentally safe alternative to current cleaners that contain chlorofluorocarbons (CFCs), thought to damage the earth's ozone layer. In addition to developing new baking soda-based products for its business

markets, Church & Dwight has created a torrent of new commercial uses for plain old baking soda. For example, it has recently begun selling the stuff as an additive to municipal drinking water. Experiments have shown that baking soda neutralizes acids in the water supply, helping to inhibit corrosion and preventing lead and other toxic metals from leaching out of the plumbing. Church & Dwight is even rumored to be experimenting with baking soda as a safe and effective fungicide for plants.

Church & Dwight battles daily with much larger competitors—consumer companies like Procter & Gamble, Lever, and Colgate, and such international heavyweights as Rhône Poulenc and Solvay. At first glance, the company may appear to be fighting a losing battle. For example, in the $3.6 billion U.S. detergent market, Arm & Hammer commands only a 4 percent market share, compared to P&G's 53 percent and Colgate's 24 percent. However, in the baking soda segment of the detergent market, Arm & Hammer dominates. In fact, when it comes to *anything* that has to do with baking soda, Church & Dwight is "king of the hill"—capturing 60 percent of the world market for sodium bicarbonate. And even if the hill is more of a molehill than a mountain, Church & Dwight outperforms many of its much larger competitors. The well-focused company has built a commanding position by concentrating on small, highly specialized market niches. During the past ten years, its annual sales have more than tripled, to $492 million, and profits have increased fourfold. Thus, Church & Dwight has proven once again what many concentrated marketers have learned — small can be beautiful.

Sources: James P. Meagher, "Church & Dwight: It Scores Big with the Brand-Name Pull of Arm & Hammer," *Barron's,* December 10, 1990, pp. 49–50; Peter Coombes, "Church & Dwight: On the Rise," *Chemical Week,* September 20, 1989, pp. 16–18; Peter Nulty, "Church & Dwight: No Product Is Too Dull to Shine," *Fortune,* July 27, 1992, pp. 95–96; and Riccardo A. Davis, "Arm & Hammer Seeks Growth Abroad," *Advertising Age,* August 17, 1992, pp. 3, 42.

At the same time, concentrated marketing involves higher than normal risks. The particular market segment can turn sour. Or larger competitors may decide to enter the same segment. For example, California Cooler's success in the wine cooler segment attracted many large competitors, causing the original owners to sell to a larger company that had more marketing resources. For these reasons, many companies prefer to diversify in several market segments.

Rapid advances in computer and communications technology are allowing many large mass marketers to act more like concentrated marketers. Using detailed customer databases, these marketers segment their mass markets into small groups of like-minded buyers. For example, using home-delivery information, Pizza Hut has developed a database containing electronic profiles of the pizza-eating habits of some nine million customers across the country. It uses this database to develop carefully targeted promotions. In a recent summer promotion, "lovers of Neapolitan-style pizza got offers for those, not for thin-crust pizza. Consumers who had been willing to try new foods got a mailing for Bigfoot, a giant-pizza innovation. Customers who had not ordered in a while got deeper discounts than others. [These targeted promotions were] very precise—and very successful."[20]

Choosing a Market-Coverage Strategy

Many factors need to be considered when choosing a market-coverage strategy. Which strategy is best depends on *company resources*. When the firm's resources are limited, concentrated marketing makes the most sense. The best strategy also depends on the degree of *product variability*. Undifferentiated marketing is more suited for uniform products such as grapefruit or steel. Products that can vary in design, such as cameras and automobiles, are more suited to differentiation or concentration. The *product's stage in the life cycle* also must be considered. When a firm introduces a new product, it is practical to launch only one version, and undifferentiated marketing or concentrated marketing makes the most sense. In the mature stage of the product life cycle, however, differentiated marketing begins to make more sense. Another factor is *market variability*. If most buyers have the same tastes, buy the same amounts, and react the same way to marketing efforts, undifferentiated marketing is appropriate. Finally, *competitors' marketing strategies* are important. When competitors use segmentation, undifferentiated marketing can be suicidal. Conversely, when competitors use undifferentiated marketing, a firm can gain an advantage by using differentiated or concentrated marketing.

POSITIONING FOR COMPETITIVE ADVANTAGE

Once a company has decided which segments of the market it will enter, it must decide what "positions" it wants to occupy in those segments.

WHAT IS MARKET POSITIONING?

Product position
The way the product is defined by consumers on important attributes—the place the product occupies in consumers' minds relative to competing products.

A **product's position** is the way the product is *defined by consumers* on important attributes—the place the product occupies in consumers' minds relative to competing products. Thus, Tide is positioned as a powerful, all-purpose family detergent; Solo is positioned as a liquid detergent with fabric softener; Cheer is positioned as the detergent for all temperatures. In the automobile market Toyota Tercel and Subaru are positioned on economy, Mercedes and Cadillac on luxury, and Porsche and BMW on performance. Volvo positions powerfully on safety.

Consumers are overloaded with information about products and services. They cannot reevaluate products every time they make a buying decision. To simplify the buying process, consumers organize products into categories—they "position" products, services, and companies in their minds. A product's position is the complex set of perceptions, impressions, and feelings that consumers hold for the product compared with competing products. Consumers position products with or without the help of marketers. But marketers do not want to leave their products' positions to chance. They must *plan* positions that will give their products the greatest advantage in selected target markets, and they must design marketing mixes to create these planned positions.

POSITIONING STRATEGIES

Marketers can follow several positioning strategies. They can position their products on specific *product attributes*—Honda Civic advertises its low price; BMW promotes performance. Products can be positioned on the needs they fill or the *benefits* they offer—Crest reduces cavities; Aim tastes good. Or products can be positioned according to *usage occasions*—in the summer, Gatorade can be positioned as a beverage for replacing athletes' body fluids; in the winter, it can be positioned as the drink to use when the doctor recommends plenty of liquids. Another approach is to position the product for certain classes of *users*—Johnson & Johnson improved the market share for its baby shampoo from 3 percent to 14 percent by repositioning the product as one for adults who wash their hair frequently and need a gentle shampoo.

A product can also be positioned directly *against a competitor*. For example, in its ads, Citibank VISA compares itself directly with American Express, saying "You'd better take your VISA card, because they don't take American Express." In its famous "We're number two, so we try harder" campaign, Avis successfully positioned itself against the larger Hertz. A product may also be positioned *away from competitors*—for many years, 7-Up has positioned itself as the "un-cola," the fresh and thirst-quenching alternative to Coke and Pepsi. And Barbasol television ads position the company's shaving cream and other products as "great toiletries for a lot less money."

Finally, the product can be positioned for different *product classes*. For example, some margarines are positioned against butter, others against cooking oils. Camay hand soap is positioned with bath oils rather than with soap. Marketers often use a *combination* of these positioning strategies. Arm & Hammer baking soda has been positioned as a deodorizer for refrigerators and garbage disposals (product class *and* usage situation).

CHOOSING AND IMPLEMENTING A POSITIONING STRATEGY

Some firms find it easy to choose their positioning strategy. For example, a firm well known for quality in certain segments will go for this position in a new segment if there are enough buyers seeking quality. But in many cases, two or more firms will go after the same position. Then, each will have to find other ways to set itself apart, such as promis-

Positioning: When you think of automobile safety, what brand comes to mind? Volvo has positioned itself powerfully on safety.

ing "high quality for a lower cost" or "high quality with more technical service." Each firm must differentiate its offer by building a unique bundle of competitive advantages that appeal to a substantial group within the segment.

The positioning task consists of three steps: identifying a set of possible competitive advantages on which to build a position, selecting the right competitive advantages, and effectively communicating and delivering the chosen position to the market.

Identifying Possible Competitive Advantages

Competitive advantage
An advantage over competitors gained by offering consumers greater value, either through lower prices or by providing more benefits that justify higher prices.

Consumers typically choose products and services that give them the greatest value. Thus, the key to winning and keeping customers is to understand their needs and buying processes better than competitors do and to deliver more value. To the extent that a company can position itself as providing superior value to selected target markets, either by offering lower prices than competitors do or by providing more benefits to justify higher prices, it gains **competitive advantage**. But solid positions cannot be built on empty promises. If a company positions its product as *offering* the best quality and service, it must then *deliver* the promised quality and service. Thus, positioning begins with actually *differentiating* the company's marketing offer so it will give consumers more value than competitors' offers do.

Not every company will find many opportunities for differentiating its offer and gaining competitive advantage. Some companies find many minor advantages that are easily copied by competitors and are, therefore, highly perishable. The solution for these companies is to keep identifying new potential advantages and to introduce them one by one to keep competitors off balance. These companies do not expect to gain a single major permanent advantage. Instead, they hope to gain many minor ones that can be introduced to win market share over a period of time.

In what specific ways can a company differentiate its offer from those of competitors? A company or market offer can be differentiated along the lines of *product, services, personnel,* or *image.*

PRODUCT DIFFERENTIATION. A company can differentiate its physical product. At one extreme, some companies offer highly standardized products that allow little variation: chicken, steel, aspirin. Yet even here, meaningful differentiation is possible. For example, Perdue claims that its branded chickens are better—fresher and more tender—and gets a 10 percent price premium based on this differentiation.

Other companies offer products that can be highly differentiated, such as automobiles, commercial buildings, and furniture. Here the company faces an abundance of design parameters. It can offer a variety of standard or optional *features* not provided by competitors. Thus, Volvo provides new and better safety features; Delta Airlines offers wider seating and free in-flight telephone use. Companies also can differentiate their products on *performance.* Whirlpool designs its dishwasher to run more quietly; Procter & Gamble formulates Liquid Tide to get clothes cleaner. *Style* and *design* also can be important differentiating factors. Thus, many car buyers pay a premium for Jaguar automobiles because of their extraordinary look, even though Jaguar has sometimes had a poor reliability record. Similarly, companies can differentiate their products on such attributes as *consistency, durability, reliability,* or *repairability.*

SERVICES DIFFERENTIATION. In addition to differentiating its physical product, the firm also can differentiate the services that accompany the product. Some companies gain competitive advantage through speedy, convenient, or careful *delivery.* Deluxe, the check supply company, has built an impressive reputation for shipping out replacement checks one day after receiving an order—without being late

Patience is indeed a virtue. Unfortunately, at some hotels it's a requirement. Not here. At The Ritz-Carlton, we realize you've got more important things to do than wait. Which is why we offer 24-hour room service, express breakfast and overnight valet services. And our highly

trained staff is second-to-none when it comes to reliability. So your suits are pressed on time. And wake-up calls happen when they're supposed to. For reservations, call your travel professional or The Ritz-Carlton at 800-241-3333.

The only thing you'll find yourself waiting for is your next business trip.

SOME THINGS ARE WORTH WAITING FOR. OF COURSE, THOSE THINGS ARE EVEN BETTER WHEN YOU GET THEM RIGHT AWAY.

THE RITZ-CARLTON
HOTELS

Atlanta · Barcelona · Boston · Buckhead · Cleveland · Dearborn · Double Bay · Hong Kong · Houston · Huntington Hotel · Kansas City · Marina del Rey
New York · Pentagon City · Philadelphia · Phoenix · San Francisco · Seoul · St. Louis · Sydney · Tysons Corner · Washington, D.C. · 1995: Singapore

Finding competitive advantage: Ritz-Carlton differentiates its hotels through outstanding service provided by carefully selected and well-trained personnel. "Our highly trained staff is second to none. . . ."

once in 12 years. And Bank One has opened full-service branches in supermarkets to provide location convenience along with Saturday, Sunday, and weekday-evening hours.

Installation also can differentiate one company from another. IBM, for example, is known for its quality installation service. It delivers all pieces of purchased equipment to the site at one time rather than sending individual components to sit and wait for others to arrive. And when asked to move IBM equipment and install it in another location, IBM often moves competitors' equipment as well. Companies can further distinguish themselves through their *repair* services. Many an automobile buyer will gladly pay a little more and travel a little farther to buy a car from a dealer that provides top-notch repair service.

Some companies differentiate their offers by providing *customer training* service. Thus, General Electric not only sells and installs expensive X-ray equipment in hospitals, but also trains the hospital employees who will use this equipment. Other companies offer free or paid *consulting services*—data, information systems, and advising services that buyers need. For example, McKesson Corporation, a major drug wholesaler, consults with its 12,000 independent pharmacists to help them set up accounting, inventory, and computer ordering systems. By helping its customers compete better, McKesson gains greater customer loyalty and sales.

Companies can find many other ways to add value through differentiated services. In fact, they can choose from a virtually unlimited number of specific services and benefits through which to differentiate themselves from the competition. Milliken & Company provides one of the best examples of a company that has gained competitive advantage through superior service. Milliken sells shop towels to industrial launderers who rent them to factories. These towels are physically similar to competitors' towels, yet Milliken charges a higher price and enjoys the leading market share. How can it charge more for what is essentially a commodity? The answer is that Milliken continuously "decommoditizes" this product through continuous service enhancements. Milliken trains its customers' salespeople, supplies them with prospect leads and sales promotional material, and lends its own salespeople to work on Customer Action Teams. It provides computer order entry and freight optimization systems, carries out marketing research for customers, and sponsors quality improvement workshops. Launderers are more than willing to buy Milliken shop towels and pay a price premium because the extra services improve their profitability.[21]

PERSONNEL DIFFERENTIATION.   Companies can gain a strong competitive advantage through hiring and training better people than their competitors do. Thus, Singapore Airlines enjoys an excellent reputation largely because of the grace of its flight attendants. McDonald's people are courteous, IBM people are professional and knowledgeable, and Disney people are friendly and upbeat. The salesforces of such companies as Connecticut General Life and Merck enjoy excellent reputations, which set their companies apart from competitors. Wal-Mart has differentiated its superstores by employing "people greeters" who welcome shoppers, give advice on where to find items, mark merchandise brought back for returns or exchanges, and give gifts to children.

Personnel differentiation requires that a company select its customer-contact people carefully and train them well. For example, guests at a Disney theme park quickly learn that every Disney employee is competent, courteous, and friendly. From the hotel check-in agents, to the monorail drivers, to the ride attendants, to the people who sweep Main Street USA, each employee understands the importance of understanding customers, communicating with them clearly and cheerfully, and responding quickly to their requests and problems. Each is carefully trained to "make a dream come true."

IMAGE DIFFERENTIATION.   Even when competing offers look the same, buyers may perceive a difference based on company or brand images. Thus, companies work to establish *images* that differentiate them from competitors. A company or brand image should convey the product's distinctive benefits and positioning. Developing a strong and distinctive image calls for creativity and hard work. A company cannot implant an image in the public's mind overnight using only a few advertisements. If "Motorola" means "quality," this image must be supported by everything the company says and does.

Symbols can provide strong company or brand recognition and image differentiation. Companies design signs and logos that provide instant recognition. They associate themselves with objects or characters that symbolize quality or other attributes, such as the Harris Bank lion, the McDonald's golden arches, the Prudential rock, or the Pillsbury doughboy. The company might build a brand around some famous person, as with perfumes such as Passion (Elizabeth Taylor) and Uninhibited (Cher). Some companies even become associated with colors, such as IBM (blue) or Campbell (red and white).

The chosen symbols must be communicated through advertising that conveys the company or brand's personality. The ads attempt to establish a storyline, a mood, a performance level—something distinctive about the company or brand. The atmosphere of the physical space in which the organization produces or delivers its products and services can be another powerful image generator. Hyatt hotels have become known for their atrium lobbies and Victoria Station restaurants for their boxcars. Thus, a bank that wants to distinguish itself as the "friendly bank" must choose the right building and interior design, layout, colors, materials, and furnishings to reflect these qualities.

A company also can create an image through the types of events it sponsors. For example, AT&T and IBM have identified themselves closely with cultural events, such as symphony performances and art exhibits. Other organizations support popular causes. For example, Heinz gives money to hospitals and Quaker gives food to the homeless.

Selecting the Right Competitive Advantages

Suppose a company is fortunate enough to discover several potential competitive advantages. It now must choose the ones on which it will build its positioning strategy. It must decide *how many* differences to promote and *which ones*.

HOW MANY DIFFERENCES TO PROMOTE?   Many marketers think that companies should aggressively promote only one benefit to the target market. Ad man Rosser Reeves, for example, said a company should develop a *unique selling proposition* (USP) for each brand and stick to it. Each brand should pick an attribute and tout itself as "number one" on that attribute. Buyers tend to remember "number one" better, especially in an overcommunicated society. Thus, Crest toothpaste consistently promotes its anticavity protection, and Volvo promotes safety. What are some of the "number one" positions to promote? The major ones are "best quality," "best service," "lowest price," "best value," and "most advanced technology." A company that hammers away at one of these positions and consistently delivers on it probably will become best known and remembered for it.

Other marketers think that companies should position themselves on more than one differentiating factor. This may be necessary if two or more firms are claiming to be best on the same attribute. Steelcase, an office furniture systems company, differentiates itself from competitors on two benefits: best on-time delivery and best installation support.

Today, in a time when the mass market is fragmenting into many small segments, companies are trying to broaden their positioning strategies to appeal to more segments. For example, Beecham promotes its Aquafresh toothpaste as offering three benefits: "anti-cavity protection," "better breath," and "whiter teeth." Clearly, many people want all three benefits, and the challenge is to convince them that the brand delivers all three. Beecham's solution was to create a toothpaste that squeezed out of the tube in three colors, thus visually confirming the three benefits.

However, as companies increase the number of claims for their brands, they risk disbelief and a loss of clear positioning. In general, a company needs to avoid three major positioning errors. The first is *underpositioning*—failing to ever really position the company at all. Some companies discover that buyers have only a vague idea of the company or that they do not really know anything special about it. The second error is *overpositioning*—giving buyers too narrow a picture of the company. Thus, a consumer might think that the Steuben glass company makes only fine art glass costing $1,000 and up, when in fact it makes affordable fine glass starting at around $50. Finally, companies must avoid *confused positioning*—leaving buyers with a confused image of a company. For example, Burger King has struggled without success for years to establish a profitable and consistent position. Since 1986, it has fielded six separate advertising campaigns, with themes ranging from "Herb the nerd doesn't eat here," and "This is a Burger King town," to "The right food for the right times," to "Sometimes you've got to break the rules" and "BK Tee Vee." This barrage of positioning statements has left consumers confused and Burger King with poor sales and profits.[22]

WHICH DIFFERENCES TO PROMOTE? Not all brand differences are meaningful or worthwhile. Not every difference makes a good differentiator. Each difference has the potential to create company costs as well as customer benefits. Therefore, the company must carefully select the ways in which it will distinguish itself from competitors. A difference is worth establishing to the extent that it satisfies the following criteria:

◆ *Important:* The difference delivers a highly valued benefit to target buyers.
◆ *Distinctive:* Competitors do not offer the difference, or the company can offer it in a more distinctive way.
◆ *Superior:* The difference is superior to other ways that customers might obtain the same benefit.
◆ *Communicable:* The difference is communicable and visible to buyers.
◆ *Preemptive:* Competitors cannot easily copy the difference.
◆ *Affordable:* Buyers can afford to pay for the difference.
◆ *Profitable:* The company can introduce the difference profitably.

Many companies have introduced differentiations that failed one or more of these tests. The Westin Stamford hotel in Singapore advertises that it is the world's tallest hotel, a distinction that is not important to many tourists—in fact, it turns many off. AT&T's original picturevision phones bombed, partly because the public did not think that seeing the other person was worth the phone's high cost. Polaroid's Polarvision, which produced instantly developed home movies, bombed too. Although Polarvision was distinctive and even preemptive, it was inferior to another way of capturing motion, namely, camcorders. Thus, choosing competitive advantages on which to position a product or service can be difficult, yet such choices may be crucial to success (see Marketing Highlight 8-4).

Some competitive advantages may be quickly ruled out because they are too slight, too costly to develop, or too inconsistent with the company's profile. Suppose that a company is designing its positioning strategy and has narrowed its list of possible competitive advantages to four. The company needs a framework for selecting the one advantage that makes the most sense to develop. Table 8-4 shows a systematic way to evaluate several potential competitive advantages and choose the right one.

In the table, the company compares its standing on four attributes—technology, cost, quality, and service—to the standing of its major competitor. Let's assume that both companies stand at 8 on technology (1 = low score, 10 = high score), which means they both have good technology. The company questions whether it can gain much by improving its technology further, especially given the high cost of new technology. The competitor has a better standing on cost (8 instead of 6), and this can hurt the company if the market gets more price sensitive. The company offers higher quality than its competitor (8 instead of 6). Finally, both companies offer below-average service (4 and 3).

At first glance, it appears that the company should go after cost or service to improve its market appeal relative to the competitor. However, it must consider other factors. First, how important are improvements in each of these attributes to the target customers? The fourth column shows that cost and service improvements would both be highly important to customers. Next, can the company afford to make the improvements? If so, how fast can it complete them? The fifth column shows that the company could improve service quickly and affordably. But if the firm decided to do this, would the competitor be able to improve its service also? The sixth column shows that the competitor's ability to improve service is low, perhaps because the competitor doesn't believe in service or is strapped for funds. The final column then shows the appropriate actions to take on each attribute. It makes the most sense for the company to invest in improving its service. Service is important to customers; the company can afford to improve its service and can do it fast, and the competitor probably will not be able to catch up.

Communicating and Delivering the Chosen Position

Once it has chosen a position, the company must take strong steps to deliver and communicate the desired position to target consumers. All the company's

TABLE 8-4 *Finding Competitive Advantage*

COMPETITIVE ADVANTAGE	COMPANY STANDING (1–10)	COMPETITOR STANDING (1–10)	IMPORTANCE OF IMPROVING STANDING (H-M-L)	AFFORD-ABILITY AND SPEED (H-M-L)	COMPETITOR'S ABILITY TO IMPROVE STANDING (H-M-L)	RECOMMENDED ACTION
Technology	8	8	L	L	M	Hold
Cost	6	8	H	M	M	Watch
Quality	8	6	L	L	H	Watch
Service	4	3	H	H	L	Invest

SCHOTT: POSITIONING FOR SUCCESS

Schott, the German manufacturer of glass for industrial and consumer products, had a problem deciding how to position its innovative product, Ceran, in the American market. The product, a glass-ceramic material made to cover the cooking surface of electric ranges, seemed to have everything going for it. It was completely nonporous (and thus stain resistant), easy to clean, and long-lasting. Best of all, when one burner was lit, the heat didn't spread; it stayed confined to the circle directly above the burner. And after ten years, cooktops made of Ceran still looked and performed like new.

Schott anticipated some difficulty igniting demand for Ceran in U.S. markets. First it would have to win over American range manufacturers, who would then have to promote Ceran to middle markets—dealers, designers, architects, and builders. These middle-market customers would, in turn, need to influence final consumers. Thus, Schott's U.S. subsidiary set out to sell Ceran aggressively to its target of 14 North American appliance manufacturers. The subsidiary positioned Ceran on its impressive technical and engineering attributes—showing cross-sections of stoves and using plenty of high-tech talk—then waited optimistically for the orders to roll in. The appliance companies listened politely to the rep's pitch, ordered sample quantities—25 or so of each available color—and then . . . nothing. Absolutely nothing.

Research by Schott's advertising agency revealed two problems. First, Schott had failed to position Ceran at all among the manufacturers' customers. The material was still virtually unknown, not only among final consumers but also among dealers, designers, architects, and builders. Second, the company was attempting to position the product on the wrong benefits. When selecting a rangetop to buy, customers seemed to care less about the sophisticated engineering that went into it and more about its appearance and cleanability. Their biggest questions were, "How does it look?" and "How easy is it to use?"

Based on these findings, Schott repositioned Ceran, shifting emphasis toward the material's inherent beauty and design versatility. And it launched an extensive promotion campaign to communicate the new position to middle-market and final buyers. Advertising to designers and remodelers revolved around lines like "Formalwear for your kitchen," which presented the black rangetop as streamlined and elegant as a tuxedo.

reinforce a weak link in the selling chain—appliance salespeople who were poorly equipped to answer customer questions about Ceran—the agency created a video that the salespeople could show customers on the TVs in their own appliance stores.

The now properly and strongly positioned Ceran is selling well. All 14 North American appliance makers are buying production quantities of Ceran and using them in their rangetops. All offer not one, but several smooth-top

Now properly positioned on their inherent beauty and design versatility, Schott's Ceran cooktops are selling very well.

As a follow-up, to persuade designers and remodelers to add Ceran to their palette of materials, Schott positioned Ceran as "More than a rangetop, a means of expression." To reinforce this beauty and design positioning, ads featured visuals, including a geometric grid of a rangetop with one glowing red burner.

In addition to advertising, Schott's agency launched a massive public relations effort that resulted in substantial coverage in home design and remodeling publications. It also produced a video news release featuring Ceran that was picked up by 150 local TV stations nationwide. To

models. Schott is the only smooth-top supplier in the United States, and smooth-tops now account for more than 15 percent of the electric stove market. And at a recent Kitchen & Bath Show, 69 percent of all range models on display were smooth-tops. To keep up with increasing demand, Schott has built a U.S. plant just to produce Ceran for the North American market.

Source: Adapted from Nancy Arnott, "Heating Up Sales: Formalware for Your Kitchen," Sales & Marketing Management, June 1994, pp. 77–78.

marketing-mix efforts must support the positioning strategy. Positioning the company calls for concrete action, not just talk. If the company decides to build a position on better quality and service, it must first *deliver* that position. Designing the marketing mix—product, price, place, and promotion—essentially involves working out the tactical details of the positioning strategy. Thus, a firm that seizes on a "high-quality position" knows that it must produce high-quality products, charge a high price, distribute through high-quality dealers, and advertise in high-quality media. It must hire and train more service people, find retailers who have a good reputation for service, and develop sales and advertising messages that broadcast its superior service. This is the only way to build a consistent and believable high-quality, high-service position.

Companies often find it easier to come up with a good positioning strategy than to implement it. Establishing a position or changing one usually takes a long time. In contrast, positions that have taken years to build can quickly be lost. Once a company has built the desired position, it must take care to maintain the position through consistent performance and communication. It must closely monitor and adapt the position over time to match changes in consumer needs and competitors' strategies. However, the company should avoid abrupt changes that might confuse consumers. Instead, a product's position should evolve gradually as it adapts to the ever-changing marketing environment.

Summary

Organizations that sell to consumer and business *markets* realize that they cannot appeal to all buyers in the market, and they cannot successfully approach all buyers in the same way. Companies generally identify the parts of the market that they can serve best, but that is not always so. There are three basic philosophies that guide a company's approach to the market. *Mass marketing* is the decision to mass-produce and mass-distribute a single product, and attempt to attract all kinds of buyers with this offering. *Product variety marketing* presents differing choices to set the seller's products apart from competitor's products. Companies following this philosophy produce two or more products that are distinctive in style, features, quality, sizes, or price. *Target marketing* is the decision to identify the different groups that compose the market and to develop specific products to appeal to a selected target audience. Sellers today are moving away from mass marketing and product variety marketing in favor of the target marketing approach. This approach is more helpful in spotting market opportunities and developing more effective products and marketing mixes.

The first step in target marketing is *market segmentation*, which is the act of dividing the market into distinct groups of buyers who might merit separate products or marketing mixes. Markets can be segmented using different variables, and marketers often try several approaches to see which yields the best opportunities. For consumer products the most commonly used segmentation variables are *geographic, demographic, psychographic,* and *behavioral.* Business markets can be segmented by *business consumer demographics, operating characteristics, purchasing approaches,* and *personal characteristics.* In both types of markets, effective segmentation requires finding segments that are *measurable, accessible, substantial,* and *actionable.*

The process of *market targeting* involves selecting the most promising segments and deciding upon a market-coverage strategy to address them. The company first *evaluates market segments* for size and growth characteristics, structural attractiveness, and compatibility with company resources and objectives. It then chooses one of three market-coverage strategies. The seller can ignore segments with an *undifferentiated marketing* approach, develop different offers for different market segments through *differentiated marketing*, or go after one or a few market segments using a *concentrated marketing* strategy. The choice of strategy depends on company resources, product variability, product life-cycle stage, and competitive marketing strategies.

Once a company has chosen what segments to enter, it approaches the market by *positioning for competitive advantage*. The market positioning strategy guides the company on which positions to occupy in its chosen segments. The positioning task consists of three steps: identifying a set of possible competitive advantages on which to build a position, selecting the right competitive advantages, and effectively communicating and delivering the chosen position to the market. The seller can position its products on *specific prod-* *uct attributes,* for certain *classes of trade,* by *product class,* or according to *usage occasion.* After these decisions are made, the company implements the strategy by *communicating and delivering the chosen position.*

Key Terms

Age and life-cycle segmentation
Behavioral segmentation
Benefit segmentation
Competitive advantage
Concentrated marketing
Demographic segmentation
Differentiated marketing

Gender segmentation
Geographic segmentation
Income segmentation
Intermarket segmentation
Market positioning
Market segmentation
Market targeting

Micromarketing
Occasion segmentation
Product position
Psychographic segmentation
Target market
Undifferentiated marketing

Discussing the Issues

1. Describe how the Ford Motor Company has moved from mass marketing to product-variety marketing to target marketing. Select some other examples of companies whose marketing approaches have evolved over time.

2. Outline what variables are used in segmenting the market for beer. Give examples.

3. Hispanics are now viewed as an attractive, distinct market segment. Can you market the same way to a Puerto Rican seamstress in New York, a Cuban doctor in Miami, and a Mexican laborer in Houston? Compare the similarities and differences that you see. What does this imply about market segments?

4. Some industrial suppliers achieve above-average profits by offering service, selection, and reliability at a premium price. Suggest ways that these suppliers can segment the market to find customers who are willing to pay more for these benefits.

5. Think about your classmates in this course. Can you segment them into different groups with specific nicknames? Explain the major segmentation variable you used. Could you effectively market products to these segments?

6. Describe the roles that product attributes and perceptions of attributes play in positioning a product. Can an attribute held by several competing brands be used in a successful positioning strategy?

Applying the Concepts

1. By looking at advertising, and at products themselves, we can often see how marketers are attempting to position their products, and what target market they hope to reach. (a) Define the positionings of and the target markets for Coca-Cola, Pepsi Cola, Mountain Dew, Dr. Pepper, and 7-Up. (b) Define the positionings of and target markets for McDonald's, Burger King, Wendy's, and a regional restaurant chain in your area such as Jack in the Box,

Bojangle's, or Friendly's. (c) Do you think the soft drinks and restaurants have distinctive positionings and target markets? Are some more clearly defined than others?

2. It is possible to market people as well as products or services [see Chapter 21 for more details]. When marketing a person, we can *position* that individual for a particular target market. Describe briefly how you would position yourself for the following target markets: (a) for a potential

employer, (b) for a potential boyfriend or girlfriend, (c) for your mother or father. Would you position yourself in different ways for these different target markets? How do the positionings differ? *Why do the positionings differ?*

References

1. Thomas Moore, "Different Folks, Different Strokes," *Fortune,* September 16, 1985, p. 65. Also see Michael Oneal, "Attack of the Bug Killers," *Business Week,* May 16, 1988, p. 81.

2. Jennifer Lawrence, "Don't Look for P&G to Pare Detergents," *Advertising Age,* May 31, 1993, pp. 1, 3.

3. Bruce Hager, "Podunk Is Beckoning," *Business Week,* December 2, 1991, p. 76.

4. Cyndee Miller, "Xers Know They're a Target Market, and They Hate That," *Advertising Age,* December 6, 1993, pp. 2, 15.

5. "Automakers Learn Better Roads to Women's Market," *Marketing News,* October 12, 1992, p. 2. Also see Betsy Sharkey, "The Many Faces of Eve," *Adweek,* June 25, 1990, pp. 44–49; Tim Triplett, "Automakers Recognizing Value of Women's Market," *Marketing News,* April 11, 1994, pp. 1, 2; and Leah Rickard, "Subaru, GMC Top Push to Win Over Women," *Advertising Age,* April 3, 1995, p. 524.

6. Raymond Serafin, "I Am Woman, Hear Me Roar . . . In My Car," *Advertising Age,* November 7, 1994, pp. 1, 8.

7. Steve Lawrence, "The Green in Blue-Collar Retailing," *Fortune,* May 27, 1985, pp. 74–77; Brian Bremner, "Looking Downscale without Looking Down," *Business Week,* October 8, 1990, pp. 62–67; Jan Larsen, "Reaching Downscale Markets," *American Demographics,* November 1991, pp. 38–40; and Cyndee Miller, "The Have-Nots: Firms with the Right Products and Services Succeed among Low-Income Consumers," *Marketing News,* August 1, 1994, pp. 1, 2.

8. Thomas Exter, "Deodorant Demographics," *American Demographics,* December 1987, p. 39.

9. For a detailed discussion of personality and buyer behavior, see Leon G. Schiffman and Leslie Lazar Kanuk, *Consumer Behavior,* 5th ed. (Englewood Cliffs, NJ: Prentice Hall, 1994), Chap. 5.

10. See Laurie Freeman and Cleveland Horton, "Spree: Honda's Scooters Ride the Cutting Edge," *Advertising Age,* September 5, 1985, pp. 3, 35.

11. Mark Maremont, "The Hottest Thing Since the Flashbulb," *Business Week,* September 7, 1992.

12. See Thomas V. Bonoma and Benson P. Shapiro, *Segmenting the Industrial Market* (Lexington, MA.: Lexington Books, 1983). For examples of segmenting business markets, see Kate Bertrand, "Market Segmentation: Divide and Conquer," *Business Marketing,* October 1989, pp. 48–54.

13. V. Kasturi Rangan, Rowland T. Moriarty, and Gordon S. Swartz, "Segmenting Customers in Mature Industrial Markets," *Journal of Marketing,* October 1992, pp. 72–82.

14. For another interesting approach to segmenting the business market, see John Berrigan and Carl Finkbeiner, *Segmentation Marketing: New Methods for Capturing Business* (New York: Harper-Business, 1992).

15. Marlene L. Rossman, "Understanding Five Nations of Latin America," *Marketing News,* October 11, 1985, p. 10; as quoted in Subhash C. Jain, *International Marketing Management,* 3rd ed. (Boston: PWS-Kent Publishing Company, 1990), p. 366.

16. Shawn Tully, "Teens: The Most Global Market of All," *Fortune,* May 16, 1994, pp. 90–97.

17. Jain, *International Marketing,* pp. 370–371.

18. See Joe Schwartz, "Southpaw Strategy," *American Demographics,* June 1988, p. 61; and "Few Companies Tailor Products for Lefties," *Wall Street Journal,* August 2, 1989, p. 2.

19. See Michael Porter, *Competitive Advantage* (New York: Free Press, 1985), pp. 4–8 and pp. 234–236.

20. Christopher Power, "How to Get Closer to Your Customers," *Business Week,* special issue on economies of scale, 1993, pp. 42–45.

21. See Tom Peters, *Thriving on Chaos* (New York: Alfred A. Knopf, Inc., 1987), pp. 56–57.

22. Mark Landler and Gail DeGeorge, "Tempers Are Sizzling Over Burger King's New Ads," *Business Week,* February 12, 1990, p. 33; Gail DeGeorge, "Turning Up the Gas at Burger King," *Business Week,* November 15, 1993, pp. 62–67; and Martha T. Moore, "Whopper of a Plan," *USA Today,* April 26, 1994, pp. 1, 2.

Company Case 8a

QUAKER OATS: DOUSING ON THE COMPETITION

Every football fan has cringed while watching two burly football players sneak up on an unsuspecting coach and douse the coach with a large cooler of icy Gatorade.

This dousing has replaced the traditional ride on the teams' shoulders as the ultimate moment following an important play. Although some 40 national and regional brands compete in the sports-drink market, Gatorade has achieved such a dominant position that the brand name has become almost a generic term for the category.

However, you may not know that Quaker Oats Company owns Gatorade. Although you associate Quaker Oats with oatmeal, cold breakfast cereals, snacks, and Willford Brimley ("It's the right thing to do"), you may be surprised to learn that Gatorade represents Quaker Oats's single most important product. For 1994, Gatorade produced about $1.2 billion in sales, about 15 percent of Quaker Oats's sales, and about 17 percent of operating profits.

Analysts estimate that Gatorade controls about 88 percent of the sports-drink market, which is the most rapidly growing beverage market. Whereas the mature traditional soft-drink category is growing annually at only a sluggish 2 percent rate, down from almost 5 percent previously, analysts predict that the sports-drink category will grow at double-digit volume rates during the 1990s.

It is not surprising, therefore, that many companies are examining and then entering the sports-drink market. It is also not surprising that Gatorade has sent clear signals that it will fight to defend its dominant market share, which was over 90 percent in the early 1990s.

QUAKER OATS AND GATORADE

Dr. Robert Cade, a kidney expert at the University of Florida, and a team of researchers who were studying heat exhaustion among the University's football players developed Gatorade in the 1960s. The researchers analyzed the players' perspiration and devised a drink that prevented severe dehydration caused by fluid and mineral loss during physical exertion in high temperatures. They tested the drink on the players, and the Florida Gators team used the drink on the sideline during all the games in the 1966 season. That year, observers designated the Gators as the "second-half team" because it consistently outplayed its opponents during the second half. The team also won the Orange Bowl; and Bobby Dodd, the losing Georgia Tech coach, noted that "We didn't have Gatorade. That made the difference." *Sports Illustrated* reported the remark, and Gatorade was on its way to creating and dominating a new product category—the isotonic beverage.

Stokely-Van Camp, a processor and marketer of fruits and vegetables, acquired Gatorade in May 1967 and began marketing it during the summer of 1968. Stokely intended to promote Gatorade not only as a sports drink but also as a health food product because of its value in replacing electrolytes lost due to colds, flu, diarrhea, and vomiting. During the 1970s, Gatorade realized rapid growth as an increasingly fitness-minded public latched on to the product and its perceived benefits. Stokely also developed a strong position for Gatorade in the institutional team sales market. Because of its lock on this market and strong consumer loyalty at the retail level, few competitors who entered the market were successful.

Quaker Oats purchased Stokely-Van Camp in 1983. Quaker saw the opportunity to grow Gatorade's sales by increasing both its distribution and promotion, and it doubled Gatorade's marketing expenditures. Between 1983 and 1990, Gatorade's sales grew at a 28 percent compound annual growth rate.

THE PRODUCT AND THE MARKET

Isotonic beverages, or sports drinks, replace fluids and minerals lost during physical activity. Research shows that an isotonic drink's effectiveness depends on several factors. The drink should provide enough carbohydrates (glucose and sucrose working in combination) to supply working muscles yet not too much to slow fluid absorption. The drink should contain the proper level of electrolytes, particularly sodium, to enhance fluid absorption. Finally, research suggests that most people prefer a noncarbonated, slightly sweet drink when they are hot and sweaty. The taste is important to encourage the person to consume enough drink to be effective in rehydration.

An 8-ounce serving of Gatorade contains few vitamins, no fat or protein, 60 calories, 15 grams of carbohydrate, 110 milligrams of sodium, and 25 milligrams of potassium. Gatorade's calories are about one-half the level contained in fruit drinks and nondiet soft drinks.

The sports-drink market is highly seasonal and regional, with most sales occurring during the summer months in the southern, southeastern, and southwestern regions. Consumers in Florida, Texas, and California account for 38 percent of Gatorade's sales.

When Quaker Oats acquired Gatorade, it found that Stokely had targeted competitive athletes and men and teenagers who were involved in competitive athletics. However, Quaker found that Stokely had not positioned the brand well and that there was no consistent focus. There was no clear message that specified the product's uses or the circumstances or occasions when consumers should use it. Quaker's market research revealed that the main users were men aged 19 to 44. These men understood the product and knew when and how to use it.

Quaker decided to develop a narrow, solid positioning for the product based on how southern consumers used it and to market the product in the North. It also decided to portray Gatorade's users as accomplished but not necessarily professional athletes. Advertisements depicted serious athletes who enjoyed their sports and enjoyed Gatorade. These were athletes that the target customer could aspire to be like.

Despite its narrow focus for Gatorade, Quaker responded to market changes by introducing Gatorade Light in 1990. This line extension targeted calorie-conscious athletes, such as those engaged in aerobics or jogging, and women. These customers exercised for short or moderate periods at low or moderate intensity. Gatorade Light had less sodium and about one-half the calories of regular Gatorade and came in three flavors. Quaker also introduced Freestyle, a more flavorful drink made with fruit juice. Freestyle targeted people who had more interest in the product's taste than in its rehydration aspects. By 1992, Quaker also offered original Gatorade in six flavors selected to appeal to different target groups.

COMPETITION TRIES TO MAKE GATORADE SWEAT

Competitors did not overlook Gatorade's success and the rapid growth of the sports-drink market. Suntory, a subsidiary of the Japanese beverage giant Suntory, introduced 10-K sports drink in the United States in 1985. Suntory made 10-K Gatorade's strongest competitor by promoting the fact that it produced the drink using salt-free spring water. 10K contained 100 percent of the recommended daily allowance of vitamin C. It also had all-natural flavors, fructose, 60 calories per serving, no caffeine, and one-half the sodium of other products. Like Gatorade, 10-K focused on grocery store distribution and targeted sports teams. Suntory claimed that 10-K beat Gatorade in taste tests and in repeat purchases.

Coca-Cola and Pepsi Cola also dabbled in the market. Coca-Cola introduced a powdered sports drink, Maxx, in 1987. Maxx never made it out of test markets, however. In 1989, Pepsi Cola joined the party by introducing Mountain Dew Sport (MDS). MDS was lightly carbonated, caffeine-free, and came in regular and two-calorie formulas. Pepsi claimed that it tasted better than Gatorade. However, consumers felt that it had too much carbonation, and Pepsi pulled the product. Pepsi subsequently introduced AllSport, a more lightly carbonated drink that came in four flavors. Pepsi distributed All-Sport through grocery and convenience stores, and it had a global distribution network in place should it decide to market the product internationally.

Although Coca-Cola and Pepsi Cola were Gatorade's main competitive threats, numerous other smaller companies attacked the market. These companies introduced products, such as PowerBurst, Workout, Workout Light, and Pro Motion, and claimed that the products had advantages over Gatorade.

In 1990, Coca-Cola reentered the market with PowerAde. Coca-Cola's second entry was noncarbonated and caffeine-free and came in three flavors. Coca-Cola planned to distribute PowerAde only through soda fountains.

By early 1992, Quaker realized that despite Gatorade's rapid growth, new sales were becoming harder to find. Quaker approached Coca-Cola with the idea that the two companies could team up to distribute Gatorade through Coca-Cola's wide network of vending machines and fountains in restaurants and convenience stores. However, in mid-1992, the two companies halted their discussions, reportedly because they could not agree on who would take the lead in making marketing decisions.

Following that development, Coca-Cola announced that it would continue to challenge Gatorade with its PowerAde product. Coca-Cola argued that PowerAde had 33% more carbohydrates for energy than Gatorade, that it was lighter, and that it "went down" easier. PowerAde quenched thirst without the heavy salt flavor, Coca-Cola suggested. Coca-Cola would focus on distributing PowerAde in vending machines, in health and fitness clubs, and in industrial plant sites—"points of sweat," as Coca-Cola called them. To help in this effort, the firm introduced canned and bottled versions of PowerAde. Coca-Cola hoped that this emphasis would also help PowerAde debut on Gatorade's turf, grocery stores. Coca-Cola had 1.5 million points of sale, including one million vending machines, as compared with Gatorade's 200,000 points of sale. Coca-Cola also started television and radio advertising and paid to make PowerAde the official drink of the 1992 Summer Olympic Games in Spain. Officials also claimed that PowerAde would be the official drink of the 1996 Olympic Games in Atlanta, Coke's hometown.

Pepsi did not stand idly by during all of this. Pepsi's managers claimed that although Gatorade dominated the category, it lacked both taste and the strong distribution system that Pepsi could provide for All-Sport. Pepsi had approximately one million points of sale and daily contact with 250,000 retailers that it could use to push AllSport. Like Coca-Cola, Pepsi had decided to confront Gatorade in supermarkets, construction sites, and health clubs. As it did with Coke, Pepsi challenged Gatorade with taste tests in stores. It also claimed that carbonated AllSport was more drinkable than Gatorade and that AllSport had one-half the sodium. Pepsi argued that consumers who ate a balanced diet did not need the extra sodium that Gatorade provided.

In response to the break in its negotiations with Coca-Cola, Quaker reorganized its operations. Previously, Quaker had relied on regional offices in North

America, Europe, Asia, and Latin America to manage the brand in 15 countries. Quaker announced that it would now form a separate division to market Gatorade world-wide. Gatorade officials also noted that they were still pursuing partnerships with other companies to expand distribution to "wherever there's thirst."

If Gatorade continues to expand internationally, however, it will find competition waiting. In Japan, Coca-Cola already offers a sports drink under the name Aquarius; and Gatorade has had problems competing with a locally produced sports beverage. In Italy, H.J. Heinz Company markets a beverage called Fitgar that it claims has 10 percent of the sports-drink market. In France, consumers seem to view bottled water as the product of choice for quenching their thirsts.

What Will the Future Bring?

Quaker Oats realizes just how important this battle is to its corporate health. Gatorade has said that it will continue to cultivate its sports image by using Michael Jordan as its spokesperson. It will also use its multi-year contracts with pro leagues from the National Football League to the Ladies Professional Golf Association. Gatorade will also resort to its time-honored scientific studies to prove that the body absorbs Gatorade faster than water or any other soft drink. Quaker understands that to maintain its dominant position it must be willing to pursue innovative marketing strategies.

Coca-Cola and Pepsi represent strong competitors with deep pockets and great determination. Although each has failed in its previous attacks on Gatorade, no one should assume they will fail in their current efforts.

Still, Quaker Oats has shown that it will be aggressively working and waiting for the opportunity to douse the competition with an orange container of icy liquid.

Questions

1. What major variables have Quaker Oats and its competitors used to segment the sports-drink market?

2. What type of market coverage strategy did Gatorade use during the early stages of the sports-drink market's life cycle? What coverage strategies are Gatorade and its competitors using now?

3. How have Gatorade and its competitors positioned their sports-drink products?

4. What competitive advantages do Gatorade and its competitors have?

5. Identify new marketing opportunities that Quaker should pursue for Gatorade, including new market segments that it should address. Develop a marketing strategy for addressing one of these opportunities.

6. Quaker Oats's reorganization—forming one division to manage Gatorade worldwide—suggests that the company wants to make Gatorade a global brand, like Coke. Is Gatorade a global brand? What changes should Quaker consider as it markets Gatorade globally?

Sources: Michael J. McCarthy and Christina Duff, "Quaker Oats Weighs Linkup With Coke for Distribution of Gatorade Beverage," *Wall Street Journal*, January 24, 1992, p. A8; Michael J. McCarthy, "Coke Hopes to Make Gatorade Sweat in Battle for U.S. Sports-Drink Market," *Wall Street Journal*, April 27, 1992, p. B6; Richard Gibson, "Gatorade Unit to Pour It On as Rivalry Rises," *Wall Street Journal*, April 28, 1992, p. B1; "Gatorade Is Cornerstone to Quaker's Growth," *Advertising Age*, May 18, 1992, p. 12; "Soft Drinks: The Thirst of Champions," *The Economist*, June 6, 1992, p. 83; Richard Gibson, "Coca-Cola and PepsiCo Are Preparing to Give Gatorade a Run for Its Money," *Wall Street Journal*, September 29, 1992, p. B1. This case also draws from Linda E. Swayne and Peter M. Ginter, "Gatorade Defends Its No. 1 Position," in Linda E. Swayne and Peter M. Ginter, *Cases in Strategic Marketing*, 2nd ed. (Englewood Cliffs, NJ: Prentice Hall, 1993), pp. 1–21. Used with permission.

Company Case 8b

RYKÄ: BE STRONG

What does it take to compete in the athletic shoe business? Some experts think you need lots of celebrities hawking products, an incredible array of products for every form of exercise and recreation, gimmicks such as lighted heels, and hundreds of millions of dollars for advertising. If so, who would believe that a young woman named Sheri Poe of Massachusetts could succeed by selling a limited line of athletic shoes with no money for advertising? Maybe no one, but after eight years of hard

work, that young woman's company, RYKÄ, is finally profitable, and its sales are growing at more than 40 percent a year. By combining niche marketing, a good understanding of customers, creative promotion, and passionate marketing, RYKÄ has more than survived.

When Sheri began exercising, she could not find an athletic shoe that fit her foot. After spending months talking to shoe salespeople, retailers, aerobics instructors, and exercise enthusiasts, she found that there was no athletic shoe designed specifically for women. Shoes sold to women were made simply by shrinking male shoes to smaller sizes. Such shoes did not accommodate women's higher arches, narrower heels, and broader forefeet.

With the help of a Texas investment banker, Sheri founded RYKÄ with just $4 million, most of which was used to design and produce shoes. Even though it had little money left over to spend on sales efforts, the company convinced Lady Foot Locker to carry the RYKÄ brand. But without funds, how could the company promote its shoes? Noting that aerobics fitness fans place much trust in aerobics instructors, the company began sending promotional materials and discount offers to U.S. fitness instructors and personal trainers. Sure enough, the instructors liked the shoes and pushed them to students, who in turn bought them. Today, RYKÄ has more than 30,000 instructors and trainers in its "RYKÄ Training Body" program. Each receives promotional materials four to six times a year.

Although RYKÄ couldn't afford to hire celebrities, Sheri sent shoes to Oprah Winfrey, who in turn invited Sheri to appear on her show. Sheri also sent shoes and a personal note to Princess Di, who was later photographed in her RYKÄ shoes. This publicity, along with the support of fitness instructors, created demand for RYKÄ shoes. And by hiring top-notch salespeople, RYKÄ secured distribution in outlets such as Foot Locker, Nordstrom, JCPenney, and Spiegel.

RYKÄ's product line now includes walking shoes, fitness training shoes, and the newest offering, aquatic fitness shoes. With over nine million participants, aquatic exercise is one of the fastest-growing forms of fitness training, and RYKÄ produces the only aquatic fitness shoe—RYKÄ's 9H2O. The shoe has mesh upper construction for quick drainage, a lightweight midsole, and a nylon tab tape for quick slip-on. Some critics question whether an aquatic shoe will be a success. Several years ago, Nike introduced AquaSocks, which have mesh uppers and rubber soles. These are so popular that imitation products, selling for as low as $6.99, have appeared at Kmart.

Nike and Reebok have noticed RYKÄ's success and have introduced their own shoes designed for women. Heavy competition could cost RYKÄ its niche in the market, but the company is now positioned as more than just an athletic shoe company. Sheri Poe, once a victim of violence, also started the RYKÄ ROSE (Regaining One's Self Esteem) Foundation to which RYKÄ donates seven percent of its pretax profits. The RYKÄ tagline, "Be Strong," encourages women to be strong physically and mentally. After suffering years of depression and mental anguish because of the attack on her, Sheri found that working out—becoming strong—helped her. In 1993, RYKÄ ran a magazine ad showing one woman pictured from behind working out and another woman facing the camera with a tear rolling down her face. The headline read "Sometimes you have to work out to work it out." Critics claim that RYKÄ and Sheri went too far with this ad, but Sheri responds "I have a commitment to bring forward the issue of violence against women, and I'm going to do that till the day I die." In 1995, RYKÄ's advertising still refers to the foundation but focuses more on fit and function.

In every box of shoes, RYKÄ places a tag with the telephone number of the National Victim Center Infolink (1-800-FYI-CALL), a set of safety rules for women, and an explanation of the company's commitment to supporting women. The tag advises:

> For some people, exercise is a form of release. For others, it can be a personal salvation. While a shoe can only offer support, the nature of that support can make all the difference. RYKÄ athletic shoes are the first to be made for women, by women. They are also the first athletic shoes to offer a support system for women, physically, mentally and spiritually.
>
> Be Strong. RYKÄ

QUESTIONS

1. Describe RYKÄ's segmentation and positioning strategies. Why would these be successful?

2. By visibly supporting causes, such as ending violence against women, Sheri Poe involves the RYKÄ company in "passion" or "cause" marketing. Is this sort of marketing appropriate? Will it be enough to carry RYKÄ in the face of increased competition from Nike and Reebok?

3. Do you agree that the RYKÄ ad described in the case goes too far in attacking violence against women? In your opinion, why would this ad be criticized?

4. In your opinion, will RYKÄ's aquatic aerobics shoe be a success? Why or why not?

Sources: "To Compete with Giants, Choose Your Niche," *Nation's Business*, July 1992, p. 6; Ron Stodghill, "What Makes RYKÄ Run? Sheri Poe and Her Story," *Business Week*, June 14, 1993, pp. 82–84; Laurel Allison Touby, "Creativity vs. Cash," November 1991, *Working Woman*, p. 73; and materials supplied by RYKÄ. The author gratefully thanks Ms. Sue Dooley for her assistance with this case.

Look Out Lipton, Here Comes Oolong!

Heating Up an Old Product

Thomas J. Lipton Company has been in the tea business for a long time. However, what seemed to Lipton to be a steady, even boring business has suddenly heated up. The beverage market is changing again.

Chalk up the change to those fickle consumers. Forget soft drinks. They were the rage of the 1980s as the cola companies added diet everything to their lines and experimented with all sorts of flavors. Forget sports drinks. They became the glamour drinks of the late 1980s and early 1990s as the soft-drink market leveled and the cola companies searched for growth opportunities. Forget those flavored sparkling waters, like Clearly Canadian. They had a wild ride in the early 1990s and became the talk of North America. Forget coffee. Sure the venerable old standby has risen from the ashes as people began to turn away from alcoholic drinks and entrepreneurs rediscovered the coffee house. However, today's hot drink is iced tea. Yes, iced tea. In fact, it's iced tea in a bottle or can, already prepared and ready to drink. No fuss, no boiling, and no tea bags.

Iced tea is not new. We can trace iced tea's invention to the 1904 World's Fair in St. Louis. Richard Blechynden, a promoter of Indian and Ceylon tea, found it impossible to peddle his hot tea in the stifling Missouri heat. In desperation, he dumped some ice cubes into his tea and discovered the spectators were willing to gulp anything cold. Iced tea in a can isn't new either. That's been around since the early 1970s, but it had never been more than a blip on the beverage market's radar screen.

Adding Flavor

Flavor is what's new. Snapple started the trend by building a regional cult following based on bottled iced teas that featured zany tea flavors like cranberry, peach, and raspberry. Snapple's flavored, hot-filled tea (the manufacturer bottles the tea while it is still warm from brewing) offered consumers a better-tasting tea. Before Snapple, Lipton and others offered iced teas in plain and lemon flavor. Young, trendsetting consumers bought Snapple directly from coolers in convenience stores and delicatessens, and chugged it straight from the bottle.

The flavored teas seemed to hit a bull's-eye with consumers who were looking for something different to drink. They were willing to move away from traditional colas in search of new flavors. Consumers seemed to have a short attention span for new products and were willing to try new drinks. They were interested in so-called "New Age" beverages, drinks that appealed to their desire for healthier, lighter refreshment. Consumers responded to the all natural, no-calorie, relaxing, and refreshing claims the new-age beverages promoted. Increasingly on the go, consumers also liked the convenience and availability of ready-to-drink teas.

As a result, ready-to-drink tea sales soared to $53 million in 1991, a 50 percent increase over 1990, but still only 5 percent of total U.S. tea sales. By comparison, the soft-drink market was $48 *billion*, and even coffee accounted for $5 billion in annual sales. But soft drinks were growing at less than a 2 percent annual rate, and the once fashionable bottled waters were trickling along at one-half percent.

Forming Teams

Despite the small size of the iced tea market, the big players noticed the growth rate and jumped in. Coca-Cola made the first move by teaming up with Nestlé to form Coca-Cola Nestlé Refreshments, combining Coca-Cola's powerful distribution network with Nestlé's tea expertise and its Nestea brand. Pepsi Cola followed by joining forces with Thomas J. Lipton Company. Barq's energized its Luzianne tea brand, A&W announced it would make and distribute Tetley tea, Cadbury Beverages uncovered little-known All Seasons to serve as its tea partner, and Perrier Group joined forces with Celestial Seasonings.

Lipton was already number one in the tea market with about a 50 percent market share of the $400 million tea market. Like Coca-Cola, Pepsi's top management argued that the company's alliance with Lipton would leverage Pepsi's distribution strength with Lipton's leadership in tea to produce a can't-miss proposition. Lipton's president observed that the new partnership would make Lipton "as widely available as Pepsi."

The entrance of Pepsi, Coca-Cola, and their competitors should invigorate the ready-to-drink tea market. One observer noted that the iced-tea market was still a Northeastern phenomenon, with the New England to Virginia corridor accounting for 65 percent of U.S. sales. By the mid-1990s, analysts saw the category growing at 20 percent annually. One Coke/Nestlé manager predicted ready-to-drink tea would equal 5 percent of the soft-drink market by 2000.

Indeed, all this attention produced almost 200 new ready-to-drink teas during 1991 and 1992. The tea category leaped another 50 percent in 1992 to $600 million and then to $1.3 billion in 1993. The competitors generated this growth by dusting off tea's boring image and recasting it as a natural, better-for-you beverage. Further, scientific evidence emerged that tea inhibited certain types of cancer in laboratory mice and seemed to be linked to lower cholesterol rates. Lipton, Nestea, and Snapple lured customers with new flavors and pointed out that lack of carbonation makes iced tea easier to drink rapidly and in quantity. Lipton used Bo Jackson to proclaim "This ain't no sippin' tea."

Although Coca-Cola/Nestlé's Nestea sales soared in 1993, Snapple's and Lipton's grew even faster. As a result, Nestea spent the summer of 1994 narrowing its promotion to target 18- to 29-year-olds with a $30 million promotional blitz consisting of sponsorships and sampling. It dispatched five 18-wheelers it called its "Cool Out Caravan" to volleyball matches, baseball games, theme parks, and beaches in 60 markets.

For its part, Pepsi continued its cola-style marketing for Lipton teas. Its radio ads argued that Snapple is "mixed up from a powder" but Lipton is "real brewed." Pepsi also promoted Lipton in supermarkets by offering customers a 99-cents "value pack" that contained one bottle each of three new drinks: Lipton Original, Ocean Spray Lemonade, and AllSport sports drink. Pepsi also pursued sponsorship of a Rolling Stones concert tour to which it would link a massive sampling program.

Because of its efforts, Lipton's teas seemed ready to unseat Snapple in late 1994; and Coca-Cola/Nestlé, despite its early market entry, was falling behind in the iced-tea wars. Lipton was taking market share from both Snapple and Nestea. One observer noted that Pepsi had done a better job with Lipton and new-age beverages than the Coke system had. Perhaps as a result, Coca-Cola and Nestlé announced they were dissolving their three-year relationship. Coca-Cola would take the primary responsibility for marketing ready-to-drink Nestea while Nestlé would focus on ready-to-drink coffees. Analysts suggested that the new arrangement would give Coca-Cola more speed and flexibility because it would not have to deal with Nestlé on every decision.

Oolong Enters from the East

Just as Lipton seems to be pulling ahead in the U.S. tea market, a threat looms in the East. Shin Shii Industrial Company, a little-known beverage company based in Tainan, a dusty industrial city in southern Taiwan, has emerged as a giant killer in the Taiwanese beverage market. In 1985, Shin Shii launched Kai Shii oolong tea, a canned ready-to-drink iced tea. Although iced tea was popular in other Pacific rim countries like Japan, the Taiwanese had never heard of iced tea. They drank only fresh-brewed hot tea.

Beginning in 1991, Shin Shii and its advertising agency Metaphysical Punctuality Advertising Company used an offbeat, multi-million-dollar advertising campaign to propel Kai Shii from back shelves in mom-and-pop stores to prominent spots in rapidly growing convenience-store chains, grocery stores, hypermarkets, and warehouse clubs. The ads proclaimed that Kai Shii was the choice of a "new breed of people in a new world" and featured "neo-people" who spanned all age groups, even the tradition-bound older generation. The ads presented Kai Shii as a natural drink that fit with people's concerns for their health and the environment. Some ads made fun of inebriated businesspeople who drank foreign liquors, picturing them along side fresh-faced Kai Shii tea drinkers.

In 1993, Kai Shii's advertising team traveled to China to film scenes of Chinese peasants clad in colorful traditional costumes. They put these scenes in Kai Shii ads that played on the emotions generated by Taiwan's growing ties with mainland China. The ads won a first place award at the Cannes Film festival.

Through aggressive advertising, Kai Shii now dominates the nearly 100 brands in the oolong sector of Taiwan's ready-to-drink tea market. Kai Shii captured 25 percent of the overall market, double its 1991 share, and 70 percent of the oolong tea segment.

Furthermore, consumer demand for ready-to-drink iced tea has cut sharply into sales of carbonated soft drinks. Soft-drink sales in Taiwan plummeted 16 percent in 1993, while ready-to-drink tea sales have more than doubled since 1991. The sales trend hit Coke and Pepsi especially hard, and Pepsi said it would move to reduce costs.

In 1994, Kai Shii's ads went global, featuring young Chinese living in New York City and Europeans living in London and Paris. These ads were just the opening salvos as Shin Shii turned its sights on foreign markets. Its managers plan to use the skills they've honed in Taiwan to enter the U.S. market.

In entering the U.S. market, Shin Shii will face the challenge of introducing American consumers to the smooth-tasting, amber-colored oolong tea. And Lipton and Pepsi will face the challenge of a new competitor that has already shown it can succeed in selling iced tea and in taking share from soft drinks.

QUESTIONS

1. What bases can companies use to segment the U.S. iced-tea market? What potential market segments can you identify?

2. How would you go about forecasting demand in the iced-tea market and in any given segment?

3. Which type of market coverage strategy should Pepsi/Lipton adopt? Why? How should they position Lipton iced teas?

4. If you were advising Shin Shii, what marketing strategy recommendations would you make concerning its entry into the U.S. market? How should it position Kai Shii?

Sources: Sally D. Goll, "Taiwan Soft Drink Sales Break for Tea," *Wall Street Journal,* July 29, 1994, p. A7B, used with permission of *Wall Street Journal.* See also: Laurie M. Grossman, "Coca-Cola, Nestlé Are Ending Venture In Tea and Coffee but Plan Other Ties, *Wall Street Journal,* August 30, 1994, p. B3; Laura Bird, "Trouble Is Brewing for Snapple As Rivals Fight for Iced Tea Sales, *Wall Street Journal,* June 9, 1994, p. B4; Eric Sfiligoj, "Ladies and Gentlemen, and Beverages of All Ages," *Beverage World,* April 1994, pp. 42–47; Gerry Khermouch, "Nestea Iced Tea Plans Summer Push," *Adweek,* March 21, 1994, p. 13; Michael J. McCarthy, "Competition Heats Up Iced-Tea Industry," *Wall Street Journal,* June 15, 1993, p. B1; Kevin Goldman, "Snapple Goes Big Time for New Age Drink," *Wall Street Journal,* April, 20, 1993, p. B6; Greg W. Prince, "Tea for All," *Beverage World,* April 1992, pp. 24–32.

Designing Products

PRODUCTS, BRANDS, PACKAGING, AND SERVICES

9

Each year, Revlon sells more than $1 billion worth of cosmetics, toiletries, and fragrances to consumers around the world. Its many successful perfume products make Revlon number one in the popular-price segment of the $4 billion fragrance market. In one sense, Revlon's perfumes are no more than careful mixtures of oils and chemicals that have nice scents. But Revlon knows that when it sells perfume, it sells much more than fragrant fluids—it sells what the fragrances can do for the women who use them.

Of course, a perfume's scent contributes to its success or failure. Fragrance marketers agree: "No smell; no sell." Most new aromas are developed by elite "perfumers" at one of many select "fragrance houses." Perfume is shipped from the fragrance houses in big, ugly drums—hardly the stuff of which dreams are made! Although a $180-an-ounce perfume may cost no more than $10 to produce, to perfume consumers the product is much more than a few dollars worth of ingredients and a pleasing smell.

Many things beyond the ingredients and scent add to a perfume's allure. In fact, when Revlon designs a new perfume, the scent may be the *last* element developed. Revlon first researches women's feelings about themselves and their relationships with others. It then develops and tests new perfume concepts that match women's changing values, desires, and lifestyles. When Revlon finds a promising new concept, it creates and names a scent to fit the idea. Revlon's research in the early 1970s showed that women were feeling more competitive with men and that they were striving to find individual identities. For this new woman of the 1970s, Revlon created Charlie, the first of the "lifestyle" perfumes. Thousands of women adopted Charlie as a bold statement of independence, and it quickly became the world's best-selling perfume.

In the late 1970s, Revlon research showed a shift in women's attitudes—"women had made the equality point, which Charlie addressed. Now women were hungering for an expression of femininity." The Charlie girls had grown up; they now wanted perfumes that were subtle rather than shocking. Thus, Revlon subtly shifted Charlie's position: The perfume still

OBJECTIVES

When you finish this chapter, you should be able to accomplish the following:

1. Define the term **product**, including the **core, actual,** and **augmented product**.

2. Explain **product classifications,** and contrast the differing **types of consumer products** and **industrial products**.

3. Outline the range of **individual product decisions** marketers make, discussing the **product attributes** of **quality, features,** and **design**.

4. Discuss **branding,** and contrast the differences among **line extensions, brand extensions, multibrands,** and **new brands**.

5. Illustrate **product line** and **product mix decisions,** describing **stretching** and **filling** the **product line length, line modernization, line featuring,** and **line width**.

6. List some of the considerations marketers face in making **international product decisions,** including whether or not to **standardize** or **adapt product** and **packaging**.

made its "independent lifestyle" statement, but with an added tinge of "femininity and romance." Revlon also launched a perfume for the woman of the 1980s, Jontue, which was positioned on a theme of romance.

Revlon continues to refine Charlie's position, now targeting the woman of the 1990s who is "able to do it all, but smart enough to know what she wants to do." After almost 20 years, aided by continuous but subtle repositioning, Charlie remains the best-selling mass market perfume.

A perfume's *name* is an important product attribute. Revlon uses such names as Charlie, Fleurs de Jontue, Ciara, Scoundrel, Guess, and Unforgettable to create images that support each perfume's positioning. Last year, it introduced Aje, which means "the power of woman," targeted toward African Americans. Competitors offer perfumes with such names as Obsession, Passion, Uninhibited, Opium, Joy, Exclamation!, White Linen, Youth Dew, and Eternity. These names suggest that the perfumes will do something more than just make you smell better. Oscar de la Renta's Ruffles perfume *began* as a name, one chosen because it created images of whimsy, youth, glamour, and femininity—all well suited to the target market of young, stylish women. Only later was a scent selected to go with the product's name and positioning.

Revlon must also carefully *package* its perfumes. To consumers, the bottle and package are the most real symbols of the perfume and its image. Bottles must feel comfortable, be easy to handle, and look impressive when displayed in stores. Most important, they must support the perfume's concept and image.

So when a woman buys perfume, she buys much, much more than simply fragrant fluids. The perfume's image, its promises, its scent, its name and package, the company that makes it, the stores that sell it—all become a part of the total perfume product. When Revlon sells perfume, it sells more than just the tangible product. It sells lifestyle, self-expression, and exclusivity; achievement, success, and status; femininity, romance, passion, and fantasy; memories, hopes, and dreams.[1]

Clearly, perfume is more than just perfume when Revlon sells it. This chapter begins with a deceptively simple question: *What is a product?* After answering this question, we look at ways to classify products in consumer and business markets, and look for links between types of products and types of marketing strategies. Next, we examine several decisions that go beyond basic product design: *branding, packaging, labeling,* and *product-support services.* Finally, we move from decisions about individual products to decisions about building product lines and product mixes.

Product
Anything that can be offered to a market for attention, acquisition, use, or consumption that might satisfy a want or need. It includes physical objects, services, persons, places, organizations, and ideas.

WHAT IS A PRODUCT?

A Sony CD player, a Supercuts haircut, a Billy Joel concert, a Hawaiian vacation, a GMC truck, H&R Block tax preparation services, and advice from an attorney are all products. We define a **product** as anything that can be offered to a market for attention, acquisition, use, or consumption and that might satisfy a want or need. Products include more than just tangible goods. Broadly defined, products include physical objects, services, persons, places, organizations, ideas, or mixes of these entities. **Services** are products that consist of activities, benefits, or satisfactions that are offered for sale, such as haircuts, tax preparation, and home repairs. Services are essentially intangible and do not result in the ownership of anything. (Because of the importance of services in the world economy, we will look at them more closely in Chapter 21.)

Service
Any activity or benefit that one party can offer to another that is essentially intangible and does not result in the ownership of anything.

Core product
The problem-solving services or core benefits that consumers are really buying when they obtain a product.

Product planners need to think about the product on three levels. The most basic level is the **core product,** which addresses the question: *What is the buyer really buying?* As Figure 9-1 illustrates, the core product stands at the center of

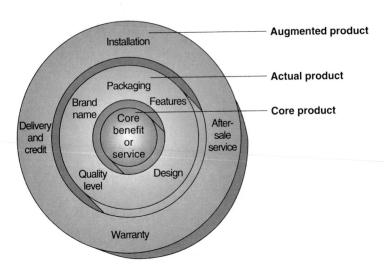

FIGURE 9-1 *Three levels of product*

Actual product
A product's parts, quality level, features, design, brand name, packaging, and other attributes that combine to deliver core product benefits.

Augmented product
Additional consumer services and benefits built around the core and actual products.

the total product. It consists of the problem-solving services or core benefits that consumers seek when they buy a product. A woman buying lipstick buys more than lip color. Charles Revson of Revlon saw this early: "In the factory, we make cosmetics; in the store, we sell hope." Theodore Levitt has pointed out that buyers "do not buy quarter-inch drills; they buy quarter-inch holes." Thus, when designing products, marketers must first define the core of *benefits* the product will provide to consumers.

The product planner must next build an **actual product** around the core product. Actual products may have as many as five characteristics: a *quality level, features, design,* a *brand name,* and *packaging.* For example, Sony's Handycam Camcorder is an actual product. Its name, parts, styling, features, packaging, and other attributes have all been combined carefully to deliver the core benefit—a convenient, high-quality way to capture important moments.

Finally, the product planner must build an **augmented product** around the core and actual products by offering additional consumer services and benefits. Sony must offer more than just a camcorder. It must provide consumers with a complete solution to their picture-taking problems. Thus, when consumers buy a Sony Handycam, Sony and its dealers also might give buyers a warranty on parts and workmanship, free lessons on how to use the camcorder, quick repair services when needed, and a toll-free telephone number to call if they have problems or questions. To the consumer, all of these augmentations become an important part of the total product.

Therefore, a product is more than a simple set of tangible features. Consumers tend to see products as complex bundles of benefits that satisfy their needs. When developing products, marketers first must identify the *core* consumer needs the product will satisfy. They must then design the *actual* product and find ways to *augment* it in order to create the bundle of benefits that will best satisfy consumers.

Today, most competition takes place at the product augmentation level. Successful companies add benefits to their offers that not only will *satisfy,* but also will *delight* the customer. Thus, hotel guests find a chocolate mint on their pillow, or a bowl of fruit, or a VCR with optional videotapes. The company is saying "we want to treat you in a special way." However, these augmentations cost money, and the marketer has to ask whether customers will pay enough to cover the extra cost. Moreover, augmentations soon become *expected* benefits: hotel guests now expect cable television, trays of toiletries, and other amenities in their rooms. This means that competitors must search for still more features and

Core, actual and augmented product: Consumers perceive this Sony camcorder as a complex bundle of tangible and intangible features and services that deliver a core benefit—a convenient, high-quality way to capture important moments.

benefits to distinguish their offers. Finally, as companies raise the prices of their augmented products, some competitors can go back to the strategy of offering a more basic product at a much lower price. Thus, along with the growth of fine hotels such as Four Seasons, Westin, and Hyatt, we see the emergence of lower-cost hotels and motels like Red Roof Inns, Fairfield Inns, and Motel 6 for clients who want only basic room accommodations.

PRODUCT CLASSIFICATIONS

In developing marketing strategies for their products and services, marketers have developed several product-classification schemes. First, marketers divide products and services into two broad classes based on the types of consumers that use them—*consumer products* and *industrial products*.

CONSUMER PRODUCTS

Consumer products
Products bought by final consumers for personal consumption.

Consumer products are those bought by final consumers for personal consumption. Marketers usually classify these goods further based on *how consumers go about buying them*. Consumer products include *convenience products, shopping products, specialty products,* and *unsought products*. These products differ in the ways consumers buy them; therefore they differ in how they are marketed (see Table 9-1).

Convenience products
Consumer products that the customer usually buys frequently, immediately, and with a minimum of comparison and buying effort.

Convenience products are consumer products and services that the customer usually buys frequently, immediately, and with a minimum of comparison and buying effort. They are usually low priced and widely available. Examples include soap, candy, and newspapers. Convenience products can be divided further into *staples, impulse products,* and *emergency products. Staples* are products that consumers buy on a regular basis, such as ketchup, toothpaste, or crackers. *Impulse products* are purchased with little planning or search effort. These products are normally widely available. Thus, candy bars and magazines are placed next to checkout counters in many stores because shoppers may not otherwise think of

TABLE 9-1 *Marketing Considerations for Consumer Products*

MARKETING CONSIDERATIONS	TYPE OF CONSUMER PRODUCT			
	Convenience	Shopping	Specialty	Unsought
Customer buying behavior	Frequent purchase, little planning, little comparison or shopping effort, low customer involvement	Less frequent purchase, much planning and shopping effort, comparison of brands on price, quality, style	Strong brand preference and loyalty, special purchase effort, little comparison of brands, low price sensitivity	Little product awareness, knowledge (or if aware, little or even negative interest)
Price	Low price	Higher price	High price	Varies
Distribution	Widespread distribution, convenient locations	Selective distribution in fewer outlets	Exclusive distribution in only one or a few outlets per market area	Varies
Promotion	Mass promotion by the producer	Advertising and personal selling by both producer and resellers	More carefully targeted promotion by both producer and resellers	Aggressive advertising and personal selling by producer and resellers
Examples	Toothpaste, magazines, laundry detergent	Major appliances, televisions, furniture, clothing	Luxury goods, such as Rolex watches or fine crystal	Life insurance, Red Cross blood donations

buying them. Customers buy *emergency products* when their need is urgent—umbrellas during a rainstorm, or boots and shovels during the year's first snowstorm. Manufacturers of emergency products place them in many outlets to make them readily available when customers need them.

Shopping products are less frequently purchased consumer products that customers compare carefully on suitability, quality, price, and style. When buying shopping products, consumers spend much time and effort in gathering information and making comparisons. Examples include furniture, clothing, used cars, and major appliances. Shopping products can be divided into *homogeneous* and *heterogeneous* products. The buyer sees homogeneous shopping products, such as major appliances, as similar in quality but different enough in price to justify shopping comparisons. The seller has to "talk price" to the buyer. However, when shopping for heterogeneous products such as clothing and furniture, customers usually find product features more important than price. If the buyer wants a new suit, the cut, fit, and look are likely to be more important than small price differences. Therefore, a seller of heterogeneous shopping products must carry a wide assortment to satisfy individual tastes and must have well-trained salespeople to give information and advice to customers.

Specialty products are consumer products with unique characteristics or brand identification for which a significant group of buyers is willing to make a special purchase effort. Examples include specific brands and types of cars, high-priced photographic equipment, and custom-made men's suits. A Rolls-Royce, for example, is a specialty product because buyers are usually willing to travel great distances to buy one. Buyers normally do not compare specialty products. They invest only the time needed to reach dealers carrying the wanted products. Although these dealers do not need convenient locations, they still must let buyers know where to find them.

Unsought products are consumer products that the consumer either does not know about or knows about but does not normally think of buying. Most major innovations are unsought until the consumer becomes aware of them through advertising. Classic examples of known but unsought products are life insurance and blood donations to the Red Cross. By their very nature, unsought products require a lot of advertising, personal selling, and other marketing efforts. Some of the most advanced personal selling methods have developed out of the challenge of selling unsought products.

INDUSTRIAL PRODUCTS

Industrial products are those purchased for further processing or for use in conducting a business. Thus, the distinction between a consumer product and an industrial product is based on the *purpose* for which the product is bought. If a consumer buys a lawn mower for use around home, the lawn mower is a consumer product. If the same consumer buys the same lawn mower for use in a landscaping business, the lawn mower is an industrial product.

There are three groups of industrial products: *materials and parts, capital items,* and *supplies and services.*

Materials and parts are industrial products that become a part of the buyer's product, through further processing or as components. They include raw materials and manufactured materials and parts.

Raw materials include farm products (wheat, cotton, livestock, fruits, vegetables) and natural products (fish, lumber, crude petroleum, iron ore). Farm products are supplied by many small producers who turn them over to marketing intermediaries that process and sell them. Natural products usually have great bulk and low unit value and require a lot of transportation to move them from pro-

---

Shopping products
Consumer goods that the customer, in the process of selection and purchase, characteristically compares on such bases as suitability, quality, price, and style.

Specialty products
Consumer products with unique characteristics or brand identification for which a significant group of buyers is willing to make a special purchase effort.

Unsought products
Consumer products that the consumer either does not know about or knows about but does not normally think of buying.

Industrial products
Products bought by individuals and organizations for further processing or for use in conducting a business.

Materials and parts
Industrial products that enter the manufacturer's product completely, including raw materials and manufactured materials and parts.

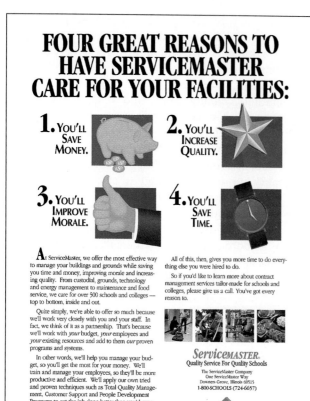

Business services: ServiceMaster supplies business services for a wide range of organizations. This advertisement to schools and colleges offers services ranging from custodial, grounds, technology, and energy management services to maintenance and food services.

ducer to user. They are supplied by fewer and larger producers, who tend to market them directly to industrial users.

Manufactured materials and parts include component materials (iron, yarn, cement, wires) and component parts (small motors, tires, castings). Component materials usually are processed further—for example, pig iron is made into steel and yarn is woven into cloth. Component parts enter the finished product completely with no further change in form, as when Hoover puts small motors into its vacuum cleaners and General Motors adds tires to its automobiles. Most manufactured materials and parts are sold directly to industrial users. Price and service are the major marketing factors; branding and advertising tend to be less important.

Capital items are industrial products that aid in the buyer's production or operations. They include installations and accessory equipment. *Installations* consist of buildings (factories, offices) and fixed equipment (generators, drill presses, large computers, elevators). Because installations are major purchases, they usually are bought directly from the producer after a long decision period.

Accessory equipment includes portable factory equipment and tools (hand tools, lift trucks) and office equipment (fax machines, desks). They have a shorter life than installations and simply aid in the production process. Most sellers of accessory equipment use middlemen because the market is spread out geographically, the buyers are numerous, and the orders are small.

Supplies and services are industrial products that do not enter the finished product at all. *Supplies* include operating supplies (lubricants, coal, computer paper, pencils) and repair and maintenance items (paint, nails, brooms). Supplies are the convenience products of the industrial field because they usually are purchased with a minimum of effort or comparison. *Business services* include maintenance and repair services (window cleaning, computer repair) and business advisory services (legal, management consulting, advertising). These services are usually supplied under contract. Maintenance services often are provided by small producers, and repair services are often available from the manufacturers of the original equipment.

INDIVIDUAL PRODUCT DECISIONS

We now look at decisions relating to the development and marketing of individual products. Figure 9-2 shows the important decisions. We will focus on decisions about *product attributes, branding, packaging, labeling,* and *product-support services.*

Product Attributes → Branding → Packaging → Labeling → Product-Support Services

FIGURE 9-2 *Individual product decisions*

PRODUCT ATTRIBUTES

Capital items
Industrial products that partly enter the finished product, including installations and accessory equipment.

Supplies and services
Industrial products that do not enter the finished product at all.

Product quality
The ability of a product to perform its functions; it includes the product's overall durability, reliability, precision, ease of operation and repair, and other valued attributes.

Developing a product involves defining the benefits that the product will offer. These benefits are communicated and delivered by product attributes such as *quality, features,* and *design.* Decisions about these attributes greatly affect consumer reactions to a product.

Product Quality

Quality is one of the marketer's major positioning tools. Quality has two dimensions—level and consistency. In developing a product, the marketer must first choose a *quality level* that will support the product's position in the target market. Here, **product quality** means the ability of a product to perform its functions. It includes the product's overall durability, reliability, precision, ease of operation and repair, and other valued attributes. Although some of these attributes can be measured objectively, from a marketing point of view, quality should be measured in terms of buyers' perceptions. Companies rarely try to offer the highest possible quality level—few customers want or can afford the high levels of quality offered in products such as a Rolls Royce, a Sub Zero refrigerator, or a Rolex watch. Instead, companies choose a quality level that matches target market needs and the quality levels of competing products.

Beyond quality level, high quality also can mean consistently *delivering* the targeted level of quality to consumers. In this sense, quality means the "absence of defects or variation." All companies should strive for high levels of *quality consistency.*

> Thus, a Chevrolet can have just as much quality as a Rolls Royce, and the service at a discount store can be equally "good"—free of variations—as at Bergdorf-Goodman. Even a perfect product can't do more than it was designed to do: Don't count on a Chevy to perform like a Rolls. Still, reducing the variations that cause defects [ensures] that customers get what they pay for.[2]

During the past decade, a renewed emphasis on quality has spawned a global quality movement. Japanese firms have long practiced "Total Quality Management" (TQM), an effort to constantly improve product and process quality in every phase of their operations. "In 40 years, a focus on quality has turned Japan from a maker of knick-knacks into an economic powerhouse—and U.S. and European companies are being forced to respond. The result: a global revolution affecting every facet of business."[3] For more than 40 years, the Japanese have awarded the Demming prize (named after quality pioneer W. Edwards Demming) to companies that have achieved outstanding quality. Recently, the U.S. Department of Commerce began granting similar awards—the annual Malcolm Baldrige National Quality Awards—to U.S. companies demonstrating outstanding quality leadership.

To some companies, improving quality means using better quality control to reduce defects that annoy consumers. To others, it means making lofty speeches about the importance of quality and passing out lapel pins with quality slogans on them. But total quality means much more than this. It requires a total-company dedication to continuous quality improvement. Quality starts with a strong commitment by top management. Then, employees at all levels of the organization must be educated and motivated to put quality first.

Rather than catching and correcting defects after the fact, good quality involves preventing defects before they occur, through better product design and improved manufacturing processes. Beyond simply reducing product defects, the ultimate goal of total quality is to improve customer value. For example, when Motorola first began its total quality program in the early 1980s, its goal was to drastically reduce manufacturing defects. In recent years, however, Motorola has adapted its quality concept to one of "customer-defined quality" and "total customer satisfaction." (See Marketing Highlight 9-1.) Customer satisfaction is the

MOTOROLA'S CUSTOMER-DEFINED, "SIX-SIGMA" QUALITY

Founded in 1928, Motorola introduced the first car radio—hence the name Motorola, suggesting "sound in motion." During World War II, it developed the first two-way radios ("walkie-talkies"), and by the 1950s, Motorola had become a household name in consumer electronics products. In the 1970s, however, facing intense competition mostly from Japanese firms, Motorola abandoned the radios and televisions that had made it famous. Instead, it focused on advanced telecommunications and electronics products—semiconductors, two-way radios, pagers, cellular telephones, and related gear. However, by the early 1980s, Japanese competitors were still beating Motorola to the market with higher-quality products at lower prices.

During the past decade, however, Motorola has come roaring back. It now leads all competitors in the global two-way mobile radio market and ranks number one in cellular telephones with a 45 percent worldwide market share. Motorola is the world's third largest semiconductor producer, behind only Intel and NEC. Once in danger of being forced out of the pager business altogether, Motorola now dominates that market with an astonishing 85 percent global market share. And rather than suffering at the hands of Japanese competitors, Motorola now has them on the run, even on their home turf. Motorola's sales in Japan now exceed $1 billion, accounting for almost 7 percent of total company sales.

"Quality means the world to us," claims Motorola. An obsession with customer-driven quality has helped the company to achieve worldwide leadership in many product markets.

How has Motorola achieved such remarkable leadership? The answer is deceptively simple: an obsessive dedication to *quality.* In the early 1980s, Motorola launched an aggressive crusade to improve product quality, first by tenfold, then by a hundredfold. It set the unheard-of goal of "six-sigma" quality. Six sigma is a statistical term that means "six standard deviations from a statistical performance average." In plain English, the six-sigma standard means that Motorola set out to slash product defects to fewer than 3.4 per million components manufactured—99.9997 percent defect free. "Six sigma" became Motorola's rallying cry. In 1988, it received one of the first annual Malcolm Baldrige National Quality Awards recognizing "preeminent quality leadership."

Motorola's initial efforts focused on manufacturing improvements. This involved much more than simply increasing the number of quality control inspectors. The goal was to prevent defects from occurring in the first place. This meant *designing* products from the onset for quality and making things right the *first* time and *every* time. For example, Motorola's highly successful MicroTAC foldable, hand-held cellular phone has only one-

most important consideration used in evaluating Baldrige Quality Award contestants.

Recently, the total quality management movement has drawn criticism. Many companies have viewed TQM as a magic cure-all, and have created token total quality programs that applied quality principles only superficially. As a result, recent surveys show that two-thirds or more of American managers think that TQM has failed in their companies, and the number of applicants for the Malcolm Baldrige Award has fallen sharply since its peak in 1991. Many companies have dropped the TQM label in favor of less trendy terms such as "continuous process improvement" or "continuous value improvement." Despite the recent backlash against TQM, basic quality principles appear sound:

> It's true that obsessively focusing on quality alone can take your eye off other critical variables—such as what your customers might want. Yes, many TQM programs have been badly executed, particularly those imposed from above in cookie cutter fashion. And, yes, TQM is, as the refrain goes, no panacea. But make no mistake, total quality's principles still represent a sound way to do business. . . . Many companies that have successfully adopted TQM don't even use the phrase "total quality" anymore; [but] it has simply become a way of doing business.[4]

Thus, companies have turned quality into a potent strategic weapon. *Strategic* quality involves gaining an edge over competitors by consistently offering prod-

eighth the number of parts contained in its original 1978 portable telephone; components snap together instead of being joined by screws or fasteners. This simpler design means fewer component defects and production errors.

Meeting the six sigma standard means that everyone in the organization must strive for quality improvement. Thus, total quality has become an important part of Motorola's basic corporate culture. Motorola spends $120 million annually to educate employees about quality, and then rewards people when they make things right. And because Motorola's products can be only as good as the components that go into them, the company forces its suppliers to meet the same exacting quality standards. Some suppliers grumble, but those that survive benefit greatly from their own quality improvements. As an executive from one of Motorola's suppliers puts it, "If we can supply Motorola, we can supply God."

More recently, as Motorola has developed a deeper understanding of the meaning of quality, its initial focus on preventing manufacturing defects has evolved into an emphasis on *customer-defined quality* and improving customer value. "Quality," notes Motorola's vice-president of quality, "has to do something for the customer." Thus, the fundamental aim of the company's quality movement is "total customer satisfaction":

> Beauty is in the eye of the user. If [a product] does not work the way that the user needs it to work, the defect is as big to the user as if it doesn't work the way the designer planned it. Our definition of a defect is "if the customer doesn't like it, it's a defect."

Instead of focusing just on manufacturing defects, Motorola now surveys customers about their quality needs, analyzes customer complaints, and studies service records in a constant quest to improve value to the customer. Motorola's executives routinely visit customers to gain better insights into their needs. As a result, Motorola's total quality management has done more than reduce product defects; it has helped the company to shift from an inwardly focused, engineering orientation to a market-driven, customer-focused one. The company has now expanded its quality program to all of its departments and processes, from manufacturing and product development to market research, finance, and even advertising.

Some skeptics are concerned that Motorola's obsession with quality might create problems. For example, the company's products sometimes have been late to the market. Others worry that building so much quality into a product might be too expensive. Not so, claims Motorola. In fact, the reverse is true—superior quality is the lowest-cost way to do things. The costs of monitoring and fixing mistakes can far exceed the costs of getting things right in the first place. Motorola estimates that its quality efforts have resulted in savings of more than $3 billion during the past six years.

And so Motorola's quest for quality continues. By the year 2001, Motorola is shooting for near perfection—a mind-boggling rate of just *one* defect per *billion.*

Sources: Quotes from "Future Perfect," *The Economist,* January 4, 1992, p. 61; Lois Therrien, "Motorola and NEC: Going for Glory," *Business Week,* Special issue on quality, 1991, pp. 60–61; and B. G. Yovovich, "Motorola's Quest for Quality," *Business Marketing,* September 1991, pp. 14–16. Also see Ronald Henkoff, "Keeping Motorola on a Roll," *Fortune,* April 18, 1994, pp. 67–78; and J. Ward Best, "The Making of Motorola," *Durham Herald Sun,* February 12, 1995, pp. A1, A11.

ucts and services that better serve customers' needs and preferences for quality. As one expert proclaims, "Quality is not simply a problem to be solved; it is a competitive opportunity."[5] Others suggest, however, that quality has now become a competitive *necessity*—that in the 1990s and beyond, only companies with the best quality will thrive.

Product Features

A product can be offered with varying features. A "stripped-down" model, one without any extras, is the starting point. The company can create higher-level models by adding more features. Features are a competitive tool for differentiating the company's product from competitors' products. Being the first producer to introduce a needed and valued new feature is one of the most effective ways to compete. Some companies are very innovative in adding new features.

How can a company identify new features and decide which ones to add to its product? The company should periodically survey buyers who have used the product and ask these questions: How do you like the product? Which specific features of the product do you like most? Which features could we add to improve the product? How much would you pay for each feature? The answers provide the company with a rich list of feature ideas. The company then can assess each feature's *customer value* versus its *company cost.* Features that customers value little in relation to costs should be dropped; those that customers value highly in relation to costs should be added.

Product Design

Product design
The process of designing a product's style and function: creating a product that is attractive; easy, safe, and inexpensive to use and service; and simple and economical to produce and distribute.

Another way to add customer value is through distinctive **product design.** Some companies have reputations for outstanding design, such as Black & Decker in cordless appliances and tools, Steelcase in office furniture and systems, Bose in audio equipment, and Ciba Corning in medical equipment. Many companies, however, lack a "design touch." Their product designs function poorly or are dull or common looking. Yet design can be one of the most powerful competitive weapons in a company's marketing arsenal.

Design is a larger concept than style. *Style* simply describes the appearance of a product. Styles can be eye-catching or yawn-inspiring. A sensational style may grab attention, but it does not necessarily make the product *perform* better. In some cases, it might even result in worse performance. For example, a chair may look great, but be very uncomfortable. Unlike style, *design* is more than skin deep—it goes to the very heart of a product. Good design contributes to a product's usefulness as well as to its looks. A good designer considers appearance but also creates products that are easy, safe, inexpensive to use and service, and simple and economical to produce and distribute.

As competition intensifies, design will offer one of the most potent tools for differentiating and positioning a company's products and services. Design investment pays off. For example, the radical design of the Ford Taurus, with its sleek styling, passenger comforts, engineering advances, and efficient manufacturing, made the car a huge success. Herman Miller, the American office furniture company, has won admiration and sales with the distinctive comfort and looks of its furniture. And Braun, a German division of Gillette which has elevated design to a high art, has had outstanding success with its coffee makers, food processors, hair dryers, electric razors, and other small appliances. Good design can attract attention, improve product performance, cut production costs, and give the product a strong competitive advantage in the target market.[6]

BRANDING

Consumers view a brand as an important part of a product, and branding can add value to a product. For example, most consumers would perceive a bottle of White Linen perfume as a high-quality, expensive product. But the same perfume in an unmarked bottle would likely be viewed as lower in quality, even if the fragrance were identical.

Branding has become a major issue in product strategy. On the one hand, developing a branded product requires a great deal of long-term marketing investment, especially for advertising, promotion, and packaging. Manufacturers often find it easier and less expensive simply to make the product and let others do the brand building. Taiwanese manufacturers have taken this course. They make a large amount of the world's clothing, consumer electronics, and computers, but these products are sold under non-Taiwanese brand names.

On the other hand, most manufacturers eventually learn that the power lies with the companies that control the brand names. For example, brand name clothing, electronics, and computer companies can replace their Taiwanese manufacturing sources with cheaper sources in Malaysia and elsewhere. The Taiwanese producers can do little to prevent the loss of sales to less expensive suppliers—consumers are loyal to the brands, not to the producers. Japanese and South Korean companies, however, have not made this mistake. They have spent heavily to build up brand names such as Sony, Panasonic, JVC, Goldstar, and Samsung for their products. Even when these companies no longer can afford to man-

Familiar brands provide consumer information, recognition, and confidence.

ufacture their products in their homelands, their brand names continue to command customer loyalty.[7]

Powerful brand names have *consumer franchise*—they command strong consumer loyalty. A sufficient number of customers demand these brands and refuse substitutes, even if the substitutes are offered at somewhat lower prices. Companies that develop brands with a strong consumer franchise are insulated from competitors' promotional strategies. Thus, companies around the world invest heavily to create strong national or even global recognition and preference for their brand names.

What Is a Brand?

Perhaps the most distinctive skill of professional marketers is their ability to create, maintain, protect, and enhance brands. A **brand** is a name, term, sign, symbol, or design, or a combination of these intended to identify the products or services of one seller or group of sellers and to differentiate them from those of competitors.[8] Thus, a brand identifies the maker or seller of a product.

A brand is a seller's promise to deliver consistently a specific set of features, benefits, and services to buyers. The best brands convey a warranty of quality. According to one marketing executive, a brand can deliver up to four levels of meaning:

Brand
A name, term, sign, symbol, or design, or a combination of these intended to identify the goods or services of one seller or group of sellers and to differentiate them from those of competitors.

- ◆ *Attributes.* A brand first brings to mind certain product attributes. For example, Mercedes suggests such attributes as "well engineered," "well built," "durable," "high prestige," "fast," "expensive," and "high resale value." The company may use one or more of these attributes in its advertising for the car. For years, Mercedes Benz advertised "Engineered like no other car in the world." This provided a positioning platform for other attributes of the car.

- ◆ *Benefits.* Customers do not buy attributes, they buy benefits. Therefore, attributes must be translated into functional and emotional benefits. For example, the attribute "durable" could translate into the functional benefit, "I won't have to buy a new car every few years." The attribute "expensive" might translate into the emotional benefit, "The car makes me feel important and admired." The attribute "well built" might translate into the functional and emotional benefit, "I am safe in the event of an accident."

◆ *Values.* A brand also says something about the buyers' values. Thus, Mercedes buyers value high performance, safety, and prestige. A brand marketer must identify the specific groups of car buyers whose values coincide with the delivered benefit package.

◆ *Personality.* A brand also projects a personality. Motivation researchers sometimes ask, "If this brand were a person, what kind of person would it be?" Consumers might visualize a Mercedes automobile as being a wealthy, middle-aged business executive. The brand will attract people whose actual or desired self-images match the brand's image.[9]

The challenge of branding is to develop a deep set of meanings for the brand. Given the four levels of a brand's meaning, marketers must decide the levels at which they will build the brand's identity. The most lasting meanings of a brand are its values and personality. They define the brand's essence. Thus, Mercedes stands for "high achievers and success." The company must build its brand strategy around creating and protecting this brand personality. Although Mercedes has recently yielded to market pressures by introducing lower-price models, this might prove risky. Marketing less expensive models might dilute the value and personality that Mercedes has built up over the decades.

Brand Equity

Brands vary in the amount of power and value they have in the marketplace. Some brands are largely unknown to most buyers. Other brands have a high degree of consumer *brand awareness*. Still others enjoy *brand preference*—buyers select them over the others. Finally, some brands command a high degree of *brand loyalty*.

Brand equity
The value of a brand, based on the extent to which it has high brand loyalty, name awareness, perceived quality, strong brand associations, and other assets such as patents, trademarks, and channel relationships.

A powerful brand has high **brand equity**. Brands have higher brand equity to the extent that they have higher brand loyalty, name awareness, perceived quality, strong brand associations, and other assets such as patents, trademarks, and channel relationships.[10] A brand with strong brand equity is a valuable asset. In fact, it can even be bought or sold for a price. For example, Grand Metropolitan acquired various Pillsbury brands, including Green Giant vegetables, Häagen-Dazs ice cream, and Burger King restaurants. Nestlé bought Rowntree (UK), Carnation (US), Stouffer (US), Buitoni-Perugina (Italy), and Perrier (France), making it the world's largest food company.

Measuring the actual equity of a brand name is difficult.[11] Because it is so hard to measure, companies usually do not list brand equity on their balance sheets. Still, they pay handsomely for it. For example, Nestlé paid $4.5 billion to buy Rowntree, five times its book value. And when Grand Metropolitan bought Heublein, it added $800 million to its assets to reflect the value of Smirnoff and other names. According to one estimate, the brand equity of Coca-Cola is $36 billion, Marlboro $33 billion, and Kodak $10 billion.[12]

The world's top brands include such superpowers as Coca-Cola, Campbell, Disney, Kodak, Sony, Mercedes-Benz, and McDonald's (see Marketing Highlight 9-2). High brand equity provides a company with many competitive advantages. Because a powerful brand enjoys a high level of consumer brand awareness and loyalty, the company will incur lower marketing costs relative to revenues. Because consumers expect stores to carry the brand, the company has more leverage in bargaining with resellers. And because the brand name carries high credibility, the company can more easily launch brand extensions. Above all, a powerful brand offers the company some defense against fierce price competition.

THE WORLD'S MOST POWERFUL BRAND NAMES

Coca-Cola, McDonald's, AT&T, Campbell, Disney, Kodak, Kellogg, Hershey—such familiar brand names are household words to most Americans. Companies around the world invest billions of dollars each year to create preference for these and hundreds of other major brands. For example, AT&T, the nation's most heavily advertised brand name, is backed by more than $500 million in advertising each year. Powerful brand names provide strong competitive advantage in the marketplace.

What are the world's most powerful brands? In a recent study, Landor Associates, an image consulting firm, surveyed 9,000 consumers in the United States, Western Europe, and Japan about their familiarity with and esteem for more than 6,000 brands. From the results, it developed brand "image-power" rankings. Listed below are the top ten brands for each part of the world.

The Landor study suggests that few brands have yet achieved true global status. Although some 20 brands were internationally known, and another 45 were poised for global prominence, no product made it onto the top-ten lists of all three markets. Only two brands—Coca-Cola and Sony—appeared in each market's top-40. And only six other brands made the top 100 in each market: Disney, Nestlé, Toyota, McDonald's, Panasonic, and Kleenex.

The study appears to counter the recent contention, summarized by former Chrysler chairman Lee Iacocca, that U.S. consumers believe "Everything from Japan is perfect. Everything from America is lousy." The study shows that Americans do like American products. The list of

top-ten American brands reads like a page out of the corporate American history book. And of the top-100 ranked brands in the United States, 97 claim American roots.

The rankings also suggest strong cultural differences among consumers in the United States, Europe, and Japan. For example, Americans appear food oriented—six of the top ten brands are food related. In the other regions, cars and high-tech brands are more revered. Based on

brand of laundry detergent. Thus, noticeably absent from the list are top brands from some of the world's most powerful marketers, including such giant consumer goods companies as Procter & Gamble, Unilever, and Philip Morris. Further, people often don't buy the brands they regard most highly—many people who hold a Mercedes in high esteem can't afford one. But no matter how you measure brand power, few marketers doubt the value of a powerful brand. As one

THE WORLD'S MOST POWERFUL BRAND NAMES

United States	Europe	Japan
Coca-Cola	Coca-Cola	Sony
Campbell	Sony	National
Disney	Mercedes-Benz	Mercedes-Benz
Pepsi-Cola	BMW	Toyota
Kodak	Philips	Takashimaya (department store)
NBC	Volkswagen	Rolls Royce
Black & Decker	Adidas	Seiko
Kellogg	Kodak	Matsushita
McDonald's	Nivea	Hitachi
Hershey	Porsche	Suntory

the top-ten list, American consumers appear satisfied with simple pleasures like a Big Mac, chocolates, and as a real self-indulgent treat, luxury ice creams. European and Japanese consumers seem to have more expensive tastes. Thus, the Landor study suggests that a global marketer may face many cultural hurdles in its attempts to create worldwide brands.

Some critics question the value of asking consumers to rate brands on such subjective factors as "esteem." People will probably hold a Mercedes in higher esteem than a

brand consultant states, almost anywhere in the world, "When you mention Kodak, I'm pretty sure everyone sees that yellow box."

Sources: Portions adapted from Cathy Taylor, "Consumers Know Native Brands Best," *Adweek,* September 17, 1990, p. 31. Also see Interbrand, *World's Greatest Brands* (New York: John Wiley & Son, 1992); Diane Crispell and Kathleen Brandenburg, "What's in a Brand?" *American Demographics,* May 1993, pp. 26–32; and Kevin Brown, "The Top 200 Mega-Brands," *Advertising Age,* May 2, 1994, p. 33.

Marketers need to manage their brands carefully in order to preserve brand equity. They must develop strategies that effectively maintain or improve brand awareness, perceived brand quality and usefulness, and positive brand associations over time. This requires continuous R&D investment, skillful advertising, and excellent trade and consumer service. Some companies, such as Canada Dry and Colgate-Palmolive, have appointed "brand equity managers" to guard their brands' images, associations, and quality. They work to prevent brand managers from overpromoting brands in order to produce short-term profits at the expense of long-term brand equity.

Companies such as Procter & Gamble, Caterpillar, IBM, and Sony have achieved outstanding *company brand strength,* measured by the proportion of product/markets in which the company markets the leading brand. For example, P&G's impressive marketing reputation in the United States rests on the fact that it markets the leading brand in 19 of the 39 categories in which it competes and has one of the top three brands in 34 of its categories. Its average brand's market share is an astounding 25 percent.

Some analysts see brands as *the* major enduring asset of a company, outlasting the company's specific products and facilities. Yet, behind every powerful brand stands a set of loyal customers. Therefore, the basic asset underlying brand equity is *customer equity.* This suggests that marketing strategy should focus on extending *loyal customer lifetime value,* with brand management serving as a major marketing tool.

Branding poses challenging decisions to the marketer. Figure 9-3 shows the key branding decisions.

FIGURE 9-3 *Major branding decisions*

To brand or not to brand	Brand name selection	Brand sponsor	Brand strategy	Brand repositioning
Brand No brand	Selection Protection	Manufacturer's brand Private brand Licensed brand Co-branding	New brands Line extensions Brand extensions Multibrands	Brand repositioning No brand repositioning

To Brand or Not to Brand

The company first must decide whether it should put a brand name on its product. Branding has become so strong that today hardly anything goes unbranded. Salt is packaged in branded containers, common nuts and bolts are packaged with a distributor's label, and automobile parts—spark plugs, tires, filters—bear brand names that differ from those of the auto makers. Even fruits and vegetables are branded—Sunkist oranges, Dole pineapples, and Chiquita bananas.

Some products, however, carry no brands. "Generic" products are unbranded, plainly packaged, less expensive versions of common products such as spaghetti, paper towels, and canned peaches. They often bear only black-stenciled labels—TOWELS, SUGAR, CAT FOOD—and offer prices as much as 40 percent lower than those of national brands. The lower price is made possible by lower-quality ingredients, lower-cost packaging, and lower advertising costs. The popularity of generics appears to have peaked in the early 1980s. Since then, the market share for generics has dropped, largely as a result of better marketing strategies by brand name manufacturers.

Despite the limited popularity of generics, the issue of whether or not to brand is very much alive today. This situation highlights some key questions: Why have branding in the first place? Who benefits? How do they benefit? At what cost? Branding helps buyers in many ways. Brand names tell the buyer something about product quality. Buyers who always buy the same brand know that they will get the same quality each time they buy. Brand names also increase the shopper's efficiency. Imagine a buyer going into a supermarket and finding thousands of generic products. Finally, brand names help call consumers' attention to new products that might benefit them. The brand name becomes the basis on which a whole story can be built about the new product's special qualities.

Branding also gives the seller several advantages. The brand name makes it easier for the seller to process orders and track down problems. Thus, Anheuser-Busch receives an order for a hundred cases of Michelob beer instead of an order for "some of your better beer." The seller's brand name and trademark provide legal protection for unique product features that otherwise might be copied by competitors. Branding lets the seller attract a loyal and profitable set of customers. Branding helps the seller to segment markets. For example, General Mills can offer Cheerios, Wheaties, Total, Lucky Charms, and many other cereal brands, not just one general product for all consumers.

Branding also adds value to consumers and society. Those who favor branding suggest that it leads to higher and more consistent product quality. Branding also increases innovation by giving producers an incentive to look for new features that can be protected against imitating competitors. Thus, branding results in more product variety and choice for consumers. Finally, branding increases shopper efficiency because it provides much more information about products and where to find them.

Brand Name Selection

The brand name should be carefully chosen. A good name can add greatly to a product's success. Most large marketing companies have developed a formal brand name selection process. Finding the best brand name is a difficult task. It begins with a careful review of the product and its benefits, the target market, and proposed marketing strategies.

Desirable qualities for a brand name include: (1) It should suggest something about the product's benefits and qualities. Examples: Beautyrest, Craftsman, Sunkist, Spic and Span, Snuggles. (2) It should be easy to pronounce, recognize, and remember. Short names help. Examples: Tide, Aim, Puffs. But longer ones are sometimes effective. Examples: "Love My Carpet" carpet cleaner, "I Can't Believe It's Not Butter" margarine, Better Business Bureau. (3) The brand name should be distinctive. Examples: Taurus, Kodak, Exxon. (4) The name should translate easily into foreign languages. Before spending $100 million to change its name to Exxon, Standard Oil of New Jersey tested the name in 54 languages in more than 150 foreign markets. It found that the name Enco referred to a stalled engine when pronounced in Japanese. (5) It should be capable of registration and legal protection. A brand name cannot be registered if it infringes on existing brand names. Also, brand names that are merely descriptive or suggestive may be unprotectable. For example, the Miller Brewing Company registered the name Lite for its low-calorie beer and invested millions in establishing the name with consumers. But the courts later ruled that the terms *lite* and *light* are generic or common descriptive terms applied to beer and that Miller could not use the Lite name exclusively.[13]

Once chosen, the brand name must be protected. Many firms try to build a brand name that will eventually become identified with the product category. Brand names such as Frigidaire, Kleenex, Levi's, Jell-O, Scotch Tape, Formica, and Fiberglas have succeeded in this way. However, their very success may threaten the company's rights to the name. Many originally protected brand names, such as cellophane, aspirin, nylon, kerosene, linoleum, yo-yo, trampoline, escalator, thermos, and shredded wheat, are now names that any seller can use.

Brand Sponsor

Manufacturer's brand (national brand)
A brand created and owned by the producer of a product or service.

Private brand (or middleman, distributor, or store brand)
A brand created and owned by a reseller of a product or service.

A manufacturer has four sponsorship options. The product may be launched as a **manufacturer's brand** (or national brand), as when Kellogg and IBM sell their output under their own manufacturer's brand names. Or the manufacturer may sell to resellers who give it a **private brand** (also called *store brand* or *distributor brand*). For example, BASF Wyandotte, the world's second-largest antifreeze maker, sells its Alugard antifreeze through middlemen who market the product under about 80 private brands, including Kmart, True Value, Pathmark, and Rite Aid. Although most manufacturers create their own brand names, others market *licensed brands*. For example, Rose Art Industries sells its children's art sets under the Kodak brand name licensed from Eastman Kodak Company. Finally, two companies can *co-brand* a product, as when General Mills and Hershey Foods combined brands to create Reese's Peanut Butter Puffs cereal.

MANUFACTURER'S BRANDS VERSUS PRIVATE BRANDS. Manufacturers' brands have long dominated the retail scene. In recent times, however, an increasing number of department and discount stores, supermarkets, service stations, clothiers, drugstores, and appliance dealers have their own brands. For example, Sears has created several names—Diehard batteries, Craftsman tools, Weatherbeater paints—that buyers look for and demand, and Sears's private-label tires are as well known as the manufacturers' brands of Goodyear and Bridgestone. Wal-Mart recently introduced its price-driven Great Value brand, which may eventually include more than 1,000 items across most major food categories. This new line joins Wal-Mart's higher-priced "Sam's American Choice" brand of colas and fruit juices to compete against major national brands. Wal-Mart claims that its own brand offers better value—"great taste at Wal-Mart's always low prices." Analysts expect that the retailer will quickly expand its Sam's Choice line to include chocolate-chip cookies, snack foods, and a slew of other products.[14]

Despite the fact that private brands are often hard to establish and are costly to stock and promote, private labels yield higher profit margins for the middleman. They also give middlemen exclusive products that cannot be bought from competitors, resulting in greater store traffic and loyalty. For example, if Sears promotes General Electric appliances, other stores that sell GE products will also benefit. Further, if Sears drops the GE brand, it loses the benefit of its previous promotion for GE. But when Sears promotes its private brand of Kenmore appliances, Sears alone benefits from the promotion, and consumer loyalty to the Kenmore brand becomes loyalty to Sears.

The competition between manufacturers' and private brands is called the *battle of the brands*. In this battle, middlemen have many advantages. They control what products they stock, where they go on the shelf, and which ones they will feature in local circulars. They charge manufacturers **slotting fees**—payments demanded by retailers before they will accept new products and find "slots" for them on the shelves. For example, Safeway required a payment of $25,000 from a small pizza roll manufacturer to stock its new product. Retailers price their store brands lower than comparable manufacturers' brands, thereby appealing to budget-conscious shoppers, especially in difficult economic times. Most shoppers know that store brands are often made by one of the larger manufacturers anyway.

As a result, the dominance of manufacturers' brands is weakening. Today's more financially squeezed consumers, hard pressed to spend wisely, are increasingly sensitive to quality, price, and value. The barrage of coupons and price specials has trained a generation of consumers to buy on price. Product proliferation and the seemingly endless stream of brand extensions and line extensions have blurred brand identity. As store brands improve in quality and as consumers gain confidence in their store chains, store brands are posing a strong challenge to manufacturers' brands. Consider the following case:

> Loblaw, the Canadian supermarket chain, is increasing the number of its store brands. Loblaw now sells the leading cookie brand in Canada, its President's Choice Decadent Chocolate Chip Cookie. It has captured 14 percent of the market, mostly from Nabisco. Loblaw also introduced its private label cola, called President's Choice cola, which racked up 50 percent of Loblaw's canned cola sales. Loblaw now sells its brand through other retailers. For example, President's Choice Decadent Chocolate Chip Cookies are now the number one seller in Chicago, where they are sold by Jewel Food Stores, beating out even Nabisco's Chips Ahoy brand.[15]

In U.S. supermarkets, store brands now capture a 13.8 percent share of dollar purchases, and this share is growing. Taken as a single brand, private-label products are the number one, two, or three brand in over 40 percent of all gro-

Slotting fees
Payments demanded by retailers from producers before they will accept new products and find "slots" for them on the shelves.

cery product categories. Private label sales are predicted to reach 25 to 30 percent of supermarket sales by the year 2000. Private labels are even more prominent in Europe, accounting for as much as 32 percent of supermarket sales in Britain and 24 percent in France. French retail giant Carrefour sells more than 3,000 in-house brands, ranging from cooking oil to car batteries.[16] Some marketing analysts predict that private brands eventually will knock out all but the strongest manufacturers' brands.

Manufacturers react by spending large amounts of money on consumer advertising and promotion to build strong brand preference. In turn, they must charge somewhat higher prices to cover this promotion. At the same time, the large retailers pressure them to spend more of their promotional money on trade allowances and deals if they want adequate shelf space. Once manufacturers start giving in to the trade, they have less to spend on consumer promotion and advertising, and their brand leadership starts slipping. This is the national brand manufacturers' dilemma.

To retain their power relative to the trade, leading brand marketers must invest in R&D to bring out new brands, new features, and continuous quality improvements. They must design strong advertising programs to maintain high brand awareness and preference. They must find ways to "partner" with major distributors in a search for distribution economies and competitive strategies that improve their joint performance. For example, P&G has assigned 20 of its managers to Wal-Mart headquarters in Bentonville, Arkansas, to work alongside Wal-Mart managers in a search for ways to improve their joint cost and competitive performance.

LICENSING. Most manufacturers take years and spend millions to create their own brand names. However, some companies license names or symbols previously created by other manufacturers, names of well-known celebrities, characters from popular movies and books—for a fee, any of these can provide an instant and proven brand name. Apparel and accessories sellers pay large royalties to adorn their products—from blouses to ties, and linens to luggage—with the names or initials of such fashion innovators as Bill Blass, Calvin Klein, Pierre Cardin, Gucci, and Halston. Sellers of children's products attach an almost endless list of character names to clothing, toys, school supplies, linens, dolls, lunch boxes, cereals, and other items. The character names range from such classics as Disney, Peanuts, Barbie, and Flintstones characters, to the Muppets, Garfield, Batman, and the Simpsons. The newest form of licensing is corporate licensing—renting a corporate trademark or logo made famous in one category and using it in a related category. Some examples include Singer sewing supplies, Caterpillar work clothes, Old Spice shaving mugs and razors, Faberge costume jewelry, Winnebago camping equipment, and Coppertone swimwear and sunglasses.

Name and character licensing has become a big business is recent years. Many companies have mastered the art of peddling their established brands and characters. For example, through savvy marketing, Warner Brothers has turned Bugs Bunny, Daffy Duck, Foghorn Leghorn, and its more than 100 other Looney Tunes characters into the world's favorite cartoon brand. The Looney Tunes license, arguably the most sought after nonsports license in the industry, generates $1 billion in annual retail sales by more than 225 licensees. And Warner Brothers has yet to tap the full potential of many of its secondary characters. The Tazmanian Devil, for example, initially appeared in only *five* cartoons. But through cross-licensing agreements with organizations like Harley-Davidson and the NFL, Taz has become something of a pop icon. He now appears again in cartoons, and consumers can expect to see more of him in commercials. Warner Brothers sees similar potential for characters like Michigan Frog, and Speedy Gonzales for the Hispanic market.[17]

Cobranding: The combined brands create broader consumer appeal and greater brand loyalty. Here, ConAgra joins Kellogg to offer Healthy Choice from Kellogg's cereals.

Co-branding
The practice of using the established brand names of two different companies on the same product.

CO-BRANDING.   Although companies have been **co-branding** products for many years, there has been a recent resurgence in co-branded products. Co-branding occurs when two established brand names of different companies are used on the same product. For example, Pillsbury joined Nabisco to create Pillsbury Oreo Bars Baking Mix. The Delicious Frookie Company combined with Musselman's to market Delicious Musselman's Apple Sauce Oatmeal Cookies. And Kellogg joined forces with ConAgra to co-brand Kellogg's Healthy Choice cereals. In most co-branding situations, one company licenses another company's well-known brand to use in combination with its own.

Co-branding offers many advantages. Because each brand dominates in a different category, the combined brands create broader consumer appeal and greater brand equity. Co-branding also allows companies to enter new markets with minimal risk or investment. For example, by co-branding with Kellogg, ConAgra entered the breakfast segment with a solid product that was backed by Kellogg's substantial marketing support. Similarly, Hershey's co-branded Reese's Peanut Butter Puffs cereal allowed Hershey to extend its best-selling Reese's brand into the supermarket cereal aisle.

Co-branding also has its limitations. Such relationships usually involve complex legal contracts and licenses. Co-branding partners must carefully coordinate their advertising, sales promotion, and other marketing efforts. Finally, when co-branding, each partner must trust the other will take good care of its brand. As one Nabisco manager puts it, "Giving away your brand is a lot like giving away your child—you want to make sure everything is perfect."[18]

FIGURE 9-4   *Four brand strategies*

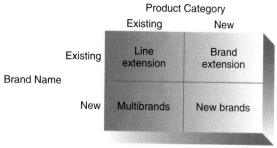

Brand Strategy

A company has four choices when it comes to brand strategy (see Figure 9-4). It can introduce *line extensions* (existing brand names extended to new forms, sizes, and flavors of an existing product category), *brand extensions* (existing brand names extended to new product categories), *multibrands* (new brand names introduced in the same product category), or *new brands* (new brand names in new product categories).

Line extension
Using a successful brand name to introduce additional items in a given product category under the same brand name, such as new flavors, forms, colors, added ingredients, or package sizes.

Brand extension
Using a successful brand name to launch a new or modified product in a new category.

Brand extensions: Fruit of the Loom has leveraged its well-known name to launch new lines of socks, women's underwear, men's fashion underwear, and even baby clothes.

LINE EXTENSIONS. Line extensions occur when a company introduces additional items in a given product category under the same brand name, such as new flavors, forms, colors, ingredients, or package sizes. Thus, Dannon recently introduced several line extensions, including seven new yogurt flavors, a fat-free yogurt, and a large economy size yogurt.

The vast majority of new product activity consists of line extensions. For example, according to *Gorman's New Product News,* of the 6,125 new products accepted by grocery stores in the first five months of 1991, only 5 percent bore new brand names, 6 percent were brand extensions, and 89 percent were line extensions. A company might introduce line extensions for any of several reasons. It might want to meet the consumer desires for variety, or it might recognize a latent consumer want and try to capitalize on it. Excess manufacturing capacity might drive the company to introduce additional items, or the company might want to match a competitor's successful line extension. Some companies introduce line extensions simply to command more shelf space from resellers.

Line extensions involve some risks. An overextended brand name might lose its specific meaning. In the past, when consumers asked for a Coke, they received a 6-ounce bottle of the classic beverage. Today the vendor has to ask: Classic or Cherry Coke? Regular or diet? Caffeine or caffeine-free? Bottle or can? Another risk is that many line extensions will not sell enough to cover their development and promotion costs. Or, even when they sell enough, the sales may come at the expense of other items in the line. A line extension works best when it takes sales away from competing brands, not when it "cannibalizes" the company's other items.[19]

Cute things
now come
in small packages.

At Fruit of the Loom, we've designed a trio of new playwear items that are as sweet and unique as your baby. Well, almost.

Fruit of the Loom. Clothes that make you feel good.

Available at your favorite mass merchandise stores.

BRAND EXTENSIONS. A **brand extension** involves the use of a successful brand name to launch new or modified products in a new category. Procter & Gamble put its Ivory name on dishwashing detergent, liquid hand soap, and shampoo with excellent results. Fruit of the Loom took advantage of its very high name recognition to launch new lines of socks, men's fashion underwear, women's underwear, and athletic apparel. Honda uses its company name to cover such different products as its automobiles, motorcycles, snowblowers, lawn mowers, marine engines, and snowmobiles. This allows Honda to advertise that it can fit "six Hondas in a two-car garage."

A brand extension strategy offers many advantages. A recent study found that brand extensions capture greater market share and realize greater advertising efficiency than individual brands.[20] A well-regarded brand name helps the company enter new product categories more easily and gives a new product instant recognition and faster acceptance. Sony puts its name on most of its new electronic products, creating an instant perception of high quality for each new product. Brand extensions also save the high advertising cost usually required to familiarize consumers with a new brand name.

At the same time, a brand extension strategy involves some risk. Brand extensions such as

Bic pantyhose, Life Savers gum, and Clorox laundry detergent met early deaths. If an extension brand fails, it may harm consumer attitudes toward the other products carrying the same brand name. Further, a brand name may not be appropriate to a particular new product, even if it is well made and satisfying—would you consider buying Texaco milk or Alpo chili? And a brand name may lose its special positioning in the consumer's mind through overuse. *Brand dilution* occurs when consumers no longer associate a brand with a specific product or even highly similar products.

Transferring an existing brand name to a new category requires great care. For example, S. C. Johnson's popular shaving cream is called Edge. This name was successfully extended to its after-shave lotion. The name Edge probably could also be used to introduce a brand of razor blades if S. C. Johnson Company wanted to do this. However, the risk would increase *if* the company tried to use the Edge brand name to launch a new shampoo or toothpaste. Then Edge would lose its meaning as a name for shaving products. Companies that are tempted to transfer a brand name must research how well the brand's associations fit the new product.[21]

Multibranding
A strategy under which a seller develops two or more brands in the same product category.

MULTIBRANDS. Companies often introduce additional brands in the same category. **Multibranding** offers a way to establish different features and appeal to different buying motives. Thus, P&G markets nine different brands of laundry detergent. Multibranding also allows a company to lock up more reseller "shelf space." Or the company may want to protect its major brand by setting up *flanker* or *fighter brands*. For example, Seiko uses different brand names for its higher priced watches (Seiko Lasalle) and lower priced watches (Pulsar) to protect the flanks of its mainstream Seiko brand. Sometimes a company inherits different brand names in the process of acquiring a competitor, and each brand name has a loyal following. Thus, Electrolux, the Swedish multinational, owns a stable of acquired brand names for its appliance lines—Frigidaire, Kelvinator, Westinghouse, Zanussi, White, and Gibson. Finally, companies may develop separate brand names for different regions or countries, perhaps to suit different cultures or languages. For example, Procter & Gamble dominates the U.S. laundry detergent market with Tide, which in all its forms captures more than a 31 percent market share. In Europe, however, P&G leads with its Ariel detergent brand, whose annual sales of $1.5 billion make it Europe's number two packaged-goods brand behind Coca-Cola.

A major drawback of multibranding is that each brand might obtain only a small market share, and none may be very profitable. The company may end up spreading its resources over many brands instead of building a few brands to a highly profitable level. These companies should reduce the number of brands they sell in a given category and set up tighter screening procedures for new brands. Ideally, a company's brands should cannibalize competitors' brands, and not each other, and net profits from multibranding should be larger, even if some cannibalism occurs.

NEW BRANDS. A company may create a new brand name when it enters a new product category for which none of the company's current brand names are appropriate. For example, Sears establishes separate family names for different product categories (Kenmore for appliances, Craftsman for tools, and Homart for major home installations). Or, the company might believe that the power of its existing brand name is waning and a new brand name is needed. Finally, the company may obtain new brands in new categories through acquisitions. For example, S. C. Johnson & Son, marketer of Pledge furniture polish, Glade air freshener, Raid insect spray, Edge shaving gel, and many other well-known brands, added several new powerhouse brands through its acquisition of Drackett Company, including Windex, Drano, and Vanish toilet bowl cleaner.

As with multibranding, offering many new brands can result in a company spreading its resources too thin. And in some industries, such as consumer packaged goods, consumers and retailers have become concerned that there are already too many brands, with too few differences between them. Thus, Procter & Gamble, Frito-Lay, and other large consumer product marketers are now pursuing *megabrand* strategies—weeding out weaker brands and focusing their marketing dollars only on brands that can achieve the number one or two market-share positions in their categories.[22]

Brand Repositioning

However well a brand is initially positioned in a market, the company may have to reposition it later. A competitor may launch a brand positioned next to the company's brand and cut into its market share. Or customer wants may shift, leaving the company's brand with less demand. Marketers should consider repositioning existing brands before introducing new ones. In this way, they can build on existing brand recognition and consumer loyalty.

Repositioning may require changing both the product and its image. For example, Arrow added a new line of casual shirts before trying to change its image. Kentucky Fried Chicken changed its menu, adding lower-fat skinless chicken and nonfried items such as broiled chicken and chicken salad sandwiches to reposition itself toward more health-conscious fast-food consumers. It's even changing its name—to KFC. A brand also can be repositioned by changing only the product's image. Ivory Soap was repositioned without a physical change from a "baby soap" to an "all natural soap" for adults who want healthy-looking skin. Similarly, Kraft repositioned Velveeta from a "cooking cheese" to a "good tasting, natural, and nutritious" snack cheese. Although the product remained unchanged, Kraft used new advertising appeals to change consumer perceptions of Velveeta. When repositioning a brand, the marketer must be careful not to lose or confuse current loyal users. When shifting Velveeta's position, Kraft made certain that the product's new position was compatible with its old one. Thus, Kraft kept loyal customers while attracting new users.[23]

PACKAGING

Many products offered to the market have to be packaged. Some marketers have called packaging a fifth *P*, along with price, product, place, and promotion. Most marketers, however, treat packaging as an element of product strategy.

Packaging includes the activities of designing and producing the container or wrapper for a product. The package may include the product's primary container (the bottle holding Old Spice After-Shave Lotion); a secondary package that is thrown away when the product is about to be used (the cardboard box containing the bottle of Old Spice); and the shipping package necessary to store, identify, and ship the product (a corrugated box carrying six dozen bottles of Old Spice). Labeling is also part of packaging and consists of printed information appearing on or with the package.

Traditionally, packaging decisions were based primarily on cost and production factors; the primary function of the package was to contain and protect the product. In recent times, however, numerous factors have made packaging an important marketing tool. An increase in self-service means that packages now must perform many sales tasks—from attracting attention, to describing the product, to making the sale. Companies are realizing the power of good packaging to create instant consumer recognition of the company or brand. For example, in an average supermarket, which stocks 15,000 to 17,000 items, the typical shopper passes by some 300 items per minute, and 53 percent of all purchases are made

Packaging
The activities of designing and producing the container or wrapper for a product.

THOSE FRUSTRATING, NOT-SO-EASY-TO-OPEN PACKAGES

The following letter from an angry consumer to Robert D. Stuart, then chairman of Quaker Oats, beautifully expresses the utter frustration all of us have experienced in dealing with so-called easy-opening packages.

Dear Mr. Stuart:

I am an 86-year-old widow in fairly good health. (You may think of this as advanced age, but for me that description pertains to the years ahead. Nevertheless, if you decide to reply to this letter I wouldn't dawdle, actuarial tables being what they are.)

As I said, my health is fairly good. Feeble and elderly, as one understands these terms, I am not. My two Doberman Pinschers and I take a brisk 3-mile walk every day. They are two strong and energetic animals and it takes a bit of doing to keep "brisk" closer to a stroll than a mad dash. But I manage because as yet I don't lack the strength. You will shortly see why this fact is relevant.

I am writing to call your attention to the cruel, deceptive and utterly [false] copy on your Aunt Jemima buttermilk complete pancake and waffle mix. The words on your package read, "to open—press here and pull back."

Mr. Stuart, though I push and press and groan and strive and writhe and curse and sweat and jab and push, poke and ram . . . . whew!—I have never once been able to do what the package instructs—to "press here and pull back" the [blankety-blank].

It can't be done! Talk about failing strength! Have you ever tried and succeeded?

My late husband was a gun collector who among other lethal weapons kept a Thompson machine gun in a locked cabinet. It was a good thing that the cabinet was locked. Oh, the number of times I was tempted to give your package a few short bursts.

An easy-to-open package?

That lock and a sense of lady-like delicacy kept me from pursuing that vengeful fantasy. Instead, I keep a small cleaver in my pantry for those occasions when I need to open a package of your delicious Aunt Jemima pancakes.

For many years that whacking away with my cleaver served a dual purpose. Not only to open the [blankety-blank] package but also to vent my fury at your sadists who willfully and maliciously did design that torture apparatus that passes for a package.

Sometimes just for the [blank] of it I let myself get carried away. I don't stop after I've lopped off the top. I whack away until the package is utterly destroyed in an outburst of rage, frustration, and vindictiveness. I wind up with a floorful of your delicious Aunt Jemima pancake mix. But that's a small price to pay for blessed release. (Anyway, the Pinschers lap up the mess.)

So many ingenious, considerate (even compassionate) innovations in package closures have been designed since Aunt Jemima first donned her red bandana. Wouldn't you consider the introduction of a more humane package to replace the example of marketing malevolence to which you resolutely cling? Don't you care, Mr. Stuart?

I'm really writing this to be helpful and in that spirit I am sending a copy to Mr. Tucker, president of Container Corp. I'm sure their clever young designers could be of immeasurable help to you in this matter. At least I feel it's worth a try.

Really, Mr. Stuart, I hope you will not regard me as just another cranky old biddy. I am The Public, the source of your fortunes.

Ms. Roberta Pavloff
Malvern, Pa.

Source: This letter was reprinted in "Some Designs Should Just Be Torn Asunder," *Advertising Age,* January 17, 1983, p. M54.

on impulse. In this highly competitive environment, the package may be the seller's last chance to influence buyers. It becomes a "five-second commercial." The Campbell Soup Company estimates that the average shopper sees its familiar red and white can 76 times a year, creating the equivalent of $26 million worth of advertising.[24]

Innovative packaging can give a company an advantage over competitors. Liquid Tide quickly attained a 10 percent share of the heavy-duty detergent market, partly because of the popularity of its container's innovative drip-proof spout and cap. The first companies to put their fruit drinks in airtight foil and paper cartons (aseptic packages), and toothpastes in pump dispensers, attracted many new customers. In contrast, poorly designed packages can cause headaches for consumers and lost sales for the company (see Marketing Highlight 9-3).

Packaging concept
What the package should *be* or *do* for the product.

In recent years, product safety has also become a major packaging concern. We have all learned to deal with hard-to-open "childproof" packages. And after the rash of product tampering scares during the 1980s, most drug producers and food makers are now putting their products in tamper-resistant packages.

Developing a good package for a new product requires making many decisions. The first task is to establish the packaging concept. The **packaging concept** states what the package should *be* or *do* for the product. Should the main functions of the package be to offer product protection, introduce a new dispensing method, suggest certain qualities about the product or the company, or something else? Decisions then must be made on specific elements of the package, such as size, shape, materials, color, text, and brand mark. These various elements must work together to support the product's position and marketing strategy. The package must be consistent with the product's advertising, pricing, and distribution.

Companies usually consider several different package designs for a new product. To select the best package, they usually test the various designs to find the one that stands up best under normal use, is easiest for dealers to handle, and receives the most favorable consumer response. After selecting and introducing the package, the company should check it regularly in the face of changing consumer preferences and advances in technology. In the past, a package design might last for 15 years before it needed changes. However, in today's rapidly changing environment, most companies must recheck their packaging every two or three years.[25]

Keeping a package up to date usually requires only minor but regular changes—changes so subtle that they may go unnoticed by most consumers. But some packaging changes involve complex decisions, drastic action, high cost, and risk. For example, Campbell has for years been searching for a new container to replace its venerable old soup can. It has experimented with a variety of containers, such as a sealed plastic bowl that can be popped into a microwave oven to produce hot soup in a hurry with no can to open and no dishes to wash. Given Campbell's 80 percent share of the canned-soup market, the potential risks and benefits of changing the package are huge. Although eliminating the can could cut Campbell's packaging costs by as much as 15 percent, revamping production facilities would cost $100 million or more. And Campbell management estimates that the change would take at least five more years to implement. Finally, and perhaps most importantly, Campbell risks alienating loyal consumers who think of the familiar red and white can as an American tradition.

In making packaging decisions, the company also must heed growing environmental concerns about packaging, and make decisions that serve society's interests as well as immediate customer and company objectives. Increasingly, companies will be asked to take responsibility for the environmental costs of their products and packaging (see Marketing Highlight 9-4).

LABELING

Labels may range from simple tags attached to products to complex graphics that are part of the package. They perform several functions, and the seller has to decide which ones to use. At the very least, the label *identifies* the product or brand, such as the name Sunkist stamped on oranges. The label might also *grade* the product—canned peaches are grade-labeled A, B, and C. The label might *describe* several things about the product—who made it, where it was made, when it was made, its contents, how it is to be used, and how to use it safely. Finally, the label might *promote* the product through attractive graphics.

Labels of well-known brands may seem old-fashioned after a while and may need freshening up. For example, the label on Ivory Soap has been redone 18 times since the 1890s, but simply with gradual changes in the lettering. In contrast, the

THE GERMAN PACKAGING ORDINANCE: MAKING THE POLLUTER PAY

The principle of "the polluter pays" once seemed farfetched, a pipe dream of radical environmentalists. But as the rest of the world watches, the notion that sellers should be responsible for the environmental costs of their products is being put to the test in Germany. The Packaging Ordinance (Verpackungsordnung), enacted in June 1991, made private industry responsible for the collecting, sorting, and ultimate recycling of packaging waste.

In Germany, as in the United States, packaging makes up a third of all solid waste. Everyone agrees that reducing it is a good idea, but the new German legislation is complex and controversial. It deals separately with three different kinds of packaging: *primary packaging*—the essential container that holds the product, like a perfume bottle; *secondary packaging*—outer material whose main function is point-of-purchase display and protection during shipping, like the box around the perfume bottle; and *transport packaging*—the carton or crate used to ship the perfume to stores. The ordinance decreed that all three types of packaging must be taken back by retailers and returned

to manufacturers—an onerous prospect for both parties. However, it allowed that if the industry could come up with an alternative, then retailers would not have to take back the first and largest category of waste, primary sales packaging.

The industry's solution was the Dual System (DSD), a nonprofit company set up by German businesses that collects waste directly from con-

In Germany, sellers are now responsible for the environmental costs of their products. This widely-used "green-dot" emblem indicates that a package is acceptable for industry collection systems.

sumers in addition to the country's municipal collection systems. DSD is funded by licensing fees for the now widely used *green dot:* a green arrow emblem indicating that a package is collectible by DSD. Now, rather than tossing their packaging out with the municipal trash, for which they must pay a fee, consumers can take it to a nearby yellow DSD bin to be collected for free.

Under the DSD system, although they must still collect secondary and transport packaging, stores are no longer required to take back huge mounds of primary sales packaging. However, there's a catch: To be eligible as DSD trash, a sales package must have the green dot. So, not surprisingly, retailers are reluctant to carry products without the green dot. Further, there is a growing preference among German consumers for recyclable packaging materials, and for less packaging in general. Thus, the Packaging Ordinance will strongly affect how companies package their products for the German market.

The ordinance puts the "polluter pays" principle to work by creating incentives rather than through direct

---

label on Orange Crush soft drink was changed substantially when its competitors' labels began to picture fresh fruits and pull in more sales. Orange Crush developed a label with new symbols and much stronger, deeper colors to suggest freshness and more orange flavor.

There has been a long history of legal concerns about labels. Labels can mislead customers, fail to describe important ingredients, or fail to include needed safety warnings. As a result, several federal and state laws regulate labeling, the most prominent being the Fair Packaging and Labeling Act of 1966. Labeling has been affected in recent times by *unit pricing* (stating the price per unit of standard measure), *open dating* (stating the expected shelf life of the product), and *nutritional labeling* (stating the nutritional values in the product). The Nutritional Labeling and Educational Act of 1990 requires sellers to provide detailed nutritional information on food products, and it regulates the use of health-related terms such as *low-fat, light,* and *high-fiber.* Sellers must ensure that their labels contain all the required information.

PRODUCT-SUPPORT SERVICES

Customer service is another element of product strategy. A company's offer to the marketplace usually includes some services, which can be a minor or a major part

regulation. Unlike other European Union (EU) countries, Germany has no ban on specific packaging materials. Instead, green dot license prices are based, in part, on the difficulty of recycling a particular material. This sets market mechanisms in motion. If a given packaging material is costly to recycle, the price of using it will rise and companies will switch to something else. Thus, the ordinance is forcing companies that do business in Germany to innovate and make their products more environmentally friendly.

The major problem with the landmark German recycling program is the lack of a market for recycled material. Notes one packaging expert:

> There seems to be widespread belief in the trash fairy, who comes overnight and turns garbage into gold for free. . . . Everything is recyclable, but that doesn't mean it's valuable. [The German ordinance] ignores the very essence of economics: supply and demand. When you're talking trash, it's difficult to believe that anyone will pay for it.

It's no secret that much of the packaging collected in DSD bins is not being recycled, but rather is piling up in warehouses or being exported. When German plastics turned up in French dumps and incinerators last year, it caused an EU-wide scandal.

All this leaves the German public skeptical. The green dot has little credibility with consumers—it's on almost all packaging, but everyone knows that the recycling structure in not yet in place. Moreover, some environmentalists are concerned that the green dot will give companies and consumers a license not to care about environmental problems. For example, they fear that the ordinance will encourage Germans to use more one-way packaging rather than reusables, which don't carry the green dot.

Still, the ordinance serves as a wake-up call to both businesses and consumers, in Germany and around the world. It says, "Hey folks, we've got a problem, and something must be done about it." And despite its flaws, the ordinance does seem to be moving the country, however timidly, toward its goal of waste reduction. The German Environmental Ministry reports that packaging recycling is at 50 to 60 percent (except for plastics), the use of reusable shipping containers is on the rise, and secondary packages (boxes for toothpaste and liquor bottles, for instance) are starting to disappear from store shelves. Producers and retailers are now working together to help solve environmental problems.

France and Austria have passed similar legislation, and France has begun using the green dot, although with a different collection system. In Germany, new ordinances are on the horizon, including ones for mandating producer take-back of cars and electronic equipment. And the European community is now working on a directive that would set minimum standards for recycling in all of its member states. "It may take another year or two, but the train is running" assures one German ministry official, "The idea of product responsibility is spreading around the world."

Source: Adapted from Marilyn Stern, "Is This the Ultimate in Recycling?" *Across the Board,* May 1993, pp. 28–31. Also see Gene Bylinsky, "Manufacturing for Reuse," *Fortune,* February 6, 1995, pp. 102–112.

Product-support services
Services that augment actual products.

of the total offer. In Chapter 21, we will discuss services as products in themselves. Here, we discuss **product-support services**—services that augment actual products. More and more companies are using product-support services as a major tool in gaining competitive advantage.

Good customer service is good for business. It costs less to keep the goodwill of existing customers than it does to attract new customers or woo back lost customers. Firms that provide high-quality service usually outperform their less service-oriented competitors. A study comparing the performance of businesses that had high and low customer ratings of service quality found that the high-service businesses managed to charge more, grow faster, and make more profits.[26] Clearly, marketers need to think carefully about their service strategies.

A company should design its product and support services to meet the needs of target customers. Customers vary in the value they assign to different services. Thus, the first step in deciding which product-support services to offer is to determine both the services valued by target consumers and the relative importance of these services. Determining customers' service needs involves more than simply monitoring complaints that come in over toll-free telephone lines or on comment cards. The company should periodically survey its customers to get ratings of current services as well as ideas for new ones. For example, Cadillac holds regular focus-group interviews with owners and carefully watches complaints that come into its dealerships. From this careful monitoring, Cadillac has learned that buyers are very upset by repairs that are not done correctly the first time. As a result, the company has set up a system directly linking each dealership with a group of ten engineers who can help walk mechanics through difficult repairs. Such actions helped Cadillac jump, in one year, from fourteenth to seventh in independent rankings of service.[27]

Products often can be designed to reduce the amount of required servicing. Thus, companies need to coordinate their product-design and service-mix decisions. For example, the Canon home copier uses a disposable toner cartridge that greatly reduces the need for service calls. Kodak and 3M are designing products that can be "plugged in" to a central diagnostic facility that performs tests, locates troubles, and fixes equipment over telephone lines. Thus, a key to successful service strategy is to design products that rarely break down and are easily fixable with little service expense.

Given the importance of customer service as a marketing tool, many companies have set up strong customer service operations to handle complaints and adjustments, credit service, maintenance service, technical service, and consumer information. For example, Whirlpool, Procter & Gamble, and many other companies have set up 1-800 telephone hotlines. By keeping records on the types of requests and complaints, the customer service group can press for needed changes in product design, quality control, and marketing efforts. An active customer service operation coordinates all the company's services, creates consumer satisfaction and loyalty, and helps the company to further set itself apart from competitors.

PRODUCT LINE DECISIONS

Product line
A group of products that are closely related because they function in a similar manner, are sold to the same customer groups, are marketed through the same types of outlets, or fall within given price ranges.

We have looked at product strategy decisions such as branding, packaging, labeling, and services for individual products. But product strategy also calls for building a product line. A **product line** is a group of products that are closely related because they function in a similar manner, are sold to the same customer groups, are marketed through the same types of outlets, or fall within given price ranges. For example, General Motors produces several lines of cars, Nike produces several lines of athletic shoes, and Motorola produces several lines of telecommunications products. In developing product line strategies, marketers face a number of tough decisions.

PRODUCT LINE LENGTH

Product line managers have to decide on product line length. The line is too short if the manager can increase profits by adding items; the line is too long if the manager can increase profits by dropping items. Product line length is influenced by company objectives. Companies that want to be positioned as full-line companies or that are seeking high market share and growth usually carry longer lines. Companies that are keen on high short-term profitability generally carry shorter lines consisting of selected items.

Product lines tend to lengthen over time. The product line manager may feel pressure to add new products to use up excess manufacturing capacity. The sales force and distributors may pressure the manager for a more complete product line to satisfy their customers. Or, the product line manager may want to add items to the product line to increase sales and profits.

However, as the manager adds items, several costs rise: design and engineering costs, inventory costs, manufacturing changeover costs, order processing costs, transportation costs, and promotional costs to introduce new items. Eventually someone calls a halt to the mushrooming product line. Top management may freeze things because of insufficient funds or manufacturing capacity. Or the controller may question the line's profitability and call for a study. The study will probably show a number of money-losing items, and they will be pruned from the line in a major effort to increase profitability. This pattern of uncontrolled product line growth followed by heavy pruning is typical and may repeat itself many times.[28]

The company must manage its product lines carefully. It can systematically increase the length of its product line in two ways: by *stretching* its line and by *filling* its line. Every company's product line covers a certain range of the products offered by the industry as a whole. For example, BMW automobiles are located in the medium-high price range of the automobile market. Toyota focuses on the low-to-medium price range. *Product line stretching* occurs when a company lengthens its product line beyond its current range. Figure 9-5 shows that the company can stretch its line downward, upward, or both ways.

Stretching Downward

Many companies initially locate at the upper end of the market and later stretch their lines downward. A company may stretch downward for any number of reasons. It may have first entered the upper end to establish a quality image and intended to roll downward later. It may respond to a competitor's attack on the upper end by invading the low end. Or a company may add a low-end product to plug a market hole that otherwise would attract a new competitor. It may find faster growth taking place at the low end. Xerox expanded into the small copier segment for all of these reasons. Although Xerox has long dominated the medium and large copier segments, by the late 1980s, the small copier segment was growing at a much faster rate. Canon, Sharp, and other Japanese competitors had entered the low-end segment, where they quickly dominated. Moreover, these competitors used their success at the low end as a base for competing with Xerox in the mid-size copier segment. Thus, to meet shifts in the market demand and to blunt competitor thrusts, Xerox introduced a line of small copiers.

In making a downward stretch, the company faces some risks. The low-end item might provoke competitors to counteract by moving into the higher end. The company's dealers may not be willing or able to handle the lower-end products. Or the new low-end item might eat away at the sales of—or *cannibalize*—the company's higher-end items, leaving the company worse off. Consider the following:

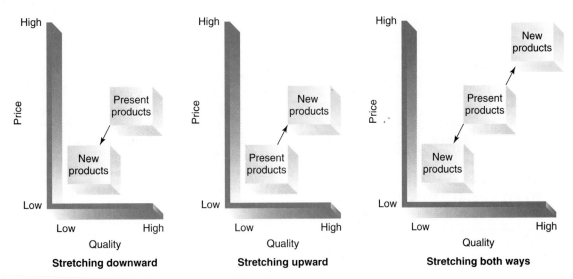

FIGURE 9-5 *Product line stretching decision*

General Electric's Medical Systems Division is the market leader in CAT scanners, expensive diagnostic machines used in hospitals. GE learned that a Japanese competitor was planning to attack its market. GE executives guessed that the new Japanese model would be smaller, more electronically advanced, and less expensive. GE's best defense would be to introduce a similar lower-priced machine before the Japanese model entered the market. But some GE executives expressed concern that this lower-priced version would hurt the sales and higher profit margins on their large CAT scanner. One manager finally settled the issue by saying: "Aren't we better off to cannibalize ourselves than to let the Japanese do it?"

Stretching Upward

Companies at the lower end of the market may want to enter the higher end. They may be attracted by a faster growth rate or higher margins at the higher end, or they may simply want to position themselves as full-line manufacturers. For example, General Electric added its Monogram line of high-quality built-in kitchen appliances targeted at the select few households earning more than $100,000 a year and living in homes valued at over $400,000. Sometimes, companies stretch upward in order to add prestige to their current products, as when Chrysler purchased Lamborghini, the maker of exotic, handcrafted sports cars.

An upward stretch decision can be risky. The higher-end competitors not only are well entrenched, but also they may strike back by entering the lower end of the market. Prospective customers may not believe that the newcomer can produce quality products. Finally, the company's salespeople and distributors may lack the talent and training to serve the higher end of the market.

Stretching Both Ways

Companies in the middle range of the market may decide to stretch their lines in both directions. Marriott did this with its hotel product line. Along with regular Marriott hotels, it added the Marriott Marquis line to serve the upper end of the market, and the Courtyard and Fairfield Inn lines to serve the lower end. Each branded hotel line is aimed at a different target market. Marriott Marquis aims to attract and please top executives; Marriotts, middle managers; Courtyards, salespeople; and Fairfield Inns, vacationers and others on a low travel budget. The major risk with this strategy is that some travelers will trade down after finding that the lower-price hotels in the Marriott chain give them pretty much everything they want. However, Marriott would rather capture its customers who move downward than lose them to competitors.

Filling in the Product Line

A product line can be lengthened by adding more items within the present range of the line. There are several reasons for *product line filling*: reaching for extra profits, trying to satisfy dealers, trying to use excess capacity, trying to be the leading full-line company, and trying to plug holes to keep out competitors. Thus, Sony filled its Walkman line by adding solar-powered and waterproof Walkmans, and an ultralight model that attaches to a sweatband for joggers, bicyclers, tennis players, and other exercisers.

However, line filling is overdone if it results in cannibalization and customer confusion. The company should ensure that new items are noticeably different from existing ones.

Product line stretching: Marriott stretched its hotel product line to include several branded hotels aimed at a different target market. Residence Inn, for example, provides a "home away from home" for people who travel for a living, who are relocating, or who are on temporary assignment and need inexpensive, temporary lodging.

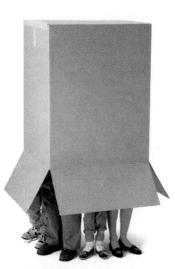

Ever wonder how an ordinary hotel room feels to a relocating family?

At Residence Inn, we haven't forgotten where relocating families are used to staying. In their homes. Their nice, big, comfortable homes. That's why our studio suites are much bigger than ordinary hotel rooms. And we not only give you more room, we also give you a living room where families can stretch out and relax. On top of that, our penthouse suites have an upstairs bath. And most of our rooms have their own fireplaces.

Families won't go hungry for home cooked meals here, either. Every room comes with a full kitchen. We'll even do all of your grocery shopping for you.

But perhaps the biggest surprise of all is the affordable price: rooms are only $60-$90 a night.* So call Residence Inn. Because families should be close. Not cramped. Toll-free 1-800-331-3131.

PRODUCT LINE MODERNIZATION

In some cases, product line length is adequate, but the line needs to be modernized. For example, a company's machine tools may have a 1970s look and lose out to better-styled competitors' lines. The central issue in product line modernization is whether to overhaul the line piecemeal or all at once. A piecemeal approach allows the company to see how customers and dealers like the new styles before changing the whole line. Piecemeal modernization also causes less drain on the company's cash flow. A major disadvantage of piecemeal modernization is that it allows competitors to see changes and start redesigning their own lines.

PRODUCT LINE FEATURING

The product line manager typically selects one or a few items in the line to feature. This is *product line featuring*. Sometimes, managers feature promotional models at the low end of the line to serve as "traffic builders." For example, Sears might advertise a special low-priced sewing machine to attract shoppers. And Rolls Royce announced an "economy model" selling for only $125,000, in contrast to its high-end model selling for over $200,000, to bring people into its showrooms.

At other times, managers feature a high-end item to give the product line "class." For example, Audimar Piguet advertises a $25,000 watch that few people buy, but that acts as a "flagship" to enhance the whole line.

PRODUCT MIX DECISIONS

Product mix (or product assortment)
The set of all product lines and items that a particular seller offers for sale to buyers.

An organization with several product lines has a product mix. A **product mix (or product assortment)** is the set of all product lines and items that a particular seller offers for sale. Avon's product mix consists of four major product lines: cosmetics, jewelry, fashions, and household items. Each product line consists of several sublines. For example, cosmetics breaks down into lipstick, rouge, powder, and so on. Each line and subline has many individual items. Altogether, Avon's product mix includes 1,300 items. In contrast, a large supermarket handles as many as 17,000 items; a typical K mart stocks 15,000 items; and General Electric manufactures as many as 250,000 items.

A company's product mix has four important dimensions: width, length, depth, and consistency. Table 9-2 illustrates these concepts with selected Procter & Gamble consumer products.

The *width* of P&G's product mix refers to the number of different product lines the company carries. Table 9-2 shows a product mix width of six lines. (In fact, P&G produces many more lines, including mouthwashes, paper towels, disposable diapers, pain relievers, and cosmetics.)

The *length* of P&G's product mix refers to the total number of items the company carries. In Table 9-2, the total number of items is 42. We can also compute the average length of a line at P&G by dividing the total length (here 42) by the number of lines (here 6). In Table 9-2, the average P&G product line consists of 7 brands.

The *depth* of P&G's product mix refers to the number of versions offered of each product in the line. Thus, if Crest comes in three sizes and two formulations (paste and gel), Crest has a depth of six. By counting the number of versions within each brand, we can calculate the average depth of P&G's product mix.

The *consistency* of the product mix refers to how closely related the various product lines are in end use, production requirements, distribution channels, or in

TABLE 9-2 *Product Mix Width and Product Line Length Shown for Selected Procter & Gamble Products*

	PRODUCT MIX WIDTH					
	Detergents	**Toothpaste**	**Bar Soap**	**Deodorants**	**Fruit Juices**	**Lotions**
PRODUCT LINE LENGTH	Ivory Snow	Gleem	Ivory	Secret	Citrus Hill	Wondra
	Dreft	Crest	Camay	Sure	Sunny Delight	Noxema
	Tide	Complete	Lava		Winter Hill	Oil of Olay
	Joy	Denquel	Kirk's		Texsun	Camay
	Cheer		Zest		Lincoln	Raintree
	Oxydol		Safeguard		Speas Farm	Tropic Tan
	Dash		Coast			Bain de Soleil
	Cascade		Oil of Olay			
	Ivory Liquid					
	Gain					
	Dawn					
	Ariel					
	Bold 3					
	Liquid Tide					

some other way. P&G's product lines are consistent insofar as they are consumer products that go through the same distribution channels. The lines are less consistent insofar as they perform different functions for buyers.

These product mix dimensions provide the handles for defining the company's product strategy. The company can increase its business in four ways. It can add new product lines, thus widening its product mix. In this way, its new lines build on the company's reputation in its other lines. The company can lengthen its existing product lines to become a more full-line company. Or it can add more product versions of each product and thus deepen its product mix. Finally, the company can pursue more product line consistency—or less—depending on whether it wants to have a strong reputation in a single field or in several fields.

INTERNATIONAL PRODUCT DECISIONS

International marketers face special product and packaging challenges. First, they must figure out what products to introduce and in which countries. Then, they must decide how much to standardize or adapt their products for world markets. On the one hand, companies would like to standardize their offerings. Standardization helps a company to develop a consistent worldwide image. It also results in lower manufacturing costs and eliminates duplication of research and development, advertising, and product design efforts. On the other hand, consumers around the world differ in their cultures, attitudes, and buying behaviors. And markets vary in their economic conditions, competition, legal requirements, and physical environments. Companies usually must respond to these differences by adapting their product offerings. Something as simple as an electrical outlet can create big product problems:

Those who have traveled to Europe know the frustration of electrical plugs, different voltages, and other annoyances of international travel. . . . Philips, the electrical appliance manufacturer, has to produce 12 kinds of irons to serve just its European market. The problem is that Europe does not have a universal [electrical] standard. The ends of irons bristle with different plugs for different countries. Some have three prongs, others two; prongs protrude straight or angled, round or rectangular, fat, thin, and sometimes sheathed. There are circular plug faces, squares, pentagons, and hexagons. Some are perforated and some are notched. One French plug has a niche like a keyhole; British plugs carry fuses.[29]

Packaging also presents new challenges for international marketers. Penn Racquet Sports found this out when it attempted to launch its line of tennis balls in Japan in a "traditional" three-ball can. After netting an initial 8 percent market share, Penn's Japanese sales quickly plummeted to less than 1 percent. The problem: poor packaging. Whereas Americans play with three balls, the Japanese use only two. Explains one Penn manager, "The Japanese thought a three-ball can was a discount, and they passed us over. Our big mistake was that we didn't know the market." Penn redesigned its package and sales recovered. It now designs its containers to fit the needs of each market: Japan gets a two-ball can, whereas Australia and Europe receive four-ball plastic tubes.[30]

Packaging issues can be subtle. For example, names, labels, and colors may not translate easily from one country to another. A firm using yellow flowers in its logo might fare well in the United States, but meet with disaster in Mexico, where a yellow flower symbolizes death or disrespect. Similarly, although "Nature's Gift" might be an appealing name for gourmet mushrooms in America, it would be deadly in Germany, where "gift" means "poison." Consumers in different countries vary in their packaging preferences. Europeans like efficient, functional, recyclable boxes with understated designs. In contrast, the Japanese often use packages as gifts. Thus, in Japan, Lever Brothers packages its Lux soap in stylish gift boxes. Packaging even may have to be tailored to meet the physical characteristics of consumers in various parts of the world. For instance, soft drinks are sold in smaller cans in Japan to better fit the smaller Japanese hand.

Companies may have to adapt their packaging to meet specific regulations regarding package design or label contents. For instance, some countries ban the use of any foreign language on labels; other countries require that labels be printed in two or more languages. Labeling laws vary greatly from country to country:

In Saudi Arabia . . . product names must be specific. "Hot Chili" will not do, it must be "Spiced Hot Chili." Prices are required to be printed on the labels in Venezuela, but in Chile, it is illegal to put prices on labels or in any way suggest retail prices. Coca-Cola ran into a legal problem in Brazil with its Diet Coke. Brazilian law interprets "diet" to have medicinal qualities. Under the law, producers must give daily recommended consumption on the label of all medicines. Coke had to get special approval to get around this restriction.[31]

Thus, although product and package standardization can produce benefits, companies usually must adapt their offerings to serve the unique needs and requirements of specific international markets.

In summary, whether domestic or international, product strategy calls for complex decisions on product mix, product line, branding, packaging, and service strategy. These decisions must be made not only with a full understanding of consumer wants and competitors' strategies but also with increasing attention to the growing public policy affecting product and packaging decisions (see Marketing Highlight 9-5).

SOCIALLY RESPONSIBLE PRODUCT AND PACKAGING DECISIONS

Product and packaging decisions are attracting increasing public attention. When making such decisions, marketers should consider carefully the following issues and regulations.

Product Decisions and Public Policy

Product Additions and Deletions. Under the Antimerger Act, the government may prevent companies from adding products through acquisitions if the effect threatens to lessen competition. Companies dropping products must be aware that they have legal obligations, written or implied, to their suppliers, dealers, and customers who have a stake in the discontinued product.

Patent Protection. A firm must obey the U.S. patent laws when developing new products. A company cannot make its product "illegally similar" to another company's established product. An example is Polaroid's successful suit to prevent Kodak from selling its new instant-picture camera on the grounds that it infringed on Polaroid's instant-camera patents.

Product Quality and Safety. Manufacturers must comply with specific laws regarding product quality and safety. The Federal Food, Drug, and Cosmetic Act protects consumers from unsafe and adulterated food, drugs, and cosmetics. Various acts provide for the inspection of sanitary conditions in the meat- and poultry-processing industries. Safety legislation has been passed to regulate fabrics, chemical substances, automobiles, toys, and drugs and poisons. The Consumer Product Safety Act of 1972 established a Consumer Product Safety Commission, which has the authority to ban or seize potentially harmful products and set severe penalties for violation of the law. If consumers have been injured by a product that has been designed defectively, they can sue manufacturers or dealers. Product liability suits now are occurring at the rate of over one million per year, with individual awards often running in the millions of dollars. This phenomenon has resulted in huge increases in product-liability insurance premiums, causing big problems in some industries. Some companies pass these higher rates along to consumers by raising prices. Others are forced to discontinue high-risk product lines.

Product Warranties. Many manufacturers offer written product warranties to convince customers of their products' quality. But these warranties are often limited and written in a language the average consumer does not understand. Too often, consumers learn that they are not entitled to services, repairs, and replacements that seem to be implied. To protect consumers, Congress passed the Magnuson-Moss Warranty Act in 1975. The act requires that full warranties meet certain minimum standards, including repair "within a reasonable time and without charge" or a replacement or full refund if the product does not work "after a reasonable number of attempts" at repair. Otherwise, the company must make it clear that it is offering only a limited warranty. The law has led several manufacturers to switch from full to limited warranties and others to drop warranties altogether as a marketing tool.

Packaging Decisions and Public Policy

Fair Packaging and Labeling. The public is concerned about false and potentially misleading packaging and

Summary

The concept of a *product* is complex, and includes three levels: the *core product,* the *actual product,* and the *augmented product.* The core product is the essential benefit that the customer is purchasing. The actual product is the tangible good itself, including such aspects as features, styling, quality, brand name, and packaging. The augmented product includes the actual product plus any additional services that come with it such as warranties, installation, maintenance or delivery.

There are three basic types of *product classifications. Durable goods* are used over an extended period of time. *Nondurable goods* are more quickly consumed, usually in a single use or a few usage occasions. *Services* are activities or benefits offered for sale which are basically intangible and do not result in ownership of anything. Each of these products can be bought by either consumer or industrial customers. *Consumer goods* are sold to the final end-user for personal consumption. *Industrial goods* are bought by individuals or organizations as goods that will receive further processing, or for use in conducting a business.

Marketers make *individual product decisions* for each product, including *product attribute decisions, brand, packaging, labeling,* and *product-support services* decisions. *Product attributes* deliver benefits through tangible aspects of the product including quality, features, and design. A *brand* is a way to identify and differentiate goods or services through use of a name or distinctive design element, resulting in long-term value known as *brand equity.* The product *package* and *labeling* are also an important element in the product decision mix, as they both carry brand equity through appearance and affect

labeling. The Federal Trade Commission Act of 1914 held that false, misleading, or deceptive labels or packages constitute unfair competition. Consumers also are concerned about confusing package sizes and shapes that make price comparisons difficult. The Fair Packaging and Labeling Act, passed by Congress in 1967, set mandatory labeling requirements, encouraged voluntary industry packaging standards, and allowed federal agencies to set packaging regulations in specific industries. The Food and Drug Administration has required processed-food producers to include nutritional labeling that clearly states the amounts of protein, fat, carbohydrates, and calories contained in products, as well as their vitamin and mineral content as a percentage of the recommended daily allowance. The FDA recently has launched a drive to control health claims in food labeling by taking action against the potentially misleading use of such descriptions as "light," "high fiber," "no cholesterol," and others. Consumerists have lobbied for additional labeling laws to require *open dating* (to describe product freshness), *unit pricing* (to

state the product cost in some standard measurement unit), *grade labeling* (to rate the quality level of certain consumer goods), and *percentage labeling* (to show the percentage of each important ingredient).

Excessive Cost. Critics have claimed that excessive packaging on some products raises prices. They point to secondary "throwaway" packaging and question its value to the consumer. They note that the package sometimes costs more than the contents; for example, Evian moisturizer consists of five ounces of natural spring water packaged as an aerosol spray selling for $5.50. Marketers respond that they also want to keep packaging costs down, but that the critics do not understand all the functions of the package.

Scarce Resources. The growing concern over shortages of paper, aluminum, and other materials suggests that marketers should try harder to reduce their packaging. For example, the growth of nonreturnable glass containers has resulted in using up to 17 times as much glass as with returnable containers. Glass and other throwaway

bottles also waste energy. Some states have passed laws prohibiting or taxing nonreturnable containers.

Pollution. As much as 40 percent of the total solid waste in this country is made up of package material. Many packages end up as broken bottles and crumpled cans littering the streets and countryside. All of this packaging creates a major problem in solid waste disposal, requiring huge amounts of labor and energy.

These packaging questions have mobilized public interest in new packaging laws. Marketers must be equally concerned. They must try to design fair, economical, and ecological packages for their products.

Sources: See Louis W. Stern and Thomas L. Eovaldi, *Legal Aspects of Marketing Strategy* (Englewood Cliffs, NJ: Prentice Hall, 1984), pp. 76–116; Marisa Manley, "Product Liability: You're More Exposed Than You Think," *Harvard Business Review,* September–October 1987, pp. 28–40; and John Carey, "Food Labeling: The FDA Has the Right Ingredients," *Business Week,* November 23, 1992, p. 42.

product performance with functionality. The level of *product-support services* provided can also have a major effect on the appeal of the product to a potential purchaser.

Product strategy goes a step beyond individual product decisions, requiring that offerings be built into a logical portfolio through *product line decisions.* A product line is a group of products that are closely related because of similar function, customers, channels of distribution, or pricing. A key dimension of the product line is the number of items it contains, referred to as the *product line length.* Profits are optimal when the line is of proper length. The product line length can be increased by *stretching upward* to a higher-priced segment, *stretching downward* to a lower-priced segment, or by *stretching both ways.* Profits can sometimes be increased by *product line filling,* adding more items within the present range of the line. Managers also keep their products current through *product line mod-*

ernization, and build volume or image through selecting specific items for *product line featuring.*

Organizations manage multiple product lines through *product mix decisions.* A company's product mix has four basic dimensions: *width, length, depth,* and *consistency.* The *width* of a product mix refers to the number of different types of product lines that a company offers. Product mix *length* is the total number of items that the company carries. *Depth* pertains to the number of versions, such as colors or flavors, offered for each product in a line. *Consistency* is a measure of how closely related different product lines are to one another. Consistency can be judged based on end use, channels of distribution, or production methods.

Marketers face complex considerations in *international product decisions.* First there must be a decision about what products to introduce in what countries. After this decision is made, the company must decide whether to *standardize* the product and packaging, or whether to *adapt* it to local conditions.

Overall, developing products and brands is a complex and demanding task. There are no firm rules that can assure success in these deci-

sions. Careful consideration of all issues in these decisions, and maintaining consistency with broad company objectives, is necessary for long-term success.

Key Terms

Actual product
Augmented product
Brand
Brand equity
Brand extension
Capital items
Co-branding
Consumer products
Convenience products
Core product
Industrial products

Line extension
Manufacturer's brand (or national brand)
Materials and parts
Multibranding
Packaging
Packaging concept
Private brand (or store brand)
Product
Product design
Product line

Product mix (or product assortment)
Product quality
Product-support services
Services
Shopping products
Slotting fees
Specialty products
Supplies and services
Unsought products

Discussing the Issues

1. List and explain the core, tangible, and augmented products of the educational experience that universities offer.

2. Decide whether you would classify the product offered by restaurants as non-durable goods or as services. Why?

3. In recent years, U.S. automakers have tried to reposition many of their brands to the high-quality end of the market. Analyze how well they have succeeded. What else could they do to change consumers' perceptions of their cars?

4. Evaluate why many people are willing to pay more for branded products than for

unbranded products. What does this tell you about the value of branding?

5. For many years there was one type of Coca-Cola, one type of Tide, and one type of Crest (in mint and regular). Now we find Coke in six or more varieties, Ultra, Liquid, and Unscented Tide, and Crest Gel with sparkles for kids. List some of the issues these brand extensions raise for manufacturers, retailers, and consumers.

6. Contrast brand extension by the brand owner with licensing a brand name for use by another company. Compare the opportunities and risks of each approach.

Applying the Concepts

1. Different areas of a town may attract different sorts of businesses. (a) Go to your local mall and find the directions kiosk. Look at the map and count the number of retail outlets for each type of consumer good: convenience, shopping, specialty, or unsought goods. (Often the map index is organized into categories that are helpful for this task.) (b) Drive down the road that serves as your local commercial "strip" and do a quick count in the same categories. (c)

Calculate what percentage of businesses fall into each category for the two areas. Do you see any differences? If so, why do you think these differences exist?

2. Go to the area of your town that has a number of fast food outlets. Compare the product mix of McDonald's to Kentucky Fried Chicken. Are there differences in width or depth? How could they stretch their lines upward or downward?

References

1. See "What Lies Behind the Sweet Smell of Success," *Business Week*, February 27, 1984, pp. 139–143; S. J. Diamond, "Perfume Equals Part Mystery, Part Marketing," *Los Angeles Times*, April 22, 1988, Section 4, p. 1; Pat Sloan, "Revlon Leads New Fragrance Charge," *Advertising Age*, July 16, 1990, p. 14; Joanne Lipman, "Big 'Outsert' Really Puts Revlon in Vogue," *Wall Street Journal*, September 17, 1992, p. B6; and "Leaders Follow Scent to Growth in Fragrances," *Advertising Age*, September 28, 1994, pp. 20, 30.

2. Otis Port, "The Quality Imperative: Questing for the Best," *Business Week*, special issue on quality, 1991, pp. 7–16.

3. Ibid., p. 7.

4. Rahul Jacob, "More Than a Dying Fad?" *Fortune*, October 18, 1993, pp. 66–72. Also see Cyndee Miller, "TQM Out; 'Continuous Process Improvement' In," *Marketing News*, May 9, 1994, pp. 5, 10; and David Greising, "Quality: How to Make It Pay," *Business Week*, August 8, 1994, pp. 54–59.

5. David A. Garvin, "Competing on Eight Dimensions of Quality," *Harvard Business Review*, November–December 1987, p. 109. Also see Robert Jacobson and David A. Aaker, "The Strategic Role of Product Quality," *Journal of Marketing*, October 1987, pp. 31–44; and Frank Rose, "Now Quality Means Service Too," *Fortune*, April 22, 1992, pp. 97–108.

6. For more on design, see Philip Kotler, "Design: A Powerful but Neglected Strategic Tool," *Journal of Business Strategy*, Fall 1984, pp. 16–21; "Competing by Design," *Business Week*, March 25, 1991, pp. 51–63; Brian Dumaine, "Design that Sells and Sells and . . . ," *Fortune*, March 11, 1991, pp. 86–94; and Stephen Potter, et al., *The Benefits and Costs of Investment in Design: Using Professional Design Expertise in Product, Engineering and Graphics Projects* (Manchester, UK: The Open University/UMIST, September 1991).

7. Pete Engardio, "Quick, Name Five Taiwanese PC Makers," *Business Week*, May 18, 1992, pp. 128–129.

8. See Peter Bennett, *Dictionary of Marketing Terms* (Chicago: American Marketing Association, 1988).

9. From a presentation delivered at Northwestern University by Larry Light, former international division chairman of Ted Bates Advertising, October 27, 1992. Also see Jean-Noel Kapferer, *Strategic Brand Management: New Approaches to Creating and Evaluating Brand Equity* (London: Kogan Page, 1992), pp. 38ff.

10. David A. Aaker, *Managing Brand Equity* (New York: The Free Press, 1991).

11. See Patrick Barwise, et al., *Accounting for Brands* (London: Institute of Chartered Accountants in England and Wales, 1990); Peter H. Farquhar, Julia Y. Han, and Yuji Ijiri, "Brands on the Balance Sheet," *Marketing Management*, Winter 1992, pp. 16–22; and Kevin Lane Keller, "Conceptualizing, Measuring, and Managing Customer-Based Brand Equity," *Journal of Marketing*, January 1993, pp. 1–22.

12. Keith J. Kelly, "Coca-Cola Shows That Top-Brand Fizz," *Advertising Age*, July 11, 1994, p. 3.

13. Thomas M. S. Hemnes, "How Can You Find a Safe Trademark?" *Harvard Business Review*, March–April 1985, p. 44.

14. Jennifer Lawrence, "Brands Beware, Wal-Mart Adds Giant House Label," *Advertising Age*, April 5, 1993, pp. 1, 45.

15. Emily DeNitto, "They Aren't Private Labels Anymore—They're Brands," *Advertising Age*, September 13, 1993, p. 8.

16. See Chip Walker, "What's in a Brand?" *American Demographics*, February 1991, pp. 54–56; Emily DeNitto, "No End to Private Label March," *Advertising Age*, November 1, 1993, p. S6; Patrick Oster, "The Eurosion of Brand Loyalty," *Business Week*, July 19, 1993, p. 22; and Marcia Mogelonsky, "When Stores Become Brands," *American Demographics*, February 1995, pp. 32–38.

17. Terry Lefton, "Warner Brothers' Not Very Looney Path to Licensing Gold," *Brandweek*, February 14, 1994, pp. 36–37.

18. Kim Cleland, "Multimarketer Melange an Increasingly Tasty Option on the Store Shelf," *Advertising Age*, May 2, 1994, p. S10. Also see Maxine S. Lans, "To Enjoin or Not to Enjoin: A Tough Question," *Marketing News*, February 13, 1995, p. 5.

19. For more on line extensions, see Kevin Lane Keller and David A. Aaker, "The Effects of Sequential Introduction of Line Extensions," *Journal of Marketing Research*, February 1992, pp. 35–50; and Srinivas K. Reddy, Susan L. Holak, and Subodh Bhat, "To Extend or Not to Extend: Success Determinants of Line Extensions," *Journal of Marketing Research*, May 1994, pp. 243–262.

20. Daniel C. Smith and C. Whan Park, "The Effects of Brand Extensions on Market Share and Advertising Efficiency," *Journal of Marketing Research*, August 1992, pp. 296–313.

21. For more on the use of brand extensions and consumer attitudes toward them, see David A. Aaker and Kevin L. Keller, "Consumer Evaluations of Brand Extensions," *Journal of Marketing*, January 1990, pp. 27–41; Julie Liesse, "Brand Extensions Take Center Stage," *Advertising Age*, March 8, 1993, p. 12, and Susan M. Broniarczyk and Joseph W. Alba, "The Importance of Brand in Brand Extension," *Journal of Marketing Research*, May 1994, pp. 214–228.

22. See Ira Teinowitz, "Brand Proliferation Attacked," *Advertising Age*, May 10, 1993, pp. 1, 49; and Jennifer Lawrence, "P&G Strategy: Build on Brands," *Advertising Age*, August 23, 1993, pp. 3, 31.

23. See Christopher Power, "And Now, Finger-Lickin' Good for Ya?" *Business Week*, February 18, 1991, p. 60; and Gary Strauss, "Building on Brand Names: Companies Freshen Old Product Lines," *USA Today*, March 20, 1992, pp. 1, 2.

24. See Bill Abrams, "Marketing," *Wall Street Journal*, May 20, 1982, p. 33; and Bernice Kanner, "Package Deals," *New York*, August 22, 1988, pp. 267–268.

25. See Alicia Swasy, "Sales Lost Their Vim? Try Repackaging," *Wall Street Journal,* October 11, 1989, p. B1.

26. Bro Uttal, "Companies That Serve You Best," *Fortune,* December 7, 1987, pp. 98–116. Also see Barry Farber and Joyce Wycoff, "Customer Service: Evolution and Revolution," *Sales & Marketing Management,* May 1991, pp. 44–51.

27. Bro Uttal, "Companies That Serve You Best," p. 116.

28. For a discussion of product line expansion issues, see

John A. Quelch and David Kenny, "Extend Profits, Not Product Lines," *Harvard Business Review,* September–October 1994, pp. 153–160.

29. Philip Cateora, *International Marketing,* 8th ed. (Homewood, IL: Irwin, 1993), p. 270.

30. David J. Morrow, "Sitting Pretty: How to Make Your Package Stand Out in a Crowd," *International Business,* November 1991, pp. 30–32.

31. Cateora, *International Marketing,* p. 426.

Company Case 9

COLGATE: SQUEEZING MORE FROM A BRAND NAME

You probably know about Colgate toothpaste—perhaps you've even used it. But what would you think of Colgate aspirin or Colgate antacid? How about Colgate laxative or Colgate dandruff shampoo?

That is exactly what Colgate-Palmolive would like to find out. Colgate wants to investigate the possibility of entering the over-the-counter (OTC) drug market. Can it use its Colgate brand name, developed in the oral-care products market, in the OTC health-care market?

Why is Colgate interested in the OTC market? The first reason is market size. The worldwide OTC market annually accounts for $27.3 billion in sales—the largest nonfood consumer products industry. Further, the $11.9 billion U.S. market is growing at a 4.4 percent annual rate, and international markets are growing at 25 percent annually! Analysts predict that the U.S. market will reach $30 billion by 2010.

Several trends are fueling this rapid growth. Consumers are becoming more sophisticated and increasingly are interested in self-medication as opposed to seeing a doctor. Companies are also switching many previously prescription-only drugs to OTC drugs. Moreover, OTC drugs tend to have very long product life cycles. Medical researchers are also discovering new drugs and new uses or benefits of existing drugs.

Colgate also knows that the OTC market can be extremely profitable. Analysts estimate that the average cost of goods sold for an OTC drug is only 29 percent, leaving a gross margin of 71 percent. Advertising and sales promotions are actually the largest expenditure categories for these products, accounting for an average of 42 percent of sales. OTC drugs produce an average 11 percent after-tax profit.

Because of the OTC market's attractiveness, Colgate conducted studies to learn the strength of its brand name with consumers. Colgate believes in the following equation: brand awareness + brand image = brand equity. Its studies found that Colgate was number one in

brand awareness, number two in brand image, and number two in brand equity among OTC consumers, even though it did not sell OTC products. The Tylenol brand name earned the number-one spot in both brand image and brand equity.

Colgate realizes that entering the OTC market will not be easy. First, its research suggests that the typical OTC product does not reach the breakeven point for four years and does not recover development costs until the seventh year. Second, OTC drugs require a high level of advertising and promotion expenditures, 25 percent of sales on year-round media alone. Third, because of the market's attractiveness, entering firms face stiff competition. Established companies like Procter & Gamble, Johnson & Johnson, and Warner-Lambert have strong sales forces and marketing organizations. Fourth, industry observers estimate that an OTC firm must have at least several hundred million dollars in sales to be large enough to afford the fixed costs of advertising and R&D and to have power versus the major retailers like Wal-Mart. So, the OTC firms are willing to fight aggressively for market share.

Given all these barriers to entry, you might wonder why Colgate would want to pursue OTC products. Colgate has adopted a strategy that aims to make it the best global consumer products company. It believes that oral-care and OTC products are very similar. Both rely on their ingredients for effectiveness; both are strictly regulated; and both have virtually identical marketing elements, including common distribution channels.

Colgate set up its Colgate Health Care Laboratories to explore product and market development opportunities in the OTC market. In the late 1980s, Colgate carried out a test market for a line of OTC products developed by its Health Care Laboratories. In cities like San Antonio, Texas, and Richmond, Virginia, it marketed a wide line of OTC products, from a nasal decongestant to a natural fiber laxative, under the brand name Ektra. The predominantly white packages featured the

Ektra name with the Colgate name in smaller letters below it.

Based on the results of that test market, Colgate quietly established a test market in Peoria, Illinois, to test a line of ten OTC health-care products, all using the Colgate name as the brand name. The line includes Colgate aspirin-free pain reliever to compete with Tylenol, Colgate ibuprofen to compete with Advil, Colgate cold tablets to compete with Contac, Colgate night-time cold medicine to compete with Nyquil, Colgate antacid to compete with Rolaids, Colgate natural laxative to compete with Metamucil, and Colgate dandruff shampoo to compete with Head and Shoulders.

Responding to inquiries, Colgate Chairman Reuben Marks suggests that "The Colgate name is already strong in oral hygiene, now we want to learn whether it can represent health care across the board. We need to expand into more profitable categories."

Colgate won't talk specifically about its new line. Peoria drugstore operators say, however, that Colgate has blitzed the town with coupons and ads. Representatives have given away free tubes of toothpaste with purchases of the new Colgate products and have handed out coupons worth virtually the full price of the new products. One store owner notes, "They're spending major money out here."

If all that promotion weren't enough, the manager of one Walgreen store points out that Colgate has priced its line well below competing brands, as much as 20 percent below in some cases. The same manager reports that the new products' sales are strong but also adds, "With all the promotion they've done, they should be. They're cheaper, and they've got Colgate's name on them. People are looking at it right now as a generic-style product. People are really price conscious, and as long as the price is cheaper, along with a name that you can trust, people are going to buy that over others."

Yet, even if Colgate's test proves a resounding success, marketing consultants say expanding the new line could prove dangerous, and ultimately, more expensive than Colgate can imagine. "If you put the Colgate brand name on a bunch of different products, if you do it willy-nilly at the lowest end, you're going to dilute what it stands for—and if you stand for nothing, you're worthless," observes Clive Chajet, chairman of Lipincott and Margulies, a firm that handles corporate identity projects.

Mr. Chajet suggests that Colgate also might end up alienating customers by slapping its name on so many products. If consumers are "dissatisfied with one product, they might be dissatisfied with everything across the board. I wouldn't risk it," he says.

Colgate's test is one of the bolder forays into line extensions by consumer products companies. Companies saddled with "mature" brands—brands that can't grow much more—often try to use those brands' solid gold names to make a new fortune, generally with a related product. Thus, Procter & Gamble's Ivory soap came up with a shampoo and conditioner.

Al Ries, chairman of Trout & Ries, a Greenwich, Connecticut, marketing consultant, questions whether any line extensions make sense—not only for Colgate, but other strong brand names. Mr. Ries argues that Colgate and the traditional over-the-counter medicine companies are basically turning their products into generic drugs instead of brands. They're losing "the power of a narrow focus," he says, adding, "If the traditional medicines maintained their narrow focus, they wouldn't leave room for an outsider such as Colgate."

If Colgate is too successful, meanwhile, it also risks cannibalizing its flagship product. Consultants note that almost all successful line extensions, and a lot of not-so-successful ones, hurt the product from which they took their name. Mr. Chajet agrees. Colgate could "save tens of millions of dollars by not having to introduce a new brand name" for its new products, he says. But in doing so, it might also "kill the goose that laid the golden egg."

Although chairman Marks admits that Colgate will continue to try to build share in its traditional cleanser and detergent markets, the company seems to consider personal care as a stronger area. But leveraging a name into new categories can be tricky, requiring patience from skeptical retailers and fickle consumers. "It isn't so much a question of where you can put the brand name," says one marketing consultant. "It's what products the consumers will let you put the brand name on."

QUESTIONS

1. What core product is Colgate selling when it sells toothpaste or the other products in its new line?

2. How would you classify these new products? What implications does this classification have for marketing the new line?

3. What brand decisions has Colgate made? What kinds of product line decisions? Are these decisions consistent?

4. If you were the marketing manager for the extended Colgate line, how would you package the new products? What risks do you see in these packaging decisions?

Source: Adapted from Joanne Lipman, "Colgate Tests Putting Its Name on Over-the-Counter Drug Line," *Wall Street Journal,* July 19, 1989. Used with permission. Also see Dan Koeppel. "Now Playing in Peoria: Colgate Generics," *Adweek's Marketing Week,* September 18, 1989, p. 5. Colgate Health Care Laboratories also cooperated in the development of this case.

Designing Products

NEW-PRODUCT DEVELOPMENT AND PRODUCT LIFE-CYCLE STRATEGIES

The 3M Company markets more than 60,000 products. These products range from sandpaper, adhesives, and laser optical disks to contact lenses, heart-lung machines, and futuristic synthetic ligaments; from coatings that sleeken boat hulls to hundreds of sticky tapes—Scotch Tape, masking tape, superbonding tape, and even refastening disposable diaper tape. 3M views *innovation* as its path to growth, and new products as its lifeblood. The company's goal is to derive an astonishing 30 percent of each year's sales from products introduced within the previous four years (recently stepped up from its longstanding goal of 25 percent in five years). More astonishing, it usually succeeds! Each year 3M launches more than 200 new products. And last year, 30 percent of its almost $15 billion in sales came from products introduced within the past four years. Its legendary emphasis on innovation has consistently made 3M one of America's most admired companies.

New products don't just happen. 3M works hard to create an environment that supports innovation. Last year, it invested $1 billion, or 7.3 percent of its annual sales, in research and development—twice as much as the average company. 3M encourages everyone to look for new products. The company's renowned "15 percent rule" allows all employees to spend up to 15 percent of their time "bootlegging"—working on projects of personal interest whether those projects directly benefit the company or not. When a promising idea comes along, 3M forms a venture team made up of the researcher who developed the idea and volunteers from manufacturing, sales, marketing, and legal. The team nurtures the product and protects it from company bureaucracy. Team members stay with the product until it succeeds or fails and then return to their previous jobs. Some teams have tried three or four times before finally making a success of an idea. Each year, 3M hands out Golden Step Awards to venture teams whose new products earned more than $2 million in U.S. sales, or $4 million in worldwide sales, within three years of introduction.

3M knows that it must try thousands of new-product ideas to hit one big jackpot. It accepts blunders and dead ends as a normal part of creativity and innovation. In fact, its

OBJECTIVES

When you finish this chapter, you should be able to accomplish the following:

1. Identify the challenges companies face in creating a **new product development strategy.**

2. List different sources for **idea generation**, and discuss how an idea moves ahead through **idea screening, concept development,** and **concept testing.**

3. Outline how a potential product advances from a concept to a product through **marketing strategy development, business analysis,** and **product development.**

4. Explain the purposes of **test marketing,** and distinguish among **standard, controlled,** and **simulated test markets.**

5. Evaluate the **product life-cycle theory,** detailing the extent to which you accept the sequence of the **introduction, growth, maturity,** and **decline stages.**

philosophy seems to be "if you aren't making mistakes, you probably aren't doing anything." But as it turns out, "blunders" have turned into some of 3M's most successful products. Old-timers at 3M love to tell the story about the chemist who accidentally spilled a new chemical on her tennis shoes. Some days later, she noticed that the spots hit by the chemical had not gotten dirty. Eureka! The chemical eventually became Scotchgard fabric protector.

And then there's the one about 3M scientist Spencer Silver. Silver started out to develop a superstrong adhesive; instead he came up with one that didn't stick very well at all. He sent the apparently useless substance on to other 3M researchers to see whether they could find something to do with it. Nothing happened for several years. Then Arthur Fry, another 3M scientist, had a problem—and an idea. As a choir member in a local church, Mr. Fry was having trouble marking places in his hymnal—the little scraps of paper he used kept falling out. He tried dabbing some of Mr. Silver's weak glue on one of the scraps. It stuck nicely and later peeled off without damaging the hymnal. Thus were born 3M's Post-It Notes, a product that is now one of the top selling office supply products in the world.[1]

A company has to be good at developing new products. It also must manage them in the face of changing tastes, technologies, and competition. Every product seems to go through a life cycle—it is born, goes through several phases, and eventually dies as newer products come along that better serve consumer needs.

This product life cycle presents two major challenges. First, because all products eventually decline, the firm must find new products to replace aging ones (the problem of *new-product development*). Second, the firm must understand how its products age and adapt its marketing strategies as products pass through life-cycle stages (the problem of *product life-cycle strategies*). We first look at the problem of finding and developing new products and then at the problem of managing them successfully over their life cycles.

NEW-PRODUCT DEVELOPMENT STRATEGY

New-product development
The development of original products, product improvements, product modifications, and new brands through the firm's own R&D efforts.

Given the rapid changes in consumer tastes, technology, and competition, companies must develop a steady stream of new products and services. A firm can obtain new products in two ways. One is through *acquisition*—by buying a whole company, a patent, or a license to produce someone else's product. The other is through **new-product development** in the company's own research and development department. As the costs of developing and introducing major new products have climbed, many large companies have acquired existing brands rather than creating new ones. Other firms have saved money by copying competitors' brands or by reviving old brands.

By *new products* we mean original products, product improvements, product modifications, and new brands that the firm develops through its own research and development efforts. In this chapter, we concentrate on new-product development.

NEW-PRODUCT SUCCESS AND FAILURE

Innovation can be very risky. Ford lost $350 million on its Edsel automobile; RCA lost $580 million on its SelectaVision videodisc player; and Texas Instruments lost a staggering $660 million before withdrawing from the home computer business. Other costly product failures from sophisticated companies include New Coke

(Coca-Cola Company), LA low-alcohol beer (Anheuser-Busch), Zap Mail electronic mail (Federal Express), Polarvision instant movies (Polaroid), Premier "smokeless" cigarettes (R. J. Reynolds), and Clorox detergent (Clorox Company).

New products continue to fail at a disturbing rate. One recent study estimated that new consumer packaged goods (consisting mostly of line extensions) fail at a rate of 80 percent. Another study found that about 33 percent of new industrial products fail at launch.[2] According to one marketing expert, "if companies can improve their effectiveness at launching new products, they could double their bottom line. It's one of the areas left with the greatest potential for improvement."[3]

Why do so many new products fail? There are several reasons. Although an idea may be good, the market size may have been overestimated. Perhaps the actual product was not designed as well as it should have been. Or maybe it was incorrectly positioned in the market, priced too high, or advertised poorly. A high-level executive might push a favorite idea despite poor marketing research findings. Sometimes the costs of product development are higher than expected, and sometimes competitors fight back harder than expected.

Because so many new products fail, companies are anxious to learn how to improve their odds of new-product success. One way is to identify successful new products and find out what they have in common. One study of 200 moderate-to high-technology new-product launches, which looked for factors shared by successful products but not by product failures, found that the number one success factor is a *unique superior product,* one with higher quality, new features, and higher value in use. Specifically, products with a high product advantage succeed 98 percent of the time, compared to products with a moderate advantage (58 percent success) or minimal advantage (18 percent success). Another key success factor is a *well-defined product concept* prior to development, in which the company carefully defines and assesses the target market, the product requirements, and the benefits before proceeding.[4] In all, to create successful new products, a company must understand its consumers, markets, and competitors and develop products that deliver superior value to customers.

Successful new-product development may be even more difficult in the future. Keen competition has led to increasing market fragmentation—companies now must aim at smaller market segments rather than the mass market, and this means smaller sales and profits for each product. New products must meet growing social and government constraints such as consumer safety and ecological standards. The costs of finding, developing, and launching new products will rise steadily due to rising manufacturing, media, and distribution costs. Many companies cannot afford the funds needed for new-product development. Instead, they introduce line extensions or "me-too" products rather than true innovations. Even when a new product is successful, rivals are so quick to copy it that the new product typically has only a short life.

THE NEW-PRODUCT DILEMMA

So companies face a problem—they must develop new products, but the odds weigh heavily against success. The solution lies in strong new-product planning. Top management is ultimately accountable for the new-product success. It cannot simply ask new-product managers to come up with great ideas. Rather, top management must define the markets and product categories that the company wants to emphasize. It must set specific criteria for new-product idea acceptance, based on the specific *strategic role* the product is expected to play. The product's role might be to help the company remain an innovator, to defend its market-share position, or to get a foothold in a new market. Or the new product might help the company to take advantage of its special strengths or exploit technology in a new way.

Another major decision facing top management is how much to budget for new-product development. New-product outcomes are so uncertain that it is difficult to use normal investment criteria for budgeting. Some companies solve this problem by encouraging as many projects as possible, hoping to achieve a few winners. Other companies set their R&D budgets as a percentage of sales or by spending what the competition spends. Still other companies decide how many successful new products they need and work backwards to estimate the required R&D investment.

Another important factor in new-product development work is to set up effective organizational structures for nurturing and handling new products. Table 10-1 presents the most common organizational arrangements for new-product development—product managers; new-product managers; and new-product committees, departments, and venture teams.

Thus, successful new-product development requires a total company effort. The most successful innovating companies make a consistent commitment of

TABLE 10-1 *Ways Companies Organize for New-Product Development*

PRODUCT MANAGERS

Many companies assign responsibility for new-product ideas to their product managers. Because these managers are close to the market and competition, they are ideally situated to find and develop new-product opportunities. In practice, however, this system has several faults. Product managers are usually so busy managing their product lines that they give little thought to new products other than brand modifications or extensions. They also lack the specific skills and knowledge needed to evaluate and develop new products.

NEW-PRODUCT MANAGERS

General Foods and Johnson & Johnson have new-product managers who report to group product managers. This position "professionalizes" the new-product function. On the other hand, new-product managers tend to think in terms of product modifications and line extensions limited to their current product and markets.

NEW-PRODUCT COMMITTEES

Most companies have a high-level management committee charged with reviewing and approving new-product proposals. It usually consists of representatives from marketing, manufacturing, finance, engineering, and other departments. Its function is not developing or coordinating new products so much as reviewing and approving new-product plans.

NEW-PRODUCT DEPARTMENTS

Large companies often establish a new-product department headed by a manager who has substantial authority and access to top management. The department's major responsibilities include generating and screening new ideas, working with the R&D department, and carrying out field testing and commercialization.

NEW-PRODUCT VENTURE TEAMS

The 3M Company, Dow, Westinghouse, and General Mills often assign major new-product development work to venture teams. A venture team is a group brought together from various operating departments and charged with developing a specific product or business. Team members are relieved of their other duties, and given a budget and a time frame. In some cases, this team stays with the product long after it is successfully introduced.

resources to new-product development, design a new-product strategy that is linked to their strategic planning process, and set up formal and sophisticated organizational arrangements for managing the new-product development process.

THE NEW-PRODUCT DEVELOPMENT PROCESS

The *new-product development process* for finding and growing new products consists of eight major steps (see Figure 10-1).

IDEA GENERATION

Idea generation
The systematic search for new-product ideas.

New-product development starts with **idea generation**—the systematic search for new-product ideas. A company typically has to generate many ideas in order to find a few good ones. The search for new-product ideas should be systematic rather than haphazard. Otherwise, although the company may find many ideas, most will not be good ones for its type of business. Top management can avoid this error by carefully defining its new-product development strategy. Major sources of new-product ideas include internal sources, customers, competitors, distributors and suppliers, and others.

Internal Sources

One study found that more than 55 percent of all new-product ideas come from within the company.[5] The company can find new ideas through formal research and development. It can pick the brains of its scientists, engineers, and manufacturing people. Or company executives can brainstorm new-product ideas. The company's salespeople are another good source because they are in daily contact with customers. Toyota claims that its employees submit two million ideas annually—about 35 suggestions per employee—and that more than 85 percent of these ideas are implemented.

Customers

Almost 28 percent of all new-product ideas come from watching and listening to customers. The company can conduct surveys or focus groups to learn about consumer needs and wants. The makers of WD-40, the multipurpose household lubricant and solvent, sponsor an annual contest to obtain new uses from customers. The company can analyze customer questions and complaints to find new products that better solve consumer problems. Company engineers or salespeople can meet with customers to get suggestions. General Electric's Video Products Division has its design engineers talk with final consumers to get ideas for new home electronics products. National Steel has a product application center where company engineers work with automotive customers to discover customer needs that might require new products.

Companies can learn a great deal from observing and listening to customers. United States Surgical Corporation (USSC) has developed most of its surgical instruments through close interaction with surgeons. By working closely with surgeons, the company was quick to pick up on early experiments in laparoscopy—surgery by inserting a tiny TV camera into the body along with slim, long-handled instruments. In recent years, USSC's focus has changed from marketing individual surgical instruments to offering a total package of products and

FIGURE 10-1 *Major stages in new-product development*

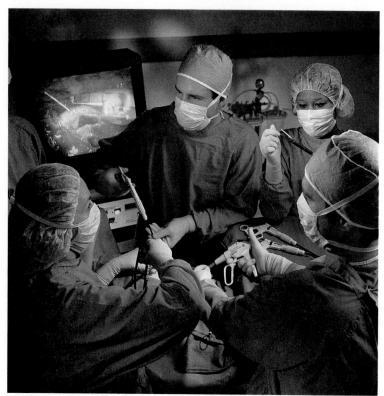

New-product ideas from customers: United States Surgical Corporation captured a lion's share of the laparoscopy market by watching and listening to surgeons, even gowning up and joining them in the operating room.

services aimed at helping hospitals achieve cost-effective surgery. Now, in addition to visiting with surgeons, the company invites representatives from materials management, financial, and other areas of customer hospitals to its corporate offices, listening and sharing information. USSC now captures about 58 percent of the single-use laparoscopy market.[6]

Finally, consumers often create new products on their own, and companies can benefit by finding these products and putting them on the market. Pillsbury gets promising new recipes through its annual Bake-Off. One of Pillsbury's four cake-mix lines and several variations of another came directly from Bake-Off winners' recipes.

Competitors

About 30 percent of new-product ideas come from analyzing competitors' products. The company can watch competitors' ads and other communications to get clues about their new products. Companies buy competing new products, take them apart to see how they work, analyze their sales, and decide whether the company should bring out a new product of its own. For example, when designing its highly successful Taurus, Ford tore down more than 50 competing models, layer by layer, looking for things to copy or improve upon. It copied the Audi's accelerator-pedal "feel," the Toyota Supra fuel gauge, the BMW 528e tire and jack storage system, and 400 other such outstanding features. Ford did this again when it redesigned the Taurus in 1992.[7]

Distributors, Suppliers, and Others

Resellers are close to the market and can pass along information about consumer problems and new-product possibilities. Suppliers can tell the company about new concepts, techniques, and materials that can be used to develop new products. Other idea sources include trade magazines, shows, and seminars; government agencies; new-product consultants; advertising agencies; marketing research firms; university and commercial laboratories; and inventors.

IDEA SCREENING

Idea screening
Screening new-product ideas in order to spot good ideas and drop poor ones as soon as possible.

The purpose of idea generation is to create a large number of ideas. The purpose of the succeeding stages is to *reduce* that number. The first idea-reducing stage is **idea screening.** The purpose of screening is to spot good ideas and drop poor ones as soon as possible. Product-development costs rise greatly in later stages. The company wants to go ahead only with the product ideas that will turn into profitable products.

Most companies require their executives to write up new-product ideas on a standard form that can be reviewed by a new-product committee. The writeup describes the product, the target market, and the competition. It makes some rough estimates of market size, product price, development time and costs, manufacturing costs, and rate of return. The committee then evaluates the idea against a set of general criteria. For example, at Kao Company, the large Japanese consumer products company, the committee asks questions such as: Is the product truly useful to consumers and society? Is it good for our particular company? Does it mesh well with the company's objectives and strategies? Do we have the people, skills, and resources to make it succeed? Does it deliver more value to customers than competing products? Is it easy to advertise and distribute?

Surviving ideas can be screened further using a simple rating process such as the one shown in Table 10-2. The first column lists factors required for the successful launching of the product in the marketplace. In the next column, management rates these factors on their relative importance. Thus, management believes that marketing skills and experience are very important (.20), and purchasing and supplies competence is of minor importance (.05).

Next, on a scale of .0 to 1.0, management rates how well the new-product idea fits the company's profile on each factor. Here, management feels that the product idea fits very well with the company's marketing skills and experience (.9), but not too well with its purchasing and supplies capabilities (.5). Finally, management multiplies the importance of each success factor by the rating of fit to obtain an overall rating of the company's ability to launch the product successfully. Thus, if marketing is an important success factor, and if this product fits the company's marketing skills, this will increase the overall rating of the product idea. In the example, the product idea scored .74, which places it at the high end of the "fair idea" level.

The checklist promotes a more systematic product idea evaluation and basis for discussion—however, it is not designed to make the decision for management.

CONCEPT DEVELOPMENT AND TESTING

Product concept
The idea that consumers will favor products that offer the most quality, performance, and features and that the organization should therefore devote its energy to making continuous product improvements. A detailed version of the new-product idea stated in meaningful consumer terms.

An attractive idea must be developed into a **product concept.** It is important to distinguish between a *product idea*, a *product concept*, and a *product image*. A product idea is an idea for a possible product that the company can see itself offering to the market. A product concept is a detailed version of the idea stated in meaningful consumer terms. A product image is the way consumers perceive an actual or potential product.

Concept Development

Suppose General Motors wants to commercialize its experimental electric car. This car can go as fast as 80 miles per hour and as far as 90 miles before needing

TABLE 10-2 *Product Idea Rating Process*

NEW-PRODUCT SUCCESS FACTORS	(A) RELATIVE IMPORTANCE	(B) FIT BETWEEN PRODUCT IDEA AND COMPANY CAPABILITIES											(A × B) IDEA RATING
		.0	.1	.2	.3	.4	.5	.6	.7	.8	.9	1.0	
Company strategy and objectives	.20									X			.160
Marketing skills and experience	.20										X		.180
Financial resources	.15								X				.105
Channels of distribution	.15									X			.120
Production capabilities	.15									X			.120
Research and development	.10								X				.070
Purchasing and supplies	.05						X						.025
Total	1.00												.780*

*Rating scale: .00–.40, poor; .50–.75, fair; .76–1.00, good. Minimum acceptance level: .70

GM's **Impact** *electric car, scheduled for introduction later this decade: This prototype goes from 0 to 60 MPH in eight seconds and travels over 90 miles at 55 MPH on a single charge.*

Concept testing
Testing new-product concepts with a group of target consumers to find out if the concepts have strong consumer appeal.

to be recharged. GM estimates that the electric car's operating costs are about half those of a regular car.

GM's task is to develop this new product into alternative product concepts, find out how attractive each concept is to customers, and choose the best one. It might create the following product concepts for the electric car:

◆ *Concept 1* An inexpensive subcompact designed as a second family car to be used around town. The car is ideal for loading groceries and hauling children, and it is easy to enter.

◆ *Concept 2* A medium-cost, medium-size car designed as an all-purpose family car.

◆ *Concept 3* A medium-cost sporty compact appealing to young people.

◆ *Concept 4* An inexpensive subcompact appealing to conscientious people who want basic transportation, low fuel cost, and low pollution.

Concept Testing

Concept testing calls for testing new-product concepts with groups of target consumers. The concepts may be presented to consumers symbolically or physically. Here, in words, is Concept 1:

> An efficient, fun-to-drive, electric-powered subcompact car that seats four. Great for shopping trips and visits to friends. Costs half as much to operate as similar gasoline-driven cars. Goes up to 80 miles per hour and does not need to be recharged for 90 miles. Priced, fully equipped, at $14,000.

For some concept tests, a word or picture description might be sufficient. However, a more concrete and physical presentation of the concept will increase the reliability of the concept test. Today, marketers are finding innovative ways to make product concepts more real to concept-test subjects (see Marketing Highlight 10-1).

After being exposed to the concept, consumers then may be asked to react to it by answering the questions in Table 10-3. The answers will help the company decide which concept has the strongest appeal. For example, the last question asks about the consumer's intention to buy. Suppose 10 percent of the consumers said they "definitely" would buy and another 5 percent said "probably." The company could project these figures to the full population in this target group to estimate sales volume. Even then, the estimate is uncertain because people do not always carry out their stated intentions.[8]

TABLE 10-3 *Questions for Electric Car Concept Test*

1. Do you understand the concept of an electric car?
2. Do you believe the claims about the electric car's performance?
3. What are the major benefits of the electric car compared with a conventional car?
4. What improvements in the car's features would you suggest?
5. For what uses would you prefer an electric car to a conventional car?
6. What would be a reasonable price to charge for the electric car?
7. Who would be involved in your decision to buy such a car? Who would drive it?
8. Would you buy such a car? (Definitely, probably, probably not, definitely not)

THE NEW WORLD OF CONCEPT TESTING: STEREOLITHOGRAPHY AND VIRTUAL REALITY

In product concept testing, the more the presentation of the concept resembles the final product or experience, the more dependable the results. Today, many firms are developing interesting new methods for product concept testing.

For example, 3D Systems, Inc., uses a technique known as 3-D printing—or "stereolithography"—to create three-dimensional models of physical products, such as small appliances and toys. The process begins with a computer-generated, three-dimensional image of the prototype. A computer first simulates a three-dimensional design and then electronically "slices" the image into wafer thin segments. The digital information that designs each of these segments is then used to guide a robotically controlled laser beam, which focuses on a soup of liquid plastic formulated to turn solid when exposed to light. The laser builds the object as it creates layer upon microthin layer of hardened plastic. Within a few hours, the process turns out plastic prototypes that would otherwise take weeks to create. Researchers can show these models to consumers to gather their comments and reactions.

Stereolithography has produced some amazing success stories. Logitech, a company that produces computer mice and other peripherals, used stereolithography to win a highly sought contract from a major computer maker. Logitech was delighted when the computer maker requested a bid to manufacture a specific mouse. The only hitch—the bid had to be submitted within only two weeks. Using stereolithography, Logitech was able to design, build, and assemble a fully functional, superior-quality prototype within the allotted time. The disbelieving customer awarded the contract to Logitech on the spot.

Beyond making prototypes, 3-D printing (also called "desktop manu-

Using stereolithography, Logitech was able to design, build, and assemble a fully-functional prototype of this computer mouse in less than two weeks.

facturing") offers exciting prospects for manufacturing custom-made products at the push of a button. In the future, 3D "factories" may churn out custom-designed parts. Companies may be able to store their entire inventories electronically in computer memory banks and possibly even "fax" solid objects to distant locations.

When a large physical product such as an automobile is involved, it can be tested using "virtual reality." Researchers use a software package to design a car on a computer. Subjects can then manipulate the simulated car as if it were a real object. By operating certain controls, a respondent can approach the simulated car, open the door, sit in the car, start the engine, hear the sound, drive away, and experience the ride. The entire experience can be enriched by placing the simulated car in a simulated showroom and having a simulated salesperson approach the customer with a certain manner and words. After completing this experience, the respondent is asked questions about what he or she liked and disliked, as well as the likelihood of buying such a car. Researchers can vary car features and salesroom encounters to see which have the greatest appeal. Although this approach may be expensive, researchers learn a great deal about designing the right car before investing millions of dollars to build the real product.

Sources: Quotes from "The Ultimate Widget: 3-D 'Printing' May Revolutionize Product Design and Manufacturing," *U.S. News & World Report,* July 20, 1992, p. 55. Also see Benjamin Wooley, *Virtual Worlds* (London: Blackwell, 1992); and "The World Leader in Senseware Orchestrates a Sales Tour de Force Using Solid Imaging," *The Edge,* 3D Systems, Inc., Spring 1993, pp. 4–5.

MARKETING STRATEGY DEVELOPMENT

Marketing strategy development
Designing an initial marketing strategy for a new product based on the product concept.

Suppose GM finds that Concept 1 for the electric car tests best. The next step is **marketing strategy development,** designing an initial marketing strategy for introducing this car to the market.

The *marketing strategy statement* consists of three parts. The first part describes the target market; the planned product positioning; and the sales, market share, and profit goals for the first few years. Thus:

The target market is households that need a second car for going shopping, running errands, and visiting friends. The car will be positioned as more economical to buy and operate, and more fun to drive, than cars now available to this market. The company will aim to sell 200,000 cars in the first year, at a loss of not more than $30 million. In the second year, the company will aim for sales of 220,000 cars and a profit of $50 million.

The second part of the marketing strategy statement outlines the product's planned price, distribution, and marketing budget for the first year:

> The electric car will be offered in three colors and will have optional air-conditioning and power-drive features. It will sell at a retail price of $14,000—with 15 percent off the list price to dealers. Dealers who sell more than ten cars per month will get an additional discount of 5 percent on each car sold that month. An advertising budget of $20 million will be split fifty-fifty between national and local advertising. Advertising will emphasize the car's economy and fun. During the first year, $100,000 will be spent on marketing research to find out who is buying the car and to determine their satisfaction levels.

The third part of the marketing strategy statement describes the planned long-run sales, profit goals, and marketing mix strategy:

> GM intends to capture a 3 percent long-run share of the total auto market and realize an after-tax return on investment of 15 percent. To achieve this, product quality will start high and be improved over time. Price will be raised in the second and third years if competition permits. The total advertising budget will be raised each year by about 10 percent. Marketing research will be reduced to $60,000 per year after the first year.

BUSINESS ANALYSIS

Business analysis
A review of the sales, costs, and profit projections for a new product to find out whether these factors satisfy the company's objectives.

Once management has decided on its product concept and marketing strategy, it can evaluate the business attractiveness of the proposal. **Business analysis** involves a review of the sales, costs, and profit projections for a new product to find out whether they satisfy the company's objectives. If they do, the product can move to the product-development stage.

To estimate sales, the company should look at the sales history of similar products and should survey market opinion. It should estimate minimum and maximum sales to assess the range of risk. After preparing the sales forecast, management can estimate the expected product costs and profits, including marketing, R&D, manufacturing, accounting, and finance costs. The company then uses the sales and costs figures to analyze the new product's financial attractiveness.

PRODUCT DEVELOPMENT

Product development
A strategy for company growth by offering modified or new products to current market segments. Developing the product concept into a physical product in order to assure that the product idea can be turned into a workable product.

So far, the product may have existed only as a word description, a drawing, or perhaps a crude mockup. If the product concept passes the business test, it moves into **product development**. Here, R&D or engineering develops the product concept into a physical product. The product-development step, however, now calls for a large jump in investment. It will show whether the product idea can be turned into a workable product.

The R&D department will develop one or more physical versions of the product concept. R&D hopes to design a prototype that will satisfy and excite consumers and that can be produced quickly and at budgeted costs. Developing a successful prototype can take days, weeks, months, or even years. The prototype must have the required functional features and also convey the intended psychological characteristics. The electric car, for example, should strike consumers as being well built and safe. Management must learn what makes consumers decide that a car is well built. Some consumers slam the door to hear its "sound." If the car does not have "solid-sounding" doors, consumers may think it is poorly built.

When the prototypes are ready, they must be tested. Functional tests are then conducted under laboratory and field conditions to make sure that the product performs safely and effectively. The new car must start easily; it must be comfortable; it must be able to withstand heavy impact in crash tests. Consumer tests are conducted, in which consumers test drive the car and rate its attributes.

TEST MARKETING

Test marketing
The stage of new-product development where the product and marketing program are tested in more realistic market settings.

If the product passes functional and consumer tests, the next step is **test marketing**, the stage at which the product and marketing program are introduced into more realistic market settings. Test marketing gives the marketer experience with marketing the product before going to the expense of full introduction. It lets the company test the product and its marketing program—positioning strategy, advertising, distribution, pricing, branding and packaging, and budget levels.

The amount of test marketing needed varies with each new product. Test marketing costs can be enormous, and test marketing takes time that may allow competitors to gain advantages. When the costs of developing and introducing the product are low, or when management is already confident about the new product, the company may do little or no test marketing. Companies often do not test market simple line extensions or copies of successful competitor products. For example, Procter & Gamble introduced its Folger's decaffeinated coffee crystals without test marketing, and Pillsbury rolled out Chewy granola bars and chocolate-covered Granola Dipps with no standard test market. However, when introducing a new product requires a big investment, or when management is not sure of the product or marketing program, a company may do a lot of test marketing.

Lever USA spent two years testing its highly-successful Lever 2000 bar soap before introducing it internationally.

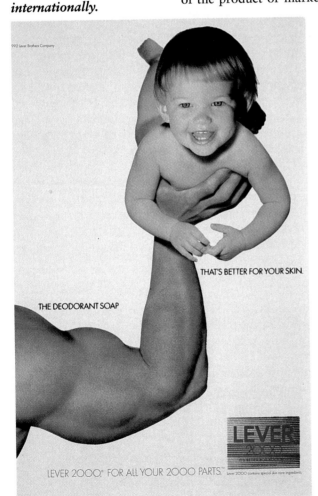

992 Lever Brothers Company

THE DEODORANT SOAP

THAT'S BETTER FOR YOUR SKIN.

LEVER 2000° FOR ALL YOUR 2000 PARTS. Lever 2000 contains special skin care ingredients.

For instance, Lever USA spent two years testing its highly successful Lever 2000 bar soap in Atlanta before introducing it internationally.

When using test marketing, consumer products companies usually choose one of three approaches—standard test markets, controlled test markets, or simulated test markets.

Standard Test Markets

Using standard test markets, the company finds a small number of representative test cities, conducts a full marketing campaign in these cities, and uses store audits, consumer and distributor surveys, and other measures to gauge product performance. The results are used to forecast national sales and profits, discover potential product problems, and fine-tune the marketing program.

Standard test markets have some drawbacks. First, they may be very costly—the average standard test market costs over $3 million, and costs can go much higher. Procter & Gamble spent $15 million developing Duncan Hines ready-to-eat cookies in test market.[9] Second, standard test markets take a long time—some last as long as three years. If the testing proves unnecessary, the company will have lost many months of sales and profits. Third, competitors often do whatever they can to make test-market results hard to read. They cut their prices in test cities, increase their promotion, or even buy up the product being tested. For example, when Pepsi tested Mountain Dew Sport drink in Minneapolis, Quaker Oats sabotaged the test with a furious advertising and couponing campaign for its Gatorade. Pepsi later pulled Mountain Dew Sport from the market. Finally, standard test markets give competitors a look at the company's new product well before it is introduced nationally. Thus, competitors may have time to develop defensive strategies, and may even beat the company's product to the market. For example, while Clorox was still test marketing its new detergent with bleach in selected markets, P&G launched Tide with Bleach nationally. Tide with Bleach quickly became the segment leader; Clorox later withdrew its detergent.

Despite these disadvantages, standard test markets are still the most widely used approach for major market testing. However, many companies today are shifting to quicker and cheaper controlled and simulated test marketing methods.

Controlled Test Markets

Several research firms keep controlled panels of stores that have agreed to carry new products for a fee. The company with the new product specifies the number of stores and geographical locations it wants. The research firm delivers the product to the participating stores and controls shelf location, amount of shelf space, displays and point-of-purchase promotions, and pricing according to specified plans. Sales results are tracked to determine the impact of these factors on demand.

Controlled test marketing systems like Nielsen's Scantrack and Information Resources Inc.'s (IRI) BehaviorScan track individual behavior from the television set to the checkout counter. IRI, for example, keeps panels of shoppers in carefully selected cities. It uses microcomputers to measure TV viewing in each panel household and can send special commercials to panel member television sets. Panel consumers buy from cooperating stores and show identification cards when making purchases. Detailed electronic scanner information on each consumer's purchases is fed into a central computer, where it is combined with the consumer's demographic and TV viewing information and reported daily. Thus, BehaviorScan can provide store-by-store, week-by-week reports on the sales of new products being tested. And because the scanners record the specific purchases of individual consumers, the system also can provide information on repeat purchases and the ways that different types of consumers are reacting to the new product, its advertising, and various other elements of the marketing program.[10]

Controlled test markets take less time than standard test markets (six months to a year) and usually cost less (a year-long BehaviorScan test might cost from $200,000 to $2,000,000). However, some companies are concerned that the limited number of small cities and panel consumers used by the research services may not be representative of their products' markets or target consumers. And, as in standard test markets, controlled test markets allow competitors to get a look at the company's new product.

Simulated Test Markets

Companies also can test new products in a simulated shopping environment. The company or research firm shows ads and promotions for a variety of products, including the new product being tested, to a sample of consumers. It gives consumers a small amount of money and invites them to a real or laboratory store where they may keep the money or use it to buy items. The researchers note how many consumers buy the new product and competing brands. This simulation provides a measure of the trial and the commercial's effectiveness against competing commercials. The researchers then ask consumers the reasons for their purchase or nonpurchase. Some weeks later, they interview the consumers by phone to determine product attitudes, usage, satisfaction, and repurchase intentions. Using sophisticated computer models, the researchers then project national sales from results of the simulated test market.

Simulated test markets overcome some of the disadvantages of standard and controlled test markets. They usually cost much less ($35,000 to $75,000), can be run in eight weeks, and keep the new product out of competitors' view. Yet, because of their small samples and simulated shopping environments, many marketers do not think that simulated test markets are as accurate or reliable as larger, real-world tests. Still, simulated test markets are used widely, often as "pretest" markets. Because they are fast and inexpensive, one or more simulated tests can be run to quickly assess a new product or its marketing program. If the pre-test results are strongly positive, the product might be introduced without further testing. If the results are very poor, the product might be dropped or substantially redesigned and retested. If the results are promising but indefinite, the product and marketing program can be tested further in controlled or standard test markets.

Test Marketing Business Products

Business marketers use different methods for test marketing their new products. For example, they may conduct *product-use tests*. Here, the business marketer selects a small group of potential customers who agree to use the new product for a limited time. The manufacturer's technical people watch how these customers use the product. From this test the manufacturer learns about customer training and servicing requirements. After the test, the marketer asks the customer about purchase intent and other reactions.

New industrial products also can be tested at *trade shows*. These shows draw a large number of buyers who view new products in a few concentrated days. The manufacturer sees how buyers react to various product features and terms, and can assess buyer interest and purchase intentions. The business marketer also can test new industrial products in *distributor and dealer display rooms,* where they may stand next to other company products and possibly competitors' products. This method yields preference and pricing information in the normal selling atmosphere of the product.

Finally, some business marketers use *standard or controlled test markets* to measure the potential of their new products. They produce a limited supply of the product and give it to the salesforce to sell in a limited number of geographical areas. The company gives the product full advertising, sales promotion, and other marketing support. Such test markets let the company test the product and its marketing program in real market situations.

COMMERCIALIZATION

Commercialization
Introducing a new product into the market.

Test marketing gives management the information needed to make a final decision about whether to launch the new product. If the company goes ahead with **commercialization**—introducing the new product into the market—it will face high costs. The company will have to build or rent a manufacturing facility. And it may have to spend, in the case of a new consumer packaged good, between $10 million and $100 million for advertising and sales promotion in the first year. For example, McDonald's spent more than $5 million *per week* on the introductory advertising campaign for its McDLT sandwich.

The company launching a new product must first decide on introduction *timing*. If the electric car will eat into the sales of the company's other cars, its introduction may be delayed. If the electric car can be improved further, or if the economy is down, the company may wait until the following year to launch it.

Next, the company must decide *where* to launch the new product—in a single location, a region, the national market, or the international market. Few companies have the confidence, capital, and capacity to launch new products into full national or international distribution. They will develop a planned *market rollout* over time. In particular, small companies may enter attractive cities or regions one

SPEEDING NEW PRODUCTS TO MARKET

Philips, the giant Dutch consumer electronics company, marketed the first practical VCR in 1972, gaining a three-year lead on its Japanese competitors. But in the seven years that it took Philips to develop its second VCR generation, Japanese manufacturers had launched at least three generations of new products. A victim of its own creaky product-development process, Philips never recovered from the Japanese onslaught. This story is typical. In today's fast-changing, fiercely competitive world, turning out new products too slowly can result in product failures, lost sales and profits, and crumbling market positions. "Speed to market" and reducing new-product development "cycle time" have become pressing concerns to companies in all industries.

Large companies traditionally have used a sequential product-development approach in which they develop new products in an orderly series of steps. In a kind of relay race, each company department completes its phase of the development process before passing the new product on. This sequential process has merits— it helps bring order to risky and complex new-product development projects. But the approach also can be fatally slow.

To speed up their product-development cycles, many companies are now adopting a faster, team-oriented approach called "simultaneous product development." Instead of passing the new product from department to department, the company assembles a team of people from various departments that stays with the new product from start to finish. Such teams usually include

A Black & Decker "fusion team" developed the highly acclaimed Quantum tool line in only 12 months. The team included 85 marketers, engineers, designers, finance people, and others from the United States, Britain, Germany, Italy, and Switzerland.

people from the marketing, finance, design, manufacturing, and legal departments, and even supplier and customer companies. Simultaneous development is more like a rugby match than a relay race—team members pass the new product back and forth as they move downfield toward the common goal of a speedy new-product launch.

Top management gives the product development team general strategic direction, but no clear-cut product idea or work plan. It challenges the team with stiff and seemingly contradictory goals—"turn out carefully planned and superior new products, but do it quickly"—and then gives the team whatever freedom and resources it needs to meet the challenge. In the sequential process, a bottleneck at one phase can seriously

---

at a time. Larger companies, however, may quickly introduce new models into several regions or into the full national market.

Companies with international distribution systems may introduce new products through global rollouts. Colgate-Palmolive uses a "lead-country" strategy. For example, it launched its Palmolive Optims shampoo and conditioner first in Australia, the Philippines, Hong Kong, and Mexico, then rapidly rolled it out into Europe, Asia, Latin America, and Africa. International companies are increasingly introducing their new products in swift global assaults. Procter & Gamble did this with its Pampers Phases line of disposable diapers. In the past, P&G typically introduced a new product in the U.S. market. If it was successful, overseas competitors would copy the product in their home markets before P&G could expand distribution globally. With Pampers Phases, however, the company introduced the new product into global markets within one month of introducing it in the United States. It planned to have the product on the shelf in 90 countries within just 12 months of introduction. Such rapid worldwide expansion solidified the brand's

slow the entire project. In the simultaneous approach, if one functional area hits snags, it works to resolve them while the team moves on.

The Allen-Bradley Company, a maker of industrial controls, provides an example of the tremendous benefits gained by using simultaneous development. Under the old sequential approach, the company's marketing department handed off a new product idea to designers. The designers, working in isolation, prepared concepts and passed them along to product engineers. The engineers, also working by themselves, developed expensive prototypes and handed them off to manufacturing, which tried to find a way to build the new product. Finally, after many years and dozens of costly design compromises and delays, marketing was asked to sell the new product, which it often found to be too high priced or sadly out of date. Now, Allen-Bradley has adopted the simultaneous product-development approach. All of the company's departments work together to develop new products. The results have been astonishing. For example, the company recently developed a new electrical control in just two years; under the old system, it would have taken six years.

Black & Decker used the simultaneous approach—what it calls "fusion teams"—to develop its Quantum line of tools targeted toward serious do-it-yourselfers. Team Quantum consisted of 85 Black & Decker

employees from around the world assigned to get the right product line to customers as quickly as possible. The team included engineers, finance people, marketers, designers, and others from the United States, Britain, Germany, Italy, and Switzerland. From idea to launch, including three months of consumer research, the team developed the highly acclaimed Quantum line in only 12 months.

The auto industry also has discovered the benefits of simultaneous product development. The approach is called "simultaneous engineering" at GM, the "team concept" at Ford, and "process-driven design" at Chrysler. The first American cars built using this process, the Ford Taurus and Mercury Sable, have been major marketing successes. Using simultaneous product development, Ford slashed development time from 60 months to less than 40. It squeezed 14 weeks from its cycle by simply getting the engineering and finance departments to review designs at the same time instead of sequentially. It claims that such actions have helped cut average engineering costs for a project by 35 percent. In an industry that has typically taken five or six years to turn out a new model, Mazda now brags about two- to three-year product-development cycles—a feat that would be impossible without simultaneous development.

However, the simultaneous approach does have it limitations.

Superfast product development can be riskier and more costly than the slower, more orderly sequential approach. And it often creates increased organizational tension and confusion. But in rapidly changing industries facing increasingly shorter product life cycles, the rewards of fast and flexible product development far exceed the risks. Companies that get new and improved products to the market faster than competitors gain a dramatic competitive edge. They can respond more quickly to emerging consumer tastes and charge higher prices for more advanced designs. As one auto industry executive states, "What we want to do is get the new car approved, built, and in the consumer's hands in the shortest time possible. . . . Whoever gets there first gets all the marbles."

Sources: Hirotaka Takeuchi and Ikujiro Nonaka, "The New New-Product Development Game," *Harvard Business Review,* January–February 1986, pp. 137–146; Bro Uttal, "Speeding New Ideas to Market," *Fortune,* March 2, 1987, pp. 62–65; John Bussey and Douglas R. Sease, "Speeding Up: Manufacturers Strive to Slice Time Needed to Develop New Products," *Wall Street Journal,* February 23, 1988, pp. 1, 24; Homer F. Hagedorn, "High Performance in Product Development: An Agenda for Senior Management," in Arthur D. Little Company, *PRISM,* First Quarter, 1992, pp. 47–58; and Susan Caminiti, "A Star Is Born," *Fortune,* November 29, 1993, pp. 45–47.

market position before foreign competitors could react. P&G has since mounted worldwide introductions of several other new products.[11]

SPEEDING UP NEW-PRODUCT DEVELOPMENT

Sequential product development
A new-product development approach in which one company department works individually to complete its stage of the process before passing the new product along to the next department and stage.

Many companies organize their new-product development process into an orderly sequence of steps, starting with idea generation and ending with commercialization. Under this **sequential product development** approach, one company department works individually to complete its stage of the process before passing the new product along to the next department and stage. This orderly, step-by-step process can help bring control to complex and risky projects. But it also can be dangerously slow. In fast-changing, highly competitive markets, such slow-but-sure product development can cost the company potential sales and profits at the hands of more nimble competitors.

Today, in order to get their new products to market more quickly, many companies are dropping the *sequential product development* method in favor of the faster, more flexible **simultaneous product development** approach. Under the new approach, various company departments work closely together, overlapping the steps in the product-development process to save time and increase effectiveness (see Marketing Highlight 10-2).

PRODUCT LIFE-CYCLE STRATEGIES

Simultaneous product development
An approach to developing new products in which various company departments work closely together, overlapping the steps in the product-development process to save time and increase effectiveness.

Product life cycle (PLC)
The course of a product's sales and profits over its lifetime. It involves five distinct stages: product development, introduction, growth, maturity, and decline.

After launching the new product, management wants the product to enjoy a long and happy life. Although it does not expect the product to sell forever, management wants to earn a decent profit to cover all the effort and risk that went into launching it. Management is aware that each product will have a life cycle, although the exact shape and length is not known in advance.

Figure 10-2 shows a typical **product life cycle (PLC)**, the course that a product's sales and profits take over its lifetime. The product life cycle has five distinct stages:

1. *Product development* begins when the company finds and develops a new-product idea. During product development, sales are zero and the company's investment costs mount.

2. *Introduction* is a period of slow sales growth as the product is being introduced in the market. Profits are nonexistent in this stage because of the heavy expenses of product introduction.

3. *Growth* is a period of rapid market acceptance and increasing profits.

4. *Maturity* is a period of slowdown in sales growth because the product has achieved acceptance by most potential buyers. Profits level off or decline because of increased marketing outlays to defend the product against competition.

5. *Decline* is the period when sales fall off and profits drop.

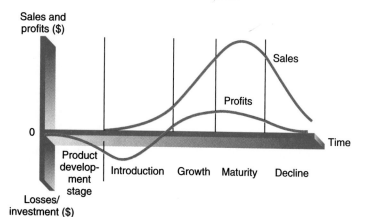

FIGURE 10-2 *Sales and profits over the product's life from inception to demise*

Not all products follow this S-shaped product life cycle. Some products are introduced and die quickly; others stay in the mature stage for a long, long time. Some enter the decline stage and are then cycled back into the growth stage through strong promotion or repositioning.

The PLC concept can describe a *product class* (gasoline-powered automobiles), a *product form* (station wagons), or a *brand* (the Ford Taurus). The PLC concept applies differently in each case. Product classes have the longest life cycles—the sales of many product classes stay in the mature stage for a long time. Product forms, in contrast, tend to have the standard PLC shape. Product forms such as "cream deodorants," the "dial telephone," and "phonograph records" passed through a regular history of introduction, rapid growth, maturity, and decline. A specific brand's life cycle can change quickly because of changing competitive attacks and responses. For example, although teeth-cleaning products (product class) and toothpastes (product form) have enjoyed fairly long life cycles, the life cycles of specific brands have tended to be much shorter.

The PLC concept also can be applied to what are known as styles, fashions, and fads. Their special life cycles are shown in Figure 10-3. A **style** is a basic and

Style
A basic and distinctive mode of expression.

FIGURE 10-3 *Styles, fashions, and fads*

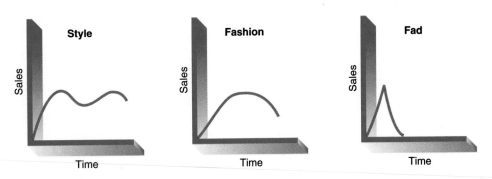

distinctive mode of expression. For example, styles appear in homes (colonial, ranch, Cape Cod); clothing (formal, casual); and art (realistic, surrealistic, abstract). Once a style is invented, it may last for generations, coming in and out of vogue. A style has a cycle showing several periods of renewed interest. A **fashion** is a currently accepted or popular style in a given field. For example, the "preppie look" in the clothing of the late 1970s gave way to the "loose and layered look" of the 1980s, which in turn yielded to the less conservative but more tailored look of the 1990s. Fashions tend to grow slowly, remain popular for a while, then decline slowly. **Fads** are fashions that enter quickly, are adopted with great zeal, peak early, and decline very fast. They last only a short time and tend to attract only a limited following. Examples include Rubik's Cubes, "pet rocks," Cabbage Patch dolls, or yo-yos. Fads do not survive for long because they normally do not satisfy a strong need or satisfy it well.

The PLC concept can be applied by marketers as a useful framework for describing how products and markets work. But using the PLC concept for forecasting product performance or for developing marketing strategies presents some practical problems.[12] For example, managers may have trouble identifying which stage of the PLC the product is in, pinpointing when the product moves into the next stage, and determining the factors that affect the product's movement through the stages. In practice, it is difficult to forecast the sales level at each PLC stage, the length of each stage, and the shape of the PLC curve.

Using the PLC concept to develop marketing strategy also can be difficult because strategy is both a cause and a result of the product's life cycle. The product's current PLC position suggests the best marketing strategies, and the resulting marketing strategies affect product performance in later life-cycle stages. Yet, when used carefully, the PLC concept can help in developing good marketing strategies for different stages of the product life cycle.

We looked at the product-development stage of the product life cycle in the first part of the chapter. We now look at strategies for each of the other life-cycle stages.

Fashion
A currently accepted or popular style in a given field.

Fads
Fashions that enter quickly, are adopted with great zeal, peak early, and decline very fast.

INTRODUCTION STAGE

Introduction stage
The product life-cycle stage when the new product is first distributed and made available for purchase.

The **introduction stage** starts when the new product is first launched. Introduction takes time, and sales growth is apt to be slow. Well-known products such as instant coffee, frozen orange juice, and powdered coffee creamers lingered for many years before they entered a stage of rapid growth.

In this stage, as compared to other stages, profits are negative or low because of the low sales and high distribution and promotion expenses. Much money is needed to attract distributors and build their inventories. Promotion spending is relatively high to inform consumers of the new product and get them to try it. Because the market is not generally ready for product refinements at this stage, the company and its few competitors produce basic versions of the product. These firms focus their selling on those buyers who are the readiest to buy.

A company might adopt one of several marketing strategies for introducing a new product. It can set a high or low level for each marketing variable, such as price, promotion, distribution, and product quality. Considering only price and promotion, for example, management might launch the new product with a high price and low promotion spending. The high price helps recover as much gross profit per unit as possible while the low promotion spending keeps marketing spending down. Such a strategy makes sense when the market is limited in size, when most consumers in the market know about the product and are willing to pay a high price, and when there is little immediate potential competition.

On the other hand, a company might introduce its new product with a low price and heavy promotion spending. This strategy promises to bring the fastest market penetration and the largest market share. It makes sense when the market is large, potential buyers are price sensitive and unaware of the product, there is strong potential competition, and the company's unit manufacturing costs fall with the scale of production and accumulated manufacturing experience.

A company, especially the *market pioneer,* must choose its launch strategy consistent with its intended product positioning. It should realize that the initial strategy is just the first step in a grander marketing plan for the product's entire life cycle. If the pioneer chooses its launch strategy to make a "killing," it will be sacrificing long-run revenue for the sake of short-run gain. As the pioneer moves through later stages of the life cycle, it will have to continuously formulate new pricing, promotion, and other marketing strategies. It has the best chance of building and retaining market leadership if it plays its cards correctly from the start.

GROWTH STAGE

Growth stage
The product life-cycle stage at which a product's sales start climbing quickly.

If the new product satisfies the market, it will enter a **growth stage,** in which sales will start climbing quickly. The early adopters will continue to buy, and later buyers will start following their lead, especially if they hear favorable word of mouth. Attracted by the opportunities for profit, new competitors will enter the market. They will introduce new product features, and the market will expand. The increase in competitors leads to an increase in the number of distribution outlets, and sales jump just to build reseller inventories. Prices remain where they are or fall only slightly. Companies keep their promotion spending at the same or a slightly higher level. Educating the market remains a goal, but now the company also must meet the competition.

Profits increase during the growth stage, as promotion costs are spread over a large volume and as unit-manufacturing costs fall. The firm uses several strategies to sustain rapid market growth as long as possible. It improves product quality and adds new product features and models. It enters new market segments and new distribution channels. It shifts some advertising from building product awareness to building product conviction and purchase, and it lowers prices at the right time to attract more buyers.

In the growth stage, the firm faces a trade-off between high market share and high current profit. By spending a lot of money on product improvement, promotion, and distribution, the company can capture a dominant position. In doing so, however, it gives up maximum current profit, which it hopes to make up in the next stage.

MATURITY STAGE

Maturity stage
The stage in the product life cycle where sales growth slows or levels off.

At some point, a product's sales growth will slow down, and the product will enter a **maturity stage.** This maturity stage normally lasts longer than the previous

The maturity stage: To sustain growth, Sony keeps adding new features and models to its Walkman and Discman lines—here the CD-ROM Discman. "From rock to rocket science, the Sony Discman takes you down whatever road you want."

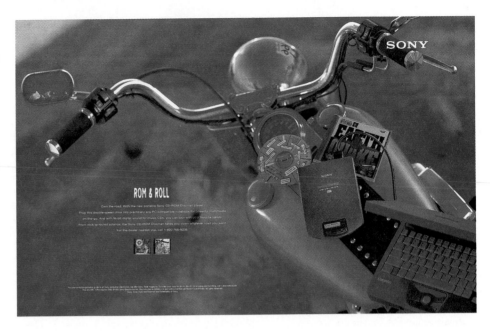

stages, and it poses strong challenges to marketing management. Most products are in the maturity stage of the life cycle, and therefore most of marketing management deals with the mature product.

The slowdown in sales growth results in many producers with many products to sell. In turn, this overcapacity leads to greater competition. Competitors begin marking down prices, increasing their advertising and sales promotions, and upping their R&D budgets to find better versions of the product. These steps lead to a drop in profit. Some of the weaker competitors start dropping out, and the industry eventually contains only well-established competitors.

Although many products in the mature stage appear to remain unchanged for long periods, most successful ones are actually evolving to meet changing consumer needs (see Marketing Highlight 10-3). Product managers should do more than simply ride along with or defend their mature products—a good offense is the best defense. They should consider modifying the market, product, and marketing mix.

Modifying the Market

During this stage, the company tries to increase the consumption of the current product. It looks for new users and market segments, as when Johnson & Johnson targeted the adult market with its baby powder and shampoo. The manager also looks for ways to increase usage among present customers. Campbell does this by offering recipes and convincing consumers that "soup is good food." Or the company may want to reposition the brand to appeal to a larger or faster-growing segment, as Arrow did when it introduced its new line of casual shirts and announced, "We're loosening our collars."

Modifying the Product

The company also can change product characteristics—such as quality, features, or style—to attract new users and to inspire more usage. It might improve the product's quality and performance—its durability, reliability, speed, taste. Or it might add new features that expand the product's usefulness, safety, or convenience. For example, Sony keeps adding new styles and features to its Walkman and Discman lines, and Volvo adds new safety features to its cars. Finally, the company can improve the product's styling and attractiveness. Thus, car

CRAYOLA CRAYONS: A LONG AND COLORFUL LIFE CYCLE

Binney & Smith Company began making crayons down by Bushkill Creek near Easton, Pennsylvania, in 1903. Partner Edwin Binney's wife, Alice, named them Crayola crayons—after the French *craie,* meaning "stick of color," and *ola,* meaning "oil." In the 90-odd years since, Crayola crayons have become a household staple, not just in the United States, but in more than 60 countries around the world, in boxes printed in 11 languages. If you placed all the Crayola crayons made in a single year end to end, they would circle the earth four and a half times.

Few people can forget their first pack of "64s"—64 beauties neatly arranged in the familiar green and yellow flip-top box with a sharpener on the back. The aroma of a freshly opened Crayola box still drives kids into a frenzy and takes members of the older generation back to some of their fondest childhood memories. Binney & Smith, now a subsidiary of Hallmark, dominates the crayon market. Sixty-five percent of all American children between the ages of 2 and 7 pick up a crayon at least once a day and color for an average of 28 minutes. Nearly eighty percent of the time, they pick up a Crayola crayon.

In some ways, Crayola crayons haven't changed much since 1903, when they were sold in an eight-pack for a nickel. Crayola has always been the number one brand, and the crayons are still made by hand in much the same way as then. But a closer look reveals that Binney & Smith has made many adjustments in order to keep the Crayola brand in the mature stage and out of decline. Over the years, the company has added a steady stream of new colors, shapes, sizes, and packages. It increased the number of colors from the original 8 in 1903 (red, yellow, blue, green, orange, black, brown, and white) to 48 in 1949, to 64 in 1958. In 1972, it added 8 fluorescent colors—with hot names like Laser Lemon, Screamin' Green, and Atomic Tangerine; and in

1993, an additional 16 new colors, including macaroni & cheese and purple mountains majesty. Most recently, it created a new line of glow in the dark colors and crayons that change colors. In all, Crayola crayons now come in 96 colors and a variety of packages, including a 96-crayon attache-like case.

Over the years, the Crayola line has grown to include many new sizes and shapes. In addition to the standard 3⅝-inch crayon, it now includes flat, jumbo, and "So Big" crayons. Crayola Washable Crayons were added in 1991. Binney & Smith also extended the Crayola brand to new markets when it developed Crayola Markers and related products. Finally, the company has added several pro-

Crayola's colorful lifecycle: Over the years, Binney & Smith has added a steady stream of new colors, shapes, sizes, and packages.

grams and services to help strengthen its relationships with Crayola customers. For example, in 1984 it began its Dream Makers art education program, a national elementary-school art program design to help students capture their dreams on paper and to support art schools. In 1986, it set up a toll-free 1-800-CRAYOLA hotline to provide better customer service.

Not all of Binney & Smith's life-cycle adjustments have been greeted with open arms by consumers. For example, facing flat sales throughout the 1980s, the company conducted

market research that showed that children were ready to break with tradition in favor of some exciting new colors. They were seeing and wearing brighter colors and wanted to be able to color with them as well. So, in 1990, Binney & Smith retired eight colors from the time-honored box of 64—raw umber, lemon yellow, maize, blue grey, orange yellow, orange red, green blue, and violet blue—into the Crayola Hall of Fame. In their place, it introduced eight more-modern shades—Cerulean, Vivid Tangerine, Jungle Green, Fuchsia, Dandelion, Teal Blue, Royal Purple, and Wild Strawberry. The move unleashed a ground-swell of protest from loyal Crayola users, who formed such organizations as the RUMPS—the Raw Umber and Maize Preservation Society—and the National Committee to Save Lemon Yellow. Binney & Smith received an average of 334 calls a month from concerned customers. Company executives were flabbergasted—"We were aware of the loyalty and nostalgia surrounding Crayola crayons," a spokesperson says, "but we didn't know we [would] hit such a nerve." Still, fans of the new colors outnumbered the protestors, and the new colors are here to stay. However, the company did revive the old standards for one last hurrah in a special collectors tin—it sold all of the 2.5 million tins made. Thus, the Crayola brand continues through its long and colorful life cycle.

Sources: Quote from "Hue and Cry Over Crayola May Revive Old Colors," *Wall Street Journal,* June 14, 1991, p. B1. Also see Margaret O. Kirk, "Coloring Our Children's World Since '03," *Chicago Tribune,* October 29, 1986, Sec. 5, p. 1; Catherine Foster, "Drawing Dreams," *Christian Science Monitor,* June 5, 1989, p. 13; Mike Christiansen, "Waxing Nostalgic: Crayola Retires a Colorful Octet," *Atlanta Constitution,* August 8, 1990, pp. B1, B4; and Ellen Neuborne, "Expansion Goes Outside Crayon Lines," *USA Today,* October 2, 1992, pp. B1, B2.

manufacturers restyle their cars to attract buyers who want a new look. The makers of consumer food and household products introduce new flavors, colors, ingredients, or packages to revitalize consumer buying.

Modifying the Marketing Mix

Marketers also can try to improve sales by changing one or more marketing-mix elements. They can cut prices to attract new users and competitors' customers. They can launch a better advertising campaign or use aggressive sales promotions—trade deals, cents-off, premiums, and contests. The company can also move into larger market channels, using mass merchandisers, if these channels are growing. Finally, the company can offer new or improved services to buyers.

DECLINE STAGE

Decline stage
The product life-cycle stage at which a product's sales decline.

The sales of most product forms and brands eventually dip. The decline may be slow, as in the case of oatmeal cereal; or rapid, as in the case of phonograph records. Sales may plunge to zero, or they may drop to a low level where they continue for many years. This is the **decline stage.**

Sales decline for many reasons, including technological advances, shifts in consumer tastes, and increased competition. As sales and profits decline, some firms withdraw from the market. Those remaining may prune their product offerings. They may drop smaller market segments and marginal trade channels, or they may cut the promotion budget and reduce their prices further.

Carrying a weak product can be very costly to a firm, and not just in profit terms. There are many hidden costs. A weak product may take up too much of management's time. It often requires frequent price and inventory adjustments. It requires advertising and salesforce attention that might be better used to make "healthy" products more profitable. A product's failing reputation can cause customer concerns about the company and its other products. The biggest cost may well lie in the future. Keeping weak products delays the search for replacements, creates a lopsided product mix, hurts current profits, and weakens the company's foothold on the future.

For these reasons, companies need to pay more attention to their aging products. The firm's first task is to identify those products in the decline stage by regularly reviewing sales, market shares, costs, and profit trends. Then, management must decide whether to maintain, harvest, or drop each of these declining products.

Management may decide to *maintain* its brand without change in the hope that competitors will leave the industry. For example, Procter & Gamble made good profits by remaining in the declining liquid-soap business as others withdrew. Or management may decide to reposition the brand in hopes of moving it back into the growth stage of the product life cycle. For instance, after watching sales of its Tostitos tortilla chips plunge 50 percent from their mid-1980s high, Frito-Lay reformulated the chips by doubling their size, changing their shape from round to triangular, and using white corn flour instead of yellow. The new Tostitos Restaurant Style Tortilla Chips have ridden the crest of the recent Tex-Mex food craze's record revenues.

Management may decide to *harvest* the product, which means reducing various costs (plant and equipment, maintenance, R&D, advertising, salesforce) and hoping that sales hold up. If successful, harvesting will increase the company's profits in the short run. Or management may decide to *drop* the product from the line. It can sell it to another firm or simply liquidate it at salvage value. If the company plans to find a buyer, it will not want to run down the product through harvesting.

Table 10-4 summarizes the key characteristics of each stage of the product life cycle. The table also lists the marketing objectives and strategies for each stage.[13]

TABLE 10-4 *Summary of Product Life-Cycle Characteristics, Objectives, and Strategies*

	INTRODUCTION	GROWTH	MATURITY	DECLINE
Characteristics				
Sales	Low sales	Rapidly rising sales	Peak sales	Declining sales
Costs	High cost per customer	Average cost per customer	Low cost per customer	Low cost per customer
Profits	Negative	Rising profits	High profits	Declining profits
Customers	Innovators	Early adopters	Middle majority	Laggards
Competitors	Few	Growing number	Stable number beginning to decline	Declining number
Marketing Objectives				
	Create product awareness and trial	Maximize market share	Maximize profit while defending market share	Reduce expenditure and milk the brand
Strategies				
Product	Offer a basic product	Offer product extensions, service, warranty	Diversify brand and models	Phase out weak items
Price	Use cost-plus	Price to penetrate market	Price to match or best competitors	Cut price
Distribution	Build selective distribution	Build intensive distribution	Build more intensive distribution	Go selective: phase out unprofitable outlets
Advertising	Build product awareness among early adopters and dealers	Build awareness and interest in the mass market	Stress brand differences and benefits	Reduce to level needed to retain hard-core loyals
Sales Promotion	Use heavy sales promotion to entice trial	Reduce to take advantage of heavy consumer demand	Increase to encourage brand switching	Reduce to minimal level

Source: Philip Kotler, *Marketing Management: Analysis, Planning, Implementation, and Control*, 8th ed. (Englewood Cliffs, NJ: Prentice Hall, 1994), p. 365.

Summary

Organizations must develop an effective new product development strategy. Their current products face limited life spans and must be replaced by newer products. But new products can fail—the risks of innovation are as great as the rewards. The key to successful innovation lies in a total-company effort, strong planning, and a systematic new-product development process.

The *new-product development process* consists of eight sequential stages, and at each stage the company must decide whether the idea should be further developed or dropped. The company wants to minimize the chances of a poor idea moving forward, but must balance this with an effort not to reject good ideas too early. A new product starts with *idea generation*, which may draw inspiration from internal sources, customers, competitors, or distributors, suppliers, and others. Next comes *idea screening*, which reduces the number of ideas based on the company's own criteria. Ideas that pass the screening phase continue through *concept development and testing.* Strong concepts will then proceed to *marketing strategy development* and *business analysis,* which are the final conceptual stages. With positive results here, the ideas become more concrete through *product development, test marketing,* and finally *commercialization.*

For each offering, a company must develop a *product life-cycle strategy.* Each product has a life cycle marked by a changing set of problems and opportunities. The sales of a typical product follow an S-shaped curve made up of five stages. The cycle begins with the *product-development stage* when the company finds and develops a new-product idea. If the product idea is pursued further, it is pushed into distribution during the *introduction stage,* which is marked by slow growth and low profits. If successful, the product enters a *growth stage* which offers rapid sales growth and increasing profits. During this stage, the company tries to improve the product, enter new market segments and distribution channels, and reduce its prices slightly. Next comes a *maturity stage* when sales growth slows down and profits stabilize. The company seeks strategies and programs to extend this stage by renewing sales growth, including market, product, and marketing-mix modification. Finally, the product enters a *decline stage* in which sales and profits dwindle. The company's task in this stage is to recognize the decline, and to decide whether the product should be maintained, harvested, or dropped. If the product is discontinued, it may be sold to another firm or liquidated for salvage value.

Key Terms

Business analysis	Idea generation	Product development
Commercialization	Idea screening	Product life cycle (PLC)
Concept testing	Introduction stage	Sequential product development
Decline stage	Marketing strategy development	Simultaneous product development
Fads	Maturity stage	Style
Fashion	New-product development	Test marketing
Growth stage	Product concept	

Discussing the Issues

1. Before videotape cameras were available for home use, Polaroid introduced Polavision, a system for making home movies that did not require laboratory processing. Like most other home-movie systems, Polavision film cassettes lasted only a few minutes and did not record sound. Despite the advantage of "instant developing" and heavy promotional expenditures by Polaroid, Polavision never gained wide acceptance. Discuss why you think Polavision flopped, given Polaroid's previous record of new product successes.

2. Less than one third of new product ideas come from the customer. Does this low percentage conflict with the marketing concept's philosophy of "find a need and fill it"? Why or why not?

3. Many companies have formal new product development systems and committees. Yet one recent study found that most successful new products were those that had been kept away from the formal system. Suggest reasons why might this be true.

4. List several factors you would consider in choosing cities for test marketing a new snack. Would where you live be a good test market? Why or why not?

5. Test market results for a new product are usually better than the business results the same brand achieves after it is launched. Name some reasons for this.

6. Recent evidence suggests that consuming oatmeal, and especially oat bran, may be helpful in reducing people's levels of cholesterol. Explain what impacts this health benefit could have on the life cycle of oatmeal and oat-based products.

Applying the Concepts

1. List at least 10 new product ideas for your favorite fast-food chain. Out of all these ideas, which ones (if any) do you think would have a good chance of succeeding? What percentage of your ideas did you rate as having a good chance of success? [Divide the number of potentially successful ideas by the total number of ideas you listed, and multiply the result by 100 to get a percentage.] Can you explain why the potentially successful ideas seem stronger?

2. Go to the grocery store and make a list of 15 items that appear to be new products. Rate each product for its level of innovation, with a 10 being extremely novel and highly innovative, and a 1 being a very minor change such as an improved package or fragrance. How truly new and innovative are these products overall? Do you think companies are being risk averse because "pioneers are the ones who get shot"?

References

1. See Russell Mitchell, "Masters of Innovation: How 3M Keeps Its New Products Coming," *Business Week,* April 10, 1989, pp. 58–64; Ronald A. Mitsch, "Three Roads to Innovation," *The Journal of Business Strategy,* September/October 1990, pp. 18–21; Gregory E. David, "Product Development: Minnesota Mining & Manufacturing," *Financial World,* September 28, 1993, p. 58; and William Keenan Jr., "Getting Customers into the Act," *Sales & Marketing Management,* February 1995, pp. 58–63.

2. Kevin J. Clancy and Robert S. Shulman, *The Marketing Revolution: A Radical Manifesto for Dominating the Marketplace* (New York: Harper Business, 1991), p. 6; and Robert G. Cooper, "New Product Success in Industrial Firms," *Industrial Marketing Management,* 1992, pp. 215–223. Also see Gary Strauss, "Building on Brand Names: Companies Freshen Old Product Lines," *USA Today,* March 20, 1992, pp. B1, B2.

3. See Christopher Power, "Flops," *Business Week,* August 16, 1993, pp. 76–82, here p. 77.

4. Robert G. Cooper and Elko J. Kleinschmidt, *New Product: The Key Factors in Success* (Chicago: American Marketing Association, 1990).

5. See Leigh Lawton and A. Parasuraman, "So You Want Your New Product Planning to Be Productive," *Business Horizons,* December 1980, pp. 29–34. The percentages in this section add to more than 100 because more than one source was named for some products in the study.

6. For this and other examples, see Jennifer Reese, "Getting Hot Ideas from Customers," *Fortune,* May 18, 1992, pp. 86–87.

7. Russell Mitchell, "How Ford Hit the Bullseye with Taurus," *Business Week,* June 30, 1986, pp. 69–70; "Copycat Stuff? Hardly!" *Business Week,* September 14, 1987, p. 112; and Jeremy Main, "How to Steal the Best Ideas Around," *Fortune,* October 19, 1992, pp. 102–106.

8. For more on product concept testing, see William L. Moore, "Concept Testing," *Journal of Business Research,* Vol. 10, 1982, pp. 279–294; and David A. Schwartz, "Concept Testing Can Be Improved—and Here's How," *Marketing News,* January 6, 1984, pp. 22–23.

9. Julie Franz, "Test Marketing: Traveling Through a Maze of Choices," *Advertising Age,* February 13, 1986, p. 11.

10. See Howard Schlossberg, "IRI, Nielsen Slug It Out in 'Scanning Wars,'" *Marketing News,* September 2, 1991, pp. 1, 47.

11. Jennifer Lawrence, "P&G Rushes on Global Diaper Rollout," *Advertising Age,* October 14, 1991, p. 6; and Bill Saporito, "Behind the Tumult at P&G," *Fortune,* March 7, 1994, pp. 75–82.

12. See George S. Day, "The Product Life Cycle: Analysis and Applications Issues," *Journal of Marketing,* Fall 1981, pp. 60–67; John E. Swan and David R. Rink, "Fitting Marketing Strategy to Varying Life Cycles," *Business Horizons,* January–February 1982, pp. 72–76; and Sak Onkvisit and John J. Shaw, "Competition and Product Management: Can the Product Life Cycle Help?" *Business Horizons,* July–August 1986, pp. 51–62.

13. For a more comprehensive discussion of marketing strategies over the course of the product life cycle, see Philip Kotler, *Marketing Management,* 8th ed. (Englewood Cliffs, NJ: Prentice Hall, 1994), Chap. 14.

Company Case 10

POLAROID: TAKING VISION TO THE MARKETPLACE

Edwin Land, Polaroid's founder, had a personal motto: "Don't do anything that someone else can do. Don't undertake a project unless it is manifestly important and nearly impossible."

Land lived by this motto. In 1937, he started Polaroid Corporation in a Cambridge, Massachusetts, garage and developed the polarization process. In 1943, as he vacationed with his family in Santa Fe, New Mexico, his three-year-old daughter asked why she could not see right away the picture he had just taken of her. Within an hour, Land had developed a mental picture of the camera, the film, and the chemistry that would allow him to solve the puzzle his daughter had presented. In 1948, Land introduced the first Polaroid instant camera. By the time he stepped down as the company's chief executive officer in 1980, at age 70, he had built Polaroid into a $1.4 billion company. When he died in 1991, he left behind 537 patents, second in number only to Thomas A. Edison.

William McCune, Jr., followed Land as Polaroid's chairman. McCune felt that the company needed to move away from its dependence on amateur instant photography. McCune led Polaroid's diversification effort, moving into disk drives, fiber optics, video recorders, inkjet printers, and floppy disks. But by the mid-1980s, some observers argued that the diversification effort was not paying off.

However, sales to amateur photographers and sales of instant cameras for business use were going strong. By 1986, these sales accounted for 55 percent of Polaroid's revenues. Consumers were still interested in instant cameras. To stimulate that demand, Polaroid introduced the Spectra camera in 1986, its first major new camera since the SX-70 in 1972. Some observers predicted that the new camera, priced at $150 to $225, was too expensive and would not sell. It sold anyway.

Edwin Land probably felt somewhat vindicated that his former company was refocusing on its core business, amateur instant photography. But Land and Polaroid knew that the company faced severe competition in this market. Video camcorders, easy-to-ease 35mm single-lens-reflex (SLR) cameras, and one-hour film developing were cutting deeply into Polaroid's market. Sales of instant cameras had fallen from a peak of 13 million units in 1978 to 4.5 million in 1990. The new 35mm cameras were outselling instant cameras five to one. Polaroid realized that it had to do something to reinvigorate the amateur photography market and to expand its base.

NEW-PRODUCT DEVELOPMENT AT POLAROID

In the 1940s and 1950s, Edwin Land gave implied approval to a product development process called "skunkworks." This process allowed maverick individuals or groups to pursue new-roduct design ideas unofficially and often in secret. These individuals or groups frequently generated technology-driven new-product designs. However, they developed these designs with little consideration for marketing or business strategy. Further, operating managers often had only limited influence over the design of machinery. Film and camera development followed parallel paths. Development of the film pack occurred after development of the film components. This development process invariably resulted in major problems when managers tried to get all the parts to work together.

In 1984, a skunkworks team from camera engineering began discussing Polaroid's next camera, and a team from film research began to work on possibilities for a new film. The two groups met unofficially to share ideas. These "blue sky" meetings focused on the big problems of picture quality, film cost, and camera size. The groups soon narrowed their discussions to a film that would fit a smaller camera. They also decided that the new camera should store pictures internally rather than automatically ejecting them as did other Polaroid cameras.

Unlike some skunkworks groups, these two groups sought marketing's input. In 1984 and 1985, Polaroid's internal market research group conducted focus groups to get consumer reactions to small, medium, and standard-sized instant cameras with picture storage features. The focus groups suggested that some customers would be interested in the smaller camera and its smaller pictures. Polaroid president MacAllister Booth asked his assistant, Roger Clapp, to investigate the idea.

THE JOSHUA STORY

Enter Joshua. Even as Polaroid introduced the Spectra camera in 1986, Booth, who had just assumed the CEO's position, realized that the company had to continue work on its next new camera. Booth asked Hal Page, Polaroid's vice-president for quality, to become program manager for the next consumer camera. For the first time, Polaroid had a single, high-level program manager responsible for all aspects of new-product development—for film as well as camera, for manufacturing as well as marketing.

Page began a year-long process of reexamination to generate ideas for a new camera. He started brainstorming sessions by showing a training film that featured a cartoon character named Joshua. In the film, Joshua finds himself trapped in a box and tries all the obvious ways to escape. Finally, in frustration, Joshua gently taps his finger against the box's wall and unexpectedly finds that his finger has poked a hole in the wall. He struggles to make the hole bigger and escapes.

Joshua sent a message to the hundreds of people from many functional groups who attended Page's brainstorming sessions. To generate truly innovative ideas for a new camera, the employees would have to attack new problems with new ways of thinking—"out-of-the-box" approaches. To create something other than an extension of Polaroid's existing cameras, people would have to think creatively and give up old prejudices.

Hal Page also showed the groups a film that dramatically illustrated the value of internal picture storage for the new camera. The film showed people at Disney World using 35mm automatic cameras to take picture after picture, while others stood around watching their one Polaroid picture develop and struggled to find a place to put it. Page and others thought consumers would take more pictures if they did not have to stop after each one to find a place to put it while it developed. Further, consumers would damage and lose fewer pictures.

Page also used outside marketing consultants. Based on studies of small cameras that Polaroid had conducted during 1984 to 1986, the consultants concluded that there would be a market for a small camera and that the camera would not cannibalize Polaroid's existing lines. Additional outside studies in 1987 and 1988 examined consumer preferences regarding camera size, camera price, and film price. Another study estimated the sales volume that Polaroid could expect from various feature combinations.

Polaroid had based these studies on the assumption that would price the new camera at $150. As the studies progressed, however, management concluded that the market at the $150 price would be too small and that it should price the camera around $100. This change required more market studies.

In 1988, Hal Page left Polaroid, and Roger Clapp took over what employees had dubbed the "Joshua Program." Although Page and his groups had made much progress, many technical and marketing hurdles remained. Design engineers faced many trade-offs between size and other features, such as performance and cost. Roger Clapp stopped the design process and ordered the developers to reconsider all trade-offs.

As Clapp's managers reviewed the Joshua project, it became apparent that they needed to clarify the lower-priced camera's market potential and to conduct new research to get marketing fully behind the program. Finally, the managers agreed that the last market research hurdle would be an "Assessor Test" conducted by Professor Glenn Urban of MIT's Sloan School of Management.

The Assessor Test involved setting up mock stores at five geographically diverse sites across the country. These stores offered 25 different cameras (both Polaroid and competing models), with prices ranging from inexpensive to expensive. Each store had a real counter, a film rack, feature cards, and sales clerks to answer questions. As a part of the interview process, the researchers created full-color sheets of print advertising for the new camera. Polaroid also developed a realistic Joshua camera model. Over a one-month period, 2,400 people participated in market interviews and testing at the five stores. Researchers carefully screened participants on factors such as age, sex, race, and economic status to make sure the group represented demographics of the U.S. population as a whole.

The studies provided convincing evidence that there was a market for a small instant camera. Polaroid gave Joshua the go-ahead in late 1989.

VISION TO REALITY

Although Polaroid had devoted an extraordinary amount of time and energy to the Joshua project before its approval in late 1989, the camera and the film were still in development. Polaroid employees throughout the company still had to solve many problems.

Manufacturing had to install a new computer-aided-design system (CAD) and to select a new material and design for the camera's mainframe. The camera would employ through-the-lens viewing, the same viewing system found on millions of 35mm cameras. The picture storage compartment would have to hold up to all ten pictures in a film package. And the camera would have to pass Polaroid's four-foot drop test.

Polaroid created a cross-functional steering committee to manage the film-manufacturing process. This team addressed problems such as how to include the battery in the film pack and how to design the film-manufacturing process itself. Like Polaroid's other instant film, Joshua's film would come in a package of ten exposures and would cost the consumer about $1.00 per picture, as compared to about $.40 for a conventional 35mm picture. The picture would be about 2 $\frac{1}{8}$" by 2 $\frac{7}{8}$", smaller than conventional 35mm prints.

Electronics engineers designed a new microcontroller to be the heart of the Joshua camera. The new controller solved many longstanding technical and manufacturing problems. Using software, it provided features to measure the light available for the picture, set the exposure, and find the distance from the camera to the subject. In other words, like many of the 35mm cameras on the market, Joshua would have "automatic everything." In all of these processes, managers insisted on meeting the highest quality and reliability standards.

By Labor Day, 1991, the Joshua team had produced 24 Joshua prototype cameras for testing by Polaroid employees over the holiday weekend. For Christmas, 1991, the team produced 300 Joshua cameras for non-Polaroid employees from coast to coast to test. This test represented the earliest time in a product's development that Polaroid had ever placed cameras with outside users. Polaroid also conducted market tests in foreign countries. Polaroid calculated that, by the time it announced the camera, more than 2,000 Polaroid and non-Polaroid consumers would have made more than 55,000 images for picture analysis.

LAUNCHING THE VISION

The company decided to introduce the new camera at the September 1992 Photokina trade show. Photokina, the world's largest photographic trade show, is held every two years in Cologne, Germany. Approximately 200,000 visitors from 150 countries attend the show. Because Polaroid had decided to market the camera first in Germany, Photokina represented the perfect place to introduce the camera. This decision itself represented a significant departure from Polaroid's previous practice of going for the big splash by selling in the United States first. After Germany, Polaroid would introduce the camera in other European countries and then in Japan in early 1993. It would not bring the camera to the U.S. market until the late summer of 1993.

This sequential introduction would allow the product team to accelerate production gradually through successive launches in discrete international markets. By the time the company took Joshua to the U.S. market, it would have had a chance to work out any production problems and to build up production quantities to the much higher volume that the U.S. market required.

Still, before introduction, the camera needed a name for the marketplace. The name had to make sense in at least 11 languages. Polaroid selected the name Vision, a name that conveyed the essence of Polaroid's spirit and mission. The company would use this name for the camera in the European market.

Reflecting on the Vision's development, Roger Clapp noted that the team approach Polaroid used in developing Vision "is part of a larger corporate initiative in which manufacturing and development has been aligned with marketing early on in the process to allow us to get high-quality products to market much quicker and with much less effort."

Clapp knows, however, that as Vision rolls across Europe and Japan toward the U.S. market, his team must continue to learn and to revise its marketing plans. Already, the team has decided to use the name, Captiva, for the camera in the U.S. market. Given that Polaroid had established distribution in the U.S. market and that it has made its other product and pricing decisions, Polaroid must still decide how to promote the Captiva so that it will spur the continued growth of the amateur instant photography market.

QUESTIONS

1. Compare Polaroid's traditional new-product development process with the process it followed for Joshua. Would you predict that Joshua (Vision) will be more successful than a product developed under the traditional system? Why or why not?

2. As it worked on the Joshua project, did Polaroid do a good job of following the text's eight-step product development process? How could Polaroid improve this process for future products?

3. Whom should Polaroid target with its U.S. promotion campaign for the Captiva, and what promotional ideas would you recommend to Polaroid for developing interest in its new product?

Sources: Subrata N. Chakravarty, "The Vindication of Edwin Land," *Forbes,* May 4, 1987, pp. 83–84; Frances Westley and Henry Mintzberg, "Visionary Leadership and Strategic Management," *Strategic Management Journal,* Vol. 10, 1989, pp. 17–32; Jane Poss, "Edwin Land Dead at 81," *Boston Globe,* March 2, 1991, p. 1; Joseph Pereira, "Polaroid Points a Smaller Instant Camera at 35mm Users," *Wall Street Journal,* September 11, 1992, p. B1. The majority of this case is adapted from articles in *Viewpoint,* a publication of Polaroid's Internal Communications department, October 1992 issue, especially "The Joshua Story: Polaroid Takes its Vision to the Marketplace." Used with permission of Polaroid Corporation.

Pricing Products

PRICING CONSIDERATIONS AND APPROACHES

Sears's pricing strategies have played a major role in the company's ups and downs over the course of ten decades. Sears originally became America's largest retailer by offering quality merchandise at affordable prices. In the late 1960s, however, the company decided to upgrade its merchandise and raise prices. When higher prices caused many loyal shoppers to switch to lower-priced competitors, Sears began using weekly price-off sales to make its prices more competitive. Despite this strategy of continuous sales, however, Sears continued to lose customers to Wal-Mart, Kmart, and other discounters. Its market share slid 33 percent during the 1980s, and America's largest retailer found itself in big trouble.

In the spring of 1989, in what it called the biggest change in its 102-year history, Sears launched a bold new pricing strategy. Scrapping its decades-old weekly sales approach, it adopted a no-sales, *everyday low-price* strategy. Sears closed all of its 824 stores for 42 hours and retagged every piece of merchandise, slashing prices by as much as 50 percent. In its biggest-ever advertising campaign, the huge retailer proclaimed, "We've lowered our prices on over 50,000 items! Sears: your money's worth and a whole lot more."

Sears bet that its new everyday low-price strategy would pull consumers back into its stores and revive sagging profits. And at first, sales did surge under the new pricing policy. But the ploy involved many risks, and after the initial fanfare died down, Sears's sales and profits began to decline once more. To be successful with everyday low *prices*, Sears first had to achieve everyday low *costs*. However, its costs traditionally had run much higher than those of its competitors. With its bloated cost structure, the price slashing left Sears with paper-thin margins, causing profits to fall. Beyond cost problems, Sears faced the even tougher problem of trying to change consumer perceptions of its prices and practices. For decades, Sears had conditioned customers to "hold out" for its traditional price-off sales. The rapid switch to a one-price policy and everyday low-price position confused consumers. Moreover, consumers who were being assaulted by everyday low-price claims from many retailers were no longer paying much attention to such claims.

OBJECTIVES

When you finish this chapter, you should be able to accomplish the following:

1. Outline the **internal factors affecting pricing decisions**, especially **marketing objectives**, **marketing-mix strategy**, **costs**, and **organizational considerations**.

2. Identify and define the **external factors affecting pricing decisions**, including the effects of the **market** and **demand**, **competitors' costs**, **prices**, and **offers**, and **other external factors**.

3. Contrast the differences in **general pricing approaches**, and be able to distinguish among **cost-plus** and **target profit pricing**, **value-based pricing**, and **going-rate** and **sealed-bid pricing**.

Worse yet, surveys showed that consumers simply did not believe Sears's new prices *were* the lowest in the marketplace.

By early 1990, after only ten months, Sears' everyday low-price strategy appeared to be on the way out. The company began to phase in a new strategy that put less emphasis on price and more on "value," returning to its traditional strengths—reliability, merchandise return, and "satisfaction guaranteed" policies. And it began again to feature major sales events in an attempt to rekindle consumer excitement and buying. In 1991, after decades as industry sales leader, Sears slid to number three behind new market leader Wal-Mart and number two Kmart. By 1994, despite deep cost cutting that resulted in improved profits, coupled with a exciting and creative new "Come see the softer side of Sears" advertising campaign, the company's price positioning remained clouded for most consumers.

Thus, Sears continues to search for the right pricing strategy. How well the huge retailer handles its pricing and related problems will dramatically affect its sales and profits—perhaps even its survival.[1]

All profit organizations and many nonprofit organizations must set prices on their products or services. *Price* goes by many names:

> Price is all around us. You pay *rent* for your apartment, *tuition* for your education, and a *fee* to your physician or dentist. The airline, railway, taxi, and bus companies charge you a *fare;* the local utilities call their price a *rate;* and the local bank charges you *interest* for the money you borrow. The price for driving your car on Florida's Sunshine Parkway is a *toll,* and the company that insures your car charges you a *premium.* The guest lecturer charges an *honorarium* to tell you about a government official who took a *bribe* to help a shady character steal *dues* collected by a trade association. Clubs or societies to which you belong may make a special *assessment* to pay unusual expenses. Your regular lawyer may ask for a *retainer* to cover her services. The "price" of an executive is a *salary,* the price of a salesperson may be a *commission,* and the price of a worker is a *wage.* Finally, although economists would disagree, many of us feel that *income taxes* are the price we pay for the privilege of making money.[2]

Price
The amount of money charged for a product or service, or the sum of the values that consumers exchange for the benefits of having or using the product or service.

In the narrowest sense, **price** is the amount of money charged for a product or service. More broadly, price is the sum of all the values that consumers exchange for the benefits of having or using the product or service.

How are prices set? Historically, prices usually were set by buyers and sellers bargaining with each other. Sellers would ask for a higher price than they expected to get, and buyers would offer less than they expected to pay. Through bargaining, they would arrive at an acceptable price. Individual buyers paid different prices for the same products, depending on their needs and bargaining skills.

Today, most sellers set *one* price for *all* buyers. This idea was helped along by the development of large-scale retailing at the end of the nineteenth century. F. W. Woolworth, Tiffany and Co., John Wanamaker, J. L. Hudson, and others advertised a "strictly one-price policy" because they carried so many items and had so many employees.

Historically, price has been the major factor affecting buyer choice. This is still true in poorer nations, among poorer groups, and with commodity products. However, nonprice factors have become more important in buyer-choice behavior in recent decades.

Price is the only element in the marketing mix that produces revenue; all other elements represent costs. Price is also one of the most flexible elements of the marketing mix. Unlike product features and channel commitments, price can be changed quickly. At the same time, pricing and price competition is the number-one problem facing many marketing executives. Yet, many companies do not handle pricing well. The most common mistakes are: pricing that is too cost oriented; prices that are not revised often enough to reflect market changes; pricing that does not take the rest of the marketing mix into account; and prices that are not varied enough for different products, market segments, and purchase occasions.

In this and the next chapter, we focus on the problem of setting prices. This chapter looks at the factors marketers must consider when setting prices and at general pricing approaches. In the next chapter, we examine pricing strategies for new-product pricing, product mix pricing, price changes, and price adjustments for buyer and situational factors.

FACTORS TO CONSIDER WHEN SETTING PRICES

A company's pricing decisions are affected both by internal company factors and external environmental factors (see Figure 11-1).[3]

INTERNAL FACTORS AFFECTING PRICING DECISIONS

Internal factors affecting pricing include the company's marketing objectives, marketing-mix strategy, costs, and organization.

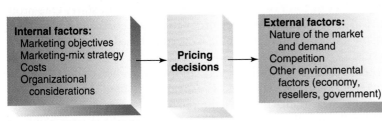

FIGURE 11-1 *Factors affecting price decisions*

Marketing Objectives

Before setting price, the company must decide on its strategy for the product. If the company has selected its target market and positioning carefully, then its marketing-mix strategy, including price, will be fairly straightforward. For example, if General Motors decides to produce a new sports car to compete with European sports cars in the high-income segment, this suggests charging a high price. Motel 6, Econo Lodge, and Red Roof Inn have positioned themselves as motels that provide economical rooms for budget-minded travelers; this position requires charging a low price. Thus, pricing strategy is largely determined by decisions on market positioning.

At the same time, the company may seek additional objectives. The clearer a firm is about its objectives, the easier it is to set price. Examples of common objectives are *survival, current profit maximization, market-share leadership,* and *product-quality leadership.*

Companies set *survival* as their major objective if they are troubled by too much capacity, heavy competition, or changing consumer wants. To keep a plant going, a company may set a low price, hoping to increase demand. In this case, profits are less important than survival. As long as their prices cover variable costs and some fixed costs, they can stay in business. However, survival is only a short-term objective. In the long run, the firm must learn how to add value or face extinction.

Many companies use *current profit maximization* as their pricing goal. They estimate what demand and costs will be at different prices and choose the price that will produce the maximum current profit, cash flow, or return on investment. In all cases, the company wants current financial results rather than long-run performance. Other companies want to obtain *market-share leadership.* They believe that the company with the largest market share will enjoy the lowest costs and highest long-run profit. To become the market-share leader, these firms set prices as low as possible. A variation of this objective is to pursue a specific market-

Sub-Zero charges a premium price for its custom-made refrigerators to attain product-quality leadership.

share gain. Suppose the company wants to increase its market share from 10 percent to 15 percent in one year. It will search for the price and marketing program that will achieve this goal.

A company might decide that it wants to achieve *product-quality leadership*. This normally calls for charging a high price to cover such quality and the high cost of R&D. For example, Sub-Zero makes the Rolls-Royce of refrigerators—custom-made, built-in units that look more like hardwood cabinets or pieces of furniture than refrigerators. By offering the highest quality, Sub-Zero sells more than $50 million worth of fancy refrigerators a year, priced at up to $3,000 each. Similarly, Pitney Bowes pursues a product-quality leadership strategy for its fax equipment. While Sharp, Canon, and other competitors fight over the low-price fax machine market with machines selling at around $500, Pitney Bowes targets large corporations with machines selling at about $5,000. As a result, it captures some 45 percent of the large-corporation fax niche.[4]

A company also might use price to attain other more specific objectives. It can set prices low to prevent competition from entering the market or set prices at competitors' levels to stabilize the market. Prices can be set to keep the loyalty and support of resellers or to avoid government intervention. Prices can be reduced temporarily to create excitement for a product or to draw more customers into a retail store. One product may be priced to help the sales of other products in the company's line. Thus, pricing may play an important role in helping to accomplish the company's objectives at many levels.

Nonprofit and public organizations may adopt a number of other pricing objectives. A university aims for *partial cost recovery,* knowing that it must rely on private gifts and public grants to cover the remaining costs. A nonprofit hospital may aim for *full cost recovery* in its pricing. A nonprofit theater company may price its productions to fill the maximum number of theater seats. A social service agency may set a *social price* geared to the varying income situations of different clients.

Marketing-Mix Strategy

Price is only one of the marketing-mix tools that a company uses to achieve its marketing objectives. Price decisions must be coordinated with product design, distribution, and promotion decisions to form a consistent and effective marketing program. Decisions made for other marketing-mix variables may affect pricing decisions. For example, producers using many resellers who are expected to support and promote their products may have to build larger reseller margins into their prices. The decision to position the product on high performance quality will mean that the seller must charge a higher price to cover higher costs.

Companies often make their pricing decisions first and then base other marketing-mix decisions on the prices they want to charge. Here, price is a crucial product positioning factor that defines the product's market, competition, and design. The intended price determines what product features can be offered and what production costs can be incurred.

Many firms support such price-positioning strategies with a technique called *target costing,* a potent strategic weapon. Target costing reverses the usual process of first designing a new product, determining its cost, and then asking "Can we sell it for that?" Instead, it starts with a target cost and works back. Compaq Computer Corporation calls this process "design to price." After being battered for years by lower-priced rivals, Compaq used this approach to create its highly successful, lower-priced Prolinea personal computer line. Starting with a price tar-

Target costing: In creating its highly successful, lower-priced Prolinea line, Compaq started with a target price set by marketing and profit-margin goals from management. Then the design team determined what costs had to be in order to charge the target price.

get set by marketing, and with profit-margin goals from management, the Prolinea design team determined what costs had to be in order to charge the target price. From this crucial calculation all else followed. To achieve target costs, the design team negotiated doggedly with all the company departments responsible for different aspects of the new product, and with outside suppliers of needed parts and materials. Compaq engineers designed a machine with fewer and simpler parts, manufacturing overhauled its factories to reduce production costs, and suppliers found ways to provide quality components at needed prices. By meeting its target *costs*, Compaq was able to set its target *price* and establish the desired price position. As a result, Prolinea sales and profits soared.[5]

Other companies deemphasize price and use other marketing-mix tools to create *nonprice* positions. Often, the best strategy is not to charge the lowest price, but rather to differentiate the marketing offer to make it worth a higher price. For example, for years Johnson Controls, a producer of climate control systems for office buildings, used initial price as its primary competitive tool. However, research showed that customers were more concerned about the total cost of installing and maintaining a system than about its initial price. Repairing broken systems was expensive, time-consuming, and risky. Customers had to shut down the heat or air conditioning in the whole building, disconnect a lot of wires, and face the dangers of electrocution. Johnson decided to change its strategy. It designed an entirely new system called Metasys. To repair the new system, customers need only pull out an old plastic module and slip in a new one—no tools required. Metasys costs more to make than the old system, and customers pay a higher initial price, but it costs less to install and maintain. Despite its higher asking price, the new Metasys system brought in $500 million in revenues in its first year.[6]

Thus, the marketer must consider the total marketing mix when setting prices. If the product is positioned on nonprice factors, then decisions about quality, promotion, and distribution will strongly affect price. If price is a crucial positioning factor, then price will strongly affect decisions made about the other marketing-mix elements. However, even when featuring price, marketers need to remember that customers rarely buy on price alone. Instead, they seek products which give them the best value in terms of benefits received for the price paid.

Thus, in most cases, the company will consider price along with all the other marketing-mix elements when developing the marketing program (see Marketing Highlight 11-1).

Costs

Costs set the floor for the price that the company can charge for its product. The company wants to charge a price that both covers all its costs for producing, distributing, and selling the product and delivers a fair rate of return for its effort and risk. A company's costs may be an important element in its pricing strategy. Many companies work to become the "low-cost producers" in their industries. Companies with lower costs can set lower prices that result in greater sales and profits.

Fixed costs
Costs that do not vary with production or sales level.

Variable costs
Costs that vary directly with the level of production.

Total costs
The sum of the fixed and variable costs for any given level of production.

TYPES OF COSTS. A company's costs take two forms, fixed and variable. **Fixed costs** (also known as overhead) are costs that do not vary with production or sales level. For example, a company must pay each month's bills for rent, heat, interest, and executive salaries, whatever the company's output.

Variable costs vary directly with the level of production. Each personal computer produced by Compaq involves a cost of computer chips, wires, plastic, packaging, and other inputs. These costs tend to be the same for each unit produced. They are called *variable* because their total varies with the number of units produced.

Total costs are the sum of the fixed and variable costs for any given level of production. Management wants to charge a price that will at least cover the total production costs at a given level of production. The company must watch its costs carefully. If it costs the company more than competitors to produce and sell its product, the company will have to charge a higher price or make less profit, putting it at a competitive disadvantage.

COSTS AT DIFFERENT LEVELS OF PRODUCTION. To price wisely, management needs to know how its costs vary with different levels of production. For example, suppose Texas Instruments (TI) has built a plant to produce 1,000 hand-held calculators per day. Figure 11-2A shows the typical short-run average cost curve (SRAC). It shows that the cost per calculator is high if TI's factory produces only a few per day. But as production moves up to 1,000 calculators per day, average cost falls. This is because fixed costs are spread over more units, with each one bearing a smaller fixed cost. TI can try to produce more than 1,000 calculators per day, but average costs will increase because the plant becomes inefficient. Workers have to wait for machines, the machines break down more often, and workers get in each other's way.

If TI believed it could sell 2,000 calculators a day, it should consider building a larger plant. The plant would use more efficient machinery and work arrangements. Also, the unit cost of producing 2,000 calculators per day would be

FIGURE 11-2 *Cost per unit at different levels of production per period*

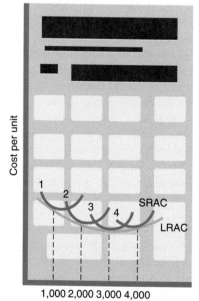

A. Cost behavior in a fixed-size plant

B. Cost behavior over different-size plants

CARMAX: GOOD PRICES AND A WHOLE LOT MORE

Would you buy a used car from this . . . er, retail store? Circuit City, the nation's leading consumer electronics and appliance retailer, thinks that you will. Its new CarMax Auto Superstores are a far cry from the usual, sometimes less than reputable, used car lot. The first CarMax, in Richmond, VA, is located on a sprawling 12-acre site filled with 500 used but still gleaming cars, trucks, and minivans. As you might expect, given Circuit City's low-price guarantees, price figures prominently into CarMax's positioning—it promises "no-haggle, below-book prices." However, unlike Circuit City stores, CarMax does not claim to charge the *lowest* prices. Instead, price is only a part—and perhaps not even the most important part—of a broader mix of values that CarMax delivers to its customers.

More than a dozen years ago, when Circuit City first opened, the highly fragmented consumer electronics industry evoked images of sleazy salespeople, bait-and-switch promotions, and high-pressure selling. Although chains like Mad Man Muntz and Crazy Eddie sold at low prices, they left many customers uneasy. Had they gotten the best value? Would the store stand behind its products? With its large and modern stores, wide selection of goods, knowledgeable salespeople, liberal returns policies, and affordable financing, Circuit City brought new respectability to consumer electronics and appliance retailing.

Now, CarMax faces a similar situation in the used car market—a highly fragmented industry and strong consumer concerns about reliability. Research shows that, when buying a used car, 40 percent of consumers have a question about the reputation of the dealer. Circuit City wants to bring the same respectability to used-car retailing that it brought to consumer electronics. It wants customers to be able to buy used cars from CarMax with the same ease and

peace of mind that they can purchase television sets, personal computers, camcorders, and refrigerators from Circuit City superstores.

Buying a used car from CarMax is a dramatically different experience. CarMax offers a large selection of cars, without a clunker in the bunch—most are less than five years old and sell for $8,000 to $15,000. Customers walk into a brightly lit showroom, where they are greeted by "sales associates" dressed in polo shirts, khakis, and sneakers. They use computer touch screens to search the CarMax inventory for cars that meet their specifications and budgets. The computer screen shows color pictures of various choices, and the customer can receive a printout listing any car's specifications, features, mileage, and price, along with what has been done to the car to get it ready for sale. The sheet even contains a photo of the car and a map showing its location on the lot.

When ready, customers are driven in golf carts to see cars on the lot, while their children enjoy the latest toys and games in the supervised KidCare Center. If the customer decides to purchase a car, financing can be arranged in less than 15 minutes through Circuit City's finance company. Moreover, CarMax will buy the customer's old car for a set price, whether or not he or she is buying a new one. The entire car-buying process, from rumbling in with the old clunker to purring out with a shiny new model, can take less than an hour.

In addition to being quick and convenient, almost everything about CarMax inspires customer confidence. CarMax gives each car a 110-point quality inspection and backs it with a 30-day comprehensive warranty. It even offers a money-back guarantee—a customer who is not 100 percent satisfied can bring the car back within five days for a full refund. CarMax allows no high-pressure selling. Salespeople are carefully

selected and trained to help people find the car that's just right for them. They receive commissions based on how many cars they sell, but not on prices. This prevents commission-hungry salespeople from steering customers to more expensive cars.

Finally, at CarMax, a price is a price. Prices are marked right on the car and no haggling is allowed. CarMax prices aren't the lowest around, but they are usually competitive—right around book value. However, these slightly higher prices don't appear to bother customers. Recent studies have shown that many customers willingly pay more to avoid the hassle of negotiating for better deals, and to ensure that they get a good car, at a fair price, backed by a reliable seller.

As one industry expert notes, the used car industry has typically "ranked from shady to illegal. The public perception [is] horrible, just horrible. People have no confidence." CarMax is setting out to change that perception. At CarMax, "You don't feel like you're going to a used-car den where you're about to be taken—you get an above-board, airy feeling." Many customers actually enjoy the used car-buying process at CarMax. "You don't have the high pressure," says one customer. "You get a quality selection, and it's no hassle." Thus, at CarMax, price is important, but so are selection and convenience. And it's hard to put a price on peace of mind.

Sources: Quotes from Michael Janofsky, "Circuit City Takes a Spin at Used Car Marketing," *The New York Times,* October 25, 1993, p. D1. Also see Bloomberg Business News, "Executive Update," *Investor's Business Daily,* October 8, 1993, p. 3; Douglas Lavin, "Cars Are Sold Like Stereos by Circuit City," *Wall Street Journal,* June 8, 1994, p. B1; and Gabrella Stern, " 'Nearly New' Autos for Sale: Dealers Buff Up Their Marketing of Used Cars," *Wall Street Journal,* February 17, 1995, p. B1.

lower than the unit cost of producing 1,000 calculators per day, as shown in the long-run average cost (LRAC) curve (Figure 11-2B). In fact, a 3,000-capacity plant would even be more efficient, according to Figure 11-2B. But a 4,000 daily production plant would be less efficient because of increasing diseconomies of scale—

too many workers to manage, paperwork slows things down, and so on. Figure 11-2B shows that a 3,000 daily production plant is the best size to build if demand is strong enough to support this level of production.

COSTS AS A FUNCTION OF PRODUCTION EXPERIENCE. Suppose TI runs a plant that produces 3,000 calculators per day. As TI gains experience in producing hand-held calculators, it learns how to do it better. Workers learn shortcuts and become more familiar with their equipment. With practice, the work becomes better organized, and TI finds better equipment and production processes. With higher volume, TI becomes more efficient and gains economies of scale. As a result, average cost tends to fall with accumulated production experience. This is shown in Figure 11-3.[7] Thus, the average cost of producing the first 100,000 calculators is $10 per calculator. When the company has produced the first 200,000 calculators, the average cost has fallen to $9. After its accumulated production experience doubles again to 400,000, the average cost is $7. This drop in the average cost with accumulated production experience is called the **experience curve** (or the **learning curve**).

If a downward-sloping experience curve exists, this is highly significant for the company. Not only will the company's unit production cost fall, but it will fall faster if the company makes and sells more during a given time period. But the market has to stand ready to buy the higher output. And to take advantage of the experience curve, TI must get a large market share early in the product's life cycle. This suggests the following pricing strategy. TI should price its calculators low; its sales will then increase, and its costs will decrease through gaining more experience, and then it can lower its prices further.

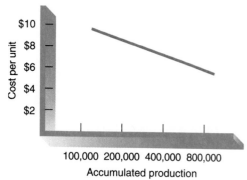

FIGURE 11-3 *Cost per unit as a function of accumulated production: the experience curve*

Experience curve (learning curve)
The drop in the average per-unit production cost that comes with accumulated production experience.

Some companies have built successful strategies around the experience curve. For example, during the 1980s, Bausch & Lomb solidified its position in the soft contact lens market by using computerized lens design and steadily expanding its one Soflens plant. As a result, its market share climbed steadily to 65 percent. However, a single-minded focus on reducing costs and exploiting the experience curve will not always work. Experience curves became somewhat of a fad during the 1970s, and like many fads, the strategy was sometimes misused. Experience curve pricing carries some major risks. The aggressive pricing might give the product a cheap image. The strategy also assumes that competitors are weak and not willing to fight it out by meeting the company's price cuts. Finally, while the company is building volume under one technology, a competitor may find a lower-cost technology that lets it start at lower prices than the market leader, who still operates on the old experience curve.

Organizational Considerations

Management must decide who within the organization should set prices. Companies handle pricing in a variety of ways. In small companies, prices often are set by top management rather than by the marketing or sales departments. In large companies, pricing typically is handled by divisional or product line managers. In industrial markets, salespeople may be allowed to negotiate with customers within certain price ranges. Even so, top management sets the pricing objectives and policies, and it often approves the prices proposed by lower-level management or salespeople. In industries in which pricing is a key factor (aerospace, railroads, oil companies), companies often will have a pricing department to set the best prices or help others in setting them. This department reports to the marketing department or top management. Others who have an influence on pricing include sales managers, production managers, finance managers, and accountants.

EXTERNAL FACTORS AFFECTING PRICING DECISIONS

External factors that affect pricing decisions include the nature of the market and demand, competition, and other environmental elements.

The Market and Demand

Whereas costs set the lower limit of prices, the market and demand set the upper limit. Both consumer and industrial buyers balance the price of a product or service against the benefits of owning it. Thus, before setting prices, the marketer must understand the relationship between price and demand for its product.

In this section, we explain how the price-demand relationship varies for different types of markets and how buyer perceptions of price affect the pricing decision. We then discuss methods for measuring the price-demand relationship.

PRICING IN DIFFERENT TYPES OF MARKETS. The seller's pricing freedom varies with different types of markets. Economists recognize four types of markets, each presenting a different pricing challenge.

Under **pure competition**, the market consists of many buyers and sellers trading in a uniform commodity such as wheat, copper, or financial securities. No single buyer or seller has much effect on the going market price. A seller cannot charge more than the going price because buyers can obtain as much as they need at the going price. Nor would sellers charge less than the market price because they can sell all they want at this price. If price and profits rise, new sellers can easily enter the market. In a purely competitive market, marketing research, product development, pricing, advertising, and sales promotion play little or no role. Thus, sellers in these markets do not spend much time on marketing strategy.

Under **monopolistic competition**, the market consists of many buyers and sellers who trade over a range of prices rather than a single market price. A range of prices occurs because sellers can differentiate their offers to buyers. Either the physical product can be varied in quality, features, or style, or the accompanying services can be varied. Buyers see differences in sellers' products and will pay different prices for them. Sellers try to develop differentiated offers for different customer segments and, in addition to price, freely use branding, advertising, and personal selling to set their offers apart. For example, H.J. Heinz, Vlasic, and several other national brands of pickles compete with dozens of regional and local brands, all differentiated by price and nonprice factors. Because there are many competi-

Pure competition
A market in which many buyers and sellers trade in a uniform commodity—no single buyer or seller has much effect on the going market price.

Monopolistic competition
A market in which many buyers and sellers trade over a range of prices rather than a single market price.

Monopolistic competition: Canadian pickle marketer Bick's sets its pickles apart from dozens of other brands using both price and nonprice factors.

Oligopolistic competition
A market in which there are a few sellers who are highly sensitive to each other's pricing and marketing strategies.

Pure monopoly
A market in which there is a single seller—it may be a government monopoly, a private regulated monopoly, or a private nonregulated monopoly.

tors, each firm is less affected by competitors' marketing strategies than in oligopolistic markets.

Under **oligopolistic competition,** the market consists of a few sellers who are highly sensitive to each other's pricing and marketing strategies. The product can be uniform (steel, aluminum) or nonuniform (cars, computers). There are few sellers because it is difficult for new sellers to enter the market. Each seller is alert to competitors' strategies and moves. If a steel company slashes its price by 10 percent, buyers will quickly switch to this supplier. The other steelmakers must respond by lowering their prices or increasing their services. An oligopolist is never sure that it will gain anything permanent through a price cut. In contrast, if an oligopolist raises its price, its competitors might not follow this lead. The oligopolist then would have to retract its price increase or risk losing customers to competitors.

In a **pure monopoly,** the market consists of one seller. The seller may be a government monopoly (the U.S. Postal Service), a private regulated monopoly (a power company), or a private nonregulated monopoly (Du Pont when it introduced nylon). Pricing is handled differently in each case. A government monopoly can pursue a variety of pricing objectives. It might set a price below cost because the product is important to buyers who cannot afford to pay full cost. Or the price might be set either to cover costs or to produce good revenue. It can even be set quite high to slow down consumption. In a regulated monopoly, the government permits the company to set rates that will yield a "fair return," one that will let the company maintain and expand its operations as needed. Nonregulated monopolies are free to price at what the market will bear. However, they do not always charge the full price for a number of reasons: a desire not to attract competition, a desire to penetrate the market faster with a low price, or a fear of government regulation.

CONSUMER PERCEPTIONS OF PRICE AND VALUE. In the end, the consumer will decide whether a product's price is right. When setting prices, the company must consider consumer perceptions of price and how these perceptions affect consumers' buying decisions. Pricing decisions, like other marketing-mix decisions, must be buyer oriented.

When consumers buy a product, they exchange something of value (the price) to get something of value (the benefits of having or using the product). Effective, buyer-oriented pricing involves understanding how much value consumers place on the benefits they receive from the product and setting a price that fits this value. These benefits can be actual or perceived. For example, calculating the cost of ingredients in a meal at a fancy restaurant is relatively easy. But assigning a value to other satisfactions such as taste, environment, relaxation, conversation, and status is very hard. And these values will vary both for different consumers and different situations.

Thus, the company often will find it hard to measure the values customers will attach to its product. But consumers do use these values to evaluate a product's price. If customers perceive that the price is greater than the product's value, they will not buy the product. If consumers perceive that the price is below the product's value, they will buy it, but the seller loses profit opportunities (see Marketing Highlight 11-2).

Marketers therefore must try to understand the consumer's reasons for buying the product and set price according to consumer perceptions of the product's value. Because consumers vary in the values they assign to different product features, marketers often vary their pricing strategies for different segments. They offer different sets of product features at different prices. For example, Sony offers small, inexpensive television models for consumers who want basic sets and larger, higher-priced models loaded with features for consumers who want the extras.

MIATA'S POPULARITY DRIVES ITS PRICES

How much would you pay for a curvaceous new two-seat convertible that has the reliability of modern engineering yet the look, feel, and sound of such classic roadsters as the 1959 Triumph TR3, the 1958 MGA, the 1962 Lotus Elan, or the Austin-Healy Sprite? That was the question facing Mazda when it introduced the hot new Mazda Miata in 1990. Not only did consumers rave about its looks, car critics passionately praised its performance. According to *Car and Driver,* if the Miata "were any more talented or tempting, driving one would be illegal." And judging on design, performance, durability and reliability, entertainment, and value, *Road & Track* named it one of the five best cars in the world. Others included in the rankings along with the Miata included the Porsche 911 Carrera, the Corvette ZR-1, the Mercedes-Benz 300 E, and the $140,000 Ferrari Testarossa. Not bad company for a car with a base sticker price of just $13,800 that was designed "just to be fun." Aside from its good looks, performance, and price, the Miata rocketed to success because it had no substitutes. Its closest competitors were the Honda CRX Si and the Toyota MR2, but they lacked its singular looks and neither came as a convertible. Thus, the Miata drove rivals to despair and customers into a covetous swoon.

Mazda had a hard time with the question of how to price its classy little car. The Japanese importer carefully controlled costs to keep the Miata's base price below $15,000. But it seems that consumers cared little about Mazda's costs, or about its intended price. When the Miata debuted, sales soared—and so did its prices. The first few thousand Miatas to arrive at Mazda dealerships sold out instantly. To make things even more interesting, Mazda planned to ship only 20,000 Miatas (in three colors—red, white, and blue) to its 844 dealers in 1989, and only 40,000 more in 1990. Thus, demand exceeded the limited supply by a reported ratio of ten to one.

The Miata was in such demand that dealers jacked up the price way beyond the sticker and still had barely enough cars to sell. Because of the car's popularity, customers were more than willing to pay the higher price. As one dealer noted, "People are offering more than what we're asking just to get [the car]." On average, dealers across the United States marked up prices $4,000; in California, they added as much as $8,000. Some enterprising owners even offered to sell their Miatas for prices ranging up to $45,000. Ads appeared daily in the *Los Angeles Times* from owners in Kansas, Nebraska, or Michigan proffering their Miatas for $32,000 plus delivery fees.

As with most hot sellers, the demand for the Miata eventually cooled down as new competitors like the Honda del Sol and the Ford Capri aimed for the same target market. Yet even today, despite its base sticker price of more that $17,000, the Miata commands intense loyalty from a core group of customers. Thirty thousand Miata fanatics across the country have formed "Miata Clubs," which hold meetings, conduct shows, and stage road rallies throughout the year. Moreover, the continuing popularity of the Miata has spawned a cottage industry of companies that produce Mazda accessories, such as specially designed luggage to fit the uniquely shaped Miata trunk.

Although many companies focus on costs as a key to setting prices, consumers rarely know of or care about the seller's costs. What really counts is what consumers are willing to pay for the benefits of owning the product. Although the Miata no longer sells at a premium, its popularity has enabled Mazda to avoid offering the rebates and discounts that have become the rule for other models in the industry. To Miata buyers, the sharp little car adds up to much more than the sum of its mechanical parts. To them, it delivers the same pleasures and prestige as cars selling at much higher prices. Therefore, even at sticker prices or above, most buyers believe they get good value when they buy a Miata. Mazda, in turn, is rewarded with satisfied customers and a steady seller that promises to remain profitable into the next century.

Thousands of Miata fanatics across the country have formed "Miata Clubs," which hold meetings, conduct shows, and stage road rallies.

Sources: Rebecca Fannin, "Mazda's Sporting Chance," *Marketing & Media Decisions,* October 1989, pp. 24–30; S. C. Gwynne, "Romancing the Roadster," *Time,* July 24, 1989, p. 39; "The Roadster Returns," *Consumer Reports,* April 1990, pp. 232–234; Michael Williams and John Bussey, "Corporate Focus: Mazda Ponders Its Route through a Bumpy Future," *The Wall Street Journal,* September 8, 1993, p. B4; and Krystal Miller, "Autos: Sports Cars Lose Their Luster," *The Wall Street Journal,* July 27, 1994, p. B1.

ANALYZING THE PRICE-DEMAND RELATIONSHIP. Each price the company might charge will lead to a different level of demand. The relation between the price charged and the resulting demand level is shown in the **demand curve** in Figure 11-4A. The demand curve shows the number of units the market will buy in a given time period, at different prices that might be charged. In the normal case, demand and price are inversely related: That is, the higher the price, the lower the demand. Thus, the company would sell less if it raised its price from P_1 to P_2. In short, consumers with limited budgets probably will buy less of something if its price is too high.

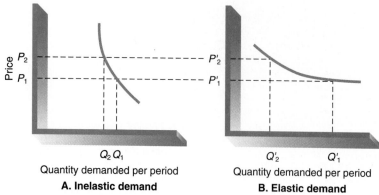

FIGURE 11-4 *Demand curves*

Demand curve
A curve that shows the number of units the market will buy in a given time period, at different prices that might be charged.

In the case of prestige goods, the demand curve sometimes slopes upward. For example, one perfume company found that by raising its price, it sold more perfume rather than less. Consumers thought the higher price meant a better or more desirable perfume. However, if the company charges too high a price, the level of demand will be lower.

Most companies try to measure their demand curves by estimating demand at different prices. The type of market makes a difference. In a monopoly, the demand curve shows the total market demand resulting from different prices. If the company faces competition, its demand at different prices will depend on whether competitors' prices stay constant or change with the company's own prices. Here, we will assume that competitors' prices remain constant. Later in this chapter, we will discuss what happens when competitors' prices change.

In measuring the price-demand relationship, the market researcher must not allow other factors affecting demand to vary. For example, if Sony increased its advertising at the same time that it lowered its television prices, we would not know how much of the increased demand was due to the lower prices and how much was due to the increased advertising. The same problem arises if a holiday weekend occurs when the lower price is set—more gift giving over the holidays causes people to buy more televisions. Economists show the impact of nonprice factors on demand through shifts in the demand curve rather than movements along it.

Price elasticity
A measure of the sensitivity of demand to changes in price.

PRICE ELASTICITY OF DEMAND. Marketers also need to know **price elasticity**—how responsive demand will be to a change in price. Consider the two demand curves in Figure 11-4. In Figure 11-4A, a price increase from P_1 to P_2 leads to a relatively small drop in demand from Q_1 to Q_2. In Figure 11-4B, however, the same price increase leads to a large drop in demand from Q'_1 to Q'_2. If demand hardly changes with a small change in price, we say the demand is *inelastic*. If demand changes greatly, we say the demand is *elastic*. The price elasticity of demand is given by the following formula:

$$\text{Price Elasticity of Demand} = \frac{\%\ \text{Change in Quantity Demanded}}{\%\ \text{Change in Price}}$$

Suppose demand falls by 10 percent when a seller raises its price by 2 percent. Price elasticity of demand is therefore −5 (the minus sign confirms the inverse relation between price and demand) and demand is elastic. If demand falls by 2 percent with a 2 percent increase in price, then elasticity is −1. In this case, the seller's total revenue stays the same: The seller sells fewer items but at a higher price that preserves the same total revenue. If demand falls by 1 percent when price is increased by 2 percent, then elasticity is $-\frac{1}{2}$ and demand is inelastic. The less elastic the demand, the more it pays for the seller to raise the price.

What determines the price elasticity of demand? Buyers are less price sensitive when the product they are buying is unique or when it is high in quality, prestige, or exclusiveness. They are also less price sensitive when substitute products are hard to find or when they cannot easily compare the quality of substitutes. Finally, buyers are less price sensitive when the total expenditure for a product is low relative to their income or when the cost is shared by another party.[8]

If demand is elastic rather than inelastic, sellers will consider lowering their price. A lower price will produce more total revenue. This practice makes sense as long as the extra costs of producing and selling more do not exceed the extra revenue.

Competitors' Costs, Prices, and Offers

Another external factor affecting the company's pricing decisions is competitors' costs and prices and possible competitor reactions to the company's own pricing moves. A consumer who is considering the purchase of a Canon camera will evaluate Canon's price and value against the prices and values of comparable products made by Nikon, Minolta, Pentax, and others. In addition, the company's pricing strategy may affect the nature of the competition it faces. If Canon follows a high-price, high-margin strategy, it may attract competition. A low-price, low-margin strategy, however, may stop competitors or drive them out of the market.

Canon needs to benchmark its costs against its competitors' costs to learn whether it is operating at a cost advantage or disadvantage. It also needs to learn the price and quality of each competitor's offer. Canon might do this in several ways. It can send out comparison shoppers to price and compare the products of Nikon, Minolta, and other competitors. It can get competitors' price lists and buy competitors' equipment and take it apart. It can ask buyers how they view the price and quality of each competitor's camera.

Once Canon is aware of competitors' prices and offers, it can use them as a starting point for its own pricing. If Canon's cameras are similar to Nikon's, it will have to price close to Nikon or lose sales. If Canon's cameras are not as good as Nikon's, the firm will not be able to charge as much. If Canon's products are better than Nikon's, it can charge more. Basically, Canon will use price to position its offer relative to the competition.

Other External Factors

When setting prices, the company also must consider other factors in its external environment. *Economic conditions* can have a strong impact on the firm's pricing strategies. Economic factors such as boom or recession, inflation, and interest rates affect pricing decisions because they affect both the costs of producing a product and consumer perceptions of the product's price and value. The company also must consider what impact its prices will have on other parties in its environment. How will *resellers* react to various prices? The company should set prices that give resellers a fair profit, encourage their support, and help them to sell the product effectively. The *government* is another important external influence on pricing decisions. Finally, *social concerns* may have to be taken into account. In setting prices, a company's short-term sales, market share, and profit goals may have to be tempered by broader societal considerations (see Marketing Highlight 11-3).

GENERAL PRICING APPROACHES

The price the company charges will be somewhere between one that is too low to produce a profit and one that is too high to produce any demand. Figure 11-5 summarizes the major considerations in setting price. Product costs set a floor to

PRICING PHARMACEUTICAL PRODUCTS: MORE THAN SALES AND PROFITS

The U.S. pharmaceutical industry historically has been the nation's most profitable industry. However, critics claim that this success has come at the expense of consumers. It is possible only because competitive forces do not operate well in the pharmaceutical market. Consumers don't usually shop around for the best deal on medicines—they simply take what the doctor orders. Because physicians who write the prescriptions don't pay for the medicines they recommend, they have little incentive to be price conscious. Moreover, third-party payers—insurance companies, health plans, and government programs—often pay all or part of the bill. Finally, in the pharmaceutical industry, the huge investment and time needed to develop and test a new drug discourages competitors from challenging the market leader and forcing lower prices.

These market factors sometimes leave pharmaceutical companies free to practice monopoly pricing, resulting in seemingly outlandish cases of price gouging. One such case involves the drug levamisole. Thirty years ago, Johnson & Johnson introduced levamisole as a drug used

to deworm sheep. When farmers using the drug noticed that dewormed sheep also suffered fewer cases of shipping fever, researchers began investigating the drug for human use. Under the sponsorship of the National Cancer Institute, and with free pills provided by Johnson & Johnson, Dr. Charles Moertel of the Mayo Comprehensive Cancer Center tested levamisole in combination with another drug as a treatment for cancer. The combination proved effective for patients with advanced colon cancer. It reduced recurrence of the disease by 40 percent and cut deaths by a third.

The FDA quickly approved levamisole for human use. In 1990, the Janssen division of Johnson & Johnson introduced the drug under the brand name Ergamisol. All went well until an Illinois farm woman noticed that her cancer pills contained the same active ingredient as the medicine she used to deworm her sheep. It wasn't the fact that both humans and sheep were using the drug that disturbed her. What really rankled her was that the sheep medicine sells for pennies a pill, whereas the human medicine sells for $5 to $6 per tablet. In a year's time, humans

may spend from $1,250 to $3,000 for Ergamisol; the cost for treating sheep may be as low as $14.95.

The price discrepancy has caused quite a stir. Doctors at the MacNeal Hospital Cancer Center in Chicago surveyed local pharmacies and found that patients paid an average of $1,200 per year for levamisole. At the annual meetings of the American Society for Clinical Oncology in May 1992, Dr. Moertel blasted Johnson & Johnson for its unconscionable pricing of the drug. His salvo marked the first time that marketplace issues had taken center stage at that scholarly forum, and it had great impact. And as if publicity from Dr. Moertel's comments were not enough, in August 1992, Chicago consumer Frank Glickman filed suit against Janssen. He claimed that he was forced to pay "an outrageous, unconscionable, and extortionate price for a life-saving drug" that is sold at a fraction of the cost for treating sheep.

Janssen replied that the cost of Ergamisol is reasonable when compared to other life-saving drugs such as AZT, which can cost $6,000 to $8,000 a year. The company also claimed that the price reflects

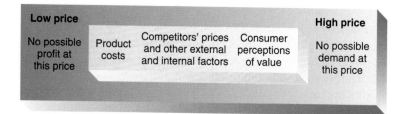

FIGURE 11-5 *Major considerations in setting price*

the price; consumer perceptions of the product's value set the ceiling. The company must consider competitors' prices and other external and internal factors to find the best price between these two extremes.

Companies set prices by selecting a general pricing approach that includes one or more of these three sets of factors. We will examine the following approaches: the *cost-based approach* (cost-plus pricing, breakeven analysis, and target profit pricing); the *buyer-based approach* (perceived-value pricing); and the *competition-based approach* (going-rate and sealed-bid pricing).

COST-BASED PRICING

Cost-Plus Pricing

Cost-plus pricing
Adding a standard markup to the cost of the product.

The simplest pricing method is **cost-plus pricing**—adding a standard markup to the cost of the product. Construction companies, for example, submit job bids by estimating the total project cost and adding a standard markup for profit. Lawyers,

decades of costly research and testing conducted to determine if levamisole could be used to treat humans. The company said it had conducted over 1,400 studies with 40,000 subjects. Dr. Moertel disagreed. He claimed that the Cancer Institute, funded by the American taxpayer, sponsored the levamisole studies. Further, he asserted, FDA approval was obtained on the basis of his research, which cost Janssen only pennies. He also pointed out that Janssen had 25 years to recoup its investment before it ever sold the drug to humans.

The levamisole example highlights many important drug pricing issues. Most consumers appreciate the steady stream of beneficial drugs produced by the U.S. pharmaceutical industry. However, there is increasing concern that the industry may be taking advantage of its monopoly pricing power—the United States remains the only country in the world that has no governmental review of pharmaceutical prices. Unlike purchases of other consumer products, drug purchases cannot be postponed. Nor can consumers shop around to save money. Because of patents and

FDA approvals, few competing brands exist, and they don't go on sale. Perhaps the most serious concern is that high drug prices may have life-and-death consequences. Without levamisole, many of the 22,000 patients diagnosed with advanced colon cancer each year would die. Thus, some critics claim that drug company profits may come at the expense of human life.

As a result, the industry is facing ever-greater pressure from the federal government, insurance companies, and consumer advocates to exercise restraint in setting prices. Legislation has been passed to curb drug pricing, and more is pending. Rather than waiting for tougher legislation on prices, some forward-thinking drug companies are taking action on their own. For example, Merck and Glaxo have agreed to keep their average price hikes at or below inflation. Bristol-Meyers Squibb has voluntarily provided discounts to agencies such as the U.S. Public Health Service and to federally funded drug- and alcohol-treatment centers. Glaxo and other companies make free drugs available to people who cannot afford them. These companies recognize

that in setting prices, their short-term sales, market share, and profit goals must be tempered by broader societal considerations. They know that in the long run, socially responsible pricing will benefit both the consumer and the company.

Sources: Quote from Marilyn Chase, "Doctor Assails J&J Price Tag on Cancer Drug," *Wall Street Journal,* May 20, 1992, p. B1. Also see "Cancer Patient Sues Johnson & Johnson over Drug Pricing," *Wall Street Journal,* August 13, 1992, p. B6; Mike King, "Colon Cancer Drug: 5 Cents for an Animal, $5 for Humans," *Atlanta Constitution,* March 11, 1991, p. E1; Joseph Weber, "For Drugmakers, the Sky's no Longer the Limit," *Business Week,* January 27, 1992, p. 68; Elyse Tanouye, "Price Rises for Drugs Cool, Manufacturer Profits Chill," *Wall Street Journal,* April 9, 1992, p. B4; Patricia Winters, "Drugmakers Portrayed as Villains, Worry about Image," *Advertising Age,* February 22, 1993, pp. 1, 42; and Shawn Tully, "The Plot to Keep Drug Prices High," *Fortune,* December 27, 1993, pp. 120–124.

accountants, and other professionals typically price by adding a standard markup to their costs. Some sellers tell their customers they will charge cost plus a specified markup; for example, aerospace companies price this way to the government.

To illustrate markup pricing, suppose a toaster manufacturer had the following costs and expected sales:

Variable cost	$10
Fixed cost	$300,000
Expected unit sales	50,000

Then the manufacturer's cost per toaster is given by:

$$\text{Unit Cost} = \text{Variable Cost} + \frac{\text{Fixed Costs}}{\text{Unit Sales}} = \$10 + \frac{\$300,000}{50,000} = \$16$$

Now suppose the manufacturer wants to earn a 20 percent markup on sales. The manufacturer's markup price is given by:[9]

$$\text{Markup Price} = \frac{\text{Unit Cost}}{(1 - \text{Desired Return on Sales})} = \frac{\$16}{1 - .2} = \$20$$

The manufacturer would charge dealers $20 a toaster and make a profit of $4 per unit. The dealers, in turn, will mark up the toaster. If dealers want to earn 50 percent on sales price, they will mark up the toaster to $40 ($20 + 50% of $40). This number is equivalent to a *markup on cost* of 100 percent ($20/$20).

Does using standard markups to set prices make sense? Generally, no. Any pricing method that ignores demand and competitor prices is not likely to lead to the best price. Suppose the toaster manufacturer charged $20 but only sold 30,000 toasters instead of 50,000. Then the unit cost would have been higher since the fixed costs are spread over fewer units, and the realized percentage markup on sales would have been lower. Markup pricing only works if that price actually brings in the expected level of sales.

Still, markup pricing remains popular for many reasons. First, sellers are more certain about costs than about demand. By tying the price to cost, sellers simplify pricing—they do not have to make frequent adjustments as demand changes. Second, when all firms in the industry use this pricing method, prices tend to be similar and price competition is thus minimized. Third, many people feel that cost-plus pricing is fairer to both buyers and sellers. Sellers earn a fair return on their investment but do not take advantage of buyers when buyers' demand becomes great.

Breakeven Analysis and Target Profit Pricing

Breakeven pricing (target profit pricing)
Setting price to break even on the costs of making and marketing a product; or setting price to make a target profit.

Another cost-oriented pricing approach is **breakeven pricing,** or a variation called **target profit pricing.** The firm tries to determine the price at which it will break even or make the target profit it is seeking. Target pricing is used by General Motors, which prices its automobiles to achieve a 15 to 20 percent profit on its investment. This pricing method is also used by public utilities, which are constrained to make a fair return on their investment.

Target pricing uses the concept of a *breakeven chart,* which shows the total cost and total revenue expected at different sales volume levels. Figure 11-6 shows a breakeven chart for the toaster manufacturer discussed here. Fixed costs are $300,000 regardless of sales volume. Variable costs are added to fixed costs to form total costs, which rise with volume. The total revenue curve starts at zero and rises with each unit sold. The slope of the total revenue curve reflects the price of $20 per unit.

The total revenue and total cost curves cross at 30,000 units. This is the *breakeven volume.* At $20, the company must sell at least 30,000 units to break even; that is, for total revenue to cover total cost. Breakeven volume can be calculated using the following formula:

FIGURE 11-6 *Break-even chart for determining target price*

$$\text{Breakeven Volume} = \frac{\text{Fixed Cost}}{\text{Price} - \text{Variable Cost}} = \frac{\$300,000}{\$20 - \$10} = 30,000$$

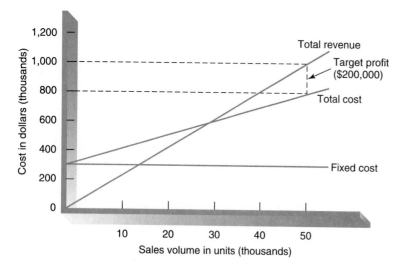

If the company wants to make a target profit, it must sell more than 30,000 units at $20 each. Suppose the toaster manufacturer has invested $1,000,000 in the business and wants to set price to earn a 20 percent return, or $200,000. In that case, it must sell at least 50,000 units at $20 each. If the company charges a higher price, it will not need to sell as many toasters to achieve its target return. But the market may not buy even this lower volume at the higher price. Much depends on the price elasticity and competitors' prices.

The manufacturer should consider different prices and estimate breakeven volumes, probable demand, and profits for

TABLE 11-1   *Breakeven Volume and Profits at Different Prices*

(1) PRICE	(2) UNIT DEMAND NEEDED TO BREAK EVEN	(3) EXPECTED UNIT DEMAND AT GIVEN PRICE	(4) TOTAL REVENUES (1) × (3)	(5) TOTAL COSTS*	(6) PROFIT (4) – (5)
$14	75,000	71,000	$ 994,000	$1,100,000	–$ 32,000
16	50,000	67,000	1,072,000	970,000	102,000
18	37,500	60,000	1,080,000	900,000	180,000
20	30,000	42,000	840,000	720,000	120,000
22	25,000	23,000	506,000	530,000	–24,000

*Assumes fixed costs of $300,000 and constant unit variable costs of $10.

each. This is done in Table 11-1. The table shows that as price increases, breakeven volume drops (column 2). But as price increases, demand for the toasters also falls off (column 3). At the $14 price, because the manufacturer clears only $4 per toaster ($14 less $10 in variable costs), it must sell a very high volume to break even. Even though the low price attracts many buyers, demand still falls below the high breakeven point, and the manufacturer loses money. At the other extreme, with a $22 price the manufacturer clears $12 per toaster and must sell only 25,000 units to break even. But at this high price, consumers buy too few toasters, and profits are negative. The table shows that a price of $18 yields the highest profits. Note that none of the prices produce the manufacturer's target profit of $200,000. To achieve this target return, the manufacturer will have to search for ways to lower fixed or variable costs, thus lowering the breakeven volume.

VALUE-BASED PRICING

Value-based pricing
Setting price based on buyers' perceptions of value rather than on the seller's cost.

An increasing number of companies are basing their prices on the product's perceived value. **Value-based pricing** uses buyers' perceptions of value, not the seller's cost, as the key to pricing. Value-based pricing means that the marketer cannot design a product and marketing program and then set the price. Price is considered along with the other marketing-mix variables *before* the marketing program is set.

Figure 11-7 compares cost-based pricing with value-based pricing. Cost-based pricing is product driven. The company designs what it considers to be a good product, totals the costs of making the product, and sets a price that covers costs plus a target profit. Marketing must then convince buyers that the product's

FIGURE 11-7 *Cost-based versus value-based pricing*

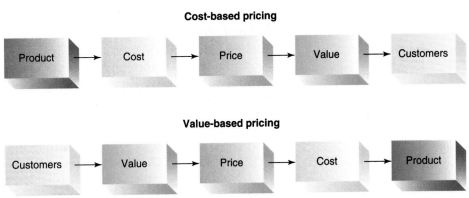

Source: Thomas T. Nagle and Reed K. Holden, *The Strategy and Tactics of Pricing,* 2nd ed. (Englewood Cliffs, NJ: Prentice Hall, 1995), p. 5.

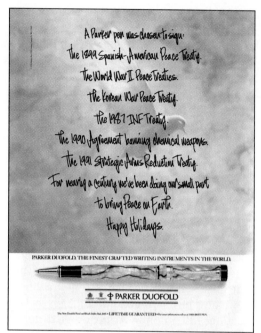

value at that price justifies its purchase. If the price turns out to be too high, the company must settle for lower markups or lower sales, both resulting in disappointing profits.

Value-based pricing reverses this process. The company sets its target price based on customer perceptions of the product value. The targeted value and price then drive decisions about product design and what costs can be incurred. As a result, pricing begins with analyzing consumer needs and value perceptions, and price is set to match consumers' perceived value.

A company using value-based pricing must find out what value buyers assign to different competitive offers. However, measuring perceived value can be difficult. Sometimes consumers are asked how much they would pay for a basic product and for each benefit added to the offer. Or a company might conduct experiments to test the perceived value of different product offers. If the seller charges more than the buyers' perceived value, the company's sales will suffer. Many companies overprice their products, and their products sell poorly. Other companies underprice. Underpriced products sell very well, but they produce less revenue than they would if price were raised to the perceived-value level.

Perceived value: A less expensive pen might write as well, but some consumers will pay much more for the intangibles. This Parker model runs $185. Others are priced as high as $3,500.

COMPETITION-BASED PRICING

Consumers will base their judgments of a product's value on the prices that competitors charge for similar products. Here, we discuss two forms of competition-based pricing—*going-rate pricing* and *sealed-bid pricing*.

Going-Rate Pricing

Going-rate pricing
Setting price based largely on following competitors' prices rather than on company costs or demand.

In **going-rate pricing**, the firm bases its price largely on *competitors'* prices, with less attention paid to its *own* costs or to demand. The firm might charge the same, more, or less than its major competitors. In oligopolistic industries that sell a commodity such as steel, paper, or fertilizer, firms normally charge the same price. The smaller firms follow the leader: They change their prices when the market leader's prices change, rather than when their own demand or costs change. Some firms may charge a bit more or less, but they hold the amount of difference constant. Thus, minor gasoline retailers usually charge a few cents less than the major oil companies, without letting the difference increase or decrease.

Going-rate pricing is quite popular. When demand elasticity is hard to measure, firms feel that the going price represents the collective wisdom of the industry concerning the price that will yield a fair return. They also feel that holding to the going price will prevent harmful price wars.

Sealed-Bid Pricing

Sealed-bid pricing
Setting price based on how the firm thinks competitors will price rather than on its own costs or demand—used when a company bids for jobs.

Competition-based pricing is also used when firms *bid* for jobs. Using **sealed-bid pricing**, a firm bases its price on how it thinks competitors will price rather than on its own costs or on the demand. The firm wants to win a contract, and winning the contract requires pricing less than other firms.

Yet the firm cannot set its price below a certain level. It cannot price below cost without harming its position. In contrast, the higher the company sets its price above its costs, the lower its chance of getting the contract.

The net effect of the two opposite pulls can be described in terms of the *expected profit* of the particular bid (see Table 11-2). Suppose a bid of $9,500 would yield a high chance (say .81) of getting the contract, but only a low profit (say $100). The expected profit with this bid is therefore $81. If the firm bid

TABLE 11-2 *Effect of Different Bids on Expected Profit*

COMPANY'S BID	COMPANY'S PROFIT (1)	PROBABILITY OF WINNING WITH THIS BID (ASSUMED) (2)	EXPECTED PROFIT [(1) × (2)]
$ 9,500	$ 100	.81	$ 81
10,000	600	.36	216
10,500	1,100	.09	99
11,000	1,600	.01	16

$11,000, its profit would be $1,600, but its chance of getting the contract might be reduced to .01. The expected profit would be only $16. Thus the company might bid the price that would maximize the expected profit. According to Table 11-2, the best bid would be $10,000, for which the expected profit is $216.

Using expected profit as a basis for setting price makes sense for the large firm that makes many bids. In playing the odds, the firm will make maximum profits in the long run. But a firm that bids only occasionally or needs a particular contract badly will not find the expected-profit approach useful. The approach, for example, does not distinguish between a $100,000 profit with a .10 probability and a $12,500 profit with an .80 probability. Yet the firm that wants to keep production going would prefer the second contract to the first.

Summary

Despite the increased role of nonprice factors in the modern marketing process, price remains an important element in the marketing mix. There are many internal and external *factors to consider when setting prices.*

One important *internal factor,* the pricing strategy, is largely determined by the company's *marketing objectives.* Pricing objectives often include survival, current profit maximization, market-share leadership, and product-quality leadership. In addition to meeting these objectives, price decisions must be carefully coordinated with the *marketing-mix strategy.* Pricing is only one of the marketing-mix tools that a company uses to accomplish its objectives, and pricing decisions affect and are affected by product design, distribution, and promotion decisions. All of these elements must be carefully coordinated when designing the marketing program.

Costs set the floor for the company's price, which must cover all the costs of making and selling the product, plus enough profit to generate a fair rate of return. There are organizational considerations that come into setting prices, and management must decide who is responsible for setting price. In large companies, some pricing decisions may be delegated to lower-level managers and salespeople. Production, finance, and accounting managers also influence pricing. Usually, however, pricing is such an important issue that top management sets pricing policies and gives final approval to proposed prices.

External factors that influence pricing decisions include the nature of the *market* and *demand; competitors' prices and offers;* and other factors such as the economy, reseller needs, and government actions. The amount of freedom a seller has in pricing varies with *different types of markets,* and markets characterized by monopolistic competition or oligopoly are especially restrictive.

Ultimately, *consumer perceptions of price and value* determine whether the company has set the right price. If the price is higher than the sum of the perceived values, consumers will not buy the product. Consumers differ in the values they assign to different product features, and marketers often vary their pricing strategies for different price segments. When assessing the market and demand, the company estimates the *price elasticity of demand* and the *demand curve,* which shows the probable quantity purchased per period at alternative price levels. The more inelastic the demand for a product, the higher the company can set the price. Demand and consumer value perceptions set the ceiling for prices.

Consumers also compare a product's price to the *prices of competitors' offers,* and choose the product that offers the best value. Marketers must carefully monitor the pricing and quality of all competitor's products, and use this information as a starting point for their own pricing.

There are three *general pricing approaches* that a company can select. *Cost-based approaches* include *cost-plus pricing, break-even analysis,* and *target profit pricing. Value-based pricing* uses the buyer's perception of value, not the seller's cost structure, to set pricing. *Competition-based pricing* has two major variations. In *going-rate pricing,* the firm sets prices based on what competitors are charging, although the absolute level may be lower, higher, or the same as competitors depending upon pricing strategy. Finally, another version of competition-based pricing is *sealed-bid pricing,* in which firms bid what they think others will charge.

Key Terms

Breakeven pricing (target profit pricing)
Cost-plus pricing
Demand curve
Experience curve (learning curve)
Fixed costs

Going-rate pricing
Monopolistic competition
Oligopolistic competition
Price
Price elasticity
Pure competition

Pure monopoly
Sealed-bid pricing
Total costs
Value-based pricing
Variable costs

Discussing the Issues

1. Certain "inexpensive" products that waste energy, provide few servings per container, or require frequent maintenance may *cost* much more to own and use than do products selling for a higher *price.* Discuss how marketers can use this information on "true cost" to gain a competitive edge in pricing and promoting their products.

2. Detergent A is priced at $2.19 for 32 ounces, and detergent B is priced at $1.99 for 26 ounces. Suggest which brand appears most attractive. Which is actually the better value, assuming equal quality? Decide if there is a psychological reason to price in this way.

3. Procter & Gamble replaced its 16-ounce packages of regular Folgers coffee with 13-ounce "fast-roast" packages. Fast-roasting allows Procter & Gamble to use fewer coffee beans per pack with no impact on flavor or the number of servings per package. Determine which pricing approach was appropriate for setting the price for the fast-roast coffee—cost-based, buyer-based, or competition-based pricing?

4. Sales of Fleischmann's gin *increased* when prices were raised 22 percent over a two-year period. Explain what this tells you about the demand curve and the elasticity of demand for Fleischmann's gin. What does this suggest about using perceived-value pricing in marketing alcoholic beverages?

5. Genentech, a high-technology pharmaceutical company, has developed a clot-dissolving drug called TPA that will halt a heart attack in progress. TPA saves lives, minimizes hospital stays, and reduces damage to the heart itself. It was initially priced at $2,200 per dose. Explain what pricing approach Genentech appeared to be using. Is demand for this drug likely to be elastic with price?

6. Columnist Dave Barry jokes that federal law requires this message under the sticker price of new cars: "Warning to stupid people: Do not pay this amount." Discuss why the sticker price is generally higher than the actual selling price of a car. Tell how you think car dealers set the actual prices of the cars they sell.

Applying the Concepts

1. Do a pricing survey of several gasoline stations in your town in different locations. If possible, check prices at: stations at an exit ramp on a major highway, stations on your local strip, convenience stores and a smaller station that is not near any other stations. Write down the brand of gasoline, prices of regular and premium grades, type of location, distance to the nearest competitor, and the competitor's prices. (a) Is there a pattern to the pricing of gasoline at various outlets? (b) Do you think that these stations are using cost-based, buyer-based, or going-rate pricing?

2. You have inherited an automatic car wash where annual fixed costs are $50,000 and variable costs are $0.50 per car washed. You think people would be willing to pay $1 to have their car washed. Determine what the break-even volume would be at that price.

References

1. See James E. Ellis and Brian Bremner, "Will the Big Markdown Get the Big Store Moving Again?" *Business Week,* March 13, 1989, pp. 110–114; Kate Fitzgerald, "Sears' Plan on the Ropes," *Advertising Age,* January 8, 1990, pp. 1, 42; Julia Flynn, "Smaller but Wiser," *Business Week,* October 12, 1992, pp. 28–29; Kevin Kelly, "The Big Store May Be on a Big Roll," *Business Week,* August 30, 1993, pp. 82–85; Ellen Neuborne, "Next Test: To Show that 1993 Was No Fluke," *USA Today,* February 9, 1994, pp. B1–B2; and Susan Chandler, "Sears' Turnaround Is For Real—For Now," *Business Week,* August 15, 1994, pp. 102–103.

2. See David J. Schwartz, *Marketing Today: A Basic Approach,* 3rd ed. (New York: Harcourt Brace Jovanovich, 1981), pp. 270–273.

3. For an excellent discussion of factors affecting pricing decisions, see Thomas T. Nagle and Reed K. Holden, *The Strategy and Tactics of Pricing,* 2nd ed. (Englewood Cliffs, NJ: Prentice Hall, Inc., 1995), Chap. 1.

4. Norton Paley, "Fancy Footwork," *Sales & Marketing Management,* July 1994, pp. 41–42.

5. Christopher Farrell, "Stuck! How Companies Cope When They Can't Raise Prices," *Business Week,* November 15, 1993, pp. 146–155. Also see John Y. Lee, "Use Target Costing to Improve Your Bottom Line," *The CPA Journal,* January 1994, pp. 68–71.

6. Brian Dumaine, "Closing the Innovation Gap," *Fortune,* December 2, 1991, pp. 56–62.

7. Here accumulated production is drawn on a semi-log scale so that equal distances represent the same percentage increase in output.

8. See Nagle and Holden, *The Strategy and Tactics of Pricing,* Chap. 4.

9. The arithmetic of markups and margins is discussed in Appendix 1, "Marketing Arithmetic."

Company Case 11

U.S. AIR: SURVIVING THE FARE WARS

A NEW FRONT

Joyce Harris and her daughter Dana pile suitcases in their car's trunk and prepare for the one-hour drive from their southern Pennsylvania home to the Baltimore Airport. Joyce and Dana are going to Cleveland to visit Joyce's sister, who just had a baby. Such visits normally would require a torturous car ride or an expensive plane trip. This morning, however, they will fly from Baltimore to Cleveland for $19 each. Only $19! Moreover, they won't fly on the dominant Baltimore carrier, U.S. Air. They will fly on upstart Southwest.

Joyce and Dana are beneficiaries of the latest skirmish in the airline fare wars. However, the continuing fare wars have meant big trouble for the industry. Between 1990 and the end of 1992, the industry lost $10 billion—more than its total profits in its 60-year history.

Since 1982, costs such as wages and fuel have doubled while the average price paid per mile flown has fallen 25 percent. Persistent overcapacity and the airlines' struggles to get out of bankruptcy have fueled suicidal price wars.

But the battle for Baltimore represents more than just another fare-war episode. The attack represents the opening round of an all-out attack on the once stable and secure East Coast air-travel market. Further, it represents a battle between lean, quick-footed, low-cost carriers and the large, full-service airlines that have charged higher fares.

THE EAST COAST MARKET

The East contains some of the nation's most important business cities and accounts for 37 percent of U.S. air travel. Executives pack the hourly shuttle flights between Washington, New York, and Boston; and northeastern families pile in to seek the Florida sun and Disney World during the winter. U.S. Air, Delta, and American Airlines, with their hubs in places like Pittsburgh, Raleigh, and Atlanta, have dominated the East Coast market. Between 1982 and 1992, short-haul fares in the East more than doubled while passenger traffic plummeted 12 percent.

In contrast, the so-called "low-cost" airlines, like Southwest, have served the Western U.S. air-travel market. These expanding airlines caused passenger travel to mushroom 75 percent while fares rose only 5 percent. One study showed that, on flights shorter than 300 miles, East Coast travelers were paying on average more than double what western travelers paid for a similar trip. For example, a passenger would pay $156 for a 190-mile flight out West. In the East, the same trip would cost $319.

ON THE ATTACK IN BALTIMORE

Given these price discrepancies, it was only natural that Southwest and 28 entrepreneurial start-ups like ValuJet (Atlanta), Reno Airline (Nevada), Kiwi (Newark), and AirSouth (Columbia, SC) would launch an attack on the established players. Southwest led the attack, selecting Baltimore as the unlikely target. U.S. Air controlled a commanding 55 percent of Baltimore's daily flights and seemed to have locked up the mid-Atlantic market with its hubs in Philadelphia, Pittsburgh, and Charlotte.

However, the Baltimore airport offered an attractive target due to its lower landing fees and reasonable gate-rental prices. Further, the airport featured easy access via interstate highways and 30 daily trains to the huge Washington, DC, Maryland, and southern Pennsylvania markets.

Southwest dispatched its "diamond team" of six planners from marketing and sales, promotion, advertising, and public relations to conduct the initial assault. The team began to develop an in-depth understanding of the Baltimore market by subscribing to the *Baltimore Sun* newspaper and analyzing specially prepared demographic data. They hunted for sports teams, special events, and cultural institutions to sponsor. Southwest joined with the Baltimore Orioles to set up advertising and joint-marketing events, including contests for Southwest tickets. Then, to position Southwest as an established carrier itself, not a "Johnny-come-lately," Southwest unleashed a flood of newspaper and television ads stressing its service, its young jet fleet, and its industry-leading profitability.

Finally, Southwest brought out its heavy artillery. It offered unheard-of fares, like the $19 one-way fare to Cleveland. Baltimore-area passengers responded, and the airport's boardings leaped 30 percent in the first three months. Southwest said that Baltimore was one of its most successful new cities and that it would add more flights.

Following Southwest's attack and forays by Continental into Baltimore, U.S. Air's market share fell to 51 percent. America West, another low-cost carrier, announced it would enter the Philadelphia market. Continental revealed that it would expand its low-fare "CALite" flights up and down the East Coast. U.S. Air decided it was time to respond.

U.S. AIR COUNTERATTACKS

U.S. Air startled the industry by slashing its ticket prices to many East Coast cities and announcing that the price cuts would be permanent. It cut business fares up to 50 percent and leisure fares up to 70 percent on about 25 percent of its flights. Business travelers account for about 60 percent of industry revenue. The airline cut the round-trip fare from Charlotte to Boston, for example, from $808 to $458.

U.S. Air followed the fare cuts with a cost-cutting program it called "Project High Ground." The project aimed to reduce costs by speeding up the time it takes U.S. Air's workers to service and "turn around" its planes at airports. The carrier wanted to imitate Southwest and cut in half the time its planes spent on the ground. For example, U.S. Air's maintenance crews would enter the rear of an unloading plane's cabin and begin cleaning up rather than waiting for all the passengers to clear. Using such techniques, the airline figured it could add one more flight per plane per day, allowing it to sell 3,500 more seats daily at no additional operating cost.

Industry analysts were concerned, however, about both U.S. Air's price and its cost-cutting strategies. Some airline specialists feared a repeat of 1992's financial disaster. That year, American Airlines introduced its value-pricing program, sparking a 50 percent-off nationwide fare war that resulted in the industry losing $2.5 billion that year alone. Further, the analysts believed that U.S. Air needed to do more than speed up its turnarounds. It needed to overhaul its entire cost structure.

Doing so, however, will be difficult. To cut its losses in 1992, U.S. Air negotiated a one-year-only deal with its unions. The unions agreed to make wage concessions for 1992; but in 1993, wages returned to normal and the unions won a no-furlough guarantee. The guarantee hindered the company from reducing it 46,000 member work force. At the same time, Delta grounded 28 planes and laid off 600 pilots.

U.S. Air knows it is in a tough battle. As one vice president noted, however, "We can't afford to let the other guy get established here." Protecting its East Coast markets will not be easy in the face of carriers with lower cost structures and less restrictive union contracts.

QUESTIONS

1. What internal and external factors affect pricing decisions in the airline industry?

2. What marketing objectives have the various airline companies selected?

3. Which airline industry costs are fixed, and which are variable? What implications does this cost structure hold for airline operations?

4. What is the nature of demand and competition in the airline industry? Does demand differ for the business and leisure segments?

5. What pricing and other marketing recommendations would you make to U.S. Air to help it protect its markets?

Sources: Adapted from M. J. McCarthy and B. O'Brian, "Lean, Nimble Airlines Head East, Targeting Region's Plump Prices," *Wall Street Journal,* February 28, 1994, p. A1. Used with permission of *Wall Street Journal.* Also see K. Labich, "What Will Save the U.S. Airlines," *Fortune,* June 14, 1993, pp. 98-101.

Pricing Products

PRICING STRATEGIES

12

Entering the 1992 summer season, American Airlines and its competitors were looking for ways to kick-start the stalled travel industry. Coming off two years of record billion-dollar-plus losses, the troubled U.S. airline industry faced many problems—an ailing economy, rising costs, industry overcapacity, and severe price competition.

One major factor contributing to the industry's woes was its convoluted pricing structure. For years, the airlines had offered a bewildering array of fares, including deep promotional discounts designed to stimulate air travel. But such promotional pricing often had erupted into costly price wars that sapped long-term industry profits. Perhaps worse, the complex fare structure and never-ending promotions resulted in customer confusion and frustration. Both business and leisure travelers were flying less, and both persisted in their long-held beliefs that the airlines were gouging them on price. As the feeble economy dragged on, even people traveling at the lowest rates were complaining about the high cost of airline travel.

In mid-April 1992, American stepped forward with a bold new fare plan that it hoped would simplify the industry's fare structure, put an end to constant price squabbling, and restore its own and the industry's profitability. The leading U.S. carrier ran four-page ads in major newspapers across the country, announcing "The Next Page in the History of Air Fares." Gone were superlow promotional fares and special discounts for children, senior citizens, the military, bereaved families, and large corporate users. In their place was a slimmed-down structure with just four fares: *anytime coach fares* (now an average of 38 percent lower than previous full-coach fares); lower-price *first class fares* (20 to 50 percent lower than before); *21-day advance-purchase fares* (at about half the price of full-coach fares); and *7-day advance-purchase fares* (running $20 to $60 more than 21-day fares).

The new plan was good for everyone, American claimed. Although some of the cheapest fares rose slightly, consumers benefitted from the overall 38 percent cut in top fares. At the same time, it helped the airlines: eliminating deep discounts meant that average fares would rise. For the plan to work,

OBJECTIVES

When you finish this chapter, you should be able to accomplish the following:

1. Identify the **new product pricing strategies** of **market-skimming pricing** and **market-penetration pricing**.

2. List and define the **product-mix pricing strategies: product line, optional-product, captive-product, by-product**, and **product-bundle pricing**.

3. Define the major **price-adjustment strategies** of **discount and allowance pricing; segmented, psychological**, and **promotional pricing**; and **value, geographical**, and **international pricing**.

4. Discuss the key issues related to **price changes**, including **initiating price cuts** and **price increases, buyer** and **competitor reactions to price changes**, and **responding to price changes**.

however, American would need help from two key groups: customers and competitors. The plan wouldn't restore industry profits unless it stimulated increased travel. And American couldn't go it alone—competitors would have to charge similar fares. Unfortunately, American got little help from either group.

The lower fares didn't cause the hoped for stampede to the ticket counter. During the high-flying 1980s, the airlines had schooled travelers to wait for special discounts and promotions. When American eliminated them in the recessionary 1990s, consumers balked. They waited to see if the new fares would stick. On the other side of the ticket counter, most major competing carriers followed American's lead—for a while. However, weaker airlines such as Trans World Airlines, America West, and Continental—all operating out of bankruptcy—began to undercut American's new prices as soon as they were announced. TWA responded immediately with fares 10 to 20 percent below American's. America West undercut fares on transcontinental trips and promoted cheaper off-peak fares. No-frills Southwest Airlines announced a kids-fly-free program for the summer. US Air discounted fares from major Northeast cities to Florida, and Continental quickly followed.

Still hoping to succeed with its simplified fare plan, powerful American Airlines responded to these breeches with remarkable restraint. It cut its fares only as necessary in markets where it competed with TWA, America West, Southwest, US Air, and the other renegade airlines. However, once the discounting started, it soon snowballed. In late April, Northwest Airlines broke ranks. To attract family travelers for the summer season, it launched an "adults-fly free" promotion, which gave a free ticket to any adult traveling with a child. Northwest ran its first ads announcing the promotion on Tuesday evening, May 26. Before the night had ended, the carrier's reservations had risen 53 percent; by mid-day Wednesday, they'd jumped an incredible 176 percent. American responded with a vengeance to Northwest's defection, slashing all of its advance-purchase fares in half. The other airlines jumped in, setting off a brutal 10-day price war.

The incredibly low fares created a tidal wave of demand. Consumers swamped travel agents and airline ticket counters, greedily buying up two, three, or more tickets for summer trips. On Sunday, May 31, at the height of the buying frenzy, reservations at Northwest were up 563 percent compared with a week earlier. On Tuesday, June 2, Delta received a mind-boggling 2.5 million calls, compared with 300,000 on a typical day. The industry sold a summer's worth of travel in a little over a week.

Although those days in May and early June marked a happy time for air travelers, they spelled disaster for the airlines. As one analyst notes, "For most of the stronger airlines . . . it wiped out chances for a profitable summer. For the weaker ones, the low fares may have been the kiss of death." When the air cleared, the industry had lost more than $3 billion dollars in 1992.

Travel agents also lost out, working harder for lower commissions. They had to reissue previously purchased tickets at the new lower prices. And although the major airlines eventually allowed the agents to keep the commissions they'd earned on the earlier purchases, prices of new tickets were often so low that the agents couldn't make enough in commissions to cover the costs of writing them. Many travel agents blamed American; some even vowed to steer future business to other carriers when possible. To make matters worse, Continental sued American, claiming that it had engaged in predatory pricing—setting fares that could not be profitable in order to drive out weaker competitors. American responded that it was only trying to establish an industry pricing discipline that would let it and other airlines earn a profit.

By fall, on many American Airlines routes, travelers were once again confronted with a complex array of fares. American's revolutionary fare plan never really had a chance to get off the ground. Instead, its attempts to bring sanity to the industry's pricing practices created even greater losses, in terms of both dollars and credibility with consumers. Laments one airline executive, "The damage done will be with us for a long, long time."[1]

In this chapter, we will look at complex dynamics of pricing. A company sets not a single price, but rather a *pricing structure* that covers different items in its line. This pricing structure changes over time as products move through their life cycles. The company adjusts product prices to reflect changes in costs and demand and to account for variations in buyers and situations. As the competitive environment changes, the company considers when to initiate price changes and when to respond to them. And as the American Airlines example demonstrates forcefully, pricing decisions are subject to an incredibly complex array of environmental and competitive forces.

This chapter examines the major dynamic pricing strategies available to management. In turn, we look at *new-product pricing strategies* for products in the introductory stage of the product life cycle, *product-mix pricing strategies* for related products in the product mix, *price-adjustment strategies* that account for customer differences and changing situations, and *strategies for initiating and responding to price changes.*[2]

NEW-PRODUCT PRICING STRATEGIES

Pricing strategies usually change as the product passes through its life cycle. The introductory stage is especially challenging. We can distinguish between pricing a product that imitates existing products and pricing an innovative product that is patent protected.

FIGURE 12-1 *Price-quality strategies*

	Price	
	Higher	Lower
Quality Higher	Premium strategy	Good-value strategy
Lower	Overcharging strategy	Economy strategy

A company that plans to develop an imitative new product faces a product-positioning problem. It must decide where to position the product versus competing products in terms of quality and price. Figure 12-1 shows four possible positioning strategies. First, the company might decide to use a *premium pricing* strategy—producing a high-quality product and charging the highest price. At the other extreme, it might decide on an *economy pricing* strategy—producing a lower quality product but charging a low price. These strategies can coexist in the same market as long as the market consists of at least two groups of buyers, those who seek quality and those who seek price. Thus, Rolex offers very high quality watches at very high prices, and Timex offers lower quality watches at more affordable prices.

The *good-value* strategy represents a way to attack the premium pricer. Its says, "We have high quality, but at a lower price." If this really is true, and quality-sensitive buyers believe the good-value pricer, they will sensibly buy the product and save money—unless the premium product offers more status or snob appeal. Using an *overcharging* strategy, the company overprices the product in relation to its quality. In the long-run, however, customers will likely feel "taken." They will stop buying the product and will complain to others about it. Thus, this strategy should be avoided.

Companies bringing out an innovative, patent-protected product face the challenge of setting prices for the first time. They can choose between two strategies: *market-skimming pricing* and *market-penetration pricing.*

Market-skimming pricing
Setting a high price for a new product to skim maximum revenues layer by layer from the segments willing to pay the high price; the company makes fewer but more profitable sales.

MARKET-SKIMMING PRICING

Many companies that invent new products initially set high prices to "skim" revenues layer by layer from the market. Intel is a prime user of this strategy, called **market-skimming pricing.** When Intel first introduces a new computer chip, it

Rolex pursues a premium pricing strategy, selling very high quality watches at a high price. In contrast, Timex uses a value-pricing strategy, offering good quality watches at more affordable prices.

charges the highest price it can given the benefits of the new chip over competing chips. It sets a price that makes it *just* worthwhile for some segments of the market to adopt computers containing the chip. As initial sales slow down, and as competitors threaten to introduce similar chips, Intel lowers the price to draw in the next price-sensitive layer of customers.

For example, when Intel first brought out its Pentium chips, it priced them at about $1,000 each. As a result, computer producers priced their first Pentium PCs at $3,500 or more, attracting as customers only serious computer users and business buyers. However, after introduction, Intel cut Pentium prices by 30 percent per year, eventually allowing the price of Pentium PCs to drop into the typical price range of home buyers. In this way, Intel skimmed a maximum amount of revenue from the various segments of the market.[3]

Market skimming makes sense only under certain conditions. First, the product's quality and image must support its higher price, and enough buyers must want the product at that price. Second, the costs of producing a smaller volume cannot be so high that they cancel the advantage of charging more. Finally, competitors should not be able to enter the market easily and undercut the high price.

MARKET-PENETRATION PRICING

Market-penetration pricing Setting a low price for a new product in order to attract a large number of buyers and a large market share.

Rather than setting a high initial price to *skim* off small but profitable market segments, some companies use **market-penetration pricing.** They set a low initial price in order to *penetrate* the market quickly and deeply—to attract a large number of buyers quickly and win a large market share. The high sales volume results in falling costs, allowing the company to cut its price even further. For example, Dell and Gateway used penetration pricing to sell high-quality computer products through lower-cost mail-order channels. Their sales soared when IBM, Compaq, Apple, and other competitors selling through retail stores could not match their prices. Home Depot, Wal-Mart, and other discount retailers also use penetration pricing. They charge low prices to attract high volume. The high volume results in lower costs which, in turn, let the discounters keep prices low.

Several conditions favor setting a low price. First, the market must be highly price sensitive so that a low price produces more market growth. Second, pro-

Home Depot practices market-penetration pricing. It charges "guaranteed low prices, day-in . . . day-out" to attract high volume, which in turn results in lower costs and still lower prices.

duction and distribution costs must fall as sales volume increases. Finally, the low price must help keep out the competition—otherwise the price advantage may be only temporary. For example, Dell and Gateway faced difficult times when IBM and Compaq established their own direct distribution channels.

PRODUCT-MIX PRICING STRATEGIES

The strategy for setting a product's price often has to be changed when the product is part of a product mix. In this case, the firm looks for a set of prices that maximizes the profits on the total product mix. Pricing is difficult because the various products have related demand and costs and face different degrees of competition. We now take a closer look at five *product-mix pricing* situations summarized in Table 12-1.

PRODUCT LINE PRICING

Companies usually develop product lines rather than single products. For example, Snapper makes many different lawn mowers, ranging from simple walk-behind versions priced at $259.95, $299.95, and $399.95, to elaborate riding mowers priced at $1,000 or more. Each successive lawn mower in the line offers more features. Kodak offers not just one type of film, but an assortment including regular Kodak film, higher-priced Kodak Royal Gold film for special occasions, and a

TABLE 12-1 *Product-Mix Pricing Strategies*

STRATEGY	DESCRIPTION
Product line pricing	Setting price steps between product line items
Optional-product pricing	Pricing optional or accessory products sold with the main product
Captive-product pricing	Pricing products that must be used with the main product
By-product pricing	Pricing low-value by-products to get rid of them
Product-bundle pricing	Pricing bundles of products sold together

Product-line pricing: Infinity offers a line of home stereo speakers at prices ranging from $275 to $50,000 per pair.

Product line pricing
Setting the price steps between various products in a product line based on cost differences between the products, customer evaluations of different features, and competitors' prices.

Optional-product pricing
The pricing of optional or accessory products along with a main product.

Captive-product pricing
Setting a price for products that must be used along with a main product, such as blades for a razor and film for a camera.

lower-priced, seasonal film called Funtime that competes with store brands. It offers each of these brands in a variety of sizes and film speeds. In **product line pricing,** management must decide on the price steps to set between the various products in a line.

The price steps should take into account cost differences between the products in the line, customer evaluations of their different features, and competitors' prices. If the price difference between two successive products is small, buyers usually will buy the more advanced product. This will increase company profits if the cost difference is smaller than the price difference. If the price difference is large, however, customers will generally buy the less advanced products.

In many industries, sellers use well-established *price points* for the products in their line. Thus, men's clothing stores might carry men's suits at three price levels: $185, $285, and $385. The customer probably will associate low-, average-, and high-quality suits with the three price points. Even if the three prices are raised a little, men normally will buy suits at their own preferred price points. The seller's task is to establish perceived quality differences that support the price differences.

OPTIONAL-PRODUCT PRICING

Many companies use **optional-product pricing**—offering to sell optional or accessory products along with their main product. For example, a car buyer may choose to order power windows, cruise control, and a radio with a CD player. Pricing these options is a sticky problem. Automobile companies have to decide which items to include in the base price and which to offer as options. Until recent years, General Motors' normal pricing strategy was to advertise a stripped-down model for, say, $12,000 to pull people into showrooms and then devote most of the showroom space to showing option-loaded cars at $14,000 or $15,000. The economy model was stripped of so many comforts and conveniences that most buyers rejected it. More recently, however, GM has followed the example of the Japanese auto makers and included in the sticker price many useful items previously sold only as options. The advertised price now often represents a well-equipped car.

CAPTIVE-PRODUCT PRICING

Companies that make products that must be used along with a main product are using **captive-product pricing.** Examples of captive products are razor blades, camera film, and computer software. Producers of the main products (razors, cameras, and computers) often price them low and set high markups on the supplies. Thus, Polaroid prices its cameras low because it makes its money on the film it sells. And Gillette sells low-priced razors but makes money on the replacement blades. Camera makers who do not sell film have to price their main products higher in order to make the same overall profit.

In the case of services, this strategy is called *two-part pricing.* The price of the service is broken into a *fixed fee* plus a *variable usage rate.* Thus, a telephone company charges a monthly rate—the fixed fee—plus charges for calls beyond some minimum number—the variable usage rate. Amusement parks charge admission plus fees for food, midway attractions, and rides over a minimum. The service firm must decide how much to charge for the basic service and how much for the variable usage. The fixed amount should be low enough to induce usage of the service, and profit can be made on the variable fees.

BY-PRODUCT PRICING

By-product pricing
Setting a price for by-products in order to make the main product's price more competitive.

In producing processed meats, petroleum products, chemicals, and other products, there are often by-products. If the by-products have no value and if getting rid of them is costly, this will affect the pricing of the main product. Using **by-product pricing**, the manufacturer will seek a market for these by-products and should accept any price that covers more than the cost of storing and delivering them. This practice allows the seller to reduce the main product's price to make it more competitive. By-products can even turn out to be profitable. For example, many lumber mills have begun to sell bark chips and sawdust profitably as decorative mulch for home and commercial landscaping.

PRODUCT-BUNDLE PRICING

Product-bundle pricing
Combining several products and offering the bundle at a reduced price.

Using **product-bundle pricing**, sellers often combine several of their products and offer the bundle at a reduced price. Thus, theaters and sports teams sell season tickets at less than the cost of single tickets; hotels sell specially priced packages that include room, meals, and entertainment; computer makers include attractive software packages with their personal computers. Price bundling can promote the sales of products consumers might not otherwise buy, but the combined price must be low enough to get them to buy the bundle.[4]

PRICE-ADJUSTMENT STRATEGIES

Companies usually adjust their basic prices to account for various customer differences and changing situations. Table 12-2 summarizes seven price-adjustment strategies: *discount and allowance pricing, segmented pricing, psychological pricing, promotional pricing, value pricing, geographical pricing,* and *international pricing.*

DISCOUNT AND ALLOWANCE PRICING

Most companies adjust their basic price to reward customers for certain responses, such as early payment of bills, volume purchases, and off-season buying. These price adjustments—called discounts and allowances—can take many forms.

Cash discount
A price reduction to buyers who pay their bills promptly.

A **cash discount** is a price reduction to buyers who pay their bills promptly. A typical example is "2/10, net 30," which means that although payment is due

TABLE 12-2   *Product Adjustment Strategies*

STRATEGY	DESCRIPTION
Discount and allowance pricing	Reducing prices to reward customer responses such as paying early or promoting the product
Segmented pricing	Adjusting prices to allow for differences in customers, products, or locations
Psychological pricing	Adjusting prices for psychological effect
Promotional pricing	Temporarily reducing prices to increase short-run sales
Value pricing	Adjusting prices to offer the right combination of quality and service at a fair price
Geographical pricing	Adjusting prices to account for the geographic location of customers
International pricing	Adjusting prices for international markets

Quantity discount
A price reduction to buyers who buy large volumes.

Functional discount
A price reduction offered by the seller to trade channel members who perform certain functions such as selling, storing, and record-keeping.

Seasonal discount
A price reduction to buyers who purchase merchandise or services out of season.

Allowance
Promotional money paid by manufacturers to retailers in return for an agreement to feature the manufacturer's products in some way.

Segmented pricing
Selling a product or service at two or more prices, where the difference in prices is not based on differences in costs.

Segmented pricing: Ramada uses customer-segment and time pricing, and other incentives, to attract family travelers during the summer season. This summer, "four adults can stay in the same room for the cost of just one, and kids always stay free."

within 30 days, the buyer can deduct 2 percent if the bill is paid within 10 days. The discount must be granted to all buyers meeting these terms. Such discounts are customary in many industries and help to improve the sellers' cash situation and reduce bad debts and credit-collection costs.

A **quantity discount** is a price reduction to buyers who buy large volumes. A typical example might be "$10 per unit for less than 100 units, $9 per unit for 100 or more units." By law, quantity discounts must be offered equally to all customers and must not exceed the seller's cost savings associated with selling large quantities. These savings include lower selling, inventory, and transportation expenses. Discounts provide an incentive to the customer to buy more from one given seller, rather than from many different sources.

A **functional discount** (also called a *trade discount*) is offered by the seller to trade channel members who perform certain functions, such as selling, storing, and recordkeeping. Manufacturers may offer different functional discounts to different trade channels because of the varying services they perform, but manufacturers must offer the same functional discounts within each trade channel.

A **seasonal discount** is a price reduction to buyers who buy merchandise or services out of season. For example, lawn and garden equipment manufacturers will offer seasonal discounts to retailers during the fall and winter to encourage early ordering in anticipation of the heavy spring and summer selling seasons. Hotels, motels, and airlines will offer seasonal discounts in their slower selling periods. Seasonal discounts allow the seller to keep production steady during an entire year.

Allowances are another type of reduction from the list price. For example, *trade-in allowances* are price reductions given for turning in an old item when buying a new one. Trade-in allowances are most common in the automobile industry, but are also given for other durable goods. *Promotional allowances* are payments or price reductions to reward dealers for participating in advertising and sales-support programs.

SEGMENTED PRICING

Companies often will adjust their basic prices to allow for differences in customers, products, and locations. In **segmented pricing,** the company sells a product or service at two or more prices, even though the difference in prices is not based on differences in costs. Segmented pricing takes several forms:

◆ *Customer-segment pricing.* Different customers pay different prices for the same product or service. Museums, for example, will charge a lower admission for students and senior citizens.

◆ *Product-form pricing.* Different versions of the product are priced differently, but not according to differences in their costs. For instance, Black & Decker prices its most expensive iron at $54.98, which is $12 more than the price of its next most expensive iron. The top model has a self-cleaning feature, yet this extra feature costs only a few more dollars to make.

◆ *Location pricing.* Different locations are priced differently, even though the cost of offering each location is the same. For instance, theaters vary their seat prices because of audience preferences for certain locations, and state universities charge higher tuition for out-of-state students.

HOW PRICE SIGNALS PRODUCT QUALITY

Heublein produces Smirnoff, America's leading brand of vodka. Some years ago, Smirnoff was attacked by another brand. Wolfschmidt, priced at one dollar less per bottle, claimed to have the same quality as Smirnoff. Concerned that customers might switch to Wolfschmidt, Heublein considered several possible counterstrategies. It could lower Smirnoff's price by one dollar to hold on to market share; it could hold Smirnoff's price but increase advertising and promotion expenditures; or it could hold Smirnoff's price and let its market share fall. All three strategies would lead to lower profits, and it seemed that Heublein faced a no-win situation.

At this point, however, Heublein's marketers thought of a fourth strategy—and it was brilliant. Heublein *raised* the price of Smirnoff by one dollar! The company then introduced a new brand, Relska, to compete with Wolfschmidt. Moreover, it introduced yet another brand, Popov, priced even *lower* than Wolfschmidt. This product line-pricing strategy positioned Smirnoff as the elite brand and Wolfschmidt as an ordinary brand. Heublein's clever strategy produced a large increase in its overall profits.

The irony is that Heublein's three brands are pretty much the same in taste and manufacturing costs. Heublein knew that a product's price signals its quality. Using price as a signal, Heublein sells roughly the same product at three different quality positions.

◆ *Time pricing.* Prices vary by the season, the month, the day, and even the hour. Public utilities vary their prices to commercial users by time of day and weekend versus weekday. The telephone company offers lower "off-peak" charges, and resorts give seasonal discounts.

For segmented pricing to be an effective strategy, certain conditions must exist. The market must be segmentable, and the segments must show different degrees of demand. Members of the segment paying the lower price should not be able to turn around and resell the product to the segment paying the higher price. Competitors should not be able to undersell the firm in the segment being charged the higher price. Nor should the costs of segmenting and watching the market exceed the extra revenue obtained from the price difference. The practice should not lead to customer resentment and ill will. Finally, the segmented pricing must be legal.

PSYCHOLOGICAL PRICING

Price says something about the product. For example, many consumers use price to judge quality. A $100 bottle of perfume may contain only $3 worth of scent, but some people are willing to pay the $100 because this price indicates something special.

Psychological pricing
A pricing approach that considers the psychology of prices and not simply the economics; the price is used to say something about the product.

In using **psychological pricing,** sellers consider the psychology of prices and not simply the economics. For example, one study of the relationship between price and quality perceptions of cars found that consumers perceive higher-priced cars as having higher quality.[5] By the same token, higher-quality cars are perceived to be even higher priced than they actually are. When consumers can judge the quality of a product by examining it or by calling on past experience with it, they use price less to judge quality. When consumers cannot judge quality because they lack the information or skill, price becomes an important quality signal (see Marketing Highlight 12-1).

Reference prices
Prices that buyers carry in their minds and refer to when they look at a given product.

Another aspect of psychological pricing is **reference prices**—prices that buyers carry in their minds and refer to when looking at a given product. The reference price might be formed by noting current prices, remembering past prices, or assessing the buying situation. Sellers can influence or use these consumers' reference prices when setting price. For example, a company could display its product next to more expensive ones in order to imply that it belongs in the same

Promotional pricing: Companies often reduce their prices temporarily to attract customers and boost sales.

class. Department stores often sell women's clothing in separate departments differentiated by price: Clothing found in the more expensive department is assumed to be of better quality. Companies also can influence consumers' reference prices by stating high manufacturer's suggested prices, by indicating that the product was originally priced much higher, or by pointing to a competitor's higher price.

Even small differences in price can suggest product differences. Consider a stereo priced at $300 compared to one priced at $299.95. The actual price difference is only 5 cents, but the psychological difference can be much greater. For example, some consumers will see the $299.95 as a price in the $200 range rather than the $300 range. Whereas the $299.95 will more likely be seen as a bargain price, the $300 price suggests more quality. Some psychologists argue that each digit has symbolic and visual qualities that should be considered in pricing. Thus, 8 is round and even and creates a soothing effect, whereas 7 is angular and creates a jarring effect.[6]

PROMOTIONAL PRICING

Promotional pricing
Temporarily pricing products below the list price, and sometimes even below cost, to increase short-run sales.

With **promotional pricing**, companies will temporarily price their products below list price and sometimes even below cost. Promotional pricing takes several forms. Supermarkets and department stores will price a few products as *loss leaders* to attract customers to the store in the hope that they will buy other items at normal markups. Sellers will also use *special-event pricing* in certain seasons to draw more customers. Thus, linens are promotionally priced every January to attract weary Christmas shoppers back into stores. Manufacturers will sometimes offer *cash rebates* to consumers who buy the product from dealers within a specified time; the manufacturer sends the rebate directly to the customer. Rebates have recently been popular with auto makers and producers of durable goods and small appliances. Some manufacturers offer *low-interest financing, longer warranties,* or *free maintenance* to reduce the consumer's "price." This practice has recently become a favorite of the auto industry. Or, the seller may simply offer *discounts* from normal prices to increase sales and reduce inventories.

VALUE PRICING

Value pricing
Offering just the right combination of quality and good service at a fair price.

During the recessionary, slow-growth 1990s, many companies have adjusted their prices to bring them into line with economic conditions and with the resulting fundamental shift in consumer attitudes toward quality and value. More and more, marketers have adopted **value pricing** strategies—offering just the right combination of quality and good service at a fair price. In many cases, this has involved the introduction of less expensive versions of established, brand name products. Thus, Campbell introduced its Great Starts Budget frozen-food line, Holiday Inn opened several Holiday Express budget hotels, Revlon's Charles of the Ritz offered the Express Bar collection of affordable cosmetics, and fast-food restaurants such as Taco Bell and McDonald's offered "value menus." In other cases, value pricing has involved redesigning existing brands in order to offer more quality for a given price or the same quality for less (see Marketing Highlight 12-2).

GEOGRAPHICAL PRICING

A company also must decide how to price its products to customers located in different parts of the country or world. Should the company risk losing the business of more distant customers by charging them higher prices to cover the higher shipping costs? Or should the company charge all customers the same prices regardless of location? We will look at five geographical pricing strategies for the following hypothetical situation:

> The Peerless Paper Company is located in Atlanta, Georgia, and sells paper products to customers all over the United States. The cost of freight is high and affects the companies from whom customers buy their paper. Peerless wants to establish a geographical pricing policy. It is trying to determine how to price a $100 order to three specific customers: Customer A (Atlanta); Customer B (Bloomington, Indiana), and Customer C (Compton, California).

FOB-origin pricing
A geographic pricing strategy in which goods are placed free on board a carrier; the customer pays the freight from the factory to the destination.

One option is for Peerless to ask each customer to pay the shipping cost from the Atlanta factory to the customer's location. All three customers would pay the same factory price of $100, with Customer A paying, say, $10 for shipping; Customer B, $15; and Customer C, $25. Called **FOB-origin pricing**, this practice means that the goods are placed *free on board* (hence, *FOB*) a carrier. At that point the title and responsibility pass to the customer, who pays the freight from the factory to the destination.

Because each customer picks up its own cost, supporters of FOB pricing feel that this is the fairest way to assess freight charges. The disadvantage, however, is that Peerless will be a high-cost firm to distant customers. If Peerless's main competitor happens to be in California, this competitor will no doubt outsell Peerless in California. In fact, the competitor would outsell Peerless in most of the West, whereas Peerless would dominate the East.

Uniform delivered pricing
A geographic pricing strategy in which the company charges the same price plus freight to all customers, regardless of their location.

Uniform delivered pricing is the exact opposite of FOB pricing. Here, the company charges the same price plus freight to all customers, regardless of their location. The freight charge is set at the average freight cost. Suppose this is $15. Uniform delivered pricing therefore results in a higher charge to the Atlanta customer (who pays $15 freight instead of $10) and a lower charge to the Compton customer (who pays $15 instead of $25). On the one hand, the Atlanta customer would prefer to buy paper from another local paper company that uses FOB-origin pricing. On the other hand, Peerless has a better chance of winning over the California customer. Other advantages of uniform delivered pricing are that it is fairly easy to administer and it lets the firm advertise its price nationally.

Zone pricing
A geographic pricing strategy in which the company sets up two or more zones. All customers within a zone pay the same total price; the more distant the zone, the higher the price.

Zone pricing falls between FOB-origin pricing and uniform delivered pricing. The company sets up two or more zones. All customers within a given zone pay a single total price; the more distant the zone, the higher the price. For example, Peerless might set up an East Zone and charge $10 freight to all customers in this zone, a Midwest Zone in which it charges $15, and a West Zone in which it charges $25. In this way, the customers within a given price zone receive no price advantage from the company. For example, customers in Atlanta and Boston pay the same total price to Peerless. The complaint, however, is that the Atlanta customer is paying part of the Boston customer's freight cost. In addition, even

VALUE PRICING: OFFERING MORE FOR LESS

Marketers have a new buzzword for the 1990s, and it's spelled V-A-L-U-E. Throughout the 1980s, marketers pitched luxury, prestige, extravagance—even expensiveness—for everything from ice cream to autos. But after the recession began, they started redesigning, repackaging, repositioning, and remarketing products to emphasize value. Now, value pricing—offering more for a lot less by underscoring a product's quality while at the same time featuring its price—has gone from a groundswell to a tidal wave.

Value pricing can mean many things to marketers. To some, it means price cutting. To others, it means special deals, such as providing more of a product at the same price. And to still others, it means a new image—one that convinces consumers they're receiving a good deal. No matter how it's defined, however, value pricing has become a prime strategy for wooing consumers. The upscale tactics that dominated the 1980s have virtually disappeared. Now, 1980s pretentiousness is used as the antithesis. Take the magazine ad for Nissan's Maxima GXE: "Today, the idea of spending thousands more on a luxury sedan for the cachet of having a hood ornament appears hopelessly unjustified. No, these are the 1990s, an era of renewed sensibility."

Marketers are finding that the flat economy and changing consumer demographics have created a new class of sophisticated, bargain-hunting shoppers who are careful of what,

Value pricing: Based on such factors as maintenance costs, fuel economy, and depreciation, Buick pitches its $25,800, top-of-the-line, full-size Park Avenue as "America's best car value."

where, and how they shop. Whereas it used to be fashionable to flaunt affluence and spend conspicuously, now it's fashionable to say you got a good deal. To convince consumers

they're getting more for their money, companies from fast-food chains to stock brokerages and car makers have revamped their marketing pitches:

- Mobil's Hefty division slashed prices as much as 20 percent and added 20 percent more plastic bags per box. Hefty also trashed its two-decade-old marketing effort centering on bag strength. The new motto: "Our strength is value." Says one Mobil manager: "People are looking for value in the 1990s, even in trash bags."
- PepsiCo's Taco Bell chain introduced an incredibly successful "value menu" offering 59-cent tacos and 15 other items for either 59 cents, 79 cents, or 99 cents. McDonald's followed suit with its Extra-Value meals, underscored by the ad theme, "Good food. Good value." Soon, Wendy's, Burger King, and other competitors entered the fray with their own value-pricing schemes.
- Stock brokerage Shearson-Lehman Hutton is searching for a new ad campaign to help it counter the low-price claims of discount stockbrokers. "People are asking, 'Am I getting what I paid for, and is there value in it?'" notes a Shearson marketing

---

Basing-point pricing
A geographic pricing strategy in which the seller designates some city as a basing point and charges all customers the freight cost from that city to the customer location, regardless of the city from which the goods are actually shipped.

though they may be within a few miles of each other, a customer just barely on the west side of the line dividing the East and Midwest pays much more than does one just barely on the east side of the line.

Using **basing-point pricing,** the seller selects a given city as a "basing point" and charges all customers the freight cost from that city to the customer location, regardless of the city from which the goods actually are shipped. For example, Peerless might set Chicago as the basing point and charge all customers $100 plus the freight from Chicago to their locations. This means that an Atlanta customer pays the freight cost from Chicago to Atlanta, even though the goods may be shipped from Atlanta. Using a basing-point location other than the factory raises the total price for customers near the factory and lowers the total price for customers far from the factory.

If all sellers used the same basing-point city, delivered prices would be the same for all customers and price competition would be eliminated. Industries such as sugar, cement, steel, and automobiles used basing-point pricing for years, but this method has become less popular today. Some companies set up multiple bas-

executive. "Companies are being challenged to [define] the value they offer versus the price they charge." The new campaign will focus on services such as investment advice and financial planning that make Shearson's full-service offering a better value, even at the higher prices it charges.

◆ In a recent world tour, General Electric Chairman Jack Welch noted that customers around the globe are now more interested in price than technology. "The value decade is upon us," he states. "If you can't sell a top-quality product at the world's lowest price, you're going to be out of the game." As a result, in products ranging from refrigerators to CAT scanners and jet engines, GE is working to offer basic, dependable units at unbeatable prices.

◆ Buick is pitching its top-of-the-line full-size Park Avenue as "America's best car value" at a suggested list price of $25,800. Buick's boast is backed by findings from IntelliChoice, an independent research firm that ranked the Park Avenue number one on factors such as maintenance costs, fuel economy, and depreciation. "We're saying that you don't have to buy [an economy car] to get value for your dollar,"

says Buick's national advertising manager. "You don't have to give up luxury, performance, or size to get great value."

Value pricing involves more than just cutting prices. It means finding the delicate balance between quality and price that gives target consumers the value they seek. To consumers, "value" is not the same as "cheap." Value pricing requires price cutting coupled with finding ways to maintain or even improve quality while still making a profit. Consumers who enjoyed high-quality brand name products during the 1980s now want the same high quality, but at much lower prices. Thus, value pricing often involves redesigning products and production processes to lower costs and preserve profit margins at lower prices. For example, before launching its value menu, Taco Bell redesigned its restaurants to increase customer traffic and reduce costs. It shrank its kitchens, expanded seating space, and introduced new menu items specifically designed for easy preparation in the new, smaller kitchens.

Although the trend toward value pricing began with the recession, its roots run much deeper. The trend reflects marketers' reactions to a fundamental change in consumer attitudes, resulting from the aging of

the baby boomers and their increased financial pressures. Today's "squeezed consumers"—saddled with debt acquired during the free-spending 1980s and facing increased expenses for child rearing, home buying, and pending retirement—will continue to demand more value long after the economy improves. Even before the economy soured, buyers were beginning to rethink the price-quality equation. Thus, value pricing will likely remain a crucial strategy throughout the 1990s and beyond. Winning over tomorrow's increasingly shrewd consumers will require finding ever-new ways to offer them more for less.

Sources: Portions adapted from Gary Strauss, "Marketers' Plea: Let's Make a Deal," *USA Today,* September 29, 1992, pp. B1–B2. The Jack Welch quote is from Stratford Sherman, "How to Prosper in the Value Decade," *Fortune,* November 30, 1992, pp. 90–104. Also see Joseph B. White, "'Value Pricing' Is Hot As Shrewd Consumers Seek Low-Cost Quality," *Wall Street Journal,* March 12, 1991, pp. A1, A9; Faye Rice, "What Intelligent Consumers Want," *Fortune,* December 28, 1992, pp. 56–60; Bill Kelley, "The New Consumer Revealed," *Sales & Marketing Management,* May 1993, pp. 46–52; and Bradford W. Morgan, "It's the Myth of the 'Value Consumer,'" *Brandweek,* February 28, 1994, p. 17.

Freight-absorption pricing
A geographic pricing strategy in which the company absorbs all or part of the actual freight charges in order to get the business.

ing points to create more flexibility: They quote freight charges from the basing-point city nearest to the customer.

Finally, the seller who is anxious to do business with a certain customer or geographical area might use **freight-absorption pricing.** Using this strategy, the seller absorbs all or part of the actual freight charges in order to get the desired business. The seller might reason that if it can get more business, its average costs will fall and more than compensate for its extra freight cost. Freight-absorption pricing is used for market penetration and to hold on to increasingly competitive markets.

INTERNATIONAL PRICING

Companies that market their products internationally must decide what prices to charge in the different countries in which they operate. In some cases, a company can set a uniform worldwide price. For example, Boeing sells its jetliners at about the same price everywhere, whether in the United States, Europe, or a Third World

International price escalation: A pair of Levi's selling for $30 in the United States goes for over $60 in a Levi's boutique in Korea and other Pacific Rim countries.

country. However, most companies adjust their prices to reflect local market conditions and cost considerations.

The price that a company should charge in a specific country depends on many factors, including economic conditions, competitive situations, laws and regulations, and development of the wholesaling and retailing system. Consumer perceptions and preferences also may vary from country to country, calling for different prices. Or the company may have different marketing objectives in various world markets, which require changes in pricing strategy. For example, Sony might introduce a new product into mature markets in highly developed countries with the goal of quickly gaining mass-market share—this would call for a penetration pricing strategy. In contrast, it might enter a less developed market by targeting smaller, less price-sensitive segments—in this case, market-skimming pricing makes sense.

Costs play an important role in setting international prices. Travelers abroad are often surprised to find that goods that are relatively inexpensive at home may carry outrageously higher price tags in other countries. A pair of Levis selling for $30 in the United States goes for about $63 in Tokyo and $88 in Paris. A McDonald's Big Mac selling for a modest $2.25 here costs $5.75 in Moscow. And an Oral-B toothbrush selling for 19 cents at home costs 90 cents in China. Conversely, a Gucci handbag going for only $60 in Milan, Italy, fetches $240 in the United States. In some cases, such *price escalation* may result from differences in selling strategies or market conditions. In most instances, however, it is simply a result of the higher costs of selling in foreign markets—the additional costs of modifying the product, higher shipping and insurance costs, import tariffs and taxes, costs associated with exchange-rate fluctuations, and higher channel and physical distribution costs.

For example, Campbell found that its distribution costs in the United Kingdom were 30 percent higher than in the United States. U.S. retailers typically purchase soup in large quantities—48-can cases of a single soup by the dozens, hundreds, or carloads. In contrast, English grocers purchase soup in small quantities—typically in 24-can cases of *assorted* soups. Each case must be hand-packed for shipment. To handle these small orders, Campbell had to add a costly extra wholesale level to its European channel. The smaller orders also mean that English retailers order two or three times as often as their U.S. counterparts, bumping up billing and order costs. These and other factors caused Campbell to charge much higher prices for its soups in the United Kingdom.[7]

Thus, international pricing presents some special problems and complexities. We discuss international pricing issues in more detail in Chapter 20.

PRICE CHANGES

After developing their pricing structures and strategies, companies often face situations in which they must initiate price changes or respond to price changes by competitors.

INITIATING PRICE CHANGES

In some cases, the company may find it desirable to initiate either a price cut or a price increase. In both cases, it must anticipate possible buyer and competitor reactions.

Initiating Price Cuts

Several situations may lead a firm to consider cutting its price. One such circumstance is excess capacity. In this case, the firm needs more business and cannot get it through increased sales effort, product improvement, or other measures. It may drop its "follow-the-leader pricing"—charging about the same price as their leading competitor—and aggressively cut prices to boost sales. But as the airline, construction equipment, and other industries have learned in recent years, cutting prices in an industry loaded with excess capacity may lead to price wars as competitors try to hold on to market share.

Another situation leading to price changes is falling market share in the face of strong price competition. Several American industries—automobiles, consumer electronics, cameras, watches, and steel, for example—lost market share to Japanese competitors whose high-quality products carried lower prices than did their American counterparts. In response, American companies resorted to more aggressive pricing action. General Motors, for example, cut its subcompact car prices by 10 percent on the West Coast, where Japanese competition was strongest.[8]

A company also may cut prices in a drive to dominate the market through lower costs. Either the company starts with lower costs than its competitors or it cuts prices in the hope of gaining market share that will further cut costs through larger volume. Bausch & Lomb used an aggressive low-cost, low-price strategy to become an early leader in the competitive soft contact lens market.

Initiating Price Increases

In contrast, many companies have had to *raise* prices in recent years. They do this knowing that the price increases may be resented by customers, dealers, and even their own salesforce. Yet a successful price increase can greatly increase profits. For example, if the company's profit margin is 3 percent of sales, a 1 percent price increase will increase profits by 33 percent if sales volume is unaffected.

A major factor in price increases is cost inflation. Rising costs squeeze profit margins and lead companies to regular rounds of price increases. Companies often raise their prices by more than the cost increase in anticipation of further inflation. Another factor leading to price increases is overdemand: When a company cannot supply all its customers' needs, it can raise its prices, ration products to customers, or both.

Companies can increase their prices in a number of ways to keep up with rising costs. Prices can be raised almost invisibly by dropping discounts and adding higher-priced units to the line. Or prices can be pushed up openly. In passing price increases on to customers, the company should avoid the image of price gouging. The price increases should be supported with a company communication program telling customers why prices are being increased. The company salesforce should help customers find ways to economize.

Where possible, the company should consider ways to meet higher costs or demand without raising prices. For example, it can shrink the product instead of raising the price, as candy bar manufacturers often do. Or it can substitute less expensive ingredients, or remove certain product features, packaging, or services. Or it can "unbundle" its products and services, removing and separately pricing elements that were formerly part of the offer. IBM, for example, now offers training and consulting as separately priced services.

Buyer Reactions to Price Changes

Whether the price is raised or lowered, the action will affect buyers, competitors, distributors, and suppliers and may interest government as well. Customers do not always interpret prices in a straightforward way. They may view a price *cut* in several ways. For example, what would you think if Sony were suddenly to cut its VCR prices in half? You might think that these VCRs are about to be replaced by newer models or that they have some fault and are not selling well. You might think that Sony is in financial trouble and may not stay in this business long enough to supply future parts. You might believe that quality has been reduced. Or you might think that the price will come down even further and that it will pay to wait and see.

Similarly, a price *increase*, which normally would lower sales, may have some positive meanings for buyers. What would you think if Sony *raised* the price of its latest VCR model? On the one hand, you might think that the item is very "hot" and may be unobtainable unless you buy it soon. Or you might think that the recorder is an unusually good value. On the other hand, you might think that Sony is greedy and charging what the traffic will bear.

Competitor Reactions to Price Changes

A firm considering a price change has to worry about the reactions of its competitors as well as its customers. Competitors are most likely to react when the number of firms involved is small, when the product is uniform, and when the buyers are well informed.

How can the firm figure out the likely reactions of its competitors? If the firm faces one large competitor, and if the competitor tends to react in a set way to price changes, that reaction can be easily anticipated. But if the competitor treats each price change as a fresh challenge and reacts according to its self-interest, the company will have to figure out just what makes up the competitor's self-interest at the time.

The problem is complex because, like the customer, the competitor can interpret a company price cut in many ways. It might think the company is trying to grab a larger market share, that the company is doing poorly and trying to boost its sales, or that the company wants the whole industry to cut prices to increase total demand.

When there are several competitors, the company must guess each competitor's likely reaction. If all competitors behave alike, this amounts to analyzing only a typical competitor. In contrast, if the competitors do not behave alike—perhaps because of differences in size, market shares, or policies—then separate analyses are necessary. However, if some competitors will match the price change, there is good reason to expect that the rest also will match it.

Buyer reactions to price changes? What would you think if the price of Joy was suddenly cut in half?

JOY
DE
JEAN PATOU
PARIS

The costliest perfume in the world.
NEIMAN-MARCUS

RESPONDING TO PRICE CHANGES

Here we reverse the question and ask how a firm should respond to a price change by a competitor. The firm needs to consider several issues: Why did the competitor change the price? Was it to take more market share, to use excess capacity, to meet changing cost conditions, or to lead an industrywide price change? Is the price change temporary or permanent? What will happen to the company's market share and profits if it does not respond? Are other companies going to respond? And what are the competitor's and other firms' responses to each possible reaction likely to be?

Besides these issues, the company must make a broader analysis. It has to consider its own product's stage in the life cycle, the product's importance in the company's product mix, the intentions and resources of the competitor, and the possible consumer reactions to price changes. The company cannot always make an extended analysis of its alternatives at the time of a price change, however. The competitor may have spent much time preparing this decision, but the company may have to react within hours or days. About the only way to cut down reaction time is to plan ahead for both possible competitor's price changes and possible responses.

Figure 12-2 shows the ways a company might assess and respond to a competitor's price cut. Once the company has determined that the competitor has cut its price and that this price reduction is likely to harm company sales and profits, it might simply decide to hold its current price and profit margin. The company might believe that it will not lose too much market share, or that it would lose too much profit if it reduced its own price. It might decide that it should wait and respond when it has more information on the effects of the competitor's price change. For now, it might be willing to hold on to good customers, while giving up the poorer ones to the competitor. The argument against this holding strategy, however, is that the competitor may get stronger and more confident as its sales increase, and that the company might wait too long to act.

If the company decides that effective action can and should be taken, it might make any of four responses. First, it could *reduce its price* to match the competitor's price. It may decide that the market is price sensitive, and that it would lose

FIGURE 12-2 *Assessing and responding to competitor's price changes*

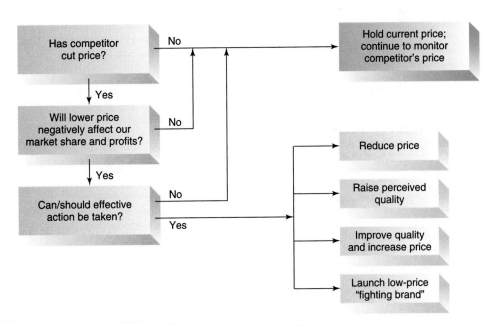

PUBLIC POLICY AND PRICING

When Russia lifted controls on bread prices as part of its dramatic move toward a free-market economy, Moscow bakers phoned around each morning to agree on regular rounds of price increases. This caused the *Wall Street Journal* to comment: "They still don't get it!" Those who have grown up under a well-regulated, free-market economy understand that such price fixing is clearly against the rules of fair competition. Setting prices is an important element of a competitive marketplace, and many federal and state laws govern the rules of fair play in pricing.

The most important pieces of legislation affecting pricing are the Sherman, Clayton, and Robinson-Patman Acts, initially adopted to curb the formation of monopolies and to regulate business practices that might unfairly restrain trade. Because these federal statutes can be applied only to interstate commerce, some states have adopted similar provisions for companies that operate locally. Public policy on pricing centers on three potentially damaging pricing practices: price fixing, price discrimination, and deceptive pricing.

Price Fixing. Federal legislation on price fixing states that sellers must set prices without talking to competitors. Otherwise, price collusion is suspected. Price fixing is illegal per se—that is, the government does not accept any excuses for price fixing. Even a simple conversation between competitors can have serious consequences. For example, during the early 1980s, American Airlines and Braniff were immersed in a price war in the Texas market. Each carrier undercut the other until both were offering absurdly low fares and each was losing money on many flights. In the heat of the battle, American's CEO, Robert Crandall, called the president of Braniff and said: "Raise your ... fares 20 percent. I'll raise mine the next morning." Fortunately for Crandall, the Braniff president warned him off, saying, "We can't talk about pricing!" As it turns out, the phone conversation had been

recorded, and the U.S. Justice Department began action against Crandall and American for price fixing. The charges were eventually dropped—the courts ruled that because Braniff had rejected Crandall's proposal, no actual collusion had occurred, and that a proposal to fix prices was not an actual violation of the law. This case and others like it have made most executives very reluctant to discuss prices in any way with competitors. In obtaining information on competitors' pricing, they rely only on openly published materials, such as trade association surveys and competitors' catalogs.

Price Discrimination. The Robinson-Patman Act seeks to ensure that sellers offer the same price terms to a given level of trade. For example, every retailer is entitled to the same price terms whether the retailer is Sears or the local bicycle shop. However, price discrimination is allowed if the seller can prove that its costs are different when selling to different retailers—for example, that it costs less per unit to sell a large volume of bicycles to Sears than to sell a few bicycles to a local dealer. Or the seller can discriminate in its pricing if the seller manufactures different qualities of the same product for different retailers. The seller has to prove that these differences are proportional. Price differentials also may be used to "match competition" in "good faith," provided the firm is trying to meet competitors at its own level of competition and the price discrimination is temporary, localized, and defensive rather than offensive.

Deceptive Pricing. Deceptive pricing occurs when a seller states prices or price savings that are not actually available to consumers. Some such deceptions are difficult for consumers to discern, as when an airline advertises a low one-way fare that is available only with the purchase of a round-trip ticket, or when a retailer sets artificially high "regular" prices, then announces "sale" prices close to its previous everyday prices. Many federal and state statutes regulate against deceptive pricing prac-

tices. For example, the Automobile Information Disclosure Act requires auto makers to attach a statement to new-car windows stating the manufacturer's suggested retail price, the prices of optional equipment, and the dealer's transportation charges. The FTC issues its *Guides Against Deceptive Pricing,* warning sellers not to advertise a price reduction unless it is a saving from the usual retail price, not to advertise "factory" or "wholesale" prices unless such prices are what they are claimed to be, and not to advertise comparable value prices on imperfect goods. Many states have developed retail advertising guidelines to ensure that locally advertised prices are accurately stated and clearly understood by consumers.

Other Regulated Pricing Practices. Sellers also are prohibited from using *predatory pricing*—selling below cost with the intention of destroying competition. Wholesalers and retailers in over half the states face laws requiring a minimum percentage markup over their cost of merchandise plus transportation. These laws attempt to protect small sellers from larger ones who might sell items below cost to attract customers. *Resale price maintenance* is also prohibited—a manufacturer cannot require dealers to charge a specified retail price for its product. Although the seller can propose a manufacturer's *suggested* retail price to dealers, it cannot refuse to sell to a dealer who takes independent pricing action, nor can it punish the dealer by shipping late or denying advertising allowances.

Sources: For more on public policy and pricing, see Louis W. Stern and Thomas L. Eovaldi, *Legal Aspects of Marketing Strategy* (Englewood Cliffs, NJ: Prentice Hall, 1984), Chap. 5; Robert J. Posch, *The Complete Guide to Marketing and the Law* (Englewood Cliffs, NJ: Prentice Hall, 1988), Chap. 28; and Thomas T. Nagle and Reed K. Holden, *The Strategy and Tactics of Pricing* (Englewood Cliffs, NJ: Prentice Hall, 1995), Chap. 14.

Fighting brands: When challenged on price by store brands and other low-priced entrants, Procter & Gamble turned a number of its brands into fighting brands, including Luvs disposable diapers.

too much market share to the lower-priced competitor. Or it might worry that recapturing lost market share later would be too hard. Cutting price will reduce the company's profits in the short run. Some companies might also reduce their product quality, services, and marketing communications to retain profit margins, but this ultimately will hurt long-run market share. The company should try to maintain its quality as it cuts prices.

Alternatively, the company might maintain its price but *raise the perceived quality* of its offer. It could improve its communications, stressing the relative quality of its product over that of the lower-price competitor. The firm may find it cheaper to maintain price and spend money to improve its perceived value than to cut price and operate at a lower margin.

Or, the company might *improve quality and increase price,* moving its brand into a higher price position. The higher quality justifies the higher price, which in turn preserves the company's higher margins. Or the company can hold price on the current product and introduce a new brand at a higher price position.

Finally, the company might launch a low-price "fighting brand." Often, one of the best responses is to add lower-price items to the line or to create a separate lower-price brand. This is necessary if the particular market segment being lost is price sensitive and will not respond to arguments of higher quality. Thus, when attacked on price by Fuji, Kodak introduced low-priced Funtime film. When challenged on price by store brands and other low-priced entrants, Procter & Gamble turned a number of its brands into fighting brands, including Luvs disposable diapers, Joy dishwashing detergent, and Camay beauty soap. In response to price pressures, Miller cut the price of its High Life brand by 20 percent in most markets, and sales jumped 9 percent in less than a year.[9]

Pricing strategies and tactics form an important element of a company's marketing mix. In setting prices, companies must carefully consider a great many internal and external factors before choosing a price that will give them the greatest competitive advantage in selected target markets. However, companies are not usually free to charge whatever prices they wish. Several laws restrict pricing practices, and a number of ethical considerations affect pricing decisions. Marketing Highlight 12-3 discusses the many public policy issues surrounding pricing.

Summary

Pricing is a dynamic process. Companies design a pricing structure that covers all their products. They change this structure over time and adjust it to account for different customers and situations.

Pricing strategies usually change as a product passes through its life cycle. Marketers face important choices when they select *new product pricing strategies.* The company can decide on one of several price-quality strategies for introducing an imitative product. In pricing innovative products, it can practice *market-skimming pricing* by initially setting high prices to "skim" the maximum amount of revenue from various segments of the market. Or it can use *market-penetration pricing* by setting a low initial price to win a large market share.

When the product is part of the product mix, the firm searches for a set of *product-mix pricing strategies* that will maximize profits from the total mix. The company decides on price steps for items in its *product line* and on the pricing of *optional products, captive products, by-products*, and sometimes *product bundles*.

Companies apply a variety of *price-adjustment strategies* to account for differences in consumer segments and situations. One is *discount and allowance* pricing, whereby the company decides on *quantity, functional*, or *seasonal discounts*, or varying types of *allowances*. A second strategy is *segmented pricing*, where the company sells a product at two or more prices to allow for differences in customers, products, or locations. Sometimes companies consider more than economics in their pricing decisions, and use *psychological pricing* to communicate about the product's quality or value. In promotional pricing, companies temporarily sell their product below list price as a *special-event* to draw more customers, sometimes even selling below cost as a *loss-leader*. With *value pricing*, the company offers just the right combination of quality and good service at a fair price. Another approach is *geographical pricing*, whereby the company decides how to price distant customers, choosing from alternatives as FOB pricing, uniform delivered pricing, zone pricing, basing-point pricing, and freight-absorption pricing. Finally, *international pricing* means that the company adjusts its price to meet different conditions and expectations in different world markets.

When a firm considers *initiating price changes*, it must consider customers' and competitors' reactions. There are different implications to *initiating price cuts* and *initiating price increases*. *Buyer reactions to price changes* are influenced by the meaning customers see in the price change. *Competitor reactions to price changes* flow from a set reaction policy or a fresh analysis of each situation. The firm initiating the price change must also anticipate probable reactions of suppliers, middlemen, and government.

There are also many factors to consider in *responding to price changes*. The firm that faces a price change initiated by a competitor must try to understand competitor's intent as well as the likely duration and impact of the change. If a swift reaction is desirable, the firm should preplan its reactions to different possible price actions by competitors. When facing a competitor's price change, the company might sit tight, reduce its own price, raise perceived quality, improve quality and raise price, or launch a fighting brand.

Key Terms

Allowances
Basing-point pricing
By-product pricing
Captive-product pricing
Cash discount
FOB-origin pricing
Freight-absorption pricing
Functional discount

Market-penetration pricing
Market-skimming pricing
Optional-product pricing
Product-bundle pricing
Product line pricing
Promotional pricing
Psychological pricing
Quantity discount

Reference prices
Seasonal discount
Segmented pricing
Uniform delivered pricing
Value pricing
Zone pricing

Discussing the Issues

1. When the dollar is weak, import prices rise, and Mercedes and Porsche prices rise with them. Yet when the dollar strengthens, the prices for these cars are kept high, yielding unusually large profits. Discuss whether Mercedes and Porsche should drop prices when costs drop. What effect would this have on used-car prices and trade-in values?

2. Describe which strategy—market skimming or market penetration—these companies use in pricing their products: (a) McDonald's, (b) Curtis Mathes (television and other home electronics), (c) Bic Corporation (pens, lighters, shavers, and related products), and (d) IBM. Are these the right strategies for these companies? Tell why or why not.

3. Carpet Fresh was the leading carpet deodorizer, priced at $2.49 for 13 ounces. Arm & Hammer launched a competitive product priced at $1.99 for 26 ounces and quickly became the number-one brand. Discuss the psychological aspects of this pricing. Does this superb-value strategy fit with Arm & Hammer's image?

4. The formula for chlorine bleach is virtually identical for all brands. Clorox charges a premium price for this same product, yet remains the unchallenged market leader. Discuss what this implies about the value of a brand name. Analyze the ethical issues involved in this type of pricing.

5. A by-product of manufacturing tennis balls is "dead" balls—ones that do not bounce high enough to meet standards (that is, they bounce less than 53 inches when dropped from 100 inches onto a concrete surface). Choose a strategy that could be used for pricing these balls.

6. A clothing store sells men's suits at three price levels—$180, $250, and $340. If shoppers use these price points as reference prices in comparing different suits, appraise the effect of adding a new line of suits at a cost of $280. Would you expect sales of the $250 suits to increase, decrease, or stay the same?

Applying the Concepts

1. List at least five examples of stores that use their pricing strategies as part of their marketing communications, such as a supermarket calling itself "the low-price leader" or even the name of Cost Plus Imports. Do any of your examples discuss offering average or high prices? Why not?

2. Go to your local supermarket and observe sizes and prices within product categories. Determine if the package sizes (the weight or number of units contained) are comparable across brands. Find at least two instances where a manufacturer seems to have made a smaller package in order to achieve a lower retail price. Does this appear effective? If your market has unit pricing labels, see whether the unit price is higher, lower, or the same as this brand's competitors. Does unit pricing information change your opinion about the effectiveness of this strategy?

References

1. Quotes from Andrea Rothman, "The Superlosers in the Supersaver War," *Business Week*, June 15, 1992, p. 44. Also see Bridget O'Brian, "Airlines Seek to Earn More from an Irritated Clientele," *Wall Street Journal*, March 16, 1992, pp. B1, B6; Bridget O'Brian and James S. Hirsch, "Flying Low: Simplifying Their Fares Proves More Difficult than Airlines Expected," *Wall Street Journal*, June 4, 1992, pp. A1, A5; Wendy Zellner, "The Airlines Are Killing Each Other Again," *Business Week*, June 8, 1992, p. 32; and Holt Hackney, "AMR: Starting Its Descent?" *Financial World*, December 7, 1993, p. 20.

2. For a comprehensive discussion of pricing strategies, see Thomas T. Nagle and Reed K. Holden, *The Strategy and Dynamics of Pricing*, 2nd ed. (Englewood Cliffs, NJ: Prentice Hall, 1995).

3. See David Kirkpatrick, "Intel Goes for Broke," *Fortune*, May 16, 1994, pp. 62–68; and Robert D. Hof, "Intel: Far Beyond the Pentium," *Business Week*, February 20, 1995, pp. 88–90.

4. See Nagle, *The Strategy and Tactics of Pricing*, pp. 225–228; and Manjit S. Yadav and Kent B. Monroe, "How Buyers Perceive Savings in a Bundle Price: An Examination of a Bundle's Transaction Value," *Journal of Marketing Research*, August 1993, pp. 350–358.

5. Gary M. Erickson and Johnny K. Johansson, "The Role of Price in Multi-Attribute Product Evaluations," *Journal of Consumer Research*, September 1985, pp. 195–199.

6. For more reading on reference prices and psychologi-

cal pricing, see Nagle and Holden, *The Strategy and Tactics of Pricing*, Chapter 12; and K. N. Rajendran and Gerard J. Tellis, "Contextual and Temporal Components of Reference Price," *Journal of Marketing*, January 1994, pp. 22–34.

7. Philip R. Cateora, *International Marketing*, 7th ed. (Homewood, IL: Irwin, 1990), p. 540.

8. For more on price cutting and its consequences, see

Kathleen Madigan, "The Latest Mad Plunge of the Price Slashers, " *Business Week*, May 11, 1992, p. 36; and Bill Saporito, "Why the Price Wars Never End," *Fortune*, March 23, 1992, pp.68–78.

9. Jonathon Berry and Zachary Schiller, "Attack of the Fighting Brands," *Business Week*, May 2, 1994, p. 125.

Company Case 12

CIRCUIT CITY: SELLING USED CARS LIKE STEREOS

A HASSLE!

Buying a used car! Just mention the subject, and anyone with experience will probably frown and immediately launch into a sad story about his or her last purchase. The used-car salesperson, in fact, is often what people have in mind when they think about marketing's excesses.

So why would Circuit City, a company that has succeeded in selling stereos, televisions, car radios, and other electronic items through its 300 superstores, suddenly decide to try selling used cars? Why, when management consultants advise companies to "stick to their knitting," would an electronics retailer try its hand at used cars?

THE USED-CAR MARKET

The answer is simple—new-car prices. During the past ten years, the average new-car price has risen 70 percent to about $19,500. Government-mandated pollution controls and safety features have driven the price increases. Over that same period, however, median family income and the consumer price index have risen only about 40 percent. For some consumers, today's new cars cost as much as their houses! Consumers also understand that new-car quality has improved and that the average used car on dealers' lots today is only 3.5 years old. Thus, they reason, they can get a low-mileage used car that will be very reliable and save $5,000 to $10,000 in the process. Moreover, surveys show that the value consumers place on new cars as a status symbol has steadily declined and that used cars have increased in status.

Besides growing demand for used cars, supply has also increased. To encourage consumers to buy new cars, many manufacturers and dealers have turned to leasing programs that allow consumers to drive new cars and turn them in after two to three years. The deal-

ers then resell the used cars. Further, the growth of the rental-car business has resulted in a growing supply of used rental cars as the companies turn over their fleets.

Moreover, although it used to be difficult to finance used cars, banks and finance companies are offering financing for used cars at interest rates only slightly above those they charge for new-car loans. Whereas lenders once saw used-car buyers as higher credit risks, today's new-car buyers actually have higher loan-default rates.

Finally, dealers may earn more net profit by selling a used car. A recent survey indicated that a used-car sale produced an average net profit of $265, versus a $130 profit for a new car.

PLUGGING IN TO A NEW WAY

Despite these changes in demand and supply, however, the process of selling and buying used cars has not changed much. Because most consumers buy cars infrequently, they often are at a disadvantage dealing with used-car salespeople. Consumers have to negotiate the price of the used car as well as the price the dealer will pay for any trade-in that is involved. Consumers worry about whether they are paying too much or getting too little. They worry about the car's quality. The process produces hassled, worried, and dissatisfied customers.

Circuit City believes it can change all this by applying the principles of electronics retailing to selling used cars. The company has started CarMax, the Auto Superstore, to carry out its vision. It opened its first CarMax store in Richmond, Virginia, and a second in Raleigh, North Carolina, in 1994. It has plans for two more stores in Atlanta, Georgia, and a fifth in Charlotte, North Carolina.

CarMax's strategy is straightforward. It located its Raleigh store, for example, on the city's outskirts where the company could buy a large piece of land on a major highway. On the nine-acre tract, CarMax displays up to 500 used cars, a selection far larger than the typical used-car lot.

Customers enter an attractive display room, similar to one in a new-car dealership. If they bring their children along, there is an attended child-care area complete with toys and video games. A sales associate clad in a blue polo shirt and khakis greets customers and escorts them to a computer kiosk. The associate finds out what type of car the consumer is seeking. Using a computer touch screen, the associate can call up a full listing of all the cars or trucks in stock that meet the customer's criteria. For example, if the customer is interested in late-model sports utility vehicles priced between $12,000 and $17,000, the computer will quickly display each such model in inventory by brand and model. The display shows a color picture of the vehicle; lists its features, such as four-wheel drive; and details its specifications, such as engine type and EPA gas-mileage estimates. The screen also presents CarMax's price for the vehicle, a price based on the average retail price in the NAPA "Blue Book" that car dealers use. The customer can print a copy of the information, including the picture and the vehicle's location on CarMax's lot. The customer is then free to look at the vehicle, which is located in a specified parking place on the lot. In addition, all similar vehicles, such as other sports utility vehicles, are located in the same area rather than being spread haphazardly across the lot. CarMax pays its salespeople commission based on the number of cars they sell, not based on the profit from each sale. Thus, the salesperson has no incentive to push the customer to look at more expensive vehicles.

Before putting cars it buys on its lot, CarMax's mechanics carry out a 110-point inspection and thorough cleaning, even cleaning the engine. The employees add new tires or make other repairs as needed. No car on the lot is over five years old. CarMax offers a five-day, money-back guarantee and a 30-day comprehensive warranty. For an additional cost, it also offers extended warranties that stretch up to three years.

If the customer decides to buy the vehicle, there is no haggling over price. The price CarMax sets is its sales price. There is no negotiation. There are no hidden or extra fees, just state sales tax, title, and tag charges. Cir-

cuit City has its own financing company, and the CarMax associate can arrange financing for the purchase in 20 minutes. If the customer wants to sell his or her current car, CarMax will make an offer based on that car's Blue Book value. The offer is not dependent on the customer purchasing a car. CarMax will purchase the car even if the customer does not want to buy another car from CarMax. The company also offers on-site car insurance service. Customers find that the entire sales process can take less than an hour.

THE BOTTOM LINE

Circuit City still considers its CarMax operation to be a test, but so far the results look good. Customers report that they like the no-pressure sales approach, and cars are flying off CarMax lots. Although the company will not reveal sales information, two employees at the Richmond store suggested that sales totaled over 400 cars per month. A typical new car dealer would sell about 700 used cars in a year!

Although Circuit City rang up sales of $4.13 billion last year, it realizes that its electronics expansion may be slowing. Perhaps the $150 to $225 billion used-car market will be its next frontier.

QUESTIONS

1. What product-mix pricing strategies do automobile dealers and manufacturers typically follow?

2. What price adjustment strategies do car dealers use?

3. How is CarMax changing the used-car industry's pricing strategies? How will buyers and competitors react to these changes?

4. What marketing recommendations would you make to CarMax?

Sources: Douglas Lavin, "Cars Are Sold Like Stereos by Circuit City," *Wall Street Journal,* June 8, 1994, p. B1; Douglas Lavin, "Stiff Showroom Prices Drive More Americans to Purchase Used Cars," *Wall Street Journal,* November 1, 1994, p. A1; J. Ward Best, "Maxed Out? Circuit City Bets Used Car Market Is Far from It," *Raleigh News and Observer,* November 6, 1994, p. F1; Gabriella Stern, "'Nearly New' Autos for Sale: Dealers Buff Up Their Marketing of Used Cars," *Wall Street Journal,* February 17, 1995, p. B1.

Placing Products

DISTRIBUTION CHANNELS AND LOGISTICS MANAGEMENT

13

For more than 60 years, Goodyear Tire & Rubber Company sold replacement tires exclusively through its powerful network of independent Goodyear dealers. Both Goodyear and its 2,500 dealers profited from this partnership. Goodyear received the undivided attention and loyalty of its single-brand dealers, and the dealers gained the exclusive right to sell the highly respected Goodyear tire line. In mid-1992, however, Goodyear shattered tradition and jolted its dealers by announcing that it would now sell Goodyear-brand tires through Sears auto centers, placing Goodyear dealers in direct competition with the giant retailer. This departure from the previously sacred dealer network left many dealers shaken and angry. Said one Goodyear dealer: "You feel like after 35 years of marriage, your [spouse] is stepping out on you." Said another, "I feel like they just stabbed me in the back."

Several factors forced the change in Goodyear's distribution system. During the late 1980s, massive international consolidation reshaped the tire industry, leaving only five competitors. Japan's Bridgestone acquired Firestone, Germany's Continental bought General Tire, Italy's Pirelli snapped up Armstrong, and France's Michelin acquired Uniroyal Goodrich. After six decades as the world's largest tire maker, Goodyear slipped to second behind Michelin. As the only remaining U.S.-owned tire company, instead of having its way with smaller domestic rivals, Goodyear now found itself battling for U.S. market share against large and newly strengthened international competitors.

To add to Goodyear's woes, consumers were changing how and where they bought tires. Tires have become more of an impulse item, and value-minded tire buyers were increasingly buying from cheaper, multibrand discount outlets, department stores, and warehouse clubs. The market share of these outlets had grown 30 percent in the previous five years, while that of tire dealers had fallen 4 percent. By selling exclusively through its dealer network, Goodyear simply wasn't putting its tires where many consumers were buying them. The shifts in consumer buying were also causing problems for dealers. Although Goodyear offered an ample variety of premium lines, it pro-

OBJECTIVES

When you finish this chapter, you should be able to accomplish the following:

1. Describe the **nature of distribution channels**, and tell why marketing intermediaries are used.

2. Discuss **channel behavior and organization**, explaining **corporate, contractual** and **administered vertical marketing systems, horizontal** and **hybrid marketing systems.**

3. Outline the **basic elements of channel design decisions** by analyzing **consumer service needs** and **setting channel objectives** and **constraints.**

4. Identify **major channel alternatives—the types** and **number of marketing intermediaries** and the **responsibilities of channel members**—and the ways of evaluating major alternatives.

5. Illustrate the **channel management decisions** of selecting, motivating, and evaluating channel members.

6. Explain the **importance** and **goals of physical distribution and logistics management,** and identify the **major logistics functions** of **order processing, warehousing, inventory** and **transportation.**

vided its dealers with none of the lower-priced lines that many consumers were demanding.

Entering the 1990s, Goodyear was foundering. Although it remained number one in the United States, its share of the U.S. replacement-tire market had fallen 3 percent in only five years. Battling a prolonged recession and vicious price competition from Michelin and Bridgestone, Goodyear suffered its first money-losing year since the Great Depression. Drastic measures were needed.

Enter new management, headed by Stanley Gault, the miracle-working manager who had transformed Rubbermaid from a sleepy Ohio rubber company into one of America's most admired market leaders. Gault took the helm in mid-1991 and moved quickly to streamline Goodyear, reducing its heavy debt, cutting costs, and selling off noncore businesses. But the biggest changes came in marketing. Under Gault, Goodyear speeded up new-product development and boosted ad spending. For example, in late 1991, it introduced four new tires simultaneously— the innovative, nonhydroplaning Aquatred, the Wrangler line for pickup trucks and vans, a fuel-efficient "green" tire, and a new high-performance Eagle model. In 1992, Goodyear brought out 12 more new tires, three times the usual number.

Gault also wasted little time in shaking up Goodyear's stodgy distribution system. In addition to selling its tires through Sears, the company beagn selling the Goodyear brand at Wal-Mart. Marketing research showed that one out of four Wal-Mart customers is a potential Goodyear buyer, and that these buyers come from a segment unlikely to be reached by independent Goodyear dealers. The company also began drumming up new private-label business. Its Kelly-Springfield unit soon inked a deal to sell private label tires through Wal-Mart, and agreements with Kmart, Montgomery Ward, and even the warehouse clubs also seem likely. Goodyear has since begun exploring other new distribution options as well. For example, it is now testing a no-frills, quick-serve discount store concept—Just Tires—designed to fend off low-priced competitors. In another test, it recently began selling Goodyear brand tires to multibrand retailers in selected U.S. cities.

The marketing, distribution, and other changes have Goodyear rolling again. In its first year under Gault, Goodyear's sales and earnings soared, its market share increased 1 percent, and its stock price quadrupled. The expanded distribution system appears to be a significant plus, at least in the short run. For example, by itself, Sears controls 10 percent of the U.S. replacement-tire market. Even a 20 percent share of Sears's business for Goodyear means three million additional tires a year, enough to erase more than half of the company's previous market-share losses.

In the long run, however, developing new channels risks eroding the loyalty and effectiveness of Goodyear's prized exclusive dealer network, one of the company's major competitive assets. To be fully effective, Goodyear and its dealers must work together in harmony for their mutual benefit. But the agreements with Sears and other retailers have created hard feelings and conflict between them. Some disgruntled dealers are striking back by taking on and aggressively promoting cheaper, private label brands, brands that offer higher margins to dealers and more appeal to some value-conscious consumers. Such dealer actions may eventually weaken the Goodyear name and the premium price that it can command.

Goodyear has taken steps to bolster anxious dealers. For example, it is now supplying dealers with a much-needed line of lower-priced Goodyear-brand tires. Goodyear sincerely believes that expanded distribution will help its dealers more than harm them. In the end, selling through Sears means better visibility for the Goodyear name, Gault contends, and the resulting expansion of business will mean more money for dealer support. However, many dealers remain skeptical. In the long run, dealer defections could lessen Goodyear's market power and offset sales gains from new channels. For example, shortly after the Sears announcement, one large Goodyear dealership in Florida adopted several lower-priced private brands, reducing its sales of Goodyear tires by 20 percent, but increasing its profit margins. The defiant dealer notes: "We [now] sell what we think will give the customer the best value, and that's not necessarily Goodyear." Thus, although Goodyear may be rolling again, the ride's not over. There are still many bumps in the road ahead.[1]

Marketing channel decisions are among the most important decisions that management faces. A company's channel decisions directly affect every other marketing decision. The company's pricing depends on whether it uses mass merchandisers or high-quality specialty stores. The firm's sales force and advertising decisions depend on how much persuasion, training, and motivation the dealers need. Whether a company develops or acquires certain new products may depend on how well those products fit the abilities of its channel members.

Companies often pay too little attention to their distribution channels, however, sometimes with damaging results. For example, automobile manufacturers have lost large shares of their parts and service business to companies like NAPA, Midas, Goodyear, and others because they have resisted making needed changes in their dealer franchise networks. In contrast, many companies have used imaginative distribution systems to *gain* a competitive advantage. Federal Express's creative and imposing distribution system made it the leader in the small-package delivery industry. And General Electric gained a strong advantage in selling its major appliances by supporting its dealers with a sophisticated computerized order processing and delivery system.

Distribution channel decisions often involve long-term commitments to other firms. For example, companies like Ford, IBM, or Pizza Hut can easily change their advertising, pricing, or promotion programs. They can scrap old products and introduce new ones as market tastes demand. But when they set up distribution channels though contracts with franchisees, independent dealers, or large retailers, they cannot readily replace these channels with company-owned stores if conditions change. Therefore, management must design its channels carefully, with an eye on tomorrow's likely selling environment as well as today's.

This chapter examines four major questions concerning distribution channels: *What is the nature of distribution channels? How do channel firms interact and organize to do the work of the channel? What problems do companies face in designing and managing their channels? What role does physical distribution play in attracting and satisfying customers?* In Chapter 14, we will look at distribution channel issues from the viewpoint of retailers and wholesalers.

THE NATURE OF DISTRIBUTION CHANNELS

Distribution channel (marketing channel)
A set of interdependent organizations involved in the process of making a product or service available for use or consumption by the consumer or business user.

Most producers use intermediaries to bring their products to market. They try to forge a **distribution channel**—a set of interdependent organizations involved in the process of making a product or service available for use or consumption by the consumer or business user.[2]

WHY ARE MARKETING INTERMEDIARIES USED?

Why do producers give some of the selling job to intermediaries? After all, doing so means giving up some control over how and to whom the products are sold. The use of intermediaries results from their greater efficiency in making goods available to target markets. Through their contacts, experience, specialization, and scale of operation, intermediaries usually offer the firm more than it can achieve on its own.

Figure 13-1 shows how using intermediaries can provide economies. Part A shows three manufacturers, each using direct marketing to reach three customers. This system requires nine different contacts. Part B shows the three manufacturers working through one distributor, who contacts the three customers. This system requires only six contacts. In this way, intermediaries reduce the amount of work that must be done by both producers and consumers.

From the economic system's point of view, the role of marketing intermediaries is to transform the assortments of products made by producers into the assortments wanted by consumers. Producers make narrow assortments of products in large quantities, but consumers want broad assortments of products in small quantities. In the distribution channels, intermediaries buy the large quantities of many producers and break them down into the smaller quantities and broader assortments wanted by consumers. Thus, intermediaries play an important role in matching supply and demand.

DISTRIBUTION CHANNEL FUNCTIONS

A distribution channel moves goods from producers to consumers. It overcomes the major time, place, and possession gaps that separate goods and services from those who would use them. Members of the marketing channel perform many key functions. Some help to complete transactions:

◆ *Information:* gathering and distributing marketing research and intelligence information about actors and forces in the marketing environment needed for planning and aiding exchange.

◆ *Promotion:* developing and spreading persuasive communications about an offer.

◆ *Contact:* finding and communicating with prospective buyers.

◆ *Matching:* shaping and fitting the offer to the buyer's needs, including such activities as manufacturing, grading, assembling, and packaging.

◆ *Negotiation:* reaching an agreement on price and other terms of the offer so that ownership or possession can be transferred.

FIGURE 13-1 *How a marketing intermediary reduces the number of channel transactions*

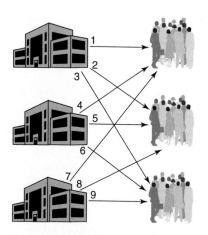

A. Number of contacts without a distributor
M x C = 3 x 3 = 9

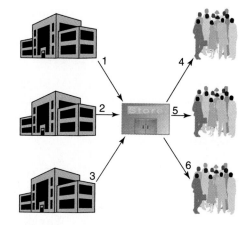

B. Number of contacts with a distributor
M + C = 3 + 3 = 6

 = Manufacturer   = Customer    = Distributor

Others help to fulfill the completed transactions:

◆ *Physical distribution:* transporting and storing goods.
◆ *Financing:* acquiring and using funds to cover the costs of the channel work.
◆ *Risk taking:* assuming the risks of carrying out the channel work.

The question is not *whether* these functions need to be performed—they must be—but rather *who* is to perform them. All the functions have three things in common: They use up scarce resources, they often can be performed better through specialization, and they can be shifted among channel members. To the extent that the manufacturer performs these functions, its costs go up and its prices have to be higher. At the same time, when some of these functions are shifted to intermediaries, the producer's costs and prices may be lower, but the intermediaries must charge more to cover the costs of their work. In dividing the work of the channel, the various functions should be assigned to the channel members who can perform them most efficiently and effectively to provide satisfactory assortments of goods to target consumers.

NUMBER OF CHANNEL LEVELS

Direct marketing channel
A marketing channel that has no intermediary levels.
Indirect marketing channels
Channels containing one or more intermediary levels.

Distribution channels can be described by the number of channel levels involved. Each layer of marketing intermediaries that performs some work in bringing the product and its ownership closer to the final buyer is a **channel level.** Because the producer and the final consumer both perform some work, they are part of every channel. We use the number of intermediary levels to indicate the length of a channel. Figure 13-2A shows several consumer distribution channels of different lengths.

Channel 1, called a **direct marketing channel,** has no intermediary levels. It consists of a company selling directly to consumers. For example, Avon, Amway, and Tupperware sell their products door to door or through home and office sales parties; Land's End sells clothing direct through mail order and by telephone; and Singer sells its sewing machines through its own stores. The remaining channels in Figure 13-2A are **indirect marketing channels.** Channel 2 contains one intermediary level. In consumer markets, this level is typically a retailer. For example, the makers of televisions, cameras, tires, furniture, major appliances, and many other products sell their goods directly to large retailers such as Wal-Mart and Sears, which then sell the goods to final consumers. Channel 3 contains two intermediary levels, a wholesaler and a retailer. This channel often is used by small manufacturers of food, drugs, hardware, and other products. Channel 4 contains three intermediary levels. In the meatpacking industry, for example, jobbers usually come between wholesalers and retailers. The jobber buys from wholesalers and sells to smaller retailers who generally are not served by larger wholesalers. Distribution channels with even more levels are sometimes found, but less often. From the producer's point of view, a greater number of levels means less control and greater channel complexity.

Direct marketing channels: Land's End sells direct through mail order and by telephone.

Figure 13-2B shows some common business distribution channels. The business marketer can use its own sales force to sell directly to business customers. It also can sell to industrial distributors, who in turn sell to business customers. It can sell through manufacturer's representatives or its own sales branches to business customers, or it can use these representatives and branches to sell through industrial distributors. Thus, business markets commonly include multilevel distribution channels.

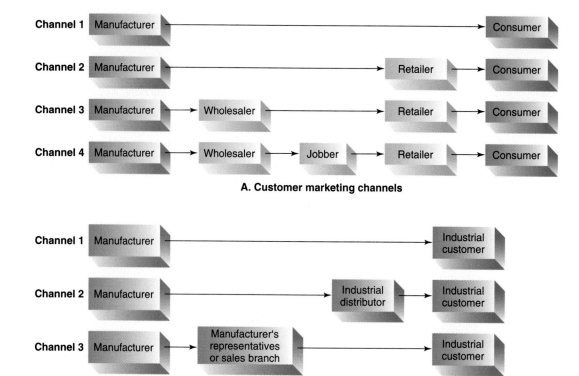

A. Customer marketing channels

B. Business marketing channels

FIGURE 13-2   *Consumer and business marketing channels*

All of the institutions in the channel are connected by several types of *flows.* These include the *physical flow* of products, the *flow of ownership,* the *payment flow,* the *information flow,* and the *promotion flow.* These flows can even make channels with only one or a few levels very complex.

CHANNELS IN THE SERVICE SECTOR

The concept of distribution channels is not limited to the distribution of physical goods. Producers of services and ideas also face the problem of making their output *available* to target populations. In the private sector, department stores, hotels, banks, and other service providers take great care to place their outlets in locations convenient to target customers. In the public sector, service organizations and agencies develop "educational distribution systems" and "health delivery systems" for reaching sometimes widely spread populations. Hospitals must be located geographically to serve various patient populations with complete medical care, and schools must be located close to the children who need to be taught. Communities must locate their fire stations to provide rapid coverage of fires in every neighborhood, and polling stations must be placed where people can vote without spending excessive time and effort.

Distribution channels also are used in "person" marketing. Before 1940, professional comedians could reach audiences through vaudeville houses, special events, nightclubs, radio, movies, carnivals, and theaters. In the 1950s, television became a strong channel and vaudeville disappeared. More recently, the comedian's channels have grown to include promotional events, product endorsements, cable television, and videotapes. Politicians must also find cost-effective channels—mass media, rallies, coffee hours—for distributing their messages to voters. We will discuss person marketing in more depth in Chapter 21.

CHANNEL BEHAVIOR AND ORGANIZATION

Distribution channels are more than simple collections of firms tied together by various flows. They are complex behavioral systems in which people and companies interact to accomplish individual, company, and channel goals. Some channel systems consist only of informal interactions among loosely organized firms; others consist of formal interactions guided by strong organizational structures. Moreover, channel systems do not stand still—new types of intermediaries surface, and whole new channel systems evolve. Here we look at channel behavior and at how members organize to do the work of the channel.

CHANNEL BEHAVIOR

A distribution channel consists of firms that have banded together for their common good. Each channel member is dependent on the others. For example, a Ford dealer depends on the Ford Motor Company to design cars that meet consumer needs. In turn, Ford depends on the dealer to attract consumers, persuade them to buy Ford cars, and service cars after the sale. The Ford dealer also depends on other dealers to provide good sales and service that will uphold the reputation of Ford and its dealer body. In fact, the success of individual Ford dealers depends on how well the entire Ford distribution channel competes with the channels of other auto manufacturers.

Each channel member plays a role in the channel and specializes in performing one or more functions. For example, IBM's role is to produce personal computers that consumers will like and to create demand through national advertising. Computerland's role is to display these IBM computers in convenient locations, to answer buyers' questions, to close sales, and to provide service. The channel will be most effective when each member is assigned the tasks it can do best.

Ideally, because the success of individual channel members depends on overall channel success, all channel firms should work together smoothly. They should understand and accept their roles, coordinate their goals and activities, and cooperate to attain overall channel goals. By cooperating, they can more effectively sense, serve, and satisfy the target market.

However, individual channel members rarely take such a broad view. They are usually more concerned with their own short-run goals and their dealings with those firms closest to them in the channel. Cooperating to achieve overall channel goals sometimes means giving up individual company goals. Although channel members are dependent on one another, they often act alone in their own short-run best interests. They often disagree on the roles each should play—on who should do what and for what rewards. Such disagreements over goals and roles generate **channel conflict** (see Marketing Highlight 13-1).

Channel conflict
Disagreement among marketing channel members on goals and roles—who should do what and for what rewards.

Horizontal conflict occurs among firms at the same level of the channel. For instance, some Ford dealers in Chicago complained about other dealers in the city who stole sales from them by being too aggressive in their pricing and advertising or by selling outside their assigned territories. Some Pizza Inn franchisees complained about other Pizza Inn franchisees cheating on ingredients, giving poor service, and hurting the overall Pizza Inn image.

Vertical conflict is even more common and refers to conflicts between different levels of the same channel. For example, General Motors came into conflict with its dealers some years ago by trying to enforce service, pricing, and adver-

CHANNEL CONFLICT: PROCTER & GAMBLE WRESTLES WITH RESELLERS

Procter & Gamble, the huge consumer packaged-goods producer, is part of a complex food-industry distribution channel consisting of producers, wholesale food distributors, and grocery retailers. Despite the immense popularity of its brands with consumers, P&G has never gotten along all that well with retailers and wholesalers. Instead, over the years, the company has acquired a reputation for wielding its market power in a somewhat high-handed fashion, without enough regard for reseller wishes. Recently, P&G's relations with many of these resellers took a decided turn for the worse. "We think that [P&G] will end up where most dictators end up—in trouble," fumes the chairman of Stop & Shop, a chain of 119 groceries in the Northeast. Hundreds of miles away, the assistant manager of Paulbeck's Super Valu in International Falls, Minnesota, shares these harsh feelings: "We should drop their top dogs—like half the sizes of Tide—and say 'Now see who put you on the shelf and who'll take you off of it.'"

The cause of the uproar is P&G's new "value pricing" policy. Under this sweeping new plan, the company is phasing out most of the large promotional discounts that it has offered resellers in the past. At the same time, it is lowering its everyday wholesale list prices for these products by 10 percent to 25 percent. P&G insists that price fluctuations and promotions have gotten out of hand. During the past decade, average trade discounts have more than tripled. Now, some 44 percent of all marketing dollars spent by manufacturers goes to trade promotions, up from 24 percent only a decade ago.

Manufacturers have come to rely on price-oriented trade promotions to differentiate their brands and boost short-term sales. In turn, wholesalers and retail chains have been conditioned to wait for manufacturers' "deals." Many have perfected "forward buying"—stocking up during manufacturers' price promotions on far more merchandise than they can sell, then reselling it to consumers at higher prices once the promotion is over. Such forward buying creates costly production and distribution inefficiencies. P&G's factories must gear up to meet the resulting huge demand swings. Meanwhile, supermarkets need more buyers to find the best prices and extra warehouses to store and handle merchandise bought "on deal." P&G claims that only 30 percent of trade promotion money actually reaches consumers in the form of lower prices, while 35 percent is lost to inefficiencies, and another 35 percent winds up in retailer's pockets. The industry's "promotion sickness" has also infected consumers. Wildly fluctuating retail prices have eroded brand loyalty by teaching consumers to shop for what's on sale, rather than to assess the merits of each brand.

Through value pricing, P&G hopes to restore the price integrity of its brands and to begin weaning the industry and consumers from discount pricing. But the strategy has created substantial conflict in P&G's distribution channels. Discounts are the bread and butter of many retailers and wholesalers, who use products purchased from P&G at special low prices for weekly sales to lure value-minded consumers into supermarkets or stores. In other cases, retailers and wholesalers rely on the discounts to pad their profits through forward buying. And although the average costs of products to resellers remain unchanged, resellers lose promotional dollars that they—not P&G—controlled. Thus, the new system gives P&G greater control over how its products are marketed, but reduces retailer and wholesaler pricing flexibility.

P&G's new strategy is risky. It alienates some of the very

---

tising policies. Coca-Cola came into conflict with some of its bottlers who agreed to bottle competitor Dr Pepper. McCulloch caused conflict when it decided to bypass its wholesale distributors and sell its chain saw directly to large retailers such as JCPenney and Kmart, which then competed directly with its smaller dealers. And Goodyear caused conflict with its dealer network when it decided to sell tires through mass merchandisers.

Some conflict in the channel takes the form of healthy competition. Such competition can be good for the channel—without it, the channel could become passive and noninnovative. But sometimes conflict can damage the channel. For the channel as a whole to perform well, each channel member's role must be specified and channel conflict must be managed. Cooperation, role assignment, and conflict management in the channel are attained through strong channel leadership. The channel will perform better if it includes a firm, agency, or mechanism that has the power to assign roles and manage conflict.

In a large company, the formal organization structure assigns roles and provides needed leadership. But in a distribution channel made up of independent firms, leadership and power are not formally set. Traditionally, distribution chan-

businesses that sell its wares to the public, and it gives competitors an opportunity to take advantage of the ban on promotions by highlighting their own specials. P&G is counting on its enormous market clout—retailers can ill afford, the company hopes, to eliminate heavily advertised powerhouse brands such as Tide detergent, Crest toothpaste, Folger's coffee, Pert shampoo, and Ivory soap. But even P&G's size and power may not be enough. Some large chains such as A&P, Safeway, and Rite-Aid drugstores are pruning out selected P&G sizes or dropping marginal brands such as Prell and Gleem. Certified Grocers, a Midwestern wholesaler, has dropped about 50 of the 300 P&G varieties it stocked. And numerous other chains are considering moving P&G brands from prime, eye-level space to less visible shelves, stocking more profitable private-label brands and competitors' products in P&G's place. SuperValu, the nation's largest wholesaler, which also runs retail stores, is adding surcharges to some P&G products and paring back orders to make up for profits it says it's losing.

Despite these strong reactions, P&G plans to stay the course with its bold new pricing approach. Once in place, the company believes, value pricing will benefit all parties—manufacturers, resellers, and consumers—through lower and more stable costs and prices. Many resellers, and even competitors, are quietly cheering P&G's actions from the sidelines, hoping that order will be restored to prices and promotions. P&G says that many of its largest retailers—especially mass merchandisers like Wal-Mart, which already employ everyday low pricing strategies—love the new system, and in fact inspired it.

P&G's struggle to reshape the industry's distorted pricing system demonstrates the dynamic forces of cooperation, power, and conflict found in distribution channels. Clearly, for the good of all parties, P&G and its resellers should work as partners to profitably market food products to consumers. But often, channels don't operate that smoothly; conflicts and power struggles sometimes flare up. In recent years, as more and more products have competed for limited supermarket shelf space, and as scanners have given retailers ever-greater leverage through market information, the balance of channel power has shifted—perhaps too far—toward grocery retailers. With its new pricing policy, P&G appears to be trying to wrestle back some of its lost marketplace control. The stakes are high: The new program stands to either empower P&G and overhaul the way most wholesalers and retailers do business—or to damage P&G's market share and force it to retreat. In the short run, the conflict will produce some bruises for all parties. In the long run, however, the struggle probably will be healthy for the channel, helping it to adapt and grow.

Sources: Portions adapted from Valerie Reitman, "Retail Resistance: Eliminated Discounts on P&G Goods Annoy Many Who Sell Them," *Wall Street Journal,* August 11, 1992, pp. A1, A3. Also see Jennifer Lawrence and Judann Dagnoli, "P&G's Low-Price Strategy Cuts Trade Fees, Irks Retailers," *Advertising Age,* December 23, 1991, p. 3; Zachary Schiller, "Not Everyone Loves a Supermarket Special," *Business Week,* February 17, 1992, pp. 64–68; "P&G Plays Pied Piper on Pricing," *Advertising Age,* March 9, 1992, p. 6; Jennifer Lawrence, "Tide, Cheer Join P&G 'Value Pricing' Plan," *Advertising Age,* February 15, 1993, p. 3; and Zachary Schiller, "Ed Artzt's Elbow Grease Has P&G Shining," *Business Week,* October 10, 1994, pp. 84–86.

nels have lacked the leadership needed to assign roles and manage conflict. In recent years, however, new types of channel organizations have appeared that provide stronger leadership and improved performance.

VERTICAL MARKETING SYSTEMS

Conventional distribution channel
A channel consisting of one or more independent producers, wholesalers, and retailers, each a separate business seeking to maximize its own profits even at the expense of profits for the system as a whole.

Historically, distribution channels have been loose collections of independent companies, each showing little concern for overall channel performance. These *conventional distribution channels* have lacked strong leadership and have been troubled by damaging conflict and poor performance. One of the biggest recent channel developments has been the *vertical marketing systems* that have emerged to challenge conventional marketing channels. Figure 13-3 contrasts the two types of channel arrangements.

A **conventional distribution channel** consists of one or more independent producers, wholesalers, and retailers. Each is a separate business seeking to maximize its own profits, even at the expense of profits for the system as a whole. No chan-

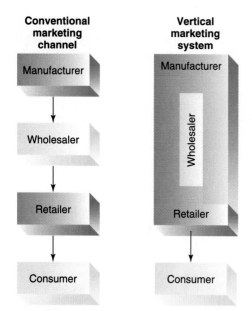

FIGURE 13-3 *A conventional marketing channel versus a vertical marketing system*

Vertical marketing system (VMS)
A distribution channel structure in which producers, wholesalers, and retailers act as a unified system. One channel member owns the others, has contracts with them, or has so much power that they all cooperate.

Corporate VMS
A vertical marketing system that combines successive stages of production and distribution under single ownership—channel leadership is established through common ownership.

nel member has much control over the other members, and no formal means exists for assigning roles and resolving channel conflict. In contrast, a **vertical marketing system (VMS)** consists of producers, wholesalers, and retailers acting as a unified system. One channel member owns the others, has contracts with them, or wields so much power that they all cooperate. The VMS can be dominated by the producer, wholesaler, or retailer. Vertical marketing systems came into being to control channel behavior and manage channel conflict. They achieve economies through size, bargaining power, and elimination of duplicated services.

We look now at the three major types of VMSs shown in Figure 13-4. Each type uses a different means for setting up leadership and power in the channel. In a *corporate VMS*, coordination and conflict management are attained through common ownership at different levels of the channel. In a *contractual VMS*, they are attained through contractual agreements among channel members. In an *administered VMS*, leadership is assumed by one or a few dominant channel members. We now take a closer look at each type of VMS.

Corporate VMS

A **corporate VMS** combines successive stages of production and distribution under single ownership. In such corporate systems, cooperation and conflict management are handled through regular organizational channels. For exam-

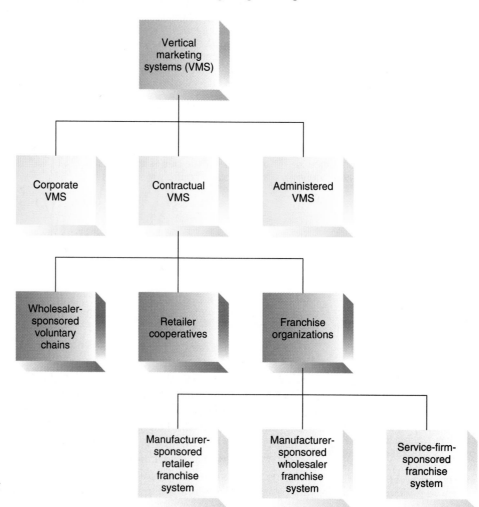

FIGURE 13-4 *Major types of vertical marketing systems*

Corporate vertical marketing systems: AT&T markets telephones and related equipment through its own chain of Phone Centers.

ple, Sears obtains more than 50 percent of its goods from companies that it partly or wholly owns. AT&T markets telephones and related equipment through its own chain of Phone Centers. Giant Food Stores operates an ice-making facility, a soft-drink bottling operation, an ice-cream-making plant, and a bakery that supplies Giant stores with everything from bagels to birthday cakes.

Gallo, the world's largest winemaker, does much more than simply turn grapes into wine. It owns Fairbanks Trucking Company, one of California's biggest intrastate trucking firms. Fairbanks trucks continuously haul wine out of Gallo wineries and raw materials back in. The raw materials include lime from Gallo's quarry near Sacramento. Gallo also makes its own bottles—more than two million a day—and its Midcal Aluminum Co. turns out bottle caps as fast as the bottles are filled. Whereas most wineries concentrate on production while neglecting marketing, Gallo participates in every aspect of selling "short of whispering in the ear of each imbiber." Gallo owns its distributors in several markets and probably would buy many more if the laws in most states did not forbid it.[3]

Contractual VMS

Contractual VMS
A vertical marketing system in which independent firms at different levels of production and distribution join together through contracts to obtain more economies or sales impact than they could achieve alone.

A **contractual VMS** consists of independent firms at different levels of production and distribution who join together through contracts to obtain more economies or sales impact than each could achieve alone. Contractual VMSs have expanded rapidly in recent years. There are three types of contractual VMSs: wholesaler-sponsored voluntary chains, retailer cooperatives, and franchise organizations.

Wholesaler-sponsored voluntary chains
Contractual vertical marketing systems in which wholesalers organize voluntary chains of independent retailers to help them compete with large corporate chain organizations.

Wholesaler-sponsored voluntary chains are systems in which wholesalers organize voluntary chains of independent retailers to help them compete with large chain organizations. The wholesaler develops a program in which independent retailers standardize their selling practices and achieve buying economies that let the group compete effectively with chain organizations. Examples include the Independent Grocers Alliance (IGA), Western Auto, and Sentry Hardwares.

Retailer cooperatives
Contractual vertical marketing systems in which retailers organize a new, jointly owned business to carry on wholesaling and possibly production.

Retailer cooperatives are systems in which retailers organize a new, jointly owned business to carry on wholesaling and possibly production. Members buy most of their goods through the retailer co-op and plan their advertising jointly.

Profits are passed back to members in proportion to their purchases. Non-member retailers also may buy through the co-op but do not share in the profits. Examples include Certified Grocers, Associated Grocers, and True Value Hardware.

Franchise organization
A contractual vertical marketing system in which a channel member, called a franchiser, links several stages in the production-distribution process.

In **franchise organizations,** a channel member called a *franchiser* links several stages in the production-distribution process. Franchising has been the fastest-growing retailing form in recent years. The more than 500,000 franchise operations in the United States now account for about one-third of all retail sales and may account for one-half by the year 2000.[4] Almost every kind of business has been franchised—from motels and fast-food restaurants to dental centers and dating services, from wedding consultants and maid services to funeral homes and fitness centers. Although the basic idea is an old one, some forms of franchising are quite new.

There are three forms of franchises. The first form is the *manufacturer-sponsored retailer franchise system,* as found in the automobile industry. Ford, for example, licenses dealers to sell its cars; the dealers are independent businesspeople who agree to meet various conditions of sales and service. The second type of franchise is the *manufacturer-sponsored wholesaler franchise system,* as found in the soft-drink industry. Coca-Cola, for example, licenses bottlers (wholesalers) in various markets who buy Coca-Cola syrup concentrate and then carbonate, bottle, and sell the finished product to retailers in local markets. The third franchise form is the *service-firm-sponsored retailer franchise system,* in which a service firm licenses a system of retailers to bring its service to consumers. Examples are found in the auto-rental business (Hertz, Avis); the fast-food service business (McDonald's, Burger King); and the motel business (Holiday Inn, Ramada Inn).

The fact that most consumers cannot tell the difference between contractual and corporate VMSs shows how successfully the contractual organizations compete with corporate chains. Chapter 14 presents a fuller discussion of the various contractual VMSs.

Administered VMS

Administered VMS
A vertical marketing system that coordinates successive stages of production and distribution, not through common ownership or contractual ties, but through the size and power of one of the parties.

An **administered VMS** coordinates successive stages of production and distribution—not through common ownership or contractual ties but through the size and power of one of the parties. Manufacturers of a top brand can obtain strong trade cooperation and support from resellers. For example, General Electric, Procter & Gamble, Kraft, and Campbell Soup can command unusual cooperation from resellers regarding displays, shelf space, promotions, and price policies. And large retailers like Wal-Mart and Toys 'R' Us can exert strong influence on the manufacturers that supply the products they sell (see Marketing Highlight 13-2).

HORIZONTAL MARKETING SYSTEMS

Horizontal marketing systems
A channel arrangement in which two or more companies at one level join together to follow a new marketing opportunity.

Another channel development is the **horizontal marketing system,** in which two or more companies at one level join together to follow a new marketing opportunity. By working together, companies can combine their capital, production capabilities, or marketing resources to accomplish more than any one company could working alone. Companies might join forces with competitors or noncompetitors.[5] They might work with each other on a temporary or permanent basis, or they may create a separate company:

◆ The Lamar Savings Bank of Texas arranged to locate its savings offices and automated teller machines in Safeway stores. Lamar gained quicker market entry at a low cost, and Safeway was able to offer in-store banking convenience to its customers.

TOYS 'R' US ADMINISTERS ITS CHANNEL

Toys 'R' Us operates 582 toy supermarkets that pull in $8 billion in annual sales and capture about 21 percent of the huge U.S. toy market. And the giant retailer is growing explosively, both in the United States and abroad. Because of its size and massive market power, Toys 'R' Us exerts strong influence on toy manufacturers—on their product, pricing, and promotion strategies, and on almost everything else they do.

Critics worry that Toys 'R' Us is *too* big and influential and that it takes unfair advantage of toy producers. The reactions of Toys 'R' Us buyers can make or break a new toy. For example, Hasbro invested some $20 million to develop Nemo—a home video game system to compete with the hugely successful Nintendo system—but then quickly canceled the project when Toys 'R' Us executives reacted negatively. Toys 'R' Us also sells its toys at everyday low prices. This sometimes frustrates toy manufacturers because Toys 'R' Us is selling toys at far below recommended retail prices, forcing producers to settle for lower margins and profits. And some analysts have accused Toys 'R' Us of placing an unfair burden on smaller toy makers by requiring all of its suppliers to pay a fee if they want their toys to be included in Toys 'R' Us newspaper advertisements.

But other industry experts think that Toys 'R' Us helps the toy industry more than hurts it. For example, whereas other retailers feature toys during the Christmas season, Toys 'R' Us has created a year-round market for toys. Moreover, its low prices cause greater overall industry sales and force producers to operate more

efficiently. Finally, Toys 'R' Us shares its extensive market data with toy producers, giving them immediate feedback on which products and marketing programs are working and which are not.

Clearly, Toys 'R' Us and the toy manufacturers need each other—the toy makers need Toys 'R' Us to market their products aggressively, and the giant retailer needs a corps of healthy producers to provide a constant stream of popular new products to fill its shelves. Through the years, both sides have recognized this inter-

Administered channels: Large retailers like Toys 'R' Us can exert strong influence on other members of the marketing channel.

dependence. For example, in the mid-1970s, when Toys 'R' Us was threatened by bankruptcy because of the financial problems of its parent company, the Toy Manufacturers Association worked directly with banks to save the troubled retailer. The banks granted credit to Toys 'R' Us largely because several major toy manufacturers were willing to grant such credit on their own. By taking

such action, the Association demonstrated a clear recognition that the entire toy industry benefited by keeping Toys 'R' Us healthy.

Similarly, Toys 'R' Us has recognized its stake in seeing that toy manufacturers succeed. In recent years, as flat toy sales have plunged many large manufacturers into deep financial trouble, Toys 'R' Us has provided a strong helping hand. For example, Toys 'R' Us often helps toy manufacturers through cash shortages and other financial difficulties by granting credit and prepaying bills. Also, its savvy buyers preview new products for toy makers, making early and valuable suggestions on possible design and marketing improvements. Such advice helped Galoob Toys convert its Army Gear line—toys that change into different weapons—from a potential flop into a top-20 seller. And following the advice of Toys 'R' Us, Ohio Arts altered the advertising strategy for its Zaks plastic building toys, increasing sales by 30 percent. The president of Tyco Toys concludes, "Toys 'R' Us gets a lot of flak for being large and taking advantage of manufacturers, but I would like to have more customers who help us as much as they do."

Sources: Amy Dunkin, "How Toys 'R' Us Controls the Game Board," Business Week, December 19, 1988, pp. 58–60; Louis W. Stern and Adel I. El-Ansary, Marketing Channels (Englewood Cliffs, NJ: Prentice Hall, 1992), pp. 14–15; Susan Caminiti, "After You Win the Fun Begins," Fortune, May 2, 1994, p. 76; and Kate Fitzgerald, "Competitors Swarm Powerful Toys 'R' Us," Advertising Age, February 21, 1995, p. 4.

◆ Coca-Cola and Nestlé formed a joint venture to market ready-to-drink coffee and tea worldwide. Coke provided worldwide experience in marketing and distributing beverages and Nestlé contributed two established brand names—Nescafé and Nestea.

◆ H&R Block and Hyatt Legal Services formed a joint venture in which Hyatt houses its legal clinics in H&R Block's tax-preparation offices. Hyatt pays a fee for office space, secretarial assistance, and office equipment usage. By working out of H&R Block's nationwide office network, Hyatt gains quick market penetration. In turn, H&R Block benefits from renting its facilities, which otherwise have a highly seasonal pattern.

◆ Such channel arrangements work well globally. Because of its excellent coverage of international markets, Nestlé sells General Mills's Cheerios brand in markets outside North America. Seiko Watch's distribution partner in Japan, K. Hattori, markets Schick's razors there, giving Schick the leading market share in Japan, despite Gillette's overall strength in many other markets.[6]

The number of such horizontal marketing systems has increased dramatically in recent years, and the end is nowhere in sight.

HYBRID MARKETING SYSTEMS

Hybrid marketing channels
Multichannel distribution systems in which a single firm sets up two or more marketing channels to reach one or more customer segments.

In the past, many companies used a single channel to sell to a single market or market segment. Today, with the proliferation of customer segments and channel possibilities, more and more companies have adopted *multichannel distribution systems*—often called **hybrid marketing channels.** Such multichannel marketing occurs when a single firm sets up two or more marketing channels to reach one or more customer segments. The use of hybrid channel systems has increased dramatically in recent years.

Figure 13-5 shows a hybrid channel. In the figure, the producer sells directly to consumer segment 1 using direct-mail catalogs and telemarketing, and reaches consumer segment 2 through retailers. It sells indirectly to business segment 1 through distributors and dealers, and to business segment 2 through its own sales force.

IBM provides a good example of a company that uses such a hybrid channel effectively. For years, IBM sold computers only through its own sales force. However, when the market for small, low-cost computers exploded, this single channel was no longer adequate. To serve the diverse needs of the many segments in the rapidly fragmenting computer market, IBM added 18 new channels in less than 10 years.[7] For example, in addition to selling through the vaunted IBM sales

Hybrid channels: For years, IBM sold computers only through its salesforce. However, it now serves the rapidly fragmenting market through a wide variety of channels, including its IBM Direct catalog and telemarketing operation.

force, the company now sells its complete line of computers and accessories through IBM Direct, its catalog and telemarketing operation. Consumers can also buy IBM personal computers from a network of independent IBM dealers, or from any of several large retailers, including Wal-Mart, Circuit City, and Office Depot. IBM dealers and value-added resellers sell IBM computer equipment and systems to a variety of special business segments.

Hybrid channels offer many advantages to companies facing large and complex markets. With each new channel, the company expands its sales and market coverage and gains opportunities to tailor its products and services to the specific needs of diverse customer segments. But such hybrid channel systems are harder to control, and they generate conflict as more channels compete for customers and sales. For example, when IBM began selling directly to customers at low prices through catalogs and telemarketing, many of its retail dealers cried "unfair competition" and threaten to drop the IBM line or to give it less emphasis.

In some cases, the multichannel marketer's channels are all under its own ownership and control. For example, Dayton-Hudson operates department stores, mass-merchandising stores, and specialty stores, each offering different product assortments to different market segments. Such arrangements eliminate conflict with outside channels, but

FIGURE 13-5 *Hybrid marketing channel*

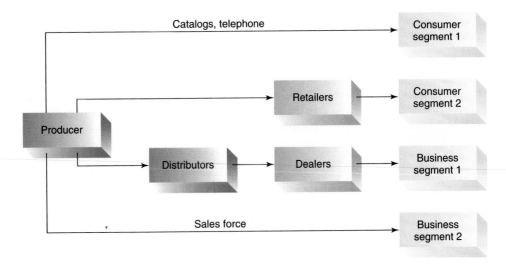

the marketer might face internal conflict over how much financial support each channel deserves.

CHANNEL DESIGN DECISIONS

We now look at several channel decisions facing manufacturers. In designing marketing channels, manufacturers struggle between what is ideal and what is practical. A new firm usually starts by selling in a limited market area. Because it has limited capital, it typically uses only a few existing intermediaries in each market—a few manufacturers' sales agents, a few wholesalers, some existing retailers, a few trucking companies, and a few warehouses. Deciding on the *best* channels might not be a problem: The problem might simply be how to convince one or a few good intermediaries to handle the line.

If the new firm is successful, it might branch out to new markets. Again, the manufacturer will tend to work through the existing intermediaries, although this strategy might mean using hybrid marketing channels. In smaller markets, the firm might sell directly to retailers; in larger markets, it might sell through distributors. In one part of the country, it might grant exclusive franchises because that is the way merchants normally work; in another, it might sell through all outlets willing to handle the merchandise.

Thus, channel systems often evolve to meet local opportunities and conditions. However, for maximum effectiveness, channel analysis and decision making should be more purposeful. Designing a channel system calls for analyzing consumer service needs, setting the channel objectives and constraints, identifying the major channel alternatives, and evaluating them.

ANALYZING CONSUMER SERVICE NEEDS

Like most marketing decisions, designing a channel begins with the customer. Marketing channels can be thought of as *customer value delivery systems* in which each channel member adds value for the customer. As noted earlier, the success of one company depends not just on its own actions, but on how well its entire channel competes with the channels of other companies. For example, Ford is just one link in a customer value delivery system that includes thousands of dealers. Even if Ford makes the best cars in the world, it will lose out to General Motors or

Toyota if these competitors have superior dealer networks. Similarly, the best Ford dealer in the world cannot do well if Ford supplies inferior cars. The company wants to design an integrated marketing channel system that will deliver superior value to its customers.

Thus, designing the distribution channel starts with finding out what values consumers in various target segments want from the channel.[8] Do consumers want to buy from nearby locations or are they willing to travel to more distant centralized locations? Would they rather buy over the phone or through the mail? Do they want immediate delivery or are they willing to wait? Do consumers value breadth of assortment or do they prefer specialization? Do consumers want many add-on services (delivery, credit, repairs, installation) or will they obtain these elsewhere? The more decentralized the channel, the faster the delivery, the greater the assortment provided, and the more add-on services supplied, the greater the channel's service level.

Consider the distribution channel service needs of business computer system buyers. The delivery of service might include such things as demonstration of the product before the sale or provision of long-term warranties and flexible financing. After the sale, there might be training programs for using the equipment and a program to install and repair it. Customers might appreciate "loaners" while their equipment is being repaired or technical advice over a telephone hot line.

But providing the fastest delivery, greatest assortment, and most services may not be possible or practical. The company and its channel members may not have the resources or skills needed to provide all the desired services. Also, providing higher levels of service results in higher costs for the channel and higher prices for consumers. The company must balance consumer service needs against not only the feasibility and costs of meeting these needs but against customer price preferences. The success of off-price and discount retailing shows that consumers are often willing to accept lower service levels if this means lower prices.

SETTING THE CHANNEL OBJECTIVES AND CONSTRAINTS

Channel objectives should be stated in terms of the desired service level of target consumers. Usually, a company can identify several segments wanting different levels of channel service. The company should decide which segments to serve and the best channels to use in each case. In each segment, the company wants to minimize the total channel cost of meeting customer service requirements.

The company's channel objectives also are influenced by the nature of its products, company policies, marketing intermediaries, competitors, and the environment. *Product characteristics* greatly affect channel design. For example, perishable products require more direct marketing to avoid delays and too much handling. Bulky products, such as building materials or soft drinks, require channels that minimize shipping distance and the amount of handling.

Company characteristics also play an important role. For example, the company's size and financial situation determine which marketing functions it can handle itself and which it must give to intermediaries. And a company marketing strategy based on speedy customer delivery affects the functions that the company wants its intermediaries to perform, the number of its outlets, and the choice of its transportation methods.

The *characteristics of intermediaries* also influence channel design. The company must find intermediaries who are willing and able to perform the needed tasks. In general, intermediaries differ in their abilities to handle promotion, customer contact, storage, and credit. For example, manufacturer's representatives who are hired by several different firms can contact customers at a low cost per

Product characteristics affect channel decisions: Fresh flowers must be delivered quickly with a minimum of handling.

customer because several clients share the total cost. However, the selling effort behind the product is less intense than if the company's own sales force did the selling.

When designing its channels, a company also must consider its *competitors' channels*. In some cases, a company may want to compete in or near the same outlets that carry competitors' products. Thus, food companies want their brands to be displayed next to competing brands; Burger King wants to locate near McDonald's. In other cases, producers may avoid the channels used by competitors. Avon, for example, decided not to compete with other cosmetics makers for scarce positions in retail stores and instead set up a profitable door-to-door selling operation.

Finally, *environmental factors,* such as economic conditions and legal constraints, affect channel design decisions. For example, in a depressed economy, producers want to distribute their goods in the most economical way, using shorter channels and dropping unneeded services that add to the final price of the goods. Legal regulations prevent channel arrangements that "may tend to lessen competition substantially or tend to create a monopoly."

IDENTIFYING MAJOR ALTERNATIVES

When the company has defined its channel objectives, it should next identify its major channel alternatives in terms of *types* of intermediaries, *number* of intermediaries, and the *responsibilities* of each channel member.

Types of Middlemen

A firm should identify the types of channel members available to carry out its channel work. For example, suppose a manufacturer of test equipment has developed an audio device that detects poor mechanical connections in any machine with moving parts. Company executives think this product would have a market in all industries where electric, combustion, or steam engines are made or used. This market includes industries such as aviation, automobile, railroad, food canning, construction, and oil. The company's current sales force is small, and the problem is how best to reach these different industries. The following channel alternatives might emerge from management discussion:

◆ *Company sales force.* Expand the company's direct sales force. Assign salespeople to territories and have them contact all prospects in the area or develop separate company salesforces for different industries.

◆ *Manufacturer's agency.* Hire manufacturer's agents—independent firms whose sales forces handle related products from many companies—in different regions or industries to sell the new test equipment.

◆ *Industrial distributors.* Find distributors in the different regions or industries who will buy and carry the new line. Give them exclusive distribution, good margins, product training, and promotional support.

Intensive distribution
Stocking the product in as many outlets as possible.

Exclusive distribution
Giving a limited number of dealers the exclusive right to distribute the company's products in their territories.

Selective distribution
The use of more than one, but fewer than all of the intermediaries who are willing to carry the company's products.

Sometimes a company must develop a channel other than the one it prefers because of the difficulty or cost of using the preferred channel. Still, the decision may turn out extremely well. For example, the U.S. Time Company first tried to sell its inexpensive Timex watches through regular jewelry stores, but most jewelry stores refused to carry them. The company then managed to get its watches into mass-merchandise outlets. This turned out to be a wise decision because of the rapid growth of mass merchandising.

Number of Marketing Intermediaries

Companies also must determine the number of channel members to use at each level. Three strategies are available: intensive distribution, exclusive distribution, and selective distribution.

Producers of convenience products and common raw materials typically seek **intensive distribution**—a strategy in which they stock their products in as many outlets as possible. These goods must be available where and when consumers want them. For example, toothpaste, candy, and other similar items are sold in millions of outlets to provide maximum brand exposure and consumer convenience. Procter & Gamble, Campbell, Coca-Cola, and other consumer goods companies distribute their products in this way.

By contrast, some producers purposely limit the number of intermediaries handling their products. The extreme form of this practice is **exclusive distribution,** in which the producer gives only a limited number of dealers the exclusive right to distribute its products in their territories. Exclusive distribution often is found in the distribution of new automobiles and prestige women's clothing. For example, Rolls-Royce dealers are few and far between—even large cities may have only one or two dealers. By granting exclusive distribution, Rolls-Royce gains stronger distributor selling support and more control over dealer prices, promotion, credit, and services. Exclusive distribution also enhances the car's image and allows for higher markups.

Between intensive and exclusive distribution lies **selective distribution**—the use of more than one, but fewer than all of the intermediaries who are willing to carry a company's products. Most television, furniture, and small appliance brands are distributed in this manner. For example, Maytag, Whirlpool, and General Electric sell their major appliances through dealer networks and selected large retailers. By using selective distribution, they do not have to spread their efforts over many outlets, including many marginal ones. They can develop good working relationships with selected channel members and expect a better-than-average selling effort. Selective distribution gives producers good market coverage with more control and less cost than does intensive distribution.

Exclusive distribution: Rolls-Royce sells exclusively through a limited number of dealerships. Such limited distribution enhances the car's image and generates stronger dealer support.

Responsibilities of Channel Members

The producer and intermediaries need to agree on the terms and responsibilities of each channel member. They should agree on price policies, conditions of sale, territorial rights, and specific services to be performed by each party. The producer should establish a list price and a fair set of discounts for intermediaries. It must define each channel member's territory, and it should be careful about where it places new resellers. Mutual services and duties need to be spelled out carefully, especially in franchise and exclusive distribution channels. For example, McDonald's provides franchisees with promotional support, a record-keeping system, training, and general management assistance. In turn, franchisees must meet company standards for physical facilities, cooperate with new promotion programs, provide requested information, and buy specified food products.

EVALUATING THE MAJOR ALTERNATIVES

Suppose a company has identified several channel alternatives and wants to select the one that will best satisfy its long-run objectives. The firm must evaluate each alternative against economic, control, and adaptive criteria. Consider the following situation: A Memphis furniture manufacturer wants to sell its line through retailers on the West Coast. The manufacturer is trying to decide between two alternatives:

◆ It could hire ten new sales representatives who would operate out of a sales office in San Francisco. They would receive a base salary plus a commission on their sales.

◆ It could use a San Francisco manufacturer's sales agency that has extensive contacts with retailers. The agency has thirty salespeople who would receive a commission based on their sales.

Economic Criteria

Each channel alternative will produce a different level of sales and costs. The first step is to figure out what sales would be produced by a company sales force compared to a sales agency. Most marketing managers believe that a company sales force will sell more. Company salespeople sell only the company's products and are better trained to handle them. They sell more aggressively because their future depends on the company. And they are more successful because customers prefer to deal directly with the company.

On the other hand, the sales agency possibly could sell more than a company sales force. First, the sales agency has thirty salespeople, not just ten. Second, the agency has many existing contacts, whereas a company sales force would have to build them from scratch. Third, the agency sales force may be just as aggressive as a direct sales force, depending on how much commission the line offers in relation to other lines carried. Fourth, some customers prefer dealing with agents who represent several manufacturers rather than with salespeople from one company.

The next step is to estimate the costs of selling different volumes through each channel. The costs are shown in Figure 13-6. The fixed costs of using a sales agency are lower than those of setting up a company sales office. But costs rise faster through a sales agency because sales agents get a larger commission than company salespeople. There is one sales level (S_B) at which selling costs are the same for the two channels. The company would prefer to use the sales agency at any sales

FIGURE 13-6 *Breakeven cost: Company sales force versus manufacturer's sales agency.*

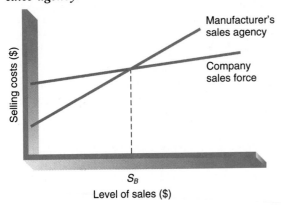

Manufacturer's sales agency

Company sales force

Selling costs ($)

S_B

Level of sales ($)

volume below S_B, and the company sales branch at any volume higher than S_B. In general, sales agents tend to be used by smaller firms, or by larger firms in smaller territories where the sales volume is too low to warrant a company sales force.

Control Criteria

Evaluation must next be broadened to consider control issues with the two channels. Using a sales agency poses more of a control problem. A sales agency is an independent business firm interested in maximizing its profits. The agent may concentrate on the customers who buy the largest volume of goods from the agency's entire mix of client companies rather than those most interested in a particular company's goods. And the agency's sales force may not master the technical details of the company's product or handle its promotion materials effectively.

Adaptive Criteria

Each channel involves some long-term commitment and loss of flexibility. A company using a sales agency may have to offer a five-year contract. During this period, other means of selling, such as a company sales force, may become more effective, but the company cannot drop the sales agency. To be considered, a channel involving a long commitment should be greatly superior on economic or control grounds.

DESIGNING INTERNATIONAL DISTRIBUTION CHANNELS

International marketers face many additional complexities in designing their channels. Each country has its own unique distribution system that has evolved over time and changes very slowly. These channel systems can vary widely from country to country. Thus, global marketers usually must adapt their channel strategies to the existing structures within each country. In some markets, the distribution system is complex and hard to penetrate, consisting of many layers and large numbers of intermediaries. Consider Japan:

The Japanese distribution system has remained remarkably traditional. A profusion of tiny retail shops are supplied by an even greater number of small wholesalers.

The Japanese distribution system stems from the early seventeenth century when cottage industries and a [quickly growing] urban population spawned a merchant class. . . . Despite Japan's economic achievements, the distribution system has remained remarkably faithful to its antique pattern. . . . [It] encompasses a wide range of wholesalers and other agents, brokers, and retailers, differing more in number than in function from their American counterparts. There are myriad tiny retail shops. An even greater number of wholesalers supplies goods to them, layered tier upon tier, many more than most U.S. executives would think necessary. For example, soap may move through three wholesalers plus a sales company after it leaves the manufacturer before it ever reaches the retail outlet. A steak goes from rancher to consumers in a process that often involves a dozen middle agents. . . . The distribution network . . . reflects the traditionally close ties among many Japanese companies . . . [and places] much greater emphasis on personal relationships with users. . . . Although [these channels appear] inefficient and cumbersome, they seem to serve the Japanese customer well. . . . Lacking much storage space in their small homes, most Japanese homemakers shop several times a week and prefer convenient [and more personal] neighborhood shops.[9]

Many Western firms have had great difficulty breaking into the closely knit, tradition-bound Japanese distribution network.

At the other extreme, distribution systems in developing countries may be scattered and inefficient, or altogether lacking. For example, China and India are huge markets, each containing hundreds of millions of people. In reality, however, these markets are much smaller than the population numbers suggest. Because of inadequate distribution systems in both countries, most companies can profitably access only a small portion of the population located in each country's most affluent cities.[10]

Thus, international marketers face a wide range of channel alternatives. Designing efficient and effective channel systems between and within various country markets poses a difficult challenge. We discuss international distribution decisions further in Chapter 20.

CHANNEL MANAGEMENT DECISIONS

Once the company has reviewed its channel alternatives and decided on the best channel design, it must implement and manage the chosen channel. Channel management calls for selecting and motivating individual channel members and evaluating their performance over time.

SELECTING CHANNEL MEMBERS

Producers vary in their ability to attract qualified marketing intermediaries. Some producers have no trouble signing up channel members. For example, Toyota had no trouble attracting new dealers for its Lexus line. In fact, it had to turn down many would-be resellers. In some cases, the promise of exclusive or selective distribution for a desirable product will draw plenty of applicants.

At the other extreme are producers who have to work hard to line up enough qualified intermediaries. When Polaroid started, for example, it could not get photography stores to carry its new cameras, and it had to go to mass-merchandising outlets. Similarly, small food producers often have difficulty getting supermarket chains to carry their products.

When selecting intermediaries, the company should determine what characteristics distinguish the better ones. It will want to evaluate the channel member's years in business, other lines carried, growth and profit record, cooperativeness, and reputation. If the intermediaries are sales agents, the company will want to evaluate the number and character of other lines carried, and the size and quality of the sales force. If the intermediary is a retail store that wants exclusive or selective distribution, the company will want to evaluate the store's customers, location, and future growth potential.

MOTIVATING CHANNEL MEMBERS

Once selected, channel members must be continuously motivated to do their best. The company must sell not only *through* the intermediaries, but *to* them. Most producers see the problem as finding ways to gain intermediary cooperation. They use the carrot-and-stick approach. At times they offer *positive* motivators such as higher margins, special deals, premiums, cooperative advertising allowances, display allowances, and sales contests. At other times they use *negative* motivators, such as threatening to reduce margins, to slow down delivery, or to end the relationship altogether. A producer using this approach usually has not done a good job of studying the needs, problems, strengths, and weaknesses of its distributors.

GENERAL ELECTRIC ADOPTS A "VIRTUAL INVENTORY" SYSTEM TO SUPPORT ITS DEALERS

Before the late 1980s, General Electric worked at selling *through* its dealers rather than *to* them or *with* them. GE operated a traditional system of trying to load up the channel with GE appliances, on the premise that "loaded dealers are loyal dealers." Loaded dealers would have less space to feature other brands and would recommend GE appliances to reduce their high inventories. To load its dealers, GE would offer the lowest price when the dealer ordered a full-truck load of GE appliances.

GE eventually realized that this approach created many problems, especially for smaller independent appliance dealers who could ill-afford to carry a large stock. These dealers were hard-pressed to meet price competition from larger multibrand dealers. Rethinking its strategy from the point of view of creating dealer satisfaction and profitability, GE created an alternative distribution model called the Direct Connect system. Under this system, GE dealers carry only display models. They rely on a "virtual inventory" to fill orders. Dealers can access GE's order-processing system 24 hours a day, check on model availability, and place orders for next-day delivery. Using the Direct Connect system, dealers also can get GE's best price, financing from GE Credit, and no interest charges for the first 90 days.

Dealers benefit by having much lower inventory costs while still having a large virtual inventory available to satisfy their customers' needs. In exchange for this benefit, dealers must commit to selling nine major GE product categories; generating 50 percent of their sales from GE products; opening their books to GE for review; and paying GE every month through electronic funds transfer.

As a result of Direct Connect, dealer profit margins have skyrocketed. GE also has benefitted. Its dealers now are more committed and dependent on GE, and the new order-entry system has saved GE substantial clerical costs. GE now knows the actual sales of its goods at the retail level, which helps it to schedule its production more accurately. It now can produce in response to demand rather than to meet inventory replenishment rules. And GE has been able to simplify its warehouse locations so as to be able to deliver appliances to 90 percent of the United States within 24 hours. Thus, by forging a partnership, GE has helped both its dealers and itself.

Creating dealer satisfaction and profitability: Using GE's Direct Connect system, dealers can access GE's order-processing system 24 hours a day, check on model availability, and place orders for next-day delivery. They can also get GE's best price, financing from GE Credit, and no interest.

Source: See Michael Treacy and Fred Wiersema, "Customer Intimacy and Other Discipline Values," *Harvard Business Review,* January–February 1993, pp. 84–93.

More advanced companies try to forge long-term partnerships with their distributors. This involves building a planned, professionally managed, vertical marketing system that meets the needs of both the manufacturer *and* the distributors.[11] Thus, Procter & Gamble and Wal-Mart work together to create superior value for final consumers. They jointly plan merchandising goals and strategies, inventory levels, and advertising and promotion plans. Similarly, General Electric works closely with its smaller independent dealers to help them be successful in selling the company's products (see Marketing Highlight 13-3). In managing its channels, a company must convince distributors that they can make their money by being part of an advanced vertical marketing system.

PUBLIC POLICY AND DISTRIBUTION DECISIONS

For the most part, companies are legally free to develop whatever channel arrangements suit them. In fact, the laws affecting channels seek to prevent the exclusionary tactics of some companies that might keep another company from using a desired channel. Of course, this means that the company must itself avoid using such exclusionary tactics. Most channel law deals with the mutual rights and duties of the channel members once they have formed a relationship.

Exclusive Dealing

Many producers and wholesalers like to develop exclusive channels for their products. When the seller allows only certain outlets to carry its products, this strategy is called *exclusive distribution.* When the seller requires that these dealers not handle competitors' products, its strategy is called *exclusive dealing.* Both parties benefit from exclusive arrangements: The seller obtains more loyal and depend-able outlets, and the dealers obtain a steady source of supply and stronger seller support. But exclusive arrangements exclude other producers from selling to these dealers. This situation brings exclusive dealing contracts under the scope of the Clayton Act of 1914. They are legal as long as they do not substantially lessen competition or tend to create a monopoly and as long as both parties enter into the agreement voluntarily.

Exclusive Territories

Exclusive dealing often includes exclusive territorial agreements. The producer may agree not to sell to other dealers in a given area, or the buyer may agree to sell only in its own territory. The first practice is normal under franchise systems as a way to increase dealer enthusiasm and commitment. It is also perfectly legal—a seller has no legal obligation to sell through more outlets than it wishes. The second practice, whereby the producer tries to keep a dealer from selling outside its territory, has become a major legal issue.

Tying Agreements

Producers of a strong brand sometimes sell it to dealers only if the dealers will take some or all of the rest of the line. This is called *full-line forcing.* Such tying agreements are not necessarily illegal, but they do violate the Clayton Act if they tend to lessen competition substantially. The practice may prevent consumers from freely choosing among competing suppliers of these other brands.

Dealers' Rights

Producers are free to select their dealers, but their right to terminate dealers is somewhat restricted. In general, sellers can drop dealers "for cause." But they cannot drop dealers if, for example, the dealers refuse to cooperate in a doubtful legal arrangement, such as exclusive dealing or tying agreements.

EVALUATING CHANNEL MEMBERS

The producer must regularly check each channel member's performance against standards such as sales quotas, average inventory levels, customer delivery time, treatment of damaged and lost goods, cooperation in company promotion and training programs, and services to the customer. The company should recognize and reward intermediaries who are performing well. Those who are performing poorly should be helped or, as a last resort, replaced.

A company may periodically "requalify" its intermediaries and prune the weaker ones. For example, when IBM first introduced its PS/2 personal computers, it reevaluated its dealers and allowed only the best ones to carry the new models. Each IBM dealer had to submit a business plan, send a sales and service employee to IBM training classes, and meet new sales quotas. Only about two-thirds of IBM's 2,200 dealers qualified to carry the PS/2 models.[12]

Finally, manufacturers need to be sensitive to their dealers. Those who treat their dealers lightly risk not only losing their support but also causing some legal problems. Marketing Highlight 13-4 describes various rights and duties pertaining to manufacturers and their channel members.

PHYSICAL DISTRIBUTION AND LOGISTICS MANAGEMENT

In today's global marketplace, selling a product is sometimes easier than getting it to customers. Companies must decide on the best way to store, handle, and move their products and services so that they are available to customers in the right assortments, at the right time, and in the right place. Logistics effectiveness will have a major impact on both customer satisfaction and company costs. A poor distribution system can destroy an otherwise good marketing effort. Here we consider the *nature and importance of marketing logistics, goals of the logistics system, major logistics functions,* and the need for *integrated logistics management.*

NATURE AND IMPORTANCE OF PHYSICAL DISTRIBUTION AND MARKETING LOGISTICS

Physical distribution (marketing logistics)
The tasks involved in planning, implementing, and controlling the physical flow of materials, final goods, and related information from points of origin to points of consumption to meet customer requirements at a profit.

To some managers, physical distribution means only trucks and warehouses. But modern logistics is much more than this. **Physical distribution**—or **marketing logistics**—involves planning, implementing, and controlling the physical flow of materials, final goods, and related information from points of origin to points of consumption to meet customer requirements at a profit.

Traditional physical distribution has typically started with products at the plant and tried to find low-cost solutions to get them to customers. However, today's marketers prefer *market logistics* thinking, which starts with the marketplace and works backwards to the factory. Logistics addresses not only the problem of outbound distribution (moving products from the factory to customers), but also the problem of inbound distribution (moving products and materials from suppliers to the factory). It involves the management of entire *supply chains,* value-added flows from suppliers to final users, as shown in Figure 13-7. Thus, the logistics manager's task is to coordinate the whole-channel physical distribution system—the activities of suppliers, purchasing agents, marketers, channel members, and customers. These activities include forecasting, information systems, purchasing, production planning, order processing, inventory, warehousing, and transportation planning.

Companies today are placing greater emphasis on logistics for several reasons. First, customer service and satisfaction have become the cornerstones of marketing strategy in many businesses, and distribution is an important customer service element. More and more, effective logistics is becoming a key to winning and keeping customers. Companies are finding that they can attract more customers by giving better service or lower prices through better physical distribution. On the other hand, companies may lose customers when they fail to supply the right products on time.

Second, logistics is a major cost element for most companies. According to one study, American companies last year "spent $670 billion—a gaping 10.5 percent of Gross Domestic Product—to wrap, bundle, load, unload, sort, reload, and transport goods."[13] About 15 percent of an average product's price is accounted for by shipping and transport alone. Poor physical distribution decisions result in high costs. Even large companies sometimes make too little use of modern decision tools for coordinating inventory levels; transportation modes; and plant, warehouse, and store locations. Improvements in physical distribution efficiency can yield tremendous cost savings for both the company and its customers.

Third, the explosion in product variety has created a need for improved logistics management. For example, in 1911, the typical A&P grocery store carried only 270 items. The store manager could keep track of this inventory on about 10 pages of notebook paper stuffed in a shirt pocket. Today, the average A&P carries a bewildering stock of more than 16,700 items, some 62 times more than in 1911.[14] Ordering, shipping, stocking, and controlling such a variety of products presents a sizable logistics challenge.

Finally, improvements in information technology have created opportunities for major gains in distribution efficiency. The increased use of computers, point-

FIGURE 13-7 *Marketing logistics: Managing supply chains*

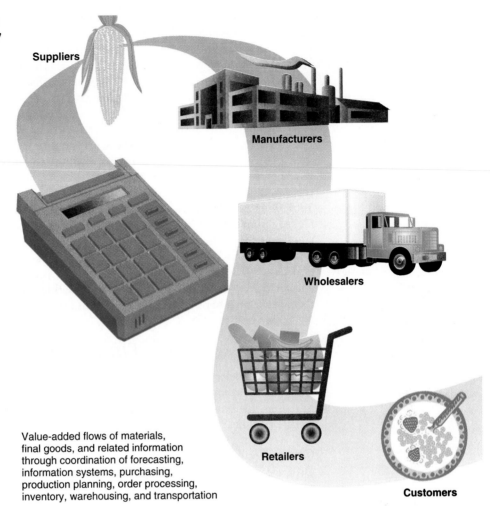

Suppliers

Manufacturers

Wholesalers

Retailers

Customers

Value-added flows of materials, final goods, and related information through coordination of forecasting, information systems, purchasing, production planning, order processing, inventory, warehousing, and transportation

of-sale scanners, uniform product codes, satellite tracking, electronic data interchange (EDI), and electronic funds transfer (EFT) has allowed companies to create advanced systems for order processing, inventory control and handling, and transportation routing and scheduling.

GOALS OF THE LOGISTICS SYSTEM

The starting point for designing a logistics system is to study the service needs of customers. Customers may want several distribution services from suppliers: fast and efficient order processing, speedy and flexible delivery, presorting and pretagging of merchandise, order tracking information, and a willingness to take back or replace defective goods.

Some companies state their logistics objective as providing maximum customer service at the least cost. Unfortunately, no logistics system can *both* maximize customer service *and* minimize distribution costs. Maximum customer service implies rapid delivery, large inventories, flexible assortments, liberal returns policies, and other services—all of which raise distribution costs. In contrast, minimum distribution costs imply slower delivery, smaller inventories, and larger shipping lots—which represent a lower level of overall customer service.

The goal of the marketing logistics system should be to provide a targeted level of customer service at the least cost. A company must first research the importance of various distribution services to its customers, and then set desired service levels for each segment. The company normally will want to offer at least the same level of service as its competitors. But the objective is to maximize *profits*, not sales. Therefore, the company must weigh the benefits of providing higher levels of service against the costs. Some companies offer less service than their competitors and charge a lower price. Other companies offer more service and charge higher prices to cover higher costs.

The company ultimately must set logistics objectives to guide its planning. For example, service-response time is very important to buyers of large photocopy machines, so Xerox developed a service-delivery standard that can "put a disabled machine anywhere in the continental United States back into operation within three hours after receiving the service request." Xerox runs a service division with 12,000 service and parts personnel. Coca-Cola's distribution standard is "to put Coke within an arm's length of desire." Some companies go further and define standards for each service factor. One appliance manufacturer has set the following service standards: to deliver at least 95 percent of the dealer's orders within two days of order receipt, to fill the dealer's order with 99 percent accuracy, to answer dealer questions on order status within three hours, and to ensure that damage to merchandise in transit does not exceed one percent.

MAJOR LOGISTICS FUNCTIONS

Given a set of logistics objectives, the company is ready to design a logistics system that will minimize the cost of attaining these objectives. The major logistics functions include *order processing, warehousing, inventory management,* and *transportation.*

Order Processing

Orders can be submitted in many ways—by mail or telephone, through salespeople, or via computer and electronic data interchange (EDI). In some cases, the suppliers might actually generate orders for their customers:

> One Kmart quick response program calls for selected suppliers to manage the retailer's inventory replenishment for their products. Kmart transmits daily records of product sales to the vendor, who analyzes the sales information, comes up with an order, and sends it back to Kmart through EDI. Once in Kmart's system, the order is treated as though Kmart itself created it. Says a Kmart executive, "We don't modify the order, and we don't question it.... Our relationship with those vendors is such that we trust them to create the type of order that will best meet our inventory needs."[15]

Once received, orders must be processed quickly and accurately. The order processing system prepares invoices and sends order information to those who need it. The appropriate warehouse receives instructions to pack and ship the ordered items. Products out of stock are back-ordered. Shipped items are accompanied by shipping and billing documents, with copies going to various departments.

Both the company and its customers benefit when the order-processing steps are carried out efficiently. Ideally, salespeople send in their orders daily, often using online computers. The order department quickly processes these orders, and the warehouse sends the goods out on time. Bills go out as soon as possible. Most companies now use computerized order-processing systems that speed up the order-shipping-billing cycle. For example, General Electric operates a computer-based system that, upon receipt of a customer's order, checks the customer's credit standing as well as whether and where the items are in stock. The computer then issues an order to ship, bills the customer, updates the inventory records, sends a production order for new stock, and relays the message back to the salesperson that the customer's order is on its way—all in less than 15 seconds.

Warehousing

Every company must store its goods while they wait to be sold. A storage function is needed because production and consumption cycles rarely match. For example, Snapper, Toro, and other lawn mower manufacturers must produce all year long and store up their product for the heavy spring and summer buying season. The storage function overcomes differences in needed quantities and timing.

A company must decide on *how many* and *what types* of warehouses it needs, and *where* they will be located. The more warehouses the company uses, the more quickly goods can be delivered to customers. However, more locations mean higher warehousing costs. The company, therefore, must balance the level of customer service against distribution costs.

Some company stock is kept at or near the plant, with the rest located in warehouses around the country. The company might own private warehouses, rent space in public warehouses, or both. Companies have more control over warehouses they own, but that ties up their capital and is less flexible if desired locations change. In contrast, public warehouses charge for the rented space and provide additional services (at a cost) for inspecting goods, packaging them, shipping them, and invoicing them. By using public warehouses, companies also have a wide choice of locations and warehouse types.

Distribution center
A large, highly automated warehouse designed to receive goods from various plants and suppliers, take orders, fill them efficiently, and deliver goods to customers as quickly as possible.

Companies may use either *storage warehouses* or *distribution centers*. Storage warehouses store goods for moderate to long periods. **Distribution centers** are designed to move goods rather than just store them. They are large and highly automated warehouses designed to receive goods from various plants and suppliers, take orders, fill them efficiently, and deliver goods to customers as quickly as possible. For example, Wal-Mart operates huge distribution centers. One center, which serves the daily needs of 165 Wal-Mart stores, contains some 28 acres of space under a single roof. Laser scanners route as many as 190,000 cases of goods per day along 11 miles of conveyer belts, and the center's 1,000 workers load or unload 310 trucks daily.[16]

Warehousing facilities and equipment technology have improved greatly in recent years. Older, multistoried warehouses with slow elevators and outdated

Automated warehouses: This sophisticated COMPAQ computer distribution center can ship any of 500 different types of COMPAQ computers and options within four hours of receiving an order.

materials-handling methods are facing competition from newer, single-storied *automated warehouses* with advanced materials-handling systems under the control of a central computer. In these warehouses, only a few employees are necessary. Computers read orders and direct lift trucks, electric hoists, or robots to gather goods, move them to loading docks, and issue invoices. These warehouses have reduced worker injuries, labor costs, theft, and breakage and have improved inventory control.

Inventory

Inventory levels also affect customer satisfaction. The major problem is to maintain the delicate balance between carrying too much inventory and carrying too little. Carrying too much inventory results in higher-than-necessary inventory carrying costs and stock obsolesence. Carrying too little may result in stock-outs, costly emergency shipments or production, and customer dissatisfaction. In making inventory decisions, management must balance the costs of carrying larger inventories against resulting sales and profits.

Inventory decisions involve knowing both *when* to order and *how much* to order. In deciding when to order, the company balances the risks of running out of stock against the costs of carrying too much. In deciding how much to order, the company needs to balance order-processing costs against inventory carrying costs. Larger average-order size results in fewer orders and lower order-processing costs, but it also means larger inventory carrying costs.

During the past decade, many companies have greatly reduced their inventories and related costs through *just-in-time* logistics systems. Through such systems, producers and retailers carry only small inventories of parts or merchandise, often only enough for a few days of operations. New stock arrives exactly when needed, rather than being stored in inventory until being used. Just-in-time systems require accurate forecasting along with fast, frequent, and flexible delivery, so that new supplies will be available when needed. However, these systems result in substantial savings in inventory carrying and handling costs.

Transportation

Marketers need to take an interest in their company's *transportation* decisions. The choice of transportation carriers affects the pricing of products, delivery performance, and condition of the goods when they arrive—all of which will affect customer satisfaction.

In shipping goods to its warehouses, dealers, and customers, the company can choose among five transportation modes: rail, water, truck, pipeline, and air. Table 13-1 summarizes the characteristics of each transportation mode.

TABLE 13-1 *Characteristics of Major Transportation Modes*

TRANSPORTATION MODE	INTERCITY CARGO VOLUME* (%)			TYPICAL PRODUCTS SHIPPED
	1970	**1980**	**1991**	
Rail	771 (39.8%)	932 (37.5%)	1078 (37.4%)	Farm products, minerals, sand, chemicals, automobiles
Truck	412 (21.3)	555 (22.3)	758 (26.3)	Clothing, food, books, computers, paper goods
Water	319 (16.5)	407 (16.4)	462 (16.0)	Oil, grain, sand, gravel, metallic ores, coal
Pipeline	431 (22.3)	588 (23.6)	578 (20.0)	Oil, coal, chemicals
Air	3.3 (0.17)	4.8 (0.19)	10 (0.3)	Technical instruments, perishable products, documents

*In billions of cargo ton-miles.
Source: Statistical Abstract of the United States, 1993.

Information At The Speed Of Light

In today's business environment speed is critical.
Roadway Express moves your shipment around the clock
and communicates your shipment's location at the speed of light.
Continuously tracked by satellite, our new sleeper tractors
keep your shipment on the road and on time.
You get reliable service and reliable information.

*Just some of the ways we're changing to offer you
exceptional service...with no exceptions.*

ROADWAY ROADWAY

ROADWAY.
Roadway Express

Roadway and other trucking firms have added many services in recent years, such as satellite tracking of shipments and sleeper tractors that keep freight moving around the clock.

RAIL. Although railroads lost market share until the mid-1970s, today they remain the nation's largest carrier, accounting for 37 percent of total cargo moved. Railroads are one of the most cost-effective modes for shipping large amounts of bulk products—coal, sand, minerals, farm and forest products—over long distances. In addition, railroads recently have begun to increase their customer services. They have designed new equipment to handle special categories of goods, provided flatcars for carrying truck trailers by rail (piggyback), and provided in-transit services such as the diversion of shipped goods to other destinations en route and the processing of goods en route. Thus, after decades of losing out to truckers, railroads appear ready for a comeback.[17]

TRUCK. Trucks have increased their share of transportation steadily and now account for 25 percent of total cargo. They account for the largest portion of transportation *within* cities as opposed to *between* cities. Each year in the United States, trucks travel more than 600 billion miles—equal to nearly 1.3 million round trips to the moon—carrying 2.5 billion tons of freight.[18] Trucks are highly flexible in their routing and time schedules. They can move goods door to door, saving shippers the need to transfer goods from truck to rail and back again at a loss of time and risk of theft or damage. Trucks are efficient for short hauls of high-value merchandise. In many cases, their rates are competitive with railway rates, and trucks can usually offer faster service. Trucking firms have added many services in recent years. For example, Roadway Express now offers satellite tracking of shipments and sleeper tractors that move freight around the clock.

WATER. A large amount of goods are moved by ships and barges on U.S. coastal and inland waterways. Mississippi River barges alone account for 15 percent of the freight shipped in the United States. On the one hand, the cost of water transportation is very low for shipping bulky, low-value, nonperishable products such as sand, coal, grain, oil, and metallic ores. On the other hand, water transportation is the slowest transportation mode and is sometimes affected by the weather.

PIPELINE. Pipelines are a specialized means of shipping petroleum, natural gas, and chemicals from sources to markets. Pipeline shipment of petroleum products costs less than rail shipment, but more than water shipment. Most pipelines are used by their owners to ship their own products.

AIR. Although air carriers transport less than one percent of the nation's goods, they are becoming more important as a transportation mode. Air-freight rates are much higher than rail or truck rates, but air freight is ideal when speed is needed or distant markets have to be reached. Among the most frequently air-freighted products are perishables (fresh fish, cut flowers) and high-value, low-bulk items (technical instruments, jewelry). Companies find that air freight also reduces inventory levels, packaging costs, and the number of warehouses needed.

Until the late 1970s, routes, rates, and service in the transportation industry were heavily regulated by the federal government. Today, most of these regulations have been eased. Deregulation has caused rapid and substantial changes. Railroads, ships and barges, trucks, airlines, and pipeline companies are now much more competitive, flexible, and responsive to the needs of their customers. These changes have resulted in better services and lower prices for shippers. But such changes also mean that marketers must do better transportation planning if they want to take full advantage of new opportunities in the changing transportation environment.

In choosing a transportation mode for a product, shippers consider as many as five criteria, as shown in Table 13-2. Thus, if a shipper needs speed, air and truck are the prime choices. If the goal is low cost, then water or pipeline might be best. Trucks appear to offer the most advantages—a fact that explains their growing share of the transportation market.

Thanks to *containerization,* shippers are increasingly combining two or more modes of transportation. **Containerization** consists of putting goods in boxes or trailers that are easy to transfer between two transportation modes. *Piggyback* describes the use of rail and trucks; *fishyback,* water and trucks; *trainship,* water and rail; and *airtruck,* air and trucks. Each combination offers advantages to the shipper. For example, not only is piggyback cheaper than trucking alone, but it also provides flexibility and convenience.

Containerization
Putting the goods in boxes or trailers that are easy to transfer between two transportation modes. They are used in multimode systems commonly referred to as piggyback, fishyback, trainship, and airtruck.

INTEGRATED LOGISTICS MANAGEMENT

Integrated logistics management
The logistics concept that emphasizes teamwork, both inside the company and among all the marketing channel organizations, to maximize the performance of the entire distribution system.

Today, more and more companies are adopting the concept of **integrated logistics management.** This concept recognizes that providing better customer service and trimming distribution costs requires *teamwork,* both inside the company and among all the marketing channel organizations. Inside the company, the various functional departments must work closely together to maximize the company's own logistics performance. The company must also integrate its logistics system with those of its suppliers and customers to maximize the performance of the entire distribution system.

Cross-Functional Teamwork Inside the Company

In most companies, responsibility for various logistics activities is assigned to many different functional units—marketing, sales, finance, manufacturing, purchasing. Too often, each function tries to optimize its own logistics performance without regard for the activities of the other functions. However, transportation, inventory, warehousing, and order processing activities interact, often in an inverse way. For example, lower inventory levels reduce inventory carrying costs. But they may also reduce customer service and increase costs from stockouts, backorders, special production runs, and costly fast-freight shipments. Because distribution activities involve strong trade-offs, decisions by different functions must be coordinated to achieve superior overall logistics performance.

Thus, the goal of integrated logistics management is to harmonize all of the company's distribution decisions. Close working relationships among functions can be achieved in several ways. Some companies have created permanent logistics committees made up of managers responsible for different physical distribution activities. These committees meet often to set policies for improving overall logistics performance. Companies can also create management positions that link the

TABLE 13-2 *Rankings of Transportation Modes (1 = Highest Rank)*

	SPEED (door-to-door delivery time)	DEPENDABILITY (meeting schedules on time)	CAPABILITY (ability to handle various products)	AVAILABILITY (no. of geographic points served)	COST (per ton-mile)
Rail	3	4	2	2	3
Water	4	5	1	4	1
Truck	2	2	3	1	4
Pipeline	5	1	5	5	2
Air	1	3	4	3	5

Source: See Carl M. Guelzo, *Introduction to Logistics Management* (Englewood Cliffs, NJ: Prentice Hall, 1986), p. 46.

logistics activities of functional areas. For example, Procter & Gamble has created "supply managers" who manage all of the supply chain activities for each of its product categories.[19] Many companies have a vice-president of logistics with cross-functional authority. In fact, according to one logistics expert, three-fourths of all major wholesalers and retailers, and a third of major manufacturing companies, have senior logistics officers at the vice president or higher level.[20] The location of the logistics functions within the company is a secondary concern. The important thing is that the company coordinate its logistics and marketing activities to create high market satisfaction at a reasonable cost.

Building Channel Partnerships

The members of a distribution channel are linked closely in delivering customer satisfaction and value. One company's distribution system is another company's supply system. The success of each channel member depends on the performance of the entire supply chain. For example, Wal-Mart can charge the lowest prices at retail only if its entire supply chain—consisting of thousands of merchandise suppliers, transport companies, warehouses, and service providers—operates at maximum efficiency.

Companies must do more than improve their own logistics. They must also work with other channel members to improve whole-channel distribution. For example, it makes little sense for Levi Strauss to ship finished jeans to its own warehouses, then from these warehouses to JCPenney warehouses, from which they are then shipped to JCPenney's stores. If the two companies can work together, Levi Strauss might be able to ship much of its merchandise directly to JCPenney's stores, saving time, inventory, and shipping costs for both. Today, smart companies are coordinating their logistics strategies and building strong partnerships with suppliers and customers to improve customer service and reduce channel costs.

These channel partnerships can take many forms. Many companies have created *cross-functional, cross-company teams*. For example, Procter & Gamble has a team of almost 100 people living in Bentonville, Arkansas, home of Wal-Mart. The P&Gers work with their counterparts at Wal-Mart to jointly find ways to squeeze costs out of their distribution system. Working together benefits not only P&G and Wal-Mart, but also their final consumers. Haggar Apparel Company has a similar system called "multiple points of contact," in which a Haggar team works with JCPenney people at corporate, divisional, and store levels. As a result of this partnership, Penney now receives Haggar merchandise within 18 days of placing an order—10 days fewer than its next best supplier. And Haggar ships the merchandise "floor ready"—hangered and pretagged—reducing the time it takes Penney to move the stock from receiving docks to the sales floor from four days to just one.[21]

Other companies partner through *shared projects*. For example, many larger retailers are working closely with suppliers on in-store programs. Home Depot allows key suppliers to use its stores as a testing ground for new merchandising programs. The suppliers spend time at Home Depot stores watching how their product sells and how customers relate to it. They then create programs specially tailored to Home Depot and its customers. Western Publishing Group, publisher of "Little Golden Books" for children, formed a similar partnership with Toys 'R' Us. Western and the giant toy retailer coordinated their marketing strategies to create mini-bookstore sections—called Books 'R' Us—within each Toys 'R' Us store. Toys 'R' Us provides the locations, space, and customers; Western serves as distributor, consolidator, and servicer for the Books 'R' Us program.[22] Clearly, both the supplier and customer benefit from such partnerships.

Channel partnerships may also take the form of *information sharing* and *continuous inventory replenishment* systems. Companies manage their supply chains through information. Suppliers link up with customers through electronic data interchange (EDI) systems to share information and coordinate their logistics decisions. Here are just two examples:

> Information sharing is at the heart of supplier-customer relationships. Increasingly, high-performance retailers are sharing point-of-sale scanner data with their suppliers through electronic data interchange. Wal-Mart was one of the first companies to provide suppliers with timely sales data. With its Retail Link system, major suppliers have "earth stations" installed by which they are directly connected to Wal-Mart's information network. Now, the same system that tells Wal-Mart what customers are buying lets suppliers know what to produce and where to ship the goods. Thus, when a teenager buys a size 10 Nike running shoe, the information goes directly to Nike's computers, triggering replacement or production. Wal-Mart no longer issues purchase orders to some of its most reliable suppliers. These suppliers automatically replenish Wal-Mart's inventory based on the retailer's scanner data and their knowledge of Wal-Mart's operations.[23]

> Bailey Controls, a manufacturer of control systems for big factories, from steel and paper mills to chemical and pharmaceutical plants, . . . treats some of its suppliers almost like departments of its own plants. Bailey has plugged two of its main electronics suppliers into itself. Future Electronics is hooked on through an electronic data interchange system. Every week, Bailey electronically sends Future its latest forecasts of what materials it will need for the next six months, so that Future can stock up in time. Bailey itself stocks only enough inventory for a few days of operation, as opposed to the three or four months worth it used to carry. Whenever a bin of parts falls below a designated level, a Bailey employee passes a laser scanner over the bin's bar code, instantly alerting Future to send the parts at once. Arrow Electronics . . . is plugged in even more closely: It has a warehouse in Bailey's factory, stocked according to Bailey's twice-a-month forecasts. Bailey provides the space, Arrow the warehouseman and the $500,000 of inventory.[24]

Today, as a result of such partnerships, many companies have switched from *anticipatory-based distribution systems* to *response-based distribution systems*.[25] In anticipatory distribution, the company produces the amount of goods called for by a sales forecast. It builds and holds stock at various supply points such as the plant, distribution centers, and retail outlets. Each supply point reorders automatically when its order point is reached. When sales are slower than expected, the company tries to reduce its inventories by offering discounts, rebates, and promotions. For example, the American auto industry produces cars far in advance of demand, and these cars often sit for months in inventory until the companies undertake aggressive promotion.

A response-based distribution system, in contrast, is *customer-triggered*. The producer continuously builds and replaces stock as orders arrive. It produces what is currently selling. For example, Japanese car makers take orders for cars, then produce and ship them within four days. Some large appliance manufacturers, such as Whirlpool and GE, are moving to this system. Benetton, the Italian fashion house, uses a *quick-response system*, dyeing its sweaters in the colors that are currently selling instead of trying to guess long in advance which colors people will want. Producing for order rather than for forecast substantially cuts down inventory costs and risks.

Summary

Understanding *the nature of distribution channels* is important, as choosing among distribution channels is one of the most challenging decisions facing the firm. *Marketing intermediaries are used* because they provide greater efficiency in making goods available to target markets. The key *distribution channel function* is moving goods from producers to consumers by helping to complete transactions and fulfilling the completed transaction. Distribution channels can be described by the *number of channel levels*, which can include no intermediaries in a direct channel, or one to several intermediaries in indirect channels.

Distribution channels can also be used in less tangible situations such as the *service sector* and even in person marketing. Each channel system creates a different level of sales and costs. Once a distribution channel has been chosen, the firm must usually stick with it for a long time. The chosen channel strongly affects, and is affected by, the other elements in the marketing mix.

There are different types of *channel behavior and organization*. Each firm needs to identify alternative ways to reach its market. Available means vary from direct selling to using one, two, three, or more intermediary channel levels. Marketing channels face continuous and sometimes dramatic change. Three of the most important trends are the growth of *vertical, horizontal, and hybrid marketing systems*. These trends affect channel cooperation, conflict, and competition.

Channel design decisions begin with assessing *customer service needs* and *setting the channel objectives and constraints*. The company then *identifies major channel alternatives* in terms of the *types of middlemen, the number of intermediaries*, and the *responsibilities of channel members*. Next managers must *evaluate the major alternatives* according to *economic, control*, and *adaptive criteria*. Special consideration must be given when *designing international distribution channels*.

Channel management decisions include *selecting* qualified intermediaries and *motivating channel members*. Individual channel members must be evaluated regularly.

Just as the marketing concept is receiving increased recognition, more business firms are paying attention to *physical distribution and logistics management*. Logistics is an area of potentially high cost savings and improves customer satisfaction. Marketing logistics involves coordinating the activities of the entire supply chain to deliver maximum value to the customers. No logistics system can both maximize customer service and minimize distribution costs. Instead, the *goal of the logistics system* is to provide a targeted level of service at the least costs. The *major logistics functions* include *order processing, warehousing, inventory management*, and *transportation*.

The *integrated logistics management* concept recognizes that improved logistics requires *cross-functional teamwork*—in the form of close working relationships across different departments inside the company, and across various organizations in the supply chain. Companies can achieve logistics harmony among functions by creating cross-functional logistics teams, integrative supply manager positions, and senior-level logistics executives with cross-functional authority. *Channel partnerships* can take the form of cross-company teams, shared projects, and information-sharing systems. Through such partnerships, many companies have switched from anticipatory-based distribution systems to customer-triggered response-based distribution systems.

Key Terms

Administered VMS
Channel conflict
Channel level
Containerization
Contractual VMS
Conventional distribution channel
Corporate VMS
Direct marketing channel
Distribution center

Distribution channel (marketing channel)
Exclusive distribution
Franchise organization
Horizontal marketing systems
Hybrid marketing channels
Indirect marketing channel
Integrated logistics management

Intensive distribution
Physical distribution (or marketing logistics)
Retailer cooperatives
Selective distribution
Vertical marketing system (VMS)
Wholesaler-sponsored voluntary chains

Discussing the Issues

1. The Book-of-the-Month Club has been successfully marketing books by mail for over 50 years. Discuss why so few publishers sell books directly by mail. Suggest reasons for how the BOMC has survived competition from B. Dalton, Waldenbooks, Borders and other large booksellers in recent years.

2. Analyze why franchising is such a fast-growing form of retail organization.

3. Why have horizontal marketing arrangements become more common in recent years? Suggest several pairs of companies that you think could have successful horizontal marketing programs.

4. Describe the channel service needs of (a) consumers buying a computer for home use, (b) retailers buying computers to resell to individual consumers, and (c) purchasing agents buying computers for company use. What channels would a computer manufacturer design to satisfy these different service needs?

5. Decide which distribution strategies—intensive, selective, or exclusive—are used for the following products, and why? (a) Piaget watches (b) Acura automobiles, (c) Snickers candy bars.

6. Identify several consequences of running out of stock that need to be considered when planning desired inventory levels.

Applying the Concepts

1. Discount malls and so-called "factory outlet centers" are increasing in popularity. Many of their stores are operated by manufacturers who normally sell only through middlemen. If you have one of these malls nearby, visit it and study the retailers. Discuss what sort of merchandise is sold in these stores. Do any of them appear to be factory owned? If so, do these factory stores compete with the manufacturer's normal retailers? Appraise the pros and cons of operating these stores.

2. Go through a camera or computer magazine, and pay special attention to large ads for mail-order retailers. Look for ads for brand-name products that use selective distribution, such as Nikon cameras or Compaq computers. Locate an ad that is clearly from an authorized dealer, and one that appears not to be. How can you judge which channel is legitimate? Are there price differences between the legitimate and the unauthorized dealers, and if so, are they what you would expect?

References

1. Quotes from Dana Milbank, "Independent Tire Dealers Rebelling Against Goodyear," *Wall Street Journal*, July 8, 1992, p. B1; and Zachary Schiller, "Goodyear Is Gunning Its Marketing Engine," *Business Week*, March 16, 1992, p. 42. Also see Nancy Hass, "CEO of the Year: Stanley Gault of Goodyear," *Financial World*, March 31, 1992, pp. 26–33; Peter Nulty, "The Bounce Is Back at Goodyear," *Fortune*, September 7, 1992, pp. 70–72; Lloyd Stoyer, "Goodyear Tires of Exclusive Relationship," *Sales & Marketing Management*, March 1994, p. 14; and Zachary Schiller, "And Fix That Flat Before You Go, Stanley," *Business Week*, January 15, 1995, p. 35.

2. Louis Stern and Adel I. El-Ansary, *Marketing Channels*, 4th. ed (Englewood Cliffs, NJ: Prentice Hall, 1992), p. 3.

3. Jaclyn Fierman, "How Gallo Crushes the Competition," *Fortune*, September 1, 1986, p. 27.

4. See Richard C. Hoffman and John F. Preble, "Franchising Into the Twenty-First Century," *Business Horizons*, November–December, 1993, pp. 35–43.

5. This has been called "symbiotic marketing." For more reading, see Lee Adler, "Symbiotic Marketing," *Harvard Business Review*, November–December 1966, pp. 59–71; P. "Rajan" Varadarajan and Daniel Rajaratnam, "Symbiotic Marketing Revisited," *Journal of Marketing*, January 1986, pp. 7–17; and Gary Hamel, Yves L. Doz, and C. D. Prahalad, "Collaborate with Your Competitors—and Win," *Harvard Business Review*, January–February 1989, pp. 133–139.

6. See Allan J. Magrath, "Collaborative Marketing Comes of Age—Again," *Sales & Marketing Management,* September 1991, pp. 61–64; and Lois Therrien, "Cafe Au Lait, A Croissant—and Trix," *Business Week,* August 24, 1992, pp. 50–51.

7. See Rowland T. Moriarity and Ursala Moran, "Managing Hybrid Marketing Systems," November–December 1990, pp. 146–155.

8. See Stern and Sturdivant, "Customer-Driven Distribution Systems," p. 35.

9. Subhash C. Jain, *International Marketing Management,* 3rd ed. (Boston, MA: PWS-Kent Publishing, 1990), pp. 489–491. Also see Emily Thronton, "Revolution in Japanese Retailing," *Fortune,* February 7, 1994, pp. 143–147.

10. See Philip Cateora, *International Marketing,* 7th ed. (Homewood, IL: Irwin, 1990), pp. 570–571.

11. See James A. Narus and James C. Anderson, "Turn Your Industrial Distributors into Partners," *Harvard Business Review,* March–April 1986, pp. 66–71; and Marty Jacknis and Steve Kratz, "The Channel Empowerment Solution," *Sales & Marketing Management,* March 1993, pp. 44–49.

12. See Katherine M. Hafner, "Computer Retailers: Things Have Gone from Worse to Bad," *Business Week,* June 8, 1987, p. 104.

13. Ronald Henkoff, "Delivering the Goods," *Fortune,* November 18, 1994, pp. 64–78. Also see Shlomo Maital, "The Last Frontier of Cost Reduction," *Across the Board,* February 1994, pp. 51–52.

14. Ibid., p. 52.

15. "Linking with Vendors for Just-In-Time Service," *Chain Store Age Executive,* June 1993, pp. 22A–24A; and Joseph Weber, "Just Get It to the Stores on Time," *Business Week,* March 6, 1995, pp. 66–67.

16. John Huey, "Wal-Mart: Will It Take Over the World?" *Fortune,* January 30, 1989, pp. 52–64.

17. Shawn Tully, "Comeback Ahead for Railroads," *Fortune,* June 17, 1991, pp. 107–113.

18. See "Trucking Deregulation: A Ten-Year Anniversary," *Fortune,* August 13, 1990, pp. 25–35.

19. "Managing Logistics in the 1990s," *Logistics Perspectives,* Anderson Consulting, Cleveland, OH, July 1990, pp. 1–6.

20. Maital, "The Last Frontier of Cost Reduction," p. 51.

21. Sandra J. Skrovan, "Partnering with Vendors: The Ties that Bind," *Chain Store Age Executive,* January 1994, pp. 6MH–9MH.

22. Ibid., p. 6MH; and Susan Caminiti, "After You Win, the Fun Begins," *Fortune,* May 2, 1994, p. 76.

23. See Skrovan, "Partnering with Vendors," p. 8MH.

24. Myron Magnet, "The New Golden Rule of Business," *Fortune,* February 21, 1994, pp. 60–64.

25. Based on an address by Professor Donald J. Bowersox at Michigan State University on August 5, 1992.

Company Case 13

ICON ACOUSTICS: BYPASSING TRADITION

THE DREAM

Like most entrepreneurs, Dave Fokos dreams a lot. He imagines customers eagerly phoning Icon Acoustics in Billerica, Massachusetts, to order his latest, custom-made stereo speakers. He sees sales climbing, cash flowing, and hundreds of happy workers striving to produce top-quality products that delight Icon's customers.

Like most entrepreneurs, Dave has taken a long time to develop his dream. While majoring in electrical engineering at Cornell, Dave discovered that he had a strong interest in audio engineering. Following graduation, Dave landed a job as a speaker designer with Conrad-Johnson, a high-end audio-equipment manufacturer. Within four years, Dave had designed 13 speaker models and decided to start his own company.

Dave identified a market niche that he felt other speaker firms had overlooked. The niche consisted of "audio-addicts"—people who love to listen to music and appreciate first-rate stereo equipment. These affluent, well-educated customers are genuinely obsessed with their stereo equipment. "They'd rather buy a new set of speakers than eat," Dave observes.

Dave faced one major problem—how to distribute Icon's products. He had learned from experience at Conrad-Johnson that most manufacturers distribute their equipment primarily through stereo dealers. Dave did not hold a high opinion of most such dealers; he felt that they too often played hardball with manufacturers, forcing them to accept thin margins. Furthermore, the dealers concentrated on only a handful of well-known producers who provided mass-produced models. This kept those firms that offered more customized products from gaining access to the market. Perhaps most disturbing, Dave felt that the established dealers often sold not what was best for customers, but whatever they had in inventory that month.

Dave dreamed of offering high-end stereo loudspeakers directly to the audio-obsessed, bypassing the established dealer network. By going directly to the customers, Dave could avoid the dealer markups and offer top-quality products and service at reasonable prices.

THE PLAN

At the age of 28, Dave set out to turn his dreams into reality. Some customers who had gotten to know Dave's work became enthusiastic supporters of his dream and invested $189,000 in Icon. With their money and $10,000 of his own, Dave started Icon in a rented facility in an industrial park.

The Market. Approximately 335 stereo-speaker makers compete for a $3 billion annual U.S. market for audio components. About 100 of these manufacturers sell to the low- and mid-range segments of the market, which account for 90 percent of the market's unit volume and about 50 percent of its value. In addition to competing with each other, U.S. manufacturers also compete with Japanese firms that offer products at affordable prices. The remaining 235 or so manufacturers compete for the remaining 10 percent of the market's unit volume and 50 percent of the value—the high end—where Dave hopes to find his customers.

Icon's Marketing Strategy. To serve the audio-addicts segment, Dave offers only the highest-quality speakers. He has developed two models: the Lumen and the Parsec. The Lumen stands 18 inches high, weighs 26 pounds, and is designed for stand mounting. The floor-standing Parsec is 47 inches high and weighs 96 pounds. Both models feature custom-made cabinets that come in natural or black oak and American walnut. Dave can build and ship two pairs of the Lumen speakers or one pair of the Parsec speakers per day by himself. In order to have an adequate parts inventory, he had to spend $50,000 of his capital on the expensive components.

Dave set the price of the Lumen and Parsec at $795 and $1,795 per pair, respectively. He selected these prices to provide a 50 percent gross margin. He believes that traditional dealers would sell equivalent speakers at retail at twice those prices. Customers can call Icon on a toll-free 800 number to order speakers or to get advice directly from Dave. Icon pays for shipping and any return freight via Federal Express—round-trip freight for a pair of Parsecs costs $486.

Dave offers to pay for the return freight because a key part of his promotional strategy is a 30-day, in-home, no-obligation trial. In his ads, Dave calls this "The 43,200 Minute, No Pressure Audition." This trial period allows customers to listen to the speakers in their actual listening environment. In a dealer's showroom, the customer must listen in an artificial environment and often feels pressure to make a quick decision.

Dave believes that typical high-end customers may buy speakers for "nonrational" reasons: They want a quality product and good sound, but they also want an image. Thus, Dave has tried to create a unique image through the appearance of his speakers and to reflect that image in all of the company's marketing. He spent over $40,000 on distinctive stationery, business cards, a brochure, and a single display ad. He also designed a laminated label he places just above the gold-plated input jack on each speaker. The label reads: "This loudspeaker was handcrafted by [the technician's name who assembled the speaker goes here in his/her own handwriting]. Made in the United States of America by Icon Acoustics, Inc., Billerica, Mass."

To get the word out, Dave concentrates on product reviews in trade magazines and on trade shows, such as the High End Hi-Fi show in New York. Attendees at the show cast ballots to select "The Best Sound at the Show." In the balloting, among 200 brands, Icon's Parsec speakers finished fifteenth. Among the top ten brands, the least expensive was a pair priced at $2,400, and six of the systems were priced from $8,000 to $18,000. A reviewer in an issue of *Stereophile* magazine evaluated Icon's speakers and noted: "The overall sound was robust and dynamic, with a particularly potent low end. Parts and construction quality appeared to be first rate. Definitely a company to watch."

Dave made plans to invest in a slick, four-color display ad in *Stereo Review,* the consumer magazine with the highest circulation (600,000). He also expected another favorable review in *Stereophile* magazine.

THE REALITY

Dressed in jeans and a hooded sweatshirt, Dave pauses in the middle of assembling a cardboard shipping carton, pulls up a chair, and leans against the concrete-block wall of his manufacturing area. Reflecting on his experiences during his first year in business, Dave realizes he's learned a lot in jumping all the hurdles the typical entrepreneur faces. Dave experienced quality problems with the first cabinet supplier. Then, he ran short of a key component after a mixup with a second supplier. Despite his desire to avoid debt, he had to borrow $50,000 from a bank. Prices for his cabinets and some components had risen, and product returns had been higher than expected (19 percent for the past six months). These price and cost increases put pressure on his margins, forcing Dave to raise his prices (to those quoted earlier). Despite the price increases, his margins remained below his 50 percent target.

Still, Dave feels good about his progress. The price increase does not seem to have affected demand. The

EXHIBIT 13-1   *Icon Acoustics's pro forma financials ($ in thousands)*

YEAR	1	2	3	4	5
Pairs of Speakers Sold	224	435	802	1,256	1,830
Total Sales Revenue	$303	$654	$1,299	$2,153	$3,338
Cost of Sales:					
Materials and Packaging	$130	$281	$561	$931	$1,445
Shipping	$43	$83	$157	$226	$322
Total Cost of Sales	$173	$364	$718	$1,157	$1,767
Gross Profit	$130	$290	$581	$996	$1,571
Gross Margin	43%	44%	45%	46%	47%
Expenses:					
New Property and Equipment	$3	$6	$12	$15	$18
Marketing	$13	$66	$70	$109	$135
General and Administrative	$51	$110	$197	$308	$378
Loan Repayment	$31	$31	$0	$0	$0
Outstanding Payables	$30	$0	$0	$0	$0
Total Expenses	$128	$213	$279	$432	$531
Pretax Profit	$2	$77	$302	$564	$1,040
Pretax Margin	1%	12%	23%	26%	31%

few ads and word-of-mouth advertising appear to be working. Dave receives about five phone calls per day, with one in seven calls leading to a sale. Dave also feels the stress of the long hours and the low pay, however. He is not able to pay himself a high salary—just $9,500 this year.

Dave reaches over and picks up his most recent financial projections from a workbench (see Exhibit 13-1). He believes that this will be a breakeven year—then he'll have it made. As Dave sets the projections back on the workbench, his mind drifts to his plans to introduce two exciting new speakers—the Micron ($2,495 per pair) and the Millennium ($7,995 per pair). He also wonders if there is a foreign market for his speakers. Should he use his same direct marketing strategy for foreign markets, or should he consider distributors? The dream continues.

QUESTIONS

1. What functions do traditional stereo dealers perform?

2. Why has Dave Fokos decided to establish a direct channel? What objectives and constraints have shaped his decision?

3. What consumer service needs do Dave's customers have?

4. What problems will Dave face as a result of his channel decisions? What changes would you recommend in Dave's distribution strategy, if any? Will his strategy work in foreign markets?

5. What other changes would you recommend in Dave's marketing strategy?

Source: Adapted from "Sound Strategy," *INC.*, May 1991, pp. 46–56. © 1991 by Goldhirsh Group, Inc. Used with permission. Dave Fokos also provided information to support development of this case.

Placing Products

RETAILING AND WHOLESALING

14

For more than 40 years, Scandinavian furniture giant IKEA (pronounced *eye-KEY-ah*) has sold its stylish, low-cost furniture worldwide. Smart targeting, careful attention to customer needs, and rock-bottom prices have made IKEA the world's largest home furnishings company.

When IKEA opened its first U.S. store in 1985, it caused quite a stir. On opening day, people flocked to the suburban Philadelphia store from as far away as Washington, DC. Traffic on the nearby turnpike backed up for six miles, and at one point the store was jammed so tightly with customers that management ordered the doors closed until the crowds thinned out. In the first week, the IKEA store packed in 150,000 people who bought over $1 million worth of furniture. When the dust had settled, the store was still averaging 50,000 customers a week. Similarly, when IKEA opened its store in Elizabeth, New Jersey, about 15 miles from Manhattan, the response bordered on a riot. On the first day of business, the New Jersey Turnpike backed up for nine miles as 26,000 shoppers converged on the new store, generating $1 million in sales and doubling IKEA's opening-day record.

IKEA is one of a new breed of retailers called "category killers." These retailers get their name from their marketing strategy: Carry a huge selection of merchandise in a single product category at such good prices that you destroy the competition. Category killers now are striking in a wide range of industries, including furniture, toys, records, sporting goods, housewares, and consumer electronics.

An IKEA store is about three football fields in size. Each store stocks more than 6,000 items—all furnishings and housewares, ranging from coffee mugs to leather sofas to kitchen cabinets. IKEA sells Scandinavian-design "knock-down" furniture—each item reduces to a flat-pack kit for assembly at home. Consumers browse through the store's comfortable display area, where signs and stickers on each item note its price, details of its construction, assembly instructions, its location in the adjacent warehouse—even which other pieces complement the item. Customers wrestle desired items from warehouse stacks, haul their choices away on large trollies, and pay at

OBJECTIVES

When you finish this chapter, you should be able to accomplish the following:

1. Discuss traditional **store retailing**, and contrast the different ways to segment stores: by **amount of service** provided, breadth and depth of **product line**, **relative price levels**, **control of outlets**, and **type of store cluster**.

2. Identify and define the types of **nonstore retailing**, including **direct marketing**, **direct selling**, and **automatic vending**.

3. Outline the key **retailer marketing decisions**: target market and positioning, product, price, promotion and place.

4. Contrast the differences among types of wholesalers, including **full-service** and **limited-service merchant wholesalers**, **brokers** and **agents**, and **manufacturers' sales branches**.

5. Explain the **wholesaler marketing decisions** of **target market** and **positioning** and **marketing mix decisions**, and describe **trends in wholesaling**.

giant-sized checkout counters. The store provides a reasonably priced restaurant for hungry shoppers and a supervised children's play area for weary parents. But best of all, IKEA's prices are low. The store operates on a simple philosophy: Provide a wide variety of well-designed home furnishings at prices that the majority of people can afford.

Although the first category killer, Toys 'R' Us, appeared during the late 1950s, other retailers only recently adopted the idea. Unlike warehouse clubs and other "off-price" retailers, which offer the lowest prices but few choices within any given category, category killers offer an exhaustive selection in one line. Toys 'R' Us stocks 18,000 different toy items in football-field-size stores. Huge Sportmart stores stock 100,000 sporting goods items, including 70 types of sleeping bags, 265 styles of athletic socks, 12,000 pairs of shoes, and 15,000 fishing lures. Tower Records stores carry up to 75,000 titles—25 times more than the average competitor. And Branden's, the housewares and home furnishings category killer, offers a choice of 30 different coffee pots, 25 irons, 100 patterns of bed sheets, and 800 kitchen gadgets. With such large assortments, category killers generate big sales that often allow them to charge prices as low as those of their discount competitors.

The category killers face a few problems, however. For example, IKEA has encountered occasional difficulty managing its huge inventory, sometimes over-promising or inconveniencing customers. The company's expansive stores also require large investments and huge markets. Some consumers find that they want more personal service than IKEA gives or that the savings aren't worth the work required to find products in the huge store, haul them out, and assemble them at home. Despite such problems, IKEA has gained worldwide prosperity beyond its founders' dreams. It now has 95 stores in 23 countries, racking up over $3.7 billion a year in sales. Since opening its initial U.S. store in Philadelphia, it has opened other stores in Washington, DC; Baltimore; Pittsburgh; Elizabeth (New Jersey); Long Island; Southern California, and other cities—12 stores in all, bringing in more than $400 million in annual sales. IKEA plans to open 60 stores around the country over the next 25 years.

Most retailing experts predict great success for stores like IKEA. One retailing analyst, Wallace Epperson, Jr., "estimates IKEA will win at least a 15 percent share of any market it enters and will expand the market as it does so. If Mr. Epperson is any indication, IKEA's prospects are good. Touring IKEA in his professional capacity, Mr. Epperson couldn't resist the store. 'I spent $400,' he said. 'It's incredible.'"[1]

This chapter looks at *retailing* and *wholesaling*. In the first section, we look at the nature and importance of retailing, major types of store and nonstore retailers, the decisions retailers make, and the future of retailing. In the second section, we discuss these same topics as they relate to wholesalers.

RETAILING

Retailing
All activities involved in selling goods or services directly to final consumers for their personal, nonbusiness use.

Retailers
Businesses whose sales come *primarily* from retailing.

What is retailing? We all know that Wal-Mart, Sears, and Kmart are retailers, but so are Avon representatives, the local Holiday Inn, and a doctor seeing patients. **Retailing** includes all the activities involved in selling goods or services directly to final consumers for their personal, nonbusiness use. Many institutions—manufacturers, wholesalers, and retailers—do retailing. But most retailing is done by **retailers**: businesses whose sales come *primarily* from retailing. And although most retailing is done in retail stores, in recent years nonstore retailing—selling by mail, telephone, door-to-door contact, vending machines, and numerous electronic means—has grown tremendously. Because store retailing accounts for most of the retail business, we discuss it first. We then look at nonstore retailing.

STORE RETAILING

Retail stores come in all shapes and sizes, and new retail types keep emerging. They can be classified by one or more of several characteristics: *amount of service, product line, relative prices, control of outlets,* and *type of store cluster.* Table 14-1 shows these classifications and the corresponding retailer types.

AMOUNT OF SERVICE

Different products require different amounts of service, and customer service preferences vary. We focus on three levels of service—self-service, limited service, and full service—and the types of retailers that use them.

Self-service retailers increased rapidly in the United States during the Great Depression of the 1930s. Customers were willing to perform their own "locate-compare-select" process to save money. Today, self-service is the basis of all discount operations and typically is used by sellers of convenience goods (such as supermarkets) and nationally branded, fast-moving shopping goods (such as catalog showrooms like Best Products or Service Merchandise).

Limited-service retailers, such as Sears or JCPenney, provide more sales assistance because they carry more shopping goods about which customers need information. Their increased operating costs result in higher prices. In *full-service retailers,* such as specialty stores and first-class department stores, salespeople assist customers in every phase of the shopping process. Full-service stores usually carry more specialty goods for which customers like to be "waited on." They provide more liberal return policies, various credit plans, free delivery, home servicing, and extras such as lounges and restaurants. More services result in much higher operating costs, which are passed along to customers as higher prices.

PRODUCT LINE

Retailers also can be classified by the length and breadth of their product assortments. Among the most important types of retailers are the *specialty store,* the *department store,* the *supermarket,* the *convenience store,* the *superstore,* and the *service business.*

TABLE 14-1   *Different Ways to Classify Retail Outlets*

AMOUNT OF SERVICE	PRODUCT LINE SOLD	RELATIVE PRICE EMPHASIS	CONTROL OF OUTLETS	TYPE OF STORE CLUSTER
Self-service	Specialty store	Discount store	Corporate chain	Central business district
Limited service	Department store	Off-price retailers	Voluntary chain and retailer cooperative	Regional shopping center
Full service	Supermarket	Catalog showroom	Franchise organization	Community shopping center
	Convenience store		Merchandising conglomerate	Neighborhood shopping center
	Combination store, superstore, and hypermarket			
	Service business			

Today, specialty stores are flourishing: they offer high-quality products, convenient locations, good hours, and excellent service.

Specialty store
A retail store that carries a narrow product line with a deep assortment within that line.

Department store
A retail organization that carries a wide variety of product lines—typically clothing, home furnishings, and household goods; each line is operated as a separate department managed by specialist buyers or merchandisers.

Specialty Store

A **specialty store** carries a narrow product line with a deep assortment within that line. Examples include stores selling sporting goods, furniture, books, electronics, flowers, or toys. Specialty stores can be classified further by the narrowness of their product lines. For example, a clothing store is a *single-line store,* a men's clothing store is a *limited-line store,* and a men's custom shirt store is a *super-specialty store.*

Today, specialty stores are flourishing for several reasons. The increasing use of market segmentation, market targeting, and product specialization has resulted in a greater need for stores that focus on specific products and segments. And because of changing consumer lifestyles and the increasing number of two-income households, many consumers have greater incomes but less time to spend shopping. They are attracted to specialty stores that provide high-quality products, convenient locations, good hours, excellent service, and quick entry and exit.

Department Store

A **department store** carries a wide variety of product lines—typically clothing, home furnishings, and household goods. Each line is operated as a separate department managed by specialist buyers or merchandisers. Examples of well-known department stores include Bloomingdale's, Marshall Field, Hudson's, and Filene's. *Specialty department stores* carry only clothing, shoes, cosmetics, luggage, and gift items—examples are Saks Fifth Avenue and I. Magnin.

Department stores grew rapidly through the first half of this century. After World War II, however, they began to lose ground to other types of retailers, including discount stores, specialty store chains, and "off-price" retailers. The heavy traffic, poor parking, and general decaying of central cities, where many department stores had made their biggest investments, made downtown shopping less appealing. As a result, many department stores closed or merged with others.

Most department stores now operate in suburban malls, and many have added "bargain basements" to meet the discount threat. Still others have remodeled their stores or set up "boutiques" and other store formats that compete with specialty stores. Many are trying mail-order and telephone selling. Still, department stores continue to have difficulty competing with more focused and flexible specialty stores on the one hand, and with more efficient, lower-priced discounters on the other.

Service remains the key differentiating factor. Many department stores, such as Nordstrom's and Neiman Marcus, are renewing their emphasis on service in an effort to keep old customers and win new ones. When it comes to service, most

NOW THAT'S DEPARTMENT STORE SERVICE

In the following account, an American visitor to Japan describes her amazing shopping experience with Odakyu Department Store.

My husband and I bought one souvenir the last time we were in Tokyo—a Sony compact-disc player. The transaction took seven minutes at the Odakyu Department Store, including time to find the right department and to wait while the salesman filled out a second charge slip after misspelling my husband's name on the first.

My in-laws, who were our hosts in the outlying city of Sagamihara, were eager to see their son's purchase, so he opened the box for them the next morning. But when he tried to demonstrate the player, it wouldn't work. We peered inside. It had no innards! My husband used the time until the Odakyu would open at 10:00 to practice for the rare opportunity in that country to wax indignant. But at a minute to 10:00 he was preempted by the store ringing us.

My mother-in-law took the call and had to hold the receiver away from her ear against the barrage of Japanese honorifics. Odakyu's vice president was on his way over with a new disc player.

A taxi pulled up 50 minutes later and spilled out the vice president and a junior employee who was laden with packages and a clipboard. In the entrance hall the two men bowed vigorously.

The younger man was still bobbing as he read from a log that recorded the progress of their efforts to rectify their mistake, beginning at 4:32 P.M. the day before, when the salesclerk alerted the store's security guards to [catch] my husband at the door. When that didn't work, the clerk turned to his supervisor, who turned to his supervisor, until a SWAT team leading all the way to the vice president was in place to work on the only clues, a name and an American Express card number. Remembering that the customer had asked him about using the disc player in the United States, the clerk called 32 hotels in and around Tokyo to ask if a Mr. Kitasei was registered. When that turned up nothing, the Odakyu commandeered a staff member to stay until 9 P.M. to call American Express headquarters in New York. American Express gave him our New York telephone number. It was after 11:00 when he reached my parents, who were staying at our apartment. My mother gave him my in-laws' telephone number.

The younger man looked up from his clipboard and gave us, in addition to the $280 disc player, a set of towels, a box of cakes, and a Chopin disk. Three minutes after this exhausted pair had arrived they were climbing back into the waiting cab. The vice president suddenly dashed back. He had forgotten to apologize for my husband having to wait while the salesman had rewritten the charge slip, but he hoped we understood that it had been the young man's first day.

Source: Reprinted from Hilary Hinds Kitasei, "Japan's Got Us Beat in the Service Department, Too," *Wall Street Journal,* July 30, 1985, p. 10.

retailers could learn a lesson from Japan's Odakyu Department Store (see Marketing Highlight 14-1).

In recent years, many large department-store chains have been joining rather than fighting the competition by diversifying into discount and specialty stores. Dayton-Hudson for example, operates Target (discount stores), Mervyn's (lower-price clothing), B. Dalton (books), and many other chains in addition to its Dayton's, Hudson's, and other department stores. These discount and specialty operations now account for more than 80 percent of the chain's total corporate sales.

Supermarket

Supermarkets Large, low-cost, low-margin, high-volume, self-service stores that carry a wide variety of food, laundry, and household products.

Supermarkets are large, low-cost, low-margin, high-volume, self-service stores that carry a wide variety of food, laundry, and household products. Most U.S. supermarket stores are owned by supermarket chains such as Safeway, Kroger, A&P, Winn-Dixie, Publix, Food Lion, Vons, and Jewel. Chains account for almost 70 percent of all supermarket sales.

The first supermarkets introduced the concepts of self-service, customer turnstiles, and checkout counters. Supermarket growth took off in the 1930s and grew rapidly for several decades. However, most supermarkets today are facing slow sales growth because of slower population growth and an increase in competition from convenience stores, discount food stores, and superstores. They also have been hit hard by the rapid growth of out-of-home eating. Thus, supermarkets are looking for new ways to build their sales. Most chains now operate fewer but larger stores. They practice "scrambled merchandising," and carry many nonfood items—

beauty aids, housewares, toys, prescriptions, appliances, videocassettes, sporting goods, garden supplies—hoping to find high-margin lines to improve profits.

Supermarkets also are improving their facilities and services to attract more customers. Typical improvements are better locations, improved decor, longer store hours, check cashing, delivery, and even child-care centers. Although consumers have always expected supermarkets to offer good prices, convenient locations, and speedy checkout, today's more sophisticated food buyer wants even more. Many supermarkets, therefore, are "moving upscale" with the market, providing "from-scratch" bakeries, gourmet deli counters, and fresh seafood departments. Others are cutting costs, establishing more efficient operations, and lowering prices in order to compete more effectively with food discounters. Finally, to attract more customers, many large supermarket chains are starting to customize their stores for individual neighborhoods. They are tailoring store size, product assortments, prices, and promotions to the economic and ethnic needs of local markets.

Convenience Store

Convenience store
A small store located near a residential area that is open long hours seven days a week and carries a limited line of high-turnover convenience goods.

Convenience stores are small stores that carry a limited line of high-turnover convenience goods. Examples include 7-Eleven, Circle K, and Stop-N-Go stores. These stores locate near residential areas and remain open long hours, seven days a week. Convenience stores must charge high prices to make up for higher operating costs and lower sales volume, but they satisfy an important consumer need. Consumers use convenience stores for "fill-in" purchases at off hours or when time is short, and they are willing to pay for the convenience.

During the 1980s, however, the convenience store industry suffered from overcapacity as its primary market of young, blue-collar men shrunk. As a result, many convenience-store operators redesigned their stores with female customers in mind. They upgraded colors, dropped video games, improved parking and lighting, and priced more competitively. The major convenience chains now are experimenting with micromarketing—tailoring each store's merchandise to the specific needs of its surrounding neighborhood. For example, a Stop-N-Go in an affluent neighborhood carries fresh produce, gourmet pasta sauces, chilled Evian water, and expensive wines. Stop-N-Go stores in Hispanic neighborhoods carry Spanish-language magazines and other goods catering to the specific needs of Hispanic consumers. Through such moves, convenience stores hope to remain strongly differentiated from other types of food stores while adapting to today's fast-paced consumer lifestyles.[2]

Superstore, Combination Store, and Hypermarket

Superstore
A store almost twice the size of a regular supermarket that carries a large assortment of routinely purchased food and nonfood items and offers such services as dry cleaning, post offices, photo finishing, check cashing, bill paying, lunch counters, car care, and pet care.

Superstores, combination stores, and hypermarkets are all larger than the conventional supermarket. **Superstores** are almost twice the size of regular supermarkets and carry a large assortment of routinely purchased food and nonfood items. They offer such services as dry cleaning, post offices, photo finishing, check cashing, bill paying, lunch counters, car care, and pet care. Because of their wider assortment, superstore prices are 5 to 6 percent higher than are those of conventional supermarkets.

Many leading chains are moving toward superstores. Examples include Safeway's Pak 'N Pay and Pathmark Super Centers. Almost 80 percent of the new Safeway stores that opened during the past several years have been superstores. Superstores now take in more than 26 percent of total food store sales and account for 39 percent of all new grocery store openings.

Combination stores
Combined food and drug stores.

Combination stores are combined food and drug stores. They average about one and a half football fields in size—about twice the size of superstores. Examples are A&P's Family Mart, Wal Mart's Supercenters, and Kmart's Super Centers.

Many convenience store operators are trying micromarketing. For example, a Stop-N-Go in an affluent neighborhood (above) carries fresh produce, gourmet pasta sauces, chilled Evian water, and expensive wines. A Stop-N-Go store in a Hispanic neighborhood (below) carries Spanish-language magazines and other items catering to the specific needs of Hispanic customers.

Combination stores take in less than 5 percent of the business done by food stores, but account for 21 percent of new grocery store openings.

Hypermarkets are even bigger than combination stores, perhaps as large as *six* football fields. They combine supermarket, discount, and warehouse retailing. A typical hypermarket may have 50 checkout counters. They carry more than just routinely purchased goods, also selling furniture, appliances, clothing, and many other things. The hypermarket operates like a warehouse. Products in wire "baskets" are stacked high on metal racks; forklifts move through aisles during selling hours to restock shelves. The store gives discounts to customers who carry their own heavy appliances and furniture out of the store.

Hypermarkets have been very successful in world markets. For example, Carrefour, the large French retailer, successfully operates hundreds of these giant stores in Europe, South America, and Asia. However, although Carrefour, Kmart, and Wal-Mart have experimented with hypermarkets in the United States, they have met with little success. The major advantage of hypermarkets—their size—

Hypermarkets
Huge stores that combine supermarket, discount, and warehouse retailing; in addition to food, they carry furniture, appliances, clothing, and many other products.

also can be a major drawback for some consumers. Many people balk at the serious walking. And despite their size and volume of sales, most hypermarkets have only limited product variety. Thus, in the United States, most retailers have abandoned hypermarkets in favor of smaller, more shoppable combination stores.[3]

Service Business

For some businesses, the "product line" is actually a service. Service retailers include hotels and motels, banks, airlines, colleges, hospitals, movie theaters, tennis clubs, bowling alleys, restaurants, repair services, hair-care shops, and dry cleaners. Service retailers in the United States are growing faster than product retailers, and each service industry has its own retailing drama. Banks look for new ways to distribute their services, including automatic tellers, direct deposit, and telephone banking. Health organizations are changing the ways consumers get and pay for health services. The amusement industry has spawned Disney World and other theme parks, and H&R Block has built a franchise network to help consumers pay as little as possible to Uncle Sam.

RELATIVE PRICES

Retailers also can be classified according to the prices they charge. Most retailers charge regular prices and offer normal-quality goods and customer service. Some offer higher-quality goods and service at higher prices. The retailers that feature low prices are discount stores, "off-price" retailers, and catalog showrooms.

Discount Store

Discount store
A retail institution that sells standard merchandise at lower prices by accepting lower margins and selling at higher volume.

A **discount store** sells standard merchandise at lower prices by accepting lower margins and selling higher volume. The use of occasional discounts or specials does not make a store a discount store. A true discount store *regularly* sells its merchandise at lower prices, offering mostly national brands, not inferior goods. The early discount stores cut expenses by operating in warehouse-like facilities in low-rent, heavily traveled districts. They slashed prices, advertised widely, and carried a reasonable width and depth of products.

In recent years, facing intense competition from other discounters and department stores, many discount retailers have "traded up." They have improved decor, added new lines and services, and opened suburban branches, which has led to higher costs and prices. As some department stores have cut their prices to compete with discounters, the distinction between many discount and department stores has blurred somewhat. As a result, many department store retailers have again upgraded their stores and services to set themselves apart from the improved discounters.

Off-Price Retailers

Off-price retailers
Retailers that buy at less than regular wholesale prices and sell at less than retail. They include factory outlets, independents, and warehouse clubs.

Factory outlets
Off-price retailing operations that are owned and operated by manufacturers and that normally carry the manufacturer's surplus, discontinued, or irregular goods.

When the major discount stores traded up, a new wave of **off-price retailers** moved in to fill the low-price, high-volume gap. Ordinary discounters buy at regular wholesale prices and accept lower margins to keep prices down. In contrast, off-price retailers buy at less than regular wholesale prices and charge consumers less than retail. They tend to carry a changing and unstable collection of higher-quality merchandise, often leftover goods, overruns, and irregulars obtained at reduced prices from manufacturers or other retailers. Off-price retailers have made the biggest inroads in clothing, accessories, and footwear. But they can be found in all areas, from no-frills banking and discount brokerages to food stores and electronics.

The three main types of off-price retailers are *factory outlets, independents,* and *warehouse clubs.* **Factory outlets** are owned and operated by manufacturers

Factory outlet malls and value-retail centers have blossomed in recent years, making them one of retailing's hottest growth areas.

and normally carry the manufacturer's surplus, discontinued, or irregular goods. Examples are The Burlington Coat Factory Warehouse, Manhattan's Brand Name Fashion Outlet, and the factory outlets of Levi Strauss, Carters, and Ship 'n Shore. Such outlets sometimes group together in *factory outlet malls* and *value-retail centers,* where dozens of outlet stores offer prices as low as 50 percent below retail on a wide range of items. Whereas outlet malls consist primarily of manufacturers' outlets, value-retail centers combine manufacturers' outlets with off-price retail stores and department store clearance outlets. The number of factory outlet malls grew from fewer than 60 in 1980 to about 280 in 1991, making them one of the hottest growth areas in retailing. The malls now are moving upscale, featuring brands such as Esprit and Liz Claiborne, causing department stores to protest to the manufacturers of these brands. Given their higher costs, the department stores have to charge more than the off-price outlets. Manufacturers counter that they send last year's merchandise and seconds to the factory outlet malls, not the new merchandise that they supply to the department stores. The malls also are located far from urban areas, making travel to them more difficult. Still, the department stores are concerned about the growing number of shoppers willing to make weekend trips to stock up on branded merchandise at substantial savings.[4]

Independent off-price retailers are either owned and run by entrepreneurs or are divisions of larger retail corporations. Although many off-price operations are run by smaller independents, most large off-price retailer operations are owned by bigger retail chains. Examples include Loehmann's (owned by Associated Dry Goods, owner of Lord & Taylor), Filene's Basement (Federated Department Stores), and T.J. Maxx (Zayre).

Warehouse clubs (or *wholesale clubs,* or *membership warehouses*) sell a limited selection of brand name grocery items, appliances, clothing, and a hodgepodge of other goods at deep discounts to members who pay $25 to $50 annual membership fees. Examples are the Sam's Wholesale Club and Costco. These wholesale clubs operate in huge, low-overhead, warehouse-like facilities and offer few frills. Often, stores are drafty in the winter and stuffy in the summer. Customers themselves must wrestle furniture, heavy appliances, and other large items into the

Independent off-price retailers
Off-price retailers that are either owned and run by entrepreneurs or are divisions of larger retail corporations.

Warehouse club (wholesale club)
Off-price retailer that sells a limited selection of brand-name grocery items, appliances, clothing, and a hodgepodge of other goods at deep discounts to members who pay annual membership fees.

Warehouse clubs operate in huge, low-overhead, warehouse-like facilities, and customers must wrestle large items to the checkout line. But such clubs offer rock-bottom prices.

checkout line. Such clubs make no home deliveries and accept no credit cards, but they do offer rock-bottom prices. Warehouse clubs took the country by storm in the 1980s, but their growth slowed considerably in the 1990s as a result of growing competition among warehouse store chains and effective reactions by supermarkets.

In general, although off-price retailing blossomed during the 1980s, competition has stiffened as more and more off-price retailers have entered the market. The growth of off-price retailing slowed a bit recently because of effective counterstrategies by department stores and regular discounters. Still, off-price retailing remains a vital and growing force in modern retailing.

Catalog Showroom

Catalog showroom
A retail operation that sells a wide selection of high-markup, fast-moving, brand name goods at discount prices.

A **catalog showroom** sells a wide selection of high-markup, fast-moving, brand-name goods at discount prices. These include jewelry, power tools, cameras, luggage, small appliances, toys, and sporting goods. Catalog showrooms make their money by cutting costs and margins to provide low prices that will attract a higher volume of sales. The catalog showroom industry is led by companies such as Best Products and Service Merchandise.

Emerging in the late 1960s, catalog showrooms became one of retailing's hottest new forms, but they have been struggling in recent years. For one thing, department stores and discount retailers now run regular sales that match showroom prices. In addition, off-price retailers consistently beat catalog showroom prices. As a result, many showroom chains are broadening their lines, doing more advertising, renovating their stores, and adding services in order to attract more business.

CONTROL OF OUTLETS

About 80 percent of all retail stores are independents, accounting for two-thirds of all retail sales. Other forms of ownership include the *corporate chain*, the *vol-*

untary chain and retailer cooperative, the *franchise organization,* and the *merchandising conglomerate.*

Corporate Chain

Chain stores
Two or more outlets that are commonly owned and controlled, have central buying and merchandising, and sell similar lines of merchandise.

The chain store is one of the most important retail developments of this century. **Chain stores** are two or more outlets that are commonly owned and controlled, employ central buying and merchandising, and sell similar lines of merchandise. Corporate chains appear in all types of retailing, but they are strongest in department stores, variety stores, food stores, drugstores, shoe stores, and women's clothing stores. Corporate chains have many advantages over independents. Their size allows them to buy in large quantities at lower prices. They can afford to hire corporate-level specialists to deal with areas such as pricing, promotion, merchandising, inventory control, and sales forecasting. And chains gain promotional economies because their advertising costs are spread over many stores and over a large sales volume.

Voluntary Chain and Retailer Cooperative

The great success of corporate chains caused many independents to band together in one of two forms of contractual associations. One is the *voluntary chain*—a wholesaler-sponsored group of independent retailers that engages in group buying and common merchandising. Examples include the Independent Grocers Alliance (IGA), Sentry Hardwares, and Western Auto. The other form of contractual association is the *retailer cooperative*—a group of independent retailers that bands together to set up a jointly owned central wholesale operation and conducts joint merchandising and promotion efforts. Examples include Associated Grocers and True Value Hardware. These organizations give independents the buying and promotion economies they need to meet the prices of corporate chains.

Franchise Organization

Franchise
A contractual association between a manufacturer, wholesaler, or service organization (a franchiser) and independent businesspeople (franchisees) who buy the right to own and operate one or more units in the franchise system.

A **franchise** is a contractual association between a manufacturer, wholesaler, or service organization (the franchiser) and independent businesspeople (the franchisees) who buy the right to own and operate one or more units in the franchise system. The main difference between a franchise and other contractual systems (voluntary chains and retail cooperatives) is that franchise systems normally are based on some unique product or service; on a method of doing business; or on the trade name, goodwill, or patent that the franchiser has developed. Franchising has been prominent in fast-food companies, motels, gas stations, video stores, health and fitness centers, auto rentals, hair cutting salons, real estate and travel agencies, and dozens of other product and service areas.

The compensation received by the franchiser may include an initial fee, a royalty on sales, lease fees for equipment, and a share of the profits. For example, McDonald's franchisees plunk down $45,000 to obtain a franchise, then pay McDonald's a royalty of 4 percent of sales, plus 8.5 percent of sales for rent and another 4 percent for advertising. McDonald's also requires franchisees to go to Hamburger University for three weeks to learn how to manage the business.[5]

Merchandising Conglomerate

Merchandising conglomerates are corporations that combine several different retailing forms under central ownership and share some distribution and management functions. Examples include Dayton-Hudson, JCPenney, and F. W. Woolworth. For example, F. W. Woolworth, in addition to its variety stores, operates 28 specialty chains, including Kinney Shoe Stores, Afterthoughts (costume jewelry and handbags), Face Fantasies (budget cosmetics), Herald Square Stationers, Frame Scene, Foot Locker (sports shoes), and Kids Mart. Diversified retailing, which provides superior management systems and economies that benefit all the separate retail operations, is likely to increase through the close of the 1990s.

TYPE OF STORE CLUSTER

Most stores today cluster together to increase their customer pulling power and to give consumers the convenience of one-stop shopping. The main types of store clusters are the *central business district* and the *shopping center.*

Central Business District

Central business districts were the main form of retail cluster until the 1950s. Every large city and town had a central business district with department stores, specialty stores, banks, and movie theaters. When people began to move to the suburbs, however, these central business districts, with their traffic, parking, and crime problems, began to lose business. Downtown merchants opened branches in suburban shopping centers, and the decline of the central business districts continued. In recent years, many cities have joined with merchants to try to revive downtown shopping areas by building malls and providing underground parking. Some central business districts have made a comeback; others remain in a slow and possibly irreversible decline.

Shopping Center

Shopping center
A group of retail businesses planned, developed, owned, and managed as a unit.

A **shopping center** is a group of retail businesses planned, developed, owned, and managed as a unit. A *regional shopping center,* the largest and most dramatic shopping center, is like a mini-downtown. It typically contains between 40 and 100 stores and attracts customers from a wide area. Larger regional malls often have several department stores and a wide variety of specialty stores on several shopping levels. Many have added new types of retailers—dentists, health clubs, and even branch libraries.

A *community shopping center* contains between 15 and 50 retail stores. It normally contains a branch of a department store or variety store, a supermarket, specialty stores, professional offices, and sometimes a bank. Most shopping centers are *neighborhood shopping centers* or *strip malls* that generally contain between 5 and 15 stores. They are close and convenient for consumers. They usually contain a supermarket, perhaps a discount store, and several service stores—dry cleaner, self-service laundry, drugstore, video-rental outlet, barber or beauty shop, hardware store, or other stores. Such neighborhood centers account for 87 percent of all shopping centers and 51 percent of all shopping center retail sales.[6]

Combined, all shopping centers now account for about one-third of all retail sales, but they may have reached their saturation point. For example, between 1986 and 1989, the number of malls increased 22 percent to 34,683. But the number of shoppers going to malls every month grew only 3 percent. Thus, many areas contain too many malls, and as sales per square foot are dropping, vacancy rates are climbing. Some experts predict a shopping mall "shakeout," with as many as 20 percent of the regional shopping malls now operating in the United States closing by the year 2000. Despite the

Shopping centers: The spectacular Mall of America near Minneapolis contains more than 800 stores, 45 restaurants, 7 theaters, and a 7-acre indoor theme park. It attracts 35 million visitors a year.

recent development of a few new "megamalls," such as the spectacular Mall of America near Minneapolis, the current trend is toward smaller malls located in medium-size and smaller cities in fast-growing areas such as the Southwest.[7]

NONSTORE RETAILING

Although most goods and services are sold through stores, nonstore retailing has been growing much faster than store retailing. Traditional store retailers are facing increasing competition from nonstore retailers who sell through catalogs, direct mail, telephone, home TV shopping shows, on-line computer shopping services, home and office parties, and other direct retailing approaches. Nonstore retailing now accounts for more than 14 percent of all consumer purchases, and it may account for a third of all sales by the end of the century. Nonstore retailing includes *direct marketing, direct selling,* and *automatic vending.*

DIRECT MARKETING

Direct marketing
Marketing through various advertising media that interact directly with consumers, generally calling for the consumer to make a direct response.

Direct marketing uses various advertising media to interact directly with consumers, generally calling for the consumer to make a direct response. Mass advertising typically reaches an unspecified number of people, most of whom are not in the market for a product or will not buy it until some future date. Direct-advertising vehicles are used to obtain immediate orders directly from targeted consumers. Although direct marketing initially consisted mostly of direct mail and mail-order catalogs, it has taken on several additional forms in recent years, including telemarketing, direct radio and television marketing, and on-line computer shopping.

Direct marketing has boomed in recent years. All kinds of organizations use direct marketing: manufacturers, retailers, service companies, catalog merchants, and nonprofit organizations, to name a few. Its growing use in consumer marketing is largely a response to the "demassification" of mass markets, which has resulted in an ever-greater number of fragmented market segments with highly individualized needs and wants. Direct marketing allows sellers to focus efficiently on these minimarkets with offers that better match specific consumer needs.

Other trends also have fueled the growth of direct marketing. The increasing number of women entering the work force has decreased the time households have to shop. The higher costs of driving, the traffic congestion and parking headaches, the shortage of retail sales help, and the longer lines at checkout counters all have promoted in-home shopping. The development of toll-free telephone numbers and the increased use of credit cards have helped sellers reach and transact with consumers outside of stores more easily. Finally, the growth of computer power and communication technology have allowed marketers to build better customer databases and communication channels with which to reach the best prospects for specific products.

Direct marketing also has grown rapidly in business-to-business marketing. It can help reduce the high costs of reaching business markets through the sales force. Lower-cost media, such as telemarketing and direct mail, can be used to identify the best prospects and prime them before making an expensive sales call.

Direct marketing provides many benefits to consumers as well. Instead of driving their cars through congested city streets to shop in crowded shopping malls, customers can use their telephones or computers to whiz along the *information superhighway.* Today's sophisticated communications networks carry voice, video, and data over fiber optic telephone lines, linking buyers and sellers in convenient, exciting ways. People who buy through direct mail or by telephone say that such shopping is convenient, hassle-free, and fun. It saves them time, and it introduces them to new lifestyles and a larger selection of merchandise. Consumers can compare products and prices from their armchairs by browsing through catalogs. They can order and receive products without having to leave their homes. Industrial customers can learn about and order products and services without tying up valuable time by meeting and listening to salespeople.

Direct marketing also provides benefits to sellers. It allows greater *selectivity*. A direct marketer can buy a mailing list containing the names of almost any group—millionaires, parents of newborn babies, left-handed people, or recent college graduates. The direct-marketing message can be *personalized* and *customized*. The marketer can search its database, select consumers with specific characteristics, and send them very individualized laser-printed letters.

With direct marketing, the seller can build a *continuous customer relationship,* tailoring a steady stream of offers to a regular customer's specific needs and interests (see Marketing Highlight 14-2). Direct marketing also can be *timed* to reach prospects at just the right moment. Moreover, because it reaches more interested prospects at the best times, direct-marketing materials receive *higher readership and response*. Direct marketing also permits easy *testing* of specific messages and media. And because results are direct and immediate, direct marketing lends itself more readily to *response measurement*. Finally, direct marketing provides *privacy*—the direct marketer's offer and strategy are not visible to competitors. We will discuss the major forms of direct marketing in detail in the next chapter.

DIRECT SELLING

Door-to-door retailing
Selling door to door, office to office, or at home-sales parties.

Door-to-door retailing, which started centuries ago with roving peddlers, has grown into a huge industry. More than 600 companies sell their products door to door, office to office, or at home-sales parties. The pioneers in door-to-door selling are the Fuller Brush Company, vacuum cleaner companies like Electrolux, and book-selling companies, such as World Book and Southwestern. The image of door-to-door selling improved greatly when Avon entered the industry with its Avon representative—the homemaker's friend and beauty consultant. Tupperware and Mary Kay Cosmetics helped to popularize home sales parties, in which several friends and neighbors attend a party at a private home where products are demonstrated and sold.

The advantages of door-to-door selling are consumer convenience and personal attention. But the high costs of hiring, training, paying, and motivating

Door-to-door and in-home selling provide customers with convenience and personal attention, but higher costs result in higher prices.

DIRECT MARKETING: FINGERHUT BUILDS STRONG CUSTOMER RELATIONSHIPS

As Betty Holmes of Detroit, Michigan, sifts through the day's stack of mail, one item in particular catches her eye. It's only a catalog, but it's speaking directly to her. A laser-printed personal message on the catalog's cover states: "Thank you, Mrs. Holmes, for your recent purchase of women's apparel. To show our thanks, we are offering you up to 50 percent savings on additional purchases, plus deferred payment until July 31st." The note goes on, with amazing accuracy, to refer Betty to specific items in the catalog that will likely interest her.

The catalog is from Fingerhut, the huge direct-mail marketer. A typical Fingerhut catalog offers between 500 and 700 products, mostly domestic and household electronics, with prices ranging from $15 to $600. Fingerhut operates on a *huge* scale. Each year, it sends out some 400 million mailings—that's well over 1 million mailings per day to a portion of the 25 million households detailed in the company's database. Betty Holmes buys regularly from Fingerhut, and the company tracks her purchases carefully. Then, it sends a steady flow of direct mail offers specially tailored to her purchasing history and interests.

When new customers first respond to a direct mail offer, Fingerhut asks them to fill out two questionnaires. One asks them about the kinds of products that interest them. The other, for Fingerhut's "Birthday Club," asks them about their families—number of children, ages, and birthdays. Using information from these two questionnaires, along with information about later purchases, Fingerhut has built an impressive marketing database that allows it to target the most likely buyers with products that interest them most. Instead of sending out the same catalogs and letters to all of its customers, Fingerhut tailors its offers based on what each customer is likely to buy. Moreover, promotions such as the Birthday Club provide opportunities to create special offers that sell

more products. A month before a child's birthday, Birthday Club customers receive a free birthday gift for their child if they agree to try any one of the products Fingerhut offers in an accompanying mailing. A customer who responds to these and other offers might become one of 12 million "promotable" customers who receive at least one Fingerhut mailing a week.

The key to Fingerhut's success is the long-term relationships that the company builds with its customers. Fingerhut carefully matches its direct-

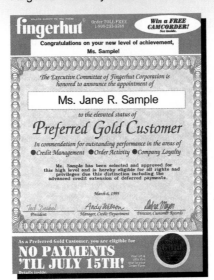

Fingerhut sends out over 1 million mailings per day to a portion of the 25 million households detailed in its database. Each mailing is specially tailored to the customer's interests and purchasing history.

mail offers to individual customer needs, characteristics, and purchasing histories, and then makes it as easy as possible for targeted customers to buy. Fingerhut tries to establish a strong relationship that goes beyond its merchandise. Credit is an important cornerstone of that relationship. The average Fingerhut customer, typically an "empty-nester" or someone just starting a family, has a household income of $18,000. The customer's median age is 38, and 90 percent of the customers are female.

Despite selling to lower-income consumers, Fingerhut controls its credit risks by what it offers to whom. The company avoids zip codes with high bad-debt levels. And when a new customer makes a first order, the item is limited to $20 to $30. If the customer pays promptly, the next mailing offers higher-ticket items. Good customers who pay their bills regularly get cards and rewards to reinforce this behavior. For example, the typical award envelope cheers "Congratulations! You've been selected to receive our 'exceptional customer award!'" and contains a certificate suitable for framing.

Fingerhut stays in continuous touch with its preferred customers through regular special promotions— an annual sweepstakes, free gifts, a deferred-billing promotion, and others. These special offers are all designed with one goal in mind: to create a reason for Fingerhut to be in the customer's mailbox. Once in the mailbox, the personalized messages and targeted offers get attention.

The skillful use of database marketing and relationship building have made Fingerhut one of the nation's largest direct-mail marketers. Founded in 1948 by brothers Manny and William Fingerhut, the company now sells more than $1.8 billion worth of merchandise each year through mail order. In fact, one in every six U.S. households has *bought* something from the company. Fingerhut's success is no accident. "Most of our competitors use a full catalog; they could care less about what the individuals want," notes a Fingerhut executive. "Fingerhut finds out what each customer wants and builds an event around each promotion."

Sources: See Eileen Norris, "Fingerhut Gives Customers Credit," *Advertising Age,* March 6, 1986, p. 19. Also see Brian Bremner, "Looking Downscale without Looking Down," *Business Week,* October 8, 1990, pp. 62–67; and Gary Levin, "Fingerhut Points to TV Shopping," *Advertising Age,* April 4, 1994, p. 20.

the sales force result in higher prices. Although some door-to-door companies are still thriving, door-to-door selling has a somewhat uncertain future. The increase in the number of single-person and working-couple households decreases the chances of finding a buyer at home. Home-party companies are having trouble finding nonworking women who want to sell products part time. And with recent advances in interactive direct-marketing technology, the door-to-door salesperson may well be replaced in the future by the household telephone, television, or home computer.

AUTOMATIC VENDING

Automatic vending
Selling through vending machines.

Automatic vending is not new—in 215 B.C. Egyptians could buy sacrificial water from coin-operated dispensers. But this method of selling soared after World War II. There are now about 4.5 million vending machines in the United States—one machine for every 55 people. Today's automatic vending uses space-age and computer technology to sell a wide variety of convenience and impulse goods—cigarettes, beverages, candy, newspapers, foods and snacks, hosiery, cosmetics, paperback books, T-shirts, insurance policies, pizza, audio tapes and videocassettes, and even shoeshines and fishing worms. Vending machines are found everywhere—in factories, offices, lobbies, retail stores, gasoline stations, airports, and train and bus terminals. Automatic teller machines provide bank customers with checking, savings, withdrawal, and funds-transfer services. Compared to store retailing, vending machines offer consumers greater convenience (available 24 hours, self-service) and fewer damaged goods. But the expensive equipment and labor required for automatic vending make it a costly channel, and prices of vended goods are often 15 to 20 percent higher than those in retail stores. Customers also must put up with aggravating machine breakdowns, out-of-stock items, and the fact that merchandise cannot be returned.[8]

RETAILER MARKETING DECISIONS

Retailers are searching for new marketing strategies to attract and hold customers. In the past, retailers attracted customers with unique products, more or better services than their competitors offered, or credit cards. Today, national brand manufacturers, in their drive for volume, have placed their branded goods everywhere. Thus, stores offer more similar assortments—national brands are found not only in department stores, but also in mass-merchandise and off-price discount stores. As a result, stores are looking more and more alike; they have become "commoditized." In any city, a shopper can find many stores, but few assortments.

FIGURE 14-1 *Retailer marketing decisions*

Service differentiation among retailers has also eroded. Many department stores have trimmed their services, whereas discounters have increased theirs. Customers have become smarter and more price sensitive. They see no reason to pay more for identical brands, especially when service differences are shrinking. And because bank credit cards are now accepted at most stores, consumers no longer need credit from a particular store. For all these reasons, many retailers today are rethinking their marketing strategies.[9]

As shown in Figure 14-1, retailers face major marketing decisions about their *target markets and positioning, product assortment and services, price, promotion,* and *place.*

TARGET MARKET AND POSITIONING DECISION

Retailers first must define their target markets and then decide how they will position themselves in these markets. Should the store focus on upscale, midscale, or downscale shoppers? Do target shoppers want variety, depth of assortment, convenience, or low prices? Until they define and profile their markets, retailers cannot make consistent decisions about product assortment, services, pricing, advertising, store decor, or any of the other decisions that must support their positions.

Too many retailers fail to define their target markets and positions clearly. They try to have "something for everyone" and end up satisfying no market well. In contrast, successful retailers define their target markets well and position themselves strongly. For example, in 1963, Leslie H. Wexner borrowed $5,000 to create *The Limited*, which started as a single store targeted to young, fashion-conscious women. All aspects of the store—clothing assortment, fixtures, music, colors, personnel—were orchestrated to match the target consumer. He continued to open more stores, but a decade later his original customers were no longer in the "young" group. To catch the new "youngs," he started the Limited Express. Over the years, he started or acquired other highly targeted store chains, including Lane Bryant, Victoria's Secret, Lerner, and others to reach new segments. Today The Limited, Inc. operates more than 4,000 stores in seven different segments of the market, with sales of more than $6.9 billion.

Even large stores such as Wal-Mart, Kmart, and Sears must define their major target markets in order to design effective marketing strategies. In fact, in recent years, thanks to strong targeting and positioning, Wal-Mart has exploded past Sears and Kmart to become the nation's largest retailer (see Marketing Highlight 14-3).

PRODUCT ASSORTMENT AND SERVICES DECISION

Retailers must decide on three major product variables: *product assortment, services mix,* and *store atmosphere.*

The retailer's *product assortment* must match target shoppers' expectations. The retailer must determine both the product assortment's *width* and its *depth.* Thus, a restaurant can offer a narrow and shallow assortment (small lunch counter), a narrow and deep assortment (delicatessen), a wide and shallow assortment (cafeteria), or a wide and deep assortment (large restaurant). Another product assortment element is the *quality* of the goods: The customer is interested not only in the range of choice but also in the quality of the products available.

No matter what the store's product assortment and quality level, there always will be competitors with similar assortments and quality. Therefore, the retailer must search for other ways to *differentiate* itself from similar competitors. It can use any of several product-differentiation strategies. For one, it can offer merchandise that no other competitor carries—its own private brands or national brands on which it holds exclusives. For example, The Limited designs most of the clothes carried by its store, and Saks gets exclusive rights to carry a well-known designer's labels. Second, the retailer can feature blockbuster merchandising events—Bloomingdale's is known for running spectacular shows featuring goods from a certain country, such as India or China. Or the retailer can offer surprise merchandise, as when Loehmann's offers surprise assortments of seconds, over-

WAL-MART: THE NATION'S LARGEST RETAILER

In 1962, Sam Walton and his brother opened the first Wal-Mart discount store in small-town Rogers, Arkansas. It was a big, flat, warehouse-type store that sold everything from apparel to automotive supplies to small appliances at very low prices. Experts gave the fledgling retailer little chance—conventional wisdom suggested that discount stores could succeed only in large cities. Yet, from these modest beginnings, the chain expanded rapidly, opening new stores in one small southern town after another. By the mid-1980s, Wal-Mart had exploded onto the national retailing scene. It began building stores in larger cities such as Dallas, St. Louis, and Kansas City. By 1990, the chain was operating 1,600 stores in 35 states and producing more than $32 billion in annual sales. Incredibly, less than 30 years after opening its first store, Wal-Mart overtook long-time industry leader Sears to become the nation's largest retailer.

Wal-Mart's phenomenal growth shows few signs of slowing. The company is now building more stores in larger cities and is expanding into the Northeast and Far West. Sales in 1994 exceeded $67 billion, and management fully expects that sales will more than double to $150 billion by the turn of the century. Over the past decade, Wal-Mart's annual return to investors has averaged more than 45 percent, rewarding investors handsomely. An investment of $1,650 in Wal-Mart stock in 1970 would be worth a whopping $3 million today!

What are the secrets behind this spectacular success? Wal-Mart listens to and takes care of its customers, treats employees as partners, and keeps a tight rein on costs.

Listening to and Taking Care of Customers

Wal-Mart positioned itself strongly in a well-chosen target market. Initially, Sam Walton focused on value-conscious consumers in small-town America. The chain built a strong everyday low-price position long before it became fashionable in retailing. It grew rapidly by bringing the lowest possible prices to towns ignored by national discounters—towns such as Van Buren, Arkansas, and Idabel, Oklahoma.

Wal-Mart knows its customers and takes good care of them. As one analyst puts it, "The company gospel . . . is relatively simple: Be an agent for customers, find out what they want, and sell it to them for the lowest possible price." Thus, the company listens carefully—for example, all top Wal-Mart executives go where their customers hang out. Each spends at least two days a week visiting stores, talking directly with customers, and getting a firsthand look at operations. Then, Wal-Mart delivers what customers want: a broad selection of carefully selected goods at unbeatable prices.

But the right merchandise at the right price isn't the only key to Wal-Mart's success. Wal-Mart also provides outstanding service that keeps customers satisfied. A sign reading "Satisfaction Guaranteed" hangs

A Wal-Mart "people greeter" lends a helping hand.

prominently at each store's entrance. Another sign inside the store reads "At Wal-Mart, our goal is: You're always next in line!" Customers are often welcomed by "people greeters" eager to lend a helping hand or just to be friendly. And, sure enough, the store opens extra checkout counters to keep waiting lines short.

Going the extra mile for customers has paid off. A recent independent survey in towns where Wal-Mart competes with Kmart and Target found that Wal-Mart's shoppers were the most satisfied; Kmart's the least. Perhaps more telling, whereas the

---

stocks, and closeouts. Finally, the retailer can differentiate itself by offering a highly targeted product assortment—Lane Bryant carries goods for larger women; Brookstone offers an unusual assortment of gadgets in what amounts to an adult toy store.

Retailers also must decide on a *services mix* to offer customers. The old "mom and pop" grocery stores offered home delivery, credit, and conversation—services that today's supermarkets ignore. The services mix is one of the key tools of nonprice competition for setting one store apart from another.

The *store's atmosphere* is another element in its product arsenal. Every store has a physical layout that makes moving around in it either hard or easy. Every

typical Kmart store rings up average sales of about $150 per square foot per year, the typical Wal-Mart store hauls in $250.

Treating Employees as Partners

Wal-Mart believes that, in the final accounting, the company's people are what really makes it better. Thus, it works hard to show employees that it cares about them. Wal-Mart calls employees "associates," a practice now widely copied by competitors. The associates work as partners, become deeply involved in operations, and share rewards for good performance.

Everyone at Wal-Mart [is] an associate—from [the CEO] . . . to a cashier named Janet at the Wal-Mart on Highway 50 in Ocoee, Florida. "We," "us," and "our" are the operative words. Wal-Mart department heads, hourly associates who look after one or more of 30-some departments ranging from sporting goods to electronics, see figures that many companies never show general managers: costs, freight charges, profit margins. The company sets a profit margin for each store, and if the store exceeds it, then the hourly associates share part of the additional profit.

The partnership concept is deeply rooted in the Wal-Mart corporate culture. It is supported by open-door policies and grass-roots meetings that give employees a say in what goes on and encourage them to bring their problems to management. Wal-Mart's concern for its employees translates into high employee satisfaction, which in turn translates into greater customer satisfaction.

Keeping a Tight Rein on Costs

Wal-Mart has the lowest cost structure in the industry: Operating expenses amount to only 16 percent of sales, compared to 23 percent at Kmart. Thus, Wal-Mart can charge lower prices but still reap higher profits, allowing it to offer better service. This creates a "productivity loop." Wal-Mart's lower prices and better service attract more shoppers, producing more sales, making the company more efficient, and enabling it to lower prices even more.

Wal-Mart's low costs result in part from superior management and more sophisticated technology. Its Bentonville, Arkansas, headquarters contains "a computer-communications system worthy of the Defense Department," giving managers around the country instant access to sales and operating information. And its huge, fully automated distribution centers employ the latest technology to supply stores efficiently. Wal-Mart also spends less than competitors on advertising—only 0.5 percent of sales, compared to 2.5 percent at Kmart and 3.8 percent at Sears. Because Wal-Mart has what customers want at the prices they'll pay, its reputation has spread rapidly by word of mouth. It has not needed more advertising.

Finally, Wal-Mart keeps costs down through good old "tough buying." Whereas the company is known for the warm way it treats customers, it is equally well known for the cold, calculated way it wrings low prices from suppliers. The following passage describes a visit to Wal-Mart's buying offices.

Don't expect a greeter and don't expect friendly. . . . Once you are ushered into one of the spartan little buyers' rooms, expect a steely eye across the table and be prepared to cut your price. "They are very, very focused people, and they use their buying power more forcefully than anyone else in America," says the marketing vice president of a major vendor. "All the normal mating rituals are [forbidden]. Their highest priority is making sure everyone at all times in all cases knows who's in charge, and it's Wal-Mart. They talk softly, but they have piranha hearts, and if you aren't totally prepared when you go in there, you'll have your [head] handed to you."

Some observers wonder whether Wal-Mart can continue to grow at such a torrid pace and still retain its focus and positioning. They wonder if an ever-larger Wal-Mart can stay close to its customers and employees. The company's managers are betting on it. Says one top executive: "We'll be fine as long as we never lose our responsiveness to the consumer."

Sources: Quoted material from Bill Saporito, "Is Wal-Mart Unstoppable?" *Fortune,* May 6, 1991, pp. 50–59; and John Huey, "Wal-Mart: Will It Take Over the World?" *Fortune,* January 30, 1989, pp. 52–61. Also see Christy Fisher, "Wal-Mart's Way," *Advertising Age,* February 18, 1991, p. 3; Bill Saporito, "David Glass Won't Crack Under Fire," *Fortune,* February 8, 1993, pp. 75–80; and Bill Saporito, "And the Winner Is Still . . . Wal-Mart," *Fortune,* May 2, 1994, pp. 62–70.

store has a "feel"; one store is cluttered, another charming, a third plush, a fourth somber. The store must have a planned atmosphere that suits the target market and moves customers to buy. A bank should be quiet, solid, and peaceful; a nightclub should be flashy, loud, and vibrating. Increasingly, retailers are working to create shopping environments that match their target markets. Chains such as the Sharper Image and Banana Republic are turning their stores into theaters that transport customers into unusual, exciting shopping environments. (See Marketing Highlight 14-4.) Even conservative Sears divides the clothing areas within each store into six distinct "shops," each with its own selling environment designed to meet the tastes of individual segments.

TODAY'S RETAILERS TAKE THEIR CUES FROM BROADWAY

Richard Melman is Chicago's preeminent restaurateur. He has designed each of his 32 restaurants around an intriguing theme: Tucci Benucch resembles an outdoor Italian village cafe, Ed Debevic is a 1950s kitsch diner, R. J. Grunts is a down-and-dirty burger-and-chili hangout, Ambria is an elegant crystal, tablecloth, and candle restaurant. According to one food-industry consultant, "Rich Melman is the Andrew Lloyd Webber of the restaurant industry. He doesn't just produce food, he produces theatre."

Turning retail establishments into theatre isn't limited just to restaurants. Toy seller F.A.O. Schwartz opened a three-story toy store on Chicago's upscale North Michigan Avenue that has customers lining up to get in. Once in, customers take an escalator to the third floor, then make their way down through various boutiques where crowds gather around spectacular Lego exhibits, Barbie Doll departments, giant stuffed zoo animals, and even a talking tree. F.A.O. Schwartz's "theatre" presents a stark contrast to the typical Toys 'R' Us store, in which nothing much seems to happen except lower prices and a senses-numbing assortment of 15,000 toys stacked high on row after row of shelves.

Even bookseller Barnes & Noble uses atmospherics to turn shopping for books into entertainment. It has found that, "to consumers, shopping is a social activity. They do it to mingle with others in a prosperous-feeling crowd, to see what's new, to enjoy the theatrical dazzle of the display, to treat themselves to something interesting or unexpected." Thus, Barnes & Noble stores are designed with "enough woody, traditional, soft-colored library to please book lovers; enough sophisticated modern architecture and graphics,

sweeping vistas, and stylish displays to satisfy fans of the theater of consumption. And for everyone, plenty of space, where they can meet other people and feel at home. . . . [Customers] settle in at heavy chairs and tables to browse through piles of books; they fill the cafes [designed] to increase the festivities." As one Barnes & Noble executive notes: "The

leisurely socializing—people-watching is big in the Philippines.

Perhaps the most dramatic conversion of stores into theatre is the Mall of America near Minneapolis. Containing more than 800 specialty stores, the Mall is a veritable playground. Under a single roof, it shelters a 7-acre Knott's Berry Farm amusement park featuring 23 rides

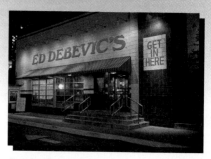 

Retail atmospheres offer a powerful differentiation tool. Ed Debevic's restaurant offers the feel of a 1950s diner.

feel-good part of the store, the quality of life contribution, is a big part of the success."

In the Philippines, the Cinderella Department Store uses theme-based, cutting-edge decor to appeal to the art-oriented Filipino market. Each store is divided into zones—or departments—each with its own flavor. The better women's apparel section has a celestial theme in which illuminated stars, planets, and zodiac constellations adorn the 10-foot high ceiling. The men's section boasts the flair of Northern Italian art, and imported goods are sold in the East India zone, where masts, wharfs, and cartons build customer anticipation. The kid's zone has the funky feel of post-modern artist Joan Miro—labels such as Osh Kosh and Esprit are contrasted under playful shapes recessed into the ceiling. A centrally located, rattan-furnished snack area encourages stopping and

and attractions, an ice-skating rink, an Underwater World featuring hundreds of marine specimens and a dolphin show, and a two-story miniature golf course. One of the stores, Oshman Supersports USA, features a basketball court, a boxing gym, a baseball batting cage, a 50-foot archery range, and a simulated ski slope.

All of this confirms that retail stores are much more than simply assortments of goods. They are environments to be experienced by the people who shop in them. Store atmospheres offer a powerful tool by which retailers can differentiate their stores from those of competitors.

Source: Quotes are from Myron Magnet, "Let's Go for Growth," *Fortune,* March 7, 1994, pp. 60–72; and "Why Rich Melman Is Really Cooking," *Business Week,* November 2, 1992, pp. 127–128. Also see Teresa Andreoli, "Cinderella Story," *Stores,* February 1994, pp. 49–51.

PRICE DECISION

A retailer's price policy is a crucial positioning factor and must be decided in relation to its target market, its product and service assortment, and its competition. All retailers would like to charge high markups and achieve high volume, but the two seldom go together. Most retailers seek *either* high markups on lower volume (most specialty stores) *or* low markups on higher volume (mass merchandisers and discount stores). Thus, Bijan's on Rodeo Drive in Beverly Hills prices men's suits starting at $1,000 and shoes at $400—it sells a low volume but makes a hefty profit on each sale. At the other extreme, T.J. Maxx sells brand name clothing at discount prices, settling for a lower margin on each sale but selling at a much higher volume.

Retailers also must pay attention to pricing tactics. Most retailers will put low prices on some items to serve as "traffic builders" or "loss leaders." On some occasions, they run storewide sales. On others, they plan markdowns on slower-moving merchandise. For example, shoe retailers may expect to sell 50 percent of their shoes at the normal markup, 25 percent at a 40 percent markup, and the remaining 25 percent at cost.

PROMOTION DECISION

Retailers use the normal promotion tools—advertising, personal selling, sales promotion, and public relations—to reach consumers. They advertise in newspapers, magazines, radio, and television. Advertising may be supported by circulars and direct-mail pieces. Personal selling requires careful training of salespeople in how to greet customers, meet their needs, and handle their complaints. Sales promotions may include in-store demonstrations, displays, contests, and visiting celebrities. Public relations activities, such as press conferences and speeches, store openings, special events, newsletters, magazines, and public service activities, are always available to retailers.

PLACE DECISION

Retailers often cite three critical factors in retailing success: *location, location,* and *location!* A retailer's location is key to its ability to attract customers. And the costs of building or leasing facilities have a major impact on the retailer's profits. Thus, site-location decisions are among the most important the retailer makes. Small retailers may have to settle for whatever locations they can find or afford. Large retailers usually employ specialists who select locations using advanced methods.

THE FUTURE OF RETAILING

Several trends will affect the future of retailing. The slowdown in population and economic growth means that retailers can no longer enjoy sales and profit growth through natural expansion in current and new markets. Growth will have to come from increasing shares of current markets. But greater competition and new types of retailers make it harder to improve market shares.

The retailing industry suffers from severe overcapacity. There is too much retail space—more than 18 square feet for every man, woman, and child, more than double that of 1972. Consumer demographics, lifestyles, and shopping patterns also are changing rapidly. Thus, the 1990s have been difficult for retailers:

> Going-out-of-business signs, bankruptcy filings, and constant sales attest to tough times in the retail industry. Such mercantile stalwarts as B. Altman and Garfinkel's have disappeared. The parent company of Bloomingdale's, Burdines, and Rich's is in [bankruptcy]. Rumors abound about R. H. Macy and other potential casualties.... "Retailing is not an area of hope," says [one retailing executive]. "It's not fun. It's almost a war." And the casualties are almost certain to keep mounting. By the end of the '90s, ... half of the nation's current retailers will be out of business.... The companies that succeed will be the ones that avoid crippling debt, focus tightly on specific customers or products, and hook into technology to hold down costs and enhance service. A tough act.[10]

To be successful, then, retailers will have to choose target segments carefully and position themselves strongly. Moreover, quickly rising costs will make more efficient operation and smarter buying essential to successful retailing. As a result, retail technologies are growing in importance as competitive tools. Progressive retailers are using computers to produce better forecasts, control inventory costs, order electronically from suppliers, communicate between stores, and even sell to consumers within stores. They are adopting checkout scanning systems, in-store television, on-line transaction processing, and electronic funds transfer.

Wheel of retailing concept
A concept of retailing that states that new types of retailers usually begin as low-margin, low-price, low-status operations but later evolve into higher-priced, higher-service operations, eventually becoming like the conventional retailers they replaced.

Many retailing innovations are partially explained by the **wheel of retailing concept.**[11] According to this concept, many new types of retailing forms begin as low-margin, low-price, low-status operations. They challenge established retailers that have become "fat" by letting their costs and margins increase. The new retailers' success leads them to upgrade their facilities and offer more services. In turn, their costs increase, forcing them to increase their prices. Eventually, the new retailers become like the conventional retailers they replaced. The cycle begins again when still newer types of retailers evolve with lower costs and prices. The wheel of retailing concept seems to explain the initial success and later troubles of department stores, supermarkets, and discount stores and the recent success of off-price retailers.

New retail forms will continue to emerge to meet new consumer needs and new situations. But the life cycle of new retail forms is getting shorter. Department stores took about 100 years to reach the mature stage of the life cycle; more recent forms, such as catalog showrooms and furniture warehouse stores, reached maturity in about ten years. In such an environment, seemingly solid retail positions can crumble quickly. For example, of the top ten discount retailers in 1962 (the year that Wal-Mart and Kmart began), not one still exists today.

Or consider the Price Club, the original warehouse store chain. When Sol Price opened his first warehouse store outside San Diego in 1976, he launched a retailing revolution. Selling everything from tires and office supplies to five-pound tubs of peanut butter at super-low prices, his store chain was generating $2.6 billion a year in sales within ten years. But Price refused to expand beyond its California base. And as the industry quickly matured, Price ran headlong into wholesale clubs run by such retail giants as Wal-Mart and Kmart. Only 17 years later, in a stunning reversal of fortune, a faltering Price sold out to competitor Costco. Price's rapid rise and fall "serves as a stark reminder to mass-market retailers that past success means little in a fiercely competitive and rapidly changing industry."[12] Thus, retailers can no longer sit back with a successful formula. To remain successful, they must keep adapting.[13]

WHOLESALING

Wholesaling
All activities involved in selling goods and services to those buying for resale or business use.
Wholesaler
A firm engaged *primarily* in wholesaling activity.

Wholesaling includes all activities involved in selling goods and services to those buying for resale or business use. A retail bakery is engaging in wholesaling when it sells pastry to the local hotel. We call **wholesalers** those firms engaged *primarily* in wholesaling activity.

Wholesalers buy mostly from producers and sell mostly to retailers, industrial consumers, and other wholesalers. But why are wholesalers used at all? For example, why would a producer use wholesalers rather than selling directly to retailers or consumers? Quite simply, wholesalers are often better at performing one or more of the following channel functions:

◆ *Selling and promoting.* Wholesalers' sales forces help manufacturers reach any small customers at a low cost. The wholesaler has more contacts and is often more trusted by the buyer than the distant manufacturer.

- *Buying and assortment building.* Wholesalers can select items and build assortments needed by their customers, thereby saving the consumers much work.

- *Bulk-breaking.* Wholesalers save their customers money by buying in carload lots and breaking bulk (breaking large lots into small quantities).

- *Warehousing.* Wholesalers hold inventories, thereby reducing the inventory costs and risks of suppliers and customers.

- *Transportation.* Wholesalers can provide quicker delivery to buyers because they are closer than the producers.

- *Financing.* Wholesalers finance their customers by giving credit, and they finance their suppliers by ordering early and paying bills on time.

- *Risk bearing.* Wholesalers absorb risk by taking title and bearing the cost of theft, damage, spoilage, and obsolescence.

- *Market information.* Wholesalers give information to suppliers and customers about competitors, new products, and price developments.

- *Management services and advice.* Wholesalers often help retailers train their salesclerks, improve store layouts and displays, and set up accounting and inventory control systems.

TYPES OF WHOLESALERS

Wholesalers fall into three major groups (see Table 14-2): *merchant wholesalers, brokers and agents,* and *manufacturers' sales branches and offices.*

MERCHANT WHOLESALERS

Merchant wholesalers
Independently owned businesses that take title to the merchandise they handle.

Merchant wholesalers are independently owned businesses that take title to the merchandise they handle. They are the largest single group of wholesalers, accounting for roughly 50 percent of all wholesaling. Merchant wholesalers include two broad types: *full-service wholesalers* and *limited-service wholesalers.*

Full-Service Wholesalers

Full-service wholesalers provide a full set of services, such as carrying stock, using a sales force, offering credit, making deliveries, and providing management assistance. They are either *wholesale merchants* or *industrial distributors.*

TABLE 14-2   *Classification of Wholesalers*

MERCHANT WHOLESALERS	BROKERS AND AGENTS	MANUFACTURERS' AND RETAILERS' BRANCHES AND OFFICES
Full-service wholesalers	Brokers	Sales branches and offices
Wholesale merchants	Agents	Purchasing offices
Industrial distributors		
Limited-service wholesalers		
Cash-and-carry wholesalers		
Truck wholesalers		
Drop shippers		
Rack jobbers		
Producers' cooperatives		
Mail-order wholesalers		

Merchant wholesalers: A typical Fleming Companies, Inc. wholesale food distribution center. The average Fleming warehouse contains 500,000 square feet of floor space (with 30-foot high ceiling), carries 16,000 different food items, and serves 150 to 200 retailers within a 500-mile radius.

Wholesale merchants sell mostly to retailers and provide a full range of services. They vary in the width of their product line. Some carry several lines of goods to meet the needs of both general-merchandise retailers and single-line retailers. Others carry one or two lines of goods in a greater depth of assortment. Examples are hardware wholesalers, drug wholesalers, and clothing wholesalers. Some specialty wholesalers carry only part of a line in great depth, such as health food wholesalers, seafood wholesalers, and automotive parts wholesalers. They offer customers deeper choice and greater product knowledge.

Industrial distributors are merchant wholesalers that sell to producers rather than to retailers. They provide inventory, credit, delivery, and other services. They may carry a broad range of merchandise, a general line, or a specialty line. Industrial distributors may concentrate on lines such as maintenance and operating supplies, original-equipment goods (such as ball bearings and motors), or equipment (such as power tools and forklift trucks).

Limited-Service Wholesalers

Limited-service wholesalers offer fewer services to their suppliers and customers. There are several types of limited-service wholesalers.

Cash-and-carry wholesalers have a limited line of fast-moving goods, sell to small retailers for cash, and normally do not deliver. A small fish store retailer, for example, normally drives at dawn to a cash-and-carry fish wholesaler and buys several crates of fish, pays on the spot, drives the merchandise back to the store, and unloads it.

Truck wholesalers (also called *truck jobbers*) perform a selling and delivery function. They carry a limited line of goods (such as milk, bread, or snack foods) that they sell for cash as they make their rounds of supermarkets, small groceries, hospitals, restaurants, factory cafeterias, and hotels.

Drop shippers operate in bulk industries such as coal, lumber, and heavy equipment. They do not carry inventory or handle the product. Once an order is received, they find a producer who ships the goods directly to the customer. The drop shipper takes title and risk from the time the order is accepted to the time it is delivered to the customer. Because drop shippers do not carry inventory, their costs are lower and they can pass on some savings to customers.

Rack jobbers serve grocery and drug retailers, mostly in the area of nonfood items. These retailers do not want to order and maintain displays of hundreds of nonfood items. Rack jobbers send delivery trucks to stores, and the delivery person sets up racks of toys, paperbacks, hardware items, health and beauty aids, or other items. They price the goods, keep them fresh, and keep inventory records. Rack jobbers sell on consignment; they retain title to the goods and bill the retailers only for the goods sold to consumers. Thus, they provide services such as delivery, shelving, inventory, and financing. They do little promotion because they carry many branded items that are already highly advertised.

Producers' cooperatives, owned by farmer-members, assemble farm produce to sell in local markets. Their profits are divided among members at the end of the year. They often try to improve product quality and promote a co-op brand name, such as Sun Maid raisins, Sunkist oranges, or Diamond walnuts.

Mail-order wholesalers send catalogs to retail, industrial, and institutional customers offering jewelry, cosmetics, special foods, and other small items. Their main customers are businesses in small outlying areas. They have no sales forces to call on customers. The orders are filled and sent by mail, truck, or other means.

BROKERS AND AGENTS

Brokers and *agents* differ from merchant wholesalers in two ways: They do not take title to goods, and they perform only a few functions. Their main function is to aid in buying and selling, and for these services they earn a commission on the selling price. Like merchant wholesalers, they generally specialize by product line or customer type. They account for 11 percent of the total wholesale volume.

Broker
A wholesaler who does not take title to goods and whose function is to bring buyers and sellers together and assist in negotiation.

Agent
A wholesaler who represents buyers or sellers on a relatively permanent basis, performs only a few functions, and does not take title to goods.

A **broker** brings buyers and sellers together and assists in negotiation. Brokers are paid by the parties hiring them. They do not carry inventory, get involved in financing, or assume risk. The most familiar examples are food brokers, real estate brokers, insurance brokers, and security brokers.

Agents represent buyers or sellers on a more permanent basis. There are several types. *Manufacturers' agents* (also called *manufacturers' representatives*) are the most common type of agent wholesaler. They represent two or more manufacturers of related lines. They have a formal agreement with each manufacturer, covering prices, territories, order-handling procedures, delivery and warranties, and commission rates. They know each manufacturer's product line and use their wide contacts to sell the products. Manufacturers' agents are used in lines such as apparel, furniture, and electrical goods. Most manufacturers' agents are small businesses, with only a few employees who are skilled salespeople. They are hired by small producers who cannot afford to maintain their own field sales forces and by large producers who want to open new territories or sell in areas that cannot support a full-time salesperson.

Selling agents contract to sell a producer's entire output—either the manufacturer is not interested in doing the selling or feels unqualified. The selling agent serves as a sales department and has much influence over prices, terms, and conditions of sale. The selling agent normally has no territory limits. Selling agents are found in product areas such as textiles, industrial machinery and equipment, coal and coke, chemicals, and metals.

Purchasing agents generally have a long-term relationship with buyers. They make purchases for buyers and often receive, inspect, warehouse, and ship goods to the buyers. One type of purchasing agent is *resident buyers* in major apparel markets—purchasing specialists who look for apparel lines that can be carried by small retailers located in small cities. They know a great deal about their product lines and provide helpful market information to clients; they also can obtain the best goods and prices available.

Commission merchants (or houses) are agents that take physical possession of products and negotiate sales. They normally are not used on a long-term basis. They are used most often in agricultural marketing by farmers who do not want to sell their own output and who do not belong to cooperatives. Typically, the commission merchant will take a truckload of farm products to a central market, sell it for the best price, deduct expenses and a commission, and pay the balance to the farmer.

MANUFACTURERS' SALES BRANCHES AND OFFICES

Manufacturers' sales branches and offices
Wholesaling by sellers or buyers themselves rather than through independent wholesalers.

The third major type of wholesaling is that done in **manufacturers' sales branches and offices** by sellers or buyers themselves rather than through independent wholesalers. Manufacturers' offices and sales branches account for about 31 percent of all wholesale volume. Manufacturers often set up their own sales branches and offices to improve inventory control, selling, and promotion. *Sales branches* carry inventory and are found in industries such as lumber and automotive equipment and parts. *Sales offices* do not carry inventory and most often are found in the dry goods and notion industries. Many retailers set up *purchasing offices* in major market centers such as New York City and Chicago. These purchasing offices perform a role similar to that of brokers or agents, but are part of the buyer's organization.

WHOLESALER MARKETING DECISIONS

Wholesalers have experienced mounting competitive pressures in recent years. They have faced new sources of competition, more demanding customers, new technologies, and more direct-buying programs on the part of large industrial, institutional, and retail buyers. As a result, they have had to improve their strategic decisions on target markets and positioning, and on the marketing mix—product assortments and services, price, promotion, and place (see Figure 14-2).

FIGURE 14-2
Wholesaler marketing decisions

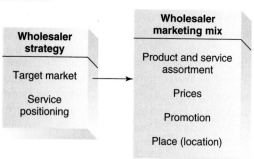

TARGET MARKET AND POSITIONING DECISION

Like retailers, wholesalers must define their target markets and position themselves effectively—they cannot serve everyone. They can choose a target group by size of customer (only large retailers), type of customer (convenience food stores only), need for service (customers who need credit), or other factors. Within the target group, they can identify the more profitable customers, design stronger offers, and build better relationships with them. They can propose automatic reordering systems, set up management-training and advising systems, or even sponsor a voluntary chain. They can discourage less profitable customers by requiring larger orders or adding service charges to smaller ones.

MARKETING MIX DECISIONS

Like retailers, wholesalers must decide on product assortment and services, prices, promotion, and place. The wholesaler's "product" is the assortment of *products and services* that it offers. Wholesalers are under great pressure to carry a full line and to stock enough for immediate delivery. But this practice can damage profits. Wholesalers today are cutting down on the number of lines they carry, choosing to carry only the more profitable ones. Wholesalers also are rethinking which services count most in building strong customer relationships and which should be dropped or charged for. The key is to find the mix of services most valued by their target customers.

Price is also an important wholesaler decision. Wholesalers usually mark up the cost of goods by a standard percentage—say, 20 percent. Expenses may run 17 percent of the gross margin, leaving a profit margin of 3 percent. In grocery wholesaling, the average profit margin is often less than 2 percent. Wholesalers are trying new pricing approaches. They may cut their margin on some lines in order to win important new customers. They may ask suppliers for special price breaks when they can turn them into an increase in the supplier's sales.

Although *promotion* can be critical to wholesaler success, most wholesalers are not promotion-minded. Their use of trade advertising, sales promotion, personal selling, and public relations is largely scattered and unplanned. Many are behind the times in personal selling—they still see selling as a single salesperson talking to a single customer instead of as a team effort to sell, build, and service major accounts. Wholesalers also need to adopt some of the nonpersonal promotion techniques used by retailers. They need to develop an overall promotion strategy and to make greater use of supplier promotion materials and programs.

Finally, *place* is important—wholesalers must choose their locations and facilities carefully. Wholesalers typically locate in low-rent, low-tax areas and tend to invest little money in their buildings, equipment, and systems. As a result, their materials-handling and order-processing systems are often outdated. In recent years, however, large and progressive wholesalers are reacting to rising costs by investing in automated warehouses and on-line ordering systems. Orders are fed from the retailer's system directly into the wholesaler's computer, and the items are picked up by mechanical devices and automatically taken to a shipping platform where they are assembled. Most large wholesalers employ computers to carry out accounting, billing, inventory control, and forecasting. Modern wholesalers are adapting their services to the needs of target customers and finding cost-reducing methods of doing business.

TRENDS IN WHOLESALING

Progressive wholesalers constantly watch for better ways to meet the changing needs of their suppliers and target customers. They recognize that, in the long run, their only reason for existence comes from increasing the efficiency and effectiveness of the entire marketing channel. To achieve this goal, they must constantly improve their services and reduce their costs.

McKesson, the nation's leading wholesaler of pharmaceuticals and healthcare products, provides an example of progressive wholesaling. To survive, McKesson had to remain more cost effective than manufacturers' sales branches. Thus, the company automated 36 of its warehouses, established direct computer links with 225 drug manufacturers, designed a computerized accounts-receivable program for pharmacists, and provided drugstores with computer terminals for ordering inventories. Retailers can even use the McKesson computer system to maintain medical profiles on their customers. Thus, McKesson has delivered better value to both manufacturers and retail customers.

Progressive wholesaling: to deliver better value to its customers, McKesson automated its warehouses, set up direct computer links with drug manufacturers, and provided drugstores with computer terminals for ordering inventories and maintaining medical profiles on their customers.

One study predicts several developments in the wholesaling industry.[14] Consolidation will significantly reduce the number of wholesaling firms. The remaining wholesaling companies will grow larger, primarily through acquisition, merger, and geographic expansion. Geographic expansion will require that distributors learn how to compete effectively over wider and more diverse areas. The increased use of computerized and automated systems will help wholesalers. By 1990, more than three-fourths of all wholesalers were using on-line order systems.

The distinction between large retailers and large wholesalers continues to blur. Many retailers now operate formats such as wholesale clubs and hypermarkets that perform many wholesale functions. In return, many large wholesalers are setting up their own retailing operations. SuperValu and Flemming, both leading food wholesalers, now operate their own retail outlets. In fact, more than 20 percent of SuperValu's $12.6 billion in sales comes from its Cub Foods, Shop 'n Save, Save-A-Lot, Laneco, and Scott's supermarket operations.[15]

Wholesalers will continue to increase the services they provide to retailers—retail pricing, cooperative advertising, marketing and management information reports, accounting services, and others. Rising costs on the one hand, and the demand for increased services on the other, will put the squeeze on wholesaler profits. Wholesalers who do not find efficient ways to deliver value to their customers will soon drop by the wayside.

Finally, facing slow growth in their domestic markets and such developments as the North American Free Trade Agreement, many large wholesalers are now going global. The National Association of Wholesaler-Distributors predicts that, by the year 2000, wholesalers will generate 18 percent of their sales outside the United States, twice the current share.[16] For example, in 1991, McKesson bought out its Canadian partner, Provigo. The company now receives about 13 percent of its total revenues from Canada.

Summary

Retailing and wholesaling consist of many organizations bringing goods and services from the point of production to the point of use. *Retailing* includes all activities involved in selling goods or services directly to final consumers for their personal, nonbusiness use. Retailers can be classified as *store retailers* and *nonstore retailers*. *Store retailers* can be further classified by the *amount of service* they provide (self-service, limited service, or full service); *product line* sold (specialty stores, department stores, supermarkets, convenience stores, combination stores, superstores, hypermarkets, and service businmsses); *relative prices* (discount stores, off-price retailers, and catalog showrooms); *control of outlets* (corporate chains, voluntary chains and retailer cooperatives, franchise organizations, and merchandising conglomerates); and *type of store cluster* (central business districts and shopping centers).

Although most goods and services are sold through stores, *nonstore retailing* has been growing much faster than store retailing. *Nonstore retailers* now account for more than 14 percent of all consumer purchases, and they may account for a third of all sales by the end of the century. Nonstore retailing consists of *direct marketing, direct selling,* and *automatic vending*.

There are many key *retailer marketing decisions*. Each retailer must choose its *target market and positioning, product assortment and service level, price, promotion,* and *place*. Retailers need to choose target markets carefully and position themselves strongly. These decisions are very important because overcapacity will sharply affect the *future of retailing*. Some future developments can be partially predicted by the *wheel of retailing concept*.

Wholesaling includes all the activities involved in selling goods or services to those who are buying for the purpose of resale or for business use. Wholesalers perform many functions, including selling and promoting, buying and assortment building, bulk-breaking, warehousing, transporting, financing, risk bearing, supplying market information, and providing management services and advice. Wholesalers fall into three groups. First, *merchant wholesalers* take the possession of the goods. They include *full-service wholesalers* (wholesale merchants, industrial distributors) and *limited-service wholesalers* (cash-and-carry wholesalers, truck wholesalers, drop shippers, rack jobbers, producers' cooperatives, and mail-order wholesalers). Second, *brokers and agents* do not take possession of the goods but are paid a commission for aiding buying and selling. Finally, *manufacturers' sales branches and offices* are wholesaling operations conducted by nonwholesalers to bypass the wholesalers.

There are important *trends in wholesaling,* including consolidation, growth of remaining firms, geographical expansion, and increasing services to retailers. Wholesaling is holding its own in the economy. Progressive wholesalers are adapting their services to the needs of target customers and are seeking cost-reducing methods of doing business.

Key Terms

Agent

Automatic vending

Broker

Catalog showroom

Chain stores

Combination stores

Convenience store

Department store

Direct marketing

Discount store

Door-to-door retailing

Factory outlets

Franchise

Hypermarkets

Independent off-price retailers

Manufacturers' sales branches and offices

Merchant wholesalers

Off-price retailers

Retailers

Retailing

Shopping center

Specialty store

Supermarkets

Superstore

Warehouse club (or wholesale club)

Wheel of retailing concept

Wholesaler

Wholesaling

Discussing the Issues

1. Explain which would do more to increase a convenience store's sales—an increase in the length or the breadth of its product assortment. Why?

2. Warehouse clubs that are restricted to members only, such as Costco and Sam's Wholesale, are growing rapidly. They offer a very broad but shallow line of products, often in institutional packaging, at very low prices. Some members buy for resale, others buy to supply a business, and still others buy for personal use. Decide whether these stores are wholesalers or retailers. How can you make a distinction?

3. Off-price retailers provide tough price competition to other retailers. Do you think that large retailers' growing power in channels of distribution will affect manufacturers' willingness to sell to off-price retailers at below regular wholesale rates? Suggest what policy Sony should have regarding selling to off-price retailers.

4. Postal-rate hikes make it more expensive to send direct mail, catalogs, and purchased products to consumers. Identify ways you would expect direct mail and catalog marketers to respond to an increase in postage rates.

5. A typical "country store" in a farming community sells a variety of food and non-food items—snacks, staples, hardware, and many other types of goods. What kinds of wholesalers do the owners of such stores use to obtain the items they sell? Are these the same suppliers that a supermarket uses?

6. Compare the fundamental differences between retailers, wholesalers, and manufacturers in the types of marketing decisions they make. Give examples of the marketing decisions made by the three groups which show their similarities and differences.

Applying the Concepts

1. Collect all the catalogs that you have received in the mail recently. (a) Sort them by type of product line. Is there some pattern to the types of direct marketers that are targeting you? (b) Where do you think these catalog companies got your name? (c) How do you think a company that was selling your name and address to a direct marketer would describe your buying habits?

2. Watch a cable television shopping channel, or tune into a late-night television-shopping show (often found on UHF stations above channel 13). (a) How are these shows attempting to target buyers? Do they mix football cleats and fine china in the same program, or are they targeting more carefully? (b) How much of the merchandise shown appears to be close-outs? How can you tell?

References

1. The quote is from Steve Weiner, "With Big Selection and Low Prices, 'Category Killer' Stores Are a Hit," *Wall Street Journal,* June 17, 1986, p. 33. Also see Bill Saporito, "IKEA's Got 'Em Lining Up," *Fortune,* March 11, 1991, p. 72; "North America's Top 100 Furniture Stores," *Furniture Today,* May 18, 1992, p. 50; Laura Loro, "IKEA," *Advertising Age,* July 4, 1994, p. S2.

2. See "Stop-N-Go Micromarkets New Upscale Mix," *Chain Store Age Executive,* January 1990, p. 145;

Christy Fisher, "Convenience Chains Pump for New Life," *Advertising Age,* April 23, 1990, p. 80; Doug Zapper, "Convenience Store Industry Embraces Change," *Chain Store Executive,* August 1993, pp. 27A–28A.

3. See Emily DeNitto, "Hypermarkets Seem to Be Big Flop in U.S.," *Advertising Age,* October 4, 1993, p. 20; and Leah Rickard, "Supercenters Entice Shoppers," *Advertising Age,* March 20, 1995, pp. 1, 10.

4. See Debra Rosenberg, "Where the Price Is Always Right," *Newsweek,* January 13, 1992, p. 45; and Adrienne Ward, "New Breed of Mall Knows: Everyone Loves a Bargain," *Advertising Age,* January 27, 1992, p. S5.

5. Andrew E. Serwer, "McDonald's Conquers the World," *Fortune,* October 17, 1994, pp. 103–116.

6. Chip Walker, "Strip Malls: Plain but Powerful," *American Demographics,* October 1991, pp. 48–50.

7. See Francesca Turchiano, "The Unmalling of America," *American Demographics,* April 1990, pp. 36–42; Kate Fitzgerald, "Mega Malls: Built for the '90s, or the '80s?" *Advertising Age,* January 27, 1992, pp. S1, S8; Eric Wieffering, "What Has the Mall of America Done to Minneapolis?" *American Demographics,* February 1994, pp. 13–15; and Kenneth Labich, "What It Will Take to Keep People Hanging Out at the Mall," *Fortune,* May 29, 1995, pp. 102–106.

8. See J. Taylor Buckley, "Machines Start New Fast-Food Era," *USA Today,* July 19, 1991, pp. B1, B2; and Laurie McLaughlin, "Vending Machines Open to New Ideas," *Advertising Age,* August 19, 1991, p. 35.

9. For a fuller discussion, see Lawrence H. Wortzel, "Retailing Strategies for Today's Mature Marketplace," *The Journal of Business Strategy,* Spring 1987, pp. 45–56.

10. Laura Zinn, "Retailing: Who Will Survive?" *Business Week,* November 26, 1990, p. 134. Also see Susan Caminiti, "The New Retailing Champs," *Fortune,* September 24, 1990, pp. 85–100.

11. See Malcolm P. McNair and Eleanor G. May, "The Next Revolution of the Retailing Wheel, *Harvard Business Review,* September–October 1978, pp. 81–91; Eleanor G. May, "A Retail Odyssey," *Journal of Retailing,* Fall 1989, pp. 356–367; and Stephen Brown, "The Wheel of Retailing: Past and Future," *Journal of Retailing,* Summer 1990, pp. 143–147.

12. Amy Barrett, "A Retailing Pacesetter Pulls Up Lame," *Business Week,* July 12, 1993, pp. 122–123.

13. Bill Saporito, "Is Wal-Mart Unstoppable?" *Fortune,* May 6, 1991, pp. 50–59. For more on retailing trends, see Eleanor G. May, C. William Ress, and Walter J. Salmon, *Future Trends in Retailing* (Cambridge, MA: Marketing Science Institute, February 1985); Daniel Sweeney, "Toward 2000," *Chain Store Age Executive,* January 1990, pp. 27–39; and Howard L. Green, "New Consumer Realities for Retailers," *Advertising Age,* April 25, 1994, pp. 4–5.

14. See Arthur Andersen & Co., *Facing the Forces of Change: Beyond Future Trends in Wholesale Distribution* (Washington, DC: Distribution Research and Education Foundation, 1987), p. 7. Also see Joseph Weber, "It's 'Like Somebody Had Shot the Postman,'" *Business Week,* January 13, 1992, p. 82.

15. *SuperValu Distribution and Retailing Handbook.* SuperValu, Inc., Minneapolis, MN, November 1993.

16. Joseph Weber, "On a Fast Boat to Anywhere," *Business Week,* January 11, 1993, p. 94.

Company Case 14

SAM'S CLUB: BULKING UP FOR COMPETITION

THE BEGINNING

In the early 1980s, Wal-Mart's founder Sam Walton wondered what Sol Price was doing on the West Coast. Price had opened a few very large stores under the name Price Club that offered businesses a narrow line of products, often in bulk sizes, at deep discounts. Walton instructed his staff to open a similar store in Oklahoma City so he could experiment with the idea to see how it worked.

This first Sam's Club opened in 1983. Apparently, Sam Walton and his staff learned the business well and quickly. By the end of the 1993 fiscal year, Sam's Club had become the largest warehouse membership club (WMC) in the United States with 419 stores generating total sales of $14.7 billion, 22 percent of Wal-Mart's revenue.

However, despite their success, Sam's managers knew they could not relax—all was not well in the WMC business. Brutal competition, price deflation, and the economic woes of the early 1990s had caused a wrenching shakeout in late 1993 and 1994. For the first time in the $39 billion industry's history, 1993 saw total industry sales decline—by one percent. To sustain growth and maintain share, Price Company and Costco Wholesale Clubs, the number-two and -three players, merged their 210 clubs to form Price/Costco. Then, the number-four player, PACE, a division of Kmart, announced it would exit the business and sell 99 stores to Sam's. The number-seven player, Wholesale Depot, filed for bankruptcy. Despite buying PACE, Sam's managers still had to explain in mid-1994 why the company had experienced 11 straight months of same-store sales that lagged behind prior-year levels.

WAREHOUSE MEMBERSHIP CLUBS

The WMC format emerged primarily to serve small-business customers who were not large enough to take advantage of lower prices suppliers offered to bigger businesses. WMCs buy in quantity and pass the lower prices on to their customers. Because target customers buy items for resale or for use as operating supplies, the WMCs sell goods in bulk, such as whole cases, or in extra-large sizes.

Most warehouse clubs require customers to become members by paying a membership fee, usually around $25. This fee provides income to the club and increases customer loyalty. Customers shop regularly because they pay a membership fee. Membership fees actually account for most of WMCs' profits. The typical Sam's Club has an average gross margin of 8.5 percent while overhead expenses average 9 percent.

From the beginning, the WMCs were operations-driven. They had to keep their costs down to attract small-business customers. As a result, the clubs offer no-frills buying, featuring no fancy buildings or expensive scanning systems for checking out. Sam's Clubs range in size from 107,000 to 135,000 square feet (about two to three football fields). The clubs carry leading brands, but typically feature only 3,000 to 4,000 SKUs (stock keeping units). For example, Sam's offers two VCR models versus the 15 an electronic specialty store might offer. The average discount store, such as a Wal-Mart, carries 70,000 to 80,000 SKUs. WMCs accept cash only, focus on high inventory turnover, and offer little customer service. Customers have to lug their own large purchases, from cases of peaches to large appliances, to the checkout line. Many are willing to put up with the inconvenience to take advantage of prices that are as much as 20 to 40 percent below regular prices. Further, Sam's and the other clubs focus on brand-name merchandise. Sam's, however, does not duplicate the merchandise in Wal-Mart stores. Its goal is to have each item in each store have gross sales revenue of $300 per week.

THE CUSTOMERS

One analyst estimates that 12.2 percent of the U.S. population over 20 years of age (about 22 million people) are primary or secondary WMC members. Although WMCs primarily target businesses, they also allow individuals to become members. As a result, about 70 percent of WMC members are retail (household) members. The 30 percent who are business members, however, account for 65 to 70 percent of WMCs' sales.

In 1992, the Babson College Retailing Research Group studied WMCs, surveying 2,150 WMC customers in 11 U.S. and Canadian cities. The group found that the average number of shoppers who used WMCs at least four times a year ranges from 5 to 41 percent, with an average of 21 percent.

The typical WMC shopper has been a member for 35 months, and one-fourth of all shoppers take a friend, neighbor, or relative shopping with them. Shoppers tend to be more upscale than the general population, with 40 percent having family incomes over $50,000. Frequent shoppers account for most WMC sales.

The Babson group examined household customer shopping habits. It found that 92 percent of cardholders buy food for their families and that the average family spends $90 on food per trip. The report estimated that WMCs capture 7 percent of all consumer food dollars. The average family also spends $75 per trip on nonfood products. Combining all purchases, the average family spends about $160 per trip, with an average shopping frequency of once every three weeks. The typical customer travels 13 miles to a WMC, as compared with traveling an average distance of one to two miles to a supermarket.

On average, business customers spend $103 on food items and $114 on nonfood items. About 40 percent of both household and business shoppers buy fresh meats and fresh-baked goods. Although conventional wisdom suggests that the typical business customer is a restaurant or convenience store, the study found that most small business members buy both food and nonfood items. Nonfood items consist primarily of office supplies and stationery.

The researchers asked both types of customers about their reactions to the WMC shopping experience. Shoppers complain about slow checkout service, security procedures, the packages' sizes, the crowds, and the lack of brand consistency from month to month.

SAM'S CHALLENGES

Sam's and the other firms face three problems. First, the once dizzying industry growth rate has slowed. Sam's must find new ways to stimulate increased business and individual buying. To attract individuals, some WMCs are featuring more one-time deals like Sony televisions, Christian Dior shirts, or Dom Perignon champagne besides their typical products. Many are also enlarging the clubs to add fresh-food departments, drug counters, bakeries, and even eyeglass departments. Sam's and Price/Costco are also looking to foreign markets. Sam's already has 10 clubs in Mexico and plans to enter Brazil, Argentina, and Chile.

Second, competition is increasing. A few years ago, a WMC might well have found a target city and have been the only WMC in town. With each firm trying to grow and with only so many markets large enough to support these large stores, increased competition is inevitable. Moreover, supermarkets are not sitting idly by as they lose market share. Many are installing "power aisles" that feature warehouse-style products. "Category-killer" stores, such as Office Depot and Office-Max, threaten to take away WMCs' business by focusing on price in certain key categories.

Finally, Sam's and the other WMCs must figure out how to differentiate themselves from each other and from the competition. With every store seemingly trying the same things, each must find ways to stand out.

QUESTIONS

1. Are warehouse membership clubs retailers or wholesalers?

2. How would you classify WMCs using the categories for classifying retail outlets discussed in the chapter?

3. What retailer/wholesaler marketing decisions have WMCs made? How are those decisions changing?

4. What do you think will happen in the WMC industry during the next five years?

5. What marketing actions should Sam's management take to deal with the challenges the chain faces?

Sources: Debra Chanil, "Wholesale Clubs: Romancing America," *Discount Merchandiser,* November 1992, pp. 26-41; and Terry Cotter, Stephen J. Arnold, and Douglas Tigert, "Warehouse Membership Clubs in North America," *Discount Merchandiser*, November 1992, pp. 42-47, used with permission. Also see: Debra Chanil, "Growing Sam's Club," *Discount Merchandiser,* August 1993, pp. 78–80; Wendy Zellner, "Why Sam's Wants Businesses to Join the Club," *Business Week,* June 27, 1994, p. 48; and "Warehouse Clubs Face Mid-Life Crisis: Industry Shakeout Leaves Two Giants," *Chain Store Age Executive,* August 1994, pp. 26A–28A.

Promoting Products

MARKETING COMMUNICATION STRATEGY

15

Founded 24 years ago at Love Field in Dallas, Southwest Airlines sees itself as the "love" airline. The company even uses LUV as its New York Stock Exchange symbol. Southwest showers most of this love on its passengers in the form of shockingly low prices for highly dependable, no-frills service. In 1992, Southwest received the Department of Transportation's first ever Triple Crown Award for best on-time service, best baggage handling, *and* best customer service. Southwest rated first in customer satisfaction among the nation's nine major airlines. It repeated this feat in 1993.

Customers have returned Southwest's love by making it the industry's most profitable airline. In an industry plagued by huge losses, Southwest has experienced 22 straight years of profits. In 1992, when the industry lost $3 billion, Southwest *made* $91 million. All this from an airline only one-quarter the size of industry leader American Airlines.

Two factors contributing to Southwest's amazing success are: a superior marketing strategy and outstanding marketing communications. The marketing strategy is a simple one—Southwest knows its niche and stays with it. It has positioned itself firmly as *the* short-haul, no-frills, low-price airline. Its average flight time is one hour; its average one-way fare just $58. In fact, its prices are so low that when it enters a new market, it actually increases total air traffic by attracting customers who might otherwise travel by car or bus. For example, when Southwest began its Louisville–Chicago flight at a one-way rate of $49 versus competitors' $250, total air passenger traffic between the two cities increased from 8,000 people weekly to 26,000.

To these practical benefits, Southwest adds one more key positioning ingredient—lots of good fun. With its happy-go-lucky CEO, Herb Kelleher, leading the charge, Southwest refuses to take itself seriously. For example, when an aviation company recently confronted Southwest for using its slogan, "Just Plane Smart," Kelleher challenged the company's CEO to a public arm-wrestling match, with the slogan going to the winner. Kelleher was quickly pinned, but the CEO showdown became a national media event, winning Southwest lots of pub-

OBJECTIVES

When you finish this chapter, you should be able to accomplish the following:

1. Outline the initial steps in developing effective communication, starting with **identifying a target audience** and **determining the response sought.**

2. Describe issues in implementing communications beginning with **choosing a message, choosing media, selecting a message source,** and **collecting feedback.**

3. Define the ways of **setting a total promotional budget: affordable, percentage-of-sales, competitive-parity,** and **objective-and-task** methods.

4. Explain each promotional tool—**advertising, personal selling, sales promotion,** and **public relations**—and the factors in setting the **promotion mix: type of product and market, push** versus **pull strategies, buyer readiness states,** and **product life-cycle stage.**

5. Discuss the **changing communications environment**—the **growth of direct marketing, integrated marketing communications,** and **socially responsible marketing communication.**

licity. And Southwest was later allowed to continue using the slogan.

In another instance, Northwest Airlines ran ads claiming that it ranked number one in customer satisfaction among the nation's seven largest airlines. Southwest, which rated number one among the *nine* major airlines, responded in classic Southwest fashion. Print ads boldly proclaimed: "After lengthy deliberation at the highest levels, and extensive consultation with our legal department, we have arrived at an official corporate response to Northwest Airlines' claim to be number one in Customer Satisfaction. Liar, liar. Pants on fire."

As the arm wrestling and "Liar, liar" incidents suggest, Southwest has little trouble communicating with consumers in a very memorable way. But beyond these special cases, the airline dispenses a carefully coordinated flow of marketing communications, ranging from media advertising, special events, and public relations to direct marketing and personal selling.

Entering a new city presents the greatest communications challenge. For example, when Southwest entered Baltimore in 1993, it had to communicate its entire positioning to East Coast consumers who knew almost nothing about the airline. The Baltimore campaign began with public relations efforts and community affairs events. Says the president of Southwest's advertising agency, "We always start out with the public relations side. . . . Then we integrate government relations, community affairs, service announcements, special events, and advertising and promotion. By the time Southwest comes into the market, the airline already is part of the community."

Five weeks before the first flight, CEO Kelleher and Maryland's Governor William Schaefer held a news conference to announce Southwest's entry into Baltimore. The governor gave Kelleher a basket of products made in Maryland; Kelleher gave the governor a flotation device—a "lifesaver" from high airfares for the people of Baltimore. Southwest next dramatized its $49 fare between Baltimore and Cleveland by flying 49 school children to Cleveland for a day to visit the Rain Forest at Cleveland Metroparks Zoo. This event garnered substantial media coverage in both Baltimore and Cleveland.

A week later, Southwest employees took to Baltimore's streets, handing out fliers on street corners promoting Southwest's "Just Plane Smart" slogan. At about the same time, Southwest sent direct mail to frequent short-haul travelers in the Baltimore area, offering a special promotion to join its Company Club frequent-flier program. Once the public relations and community affairs efforts had set the stage, the company began running "Just Plane Smart" television and print commercials, which praised the people of Baltimore for their wisdom in allowing Southwest to come to the city. Outdoor ads shouted "Hello, Baltimore, Goodbye High Fares." The integrated communications campaign was incredibly successful. In all, 90,000 Baltimore passengers purchased tickets before the start of service— a company record for advance bookings.

When the introductory fanfare had settled down, Southwest set up a Baltimore marketing office to continue working on local advertising, promotions, and community events. And now, of course, Baltimore travelers will be treated to the unique brand of more personal communication dispensed by Southwest's cheerful employees.

> Southwest workers often go out of their way to amuse, surprise, or somehow entertain passengers. During delays at the gate, ticket agents will award prizes to the passenger with the largest hole in his or her sock. Flight attendants have been known to hide in overhead luggage bins and then pop out when passengers start filing onboard. Veteran Southwest fliers looking for a few yuks have learned to listen up to announcements over the intercom. A recent effort: "Good morning ladies and gentlemen. Those of you who wish to smoke will please file out to our lounge on the wing, where you can enjoy our feature film, *Gone With the Wind*." On that same flight, an attendant later made this

announcement: "Please pass all plastic cups to the center aisle so that we can wash them out and use them for the next group of passengers."

Southwest owes much of its success to its ability to deliver dependable no-frills, low-cost service to its customers. But success also depends on Southwest's skill at blending all of its promotion tools—advertising, sales promotion, public relations, and personal selling—into an integrated program that communicates the Southwest story.[1]

Promotion mix
The specific mix of advertising, personal selling, sales promotion, and public relations a company uses to pursue its advertising and marketing objectives.

Advertising
Any paid form of nonpersonal presentation and promotion of ideas, goods, or services by an identified sponsor.

Personal selling
Personal presentation by the firm's sales force for the purpose of making sales and building customer relationships.

Sales promotion
Short-term incentives to encourage purchase or sales of a product or service.

Public relations
Building good relations with the company's various publics by obtaining favorable publicity, building up a good "corporate image," and handling or heading off unfavorable rumors, stories, and events.

Modern marketing calls for more than just developing a good product, pricing it attractively, and making it available to target customers. Companies also must *communicate* with their customers, and what they communicate should not be left to chance. For most companies, the question is not *whether* to communicate, but *how much to spend* and *in what ways*.

A modern company manages a complex marketing communications system (see Figure 15-1). The company communicates with its middlemen, consumers, and various publics. In turn, middlemen communicate with their consumers and publics. Consumers have word-of-mouth communication with each other and with other publics. Meanwhile, each group provides feedback to every other group.

A company's total marketing communications program—called its **promotion mix**—consists of the specific blend of advertising, personal selling, sales promotion, and public relations tools that the company uses to pursue its advertising and marketing objectives. Definitions of the four major promotion tools follow:

◆ **Advertising:** Any paid form of nonpersonal presentation and promotion of ideas, goods, or services by an identified sponsor.

◆ **Personal selling:** Personal presentation by the firm's sales force for the purpose of making sales and building customer relationships.

◆ **Sales promotion:** Short-term incentives to encourage the purchase or sale of a product or service.

◆ **Public relations:** Building good relations with the company's various publics by obtaining favorable publicity, building up a good "corporate image," and handling or heading off unfavorable rumors, stories, and events.[2]

Each category consists of specific tools. For example, advertising includes print, broadcast, outdoor, and other forms. Personal selling includes sales presentations, trade shows, and incentive programs. Sales promotion includes point-of-

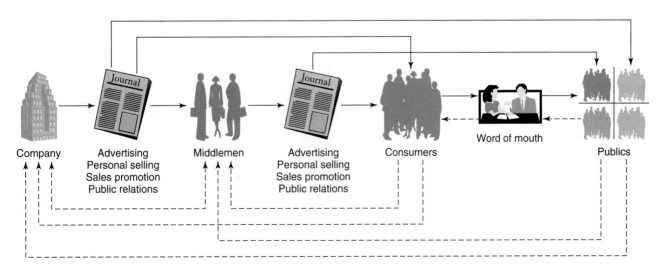

FIGURE 15-1 *The marketing communications system*

purchase displays, premiums, discounts, coupons, specialty advertising, and demonstrations. At the same time, communication goes beyond these specific promotion tools. The product's design, its price, the shape and color of its package, and the stores that sell it—*all* communicate something to buyers. Thus, although the promotion mix is the company's primary communication activity, the entire marketing mix—promotion *and* product, price, and place—must be coordinated for greatest communication impact.

In this chapter, we begin by examining two questions: First, *what are the major steps in developing effective marketing communication?* Second, *how should the promotion budget and mix be determined?* We then look at recent dramatic changes in marketing communications that have resulted from shifting marketing strategies and advances in computers and information technologies. Next, we review the fast-growing field of *direct marketing communications.* Finally, we summarize the legal, ethical, and social responsibility issues in marketing communications. In Chapter 16, we look at *mass-communication tools*—advertising, sales promotion, and public relations. Chapter 17 examines the *sales force* as a communication and promotion tool.

STEPS IN DEVELOPING EFFECTIVE COMMUNICATION

Marketers need to understand how communication works. Communication involves the nine elements shown in Figure 15-2. Two of these elements are the major parties in a communication—the *sender* and the *receiver*. Another two are the major communication tools—the *message* and the *media.* Four more are major communication functions—*encoding, decoding, response,* and *feedback.* The last element is *noise* in the system. Definitions of these elements follow and are applied to a McDonald's television ad:

◆ *Sender:* The *party sending the message* to another party—McDonald's.

◆ *Encoding:* The process of *putting thought into symbolic form*—McDonald's advertising agency assembles words and illustrations into an advertisement that will convey the intended message.

◆ *Message:* The *set of symbols* that the sender transmits—the actual McDonald's advertisement.

◆ *Media:* The *communication channels* through which the message moves from sender to receiver—in this case, television and the specific television programs McDonald's selects.

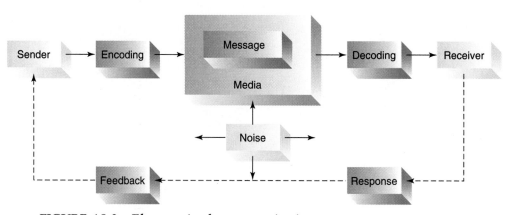

FIGURE 15-2 *Elements in the communication process*

◆ *Decoding:* The process by which the receiver *assigns meaning to the symbols* encoded by the sender—a consumer watches the McDonald's ad and interprets the words and illustrations it contains.

◆ *Receiver:* The *party receiving the message* sent by another party—the consumer who watches the McDonald's ad.

◆ *Response:* The *reactions of the receiver* after being exposed to the message—any of hundreds of possible responses, such as the consumer likes McDonald's better, is more likely to eat at McDonald's next time he or she eats fast food, or does nothing.

◆ *Feedback:* The part of the *receiver's response communicated back to the sender*—McDonald's research shows that consumers like and remember the ad, or consumers write or call McDonald's praising or criticizing the ad or McDonald's products.

◆ *Noise:* The *unplanned static or distortion* during the communication process, which results in the receiver's getting a different message than the one the sender sent—the consumer has poor TV reception or is distracted by family members while watching the ad.

This model points out several key factors in good communication. Senders need to know what audiences they wish to reach and what responses they want. They must be good at encoding messages that take into account how the target audience decodes them. They must send messages through media that reach target audiences, and they must develop feedback channels so that they can assess the audience's response to the message.

Thus, the marketing communicator must do the following: identify the target audience; determine the response sought; choose a message; choose the media through which to send the message; select the message source; and collect feedback.

IDENTIFYING THE TARGET AUDIENCE

A marketing communicator starts with a clear target audience in mind. The audience may be potential buyers or current users, those who make the buying decision or those who influence it. The audience may be individuals, groups, special publics, or the general public. The target audience will heavily affect the communicator's decisions on *what* will be said, *how* it will be said, *when* it will be said, *where* it will be said, and *who* will say it.

DETERMINING THE RESPONSE SOUGHT

Buyer-readiness stages
The stages consumers normally pass through on their way to purchase, including awareness, knowledge, liking, preference, conviction, and purchase.

Once the target audience has been defined, the marketing communicator must decide what response is sought. Of course, in most cases, the final response is *purchase*. But purchase is the result of a long process of consumer decision making. The target audience may be in any of six **buyer-readiness stages**, the stages consumers normally pass through on their way to making a purchase. The marketing communicator needs to know where the target audience now stands and to what stage it needs to be moved. These stages include *awareness, knowledge, liking, preference, conviction,* or *purchase* (see Figure 15-3).

The marketing communicator's target market may be totally unaware of the product, know only its name, or know one or a few things about it. The communicator must first build *awareness* and *knowledge*. For example, when Nissan introduced its Infiniti automobile line, it began with an extensive "teaser" advertising campaign to create name familiarity. Initial ads for the Infiniti created curiosity and awareness by showing the car's name but not the car. Later ads created

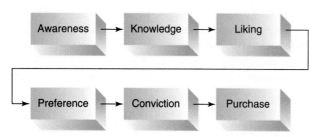

FIGURE 15-3 *Buyer-readiness stages*

knowledge by informing potential buyers of the car's high quality and many innovative features.

Assuming target consumers *know* the product, how do they *feel* about it? Once potential buyers know about the Infiniti, Nissan's marketers want to move them through successively stronger stages of feelings toward the car. These stages include *liking* (feeling favorable about the Infiniti), *preference* (preferring Infiniti to other car brands), and *conviction* (believing that Infiniti is the best car for them). Infiniti marketers can use a combination of the promotion mix tools to create positive feelings and conviction. Advertising extols the Infiniti's advantages over competing brands. Press releases and other public relations activities stress the car's innovative features and performance. Dealer salespeople tell buyers about options, value for the price, and after-sale service.

Finally, some members of the target market might be convinced about the product, but not quite get around to making the *purchase*. Potential Infiniti buyers may decide to wait for more information, or for the economy to improve. The communicator must lead these consumers to take the final step. Actions might include offering special promotional prices, rebates, or premiums. Salespeople might call or write to selected customers, inviting them to visit the dealership for a special showing.

Of course, marketing communications alone cannot create positive feelings and purchases for Infiniti. The car itself must provide superior value for the customer. In fact, outstanding marketing communications can actually speed the demise of a poor product. The more quickly potential buyers learn about the poor product, the more quickly they become aware of its faults. Thus, good marketing communication calls for "good deeds followed by good words."

In discussing buyer readiness states, we have assumed that buyers pass through cognitive (awareness, knowledge); affective (liking, preference, conviction); and behavioral (purchase) stages, in that order. This "learn-feel-do" sequence is appropriate when buyers have high involvement with a product category and perceive brands in the category to be highly differentiated, as is the case when they purchase a product such as an automobile. But consumers often follow other sequences. For example, they might follow a "do-feel-learn" sequence for high-involvement products with little perceived differentiation, such as aluminum siding. Still a third sequence is the "learn-do-feel," where consumers have low involvement and perceive little differentiation, as is the case when they buy a product such as salt. By understanding consumers' buying stages and their sequence, the marketer can do a better job of planning communications.

CHOOSING A MESSAGE

Having defined the desired audience response, the communicator turns to developing an effective message. Ideally, the message should get *Attention*, hold *Interest*, arouse *Desire*, and obtain *Action* (a framework known as the *AIDA model*). In practice, few messages take the consumer all the way from awareness to purchase, but the AIDA framework suggests the qualities of a good message.

In putting the message together, the marketing communicator must solve three problems: what to say (*message content*), how to say it logically (*message structure*), and how to say it symbolically (*message format*).

Message Content

The communicator has to figure out an appeal or theme that will produce the desired response. There are three types of appeals: rational, emotional, and moral.

Rational appeals
Message appeals that relate to the audience's self-interest and show that the product will produce the claimed benefits; examples include appeals of product quality, economy, value, or performance.

Emotional appeals
Message appeals that attempt to stir up negative or positive emotions that will motivate purchase; examples include fear, guilt, shame, love, humor, pride, and joy appeals.

Moral appeals
Advertising messages directed to the audience's sense of what is "right" or "proper."

Rational appeals relate to the audience's self-interest. They show that the product will produce the desired benefits. Examples are messages showing a product's quality, economy, value, or performance. Thus, in its ads, Mercedes offers automobiles that are "engineered like no other car in the world," stressing engineering design, performance, and safety. When pitching computer systems to business users, IBM salespeople talk about quality, value, improved productivity, and service.

Emotional appeals attempt to stir up either negative or positive emotions that can motivate purchase. These include fear, guilt, and shame appeals that get people to do things they should (brush their teeth, buy new tires), or to stop doing things they shouldn't (smoke, drink too much, eat fatty foods). For example, a Crest ad invokes mild fear when it claims, "There are some things you just can't afford to gamble with" (cavities). So does a Michelin tire ad that features cute babies and suggests, "Because so much is riding on your tires."[3] Communicators also use positive emotional appeals such as love, humor, pride, and joy. Thus, AT&T's long-running ad theme, "Reach out and touch someone," arouses strong, positive emotions.

Moral appeals are directed to the audience's sense of what is "right" and "proper." They often are used to urge people to support social causes such as a cleaner environment, better race relations, equal rights for women, and aid to the needy. An example of a moral appeal is the March of Dimes appeal: "God made you whole. Give to help those He didn't."

Message Structure

The communicator also must decide how to handle three message-structure issues. The first is whether to draw a conclusion or leave it to the audience. Early research showed that drawing a conclusion was usually more effective. More recent research, however, suggests that in many cases the advertiser is better off asking questions and letting buyers come to their own conclusions. The second message-structure issue is whether to present a one-sided argument (mentioning only the product's strengths), or a two-sided argument (touting the product's strengths while also admitting its shortcomings). Usually, a one-sided argument is more effective in sales presentations—except when audiences are highly educated, negatively disposed, or likely to hear opposing claims. In these cases, two-sided messages can enhance the advertiser's credibility and make buyers more resistant to competitor attacks. The third message-structure issue is whether to present the strongest arguments first or last. Presenting them first gets strong attention, but may lead to an anticlimactic ending.[4]

A mild fear appeal: "When you get a cavity, there's no second chance."

Message Format

The marketing communicator also needs a strong *format* for the message. In a print ad, the communicator has to decide on the headline, copy, illustration, and color. To attract attention, advertisers can use novelty and contrast; eye-catching pictures and headlines; distinctive formats; message size and position; and color, shape, and movement. If the message is to be carried over the radio, the communicator has to choose words, sounds, and voices. The "sound" of an announcer promoting banking services should be different from one promoting quality furniture.

To capture attention and communicate persuasively, advertisers often use eye-catching pictures and headlines, novelty and contrast. This General Motors ad ran in Seventeen *magazine.*

If the message is to be carried on television or in person, then all these elements plus body language have to be planned. Presenters plan their facial expressions, gestures, dress, posture, and hair style. If the message is carried on the product or its package, the communicator has to watch texture, scent, color, size, and shape. For example, color plays a major communication role in food preferences. When consumers sampled four cups of coffee that had been placed next to brown, blue, red, and yellow containers (all the coffee was identical, but the consumers did not know this), 75 percent felt that the coffee next to the brown container tasted too strong; nearly 85 percent judged the coffee next to the red container to be the richest; nearly everyone felt that the coffee next to the blue container was mild; and the coffee next to the yellow container was seen as weak. Thus, if a coffee company wants to communicate that its coffee is rich, it should probably use a red container along with label copy boasting the coffee's rich taste.

CHOOSING MEDIA

The communicator now must select *channels of communication*. There are two broad types of communication channels—*personal* and *nonpersonal*.

Personal Communication Channels

Personal communication channels
Channels through which two or more people communicate directly with each other, including face to face, person to audience, over the telephone, or through the mail.

In **personal communication channels,** two or more people communicate directly with each other. They might communicate face to face, over the telephone, or even through the mail. Personal communication channels are effective because they allow for personal addressing and feedback.

Some personal communication channels are controlled directly by the company. For example, company salespeople contact buyers in the target market. But other personal communications about the product may reach buyers through channels not directly controlled by the company. These might include independent experts—consumer advocates, consumer buying guides, and others—making statements to target buyers. Or they might be neighbors, friends, family members, and associates talking to target buyers. This last channel, known as **word-of-mouth influence,** has considerable effect in many product areas.

Word-of-mouth influence
Personal communication about a product between target buyers and neighbors, friends, family members, and associates.

Personal influence carries great weight for products that are expensive, risky, or highly visible. For example, buyers of automobiles and major appliances often go beyond mass-media sources to seek the opinions of knowledgeable people.

Companies can take several steps to put personal communication channels to work for them. They can devote extra effort to selling their products to well-known people or companies, who may in turn influence others to buy. They can create *opinion leaders*—people whose opinions are sought by others—by supplying certain people with the product on attractive terms. For example, companies can work through community members such as local radio personalities, class presidents, and heads of local organizations. And they can use influential people in their advertisements or develop advertising that has high "conversation value." Finally, the firm can attempt to manage word-of-mouth communications by finding out what consumers are saying to others, by taking appropriate actions to satisfy consumers and correct problems, and by helping consumers seek information about the firm and its products.[5]

Nonpersonal Communication Channels

Nonpersonal communication
channels
Media that carry messages without personal contact or feedback, including major media, atmospheres, and events.

Nonpersonal communication channels are media that carry messages without personal contact or feedback. They include major media, atmospheres, and events. Major *media* include print media (newspapers, magazines, direct mail); broadcast media (radio, television); and display media (billboards, signs, posters). *Atmospheres* are designed environments that create or reinforce the buyer's leanings toward buying a product. Thus, lawyers' offices and banks are designed to communicate confidence and other qualities that might be valued by their clients. *Events* are staged occurrences that communicate messages to target audiences. For example, public relations departments arrange press conferences, grand openings, shows and exhibits, public tours, and other events.

Celebrities impart some of their own likability and trustworthiness to the products they endorse. Here, Shaquille O'Neill speaks powerfully for Pepsi.

Nonpersonal communication affects buyers directly. In addition, using mass media often affects buyers indirectly by causing more personal communication. Communications first flow from television, magazines, and other mass media to opinion leaders and then from these opinion leaders to others. Thus, opinion leaders step between the mass media and their audiences and carry messages to people who are less exposed to media. This suggests that mass communicators should aim their messages directly at opinion leaders, letting them carry the message to others.

BETTER GET YOURS BEFORE SHAQ GETS IT ALL.

BE YOUNG
HAVE FUN
DRINK PEPS

SELECTING THE MESSAGE SOURCE

The message's impact on the audience also is affected by how the audience views the sender. Messages delivered by highly credible sources are more persuasive. For example, pharmaceutical companies want doctors to tell about their products' benefits because doctors are very credible figures. Many food companies now are promoting to doctors, dentists, and other health-care providers to motivate these professionals to recommend their products to patients (see Marketing Highlight 15-1). Marketers also hire well-known actors, athletes, and even cartoon characters to deliver their messages. Basketball star Michael Jordan speaks for Gatorade, McDonald's, and Nike, and giant Shaquille O'Neal towers for Pepsi. Fred Flintstone teams with TV weatherman Willard Scott to pitch for Days Inns.

What factors make a source credible? The three factors most often found are expertise, trustworthiness, and likabil-

PROMOTING PRODUCTS THROUGH DOCTORS AND OTHER PROFESSIONALS

Food marketers are discovering that the best way to a consumer's stomach may be through a doctor's recommendation. Today's more nutrition-conscious consumers often seek advice from doctors and other health-care professionals about which products are best for them. Kellogg, Procter & Gamble, Quaker, and other large food companies are increasingly recognizing what pharmaceutical companies have known for years—professional recommendations can strongly influence consumer buying decisions. So they are stepping up promotion to doctors, dentists, and others, hoping to inform them about product benefits and motivate them to recommend the promoted brands to their patients.

Doctors receive the most attention from food marketers. For example, Cumberland Packing runs ads in medical journals for its Sweet 'N Low sugar substitute, saying, "It's one thing you can do to make your patient's diet a little easier to swallow." And Kellogg launched its "Project Nutrition" promotion to sell doctors on the merits of eating high-fiber cereal breakfasts. The promotion consists of cholesterol screenings of 100,000 Americans around the country, ads targeting doctors in the *Journal of the American Medical Association* and the *New England Journal of Medicine*, and a new quarterly newsletter called *Health Vantage* mailed to 50,000 U.S. medical professionals. Similarly, Quaker sends out to doctors nationwide a quarterly newsletter, *Fiber Report*, which includes articles, research reports, and feature stories about the importance of fiber in diets.

Procter & Gamble provides literature about several of its products that doctors can pass along to patients. And P&G actively seeks medical endorsements. Years ago, a heavily promoted American Dental Association endorsement helped make P&G's Crest the leading brand of toothpaste. The recent Crest Guarantee offer continues this tradition. In this program, a Crest user first visits the dentist, who rates the patient's dental condition and returns an enrollment card to P&G. The buyer then uses Crest for six months and once

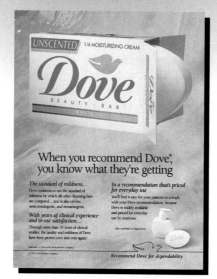

Promoting through professionals: Lever promotes its Dove soap to doctors— "Recommend Dove for dependability."

again visits the dentist, who verifies the visit. If the user (or the user's parent) isn't satisfied with the results of the second visit, P&G will refund six months' worth of Crest purchases, up to $15. Clearly, this program is designed to build loyalty among both customers *and* dentists.

P&G isn't the only marketer targeting dentists. The makers of Trident gum, Equal sugar substitute, Plax mouth rinse, and dozens of other products reach dentists through colorful brochures, samples, and ads in dental journals. As part of its Wrigley Dental Programs, Wrigley advertises Extra sugar-free gum to dentists as a preventive dentistry tool for their patients. Other professionals targeted by food companies include veterinarians, teachers, and even high school coaches. Quaker does extensive product sampling of its Gaines and Ken-L Ration pet foods through veterinarians. It also runs ads for Gatorade in magazines read by high school sports trainers and coaches, and sponsors a fleet of vans that comb the country, offering Gatorade information and samples in key markets. Thus, food companies actively court as spokespeople any professionals who provide health or nutrition advice to their customers.

Many doctors and other health-care providers welcome the promotions as good sources of information about healthy foods and nutrition that can help them give better advice to their patients. Others, however, do not feel comfortable recommending specific food brands; some even resent attempts to influence them through promotion. Although it may take a lot of time and investment to get these professionals to change their habits, the results probably will justify the effort and expense. If a company can convince key health-care providers that the product is worthy of endorsement, it will gain powerful marketing allies. As one marketer puts it, "If a doctor hands you a product to use, that recommendation carries a lot of weight."

Sources: See Laurie Freeman and Julie Liesse Erickson, "Doctored Strategy: Food Marketers Push Products Through Physicians," *Advertising Age,* March 28, 1988, p. 12; and Jennifer Lawrence, "P&G Polishes Guarantee for Crest," *Advertising Age,* September 1, 1992, pp. 1, 34.

ity. *Expertise* is the degree to which the communicator has the authority to back the claim. Doctors, scientists, and professors rank high on expertise in their fields. *Trustworthiness* is related to how objective and honest the source appears to be. Friends, for example, are more trusted than salespeople. *Likability* is how attractive the source is to the audience; people like open, humorous, and natural sources. Not surprisingly, the most highly credible source is a person who scores high on all three factors.

COLLECTING FEEDBACK

After sending the message, the communicator must research its effect on the target audience. This involves asking the target audience members whether they remember the message, how many times they saw it, what points they recall, how they felt about the message, and their past and present attitudes toward the product and company. The communicator also would like to measure behavior resulting from the message—how many people bought a product, talked to others about it, or visited the store.

Feedback on marketing communications may suggest changes in the promotion program or in the product offer itself. For example, when the new Boston Chicken restaurant chain enters new market areas, it uses television advertising and coupons in newspaper inserts to inform area consumers about the restaurant and to lure them in. Suppose feedback research shows that 80 percent of all consumers in an area recall seeing Boston Chicken ads and are aware of what the restaurant offers. Sixty percent of those aware of it have eaten at the restaurant, but only 20 percent of those who tried it were satisfied. These results suggest that although the promotion program is creating *awareness,* the restaurant isn't giving consumers the *satisfaction* they expect. Therefore, Boston Chicken needs to improve its food or service while staying with the successful communication program. In contrast, suppose the feedback research shows that only 40 percent of area consumers are aware of the restaurant, that only 30 percent of those aware of it have tried it, but 80 percent of those who have tried it return. In this case, Boston Chicken needs to strengthen its promotion program to take advantage of the restaurant's power to create customer satisfaction.

SETTING THE TOTAL PROMOTION BUDGET AND MIX

We have looked at the steps in planning and sending communications to a target audience. But how does the company decide on the total *promotion budget* and its division among the major promotional tools to create the *promotion mix?* We now look at these questions.

SETTING THE TOTAL PROMOTION BUDGET

One of the hardest marketing decisions facing a company is how much to spend on promotion. John Wanamaker, the department store magnate, once said: "I know that half of my advertising is wasted, but I don't know which half. I spent $2 million for advertising, and I don't know if that is half enough or twice too much." Thus, it is not surprising that industries and companies vary widely in how much they spend on promotion. Promotion spending may be 20 to 30 percent of sales in the cosmetics industry and only 2 or 3 percent in the industrial machinery industry. Within a given industry, both low and high spenders can be found.

How does a company decide on its promotion budget? We look at four common methods used to set the total budget for advertising: the *affordable method,* the *percentage-of-sales method,* the *competitive-parity method,* and the *objective-and-task method.*[6]

Affordable method
Setting the promotion budget at the level management thinks the company can afford.

Affordable Method

Some companies use the **affordable method:** They set the promotion budget at the level they think the company can afford. Small businesses often use this method, reasoning that the company cannot spend more on advertising than it has. They start with total revenues, deduct operating expenses and capital outlays, and then devote some portion of the remaining funds to advertising.

Unfortunately, this method of setting budgets completely ignores the effects of promotion on sales. It tends to place advertising last among spending priorities, even in situations where advertising is critical to the firm's success. It leads to an uncertain annual promotion budget, which makes long-range market planning difficult. Although the affordable method can result in overspending on advertising, it more often results in underspending.

Percentage-of-Sales Method

Percentage-of-sales method
Setting the promotion budget at a certain percentage of current or forecasted sales or as a percentage of the sales price.

Other companies use the **percentage-of-sales method,** setting their promotion budget at a certain percentage of current or forecasted sales. Or they budget a percentage of the unit sales price. The percentage-of-sales method has a number of advantages. First, using this method means that promotion spending is likely to vary with what the company can "afford." It also helps management think about the relationship between promotion spending, selling price, and profit per unit. Finally, this method supposedly creates competitive stability because competing firms tend to spend about the same percent of their sales on promotion.

Despite these claimed advantages, however, the percentage-of-sales method has little to justify it. It wrongly views sales as the *cause* of promotion rather than as the *result.* The budget is based on availability of funds rather than on opportunities. It may prevent the increased spending sometimes needed to turn around falling sales. Because the budget varies with year-to-year sales, long-range planning is difficult. Finally, the method does not provide any basis for choosing a *specific* percentage, except what has been done in the past or what competitors are doing.

Competitive-Parity Method

Competitive-parity method
Setting the promotion budget to match competitors' outlays.

Still other companies use the **competitive-parity method,** setting their promotion budgets to match competitors' outlays. They monitor competitors' advertising or get industry promotion-spending estimates from publications or trade associations, and then set their budgets based on the industry average.

Two arguments support this method. First, competitors' budgets represent the collective wisdom of the industry. Second, spending what competitors spend helps prevent promotion wars. Unfortunately, neither argument is valid. There are no grounds for believing that the competition has a better idea of what a company should be spending on promotion than does the company itself. Companies differ greatly, and each has its own special promotion needs. Finally, there is no evidence that budgets based on competitive parity prevent promotion wars.

Objective-and-Task Method

Objective-and-task method
Developing the promotion budget by (1) defining specific objectives; (2) determining the tasks that must be performed to achieve these objectives; and (3) estimating the costs of performing these tasks. The sum of these costs is the proposed promotion budget.

The most logical budget setting method is the **objective-and-task method,** whereby the company sets its promotion budget based on what it wants to accomplish with promotion. This budgeting method entails (1) defining specific promotion objectives, (2) determining the tasks needed to achieve these objectives, and (3) estimating the costs of performing these tasks. The sum of these costs is the proposed promotion budget.

The objective-and-task method forces management to spell out its assumptions about the relationship between dollars spent and promotion results. But it is also the most difficult method to use. Often, it is hard to figure out which specific tasks will achieve specific objectives. For example, suppose Sony wants 95 percent awareness for its latest camcorder model during the six-month introductory period. What specific advertising messages and media schedules should Sony use to attain this objective? How much would these messages and media schedules cost? Sony management must consider such questions, even though they are hard to answer.

SETTING THE PROMOTION MIX

The company now must divide the total promotion budget among the major promotion tools—advertising, personal selling, sales promotion, and public relations. It must blend the promotion tools carefully into a coordinated *promotion mix*. Companies within the same industry differ greatly in the design of their promotion mixes. For example, Avon spends most of its promotion funds on personal selling and direct marketing, whereas Helene Curtis Industries spends heavily on consumer advertising. Electrolux sells most of its vacuum cleaners door to door, whereas Hoover relies more on advertising and promotion to retailers. We now look at the many factors that influence the marketer's choice of promotion tools.

The Nature of Each Promotion Tool

Each promotion tool—*advertising, personal selling, sales promotion,* and *public relations*—has unique characteristics and costs. Marketers have to understand these characteristics in selecting their tools.

ADVERTISING. The many forms of advertising contribute uniquely to the overall promotion mix. Advertising can reach masses of geographically dispersed buyers at a low cost per exposure. It enables the seller to repeat a message many times, and it lets the buyer receive and compare the messages of various competitors. Because of advertising's public nature, consumers tend to view advertised products as standard and legitimate—buyers know that purchasing advertised products will be understood and accepted publicly. Large-scale advertising says something positive about the seller's size, popularity, and success.

Advertising is also very expressive—it allows the company to dramatize its products through the artful use of visuals, print, sound, and color. On the one hand, advertising can be used to build up a long-term image for a product (such as Coca-Cola ads). On the other hand, advertising can trigger quick sales (as when Sears advertises a weekend sale).

Advertising also has some shortcomings. Although it reaches many people quickly, advertising is impersonal and cannot be as persuasive as company salespeople. For the most part, advertising can carry on only a one-way communication with the audience, and the audience does not feel that it has to pay attention or respond. In addition, advertising can be very costly. Although some advertising forms, such as newspaper and radio advertising, can be done on small budgets, other forms, such as network TV advertising, require very large budgets.

PERSONAL SELLING. Personal selling is the most effective tool at certain stages of the buying process, particularly in building up buyers' preferences, convictions, and actions. Compared to advertising, personal selling has several unique qualities. It involves personal interaction between two or more people, so each person can observe the other's needs and characteristics and make quick adjustments. Personal selling also allows all kinds of relationships to spring up, ranging from a matter-of-fact selling relationship to a deep personal friendship. The effective salesperson keeps the customer's interests at heart in order to build a long-term relationship. Finally, with personal selling the buyer usually feels a greater need to listen and respond, even if the response is a polite "no thank you."

These unique qualities come at a cost, however. A sales force requires a longer-term commitment than does advertising—advertising can be turned on and off, but sales force size is harder to change. Personal selling is also the company's most expensive promotion tool, costing industrial companies an average of over

$200 per sales call.[7] U.S. firms spend up to three times as much on personal selling as they do on advertising.

SALES PROMOTION. Sales promotion includes a wide assortment of tools—coupons, contests, cents-off deals, premiums, and others—all of which have many unique qualities. They attract consumer attention and provide information that may lead to a purchase. They offer strong incentives to purchase by providing inducements or contributions that give additional value to consumers. And sales promotions invite and reward quick response. Whereas advertising says "buy our product," sales promotion says "buy it now."

Companies use sales-promotion tools to create a stronger and quicker response. Sales promotion can be used to dramatize product offers and to boost sagging sales. Sales promotion effects are usually short-lived, however, and are not effective in building long-run brand preference.

PUBLIC RELATIONS. Public relations offers several unique qualities. It is very believable—news stories, features, and events seem more real and believable to readers than ads do. Public relations also can reach many prospects who avoid salespeople and advertisements—the message gets to the buyers as "news" rather than as a sales-directed communication. And, like advertising, public relations can dramatize a company or product.

Marketers tend to underuse public relations or to use it as an afterthought. Yet a well thought out public relations campaign used with other promotion mix elements can be very effective and economical.

Factors in Setting the Promotion Mix

Companies consider many factors when developing their promotion mixes, including type of product/market, the use of a push or pull strategy, the buyer readiness stage, and the product life-cycle stage.

TYPE OF PRODUCT/MARKET. The importance of different promotion tools varies between consumer and business markets (see Figure 15-4). Consumer goods companies usually put more of their funds into advertising, followed by sales promotion, personal selling, and then public relations. In contrast, industrial goods companies put most of their funds into personal selling, followed by sales promotion, advertising, and public relations. In general, personal selling is used more heavily with expensive and risky goods and in markets with fewer and larger sellers.

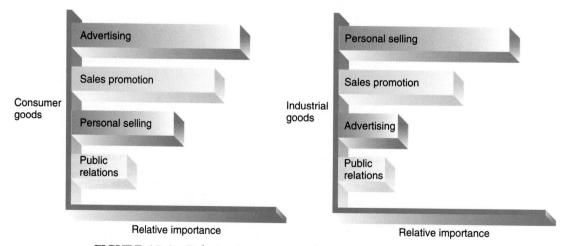

FIGURE 15-4 *Relative importance of promotion tools in consumer versus industrial markets*

Although advertising is less important than sales calls in business markets, it still plays an important role. Business-to-business advertising can build product awareness and knowledge, develop sales leads, and reassure buyers. Similarly, personal selling can add a lot to consumer goods marketing efforts. It is simply not the case that "salespeople put products on shelves and advertising takes them off." Well-trained consumer goods salespeople can sign up more dealers to carry a particular brand, convince them to give the brand more shelf space, and urge them to use special displays and promotions.

PUSH VERSUS PULL STRATEGY. The promotional mix is affected heavily by whether the company chooses a *push* or *pull* strategy. Figure 15-5 contrasts the two strategies. A **push strategy** involves "pushing" the product through distribution channels to final consumers. The producer directs its marketing activities (primarily personal selling and trade promotion) toward channel members to induce them to carry the product and to promote it to final consumers. Using a **pull strategy**, the producer directs its marketing activities (primarily advertising and consumer promotion) toward final consumers to induce them to buy the product. If the pull strategy is effective, consumers then will demand the product from channel members, who will in turn demand it from producers. Thus, under a pull strategy, consumer demand "pulls" the product through the channels.

Some small industrial goods companies use only push strategies; some direct-marketing companies use only pull. Most large companies use some combination of both. For example, RJR/Nabisco uses mass-media advertising to pull its products, and a large sales force and trade promotions to push its products through the channels. In recent years, consumer goods companies have been decreasing the pull portions of their promotion mixes in favor of more push (see Marketing Highlight 15-2).

BUYER READINESS STAGE. The effects of the promotional tools vary for the different buyer readiness stages. Advertising, along with public relations, plays the major role in the awareness and knowledge stages, more important than that played by "cold calls" from salespeople. Customer liking, preference, and conviction are more affected by personal selling, which is closely followed by advertising. Finally, closing the sale is mostly done with sales calls and sales promotion. Clearly, personal selling, given its high costs, should focus on the later stages of the customer buying process.

Push strategy
A promotion strategy that calls for using the sales force and trade promotion to push the product through channels. The producer promotes the product to wholesalers, the wholesalers promote to retailers, and the retailers promote to consumers.

Pull strategy
A promotion strategy that calls for spending a lot on advertising and consumer promotion to build up consumer demand. If the strategy is successful, consumers will ask their retailers for the product, the retailers will ask the wholesalers, and the wholesalers will ask the producers.

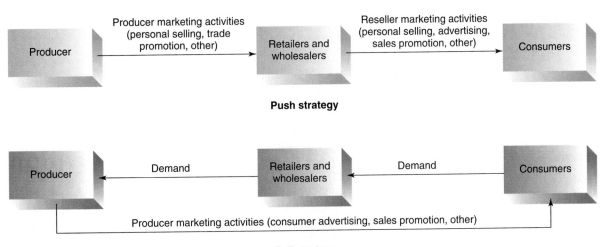

FIGURE 15-5 *Push versus pull promotion strategy*

ARE CONSUMER GOODS COMPANIES GETTING TOO "PUSHY"?

Consumer packaged-goods companies like Kraft/General Foods, Procter & Gamble, RJR/Nabisco, Campbell, and Gillette grew into giants by using mostly pull promotion strategies. They used massive doses of national advertising to differentiate their products, build market share, and maintain customer loyalty. But during the past two decades, these companies have gotten more "pushy," deemphasizing national advertising and putting more of their promotion budgets into personal selling and sales promotions. Trade promotions (trade allowances, displays, cooperative advertising) now account for about 47 percent of total consumer product company marketing spending; consumer promotions (coupons, cents-off deals, premiums) account for another 28 percent. That leaves only 25 percent of total marketing spending for media advertising, down from 42 percent just 15 years ago.

Why have these companies shifted so heavily toward push strategies? One reason is that mass-media campaigns have become more expensive and less effective in recent years. Network television costs have risen sharply while audiences have fallen off, making national advertising less cost effective. Companies also have increased their market segmentation efforts and are tailoring their marketing programs more narrowly, making national advertising less suitable than localized retailer promotions. And in these days of brand extensions and me-too products, companies sometimes have trouble finding meaningful product differences to feature in advertising. So they have differentiated their products through price reductions, premium offers, coupons, and other push techniques.

Another factor speeding the shift from pull to push has been the greater strength of retailers. Today's retailers are larger and have more access to product sales and profit information. They now have the power to demand and get what they want—and what they want is more push. Whereas national advertising bypasses them on its way to the masses, push promotion benefits them directly. Consumer promotions give retailers an immediate sales boost, and cash from trade allowances pads retailer profits. Thus, producers often must use push just to obtain good shelf space and advertising support from important retailers.

However, many marketers are concerned that the reckless use of push will lead to fierce price competition and a never-ending spiral of price slashing and deal making. This situation would mean lower margins, and companies would have less money to invest in the research and development, packaging, and advertising needed to improve products and maintain long-run consumer preference and loyalty. If used improperly, push promotion can mortgage a brand's future for short-term gains. Sales promotion buys short-run reseller support and consumer sales, but advertising builds long-run brand value and consumer preference. By robbing the advertising budget to pay for more sales promotion, companies might win the battle for short-run earnings but lose the war for long-run consumer loyalty and market share.

Thus, many consumer companies now are rethinking their promotion strategies and reversing the trend by shifting their promotion budgets back slightly toward advertising. Push strategies remain very important. In packaged-goods marketing, short-run success often depends more on retailer support than on the producer's advertising. But many companies have realized that it's not a question of sales promotion versus advertising, or of push versus pull. Success lies in finding the best mix of the two: consistent advertising to build long-run brand value and consumer preference, and sales promotion to create short-run trade support and consumer excitement. The company needs to blend both push and pull elements into an integrated promotion program that meets immediate consumer and retailer needs as well as long-run strategic needs.

Sources: James C. Schroer, "Ad Spending: Growing Marketing Share," *Harvard Business Review,* January–February 1990, pp. 44–48; John Philip Jones, "The Double Jeopardy of Sales Promotions," *Harvard Business Review,* September–October 1990, pp. 145–152; Zachary Schiller, "Not Everyone Loves a Supermarket Special," *Business Week,* February 17, 1992, pp. 64–68; Lois Therrien, "Brands on the Run," *Business Week,* April 19, 1993, pp. 26–29; and *16th Annual Survey of Promotional Practices,* Donnelly Marketing Inc., Oakbrook Terrace, IL, June 1994, p. 9.

PRODUCT LIFE-CYCLE STAGE. The effects of different promotion tools also vary with stages of the product life cycle. In the introduction stage, advertising and public relations are good for producing high awareness, and sales promotion is useful in promoting early trial. Personal selling must be used to get the trade to carry the product. In the growth stage, advertising and public relations continue to be powerful influences, whereas sales promotion can be reduced because fewer incentives are needed. In the mature stage, sales promotion again becomes important relative to advertising. Buyers know the brands, and advertising is needed only to remind them of the product. In the decline stage, advertising is kept at a reminder level, public relations is dropped, and salespeople give the product only a little attention. Sales promotion, however, might continue strong.

THE CHANGING FACE OF MARKETING COMMUNICATIONS

During the past several decades, companies around the world have perfected the art of mass marketing—selling highly standardized products to masses of customers. In the process, they have developed effective mass media advertising techniques to support their mass marketing strategies. These companies routinely invest millions of dollars in the mass media, reaching tens of millions of customers with a single ad. However, as we move toward the twenty-first century, marketing managers are facing some new marketing communications realities.

THE CHANGING COMMUNICATIONS ENVIRONMENT

Two major factors are changing the face of today's marketing communications. First, as mass markets have fragmented, marketers are shifting away from mass marketing. More and more, they are developing focused marketing programs designed to build closer relationships with customers in more narrowly defined micromarkets. Second, vast improvements in computer and information technology are speeding the movement toward segmented marketing. Today's information technology helps marketers to keep closer track of customer needs—more information about consumers at the individual and household levels is available than ever before. New technologies also provide new communications avenues for reaching smaller customer segments with more tailored messages.

The shift from mass marketing to segmented marketing has had a dramatic impact on marketing communications. Just as mass marketing gave rise to a new generation of mass media communications, the shift toward one-on-one marketing is spawning a new generation of more specialized and highly targeted communications efforts.[8]

Given this new communications environment, marketers must rethink the roles of various media and promotion mix tools. Mass media advertising has long dominated the promotion mixes of consumer product companies. However,

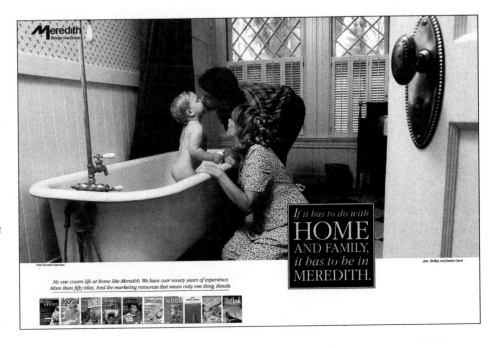

Thousands of specialized magazines match today's targeting strategies. Meredith Corporation alone publishes more than 50 magazines targeting home and family, including Better Homes and Gardens, Ladies' Home Journal, *and* Country Home.

although television, magazines, and other mass media remain very important, their dominance is now declining. *Market* fragmentation has resulted in *media* fragmentation—in an explosion of more focused media that better match today's targeting strategies. For example, in 1960, by purchasing commercial time on the three major television networks, an advertiser could reach 90 percent of the U.S. population during an average week. Today, that number has fallen to less than 60 percent, as cable television systems now offer advertisers dozens or even hundreds of alternative channels that reach smaller, specialized audiences. Similarly, the relatively few mass magazines of the 1940s and 1950s—*Look, Life, Saturday Evening Post*—have been replaced by more than 11,000 special-interest magazines reaching smaller, more focused audiences. And, beyond these channels, advertisers are making increased use of new, highly targeted media, ranging from video screens on supermarket shopping carts to on-line computer services and CD-ROM catalogs.

More generally, advertising appears to be giving way to other elements of the promotion mix. In the glory days of mass marketing, consumer product companies spent a lion's share of their promotion budgets on mass media advertising. Today, media advertising captures only about 25 percent of total promotion spending.[9] The rest goes to various sales promotion activities, which can be focused more effectively on individual consumer and trade segments. In all, companies are doing less *broadcasting* and more *narrowcasting*. They are using a richer variety of focused communication tools in an effort to reach their many and diverse target markets. Some observers envision a future in which today's advertising-supported mass media will be replaced almost entirely by one-on-one, interactive marketing media such as on-line computer services and two-way television.

GROWTH OF DIRECT MARKETING

The new face of marketing communications is most apparent in the rapidly growing field of direct marketing. Now the fastest growing form of marketing, direct marketing reflects the trend toward targeted or one-on-one marketing communications. As discussed in the previous chapter, **direct marketing** consists of direct communications with carefully targeted consumers to obtain an immediate response. Through direct marketing, sellers can closely match their marketing offers and communications to the needs of narrowly defined segments. All kinds of consumer and business-to-business marketers use direct marketing— producers, wholesalers, retailers, nonprofit organizations, and government agencies. Direct marketers employ a variety of communications tools. In addition to old favorites such as television, direct mail, and telephone marketing, direct marketers employ powerful new forms of telecommunications and computer-based media. These tools are often used in combinations that move the customer from initial awareness of an offer to purchase and aftersale service.

Forms of Direct Marketing Communication

The four major forms of direct marketing are *direct mail and catalog marketing, telemarketing, television marketing,* and *on-line shopping.*

DIRECT-MAIL AND CATALOG MARKETING. **Direct-mail marketing** involves mailings of letters, ads, samples, foldouts, and other "salespeople on wings" sent to prospects on mailing lists. The mailing lists are developed from customer lists or obtained from mailing-list houses that provide names of people fitting almost any description—the superwealthy, mobile-home owners, veterinarians, pet owners, or about anything else.

Direct mail is well suited to direct, one-on-one communication. Direct mail permits high target-market selectivity, can be personalized, is flexible, and allows easy measurement of results. Whereas the cost per thousand people reached is

Direct marketing
Marketing through various advertising media that interact directly with consumers, generally calling for the consumer to make a direct response.

Direct-mail marketing
Direct marketing through single mailings that include letters, ads, samples, foldouts, and other "salespeople on wings" sent to prospects on mailing lists.

Billions of catalogs are mailed out each year; the average household receives 50 catalogs annually.

Catalog marketing
Direct marketing through catalogs that are mailed to a select list of customers or made available in stores.

higher than with mass media such as television or magazines, the people who are reached are much better prospects. Direct mail has proved very successful in promoting books, magazine subscriptions, and insurance. Increasingly, it is being used to sell novelty and gift items, clothing, gourmet foods, and industrial products. Direct mail also is used heavily by charities, which raise billions of dollars each year and account for about 25 percent of all direct-mail revenues.

Catalog marketing involves selling through catalogs mailed to a select list of customers or made available in stores. Some huge general-merchandise retailers—such as JCPenney and Spiegel—sell a full line of merchandise through catalogs. But recently, the giants have been challenged by thousands of specialty catalogs that serve highly specialized market niches. As a result, Sears discontinued its 97-year-old annual "Big Book" catalog in 1993 after years of unprofitable operation.[10]

Over 14 billion copies of more than 8,500 different consumer catalogs are mailed out annually, and the average household receives some 50 catalogs a year. Consumers can buy just about anything from a catalog. Hanover House sends out 22 different catalogs selling everything from shoes to decorative lawn birds. Sharper Image sells $2,400 jet-propelled surf boards. The Banana Republic Travel and Safari Clothing Company features everything you would need to go hiking in the Sahara or the rain forest.

Recently, specialty department stores, such as Neiman Marcus, Bloomingdale's, and Saks Fifth Avenue, have begun sending catalogs to cultivate upper-middle-class markets for high-priced, often exotic, merchandise. Several major corporations also have developed or acquired mail-order divisions. For example, Avon now issues ten women's fashion catalogs along with catalogs for children's and men's clothes. And Walt Disney Company mails out over 6 million catalogs each year featuring videos, stuffed animals, and other Disney items.

Most consumers enjoy receiving catalogs and will sometimes even pay to get them. Many catalog marketers are now even selling their catalogs at book stores and magazine stands. Some companies, such as Royal Silk, Neiman Marcus, Sears, and Spiegel, are also experimenting with videotape, computer diskette, and CD-ROM catalogs. Royal Silk sells a 35-minute video catalog to its customers for $5.95. The tape contains a polished presentation of Royal Silk products, tells customers how to care for silk, and provides ordering information. Soloflex uses a video brochure to help sell its $1,000 in-home exercise equipment. The 22-minute video shows an attractive couple demonstrating the exercises possible with the system. Soloflex claims that almost half of those who view the video brochure later place an order via telephone, compared with only a 10 percent response from those receiving regular direct mail.[11]

Many business-to-business marketers also rely heavily on catalogs. Whether in the form of a simple brochure, three-ring binder, or book, or encoded on a videotape or computer disk, catalogs remain one of today's hardest-working sales tools. For some companies, in fact, catalogs have even taken the place of salespeople. In all, companies mail out more than 1.1 *billion* business-to-business catalogs each year, reaping more than $50 billion worth of catalog sales.[12]

Telemarketing
Using the telephone to sell directly to consumers.

TELEMARKETING. Telemarketing—using the telephone to sell directly to consumers—has become the major direct-marketing communication tool. Marketers use *outbound* telephone marketing to sell directly to consumers and businesses. *Inbound* toll-free 800 numbers are used to receive orders from television and radio ads, direct mail, or catalogs. The average household receives 19 telephone sales calls each year and makes 16 calls to place orders. During 1990, AT&T logged more than 7 billion 800-number calls.[13]

Other marketers use 900 numbers to sell consumers information, entertainment, or the opportunity to voice an opinion. For example, for a charge, consumers can obtain weather forecasts from American Express (1-900-WEATHER—75 cents a minute); pet care information from Quaker Oats (1-900-990-PETS—95 cents a minute); advice on snoring and other sleep disorders from Somnus (1-900-USA-SLEEP—$2 for the first minute, then $1 a minute); or golf lessons from *Golf Digest* (1-900-454-3288—95 cents a minute). Altogether, the 900-number industry now generates $860 million in annual revenues.[14]

Business-to-business marketers use telemarketing extensively. In fact, more than $115 billion worth of industrial products were marketed by phone last year. For example, General Electric uses telemarketing to generate and qualify sales leads and to manage small accounts. Raleigh Bicycles uses telemarketing to reduce the amount of personal selling needed for contacting its dealers; in the first year, sales force travel costs were reduced 50 percent, and sales in a single quarter increased 34 percent.[15]

Most consumers appreciate many of the offers they receive by telephone. Properly designed and targeted telemarketing provides many benefits, including purchasing convenience and increased product and service information. However, the recent explosion in unsolicited telephone marketing has annoyed many consumers who object to the almost daily "junk phone calls" that pull them away from the dinner table or clog up their answering machines. Lawmakers around the country are responding with legislation ranging from banning unsolicited telemarketing calls during certain hours to letting households sign up for a national "Don't Call Me" list. Most telemarketers support some action against random and poorly targeted telemarketing. As a Direct Marketing Association executive notes, "We want to target people who want to be targeted."[16]

Television marketing
Direct marketing via television using direct-response advertising or home shopping channels.

TELEVISION MARKETING. Television marketing takes one of two major forms. The first is *direct-response advertising*. Direct marketers air television spots, often 60 or 120 seconds long, that persuasively describe a product and give customers a toll-free number for ordering. Television viewers often encounter 30-minute advertising programs, or *infomercials*—for a single product. Such direct-response advertising works well for magazines, books, small appliances, tapes and CDs, collectibles, and many other products.

Some successful direct-response ads run for years and become classics. For example, Dial Media's ads for Ginsu knives ran for seven years and sold almost 3 million sets of knives worth more than $40 million in sales; its Armourcote cookware ads generated more than twice that much. And the now-familiar 30-minute Psychic Friends infomercials have aired more than 12,000 times during the past two years, offering callers access to its national network of psychics and generating more than $100 million worth of business. For years, infomercials have been associated with somewhat questionable pitches for juicers, get-rich-quick schemes, and nifty ways to stay in shape without working very hard at it. Recently, however, a number of top marketing companies—GTE, Johnson & Johnson, MCA Universal, Sears, Revlon, Philips Electronics, and others—have begun using infomercials to sell their wares over the phone, refer customers to retailers, or send out coupons and product information. In all, infomercials produced almost $1 billion in sales in 1994.[17]

Home shopping channels, another form of television direct marketing, are television programs or entire channels dedicated to selling goods and services. Some home shopping channels, such as the Quality Value Channel (QVC) and the Home Shopping Network (HSN), broadcast 24 hours a day. On HSN, the program's hosts offer bargain prices on products ranging from jewelry, lamps, collectible dolls, and clothing to power tools and consumer electronics—usually obtained by the home shopping channel at closeout prices. The show is upbeat, with the hosts honking horns, blowing whistles, and praising viewers for their good taste. Viewers call an 800 number to order goods. At the other end of the operation, 400 operators handle more than 1,200 incoming lines, entering orders directly into computer terminals. Orders are shipped within 48 hours.

Sales through home shopping channels grew from $450 million in 1986 to an estimated $2 billion in 1994. More than half of all U.S. homes have access to QVC, HSN, or other home shopping channels such as Value Club of America, Home Shopping Mall, or TelShop. Sears, Kmart, JCPenney, Spiegel, and other major retailers are now looking into the home shopping industry. Many experts think that advances in two-way, interactive television will make video shopping one of the major forms of direct marketing by the end of the century.[18]

ON-LINE SHOPPING.   **On-line computer shopping** is conducted through interactive on-line computer services, two-way systems that link consumers with sellers electronically. These services create computerized catalogs of products and services offered by producers, retailers, banks, travel organizations, and others. Consumers use a home computer to hook into the system through cable or telephone lines. For example, a consumer wanting to buy a new compact-disc player could request a list of all brands in the computerized catalog, compare the brands, then order one using a charge card—all without leaving home.

Such on-line services are still in their infancy. In recent years, several large systems have failed because of a lack of subscribers or too little use. Three currently successful systems in the United States, however, are CompuServe, Prodigy, and America Online. Prodigy, developed through a partnership by IBM and Sears, offers in-home shopping services and much more. Through Prodigy, subscribers can order thousands of products and services electronically from dozens of major stores and catalogs. They also can do their banking with local banks; buy and sell investments through a discount brokerage service; book airline, hotel, and car-rental reservations; play games, quizzes, and contests; check *Consumer Reports* ratings of various products; receive the latest sports scores and statistics; obtain weather forecasts; and exchange messages with other subscribers around the country.

Although relatively few consumers now subscribe to such electronic systems, the number is expected to grow in future years. In fact, some experts predict that computers, televisions, and telephones will soon mutate into a single "smart box," which users will manipulate to receive entertainment, information, and direct access to "video shopping malls." By the turn of the century, they assert, all of us will enjoy the wonders of interactive, on-line shopping.[19]

On-line shopping
Shopping through interactive on-line computer services, two-way systems that link consumers with sellers electronically.

Marketing database
An organized set of data about individual customers or prospects that can be used to generate and qualify customer leads, sell products and services, and maintain customer relationships.

Electronic shopping: Prodigy offers in-home shopping services and much more.

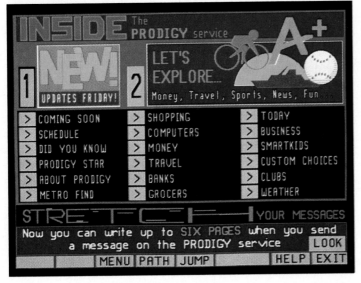

Direct Marketing Databases

Successful direct marketing begins with a good customer database. A **marketing database** is an organized set of data about individual customers or prospects, including geographic, demographic, psychographic, and buying behavior data. The database can be used to locate good potential customers, tailor products and services to the special needs of targeted consumers, and maintain long-term customer relationships. Many companies are now building and using customer databases for targeting marketing communications and selling efforts. A recent survey found that more than one-half of all large consumer products companies are currently building such databases.[20]

Building a marketing database takes time and involves much cost, but it can pay handsome dividends. For example, a General Electric customer database contains each customer's demographic and psychographic characteristics along with an appliance purchasing history. GE direct marketers use this database to assess how long specific customers have owned their current appliances and which past customers might be ready to purchase again. They can determine which customers need a new GE videorecorder, compact-disc player, stereo receiver, or something else to go with other recently purchased electronics products. Or they can identify the best past GE purchasers and send them gift certificates or other promotions to apply against their next GE purchases. Clearly, a rich customer database allows GE to build profitable new business by locating good prospects, anticipating customer needs, cross-selling products and services, and rewarding loyal customers.[21]

Integrated Direct Marketing

Integrated direct marketing Direct marketing campaigns that use multiple vehicles and multiple stages to improve response rates and profits.

Many direct marketers use only a "one-shot" effort to reach and sell a prospect, or a single vehicle in multiple stages to trigger purchases. For example, a magazine publisher might send a series of four direct-mail notices to a household to get a subscriber to renew before giving up. A more powerful approach is **integrated direct marketing**, which involves using multiple-vehicle, multiple-stage campaigns. Such campaigns can greatly improve response. Whereas a direct mail piece alone might generate a 2 percent response, adding a toll-free 800-number can raise the response rate by 50 percent. A well-designed outbound telemarketing effort might lift response by an additional 50 percent. A 2 percent response has grown to 13 percent or more by adding interactive marketing channels to a regular mailing.[22]

More elaborate integrated direct marketing campaigns can be used. Consider the following multimedia, multistage campaign:

Paid ad with a response channel $\longrightarrow$ Direct mail $\longrightarrow$ Outbound telemarketing $\longrightarrow$ Face-to-face sales call

Here, the paid ad creates product awareness and stimulates inquiries. The company immediately sends direct mail to those who inquire. Within a few days, the company follows up with a phone call seeking an order. Some prospects will order by phone; others might request a face-to-face sales call. In such a campaign, the marketer seeks to improve response rates and profits by adding media and stages that contribute more to additional sales than to additional costs.

INTEGRATED MARKETING COMMUNICATIONS

The recent shifts from mass marketing to targeted marketing, along with innovations in information technology and the rapid growth of direct marketing, have had a major impact on the nature of marketing communications. In their efforts to communicate with more fragmented and diverse target segments, marketers are employing a richer variety of more focused promotional tools. As a result, consumers are being exposed to a greater variety of marketing communications from and about the company.

However, customers don't distinguish between message sources the way marketers do. In the consumer's mind, advertising messages from different media such as television, magazines, or on-line computer shopping services blur into one. Messages delivered via different promotional approaches—such as advertising, personal selling, sales promotion, public relations, or direct marketing—all become part of a single overall message about the company. Conflicting messages from these different sources can result in confused company images and brand positions.

All too often, companies fail to integrate these various communications channels. The result is a hodgepodge of communications to the consumer—"a mass message saying one thing, a price promo creating a different signal, a product label creating still another message, sales literature having an entirely different vocabulary, a sales force doing nothing but pitching price, price, price to the retailer."[23]

The problem is that these communications often come from different company sources. Advertising messages are planned and implemented by the advertising department or advertising agency. Personal selling communications are developed by sales management. Other functional specialists are responsible for public relations, sales promotion, direct marketing, and other forms of marketing communications. Moreover, members of various departments often differ in their views on how to split the promotion budget. The sales manager would rather hire a few more salespeople than spend $150,000 on a single television commercial. The public relations manager feels that he or she can do wonders with some money shifted from advertising to public relations.

Integrated marketing communications
The concept under which a company carefully integrates and coordinates its many communications channels to deliver a clear, consistent, and compelling message about the organization and its products.

In the past, no one person was responsible for thinking through the communication roles of the various promotion tools and coordinating the promotion mix. Today, however, more companies are adopting the concept of **integrated marketing communications**. Under this concept, the company carefully integrates and coordinates its many communications channels—mass media advertising, personal selling, sales promotion, public relations, direct marketing, packaging, and others—to deliver a clear, consistent, and compelling message about the organization and its products.[24] (See Marketing Highlight 15-3 for examples.) The company works out the roles that the various promotional tools will play and the extent to which each will be used. It carefully coordinates the promotional activities and the timing of when major campaigns take place. It keeps track of its promotional expenditures by product, promotional tool, product life-cycle stage, and observed effect in order to improve future use of the promotion mix tools. Finally, to help implement its integrated marketing strategy, the company appoints a marketing communications director who has overall responsibility for the company's communications efforts.

Integrated marketing communications produces better communications consistency and greater sales impact. It places the responsibility in someone's hands—where none existed before—to unify the company's image as it is shaped by thousands of company activities. It leads to a total marketing communication strategy aimed at showing how the company and its products can help customers solve their problems.

SOCIALLY RESPONSIBLE MARKETING COMMUNICATION

Whoever is in charge, people at all levels of the organization must be aware of the growing body of legal and ethical issues surrounding marketing communications. Most marketers work hard to communicate openly and honestly with consumers and resellers. Still, abuses may occur, and public policy makers have developed a substantial body of laws and regulations to govern advertising, personal selling, and direct marketing activities.

INTEGRATED MARKETING COMMUNICATIONS AT HEWLETT-PACKARD AND HALLMARK

An ever-increasing number of companies are learning that carefully integrated marketing communications can pay big dividends. Here are just two examples.

Hewlett-Packard: Integrated Business-to-Business Marketing

Hewlett-Packard puts integrated marketing communications to work in its business-to-business markets. H-P uses a closely coordinated mix of advertising, event marketing, direct marketing, and personal selling to sell workstations to high-level corporate buyers. At the broadest level, corporate image television ads, coupled with targeted ads in trade magazines, position H-P as a supplier of high-quality solutions to customers' workstation problems. Beneath this broad advertising umbrella, H-P then uses direct marketing to polish its image, update its customer database, and generate leads for the sales force. Finally, company sales reps follow up to close sales and build customer relationships.

H-P's highly successful program of "interactive audio teleconferences" illustrates the company's mastery of integrated communications. These teleconferences are like mammoth conference calls in which

H-P representatives discuss key industry issues and H-P practices with current and potential customers. To garner participation in the program, H-P employs a five-week, seven-step "registration process." First, four weeks before a teleconference, H-P mails out an introductory direct-mail package, complete with an 800 number and business reply cards. One or two days after the mail package is

Integrated Marketing Communications: To rebuild relationships with working women, Hallmark developed a major marketing effort called "The Very Best." Hallmark's most frequent and loyal customers receive personalized mailings with product information.

received, H-P telemarketers call prospects to register them for the conference, and registrations are confirmed immediately by direct mail. A week before the teleconference, H-P mails out detailed briefing packages, and three days before the event, calls are made again to confirm participation. A final confirmation call is made the day before the teleconference. Finally, one week after the event, H-P uses follow-up direct mail and telemarketing to qualify sales leads and develop account profiles for sales reps.

What is the result of this integrated marketing communications effort? A response rate of 12 percent, compared with just 1.5 percent using a traditional mail and telemarketing approach. Moreover, 82 percent of those who say they'll participate actually take part, compared with only 40 percent for past, nonsynchronized efforts. The program has generated qualified sales leads at 200 percent above the forecasted level, and the average workstation sale has increased 500 percent.

Not surprisingly, Hewlett-Packard is sold on integrated marketing communications. However, H-P managers warn that integrated marketing requires great dedication and practical rigor. Perhaps the toughest

ADVERTISING

By law, companies must avoid false or deceptive advertising. Advertisers must not make false claims, such as stating that a product cures something when it does not. They must avoid false demonstrations, as when a soup marketer put clear marbles in the bottom of the bowl to make the soup appear to have more noodles in advertising.

Advertisers must not create ads that have the capacity to deceive, even though no one actually may be deceived. An automobile cannot be advertised as giving 32 miles per gallon unless it does so under typical conditions, and a diet bread cannot be advertised as having fewer calories simply because its slices are thinner. The problem is how to tell the difference between deception and "puffery"—simple acceptable exaggerations not intended to be believed.

Sellers must avoid bait-and-switch advertising that attracts buyers under false pretenses. For example, a large retailer advertised a sewing machine at $79. However, when consumers tried to buy the advertised machine, the seller downplayed

challenge is the fact that success results from the intense and detailed coordination of the efforts of many company departments. To achieve coordination, H-P assigns cross-functional teams made up of representatives from sales, advertising, marketing, production, and information systems to oversee its integrated communications efforts.

Hallmark Cards: Integrated Consumer Marketing

Hallmark's general brand advertising and program sponsorship are well known. Over the years, the company has relied heavily on mass-media television and print advertising to position Hallmark as the card to give "When you care enough to send the very best." It has also sponsored the highly regarded *Hallmark Hall of Fame* TV specials to reinforce its wholesome, family-oriented image.

Over the past five years, however, Hallmark has transformed itself from a traditional advertiser to a leader in state-of-the-art integrated marketing communications. Hallmark now uses a well-engineered combination of network TV, print advertising, newspaper-distributed coupons, in-store promotions, point-of-sale materials, and direct marketing to lure customers into its stores.

In the late 1980s, the No. 1 greeting card marketer realized that its core group of consumers—working women—was changing. These women had become busier than ever and therefore harder to reach through traditional mass-media advertising. Also, Hallmark's product line had expanded beyond greeting cards to include gifts, collectibles, and home entertaining and decorating products. To rebuild relationships with working women, Hallmark developed a major database marketing effort called "The Very Best," which tied directly into its overall advertising program.

"The Very Best" cultivates Hallmark's most frequent and loyal customers, who receive regular personalized mailings filled with information about new products, including coupons and incentives to pull them into Hallmark's 5,000 Gold Crown stores. "The Very Best" mailings also provide information about holiday entertaining and gift giving. Hallmark's goal is to build closer, more personal relationships with important customers. "We want our communications to be very warm and relevant," says Ira Stolzer, Hallmark's director of advertising. "We want each woman on our 'Very Best' list to feel like she's getting a mailing from her sister." According to Mr. Stolzer, the results

have been "absolutely phenomenal. People really enjoy being on our mailing lists, and in focus groups we've had incredible feedback from them." In each mailing, Hallmark invites comments about the program. This has created a positive dialogue between Hallmark and its customers.

Hallmark is careful to see that all the different parts of its marketing communications work together. The same team oversees media advertising, in-store marketing, and direct mailings. The integrated effort has put many new weapons in Hallmark's communications arsenal. "In the old days we might have said, 'Here's a marketing problem, let's solve it with some TV and print advertising,' and that was all there was to it," Mr. Stolzer says. "Today, we have . . . multiple solutions and [can be] extremely creative [in finding] effective ways to reach our target customers."

Sources: Portions based on Mark Suchecki, "Integrated Marketing: Making It Pay," *Direct,* October 1993, p. 43; and Kate Fitzgerald, "In Line for Integrated Hall of Fame," *Advertising Age,* November 8, 1993, p. S12. Also see Kate Fitzgerald, "Hallmark Alters Focus as Lifestyles Change," *Advertising Age,* October 31, 1994, p. 4.

its features, placed faulty machines on showroom floors, downplayed the machine's performance, and took other actions in an attempt to switch buyers to a more expensive machine. Such actions are both unethical and illegal.

A company's trade promotion activities also are closely regulated. For example, under the Robinson-Patman Act, sellers cannot favor certain customers through their use of trade promotions. They must make promotional allowances and services available to all resellers on proportionately equal terms.

Beyond simply avoiding legal pitfalls, such as deceptive or bait-and-switch advertising, companies can use advertising to encourage and promote socially responsible programs and actions. For example, State Farm joined with the National Council for Social Studies, National Science Teachers Association, and other national teachers organizations to create a Good Neighbor Award, to recognize primary and secondary teachers for innovation, leadership, and involvement in their profession. State Farm promotes the award through a series of print advertisements.

HER STUDENTS BECOME LAWYERS AND JUDGES.
EVEN BEFORE THEY GRADUATE.

Lori Urogdy Eiler frequently holds court in her high school law class. Her students stage mock trials, playing the roles of defendant, prosecutor, and public defender.

Why? Because Lori feels her students best achieve by doing. That's important in a school where creative resources must far exceed budgets.

By thinking in new and different ways, they become better students. Better citizens. Not to mention better lawyers and judges.

For educational methods that truly inspire achievement, Lori receives the Good Neighbor Award, along with a contribution of $5,000 to Shaw High School of East Cleveland, Ohio.

GOOD
NEIGHBOR
AWARD

Social responsibility: State Farm encourages and promotes social responsibility with its Good Neighbor Award ads.

PERSONAL SELLING

Companies that market products directly through their own sales forces must ensure that their salespeople follow the rules of "fair competition." Most states have enacted deceptive sales acts that spell out what is not allowed. For example, salespeople may not lie to consumers or mislead them about the advantages of buying a product. To avoid bait-and-switch practices, salespeople's statements must match advertising claims.

From a public policy viewpoint, different rules apply to consumers who are called on at home versus those who go to a store in search of a product. Because people called on at home may be taken by surprise and may be especially vulnerable to high-pressure selling techniques, the Federal Trade Commission (FTC) has adopted a *three-day cooling off rule* to give special protection to customers who are not seeking products. Under this rule, customers who agree in their own homes to buy something costing more than $25 have 72 hours in which to cancel a contract or return merchandise and get their money back, no questions asked.

Much personal selling involves business-to-business trade. In selling to businesses, salespeople may not offer bribes to purchasing agents or to others who can influence a sale. They may not obtain or use technical or trade secrets of competitors through bribery or industrial espionage. Finally, salespeople must not disparage competitors or competing products by suggesting things that are not true.[25]

DIRECT MARKETING

Direct marketers and their customers usually enjoy mutually rewarding relationships. Occasionally, however, a darker side emerges. The aggressive and sometimes shady tactics of a few direct marketers can bother or harm consumers, giving the entire industry a black eye. Abuses range from simple excesses that irritate consumers to instances of unfair practices or even outright deception and fraud. During the past few years, the direct marketing industry also has faced growing concerns about invasion of privacy issues.[26]

Irritation, Unfairness, Deception, and Fraud

Direct marketing excesses sometimes annoy or offend consumers. Many people find the increasing number of hard-sell solicitations to be a nuisance. Most of us dislike direct-response TV commercials that are too loud, too long, and too insistent. Especially bothersome are dinner-time or late-night phone calls, poorly trained callers, and computerized calls placed by an ADRMP (auto-dial recorded message player).

Beyond irritating consumers, some direct marketers have become so skilled at targeting audiences and putting together effective appeals that they have been accused of taking unfair advantage of impulsive or less sophisticated buyers. TV shopping shows and program-long "infomercials" seem to be the worst culprits. They feature smooth-talking hosts, elaborately staged demonstrations, claims of drastic price reductions, "while they last" time limitations, and unequaled ease of purchase to inflame buyers who have low sales resistance.

Worse yet, so-called "heat merchants" design mailers and write copy intended to mislead buyers. Political fundraisers, among the worst offenders, sometimes use gimmicks such as "look-alike" envelopes that resemble official documents, simulated newspaper clippings, and fake honors and awards. Other direct marketers, including some nonprofit organizations, pretend to be conducting research surveys when they are actually asking leading questions to screen or persuade consumers. Still other problems of potential deception include greatly exaggerated product size and performance claims, and reference to much higher "retail" or regular prices that may never really have existed.

Fraudulent schemes, such as investment scams or phony collections for charity, have multiplied in recent years. The Federal Trade Commission receives thousands of complaints each year, and the number is rising. Irate consumers flood their local Better Business Bureaus with additional complaints of local abuses. Crooked direct marketers can be hard to catch: direct marketing customers often respond quickly, do not interact personally with the seller, and usually expect to wait for delivery. By the time buyers realize that they have been bilked, the thieves are usually somewhere else plotting new schemes.

Invasion of Privacy

Invasion of privacy is perhaps the toughest public policy issue now confronting the direct marketing industry. These days, it seems that almost every time consumers order products by mail or telephone, enter a sweepstakes, apply for a credit card, or take out a magazine subscription, their names are entered into some company's already bulging database. Using sophisticated computer technologies, direct marketers can use these databases to "microtarget" their selling efforts.

Consumers often benefit from such database marketing—they receive more offers that are closely matched to their interests. However, direct marketers sometimes find it difficult to walk the fine line between their desires to reach carefully targeted audiences and consumer rights to privacy.

Many critics worry that marketers may know *too* much about consumers' lives, and that they may use this knowledge to take unfair advantage of consumers. At some point, they claim, the extensive use of databases intrudes on consumer privacy. For example, they ask, should AT&T be allowed to sell marketers the names of customers who frequently call the 800 numbers of catalog companies? Is it right for credit bureaus to compile and sell lists of people who have recently applied for credit cards—people who are considered prime direct marketing targets because of their spending behavior? Or is it right for states to sell the names and addresses of driver's license holders, along with height, weight, and gender information, allowing apparel retailers to target tall or overweight people with special clothing offers? Such practices have spawned a quiet but determined "privacy revolt" among consumers and public policy makers.

In a recent survey of consumers, 78 percent of respondents said that they were concerned about threats to their personal privacy. In another survey, *Advertising Age* asked advertising industry executives how they felt about database marketing and the privacy issue. The responses of three executives show that even industry insiders have mixed feelings:[27]

> There are profound ethical issues relating to the marketing of specific household data—financial information, for instance. . . . For every household in the United States, the computer can guess with amazing accuracy . . . things like credit use, net worth, and investments, the kind of information most people would never want disclosed, let alone sold to any marketer.

I'm a big believer in getting as close to your customer as you can. . . . [For example,] I love to garden; [I order seeds from the Burpee's catalog and] Burpee's sells my name—that [results in my receiving] the kind of stuff I like to look at. . . . Credit card solicitations I don't. Travel-related information I do if I'm interested in the destination.

It doesn't bother me that people know I live in a suburb of Columbus, Ohio, and have X number of kids. It [does] bother me that these people know the names of my wife and kids and where my kids go to school. They . . . act like they know me when the bottom line is they're attempting to sell me something. I do feel that database marketing has allowed companies to cross the fine line of privacy. . . . In some cases, it's difficult to know when the line's crossed. But in a lot of cases, I think they know they have crossed it.

The direct marketing industry is working to address issues of ethics and public policy. They know that, left untended, such problems will lead to increasingly negative consumer attitudes, lower response rates, and calls for greater state and federal legislation to further restrict direct marketing practices. More importantly, most direct marketers want the same thing that consumers want: honest and well-designed marketing offers targeted only toward consumers who will appreciate and respond to them. Direct marketing is just too expensive to waste on consumers who don't want it.

Summary

Promotion is one of the four major elements of the company's marketing mix. The main promotion tools—advertising, sales promotion, public relations, and personal selling—work together to achieve the company's communications objectives.

In preparing marketing communications, the communicator needs to understand the *steps in developing effective communication* and the nine elements of any communication process: *sender, receiver, encoding, decoding, message, media, response, feedback,* and *noise.* The communicator's first task is to *identify the target audience* and its characteristics. Next, the communicator has to define the *response sought,* whether it be *awareness, knowledge, liking, preference, conviction,* or *purchase.* Then the company must *choose a message* constructed with an effective *content, structure,* and *format. Media* must be selected, both for *personal communication* and *nonpersonal communication channels.* The message must be delivered by a credible *message source*—someone who is an expert and is trustworthy and likable. Finally, the communicator must *collect feedback* by watching how much of the market becomes aware, tries the product, and is satisfied in the process.

The company also has to decide how to *set the total promotion budget* and the *promotion mix.* The most popular approaches are to spend what the company can afford via the *affordable method,* to use a *percentage of sales,* to base promotion spending on a *competitive-parity* basis, or to base it on an analysis and costing of the communication *objectives and tasks.*

The company has to divide the promotion budget among the major tools to *set the promotion mix.* Companies are guided by the *nature of each promotion tool,* the *type of product/market,* the desirability of a *push or pull strategy,* the *buyer readiness stage,* and the *product life-cycle stage.*

Recent shifts from mass marketing to one-on-one marketing, coupled with advances in computers and information technology, have had a dramatic impact on the *marketing communications environment.* Although still important, the mass media are giving way to a profusion of smaller, more focused media. Companies are doing less broadcasting and more narrowcasting.

This shift is most evident in the rapid *growth of direct marketing,* which employs direct, one-on-one communications channels to obtain an immediate buying response. Major forms of direct marketing include *direct-mail and catalog marketing, telemarketing, television marketing,* and *on-line shopping.* Successful direct marketing begins with a good *direct marketing database,* which can be used to locate potential customers, tailor products and services, and target marketing communications. Although many direct marketers use only one-shot efforts to reach and sell prospects, multimedia, multistage *integrated direct marketing* campaigns can boost impact and consumer response.

As marketing communicators adopt richer but more fragmented media and promotion mixes to reach their diverse markets, they run the danger of creating a communications hodgepodge for consumers. To prevent this, more companies are adopting the concept of *integrated*

marketing communications, which calls for integrating all sources of company communication to deliver a clear and consistent message to target markets.

Finally, people at all levels of the organization must be aware of the many legal and ethical issues surrounding marketing communications. Much work is required to produce *socially responsible marketing communication* in advertising, personal selling, and direct selling. Companies must work hard and proactively at communicating openly, honestly, and agreeably with their customers and resellers.

Key Terms

Advertising
Affordable method
Buyer-readiness stages
Catalog marketing
Competitive-parity method
Direct marketing
Direct mail marketing
Emotional appeals
Integrated direct marketing
Integrated marketing
   communications

Marketing database
Moral appeals
Nonpersonal communication
   channels
Objective-and-task method
On-line shopping
Percentage-of-sales method
Personal communication channels
Personal selling
Promotion mix

Public relations
Pull strategy
Push strategy
Rational appeals
Sales promotion
Telemarketing
Television marketing
Word-of-mouth influence

Discussing the Issues

1. Name which form of marketing communications each of the following represents: (a) a U2 T-shirt sold at a concert, (b) a *Rolling Stone* interview with Eric Clapton arranged by his manager, (c) a scalper auctioning tickets at a Pearl Jam concert, and (d) a record store selling Boyz II Men albums for $2 off the week their latest music video debuts on network television.

2. Bill Cosby has appeared in ads for such products and companies as Jell-O, Coke, Texas Instruments, and E.F. Hutton. Is he a credible source for all these companies, or does his credibility vary? Is he chosen for his credibility as a spokesperson or for some other characteristic?

3. How can an organization get feedback on the effects of its communication efforts? Describe how (a) the March of Dimes and

(b) Procter & Gamble can get feedback on the results of their communications.

4. Companies spend billions of dollars on advertising to build a quality image for their products. At the same time they spend billions more on discount-oriented sales promotions, offering lower price as a main reason to purchase. Discuss whether promotion is enhancing or reducing the effect of advertising. Can you find an example where they enhance one another?

5. Recently, pharmaceutical companies have begun to communicate directly with consumers via the mass media, even though they cannot mention prescription product names and benefits in the same television ad. Ads promise that doctors have some unspecified help available for baldness. Nicoderm, Habitrol, and Prostep nicotine

patches battle for consumers' awareness, but they cannot mention cigarette addiction. Decide whether you consider this to be advertising or public relations. Do you think it would be effective?

6. Why do some industrial marketers advertise on national television, when their target audience is only a fraction of the people they have paid to reach with their message? List some nonconsumer-oriented commercials you have seen on TV and describe what the marketers were trying to accomplish with them.

Applying the Concepts

1. Think of a nationally advertised product or service that has been running a consistent advertising message for a number of years. Go to the library and copy several examples of print advertising for this brand from back issues of magazines. (a) When you examine these ads closely, how consistent are the message content, structure, and format? (b) Which response(s) do you think this campaign is seeking: awareness, knowledge, liking, preference, conviction, or purchase? (c) Do you think the advertising campaign is successful in getting the desired response? Why or why not?

2. Consider an automobile brand you are familiar with. (a) List examples of how this brand uses advertising, personal selling, sales promotion, and public relations. (Public relations examples may be difficult to spot, but consider how cars are used in movies or television programs, or as celebrity vehicles for sports tournaments or parades.) (b) Does this auto maker use promotion tools in a coordinated way that builds a consistent image, or are the efforts fragmented? Explain.

References

1. Based on information from Charles Butler, "General Excellence: Southwest Airlines," *Sales & Marketing Management*, August 1993, p. 38; and Jennifer Lawrence, "Integrated Mix Makes Expansion Fly," *Advertising Age*, November 8, 1993, pp. S10, S12. Extract from Kenneth Labich, "Is Herb Kelleher America's Best CEO?" *Fortune*, May 2, 1994, pp. 44–52. Also see "Southwest's New Deal," *Fortune*, January 16, 1995, p. 94; and Michael Wilke, "United Lands Brighter Image with Shuttle," *Advertising Age*, April 10, 1995, p. 4.

2. For these and other definitions, see Peter D. Bennett, *Dictionary of Marketing Terms* (Chicago: American Marketing Association, 1988).

3. For more on fear appeals, see John F. Tanner, James B. Hunt, and David R. Eppright, "The Protection Motivation Model: A Normative Model of Fear Appeals," *Journal of Marketing*, July 1991, pp. 36–45.

4. For more on message content and structure, see Leon G. Schiffman and Leslie Lazar Kanuk, *Consumer Behavior*, 5th ed. (Englewood Cliffs, NJ: Prentice Hall, 1994), Chap. 10; Alan G. Sawyer and Daniel J. Howard, "Effects of Omitting Conclusions in Advertisements to Involved and Uninvolved Audiences," *Journal of Marketing Research*, November 1991, pp. 467–474; Cornelia Pechmann, "Predicting When Two-Sided Ads Will Be More Effective Than One-Sided Ads: The Role of Correlational and Correspondent Inferences," *Journal of Marketing*, November 1992, pp. 441–453; and Ayn E. Crowley and Wayne D. Hoyer, "An Integrative Framework for Understanding Two-Sided Persuasion," *Journal of Consumer Research*, March 1994, pp. 561–574.

5. See K. Michael Haywood, "Managing Word of Mouth Communications," *Journal of Services Marketing*, Spring 1989, pp. 55–67.

6. For a more comprehensive discussion on setting promotion budgets, see J. Thomas Russell and W. Ronald Lane, *Kleppner's Advertising Procedure* (Englewood Cliffs, NJ: Prentice Hall, 1993), pp. 138–141.

7. See "Median Costs Per Call By Industry," *Sales & Marketing Management*, June 28, 1993, p. 65.

8. For more discussion, see Don E. Schultz, Stanley I. Tannenbaum, and Robert F. Lauterborn, *Integrated Marketing Communication* (Chicago, IL: NTC Publishing, 1992), pp. 11, 17.

9. *16th Annual Survey of Promotional Practices*, Donnelly Marketing Inc., Oakbrook Terrace, IL, June 1994, p. 9.

10. Kate Fitzgerald, "With 'Big Book' Buried, Rivals See Opportunity," *Advertising Age*, February 1, 1993, p. 36.

11. Richard L. Bencin, "Telefocus: Telemarketing Gets Synergized," *Sales & Marketing Management*, February 1992, pp. 49–53, here p. 50.

12. Bristol Voss, "Calling All Catalogs!" *Sales & Marketing Management*, December 1990, pp. 32–37.

13. Rudy Oetting, "Telephone Marketing: Where We've Been and Where We Should Be Going," *Direct Marketing*, February 1987, p. 98.

14. For more discussion, see Junu Bryan Kim, "800/900: King of the Road in Marketing Value, Usage," *Advertising Age*, February 17, 1992, pp. S1, S4.

15. See Bill Kelley, "Is There Anything that Can't Be Sold by Phone?" *Sales & Marketing Management*, April 1989, pp. 60–64; Rudy Oetting and Geri Gantman, "Dial M for Maximize," *Sales & Marketing Management*, June 1991, pp. 100–106; Richard L. Bencin, "Telefocus: Telemarketing Gets Synergized," *Sales & Marketing Management*, February 1992, pp. 49–57; and Martin Everett, "Selling By Telephone," *Sales & Marketing Management*, December 1993, pp. 75–79.

16. See Dan Fost, "Privacy Concerns Threaten Database Marketing," *American Demographics*, May 1990, pp. 18–21; and Michael W. Miller, "Lawmakers Are Hoping to Ring Out Era of Unrestricted Calls by Telemarketers," *Wall Street Journal*, May 28, 1991, pp. B1, B5.

17. Jim Auchmute, "But Wait There's More!" *Advertising Age*, October 17, 1985, p. 18; Julie Steenhuysen, "Adland's New Billion-Dollar Baby," *Advertising Age*, April 11, 1994, pp. S8, S14; and Kathy Haley, "Infomercials Lure More Top Marketers," *Advertising Age*, May 9, 1994, pp. IN2, IN8.

18. See Rebecca Piirto, "The TV Beast," *American Demographics*, May 1993, pp. 34–42.

19. See Rebecca Piirto, "Over the Line," *American Demographics*, July 1992, p. 6; Scott Donaton, "In Fast-Changing World, a Sense of Urgency at Prodigy," *Advertising Age*, April 15, 1993, p. S1; and Paul M. Eng, "Prodigy Is in that Awkward Stage," *Business Week*, February 13, 1995, pp. 90–91.

20. *The 16th Annual Survey of Promotional Practices* (Oakbrook, IL: Donnelly Marketing Inc., 1994), p. 11.

21. See Joe Schwartz, "Databases Deliver the Goods," *American Demographics*, September 1989, pp. 23–25; Lynn G. Coleman, "Data-Base Masters Become King in the Marketplace," *Marketing News*, February 18, 1991, pp. 13, 18; Laura Loro, "Data Bases Seen As Driving Force," *Advertising Age*, March 18, 1991, p. 39; and Gary Levin, "Database Draws Fevered Interest," *Advertising Age*, June 8, 1992, p. 31.

22. See Ernan Roman, *Integrated Direct Marketing* (New York: McGraw-Hill, 1988), p. 108; and Mark Suchecki, "Integrated Marketing: Making It Pay," *Direct*, October 1993, p. 43.

23. Schultz, Tannenbaum, and Lauterborn, *Integrated Marketing Communication*, p. 65.

24. See Schultz, Tannenbaum, and Lauterborn, *Integrated Marketing Communication*, Chaps. 3 and 4; and Don Schultz, "It's Time to Come Up with Strategies, Not Just Tactics," *Marketing News*, August 20, 1990, p. 11.

25. For more on the legal aspects of promotion, see Louis W. Stern and Thomas I. Eovaldi, *Legal Aspects of Marketing Policy* (Englewood Cliffs, NJ: Prentice Hall, 1984), Chaps. 7 and 8; Robert J. Posch, *The Complete Guide to Marketing and the Law* (Englewood Cliffs, NJ: Prentice Hall, 1988), Chaps. 15 to 17; and Kevin Kelly, "When a Rival's Trade Secret Crosses Your Desk . . ." *Business Week*, May 20, 1991, p. 48.

26. Portions of this section are based on Terrence H. Witkowski, "Self-Regulation Will Suppress Direct Marketing's Downside," *Marketing News*, April 24, 1989, p. 4. Also see Evan I. Schwartz, "The Rush to Keep Mum," *Business Week*, June 8, 1992, pp. 36–38; and Cyndee Miller, "Privacy vs. Direct Marketing," *Marketing News*, March 1, 1993, pp. 1, 14.

27. Melanie Rigney, "Too Close for Comfort, Execs Warn," *Advertising Age*, January 13, 1992, p. 31.

Company Case 15

AVON: A PROMOTIONAL STRATEGY MAKEOVER

"Ding-dong, Avon calling." With that simple advertising message for over 100 years, Avon Products built a $3.5 billion worldwide beauty-products business. Founded in 1886, and incorporated as California Perfume Products in 1916, Avon deployed an army of women to sell its products. These "Avon ladies," 40 million of them in the company's history, met with friends and neighbors in their homes, showed products, took and delivered orders, and earned sales commissions.

Through direct selling, Avon bypassed the battle for space and attention waged by its competitors in department stores, and later in discount drugstores and supermarkets. Direct selling also offered convenience for the customer, coupled with personal beauty-care advice from a friend.

Avon's plan worked well. Most members of its up to 500,000-member sales force were homemakers who did not want a full-time job outside the home. They developed client lists of friends and neighbors. Recruiting salespeople was easy, and a good salesperson could develop a loyal core of customers.

However, during the 1970s and 1980s, the environment changed. First, more women found that they needed to work outside the home. As a result, when Avon ladies rang the doorbell, often no one answered. Second, many Avon ladies decided that they needed more than part-time jobs. Avon experienced annual sales force turnover rates of more than 200 percent for some positions. Third, because of sales force turnover, many Avon customers who did want to see a salesperson could not find one. Fourth, more competitors, such as Amway, Mary Kay Cosmetics, and Tupperware, were competing for the pool of people interested in full- or part-time direct-selling jobs. Finally, the increasing mobility of the U.S. population meant that both customers and salespeople were moving. This made it difficult for salespeople to establish loyal, stable customer bases.

To deal with these issues, Avon Products tapped James E. Preston to serve as its chairman and chief executive. Preston first had to wrestle with the economic downturn of the early 1990s, which slammed door-to-door sales. Compared with a 5- to 7-percent growth rate for the cosmetics industry as a whole, door-to-door sales had been flat since 1989. Even Avon's international sales, which came from over 100 countries and made up 55 percent of its total sales, were sluggish. Although there were some bright spots, such as China, sales in key markets such as Brazil and Japan dropped sharply.

Preston decided that Avon needed to overhaul its marketing strategy. First, he wanted to refocus the company on its core business—selling cosmetics, fragrances, and toiletries. Therefore, he sold Avon's holdings in health care and retirement homes, ending a diversification strategy. Next, he cut prices on Avon products, some up to 75 percent. Finally, he tried a new compensation program that allowed sales representatives to earn up to 21 percent in bonuses based on the sales of new representatives they recruited. However, this price cutting and market expansion reduced gross margins and increased costs. Between 1990 and 1991, earnings dropped from $195 million to $135 million. Marketing, distribution, and administrative expenses during this period increased from $1.682 billion to $1.746 billion.

Preston next turned his attention to Avon's promotional strategy. Beginning in 1988, Avon had cut advertising spending, in part to cut costs during three unfriendly takeover attempts. It had reduced its $22 million advertising budget to $11 million in 1989, and then to $4.6 million in 1990. Preston decided that Avon now needed to restore the ad budget and pay for it by reducing the level of premiums and other sales-promotion activities.

Preston believed that Avon had left as many as 10 million former or potential customers stranded. These customers wanted to buy Avon products, but because of sales force turnover, they did not know how to find a salesperson or order products. Fourteen percent of American women accounted for one-third of Avon's sales. Another 62 percent were fringe customers. These customers viewed Avon positively but did not buy regularly. Another 15 percent of American women were potentially receptive to Avon but were not necessarily interested in dealing with a traditional Avon sales representative.

Thus, the second step in the revamped promotion strategy was to develop a catalog and try direct-mail selling. Avon's research revealed that its median customer was 45 years old and had an average household income of under $30,000. The catalog would reach younger, higher-income customers. Preston believed that by using a catalog, the company could cut the median age of customers to 38 while at the same time increasing average household income.

Under Avon's plan, its salespeople would supply names of customers who had moved or were no longer active buyers. Avon planned to mail up to one million catalogs, and recipients could then order directly from Avon or from salespeople. If they ordered from the company, Avon would pay sales representatives a 20-percent commission, about half the standard commission. Avon mailed orders directly to the customers rather than having the sales representative deliver the orders.

Avon supported the catalog program by kicking off a print-advertising campaign that featured the slogan "Avon—The Smartest Shop in Town." Ads provided customers with a toll-free telephone number that they could call to order the catalog. When people called, Avon assigned them to the nearest Avon representative, who received commissions on any orders the customer placed directly with Avon. Avon hoped that the catalog project would generate $20 to $25 million in sales in its first year. Preston predicted the direct-mail business would generate sales of $300 to $500 million within three to five years.

For the third phase of its revised promotional strategy, Avon planned to launch a series of television commercials in 1993, something it had not done since 1988. The new television ads would encourage women to use the toll-free number to buy Avon products. Avon would back the ads with a new print-media campaign. Analysts estimated that Avon would spend $34 million on advertising in 1993, funding the program with cost cuts and with the reduction of some incentive programs for sales representatives. Avon also planned to spend about $70 million on advertising outside the United States, up from $35 million in 1992.

Underlying all of the advertising, selling, and sales promotions, Avon had continued its key public relations program, the Women of Enterprise Awards. Avon had been sponsoring tennis and running events. However, each year since 1987, Avon had solicited nominations for its awards from several hundred women's organizations. It sought the names of women who had overcome tragedy, prejudice, or personal handicap to become successful in business. Avon presented awards to five winners each year at a gala luncheon in New York City attended by 1,200 entrepreneurs, businesspeople, Avon staff members, and media representatives.

Advertising executives believe that Avon is on the right track. As one analyst notes, several companies have shown that selling cosmetics on television works. However, another adds that the advertising and toll-free numbers may cause some concern among members of the sales force—suggesting that Avon runs the risk of alienating its army of Avon ladies.

Whether the strategy is risky or not, Avon and Preston realize that they must act. Last year, Avon's U.S. sales revenue fell 2 percent to $1.36 billion, and profits declined 3 percent to $182 million. In addition, Avon's sales force shrank 4 percent to 425,000. Meanwhile, Mary Kay Cosmetics had a good year, perhaps sparked by a new incentive compensation plan that enabled some Mary Kay sales managers to earn as much as $1 million.

QUESTIONS

1. How does Avon's new strategy change the promotion mix? How do the elements of the new promotion mix support each other?

2. What are Avon's objectives for its catalog, print, and television campaigns?

3. What advertising message(s) should Avon communicate with its new programs, and what message execution style(s) would you recommend? How would you measure the effect of the new campaigns?

4. What consumer or sales force promotions would you recommend to Avon?

5. Is the Women of Enterprise Award public relations activity appropriate for Avon?

6. In foreign markets, should Avon stick with its traditional personal-selling strategy, or should it employ the newer strategy it is developing for the United States?

Sources: Jeffrey A. Trachtenberg, "Catalogs Help Avon Get a Foot in the Door," *Wall Street Journal,* February 28, 1992, p. B1; and Jeffrey A. Trachtenberg, "Avon's New TV Campaign Says, 'Call Us,' " *Wall Street Journal,* December 28, 1992, p. B1. Used with permission of *Wall Street Journal.* See also: Pat Sloan, "Avon Is Calling on New Tactics, FCB," *Advertising Age,* January 7, 1991, p. 3; Andrew Tanzer, "Ding-Dong, Capitalism Calling," *Forbes,* October 14, 1991, pp. 184–185; Wendy Zellner, "Despite the Face-Lift, Avon Is Sagging," *Business Week,* December 2, 1991, pp. 101–102; Julie C. Mason, "Corporate Sponsorships Help Target the Right Audience," *Management Review,* November 1992, pp. 58–61.

Promoting Products

ADVERTISING, SALES PROMOTION, AND PUBLIC RELATIONS

16

ALWAYS HAPPENING. ALWAYS COCA-COLA.

In 1992, fed up after years of being out-advertised by rival Pepsi, Coca-Cola did the unthinkable. It abandoned Madison Avenue and went Hollywood. Forsaking its 38-year relationship with McCann-Erickson, the huge Madison Avenue advertising agency, Coca-Cola awarded creative control over its flagship Coke brand to—of all things—a Hollywood talent agency called Creative Artists Agency (CAA). The result: a breathtaking but highly controversial new ad campaign—Always Coca-Cola.

Going into the 1990s, Coca-Cola's advertising had gone stale. Pepsi's snazzier ads consistently outranked Coke's more sedate entries in consumer awareness surveys. Coca-Cola executives worried that Coke's brand personality was becoming blurred or dated. Moreover, the advertising environment was changing rapidly. Consumer markets and media had grown fragmented and diverse. And consumers had become practiced ad ignorers, using their remote controls to avoid ads by zipping around channels during commercial breaks or zapping unwanted commercials from recorded programs.

In 1989, Coca-Cola had tapped a panel of ten unconventional marketing thinkers for their views on reaching this fractured and fickle marketplace. The panel's conclusion: "A brand advertised in the normal way, with normal media, is likely to develop a normal image, and not something special." Their advice: "Don't be normal."[1] Yet, in Coke's view, the big Madison Avenue agencies were stamping out the same old cookie-cutter ad campaigns that they'd been producing for decades.

So, in a radical effort to revitalize its advertising, Coca-Cola hired Creative Artists Agency, Hollywood's premier talent agency. Why CAA? For one thing, CAA gave Coke access to many first-rate Hollywood stars, writers, and directors. But most importantly, CAA provided a pipeline into the pop culture. The talent agency knows what's hot in Hollywood—the talk, music, fashions, sports—and what's hot in Hollywood will soon be hot everywhere.

Coca-Cola initially hired Creative Artists Agency as a "creative consultant." Within months, however, CAA was competing head to head with McCann-Erickson—Hollywood against Madison Avenue—for creative control of the 1993 Coke Classic campaign, scheduled to be one of Coke's biggest advertising efforts ever. On presentation day, McCann-Erickson proposed the usual—a half-dozen ads positioning Coke as the all-world, something-for-everyone soft drink. In refreshing contrast, CAA dazzled Coke executives with a whirlwind 60-minute show in which it pitched some 50 excitingly different contemporary ad ideas. When the lights came up, CAA got more than two dozens ads to produce. McCann got two.

Coca-Cola launched CAA's groundbreaking "Always Coca-Cola" ads in spring 1993. The new campaign was anything but normal, anything but Madison Avenue. For the first time, Coke dropped its longstanding "one sight, one sound, one sell" approach, in which a few standardized, broadly targeted ads celebrated Coke's universal appeal. Instead, following the global trend toward media and market fragmentation, the Always Coca-Cola campaign featured a large number of ads narrowly targeted to specific media, audiences, and seasons.

The ads themselves were wildly different from the usual Coke fare. They also varied dramatically from one ad to the next in tone and approach, with no apparent connecting theme—a Coke bottle sweating to the sounds of summer; a global Coke orchestra making music with only Coke bottles; dancers rhythmically attacking a giant block of ice and reducing it to shavings; a Harry-Met-Sally-like couple tracking Coke's role in their relationship from the 1920s through their 50th anniversary; animated polar bears massing on an ice flow, watching the northern lights, and blissfully chugging Coca-Cola. Some ads were concrete, others highly abstract. Some had story lines, others had no clear theme. Some were refined, others bawdy. About all they had in common was the Always slogan and the red Coke-button icon.

In producing the trendier ads, CAA enlisted the talents of some of Hollywood's best known producers—Rob Reiner (known for such movies as *Stand by Me, When Harry Met Sally,* and *A Few Good Men*), Francis Coppola (*Dracula, Apocalypse Now,* and *The Godfather I–III*), David Lynch (*Dune, Twin Peaks,* and *Elephant Man*), and Richard Donner (*Lethal Weapons 1–3* and *Superman*).

The new Always Coca-Cola campaign clearly broke new ground; it also created much controversy. Although some industry insiders praised the CAA ads as innovative, clever, playful, and even sexy, most Madison Avenue regulars bashed the campaign as all technique and no strategy. Many experts had mixed feelings, as reflected in this assessment by advertising critic Bob Garfield:

> [CAA] delivered a substantially, sometimes maddeningly, flawed pool of two dozen commercials that nonetheless represent the best Coca-Cola advertising campaign in at least a decade. Sometimes ingenious. Sometimes surprising. Sometimes delightful. Sometimes extraordinary. Sometimes, my goodness, breathtaking. Not always, but some of the time."[2]

While the new spots were intriguing and very entertaining, they appeared to lack overall strategic direction. Many observers, even Coca-Cola insiders, worried that the campaign was little more than a grab bag of contemporary and very clever but loosely connected short features.

Despite the controversy, the Always Coca-Cola campaign endured. The memorable, Coke-guzzling polar bears became the centerpiece of a winter holiday ad campaign and Coke's mascots for the 1994 Winter Olympics. And in 1994, Coke gave CAA a giant bear hug when it commissioned another 30 ads for its 1994 campaign. Whereas the initial Always Coca-Cola ads drew mixed reviews, the 1994 encore drew consistently high praise. According to Garfield:

> The new pool of 30 spots is the best Coke advertising, and maybe the best soft-drink advertising, in decades. The collaboration of Coca-Cola Co. and CAA, having produced some startlingly good and startlingly bad results a year

ago, seems to have . . . coalesced around the strongest elements of the introductory campaign. The contour bottle, . . . [the red Coke button] logo, and the irresistible jingle . . . are leveraged to the max. The wonderfully resonant Always Coca-Cola slogan, instead of being a tagline in a series of . . . unrelated ministries, is now central to nearly every spot. . . . These spots are as cohesive and integrated as the first ones were haphazard and unfocused. . . . They manage to be both contemporary and classic while addressing diverse audiences in differing language and style. . . . And around the world, people are getting thirsty.[3]

Coca-Cola executives claim that the Coke/CAA relationship sets a new paradigm for the advertising creative process. And although the debate continues about whether the controversial new ads will sell more Coke, few debate that the breakthrough campaign has left an indelible impression on the advertising industry. Perhaps the highest praise for CAA comes from a high-level McCann-Erickson executive. He says: "What I believe [CAA's Always Coca-Cola commercials] have done most effectively is shout out the news that this 107-year-old [brand] isn't about to act like a 107-year-old. Creatively, they threw away the book, risked the rancor of old creative pros and old consumers, and cranked out a whole new regimen of [ads]."[4]

Companies must do more than make good products—they must inform consumers about product benefits and carefully position products in consumers' minds. To do this, they must skillfully use the mass-promotion tools of *advertising, sales promotion,* and *public relations.* We take a closer look at each of these tools in this chapter.

ADVERTISING

Advertising
Any paid form of nonpersonal presentation and promotion of ideas, goods, or services by an identified sponsor.

We define **advertising** as any paid form of nonpersonal presentation and promotion of ideas, goods, or services by an identified sponsor. Advertising can be traced back to the very beginnings of recorded history. Archaeologists working in the countries around the Mediterranean Sea have dug up signs announcing various events and offers. The Romans painted walls to announce gladiator fights, and the Phoenicians painted pictures promoting their wares on large rocks along parade routes. A Pompeii wall painting praised a politician and asked for votes. During the Golden Age in Greece, town criers announced the sale of cattle, crafted items, and even cosmetics. An early "singing commercial" went as follows: "For eyes that are shining, for cheeks like the dawn / For beauty that lasts after girlhood is gone / For prices in reason, the woman who knows / Will buy her cosmetics from Aesclyptos."

Modern advertising, however, is a far cry from these early efforts. In 1993, advertisers ran up a bill of more than $138 billion. Although advertising is used mostly by business firms, it also is used by a wide range of nonprofit organizations, professionals, and social agencies that advertise their causes to various target publics. In fact, the thirty-fourth largest advertising spender is a nonprofit organization—the U.S. government. Advertising is a good way to inform and persuade, whether the purpose is to sell Coca-Cola worldwide or to get consumers in a developing nation to drink milk or use birth control.

The top 100 national advertisers account for about one-fourth of all advertising.[5] Table 16-1 lists the top ten advertisers in 1993. Procter & Gamble is the leader with more than $2.4 billion, or about 15.5 percent of its total U.S. sales. P&G is also the *world's* largest advertiser, spending a whopping $3.6 billion globally. The other major spenders are found in the retailing, auto, and food industries. Advertising as a percentage of sales varies greatly by industry. For example, percentage spending is low in the auto industry but high in food, drugs, toiletries,

How Does an Advertising Agency Work?

Madison Avenue is a familiar name to most Americans. It's a street in New York City where some major advertising agency headquarters are located. But most of the nation's 10,000 agencies are found outside New York, and almost every city has at least one agency, even if it's a one-person shop. Some ad agencies are huge—the largest U.S. agency, McCann-Erickson, has annual worldwide billings (the dollar amount of advertising placed for clients) of more than $6.5 billion. Dentsu, a Japanese agency, is the world's largest agency, with billings of more than $10 billion.

Advertising agencies were started in the mid-to-late 1800s by salespeople and brokers who worked for the media and received a commission for selling advertising space to various companies. As time passed, the salespeople began to help customers prepare their ads. Eventually, they formed agencies and grew closer to the advertisers than to the media. Agencies offered both more advertising and more marketing services to their clients.

Even companies with strong advertising departments use advertising agencies. Agencies employ specialists who can often perform advertising tasks better than the company's own staff. Agencies also bring an outside point of view to solving the company's problems, along with lots of experience from working with different clients and situations. Agencies are paid partly from media discounts and often cost the firm very little. And because the firm can drop its agency at any time, an agency works hard to do a good job.

Advertising agencies usually have four departments: *creative,* which develops and produces ads; *media,* which selects media and places ads; *research,* which studies audience characteristics and wants; and *business,* which handles the agency's business activities. Each account is supervised by an account executive, and people in each department are usually assigned to work on one or more accounts.

Agencies often attract new business through their reputation or size. Generally, however, a client invites a few agencies to make a presentation for its business and then selects one.

Ad agencies traditionally have been paid through commissions and some fees. Under this system, the agency usually receives 15 percent of the media cost as a rebate. Suppose the agency buys $60,000 of magazine space for a client, for example. The magazine bills the advertising agency for $51,000 ($60,000 less 15 percent), and the agency bills the client for $60,000, keeping the $9,000 commission. If the client bought space directly from the magazine, it would have paid $60,000 because commissions are only paid to recognized advertising agencies.

However, both advertisers and agencies have become more and more unhappy with the commission system. Larger advertisers complain that they pay more for the same services received by smaller ones simply because they place more advertising. Advertisers also believe that the commission system drives agencies away from low-cost media and short advertising campaigns. Agencies are unhappy because they perform extra services for an account without getting any more pay. As a result, the trend is now toward paying either a straight fee or a combination commission and fee. And some large advertisers are tying agency compensation to the performance of the agency's advertising campaigns. Today, only about 35 percent of companies still pay their agencies on a commission-only basis.

Another trend is hitting the advertising agency business: In recent years, as growth in advertising spending has slowed, many agencies have tried to keep growing by gobbling up other agencies, thus creating huge agency holding companies. The largest of these agency "mega-groups," WPP Group, includes several large agencies—Ogilvy & Mather, J. Walter Thompson, Fallon McElligott, and others—with combined billings exceeding $20 billion. Many agencies also have sought growth by diversifying into related marketing services. These new diversified agencies offer a complete list of integrated marketing and promotion services under one roof, including advertising, sales promotion, public relations, direct marketing, and marketing research. Some have even added marketing consulting, television production, and sales training units in an effort to become full "marketing partners" to their clients.

However, most agencies are finding that advertisers don't want much more from them than traditional media advertising services plus direct marketing, sales promotion, and sometimes public relations. Thus, many agencies recently have dropped unrelated activities in order to focus more on traditional advertising services. Some have even started their own "creative boutiques," smaller and more independent agencies that can develop creative campaigns for clients free of large-agency bureaucracy.

Sources: See R. Craig Endicott, "Ad Age 500 Grows 9.7%," *Advertising Age,* March 26, 1990, pp. S1–S2; Gary Levin, "Ad Agencies Ax Side Ventures," *Advertising Age,* March 18, 1991, p. 4; Mark Landler, "Advertising's 'Big Bang' Is Making Noise at Last," *Business Week,* April 1, 1991, pp. 62–63; Patricia Sellers, "Do You Need Your Ad Agency?" *Fortune,* November 15, 1993, pp. 147–164; and "World's Top 50 Advertising Organizations," *Advertising Age,* April 10, 1995, p. S18.

and cosmetics. The company spending the largest percentage of its sales on advertising was Warner-Lambert (27 percent).

Different organizations handle advertising in different ways. In small companies, advertising might be handled by someone in the sales department. Large companies set up advertising departments whose job it is to set the advertising budget; work with the ad agency; and handle direct-mail advertising, dealer dis-

TABLE 16-1 *Top Ten National Advertisers*

RANK	COMPANY	TOTAL U.S. ADVERTISING (Millions)	TOTAL U.S. SALES (Millions)	ADVERTISING AS A PERCENT OF SALES
1	Procter & Gamble	$2,397	$ 15,519	15.5
2	Philip Morris	1,844	38,387	4.8
3	General Motors	1,539	109,668	1.4
4	Sears	1,310	50,838*	
5	PepsiCo	1,039	18,308	5.7
6	Ford	958	75,661	1.3
7	AT&T	812	61,580	1.3
8	Nestlé	794	3,749	21.2
9	Johnson & Johnson	763	7,203	10.6
10	Chrysler	761	37,847	2.0

*Worldwide sales—U.S. sales not available. Percent of sales not calculated.
Sources: Reprinted with permission from "100 Leading National Advertisers," *Advertising Age,* September 28, 1994. Also see "Advertising Factbook," *Advertising Age,* January 2, 1995, p. 12.

plays, and other advertising not done by the agency. Most large companies use outside advertising agencies because they offer several advantages (see Marketing Highlight 16-1).

MAJOR DECISIONS IN ADVERTISING

Marketing management must make five important decisions when developing an advertising program (see Figure 16-1).

SETTING OBJECTIVES

The first step in developing an advertising program is to set *advertising objectives*. These objectives should be based on past decisions about the target market, positioning, and marketing mix. The marketing positioning and mix strategy define the job that advertising must do in the total marketing program.

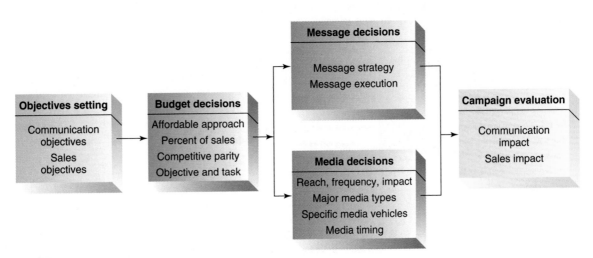

FIGURE 16-1 *Major advertising decisions*

TABLE 16-2   *Possible Advertising Objectives*

TO INFORM	
Telling the market about a new product	Describing available services
Suggesting new uses for a product	Correcting false impressions
Informing the market of a price change	Reducing buyers' fears
Explaining how the product works	Building a company image

TO PERSUADE	
Building brand preference	Persuading buyers to purchase now
Encouraging switching to your brand	Persuading buyers to receive a sales call
Changing buyer perceptions of product attributes	

TO REMIND	
Reminding buyers that the product may be needed in the near future	Keeping the product in buyers' minds during off seasons
Reminding buyers where to buy the product	Maintaining top-of-mind product awareness

Advertising objective
A specific communication *task* to be accomplished with a specific *target* audience during a specific period of *time*.

Informative advertising
Advertising used to inform consumers about a new product or feature and to build primary demand.

Persuasive advertising
Advertising used to build selective demand for a brand by persuading consumers that it offers the best quality for their money.

Comparison advertising
Advertising that compares one brand directly or indirectly to one or more other brands.

An **advertising objective** is a specific communication *task* to be accomplished with a specific *target* audience during a specific period of *time*. Advertising objectives can be classified by primary purpose—whether the aim is to *inform, persuade,* or *remind.* Table 16-2 lists examples of each of these objectives.

Informative advertising is used heavily when introducing a new product category. In this case, the objective is to build primary demand. Thus, producers of compact-disc players first informed consumers of the sound and convenience benefits of CDs. **Persuasive advertising** becomes more important as competition increases. Here, the company's objective is to build selective demand. For example, when compact-disc players became established, Sony began trying to persuade consumers that its brand offered the best quality for their money.

Some persuasive advertising has become **comparison advertising,** in which a company directly or indirectly compares its brand with one or more other brands. For example, in its classic comparison campaign, Avis positioned itself against market-leading Hertz by claiming, "We're number two, so we try harder." Procter & Gamble positioned Scope mouthwash against Listerine, claiming that minty-fresh Scope "fights bad breath and doesn't give medicine breath." Comparison advertising also has been used

Comparison advertising: Visa compares its card directly to those of major competitors—"Of all the cards in all the wallets of all the men and women in America, there's one that towers over all the others. The Visa card."

for products such as soft drinks, computers, deodorants, toothpastes, automobiles, pain relievers, and long-distance telephone service.[6]

Reminder advertising is important for mature products—it keeps consumers thinking about the product. Expensive Coca-Cola ads on television are designed primarily to remind people about Coca-Cola, not to inform or persuade them.

Reminder advertising
Advertising used to keep consumers thinking about a product.

Setting the Advertising Budget

After determining its advertising objectives, the company next sets its *advertising budget* for each product. The role of advertising is to affect demand for a product. The company wants to spend the amount needed to achieve the sales goal. Four commonly used methods for setting the advertising budget are discussed in Chapter 15. Here we describe some specific factors that should be considered when setting the advertising budget:

◆ *Stage in the product life cycle.* New products typically need large advertising budgets to build awareness and to gain consumer trial. Mature brands usually require lower budgets as a ratio to sales.

◆ *Market share.* High-market-share brands usually need more advertising spending as a percent of sales than low-share brands. Building the market or taking share from competitors requires larger advertising spending than simply maintaining current share.

◆ *Competition and clutter.* In a market with many competitors and high advertising spending, a brand must advertise more heavily to be heard above the noise in the market.

◆ *Advertising frequency.* When many repetitions are needed to present the brand's message to consumers, the advertising budget must be larger.

◆ *Product differentiation.* A brand that closely resembles other brands in its product class (beer, soft drinks, laundry detergents) requires heavy advertising to set it apart. When the product differs greatly from competitors, advertising can be used to point out the differences to consumers.[7]

Setting the advertising budget is no easy task. How does a company know if it is spending the right amount? Some critics charge that large consumer packaged-goods firms tend to spend too much on advertising and industrial companies generally underspend on advertising. They claim that, on the one hand, the large consumer companies use lots of image advertising without really knowing its effects. They overspend as a form of "insurance" against not spending enough. On the other hand, industrial advertisers tend to rely too heavily on their sales forces to bring in orders. They underestimate the power of company and product image in preselling industrial customers. Thus, they do not spend enough on advertising to build customer awareness and knowledge.

How much impact does advertising really have on consumer buying and brand loyalty? A research study analyzing household purchases of frequently bought consumer products came up with the following surprising conclusion:

> Advertising appears effective in increasing the volume purchased by loyal buyers but less effective in winning new buyers. For loyal buyers, high levels of exposure per week may be unproductive because of a leveling off of ad effectiveness. . . . Advertising appears unlikely to have some cumulative effect that leads to loyalty. . . . Features, displays, and especially price have a stronger impact on response than does advertising.[8]

These findings did not sit well with the advertising community, and several people attacked the study's data and methodology. They claimed that the study measured mostly short-run sales effects. Thus, it favored pricing and sales-promotion activities, which tend to have more immediate impact. In contrast, most advertising takes many months, or even years, to build strong brand positions and consumer loyalty. These long-run effects are difficult to measure. However, a more recent study of BehaviorScan data over a ten-year period found that advertising does produce long-term sales growth, even two years after a campaign ends.[9] This debate underscores the fact that measuring the results of advertising spending remains a poorly understood subject.

ADVERTISING STRATEGY

Advertising strategy consists of two major elements—creating advertising *messages* and selecting advertising *media*. In the past, most companies developed messages and media plans independently. Media planning often was seen as secondary to the message creation process. The creative department first created good advertisements; then the media department selected the best media for carrying these advertisements to desired target audiences. This often caused friction between creatives and media planners.

Today, however, media fragmentation, soaring media costs, and more focused target marketing strategies have promoted the importance of the media planning function. In some cases, an advertising campaign might start with a great message idea, followed by the choice of appropriate media. In other cases, however, a campaign might begin with a good media opportunity, followed by advertisements designed to take advantage of that opportunity. Increasingly, companies are realizing the benefits of planning these two important elements *jointly*. Messages and media should blend harmoniously to create an effective overall advertising campaign. This realization has resulted in greater cooperation between the creative and media functions. (See Marketing Highlight 16-2.)

Creating the Advertising Message

A large advertising budget does not guarantee a successful advertising campaign. Two advertisers can spend the same amount on advertising, yet have very different results. Studies show that creative advertising messages can be more important to advertising success than the number of dollars spent. No matter how big the budget, advertising can succeed only if commercials gain attention and communicate well.

THE CHANGING MESSAGE ENVIRONMENT. Good advertising messages are especially important in today's costly and cluttered advertising environment. The average consumer has 22 television stations and 11,500 magazines from which to choose. Add the countless radio stations and a continuous barrage of catalogs, direct-mail ads, and out-of-home media, and consumers are bombarded with ads at home, at work, and at all points in between.

All this advertising clutter bothers some consumers; it also causes big problems for advertisers. Take the situation facing network television advertisers. They typically pay an average of about $140,000 for 30 seconds of advertising time during a popular prime-time TV program—even more if it's an especially popular program such as "Home Improvement" ($350,000 per spot); "Roseanne" ($310,000); or an event like the Super Bowl ($1 million). In such cases, their ads are sandwiched in with a clutter

Breaking through advertising clutter: How would you advertise an ordinary bathroom fixture? American Standard notes: "Designing a toilet or a sink may not be as glamorous as, say, designing a Maserati. . . . but more people will be sitting on our seats than theirs."

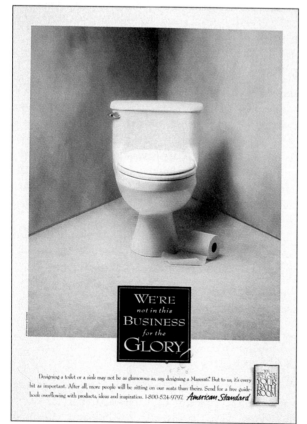

THE MEDIUM AND THE MESSAGE: A NEW HARMONY

There's a creative revolution taking place in ad agencies today, but it isn't necessarily coming from the creatives. More and more, creative directors are turning to the media departments to make their best ideas work harder. Media planning is no longer an after-the-fact complement to a new ad campaign. Media planners are now working more closely than ever with creatives to allow media selection to help shape the creative process, often before a single ad is written. In some cases, media people are even initiating ideas for new campaigns.

Among the more noteworthy ad campaigns based on tight media-creative partnerships is the one for Vin & Sprit AB's Absolut vodka. V & S and TBWA, its New York ad agency, meet once each year with a slew of magazines to set Absolut's media schedule. The schedule consists of up to 100 magazines, ranging from consumer and business magazines to theater playbills. The agency's creative department is charged with creating media-specific ads.

The result is a wonderful assortment of very creative ads for Absolut, tightly targeted to audiences of the media in which they appear. For example, an "Absolut Bravo" ad in playbills has roses adorning a clear bottle, while business magazines contain an "Absolut Merger" foldout. Los Angeles-area magazines carry "Absolut LA" ads featuring an LA-style swimming pool in the shape of an Absolut bottle. In New York-area magazines, "Absolut Manhattan" ads feature a satellite photo of Manhattan, with Central Park assuming the dis-

tinctive outline of an Absolut bottle. In Chicago, the windy city, ads show an Absolut bottle with the letters on the label blown askew. In some cases, the creatives even developed ads for magazines not yet on the schedule, as was the case with a clever "Absolut Centerfold" ad for *Playboy* magazine. The ad portrayed a clear,

and put more demand on all departments to be creative in their ideas than might be the case otherwise." And closer cooperation between creative and media people has paid off handsomely for V & S. Largely as a result of its breakthrough advertising, V & S now captures a 58 percent share of the imported vodka market.

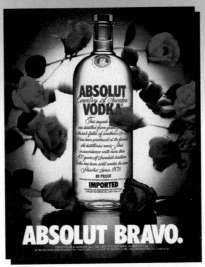 

Media planners for Absolut Vodka work with creatives to design ads targeted to specific media audiences. "Absolut Bravo" appears in theater playbills. "Absolut Chicago" targets consumers in the Windy City.

unadorned playmate bottle ("11-inch bust, 11-inch waist, 11-inch hips").

At a time of soaring media costs and cluttered communication channels, increased creative-media harmony can pay big dividends. The Absolut experience has had a positive impact on TBWA's approach to the advertising creative process. Says the agency's CEO, "What V & S has done for us is to give us a more open mind

Sales rocketed from just 12,000 cases in 1980 to more than 2.7 million cases in 1990.

Sources: Adapted from Gary Levin, " 'Meddling' in Creative More Welcome," *Advertising Age,* April 9, 1990, pp. S4, S8. Also see William Wells, John Burnett, and Sandra Moriarty, *Advertising: Principles and Practice,* 2nd ed. (Englewood Cliffs, NJ: Prentice Hall, 1992), p. 266.

of some 60 other commercials, announcements, and network promotions per hour.

But things get even worse. Until recently, television viewers were pretty much a captive audience for advertisers. Viewers had only a few channels from which to choose. Those who found the energy to get up and change channels during boring commercial breaks usually found only more of the same on the other channels. But with the growth in cable TV, VCRs, and remote-control units, today's viewers have many more options. They can avoid ads by watching commercial-free cable channels. They can "zap" commercials by pushing the fast-forward button during taped programs. With remote control, they can instantly turn off the sound during a commercial or "zip" around the channels to see what else is on.

Advertisers take such "zipping" and "zapping" very seriously. One expert predicts that by the year 2000, 60 percent of all TV viewers may be regularly tuning out commercials.[10]

Thus, just to gain and hold attention, today's advertising messages must be better planned, more imaginative, more entertaining, and more rewarding to consumers. Creative strategy therefore will play an increasingly important role in advertising success.

MESSAGE STRATEGY. The first step in creating effective advertising messages is to decide what general message will be communicated to consumers—to plan a *message strategy*. The purpose of advertising is to get consumers to think about or react to the product or company in a certain way. People will react only if they believe that they will benefit from doing so. Thus, developing an effective message strategy begins with identifying customer *benefits* that can be used as advertising appeals. In the search for benefits to feature, many creative people start by talking to consumers, dealers, experts, and competitors. Others try to imagine consumers buying or using the product to figure out the benefits they seek. Ideally, advertising message strategy will follow directly from the company's broader positioning strategy.

Message strategy statements tend to be plain, straightforward outlines of benefits and positioning points that the advertiser wants to stress. These strategy statements must be turned into advertisements that will persuade consumers to buy or believe something. The advertiser must now develop a compelling *creative concept*—or *"big idea"*—that will bring the message strategy to life in a distinctive and memorable way. At this stage, simple message ideas become great ad campaigns. Usually, a copywriter and art director will team up to generate many creative concepts, hoping that one of these concepts will turn out to be the big idea. The creative concept may emerge as a visualization, a phrase, or a combination of the two.

The creative concept will guide the choice of specific appeals to be used in an advertising campaign. Advertising appeals should have three characteristics. First, they should be *meaningful,* pointing out benefits that make the product more desirable or interesting to consumers. Second, appeals must be *believable*—consumers must believe that the product or service will deliver the promised benefits. However, the most meaningful and believable benefits may not be the best ones to feature. Appeals should also be *distinctive*—they should tell how the product is better than the competing brands. For example, the most meaningful benefit of owning a wrist watch is that it keeps accurate time, yet few watch ads feature this benefit. Instead, based on the distinctive benefits they offer, watch advertisers might select any of a number of advertising themes. For years, Timex has been the affordable watch that "Took a lickin' and kept on tickin'." In contrast, Swatch has featured style and fashion, whereas Rolex stresses luxury and status.

MESSAGE EXECUTION. The impact of the message depends not only on *what* is said, but also on *how* it is said. The advertiser now has to turn the "big idea" into an actual ad execution that will capture the target market's attention and interest. The creative people must find the best style, tone, words, and format for executing the message. Any message can be presented in different *execution styles,* such as the following:

◆ *Slice of life*. This style shows one or more "typical" people using the product in a normal setting. For example, two mothers at a picnic discuss the nutritional benefits of Jif peanut butter.

◆ *Lifestyle*. This style shows how a product fits in with a particular lifestyle. For example, a National Dairy Board ad shows women exercising and talks about how milk adds to a healthy, active lifestyle.

Accepted at
more schools
than you were.

VISA

It's everywhere
you want to be.

© Visa U.S.A. Inc. 1994

Visa uses humor to set the right tone for its student market.

◆ *Fantasy.* This style creates a fantasy around the product or its use. For instance, Revlon's first ad for Jontue showed a barefoot woman in a chiffon dress coming out of an old French barn, crossing a meadow, meeting a handsome young man on a white horse, and riding away with him.

◆ *Mood or image.* This style builds a mood or image around the product, such as beauty, love, or serenity. No claim is made about the product except through suggestion. Bermuda tourism ads create such moods.

◆ *Musical.* This style shows one or more people or cartoon characters singing a song about the product. Sears intones, "Come see the softer side of Sears."

◆ *Personality symbol.* This style creates a character that represents the product. The character might be *animated* (the Jolly Green Giant, Cap'n Crunch, Garfield the Cat) or *real* (the Marlboro man, Betty Crocker, Morris the 9-Lives Cat).

◆ *Technical expertise.* This style shows the company's expertise in making the product. Thus, Maxwell House shows one of its buyers carefully selecting the coffee beans, and Gallo tells about its many years of wine-making experience.

◆ *Scientific evidence.* This style presents survey or scientific evidence that the brand is better or better liked than one or more other brands. For years, Crest toothpaste has used scientific evidence to convince buyers that Crest is better than other brands at fighting cavities.

◆ *Testimonial evidence.* This style features a highly believable or likable source that endorses the product. It could be a celebrity like Bill Cosby (Jell-O Pudding or Kodak film) or ordinary people saying how much they like a given product ("My doctor said Mylanta").

The advertiser also must choose a *tone* for the ad. Procter & Gamble always uses a positive tone: Its ads say something very positive about its products. P&G also avoids humor that might take attention away from the message. In contrast, Little Caesar's "pizza, pizza" ads use humor—in the form of the comical Little Caesar character—to drive home the advertiser's "two for the price of one" message.

The advertiser must use memorable and attention-getting *words* in the ad. For example, the following themes on the left would have much less impact without the creative phrasing on the right:

Message Theme	Creative Copy
7-Up is not a cola.	"The Uncola."
A BMW is a well-engineered automobile.	"The Ultimate Driving Machine."
If you drink a lot of beer, Schaefer is a good beer to drink.	"The one beer to have when you're having more than one."
We don't rent as many cars, so we have to do more for our customers.	"We're number two, so we try harder." (Avis)
Hanes socks last longer than less expensive ones.	"Buy cheap socks and you'll pay through the toes."
Through the United Way, you can give to many charities with one donation.	"We're putting all our begs in one ask it."

Finally, *format* elements make a difference on an ad's impact as well as its cost. A small change in ad design can make a big difference on its effect. The *illustration* is the first thing the reader notices—it must be strong enough to draw attention. Next, the *headline* must effectively entice the right people to read the copy. Finally, the *copy*—the main block of text in the ad—must be simple but strong and convincing. Moreover, these three elements must effectively work *together*. Even then, less than 50 percent of the exposed audience might notice a truly outstanding ad; 30 percent might recall the main point of the headline; 25 percent might remember the advertiser's name; and less than 10 percent might have read most of the body copy. Less than outstanding ads, unfortunately, will not achieve even these results.

Selecting Advertising Media

The major steps in media selection are (1) deciding on *reach, frequency,* and *impact;* (2) choosing among major *media types;* (3) selecting specific *media vehicles;* and (4) deciding on *media timing.*

DECIDING ON REACH, FREQUENCY, AND IMPACT.   To select media, the advertiser must decide what reach and frequency are needed to achieve advertising objectives. **Reach** is a measure of the *percentage* of people in the target market who are exposed to the ad campaign during a given period of time. For example, the advertiser might try to reach 70 percent of the target market during the first three months of the campaign. **Frequency** is a measure of how many *times* the average person in the target market is exposed to the message. For example, the advertiser might want an average exposure frequency of three. The advertiser also must decide on the desired **media impact**—the *qualitative value* of a message exposure through a given medium. For example, for products that need to be demonstrated, messages on television may have more impact than messages on radio because television uses sight *and* sound. The same message in one magazine (say, *Newsweek*) may be more believable than in another (say, *The National Enquirer*).

Suppose that the advertiser's product might appeal to a market of 1 million consumers. The goal is to reach 700,000 consumers (70 percent of 1,000,000). Because the average consumer will receive three exposures, 2,100,000 exposures (700,000 × 3) must be bought. If the advertiser wants exposures of 1.5 impact (assuming 1.0 impact is the average), a rated number of exposures of 3,150,000 (2,100,000 × 1.5) must be bought. If a thousand exposures with this impact cost $10, the advertising budget will have to be $31,500 (3,150 × $10). In general, the more reach, frequency, and impact the advertiser seeks, the higher the advertising budget will have to be.

CHOOSING AMONG MAJOR MEDIA TYPES.   The media planner has to know the reach, frequency, and impact of each of the major media types. As summarized in Table 16-3, the major media types are newspapers, television, direct mail, radio, magazines, and outdoor. Each medium has advantages and limitations.

Media planners consider many factors when making their media choices. The *media habits of target consumers* will affect media choice—for example, radio and television are the best media for reaching teenagers. So will the *nature of the product*—fashions are best advertised in color magazines, and Polaroid cameras are best demonstrated on television. Different *types of messages* may require different media. A message announcing a major sale tomorrow will require radio or newspapers; a message with a lot of technical data might require magazines or direct mailings. *Cost* is also a major factor in media choice. Whereas television is very expensive, for example, newspaper advertising costs much less. The media planner looks at both the total cost of using a medium and at the cost per thousand exposures—the cost of reaching 1,000 people using the medium.

Reach
The percentage of people in the target market exposed to an ad campaign during a given period.

Frequency
The number of times the average person in the target market is exposed to an advertising message during a given period.

Media impact
The qualitative value of a message exposure through a given medium.

TABLE 16-3 *Profiles of Major Media Types*

MEDIUM	VOLUME IN BILLIONS	PERCENTAGE	EXAMPLES OF COST	ADVANTAGES	LIMITATIONS
Newspapers	32.0	23.2%	$45,990 for one page, weekday *Chicago Tribune*	Flexibility; timeliness; good local market coverage; broad acceptance; high believability	Short life; poor reproduction quality; small pass-along audience
Television	30.6	22.2	$1,900 for 30 seconds of prime time in Chicago	Combines sight, sound, and motion; appealing to the senses; high attention; high reach	High absolute cost; high clutter; fleeting exposure; less audience selectivity
Direct Mail	27.3	19.8	$1,520 for the names and addresses of 40,000 veterinarians	Audience selectivity; flexibility; no ad competition within the same medium; personalization	Relatively high cost; "junk mail" image
Radio	9.6	6.9	$400 for one minute of drive time (during commuting hours, A.M. and P.M.) in Chicago	Mass use; high geographic and demographic selectivity; low cost	Audio presentation only; lower attention than television; nonstandardized rate structures; fleeting exposure
Magazines	7.4	5.3	$126,755 for one page, four-color, in *Newsweek*	High geographic and demographic selectivity; credibility and prestige; high-quality reproduction; long life; good pass-along readership	Long ad purchase lead time; some waste circulation; no guarantee of position
Outdoor	1.1	0.8	$25,500 per month for 71 billboards in metropolitan Chicago	Flexibility; high repeat exposure; low cost; low competition	No audience selectivity; creative limitations
Other	30.1	21.8			
Total	138.1	100.0			

Source: Columns 1 and 2 are reprinted with permission from Robert J. Coen, "Ad Gain of 5.2% in '93 Marks Downturn's End," *Advertising Age*, May 2, 1994, p. 4.

Media impact and cost must be reexamined regularly. For a long time, television and magazines have dominated in the media mixes of national advertisers, with other media often neglected. Recently, however, the costs and clutter of these media have gone up, audiences have dropped, and marketers are adopting strategies beamed at narrower segments. As a result, TV and magazine advertising revenues have leveled off or declined.[11] Advertisers are increasingly turning to alternative media, ranging from cable TV and outdoor advertising to parking meters and shopping carts (see Marketing Highlight 16-3).

Given these and other media characteristics, the media planner must decide how much of each media type to buy. For example, in launching a new biscuit product, Pillsbury might decide to spend $6 million advertising in daytime network television, $4 million in women's magazines, and $2 million in daily newspapers in 20 major markets.

Media vehicles
Specific media within each general media type, such as specific magazines, television shows, or radio programs.

SELECTING SPECIFIC MEDIA VEHICLES. The media planner now must choose the best **media vehicles**—specific media within each general media type. For example, television vehicles include "Roseanne," "Murphy Brown," "60 Minutes," and "ABC World News Tonight." Magazine vehicles include *Newsweek, People,* and

ADVERTISERS SEEK ALTERNATIVE MEDIA

As network television costs soar and audiences shrink, many advertisers are looking for new ways to reach consumers. And the move toward micromarketing strategies, focused more narrowly on specific consumer groups, also has fueled the search for alternative media to replace or supplement network television. Advertisers are shifting larger portions of their budgets to media that cost less and target more effectively.

Two media benefiting most from the shift are outdoor advertising and cable television. Billboards have undergone a resurgence in recent years. Although outdoor advertising spending recently has leveled off, advertisers now spend more than $1.1 billion annually on outdoor media, a 25 percent increase over ten years ago. Gone are the ugly eyesores of the past; in their place we now see cleverly designed, colorful attention-grabbers. Outdoor advertising provides an excellent way to reach important local consumer segments.

Cable television is also booming. Today, more than 60 percent of all U.S. households subscribe to cable, up from just 20 percent in 1980, and cable TV advertising revenues now exceed $3 billion a year, compared to a mere $58 million in 1980. Industry experts expect that cable television advertising will continue to grow explosively through the 1990s. Cable systems allow narrow programming formats such as all sports, all news, nutrition programs, arts programs, and others that target select groups. Advertisers can take advantage of such "narrowcasting" to "rifle in" on special market segments rather than the "shotgun" approach offered by network broadcasting.

Cable TV and outdoor advertising seem to make good sense. But, increasingly, ads are popping up in far less likely places. In their efforts to find less costly and more highly targeted ways to reach consumers, advertisers have discovered a dazzling collection of "alternative media." As consumers, we're used to ads on television, in magazines and newspapers, on the radio, and along the

roadways. But these days, no matter where you go or what you do, you probably will run into some new form of advertising.

Tiny video screens attached to shopping carts, triggered by the aisle in which the consumer is shopping, show ads from national advertisers and flash messages about store specials. As you wait in line to buy your

Marketers have discovered a dazzling array of "alternative media."

groceries, television screens tuned to the "Checkout Channel" treat you to the latest news interspersed with food-product ads. As you approach your car, signs atop parking meters hawk everything from Jeeps to Minolta cameras to Recipe dog food. You escape to the ballpark, only to find billboard-size video screens running Budweiser ads while a blimp with an electronic message board

circles lazily overhead.

You pay to see a movie at your local theater, but first you see a two-minute science-fiction fantasy that turns out to be an ad for General Electric portable stereo boxes. Then the movie itself is full of not-so-subtle promotional plugs for Pepsi, Domino's Pizza, Alka-Seltzer, MasterCard, Fritos, or any of a dozen other products. At the airport you're treated to the CNN Airport Network; at the local rail station, it's the Commuter Channel. Boats cruise along public beaches flashing advertising messages for Sundown Sunscreen or Gatorade to sunbathers. Even church bulletins carry ads for Campbell's Soup. Advertisers seeking a really out-of-this-world alternative can pay $500,000 for 58 feet of prime advertising space on the hull of a Conestoga 1620 expendable rocket scheduled for launch by NASA this spring.

Some of these alternative media seem a bit far-fetched, and they sometimes irritate consumers. But for many marketers, these media can save money and provide a way to hit selected consumers where they live, shop, work, and play. Of course, this may leave you wondering if there are any commercial-free havens remaining for ad-weary consumers. The back seat of a taxi, perhaps, or public elevators, or stalls in a public restroom? Forget it! Each has already been invaded by innovative marketers.

Sources: See Alison Leigh Cowan, "Marketers Worry as Ads Crop Up in Unlikely Places," *Raleigh News and Observer,* February 21, 1988, p. 11; Kathy Martin, "What's Next? Execs Muse Over Boundless Ad Possibilities," *Advertising Age,* August 27, 1990; John P. Cortez, "Ads Head for the Bathroom," *Advertising Age,* May 18, 1992, p. 24; Ronald Grover, Laura Zinn, and Irene Recio, "Big Brother Is Grocery Shopping with You," *Business Week,* March 29, 1993, p. 60; Richard Szathmary, "The Great (and Not So Great) Outdoors," *Sales & Marketing Management,* March 1992, pp. 75–81; Riccardo A. Davis, "More Ads Go Outdoors," *Advertising Age,* November 9, 1992, p. 36; and "Special Report: Cable TV," *Advertising Age,* March 27, 1995, pp. 51–53.

Sports Illustrated. If advertising is placed in magazines, the media planner must look up circulation figures and the costs of different ad sizes, color options, ad positions, and frequencies for specific magazines. Then the planner must evaluate each magazine on factors such as credibility, status, reproduction quality, editorial focus, and advertising submission deadlines. The media planner ultimately decides which vehicles give the best reach, frequency, and impact for the money.

Media planners also compute the cost per thousand persons reached by a vehicle. For example, if a full-page, four-color advertisement in *Newsweek* costs $126,000 and *Newsweek's* readership is 3.1 million people, the cost of reaching each group of 1,000 persons is about $40. The same advertisement in *Business Week* may cost only $64,400 but reach only 870,000 persons—at a cost per thousand of about $74. The media planner would rank each magazine by cost per thousand and favor those magazines with the lower cost per thousand for reaching target consumers.

The media planner also must consider the costs of producing ads for different media. Whereas newspaper ads may cost very little to produce, flashy television ads may cost millions. On average, advertisers must pay $222,000 to produce a single 30-second television commercial. Nike recently paid a cool $2 million to make a single ad called "The Wall."[12]

Thus, the media planner must balance media cost measures against several media impact factors. First, the planner should balance costs against the media vehicle's *audience quality.* For a baby lotion advertisement, for example, *New Parents* magazine would have a high-exposure value; *Gentlemen's Quarterly* would have a low-exposure value. Second, the media planner should consider *audience attention.* Readers of *Vogue,* for example, typically pay more attention to ads than do *Newsweek* readers. Third, the planner should assess the vehicle's *editorial quality*—*Time* and *The Wall Street Journal* are more believable and prestigious than *The National Enquirer.*

DECIDING ON MEDIA TIMING. The advertiser also must decide how to schedule the advertising over the course of a year. Suppose sales of a product peak in December and drop in March. The firm can vary its advertising to follow the seasonal pattern, to oppose the seasonal pattern, or to be the same all year. Most firms do some seasonal advertising. Some do *only* seasonal advertising: For example, Hallmark advertises its greeting cards only before major holidays.

Finally, the advertiser has to choose the pattern of the ads. *Continuity* means scheduling ads evenly within a given period. *Pulsing* means scheduling ads unevenly over a given time period. Thus, 52 ads could either be scheduled at one per week during the year or pulsed in several bursts. The idea is to advertise heavily for a short period to build awareness that carries over to the next advertising period. Those who favor pulsing feel that it can be used to achieve the same impact as a steady schedule, but at a much lower cost. However, some media planners believe that although pulsing achieves minimal awareness, it sacrifices depth of advertising communications.

ADVERTISING EVALUATION

The advertising program should evaluate both the *communication effects* and the *sales effects* of advertising regularly.

Measuring the Communication Effect

Measuring the communication effect of an ad—*copy testing*—tells whether the ad is communicating well. Copy testing can be done before or after an ad is printed or broadcast. There are three major methods of advertising *pretesting*. The first is through *direct rating,* where the advertiser exposes a consumer panel to alternative ads and asks them to rate the ads. These direct ratings indicate how well the ads get attention and how they affect consumers. Although this is an imperfect measure of an ad's actual impact, a high rating indicates a potentially more effective ad. In *portfolio tests,* consumers view or listen to a portfolio of advertisements, taking as much time as they need. They then are asked to recall all the ads and their content, aided or unaided by the interviewer. Their recall level indicates the ability of an ad to stand out and its message to be understood and remembered. *Laboratory tests* use equipment to measure consumers' physiological reactions to an ad—heartbeat, blood pressure, pupil dilation, perspiration. These tests measure an ad's attention-getting power, but reveal little about its impact on beliefs, attitudes, or intentions.

There are two popular methods of *posttesting* ads. Using *recall tests,* the advertiser asks people who have been exposed to magazines or television programs to recall everything they can about the advertisers and products they saw. Recall scores indicate the ad's power to be noticed and retained. In *recognition tests,* the researcher asks readers of a given issue of, say, a magazine to point out what they recognize as having seen before. Recognition scores can be used to assess the ad's impact in different market segments and to compare the company's ads with competitors' ads.

Measuring the Sales Effect

What sales are caused by an ad that increases brand awareness by 20 percent and brand preference by 10 percent? The sales effect of advertising is often harder to measure than the communication effect. Sales are affected by many factors besides advertising—such as product features, price, and availability.

One way to measure the sales effect of advertising is to compare past sales with past advertising expenditures. Another way is through experiments. For example, to test the effects of different advertising spending levels, Pizza Hut could vary the amount it spends on advertising in different market areas and measure the differences in the resulting sales levels. It could spend the normal amount in one market area, half the normal amount in another area, and twice the normal amount in a third area. If the three market areas are similar, and if all other marketing efforts in the area are the same, then differences in sales in the three cities could be related to advertising level. More complex experiments could be designed to include other variables, such as difference in the ads or media used.

INTERNATIONAL ADVERTISING DECISIONS

International advertisers face many complexities not encountered by domestic advertisers. The most basic issue concerns the degree to which global advertising should be adapted to the unique characteristics of various country markets. Some large advertisers have attempted to support their global brands with highly standardized worldwide advertising. Standardization produces many benefits—lower advertising costs, greater coordination of global advertising efforts, and a more consistent worldwide company or product image. However, standardization also has drawbacks. Most importantly, it ignores the fact that country markets differ greatly in their cultures, demographics, and economic conditions. Thus, most international advertisers think globally but act locally. They develop global advertising *strategies* that bring efficiency and consistency to their worldwide advertising efforts. Then they adapt their advertising *programs* to make them more responsive to consumer needs and expectations within local markets.

Kellogg's Frosted Flakes commercials are almost identical worldwide, with only minor adjustments for local cultural differences.

Companies vary in the degree to which they adapt their advertising to local markets. For example, Kellogg's Frosted Flakes commercials are almost identical worldwide, with only minor adjustments for local cultural differences.[13] The advertising uses a tennis theme that has worldwide appeal and features teenage actors with generic good looks—neither too Northern European nor too Latin American. Of course, Kellogg translates the commercials into different languages. In the English version, for example, Tony growls "They're Gr-r-reat!" whereas in the German version it's "Gr-r-rossartig!" Other adaptations are more subtle. In the American ad, after winning the match, Tony leaps over the net in celebration. In other versions, he simply "high fives" his young partner. The reason: Europeans do not jump over the net after winning at tennis.

In contrast, Parker Pen Company changes its advertising substantially from country to country.

> Print ads in Germany simply show the Parker Pen held in a hand that is writing a headline—"This is how you write with precision." In the United Kingdom, where it is the brand leader, [ads emphasize] the exotic processes used to make pens, such as gently polishing the gold nibs with walnut chips. . . . In the United States, the ad campaign's theme is status and image. The headlines are . . . "Here's how you tell who's boss," and "There are times when it has to be Parker." The company considers the different themes necessary because of different product images and . . . customer motives in each market.[14]

Global advertisers face several additional problems. For instance, advertising media costs and availability differ considerably from country to country. Some countries have too few media to handle all of the advertising offered to them. Other countries are peppered with so many media that an advertiser cannot gain national coverage at a reasonable cost. Media prices often are negotiated and may vary greatly. For example, one study found that the cost of reaching 1,000 consumers in 11 different European countries ranged from $1.58 in Belgium to $5.91 in Italy. For women's magazines, the advertising cost per page ranged from $2.51 per thousand circulation in Denmark to $10.87 in Germany.[15]

Countries also differ in the extent to which they regulate advertising practices. Many countries have extensive systems of laws restricting how much a company can spend on advertising, the media used, the nature of advertising claims, and other aspects of the advertising program. Such restrictions often require that advertisers adapt their campaigns from country to country. Consider the following examples:

> When General Mills Toy Group's European subsidiary launched a product line of G.I. Joe-type war toys and soldiers, it had to develop two television com-

mercials, a general version for most European countries and another for countries that bar advertisements for products with military or violent themes. As a result, in the version running in Germany, Holland, and Belgium, jeeps replaced the toy tanks, and guns were removed from the hands of toy soldiers.[16]

A 30-second Kellogg commercial produced for British TV would have to have [several] alterations to be acceptable [elsewhere] in Europe: Reference to iron and vitamins would have to be deleted in the Netherlands. A child wearing a Kellogg's T-shirt would be edited out in France where children are forbidden from endorsing products on TV. In Germany, the line "Kellogg makes cornflakes the best they've ever been" would be cut because of rules against making competitive claims. After alterations, the 30-second commercial would be [only] about five seconds long.[17]

Thus, although advertisers may develop global strategies to guide their overall advertising efforts, specific advertising programs usually must be adapted to meet local cultures and customs, media characteristics, and advertising regulations.

SALES PROMOTION

Sales promotion
Short-term incentives to encourage purchase or sales of a product or service.

Advertising is joined by two other mass-promotion tools—*sales promotion* and *public relations*. **Sales promotion** consists of short-term incentives to encourage purchase or sales of a product or service. Whereas advertising offers reasons to buy a product or service, sales promotion offers reasons to buy *now*. Examples are found everywhere. A freestanding insert in the Sunday newspaper contains a coupon offering 50 cents off on Folger's coffee. The end-of-the-aisle display in the local supermarket tempts impulse buyers with a wall of Coke cartons. An executive buys a new Compaq laptop computer and gets a free carrying case, or a family buys a new Taurus and receives a rebate check for $500. A hardware store chain receives a 10 percent discount on selected Black & Decker portable power tools if it agrees to advertise them in local newspapers.

Sales promotion includes a wide variety of promotion tools designed to stimulate earlier or stronger market response. It includes **consumer promotion**—samples, coupons, rebates, prices-off, premiums, contests, and others; **trade promotion**—buying allowances, free goods, merchandise allowances, cooperative advertising, push money, dealer sales contests; and **sales force promotion**—bonuses, contests, sales rallies.

Consumer promotion
Sales promotion designed to stimulate consumer purchasing, including samples, coupons, rebates, prices-off, premiums, patronage rewards, displays, and contests and sweepstakes.

Trade promotion
Sales promotion designed to gain reseller support and to improve reseller selling efforts, including discounts, allowances, free goods, cooperative advertising, push money, and conventions and trade shows.

Sales force promotion
Sales promotion designed to motivate the sales force and make sales force selling efforts more effective, including bonuses, contests, and sales rallies.

RAPID GROWTH OF SALES PROMOTION

Sales-promotion tools are used by most organizations, including manufacturers, distributors, retailers, trade associations, and nonprofit institutions. Estimates of annual sales-promotion spending run as high as $125 billion, and this spending has increased rapidly in recent years. Today in many consumer packaged-goods companies, sales promotion accounts for 75 percent or more of all marketing expenditures. Sales-promotion expenditures have been increasing 12 percent annually, compared to advertising's increase of only 7.6 percent.[18]

Several factors have contributed to the rapid growth of sales promotion, particularly in consumer markets. First, inside the company, product managers face greater pressures to increase their current sales, and promotion now is accepted more by top management as an effective sales tool. Second, externally, the company faces more competition, and competing brands are less differentiated. Competitors are using more promotions, and consumers have become more deal oriented. Third, advertising efficiency has declined because of rising costs, media clutter, and legal restraints. Finally, retailers are demanding more deals from manufacturers.

The growing use of sales promotion has resulted in *promotion clutter,* similar to advertising clutter. Consumers are increasingly tuning out promotions, weakening their ability to trigger immediate purchase. In fact, the extent to which U.S. consumers have come to take promotions for granted was illustrated dramatically by the reactions of Eastern European consumers when Procter & Gamble recently gave out samples of a newly introduced shampoo. To P&G, the sampling campaign was just business as usual. To consumers in Poland and Czechoslovakia, however, it was little short of a miracle:

> With nothing expected in return, Warsaw shoppers were being handed free samples of Vidal Sassoon Wash & Go shampoo. Just for the privilege of trying the new product; no standing in line for a product that may not even be on the shelf. Some were so taken aback that they were moved to tears. In a small town in Czechoslovakia, the head of the local post office was so pleased to be part of the direct-mail sampling program, he sent the P&G staffer roses to express his thanks. The postmaster told the P&G'er: "This is the most exciting thing that's ever happened in this post office—it's a terrific experience to be part of this new market economy that's coming."[19]

Although no sales promotion is likely to create such excitement among promotion-prone consumers in the United States and other Western countries, manufacturers now are searching for ways to rise above the clutter, such as offering larger coupon values or creating more dramatic point-of-purchase displays.

PURPOSE OF SALES PROMOTION

Sales-promotion tools vary in their specific objectives. For example, a free sample stimulates consumer trial; a free management advisory service cements a long-term relationship with a retailer. Sellers use sales promotions to attract new triers, to reward loyal customers, and to increase the repurchase rates of occasional users.

There are three types of new triers—nonusers of the product category, loyal users of another brand, and users who frequently switch brands. Sales promotions often attract the last group—brand switchers—because nonusers and users of other brands do not always notice or act on a promotion. Brand switchers mostly are looking for low price or good value. Sales promotions are unlikely to turn them into loyal brand users. Thus, sales promotions used in markets where brands are very similar usually produce high short-run sales response but little permanent market-share gain. In markets where brands differ greatly, however, sales promotions can alter market shares more permanently.

Many sellers think of sales promotion as a tool for breaking down brand loyalty and advertising as a tool for building up brand loyalty. Thus, an important issue for marketing managers is how to divide the budget between sales promotion and advertising. There is a danger in letting advertising take a back seat to sales promotion. Reduced advertising spending can result in lost consumer brand loyalty. One recent study of loyalty toward 45 major packaged-goods brands showed that when share of advertising drops, so does brand loyalty. Since 1975, brand loyalty for brands with increased advertising spending fell 5 percent. However, for brands with decreased ad spending, brand loyalty fell 18 percent.[20]

When a company price-promotes a brand too much of the time, consumers begin to think of it as a cheap brand. Soon, many consumers will buy the brand only when it is on special. Most analysts believe that sales-promotion activities do not build long-term consumer preference and loyalty, as does advertising. Instead, promotion usually produces only short-term sales that cannot be maintained.

The upshot is that many consumer packaged-goods companies feel that they are forced to use more sales promotion than they would like. Recently, Kellogg, Kraft, Procter & Gamble, and several other market leaders have announced that they will put growing emphasis on pull promotion and increase their advertising budgets. They blame the heavy use of sales promotion for decreased brand loyalty, increased consumer price sensitivity, a focus on short-run marketing planning, and an erosion of brand-quality image.

Some marketers dispute this criticism, however. They argue that the heavy use of sales promotion is a symptom of these problems, not a cause. They point to more basic causes, such as slower population growth, more educated consumers, industry overcapacity, the decreasing effectiveness of advertising, the growth of reseller power, and U.S. businesses' emphasis on short-run profits. These marketers assert that sales promotion provides many important benefits to manufacturers as well as to consumers. Sales promotions let manufacturers adjust to short-term changes in supply and demand and to differences in customer segments. They let manufacturers charge a higher list price to test "how high is high." Sales promotions encourage consumers to try new products instead of always staying with their current ones. They lead to more varied retail formats, such as the everyday-low-price store or the promotional-pricing store, which gives consumers more choice. Finally, sales promotions lead to greater consumer awareness of prices, and consumers themselves enjoy the satisfaction of feeling like smart shoppers when they take advantage of price specials.[21]

Sales promotions usually are used together with advertising or personal selling. Consumer promotions usually must be advertised and can add excitement and pulling power to ads. Trade and sales force promotions support the firm's personal selling process. In using sales promotion, a company must set objectives, select the right tools, develop the best program, pretest and implement it, and evaluate the results.

SETTING SALES-PROMOTION OBJECTIVES

Sales-promotion objectives vary widely. Sellers may use *consumer promotions* to increase short-term sales or to help build long-term market share. The objective may be to entice consumers to try a new product, lure consumers away from competitors' products, get consumers to "load up" on a mature product, or hold and reward loyal customers. Objectives for *trade promotions* include getting retailers to carry new items and more inventory, getting them to advertise the product and give it more shelf space, and getting them to buy ahead. For the *sales force*, objectives include getting more sales force support for current or new products or getting salespeople to sign up new accounts.

In general, sales promotions should be *consumer relationship building*. Rather than creating only short-term sales volume or temporary brand switching, they should help to reinforce the product's position and build long-term relationships with consumers. Increasingly, marketers are avoiding "quick fix," price-only promotions in favor of promotions designed to build brand equity. For example, in France, Nestlé set up roadside Relais Bébé centers, where travelers can stop to feed and change their babies. At each center, Nestlé hostesses provide free disposable diapers, changing tables, high chairs, and free samples of Nestlé baby food. Each summer, 64 hostesses welcome 120,000 baby visits and dispense 6,000,000 samples of baby food. This ongoing promotion provides real value to parents and an ideal opportunity to build relationships with customers. At key meal-time moments, Nestlé hostesses are in direct contact with mothers in a unique, brand-related relationship. Nestlé also provides a toll-free phone number for free baby-nutrition counseling.[22]

Even price promotions can be designed to help build customer relationships. Examples include all of the "loyalty marketing programs" that have mushroomed in recent years. For instance, Waldenbooks sponsors a Preferred Reader Program through which more than five million regular customers receive a 10 percent discount on book purchases along with toll-free ordering, mailings about new books, and other services. Thus, if properly designed, every sales-promotion tool has consumer-relationship-building potential.

SELECTING SALES-PROMOTION TOOLS

Many tools can be used to accomplish sales-promotion objectives. Descriptions of the main consumer- and trade-promotion tools follow.

Consumer-Promotion Tools

The main consumer-promotion tools include samples, coupons, cash refunds, price packs, premiums, advertising specialties, patronage rewards, point-of-purchase displays and demonstrations, and contests, sweepstakes, and games.

Samples
Offers to consumers of a trial amount of a product.

Samples are offers of a trial amount of a product. Some samples are free; for others, the company charges a small amount to offset its cost. The sample might be delivered door to door, sent by mail, handed out in a store, attached to another product, or featured in an ad. Sampling is the most effective—but most expensive—way to introduce a new product. For example, Lever Brothers had so much confidence in its Surf detergent that it spent $43 million to distribute free samples to four of every five American households. Sometimes, samples are combined into sample packs, which can then be used to promote other products and services. An example is Blockbuster Video's "Bonus Box" promotion, in which customers who rent at least three movies receive a box containing samples of Triples and other General Mills cereals, Hawaiian Punch from Procter & Gamble, Hidden Valley dip from Clorox, and Lever 2000 soap from Lever Brothers. Blockbuster hands out more than four million of these boxes over a typical July Fourth weekend.[23]

Coupons
Certificates that give buyers a saving when they purchase a specified product.

Coupons are certificates that give buyers a saving when they purchase specified products. More than 322 billion coupons are distributed in the United States each year. Consumers redeem almost eight billion of these coupons at an average face value of 59 cents per coupon, saving over $4.7 billion on their shopping bills.

Consumer-promotion tools: Here NutraSweet tries to stimulate immediate purchase with a combination of incentives, including a sample offer (free trial size), a coupon offer ($1 off larger sizes), and a premium offer (a recipe collection). On the right, it celebrates its tenth anniversary with a sweepstakes offer.

Point-of-sale couponing: Using Checkout Direct technology, marketers can dispense personalized coupons to carefully targeted buyers at the checkout counter. This avoids the waste of poorly targeted coupons delivered through FSIs (coupon pages inserted into newspapers).

Coupons can be mailed, included with other products, or placed in ads. They can stimulate sales of a mature brand or promote early trial of a new brand. Stores now feature electronic point-of-sale coupon printers as well as "paperless coupon systems" which dispense personalized discounts to targeted buyers at the checkstand in stores. Early tests using instant coupon machines have produced average redemption rates of 24 percent and boosted sales about 32 percent.[24]

Cash refund offers (rebates)
Offers to refund part of the purchase price of a product to consumers who send a "proof of purchase" to the manufacturer.

Cash refund offers (or **rebates**) are like coupons except that the price reduction occurs after the purchase rather than at the retail outlet. The consumer sends a "proof of purchase" to the manufacturer, who then refunds part of the purchase price by mail. For example, Toro ran a clever preseason promotion on some of its snowblower models, offering a rebate if the snowfall in the buyer's market area turned out to be below average. Competitors were not able to match this offer on such short notice, and the promotion was very successful. In contrast, rebates have become so common in the automotive industry that many car buyers postpone purchasing until a rebate is announced. Because most auto companies match each other's rebates, each company gains little. The money could be better spent on advertising to build stronger brand images.

Price packs (cents-off deals)
Reduced prices that are marked by the producer directly on the label or package.

Price packs (also called **cents-off deals**) offer consumers savings off the regular price of a product. The reduced prices are marked by the producer directly on the label or package. Price packs can be single packages sold at a reduced price (such as two for the price of one), or two related products banded together (such as a toothbrush and toothpaste). Price packs are very effective—even more so than coupons—in stimulating short-term sales.

Premiums
Goods offered either free or at low cost as an incentive to buy a product.

Premiums are goods offered either free or at low cost as an incentive to buy a product. In its "Treasure Hunt" promotion, for example, Quaker Oats inserted $5 million worth of gold and silver coins in Ken-L Ration dog-food packages. In its recent premium promotion, Cutty Sark scotch offered a brass tray with the purchase of one bottle of Cutty and a desk lamp with the purchase of two. A premium may come inside the package (in-pack) or outside the package (on-pack). If reusable, the package itself may serve as a premium—such as a decorative tin. Premiums are sometimes mailed to consumers who have sent in a proof of purchase, such as a box top. A *self-liquidating premium* is a premium sold below its normal retail price to consumers who request it. For example, manufacturers now offer consumers all kinds of premiums bearing the company's name: Budweiser fans can order T-shirts, hot-air balloons, and hundreds of other items with Bud's name on them at unusually low prices.

Advertising specialties

Useful articles imprinted with an advertiser's name, given as gifts to consumers.

Advertising specialties are useful articles imprinted with an advertiser's name given as gifts to consumers. Typical items include pens, calendars, key rings, matches, shopping bags, T-shirts, caps, nail files, and coffee mugs. U.S. companies spend over $4.5 billion each year on advertising specialties. Such items can be very effective. In a recent study, 63 percent of all consumers surveyed were either carrying or wearing an ad specialty item. More than three quarters of those who had an item could recall the advertiser's name or message before showing the item to the interviewer.[25]

Patronage rewards

Cash or other awards for the regular use of a certain company's products or services.

Patronage rewards are cash or other awards offered for the regular use of a certain company's products or services. For example, airlines offer "frequent flyer plans," awarding points for miles traveled that can be turned in for free airline trips. Marriott Hotels has adopted an "honored guest" plan that awards points to users of their hotels. Baskin-Robbins offers frequent-purchase awards—for every ten purchases, customers receive a free quart of ice cream. Trading stamps are also patronage rewards in that customers receive stamps when buying from certain merchants, which can be redeemed for goods either at redemption centers or through mail-order catalogs.

Point-of-purchase (POP) promotions

Displays and demonstrations that take place at the point of purchase or sale.

Point-of-purchase (POP) promotions include displays and demonstrations that take place at the point of purchase or sale. An example is a five-foot-high cardboard display of Cap'n Crunch next to Cap'n Crunch cereal boxes. Unfortunately, many retailers do not like to handle the hundreds of displays, signs, and posters they receive from manufacturers each year. Manufacturers have responded by offering better POP materials, tying them in with television or print messages, and offering to set them up. A good example is the award-winning Pepsi "tipping can" display. From an ordinary display of Pepsi six-packs along a supermarket aisle, a mechanically rigged six-pack begins to tip forward, grabbing the attention of passing shoppers who think the six-pack is falling. A sign reminds shoppers, "Don't forget the Pepsi!" In test-market stores, the display helped get more trade support and greatly increased Pepsi sales.

Contests, sweepstakes, games

Promotional events that give consumers the chance to win something—such as cash, trips, or goods—by luck or through extra effort.

Contests, sweepstakes, and **games** give consumers the chance to win something, such as cash, trips, or goods, by luck or through extra effort. A *contest* calls for consumers to submit an entry—a jingle, guess, suggestion—to be judged by a panel that will select the best entries. A *sweepstakes* calls for consumers to submit their names for a drawing. A *game* presents consumers with something—bingo numbers, missing letters—every time they buy, which may or may not help them win a prize. A sales contest urges dealers or the sales force to increase their efforts, with prizes going to the top performers.

Trade-Promotion Tools

More sales-promotion dollars are directed to retailers and wholesalers (63 percent) than to consumers (37 percent). Trade promotion can persuade retailers or wholesalers to carry a brand, give it shelf space, promote it in advertising, and push it to consumers. Shelf space is so scarce these days that manufacturers often have to

Discount
A straight reduction in price on purchases during a stated period of time.

Allowance
Promotional money paid by manufacturers to retailers in return for an agreement to feature the manufacturer's products in some way.

offer price-offs, allowances, buy-back guarantees, or free goods to retailers and wholesalers to get on the shelf and, once there, to stay on it.

Manufacturers use several trade-promotion tools. Many of the tools used for consumer promotions—contests, premiums, displays—also can be used as trade promotions. Or the manufacturer may offer a straight **discount** off the list price on each case purchased during a stated period of time (also called a *price-off, off-invoice,* or *off-list*). The offer encourages dealers to buy in quantity or to carry a new item. Dealers can use the discount for immediate profit, for advertising, or for price reductions to their customers.

Manufacturers also may offer an **allowance** (usually so much off per case) in return for the retailer's agreement to feature the manufacturer's products in some way. An *advertising allowance* compensates retailers for advertising the product. A *display allowance* compensates them for using special displays.

Manufacturers may offer *free goods,* which are extra cases of merchandise, to middlemen who buy a certain quantity or who feature a certain flavor or size. They may offer *push money*—cash or gifts to dealers or their sales force to "push" the manufacturer's goods. Manufacturers may give retailers free *specialty advertising items* that carry the company's name, such as pens, pencils, calendars, paperweights, matchbooks, memo pads, ashtrays, and yardsticks.

Business-Promotion Tools

Companies spend billions of dollars each year on promotion to industrial customers. These business promotions are used to generate business leads, stimulate purchases, reward customers, and motivate salespeople. Business promotion includes many of the same tools used for consumer or trade promotions. Here, we focus on two major business-promotion tools—conventions and trade shows, and sales contests.

Many companies and trade associations organize *conventions and trade shows* to promote their products. Firms selling to the industry show their products at the trade show. More than 5,800 trade shows take place every year, drawing approximately 80 million people. Vendors receive many benefits, such as opportunities to find new sales leads, contact customers, introduce new products, meet new customers, sell more to present customers, and educate customers with publications and audiovisual materials. Trade shows also help companies reach many prospects not reached through their sales forces. About 90 percent of a trade show's visitors see a company's salespeople for the first time at the show.

Business marketers may spend as much as 35 percent of their annual promotion budgets on trade shows. They face several decisions, including which trade shows to participate in, how much to spend on each trade show, how to build dramatic exhibits that attract attention, and how to follow up on sales leads effectively.[26]

A *sales contest* is a contest for salespeople or dealers to motivate them to increase their sales performance over a given period. Most companies sponsor annual or more frequent sales contests for their sales force. Called "incentive programs," these contests motivate and recognize good company performers, who may receive trips, cash prizes, or other gifts. Some companies award points for performance, which the receiver can turn in for any of a variety of prizes. Sales contests work best when they are tied to measurable and achievable sales objectives (such as finding new accounts, reviving old accounts, or increasing account profitability) and when employees believe they have an equal chance of winning. Otherwise, employees who do not think the contest's goals are reasonable or equitable will not take up the challenge.

DEVELOPING THE SALES-PROMOTION PROGRAM

The marketer must make several other decisions in order to define the full sales-promotion program. First, the marketer must decide on the *size of the incentive*. A certain minimum incentive is necessary if the promotion is to succeed; a larger incentive will produce more sales response. The marketer also must set *conditions for participation*. Incentives might be offered to everyone or only to select groups. The marketer must decide how to *promote and distribute the promotion* program itself. A 50-cents-off coupon could be given out in a package, at the store, by mail, or in an advertisement. Each distribution method involves a different level of reach and cost. Increasingly, marketers are blending several media into a total campaign concept:

> A sports trivia game to create pull-through at taverns for a premium beer brand would use TV to reach consumers, direct mail to incentivize distributors, point-of-purchase for retail support, telephones for consumer call-ins, a service bureau for call processing, live operators for data entry, and computer software and hardware to tie it all together. . . . Companies use telepromotions not only to pull product through at retail but also to identify customers, generate leads, build databases and deliver coupons, product samples and rebate offers.[27]

The *length of the promotion* is also important. If the sales-promotion period is too short, many prospects (who may not be buying during that time) will miss it. If the promotion runs too long, the deal will lose some of its "act now" force.

Finally, the marketer must determine the *sales-promotion budget*. The most common way is to use a percentage of the total budget for sales promotion. A better way is the objective-and-task method discussed in the previous chapter. Whatever method is used, marketers need to consider the cost effectiveness of their sales promotion programs carefully.

Whenever possible, sales-promotion tools should be *pretested* to find out if they are appropriate and of the right incentive size. Yet few promotions are ever tested ahead of time—70 percent of companies do not test sales promotions before starting them.[28] Nevertheless, consumer sales promotions can be pretested quickly and inexpensively. For example, consumers can be asked to rate or rank different possible promotions, or promotions can be tried on a limited basis in selected geographic areas.

Evaluation is also very important. Yet many companies fail to evaluate their sales-promotion programs, and others evaluate them only superficially. Manufacturers can use one of many evaluation methods. The most common method is to compare sales before, during, and after a promotion. Suppose a company has a 6 percent market share before the promotion, which jumps to 10 percent during the promotion, falls to 5 percent right after, and rises to 7 percent later on. The promotion seems to have attracted new triers and more buying from current customers. After the promotion, sales fell as consumers used up their inventories. The long-run rise to 7 percent means that the company gained some new users. If the brand's share had returned to the old level, then the promotion would have changed only the *timing* of demand rather than the *total* demand.

Consumer research also would show the kinds of people who responded to the promotion and what they did after it ended. *Surveys* can provide information on how many consumers recall the promotion, what they thought of it, how many took advantage of it, and how it affected their buying. Sales promotions also can be evaluated through *experiments* that vary factors such as incentive value, length, and distribution method.

AWARD-WINNING SALES PROMOTIONS

Each year, American companies bombard consumers with thousands upon thousands of assorted sales promotions. Some fizzle badly, never meeting their objectives; others yield blockbuster returns. Here are examples of some award-winning sales promotions.

9-Lives "Free Health Exam for Your Cat" Offer

In this unusual premium promotion, Star-Kist Foods teamed with the American Animal Hospital Association to offer cat owners a free $15 cat physical in exchange for proofs of purchase from 9-Lives cat food products. The 1,500 AAHA members donated their services to encourage cat owners to bring in their cats for regular checkups. Star-Kist supported the premium offer with 63 million coupons and trade discounts to boost retailer support. The promotion cost about $600,000 (excluding media). Consumers redeemed coupons at a rate 40 percent higher than normal, and

Star-Kist gave out more than 50,000 free exam certificates. During the promotion, 9-Lives canned products achieved their highest share of the market in two years.

NutraSweet's Tenth Anniversary Sweepstakes

To celebrate its tenth anniversary, NutraSweet developed an innovative call-in sweepstakes. The objective: to increase sales and awareness of NutraSweet's broad acceptance since its introduction ten years earlier. The company also wanted to salute its many corporate customers. Because it has no sales force to place in-store materials, NutraSweet designed a promotion using the Universal Product Codes on products containing NutraSweet as "lucky numbers" in its sweepstakes. Customers entered by calling a toll-free number and punching in the UPC. Callers received immediate "you win" or "try again" messages. The promotion featured 18,000 prizes ranging from gumball

machines to trips to one of the 50 countries where products containing NutraSweet are sold. The UPCs of key NutraSweet customers also triggered customized messages, such as "Thanks for choosing Diet Pepsi." The sweepstakes was promoted using national free-standing inserts. It generated more than 1.5 million calls, triple the number projected. Corporate customers were pleased and the agency that designed the promotion was voted *Advertising Age*'s Promotion Agency of the Year.

The "Red Baron Fly-In" Promotion

Red Baron Pizza Service used an imaginative combination of special events, couponing, and charitable activities to boost sales of its frozen pizza. The company recreated World War I flying ace Baron Manfred von Richtofen—complete with traditional flying gear and open-cockpit Stearman biplanes—as its company spokesperson. Red Baron pilots barn-

Clearly, sales promotion plays an important role in the total promotion mix. To use it well, the marketer must define the sales-promotion objectives, select the best tools, design the sales-promotion program, pretest and implement the program, and evaluate the results. Marketing Highlight 16-4 describes some award-winning sales-promotion campaigns.

PUBLIC RELATIONS

Public relations
Building good relations with the company's various publics by obtaining favorable publicity, building up a good "corporate image," and handling or heading off unfavorable rumors, stories, and events. Major PR tools include press relations, product publicity, corporate communications, lobbying, and counseling.

Publicity
Activities to promote a company or its products by planting news about it in media not paid for by the sponsor.

Another major mass-promotion tool is **public relations**—building good relations with the company's various publics by obtaining favorable publicity, building up a good "corporate image," and handling or heading off unfavorable rumors, stories, and events. The old name for marketing public relations was **publicity,** which was seen simply as activities to promote a company or its products by planting news about it in media not paid for by the sponsor. Public relations is a much broader concept that includes publicity as well as many other activities. Public relations departments may perform any or all of the following functions:

◆ *Press relations or press agentry:* Creating and placing newsworthy information in the media to attract attention to a person, product, or service.

◆ *Product publicity:* Publicizing specific products.

◆ *Public affairs:* Building and maintaining national or local community relations.

◆ *Lobbying:* Building and maintaining relations with legislators and government officials to influence legislation and regulation.

◆ *Investor relations:* Maintaining relationships with shareholders and others in the financial community.

stormed 13 markets, showed the plane, performed stunts, gave out coupons, and invited consumers to "come fly with the Red Baron." The company donated $500 to a local youth organization in each market and urged consumers to match the gift. Trade promotions and local tie-in promotions boosted retailer support. The total budget: about $1 million. The results: For the four-week period during and after the fly-ins, unit sales in the 13 markets jumped an average of 100 percent. In the 90 days following the fly-in, sales in some markets increased as much as 400 percent.

Georgia-Pacific's "World's Fastest Roofer" Contest

Georgia-Pacific developed this creative business promotion to acquaint its roofing contractor target market with the full range of G-P's products and to celebrate the industry's "unsung heroes"—roofers. Most importantly, the contest would give roofers hands-on experience with Summit, a

new high-quality shingle whose key feature was its ease of installation. Contestants installed 100 square feet of shingles. Judges chose the winner based on a combination of roofing speed and job quality. First prize was an all-expenses-paid trip to Hawaii for two. The contest began with eight regional eliminations held at G-P distribution centers around the country. Months in advance, each distribution center promoted the contest to area roofers using direct-mail promotional materials furnished by the G-P public relations department. In all, more than 150 roofers competed in the local contests. The eight regional winners were flown to Atlanta to compete in the national contest, timed to coincide with National Roofing Week. Tie-ins with a home-oriented Atlanta radio station resulted in widespread on-air promotion and raised several thousand dollars for an Atlanta children's hospital. The mayor of Atlanta issued a proclamation recognizing roofers, National Roofing Week, and

Georgia-Pacific. Caps, T-shirts, and posters were used to merchandise the event both locally and nationally. After the contest, G-P sent a print and video media kit to key national media, Atlanta media, and media in the hometowns of contest participants. The budget: only $50,000 to $75,000. The results: The promotion generated more than 2.5 million media impressions and increased sales in Georgia-Pacific's targeted markets by 90 percent.

Sources: See William A. Robinson, "Event Marketing at the Crossroads," *Promote,* November 14, 1988, pp. P11–P23; Alison Fahey, "CBS, Kmart Lead Reggie Winners," *Advertising Age,* March 19, 1990, p. 47; Jon Lafayette, "Hadley Group Sweeps Competition," *Advertising Age,* January 20, 1992, p. 43; and "7-Eleven Cups Supper Reggie," *Advertising Age,* March 16, 1992, p. 39.

◆ *Development*: Public relations with donors or members of nonprofit organizations to gain financial or volunteer support.[29]

Public relations is used to promote products, people, places, ideas, activities, organizations, and even nations. Trade associations have used public relations to rebuild interest in declining commodities such as eggs, apples, milk, and potatoes. New York City turned its image around when its "I Love New York" campaign took root, bringing millions more tourists to the city. Johnson & Johnson's masterly use of public relations played a major role in saving Tylenol from extinction after its product-tampering scare. Nations have used public relations to attract more tourists, foreign investment, and international support.

Public relations can have a strong impact on public awareness at a much lower cost than advertising. The company does not pay for the space or time in the media. Rather, it pays for a staff to develop and circulate information and to manage events. If the company develops an interesting story, it could be picked up by several different media, having the same effect as advertising that would cost millions of dollars. And it would have more credibility than advertising. Public relations results can sometimes be spectacular. Consider the classic case of Cabbage Patch dolls:

Public relations played a major role in making Coleco's Cabbage Patch dolls an overnight sensation. The dolls were formally introduced at a Boston press conference where local school children performed a mass-adoption ceremony for the press. Thanks to Coleco's public relations machine, child psychologists publicly endorsed the Cabbage Patch Kids, and Dr. Joyce Brothers and other newspaper columnists proclaimed that the Kids were healthy playthings. Major women's magazines featured the dolls as ideal Christmas gifts, and after a 5-minute feature on the *Today* show, the Kids made the complete talk-show circuit. Marketers of other products used the hard-to-get Cabbage Patch dolls as premiums, and retailers used them to lure customers into their stores. The word spread, and every child just *had* to have one. The dolls were quickly sold out, and the great "Cabbage Patch Panic" began.

Despite its potential strengths, public relations often is described as a marketing stepchild because of its limited and scattered use. The public relations department is usually located at corporate headquarters. Its staff is so busy dealing with various publics—stockholders, employees, legislators, city officials—that public relations programs to support product marketing objectives may be ignored. And marketing managers and public relations practitioners do not always talk the same language. Many public relations practitioners see their job as simply communicating. In contrast, marketing managers tend to be much more interested in how advertising and public relations affect sales and profits.

This situation is changing, however. Many companies now want their public relations departments to manage all of their activities with a view toward marketing the company and improving the bottom line. Some companies are setting up special units called *marketing public relations* to support corporate and product promotion and image making directly. Many companies hire marketing public relations firms to handle their PR programs or to assist the company public relations team.

MAJOR PUBLIC RELATIONS TOOLS

Public relations professionals use several tools. One of the major tools is *news*. PR professionals find or create favorable news about the company and its products or people. Sometimes news stories occur naturally, and sometimes the PR person can suggest events or activities that would create news. *Speeches* can also create product and company publicity. Increasingly, company executives must field questions from the media or give talks at trade associations or sales meetings, and these events can either build or hurt the company's image. Another common PR

Attractive, distinctive, memorable company logos become strong marketing tools.

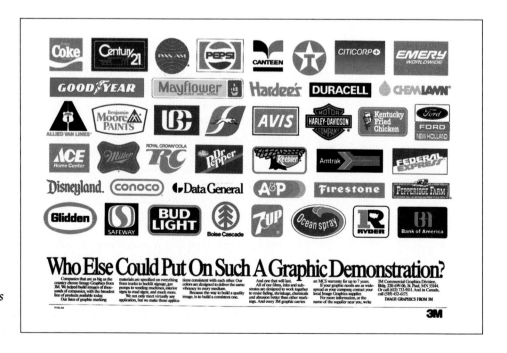

tool is *special events,* ranging from news conferences, press tours, grand openings, and fireworks displays to laser shows, hot-air balloon releases, multimedia presentations, and star-studded spectaculars designed to reach and interest target publics.

Public relations people also prepare *written materials* to reach and influence their target markets. These materials include annual reports, brochures, articles, and company newsletters and magazines. *Audiovisual materials,* such as films, slide-and-sound programs, and video and audio cassettes, are being used increasingly as communication tools. *Corporate-identity materials* also can help create a corporate identity that the public immediately recognizes. Logos, stationery, brochures, signs, business forms, business cards, buildings, uniforms, and company cars and trucks—all become marketing tools when they are attractive, distinctive, and memorable.

Companies also can improve public goodwill by contributing money and time to *public-service activities.* For example, Procter & Gamble and Publishers' Clearing House held a joint promotion to raise money for the Special Olympics. The Publishers' Clearing House mailing included product coupons, and Procter & Gamble donated ten cents per redeemed coupon to the Special Olympics. In another example, B. Dalton Booksellers donated $3 million during a four-year period to the fight against illiteracy.

MAJOR PUBLIC RELATIONS DECISIONS

In considering when and how to use product public relations, management should set PR objectives, choose the PR messages and vehicles, implement the PR plan, and evaluate the results.

Setting Public Relations Objectives

The first task is to set *objectives* for public relations. Some years ago, the Wine Growers of California hired a public relations firm to develop a program to support two major marketing objectives: Convince Americans that wine drinking is a pleasant part of good living, and improve the image and market share of California wines among all wines. The following public relations objectives were set: Develop magazine stories about wine and get them placed in top magazines (such as *Time* and *House Beautiful*) and in newspapers (food columns and feature sections); develop stories about the many health values of wine and direct them to the medical profession; and develop specific publicity for the young adult market, the college market, governmental bodies, and various ethnic communities. These objectives were turned into specific goals so that final results could be evaluated.

Choosing Public Relations Messages and Vehicles

The organization next finds interesting stories to tell about the product. Suppose a little-known college wants more public recognition. It will search for possible stories: Do any faculty members have unusual backgrounds or are any working on unusual projects? Are any interesting new courses being taught or any interesting events taking place on campus? Usually, this search will uncover hundreds of stories that can be fed to the press. The chosen stories should reflect the image sought by the college.

If there are not enough stories, the college could sponsor newsworthy events. Here, the organization *creates* news rather than finds it. Ideas might include hosting major academic conventions, inviting well-known speakers, and holding news conferences. Each event creates many stories for many different audiences.

Creating events is especially important in publicizing fund-raising drives for nonprofit organizations. Fund-raisers have developed a large set of special events such as art exhibits, auctions, benefit evenings, book sales, contests, dances, dinners, fairs, fashion shows, phonathons, rummage sales, tours, and walkathons. No sooner is one type of event created, such as a walkathon, than competitors create new versions, such as readathons, bikeathons, and jogathons.

Implementing the Public Relations Plan

Implementing public relations requires care. Take the matter of placing stories in the media. A *great* story is easy to place—but most stories are not great and may not get past busy editors. Thus, one of the main assets of public relations people is their personal relationships with media editors. In fact, PR professionals are often former journalists who know many media editors and know what they want. They view media editors as a market to be satisfied so that editors will continue to use their stories.

Evaluating Public Relations Results

Public relations results are difficult to measure because PR is used with other promotion tools and its impact is often indirect. If PR is used before other tools come into play, its contribution is easier to evaluate.

The easiest measure of publicity effectiveness is the number of exposures in the media. Public relations people give the client a "clippings book" showing all the media that carried news about the product. Such exposure measures are not very satisfying, however. They do not tell how many people actually read or heard the message, nor what they thought afterward. In addition, because the media overlap in readership and viewership, it does not give information on the *net* audience reached.

A better measure is the change in product awareness, knowledge, and attitude resulting from the publicity campaign. Assessing the change requires measuring the before-and-after levels of these measures. The Potato Board learned, for example, that the number of people who agreed with the statement "Potatoes are rich in vitamins and minerals" went from 36 percent before its public relations campaign to 67 percent after the campaign. That change represented a large increase in product knowledge.

Sales and profit impact, if obtainable, is the best measure of public relations effort. For example, 9-Lives sales increased 43 percent at the end of a major "Morris the Cat" publicity campaign. However, advertising and sales promotion also had been stepped up, and their contribution has to be considered.

Summary

Three major tools of mass promotion are *advertising, sales promotion,* and *public relations.* They are mass-marketing tools as opposed to personal selling, which targets specific buyers.

Advertising—the use of paid media by a seller to inform, persuade, and remind about its product or organization—is a strong promotion tool. American marketers spend more than $131 billion each year on advertising, and it takes many forms and has many uses. Advertising decision making is a five-step process consisting of decisions about the *objectives,* the *budget,* the *message,* the *media,* and finally, the *evaluation of results.* Advertisers should set clear *objectives* as to whether the advertising budget is supposed to *inform, persuade,* or *remind* buyers. The *advertising budget* is based on what is *affordable,* on a *percentage of sales,* on *competitors' spending,* or on the *objectives and tasks.* The *message decision* calls for defining *reach, frequency,* and *impact* goals; *choosing major media types; selecting media vehicles* and scheduling the media *timing.* Message and media decisions must be closely coordinated for maximum campaign effectiveness.

Finally, *advertising evaluation* calls for *measuring the communication effect* and *measuring the sales effects* of advertising before, during, and after the advertising is placed. Although similar considerations are required in making *international advertising decisions*, these situations have many complexities not found in domestic decisions.

Recent years have shown *rapid growth in sales promotion*. Sales promotion covers a wide variety of short-term incentive tools—coupons, premiums, contents, buying allowances—designed to stimulate consumers, the trade, and the company's own sales force. Sales-promotion spending calls for *setting sales-promotion objectives; selecting sales-promotion tools; developing, pretesting, and implementing the sales-promotion program;* and *evaluating the results.*

Public relations—gaining favorable publicity and creating a favorable company image—is the least used of the major promotion tools, although it has great potential for building awareness and preference. The *major public relations decisions* are *setting objectives, choosing messages and vehicles, implementing the plan,* and *evaluating public relations results.*

Key Terms

Advertising	Frequency	Public relations
Advertising objective	Informative advertising	Publicity
Advertising specialties	Media impact	Reach
Allowance	Media vehicles	Reminder advertising
Cash refund offers (rebates)	Patronage rewards	Sales promotion
Comparison advertising	Persuasive advertising	Sales force promotion
Consumer promotion	Point-of-purchase promotions	Samples
Contests, sweepstakes, games	(POP)	Trade promotion
Coupons	Premiums	
Discount	Price packs (cents-off deals)	

Discussing the Issues

1. Contrast the benefits and drawbacks of comparison advertising. Which has more to gain from using comparison advertising—the leading brand in a market or a lesser brand? Why?

2. Surveys show that many Americans are skeptical of advertising claims. Do you mistrust advertising? Analyze why or why not. Suggest some things advertisers could do to increase credibility.

3. Explain what factors call for more *frequency* in an advertising media schedule, and what factors call for more *reach*. How can you increase one without sacrificing the other or increasing the advertising budget?

4. An ad states that Almost Home cookies are the "moistest, chewiest, most perfectly baked cookies the world has ever tasted," besides homemade cookies. If you think some other brand of cookies is moister or chewier, is the Almost Home claim false? Should this type of claim be regulated?

5. Companies often run advertising, sales promotion, and public relations efforts at the same time. Can their effects be separated? Discuss how a company might evaluate the effectiveness of each element in this mix.

6. Assess why many companies are spending more on trade promotions and consumer promotions than on advertising. Is heavy spending on sales promotions a good strategy for long-term profits? Why or why not?

Applying the Concepts

1. Buy a Sunday paper and sort through the color advertising and coupon inserts. Find several examples that combine advertising, sales promotion, and/or public relations. For instance, a manufacturer may run a full-page ad that also includes a coupon and information on its sponsorship of a charity event, such as Easter Seals or Special Olympics. (a) Do you think these approaches using multiple tools are more or less effective than a simple approach? Why? (b) Try to find ads from two direct competitors. Are these brands using similar promotional tools in similar ways?

2. Find two current television advertisements that you think are particularly effective, and two more that you feel are ineffective. (a) Describe precisely why you think the better ads are effective, and why the ineffective ads fall short. (b) How would you improve the less effective ads? If you feel they are too poor to be improved, write a rough draft of an alternate ad for each.

References

1. Patricia Sellers, "How CAA Bottled Coca-Cola," *Fortune,* November 15, 1993, p. 156.

2. Bob Garfield, "Coke Ads Great, But Not Always," *Advertising Age,* February 22, 1993, pp. 1, 60.

3. Bob Garfield, "CAA Casts Perfect Spell in Latest Coca-Cola Ads," *Advertising Age,* February 14, 1994, p. 40.

4. Larry Jabbonsky, "The Return of a Lightning Rod," *Beverage World,* August 1993, p. 6. For more on the development of the Always Coca-Cola campaign, see "Soda-Pop Celebrity," *The Economist,* September 14, 1991, pp. 75–76; Betsy Sharkey, "CAA's Casting Call for Coke," *Adweek,* February 8, 1993, pp. 38–40; Melanie Wells and Marcy Magiera, "Coke Features Classic Images," *Advertising Age,* February 14, 1994, p. 5; Melanie Wells, "No Cataclysm, Just Hollywood Dabble-On," *Advertising Age,* January 16, 1995, pp. 1, 8; and Dottie Enrico, "Coca-Cola's Polar Bears Make for Hottest Ads," *USA Today,* March 17, 1995, p. 2.

5. Statistical information in this section on advertising's size and composition draws on Julie Skur Hill, "Top Ad Spenders: Unilever, P&G," *Advertising Age,* October 28, 1991, p. 1; "Ad Dollars Outside the U.S.," *Advertising Age,* December 14, 1992, p. S1; Robert J. Coen, "Ad Gains of 5.2% in '93 Mark Downturn's End," *Advertising Age,* May 2, 1994, p.4; "100 Leading National Advertisers," *Advertising Age,* September 28, 1994; and "Advertising Fact Book," *Advertising Age,* January 2, 1995, pp. 11–17.

6. Leah Rickard, "New Ammo for Comparative Ads," *Advertising Age,* February 14, 1994, p. 26.

7. See Donald E. Schultz, Dennis Martin, and William P. Brown, *Strategic Advertising Campaigns* (Chicago: Crain Books, 1984), pp. 192–197; and Philip Kotler, *Marketing Management: Analysis, Planning, Implementation, and Control,* 8th ed. (Englewood Cliffs, NJ: Prentice Hall, 1994), pp. 630–631.

8. Gerard J. Tellis, "Advertising Exposure, Loyalty, and Brand Purchase: A Two-Stage Model of Choice," *Journal of Marketing Research,* May 1988, pp. 134–135. For counterpoints, see Magid M. Abraham and Leonard M. Lodish, "Getting the Most Out of Advertising and Promotion," *Harvard Business Review,* May–June 1990, pp. 50–60.

9. Gary Levin, "Tracing Ads' Impact," *Advertising Age,* November 4, 1991, p. 49.

10. Christine Dugas, "And Now, A Wittier Word from Our Sponsors," *Business Week,* March 24, 1986, p. 90. Also see Sam Alfstad, "Don't Shrug Off Zapping," *Advertising Age,* September 9, 1991, p. 20; and Adrienne Ward Fawcett, "Even Ad Pros Hate Ad Clutter," *Advertising Age,* February 8, 1993, p. 33. For more on media costs, see "Agency Estimates of Prices for Fall Prime-Time Schedule," *Advertising Age,* September 19, 1994, p. 35; and Dottie Enrico and Laura Petrecca, "Super Bowl Ad Watch," *USA Today,* January 27, 1995, p. 8B.

11. See Mark Landler, "Neck and Neck at the Networks," *Business Week,* May 20, 1991, pp. 36–37; Faye Rice, "A Cure for What Ails Advertising," *Fortune,* December 16, 1991, pp. 119–122; and Allan J. Magrath, "The Death of Advertising Has Been Greatly Exaggerated," *Sales & Marketing Management,* February 1992, pp. 23–24.

12. Joe Mandese, "Cost to Make TV Ad Nears Quarter Million," *Advertising Age,* July 4, 1994, pp. 3, 6.

13. Michael Lev, "Advertisers Seek Global Messages," *New York Times,* November 18, 1991, p. D9.

14. Philip R. Cateora, *International Marketing,* 7th ed. (Homewood, IL: Irwin, 1990), p. 462.

15. Ibid., p. 475.

16. Michael R. Czinkota and Ilkka A. Ronkainen, *International Marketing,* 2nd ed. (Chicago: Dryden, 1990), p. 615.

17. Cateora, *International Marketing,* pp. 466–467.

18. Alison Fahey, "Shops See Surge in Promotion Revenues," *Advertising Age,* February 20, 1989, p. 20; Scott Hume, "Sales Promotion: Agency Services Take on Exaggerated Importance for Marketers," *Advertising Age,* May 4, 1992, pp. 29, 32; and *16th Annual Survey of Promotional Practices,* Donnelly Marketing Inc., Oakbrook Terrace, IL, June 1994, p. 9.

19. Jennifer Lawrence, "Free Samples Get Emotional Reception," *Advertising Age,* September 30, 1991, p. 10.

20. Scott Hume, "Brand Loyalty Steady," *Advertising Age,* March 2, 1992, p. 19.

21. For more on the use of sales promotion versus advertising, see Paul W. Farris and John A. Quelch, "In Defense of Price Promotion," *Sloan Management Review,* Fall 1987; and John Philip Jones, "The Double Jeopardy of Sales Promotions," *Harvard Business Review,* September–October, 1990, pp. 145–152.

22. "Nestlé Banks on Databases," *Advertising Age,* October 25, 1993, pp. S6–S10.

23. Terry Lefton, "Blockbuster Re-Ups 'Bonus Box,'" *Brandweek,* August 9, 1994, p. 3.

24. See Scott Hume, "Coupons: Are They Too Popular?" *Advertising Age,* February 15, 1993, p. 32; Jeanne Whalen, "Coupon Marketers Felt Chill in '93," *Advertising Age,* January 17, 1994, p. 26; and Larry Armstrong, "Coupon Clippers, Save Your Scissors," *Business Week,* June 20, 1994, pp. 164–166.

25. See "Power to the Key Ring and T-Shirt," *Sales & Marketing Management,* December 1989, p. 14; and J. Thomas Russell and W. Ronald Lane, *Kleppner's Advertising Procedure,* 12th ed. (Englewood Cliffs, NJ: Prentice Hall, 1993), pp. 408–410.

26. See Thomas V. Bonoma, "Get More Out of Your Trade Shows," *Harvard Business Review,* January–February 1983, pp. 75–83; Jonathan M. Cox, Ian K. Sequeira, and Alissa Eckstein, "1988 Trade Show Trends: Shows Grow in Size; Audience Quality Remains High," *Business Marketing,* June 1989, pp. 57–60; and Richard Szathmary, "Trade Shows," *Sales & Marketing Management,* May 1992, pp. 83–84.

27. Quoted from Kerry E. Smith, "Media Fusion," *PROMO,* May 1992, p. 29.

28. "Pretesting Phase of Promotions Is Often Overlooked," *Marketing News,* February 29, 1988, p. 10.

29. Adapted from Scott M. Cutlip, Allen H. Center, and Glen M. Brown, *Effective Public Relations,* 7th ed. (Englewood Cliffs, NJ: Prentice Hall, 1994), pp. 8–21.

Company Case 16

BURGER KING: SEARCHING FOR THE RIGHT MESSAGE

ADVERTISING'S UPS AND DOWNS

Burger King has shown how powerful and yet ineffective advertising can be. In 1974, with its market share hovering at about 4 percent, Burger King introduced the "Have It Your Way" advertising campaign. The ads focused on Burger King's strategy of making burgers according to customer requests instead of serving already prepared, standardized burgers. Many people still consider this campaign to be Burger King's best ever.

In the early 1980s, however, Burger King began to flip from one advertising campaign to another, trying to keep its sales growing. In 1982, it introduced the "Battle of the Burgers" campaign, featuring the slogan "Aren't you hungry for Burger King now?" The "Broiling vs. Frying" campaign followed in 1983, driving home the point that Burger King flame-broiled its burgers rather than frying them. "The Big Switch" theme guided advertising until 1985. All of these campaigns centered on Burger King's advantages over McDonald's, and they helped increase market share from 7.6 percent in 1983 to 8.3 percent in 1985.

Then, disaster struck. With its market share peaking at 8.7 percent, Burger King unveiled its now infamous "Search for Herb" ad campaign. The campaign centered on Herb, an eccentric nerd who was supposedly the only person never to have tasted a Burger King Whopper. Consumers were supposed to search for Herb and earn a chance to win valuable prizes. The campaign flopped. Sales inched up only one percent—far short of executives' 10-percent projections. The campaign led consumers to focus on Herb, rather than the Whopper, and Burger King found itself in the uncomfortable position of associating its image with a "nerdy" personality.

Following "Herb," Burger King's market share began a steady decline. Burger King tried to reverse its slide with its "This Is a Burger King Town" theme in 1986–87, and followed it with a "Best Food for Fast Times" message. In 1988, the chain tried the "We Do It Like You'd Do It" campaign, which again focused on flame broiling. However, because of confusing situations, bad humor, and bad acting, the campaign never succeeded in increasing sales. In 1989, Burger King launched its "Sometimes You Gotta Break the Rules" campaign. Burger King wanted this slogan to convey the idea that it was "breaking the rules" of the burger industry by flame broiling, not frying its burgers, and by making the burgers to meet individual customer requests.

The most recent and most disappointing campaign, "BK Tee Vee," featured MTV personality Dan Cortese, rapid editing, and a voice-over that shrieked, "I love this place." The ads targeted teenage males, but the majority of Burger King's customers—parents and people on the go—found the commercials to be loud and irritating.

Thus, since the mid-1980s, Burger King has had trouble persuading consumers that they should prefer its restaurants to those of McDonald's and other competitors. With its long string of lackluster, quick-changing advertising campaigns, Burger King has failed to establish a solid image that would differentiate it from competitors. If anything, the ads only confused consumers as to what advantages Burger King offered.

By 1993, Burger King held a 6.1 percent market share, barely ahead of Hardee's 4.4 percent and Wendy's 4.1 percent. It lagged far behind McDonald's, which dominates the industry with a 15.6 percent market share. Moreover, Burger King's sales were growing more slowly than those of its rivals. So, for the fourth time in five years, Burger King's managers decided to put its advertising account up for review, seeking a new agency and a new ad campaign.

Not the Only Problems

Failed advertising campaigns are only the most visible of Burger King's problems. Its marketing stumbles involve other, deeper issues. Since the 1980s, Burger King has also wrestled with internal problems. Management has lacked focus and direction and has struggled with marketing-mix decisions. Franchisees, who often felt that headquarters had no well-thought-out strategy, became confused and angered. To make matters worse, in-store operations were less than spectacular—service in many

Burger King restaurants was slow, and food preparation was inconsistent. Many stores needed remodeling.

Burger King lost its focus on its core product—flame-broiled burgers, made the way the customer wanted them. It introduced a variety of unrelated products, ranging from pizza and tacos to ice-cream bars. A failure to concentrate on its leading product, the Whopper, confused consumers. Many customers also believed that Burger King served lower-quality food.

In the age of the price-conscious consumer, McDonald's and Wendy's listened and responded with lower-priced combo meals. Burger King's higher prices and its refusal to provide discounts contributed to its below-average sales growth.

Burger King's promotion problems also involved more than just its television commercials. Many in-store promotions failed. And the dinner-basket program—combo meals along with table service—showed that Burger King was not listening to its customers. Fast-food patrons really wanted low prices and quick but high-quality food, not a higher-priced, sit-down meal. In addition to chewing up a number of advertising agencies, the company also tossed out several marketing managers.

Back to the Basics

With the help of CEO Jim Adamson, a former marketer from Revco Drug Stores who came to Burger King in July 1991, Burger King has begun a turnaround. Adamson came to Burger King as president of company-owned outlets. In 1993, he moved up to become the eighth Burger King CEO since 1980. Adamson took a hands-on approach that pleased franchisees. He listened and responded to franchisee problems and recommendations. For example, Burger King initiated Operation Phoenix, a program to improve sales, service, and quality by offering franchisees help with menus, pricing, and local advertising.

Management finally locked into a strategy of concentrating on Burger King's core product—flame-broiled, bigger burgers. Since last year, the company has pruned thirty items from the menu. It also launched a new pricing structure featuring $.99, $1.99, and $2.99 value meals that allow it to compete with McDonald's on price.

In addition to resolving its internal problems, Burger King is also attending to its major external problem—the lack of effective advertising. It has hired a new advertising agency, Ammirati and Puris/Lintas, to communicate a new "Back to the Basics" positioning. Ammirati's Helayne Spivak describes Burger King's image as "The Voice of the People," as opposed to McDonald's image as the "Voice of a Corporation," and Wendy's image as the "Voice of Dave." Burger King is a company that listens to its customers. To communicate this message, the advertising agency will use about $180 million of Burger King's total $250 million promotion budget. Burger King has been spending the $180 million on television and radio, with about 40 percent going for national advertising and 60 percent to local. Ammirati and Puris/Lintas must now create an advertising campaign that will successfully communicate Burger King's competitive advantages and pull more customers into its 5,700 restaurants.

QUESTIONS

1. What are the objectives of Burger King's advertising?

2. Why did Burger King's corporate strategy and past advertising fail to achieve these objectives?

3. What suggestions do you have for Burger King's new advertising campaign?

4. What recommendations would you make regarding future sales promotions for Burger King?

Sources: Jeanne Whalen, Gary Levin, and Melanie Wells, "Ammirati's Big Win: It's a $180M Whopper," *Advertising Age,* March 28, 1994, pp. 1, 40–41; Gail DeGorge and Julia Flynn, "Turning Up the Gas at Burger King," *Business Week,* Nov. 15, 1993, pp. 62, 66–67; Kevin Goldman, "Burger King Training Its Sights on McDonald's with Campaign," *Wall Street Journal,* Sept. 1, 1994, p. B2; Bob Garfield, "BK Finally Catches Fire with Ammirati's Quirky Ads," *Advertising Age,* Sept. 5, 1994; Jeanne Whalen and Gary Levin, "BK Puts Basics on Center Stage in Huge Ad Blitz," *Advertising Age,* Sept. 5, 1994, p. 37; Kevin Goldman, "Burger King Reviews Account . . . Again," *Wall Street Journal,* Oct. 21, 1993, p. B9.

Promoting Products
PERSONAL SELLING AND SALES MANAGEMENT

In 1982, Eastman Chemical Company in Kingsport, Tennessee, began a customer-driven quality program called "Customers and Us." As a result, little more than a decade later, Eastman captured the 1993 Malcolm Baldrige National Quality Award for outstanding quality leadership. Eastman's quality program is deceptively simple—it focuses on doing everything possible to improve the quality of the company's relationships with its customers.

Not surprisingly, Eastman's 500 salespeople have played a prominent role in the company's customer-driven quality program, and in its winning the Baldrige Award. Eastman knows that its salespeople have to be good at performing the basic selling tasks—finding qualified customers, presenting Eastman's products, and getting orders. And its sales managers must be good at hiring outstanding sales prospects, training them to sell effectively, and motivating them to perform at a high level. Each year, the sales force generates more than $4 billion in sales for Eastman's ten different business units, ranging from packaging plastics and coatings to fine chemicals. However, at Eastman, salespeople do more than simply travel their territories hawking the company's wares. What makes Eastman's sales force so special is its penchant for building long-term, mutually profitable *relationships* with the company's 7,000 customers worldwide.

Building strong customer relationships is an important criterion for the Baldrige Award. Among other things, Baldrige examiners look at how a company uses sales contacts to manage customer relationships; how it trains salespeople to understand products, listen to customers, and deal with customer problems and complaints; how it gets information from customers; and how it manages customers' expectations. Eastman's carefully selected, extensively trained salespeople excel at keeping customers satisfied.

The sales force forms a critical link between Eastman and its customers. Given the company's deep dedication to customer satisfaction, the sales force often finds itself in the position of coordinating many of Eastman's 18,000 employees in team efforts focused on improving customer relationships. The

OBJECTIVES

When you finish this chapter, you should be able to accomplish the following:

1. Explain the **role** and **nature of personal selling** and the **role of the sales force**.

2. Describe the basics of **managing the sales force**, and tell how to set **sales force strategy**, how to pick a **structure—territorial, product, customer, or complex**—and how to ensure that **sales force size** is appropriate.

3. Identify the key issues in **recruiting, selecting, training, and compensating salespeople**.

4. Discuss **supervising salespeople**, including **directing, motivating**, and **evaluating performance**.

5. Apply the **principles of personal selling** process, and outline the **steps in the selling process—qualifying, preapproach** and **approach, presentation** and **demonstration, handling objectives, closing** and **follow-up**.

acronym for Eastman's customer-driven, team-oriented problem-solving approach is MEPS, which stands for "Making Eastman the Preferred Supplier." The objective of the MEPS program is to improve the processes that link Eastman to its customers. When specific customer problems are found, MEPS teams are formed to solve them. MEPS projects vary widely, but they are all sales driven and customer focused.

One Eastman sales rep, for instance, initiated a MEPS project when a customer was having a persistent problem with black specks in one of its chemical products. The sales rep put together a cross-functional team to study the problem, including people from Eastman's supply and distribution, manufacturing, and product support services groups. The MEPS team solved the problem by recommending that new equipment be installed at the customer's facility. Another project arose when customers complained that they found Eastman's standard "conditions of sale," printed on the back of order sheets, somewhat offensive. The conditions made it sound as though Eastman was saying, "We know you're out to get us, and we're going to make sure you don't." The MEPS team refined and shortened the terms of sale and made them more friendly.

To resolve customer problems, Eastman must first know what they are, so the company tries to make it easy for customers to complain. It asks about complaints on frequent customer satisfaction surveys, encourages salespeople to ask about problems, and provides a 24-hour, toll-free number for receiving complaints. The sales organization is responsible for managing the customer satisfaction survey, which is printed in nine different languages and administered to customers around the world. On the survey, customers rate Eastman on 25 performance factors, including such things as product quality, pricing practices, on-time and correct delivery, and sharing market information. Salespeople take the survey seriously. Trainees are taught that "the second most important thing they have to do is get their customer satisfaction surveys out to and back from customers," says Eastman's sales training manager. "Number one, of course, is getting orders."

The customer survey provides important feedback, but it has also become one of the sales force's most powerful marketing tools. It's the sales reps' responsibility to discuss survey results with customers. It's also the reps' job to let customers know what Eastman is doing to fix problems detected by the survey. Thus, according to an Eastman sales executive, "The survey results give you something you can go back and talk about to customers over three or four visits." More importantly, customers appreciate the survey. It shows that Eastman is listening to them, and working hard to satisfy their needs. As one customer notes, "The survey is just a piece of paper. . . . What I value is the professional courtesy, the fact that [Eastman] follows up continually."

Thus, Eastman's salespeople have learned that the best way to keep getting orders is to build long-term relationships with customers. The company's focus on quality and customer satisfaction has given its sales force renewed energy and a new sense of purpose. "At one time, I would have called them stodgy," says the buyer at Tectonic Industries, which does about $3 million in business with Eastman each year. "Now they're aggressive, eager to do a good job, and you don't have to chase after them."[1]

Robert Louis Stevenson once noted that "everyone lives by selling something." We are all familiar with the sales forces used by business organizations to sell products and services to customers around the world. But sales forces are also found in many other kinds of organizations, in both the public and private sectors. For example, colleges use recruiters to attract new students, and churches use membership committees to attract new members. Hospitals and museums use fundraisers to contact donors and raise money. Even governments use sales forces. The U.S. Postal Service, for instance, uses a sales force to sell Express Mail and other services to corporate customers, and the Agricultural Extension Service sends agricultural specialists to sell farmers on new farming methods. In this chapter, we examine the role of personal selling in the organization, sales force management decisions, and basic principles of personal selling.

THE ROLE OF PERSONAL SELLING

There are many types of personal selling jobs, and the role of personal selling can vary greatly from one company to another. Here, we look at the nature of personal selling positions and at the role the sales force plays in modern marketing organizations.

THE NATURE OF PERSONAL SELLING

Selling is one of the oldest professions in the world. The people who do the selling go by many names: *salespeople, sales representatives, account executives, sales consultants, sales engineers, agents, district managers,* and *marketing representatives,* to name just a few.

People hold many stereotypes of salespeople—including some unfavorable ones. "Salesman" may bring to mind the image of Arthur Miller's pitiable Willy Loman in *Death of a Salesman.* Or you might think of Meredith Willson's cigar-smoking, back-slapping, joke-telling Harold Hill in *The Music Man.* Both examples depict salespeople as loners, traveling their territories trying to foist their wares on unsuspecting or unwilling buyers.

However, modern salespeople are a far cry from these unfortunate stereotypes. Today, most salespeople are well-educated, well-trained professionals who work to build and maintain long-term relationships with customers. They build these relationships by listening to their customers, assessing customer needs, and organizing the company's efforts to solve customer problems and satisfy customer needs. For example, consider Boeing, the aerospace giant that dominates the worldwide commercial aircraft market with a 55 percent market share. It takes more than a friendly smile and a firm handshake to sell expensive airplanes:

> Selling high-tech aircraft at $70 million or more a copy is complex and challenging. A single big sale can easily run into the billions of dollars. Boeing salespeople head up an extensive team of company specialists—sales and service technicians, financial analysts, planners, engineers—all dedicated to finding ways to satisfy airline customer needs. The salespeople begin by becoming experts on the airlines, much like Wall Street analysts would. They find out where each airline wants to grow, when it wants to replace planes, and details of its financial situation. The team runs Boeing and competing planes through computer systems, simulating the airline's routes, cost per seat, and other factors to show that their planes are most efficient. Then the high-level negotiations begin. The selling process is nerve-rackingly slow—it can take two or three years from the first sales presentation to the day the sale is announced. Sometimes top executives from both the airline and Boeing are brought in to close the deal. After getting the order, salespeople then must stay in almost constant touch to keep track of the account's equipment needs and to make certain the customer stays satisfied. Success depends on building solid, long-term relationships with customers, based on performance and trust. According to one analyst, Boeing's salespeople "are the vehicle by which information is collected and contacts are made so all other things can take place."[2]

Salesperson
An individual acting for a company by performing one or more of the following activities: prospecting, communicating, servicing, and information gathering.

The term **salesperson** covers a wide range of positions. At one extreme, a salesperson might be largely an *order taker,* such as the department store salesperson standing behind the counter. At the other extreme are *order getters,* salespeople whose positions demand the *creative selling* of products and services ranging from appliances, industrial equipment, or airplanes to insurance, advertising,

The term "salesperson" covers a wide range of positions, from the clerk selling in a retail store to the engineering salesperson who consults with client companies.

or consulting services. Other salespeople engage in *missionary selling:* These salespeople are not expected or permitted to take an order, but only build goodwill or educate buyers. An example is a salesperson for a pharmaceutical company who calls on doctors to educate them about the company's drug products and to urge them to prescribe these products to their patients.[3] In this chapter, we focus on the more creative types of selling and on the process of building and managing an effective sales force.

THE ROLE OF THE SALES FORCE

Personal selling is the interpersonal arm of the promotion mix. Advertising consists of one-way, nonpersonal communication with target consumer groups. In contrast, personal selling involves two-way, personal communication between salespeople and individual customers—whether face-to-face, by telephone, through video conferences, or by other means. This means that personal selling can be more effective than advertising in more complex selling situations. Salespeople can probe customers to learn more about their problems. They can adjust the marketing offer to fit the special needs of each customer and can negotiate terms of sale. They can build long-term personal relationships with key decision makers.

The role of personal selling varies from company to company. Some firms have no salespeople at all—for example, companies that sell only through mail-order catalogs, or companies that sell through manufacturer's reps, sales agents, or brokers. In most firms, however, the sales force plays a major role. In companies that sell business products, such as Xerox or Du Pont, the company's salespeople work directly with customers. In fact, to many customers, salespeople may be the only contact. To these customers, the sales force *is* the company. In consumer product companies such as Procter & Gamble or Wilson Sporting Goods that sell through intermediaries, final consumers rarely meet salespeople or even know about them. Still, the sales force plays an important behind-the-scenes role. It works with wholesalers and retailers to gain their support and to help them be more effective in selling the company's products.

The sales force serves as a critical link between a company and its customers.

In many cases, salespeople serve both masters—the seller and the buyer. First, they *represent the company to customers*. They find and develop new customers and communicate information about the company's products and services. They sell products by approaching customers, presenting their products, answering objections, negotiating prices and terms, and closing sales. In addition, salespeople provide services to customers, carry out market research and intelligence work, and fill out sales call reports.

At the same time, salespeople *represent customers to the company*, acting inside the firm as "champions" of customers' interests. Salespeople relay customer concerns about company products and actions back to those who can handle them. They learn about customer needs, and work with others in the company to develop greater customer value. Thus, the salesperson often acts as an "account manager" who manages the relationship between the seller and buyer.

As companies move toward a stronger market orientation, their sales forces are becoming more market focused and customer oriented. The old view was that salespeople should worry about sales and the company should worry about profit. However, the current view holds that salespeople should be concerned with more than just producing *sales*—they also must know how to produce *customer satisfaction* and *company profit*. They should be able to look at sales data, measure market potential, gather market intelligence, and develop marketing strategies and plans. They should know how to orchestrate the firm's efforts toward delivering customer value and satisfaction. A market-oriented rather than a sales-oriented sales force will be more effective in the long run. Beyond winning new customers and making sales, it will help the company to create long-term, profitable relationships with customers.

MANAGING THE SALES FORCE

Sales force management
The analysis, planning, implementation, and control of sales force activities. It includes designing sales force strategy and structure; and recruiting, selecting, training, compensating, supervising, and evaluating the firm's salespeople.

We define **sales force management** as the analysis, planning, implementation, and control of sales force activities. It includes designing sales force strategy and structure, and recruiting, selecting, training, compensating, supervising, and evaluating the firm's salespeople. These major sales force management decisions are shown in Figure 17-1 and are discussed in the following sections.

DESIGNING SALES FORCE STRATEGY AND STRUCTURE

Marketing managers face several sales force strategy and design questions. How should salespeople and their tasks be structured? How big should the sales force be? Should salespeople sell alone or work in teams with other people in the company? Should they sell in the field or by telephone? We address these issues next.

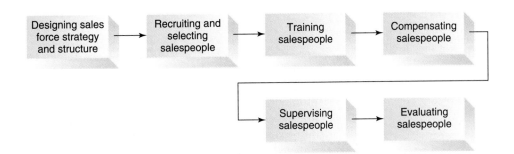

FIGURE 17-1 *Major steps in salesforce management*

Sales Force Structure

A company can divide up sales responsibilities along any of several lines. The decision is simple if the company sells only one product line to one industry with customers in many locations. In that case the company would use a *territorial sales force structure*. However, if the company sells many products to many types of customers, it might need a *product sales force structure*, a *customer sales force structure*, or a combination of the two.

TERRITORIAL SALES FORCE STRUCTURE. In the **territorial sales force structure**, each salesperson is assigned to an exclusive geographic territory and sells the company's full line of products or services to all customers in that territory. This sales organization has many advantages. It clearly defines the salesperson's job, and because only one salesperson works the territory, he or she gets all the credit or blame for territory sales. The territorial structure also increases the salesperson's desire to build local business relationships that, in turn, improve selling effectiveness. Finally, because each salesperson travels within a limited geographic area, travel expenses are relatively small.

A territorial sales organization often is supported by many levels of sales management positions. For example, Campbell Soup recently changed from a product sales force structure to a territorial one, whereby each salesperson is now responsible for selling all Campbell Soup products. Starting at the bottom of the organization, *sales merchandisers* report to *sales representatives,* who report to *retail supervisors,* who report to *directors of retail sales operations,* who report to one of twenty-two *regional sales managers*. Regional sales managers, in turn, report to one of four *general sales managers* (West, Central, South, and East), who report to a *vice-president and general sales manager*.[4]

PRODUCT SALES FORCE STRUCTURE. Salespeople must know their products—especially when the products are numerous and complex. This need, together with the trend toward product management, has led many companies to adopt a **product sales force structure,** in which the sales force sells along product lines. For example, Kodak uses different sales forces for its film products than for its industrial products. The film products sales force deals with simple products that are distributed intensively, whereas the industrial products sales force deals with complex products that require technical understanding.

The product structure can lead to problems, however, if a single large customer buys many different company products. For example, Baxter International, a hospital supply company, has several product divisions, each with a separate sales force. Several Baxter salespeople might end up calling on the same hospital on the same day. This means that the salespeople travel over the same routes and wait to see the same customer's purchasing agents. These extra costs must be compared with the benefits of better product knowledge and attention to individual products.

CUSTOMER SALES FORCE STRUCTURE. More and more companies are now using a **customer sales force structure,** in which they organize the sales force along customer or industry lines. Separate sales forces may be set up for different industries, for serving current customers versus finding new ones, and for major accounts versus regular accounts. Xerox classifies its customers into four major groups, each served by a different sales force. The top group consists of large national accounts with multiple and scattered locations. These customers are handled by 250 to 300 *national account managers*. Next are major accounts that, although not national in scope, may have several locations within a region; these are handled by one of Xerox's 1,000 or so *major account managers*. The third customer group consists of standard commercial accounts with annual sales potential of $5,000 to $10,000; they are served by *account representatives*. All other customers are handled by *marketing representatives*.[5]

Territorial sales force structure
A sales force organization that assigns each salesperson to an exclusive geographic territory in which that salesperson carries the company's full line.

Product sales force structure
A sales force organization under which salespeople specialize in selling only a portion of the company's products or lines.

Customer sales force structure
A sales force organization under which salespeople specialize in selling only to certain customers or industries.

Organizing the sales force around customers can help a company become more customer focused and build closer relationships with important customers. For example, giant ABB, the $29-billion-a-year Swiss-based industrial equipment maker, recently changed from a product-based to a customer-based sales force. The new structure resulted in a stronger customer orientation and improved service to clients:

> Until four months ago, David Donaldson sold boilers for ABB.... After 30 years, Donaldson sure knew boilers, but he didn't know much about the broad range of other products offered by ABB's U.S. Power Plant division. Customers were frustrated because as many as a dozen ABB salespeople called on them at different times to peddle their products. Sometimes representatives even passed each other in customers' lobbies without realizing that they were working for the same company. ABB's bosses decided that this was a poor way to run a sales force. So [recently], David Donaldson and 27 other power plant salespeople began new jobs. [Donaldson] now also sells turbines, generators, and three other product lines. He handles six major accounts . . . instead of a [mixed batch] of 35. His charge: Know the customer intimately and sell him the products that help him operate productively. Says Donaldson: "My job is to make it easy for my customer to do business with us. . . . I show him where to go in ABB whenever he has a problem." The president of ABB's power plant businesses [adds]: "If you want to be a customer-driven company, you have to design the sales organization around individual buyers rather than around your products."[6]

COMPLEX SALES FORCE STRUCTURES. When a company sells a wide variety of products to many types of customers over a broad geographical area, it often combines several types of sales force structures. Salespeople can be specialized by customer and territory, by product and territory, by product and customer, or by territory, product, and customer. No single structure is best for all companies and situations. Each company should select a sales force structure that best serves the needs of its customers and fits its overall marketing strategy.

Sales Force Size

Once the company has set its structure, it is ready to consider *sales force size*. Salespeople constitute one of the company's most productive—and most expensive—assets. Therefore, increasing their number will increase both sales and costs.

Workload approach
An approach to setting sales force size in which the company groups accounts into different size classes and then determines how many salespeople are needed to call on them the desired number of times.

Many companies use some form of **workload approach** to set sales force size. Using this approach, a company first groups accounts into different classes according to size, account status, or other factors related to the amount of effort required to maintain them. It then determines the number of salespeople needed to call on each class of accounts the desired number of times. The company might think as follows: Suppose we have 1,000 Type-A accounts and 2,000 Type-B accounts. Type-A accounts require 36 calls a year and Type-B accounts require 12 calls a year. In this case, the sales force's *workload*—the number of calls it must make per year—is 60,000 calls [(1,000 × 36) + (2,000 × 12) = 36,000 + 24,000 = 60,000]. Suppose our average salesperson can make 1,000 calls a year. Thus, the company needs 60 salespeople (60,000 ÷ 1,000).

Other Sales Force Strategy and Structure Issues

Sales management must also decide who will be involved in the selling effort and how various sales and sales-support people will work together.

Outside sales force
(or *field sales force*) Outside salespeople who travel to call on customers.

Inside sales force
Salespeople who conduct business from their offices via telephone or visits from prospective buyers.

OUTSIDE AND INSIDE SALES FORCES. The company may have an **outside sales force** (or *field sales force*), an **inside sales force,** or both. Outside salespeople travel to call on customers. Inside salespeople conduct business from their offices via telephone or visits from prospective buyers.

To reduce time demands on their outside sales forces, many companies have increased the size of their inside sales forces. Inside salespeople include technical support people, sales assistants, and telemarketers. *Technical support people* provide technical information and answers to customers' questions. *Sales assistants* provide clerical backup for outside salespeople. They call ahead and confirm appointments, conduct credit checks, follow up on deliveries, and answer customers' questions when outside salespeople cannot be reached. *Telemarketers* use the phone to find new leads and qualify prospects for the field sales force, or to sell and service accounts directly.

The inside sales force frees outside salespeople to spend more time selling to major accounts and finding major new prospects. Depending on the complexity of the product and customer, a telemarketer can make from 20 to 33 decision-maker contacts a day, compared to the average of four that an outside salesperson can see. And for many types of products and selling situations, **telemarketing** can be as effective as a personal call but much less expensive. For example, whereas a typical personal sales call can cost well over $200, a routine industrial telemarketing call costs only about $5 and a complex call about $20.[7] Telemarketing can be used successfully by both large and small companies:

> Du Pont uses experienced former field salespeople as telemarketing reps to help sell some of the company's complex chemical products. Housed in Du Pont's state-of-the-art Customer Telecontact Center, the telemarketers handle technical questions from customers, smooth out product and distribution problems, and find and cultivate hot prospects. The teamwork pays off—50 percent of the leads passed on to the field force are converted into sales. Notes one Du Pont telemarketer: "I'm more effective on the phone. [When you're in the field], if some guy's not in his office, you lose an hour. On the phone, you lose 15 seconds. . . . Through my phone calls, I'm in the field as much as the rep is." There are other advantages, quips the rep. "Customers can't throw things at you, . . . and you don't have to outrun the dogs."[8]

Climax Portable Machine Tools has proven that a small company can use telemarketing to save money and still lavish attention on buyers. Under the old system, Climax sales engineers spent one-third of their time on the road, training distributor salespeople and accompanying them on calls. They could make about four contacts a day. Now, each of five sales engineers on Climax's telemarketing team calls about 30 prospects a day, following up on leads generated by ads and direct mail. Because it takes about five calls to close a sale, the sales engineers update a prospect's computer file after each contact, noting the degree of commitment, requirements, next call date, and personal comments. "If anyone mentions he's going on a fishing trip, our sales engineer enters that in the computer and uses it to personalize the next phone call," says Climax's president, noting that's just one way to build good relations. Another is that the first mailing to a prospect includes the sales engineer's business card with his picture on it. Of course, it takes more than friendliness to sell $15,000 machine tools (special orders may run $200,000) over the phone, but the telemarketing approach is working well. When Climax customers were asked, "Do you see the sales engineer often enough?" the response was overwhelmingly positive. Obviously, many people didn't realize that the only contact they'd had with Climax had been on the phone.[9]

TEAM SELLING. The days when a single salesperson handled a large and important customer are vanishing rapidly. Today, as products become more complex, and as customers grow larger and more demanding, one person simply cannot handle all of a large customer's needs anymore. Instead, most companies now

Telemarketing
Using the telephone to sell directly to consumers.

Experienced telemarketers sell complex chemical products by phone at DuPont's Corporate Telemarketing Center. Says one: "I'm more effective on the phone . . . and you don't have to outrun the dogs."

Team selling
Using teams of people from sales, marketing, engineering, finance, technical support, and even upper management to service large, complex accounts.

are using **team selling** to service large, complex accounts. Sales teams might include people from sales, marketing, engineering, finance, technical support, and even upper management. For example, Procter & Gamble assigns teams consisting of salespeople, marketing managers, technical service people, and logistics and information-systems specialists to work closely with large retail customers such as Wal-Mart, Kmart, and Target. In such team-selling situations, salespeople become "orchestrators" who help coordinate a whole-company effort to build profitable relationships with important customers (see Marketing Highlight 17-1).[10]

Yet companies recognize that just asking their people for teamwork does not produce it. They must revise their compensation and recognition systems to give credit for work on shared accounts, and they must set up better goals and measures for sales force performance. They must emphasize the importance of teamwork in their training programs while at the same time honoring the importance of individual initiative.

RECRUITING AND SELECTING SALESPEOPLE

At the heart of any successful sales force operation is the recruiting and selection of good salespeople. The performance difference between an average salesperson and a top salesperson can be substantial. According to one study, sales superstars sell an average of 1.5 to 2 times more than the average salesperson.[11] In a typical sales force, the top 30 percent of the salespeople might bring in 60 percent of the sales. Thus, careful salesperson selection can greatly increase overall sales force performance.

Beyond the differences in sales performance, poor selection results in costly turnover. One study found an average annual sales force turnover rate of 27 percent for all industries. The costs of high turnover can be great. When a salesperson quits, the costs of finding and training a new salesperson—plus the costs of lost sales—can run as high as $50,000 to $75,000. And a sales force with many new people is less productive.[12]

What Makes a Good Salesperson?

Selecting salespeople would not be a problem if the company knew what traits to look for. If it knew that good salespeople were outgoing, aggressive, and energetic, for example, it could simply check applicants for these characteristics. But many successful salespeople are also bashful, soft-spoken, and laid back. Some are tall and others are short; some speak well and others poorly; some dress fashionably and others shabbily.

Still, the search continues for the magic list of traits that spells sure-fire sales success. One survey suggests that good salespeople have a lot of enthusiasm, persistence, initiative, self-confidence, and job commitment. They are committed to sales as a way of life and have a strong customer orientation. Another study suggests that good salespeople are independent and self-motivated, and are excellent listeners. Still another study advises that salespeople should be a friend to the customer as well as persistent, enthusiastic, attentive, and—above all—honest. They must be internally motivated, disciplined, hard-working, and able to build strong relationships with customers.[13]

How can a company find out what traits salespeople in its industry should have? Job *duties* suggest some of the traits a company should look for. Is a lot of planning and paperwork required? Does the job call for much travel? Will the

TEAM SELLING: SHIFTING SALESPEOPLE FROM "SOLOISTS" TO "ORCHESTRATORS"

For years, the customer has been solely in the hands of the salesperson. The salesperson identified the prospect, arranged the call, explored the customer's needs, created and proposed a solution, closed the deal, and turned cheerleader as others delivered what he or she promised. For selling relatively simple products, this approach can work well. But if the products are more complex and the service requirements greater, the salesperson simply can't go it alone. Consider the following example:

> This was Michael Quintano's big chance. The 23-year-old, up-and-coming MCI sales rep had only called on customers billing less than $2,000 a month. Then, from out of the blue, he hit upon Nat Schwartz and Company (NS&C), a china and crystal retail-telemarketer with monthly telephone billings exceeding $7,000. In over his head, he offered MCI veteran Al Rodriguez a split on the commission in return for some help. When the pair visited NS&C headquarters, they found a store filled with nothing but china and crystal. "No way does this store bill $7,000. We'll close this deal in one or two calls," Quintano thought. However, when they were led to a bustling back room filled with telemarketers working the phones, their visions of a quick close were swiftly put on hold. Quintano and Rodriguez realized they would have to expand their sales team. They called on sales manager Stephen Smith and MCI Telecommunications consultant Tom Mantone, who during two meetings with NS&C cleared up questions about technical details such as phone line installations. That smoothed the way for Quintano and Rodriguez to close the deal. Thus, by relying on team selling, Michael Quintano landed the largest account of his career.

More and more, companies are finding that sales teams can unearth problems, solutions, and sales opportunities that no individual salesperson could. Such teams might include experts from any area or level of the selling firm—sales, marketing, technical and support services, R&D, engineering, operations, finance, and others. In team selling situations, the salesperson shifts from "soloist" to "orchestrator." One such salesperson puts it in sports terms. "It's my job to be the quarterback. [Taking care of a large customer] gets farmed out to different areas of the company, and different questions have to be answered by different people. We set up a game plan and then go in and make the call."

Some companies, like IBM and Xerox, have used teams for a long time. Others have only recently reorganized to adopt the team concept. John Hancock, for example, recently set up sales-and-service teams in six territories. Each team is led by a director of sales who acts as a mini-CEO, managing all aspects of customer contact: sales, service, and technical support. The result is an informed, dedicated team that is closer to the customer.

When a customer's business becomes so complex that a single company's sales organization can't provide a complete solution, firms might even create multi-company sales teams. For example, teams from MCI, IBM, and Rohm recently joined forces in an effort to provide solutions to a large customer that was setting up a complex data-application network. MCI's team provided information on data communication, IBM's on computer hardware and software, and Rohm's on switching equipment. "The meeting provided the customer with one point of contact to solve a variety of needs," said an MCI sales executive.

Some companies have even opened special sites for team sales meetings, called *executive briefing centers.* Xerox runs six of these centers. Xerox sales teams invite key people from important accounts to one of the centers, where center staff conduct briefings, arrange video conferences with experts in other parts of the country, and provide other services that help the team build business and improve customer service.

Team selling does have some pitfalls. For example, selling teams can confuse or overwhelm customers who are used to working with only one saleperson. Salespeople who are used to having customers all to themselves may have trouble learning to work with and trust others on a team. Finally, difficulties in evaluating individual contributions to the team-selling effort can create some sticky compensation issues.

Still, team selling can produce dramatic results. For example, Dun & Bradstreet, the world's largest marketer of business information and related services, recently established sales teams made up of representatives from its credit, collection, and marketing business units, which up to then had worked separately. Their mission was to work as a team to call on higher-ups in customer organizations, learn about customer needs, and offer solutions. The teams concentrated on D&B's top 50 customers. When one of the D&B sales teams asked to meet with the chief financial officer of a major telecommunications company, the executive responded, "I'm delighted you asked, but why talk?" He found out after a one-hour meeting. The D&B team listened as he discussed problems facing his organization, and by the end of the information-seeking session, the team had come up with several solutions for the executive, and had identified $1.5 million in D&B sales opportunities from what had been a $700,000 customer. More teams met with more clients, creating more opportunities. About a year after the program started, D&B's marketing department had targeted $200 million in sales opportunities, about half of which would not have been found under the old system. Now these teams are getting together with D&B's top 200 customers.

Sources: Portions adapted from Joseph Conlin, "Teaming Up," *Sales & Marketing Management,* October 1993, pp. 98–104; and Richard C. Whiteley, "Orchestrating Service," *Sales & Marketing Management,* April 1994, pp. 29–30. Also see Christopher Meyer, "How the Right Measures Help Teams Excel," *Harvard Business Review,* May–June 1994, pp. 95–103.

salesperson face a lot of rejections? Will the salesperson be working with high-level buyers? The successful salesperson should be suited to these duties. The company also should look at the characteristics of its most successful salespeople for clues to needed traits.

Recruiting Procedures

After management has decided on needed traits, it must *recruit* salespeople. The human resources department looks for applicants by getting names from current salespeople, using employment agencies, placing classified ads, and contacting college students. Until recently, companies sometimes found it hard to sell college students on selling. Many thought that selling was a job and not a profession, that salespeople had to be deceitful to be effective, and that selling involved too much insecurity and travel. In addition, some women believed that selling was a man's career. To counter such objections, recruiters now offer high starting salaries and income growth and tout the fact that more than one-fourth of the presidents of large U.S. corporations started out in marketing and sales. They point out that more than 28 percent of the people now selling industrial products are women. Women account for a much higher percentage of the sales force in some industries, such as textiles and apparel (61 percent), banking and financial services (58 percent), communications (51 percent), and publishing (49 percent). See Marketing Highlight 17-2.

Selecting Salespeople

Recruiting will attract many applicants, from which the company must select the best. The selection procedure can vary from a single informal interview to lengthy testing and interviewing. Many companies give formal tests to sales applicants. Tests typically measure sales aptitude, analytical and organizational skills, personality traits, and other characteristics. Test results count heavily in such companies as IBM, Prudential, Procter & Gamble, and Gillette. Gillette claims that tests have reduced turnover by 42 percent and that test scores have correlated well with the later performance of new salespeople. But test scores provide only one piece of information in a set that includes personal characteristics, references, past employment history, and interviewer reactions.[14]

TRAINING SALESPEOPLE

Many companies used to send their new salespeople into the field almost immediately after hiring them. They would be given samples, order books, and general instructions ("sell west of the Mississippi"). Training programs were luxuries. To many companies, a training program translated into much expense for instructors, materials, space, and salary for a person who was not yet selling, and a loss of sales opportunities because the person was not in the field.

Today's new salespeople, however, may spend anywhere from a few weeks or months to a year or more in training. The average training period is four months. Norton Company, the industrial abrasives manufacturer, puts its new salespeople through a 12-month training program. The first six months are spent at company headquarters, with the remaining time spent out in the field. The initial period focuses on selling skills, product knowledge, the company, and the distributors that sell Norton products. Salespeople even spend two weeks with a Norton distributor. Among other things, they learn that distributors have dozens of salespeople calling on them all the time. After initial training, every year Norton brings back about a third of its 200 salespeople to company headquarters for follow-up training.[15]

ON THE JOB WITH TWO SUCCESSFUL SALESWOMEN

The word *salesman* now has an archaic ring. The entry of women into what was once the male bastion of professional selling has been swift and dramatic. More than 28 percent of people selling industrial products are women, compared to just 7 percent in 1975. In some industries this percentage reaches as high as 60 percent. Here are two examples of highly successful technical saleswomen.

Catherine Hogan, Account Manager, Bell Atlantic Network Services

As an undergraduate student, Catherine Hogan had few thoughts about a career in sales, especially *technical* sales. "I was a warm, fuzzy person," she says, "artsy-craftsy." Now, just six years later, she's in the thick of it, successfully handling a complex line of technical products in what was once a male-dominated world. Why the change? "I needed to get out there and feel the heat—take risks, handle customers, and be responsible for their complaints," says Hogan. Still far from being a technical person, she has quickly acquired a working knowledge of modern communications services and the ways they can be delivered to businesses through Bell Atlantic's phone network.

So rapidly is the company diversifying that, artsy-craftsy or not, Hogan finds herself studying up on new hardware, software, and leasing programs so she can explain them both to business customers and to Bell's own account executives, who have ongoing responsibilities for those customers. The account executives can handle their customers' local applications by themselves, but they team up with Hogan when customers want long-distance voice or data services. This sort of team selling requires empathy and skill. On joint calls, Hogan is careful not to interfere when the account executive is negotiating with a customer.

On a more personal level, Hogan has worked through the pros and cons of being something of a novelty in an industry undergoing wrenching change. "People are used to seeing middle-age, white males with a technical background in this industry," she says. "It's challenging being young, female, and ethnic." Her advice to others in similar situations? "Go beyond what the world prescribes

for you. Be strong enough to lance the dragon but soft enough to wear silk."

Joyce Nardone, Sales Manager, Facsimile Division, Amfax America

For a vivid picture of what it takes to succeed in sales, listen to Joyce Nardone exclaim about the terrors and triumphs of selling to strangers who've never heard your name before you walk in the door. "I'm good at cold-calling, but it takes a long time to learn to take rejection," she says. "Sometimes just getting out of the car is a feat in itself."

So resilient is the 24-year-old Joyce, however, that prior to her recent promotion to management, she compiled an impressive record of knocking on doors for Amfax America, an office equipment dealer whose main line is Sharp facsimile machines and copiers. "You have to be friendly and upbeat," she says. "If you look like a winner, they'll buy from you."

As good as she is at cold-calling, Nardone adds a special ingredi-

ent in a business that traditionally has been built around the one-time sale: She keeps up with her customers and makes sure they're satisfied with the product. "I have over 100 clients, and I consider them my friends," she says. "Most people don't bother to go back, but I'll bring them a free roll of paper or fax them a Hanukkah or Christmas

Successful saleswomen Catherine Hogan and Joyce Nardone—the word "salesman" now has an archaic ring.

card." As a result, customers often refer other companies to Nardone, so she has a steady stream of new business.

Fortunately, management recognizes her talents, too. Nardone is now in charge of the sales force for Amfax's Facsimile Division. As manager, she is responsible for training, motivation, and overall performance of eight direct salespeople. She also coordinates advertising and trade show exhibits. Her advice to new salespeople? "To discover customers' needs, *listen* to them!"

Sources: Adapted from portions of Martin Everett, "Selling's New Breed: Smart and Feisty," Sales & Marketing Management, October 1989, pp. 52–64. Also see Bill Kelley, "Selling in a Man's World," Sales & Marketing Management, January 1991, pp. 28–35; "What's Selling? Sales Jobs," Sales & Marketing Management, September 1993, p. 11; and Nancy Arnott, "It's a Woman's World," Sales & Marketing Management, March 1995, pp. 55–59.

Training programs have several goals. Salespeople need to know and identify with the company, so most training programs begin by describing the company's history and objectives, its organization, its financial structure and facilities, and its chief products and markets. Salespeople also need to know the company's products, so sales trainees are shown how products are produced and how they work. They also need to know customers' and competitors' characteristics, so the training program teaches them about competitors' strategies and about different types of customers and their needs, buying motives, and buying habits. Because salespeople must know how to make effective presentations, they are trained in the principles of selling. Finally, salespeople need to understand field procedures and responsibilities. They learn how to divide time between active and potential accounts and how to use an expense account, prepare reports, and route communications effectively.

COMPENSATING SALESPEOPLE

To attract salespeople, a company must have an appealing compensation plan. These plans vary greatly both by industry and by companies within the same industry. The level of compensation must be close to the "going rate" for the type of sales job and needed skills. For example, the average earnings of an experienced, middle-level industrial salesperson amount to about $47,000.[16] To pay less than the going rate would attract too few quality salespeople; to pay more would be unnecessary.

Compensation is made up of several elements—a fixed amount, a variable amount, expenses, and fringe benefits. The fixed amount, usually a salary, gives the salesperson some stable income. The variable amount, which might be commissions or bonuses based on sales performance, rewards the salesperson for greater effort. Expense allowances, which repay salespeople for job-related expenses, let salespeople undertake needed and desirable selling efforts. Fringe benefits, such as paid vacations, sickness or accident benefits, pensions, and life insurance, provide job security and satisfaction.

Management must decide what *mix* of these compensation elements makes the most sense for each sales job. Different combinations of fixed and variable compensation give rise to four basic types of compensation plans—straight salary, straight commission, salary plus bonus, and salary plus commission. A study of sales force compensation plans showed that about 14 percent of companies paid straight salary, 19 percent paid straight commission, 26 percent paid salary plus bonus, 37 percent paid salary plus commission, and 10 percent paid salary plus commission plus bonus.[17]

The sales force compensation plan can be designed both to motivate salespeople and to direct their activities. For example, if sales management wants salespeople to emphasize new account development, it might pay a bonus for opening new accounts. Thus, the compensation plan should direct the sales force toward activities that are consistent with overall marketing objectives. Table 17-1 illustrates how a company's compensation plan should reflect its overall marketing strategy. For example, if the overall strategy is to grow rapidly and gain market share, the compensation plan should reward high sales performance and encourage salespeople to capture new accounts. This might suggest a larger commission component coupled with new account bonuses. By contrast, if the marketing goal is to maximize profitability of current accounts, the compensation plan might contain a larger base salary component, with additional incentives based on current account sales or customer satisfaction.[18]

SUPERVISING SALESPEOPLE

New salespeople need more than a territory, compensation, and training—they need *supervision*. Through supervision, the company *directs* and *motivates* the sales force to do a better job.

TABLE 17-1   *The Relationship between Overall Marketing Strategy and Sales Force Compensation*

	STRATEGIC GOAL		
	To Rapidly Gain Market Share	**To Solidify Market Leadership**	**To Maximize Profitability**
Ideal Salesperson	• An independent self-starter	• A competitive problem solver	• A team player • A relationship manager
Sales Focus	• Deal making • Sustained high effort	• Consultative selling	• Account penetration
Compensation Role	• To capture accounts • To reward high performance	• To reward new and existing account sales	• To manage the product mix • To encourage team selling • To reward account management

Source: Adapted from Sam T. Johnson, "Sales Compensation: In Search of a Better Solution," *Compensation & Benefits Review,* November–December 1993, pp. 53–60.

Directing Salespeople

How much should sales management be involved in helping salespeople manage their territories? It depends on everything from the company's size to the experience of its sales force. Thus, companies vary widely in how closely they supervise their salespeople. And what works for one company may not work for another.

Developing Customer Targets and Call Norms

Most companies classify customers based on sales volume, profit, and growth potential, and then they set call norms accordingly. Thus, salespeople may call weekly on accounts with large sales or potential, but only infrequently on small accounts. Beyond account size and potential, call norms also may depend on other factors such as competitive call activity and account development status.

Companies often specify how much time their sales forces should spend prospecting for new accounts. For example, Spector Freight wants its salespeople to spend 25 percent of their time prospecting and to stop calling on a prospect after three unsuccessful calls. Companies set up prospecting standards for several reasons. For example, if left alone, many salespeople will spend most of their time with current customers, who are better-known quantities. Moreover, whereas a prospect may never deliver any business, salespeople can depend on current accounts for some business. Therefore, unless salespeople are rewarded for opening new accounts, they may avoid new-account development. Some companies even rely on a special sales force to open new accounts.

Using Sales Time Efficiently

Salespeople need to know how to use their time efficiently. One tool is the *annual call plan* that shows which customers and prospects to call on in which months and which activities to carry out. Activities include taking part in trade shows, attending sales meetings, and carrying out marketing research. Another tool is *time-and-duty analysis*. In addition to time spent selling, the salesperson spends time traveling, waiting, eating, taking breaks, and doing administrative chores.

Figure 17-2 shows how salespeople spend their time. On average, actual face-to-face selling time accounts for only 30 percent of total working time! If selling time could be raised from 30 percent to 40 percent, this would be a 33 percent increase in the time spent selling. Companies always are trying to find ways to save time—using phones instead of traveling, simplifying record-keeping forms, finding better call and routing plans, and supplying more and better customer information.

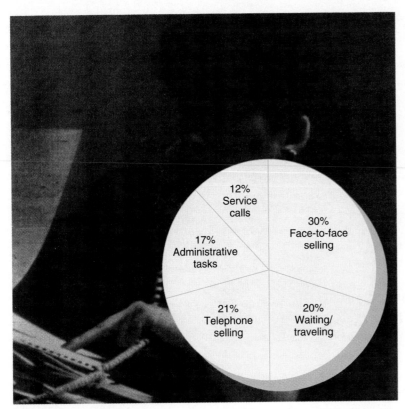

12%
Service
calls

17%
Administrative
tasks

30%
Face-to-face
selling

21%
Telephone
selling

20%
Waiting/
traveling

FIGURE 17-2   *How salespeople spend their time*

Source: Dartnell Corporation; 27th Survey of Sales Force Compensation. ©1992; Dartnell Corporation

Advances in information and computer technology—laptop computers, telecommunications, personal selling software, videodisc players, and others—have encouraged many firms to go "electronic." They have adopted *sales force automation systems,* computerized sales operations for more efficient order-entry transactions, improved customer service, and better salesperson decision-making support. A recent study of 100 large companies found that 48 percent are "actively pursuing" sales force automation; another 34 percent are planning or considering it.[19]

Salespeople use computers to profile customers and prospects, analyze and forecast sales, manage accounts, schedule sales calls, enter orders, check inventories and order status, prepare sales and expense reports, process correspondence, and carry out many other activities. Sales force automation not only lowers sales force costs and improves productivity, it also improves the quality of sales management decisions. Here is an example of successful sales force automation:[20]

Owens-Corning recently put its sales force on-line with FAST—its newly-developed Field Automation Sales Team system. FAST gives Owens-Corning salespeople a constant supply of information about their company and the people they're dealing with. Using laptop computers, each salesperson can access three types of programs. First, FAST gives them a set of *generic tools,* everything from word processing to fax transmission to creating presentations on-line. Second, it provides *product information*—tech bulletins, customer specifications, pricing information, and other data that can help close a sale. Finally, it offers up a wealth of *customer information*—buying history, types of products ordered, and preferred payment terms. Reps previously stored such information in loose-leaf books, calendars, and account cards. FAST makes working directly with customers easier than ever. Salespeople can prime themselves on backgrounds of clients; call up prewritten sales letters; transmit orders and resolve customer-service issues on the spot during customer calls; and have samples, pamphlets, brochures, and other materials sent to clients with a few keystrokes.

Motivating Salespeople

Some salespeople will do their best without any special urging from management. To them, selling may be the most fascinating job in the world. But selling can also be frustrating. Salespeople often work alone, and they must sometimes travel away from home. They may face aggressive, competing salespeople and difficult customers. They sometimes lack the authority to do what is needed to win a sale and may thus lose large orders they have worked hard to obtain. Therefore, salespeople often need special encouragement to do their best. Management can boost sales force morale and performance through its *organizational climate, sales quotas,* and *positive incentives.*

Sales force automation: Owens-Corning's FAST sales force automation system makes working directly with customers easier than ever.

ORGANIZATIONAL CLIMATE. Organizational climate describes the feeling that salespeople have about their opportunities, value, and rewards for a good performance within the company. Some companies treat salespeople as if they are not very important. Other companies treat their salespeople as their prime movers and allow virtually unlimited opportunity for income and promotion. Not surprisingly, a company's attitude toward its salespeople affects their behavior. If they are held in low esteem, there is high turnover and poor performance. If they are held in high esteem, there is less turnover and higher performance.

Treatment from the salesperson's immediate superior is especially important. A good sales manager keeps in touch with the sales force through letters and phone calls, visits in the field, and evaluation sessions in the home office. At different times, the sales manager acts as the salesperson's boss, companion, coach, and confessor.

Sales quotas
Standards set for salespeople, stating the amount they should sell and how sales should be divided among the company's products.

SALES QUOTAS. Many companies set **sales quotas** for their salespeople—standards stating the amount they should sell and how sales should be divided among the company's products. Compensation often is related to how well salespeople meet their quotas.

Sales quotas are set at the time the annual marketing plan is developed. The company first decides on a sales forecast that is reasonably achievable. Based on this forecast, management plans production, work-force size, and financial needs. It then sets sales quotas for its regions and territories. Generally, sales quotas are set higher than the sales forecast to encourage sales managers and salespeople to give their best effort. If they fail to make their quotas, the company may still make its sales forecast.

POSITIVE INCENTIVES. Companies also use several incentives to increase sales force effort. *Sales meetings* provide social occasions, breaks from routine, chances to meet and talk with "company brass," and opportunities to air feelings and to identify with a larger group. Companies also sponsor *sales contests* to spur the sales force to make a selling effort above what would normally be expected. Other incentives include honors, merchandise and cash awards, trips, and profit-sharing plans.

EVALUATING SALESPEOPLE

We have thus far described how management communicates what salespeople should be doing and how it motivates them to do it. This process requires good feedback. And good feedback means getting regular information from salespeople to evaluate their performance.

Sources of Information

Management gets information about its salespeople in several ways. The most important source is the *sales report.* Additional information comes from personal observation, customers' letters and complaints, customer surveys, and talks with other salespeople.

Sales reports are divided into plans for future activities and writeups of completed activities. The best example of the plan for future activities is the *work plan* that salespeople submit a week or month in advance. The work plan describes intended calls and routing. From this report, the sales force plans and schedules activities. It also informs management of the salespeople's whereabouts and provides a basis for comparing plans and performance. Salespeople can then be evaluated on their ability to "plan their work and work their plan." Sometimes, managers contact individual salespeople to suggest improvements in work plans.

Sales force incentives: Many companies award cash, merchandise, trips, or other gifts as incentives for outstanding sales performance.

Companies also are beginning to require their salespeople to draft *annual territory marketing plans* in which they outline their plans for building new accounts and increasing sales from existing accounts. Formats vary greatly—some ask for general ideas on territory development; others ask for detailed sales and profit estimates. Such reports cast salespeople as territory marketing managers. Sales managers study these territory plans, make suggestions, and use the plans to develop sales quotas.

Salespeople write up their completed activities on *call reports.* Call reports keep sales management informed of the salesperson's activities, show what is happening with each customer's account, and provide information that might be useful in later calls. Salespeople also turn in *expense reports* for which they are partly or wholly repaid. Some companies also ask for reports on new business, lost business, and local business and economic conditions.

These reports supply the raw data from which sales management can evaluate sales force performance. Are salespeople making too few calls per day? Are they spending too much time per call? Are they spending too much money on entertainment? Are they closing enough orders per hundred calls? Are they finding enough new customers and holding onto enough old customers?

Formal Evaluation of Performance

Using sales force reports and other information, sales management formally evaluates members of the sales force. Formal evaluation produces four benefits. First, management must develop and communicate clear standards for judging performance. Second, management must gather well-rounded information about each salesperson. Third, salespeople receive constructive feedback that helps them to improve future performance. Finally, salespeople are motivated to perform well because they know they will have to sit down with the sales manager and explain their performance.

COMPARING SALESPEOPLE'S PERFORMANCE. One type of evaluation compares and ranks the sales performance of different salespeople. Such comparisons can be misleading, however. Salespeople may perform differently because of differences in territory potential, workload, level of competition, company promotion effort, and other factors. Furthermore, sales are not usually the best indicator of achievement. Management should be more interested in how much each salesperson contributes to net profits, a concern that requires looking at each salesperson's sales mix and expenses.

COMPARING CURRENT SALES WITH PAST SALES. A second type of evaluation is to compare a salesperson's current performance with past performance. Such a comparison should directly indicate the person's progress. Table 17-2 provides an example.

The sales manager can learn many things about Chris Bennett from this table. Bennett's total sales increased every year (line 3). This does not necessarily mean that Bennett is doing a better job. The product breakdown shows that Bennett has been able to push the sales of product B further than those of product A (lines 1 and 2). According to the quotas for the two products (lines 4 and 5), the success in increasing product B sales may be at the expense of product A sales. According to gross profits (lines 6 and 7), the company earns twice as much gross profit (as a ratio to sales) on A as it does on B. Bennett may be pushing the higher-volume, lower-margin product at the expense of the more profitable product. Although Bennett increased total sales by $1,100 between 1992 and 1993 (line 3), the gross profits on these total sales actually decreased by $580 (line 8).

Sales expense (line 9) shows a steady increase, although total expense as a percentage of total sales seems to be under control (line 10). The upward trend in Bennett's total dollar expenses does not seem to be explained by any increase in the number of calls (line 11), although it may be related to his success in acquiring new customers (line 14). However, there is a possibility that in prospecting for

TABLE 17-2 *Evaluating Salespeople's Performance*

TERRITORY: MIDLAND	1992	SALESPERSON: CHRIS BENNETT 1993	1994	1995
1. Net sales product A	$251,300	$253,200	$270,000	$263,100
2. Net sales product B	$423,200	$439,200	$553,900	$561,900
3. Net sales total	$674,500	$692,400	$823,900	$825,000
4. Percent of quota product A	95.6	92.0	88.0	84.7
5. Percent of quota product B	120.4	122.3	134.9	130.8
6. Gross profits product A	$ 50,260	$ 50,640	$ 54,000	$ 52,620
7. Gross profits product B	$ 42,320	$ 43,920	$ 53,390	$ 56,190
8. Gross profits total	$ 92,580	$ 94,560	$109,390	$108,810
9. Sales expense	$ 10,200	$ 11,100	$ 11,600	$ 13,200
10. Sales expense to total sales (%)	1.5	1.6	1.4	1.6
11. Number of calls	1,675	1,700	1,680	1,660
12. Cost per call	$ 6.09	$ 6.53	$ 6.90	$ 7.95
13. Average number of customers	320	324	328	334
14. Number of new customers	13	14	15	20
15. Number of lost customers	8	10	11	14
16. Average sales per customer	$ 2,108	$ 2,137	$ 2,512	$ 2,470
17. Average gross profit per customer	$ 289	$ 292	$ 334	$ 326

new customers, Bennett is neglecting present customers, as indicated by an upward trend in the annual number of lost customers (line 15).

The last two lines on the table show the level and trend in Bennett's sales and gross profits per customer. These figures become more meaningful when they are compared with overall company averages. If Chris Bennett's average gross profit per customer is lower than the company's average, Chris may be concentrating on the wrong customers or may not be spending enough time with each customer. Looking back at the annual number of calls (line 11), Bennett may be making fewer calls than the average salesperson. If distances in the territory are not much different, this may mean he is not putting in a full workday, he is poor at planning his routing or minimizing his waiting time, or he spends too much time with certain accounts.

QUALITATIVE EVALUATION OF SALESPEOPLE.   A *qualitative evaluation* usually looks at a salesperson's knowledge of the company, products, customers, competitors, territory, and tasks. Personal traits—manner, appearance, speech, and temperament—can be rated. The sales manager also can review any problems in motivation or compliance. Each company must decide what would be most useful to know. It should communicate these criteria to salespeople so that they understand how their performance is evaluated and can make an effort to improve it.

PRINCIPLES OF PERSONAL SELLING

We now turn from designing and managing a sales force to the actual personal selling process. Personal selling is an ancient art that has spawned a large literature and many principles. Effective salespeople operate on more than just instinct—they are highly trained in methods of territory analysis and customer management.

THE PERSONAL SELLING PROCESS

Companies spend hundreds of millions of dollars on seminars, books, cassettes, and other materials to teach salespeople the "art" of selling. Millions of books on selling are purchased every year, with tantalizing titles such as *How to Sell Anything to Anybody, How I Raised Myself from Failure to Success in Selling, The Four-Minute Sell, The Best Seller, The Power of Enthusiastic Selling, Where Do You Go from No. 1?,* and *Winning Through Intimidation.* One of the most popular and enduring books on selling is Dale Carnegie's *How to Win Friends and Influence People.*

Most companies take a *customer-oriented approach* to personal selling. They train salespeople to identify customer needs and to find solutions. This approach assumes that customer needs provide sales opportunities, that customers appreciate good suggestions, and that customers will be loyal to salespeople who have their long-term interests at heart. One recent survey found that purchasing agents appreciate salespeople who understand their needs and meet them. As one purchasing agent states:

> My *expectation* of salespeople is that they've done their homework, uncovered some of our needs, probed to uncover other needs, and presented convincing arguments of mutual benefits for both organizations. . . . [The problem is that] I don't always see that.[21]

The problem-solver salesperson fits better with the marketing concept than does the hard-sell salesperson. The qualities that purchasing agents *dislike most* in salespeople included being pushy, late, and unprepared or disorganized. The qualities they *value most* included honesty, dependability, thoroughness, and follow-through.

STEPS IN THE SELLING PROCESS

Selling process
The steps that the salesperson follows when selling, which include prospecting and qualifying, preapproach, approach, presentation and demonstration, handling objections, closing, and follow-up.

Prospecting
The step in the selling process in which the salesperson identifies qualified potential customers.

Most training programs view the **selling process** as consisting of several steps that the salesperson must master (see Figure 17-3). These steps focus on the goal of getting new customers and obtaining orders from them. However, most salespeople spend much of their time maintaining existing accounts and building long-term customer *relationships*. We discuss the relationship aspect of the personal selling process in the final section of the chapter.

Prospecting and Qualifying

The first step in the selling process is **prospecting**—identifying qualified potential customers. The salesperson often must approach many prospects to get just a few sales. In the insurance industry, for example, only one out of nine prospects becomes a customer. In the computer business, 125 phone calls result in 25 interviews leading to five demonstrations and one sale.[22] Although the company supplies some leads, salespeople need skill in finding their own. They can ask current customers for the names of prospects. They can build referral sources, such as suppliers, dealers, noncompeting salespeople, and bankers. They can join organizations to which prospects belong or can engage in speaking and writing activities that will draw attention. They can search for names in newspapers or directories and use the telephone and mail to track down leads. Or they can drop in unannounced on various offices (a practice known as "cold calling").

Salespeople need to know how to *qualify* leads—that is, how to identify the good ones and screen out the poor ones. Prospects can be qualified by looking at their financial ability, volume of business, special needs, location, and possibilities for growth.

Preapproach

Preapproach
The step in the selling process in which the salesperson learns as much as possible about a prospective customer before making a sales call.

Before calling on a prospect, the salesperson should learn as much as possible about the organization (what it needs, who is involved in the buying) and its buyers (their characteristics and buying styles). This step is known as the **preapproach.** The salesperson can consult standard sources (*Moody's, Standard & Poor's, Dun & Bradstreet*), acquaintances, and others to learn about the company. The salesperson should set *call objectives,* which may be to qualify the prospect, to gather information, or to make an immediate sale. Another task is to decide on the best approach, which might be a personal visit, a phone call, or a letter. The best timing should be considered carefully because many prospects are busiest at certain times. Finally, the salesperson should give thought to an overall sales strategy for the account.

Approach

Approach
The step in the selling process in which the salesperson meets and greets the buyer to get the relationship off to a good start.

During the **approach** step, the salesperson should know how to meet and greet the buyer and to get the relationship off to a good start. This step involves the

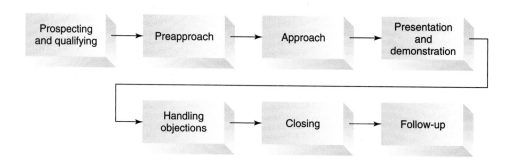

FIGURE 17-3 *Major steps in effective selling*

salesperson's appearance, opening lines, and the follow-up remarks. The opening lines should be positive, such as "Mr. Johnson, I am Chris Bennett from the All-tech Company. My company and I appreciate your willingness to see me. I will do my best to make this visit profitable and worthwhile for you and your company." This opening might be followed by some key questions to learn more about the customer's needs or the showing of a display or sample to attract the buyer's attention and curiosity.

Presentation and Demonstration

Presentation
The step in the selling process in which the salesperson tells the product "story" to the buyer, showing how the product will make or save money for the buyer.

During the **presentation** step of the selling process, the salesperson tells the product "story" to the buyer, showing how the product will make or save money. The salesperson describes the product features but concentrates on presenting customer benefits. Using a *need-satisfaction approach*, the salesperson starts with a search for the customer's needs by getting the customer to do most of the talking. This approach calls for good listening and problem-solving skills. One marketing director describes the approach this way:

> [High-performing salespeople] make it a point to understand customer needs and goals before they pull anything out of their product bag. . . . Such salespeople spend the time needed to get an in-depth knowledge of the customer's business, asking questions that will lead to solutions our systems can address.[23]

Sales presentations can be improved with demonstration aids, such as booklets, flip charts, slides, videotapes or videodiscs, and product samples. If buyers can see or handle the product, they will better remember its features and benefits.

Handling Objections

Handling objections
The step in the selling process in which the salesperson seeks out, clarifies, and overcomes customer objections to buying.

Customers almost always have objections during the presentation or when asked to place an order. The problem can be either logical or psychological, and objections are often unspoken. In **handling objections**, the salesperson should use a positive approach, seek out hidden objections, ask the buyer to clarify any objections, take objections as opportunities to provide more information, and turn the objections into reasons for buying. Every salesperson needs training in the skills of handling objections.

Closing

Closing
The step in the selling process in which the salesperson asks the customer for an order.

After handling the prospect's objections, the salesperson now tries to close the sale. Some salespeople do not get around to **closing** or do not handle it well. They may lack confidence, feel guilty about asking for the order, or fail to recognize the right moment to close the sale. Salespeople should know how to recognize closing signals from the buyer, including physical actions, comments, and questions. For example, the customer might sit forward and nod approvingly or ask about prices and credit terms. Salespeople can use one of several closing techniques. They can ask for the order, review points of agreement, offer to help write up the order, ask whether the buyer wants this model or that one, or note that the buyer will lose out if the order is not placed now. The salesperson may offer the buyer special reasons to close, such as a lower price or an extra quantity at no charge.

In the sales presentation, the salesperson tells the product story to the buyers.

GREAT SALESPEOPLE: DRIVE, DISCIPLINE, AND RELATIONSHIP-BUILDING SKILLS

What sets great salespeople apart from all the rest? What separates the masters from the merely mediocre? In an effort to profile top sales performers, Gallup Management Consulting, a division of the well-known Gallup polling organization, has interviewed as many as a half million salespeople. Its research suggests that the best salespeople possess four key talents: intrinsic motivation, disciplined work style, the ability to close a sale, and perhaps most importantly, the ability to build relationships with customers.

Intrinsic Motivation

"Different things drive different people—pride, happiness, money, you name it," says one expert. "But all great salespeople have one thing in common: an unrelenting drive to excel." This strong, internal drive can be shaped and molded, but it can't be taught. The source of the motivation varies—some are driven by money, some by hunger for recognition, some

by a yearning to build relationships. The Gallup research revealed four general personality types, all high performers, but each with different sources of motivation. *Competitors* are people who not only want to win, but crave the satisfaction of beating specific rivals—other companies *and* their fellow salespeople. They'll come right out and say to a colleague, "With all due respect, I know you're salesperson of the year, but I'm going after your title." The *ego-driven* are salespeople who just want to experience the glory of winning. They want to be recognized as being the best, regardless of the competition. *Achievers* are a rare breed who are almost completely self-motivated. They like accomplishment, and routinely set goals that are higher than what is expected of them. They often make the best sales managers because they don't mind seeing other people succeed, as long as the organization's goals are met. Finally, *service-oriented* salespeople are those whose strength lies

in their ability to build and cultivate relationships. They are generous, caring, and empathetic. "These people are golden," says the national training manager of Minolta Corporation's business equipment division. "We need salespeople who will take the time to follow up on the ten questions a customer might have, salespeople who love to stay in touch."

No one is purely a competitor, an achiever, ego-driven, or service-driven. There's at least some of each in most top performers. "A *competitor* with a strong sense of *service* will probably bring in a lot of business, while doing a great job of taking care of customers," observes the managing director of the Gallup Management Consulting Group. "Who could ask for anything more?"

Disciplined Work Style

Whatever their motivation, if salespeople aren't organized and focused, and if they don't work hard, they can't meet the ever-increasing demands

---

Follow-up
The last step in the selling process in which the salesperson follows up after the sale to ensure customer satisfaction and repeat business.

Follow-Up

The last step in the selling process—**follow-up**—is necessary if the salesperson wants to ensure customer satisfaction and repeat business. Right after closing, the salesperson should complete any details on delivery time, purchase terms, and other matters. The salesperson then should schedule a follow-up call when the initial order is received to make sure there is proper installation, instruction, and servicing. This visit would reveal any problems, assure the buyer of the salesperson's interest, and reduce any buyer concerns that might have arisen since the sale.

RELATIONSHIP MARKETING

The principles of personal selling as just described are *transaction oriented*—their aim is to help salespeople close a specific sale with a customer. But in many cases, the company is not seeking simply a sale: it has targeted a major customer that it would like to win and serve. The company would like to show the customer that it has the capabilities to serve the customer's needs in a superior way over the long haul, in a mutually profitable *relationship*.

Relationship marketing
The process of creating, maintaining, and enhancing strong, value-laden relationships with customers and other stakeholders.

Most companies today are moving away from transaction marketing, with its emphasis on making a sale. Instead, they are practicing **relationship marketing,** which emphasizes building and maintaining profitable long-term relationships with customers by creating superior customer value and satisfaction. Recognition of the importance of relationship marketing has increased rapidly in the past few years. Companies are realizing that when operating in maturing markets and facing stiffer competition, it costs a lot more to wrest new customers from competitors than to keep current customers.

customers are making these days. Great salespeople are tenacious about laying out detailed, organized plans, then following through in a timely, disciplined way. There's no magic here, just solid organization and hard work. "Our best sales reps never let loose ends dangle," says the president of a small business equipment firm. "If they say they're going to make a follow-up call on a customer in six months, you can be sure that they'll be on the doorstep in six months." Top sellers rely on hard work, not luck or gimmicks. "Some people says it's all technique or luck," notes one sales trainer. "But luck happens to the best salespeople when they get up early, work late, stay up till two in the morning working on a proposal, or keep making calls when everyone is leaving at the end of the day."

The Ability to Close the Sale

Other skills mean little if a seller can't ask for the sale. No close, no sale.

Period. So what makes for a great closer? For one thing, an unyielding persistence, say managers and sales consultants. Claims one, "Great closers are like great athletes. They're not afraid to fail, and they don't give up until they close." Part of what makes the failure rate tolerable for top performers is their deep-seated belief in themselves and what they are selling. Great closers have a high level of self-confidence and believe that they are doing the right thing. And they've got a burning need to make the sale happen—to do whatever it takes within legal and ethical standards to get the business.

The Ability to Build Relationships

Perhaps most important in today's relationship-marketing environment, top salespeople are customer-problem solvers and relationship builders. They have an instinctive understanding of their customers' needs. Talk to sales executives and they'll describe

top performers in these terms: Empathetic. Patient. Caring. Responsive. Good listeners. Even *honest.* Top sellers can put themselves on the buyer's side of the desk and see the world through their customers' eyes. Today, customers are looking for business partners, not golf partners. "At the root of it all," says a Dallas sales consultant, "is an integrity of intent. High performers don't just want to be liked, they want to add value." High-performing salespeople, he adds, are "always thinking about the big picture, where the customer's organization is going, and how they can help them get there."

Source: Adapted from Geoffrey Brewer, "Mind Reading: What Drives Top Salespeople to Greatness?" *Sales & Marketing Management,* May 1994, pp. 82–88.

Today's customers are large and often global. They prefer suppliers who can sell and deliver a coordinated set of products and services to many locations; who can quickly solve problems that arise in their different parts of the nation or world; and who can work closely with customer teams to improve products and processes. For these customers, the sale is only the beginning of the relationship.

Unfortunately, some companies are not set up for these developments. They often sell their products through separate sales forces, each working independently to close sales. Their technical people may not be willing to lend time to educate a customer. Their engineering, design, and manufacturing people may have the attitude that "it's our job to make good products and the salesperson's to sell them to customers." However, companies increasingly are recognizing that winning and keeping accounts requires more than making good products and directing the sales force to close lots of sales. It requires a carefully coordinated, whole-company effort to create value-laden, satisfying relationships with important customers.

Relationship marketing is based on the premise that important accounts need focused and continuous attention. Studies have shown that the best salespeople are those who are highly motivated and good closers, but more than this, they are customer-problem solvers and relationship builders (see Marketing Highlight 17-3). Good salespeople working with key customers do more than call when they think a customer might be ready to place an order. They also study the account and understand its problems. They call or visit frequently, work with the customer to help solve the customer's problems and improve its business, and take an interest in customers as people. We discuss relationship marketing further in Chapter 18.

Summary

Most companies use salespeople, and many companies assign a key *role to personal selling* in the marketing mix. The high cost of personal selling calls for an effective process of *managing the sales force,* consisting of multiple steps: designing sales force strategy and structure, recruiting and selecting, training, compensating, supervising, and evaluating salespeople.

As an element of the marketing mix, the sales force is very effective in achieving certain marketing objectives and carrying out such objectives as prospecting, communicating, selling and servicing, and information gathering. A market-oriented sales force needs skills in marketing analysis and planning in addition to the traditional selling skills.

In *designing a sales force strategy and structure,* sales management must address issues such as what type of *sales force structure* will work best (*territorial, product,* or *customer structured* and *complex structures*); how large the *sales force size* should be; and who will be involved in the selling effort and how its various sales and sales-support people will work together (*inside or outside sales forces* and *team selling*).

To hold down the high costs of hiring the wrong people, companies must use careful *recruiting and selecting of salespeople. Training* programs familiarize new salespeople not only with the art of selling, but with the company's history, its products and policies, and the characteristics of its market and competitors. The *sales force compensation system* helps to reward, motivate, and direct salespeople. All salespeople need *supervision,* and many need continuous encouragement because they must make many decisions and face many frustrations. Periodically, the company must *evaluate salespeople's performance* to help them do a better job.

The art of selling involves a seven-step *selling process: prospecting and qualifying, preapproach, approach, presentation and demonstration, handling objections, closing,* and *follow-up.* These steps help marketers close a specific sale. However, a seller's dealings with customers should be guided by the larger concept of *relationship marketing.* The company's sales force should help orchestrate a whole-company effort to develop profitable long-term relationships with key customers based on superior customer value and satisfaction.

Key Terms

Approach	Preapproach	Sales quotas
Closing	Presentation	Selling process
Customer sales force structure	Product sales force structure	Team selling
Follow-up	Prospecting	Telemarketing
Handling objections	Relationship marketing	Territorial sales force structure
Inside sales force	Sales force management	Workload approach
Outside sales force	Salesperson	

Discussing the Issues

1. Grocery stores require their suppliers' salespeople not only to sell but also to serve as aisle clerks. These salespeople must arrange and restock shelves, build special displays, and set up point-of-purchase material. Decide whether it is important for a manufacturer to meet these demands. Are there creative ways to free the salesperson's time for more productive uses?

2. Explain why so many sales force compensation plans combine salary with bonus or commission. What are the advantages and disadvantages of using bonuses as incentives, rather than using commissions?

3. Many people feel they do not have the ability to be a successful salesperson. Suggest what role training plays in helping someone develop selling ability.

4. Some companies have installed computerized inventory tracking that automatically sends reorders to the supplier's computer as needed. Predict whether this process is likely to expand. Discuss the effects this could have on the role of the salesperson.

5. The surest way to become a sales force manager is to be an outstanding salesperson. Name some advantages and disadvantages of promoting top salespeople to management positions. Why might an outstanding salesperson refuse to be promoted?

6. Good salespeople are familiar with their competitors' products as well as their own. Analyze what you would do if your company expected you to sell a product that you thought was inferior to the competition's. Why?

Applying the Concepts

1. Experience a sales pitch. Go to a retailer where the salespeople are likely to be working on commission, such as a car dealership, an appliance and electronics dealer, or a clothing store. (a) Rate your salesperson. Was their approach, presentation and demonstration effective? (b) Consider your emotional response to the sales pitch. Did you enjoy the experience, or find it hard to endure? Why did you react this way?

2. Go to a retailer that specializes in complex products such as computers and software, stereo, or video equipment. Get a salesperson to explain a product to you, and ask specific questions. (a) Was the salesperson knowledgeable, and able to answer your questions in a helpful and believable way? (b) Did you feel the salesperson's expertise added value to the product, or not? (c) Would you rather buy this product from the salesperson you spoke with, or purchase it by mail order for a slightly lower price?

References

1. Based on William Keenan, Jr., "What's Sales Got to Do With It?" *Sales & Marketing Management,* March 1994, pp. 66–73. Also see Melissa Campanelli, "Eastman Chemical: A Formula for Quality," *Sales & Marketing Management,* October 1994, p. 88.

2. See Bill Kelley, "How to Sell Airplanes, Boeing-Style," *Sales & Marketing Management,* December 9, 1985, pp. 32–34. Also see Dori Jones Yang and Andrea Rothman, "Boeing Cuts Its Altitude as the Clouds Roll In," *Business Week,* February 8, 1993, p. 25.

3. For a comparison of several classifications, see William C. Moncrief III, "Selling Activity and Sales Position Taxonomies for Industrial Sales Forces," *Journal of Marketing Research,* August 1986, pp. 261–270.

4. See Rayna Skolnik, "Campbell Stirs Up Its Sales Force," *Sales & Marketing Management,* April 1986, pp. 56–58.

5. See Thayer C. Taylor, "Xerox's Sales Force Learns a New Game," *Sales & Marketing Management,* July 1, 1986, pp. 48–51; Thayer C. Taylor, "Xerox's Makeover," *Sales & Marketing Management,* June 1987, p. 68; and "Restructuring Your Sales Force," *Sales & Marketing Management,* February 1994, p. 40.

6. Patricia Sellers, "How to Remake Your Sales Force," *Fortune,* May 4, 1992, pp. 96–103, here p. 96. Also see Melissa Campanelli, "Reshuffling the Deck," *Sales & Marketing Management,* June 1994, pp. 83–89.

7. See Rudy Oetting and Geri Gantman, "Dial 'M' for Maximize," *Sales & Marketing Management,* June 1991, pp. 100–106; and "Median Costs Per Call By Industry," *Sales & Marketing Management,* June 28, 1993, p. 65.

8. See Martin Everett, "Selling By Telephone," *Sales & Marketing Management,* December 1993, pp. 75–79.

9. See "A Phone Is Better Than a Face," *Sales & Marketing Management,* October 1987, p. 29. Also see Aimee L. Stern, "Telemarketing Polishes Its Image," *Sales & Marketing Management,* June 1991, pp. 107–110; and Richard L. Bencin, "Telefocus: Telemarketing Gets Synergized," *Sales & Marketing Management,* February 1992, pp. 49–57.

10. See Frank V. Cespedes, Stephen X. Doyle, and Robert J. Freedman, "Teamwork for Today's Selling," *Harvard Business Review,* March–April 1989, pp. 44–54, 58; Joseph Conlin, "Teaming Up," *Sales & Marketing Management,* October 1993, pp. 98–104; and Richard C. Whiteley, "Orchestrating Service," *Sales &*

Marketing Management, April 1994, pp. 29–30.

11. See Perri Capel, "Are Good Salespeople Born or Made?" *American Demographics,* July 1993, pp. 12–13.

12. See George H. Lucas, Jr., A. Parasuraman, Robert A. Davis, and Ben M. Enis, "An Empirical Study of Sales Force Turnover," *Journal of Marketing,* July 1987, pp. 34–59; Lynn G. Coleman, "Sales Force Turnover Has Managers Wondering Why," *Marketing News,* December 4, 1989, p. 6; and Thomas R. Wotruba and Pradeep K. Tyagi, "Met Expectations and Turnover in Direct Selling," *Journal of Marketing,* July 1991, pp. 24–35.

13. See Geoffrey Brewer, "Mind Reading: What Drives Top Salespeople to Greatness?" *Sales & Marketing Management,* May 1994, pp. 82–88.

14. See "To Test or Not to Test," *Sales & Marketing Management,* May 1994, p. 86.

15. See Matthew Goodfellow, "Hiring and Training: A Call for Action," *Sales & Marketing Management,* May 1992, pp. 87–88; and Bill Kelley, "Training: 'Just Plain Lousy' or 'Too Important to Ignore'?" *Sales & Marketing Management,* March 1993, pp. 66–70.

16. See *1993 Sales Manager's Budget Planner, Sales & Marketing Management,* June 28, 1993, p. 72.

17. The percentages add to more than 100 percent because some companies use more than one type of plan. See "1989 Survey of Selling Costs," *Sales & Marketing Management,* February 20, 1989, p. 26.

18. For a good discussion of sales force compensation, see

Sam T. Johnson, "Sales Compensation: In Search of a Better Solution," *Compensation & Benefits Review,* November–December 1993, pp. 53–60.

19. Thayer C. Taylor, "SFA: The Newest Orthodoxy," *Sales & Marketing Management,* February 1993, pp. 26–28. Also see Rowland T. Moriarty and Gordon S. Swartz, "Automation to Boost Sales and Marketing," *Harvard Business Review,* January–February 1989, pp. 100–108; Thayer C. Taylor, "Going Mobile," *Sales & Marketing Management,* May 1994, pp. 94–101; and "Road Warrior: A Special Focus on Sales Automation," *Sales & Marketing Management,* June 1994, Part 2.

20. Tony Seideman, "Who Needs Managers?" *Sales & Marketing Management,* Part 2, June 1994, pp. 15–17.

21. Derrick C. Schnebelt, "Turning the Tables," *Sales & Marketing Management,* January 1993, pp. 22–23.

22. Vincent L. Zirpoli, "You Can't 'Control' the Prospect, So Manage the Presale Activities to Increase Performance," *Marketing News,* March 16, 1984, p. 1.

23. Thayer C. Taylor, "Anatomy of a Star Salesperson," *Sales & Marketing Management,* May 1986, p. 50. Also see Barry J. Farber and Joyce Wycoff, "Relationships: Six Steps to Success," *Sales & Marketing Management,* April 1992, pp. 50–58; and Stephen B. Castleberry and C. David Shepherd, "Effective Interpersonal Listening and Personal Selling," *Journal of Personal Selling and Sales Management,* Winter 1993, pp. 35–49.

Company Case 17

IBM: RESTRUCTURING THE SALES FORCE

TAKING OVER

In early 1993, IBM's Board of Directors decided the time was right for dramatic action. The once-proud company had seen its sales fall from almost $69 billion in 1990 to $64.5 billion in 1992. Moreover, in the same period, profits had plunged from $5.9 billion to a loss of $4.96 billion. In April, the Board hired Louis V. Gerstner, Jr., a former McKinsey Company consultant and R. J. Reynolds CEO, to serve as its new Chairman and Chief Executive Officer and to turn the company around.

In July 1993, just three months into his new job, Gerstner announced his first major strategic decision. Gerstner identified IBM's sales force as a key source of the company's problems. Many observers had expected that he would restructure the sales force in his efforts to refocus the company. These observers felt that IBM's sales force was too large and unwieldy and that it was

too slow to change to meet changing customer needs. However, Gerstner surprised many people by announcing that he would postpone his decision as to what to do about IBM's sales force.

In an internal memo to his 13 top managers, Gerstner concluded that, "It is clear to me that our current [marketing] organization doesn't always function well, *i.e.,* doesn't always permit us to serve our customer in the most efficient and effective way." However, he noted, "I don't want to undertake a major reorganization of IBM at this time." Gerstner argued that radical reform would pose unacceptable risks to customer loyalty. Therefore, he had decided to try to make IBM's current sales and marketing systems work better.

GETTING INTO TROUBLE

You might wonder how IBM, one of the largest and most successful companies in the world, had gotten into such a fix. In early 1994, in his introduction to the *1993 IBM Annual Report,* Gerstner wrote that IBM's problems resulted from the company's failure to keep pace with rapid industry change. He also argued that IBM had been too bureaucratic and too preoccupied with its own view of the world. He suggested that the company had been too slow to take new products to market and had missed the higher profit margins that are typical of the computer industry early in a product's life cycle.

Although bureaucracy and slowness were significant problems, IBM's customers and industry observers identified IBM's preoccupation with its own view of the world as the real problem. They argued that the company stopped listening to its customers. It peddled mainframe computers to customers who wanted midrange systems and personal computers. It pushed products when customers wanted solutions. One former salesperson noted that, "We were so well trained, we could sell anything, good or bad. So, under quota pressures, we sold systems that our customers didn't need, didn't want, and couldn't afford."

IBM had designed its sales compensation system to encourage and reward selling mainframe systems. Another former salesperson observed that, "You could sell a PC and get a pat on the back. You could sell a midrange system and get a lot of dollars. But when you sold a mainframe, you would walk on water. You were a hero."

The salespeople also often insisted that customers buy all of their products from IBM and became indignant when a customer used another vendor. Also, the salespeople were often inflexible. They made "one-size-fits-all" presentations using canned, off-the-shelf marketing programs. One customer added, "They wouldn't tailor their programs to what you needed as a customer." It was ". . . this is our canned package. We know this works. Trust us."

TURNING THINGS AROUND

Despite these problems, Gerstner's decision not to make strategic changes to the 40,000-person sales force meant that he would continue to carry out changes that former CEO John Akers had begun. Beginning in 1991, Akers had restructured the sales force using a geographic focus. Senior managers acted as account executives for the top IBM clients in their regions. These account executives managed the full breadth of client relationships including understanding the customer's company and its industry. These managers could call on a pool of regional product specialists and service representatives to satisfy customer needs. The account executives reported to branch managers who reported to "trading area" managers who ultimately reported to regional managers. In foreign countries, a country manager had full control over that country's sales force.

Akers' approach continued IBM's traditional focus on presenting "one face to the customer." The account executive structure allowed the customer to deal with one IBM interface rather than dealing with salespeople from each of IBM's product and service areas. Gerstner's reluctance to make changes probably resulted from a meeting where the company's top 200 customers told him they did not want to be confused by 20 different IBM salespeople calling on them. However, it was also hard for any IBM salesperson to be familiar with the wide range of products and services the company offered. One manager pointed out that, "We have an awfully broad sales manual. . . .You can't be a generalist."

Nevertheless, IBM had already begun to tinker with its sales approach. In response to increasing competition, declining sales, and changing corporate buying habits, the company had already developed "fighter pilots." These salespeople were specialists who tried to increase sales by pushing neglected products. Further, Akers had allowed some product lines, like the personal computer and printer divisions, to develop their own sales forces. He had also allowed some experimentation with salespeople who specialized in certain industries.

As for compensating the sales force, IBM adjusted the compensation plan each January. The company modified the plan to promote sales of certain products or increase market share in targeted areas. One analyst noted that it was not unusual for a branch manager to have 240 separate measurements because different product groups would set quotas to encourage salespeople to sell their offerings. Until 1993, only 6 percent of a salesperson's salary above the base salary (the bulk of a person's pay) reflected the profitability of his or her sales. In 1993, the company increased the portion based on profitability to 20 percent.

PURSUING THE IDEAL SALES FORCE

Many industry observers argued that Gerstner's decision to forego any major sales force changes merely reflected his desire to continue to study the problem. One consultant noted that Gerstner wanted to wait until the dust settled from personnel cutbacks that had reduced IBM's employment from 344,000 to 256,000 between 1991 and 1993. Microsoft Chairman William Gates suggested that although IBM was known for its unified sales force, ". . . I think it's inevitable that they'll get rid of it."

The question was: What sales force strategy should IBM use to revive its sagging sales and profits while satisfying customer and employee requirements?

QUESTIONS

1. What problems do you see in IBM's sales force's objectives, strategy, structure, and compensation?

2. What objectives would you set for IBM's sales force, and what strategy, structure, and compensation plan would you establish to accomplish your objectives? Identify the tradeoffs involved as you make each of these decisions.

3. Given your recommendations, how would you recruit, train, supervise, motivate, and evaluate IBM's sales force?

Sources: Laurie Hays, "IBM's Gerstner Holds Back from Sales Force Shake-Up," *Wall Street Journal,* July 7, 1993, p. B1. Used with permission of *Wall Street Journal.* Also see Geoffrey Brewer, "Abort, Retry, Fail?" *Sales and Marketing Management,* October 1993, pp. 80–86; and IBM Corporation, *1993 Annual Report.*

Video Case 4

ROLLERBLADE: THE ASPHALT IS CALLING

Legend has it that a Dutchman made the first in-line skates in the 1700s when he nailed wooden spools to strips of wood attached to his shoes. Later, the Victorians of the 1860s tried them. But in-line skates never really took off until two brothers, Brennan and Scott Olson, got the idea to sell them to hockey players during the off-season in the early 1980s. Since then, millions of Americans have answered the call of the asphalt, making in-line skating one of the fastest growing sports in the United States (see Table 17-1). Who uses them? Just about everyone—kids, hockey players, college students, grandmothers (see Table 17-2). Why do these folks skate? FUN, FUN, FUN! Of course, many have more pedestrian reasons, such as exercise, hockey, and cross-training; but mostly, it's just for fun.

Rollerblade, Inc., founded by the Olson brothers, is the premier in-line skate company with roughly 50 percent of the market, a position that most would think highly enviable. However, Rollerblade's success in promoting skating has caused it a few major headaches. First, competition has increased as a few dozen other firms have entered the market, making it increasingly difficult for Rollerblade to maintain its market share. Second, some analysts contend that in-line skating is just a fad that will inevitably decline. That could be devastating for a firm like Rollerblade that has only one product. Finally, many Americans use the name Rollerblade when referring to any and all in-line skates, and they refer to in-line skating as rollerblading. To be correct, however, you should say "Rollerblade Skates," and the sport is in-line skating, not rollerblading. If the

Rollerblade name becomes generic, the company risks losing its rights to exclusive use of the brand name.

How is Rollerblade responding to these challenges? To distinguish its product from that of the competition, it engages in product design and development. For example, in 1994 Rollerblade introduced a new braking system—the Active Brake Technology (ABT)—that enables skaters greater speed control and stopping power. To reduce dependence on a single product line, the company is adding protective gear—knee and elbow pads, wristguards, and the first helmet designed for in-line skaters.

To protect its brand name, Rollerblade sends information to the media and dealers detailing correct spelling and use of the name. For example, brand names should not be used as verbs—saying or writing "rollerblading" is improper. Rollerblade also asks dealers to avoid using slang terms such as "blader(s)" and "blading."

To counter the predicted decline of in-line skating, Rollerblade is working to attract more skaters through safety campaigns and by offering instruction videos to dealers who give interested skaters free trials and lessons. The company is also the first to introduce television advertising to increase awareness of the sport and to promote the Rollerblade brand.

Between 1992 and 1993, in-line skating did not grow as rapidly as it has in the past. Therefore, Rollerblade has attempted to expand the market by reaching new segments of consumers. Based on consumer information like that in Table 17-2, Rollerblade is targeting the in-line hockey, youth, and fitness markets. For example, it pitches in-line hockey to ice hockey players in the off-season and to individuals in areas where ice hockey is not well established. And based on a University of Massachusetts study proving that in-line skating is a highly effective, low-impact aerobic workout (it burns 360 calories in 30 minutes for a 150-pound person), the company has developed the "Rollerblade

TABLE 17-1   *Growth of In-Line Skating*

	1989	1990	1991	1992	1993
No. of participants (in thousands)	3,065	4,307	6,212	9,364	12,559
Percentage	—	40%	44%	51%	34%

TABLE 17-2 *Characteristics of Skaters (Numbers in thousands)*

		1989	1990	1991	1992	1993
Age	6–11	759	1,066	2,154	3,423	4,866
	12–17	928	1,348	1,267	2,694	3,240
	18–24	598	841	1,021	1,183	1,565
	25–34	409	647	1,220	1,487	1,822
	35–54	285	345	542	495	1,001
	55+	86	60	80	80	65
Gender	Male	1,444	2,237	3,432	5,035	6,280
	Female	1,621	2,070	2,780	4,329	6,279
Income	Under $25,000	1,546	1,647	2,161	3,044	3,136
	$25–$50,000	1,023	1,422	2,169	3,481	4,816
	Over $50,000	496	1,238	1,882	2,839	4,607
Geographic location	Northeast	651	831	1,469	1,720	2,889
	North Central	849	1,275	1,435	2,646	3,963
	South	1,048	1,458	1,749	2,306	2,899

Roll & Tone—An In-Line Skate Workout" brochure for fitness buffs. It contains workouts for beginner, intermediate, and advanced skaters along with tips for beginners on how to get started skating.

QUESTIONS

1. What trends can you detect in Tables 17-1 and 17-2?
2. Using the information in the tables, evaluate the various age, gender, and income groups as potential consumer targets for Rollerblade. In your opinion, are the exercise, youth, and in-line hockey groups good choices for Rollerblade to target?
3. What stage of the product life cycle is Rollerblade in? Is the company taking the appropriate actions to increase sales in this stage?
4. Evaluate the effectiveness of the actions Rollerblade has taken to protect its brand name and maintain its market position.

Sources: David Biemesderfer, "Fast Track," *World Traveler,* Northwest Airlines publication, 1993; Lois Therrien, "Rollerblade Is Skating in Heavier Traffic," *Business Week,* June 24, 1992, pp. 114–115; and numerous materials provided by Rollerblade. The author would like to thank Rollerblade, Inc., for its help with this case.

Video Case 5

TERRA CHIPS: EAT YOUR VEGGIES!

Consumer, browsing in store: "What are these? Multicolored chips? They are really pretty. Wonder what they're made of—taro, batata . . . What on earth is that? Sweet potatoes from Cuba? Gee, I wonder if they're any good. What's the price? $3.99 for a 6-ounce bag! Could they be worth that . . .?

This consumer's pricing question was a major concern of Dana Sinkler and Alex Dzieduszycki when they introduced Terra Chips. Although they knew they had a good product, given the speed with which guests gobbled down the chips at functions catered by the young entrepreneurs, marketing the chips posed many challenges.

Because of the high costs of ingredients, the chips had to be priced higher. If sold in grocery stores, they would not compete well on price with much cheaper chips. Even in higher-priced outlets, placing Terra Chips in snack sections next to other chips might result in consumer price shock. Therefore, Terra Chips were initially sold only as a food-service product. It was almost by a fluke (an order from Saks) that they ended up on retail shelves.

Terra Chips faced other marketing challenges. For example, the product needed packaging and distribution channels that would support its high-price image. Also, Dana and Alex were concerned about whether their new product would appeal to broader markets. Although New Yorkers liked Terra Chips, there were questions of whether they would sell in less cosmopolitan markets.

To deal with these issues, the entrepreneurs hired Keith Bright and Associates of Venice, California, to create a sophisticated silver-and-black package with a colorful picture of the chips on the front. They distributed the chips through upscale outlets such as Saks and Neiman Marcus and eventually sold them through delicatessens, natural food stores, and, finally, a few select grocery chains. After only four short years, Terra Chips are reported to be a $10 million business.

Why have Terra Chips been so successful? The answer can't be advertising—they haven't done any. Instead, Terra Chips created an exciting new category with strong, demonstrated consumer appeal. Although it now has many imitators, Terra really did forge new ground and is now widely recognized throughout the food industry as the "pioneer of the vegetable chip category." In addition to having no additives, Terra Chips are also lower in sodium and fat than regular potato chips, which is probably of more interest to most consumers.

Terra Chips are also beautiful. Sweet potato chips are orange, yucca chips are light colored, and taro chips have thin purple markings. Ruby taro chips come in a beautiful red (with beet juice added), and parsnip chips have a light brown color. A bowl of Terra Chips is extremely eye-catching, making hostesses proud to serve them. Their subtle blend of tastes provides a welcome change from potato chips. The high price creates an image of exclusivity, and the use of "exotic" vegetables has created a cosmopolitan aura.

A gold, ribbon-shaped symbol on the front of each bag informs consumers that Terra Chips were the 1992 and 1993 winners at NASFT's (National Association for the Specialty Food Trade) trade show. In addition, the chips were served backstage at *The Tonight Show*, generating publicity that reinforced the exclusive image. It seems that lots of consumers want to eat the same chips as Jay Leno!

Terra Chips are so popular that Dana and Alex have introduced line extensions: Terra Sweet Potato Chips, Terra Spiced Sweet Potato Chips, and Terra

Spiced Taro Chips. The Spiced Sweet Potato Chips are a vibrant orange-red color and have a fiery taste. Seasoned with cumin, cilantro, garlic, and red cayenne, they are the perfect complement to beer. The Spiced Taro Chips, covered with a peppery mix of lemongrass, Thai chilis, lime leaves, and coriander, are the perfect complement for Asian cuisine and seafood, as well as for salads and soups. The extensions are priced lower than mixed Terra Chips, selling for $.99 for a 1.5-ounce bag and $2.99 for a 6-ounce bag.

Even as the chips grow in popularity, Dana and Alex are looking for new ways to increase sales. For example, they plan to sell Terra Chips abroad. However, the chips could suffer image problems in other countries. Although taro may be uncommon in the United States, it is fairly common to consumers in other parts of the world, especially those familiar with Asian foods. Another growth strategy would be to produce private-label chips. However, if consumers recognize private-label chips as Terra Chips, private-label sales could cannibalize sales of the higher-margin Terra Chips.

Another issue is the narrowness of the company's product mix. If veggie chips turn out to be a fad, Dana and Alex understand that Terra Chips will need another product line to sustain sales and profits. For now, however, they are building on their current success while exploring options for the future.

QUESTIONS

1. Are the Sweet Potato, Spiced Sweet Potato, and Spiced Taro Chips true line extensions?

2. Do you think veggie chips are a fad? Why or why not?

3. In your opinion, would Terra Chips be successful in other countries?

4. Should Dana and Alex make private-label chips? Explain.

5. If you were Dana and Alex, what would your next product be? Why? What other marketing steps would you recommend?

Sources: "How to Veg Out and Live Life," *Brandweek,* June 27, 1994; Toddi Gunter, "Chip Mania," *Forbes,* July 19, 1993, pp. 196–198; and numerous company-supplied materials. The author gratefully acknowledges the assistance of Andrew Friedman in the writing of this case.

Video Case 6

MOUNTAIN TRAVEL SOBEK: ALL OVER THE WORLD

Would you like to take a trek to Nepal? Raft rivers in Chile? Walk the Great Wall of China? Inspect icebergs

and penguins in the Antarctic—up close? If you answered yes, you're not alone. Over seven million Americans engage in adventure travel annually, making it the fastest growing form of travel (30 percent annual growth).

Mountain Travel Sobek (MT-S) is the premier adventure-travel firm, offering trips to seven continents. It was formed in 1991 when the two most venerable firms in adventure travel, Mountain Travel and Sobek Expeditions, joined operations. Mountain Travel, founded by Leo Le Bon, Allen Steck, and Barry Bishop, specialized in trekking and mountain expeditions. It was the first company to offer treks to Everest Base Camp, walking safaris in East Africa, expeditions to Kilimanjaro and Mt. Anyemaquen in China (1981), and the cross-country ski expeditions to the South Pole (1989).

Sobek Expeditions was founded by two river rafters from Bethesda, Maryland—Richard Bangs and John Yost. Their last fling before entering the working world was a rafting trip on the Awash, a little-known and unrun African river. They recruited clients to pay for the trip and, upon successfully completing the adventure, formed Sobek, named for the Egyptian crocodile god who seemed to have guided them through the croc-infested waters of the Awash. Sobek went on to lead the first descents of 35 rivers around the world, including the Bio-Bio (Chile), Bashkaus (USSR), Blue Nile (Ethiopia), and Tatshenshini (Alaska).

During the 1980s, both Mountain Travel and Sobek prospered. Mountain Travel increased its annual departures by 50 percent to 478, and Sobek upped its departures by 70 percent to 415. Annual revenues climbed to more than $7 million for Mountain Travel and to $5 million for Sobek. However, this success disguised deteriorating profitability resulting from the offering of less-profitable trips. With the help of Hap Klopp, former owner of North Face, the companies merged. The new company has improved profitability by combining trekking and rafting trips to the same parts of the world and by eliminating 180 money-losing trips to 100 destinations.

What is an MT-S trip like? If you envision hardship, cold food, and primitive facilities, forget it. Accommodations are actually quite pleasant, with comfortable cabins and spacious tents, and local chefs prepare delicious food. What sets MT-S trips apart is the high-quality amenities, staff who are knowledgeable about local conditions and cultures, and the small size of groups, limited to 15 or fewer. But all this doesn't come cheaply. Trips through the Northeast passage cost more than $10,000, and safaris in Africa can cost more than $4,000. However, not all MT-S trips are this expensive. A trip to the Galapagos may cost less than $2,500, and kayaking in the Sea of Cortez costs only about $1,000.

Who takes these trips? It's mostly men and women aged 30 to 60 years old. However, the average age of ad-

venture travelers is likely to increase in the future. The population of 55-year-old and older Americans will increase from 53 million in 1990 to 75 million by 2010. Older people have higher buying power, greater leisure time, and, lately, a greater inclination to explore. Seniors account for $60 billion of the $293.7 billion travel market, and close to 50 percent of Mountain Travel Sobek's business comes from seniors. In "soft" adventure travel, the army jeeps of the past have been replaced by more comfortable land rovers and minivans.

Leo Le Bon claims that the company has changed: "Adventure travel does not lend itself to commercialization; it's most successful when the company is small, specialized, high spirited, hands-on. When corporate America comes to it, it doesn't work." But Richard Weiss, the new president of Mountain Travel Sobek, is more upbeat. While it is true that MT-S offers more easy trips than in the past, the trips still consist of small groups led by enthusiastic guides. Participants can get into the countryside, see wildlife, meet the local population, and experience the feeling of leaving the beaten path.

To appeal to the changing market, MT-S expanded its product offerings by introducing Quick Escapes, short trips to Canada or Baja, and longer programs to destinations such as Morocco, Vietnam, and Bhutan. MT-S has also tried new forms of promotion. One is The Adventure Disc (1993), an interactive Photo CD on which you can hear the calls of wildlife, listen to voices of explorers such as Edmund Hillary, look at hundreds of spectacular photos of the world's wonders, and view shots of MT-S trips. In 1994, the company developed The Traveler, an interactive CD-ROM catalog for the Macintosh and Windows systems produced by Magellan Systems. In addition, MT-S trip information is now available on the Internet. Prospective travelers can examine full itineraries of tours, read the history of the company, and look at video clips. However, there is a question about whether these promotions reach targeted older consumers or younger, more computer-oriented ones.

Competition is increasing. New adventure firms are entering the industry and some travel agencies now specialize in adventure trips. MT-S's new product offerings and promotional efforts may help distinguish it and perhaps will give it an edge over competitors. This could be very important if an industry shakeout occurs.

Questions

1. Where is Mountain Travel Sobek in its product life cycle? Is the company following appropriate strategies for this stage? What might it do in the future?

2. Do you agree with Mr. Le Bon that adventure travel does not lend itself to commercialization?

3. Evaluate the usefulness of MT-S's CD-ROM and Internet promotions. Why would or wouldn't these be effective means of promotion?

Sources: James M. Clash, "Survivalists," *Forbes*, November 22, 1993, pp. 154–156; Jeffery D. Zbar, "More Than a Cool Bus Ride Needed to Sway Seniors," *Advertising Age*, June 27, 1994, pp. 34–37; and numerous company-supplied materials. The author gratefully acknowledges the help of Liz Longstreth in preparing this case.

Video Case 7

MALL OF AMERICA: THE ULTIMATE DESTINATION FOR FUN

Question: Who has . . .

A Wilderness Theater with a variety of wildlife?

Five classrooms, a multipurpose room, and a computer lab?

The site where Harmon Killebrew hit a 520-foot home run?

Forty-five restaurants, nine nightclubs, and 14 theater screens?

Some 4.2 million square feet of enclosed space and 13,000 parking spaces?

The third-largest number of visitors among U.S. tourist attractions?

Answer: Believe it or not . . . *Mall of America!*

When the Mall of America opened near Minneapolis in 1992, skeptics questioned whether it could attract a projected 35 million visitors a year to spend over $600 million. Local retailers worried that the Mall's success would mean their own decline. So, two years later, how has the mammoth mall done?

According to reports, Mall of America has met most of its projections. It attracted more than 35 million visitors in its first 12 months and 60 million within the first 20 months. Weekly visitors vary in number from 600,000 to 900,000 depending on the season, and 30 percent of visitors come from outside a 150-mile radius. Moreover, these results were achieved during the worst retail slump of the last decade.

The Mall's impact on other area retailers, however, was not what they expected. The area's total retail pie seems to have expanded—partly because of an increase in tourists attracted by the Mall. Mall of America actually creates *more* business for other retailers and increases receipts for hotels, restaurants, and other travel-related services. In addition, the Mall has created 12,000 new jobs in Minneapolis, which means additional spendable income.

What can visitors see and do at Mall of America? For shopping, the Mall offers four major anchors: Macy's, Nordstrom, Bloomingdale's, and Sears. It contains several junior anchors such as Oshman's Super-Sports USA, Filene's Basement, Service Merchandise,

and Linens 'N' Things. It also contains more than 400 specialty shops where visitors can purchase specialized clothing, such as grunge-look merchandise at the Junkyard; gardening supplies at Gardener's Paradise; or anything and everything for a left-handed person at The Leftorium.

For food, customers can choose from 45 restaurants. They can grab a quick bite at a fast-food restaurant such as TacoTime or Dairy Queen. For slower-paced dining, there's the California Cafe and the Twin City Diner. For something different, the Rainforest Cafe features a menu of foods from rainforest countries and a 5,500-gallon fish tank. Or shoppers can stargaze at Planet Hollywood, where they might see Roseanne or Whoopi while sampling California cuisine.

For the family, there's Knott's Camp Snoopy—a seven-acre, indoor theme park with 16 rides, nine restaurants, and entertainments such as panning for gold, visiting the wilderness ranger station, the Peanuts gallery (a cutting-edge video game arcade), and 3D films and musical reviews at The Ford Playhouse. The Peanuts Gang—Snoopy, Lucy, and Charlie Brown—are the hosts. For adults, there's America's Original Sports Bar, Knuckleheads Comedy Club, and the Gatlin Brothers Music City with free line-dancing lessons.

Families and singles also like the LEGO Imagination Center with its millions of LEGO blocks to play with and models to look at and buy. Golf Mountain is a state-of-the-art miniature golf course, complete with waterfalls, streams, and trees. At StarBase Omega, an interactive laser game, players are trained in the latest high-tech equipment and transported to StarBase Omega or Planet Previa to fight it out with the Kytefs. The Mall also offers a 14-screen General Cinema Theater showing first-run movies.

Unusual features include the Chapel of Love (the first wedding chapel in an enclosed mall); classrooms from the Metropolitan Learning Alliance (a cooperative effort between local schools and the University of St. Thomas); and a plaque marking the spot of Killebrew's famous home run (Mall sits atop the old site of Metropolitan Stadium).

To attract both customers *and* tourists, the Mall distributes hundreds of brochures, newspaper inserts, and maps in the Minneapolis–St. Paul region; runs joint promotions with local radio stations; runs ads in a local newspaper and commercials on local television; buys billboard space; and works with over 200 tour operators to develop travel packages and with Northwest Airlines to create tie-in packages. It holds major holiday and sales events, attractions at the Events Center, entertainment events in nightclubs, and events to celebrate the addition of new retailers. It has used contests such as the one featured in an insert in *USA Today,* in which the prize was a trip to the Mall. WCCO-AM, a local radio station and the Mall's official information station, relays the latest scoop about what's happening at the Mall to listeners. The Mall's advertising campaign theme is "There's a place for fun in your life."

The good news for Mall of America is that merchant occupancy levels have hovered around 92 percent (right on track). The bad news is that some shoppers have been scared away by rumors of long lines at restaurants, rest-room facilities, and parking lots. To help shoppers deal with the Mall's massive size and find their way around, the Mall provides maps and directories. In addition, it is organized into four "neighborhoods," each of which might be a mini–shopping expedition. To help drivers, exit ramps off freeways guide shoppers into the Mall's parking lots.

Thus, although the size of the Mall of America entices many shoppers, it intimidates others. As an exhilarating shopping, dining, and entertainment experience, the Mall is tops. But the serious question remains: will shoppers use it on an everyday basis?

QUESTIONS

1. What are Mall of America's target markets? How does it attempt to serve each one?

2. How does the Mall promote itself to each of its target markets? Why do you think it picked a theme that focuses on fun?

3. Make a list of all the disadvantages consumers face when visiting Mall of America. How does the Mall try to overcome each of those? What else might it do?

4. In your opinion, is the Mall likely to be a long-run success? Why or why not?

Sources: William Stern, "Bumpbacks in Minneapolis," *Forbes,* April 11, 1994, pp. 48–49; Eric Wieffering, "What Has the Mall of America Done to Minneapolis?" *American Demographics,* February 1994, pp. 13–16; and numerous materials supplied by the Mall of America. The author gratefully thanks Jayne Lopez for her assistance with this case.

SMITH'S HOME FOODS:
BRINGING HOME THE BACON

Ronald Smith, president of Smith's Country Hams in Ashton, North Carolina, walked into his daughter's office and plopped down in one of the chairs across from her desk. "Christy," he said, "I've just been looking at last month's numbers, and they are pretty discouraging. We've got to find a way to get the home foods business moving. I'm not sure what's wrong, but I think we've somehow got the cart before the horse. I'm convinced that if we could just find the right button, and push it, everything would work well."

Christy Smith looked across the desk at her casually dressed father. "Dad, I am just as frustrated as you are," she replied. "Nothing we try seems to work right. Even when we do attract new customers, they are the wrong kind."

Christy was a very busy person. In addition to her duties at Smith's, she commuted daily to a major university located in a neighboring city, where she was a senior business major. Although she had worked in the family business for as long as she could remember, she had been pleased and surprised when her father had asked her to take over the newly formed Smith's Home Foods operation. Glancing at the calendar on her desk, she noted the date—April 4, 1994. She could hardly believe that five months had passed since taking on the assignment. Although pleased with her father's confidence in her, she knew that he felt frustrated about the slow development of the Smith's Home Foods business.

As Christy and her father talked, Sonny Jones, one of Home Foods' two full-time salespeople, entered the office and joined the conversation. He seemed upset. "We just got two more turn-downs from the finance company," he grumbled. "They rejected both of the families I sold plans to last night. We just can't seem to get onto the right side of the street."

"What do you mean?" Ronald asked.

"It's the same old story," Sonny replied. "Both families I called on last night live in Dogwood Acres—they're nice people and all, but they don't have very high incomes. We have to find a way to attract the higher-income folks who live across the road in Ashton Estates."

Ronald Smith rose to leave. "Whatever the problem is, I'm depending on the two of you to figure it out and tell me what we need to do. And you need to get moving quickly."

BACKGROUND

Smith's Country Hams, a 25-year-old family business that focuses on wholesale meat products such as ham, bacon, and other pork products, sells to restaurants and fast-food operations in eastern North Carolina. In July 1993, seeking growth opportunities, Ronald Smith started a new division—Smith's Home Foods. He got the idea from an employee who had previously worked for another home-delivered foods company. Ronald, who is always looking for new ways to make money, believed the idea had potential. He knew that people these days are seeking more convenience. Therefore, a service that provides home-delivered meats, vegetables, and fruits should be in considerable demand. He also realized that he could use his own meat products in the business, thereby providing new sales for Smith's Country Hams.

Ronald reconditioned an old production facility that had been idle and set up offices there for Smith's Home Foods. He put the employee who had the idea in charge of the business. However, by October 1993, the employee had failed to meet Ronald's expectations and had resigned. Ronald then asked Christy to take over. He knew this would be a challenging assignment for her. She was still a full-time university student. As a result, she could devote only afternoons and whatever time she could squeeze from her evenings to manage Smith's Home Foods.

The Home Foods Business. The home-delivered foods business centers on providing families with pre-arranged assortments of foods that are delivered to their homes. Smith's Home Foods offers 11 standard packages, containing various combinations of frozen meats, vegetables, and fruits. The packages differ in size and cost, but each provides a four-month food supply. Exhibit IV-1 shows the items in a typical package. Exhibit IV-2 summarizes the characteristics of each of the 11 packages.

When Christy first assumed management of the operation, she wondered why everything was sold in

EXHIBIT IV-1 Contents of a Typical Smith's Home Foods Package

107 Pounds Net Weight Beef
  6 Chuck Roasts (2 lb avg.)
  4 Shoulder Roasts (2 lb avg.)
  1 Sirloin Tip Roast (3 lb avg.)
  1 Eye of Round Roast (3 lb avg.)
  1 Bottom Round Roast (3 lb avg.)
 20 Ribeye Steaks (8 oz)
 12 T-Bone Steaks (12 oz)
    Cube Steak (8 lb)
    BLS Stew Beef (10 lb)
 18 Chopped Beef Steaks (8 oz; 9 lb case)
    Ground Beef (32 lb; 1 lb rolls or 4 oz patties)
    Pork Chops (6 lb)
    BLS Pork Chops (6 lb)
    Dinner Ham (5 lb)
 30 Misc. Meats
 20 Fryers
  1 Seafood
 60 Vegetables (16 oz)
 12 Fruits
 32 Juices (12 oz)
    Cheese (6 lb)
    Margarine (6 lb)

Bank	$1,094.38
Tax	54.71
	1,149.09
Deposit	35.00
Amount Financed	1,114.09
Finance Charge	56.23
Deferred Payment	1,170.32
Total Price	1,205.32

Four Payments at $292.58
$68.04 per Week

EXHIBIT IV-2 *Characteristics of Smith's Home Foods Packages*

FOOD PACKAGE NUMBER	POUNDS OF MEAT PER WEEK	MINIMUM FREEZER SIZE	FAMILY SIZE	PACKAGE PRICE*
1	14	21 cu ft	3–4	$1,205
2	12	18	3–4	1,088
3	12	18	3	1,070
4	10	15	2–3	940
5	17	21	4–5	1,532
6	6.5	12	2	655
7	8	15	2–3	1,093
8	9.5	12	2–3	825
9	11	15	2–3	809
10	11	15	2–3	834
11	13	21	4–5	958

*Price for four-month package, including tax and finance charges.

four-month packages. According to Sonny Jones, who had once worked with a competing food service, most competitors offer similar four-month packages. As a result, the quantity of food delivered with each package requires that customers own a freezer or purchase one. Therefore, Smith's Home Foods, like other home-foods companies, also sells a 21-cubic-foot freezer on an installment payment plan. In general, the requirement of having a freezer does not appear to be a barrier to food-package sales.

Christy believes that customers gain many benefits from the home delivery of food. First, it's convenient—customers can make fewer trips to the store because Smith's Home Foods packages make a large variety of foods readily available in the home. Therefore, the person who does the cooking has fewer worries about whether enough food is available. Second, Christy believes that Smith's offers superior quality products, especially meats, compared with those consumers typically find at grocery stores. She and her father carefully select the meat offered in the packages. Of course, they supply their own high-quality Smith's Country Ham products. All other meats are purchased from other quality wholesalers, either in individually wrapped portions, such as eight-ounce T-bone steaks, or in "family portions," such as five-pound rib roasts. The wholesalers vacuum pack the meats with plastic shrink wrap to protect their freshness and flavor. Meats packed this way and frozen will maintain their freshness indefinitely. Smith's Home Foods packages feature brand-name meats, such as Morrell, Armour, Jimmy Dean, and Fishery products. The packages also include brand-name fruits and vegetables, such as Dulany and McKenzie, which are purchased from wholesalers. Smith's guarantees the quality of its food, stating that it will replace any food that fails to completely satisfy the customer.

Finally, Christy argues, purchasing food through a home food service saves consumers money. Because customers buy in large quantities, they receive lower prices. And they escape any price increases that occur during the four-month period covered by their food packages. Making fewer trips to the store also helps customers avoid expensive impulse purchases.

SMITH'S HOME FOODS'S MARKETING PROGRAM

Smith's priced its food packages at $655 to $1,532, including tax and finance charges, with an average price of $1,000. Smith's cost of goods sold averages 48 percent for the 11 packages, not including a variable cost of $30 per package for delivery. Customers can pay cash, or they can charge or finance their purchases. Although Smith's accepts Visa and MasterCard, customers seldom use these cards to purchase the food packages. Another option allows customers to pay one half in cash on signing the contract and the final half within 30 days without an interest charge.

Smith's provides credit to qualified customers through the Fair Finance Company of Akron, Ohio, one of the few finance companies that finances food purchases. Customers who opt for financing make a $35 down payment and fill out a credit application. If Fair approves the application, the customer makes the first payment—one-fourth of the amount financed—30 days after the delivery of the food. Thus, on a $1,200 food package financed by Fair, the customer makes four $300 payments. Because the first payment is not due until a month after delivery, the financing plan allows this customer to save $75 a week for food in each of the four weeks leading up to the first payment, and so forth for the remaining three payments. Although the finance company absorbs the risks of the purchase, Smith's assumes the risk until the first payment is made. That is, if a customer receives the food but does not make the first payment, Smith's accepts responsibility for the entire amount financed and must take whatever action it can to obtain payment or reclaim the food.

When a salesperson submits an order for a food package, if the customer wants to finance it, Smith's faxes a copy of the order to Fair Finance Company. Typically, the finance company approves or rejects the application within one business day. If credit is approved, a clerk completes a "pull sheet," which tells warehouse employees which package the customer purchased and what items are included. Typically, the warehouse manager holds orders until five or six are ready to be pulled and then sets a delivery date with the customer.

For customers who want to purchase freezers,

Smith's sells a 21-cubic-foot freezer for approximately $800, with a cost of goods sold of $435. This freezer can also be financed through a separate finance company—consumers pay $12.95 down and make 24 monthly payments of about $33. When a customer orders a freezer and credit is approved, Smith's calls a local appliance store that delivers the freezer to the customer and installs it. Once installed, the freezer must run for about three days before it reaches the appropriate temperature to receive the food. Therefore, Smith's must coordinate food delivery with delivery of the freezer.

Smith's stores its inventory in the Smith's Country Hams warehousing and cold-storage facilities. It has a one-ton pickup truck equipped with a freezer box to make the delivery to customers. Two Smith's Country Hams employees make the deliveries, personally placing the food in the customer's freezer.

Smith's Home Foods uses both personal and mass selling techniques to promote its service. Its two full-time salespeople, Sonny Jones and Barbara Johnson, both earn salaries plus commission on their own sales. Sonny and Barbara have also recruited four other part-time, commission-only salespeople. Smith's pays its salespeople a $100 commission on each package sold. It also pays an additional $25 commission to both Sonny and Barbara for each sale made by the part-time salespeople. The same commissions are paid on each freezer sold.

When the salespeople make a call, they must often meet with the customers in the evening, spending as long as two hours discussing the service and completing the applications. Each salesperson carries a three-ring binder that contains all the information needed for a sales presentation. The binder includes 12 pages of beef and pork product pictures, six pages of poultry and fish product pictures, three pages of vegetable and fruit product pictures, and one page of dessert pictures. Additional pages describe the costs and terms for each of the 11 packages. The binder also contains pictures of freezers and lists substitutions allowed in the packages.

To generate leads for the sales force, Smith's uses several mass-selling techniques. First, it has advertised three times recently in the local Ashton paper, which also serves the small adjoining community of Wolfsburg and the surrounding county with a total population of about 100,000. Each insert costs about $.04. The inserts stress the money-saving features of the service and include a detachable postcard that consumers can mail, postage paid, to the company.

More recently, the company has contracted with the local Welcome Wagon to distribute a $10-off coupon for Smith's products along with the other promotions that it gives to newlyweds, families who have just had babies, and new arrivals to the community. Finally, Christy also prepared a flyer that outlines the service. Salespeople place these flyers in various locations around the community, such as beauty parlors.

Christy does not feel that Smith's Home Foods faces any direct competition in the Ashton area. Another large, well-established company, Southern Foods of Greensboro, NC, operates a home foods service very similar to Smith's. However, although Southern Foods also operates in some other states and has customers throughout North Carolina, it does not directly target the Ashton area. In fact, Christy feels that Southern Foods has probably helped her business—it has developed the market generally and acquainted potential customers with the kinds of services that Smith's offers.

When Christy took over, she made a number of immediate changes in an effort to improve performance. She redesigned the food packages to make them more attractive and developed the newspaper insert, flyer, and sales book. Despite these efforts, however, the business has developed very slowly.

Although only about eight families had contracted for the service when Christy took over, Smith's now has 60 customers. However, many of the families who signed up since she arrived would soon be finishing their first package. Christy was concerned about how many of these customers would reorder. She was also worried about how long her father's patience would last. He had told her that he would invest as much as $250,000 to get this business going. He had already invested $25,000 in inventory. Furthermore, she estimated that Smith's Home Foods annual fixed costs amounted to $57,000, including salaries, rent and utilities, and other overhead. Christy wondered about the business's profitability and about how many customers she needed to reach to break even.

QUESTIONS

1. Outline Smith's Home Foods' marketing strategy. What is Smith's Home Foods really selling?

2. What problems, if any, do you see with each element of the strategy?

3. Using information given in the case, calculate the average contribution per food package and the number of customers Smith's Home Foods needs to break even.

4. Based on your analysis, what steps would you recommend that Christy take to improve her marketing strategy and Smith's performance?

Building Customer Relationships Through Satisfaction, Value, and Quality

18

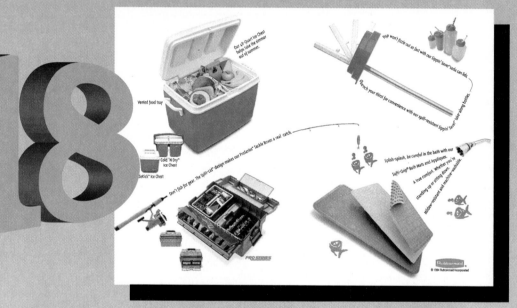

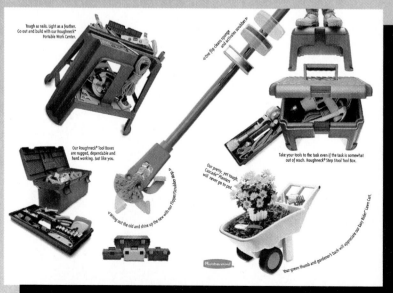

In 1934, the Wooster Rubber Company made a little-noticed addition to its line of balloons: a rubber dustpan. It sold the new dustpan door to door for $1, much more than the $.39 that competitors were charging for their metal versions. But this dustpan was special—it was well-designed, long-lasting, and very high in quality. Even at the $1 price, it was a good value. The Wooster Rubber Company now is called Rubbermaid, and that lowly dustpan turned out to be a real winner. Since then, the same concepts that led to the development of the rubber dustpan have transformed Rubbermaid from a sleepy, small-town rubber-products company into a dynamic market leader.

Today, Rubbermaid thoroughly dominates its fragmented industry, without serious competition. It produces a dazzling array of more than 5,000 products, ranging from food containers, garbage cans, dust mitts, and spatulas to toy cars, mailboxes, snap-together furniture, playground equipment, and molded plastic bird feeders. It sells $1.7 billion worth of rubber and plastic housewares, toys, outdoor furniture, and office products each year. Rubbermaid's rise to the top has been nothing short of spectacular. In only the past decade or so, its sales have quadrupled and profits have grown sixfold. It has achieved 54 consecutive years of profits, 44 consecutive quarters of sales and earnings growth, and 18 percent average earnings per share since 1985. *Fortune* magazine has rated Rubbermaid first or second among the nation's top most admired corporations for five years running.

Rubbermaid's success results from a simple but effective competitive marketing strategy: to consistently offer the best value to customers. First, the company carefully studies and listens to consumers. It uses demographic and lifestyle analysis to spot consumer trends, and conducts focus groups, interviews, and in-home product tests to learn about consumer problems and needs, likes and dislikes. Then, it gives consumers what they want—a continuous flow of useful, innovative, and high-quality products.

Rubbermaid has forged a strong market position. To most consumers, the Rubbermaid name has become the gold standard of good value and quality. Customers know that

OBJECTIVES

When you finish this chapter, you should be able to accomplish the following:

1. Define **customer value** and **customer satisfaction**.

2. Explain how companies deliver **value** and **satisfaction** through a **value chain** and a **value delivery system**.

3. Discuss **attracting new users** and **retaining current customers** by developing **relationship marketing**.

4. Clarify the concept of **total quality marketing**, defining quality and discussing the importance of building profitable relationships with customers.

Rubbermaid products are well designed and well made, and they willingly pay premium prices to own them. Rubbermaid management jealously protects this reputation. The company has an obsession for quality. Under its strict quality-control program, no product with so much as a scratch ever leaves the factory floor.

Rubbermaid thrives on finding new ways to serve customers. Innovation and new-product development have become a kind of religion in the company. Rubbermaid introduces a staggering 365 new products each year. Its goal is to generate at least 33 percent of its total sales from products less than five years old, a goal that it usually meets or exceeds. The company even bases part of its executive compensation on new products' share of sales. Despite the hectic pace of new introductions, Rubbermaid has met with astonishing success. In a fiercely competitive industry where 90 percent of all new products typically fail, Rubbermaid boasts an amazing 90 percent *success* rate for its new products.

To speed up the flow of new products, Rubbermaid assigns small teams—made up of experts from marketing, design, manufacturing, and finance—to each of its 50 or so product categories. These teams identify new product ideas and usher them through design, development, and introduction. The teams tackle the new-product development challenge with enthusiasm. For example, the manager of Rubbermaid's bath accessories, decorative coverings, and home organizational products notes that her "bath team" lives and breathes soap dishes, vanity wastebaskets, and shower caddies. Team members go to trade shows, scour magazines, scan supermarket shelves, and travel the globe searching for new product ideas. "We are like sponges," she says.

Rubbermaid's versions of ordinary products usually offer simple but elegant improvements. For example, it added an antimicrobial agent to the plastic in its mop bucket to come up with the only antimicrobial mop bucket on the market. Its new, wider mailbox allows magazines to lie flat, doesn't rust, prevents water from seeping in when opened, and raises a yellow flag to let you know when the mail has been delivered. And its simple yet stylish line of Litterless Lunch lunch pails feature plastic containers that hold a sandwich, a drink, and another item, eliminating the need for plastic wrapping, milk cartons, cans, and other potential litter. The soft and hard side Litterless Lunch kits are priced between $6.99 and $10.99, higher than competing products. The colorful lunch boxes have become all the rage among parents worried about the nation's garbage glut and grade-school children who've had environmental messages pounded into them at school.

Rubbermaid also has built strong relationships with its "other customers"—retailers who operate the more than 120,000 outlets that sell Rubbermaid products. Retailers appreciate the company's consistent high quality, larger margins, outstanding service, and strong consumer appeal. In fact, Rubbermaid recently received "Vendor of the Year" honors from the mass-merchandising industry. It has built alliances aggressively with fast-growing discount stores such as Wal-Mart and Kmart, which account for the bulk of housewares sales. It created "Rubbermaid boutiques," whole sections within stores that stock only Rubbermaid products. For example, Twin Valu stores set up ten 24-foot long shelves with Rubbermaid products, displacing 20 to 490 feet of competing products. As a result, most of Rubbermaid's competitors have trouble simply getting shelf space.

Thus, Rubbermaid has done all of the things that an outstanding marketing company must do to establish and retain its leadership. As one industry analyst notes: "[Rubbermaid has] the ability to execute strategy flawlessly. There's something about Rubbermaid that's magical, that is so difficult for competitors to replicate." Rubbermaid has positioned itself strongly and gained competitive advantage by providing the best value to consumers. It has set the pace for its industry and kept competitors at bay through continuous innovation. Finally, it has developed a constant stream of useful, high-quality products in a constant quest to deliver ever more value to consumers. In fact, some observers wonder if

Rubbermaid can maintain its current torrid pace. How many more new products and approaches, they ask, can the company find? "It's a little like in 1900, when there was legislation to close the patent office," answers a Rubbermaid executive. "The country was convinced that everything that could be invented already was. [But when it comes to fresh and salable new ways to serve our customers], we're never going to run out of ideas."[1]

Today's companies face their toughest competition in decades, and things will only get tougher in years to come. In previous chapters, we have argued that to succeed in today's fiercely competitive marketplace, companies will have to move from a *product and selling philosophy* to a *customer and marketing philosophy*. This chapter spells out in more detail how companies can go about winning customers and outperforming competitors. The answer lies in the marketing concept—in doing a better job of *meeting and satisfying customer needs.*

In sellers' markets—those characterized by shortages and near-monopolies—companies do not make special efforts to please customers. Today in Eastern Europe, for example, millions of consumers stand sullenly in line for hours only to receive poorly made clothes, toiletries, appliances, and other products at high prices. Producers and retailers show little concern for customer satisfaction with goods and services. Sellers pay relatively little heed to marketing theory and practice.

In buyers' markets, in contrast, customers can choose from a wide array of goods and services. In these markets, if sellers fail to deliver acceptable product and service quality, they will quickly lose customers to competitors. And what is considered acceptable today may not be acceptable to tomorrow's ever-more-demanding consumers. Consumers are becoming more educated and demanding, and their quality expectations have been raised by the practices of superior manufacturers and retailers. The decline of many U.S. industries in recent years—autos, cameras, machine tools, consumer electronics—offers dramatic evidence that firms offering only average quality lose their consumer franchises when attacked by superior competitors.

Customer-centered company
A company that focuses on customer developments in designing its marketing strategies and on delivering superior value to its target customers.

To succeed, or simply to survive, companies need a new philosophy. To win in today's marketplace, companies must be **customer-centered**—they must deliver superior value to their target customers. They must become adept in *building customers,* not just *building products.*

Too many companies think that winning and keeping customers is the job of the marketing or sales department. But successful companies have come to realize that marketing cannot do this job alone. In fact, although it plays a leading role, marketing can be only a partner in attracting and keeping customers. The world's best marketing department cannot successfully sell poorly made products that fail to meet consumer needs. The marketing department can be effective only in companies in which all departments and employees have teamed up to form a competitively superior *customer value-delivery system.*

Consider McDonald's. People do not swarm to the world's 11,000 McDonald's restaurants only because they love the chain's hamburgers. Many other restaurants make better-tasting hamburgers. Consumers flock to the McDonald's *system,* not just to its food products. Throughout the world, McDonald's finely tuned system delivers a high standard of what the company calls QSCV—quality, service, cleanliness, and value. The system consists of many components, both internal and external. McDonald's is only effective to the extent that it successfully partners with its employees, franchisees, suppliers, and others to jointly deliver exceptionally high customer value.

This chapter discusses the philosophy of customer-value-creating marketing and the customer-focused firm. It addresses several important questions: What are customer value and customer satisfaction? How do leading companies organize to create and deliver high value and satisfaction? How can companies keep current customers as well as get new ones? How can companies practice total quality marketing?

DEFINING CUSTOMER VALUE AND SATISFACTION

More than 35 years ago, Peter Drucker insightfully observed that a company's first task is "to create customers." However, creating customers can be a difficult task. Today's customers face a vast array of product and brand choices, prices, and suppliers. The company must answer a key question: How do customers make their choices?

The answer is that customers choose the marketing offer that gives them the most value. Customers are value-maximizers, within the bounds of search costs and limited knowledge, mobility, and income. They form expectations of value and act upon them. Then they compare the actual value they receive in consuming the product to the value expected, and this affects their satisfaction and repurchase behavior. We will now examine the concepts of customer value and customer satisfaction more carefully.

CUSTOMER VALUE

Customer delivered value
The consumer's assessment of the product's overall capacity to satisfy his or her needs. The difference between total customer value and total customer cost of a marketing offer—"profit" to the customer.

Total customer value
The total of all of the product, services, personnel, and image values that a buyer receives from a marketing offer.

Total customer cost
The total of all the monetary, time, energy, and psychic costs associated with a marketing offer.

Consumers buy from the firm that they believe offers the highest **customer delivered value**—the difference between *total customer value* and *total customer cost* (see Figure 18-1). For example, suppose that a large construction firm wants to buy a bulldozer to use in residential construction work. It wants a reliable, durable bulldozer that performs well. It can buy the bulldozer from either Caterpillar or Komatsu. The salespeople for the two companies carefully describe their respective offers to the buyer.

The construction firm now evaluates the two competing bulldozer offers to assess which one offers the greatest value. It adds all the values from four sources—*product, services, personnel,* and *image*. First, it judges that Caterpillar's bulldozer provides higher reliability, durability, and performance. It also decides that Caterpillar has better accompanying services—delivery, training, and maintenance. The customer views Caterpillar personnel as more knowledgeable and responsive. Finally, it places higher value on Caterpillar's reputation. Thus, the customer decides that Caterpillar offers more **total customer value** than does Komatsu.

Does the construction firm buy the Caterpillar bulldozer? Not necessarily. The firm also will examine the **total customer cost** of buying Caterpillar's bulldozer versus Komatsu's. First, the buyer will compare the prices it must pay for each of the competitors' products. If Caterpillar's bulldozer costs a lot more than Komatsu's does, the higher price might offset the higher total customer value.

FIGURE 18-1 *Customer delivered value*

	Total customer value	(Product, services, personnel, and image values)
minus	Total customer cost	(Monetary, time, energy, and psychic costs)
equals	Customer delivered value	("Profit" to the consumer)

Moreover, total customer cost consists of more than just monetary costs. As Adam Smith observed more than two centuries ago, "The real price of anything is the toil and trouble of acquiring it." Total customer cost also includes the buyer's anticipated time, energy, and psychic costs. The construction firm will evaluate these costs along with monetary costs to form a complete estimate of its costs.

Caterpillar must convince customers that its products offer greater value than competitors' products. It makes "serious machines," and a "serious commitment" to customer satisfaction.

The buying firm now compares total customer value to total customer cost and determines the total delivered value associated with Caterpillar's bulldozer. In the same way, it assesses the total delivered value for the Komatsu bulldozer. The firm then will buy from the competitor that offers the highest delivered value.

How can Caterpillar use this concept of buyer decision making to help it succeed in selling its bulldozer to this buyer? Caterpillar can improve its offer in three ways. First, Caterpillar can increase total customer value by improving product, services, personnel, or image benefits. Second, Caterpillar can reduce the buyer's nonmonetary costs by lessening the buyer's time, energy, and psychic costs. Third, Caterpillar can reduce the buyer's monetary costs by lowering its price, providing easier terms of sale, or, in the longer term, lowering its bulldozer's operating or maintenance costs.

Suppose Caterpillar carries out a *customer value assessment* and concludes that buyers see Caterpillar's offer as worth $200,000. Further suppose that it costs Caterpillar $140,000 to produce the bulldozer. This means that Caterpillar's offer potentially generates $60,000 ($200,000 minus $140,000) of *total added value*. Caterpillar needs to price its bulldozer between $140,000 and $200,000. If it charges less than $140,000, it won't cover its costs. If it charges more than $200,000, the price will exceed the total customer value. The price Caterpillar charges will determine how much of the total added value will be delivered to the buyer and how much will flow to Caterpillar. For example, if Caterpillar charges $160,000, it will grant $40,000 of total added value to the customer and keep $20,000 for itself as profit. If Caterpillar charges $190,000, it will grant only $10,000 of total added value to the customer and keep $50,000 for itself as profit. Naturally, the lower Caterpillar's price, the higher the delivered value of its offer will be, and, therefore, the higher the customer's incentive to purchase from Caterpillar. Delivered value should be viewed as "profit to the customer." Given that Caterpillar wants to win the sale, it must offer more delivered value than Komatsu does.

Some marketers might rightly argue that this concept of how buyers choose among product alternatives is too rational. They might cite examples in which buyers did not choose the offer with an objectively measured highest delivered value. For example, suppose that the Caterpillar salesperson convinces the construction firm that, considering the benefits relative to the purchase price, Caterpillar's bulldozer offers a higher delivered value. The customer still might decide to buy the Komatsu bulldozer. Why would the buyer make this apparent non-value-maximizing purchase? There are many possible explanations. For example, perhaps the construction firm's buyers enjoy a long-term friendship with the Komatsu salesperson. Or the firm's buyers might be under strict company orders to buy at the lowest price. Or perhaps the construction firm rewards its buyers for short-term performance, causing them to choose the less expensive Komatsu bulldozer, even though the Caterpillar machine will perform better and be less expensive to operate in the long run.

Clearly, buyers operate under various constraints and sometimes make choices that give more weight to their personal benefit than to company benefit. However, the customer-delivered-value framework applies to many situations and yields rich insights. The framework suggests that sellers must first assess the total customer value and total customer cost associated with their own and competing marketing offers to determine how their own offers measure up in terms of customer delivered value. If a seller finds that competitors deliver greater value, it has two alternatives. It can try to increase total customer value by strengthening or augmenting the product, services, personnel, or image benefits of the offer. Or it can decrease total customer cost by reducing its price and simplifying the ordering and delivery process.[2]

CUSTOMER SATISFACTION

Thus, consumers form judgments about the value of marketing offers and make their buying decisions based upon these judgments. *Customer satisfaction* with a purchase depends on the product's performance relative to a buyer's expectations. A customer might experience various degrees of satisfaction. If the product's performance falls short of expectations, the customer is dissatisfied. If performance matches expectations, the customer is satisfied. If performance exceeds expectations, the customer is highly satisfied or delighted.

But how do buyers form their expectations? Expectations are based on the customer's past buying experiences, the opinions of friends and associates, and marketer and competitor information and promises. Marketers must be careful to set the right level of expectations. If they set expectations too low, they may satisfy those who buy but fail to attract enough buyers. In contrast, if they raise expectations too high, buyers are likely to be disappointed. For example, Holiday Inn ran a campaign a few years ago called "No Surprises," which promised consistently trouble-free accommodations and service. However, Holiday Inn guests still encountered a host of problems, and the expectations created by the campaign only made customers more dissatisfied. Holiday Inn had to withdraw the campaign.

Still, some of today's most successful companies are raising expectations—and delivering performance to match. These companies embrace *total customer satisfaction*. For example, Honda claims "One reason our customers are so satisfied is that we aren't." And Cigna vows "We'll never be 100 percent satisfied until you are, too." These companies aim high because they know that customers who are *only* satisfied will still find it easy to switch suppliers when a better offer comes along. For example, a study by AT&T showed that 70 percent of customers who say they are satisfied with a product or service would still be willing to switch to a competitor. In contrast, customers who are *highly* satisfied are much less ready to switch. One study showed that 75 percent of Toyota buyers were highly satisfied and about 75 percent said they intended to buy a Toyota again.[3] Thus, customer *delight* creates an emotional affinity for a product or service, not just a rational preference, and this creates high customer loyalty.

Today's winning companies track their customers' expectations, perceived company performance, and customer satisfaction. However, customer satisfaction measures are meaningful only in a competitive context. For example, a company might be pleased to find that 80 percent of its customers say they are satisfied with its products. However, if a competitor is attaining 90 percent customer satisfaction and aiming for 100 percent, the company may find that it is losing customers to the competitor. Thus, companies must monitor both their own and competitors' customer satisfaction performance. Marketing Highlight 18-1 describes the ways in which companies can track customer satisfaction.

Total customer satisfation: Cigna vows, "We'll never be 100 percent satisfied until you are, too."

Are we aiming too high? Or is everyone else aiming too low?

At the CIGNA Group Pension Division, customer satisfaction is our number one priority. Sounds good in an ad. But how do we achieve it? By giving the customer a voice. And then listening to it. When our customers told us that simplifying participant financial statements was a major priority, we listened. Then, using their input we designed more user-friendly reports.

When customers told us they wanted more investment options, we listened, too. Responding to their request with new accounts—six investing in mutual funds. Including highly rated funds from well-known outside investment companies.

And because even a little thing can often be a big thing, we listen to everything. For example, when customers told us they preferred talking to people rather than computers, we eliminated recorded messages in our customer service areas.

The point is, when the customer talks, we listen. To find out precisely how well, call CIGNA Group Pension Division, 1-800-238-2525.

Of course, we're not saying that we're perfect. But what we are saying is that we'll never be 100% satisfied until you are, too.

100% SATISFACTION. 100% OF THE TIME.

CIGNA

TRACKING CUSTOMER SATISFACTION

Tools for tracking and measuring customer satisfaction range from the primitive to the sophisticated. Companies use the following methods to measure how much customer satisfaction they are creating.

Complaint and Suggestion Systems

A customer-centered organization makes it easy for customers to make suggestions or complaints. Restaurants and hotels provide forms on which guests can check off their likes and dislikes. Hospitals place suggestion boxes in the corridors, supply comment cards to exiting patients, and employ patient advocates to solicit grievances. Some customer-centered companies, such as P&G, General Electric, and Whirlpool, set up customer hotlines with 800 numbers to make it easy for customers to inquire, suggest, or complain. Such systems not only help companies to act more quickly to resolve problems, they also provide companies with many good ideas for improved products and service.

Customer Satisfaction Surveys

Simply running complaint and suggestion systems may not give the company a full picture of customer satisfaction and dissatisfaction. Studies show that one of every four purchases results in consumer dissatisfaction, but that less than 5 percent of dissatisfied customers bother to complain—most customers simply switch suppliers. As a result, the company needlessly loses customers.

Responsive companies take direct measures of customer satisfaction by conducting regular surveys. They send questionnaires or make telephone calls to a sample of recent customers to find out how they feel about various aspects of the company's performance. They also survey buyers' views on competitor performance. Whirlpool surveys customer satisfaction on a massive scale, then acts on the results:

When customers talk, Whirlpool listens. Each year the company mails its Standardized Appliance Measurement of Satisfaction (SAMS) survey to 180,000 households, asking people to rate all its appliances on dozens of attributes. When a competitor's product ranks higher, Whirlpool engineers rip it apart to see why. The company [also] pays hundreds of consumers to fiddle with computer-simulated products at the company's Usability Lab while engineers record the users' reactions on videotape.

A company can measure customer satisfaction in a number of ways. It can measure satisfaction directly by asking: "How satisfied are you with this product? Are you highly dissatisfied, somewhat dissatisfied, neither satisfied nor dissatisfied, somewhat satisfied, or highly satisfied?" Or it can ask respondents to rate how

Tracking customer satisfaction: Each year Whirlpool mails its Standardized Appliance Measurement of Satisfaction survey to 180,000 households, asking them to rate all of its appliances.

much they expected of certain attributes and how much they actually experienced. Finally, the company can ask respondents to list any problems they have had with the offer and to suggest improvements.

While collecting customer satisfaction data, companies often ask additional useful questions. They often measure the customer's *repurchase intention;* this will usually be high if customer satisfaction is high. According to CEO John Young at Hewlett-Packard, nine out of ten customers in H-P surveys who rank themselves as highly satisfied say they would definitely or probably buy from H-P again. The company also might ask about the customer's likelihood or willingness to recommend the company and brand to other people. A strongly positive word-of-mouth rating suggests high customer satisfaction.

Ghost Shopping

Another useful way of assessing customer satisfaction is to hire people to pose as buyers to report their experiences in buying the company's and competitors' products. These "ghost shoppers" can even present specific problems to test whether the company's personnel handle difficult situations well. For example, ghost shoppers can complain about a restaurant's food to see how the restaurant handles this complaint. Not only should companies hire ghost shoppers, but managers themselves should leave their offices from time to time and experience first-hand the treatment they receive as "customers."

Lost Customer Analysis

Companies should contact customers who have stopped buying, or those who have switched to a competitor, to learn why this happened. When IBM loses a customer, it mounts a thorough effort to learn how it failed: Was IBM's price too high, its service poor, or its products substandard? Not only should the company conduct such *exit interviews,* it should also monitor the *customer loss rate.* A rising loss rate indicates that the company is failing to satisfy its customers.

Some Cautions in Measuring Customer Satisfaction

Customer satisfaction ratings are sometimes difficult to interpret. When customers rate their satisfaction with some element of the company's performance, say delivery, they can vary greatly in how they define good delivery. It might mean early delivery, on-time delivery, order completeness, or something else. Yet, if the company tried to define every element in detail, customers would face a huge questionnaire.

Companies also must recognize that two customers can report

being "highly satisfied" for different reasons. One might be easily satisfied most of the time, whereas the other might be hard to please but was pleased on this occasion. Further, managers and salespeople can manipulate their ratings on customer satisfaction. They can be especially nice to customers just before the survey or try to exclude unhappy customers from being included in the survey. Finally, if customers know that the company will go out of its way to please customers, even if they are satisfied, some customers may express high dissatisfaction in order to receive more concessions.

Source: Quote from Sally Solo, "Whirlpool: How to Listen to Consumers," *Fortune,* January 11, 1993, pp. 77–79. Also see Howard Schlossberg, "Measuring Customer Satisfaction Is Easy to Do—Until You Try It," *Marketing News,* April 26, 1993, pp. 5, 8; and John W. Verity, "The Gold Mine of Data in Customer Service," *Business Week,* March 21, 1994, pp. 113–114.

For customer-centered companies, customer satisfaction is both a goal and a major factor in company success. These and other companies realize that highly satisfied customers produce several benefits for the company. They are less price sensitive and they remain customers for a longer period. They buy additional products over time as the company introduces related products or improvements. And they talk favorably to others about the company and its products.

Although the customer-centered firm seeks to deliver high customer satisfaction relative to competitors, it does not attempt to *maximize* customer satisfaction. A company can always increase customer satisfaction by lowering its price or increasing its services, but this may result in lower profits. In addition to customers, the company has many stakeholders, including employees, dealers, suppliers, and stockholders. Spending more to increase customer satisfaction might divert funds from increasing the satisfaction of these other "partners." Thus, the purpose of marketing is to generate customer value profitably. Ultimately, the company must deliver a high level of customer satisfaction while at the same time delivering at least acceptable levels of satisfaction to the firm's other stakeholders. This requires a very delicate balance: the marketer must continue to generate more customer value and satisfaction but not "give away the house."[4]

DELIVERING CUSTOMER VALUE AND SATISFACTION

Customer value and satisfaction are important ingredients in the marketer's formula for success. But what does it take to produce and deliver customer value? To answer this, we will examine the concepts of a *value chain* and a *value delivery system.*

VALUE CHAIN

Value chain
A major tool for identifying ways to create more customer value.

Michael Porter proposed the **value chain** as the major tool for identifying ways to create more customer value (see Figure 18-2).[5] Every firm consists of a collection of activities performed to design, produce, market, deliver, and support the firm's products. The value chain breaks the firm into nine value-creating activities in an effort to understand the behavior of costs in the specific business and the potential sources of competitive differentiation. The nine value-creating activities include five primary activities and four support activities.

The primary activities involve the sequence of bringing materials into the business (inbound logistics), operating on them (operations), sending them out

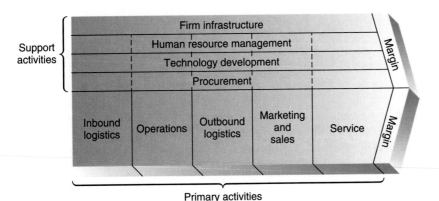

FIGURE 18-2 *The generic value chain*
Source: Michael E. Porter, *Competitive Advantage* (New York: Free Press, 1985), p. 37.

(outbound logistics), marketing them (marketing and sales), and servicing them (service). The support activities occur within each of these primary activities. For example, procurement involves obtaining the various inputs for each primary activity—only a fraction of procurement is done by the purchasing department. Technology development and human-resource management also occur in all departments. The firm's infrastructure covers the overhead of general management, planning, finance, accounting, and legal and government affairs borne by all the primary and support activities.

Under the value-chain concept, the firm should examine its costs and performance in each value-creating activity to look for improvements. It also should estimate its competitors' costs and performances as benchmarks. To the extent that the firm can perform certain activities better than its competitors, it can achieve a competitive advantage.

The firm's success depends not only on how well each department performs its work, but also on how well the activities of various departments are coordinated. Too often, individual departments maximize their own interests rather than those of the total company and the customer. For example, a credit department might attempt to reduce bad debts by raising credit standards; meanwhile, salespeople get frustrated and customers must buy elsewhere. A distribution department might decide to save money by shipping goods by rail; meanwhile, the customer waits. In each case, individual departments have erected walls that impede the delivery of quality customer service.

To overcome this problem, companies should place more emphasis on the smooth management of *core business processes,* most of which involve inputs and cooperation from many functional departments. Among other things, these core business processes include the following:

◆ *Product development process:* all the activities involved in identifying, researching, and developing new products with speed, high quality, and reasonable cost.

◆ *Inventory management process:* all the activities involved in developing and managing the right inventory levels of raw materials, semifinished materials, and finished goods so that adequate supplies are available while avoiding the costs of high overstocks.

◆ *Order-to-payment process:* all the activities involved in receiving orders, approving them, shipping the goods on time, and collecting payment.

◆ *Customer service process:* all the activities involved in making it easy for customers to reach the right parties within the company to obtain service, answers, and resolutions of problems.

Successful companies develop superior capabilities in managing these and other core processes. In turn, mastering core business processes gives these companies a substantial competitive edge.[6] For example, one of Wal-Mart's great strengths is its superiority in handling the inventory management and order flow process. As individual Wal-Mart stores sell their goods, sales information flows not only to Wal-Mart's headquarters but to Wal-Mart's suppliers, who ship replacement goods to Wal-Mart stores almost as fast as the products move off the shelf.

VALUE DELIVERY SYSTEM

Customer value delivery system
The system made up of the value chains of the company and its suppliers, distributors, and ultimately customers who work together to deliver value to customers.

In its search for competitive advantage, the firm needs to look beyond its own value chain and into the value chains of its suppliers and distributors, and ultimately, its customers. More companies today are "partnering" with the other members of the supply chain to improve the performance of the **customer value delivery system**. For example, Campbell Soup operates a qualified supplier program in which it sets high standards for suppliers and chooses only the few who are willing to meet its demanding requirements for quality, on-time delivery, and continuous improvement. Campbell then assigns its own experts to work with suppliers to constantly improve their joint performance.

Similarly, Honda has designed a program for working closely with its suppliers to help them reduce their costs and improve quality. For example, when Honda chose Donnelly Corporation to supply all of the mirrors for its U.S.-made cars, it sent engineers swarming over Donnelly's plants, looking for ways to improve its products and operations. This helped Donnelly reduce its costs by 2 percent in the first year. As a result of its improved performance, Donnelly's sales to Honda have grown from $5 million annually to more than $60 million in less than 10 years. In turn, Honda has gained an efficient, low-cost supplier of quality components. And as a result of Honda's partnerships with Donnelly and other suppliers, Honda customers benefit from lower cost, higher quality cars.[7]

An excellent value delivery system connects jeans maker Levi Strauss with its suppliers and distributors (see Figure 18-3). One of Levi's major retailers is Sears. Every night, through electronic data interchange (EDI), Levi's learns the sizes and styles of its blue jeans that sold through Sears and other major outlets. Levi's then electronically orders more fabric from the Milliken Company, its fabric supplier. In turn, Milliken relays an order for more fiber to Du Pont, the fiber supplier. In this way, the partners in the supply chain use the most current sales information to manufacture what is selling, rather than to manufacture based on potentially inaccurate sales forecasts. This is known as a *quick response* system, in which goods are pulled by demand, rather than pushed by supply.

As companies struggle to become more competitive, they are turning, ironically, to greater cooperation. Companies used to view their suppliers and distributors as cost centers, and in some cases, as adversaries. Today, however, they are selecting partners carefully and working out mutually profitable strategies. Increasingly in today's marketplace, competition no longer takes place between individual competitors. Rather, it takes place between the value delivery systems created by these competitors. Thus, if Levi Strauss has built a more potent value delivery system than Wrangler or another competitor, it will win more market share and profit.

Therefore, marketing can no longer be thought of as only a selling department. That view of marketing would give it responsibility only for formulating a promotion-oriented marketing mix, without much say about product features, costs, and other important elements. Under the new view, marketing is responsi-

FIGURE 18-3 *Levi Strauss's value delivery system*

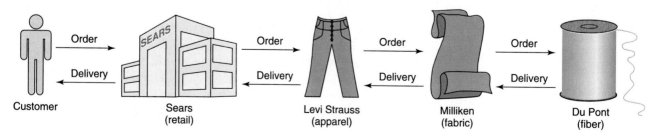

| Customer | | Sears (retail) | | Levi Strauss (apparel) | | Milliken (fabric) | | Du Pont (fiber) |

Customer value delivery system: Campbell operates a qualified supplier program in which it chooses only the few suppliers who can meet its demanding quality requirements. Campbell's experts then work with suppliers to constantly improve their joint performance.

ble for *designing and managing a superior value delivery system to reach target customer segments.* Today's marketing managers must think not only about selling today's products but also about how to stimulate the development of improved products, how to work actively with other departments in managing core business processes, and how to build better external partnerships.[8]

RETAINING CUSTOMERS

Beyond building stronger relations with their partners in the supply chain, companies today must work to develop stronger bonds and loyalty with their ultimate customers. In the past, many companies took their customers for granted. Customers often did not have many alternative suppliers, or the other suppliers were just as poor in quality and service, or the market was growing so fast that the company did not worry about fully satisfying its customers. A company could lose 100 customers a week but gain another 100 customers and consider its sales to be satisfactory. Such a company, operating on a "leaky bucket" theory of business, believes that there will always be enough customers to replace the defecting ones. However, this high *customer churn* involves higher costs than if a company retained all 100 customers and acquired no new ones.

THE COST OF LOST CUSTOMERS

Companies must pay close attention to their customer defection rate and undertake steps to reduce it. First, the company must define and measure its customer retention rate. Then, the company must identify the causes of customer defection and determine which of these can be reduced or eliminated. The company needs to prepare a frequency distribution showing the percentage of customers who defect for different reasons. Not much can be done about customers who leave the region, or about business customers who go out of business. But much can be done about customers who leave because of shoddy products, poor service, or prices that are too high.

Companies can estimate how much profit they lose when customers defect unnecessarily. For an individual customer, this is the same as the *customer's lifetime value*. For a group of lost customers, a major transportation firm estimated the profit loss as follows: The company had 64,000 accounts. It lost 5 percent of its accounts (3,200 accounts) this year as a result of poor service. The average lost account represented $40,000 in lost revenue. Therefore, the company lost 3,200 × $40,000 = $128,000,000 in revenue. Given its 10 percent profit margin, the company lost $12,800,000 unnecessarily in a single year.

The company needs to figure out how much it would cost to reduce the defection rate. If the cost is less than the lost profits, the company should spend that amount to reduce customer defections. In this example, if the transportation firm can spend less than $12,800,000 to retain all of these accounts, it would be wise to do so.

THE NEED FOR CUSTOMER RETENTION

Today, outstanding companies go all out to retain their customers. Many markets have settled into maturity, and there are not many new customers entering most categories. Competition is increasing, and the costs of attracting new customers are rising. In these markets, it might cost five times as much to attract a new customer as to keep a current customer happy.[9] Offensive marketing typically costs more than defensive marketing, because it takes a great deal of effort and spending to coax satisfied customers away from competitors.

Unfortunately, classic marketing theory and practice centers on the art of attracting new customers rather than retaining existing ones. The emphasis has been on creating *transactions* rather than *relationships*. Discussion has focused on *presale activity* and *sale activity* rather than on *postsale activity*. Today, however, more companies recognize the importance of retaining current customers. According to one report, by reducing customer defections by only 5 percent, companies can improve profits anywhere from 25 to 85 percent.[10] Unfortunately, however, most company accounting systems fail to show the value of loyal customers.

Thus, although much current marketing focuses on formulating marketing mixes that will create sales and new customers, the firm's first line of defense lies in customer retention. And the best approach to customer retention is to deliver high customer satisfaction and value that result in strong customer loyalty.

THE KEY: CUSTOMER RELATIONSHIP MARKETING

Relationship marketing
The process of creating, maintaining, and enhancing strong, value-laden relationships with customers and other stakeholders.

Relationship marketing involves creating, maintaining, and enhancing strong relationships with customers and other stakeholders. Increasingly, marketing is moving away from a focus on individual transactions and toward a focus on building value-laden relationships and value delivery networks. Relationship marketing is oriented more toward the long term. The goal is to deliver long-term value to customers, and the measure of success is long-term customer satisfaction. Relationship marketing requires that all of the company's departments work together with marketing as a team to serve the customer. It involves building relationships at many levels—economic, social, technical, and legal—resulting in high customer loyalty.

We can distinguish five different levels of relationships that can be formed with customers who have purchased a company's product, such as an automobile or a piece of industrial machinery:

Relationship marketing: Increasingly, companies are moving away from a focus on individual transactions and toward a focus on building value-laden relationships with customers. Here PaineWebber declares, "We invest in relationships."

◆ *Basic:* The company salesperson sells the product but does not follow up in any way.

◆ *Reactive:* The salesperson sells the product and encourages the customer to call whenever he or she has any questions or problems.

◆ *Accountable:* The salesperson phones the customer a short time after the sale to check whether the product is meeting the customer's expectations. The salesperson also solicits from the customer any product improvement suggestions and any specific disappointments. This information helps the company to continuously improve its offering.

◆ *Proactive:* The salesperson or others in the company phone the customer from time to time with suggestions about improved product use or helpful new products.

◆ *Partnership:* The company works continuously with the customer and with other customers to discover ways to deliver better value.

Figure 18-4 shows that a company's relationship marketing strategy will depend on how many customers it has and their profitability. For example, companies with many low-margin customers will practice *basic* marketing. Thus, H. J. Heinz will not phone all of its ketchup buyers to express its appreciation for their business. At best, Heinz will be reactive by setting up a customer information service. At the other extreme, in markets with few customers and high margins, most sellers will move toward partnership marketing. Boeing, for example, will work closely with United Airlines in designing its airplanes and insuring that Boeing airplanes fully satisfy United's requirements. In between these two extreme situations, other levels of relationship marketing are appropriate.

What specific marketing tools can a company use to develop stronger customer bonding and satisfaction? It can adopt any of three customer value-building approaches: financial, social, or structural.[11]

Financial Benefits

The first value-building approach relies primarily on adding *financial benefits* to the customer relationship. For example, airlines offer frequent-flyer programs, hotels give room upgrades to their frequent guests, and supermarkets give patronage refunds. (See Marketing Highlight 18-2 for examples of these and other such relationship programs.)

Procter & Gamble recently offered a unique money-back guarantee on its Crest toothpaste in an effort to build a long-term bond with customers. P&G advertises a toll-free number customers can call to join the Crest money-back guarantee program. It then supplies dental patients with evaluation forms that they take to their local dentists. Dentists check for cavities and tartar buildup. After using Crest for six months, buyers return to the dentist for another checkup. Those who haven't improved can receive a refund on the money they spent on Crest.[12] Beyond assuring customers that Crest delivers value, this promotion helps P&G build a customer database containing the dental histories of families that sign up. Using this database,

FIGURE 18-4
Relationship levels as a function of profit margin and number of customers

	Profit margins		
	High	Medium	Low
Many	Accountable	Reactive	Basic
Medium	Proactive	Accountable	Basic
Few	Partnership	Accountable	Reactive

Number of customers

BUILDING CUSTOMER RELATIONSHIPS: FREQUENCY MARKETING PROGRAMS AND CLUBS

In moving from transaction-oriented marketing to relationship building, many companies have created programs that keep their customers coming back, buying more, and staying loyal. They work at building a special relationship in which their best customers experience a value-laden dialogue and receive special privileges and awards. Among the most common efforts are *frequency marketing programs* and *club marketing programs.*

Frequency Marketing Programs

Frequency marketing programs (FMPs) reward customers who buy frequently or in large amounts. *Colloquy,* a quarterly frequency-marketing newsletter, defines frequency marketing as the effort "to identify, maintain, and increase the yield from best customers through long-term, interactive, value-added relationships."

American Airlines was one of the first companies to pioneer a frequency marketing program when it offered free mileage credits to its best customers in the early 1980s. A customer simply joined the AAdvantage program at no cost, accumulated credits for miles flown, and turned them in for a free airline ticket, seat upgrade, or other benefits. As more flyers switched to American, the other airlines were compelled to offer similar programs.

Hotels soon adopted FMP. Marriott took the lead with its Honored Guest Program, quickly followed by Hyatt (with its Gold Passport Program) and other hotel chains. Frequent guests receive room upgrades or free rooms after earning enough points. Next, car rental firms spon-

Exclusive savings day just for you...
Sears Best Customer
ADDITIONAL
10% OFF ALL SALE PRICES
Plus 10% off all regular prices, too!
Feb. 1st is your bonus savings day.
Sale goes public Feb. 2nd, 3rd & 4th.

SBC
SEARS BEST CUSTOMER

Frequency marketing programs: The Sears Best Customer Program boosted customer retention by 11 percent and increased sales from the retailer's best customers by 9 percent.

sored FMPs, and credit card companies began to offer points based on their cards' usage level. For example, Sears offers rebates to their Discover cardholders on charges made against the card, and Shell Oil card users can earn free gasoline.

Typically, the first company to introduce an FMP gains the most benefit. However, after competitors respond, FMPs can become a burden to all the offering companies. Soon, many customers belong to several competing FMP's, accumulating credit with whomever they patronize. Companies may find that they are giving away many flights, rooms, and merchandise without gaining much advantage. The winning companies, if any, are those that run their programs most efficiently, attract the most business based on their program's distinctive benefits, or build sophisticated database systems to present personalized offers to targeted customers. Despite these problems, frequency marketing programs remain an important tool for building long-term relationships with customers.

Club Marketing Programs

Many companies have created club concepts around their products. Club membership may be offered automatically on purchase of a product or by paying a fee. Some clubs have been spectacularly successful:

P&G can expand its relationships with customers by offering additional related products and services to them.

Social Benefits

Although such programs and other financial incentives build customer preference, they can be easily imitated by competitors and thus may fail to differentiate the company's offer permanently. The second approach is to add *social benefits* as well as financial benefits. Here company personnel work to increase their social bonds with customers by learning individual customers' needs and wants and then individualizing and personalizing their products and services. For example, Ritz-Carlton employees treat customers as individuals, not as nameless, faceless members of a mass market. Whenever possible, they refer to guests by name and give each guest a warm welcome every day. They record specific guest preferences into the company's customer database, accessible by all hotels in the worldwide Ritz

Nintendo, the Japanese game company, has enrolled two million members in its Nintendo Club. For $16 a year, members receive a monthly magazine, *Nintendo Power,* which previews Nintendo games and discusses the latest developments in home video entertainment systems. The club also offers one of the most extensive telephone hotline systems in the country. Club members can dial in and talk to one of 250 Nintendo game counselors to receive tips on game strategy. The club not only cements customer relationships, it also provides Nintendo with valuable marketing information—the company learns firsthand what's hot and what's not.

Waldenbooks sponsors a Preferred Reader Program which has attracted over four million members, each paying $5 to receive mailings about new books, a 10 percent discount on book purchases, toll-free ordering, and many other services.

Lladró, maker of fine porcelain figurines, sponsors a "Collectors Society" with an annual membership fee of $35. Members receive a free subscription to a quarterly magazine, a bisque plaque, free enrollment in the Lladró Museum of New York, and member-only tours to visit the company and Lladró family in Valencia, Spain.

Gateway Federal, a Cincinnati thrift bank, sponsors "The Stateman's Club" for customers who maintain a minimum deposit of $10,000. Its 10,000 members receive over 26 benefits including free checking, money orders, and traveler's checks; social gatherings and guest lecturers; and complimentary refreshments. Members have access to IBM computers and other equipment, and they can reserve the Club room for private receptions after regular hours.

Burger King sponsors the Burger King Kids Club, which now numbers over 1.6 million members. Kids receive free membership, a secret code name, a newsletter, and a variety of premiums. Other companies targeting kids through clubs include Kraft, LEGO, and Toys 'R' Us.

Harley-Davidson sponsors the Harley Owners Group (HOG) that now numbers 127,000 members. The first-time buyer of a Harley-Davidson motorcycle gets a free one-year membership with annual renewal costing $35. HOG benefits include a magazine (*Hog Tales*), a touring handbook, an emergency pick-up service, a specially designed insurance program, theft reward service, discount hotel rates, and a Fly & Ride program enabling members to rent Harleys while on vacation.

If properly done, such programs can help bond customers to the company, creating strong and lasting relationships.

Well-executed clubs and frequency marketing programs can produce significant results. For example, when Sears found that it was losing too many of its best customers to competitors, it launched its Best Customer Program. It defined its best customers as those who shop at Sears frequently and in a variety of departments, and who spend a large amount of money annually at the store. About 7.2 million Sears customers fit this definition, and the retailer estimates that each is worth about six times more to Sears than the average new customer. Best Customers receive special benefits and privileges, such as guaranteed response to a service call within 24 hours. The program has improved Sears's customer retention rate by 11 percent and increased sales from best customers by 9 percent.

Sources: See Cyndee Miller, "Rewards for the Best Customers," *Marketing News,* July 5, 1993, pp. 1, 6; Gary Levin, "Marketers Flock to Loyalty Offers," *Advertising Age,* May 24, 1993, p. 13; and Louise O'Brien and Charles Jones, "Do Rewards Really Create Loyalty?" *Harvard Business Review,* May–June 1995, pp. 75–82.

chain. A guest who requests a foam pillow at the Ritz in Montreal will be delighted to find one waiting in the room when he or she checks into the Atlanta Ritz months later.[13]

To build better relationships with its customers, during the summer of 1994 Saturn invited all of its almost 700,000 owners to a "Saturn Homecoming" at its manufacturing facility in Spring Hill, Tennessee. The two-day affair included family events, plant tours, and physical challenge activities designed to build trust and a team spirit. Says Saturn's manager of corporate communications, "The Homecoming party is another way of building . . . relationships, and it shows that we treat our customers differently than any other car company."[14]

Structural Ties

The third approach to building strong customer relationships is to add *structural ties* as well as financial and social benefits. For example, a business marketer might supply customers with special equipment or computer linkages that help them manage their orders, payroll, or inventory. McKesson Corporation, a leading pharmaceutical wholesaler, has invested millions of dollars in its electronic data interchange (EDI) system to help small pharmacies manage their inventory, their order entry, and their shelf space. As another example, Federal Express uses its Powership Program, which it offers to more than 20,000 customer companies, to keep its best customers from defecting to competitors like UPS. It provides Powership customers with free computers linked to Federal Express headquarters. Customer firms can use the machines to check the status of their own Federal Express packages or those that they ship for their customers. To further enhance its relationships with important customers, Federal Express polls 1,000 of its Powership customers each month seeking ways to improve service to them.[15]

Relationship marketing means that organizations must focus on managing their customers as well as their products. At the same time, although many companies are moving strongly toward relationship marketing, companies don't want relationships with every customer. In fact, there are undesirable customers for every company. The objective is to determine which customers the company can serve most effectively relative to competitors. Companies must judge which segments and which specific customers will be profitable.

THE ULTIMATE TEST: CUSTOMER PROFITABILITY

Ultimately, marketing is the art of attracting and keeping *profitable customers*. However, companies often discover that between 20 and 40 percent of their customers are unprofitable. Further, many companies report that their most profitable customers are not their largest customers, but their mid-size customers. The largest customers demand greater service and receive the deepest discounts, thereby reducing the company's profit level. The smallest customers pay full price and receive less service, but the cost of transacting with small customers reduces their profitability. In many cases, mid-size customers who pay close to full price and receive good service are the most profitable. This helps to explain why many large firms that once targeted only large customers now are invading the middle market.

A company should not try to pursue and satisfy every customer. Moreover, companies should not try to satisfy every customer whim. Some organizations attempt to provide anything and everything that customers suggest. However, although customers often make good suggestions, they also suggest actions that a company cannot undertake profitably. A market focus does not mean blindly following such suggestions. Instead, it means making disciplined choices of which customers to serve and which specific benefits to deliver or deny.[16] For example, if business customers of Courtyard (Marriott's less expensive motel) start asking for Marriott-level business services, Courtyard should say "no." Providing such services would only confuse the respective positionings of the Marriott and Courtyard systems.

What makes a customer profitable? A profitable customer is a person, household, or company whose revenues over time exceed, by an acceptable amount, the company costs of attracting, selling, and servicing that customer. This definition emphasizes lifetime revenues and costs, not profits from a single transaction. Here are some dramatic illustrations of **customer lifetime value**:

Customer lifetime value The amount by which revenues from a given customer over time will exceed the company's costs of attracting, selling, and servicing that customer.

> Stew Leonard, who operates a highly profitable single-store supermarket, says that he sees $50,000 flying out of his store every time he sees a sulking customer. Why? Because his average customer spends about $100 a week, shops 50 weeks a year, and remains in the area for about 10 years. If this customer has an unhappy experience and switches to another supermarket, Stew Leonard

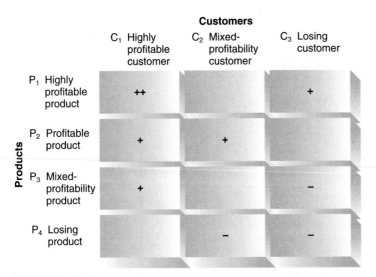

Customers

	C_1 Highly profitable customer	C_2 Mixed-profitability customer	C_3 Losing customer
P_1 Highly profitable product	++		+
P_2 Profitable product	+	+	
P_3 Mixed-profitability product	+		−
P_4 Losing product		−	−

FIGURE 18-5
Customer/product profitability analysis

has lost $50,000 in revenue. The loss can be much greater if the disappointed customer shares the bad experience with other customers and causes them to defect.

Tom Peters, noted author of several books on managerial excellence, runs a business that spends $1,500 a month on Federal Express service. His company spends this amount 12 months a year and expects to remain in business for at least another 10 years. Therefore, he expects to spend more than $180,000 on future Federal Express service. If Federal Express makes a 10 percent profit margin, Peters' lifetime business will contribute $18,000 to Federal Express's profits. Federal Express risks all of this profit if Peters receives poor service from a Federal Express driver or if a competitor offers better service.

Companies should actively measure individual customer value and profitability. Figure 18-5 shows a useful type of profitability analysis.[17] Customers make up the columns of the figure and products or services make up the rows. Each cell contains a symbol for the profitability of selling a given product or service to a given customer. Customer C_1 is very profitable—he or she buys three profit-making products, products P_1, P_2, and P_3. Customer C_2 yields mixed profitability, buying one profitable product and one unprofitable product. Customer C_3 generates losses by purchasing one profitable product and two unprofitable ones ("loss leaders"). What can the company do about consumers like C_3? First, the company should consider raising the prices of its less profitable products or eliminating them. Second, the company also can try to cross-sell its profit-making products to its unprofitable customers. If these actions cause customers like C_3 to defect, it may be for the good. In fact, the company might benefit by *encouraging* its unprofitable customers to switch to competitors.

IMPLEMENTING TOTAL QUALITY MARKETING

Customer satisfaction and company profitability are linked closely to product and service quality. Higher levels of quality result in greater customer satisfaction, while at the same time supporting higher prices and often lower costs. Therefore, *quality improvement programs* normally increase profitability. The well-known Profit Impact of Marketing Strategies (PIMS) studies show a high correlation between relative product quality and profitability.[18]

The task of improving product and service quality should be a company's top priority. Much of the striking global successes of Japanese companies has resulted from their building exceptional quality into their products. Most customers will no longer tolerate poor or average quality. Companies today have no choice but to adopt quality concepts if they want to stay in the race, let alone be profitable. According to GE's Chairman, John F. Welch, Jr.: "Quality is our best assurance of customer allegiance, our strongest defense against foreign competition, and the only path to sustained growth and earnings."[19] (See Marketing Highlight 18-3.)

Quality has been variously defined as "fitness for use," "conformance to requirements," and "freedom from variation."[20] The American Society for Quality Control defines **quality** as the totality of features and characteristics of a product or service that bear on its ability to satisfy stated or implied needs. This is

Quality
The totality of features and characteristics of a product or service that bear on its ability to satisfy stated or implied needs.

THE MALCOLM BALDRIGE NATIONAL QUALITY AWARD: A SPUR TO WORLD-CLASS QUALITY

For a growing number of companies, competition is no longer just local—it has become global. Therefore, a nation's companies must strive to produce goods that are competitive or superior in world markets. As a result, to spur their firms to world-class quality, some countries have established national prizes that are awarded to companies that exemplify the best quality practices and improvements.

Japan was the first country to award a national quality prize, the Deming prize, named after the American statistician who taught the importance of quality to post-war Japan. In the mid-1980s, the United States established the Malcolm Baldrige National Quality Award in honor of the late Secretary of Commerce. The award encourages U.S. firms to implement quality practices. When quality results justify it, companies can submit applications and evidence for a Baldrige Award.

The Baldrige Board of Examiners may give up to two Awards each year in each of three categories: manufacturing companies, service companies, and small businesses. The award criteria consist of seven measures, ranging from the extent of quality leadership provided by the company's top executives, to how well the firm develops its human resources to support quality, to the degree of customer focus and satisfaction achieved by the firm. Each of the seven measures carries a certain number of award points, which total to 1,000 points. Of these measures, *customer focus and satisfaction* gets the most points (300). The 300 points are further broken down into points for understanding customer expectations, managing customer relation-

ships well, and determining customer satisfaction. Thus far, Baldrige Awards have gone to such well-known giants as AT&T, Texas Instruments, Xerox, Motorola, Federal Express, IBM, and the Cadillac Division of General Motors, but also to lesser known, smaller businesses such as the Granite Rock Company

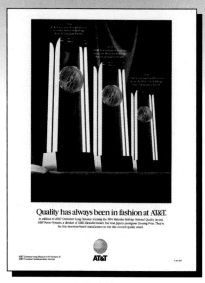

Quality has always been in fashion at AT&T.

In addition to AT&T Consumer Long Distance winning the 1994 Malcolm Baldrige National Quality Award, AT&T Power Systems, a division of AT&T Microelectronics, has won Japan's prestigious Deming Prize. They're the first American-based manufacturer to win this coveted quality award.

AT&T
AT&T Consumer Long Distance is the business of AT&T Consumer Communications Services

Many U.S. firms have closed the quality gap. Here, AT&T notes that it has won three Baldrige Awards since 1992. It is also the first American-based firm to win Japan's prestigious Deming Prize.

of Watsonville, California, and Globe Metallurgical of Cleveland, Ohio.

One company that is currently competing for a Baldrige National Quality Award in the small-business category is a marketing research firm, Custom Research Incorporated (CRI), headquartered in Minneapolis. In 1990, CRI began using the Baldrige criteria as a framework for developing its quality system. It applied for the

award in 1991 and received feedback that led to further improvements. In 1992, CRI was selected to receive a site visit. CRI believes that it earned a site visit because it fervently applies the following quality principles:

◆ Focus on building major customer relationships.

◆ Organize into cross-functional, client-centered teams—get everyone working toward customer satisfaction.

◆ Develop high-quality processes and procedures to get work done, then measure the results.

◆ Explicitly ask customers what they expect from a partnering relationship.

◆ Seek customer feedback on individual projects and the overall relationship.

◆ Hire the best people and invest in their development.

◆ Stay flexible, agile, fast moving—empower everyone in the company to "just do it."

◆ Have fun with hoopla and recognition.

◆ Build quality continuously.

◆ Never be satisfied.

All companies would do well to emulate this excellent statement of modern business and marketing thinking.

Source: See *1993 Award Criteria,* Malcolm Baldrige National Quality Award brochure, United States Department of Commerce, National Institute of Standards and Technology, Gaithersburg, Maryland.

clearly a customer-centered definition of quality. It suggests that a company has delivered quality whenever its product and service meet or exceed customers' needs, requirements, and expectations. A company that satisfies most of its customers' needs most of the time is a quality company.

It is important to distinguish between performance quality and conformance quality. *Performance quality* refers to the *level* at which a product performs its functions. For example, a Mercedes provides higher performance quality than a Volkswagen: it has a smoother ride, handles better, and lasts longer. It is more expensive and sells to a market with higher means and requirements. *Conformance quality* refers to freedom from defects and the *consistency* with which a product delivers a specified level of performance. Thus, a Mercedes and a Volkswagen can be said to offer equivalent conformance quality to their respective markets to the extent that each consistently delivers what its market expects. A $50,000 car that meets all of its requirements is a quality car; so is a $15,000 car that meets all of its requirements. But if the Mercedes handles badly, or if the Volkswagen gives poor fuel efficiency, then both cars have failed to deliver quality, and customer satisfaction suffers accordingly.

TOTAL QUALITY MANAGEMENT

Total quality management (TQM) swept the corporate boardrooms of the 1980s. Many companies adopted the language of TQM but not the substance. Others viewed TQM as a cure-all for all the company's problems. Still others became obsessed with narrowly defined TQM principles and lost sight of broader concerns for customer value and satisfaction. As a result, many TQM programs begun in the 1980s failed, causing a recent backlash against TQM. Still, when applied in the context of creating customer satisfaction, total quality principles remain a requirement for success. Although many firms don't use the TQM label anymore, for most top companies customer-driven quality has become a way of doing business. They apply the notion of "return on quality (ROQ)," and they make certain that the quality they offer is the quality that customers want. This quality, in turn, results in improved sales and profits.[21]

Total quality is the key to creating customer value and satisfaction. Just as marketing is everyone's job, total quality is everyone's job:

> Marketers who don't learn the language of quality improvement, manufacturing, and operations will become as obsolete as buggy whips. The days of functional marketing are gone. We can no longer afford to think of ourselves as market researchers, advertising people, direct marketers, marketing strategists—we have to think of ourselves as customer satisfiers—customer advocates focused on whole processes.[22]

MARKETING'S ROLE IN TOTAL QUALITY

Marketing management has two responsibilities in a quality-centered company. First, marketing management must participate in formulating strategies and policies designed to help the company win through total quality excellence. Second, marketing must deliver marketing quality as well as production quality. It must perform each marketing activity—marketing research, sales training, advertising, customer service, and others—to high standards.

Marketers play several major roles in helping their companies define and deliver high-quality goods and services to target customers. First, marketers bear the major responsibility for correctly identifying the customers' needs and requirements and for communicating customer expectations correctly to product designers. Second, marketers must make sure that the customers' orders are filled correctly and on time, and must check to see that customers have received proper instructions, training, and technical assistance in the use of the product. Third, marketers must stay in touch with customers after the sale to make sure that they remain satisfied. Finally, marketers must gather and convey customer ideas for product and service improvements to the appropriate company departments.

At the same time, ironically, one study found that marketing people were responsible for more customer complaints than any other department (35 percent). Marketing mistakes included cases in which the sales force ordered special prod-

PURSUING A TOTAL QUALITY MARKETING STRATEGY

The Japanese have long taken to heart consultant W. Edwards Deming's lessons about winning through *total quality management* (TQM). This quest for quality paid off handsomely. Consumers around the world flocked to buy high-quality Japanese products, leaving many American firms playing catch-up.

In recent years, many U.S. firms have closed the quality gap. Many have started their own quality programs in an effort to compete both globally and domestically with the Japanese. A growing number of U.S. companies have appointed a "Vice-President of Quality" to spearhead total quality. Total quality stems from the following premises about quality improvement:

1. *Quality is in the eyes of the customer.* Quality must begin with customer needs and end with customer perceptions. As Motorola's vice-president of quality suggests, "Quality has to do something for the customer. . . . Beauty is in the eye of the beholder. If [a product] does not work the way that the user needs it to work, the defect is as big to the user as if it doesn't work the way the designer planned it. Our defini-

tion of a defect is 'if the customer doesn't like it, it's a defect.'" Thus, the fundamental aim of today's quality movement has now become "total

Ford recognizes that quality requires a total employee commitment.

customer satisfaction." Quality improvements are meaningful only when they are perceived by customers.

2. *Quality must be reflected not just in the company's products, but in every company activity.* Leonard A. Morgan of GE says: "We are not just concerned with the quality of the product, but with the quality of our advertising, service, product literature, delivery, and after-sales support."

3. *Quality requires total employee commitment.* Quality can be delivered only by companies in which all employees are committed to quality and motivated and trained to deliver it. Successful companies remove the barriers between departments. Their employees work as teams to carry out core business processes and to create desired outcomes. Employees work to satisfy their internal customers as well as external customers.

4. *Quality requires high-quality partners.* Quality can be delivered only by companies whose value-chain partners also deliver quality. Therefore, a quality-driven company must find and align itself with high-quality suppliers and distributors.

uct features for customers but failed to notify manufacturing of the changes; in which incorrect order processing resulted in the wrong product being made and shipped; and in which customer complaints were not properly handled.[23]

The implication here is that marketers must spend time and effort not only to improve external marketing, but also to improve internal marketing. Marketers must be the customer's watchdog or guardian, complaining loudly for the customer when the product or the service is not right. Marketers must constantly uphold the standard of "giving the customer the best solution." Marketing Highlight 18-4 presents some important conclusions about total marketing quality strategy.

Summary

Today's customers face a growing range of choices in the products and services they can buy. They base their choices on perceptions of quality, value, and service. Companies need to understand the determinants of *customer value and satisfaction. Customer delivered value* is the difference between *total customer value* and *total customer cost*. Customers will normally choose the offer that maximizes their delivered value.

Customer satisfaction is the outcome felt

5. *A quality program cannot save a poor product.* The Pontiac Fiero launched a quality program, but because the car didn't have a performance engine to support its performance image, the quality program did not save the car. A quality drive cannot compensate for product deficiencies.

6. *Quality can always be improved.* The best companies believe in the Japanese concept of *kaizen,* "continuous improvement of everything by everyone." The best way to improve quality is to benchmark the company's performance against the "best-of-class" competitors or the best performers in other industries, striving to equal or even surpass them.

7. *Quality improvement sometimes requires quantum leaps.* Although the company should strive for continuous quality improvement, it must at times seek a quantum quality improvement. Companies sometimes can obtain small improvements by working harder. But large improvements call for fresh solutions and for working smarter. For example, John Young of Hewlett-Packard did not ask for a 10 percent reduction in defects, he asked for a *tenfold* reduction and got it.

8. *Quality does not cost more.* Managers once argued that achieving more quality would cost more and slow down production. But improving quality involves learning ways to "do things right the first time." Quality is not *inspected* in; it must be *designed* in. Doing things right the first time reduces the costs of salvage, repair, and redesign, not to mention losses in customer goodwill. Motorola claims that its quality drive has saved $700 million in manufacturing costs during the last five years.

9. *Quality is necessary but may not be sufficient.* Improving a company's quality is absolutely necessary to meet the needs of more demanding buyers. At the same time, higher quality may not ensure a winning advantage, especially as all competitors increase their quality to more or less the same extent. For example, Singapore Airlines enjoyed a reputation as the world's best airline. However, competing airlines have attracted larger shares of passengers recently by narrowing the perceived gap between their service quality and Singapore's service quality.

Sources: Quotes from Lois Therrien, "Motorola and NEC: Going for Glory," *Business Week,* Special issue on quality, 1991, pp. 60–61. Also see David A. Garvin, "Competing on Eight Dimensions of Quality," *Harvard Business Review,* November–December 1987, p. 109; Frank Rose, "Now Quality Means Service Too," *Fortune,* April 22, 1992, pp. 97–108; Cyndee Miller, "TQM Out; 'Continuous Process Improvement' In," *Marketing News,* May 9, 1994, pp. 5, 10; and David Greising, "Quality: How to Make It Pay," *Business Week,* August 8, 1994, pp. 54–59.

---

by buyers who experience a company performance that fulfills expectations. Customers are satisfied when their expectations are met, and delighted when their expectations are exceeded. Satisfied customers tend to remain loyal longer, buy more, are less price sensitive, and talk favorably about the company.

To *deliver customer value and satisfaction,* companies must manage their own *value chains* and the entire *value delivery system* in a customer-centered way. The company's goal is not only to get customers but, even more importantly, to *retain customers.* There is a very *high cost from lost customers. Customer relationship marketing* provides the key to retaining customers and involves building financial and social benefits as well as structural ties to customers. Companies must decide the level at which they want to build relationships with different market segments and individual customers, from such levels as basic, reactive, accountable, and proactive to full partnership. Which is best depends on *customer profitability* measured over a lifetime, and whether the costs required to attract and retain that customer provide value to the firm.

Total quality management has become a major approach to providing customer satisfaction and company profitability. Companies must understand how their customers perceive quality and how much quality they expect. Companies must then do a better job of meeting consumer quality expectations than their competitors do. Delivering quality requires total management and employee commitment as well as measurement and reward systems. Marketers play an especially critical role in their company's drive toward higher quality.

Key Terms

Customer-centered company	Customer value delivery system	Total customer cost
Customer delivered value	Quality	Total customer value
Customer lifetime value	Relationship marketing	Value chain

Discussing the Issues

1. Imagine that your instructor is your customer. *You*, in your role as a student, are the main product of your firm. You are attempting to create added value for yourself with the instructor. (a) Name the student tasks you would consider to be inbound logistics, operations, outbound logistics, marketing and sales, and service. (b) How would you perform these tasks to maximize customer value?

2. Recall an activity in which you went beyond the normal effort and "gave your all" to produce the utmost in quality. How much of your improvement in quality did other people notice—all, some, or none? Analyze whether there is a balance point that provides the right mix of quality and effort.

3. Describe a situation in which you became a "lost customer." Did you leave because of poor product quality, poor service quality, or both?

4. Who should define quality standards: research and development, engineering, manufacturing, or marketing? Explain your choice(s).

5. Health care reform remains a major issue in the United States. One concern is a lack of value: the costs of medical care often seem to outweigh the benefits. Propose some meaningful ways to measure health-care quality that could be used in efforts to improve value.

6. "Just in time" inventory management makes suppliers responsible for delivering parts in exact quantities at precisely the right time. Companies that succeed with "JIT" find that benefits often go beyond inventory cost savings, and that many quality improvements come from the process of working very closely with suppliers. Assess whether the ideas of a value chain are used in "JIT" management. Can "JIT" succeed *without* using the concepts in the value chain?

Applying the Concepts

1. Write a complaint letter to a firm about one of their products or services. Did you receive a refund or replacement product, a response letter, or no reply at all? How does the type of response affect your attitude toward the company?

2. Find some product, service, or activist person that has clearly established a strong relationship with its customers. Some examples include: BMW automobiles or Harley Davidson motorcycles; reruns of *The Lawrence Welk Show* or a Grateful Dead concert; Jesse Jackson or Rush Limbaugh. Talk to several customers that strongly identify with one such "product." How do they see their relationship to the product? What are the key values they receive? What, if anything, does the "manufacturer" do to maintain this relationship?

References

1. Quotes from Valerie Reitman, "Rubbermaid Turns Up Plenty of Profit in the Mundane," *Wall Street Journal*, March 27, 1992, p. B4. Also see Cristy Marshall, "Rubbermaid: Yes, Plastic," *Business Month*, December 1988, p. 38; Maria Mallory, "Profits on Everything but the Kitchen Sink," *Business Week*, Special is-

sue on innovation, 1991, p.122; Zachary Schiller, "At Rubbermaid, Little Things Mean a Lot," *Business Week,* November 11, 1991; "Rubbermaid: Breaking All the Molds," *Sales & Marketing Management,* August 1992, p. 42; and Alan Farnham, "America's Most Admired Company: It's Rubbermaid," *Fortune,* February 7, 1994, pp. 50–54.

2. For an interesting discussion of alternative strategies for delivering customer value, see Michael Treacy and Fred Wiersema, "Customer Intimacy and Other Value Disciplines," *Harvard Business Review,* January–February 1993, pp. 84–93.

3. Richard Whitely, "Do Selling and Quality Mix?" *Sales & Marketing Management,* October 1993, p. 70.

4. Thomas E. Caruso, "Got a Marketing Topic? Kotler Has an Opinion," *Marketing News,* June 8, 1992, p. 21.

5. Michael E. Porter, *Competitive Advantage: Creating and Sustaining Superior Performance* (New York: Free Press, 1985). For more discussion on value chains and strategies for creating value, see Richard Normann and Rafael Ramirez, "From Value Chain to Value Constellation: Designing Interactive Strategy," *Harvard Business Review,* July–August, 1993, pp. 65–77; and "Strategy and the Art of Reinventing Value," *Harvard Business Review,* September–October, 1993, pp. 39–51.

6. See George Stalk, Philip Evans, and Laurence E. Shulman, "Competing Capabilities: the New Rules of Corporate Strategy," *Harvard Business Review,* March–April 1992, pp. 57–69; and Benson P. Shapiro, V. Kasturi Rangan, and John J. Sviokla, "Staple Yourself to an Order," *Harvard Business Review,* July–August 1992, pp. 113–122.

7. Myron Magnet, "The New Golden Rule of Business," *Fortune,* February 21, 1994, pp. 60–63.

8. For more discussion, see Frederick E. Webster, Jr., "The Changing Role of Marketing in the Corporation," *Journal of Marketing,* October 1992, pp. 1–17.

9. See Kevin J. Clancy and Robert S. Shulman, "Breaking the Mold," *Sales & Marketing Management,* pp. 82–84.

10. Frederick F. Reichheld and W. Earl Sasser, Jr., "Zero Defections: Quality Comes to Services," *Harvard Business Review,* September–October 1990, pp. 301–307.

11. Leonard L. Berry and A. Parasuraman, *Marketing Services: Competing Through Quality* (New York: The Free Press, 1991), pp. 136–142.

12. Aimee L. Stern, "Courting Consumer Loyalty with the Feel-Good Bond," *New York Times,* January 17, 1993, p. F10.

13. Edwin McDowell, "Ritz-Carlton's Keys to Good Service," *New York Times,* March 31, 1993, p. 1.

14. Andy Cohen, "It's Party Time for Saturn," *Sales & Marketing Management,* June 1994, p. 19.

15. David Greising, "Watch Out for Flying Packages," *Business Week,* November 14, 1994, p. 40.

16. See Michael J. Lanning and Lynn W. Phillips, "Strategy Shifts Up a Gear," *Marketing,* October 1991, p. 9.

17. See Thomas M. Petro, "Profitability: The Fifth 'P' of Marketing," *Bank Marketing,* September 1990, pp. 48–52.

18. Robert D. Buzzell and Bradley T. Gale, *The PIMS Principles: Linking Strategy to Performance* (New York: The Free Press, 1987), Chapter 6.

19. "Quality: The U.S. Drives to Catch Up," *Business Week,* November, 1982, pp. 66–80, here p. 68. For a recent assessment of progress, see "Quality Programs Show Shoddy Results," *Wall Street Journal,* May 14, 1992, p. B1.

20. See "The Gurus of Quality: American Companies Are Hearing the Quality Gospel Preached by Deming, Juran, Crosby, and Taguchi," *Traffic Management,* July 1990, pp. 35–39.

21. See David Greising, "Quality: How to Make It Pay," *Business Week,* August 8, 1994, pp. 54–59; and Cyndee Miller, "TQM Out; 'Continuous Process Improvement' In," *Marketing News,* May 9, 1994, pp. 5, 10.

22. J. Daniel Beckham, "Expect the Unexpected in Health Care Marketing Future," in *The Academy Bulletin,* July 1992, p. 3.

23. Kenneth Kivenko, *Quality Control for Management* (Englewood Cliffs, NJ: Prentice Hall, 1984). Also see Kate Bertrand, "Marketing Discovers What 'Quality' Really Means," *Business Marketing,* April 1987, pp. 58–72.

Company Case 18

OUTBACK STEAKHOUSE: BREAKING THE RULES

NEW RULES

Most people will include restaurants on their list of the toughest businesses in which to be successful. Thousands of restaurants compete for customers, ranging from giant chains to mom-and-pop, hole-in-the-wall eateries. Moreover, restaurant owners have tried everything. Catchy new ideas often spawn too-rapid growth or encourage imitators who steal customers.

Restaurant owners have learned from all the successes and failures, however, and certain rules for success have emerged. Find a good location, operate as many hours as possible to spread fixed costs, and keep food costs as low as possible. Control personnel costs.

Design a highly centralized management structure that leaves nothing to chance. Following these rules, so the conventional wisdom goes, increases chances for success.

Given this wisdom, it is surprising that *Inc.* magazine recently chose Outback Steakhouse's developers as the "Entrepreneurs of the Year." Outback seems to violate all the established rules. In fact, the chain uses the phrase, "No Rules. Just Right." in its advertising. One might characterize its strategy, however, as, "*New* Rules. Just Right."

MODEST AMBITIONS

When Chris Sullivan and Robert Basham began to toy with the idea of starting a restaurant, they knew the industry's conventional wisdom well. Over a 16-year period, they had learned the business by working with the Steak & Ale chain, guiding Bennigan's growth from 32 to 140 units, and opening 17 Chili's restaurants. In 1987, they had modest ambitions when they used their own resources to open five restaurants in the Tampa area. They believed these units, if successful, would support their lifestyles, leaving plenty of time for golf and boating.

Sullivan and Basham's research identified an opportunity in the steakhouse business. Despite consumers' widely publicized decisions to eat less red meat, both upscale steak houses and budget-priced chains, like Golden Corral, were doing well. Consumers still liked to splurge by eating good steaks, and they wanted to eat those steaks in casual restaurants, not at home. Sullivan and Basham saw an opening for a midrange steakhouse with a casual atmosphere that targeted adults aged 25 to 54.

The two founders realized, however, that they needed to beef up their management team. They knew restaurant operations and how to cut real estate deals, but they needed a "food guy." They found him in Tim Gannon, a friend who had been successful in the New Orleans restaurant business. Gannon brought with him a collection of great recipes that he could teach young chefs to prepare quickly.

Finally, they needed a name. The movie *Crocodile Dundee II* was popular at the time, and Australia had a mystique that implied a friendly, casual approach to life. The team settled on Outback because consumers could remember the name easily, and it suggested a rugged, outdoorsy quality that would give the chain a point of differentiation.

STRATEGIC DECISIONS

Having settled on the team, target market, concept, and name, the founders were ready to complete their strat-egy. First, they considered location. One major factor dictated location: Outback would offer only dinner—no breakfast, no lunch. This meant that Outback did not need to build in the high-rent, center-city areas needed to attract the business lunch crowd. Instead, Outback searched for sites in suburban locations where people were at night. Because Outback was a destination, it could occupy a *B* location in an *A* market.

The dinner-only decision also meant that employees had to work only one shift a day. Managers could come in at 3 P.M. and leave by midnight. Many other restaurants experienced rapid turnover of managers because of six- to seven-day weeks and sweatshop hours. Outback prohibited its managers from working more than five days a week. The founders wanted the managers to have fuller personal lives and not to destroy their marriages.

Waiters, waitresses, and bartenders liked the plan also because they depended on tips, and they typically earned little tip money at lunch. Outback servers handled only three tables at a time so they could provide excellent service. With tables that turned over in about an hour and an average $16 per person "ticket" including the bar tab, a server could earn up to $30 an hour in tips and $125 a night.

Serving only dinner also meant that cooks focused on just that meal. Tim Gannon observed that "when you're preparing food all day long, it diminishes the quality. When you have to prepare for only one shift, you can be flawless." Outback's limited menu also meant that it could focus on food quality. For example, the chain bought meat from only one supplier, and it demanded that the supplier purchase meat only from selected areas in Nebraska and Colorado. Gannon believed that these two areas produced the best steers. The chain used chicken that had never been frozen. It knew where to get the best onions, potatoes, and lettuce. Each restaurant made its own salad dressings, bread, and other items from scratch. This emphasis on food quality produced higher-than-average food costs of 39 percent versus 36 percent or less for most restaurants. However, Outback provided generous portions and maintained its philosophy of moderately priced entrees.

The managers designed the typical Outback to occupy about 6,000 square feet, with the roomy kitchen accounting for more than half the space. The restaurants had only 220 seats. If they had more, the managers reasoned, food requests could swamp the kitchen and negatively affect service. Outback's logistics meant that a server could deliver a properly cooked steak 12 minutes after the steak order reached the kitchen, just as other waitstaff picked up the salad plates.

Outback designed a restaurant management system that would make managers act like owners and enable decentralized control. Each restaurant's manager invested $25,000 and signed a 5-year contract. The manager earned a base salary of $45,000 plus 10 percent of the unit's cash flow, defined as earnings before taxes, interest, and depreciation/amortization. With the average unit serving 3,800 customers per week, reaping annual sales of $3.2 million, and generating cash flow of $736,000, the average Outback manager made $118,000 per year, well above industry averages. Thus, Outback's management turnover was only 5.4 percent versus 30 to 40 percent for the industry.

Being an owner also meant that managers were picky about whom they hired. Instead of hiring experienced cooks and waitstaff they had to train to be friendly, they focused on hiring 75 to 80 friendly people they could train. There was no corporate-level human-resources department. Corporate headquarters had only 55 people to oversee the 210 steak houses—only one management layer between manager and founders, versus an industry average of four to five layers.

Outback promoted its restaurants with extensive advertising on college campuses and at professional football, basketball, hockey, and golf events. The ads featured supermodel Rachael Hunter.

PAYING OFF

Conventional or not, Outback's strategy has paid off. In a recent survey, *Restaurants & Institutions* magazine gave Outback top honors for food quality and service. Outback also posted the strongest sales and unit growth rates for the casual steakhouse sector. The number-two player, Lone Star Steakhouse, had only 104 units and average unit sales of $2.6 million, even though it offered both lunch and dinner. The strategy has also paid off for investors, who have seen the stock price jump from $3.50 per share at the initial public offering in 1991 to $30 in 1994.

By the end of 1996, Outback wants to have 350 units and sales of almost $1 billion—not bad for three guys with modest ambitions.

QUESTIONS

1. Who are Outback's customers? Who are its other stakeholders?

2. Using the value-chain concept, analyze how Outback delivers value.

3. What factors account for Outback's profitability? What is the most important factor?

4. What risks does the Outback chain face? What recommendations would you make to help it deal with those risks?

Source: Adapted from Jay Finegan, "Unconventional Wisdom," *Inc.*, December 1994, pp. 44–54. Copyright 1994 by Goldhirsh Group, Inc. Used with permission.

Creating Competitive Advantage

COMPETITOR ANALYSIS AND COMPETITIVE MARKETING STRATEGIES

Federal Express almost single-handedly created the express-package delivery industry as we now know it. Founded in 1973, the company got off to a slow start—it took time to educate the American public about the value of overnight delivery. However, building doggedly on the advertising promise, "when it absolutely, positively *has* to be there on time," made possible by the company's innovative and now much-copied "hub-and-spoke" distribution system, FedEx went on to become one of the fastest start-ups in American history. After three years of losses, it grew explosively. At a compound growth rate of more than 40 percent per year, annual sales reached $1 billion by 1983, $5 billion by 1989, and almost $8 billion by 1993. And despite strong challenges from a glut of imitators over the years, Federal Express remains the undisputed market leader. It now commands a 45 percent U.S. market share, comfortably ahead of major challengers UPS at 25 percent, Airborne at 14 percent, and the U.S. Postal Service at about 8 percent.

Staying atop the overnight package delivery business will require a well-designed and well-executed competitive strategy. Although the market is large and growing, competition is torrid. Federal Express is now streetfighting with competitors on price, looking for ways to boost productivity in order to stay price competitive. But FedEx is not, and may never be, the lowest-priced express-delivery service. Federal Express traditionally has differentiated itself not by luring customers with low prices, but by giving them unbeatable reliability and service. Even in the face of cutthroat pricing by competitors, the company has been careful not to let cost-cutting undermine its main source of competitive advantage—superior quality.

At Federal Express, quality goes far beyond slogans and idle talk. In 1987, it established a formal Quality Improvement Process, which set simple yet lofty quality goals: 100 percent on-time deliveries, 100 percent accurate information on every shipment to every location in the world, and 100 percent customer satisfaction. A few years later, FedEx became the first service organization to receive the Malcolm Baldrige National Quality Award for outstanding quality leadership. It developed a Service Quality Index (SQI—pronounced "sky"), made up of twelve things that it knows disappoint customers—how many packages were late, how many were delivered on the wrong day, how many were damaged, how many billing corrections the company had to make, and other such mistakes. "Quality action teams" study SQI results daily, looking for trouble spots and ways to eliminate them. Even management bonuses are keyed to achieving SQI goals. Each year, the company invests more than $200 on each of its 96,000 employees in 185 countries for quality initiatives.

Federal Express believes that top-flight quality is well worth the heavy investment, even if it results in higher prices. In an industry where late delivery can spell disaster, most customers will gladly pay a little more for the added peace of mind that comes with unwavering reliability. Although raising service quality can be expensive, losses of customers resulting from poor quality can cost a great deal more. Federal Express's obsession with quality has paid big dividends. In recent years, despite a sluggish economy and the long-running price war, the company has experienced healthy growth.

In the early 1980s, flush with domestic success, Federal Express decided that the time had come to go global. It began to buy up foreign competitors, invested heavily to set up a European version of its venerable hub-and-spoke system, and prepared to launch a full frontal assault on Europe. In 1989, it capped its global network building with the acquisition of the legendary Flying Tigers, the world's largest carrier of heavyweight cargo. With this acquisition, it could now move freight of any size. By the early 1990s, Federal Express had become the world's largest express transportation company, with 441 aircraft and 30,000 pickup and delivery vans serving 173 countries. Its new global goal: to be able to deliver freight anywhere in a global network within just two days.

Despite its high hopes and heavy investment, however, the global effort turned out to be a disaster. Flying Tigers became an albatross, and although international sales doubled in only a year, earnings plummeted. After eight long years and losses of more than $1 billion, FedEx finally turned a modest profit on its international operations in 1994. What went wrong? For one thing, Federal Express appears to have overestimated the European market for overnight delivery, which stalled out at only 100,000 packages daily. For another, the company may have underestimated the competition. Whereas FedEx is the clear market leader in the United States, in Europe it is a challenger. To win in Europe, it had to take on a well-entrenched competitor, DHL, the world leader in international express delivery. FedEx's aggressive attack on international markets provoked an equally aggressive defense, not just from DHL, but also from UPS, Australian-based TNT, and other large international rivals. For example, DHL strengthened its international base by forging new relationships with Lufthansa and Japan Airlines. UPS invested heavily to beef up its global delivery network, expanding coverage to 175 countries. The result: too many competitors chasing too little business, driving down prices and profits for all.

In May 1992, Federal Express began a decisive retreat from its disastrous European campaign. It closed down operations in more than 100 countries, fired 6,600 employees, and contracted with other companies to handle its deliveries to all but 16 major European cities—such as London, Paris, and Milan—that it still serves directly. FedEx executives insist that the retreat doesn't mean surrender. The company still leads in the U.S. market, and it has retained a strong base for building more solid international operations. The European retrenchment simply signals a new, more cautious approach to international expansion. Despite its losses, Federal Express has learned from its international misfortune. Perhaps the most important lesson: A blockbuster competitive strategy that makes a company "lord of the skies" at home won't necessarily fly abroad.[1]

Competitive advantage
An advantage over competitors gained by offering consumers greater value, either through lower prices or by providing more benefits that justify higher prices.

Today, understanding customers is not enough. Under the marketing concept, companies gain **competitive advantage** by designing offers that satisfy target consumer needs *better than competitors' offers*. They might deliver more customer value by offering consumers lower prices for similar products and services, or by providing more benefits that justify higher prices. Thus, marketing strategies must consider not only the needs of target consumers, but also the strategies of competitors. The first step is **competitor analysis**, the process of identifying and assessing key competitors. The second step is developing **competitive marketing strategies** that strongly position the company against competitors and give it the greatest possible competitive advantage.

COMPETITOR ANALYSIS

Competitor analysis
The process of identifying key competitors; assessing their objectives, strategies, strengths and weaknesses, and reaction patterns; and selecting which competitors to attack or avoid.

Competitive marketing strategies
Strategies that strongly position the company against competitors and that give the company the strongest possible strategic advantage.

To plan effective competitive marketing strategies, the company needs to find out all it can about its competitors. It must constantly compare its products, prices, channels, and promotion with those of close competitors. In this way the company can find areas of potential competitive advantage and disadvantage. And it can launch more effective marketing campaigns against its competitors and prepare stronger defenses against competitors' actions.

But what do companies need to know about their competitors? They need to know: Who are our competitors? What are their objectives? What are their strategies? What are their strengths and weaknesses? What are their reaction patterns? Figure 19-1 shows the major steps in analyzing competitors.

IDENTIFYING THE COMPANY'S COMPETITORS

Normally, it would seem a simple task for a company to identify its competitors. Coca-Cola knows that Pepsi is its major competitor; and Caterpillar knows that it competes with Komatsu. At the narrowest level, a company can define its competitors as other companies offering a similar product and services to the same customers at similar prices. Thus, Buick might see Ford as a major competitor, but not Mercedes or Hyundai.

But companies actually face a much wider range of competitors. The company might define competitors as all firms making the same product or class of products. Thus, Buick would see itself as competing against all other automobile makers. Even more broadly, competitors might include all companies making products that supply the same service. Here Buick would see itself competing against not only other automobile makers, but also companies that make trucks, motorcycles, or even bicycles. Finally, and still more broadly, competitors might include all companies that compete for the same consumer dollars. Here Buick would see itself competing with companies that sell major consumer durables, new homes, or vacations abroad.

Companies must avoid "competitor myopia." A company is more likely to be "buried" by its latent competitors than its current ones. For example, Kodak, in its film business, has been worrying about the growing competition from Fuji, the Japanese film maker. But Kodak faces a much greater threat from the recent advances in "filmless camera" technology. These cameras, already sold by Canon and Sony, take video still pictures that can be shown on a

FIGURE 19-1 *Steps in analyzing competitors*

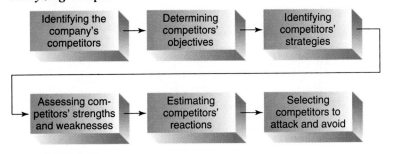

TV set, turned into hard copy, and later erased. What greater threat is there to a film business than a filmless camera?

Companies can identify their competitors from the *industry* point of view. They might see themselves as being in the oil industry, the pharmaceutical industry, or the beverage industry. A company must understand the competitive patterns in its industry if it hopes to be an effective "player" in that industry. Companies can also identify competitors from a *market* point of view. Here they define competitors as companies that are trying to satisfy the same customer need or serve the same customer group. From an industry point of view, Coca-Cola might see its competition as Pepsi, Dr Pepper, 7-Up, and other soft-drink manufacturers. From a market point of view, however, the customer really wants "thirst quenching." This need can be satisfied by iced tea, fruit juice, bottled water, or many other fluids. Similarly, Binney & Smith, maker of Crayola crayons, might define its competitors as other makers of crayons and children's drawing supplies. But from a market point of view, it would include all firms making recreational products for children. In general, the market concept of competition opens the company's eyes to a broader set of actual and potential competitors. This leads to better long-run market planning.

The key to identifying competitors is to link industry and market analysis by mapping out *product/market segments.* Figure 19-2 shows the product/market segments in the toothpaste market by product types and customer age groups. We see that P&G (with several versions of Crest and Gleem) and Colgate-Palmolive (with Colgate) occupy nine of the segments; Lever Brothers (Aim), three; and Beecham (Aqua Fresh) and Topol, two. If Topol wanted to enter other segments, it would need to estimate the market size of each segment, the market shares of the current competitors, and their current capabilities, objectives, and strategies. Clearly each product/market segment would pose different competitive problems and opportunities.

FIGURE 19-2
Product/market segments for toothpaste
Source: William A. Cohen, *Winning on the Marketing Front* (New York: John Wiley & Sons, 1986), p. 63.

DETERMINING COMPETITORS' OBJECTIVES

Having identified the main competitors, marketing management now asks: What does each competitor seek in the marketplace? What drives each competitor's behavior?

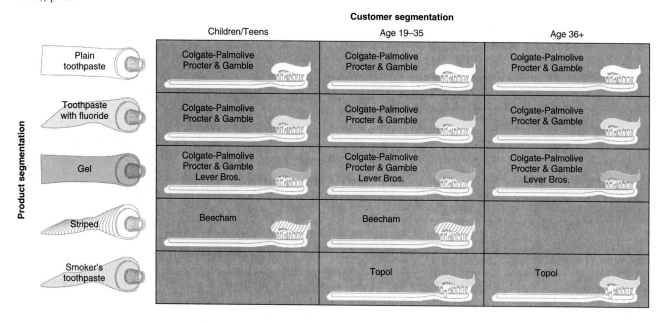

The marketer might at first assume that all competitors will want to maximize their profits and will choose their actions accordingly. But companies differ in the emphasis they put on short-term versus long-term profits. And some competitors might be oriented toward "satisfying" rather than "maximizing" profits. They have target profit goals and are satisfied in achieving them, even if more profits could have been produced by other strategies.

Thus, marketers must look beyond competitors' profit goals. Each competitor has a mix of objectives, each with differing importance. The company wants to know the relative importance that a competitor places on current profitability, market share growth, cash flow, technological leadership, service leadership, and other goals. Knowing a competitor's mix of objectives reveals whether the competitor is satisfied with its current situation and how it might react to different competitive actions. For example, a company that pursues low-cost leadership will react much more strongly to a competitor's cost-reducing manufacturing breakthrough than to the same competitor's advertising increase.

A company also must monitor its competitors' objectives for various product/market segments. If the company finds that a competitor has discovered a new segment, this might be an opportunity. If it finds that competitors plan new moves into segments now served by the company, it will be forewarned and, hopefully, forearmed.

IDENTIFYING COMPETITORS' STRATEGIES

Strategic group
A group of firms in an industry following the same or a similar strategy.

The more that one firm's strategy resembles another firm's strategy, the more the two firms compete. In most industries, the competitors can be sorted into groups that pursue different strategies. A **strategic group** is a group of firms in an industry following the same or a similar strategy in a given target market. For example, in the major appliance industry, General Electric, Whirlpool, and Maytag all belong to the same strategic group. Each produces a full line of medium-price appliances supported by good service. Sub Zero and KitchenAid, on the other hand, belong to a different strategic group. They produce a narrower line of higher quality appliances, offer a higher level of service, and charge a premium price.

Some important insights emerge from identifying strategic groups. For example, if a company enters one of the groups, the members of that group become its key competitors. Thus, if the company enters the first group against General Electric, Whirlpool, and Maytag, it can succeed only if it develops some strategic advantages over these competitors.

Although competition is most intense within a strategic group, there is also rivalry among groups. First, some of the strategic groups may appeal to overlapping customer segments. For example, no matter what their strategy, all major appliance manufacturers will go after the apartment and home-builders segment. Second, the customers may not see much difference in the offers of different groups—they may see little difference in quality between Whirlpool and KitchenAid. Finally, members of one strategic group might expand into new strategy segments. Thus, General Electric now offers a premium quality, premium price line to compete with KitchenAid and Sub Zero.

Expanding into a new strategy segment: General Electric offers a premium-quality, premium-price line of kitchen appliances.

The company needs to look at all of the dimensions that identify strategic groups within the industry. It needs to know each competitor's product quality, features, and

HOW BENCHMARKING HELPS IMPROVE COMPETITIVE PERFORMANCE

Benchmarking is the art of finding out how and why some companies perform tasks much better than others. The benchmarking company aims to imitate, or better yet, to improve on the best practices of other companies.

The Japanese used benchmarking extensively after World War II, copying many American products and practices. In 1979, Xerox undertook one of the first major U.S. benchmarking projects. It wanted to learn how Japanese competitors were able to produce more reliable copiers and charge prices below Xerox's production costs. By buying Japanese copiers and analyzing them through "reverse engineering," Xerox learned how to greatly improve its own copiers' reliability and costs. But Xerox didn't stop there. It went on to ask additional questions: Are Xerox scientists and engineers among the best in their respective specialties? Are Xerox marketing people and practices among the best in the world? To answer these questions, the company had to identify world-class, "best practices" companies and learn from them. Although benchmarking initially focused on studying other companies' products and services, it later expanded to include benchmarking work processes, staff functions, and the entire customer value delivery process.

Another early benchmarking pioneer was Ford. Ford was losing sales to Japanese and European car makers. Ford's CEO instructed his engineers and designers to build a new car that combined the 400 features that Ford customers said were the most important. If Saab made the best seats, then Ford should copy Saab's seats. If Toyota had the best fuel gauge and BMW had the best tire and jack storage system, then Ford should copy these features also. More than this, the CEO asked Ford's engineers to "better the best" where possible. When the new car—the highly successful Taurus—was finished, Ford claimed that it had improved on, not just copied, the best features found in competing cars.

In a later benchmarking project, Ford discovered that it employed 500 people to manage its accounts payable operation, whereas its partly owned Japanese partner, Mazda, handled the same task with only 10 people. After studying Mazda's system, Ford installed an "invoiceless system" and reduced its staff to 200.

Today many companies such as AT&T, IBM, Kodak, Du Pont, Intel, Marriott, and Motorola use benchmarking as a standard tool. Benchmarking usually goes beyond simply analyzing competitors. Motorola, for example, starts each benchmarking project with a search for "best of breed" in the world. According to one executive, "The further away from our industry we reach for comparisons, the happier we are. We are seeking competitive superiority, after all, not just competitive parity."

As an example of seeking "best of breed" practices, Xerox benchmarked L. L. Bean, the "outdoors" catalog company, to find out how L. L. Bean's warehouse workers managed to "pick and pack" items three times faster than Xerox. As a noncompetitor, L. L. Bean was happy to show off its practice, and Xerox ended up redesigning its warehouses and software system. On later occasions, Xerox benchmarked American Express for its billing expertise and Cummins Engine for its production scheduling expertise.

How can a company identify "best-practice" companies? As a good starting point, it can ask customers, suppliers, and distributors who they rate as doing the best job. Or it can contact consulting firms that have built large files of "best practices." An important point is that benchmarking can be done without resorting to industrial espionage.

Once a company commits to benchmarking, it may get carried away with trying to benchmark every activity. Yet benchmarking takes time and costs money. Companies should confine their benchmarking only to critical tasks that deeply affect customer satisfaction and company costs, and for which much better performers are known to exist. Some critics suggest that companies must be careful not to rely *too* much on benchmarking. They warn that because benchmarking takes other companies' performance as a starting

mix; customer services; pricing policy; distribution coverage; sales force strategy; and advertising and sales promotion programs. And it must study the details of each competitor's R&D, manufacturing, purchasing, financial, and other strategies.

ASSESSING COMPETITORS' STRENGTHS AND WEAKNESSES

Marketers need to carefully assess each competitor's strengths and weaknesses in order to answer the critical question: What *can* our competitors do? As a first step, companies can gather data on each competitor's goals, strategies, and per-

point, it might hamper real creativity. Or, too often, benchmarking studies take many months, and by that time, better practices may have emerged elsewhere. Benchmarking might cause the company to focus too much on competitors while losing touch with customers' changing needs. Finally, benchmarking might distract from making further improvements in the company's core competencies.

Nevertheless, a company must do more than simply look inside when trying to continuously improve its performance. To gain competitive advantage, it must compare its products and processes to those of its competitors and leading companies in other industries. Thus, benchmarking remains one of the most powerful tools for improving quality and competitive performance.

Sources: Robert C. Camp, *Benchmarking: The Search for Industry-Best Practices That Lead to Superior Performance* (White Plains, NY: Quality Resources, 1989); A. Steven Walleck, et al., "Benchmarking World Class Performance," McKinsey Quarterly, No. 1, 1990, pp. 3–24; Michael J. Spendolini, *The Benchmarking Book* (New York: AMACOM, 1992); Jeremy Main, "How to Steal the Best Ideas Around," Fortune, October 19, 1992; Betsy Weisendanger, "Benchmarking for Beginners," *Sales & Marketing Management,* November 1992, pp. 59–64; and Stanley Brown, "Don't Innovate—Imitate!" *Sales & Marketing Management,* January 1995, pp. 24–25.

When Ford redesigned Taurus, it benchmarked these features and more than 200 others against major competitors. Benchmarking helped Ford make Taurus the best-selling car in the world.

Benchmarking
The process of comparing the company's products and processes to those of competitors or leading firms in other industries to find ways to improve quality and performance.

formance over the last few years. Admittedly, some of this information will be hard to obtain. For example, business products companies find it hard to estimate competitors' market shares because they do not have the same syndicated data services that are available to consumer packaged-goods companies.

Companies normally learn about their competitors' strengths and weaknesses through secondary data, personal experience, and hearsay. They also can conduct primary marketing research with customers, suppliers, and dealers. Recently, a growing number of companies have turned to **benchmarking,** comparing the company's products and processes to those of competitors or leading firms in other industries to find ways to improve quality and performance. Benchmarking has become a powerful tool for increasing a company's competitiveness (see Marketing Highlight 19-1).

ESTIMATING COMPETITORS' REACTIONS

Next, the company wants to know: What *will* our competitors do? A competitor's objectives, strategies, and strengths and weaknesses go a long way toward explaining its likely actions, as well as its likely reactions to company moves such as price cuts, promotion increases, or new-product introductions. In addition, each competitor has a certain philosophy of doing business, a certain internal culture and guiding beliefs. Marketing managers need a deep understanding of a given competitor's mentality if they want to anticipate how the competitor will act or react.

Each competitor reacts differently. Some do not react quickly or strongly to a competitor's move. They may feel their customers are loyal; they may be slow in noticing the move; they may lack the funds to react. Some competitors react only to certain types of moves and not to others. They might always respond strongly to price cuts in order to signal that these will never succeed. But they might not respond at all to advertising increases, believing these to be less threatening. Other competitors react swiftly and strongly to any action. Thus, P&G does not let a new detergent come easily into the market. Many firms avoid direct competition with P&G and look for easier prey, knowing that P&G will react fiercely if challenged. Finally, some competitors show no predictable reaction pattern. They might or might not react on a given occasion, and there is no way to foresee what they will do based on their economics, history, or anything else.

In some industries, competitors live in relative harmony; in others, they fight constantly. Knowing how major competitors react gives the company clues on how best to attack competitors or how best to defend the company's current positions.[2]

SELECTING COMPETITORS TO ATTACK AND AVOID

A company has already largely selected its major competitors through prior decisions on customer targets, distribution channels, and marketing-mix strategy. These decisions define the strategic group to which the company belongs. Management now must decide which competitors to compete against most vigorously. The company can focus on one of several classes of competitors.

Strong or Weak Competitors

Most companies prefer to aim their shots at their weak competitors. This requires fewer resources and less time. But in the process, the firm may gain little. The argument could be made that the firm also should compete with strong competitors in order to sharpen its abilities. Furthermore, even strong competitors have some weaknesses, and succeeding against them often provides greater returns.

Customer value analysis
Analysis conducted to determine what benefits target customers value and how they rate the relative value of various competitors' offers.

A useful tool for assessing competitor strengths and weaknesses is **customer value analysis.** The aim of customer value analysis is to determine the benefits that target customers value and how customers rate the relative value of various competitors' offers. In conducting a customer value analysis, the company first identifies the major attributes that customers value and the importance customers place on these attributes. Next, it assesses the company's and competitors' performance on the valued attributes. The key to gaining competitive advantage is to take each customer segment and examine how the company's offer compares to that of its major competitor. If the company's offer exceeds the competitor's offer on all important attributes, the company can charge a higher price and earn higher profits, or it can charge the same price and gain more market share. But if the company is seen as performing at a lower level than its major competitor on some important attributes, it must invest in strengthening those attributes or finding other important attributes where it can build a lead on the competitor.

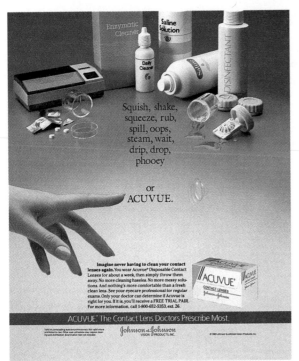

Squish, shake,
squeeze, rub,
spill, oops,
steam, wait,
drip, drop,
phooey

or
ACUVUE.

*After driving smaller
competitors from the
market, Bausch & Lomb
faced larger, more
resourceful ones, such as
Johnson & Johnson's
Vistakon division.
Vistakon's Acuvue
disposable lenses forced
Bausch & Lomb to take
some of its own medicine.*

Close or Distant Competitors

Most companies will compete with competitors who resemble them most. Thus, Chevrolet competes more against Ford than against Jaguar. At the same time, the company may want to avoid trying to "destroy" a close competitor. For example, in the late 1970s, Bausch & Lomb moved aggressively against other soft lens manufacturers with great success. However, the conquests turned out to be questionable victories. One after another, competitors were forced to sell out to larger firms such as Revlon, Schering-Plough, and Johnson & Johnson. As a result, Bausch & Lomb now faced much larger competitors—and it suffered the consequences.

For example, Johnson & Johnson acquired Vistakon, a small nicher with only $20 million in annual sales, which served the tiny portion of the contact-lens market for people with astigmatism. Backed by J&J's deep pockets, however, Vistakon proved a formidable opponent. When the small but nimble Vistakon unit introduced its innovative Acuvue disposable lenses, the much larger Bausch & Lomb was forced to take some of its own medicine. According to one analyst, "The speed of the [Acuvue] rollout and the novelty of [J&J's] big-budget ads left giant Bausch & Lomb . . . seeing stars." By 1992, J&J's Vistakon was No. 1 in the fast-growing disposable segment and had captured about 25 percent of the entire U.S. contact-lens market.[3] In this case, success in hurting a close rival brought in tougher competitors.

"Well-Behaved" or "Disruptive" Competitors

A company really needs and benefits from competitors. The existence of competitors results in several strategic benefits. Competitors may help increase total demand. They may share the costs of market and product development and help to legitimize new technologies. They may serve less attractive segments or lead to more product differentiation. Finally, they lower the antitrust risk and improve bargaining power versus labor or regulators.

However, a company may not view all of its competitors as beneficial. An industry often contains "well-behaved" competitors and "disruptive" competitors.[4] Well-behaved competitors play by the rules of the industry. They favor a stable and healthy industry, set reasonable prices in relation to costs, motivate others to lower costs or improve differentiation, and accept reasonable levels of market share and profits. Disruptive competitors, on the other hand, break the rules. They try to buy share rather than earn it, take large risks, and in general shake up the industry. For example, American Airlines finds Delta and United to be well-behaved competitors because they play by the rules and attempt to set their fares sensibly. But American finds TWA, Continental, and America West disruptive competitors because they destabilize the airline industry through continual heavy price discounting and wild promotional schemes. A company might be smart to support well-behaved competitors, aiming its attacks at disruptive competitors. Thus, some analysts claim that American's huge fare discounts during the summer of 1992 were intentionally designed to teach the disruptive airlines a lesson or to drive them out of business altogether.[5]

The implication is that "well-behaved" companies would like to shape an industry that consists of only well-behaved competitors. Through careful licensing, selective retaliation, and coalitions, they can shape the industry so that the competitors behave rationally and harmoniously, follow the rules, try to earn share rather than buy it, and differentiate to compete less directly.

DESIGNING A COMPETITIVE INTELLIGENCE SYSTEM

We have described the main types of information that companies need about their competitors. This information must be collected, interpreted, distributed, and used. The cost in money and time of gathering competitive intelligence is high, and the company must design its competitive intelligence system in a cost-effective way.

The competitive intelligence system first identifies the vital types of competitive information and the best sources of this information. Then, the system continuously collects information from the field (sales force, channels, suppliers, market research firms, trade associations) and from published data (government publications, speeches, articles). Next the system checks the information for validity and reliability, interprets it, and organizes it in an appropriate way. Finally, it sends key information to relevant decision makers and responds to inquiries from managers about competitors.

With this system, company managers will receive timely information about competitors in the form of phone calls, bulletins, newsletters, and reports. In addition, managers can connect with the system when they need an interpretation of a competitor's sudden move, or when they want to know a competitor's weaknesses and strengths, or when they need to know how a competitor will respond to a planned company move.

Smaller companies that cannot afford to set up formal competitive intelligence offices can assign specific executives to watch specific competitors. Thus, a manager who used to work for a competitor might follow that competitor closely; he or she would be the "in-house expert" on that competitor. Any manager needing to know the thinking of a given competitor could contact the assigned in-house expert.[6]

COMPETITIVE STRATEGIES

Having identified and evaluated its major competitors, the company now must design broad competitive marketing strategies that will best position its offer against competitors' offers and give the company the strongest possible competitive advantage. But what broad marketing strategies might the company use? Which ones are best for a particular company, or for the company's different divisions and products?

No one strategy is best for all companies. Each company must determine what makes the most sense given its position in the industry and its objectives, opportunities, and resources. Even within a company, different strategies may be required for different businesses or products. Johnson & Johnson uses one marketing strategy for its leading brands in stable consumer markets and a different marketing strategy for its new high-tech health-care businesses and products. We now look at broad competitive marketing strategies companies can use.

BASIC COMPETITIVE STRATEGIES

More than a decade ago, Michael Porter suggested four basic competitive positioning strategies that companies can follow—three winning strategies and one losing one.[7] The three winning strategies include:

◆ *Overall cost leadership.* Here the company works hard to achieve the lowest costs of production and distribution so that it can price lower than its competitors and win a large market share. Texas Instruments and Wal-Mart are leading practitioners of this strategy.

◆ *Differentiation.* Here the company concentrates on creating a highly differentiated product line and marketing program so that it comes across as the class leader in the industry. Most customers would prefer to own this brand if its price is not too high. IBM and Caterpillar follow this strategy in computers and heavy construction equipment, respectively.

◆ *Focus.* Here the company focuses its effort on serving a few market segments well rather than going after the whole market. Thus, glass-maker AFG Industries focuses on users of tempered and colored glass—it makes 70 percent of the glass for microwave oven doors and 75 percent of the glass for shower doors and patio table tops. And U.S. Surgical focuses on making instruments for laparoscopic surgery—surgery by inserting a tiny TV camera into the body along with slim, long-handled surgical instruments. U.S. Surgical captures an 80 percent share of this market.[8]

Companies that pursue a clear strategy—one of the above—are likely to perform well. The firm that carries out that strategy best will make the most profits. But firms that do not pursue a clear strategy—*middle-of-the-roaders*—do the worst. Sears, Chrysler, and International Harvester all encountered difficult times because they did not stand out as the lowest in cost, highest in perceived value, or best in serving some market segment. Middle-of-the-roaders try to be good on all strategic counts, but end up being not very good at anything.

More recently, two marketing consultants, Michael Treacy and Fred Wiersema, offered a new classification of competitive marketing strategies.[9] They suggest that companies gain leadership positions by delivering superior value to their customers. Companies can pursue any of three strategies—called *value disciplines*—for delivering superior customer value. These are:

◆ *Operational excellence:* The company provides superior value by leading its industry in price and convenience. It works to reduce costs and to create a lean and efficient value delivery system. It serves customers who want reliable, good quality products or services, but who want them cheaply and easily. Examples include Wal-Mart and Dell Computer.

◆ *Customer intimacy:* The company provides superior value by precisely segmenting its markets and then tailoring its products or services to match exactly the needs of targeted customers. It builds detailed customer databases for segmenting and targeting, and empowers its marketing people to respond quickly to customer needs. It serves customers who are willing to pay a premium to get precisely what they want, and it will do almost anything to build long-term customer loyalty and to capture customer lifetime value. Examples include Nordstrom department stores, Land's End outfitters, and Kraft Foods (see Marketing Highlight 19-2).

◆ *Product leadership:* The company provides superior value by offering a continuous stream of leading-edge products or services that make their own and competing products obsolete. It is open to new ideas, relentlessly pursues new solutions, and works to reduce cycle times so that it can get new products to market quickly. It serves customers who want state-of-the-art products and services, regardless of the costs in terms of price or inconvenience. Examples include Intel and Motorola.

Product leadership: Motorola provides superior value through a continuous stream of leading-edge products. It developed the first wireless two-way radio (walkie-talkie) during World War II and now leads the world market with innovative cellular phones.

Daddy fought in the war.

The Motorola MicroTAC Ultra Lite™ comes from a long line of heroes. Like the original SCR 536 hand-held wireless radio, which cut our boys loose from the wires of war. Lives depended on us then. Busy lives depend on us now. Motorola. The best-selling, most-preferred cellular phones in the world.

Ⓜ **MOTOROLA**

KRAFT FOODS: IN PURSUIT OF CUSTOMER INTIMACY

An investigation of your pantry or refrigerator will likely unearth a dozen or more Kraft Foods products. Well-known Kraft brands such as Miracle Whip, Kool-Aid, Jell-O, Maxwell House, Log Cabin, Velveeta, Cracker Barrel, Philadelphia, and Oscar Mayer have become household words to most of us. Not surprisingly, Kraft Foods pursues a strategy of customer intimacy. It gets to know its customers well, segments and targets its markets precisely, and tailors its products and merchandising programs closely to match the needs of targeted customers.

At the heart of Kraft's customer-intimacy strategy is an extensive, centralized customer information system, which keeps track of the whos, whats, and hows of customer buying. The information system consists of three databases. The first database contains customer-purchase information collected from individual stores, broken out by store, category, and product. It also shows how purchases are affected by displays, price promotions, and other merchandising factors. A second data base, supplied by an outside research firm, contains geo-demographic data by zip code. The final and most extensive database contains demographic and purchasing information on more than 30 million Kraft customers who have supplied their names when sending in coupons or responding to some other Kraft promotion.

Kraft's marketers use this information to create carefully tailored and targeted marketing offers. They develop direct marketing programs—clubs, newsletters, premium offers, and coupon mailings—to increase customer purchasing and loyalty. For example, based on the interests they express in surveys, Kraft customers receive regular tips on such topics as exercise and nutrition, along with recipes and coupons for specific brands. Kraft also uses its information system to shape individual retail store assortments and merchandising programs.

Like most other customer-intimate companies, Kraft has decentralized its marketing organization, empowering its marketers and salespeople with the information, authority, and merchandising tools required to meet customer needs in specific segments.

[Kraft] has created the capacity to tailor its advertising, merchandising, and operations in a single store, or in several stores within a supermarket chain, to the needs of those stores' particular customers. Kraft has the information systems, analytical capability, and educated sales force to allow it to develop as many different so-called micro-merchandising programs for a chain . . . as the chain has stores. The program can be different for every neighborhood outlet. . . . Instead of pushing one-size-fits-all sales promotion programs, Kraft salespeople now work with individual store managers and regional managers to create customized promotional programs from an extensive computerized menu of program models.

At . . . headquarters, [Kraft's] trade marketing team sorts and integrates the information from [its] databases and uses the results to supply sales teams with [an assortment] of usable programs, products, value-added ideas, and selling tools. For instance, the . . . team sorted all shoppers into six distinct groups, with names such as full-margin shoppers, planners and dine-outs, and commodity shoppers. Kraft then determined for its major accounts which shopper groups frequented each of their stores. A Kraft sales team even persuaded one chain to create a drive-through window in stores where planners and dine-outs—people who plan their shopping trips and dine out often—were a large segment, making it more convenient for them to pick up staples between big shopping trips.

Kraft is also able to develop promotion packages for store clusters for special events like the Superbowl. It can design a product mix more likely to succeed in one cluster than another. Pinpointing which store gets which products reduces inventory and delivers the right product to the right place at the right time.

Thus, in pursuit of customer intimacy, Kraft Foods delivers superior customer value by first acquiring a detailed understanding of customer needs in precisely defined segments, and then developing a flexible and responsive organization that closely meets those needs.

Sources: Excerpts from Michael Treacy and Fred Wiersema, "Customer Intimacy and Other Value Disciplines," *Harvard Business Review*, January–February 1993, pp. 84–93. Copyright © 1993 by the President and Fellows of Harvard College; all rights reserved. Also see Scott A. Spry, "Customer-Based Marketing and Packaged Goods," *DM News*, July 12, 1993, p. 30; Jonathan Berry, "Database Marketing," *Business Week*, September 5, 1994, pp. 56–67; and Julie Liesse, "Kraft Retires General in Reorganization," *Advertising Age*, January 9, 1995, p. 4.

Some companies successfully pursue more than one value discipline at the same time. For example, Federal Express excels at both operational excellence and customer intimacy. However, such companies are rare—few firms can be the best at more than one of these disciplines. By trying to be *good at all* of the value disciplines, a company usually ends up being *best at none*.

Treacy and Wiersema have found that leading companies focus on and excel at a single value discipline, while meeting industry standards on the other two. They design their entire value delivery system to single-mindedly support the chosen discipline. For example, Wal-Mart knows that customer intimacy and product leadership are important. Compared with other discounters, it offers very good customer service and an excellent product assortment. Still, it offers less customer service and less depth in its product assortment than specialty and department stores that pursue customer intimacy or product leadership strategies. Instead, it focuses obsessively on operational excellence—on reducing costs and streamlining its order-to-delivery process in order to make it convenient for customers to buy just the right products at the lowest prices.

Classifying competitive strategies as value disciplines is appealing. It defines marketing strategy in terms of the single-minded pursuit of delivering value to customers. It recognizes that management must align every aspect of the company with the chosen value discipline—from its culture, to its organization structure, to its operating and management systems and processes.

COMPETITIVE POSITIONS

Firms competing in a given target market will, at any point in time, differ in their objectives and resources. Some firms will be large, others small. Some will have many resources, others will be strapped for funds. Some will be old and established, others new and fresh. Some will strive for rapid market share growth, others for long-term profits. And the firms will occupy different competitive positions in the target market.

We will adopt a classification of competitive strategies based on the roles firms play in the target market—that of leading, challenging, following, or niching. Suppose that an industry contains the firms shown in Figure 19-3. Forty percent of the market is in the hands of the **market leader,** the firm with the largest market share. Another 30 percent is in the hands of a **market challenger,** a runner-up that is fighting hard to increase its market share. Another 20 percent is in the hands of a **market follower,** another runner-up that wants to hold its share without rocking the boat. The remaining 10 percent is in the hands of **market nichers,** firms that serve small segments not being pursued by other firms.

We now look at specific marketing strategies that are available to market leaders, challengers, followers, and nichers. You should remember, however, that these classifications often do not apply to a whole company, but only to its position in a specific industry. For example, large and diversified companies such as IBM, Sears, or Procter & Gamble might be leaders in some markets and nichers in others. For example, Procter & Gamble leads in many segments, such as dishwashing and laundry detergents, disposable diapers, and shampoo, but it challenges Lever in the hand soaps. Such companies often use different strategies for different business units or products, depending on the competitive situations of each.

Market leader
The firm in an industry with the largest market share; it usually leads other firms in price changes, new product introductions, distribution coverage, and promotion spending.

Market challenger
A runner-up firm in an industry that is fighting hard to increase its market share.

Market follower
A runner-up firm in an industry that wants to hold its share without rocking the boat.

Market nicher
A firm in an industry that serves small segments that the other firms overlook or ignore.

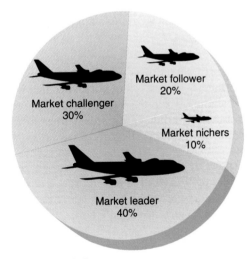

FIGURE 19-3
Hypothetical market structure

MARKET-LEADER STRATEGIES

Most industries contain an acknowledged market leader. The leader has the largest market share and usually leads the other firms in price changes, new product introductions, distribution coverage, and promotion spending. The leader may or may not be admired or respected, but other firms concede its dominance. Competitors focus on the leader as a company to challenge, imitate, or avoid. Some of the best-known market leaders are General Motors (autos), Kodak (photography), IBM (computers), Caterpillar (earth-moving equipment), Coca-Cola (soft drinks),

Campbell's (soups), Wal-Mart (retailing), McDonald's (fast food), and Gillette (razors and blades).

A leader's life is not easy. It must maintain a constant watch. Other firms keep challenging its strengths or trying to take advantage of its weaknesses. The market leader can easily miss a turn in the market and plunge into second or third place. A product innovation may come along and hurt the leader (as when Tylenol's nonaspirin painkiller took the lead from Bayer Aspirin). Or the leading firm might grow fat and slow, losing out against new and peppier rivals (Xerox's share of the world copier market fell from over 80 percent to less than 35 percent in just five years when Japanese producers challenged with cheaper and more reliable copiers).

To remain number one, leading firms can take any of three actions. First, they can find ways to expand total demand. Second, they can protect their current market share through good defensive and offensive actions. Third, they can try to expand their market share further, even if market size remains constant.

Expanding the Total Market

The leading firm normally gains the most when the total market expands. If Americans take more pictures, Kodak stands to gain the most because it sells more than 80 percent of this country's film. If Kodak can convince more Americans to take pictures, or to take pictures on more occasions, or to take more pictures on each occasion, it will benefit greatly. In general, the market leader should look for new users, new uses, and more usage of its products.

NEW USERS. Every product class can attract buyers who are still unaware of the product, or who are resisting it because of its price or its lack of certain features. A seller usually can find new users in many places. For example, Revlon might find new perfume users in its current markets by convincing women who do not use perfume to try it. It might find users in new demographic segments, such as by producing cologne for men. Or it might expand into new geographic segments, perhaps by selling its perfume in other countries.

Johnson's Baby Shampoo provides a classic example of developing new users. When the baby boom had passed and the birth rate slowed down, the company grew concerned about future sales growth. But J&J's marketers noticed that other family members sometimes used the baby shampoo for their own hair. Management developed an advertising campaign aimed at adults. In a short time, Johnson's Baby Shampoo became a leading brand in the total shampoo market.

NEW USES. The marketer can expand markets by discovering and promoting new uses for the product. For example, the makers of WD-40, the multipurpose household lubricant and solvent, sponsors an annual contest to discover new uses (see Marketing Highlight 19-3). Du Pont's nylon provides a classic example of new-use expansion. Every time nylon became a mature product, some new use was discovered. Nylon was first used as a fiber for parachutes; then for women's stockings; later as a major material in shirts and blouses; and still later in automobile tires, upholstery, and carpeting. Another example of new-use expansion is Arm & Hammer baking soda. Its sales had flattened after 125 years. Then the company discovered that consumers were using baking soda as a refrigerator deodorizer. It launched a heavy advertising and publicity campaign focusing on this use and persuaded consumers in half of America's homes to place an open box of baking soda in their refrigerators and to replace it every few months.

MORE USAGE. A third market expansion strategy is to convince people to use the product more often or to use more per occasion. Campbell encourages people

WD-40: SLICK WAYS TO CREATE NEW USES

Along with duct tape and the trusty hammer, WD-40 has become one of the truly essential survival items in most American homes. Originally developed in 1953 to prevent rust and corrosion on Atlas missiles, it takes its name from the 40th and final attempt at creating a *water displacement* formula. Over the past 40 years, WD-40 has achieved a kind of "cult" status and is now found in more than 80 percent of American households.

The WD-40 Company has shown a real knack for expanding the market by finding new uses for its popular substance. Many new ideas come from current users, who enter the company's annual contests. Winners of last year's "Invent Your Own Use" contest received cash prizes and many had their ideas featured in the company's "There's Always Another Use" advertising campaign.

Some entrants suggest simple and practical uses. This year's winning entry came from a teacher who used WD-40 to clean old chalk boards in her classroom. "Amazingly, the boards started coming to life again," she reports. "Not only were they restored, but years of masking and scotch tape residue came off as well." Other entrants report some pretty unusual uses. First place last year went to a California woman whose parakeet, "Cookie," fell off her shoulder and landed on sticky mouse-trap paper. When she tried to free the bird, she got both her hands stuck. The vet used good old WD-40 to free both victims. Still other reported uses seem highly improbable—one entrant claims that after spraying his Frisbee with WD-40, it flew out of sight, never to be seen again.

By now, almost everyone has discovered that WD-40 comes in handy for lubricating machinery, protecting tools from rust, loosening nuts and bolts, quieting squeaky hinges, and freeing stuck doors, drawers, windows, and zippers. And many fans know that you can use WD-40 to remove sticky-back labels from glassware, plastic, and metal items; bubble gum from hair and carpets; scuff marks from vinyl floors; and crayon marks from just about anywhere. Whether it be crayon or bubble gum on walls or in hair, WD-40 is a lifesaver for the parents of precocious mess-makers. For example, when one user's two-year-old daughter took crayons in hand to create a colorful rainbow on the living room wall, a few squirts of WD-40 took care of the problem.

Such common uses make good sense, but did you hear about the nude burglary suspect who had wedged himself in a vent at a café in Denver? The fire department extracted him with a large dose of WD-40. Or how about the Mississippi naval officer who used WD-40 to repel an angry bear? Then there's the college student who wrote to say that a friend's nightly amorous activities in the next room were causing everyone in his dorm to lose sleep—he solved the problem by treating the squeaky bedsprings with WD-40.

Others report using WD-40 to clean paint brushes, renew old printer and typewriter ribbons, keep snow from sticking to snow shovels, and clean hard water stains and soap scum off shower doors and bathroom tiles. One inventive cemetery grounds keeper even uses WD-40 to clean and polish headstones. Many fishermen report that spraying a little WD-40 on bait helps them catch more fish. Some recreational users claim that spraying their golf clubs, golf balls, or bowling balls has greatly improved their games.

WD-40 has been used to unstick just about everything, including a repairman's finger from a toilet fitting, a little boy's head from his potty training seat, and a cow's head from a fence. Reports the farmer, "We just sprayed a little WD-40 on his head, and he slipped right out. . . ." Ranchers and race horse trainers say they use WD-40 to untangle manes and tails and to repel mud from hooves. And then there's the Florida man who found an entirely different way to use the product. When modern-day pirates boarded his boat, he hit one of the would-be hijackers over the head with a can of WD-40, which knocked him off the boat and saved the day.

Source: Numerous WD-40 Company press releases created by Phillips-Ramsey Advertising & Public Relations, San Diego, California. Also see John Hahn, "A Little Squirt Comes to the Rescue," *The Seattle Post-Intelligencer,* September 2, 1994, p. C2.

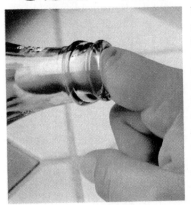

USE #722

WD-40® gets kid out of sticky situation. *A relieved mom (and daughter) from Washington state discovered that WD-40 is as good on stuck fingers as it is on stuck drawers. It's great for lubricating sliding glass doors, windows and anything else that sticks or squeaks.*

WD-40. THERE'S ALWAYS ANOTHER USE.

WD-40 Company has shown a real knack for expanding the market by finding new uses.

to eat soup more often by running ads containing new recipes in *Better Homes and Gardens* and other home magazines. Procter & Gamble advises users that its Head and Shoulders shampoo is more effective with two applications instead of one per shampoo.

Years ago, the Michelin Tire Company found a creative way to increase usage per occasion. It wanted French car owners to drive more miles per year, resulting in more tire replacement. Michelin began rating French restaurants on a three-star system. It reported that many of the best restaurants were in the south of France, leading many Parisians to take weekend drives south. Michelin also published guidebooks with maps and sights along the way to encourage additional travel.

Protecting Market Share

While trying to expand total market size, the leading firm also must constantly protect its current business against competitors' attacks. Coca-Cola must constantly guard against Pepsi-Cola; Gillette against Bic; Kodak against Fuji; McDonald's against Wendy's; General Motors against Ford.

What can the market leader do to protect its position? First, it must prevent or fix weaknesses that provide opportunities for competitors. It needs to keep its costs down and its prices in line with the value the customers see in the brand. The leader should "plug holes" so that competitors do not jump in. But the best defense is a good offense, and the best response is *continuous innovation*. The leader refuses to be content with the way things are and leads the industry in new products, customer services, distribution effectiveness, and cost cutting. It keeps increasing its competitive effectiveness and value to customers. It takes the offensive, sets the pace, and exploits competitors' weaknesses.

Figure 19-4 shows six defense strategies that a market leader can use.[10] The most basic defense is a *position defense* in which a company builds fortifications around its current position. But simply defending a current position or product rarely works. Even lasting brands such as Coca-Cola and Bayer Aspirin must be continuously improved and adapted to meet changing conditions, and new brands must be developed. For example, despite its dominating 40 percent share of the U.S. soft drink market, Coca-Cola is aggressively extending its beverage lines and has diversified into desalinization equipment and plastics.

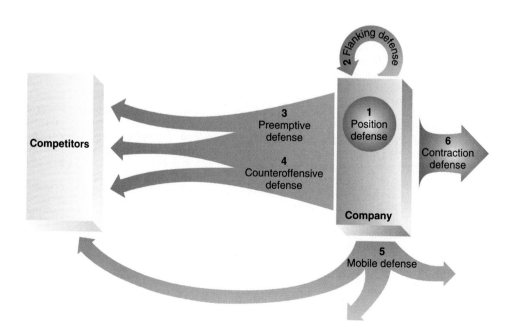

FIGURE 19-4 *Defense strategies*

Smart competitors normally will attack the leader's weaknesses. Thus, the Japanese successfully entered the small car market because U.S. auto makers left a gaping hole in that submarket. Using a *flanking defense,* the company carefully checks its flanks and protects the weaker ones. By contrast, the leader can launch a more aggressive *preemptive defense,* striking competitors before they can move against the company. Thus, when threatened in the mid-1980s by the impending entry of Japanese manufacturers into the U.S. market, Cummins Engine slashed its prices by almost a third to save its number-one position in the $2 billion heavy-duty truck engine market. Today, Cummins claims a commanding 50 percent market share in North America, and not a single U.S.-built tractor-trailer truck contains a Japanese engine.[11]

When a market leader is attacked despite its flanking or preemptive efforts, it can launch a *counteroffensive defense.* When Fuji attacked Kodak in the U.S. film market, Kodak counterattacked by greatly increasing its promotion and introducing several innovative new film products. And when attacked by Clorox's detergent with bleach, P&G responded with Tide With Bleach, which drove the Clorox brand from the market and captured a 17 percent share of all U.S. detergent sales.[12]

A *mobile defense* involves more than aggressively defending a current market position. The leader stretches to new markets that can serve as future bases for defense and offense. For example, Armstrong Cork redefined its focus from "floor covering" to "decorative room covering" (including walls and ceilings) and expanded into related businesses that were balanced for growth and defense. Similarly, Wal-Mart is currently muscling its way into the grocery business with new Wal-Mart Supercenters—huge combination grocery and discount stores.

Finally, if a large company finds that its resources are spread too thin and competitors are nibbling away on several fronts, the best action might be a *contraction defense.* For example, in recent years, ITT, Georgia Pacific, and General Mills have pruned their portfolios to concentrate resources. These companies now serve fewer markets, but serve them much better.

Expanding Market Share

Market leaders also can grow by increasing their market shares further. In many markets, small market share increases mean very large sales increases. For example, in the coffee market, a one-percent increase in market share is worth $48 million; in soft drinks, $490 million!

Studies have shown that, on average, profitability rises with increasing market share.[13] Because of these findings, many companies have sought expanded market shares to improve profitability. General Electric, for example, declared that it wants to be at least number one or two in each of its markets or else get out. GE shed its computer, air-conditioning, small appliances, and television businesses because it could not achieve top-dog position in these industries.

However, some studies have found that many industries contain one or a few highly profitable large firms, several profitable and more focused firms, and a large number of medium-sized firms with poorer profit performance. It appears that profitability increases as a business gains share relative to competitors in its *served market.* For example, Mercedes holds only a small share of the total car market, but it earns high profit because it is a high-share company in its luxury car segment. And it has achieved this high share in its served market because it does other things right, such as producing high quality, giving good service, and holding down its costs.

Companies must not think, however, that gaining increased market share will improve profitability automatically. Much depends on their strategy for gaining increased share. There are many high-share companies with low profitability and many low-share companies with high profitability. The cost of buying higher market share may far exceed the returns. Higher shares tend to produce higher profits only when unit costs fall with increased market share, or when the company offers a superior-quality product and charges a premium price that more than covers the cost of offering higher quality.

MARKET-CHALLENGER STRATEGIES

Firms that are second, third, or lower in an industry are sometimes quite large, such as Colgate, Ford, Kmart, Avis, Westinghouse, and PepsiCo. These runner-up firms can adopt one of two competitive strategies. They can challenge the leader and other competitors in an aggressive bid for more market share (market challengers). Or they can play along with competitors and not rock the boat (market followers). We now look at competitive strategies for market challengers.

Defining the Strategic Objective and the Competitor

A market challenger must first define its strategic objective. Most market challengers seek to increase their profitability by increasing their market shares. But the strategic objective chosen depends on which competitors the company will challenge.

The challenger can attack the market leader, a high-risk but potentially high-gain strategy that makes good sense if the leader is not serving the market well. To succeed with such an attack, a company must have some sustainable competitive advantage over the leader—a cost advantage leading to lower prices or the ability to provide better value at a premium price. In the construction equipment industry, Komatsu successfully challenged Caterpillar by offering the same quality at much lower prices. And Kimberly Clark's Huggies grabbed a big share of the disposable diaper market from P&G by offering a better-fitting diaper with reusable fasteners. If the company goes after the market leader, its objective may be to wrest a certain market share. Bic knows that it can't topple Gillette in the razor market—it simply wants a larger share. Or the challenger's goal might be to take over market leadership. IBM entered the personal computer market late, as a challenger, but quickly became the market leader.

The challenger can avoid the leader and instead challenge firms its own size, or smaller local and regional firms. These smaller firms may be underfinanced and not serving their customers well. Several of the major beer companies grew to their present size not by challenging large competitors, but by gobbling up small local or regional competitors. If the company goes after a small local company, its objective may be to put that company out of business. The important point remains: The challenger must choose its opponents carefully and have a clearly defined and attainable objective.

Market challenger Nissan attacks more expensive competitors, claiming that the Nissan Altima can do what a $40,000 car can do. Properly equipped, the Altima can "out-slalom an Acura Legend L Sedan," "out-brake a BMW 325si," and "provide more freeway power than a Mercedes-Benz 190E 2.3."

Choosing an Attack Strategy

How can the market challenger best attack the chosen competitor and achieve its strategic objectives? Figure 19-5 shows five possible attack strategies. In a full *frontal attack,* the challenger matches the competitor's product, advertising, price, and distribution efforts. It attacks the competitor's strengths rather than its weaknesses. The outcome depends on who has the greater strength and endurance. If the market chal-

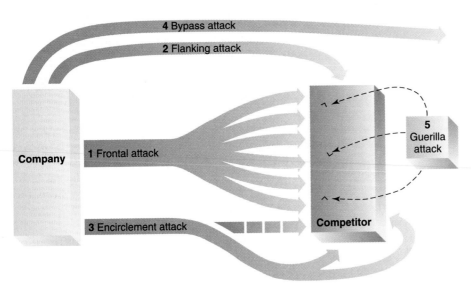

FIGURE 19-5 *Attack strategies*

lenger has fewer resources than the competitor, a frontal attack makes little sense.

Even great size and strength may not be enough to challenge a firmly entrenched, resourceful competitor successfully. For example, Unilever has twice the worldwide sales of Procter & Gamble and five times the sales of Colgate-Palmolive. Yet its American subsidiary, Lever Brothers, trails P&G in the United States. A while back, Lever launched a full frontal assault against P&G in the detergent market. Lever's Wisk was already the leading liquid detergent. In quick succession, it added a barrage of new products—Sunlight dishwashing detergent, Snuggle fabric softener, Surf laundry powder—and backed them with aggressive promotion and distribution efforts. But P&G spent heavily to defend its brands and held on to most of its business. And it counterattacked with Liquid Tide, which came from nowhere in just 17 months to run neck-and-neck with Wisk. Lever did gain market share, but most of it came from smaller competitors.[14]

Rather than attacking head on, the challenger can launch a *flanking attack,* concentrating its strength against the competitor's weaker flanks or on gaps in the competitor's market coverage. For example, during the 1960s and 1970s, German and Japanese auto makers chose not to enter the U.S. market by competing directly with American auto makers producing large, flashy, gas-guzzling automobiles. Instead they found an unserved consumer segment that wanted small, fuel-efficient cars and moved to fill this hole. To their satisfaction and Detroit's surprise, the segment grew to be a large part of the market. Flank attacks make good sense when the company has fewer resources than the competitor.

An *encirclement attack* involves attacking from the front, sides, and rear at the same time. The encirclement strategy makes sense when the challenger has superior resources and believes that it can break the competitor's hold on the market quickly. For example, Seiko attacked the watch market by gaining distribution in every major watch outlet and overwhelming competitors with constantly changing variety. In the United States alone it offers some four hundred models, but it makes and sells 2,300 models worldwide.

Using a *bypass attack,* the challenger bypasses the competitor and targets easier markets. It might diversify into unrelated products, move into new geographic markets, or leapfrog into new technologies to replace existing products. With technological leapfrogging, instead of copying the competitor's product and mounting a costly frontal attack, the challenger passes by the competitor with the next technology. Thus, Minolta toppled Canon from the lead in the 35mm SLR camera market when it introduced its technologically advanced auto-focusing Maxxum camera. Canon's market share dropped toward 20 percent while Minolta's zoomed past 30 percent. It took Canon three years to introduce a matching technology.

Finally, smaller or poorly financed challengers can mount *guerrilla attacks.* These are small, periodic attacks to harass and demoralize the competitor, with the goal of eventually establishing permanent footholds. The challenger might use selective price cuts, executive raids, intense promotional outbursts, or assorted legal actions. Specific guerrilla actions can be cheap, but continuous guerrilla campaigns can be expensive. And they eventually must be followed up by stronger attacks if the challenger wishes to gain ground against competitors.

MARKET-FOLLOWER STRATEGIES

Not all runner-up companies want to challenge the market leader. Challenges are never taken lightly by the leader. If the challenger's lure is lower prices, improved service, or additional product features, the leader can quickly match these to defuse the attack. The leader probably has more staying power in an all-out battle for customers. A hard fight might leave both firms worse off. Thus, many firms prefer to follow rather than challenge the leader.

A follower can gain many advantages. The market leader often bears the huge expenses of developing new products and markets, expanding distribution, and educating the market. The market follower, on the other hand, can learn from the leader's experience and copy or improve on the leader's products and programs, usually with much less investment. Although the follower probably will not overtake the leader, it often can be as profitable. A good example of a follower is Dial Corporation, maker of such well-known brands as Dial, Tone, and Pure&Natural hand soaps, Armour Star canned meats, Purex laundry products, StaPuf fabric softener, SnoBol toilet cleaner, and Brillo scouring pads:

> Flashy it isn't. Dial doesn't try to come up with innovative new products. . . . It doesn't spend zillions to make its offerings household names across the nation. Instead, Dial prefers to coast in the slipstream of giant rivals, such as Procter & Gamble. [Its] lineup consists largely of me-too products and second-tier regional brands. . . . Instead of spending big on research and development or marketing, Dial leaves it to others. . . . And Dial lets other companies educate consumers about new products. P&G, for instance, introduced concentrated powder detergents in 1990. Dial followed over a year later with its own concentrated version, Purex—priced as much as one-third lower than P&G's Tide.[15]

Following is not the same as being passive or a carbon copy of the leader. The follower has to define a growth path, but one that does not create competitive retaliation. A market follower must know how to hold current customers and win a fair share of new ones. Each follower tries to bring distinctive advantages to its target market—location, services, financing. The follower is often a major target of attack by challengers. Therefore, the market follower must keep its manufacturing costs low and its product quality and services high. It must also enter new markets as they open up.

MARKET-NICHER STRATEGIES

Almost every industry includes firms that specialize in serving market niches. Instead of pursuing the whole market, or even large segments, these firms target subsegments, or niches. Nichers are often smaller firms with limited resources. But smaller divisions of larger firms also may pursue niching strategies. Firms with low shares of the total market can be highly profitable through smart niching (see Marketing Highlight 19-4).

One study of highly successful midsize companies found that, in almost all cases, these companies niched within a larger market rather than going after the whole market.[16] An example is A. T. Cross, which niches in the high-price pen and pencil market. It makes the famous gold writing instruments that many executives own or want to own. By concentrating in the high-price niche, Cross has

CONCENTRATED MARKETING: TERRY BIKES FIND SPECIAL NICHE

Is there room for a budding new competitor alongside the giants in the bicycle industry? Georgena Terry thinks so. And so do the hundreds of people now riding Terry bikes. Terry has developed a small but promising niche in the bicycle market—high-performance bikes for women.

There was nothing astonishing about the idea. Three years ago, Terry, then a 34-year-old MBA student, decided to start building bicycles. Oh, sure, she'd specialize in high-priced women's bikes, carving out a niche just as they had taught her at The Wharton Business School. But the $1.3 billion bicycle industry didn't tremble at the thought of diminutive Terry picking up a wrench. True, she might have an interesting twist: her bikes would have a shorter top tube and a slightly smaller front wheel that would provide a more comfortable ride for women cyclists who put in 40 or 50 miles at a clip—but who rides that far? Most folks just use their bikes to pedal down to the Dairy Queen or tool around the neighborhood on Sunday afternoons. Besides, if it turned out she had something, the industry could always wheel out a knockoff.

So when Terry set up shop, no one noticed. But they are noticing now. In its first year, Terry Precision Bicycles for Women, Inc., sold 20 bikes. In the second year it shipped 1,300, and in the third year it sold 2,500 more. Suddenly, her banker is more friendly, and the bicycle magazines are calling to see what she thinks of this or that. Terry has succeeded by concentrating on serving the special needs of serious women cyclists.

The idea began when Terry herself became interested in biking. She found that she had trouble finding a comfortable riding position. "The standard bicycle—even a woman's bike—is designed for a man. To fit women, who have longer legs and shorter torsos, bike shops shove the seat forward and tilt the handlebars back." That didn't help the five-foot-two, 98-pound Terry. She began wondering if shortening the frame would improve things. So she picked up a blowtorch—"a friend showed me how to use it so I wouldn't kill myself"—and headed for the basement. She

came back up with a bike that had a smaller frame. Friends saw it, borrowed it, and asked if she'd make frames for them. Two years later she was still turning out frames and making a living—sort of.

Finally, she got tired of just getting by and started a company. Bicycling was undergoing a mini-boom and 70 percent of all new riders were women, so she'd specialize in women's bikes. She hauled seven or eight of her bikes to a New England Area Rally in Amherst, Massachusetts. "I figured we'd do very well or

Concentrated marketing: Georgena Terry has shown how a small company can succeed against larger competitors.

very badly. Women would either go 'who cares?' or love it." She sold three bikes that weekend (at $775 each) and took orders for four more. Says Terry, "I have never been more excited in my life."

To her credit, Terry moved deliberately. Her major innovation was the frame, so she concentrated on that and didn't set out to reinvent the (bicycle) wheel. Her marketing plan was equally careful. As word spread, people would call up and ask to buy a bike. "We were thrilled, but always asked the name of their local bicycle shop. We'd then call the shop and say, 'Congratulations, you've just sold a Terry bike.'" Retailers, who found themselves making a quick couple of hundred dollars, usually asked for a few more bikes. That's how Terry put together a dealer network.

With almost no money for advertising, Terry concentrated on promotion. She hired a public relations firm that was quick to position her as a female David taking on bicycling's Goliaths. The approach paid off—the bicycle press discovered Terry and gave her bikes enthusiastic endorsements. That got customers into the stores and bikes out the door. Terry's professional business approach makes her stand out from competitors in a high-end bicycling industry filled with scores of tiny manufacturers that can take months to fill orders and are often unresponsive to both customers and shop owners. Terry, who ships on time, courts retailers, and answers questions from customers, quickly became a favorite.

But even as the marketing plan got her up and pedaling, Terry was moving to forestall competition. Recognizing that her high price would scare off many customers, Terry almost immediately began to segment. She was soon selling her high-end models for $1,200 and, to preempt the foreign competition that she knew would be coming, she signed two Asian companies to build versions of her bike that retail for $450 to $850. The strategy has worked so far. Although six companies, including Fuji America, now market bicycles to women, Terry is holding her own. Competitors' bikes just aren't as good. As one customer asserts, "Women can tell the difference on a ride around the block. My feet reach the pedals more comfortably, and it is easier to reach the hand brakes. You feel more in control on one of her bikes."

Continued success is far from assured. Over time, her competitors will improve their designs. And the more successful Terry becomes, the more competition she is likely to attract. Yet, she has shown how a company with fewer resources can succeed against larger competitors by concentrating on a small, high-quality segment. At some point, as with many small nichers, Terry may have to think about selling out or joining forces with a bigger company to survive. But that is still a long way off. For now, Terry says, "This is wonderful."

Source: Adapted from Paul B. Brown, "Spokeswoman," *Career Futures,* Spring–Summer 1989, pp. 30–32.

Quality nicher: Hewlett-Packard specializes in the high-quality, high-price end of the hand-calculator market.

enjoyed great sales growth and profit. Of course, the study found other features shared by successful smaller companies—offering high value, charging a premium price, and having strong corporate cultures and vision.

Why is niching profitable? The main reason is that the market nicher ends up knowing the target customer group so well that it meets their needs better than other firms that casually sell to this niche. As a result, the nicher can charge a substantial markup over costs because of the added value. Whereas the mass marketer achieves *high volume,* the nicher achieves *high margins.*

Nichers try to find one or more market niches that are safe and profitable. An ideal market niche is big enough to be profitable and has growth potential. It is one that the firm can serve effectively. Perhaps most importantly, the niche is of little interest to major competitors. And the firm can build the skills and customer goodwill to defend itself against a major competitor as the niche grows and becomes more attractive.

The key idea in nichemanship is specialization. A market nicher can specialize along any of several market, customer, product, or marketing mix lines. For example, it can specialize in serving one type of *end-user,* as when a law firm specializes in the criminal, civil, or business law markets. The nicher can specialize in serving a given *customer-size* group—many nichers specialize in serving small customers who are neglected by the majors. Some nichers focus on one or a few *specific customers,* selling their entire output to a single company, such as Wal-Mart or General Motors. *Geographic nichers* sell only in a certain locality, region, or area of the world. *Quality-price nichers* operate at the low or high end of the market. For example, Hewlett-Packard specializes in the high-quality, high-price end of the hand-calculator market. Finally, *service nichers* offer services not available from other firms. An example is a bank that takes loan requests over the phone and hand delivers the money to the customer.

Niching carries some major risks. For example, the market niche may dry up, or it might grow to the point that it attracts larger competitors. That is why many companies practice *multiple niching.* By developing two or more niches, the company increases its chances for survival. Even some large firms prefer a multiple-niche strategy to serving the total market. One large law firm has developed a national reputation in the three areas of mergers and acquisitions, bankruptcies, and prospectus development, and it does little else.

BALANCING CUSTOMER AND COMPETITOR ORIENTATIONS

Competitor-centered company
A company whose moves are mainly based on competitors' actions and reactions; it spends most of its time tracking competitors' moves and market shares and trying to find strategies to counter them.

Whether a company is a market leader, challenger, follower, or nicher, it must watch its competitors closely and find the competitive marketing strategy that positions it most effectively. And it must continually adapt its strategies to the fast-changing competitive environment.

This question now arises: Can the company spend too much time and energy tracking competitors, damaging its customer orientation? The answer is yes! A company can become so competitor-centered that it loses its even more important customer focus.

A **competitor-centered company** is one that spends most of its time tracking competitors' moves and market shares and trying to find strategies to counter

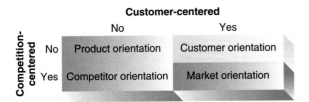

FIGURE 19-6 *Evolving company orientations*

Customer-centered company
A company that focuses on customer developments in designing its marketing strategies and on delivering superior value to its target customers.

Market-centered company
A company that pays balanced attention to both customers and competitors in designing its marketing strategies.

them. This approach has some pluses and minuses. On the positive side, the company develops a fighter orientation. It trains its marketers to be on a constant alert, watching for weaknesses in their own position, and searching out competitors' weaknesses. On the negative side, the company becomes too reactive. Rather than carrying out its own customer-oriented strategy, it bases its own moves on competitors' moves. As a result, because so much depends on what the competitors do, the company does not move in a planned direction toward a goal.

A **customer-centered company,** by contrast, focuses more on customer developments in designing its strategies. Clearly, the customer-centered company is in a better position to identify new opportunities and set long-run strategies that make sense. By watching customer needs evolve, it can decide what customer groups and what emerging needs are the most important to serve, given its resources and objectives.

In practice, today's companies must be **market-centered companies,** watching both their customers and their competitors. They must not let competitor watching blind them to customer focusing. Figure 19-6 shows that companies have moved through four orientations over the years. In the first stage, they were product-oriented, paying little attention to either customers or competitors. In the second stage, they became customer-oriented and started to pay attention to customers. In the third stage, when they started to pay attention to competitors, they became competitor-oriented. Today, companies need to be market-oriented, paying balanced attention to both customer and competitors. A market orientation pays big dividends—one recent study found a substantial positive relationship between a company's marketing orientation and its profitability, a relationship that held regardless of type of business or market environment.[17]

Summary

In order to prepare an effective marketing strategy, a company must consider its competitors as well as its customers. It must continuously engage in *competitor analysis* and develop *competitive marketing strategies* that effectively position it against competitors and give it the strongest possible competitive advantage.

Competitor analysis first involves identifying the company's major competitors, using both an industry and a market-based analysis. The company then gathers information on competitors' *objectives, strategies, strengths and weaknesses,* and *reaction patterns.* With this information in hand, it can *select competitors to attack or avoid. Competitive intelligence* must be collected, interpreted, and distributed continuously through a formal system. Company marketing managers should be able to obtain full and reliable information about any competitor affecting their decisions.

Which competitive marketing strategy makes the most sense depends on the company's industry position and its objectives, opportuni-

ties, and resources. The company's competitive marketing strategy depends on whether it is a market leader, challenger, follower, or nicher.

A *market leader* faces three challenges: *expanding the total market, protecting market share,* and *expanding market share.* The market leader is interested in finding ways to expand the total market because it will benefit most from any increased sales. To expand market size, the leader looks for new users of the product, new uses, and more usage. To protect its existing market share, the market leader has several defenses: *position defense, flanking defense, preemptive defense, counteroffensive offense, mobile defense,* and *contraction defense.* The most sophisticated leaders cover themselves by doing everything right, leaving no openings for competitive attack. Leaders can also try to increase their market shares. This makes sense if profitability increases at higher market-share levels.

A *market challenger* is a firm that aggressively tries to expand its market share by attacking the leader, other runner-up firms, or smaller firms in the industry. The challenger can choose from a variety of attack strategies, including a frontal attack, flanking attack, encirclement attack, bypass attack, and guerrilla attack.

A *market follower* is a runner-up firm that chooses not to rock the boat, usually out of fear that it stands more to lose than it might gain. The follower is not without a strategy, however, and seeks to use its particular skills to gain market growth. Some followers enjoy a higher rate of return than the leaders in their industry.

A *market nicher* is a smaller firm that serves some part of the market that is not likely to at- tract the larger firms. Market nichers often be- come specialists in some end use, vertical level, customer size, specific customer, geographic area, product or product feature, or service.

A competitive orientation is important in today's markets, but companies should not overdo their focus on competitors. Companies are more likely to be hurt by emerging consumer needs and new competitors than by existing com- petitors. Companies that *balance consumer and competitor considerations* are practicing a true market orientation.

Key Terms

Benchmarking	Customer-centered company	Market leader
Competitive advantage	Customer value analysis	Market nicher
Competitive marketing strategies	Market-centered company	Strategic group
Competitor analysis	Market challenger	
Competitor-centered company	Market follower	

Discussing the Issues

1. "Well-behaved" companies prefer well-be- haved competition. Decide whether it should make any difference to consumers whether competition is "well-behaved" or "disruptive." Why or why not?

2. Hewlett-Packard, a market leader in the high-priced end of the calculator market, has found itself in a squeeze between ag- gressively promoted portable computers and less expensive calculators with increas- ingly sophisticated features. Suggest a mar- ket leader strategy you would recommend for Hewlett-Packard. Explain why.

3. Invent some ways Morton Salt could ex- pand the total market for table salt. Iden- tify the roles sales promotion would play in getting new users, communicating new uses, or increasing usage of table salt.

4. Many medium-sized firms are in an un- profitable middle ground between large firms and smaller, more focused firms. Discuss how medium-sized firms could use market nicher strategies to improve their profitability.

5. The goal of the marketing concept is to sat- isfy customer wants and needs. What is the goal of a competitor-centered strategy? De- termine whether the marketing concept and competitor-centered strategy are in conflict.

6. Assume you are the product manager in charge of Lysol Disinfectant or Woolite Fine Fabric Wash. Your brand has over 60 percent of the market, and no competing brand has ever succeeded in gaining signifi- cant market share. What would your strat- egy be for growing your business?

Applying the Concepts

1. Study a new-car purchasing guide, avail- able at the library or for sale at newsstands. Examine different aspects of the cars, in- cluding features, style and image, and price. (a) Identify companies that you think are competing, based on the market point of view. (b) What sort of competitive strate- gies do you see being used by market-lead- ers, -followers, -challengers, and -nichers? (c) What different strategic groups can you identify in the automobile industry? Which groups compete with which other groups?

2. Market-leaders often attempt to expand the total market, especially in slower-growing, mature markets. (a) Look at the ads in several issues of women's magazines such as *Family Circle* or *Ladies' Home Journal*. Find examples in which manufacturers are attempting to expand total market demand for their products. (b) Look for similar examples in your local supermarket. (c) What specific strategies are these expansion attempts trying: new users, new uses, or more usage? Rate the chances of success for each example you have found.

References

1. Chuck Hawkins, "FedEx: Europe Nearly Killed the Messenger," *Business Week*, May 25, 1992, pp. 124–126; Erik Calonius, "Federal Express's Battle Overseas," *Fortune*, December 3, 1990, pp. 137–140; Shlomo Maital, "When You Absolutely, Positively Have to Give the Better Service," *Across the Board*, March 1991, pp. 8–12; "Pass the Parcel," *The Economist*, March 21, 1992, pp. 73–74; "ATW Awards 20 Years of Excellence in Cargo Service: Federal Express," *Air Transport World*, February 1994, pp. 48–52; and Alan Solomon, "UPS Rewraps Image as Problem Solver," *Advertising Age*, February 6, 1995, p. 4.

2. For a good discussion of the underlying rules of competitive interaction and reaction, see Gloria P. Thomas and Gary F. Soldow, "A Rules-Based Approach to Competitive Interaction," *Journal of Marketing*, April 1988, pp. 63–74. Also see Walter D. Brandt, Jr., "Profiling Rival Decision Makers," *The Journal of Business Strategy*, January/February 1991, pp. 8–11.

3. See Michael E. Porter, *Competitive Advantage* (New York: The Free Press, 1985), pp. 226–227; Joseph Weber, "How J&J's Foresight Made Contact Lenses Pay," *Business Week*, May 4, 1992, p. 132.

4. See Porter, *Competitive Advantage,* Chap. 6.

5. Wendy Zellner, "The Airline Mess," *Business Week,* July 6, 1992, pp. 50–55.

6. For more discussion, see Leonard M. Fuld, *Monitoring the Competition* (New York: John Wiley & Sons, 1988); Howard Schlossberg, "Competitive Intelligence Pros Seek Formal Role in Marketing," *Marketing News*, March 5, 1990, pp. 2, 28; Michele Galen, "These Guys Aren't Spooks, They're 'Competitive Analysts,'" *Business Week*, October 14, 1991, p. 97; and Norton Paley, "Choose Competitors Carefully," *Sales & Marketing Management*, June 1994, pp. 57–58.

7. Michael E. Porter, *Competitive Strategy: Techniques for Analyzing Industries and Competitors* (New York: Free Press, 1980), Ch. 2.

8. See Stuart Gannes, "The Riches in Market Niches," *Fortune*, April 27, 1987, p. 228; and Tim Smart, "Will U.S. Surgical's Cutting Edge Be Enough?" *Business Week*, September 21, 1992, pp. 50–51.

9. Michael Treacy and Fred Wiersema, "Customer Intimacy and Other Value Disciplines," *Harvard Business Review*, January–February 1993, pp. 84–93; and Michael Treacy and Fred Wiersema, "How Market Leaders Keep Their Edge," *Fortune*, February 6, 1995, pp. 88–98.

10. For more discussion on defense and attack strategies, see Philip Kotler, *Marketing Management: Analysis, Planning, Implementation, and Control* (Englewood Cliffs, NJ: Prentice Hall, 1994), Chap. 14.

11. See Lois Therrien, "Mr. Rust Belt," *Business Week*, October 17, 1988, pp. 72–80.

12. See Bradley Johnson, "Wash-Day Washout," *Advertising Age*, June 3, 1991, p. 54.

13. See David M. Szymanski, Sundar G. Bharadwaj, and P. Rajan Varadarajan, "An Analysis of the Market Share-Profitability Relationship," *Journal of Marketing*, July 1993, pp. 1–18.

14. See Andrew C. Brown, "Unilever Fights Back in the U.S.," *Fortune*, May 26, 1986, pp. 32–38.

15. Amy Barrett, "Dial Succeeds by Stepping in Bigger Footsteps," *Business Week*, June 13, 1994, pp. 82–83.

16. Donald K. Clifford and Richard E. Cavanagh, *The Winning Performance: How America's High- and Midsize Growth Companies Succeed* (New York: Bantam Books, 1985).

17. See John C. Narver and Stanley F. Slater, "The Effect of a Market Orientation on Business Profitability," *Journal of Marketing*, October 1990, pp. 20–35.

Company Case 19

PROCTER & GAMBLE: GOING GLOBAL—A NEW WRINKLE IN COSMETICS

Procter & Gamble, the Cincinnati-based, multinational company known for its household products, has decided to get serious about the cosmetics business. The question is, can the firm that has gotten us to Pamper-away our babies' wetness, Crest-away our cavities, and Tide-away the grime in our clothes now use its potent marketing skills to get us to make up our faces?

STEP 1: DIVERSIFYING

P&G's aggressive chairman, Edwin L. Artzt, thinks it can. The company tiptoed into the skin-care business in 1985 when it purchased the Oil of Olay skin-care line. Under Artzt's leadership, P&G then drove headlong into the cosmetics business. In 1989, it bought Noxell Corporation and its Cover Girl and Clarion brand cosmetics lines for $1.3 billion in stock.

Artzt saw the opportunity to strengthen Noxell's marketing support with P&G's considerable resources while at the same time providing P&G with new growth opportunities outside its stable of mature products. Artzt also recognized that cosmetics carried high gross margins and resisted recessions. As of June 1990, P&G obtained 47.7 percent of its $24.08 billion in total sales from personal-care products. About half of these sales came from paper products, including diapers. Another 32.2 percent of its total sales came from laundry and cleaning products, 13.4 percent from food and beverages, and 6.7 percent from pulp and chemicals.

After acquiring Noxell, Artzt turned P&G's marketers loose. They quickly redesigned Cover Girl's packaging, giving it a ritzier look, but retained the brand's budget-pricing strategy. P&G also speeded up new-product development. It backed these changes with a 58 percent increase in advertising, spending $47.5 million on Cover Girl in the first nine months of 1990 alone. Ads spotlighted famous models of various ages who featured a more natural look. By 1991, Cover Girl's market share had increased to 23 percent, up from 21 percent in 1986. Meanwhile, number-two Maybelline's share had fallen to 17 percent, down from 19 percent in 1986.

STEP 2: GROWING BIGGER

P&G realized that it could not rest on its success. The cosmetics industry was changing, and P&G would have to change if it wanted to become a serious contender. Consumers were deserting department stores in droves, looking for distinct brands offered by specialty clothing chains and cosmetics boutiques, such as the Body Shop. Analysts believed that women were tired of being assaulted as they entered department stores' cosmetics sections. Women wanted to buy cosmetics where they bought other items, which was increasingly in specialty shops. As a result of this, department store cosmetics sales were declining and mass merchandiser shares were increasing.

The Cover Girl brand also faced problems. For example, the Cover Girl name suggested that the brand was designed for young, glamorous women, giving the line a built-in problem when appealing to career

women, homemakers, and older women. In addition, Cover Girl generated 90 percent of its sales in the United States, whereas the rest of the industry was increasingly going global. For these reasons, Artzt went shopping again.

At the same time, New York financier Ronald Perelman had decided that he might need to sell Revlon, his beauty-products company. Revlon's brands included Max Factor, Betrix, and Almay cosmetics, Charlie and Jontou perfumes, and Flex shampoo.

Several big firms besides P&G expressed an interest in Revlon. Like P&G, these other companies wanted to expand their cosmetics businesses through acquisitions. Unilever, a Dutch multinational company, had begun buying personal-care brands in the United States in 1989. As a result of its Faberge and Elizabeth Arden acquisitions, Unilever held the number-three spot behind Estee Lauder and L'Oreal in sales at U.S. department store cosmetics counters. Unilever had worldwide personal-care sales of $4.7 billion in 1990. Gesparal, S.A., owned the majority of Cosmair's L'Oreal, which had 1989 worldwide revenues of $5.3 billion. In turn, Nestlé, the Swiss food conglomerate, owned 49 percent of Gesparal.

P&G was especially interested in Revlon's Max Factor and Betrix lines, because 80 percent of their sales were outside the United States. These two brands would fit well with P&G's other lines and give the company a good basis to compete for a bigger share of the $16 billion worldwide cosmetics and fragrance business. In April 1991, Artzt announced that P&G would pay $1.1 billion for the two Revlon lines, which together captured $800 million in sales. Artzt decided not to purchase Revlon's other major brands, which sold at higher prices in department stores.

It turned out, however, that Artzt had more in mind that simply buying lines that would give P&G an international presence. He also saw opportunities to use the new brands' distribution and marketing networks to speed Cover Girl's transition from a U.S. brand to an international brand. Max Factor and Betrix gave P&G immediate access to Europe and Japan. Before the acquisitions, P&G had no cosmetics or fragrance sales in Japan and only $28 million in Europe. After the acquisition, P&G had annual sales of $237 million in Japan and $340 million in Europe. About 75 percent of Max Factor's $600-million sales came from outside the United States, whereas all of Betrix's $200 million came from other countries. One analyst estimated that Procter & Gamble had shortened by three years the time it would have taken to go global with its U.S. brands.

Just as the Max Factor and Betrix lines helped P&G, acquisition by P&G helped the two brands immensely. Betrix, especially, had learned that it took deep pockets to compete in the international cosmetics business. It achieved about 62.5 percent of its sales in its home market, Germany, with the remainder coming from Switzerland, Spain, Italy, and Sweden. Betrix wanted to crack the French market but had not been successful against powerful L'Oreal, which dominated that market. P&G's marketing muscle would now allow it to elbow its way into the French market. Betrix's major brands were the mid-priced Ellen Betrix women's skin-care products and cosmetics, and Henry M. Betrix men's toiletries. Its Eurocos Cosmetic subsidiary marketed upscale cosmetics under the Hugo Boss and Laura Biagiotti brand names.

STEP 3: REVIVING MAX FACTOR IN THE U.S. MARKET

P&G felt that it could make Max Factor more competitive in the United States because it would not be under Revlon's umbrella. As it had done with Cover Girl, P&G quickly learned Max Factor's business and plotted strategies to improve its performance. P&G's managers revamped Max Factor with new products and technological improvements, and they beefed up the brand's promotion and advertising support.

Revlon, however, did not stand still after selling Max Factor to P&G. It hired a new management team for its Revlon brand, cut its manufacturing costs, and introduced a $200-million advertising barrage that featured a jazzy "Shake Your Body" message.

Both firms realized that they had to find ways to attract younger women, including teenagers, without alienating older customers. Mass-market sales, such as sales through drugstores and discounters, grew only 2 percent in 1991, compared with 6 percent in 1990. Changing consumer demographics and shopping habits seemed to account for this slowdown. Aging baby boomers had decided to invest in skin-care products and were buying fewer cosmetics like mascara, nail polish, and lipstick.

These changes meant that attracting younger women had become even more important if the cosmetics companies were to revive sales growth. One college sophomore suggested that she could understand the companies' interest in younger consumers. She felt that younger women often wanted to look older and might even use more cosmetics than they needed. "Putting on makeup," she added, "is a big part of growing up." An industry consultant noted that "younger women are constantly changing and reapplying their nail polish, something older women don't do."

Yet, the companies faced problems in attracting younger customers. First, there were fewer younger women than baby boomers. Second, all cosmetics manufacturers were fighting for shelf space and the attention of younger buyers. One analyst noted that there were simply too many manufacturers and too many products chasing too few customers. Competition was intense. The analyst noted that even at the prestige end of the mass market, L'Oreal had dropped its emphasis on quality and had begun emphasizing having fun in order to lure more young customers. Additional competition was coming from department store product lines, specialty shops, direct marketers such as Avon, and even home-shopping networks.

As a result, P&G's cosmetics sales remained flat in 1991 at $722 million, and its market share slipped slightly to 34 percent, down from 34.4 percent in 1990. Revlon's share increased to 22.5 percent, up from 20.4 percent in 1990, partly at P&G's expense.

Even with the slowdown, however, P&G remained the nation's largest seller of cosmetics sold through drug and mass merchandise stores. P&G admitted that it was still learning the cosmetics business. It faced distribution problems, being slow to fill orders and slow to deliver promised new products. In addition, the company had consolidated its cosmetics salesforce. Its salespeople now sold all three lines Cover Girl, Clarion, and Max Factor. Some distributors argued that P&G was expecting too much from a single salesperson the product lines were simply too wide to expect one person to know much about all the products. P&G countered that the new system would reduce the number of salespeople with whom retailers had to deal.

STEP 4: GOING GLOBAL

Most recently, P&G has decided to overhaul the Max Factor line and launch its first simultaneous worldwide product introduction. The company introduced the new Max Factor line during the spring of 1993. The new products feature more elegant styling and more colors. P&G first produced new eyeshadows, blushes, and lipsticks. In 1994, it introduced new foundations, face powders, and mascaras.

All of these products are the same, no matter where in the world P&G sells them. Previously, P&G had used different products and strategies in different markets, often using local manufacturers. In Japan, for example, the Max Factor line had consisted primarily of skin-care products sold at high prices in department stores. Max Factor had accounted for 28 percent of Revlon's Japanese sales of $507 million in 1990. However, the brand had not kept up with changing Japanese lifestyles and tastes, and it was steadily losing market share. Kao Corporation and Shiseido Company were emerging as powerful competitors in the Japanese market. In Europe, P&G sold Max Factor products in chain stores and pharmacies at lower prices.

The new line features similar styles, colors, and images across all international markets. Packages are a deep blue color with gold trim. The products come in a variety of colors to meet the needs of women with differing skin tones. P&G has also revised its in-store displays. To support such changes, it will increase prices to between 8 and 10 percent above previous Max Factor prices.

P&G is following the successful strategies of Estee Lauder's Clinique and Chanel, which have both been successful with standardized global marketing. Consumers around the globe recognize Clinique's blue-green packaging and Chanel's classic black compacts. P&G hopes that the standardized strategy will allow it to save money by unifying and consolidating many of its marketing efforts.

STEP 5: WATCHING THE COMPETITION

Despite Artzt's perpetual optimism, however, P&G knows it is making a bold move. No other company has tried to develop a worldwide, mass-market cosmetics brand. The company has already learned from its experiences in the U.S. market that the cosmetics business is complicated. P&G also knows that Revlon will be right behind with its own global strategy. Revlon already receives between 30 and 35 percent of its revenue from 126 foreign countries, and P&G expects that Revlon will try to take more of its regional brands global.

P&G also knows that it must watch its home market. Noting all the attention being paid to younger women, Maybelline is now focusing on aging baby boomers. It plans to introduce a new line, called Maybelline Revitalizing, that targets women 35 and older. Maybelline claims that these products will help mature women look younger, and it plans to sell the products through mass-market outlets. To stay ahead of the competitors in cosmetics, Procter & Gamble will have to find some new marketing wrinkles.

QUESTIONS

1. Who are Procter & Gamble's competitors, from an industry point of view and from a market point of view? Are there strategic groups in the industry? Why are these questions important for P&G?

2. What trends are shaping competitors' objectives in the cosmetics industry?

3. Based on information in the case, which of Michael Porter's competitive positions have the various cosmetics competitors pursued to gain competitive advantage?

4. What actions should P&G take in order to expand the total cosmetics market and to protect and expand its market share?

5. What competitive strategies would you recommend for P&G's competitors?

Sources: Randall Smith, Kathleen Deveny, and Alecia Swasy, "Sale of Revlon Beauty Line Is Considered by Perelman," *Wall Street Journal,* March 1, 1991, p. B4; Alecia Swasy, "Cover Girl Is Growing Up and Moving Out as Its New Parent, P&G, Takes Charge," *Wall Street Journal,* March 28, 1991, p. B1; Pat Sloan and Jennifer Lawrence, "What P&G Plans for Cosmetics," *Advertising Age,* April 15, 1991, pp. 3, 46; Zachary Schiller and Larry Light, "Proctor & Gamble Is Following Its Nose," *Business Week,* April 22, 1991, p. 28; Valerie Reitman and Jeffrey A. Trachenberg, "Battle to Make Up the Younger Woman Pits Revlon Against Its New Rival, P&G," *Wall Street Journal,* July 10, 1992; Valerie Reitman, "P&G Planning a Fresh Face for Max Factor," *Wall Street Journal,* December 29, 1992, p. B1; Marilyn Much, "Cosmetic War Gets Ugly as Front Moves Abroad," *Investor's Business Daily,* January 14, 1993, p. 4; and Gabriella Stern, "Aging Boomers Are New Target for Maybelline," *Wall Street Journal,* April 13, 1993, p. B1.

Video Case 8

RITZ-CARLTON: SIMPLY THE BEST

When introducing himself to new employees, the president of The Ritz-Carlton Hotel Company says "My name is Horst Schulze. I'm the president, and I'm a very important person around here." After a few seconds he continues, "But so are you. In fact, you are more important to customers than I am. If you don't show up, we are in trouble. If I don't show up, hardly anyone would notice."

These comments reflect Mr. Schulze's attitude that employees are the crucial component in quality service. Therefore, The Ritz-Carlton very carefully selects only those applicants with an appropriate caring attitude. For every new employee at an introductory orientation session, ten others applied, and employees are told that they were not hired, they were selected. Once selected, each employee learns the Ritz-Carlton corporate culture in a two-day orientation, followed by extensive on-the-job training that results in job certification.

Each employee learns The Ritz-Carlton Gold Standards, which include a credo, 20 basics of service, and the three steps of service. The steps include: (1) a warm and sincere greeting; (2) anticipation and compliance with guest needs; and (3) a fond farewell, using the guest's name if possible. Employees may even have to modify their language. They should say "Good morning," or "Good afternoon," not "Hi, how's it going?" When asked to do something, they should respond "Certainly," or "My pleasure." In addition, all employees should learn the 20 Ritz-Carlton basics of quality service, which range from knowledge of one's work area and The Ritz-Carlton Credo to answering the telephone with a smile and wearing immaculate uniforms. At The Ritz-Carlton employees are not servants, they are "ladies and gentlemen serving ladies and gentlemen."

To back up all this training, employees are empowered to handle any customer complaint on the spot and can spend up to $2,000 doing so. And they can demand the immediate assistance of other employees. Twenty minutes later, they should telephone the guest to make sure that the complaint was handled properly. In addition, once employees learn of particular customer wants, such as foam pillows or a desire for a particular newspaper, that information goes into a 240,000 person database so that the customer will automatically get the desired service the next time he or she stays at a Ritz-Carlton.

This attention to quality is not confined to hotel staff. Mr. Schulze and the other senior executives meet weekly to review measures of product and service quality, guest satisfaction, market growth and development, and other business indicators. From top management down, Ritz-Carlton's approach to quality management is characterized by detailed planning. Quality teams at all levels set objectives and devise action plans, and each hotel has a quality leader and work-area teams responsible for problem solving, strategic planning, and setting quality-certification standards for each position.

Each hotel aims to create a two-to-one ratio of internal to external complaints. Internal complaints are made by employees who spot problems in service delivery. By eliminating internal problems, Ritz-Carlton removes the causes of external complaints by customers. Management thinks that solving problems before they arise is cost-effective. Once a problem has occurred, there are additional costs of employee time to fix the problem plus hotel remedies such as complimentary cocktails and a follow-up letter, not to mention the possible cost of losing a customer. Patrick Mene, Vice President of Quality, expresses this as the 1–10–100 rule: "What costs a dollar to fix today will cost $10 to fix tomorrow and $100 to fix downstream."

To ensure that quality standards are maintained, Ritz-Carlton collects daily reports from each of the 720 work areas in each of the 30 hotels it manages. The company tracks measures such as annual guest-room preventive-maintenance cycles, percentage of check-ins with no queuing, time spent to achieve industry-best clean-room appearance, and time to service an occupied room.

Not surprisingly, Ritz-Carlton won the prestigious Malcolm Baldrige National Quality Award in 1992. This moved the firm into very select company—only one service firm had ever won this award. You might think Ritz-Carlton would be satisfied with a customer satisfaction rating of 97 percent, one of the lowest employee turnover rates in the hotel industry (30 percent). But not Ritz-Carlton! Mr. Schulze has set new quality performance standards to be reached by 1996: a 100-percent customer satisfaction rating and a reduction of defects to just four for every million customer encounters.

Eliminating virtually all problems, however, is a costly process that can reduce company profits, and some critics believe that Ritz-Carlton is not sensitive enough to its bottom line. For example, to improve customer satisfaction from 97 percent to 98 percent, some would say, is a marginal improvement that could require a great deal of employee effort and expense for a low dollar return. Besides, how can any firm anticipate all possible problems in order to eliminate complaints? Should it even desire to do so?

QUESTIONS

1. Why is it important for Ritz-Carlton to insist that employees not think of themselves as servants, but rather as ladies and gentlemen?

2. In what ways does Ritz-Carlton engage in relationship marketing?

3. Is quality at Ritz-Carlton cost-effective? Even if it costs $2,000 an incident?

4. Should Ritz-Carlton attempt to move toward Mr. Schulze's latest goals? Why or why not?

Sources: Patricia A. Galagan, "Putting on the Ritz," *Training & Development,* December 1993, pp. 41–45; Charles G. Partlow, "How Ritz-Carlton Applies 'TQM,'" *The Cornell H.R.A. Quarterly,* August 1993; and numerous company-supplied materials. The author would like to thank Stephanie Platt, Manager of Communications, Ritz-Carlton Hotels, for help with this case.

NEW BALANCE: RUNNING IN THE BUSINESS MARATHON

Making a profit is important, but it's not the most important thing. To me, what matters most is making a product you believe in.

That motto has shaped Jim Davis's approach to business since he purchased New Balance Athletic Shoe, Inc., on the day of the 1972 Boston Marathon. Whereas the winner of the Boston Marathon broke the tape in a little over two hours, Jim Davis's business marathon is still going. The question is whether Jim and his company will "hit the wall" and falter on business's equivalent of "heartbreak hill." Or can New Balance sprint to the finish line ahead of bigger and stronger rivals Nike and Reebok?

New Balance had been in business in Watertown, Massachusetts, since 1906 as an orthopedic-shoe maker and had begun making athletic shoes in 1962. When Davis purchased New Balance, the company employed only six people, who operated from a garage and crafted only 30 pairs of shoes a day.

Sensing that more people were becoming interested in jogging and running, Davis scraped together $100,000 to buy the company, an amount equal to the company's annual sales. His timing was superb—the running boom ignited in 1974. In 1976, *Runner's World* magazine selected one of New Balance's shoe models as the best and rated four of its models among the top ten running shoes.

With that kind of endorsement, sales exploded. Davis's major problem became getting enough products out of the factory. By 1982, sales topped $60 million. By the mid-1980s, sales reached $85 million, with good profitability.

Then New Balance "hit the wall." In marathon running, the *wall* is an imaginary point about 18 miles into the race where runners may suddenly find that, although they have been running well, they can't go any further. Even though the athletic-shoe industry continued to expand, New Balance's sales growth vanished. Davis blamed himself. "We lost our focus," he said. "We didn't execute well. And we tried to chase Nike and Reebok in terms of design, which we never should have done. The result was a lot of closeouts, a lot of selling below the recommended wholesale price.

"What always sold," he added, "were our core running products and our tennis shoes. But we never had enough of them because we had spread ourselves too thin in all the peripheral areas. We knew our brand awareness was low, but even if we'd had money to advertise, we wouldn't have spent it because of our failure to execute effectively."

In 1989, Davis's top managers urged him to stop U.S. manufacturing and to join the rush to manufacture in the Far East. They pointed out that Nike, which started the same year as New Balance, had already shot past the $1 billion mark in sales. With low labor costs and economies of scale, Nike could feed its huge advertising and marketing machine. New Balance, they argued, was struggling to break even on sales of $95 million. Moreover, managers questioned how a company paying $12 to $13 an hour, including benefits, could compete with companies using Chinese workers who made $80 a month. With lower labor costs generating higher margins, industry leaders could afford to carpet-bomb the country with advertising, enforcing their dominance.

However, despite his managers' advice, Davis held fast to his philosophy. Although New Balance did make some shoes and components overseas, Davis had always felt strongly that the advantages of domestic manufacturing outweighed the benefits of cheap labor overseas. "Initially, we manufactured here because when I bought the company, it was making shoes here," he says. "Then we realized that you can control the quality better from here. You can establish proprietary techniques to improve product quality. [But] we'd be a bigger, more profitable company if we made everything overseas."

However, as Davis's motto suggests, profit isn't everything. Actually, until the early 1990s, making a profit was not very difficult for most athletic shoe companies. The industry had surged with the onset of the fitness craze in the 1970s. Sales had skyrocketed in the 1980s, with annual growth rates as high as 20 percent. By 1992, footwear for running, tennis, basketball, and other sports accounted for 40 percent of all U.S. shoe sales. Throughout this rapid growth phase, there had been plenty of room for the top 25 brand name manufacturers.

Then, suddenly, the party was over. In the second half of 1991 and the first half of 1992, the U.S. athletic-footwear market contracted. Annual unit volume dropped from 398 million pairs to 381 million. Retail sales dipped by 2.6 percent. Industry analysts blamed the recession, market saturation, and a shift in consumer tastes for the stall.

As a result, for all but the biggest names, a bare-knuckled brawl began. Nike and Reebok still dominate the industry, racking up combined 1992 sales of $3.3 billion, more than half the total market. However, the smaller players, like New Balance, who had less than a 3 percent market share, found themselves facing an uphill battle. Some analysts speculated that many smaller competitors would fade away.

TURNING THINGS AROUND

To attack the industry's heartbreak hill, which like its Boston Marathon counterpart would exhaust competitors lacking sufficient resources, Davis crafted a new strategy. First, he focused on manufacturing. New Balance operated four factories, two in Massachusetts and two in Maine. The 800 workers at these plants produced 10,000 pairs of shoes a day. Davis wanted to double that number by 1994. He also wanted to cut the time from starting to cut material for a pair of shoes to putting them in the box from six weeks to two days!

To help speed up the manufacturing process, Davis scrapped New Balance's old-style piecework manufacturing system in favor of a team approach he called modular manufacturing. Everyone worked on fewer pieces that moved through more quickly, instead of working on many shoes that moved more slowly. In addition to cutting inventory costs, the new process slashed new-product development time. It had been taking New Balance a year from new-product idea to delivery of a new shoe model. Davis wanted to cut the time to four months. "That's very aggressive, but it's important because when you get retailers excited about a product, they want it now, not a year from now." By involving the teams at the beginning of the process, Davis believed he could reach his four-month target.

These early steps toward revitalization helped increase New Balance's sales to $100 million in 1991 and restored the company's profitability. Davis also spent $2 million on new plant and equipment in both 1991 and 1992 and planned to spend $3 million in 1993.

THE NEW STRATEGY

With the first steps taken, Davis now wants to implement a new, multistep strategy to reestablish New Balance's position, sales growth, and profitability.

Continue Width Sizing

New Balance had always made shoes comparable in quality to any competing shoe. Its competitive advantage has stemmed from its focus on width sizing. All of its shoes come in true widths; some range from AA to EEEE. Few competitors make anything beyond narrow or wide versions of selected products. For men's shoes, competitors make a D width; for women's shoes, they make a B width. When competitors offer different widths, they often simply cut the upper shoe materials tighter or looser and then glue them onto average-width soles.

Width sizing is difficult and expensive. The process complicates production because it requires shorter runs and more flexible production. It also requires workers to use multiple lasts, the molds used to build shoes. With the many widths, and with lengths that varied from sizes 6 to 16, New Balance could have more than 80 sizes for a single model. Despite these problems, width sizing provides the most customized athletic footwear available. Davis believes that well-fitting shoes will become more important to consumers as the population ages.

Maintain Production Control

Although manufacturing domestically has some drawbacks, it has one major advantage. New Balance controls its own production in its own factories, rather than depending on foreign firms to do the work. Thus, Davis eliminates the problem that some companies face of finding enough factory time to manufacture shoes when more are needed. The ability to respond to market changes affects retailers. One retailer points out that his firm bought some of its shoes from Japanese-owned ASICS Tiger Corporation. He said that there had been times when his company had been out of ASICS's shoes and could not get more for three or four months. "They can't control the factories the way New Balance does, because they don't own them," he noted.

Pursue Just-in-Time Retailing

Having his own factories fits well with Davis's emphasis on serving retail customers better. The use of teams allows New Balance to respond faster to retailer needs. Like other athletic-shoe manufacturers, New Balance wants retailers to place their orders six months in advance. This helps in production planning. With faster production speed, however, New Balance can fill orders in fewer than 30 days. The company also plans to keep its 14 best-selling models always in stock.

Davis argues that such a quick-response capability is important. A senior buyer for a 58-store, Florida-based chain supported Davis's assertion. "When you buy from Nike or Reebok, you have to order six months in advance. Without a crystal ball, it's tough to project your business that far out. With New Balance, we're able to order 30 days out, and we're getting a 90 percent [order] fill rate or better. That's fantastic. When you have 58 stores, a fill-in order can be $200,000. By having New Balance deliver as fast as on a weekly basis, we can buy to match our current needs. So we're not losing any sales, and we don't have to carry a big inventory."

Davis calls this "sharing the risk" with the retailer, a kind of partnership that is important to his growth plans. "We feel that with the better retailers around the country, we can take more business just by virtue of working more closely with them, making a better product, with better service," he says. "That means higher margins for them."

Continue Capital Improvements

By the end of 1994, Davis had spent $6 million over a three-year period on high-tech equipment to enhance operational flexibility and speed. A new computer-aided design system helped research and development cut the time required to introduce a new model. Computerized cutting and stitching machines increased factory productivity. These investments helped boost gross margins from the mid-30-percent range to a target of 40 percent. This target margin compares well with what New Balance's competitors get by manufacturing abroad. Nike had a 38.7 percent gross margin in 1992.

Increase Domestic Production

The capital improvements tie in with Davis's plan to make more shoes domestically. With New Balance's cost structure, it cannot price a domestically produced pair of shoes below $50 at retail. The company imports some 36 percent of its finished goods, 1.3 million pair, to provide lower-priced shoes. As domestic margins increase, Davis plans to make more shoes in the United States.

Exploit the "Buy American" Trend

Davis wants to take advantage of this trend. He plans to play up New Balance's preference for domestic production in new advertising and point-of-purchase displays.

Some retailers believe that more customers are requesting American-made shoes, especially in blue-collar areas. Others suggest that consumers have learned that the fit is more consistent with American-made shoes. Shoes made in different foreign countries can each fit a little differently, causing problems for retailers and customers.

Stress Product Quality

New Balance's defect rate had risen as high as 8 percent. Alarmed, Davis has restructured the factory workers' compensation system so that 70 percent of their pay hinges on quality and 30 percent on volume. As a result, 99.9 percent of the shoes now arrive at the packing point ready for shipping. New Balance will also continue to use top-notch materials and components. A brochure on the shoes' "suspension system" touts such ingredients as a "roll bar" that resists back-and-forth foot motion; the Encap mid-sole cushioning pad, which "disperses shock"; and the contrabalance heel design, which "like an inverted trampoline, . . . adds spring to your step."

Davis knows that quality is important, but price is also becoming increasingly important. In *Consumer Reports'* May 1992 analysis of running shoes, the Saucony Jazz 3000 model placed first in both the men's and women's categories. The magazine judged the shoes "best buys" at $68 a pair. New Balance's highest rating was the eighth-ranked M997 model at $120. The M997 was beaten by shoes from Nike (at $125, retail), Avia ($70), ASICS ($85 and $55), Adidas ($85), and even another Saucony model, the Azura II ($82). New Balance fared better in the women's category, with the judges ranking the W997 model second. One analyst noted that retailers discounted 64 percent of athletic footwear last year, up from 62 percent in 1991.

Introduce New Products

For 1993, New Balance introduced 30 new models in its 78-model line, including an off-track, deep-treaded running shoe; a brightly hued racing spike; four basketball models; and two hiking boots. A volleyball shoe is under development.

However, Davis seems most excited about the American Classic line of men's dress shoe. The line features six styles of bucks, wing tips, and casuals. "They're as comfortable as any athletic shoe we have," Davis boasted. American Classics competes with the Reebok-owned Rockport line, the titan of the dress-comfort class. Davis projected that the company would sell 200,000 pairs—$10 million worth—in 1993.

The new line is part of New Balance's growing line of walking shoes. In fact, New Balance offers 28 walking models versus 24 for running. Davis believes that the walking shoes will outsell his running shoes in five years. He argues that many baby boomers will be giving up running as their knees start to go. These consumers will take up exercise walking as a good alternative, and they will need appropriate shoes.

Increase Advertising

Finally, Davis realizes that he must raise brand awareness. Although consumers associate the New Balance name with quality, too few consumers know about the company and its products. A 1991 market research study revealed that only 4 percent of Americans could identify the company as an athletic-shoe maker.

Moreover, advertising has become critical in the industry. In 1993 alone, Nike spent about $120 million on advertising and millions more in promotional payments to athletes like Michael Jordon and Bo Jackson. Reebok countered with a $100-million ad budget, including $20 million to promote Shaquille O'Neal, the Orlando Magic rookie.

New Balance has been hard pressed to compete. These competitors spend more on *advertising* than New Balance has in *sales revenue*! A few years ago, New Balance ran ads proclaiming that it was "endorsed by no one." The company felt that quality alone would sell the shoes.

To send the message that a shoe that fits better performs better, Davis spent $6 million for advertising in 1993, up from $1 million in 1990. The company spent money on cooperative print and radio advertising in partnership with its retailers. For the first time, however, New Balance will buy time on national television, spending $700,000 for commercials on ESPN, TNT, the Sports Channel, and the Discovery Channel.

Davis placed advertisements in magazines such as *Runner's World, Tennis, Esquire, Travel and Leisure, Sierra,* and *Outside.* He also bought pages in women's magazines such as *Self, Glamour,* and *Working Woman.*

Finally, the company spent $500,000 on point-of-purchase displays and other devices to enhance brand identity.

THE FINISH LINE

The question is, will Davis's strategy, which he calls Operation Quick Strike, work? Is the strategy strong enough to guarantee New Balance's survival as it races Nike, Reebok, and the myriad of other smaller companies toward the finish line? Can Davis double New Balance's sales to $200 million in the next three years? Can a small-share competitor really survive in the big leagues?

QUESTIONS

1. Outline New Balance's marketing strategy, including the new strategic steps it wants to take. Who is its target market? What is its marketing mix? What is its competitive strategy?

2. How does New Balance enhance the total delivered value to its customers? How does it influence customer expectations? How will New Balance's new strategy affect its value chain activities?

3. What threats and opportunities does New Balance face? What are its objectives, and what issues do those objectives raise?

4. What changes would you recommend in the company's marketing strategy?

5. How do you react to Jim Davis's quote that begins the case? Is profit the most important thing, or is it making something in which you believe?

Source: Adapted from Jay Finegan, "Surviving the Nike/Reebok Jungle," *INC. Magazine,* May 1993, pp. 98–108. Used with permission.

The Global Marketplace

20

In the late 1970s, Apple Computer invaded Japan. The $7 billion Japanese personal computer market, second only to the huge U.S. market, offered very attractive growth opportunities. If Apple had made the right moves then, it might well have sewn up Japan before the competition could establish itself. However, more than a decade later, Apple had achieved little more than novelty sales and a tiny 1.4 percent market share.

Looking back, far from making all the right moves in Japan, Apple did just about everything wrong. Its mostly American managers never really took the time to understand the Japanese market. Instead, they treated Japan largely as an extension of Apple's U.S. market. For example, repeated requests from Japanese dealers to tailor the Macintosh computer for Japanese use fell on deaf ears. Even though the Mac's powerful graphics capabilities made it ideal for handling Kanji, the complex Chinese characters used in written Japanese, Apple insisted on selling its American version in Japan pretty much as is. To make matters worse, the first Macs arrived in Japan with shoddy packaging and keyboards that didn't work. Apple didn't even provide a Japanese-language operating manual.

Japanese buyers were also put off by the Mac's high prices—almost double those of comparable Japanese machines. Moreover, Apple's machines were distributed poorly and the company seldom advertised its products in Japan or displayed them at trade shows. Finally, when Apple entered Japan, it quickly acquired a reputation among local software houses for "Yankee arrogance." Rather than pay software developers to convert their packages to run on Macs, a common practice in Japan, Apple *charged* them for technical information. It also refused to join any Japanese trade associations or even to loan Macs to the software developers. In contrast, when NEC entered the personal computer market in the early 1980s, it did all it could to court software houses. As a result, by the late 1980s, only 15 Japanese software packages existed for the Mac, compared to more than 5,000 for NEC computers, helping NEC to corner a staggering 60 percent market share.

OBJECTIVES

When you finish this chapter, you should be able to accomplish the following:

1. Discuss the **global marketing environment**, the **international trade system**, and the **economic, political-legal,** and **cultural environments** that affect marketing decisions.

2. Outline the key elements of **deciding whether to go international, deciding which markets to enter,** and **deciding how to enter the market,** either through **exporting, joint venturing,** or **direct investment**.

3. Explain the primary issue of **deciding on the global marketing program,** whether to use a **standardized** or **adapted marketing mix,** or some combination of the two.

4. Distinguish among the three ways companies manage their **global marketing organizations,** through **export departments, international divisions,** and becoming a **global organization**.

By 1988, Apple Computer Japan had become an embarrassment. Mac sales were paltry and Japan's hard-line America-bashers were pointing to Apple Computer Japan as a classic example of "ugly American" incompetence. Apple finally saw the light. With newfound insight, it set out to reverse its fortunes in Japan. As a first step, Apple recruited an all-Japanese executive team—a new president from Toshiba, an engineering manager from Sony, and a support services manager from NCR Japan. The new team moved quickly to slash prices, broaden distribution, and repair its reputation with Japanese software developers, dealers, and consumers.

Apple introduced three lower-priced Macs. The least expensive of these, a machine selling for less than $1,500, would later grow to account for more than half of Apple's unit sales in Japan. The company also prepared to offer a family of Japanese-language products, including a new Japanese-character version of its highly acclaimed Postscript laser printer and KanjiTalk, a Japanese-language operating system. To strengthen distribution, Apple recruited several major blue-chip Japanese companies to sell Macs, including business equipment giant Brother Industries, stationery leader Kokuyo, Mitsubishi, Sharp, and Minolta. And it began to open Apple Centers, outlets that sell only Apple products targeted at the corporate market.

Perhaps most importantly, Apple Computer Japan set out to patch up relations with Japanese software houses. It joined the Japan Personal Computer Software Association (JPSA) and began to aggressively recruit software developers. It even brought in engineers from top U.S. software firms to work as partners with the Japanese firms in developing Japanese versions of proven American packages. The software houses responded. By 1992, 200 Mac-compatible software programs were available, and the number was increasing daily. Some of Japan's largest software developers now endorse and distribute Macs. And a recent JPSA survey shows that Macs are the number-two choice behind NEC among Japanese software writers as the machine they hope to buy next.

To complete the makeover and repair its tarnished image, Apple launched a full-scale promotion campaign, including heavy TV and print advertising that portrayed the Mac as a creative, easy-to-use tool. Apple also sponsored several high-profile events, such as the first Japanese Ladies Professional Golf Association tournament and a Janet Jackson concert in Tokyo. The concert drew 60,000 fans, each of whom found a bag of Apple literature on his or her chair. To further enhance its new image, Apple marketed the "Apple Collection" of T-shirts, coffee mugs, key chains, hats, and other merchandise emblazoned with the colorful Apple logo through Tokyo retailers.

Apple's overhaul produced amazing results—Macs now are sprouting up everywhere in Japan. Apple dominates in the desk-top publishing and graphics design segments and is grabbing share from Japanese competitors in several other important areas. More and more, Macs are popping into college classrooms, and into primary and secondary schools, where Apple has earned a reputation as easy to use. Whereas Apple is struggling in the United States, Japan now has become its fastest-growing market. Its market share has grown to 16 percent, making it second only to the still dominant NEC (53.4 percent). Apple's outstanding success in Japan may provide the model for the ailing company's worldwide revival.

Its experiences in Japan have taught Apple that international marketing involves more than simply taking what's successful at home and exporting it abroad. Rather, entering a foreign market requires a strong commitment and a keen understanding of sometimes very different cultures and marketing environments. It usually means adapting the company's products, programs, and approaches to the special needs and circumstances of each new global market. For an ever-growing number of Japanese, Apple's new, more fitting approach has transformed the old "rotten Apple" to a new "Apple of their eye."[1]

In the past, U.S. companies paid little attention to international trade. If they could pick up some extra sales through exporting, that was fine. But the big market was at home, and it teemed with opportunities. The home market was also much safer. Managers did not need to learn other languages, deal with strange and changing currencies, face political and legal uncertainties, or adapt their products to different customer needs and expectations. Today, however, the situation is much different.

GLOBAL MARKETING INTO THE TWENTY-FIRST CENTURY

The 1990s mark the first decade in which companies around the world must start thinking globally. Time and distance are shrinking rapidly with the advent of faster communication, transportation, and financial flows. Products developed in one country are finding enthusiastic acceptance in other countries.

True, many companies have been carrying on international activities for decades. Coca-Cola, IBM, Kodak, Nestlé, Shell, Bayer, Toshiba, Sony, and other companies are familiar to most consumers around the world. But today global competition is intensifying. Foreign firms are expanding aggressively into new international markets, and home markets are no longer as rich in opportunity. Domestic companies that never thought about foreign competitors suddenly find these competitors in their own backyards. The firm that stays at home to play it safe not only might lose its chance to enter other markets but also risks losing its home market.

In the United States, names such as Sony, Toyota, Nestlé, Norelco, Mercedes, and Panasonic have become household words. Other products and services that appear to be American really are produced or owned by foreign companies: Bantam books, Baskin-Robbins ice cream, GE and RCA televisions, Firestone tires, Kiwi shoe polish, Lipton tea, Carnation milk, Pillsbury products, and Motel 6, to name just a few. The United States also has attracted huge foreign investments in basic industries such as steel, petroleum, tires, and chemicals, and in tourist and real estate ventures, illustrated by Japanese land purchases in Hawaii and California, Kuwait's resort development off the South Carolina coast, and Arab and Japanese purchases of Manhattan office buildings. Few U.S. industries are now safe from foreign competition.

Although some companies would like to stem the tide of foreign imports through protectionism, this response would be only a temporary solution. In the long run, it would raise the cost of living and protect inefficient U.S. firms. The answer is that more U.S. firms must learn how to enter foreign markets and increase their global competitiveness. Many U.S. companies have been successful at international marketing: Gillette, Colgate, IBM, Xerox, Corning, Coca-Cola, McDonald's, General Electric, Caterpillar, Du Pont, Ford, Kodak, 3M, Boeing, Motorola, and dozens of other American firms have made the world their market. But there are too few like them. In fact, just five U.S. companies account for 12 percent of all exports; 1,000 manufacturers (out of 300,000) account for 60 percent.[2]

Every government runs an export promotion program, trying to persuade its local companies to export. The government in Denmark pays more than half the salary of marketing consultants who help small and medium-size Danish companies get into exports. Many countries go even farther and subsidize their companies by granting preferential land and energy costs—they even supply cash outright so that their companies can charge lower prices than their foreign competitors.

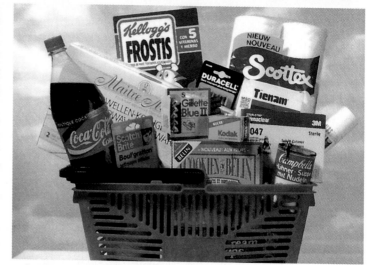

Many American companies have made the world their market.

The longer companies delay taking steps toward internationalizing, the more they risk being shut out of growing markets in Western Europe, Eastern Europe, the Pacific Rim, and elsewhere. Domestic businesses that thought they were safe now find companies from neighboring countries invading their home markets. All companies will have to answer some basic questions: What market position should we try to establish in our country, in our economic region, and globally? Who will our global competitors be, and what are their strategies and resources? Where should we produce or source our products? What strategic alliances should we form with other firms around the world?

Ironically, although the need for companies to go abroad is greater today than in the past, so are the risks. Companies that go global confront several major problems. First, high debt, inflation, and unemployment in many countries have resulted in highly unstable governments and currencies, which limit trade and expose U.S. firms to many risks. Second, governments are placing more regulations on foreign firms, such as requiring joint ownership with domestic partners, mandating the hiring of nationals, and limiting profits that can be taken from the country. Third, foreign governments often impose high tariffs or trade barriers in order to protect their own industries. Finally, corruption is an increasing prob-

Global industry
An industry in which the strategic positions of competitors in given geographic or national markets are affected by their overall global positions.

Global firm
A firm that, by operating in more than one country, gains R&D, production, marketing, and financial advantages that are not available to purely domestic competitors.

FIGURE 20-1 *Major decisions in international marketing*

lem—officials in several countries often award business not to the best bidder but to the highest briber.

You might conclude that companies are doomed whether they stay at home or go abroad. But companies selling in global industries have no choice but to internationalize their operations. A **global industry** is one in which the competitive positions of firms in given local or national markets are affected by their overall global positions. Therefore, a **global firm** is one that, by operating in more than one country, gains marketing, production, R&D, and financial advantages that are not available to purely domestic competitors. The global company sees the world as one market. It minimizes the importance of national boundaries and raises capital, source materials and components, and manufactures and markets its goods wherever it can do the best job. For example, Ford's "world truck" sports a cab made in Europe and a chassis built in North America. It is assembled in Brazil and imported to the United States for sale. Thus, global firms gain advantages by planning, operating, and coordinating their activities on a worldwide basis.

Because firms around the world are globalizing at a rapid rate, domestic firms in global industries must act quickly before the window closes on them. This does not mean that small and medium-size firms must operate in a dozen countries to succeed. These firms can practice global nichemanship. But the world is becoming smaller, and every company operating in a global industry—whether large or small—must assess and establish its place in world markets.

As shown in Figure 20-1, a company faces six major decisions in international marketing. Each decision will be discussed in detail in this chapter.

LOOKING AT THE GLOBAL MARKETING ENVIRONMENT

Before deciding whether to operate internationally, a company must thoroughly understand the international marketing environment. That environment has changed a great deal in the last two decades, creating both new opportunities and new problems. The world economy has globalized. World trade and investment have grown rapidly, with many attractive markets opening up in Western and Eastern Europe, China and the Pacific Rim, Russia, and elsewhere. There has been a growth of global brands in automobiles, food, clothing, electronics, and many other categories. The number of global companies has grown dramatically. Meanwhile, the dominant position of the United States has declined. Other countries, such as Japan and Germany, have increased their economic power in world markets (see Marketing Highlight 20-1). The international financial system has become more complex and fragile, and U.S. companies face increasing trade barriers erected to protect domestic markets from outside competition.

THE INTERNATIONAL TRADE SYSTEM

Tariff
A tax levied by a government against certain imported products. Tariffs are designed to raise revenue or to protect domestic firms.

Quota
A limit on the amount of goods that an importing country will accept in certain product categories; it is designed to conserve on foreign exchange and to protect local industry and employment.

The U.S. company looking abroad must start by understanding the international *trade system*. When selling to another country, the U.S. firm faces various trade restrictions. The most common is the **tariff**, which is a tax levied by a foreign government against certain imported products. The tariff may be designed either to raise revenue or to protect domestic firms. The exporter also may face a **quota,**

WORLD-CLASS MARKETING: THE JAPANESE

Few dispute that the Japanese have performed an economic miracle since World War II. In a very short time, they've risen from economic ruin to achieve global market leadership in many industries: automobiles, motorcycles, watches, cameras, optical instruments, steel, shipbuilding, computers, and consumer electronics. They have made strong inroads into tires, chemicals, machine tools, and even designer clothes, cosmetics, and food. Some credit the global success of Japanese companies to their unique business and management practices. Others point to the help they get from Japan's government, powerful trading companies, and banks. Still others say Japan's success is based on low wage rates and unfair dumping policies.

In any case, one of the main keys to Japan's success is certainly its skillful use of marketing. Japanese managers came to the United States to study marketing and went home understanding it better than many U.S. companies. They know how to select a market, enter it in the right way, build market share, and protect that share against competitors.

Selecting Markets
The Japanese work hard to identify attractive global markets. First, they look for industries that require high skills and high labor intensity, but few natural resources. These include consumer electronics, cameras, watches, motorcycles, and pharmaceuticals. Second, they prefer markets in which consumers around the world would be willing to buy the same product designs. Finally, they look for industries in which the market leaders are weak or complacent.

Entering Markets
Japanese study teams spend several months evaluating a target market and searching for market niches that are not being satisfied. Sometimes they start with a low-priced, stripped-down version of a product; other times they create a product that is as good as the competition's but priced lower; and still other times, they produce a product with higher quality or new features. The Japanese line up good distribution channels in order to provide quick service. They also use effective advertising to bring their products to the consumers' attention. Their basic entry strategy is to build market share rather than early profits. The Japanese often are willing to wait as long as a decade before realizing their profits.

Building Market Share
Once Japanese firms gain a market foothold, they begin to expand their market share. They pour money into product improvements and new models so that they can offer more and better products than the competition. They spot new opportunities through market segmentation, develop markets in new countries, and work to build a network of world markets and production locations.

Protecting Market Share
Once the Japanese achieve market leadership, they become defenders rather than attackers. Their defense strategy is continuous product development and refined market segmentation. Their philosophy is to make "tiny improvements in a thousand places."

Recently, some experts have questioned whether Japanese companies can sustain their push toward global marketing dominance. They suggest that the Japanese emphasis on the long-term market share over short-term profits and its ability to market high-quality products at low prices have come at the expense of Japan's employees, stockholders, and communities. They note that, compared to Western firms, Japanese companies work their employees longer hours for lower wages, pay their stockholders lower dividends, and contribute less to community and environmental causes. Other analysts, however, predict that Japan's marketing success will likely continue.

American firms have fought back by adding new product lines, improving quality, pricing more aggressively, streamlining production, and forming strategic partnerships with foreign companies. With the help of a weakened Japanese economy, a soaring yen, and strong political trade pressures, American companies are winning back U.S. market share in industries ranging from automobiles and earthmovers to semiconductors and computers. Many U.S. companies are also gaining ground in Japan. In fact, U.S. companies sell more than 50,000 different products in Japan, and many hold leading market shares—Coke leads in soft drinks (60 percent share), Schick in razors (71 percent), Polaroid in instant cameras (66 percent), and McDonald's in fast food. Procter & Gamble markets the leading brand in several categories, ranging from disposable diapers and liquid laundry detergents to acne treatments. Apple, Motorola, Levi Strauss, Dow, and scores of other U.S. companies have found that Japan offers large and profitable market opportunities. For example, since the early 1980s, U.S. companies have increased their Japanese computer sales by 48 percent, pharmaceutical sales by 41 percent, and electronic parts sales by 63 percent.

Sources: See Philip Kotler, Liam Fahey, and Somkid Jatusripitak, *The New Competition* (Englewood Cliffs, NJ: Prentice Hall, 1985); Vernon R. Alden, "Who Says You Can't Crack Japanese Markets?" *Harvard Business Review,* January–February 1987, pp. 52–56; Howard Schlossberg, "Japan Market Hardly Closed to U.S. Firms," *Marketing News,* July 9, 1990, pp. 1, 12; "Why Japan Must Change," *Fortune,* March 9, 1992, pp. 66–67; and Kevin Kelly, "Besting Japan," *Business Week,* June 7, 1993, pp. 26–28.

Embargo
A ban on the import of a certain product.

which sets limits on the amount of goods the importing country will accept in certain product categories. The purpose of the quota is to conserve on foreign exchange and to protect local industry and employment. An **embargo,** or boycott, is the strongest form of quota, which totally bans some kinds of imports.

Exchange controls
Government limits on the amount of its foreign exchange with other countries and on its exchange rate against other currencies.

Nontariff trade barriers
Nonmonetary barriers to foreign products, such as biases against a foreign company's bids or product standards that go against a foreign company's product features.

American firms may face **exchange controls** that limit the amount of foreign exchange and the exchange rate against other currencies. The company also may face **nontariff trade barriers,** such as biases against U.S. company bids or restrictive product standards that go against American product features:

> One of the cleverest ways the Japanese have found to keep foreign manufacturers out of their domestic market is to plead "uniqueness." Japanese skin is different, the government argues, so foreign cosmetics companies must test their products in Japan before selling there. The Japanese say their stomachs are small and have room for only the *mikan,* the local tangerine, so imports of U.S. oranges are limited. Now the Japanese have come up with what may be the flakiest argument yet: Their snow is different, so ski equipment should be too.[3]

At the same time, certain forces *help* trade between nations. Examples are the General Agreement on Tariffs and Trade and various regional free trade agreements.

The General Agreement on Tariffs and Trade

The General Agreement on Tariffs and Trade (GATT) is a 45-year-old treaty designed to promote world trade by reducing tariffs and other international trade barriers. Since the treaty's inception in 1948, member nations (currently numbering 117) have met in eight rounds of GATT negotiations to reassess trade barriers and set new rules for international trade. The first seven rounds of negotiations reduced the average worldwide tariffs on manufactured goods from 45 percent to just 5 percent.

The most recent GATT negotiations, dubbed the Uruguay Round, dragged on for seven long years before concluding in 1993. Although the benefits of the Uruguay Round won't be felt for many years, the new accord should promote robust long-term global trade growth. It reduces the world's remaining merchandise tariffs by 30 percent, which could boost global merchandise trade by up to 10 percent, or $270 billion in current dollars, by the year 2002. The new agreement also extends GATT to cover trade in agriculture and a wide range of services, and it toughens international protection of copyrights, patents, trademarks, and other intellectual property.[4] Beyond reducing trade barriers and setting standards for trade, GATT also provides a forum for resolving international trade disputes. When member nations fail to resolve trade disputes among themselves, special GATT panels can be set up to recommend action.

Regional Free Trade Zones

Economic community
A group of nations organized to work toward common goals in the regulation of international trade.

Certain countries have formed *free trade zones* or **economic communities**—groups of nations organized to work toward common goals in the regulation of international trade. One such community is the *European Union (EU).* The EU's members are the major Western European nations, with a combined population exceeding 320 million people. The EU works to create a single European market by reducing physical, financial, and technical barriers to trade among member nations. Founded in 1957, the European Union has yet to achieve the true "common market" originally envisioned. In 1985, however, member countries renewed their push to integrate economically (see Marketing Highlight 20-2).

In North America, the United States and Canada phased out trade barriers in 1989. In January 1994, the *North American Free Trade Agreement (NAFTA)* established a free trade zone with the United States, Mexico, and Canada. The agreement creates a single market of 360 million people who produce and consume $6.7 trillion worth of goods and services. As it is implemented over the next fifteen years, NAFTA will eliminate all trade barrier and investment restrictions among the three countries. Prior to NAFTA, tariffs on American products entering Mexico averaged 13 percent, while U.S. tariffs on Mexican goods averaged 6 percent.

RESHAPING THE EUROPEAN UNION

Formed in 1957, the European Union (EU)—or Common Market—set out to create a single European market by reducing trade barriers among its member nations and by developing European-wide policies on trade with nonmember nations. However, the dream of a true "common market" was buried quickly under heaps of regulations and nationalistic squabbling. Despite early common market initiatives, Europe remained a fragmented maze of isolated and protected national markets, making it a difficult and confusing place to do business. In 1985, however, the European Union countries renewed their push for a common market. They jointly enacted the Single European Act, which called for sweeping deregulation to eliminate barriers to the free flow of products, services, finances, and labor among member countries.

The European Union represents one of the world's single largest markets. It contains 340 million consumers and accounts for 20 percent of the world's exports, compared to 14 percent for the United States and 12 percent for Japan. By the year 2000, the EU could contain as many as 450 million people in 25 countries, as more European nations seek admission to the free trade area. Thus, European economic unification promises tremendous opportunities for U.S. firms—as trade barriers drop, lower costs will result in greater operating efficiency and productivity. European markets will grow and become more accessible. As a result, most U.S. companies have drafted new strategies for cultivating the invigorated European market.

Yet, many U.S. managers have mixed reactions: Just as European unification has created many opportunities, it also poses threats. As a result of increased unification, European companies will grow bigger and more competitive. Thus, many companies from the United States, Japan, and other non-European countries are bracing for an onslaught of new European competition, both in Western Europe and in other world markets. Perhaps an even bigger concern, however, is that lower barriers *inside* Europe will only create thicker *outside* walls. Some observers envision a "Fortress Europe" that

heaps favors on firms from EU countries but hinders outsiders by imposing obstacles such as stiffer import quotas, local content requirements, and other nontariff barriers. Companies that already operate in Europe will be shielded from such protectionist moves. Thus, companies that sell to Europe but are not now operating there are rushing to become insiders before unification threatens to close them out. They are building their own operations in Europe, acquiring existing businesses there, or forming strategic alliances with established European firms.

Renewed unification efforts have created much excitement within the European Union, but they also have drawn criticism. There is still confusion and disagreement among Europeans as to the scope and nature of the changes they want. Thus, progress toward unification has been slow—many doubt that complete unification ever will be achieved. By mid-1993, of 219 EU laws called for in the original blueprint for a single market, only 106 had been implemented with the needed legislation in all 12 EU countries. The most difficult issues—those involving the free flow of money, people, and goods—are still unresolved. For example, in December 1991, European Union leaders approved the Maastricht Treaty, an amendment to the original EU charter, which calls for establishing a single European currency and central bank by 1999. Before the treaty can become law, however, all 12 member states must approve it by legislative vote or by referendum. So far, the treaty is off to a rocky start—in 1992 Danish voters rejected the treaty, and the French passed it by only a narrow margin. Thus, although the creation of a common currency would greatly ease trade, such a measure is unlikely to be a reality for at least another decade, if at all.

Beyond these currency issues, actions such as standardizing taxes, abolishing border checks, and forging other European-wide efforts will require changing the entire economic makeup of Europe. Individual countries will have to give up some of their independence for the common good, pushing aside the nationalism that has ruled European history for centuries. For these reasons, the odds

are low that Europe ever will realize the full unification vision.

Even if the European Union does manage to standardize its general trade regulations, creating an economic community will not create a homogeneous market. With nine different languages and distinctive national customs, Europe will be anything but a "common market." Although economic and political boundaries may fall, social and cultural differences will remain. And although the unification effort may create common general standards, companies marketing in Europe still will face a daunting mass of local rules. Take advertising for example. One large advertising agency has prepared a 52-page book containing dense statistics on country-by-country restrictions. Ireland, for example, forbids ads for liquor but allows them for beer and wine—as long as they run after 7 P.M.; Spain allows ads only for drinks with less than 23 percent alcohol, and they can run only after 9:30 P.M. In Holland, ads for sweets have to show a toothbrush in the corner of the television screen. European unification will have little effect on such local rules.

Thus, the European market will always be far more diverse than either the U.S. or Japanese markets. It is unlikely that the European Union will ever become the "United States of Europe." Nonetheless, great changes are occurring in Europe. Even if only partly successful, European unification will make a more efficient and competitive Europe a global force to be reckoned with. The best prepared companies will benefit most. Thus, whether they cheer it or fear it, all companies must prepare now for the New Europe or risk being shut out later.

Sources: See Cyndee Miller, "Marketers Optimistic About EC Despite Monetary Muddle," *Marketing News,* October 26, 1992, p. 2; Andrew Hilton, "Mythology, Markets, and the Emerging Europe," *Harvard Business Review,* November–December 1992, pp. 50–54; several articles in a special section of *The Economist,* July 3, 1993, pp. SS12–SS17; and Bill Javetski, "The Single Market Itself Is in Question," *Business Week,* November 1, 1993, p. 52.

Wal-Mart and other companies are expanding rapidly in Mexico and Canada to take advantage of the many opportunities presented by NAFTA. The trade agreement establishes a single market of 360 million people in Mexico, Canada, and the United States.

Other free trade areas are forming in Latin America and South America. For example, MERCOSUL now links Brazil, Colombia, and Mexico, and Chile and Mexico have formed a successful free trade zone. Venezuela, Colombia, and Mexico—the "Group of Three"—are negotiating a free trade area as well. It is likely that NAFTA will eventually merge with this and other arrangements to form an all-Americas free trade zone.[5]

Although the recent trend toward free trade zones has caused great excitement and new market opportunities, this trend also raises some concerns. For example, groups of countries that trade freely among themselves may tend to increase barriers to outsiders (for example, creating a "Fortress Europe"). Stricter local-content rules may add a new kind of bureaucracy and will once again limit international trade. In the United States, unions fear that NAFTA will lead to the further exodus of manufacturing jobs to Mexico, where wage rates are much lower. And environmentalists worry that companies that are unwilling to play by the strict rules of the U.S. Environmental Protection Agency will relocate in Mexico, where pollution regulation has been lax.

Each nation has unique features that must be understood. A nation's readiness for different products and services and its attractiveness as a market to foreign firms depend on its economic, political-legal, and cultural environments.

ECONOMIC ENVIRONMENT

The international marketer must study each country's economy. Two economic factors reflect the country's attractiveness as a market: the country's industrial structure and its income distribution.

The country's *industrial structure* shapes its product and service needs, income levels, and employment levels. The four types of industrial structures are as follows:

◆ *Subsistence economies.* In a subsistence economy, the vast majority of people engage in simple agriculture. They consume most of their output and barter the rest for simple goods and services. They offer few market opportunities.

♦ *Raw-material-exporting economies.* These economies are rich in one or more natural resources but poor in other ways. Much of their revenue comes from exporting these resources. Examples are Chile (tin and copper); Zaire (copper, cobalt, and coffee); and Saudi Arabia (oil). These countries are good markets for large equipment, tools and supplies, and trucks. If there are many foreign residents and a wealthy upper class, they are also a market for luxury goods.

♦ *Industrializing economies.* In an industrializing economy, manufacturing accounts for 10 to 20 percent of the country's economy. Examples include Egypt, the Philippines, India, and Brazil. As manufacturing increases, the country needs more imports of raw textile materials, steel, and heavy machinery, and fewer imports of finished textiles, paper products, and automobiles. Industrialization typically creates a new rich class and a small but growing middle class, both demanding new types of imported goods.

♦ *Industrial economies.* Industrial economies are major exporters of manufactured goods and investment funds. They trade goods among themselves and also export them to other types of economies for raw materials and semifinished goods. The varied manufacturing activities of these industrial nations and their large middle class make them rich markets for all sorts of goods.

The second economic factor is the country's *income distribution.* The international marketer might find countries with one of five different income distribution patterns: (1) very low family incomes; (2) mostly low family incomes; (3) very low/very high family incomes; (4) low/medium/high family incomes; and (5) mostly medium family incomes.

However, even people in low-income countries may find ways to buy products that are important to them, or sheer population numbers can counter low average incomes. Also, in many cases, poorer countries may have small but wealthy segments of upper-income consumers:

> Recall that in the U.S. the first satellite dishes sprang up in the poorest parts of Appalachia. . . . The poorest slums of Calcutta are home to 70,000 VCRs. In Mexico, homes with color televisions out-number those with running water. Remember also that low average-income figures may conceal a lively luxury

Income distribution: Even poorer countries may have small but wealthy segments. Although citizens of Budapest, Hungary have relatively low annual incomes, well-dressed shoppers flock to elegant stores like this one, stocked with luxury goods.

market. In Warsaw (average annual income: $2,500) well-dressed shoppers flock to elegant boutiques stocked with Christian Dior perfume and Valentino shoes. . . . In China, where per capita income is less than $600, the Swiss company Rado is selling thousands of its $1,000 watches.[6]

Thus, international marketers face many challenges in understanding how the economic environment will affect decisions about which global markets to enter and how.

POLITICAL-LEGAL ENVIRONMENT

Nations differ greatly in their political-legal environments. At least four political-legal factors should be considered in deciding whether to do business in a given country: attitudes toward international buying, political stability, monetary regulations, and government bureaucracy.

Attitudes toward International Buying

Some nations are quite receptive to foreign firms, and others are quite hostile. For example, Mexico has been attracting foreign businesses for many years by offering investment incentives and site-location services. In contrast, India has bothered foreign businesses with import quotas, currency restrictions, and limits on the percentage of the management team that can be nonnationals. As a result, many U.S. companies left India because of all the hassles. For example, despite holding 80 percent of India's soft-drink market, Coca-Cola left the country in 1977 rather than comply with a law that would require it to give 60 percent control to an Indian company.[7] Pepsi, however, took positive steps to persuade the Indian government to allow it to do business on reasonable terms there (see Marketing Highlight 20-3).

Political Stability

Stability is another issue. Governments change hands, sometimes violently. Even without a change, a government may decide to respond to new popular feelings. The foreign company's property may be taken, its currency holdings may be blocked, or import quotas or new duties may be set. International marketers may find it profitable to do business in an unstable country, but the unsteady situation will affect how they handle business and financial matters.

Monetary Regulations

Sellers want to take their profits in a currency of value to them. Ideally, the buyer can pay in the seller's currency or in other world currencies. Short of this, sellers might accept a blocked currency—one whose removal from the country is restricted by the buyer's government—if they can buy other goods in that country that they need themselves or can sell elsewhere for a needed currency. Besides currency limits, a changing exchange rate also creates high risks for the seller.

Countertrade
International trade involving the direct or indirect exchange of goods for other goods instead of cash. Forms include barter, compensation (buyback), and counterpurchase.

Most international trade involves cash transactions. Yet many nations have too little hard currency to pay for their purchases from other countries. They may want to pay with other items instead of cash, which has led to a growing practice called **countertrade**, which now accounts for about 25 percent of all world trade. Countertrade takes several forms. *Barter* involves the direct exchange of goods or services, as when the Germans built a steel plant in Indonesia in exchange for oil. Another form is *compensation* (or *buyback*), whereby the seller sells a plant, equipment, or technology to another country and agrees to take payment in the resulting products. Thus, Goodyear provided China with materials and training for a printing plant in exchange for finished labels. Another form is *counterpurchase*, in which the seller receives full payment in cash but agrees to spend

THE FOUR *P*S PLUS TWO: "POLITICS" AND "PUBLIC OPINION"

It's one thing to want to do business in a particular country; it's quite another to be allowed into the country on reasonable terms. The problem of entering an unreceptive or blocked country calls for using the traditional four *P*s plus economic, psychological, political, and public relations skills to gain the cooperation of several parties in the country.

For example, in its attempt to enter the huge India market, PepsiCo worked with an Indian business group to seek government approval for its entry. Both domestic soft-drink companies and anti-multinational legislators objected to letting Pepsi into India, so Pepsi had to make an offer that the Indian government would find hard to refuse. With this in mind, Pepsi offered to help India export enough of its agricultural products to more than offset the outlay for import-

ing soft-drink syrup. Pepsi also promised to focus a good deal of selling effort on rural areas to help in their economic development. It further offered to construct an agricultural research center and to give food processing, packaging, and water-treatment technology to India. After three years of haggling, the Indian bureaucracy finally approved Pepsi's extensive proposal.

Clearly, Pepsi's strategy was to bundle a set of benefits that would win the support of the various interest groups influencing the entry decision. Pepsi's marketing problem was not one of simply applying the four *P*s in a new market, but rather one of just getting into the market in the first place. In trying to win over the government and public groups—and to maintain a reasonable relationship once admitted—Pepsi had to add

two more *P*s: "politics" and "public opinion."

Many other large companies have learned that it pays to build good relations with host governments. Olivetti, for example, enters new markets by building housing for workers, supporting local arts and charities, and hiring and training local managers. IBM sponsors nutrition programs for Latin American children and gives agricultural advice to the Mexican government. And Polaroid is helping Italy restore Leonardo da Vinci's *Last Supper.*

Sources: See Philip Kotler, "Mega-marketing," *Harvard Business Review,* March–April 1986, pp. 117–124; Sheila Tefft, "The Mouse That Roared at Pepsi," *Business Week,* September 7, 1987, p. 42; and Anthony Spaeth, "India Beckons—and Frustrates," *Wall Street Journal,* September 22, 1989, pp. R23–25.

some portion of the money in the other country within a stated time period. For example, Pepsi sells its cola syrup to Russia for rubles and agrees to buy Russian-made Stolichnaya vodka for sale in the United States.

Countertrade deals can be very complex. For example, Daimler-Benz recently agreed to sell 30 trucks to Romania in exchange for 150 Romanian jeeps, which it then sold to Ecuador for bananas, which were in turn sold to a German supermarket chain for German currency. Through this roundabout process, Daimler-Benz finally obtained payment in German money. In another case, when Occidental Petroleum Company wanted to sell oil to Yugoslavia, it hired a trading firm, SGD International, to arrange a countertrade. SGD arranged for a New York City automobile dealer-distributor, Global Motors Inc., to import more than $400 million worth of Yugoslavian Yugo automobiles, paid for by Occidental oil. Global then paid Occidental in cash. SGD, however, was paid in Yugos, which it peddled piecemeal by trading them for everything from cash to Caribbean resort hotel rooms, which it in turn sold to tour packagers and travel agencies for cash.[8]

Government Bureaucracy

A fourth factor is the extent to which the host government runs an efficient system for helping foreign companies: efficient customs handling, good market information, and other factors that aid in doing business. A common shock to Americans is how quickly barriers to trade disappear in some countries if a suitable payment (bribe) is made to some official.

CULTURAL ENVIRONMENT

Each country has its own folkways, norms, and taboos. The seller must examine the way consumers in different countries think about and use certain products before planning a marketing program. There are often surprises. For example, the average French man uses almost twice as many cosmetics and beauty aids as his wife. The Germans and the French eat more packaged, branded spaghetti than do Italians. Italian children like to eat chocolate bars between slices of bread as a snack. And women in Tanzania will not give their children eggs for fear of making them bald or impotent.

Business norms and behavior also vary from country to country. American business executives need to be briefed on these factors before conducting business in another country. Here are some examples of different global business behavior:

◆ South Americans like to sit or stand very close to each other when they talk business—in fact, almost nose-to-nose. The American business executive tends to keep backing away as the South American moves closer. Both may end up being offended.

◆ In face-to-face communications, Japanese business executives rarely say no to an American business executive. Thus, Americans tend to be frustrated, and they may not know where they stand. However, when Americans come to the point quickly, Japanese business executives may find this behavior offensive.

◆ In France, wholesalers don't want to promote a product. They ask their retailers what they want and deliver it. If an American company builds its strategy around the French wholesaler's cooperation in promotions, it is likely to fail.

◆ When American executives exchange business cards, each usually gives the other's card a cursory glance and stuffs it in a pocket for later reference. In Japan, however, executives dutifully study each other's cards during a greeting, carefully noting company affiliation and rank. They hand their card to the most important person first.

Thus, each country and region has cultural traditions, preferences, and behaviors that the marketer must study.

DECIDING WHETHER TO GO INTERNATIONAL

Not all companies need to venture into international markets to survive. For example, many companies are local businesses that need to market well only in the local marketplace. However, companies that operate in global industries, where their strategic positions in specific markets are affected strongly by their overall global positions, must think and act globally. Thus, IBM must organize globally if it is to gain purchasing, manufacturing, financial, and marketing advantages. Firms in a global industry must be able to compete on a worldwide basis if they are to succeed.

Any of several factors might draw a company into the international arena. Global competitors might attack the company's domestic market by offering better products or lower prices. The company might want to counterattack these competitors in their home markets to tie up their resources. Or the company might discover foreign markets that present higher profit opportunities than the domestic market does. The company's domestic market might be shrinking, or the company might need an enlarged customer base in order to achieve economies of scale. Or it might want to reduce its dependence on any one market so as to reduce its risk. Finally, the company's customers might be expanding abroad and require international servicing.

Before going abroad, the company must weigh several risks and answer many questions about its ability to operate globally. Can the company learn to understand the preferences and buyer behavior of consumers in other countries? Can it offer competitively attractive products? Will it be able to adapt to other countries' business cultures and deal effectively with foreign nationals? Do the company's managers have the necessary international experience? Has management considered the impact of regulations and the political environments of other countries?

Because of the risks and difficulties of entering international markets, most companies do not act until some situation or event thrusts them into the global arena. Someone—a domestic exporter, a foreign importer, a foreign government—may ask the company to sell abroad. Or the company may be saddled with overcapacity and must find additional markets for its goods.

DECIDING WHICH MARKETS TO ENTER

Before going abroad, the company should try to define its international *marketing objectives and policies*. First, it should decide what *volume* of foreign sales it wants. Most companies start small when they go abroad. Some plan to stay small, seeing international sales as a small part of their business. Other companies have bigger plans, seeing international business as equal to or even more important than their domestic business.

Second, the company must choose *how many* countries it wants to market in. For example, the Bulova Watch Company decided to operate in many international markets and expanded into more than 100 countries. As a result, it spread itself too thin, made profits in only two countries, and lost around $40 million. Generally, it makes better sense to operate in fewer countries with deeper penetration in each.

Third, the company must decide on the *types* of countries to enter. A country's attractiveness depends on the product, geographical factors, income and population, political climate, and other factors. The seller may prefer certain country groups or parts of the world.

After listing possible international markets, the company must screen and rank each one. Consider the following example:

> Many mass marketers dream of selling to China's 1 billion people. Some think of the market less elegantly as 2 billion armpits. To PepsiCo, though, the market is mouths, and the People's Republic is especially enticing: it is the most populous country in the world, and Coca-Cola does not yet dominate it.[9]

Pepsi in China—a huge but risky market.

TABLE 20-1   *Indicators of Market Potential*

1. DEMOGRAPHIC CHARACTERISTICS	4. TECHNOLOGICAL FACTORS
Size of population	Level of technological skill
Rate of population growth	Existing production technology
Degree of urbanization	Existing consumption technology
Population density	Education levels
Age structure and composition of the population	
2. GEOGRAPHIC CHARACTERISTICS	**5. SOCIOCULTURAL FACTORS**
Physical size of a country	Dominant values
Topographical characteristics	Lifestyle patterns
Climate conditions	Ethnic groups
	Linguistic fragmentation
3. ECONOMIC FACTORS	**6. NATIONAL GOALS AND PLANS**
GNP per capita	Industry priorities
Income distribution	Infrastructure investment plans
Rate of growth of GNP	
Ratio of investment to GNP	

Source: Susan P. Douglas, C. Samuel Craig, and Warren Keegan, "Approaches to Assessing International Marketing Opportunities for Small and Medium-Sized Business," *Columbia Journal of World Business,* Fall 1982, pp. 26–32.

PepsiCo's decision to enter the Chinese market seems fairly simple and straightforward: China is a huge market without established competition. In addition to selling Pepsi soft drinks, the company hopes to build many of its Pizza Hut restaurants in China. Yet we still can question whether market size *alone* is reason enough for selecting China. PepsiCo also must consider other factors: Will the Chinese government be stable and supportive? Does China provide for the production and distribution technologies needed to produce and market Pepsi products profitably? Will Pepsi and pizza fit Chinese tastes, means, and lifestyles?

Possible global markets should be ranked on several factors, including market size, market growth, cost of doing business, competitive advantage, and risk level. The goal is to determine the potential of each market, using indicators like those shown in Table 20-1. Then the marketer must decide which markets offer the greatest long-run return on investment.

DECIDING HOW TO ENTER THE MARKET

Once a company has decided to sell in a foreign country, it must determine the best mode of entry. Its choices are *exporting, joint venturing,* and *direct investment.* Figure 20-2 shows three market entry strategies, along with the options each one offers. As the figure shows, each succeeding strategy involves more commitment and risk, but also more control and potential profits.

Exporting
Entering a foreign market by sending products and selling them through international marketing middlemen (indirect exporting) or through the company's own department, branch, or sales representatives or agents (direct exporting).

EXPORTING

The simplest way to enter a foreign market is through **exporting.** The company may passively export its surpluses from time to time, or it may make an active commitment to expand exports to a particular market. In either case, the company produces all its goods in its home country. It may or may not modify them for the export market. Exporting involves the least change in the company's product lines, organization, investments, or mission.

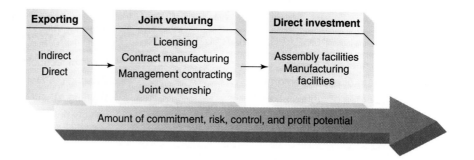

FIGURE 20-2 *Market entry strategies*

Companies typically start with *indirect exporting,* working through independent international marketing intermediaries. Indirect exporting involves less investment because the firm does not require an overseas sales force or set of contacts. It also involves less risk. International marketing middlemen—domestic-based export merchants or agents, cooperative organizations, and export-management companies—bring know-how and services to the relationship, so the seller normally makes fewer mistakes.

Sellers may eventually move into *direct exporting,* whereby they handle their own exports. The investment and risk are somewhat greater in this strategy, but so is the potential return. A company can conduct direct exporting in several ways. It can set up a domestic export department that carries out export activities. It can also set up an overseas sales branch that handles sales, distribution, and perhaps promotion. The sales branch gives the seller more presence and program control in the foreign market and often serves as a display center and customer service center. The company also can send home-based salespeople abroad at certain times in order to find business. Finally, the company can do its exporting either through foreign-based distributors who buy and own the goods or through foreign-based agents who sell the goods on behalf of the company.

JOINT VENTURING

Joint venturing
Entering foreign markets by joining with foreign companies to produce or market a product or service.

A second method of entering a foreign market is **joint venturing**—joining with foreign companies to produce or market products or services. Joint venturing differs from exporting in that the company joins with a partner to sell or market abroad. It differs from direct investment in that an association is formed with someone in the foreign country. There are four types of joint ventures: licensing, contract manufacturing, management contracting, and joint ownership.

Licensing

Licensing
A method of entering a foreign market in which the company enters into an agreement with a licensee in the foreign market, offering the right to use a manufacturing process, trademark, patent, trade secret, or other item of value for a fee or royalty.

Licensing is a simple way for a manufacturer to enter international marketing. The company enters into an agreement with a licensee in the foreign market. For a fee or royalty, the licensee buys the right to use the company's manufacturing process, trademark, patent, trade secret, or other item of value. The company thus gains entry into the market at little risk; the licensee gains production expertise or a well-known product or name without having to start from scratch.

Coca-Cola markets internationally by licensing bottlers around the world and supplying them with the syrup needed to produce the product. In Japan, Budweiser beer flows from Kirin breweries, Lady Borden ice cream is churned out at Meiji Milk Products dairies, and Marlboro cigarettes roll off production lines at Japan Tobacco, Inc. Tokyo Disneyland is owned and operated by Oriental Land Company under license from the Walt Disney Company. The 45-year license gives Disney licensing fees plus 10 percent of admissions and 5 percent of food and merchandise sales. In Mexico, Wal-Mart is joining with Cifra, the country's

Licensing: Tokyo Disney-land is owned and operated by the Oriental Land Co., Ltd. (a Japanese development company), under license from Walt Disney Company.

Contract manufacturing
A joint venture in which a company contracts with manufacturers in a foreign market to produce the product.

Management contracting
A joint venture in which the domestic firm supplies the management know-how to a foreign company that supplies the capital; the domestic firm exports management services rather than products.

Joint ownership
A joint venture in which a company joins investors in a foreign market to create a local business in which the company shares joint ownership and control.

Direct investment
Entering a foreign market by developing foreign-based assembly or manufacturing facilities.

top retailer, to open Wal-Mart Supercenters and Sam's Clubs.[10]

Licensing has potential disadvantages, however. The firm has less control over the licensee than it would over its own production facilities. Furthermore, if the licensee is very successful, the firm has given up these profits, and if and when the contract ends, it may find it has created a competitor.

Contract Manufacturing

Another option is **contract manufacturing**—the company contracts with manufacturers in the foreign market to produce its product or provide its service. Sears used this method in opening up department stores in Mexico and Spain, where it found qualified local manufacturers to produce many of the products it sells. The drawbacks of contract manufacturing are the decreased control over the manufacturing process and the loss of potential profits on manufacturing. The benefits are the chance to start faster, with less risk, and the later opportunity either to form a partnership with or to buy out the local manufacturer.

Management Contracting

Under **management contracting**, the domestic firm supplies management know-how to a foreign company that supplies the capital. The domestic firm exports management services rather than products. Hilton uses this arrangement in managing hotels around the world.

Management contracting is a low-risk method of getting into a foreign market, and it yields income from the beginning. The arrangement is even more attractive if the contracting firm has an option to buy some share in the managed company later on. The arrangement is not sensible, however, if the company can put its scarce management talent to better uses or if it can make greater profits by undertaking the whole venture. Management contracting also prevents the company from setting up its own operations for a period of time.

Joint Ownership

Joint ownership ventures consist of one company joining forces with foreign investors to create a local business in which they share joint ownership and control. A company may buy an interest in a local firm, or the two parties may form a new business venture. Joint ownership may be needed for economic or political reasons. The firm may lack the financial, physical, or managerial resources to undertake the venture alone, or a foreign government may require joint ownership as a condition for entry.

Joint ownership has certain drawbacks. The partners may disagree over investment, marketing, or other policies. Whereas many U.S. firms like to reinvest earnings for growth, local firms often like to take out these earnings. Furthermore, whereas U.S. firms emphasize the role of marketing, local investors may rely on selling.

DIRECT INVESTMENT

The biggest involvement in a foreign market comes through **direct investment**—the development of foreign-based assembly or manufacturing facilities. If a company has gained experience in exporting and if the foreign market is large enough, foreign production facilities offer many advantages. The firm may have lower costs in the form of cheaper labor or raw materials, foreign government investment incentives, and freight savings. The firm may improve its image in the host country because it creates jobs. Generally, a firm develops a deeper relationship with government, customers, local suppliers, and distributors, allowing it to better adapt its products to the local market. Finally, the firm keeps full control over the investment and therefore can develop manufacturing and marketing policies that serve its long-term international objectives.

The main disadvantage of direct investment is that the firm faces many risks, such as restricted or devalued currencies, falling markets, or government takeovers. In some cases, a firm has no choice but to accept these risks if it wants to operate in the host country.

DECIDING ON THE GLOBAL MARKETING PROGRAM

Standardized marketing mix
An international marketing strategy for using basically the same product, advertising, distribution channels, and other elements of the marketing mix in all the company's international markets.

Adapted marketing mix
An international marketing strategy for adjusting the marketing-mix elements to each international target market, bearing more costs but hoping for a larger market share and return.

Companies that operate in one or more foreign markets must decide how much, if at all, to adapt their marketing mixes to local conditions. At one extreme are companies that use a **standardized marketing mix** worldwide. Proponents of global standardization claim that it results in lower production, distribution, marketing, and management costs, letting companies offer consumers higher quality and more reliable products at lower prices. This is the thinking behind Coca-Cola's decision that Coke should taste about the same around the world and Ford's production of a "world car" that suits the needs of most consumers in most countries.

At the other extreme is an **adapted marketing mix.** In this case, the producer adjusts the marketing mix elements to each target market, bearing more costs but hoping for a larger market share and return. Nestlé, for example, varies its product line and its advertising in different countries. Proponents argue that consumers in different countries vary greatly in their geographic, demographic, economic, and cultural characteristics, resulting in different needs and wants, spending power, product preferences, and shopping patterns. Therefore, companies should adapt their marketing strategies and programs to fit the unique consumer needs in each country.

The question of whether to adapt or standardize the marketing mix has been much debated in recent years. However, global standardization is not an all-or-nothing proposition, but rather a matter of degree. Companies should look for more standardization to help keep down costs and prices and to build greater global brand power. But they must not replace long-run marketing thinking with short-run financial thinking. Although standardization saves money, marketers must make certain that they offer what consumers in each country want.[11]

Many possibilities exist between the extremes of standardization and complete adaptation. For example, Coca-Cola sells virtually the same Coke beverage worldwide, and it pulls advertisements for specific markets from a common pool of ads designed to have cross-cultural appeal. However, the company sells a variety of other beverages created specifically for the tastebuds of local markets. Prices and distribution channels may also vary widely from market to market.

PRODUCT

Straight product extension
Marketing a product in a foreign market without any change.

Five strategies allow for adapting products and promotions to a foreign market (see Figure 20-3).[12] We first discuss the three product strategies and then turn to the two promotion strategies.

Straight product extension means marketing a product in a foreign market without any change. Top management tells its marketing people: "Take the prod-

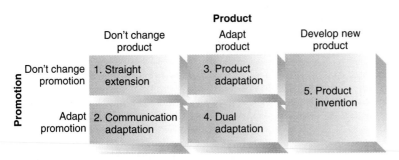

FIGURE 20-3 *Five international product and promotion strategies*

uct as is and find customers for it." The first step, however, should be to find out whether foreign consumers use that product and what form they prefer.

Straight extension has been successful in some cases and disastrous in others. Coca-Cola, Kellogg cereals, Heineken beer, and Black & Decker tools are all sold successfully in about the same form around the world. But General Foods introduced its standard powdered Jell-O in the British market only to find that British consumers prefer a solid-wafer or cake form. Likewise, Philips began to make a profit in Japan only after it reduced the size of its coffee makers to fit into smaller Japanese kitchens and its shavers to fit smaller Japanese hands. Straight extension is tempting because it involves no additional product-development costs, manufacturing changes, or new promotion. But it can be costly in the long run if products fail to satisfy foreign consumers.

Product adaptation

Adapting a product to meet local conditions or wants in foreign markets.

Product adaptation involves changing the product to meet local conditions or wants. For example, McDonald's serves beer in Germany and coconut, mango, and tropic mint shakes in Hong Kong. General Foods blends different coffees for the British (who drink their coffee with milk), the French (who drink their coffee black), and Latin Americans (who prefer a chicory taste). In Japan, Mister Donut serves coffee in smaller and lighter cups that better fit the fingers of the average Japanese consumer; even the doughnuts are a little smaller. In Brazil, Levi's developed its Femina jeans featuring curvaceous cuts that provide the ultratight fit traditionally favored by Brazilian women. Campbell serves up soups that match unique tastes of consumers in different countries. For example, it sells duck-gizzard soup in the Guangdong Province of China; in Poland, it features *flaki*, a peppery tripe soup. And IBM adapts its worldwide product line to meet local needs. For example, IBM must make dozens of different keyboards—20 for Europe alone—to match different languages.[13]

Product invention

Creating new products or services for foreign markets.

Product invention consists of creating something new for the foreign market. This strategy can take two forms. It might mean reintroducing earlier product forms that happen to be well adapted to the needs of a given country. For example, the National Cash Register Company reintroduced its crank-operated cash register at half the price of a modern cash register and sold large numbers in the Orient, Latin America, and Spain. Or a company might create a new product to meet a need in another country. For example, an enormous need exists for low-cost, high-protein foods in less developed countries. Companies such as Quaker Oats, Swift, Monsanto, and Archer Daniels Midland are researching the nutrition needs of these countries, creating new foods, and developing advertising campaigns to gain product trial and acceptance. Product invention can be costly, but the payoffs are worthwhile.

PROMOTION

Companies can either adopt the same promotion strategy they used in the home market or change it for each local market.

Consider advertising messages. Some global companies use a standardized advertising theme around the world. Exxon used "Put a tiger in your tank," which gained international recognition. Of course, the copy may be varied in minor ways to adjust for language differences. In Japan, for instance, where consumers have trouble pronouncing "snap, crackle, pop," the little Rice Crispies critters say "patchy, pitchy, putchy." Colors also are changed sometimes to avoid taboos in other countries. Purple is associated with death in most of Latin America; white

WATCH YOUR LANGUAGE!

Many U.S. multinationals have had difficulty crossing the language barrier, with results ranging from mild embarrassment to outright failure. Seemingly innocuous brand names and advertising phrases can take on unintended or hidden meanings when translated into other languages. Careless translations can make a marketer look downright foolish to foreign consumers. We've all run across examples when buying products from foreign countries—here's one from a firm in Taiwan attempting to instruct children on how to install a ramp on a garage for toy cars:

> Before you play with, please fix the waiting plate by yourself as per below diagram. But after you once fixed it, you can play with as is and no necessary to fix off again.

Many U.S. firms are guilty of similar atrocities when marketing abroad.

The classic language blunders involve standardized brand names that do not translate well. When Coca-Cola first marketed Coke in China in the 1920s, it developed a group of Chinese characters that, when pronounced, sounded like the product name. Unfortunately, the characters actually translated to mean "bite the wax tadpole." Today, the characters on Chinese Coke bottles translate as "happiness in the mouth."

Several car makers have had similar problems when their brand names crashed into the language barrier. Chevy's Nova translated into Spanish as *no va*—"It doesn't go." GM changed the name to Caribe and sales increased. Ford introduced its Fiera truck only to discover that the name means "ugly old woman" in Spanish. And it introduced its Comet car in Mexico as the Caliente—slang for "streetwalker." Rolls-Royce avoided the name Silver Mist in German markets, where "mist" means "manure." Sunbeam, however, entered the German market with its Mist-Stick hair curling iron. As should have been expected, the Germans had little use for a "manure wand."

One well-intentioned firm sold its shampoo in Brazil under the name Evitol. It soon realized it was claiming to sell a "dandruff contraceptive." An American company reportedly had trouble marketing Pet milk in French-speaking areas. It seems that the word "pet" in French means, among other things, "to break wind."

Advertising themes often lose—or gain—something in the translation. The Coors beer slogan "get loose with Coors" in Spanish came out as "get the runs with Coors." Coca-Cola's "Coke adds life" theme in Japanese translated into "Coke brings your ancestors back from the dead."

Such classic boo-boos are soon discovered and corrected, and they may result in little more than embarrassment for the marketer. But countless other more subtle blunders may go undetected and damage product performance in less obvious ways. The multinational company must carefully screen its brand names and advertising messages to guard against those that might damage sales, make it look silly, or offend consumers in specific international markets.

Sources: Some of these and many other examples of language blunders are found in David A. Ricks, "Products That Crashed into the Language Barrier," *Business and Society Review,* Spring 1983, pp. 46–50. Also see Marty Westerman, "Death of the Frito Bandito," *American Demographics,* March 1989, pp. 28–32; and David W. Helin, "When Slogans Go Wrong," *American Demographics,* February 1992, p. 14.

is a mourning color in Japan; and green is associated with jungle sickness in Malaysia. Even names must be changed. In Sweden, Helene Curtis changed the name of its Every Night Shampoo to Every Day because Swedes usually wash their hair in the morning. Kellogg also had to rename Bran Buds cereal in Sweden, where the name roughly translates as "burned farmer." (See Marketing Highlight 20-4 for more on language blunders in international marketing.)

Communication adaptation
A global communication strategy of fully adapting advertising messages to local markets.

Other companies follow a strategy of **communication adaptation,** fully adapting their advertising messages to local markets. The Schwinn Bicycle Company might use a pleasure theme in the United States and a safety theme in Scandinavia. Kellogg ads in the United States promote the taste and nutrition of Kellogg's cereals versus competitors' brands. In France, where consumers drink little milk and eat little for breakfast, Kellogg's ads must convince consumers that cereals are a tasty and healthful breakfast.

Media also need to be adapted internationally because media availability varies from country to country. TV advertising time is very limited in Europe, for instance, ranging from four hours a day in France to none in Scandinavian countries. Advertisers must buy time months in advance, and they have little control over airtimes. Magazines also vary in effectiveness. For example, magazines are a major medium in Italy and a minor one in Austria. Newspapers are national in the United Kingdom but are only local in Spain.

Standardized advertising messages: Cross pens uses the same promotion approach in many different countries.

PRICE

Companies also face many problems in setting their international prices. For example, how might Black & Decker price its power tools globally? It could set a uniform price all around the world, but this amount would be too high a price in poor countries and not high enough in rich ones. It could charge what consumers in each country would bear, but this strategy ignores differences in the actual costs from country to country. Finally, the company could use a standard markup of its costs everywhere, but this approach might price Black & Decker out of the market in some countries where costs are high.

Regardless of how companies go about pricing their products, their foreign prices probably will be higher than their domestic prices. A Gucci handbag may sell for $60 in Italy and $240 in the United States. Why? Gucci faces a *price escalation* problem. It must add the cost of transportation, tariffs, importer margin, wholesaler margin, and retailer margin to its factory price. Depending on these added costs, the product may have to sell for two to five times as much in another country to make the same profit. For example, a pair of Levi's jeans that sells for $30 in the United States typically fetches $63 in Tokyo and $88 in Paris. A computer that sells for $1,000 in New York may cost £1,000 in the United Kingdom. A Chrysler automobile priced at $10,000 in the United States sells for more than $47,000 in South Korea.[14]

Another problem involves setting a price for goods that a company ships to its foreign subsidiaries. If the company charges a foreign subsidiary too much, it may end up paying higher tariff duties even while paying lower income taxes in that country. If the company charges its subsidiary too little, it can be charged with *dumping*. Dumping occurs when a company either charges less than its costs or less than it charges in its home market. Thus, Harley-Davidson accused Honda and Kawasaki of dumping motorcycles on the U.S. market. The U.S. International Trade Commission agreed and responded with a special five-year tariff on Japanese heavy motorcycles, starting at 45 percent in 1983 and gradually dropping to 10 percent by 1988.[15] The commission also ruled recently that Japan was dumping computer memory chips in the United States and laid stiff duties on future imports. Various governments are always watching for dumping abuses, and they often force companies to set the price charged by other competitors for the same or similar products.

Last but not least, many global companies face a *grey market* problem. For example, Minolta sold its cameras to Hong Kong distributors for less than it charged German distributors because of lower transportation costs and tariffs. Minolta cameras ended up selling at retail for $174 in Hong Kong and $270 in Germany. Some Hong Kong wholesalers noticed this price difference and shipped Minolta cameras to German dealers for less than the dealers were paying their German distributor. The German distributor couldn't sell its stock and complained to Minolta. Thus, a company often finds some enterprising distributors buying more than they can sell in their own country, then shipping goods to another country to take advantage of price differences. International companies try to prevent grey markets by raising their prices to lower cost distributors, dropping those who cheat, or altering the product for different countries.

DISTRIBUTION CHANNELS

Whole-channel view
Designing international channels that take into account all the necessary links in distributing the seller's products to final buyers, including the seller's headquarters organization, channels between nations, and channels within nations.

The international company must take a **whole-channel view** of the problem of distributing products to final consumers. Figure 20-4 shows the three major links between the seller and the final buyer. The first link, the *seller's headquarters organization,* supervises the channels and is part of the channel itself. The second link, *channels between nations,* moves the products to the borders of the foreign nations. The third link, *channels within nations,* moves the products from their foreign entry point to the final consumers. Some U.S. manufacturers may think their job is done once the product leaves their hands, but they would do well to pay more attention to its handling within foreign countries.

Channels of distribution within countries vary greatly from nation to nation. First, there are the large differences in the *numbers and types of middlemen* serving each foreign market. For example, a U.S. company marketing in China must operate through a frustrating maze of state-controlled wholesalers and retailers. Chinese distributors often carry competitors' products and frequently refuse to share even basic sales and marketing information with their suppliers. Hustling for sales is an alien concept to Chinese distributors, who are used to selling all they can obtain. Working with or getting around this system sometimes requires substantial time and investment. When Coke and Pepsi first entered China, for example, customers bicycled up to bottling plants to get their soft drinks. Now, both companies have set up direct-distribution channels, investing heavily in trucks and refrigeration units for retailers.[16]

Another difference lies in the *size and character of retail units* abroad. Whereas large-scale retail chains dominate the U.S. scene, much retailing in other

FIGURE 20-4   *Whole-channel concept for international marketing*

countries is done by many small independent retailers. In India, millions of retailers operate tiny shops or sell in open markets. Their markups are high, but the actual price is lowered through price haggling. Supermarkets could offer lower prices, but supermarkets are difficult to build and open because of many economic and cultural barriers. Incomes are low, and people prefer to shop daily for small amounts rather than weekly for large amounts. They also lack storage and refrigeration to keep food for several days. Packaging is not well developed because it would add too much to the cost. These factors have kept large-scale retailing from spreading rapidly in developing countries.

DECIDING ON THE GLOBAL MARKETING ORGANIZATION

Companies manage their international marketing activities in at least three different ways. Most companies first organize an export department, then create an international division, and finally become a global organization.

A firm normally gets into international marketing by simply shipping out its goods. If its international sales expand, the company organizes an *export department* with a sales manager and a few assistants. As sales increase, the export department then can expand to include various marketing services so that it can actively go after business. If the firm moves into joint ventures or direct investment, the export department no longer will be adequate.

Many companies get involved in several international markets and ventures. A company may export to one country, license to another, have a joint ownership venture in a third, and own a subsidiary in a fourth. Sooner or later it will create an *international division* or subsidiary to handle all its international activity.

International divisions are organized in a variety of ways. The international division's corporate staff consists of marketing, manufacturing, research, finance, planning, and personnel specialists. They plan for and provide services to various operating units, which can be organized in one of three ways. They may be *geographical organizations,* with country managers who are responsible for salespeople, sales branches, distributors, and licensees in their respective countries. Or the operating units can be *world product groups,* each responsible for worldwide sales of different product groups. Finally, operating units can be *international subsidiaries,* each responsible for its own sales and profits.

Several firms have passed beyond the international division stage and become truly *global organizations.* They stop thinking of themselves as national marketers who sell abroad and start thinking of themselves as global marketers. The top corporate management and staff plan worldwide manufacturing facilities, marketing policies, financial flows, and logistical systems. The global operating units report directly to the chief executive or executive committee of the organization, not to the head of an international division. Executives are trained in worldwide operations, not just domestic *or* international. The company recruits management from many countries, buys components and supplies where they cost the least, and invests where the expected returns are greatest.

Moving into the twenty-first century, major companies must become more global if they hope to compete. As foreign companies successfully invade their domestic markets, companies must move more aggressively into foreign markets. They will have to change from companies that treat their international operations as secondary concerns to companies that view the entire world as a single borderless market.[17]

Summary

Companies can no longer afford to pay attention only to their domestic market, no matter how large it is. Many industries are global industries, and those firms that operate globally achieve lower costs and higher brand awareness. At the same time, global marketing is risky because of variable exchange rates, unstable governments, protectionist tariffs and trade barriers, and several other factors. Given the potential gains and risks of international marketing, companies need a systematic way to make their international marketing decisions.

As a first step, a company must understand the *global marketing environment*, especially the *international trade system*. It must assess each foreign market's *economic, political-legal,* and *cultural characteristics.* Second, the company must *decide whether to go international* and consider the potential risks and benefits. Third, the company must decide the volume of international sales it wants, how many countries it wants to market in, and *which markets to enter.* This decision calls for weighing the probable rate of return on investment against the level of risk. Fourth, the company must decide *how to enter each market*—whether through *exporting, joint venturing,* or *direct investment.* Many companies start as exporters, move to joint ventures, and finally make a direct investment in foreign markets. Companies must next *decide on the global marketing program,* and how much their *products, promotion, price* and *distribution channels* should be adapted for each foreign market.

Finally, the company must develop an effective *global marketing organization.* Most firms start with an export department and graduate to an international division. A few will go on to become global organizations, with worldwide marketing planned and managed by the top officers of the company. Global organizations view the entire world as a single borderless market.

Key Terms

Adapted marketing mix	Exporting	Product adaptation
Communication adaptation	Global firm	Product invention
Contract manufacturing	Global industry	Quota
Countertrade	Joint ownership	Standardized marketing mix
Direct investment	Joint venturing	Straight product extension
Economic community	Licensing	Tariff
Embargo	Management contracting	Whole-channel view
Exchange controls	Nontariff trade barriers	

Discussing the Issues

1. With all the problems facing companies that "go global," explain why so many companies are choosing to expand internationally. What are the advantages of expanding beyond the domestic market?

2. When exporting goods to a foreign country, a marketer may be faced with various trade restrictions. Discuss the effects these restrictions might have on an exporter's marketing mix: (a) tariffs, (b) quotas, and (c) embargoes.

3. The first Honda automobile exported here was described by a U.S. car magazine as "a shopping cart with a motor"; the first Subaru exported to the United States was voted "Worst New Car of the Year." Both companies have become highly successful over the years, however. Discuss the Japanese strategy of long-term commitment to

international business objectives. Would the Japanese have left India, as IBM and Coca-Cola did, because of "hassles"?

4. Imported products are usually more expensive, but not always: A Nikon camera is cheaper in New York than in Tokyo. Assess why foreign prices are sometimes higher and sometimes lower than domestic prices for exports.

5. "Dumping" leads to price savings to the consumer. Determine why governments make dumping illegal. What are the *disadvantages* to the consumer of dumping by foreign firms?

6. Which type of international marketing organization would you suggest for the following companies? (a) Cannondale Bicycles, selling three models in the Far East; (b) a small U.S. manufacturer of toys, marketing its products in Europe; and (c) Dodge, planning to sell its full line of cars and trucks in Kuwait.

Applying the Concepts

1. Go to a large electronics and appliance store that sells products such as televisions, stereos, and microwaves. Pick one or two product categories to examine. (a) Make a list of brand names in the category, and classify each name as being either "American" or "foreign." How did you decide whether a brand was American or foreign? (b) Look at where these different brands were manufactured. Are any of the "American" brands manufactured abroad, and are any of the "foreign" brands made in the United States? What does this tell you about how much international marketing is being done? Is "global" a better term to describe some of these brands?

2. Entertainment, including movies, television programs, and music recordings, is America's second largest export category—only aircraft is larger. (a) Go to your college library and find several foreign magazines. Locate pictures, stories, or ads featuring American entertainers. Study what you find. Look at the size and layout of the stories, and see if you can understand basically what is being said. Does American entertainment seem to be interesting or important to people abroad? What, if anything, do you think is appealing to them? (b) India has the largest movie industry in the world, yet few Indian films are ever shown in the United States. Why do you think this is so? Suggest some ways that Indian movie companies might make a bigger impact in America.

References

1. Stephen K. Yoder, "Apple, Loser in Japan Computer Market, Tries to Recoup by Redesigning Its Models," *Wall Street Journal,* June 21, 1985; Neil Gross, "Is It Finally Time for Apple to Blossom in Japan?" *Business Week,* May 28, 1990, pp. 100–101; Andrew Tanzer, "How Apple Stormed Japan," *Forbes,* May 27, 1991, pp. 40–41; Larry Holyoke, "Apple's Man in Japan Steps Up the Mac Attack," *Business Week,* October 31, 1994, pp. 117–118; and Bradley Johnson, "Apple Gets Bruised By Shrinking Share," *Advertising Age,* April 24, 1995, p. 44.

2. See Therese Eiben, "50 Leading U.S. Exporters," *Fortune,* June 14, 1993, p. 131; and Edmund Faltermayer, "Competitiveness: How U.S. Companies Stack Up Now," *Fortune,* April 18, 1994, pp. 52–64.

3. "The Unique Japanese," *Fortune,* November 24, 1986, p. 8. For more on nontariff and other barriers, see Philip R. Cateora, *International Marketing,* 8th ed. (Homewood, IL: Irwin, 1993), pp. 44–45.

4. Douglas Harbrecht and Owen Ullmann, "Finally GATT May Fly," *Business Week,* December 29, 1993, pp. 36–37. Also see Cateora, *International Marketing,* pp. 49–51; and Louis S. Richman, "What's Next After GATT's Victory?" *Fortune,* January 10, 1994, pp. 66–70.

5. For more reading on free-trade zones, see Blayne Cutler, "North American Demographics," *American Demographics,* March 1992, pp. 38–42; Andrew Hilton, "Mythology, Markets, and the Emerging Europe," *Harvard Business Review,* November–December 1992, pp. 50–54; Geoffrey Brewer, "New World Orders," *Sales & Marketing Management,* January 1994, pp. 59–63; Roberto E. Batres, "Benefiting from NAFTA: New Opportunities in North America," *Prizm,* Arthur D. Little, Inc., Cambridge, MA, First Quarter, 1994, pp. 17–29; and William C. Symonds, "Meanwhile, to the North, NAFTA Is a Smash," *Business Week,* February 27, 1995, p. 66.

6. Bill Saporito, "Where the Global Action Is," *Fortune,* Special Issue on "The Tough New Consumer," Autumn-Winter 1993, pp. 62–65.

7. "Coca-Cola Returns to India," *USA Today,* September 22, 1993, p. B1.

8. For these and other examples, see Louis Kraar, "How to Sell to Cashless Buyers," *Fortune,* November 7, 1988, pp. 147–154; Cyndee Miller, "Worldwide Money Crunch Fuels More International Barter," *Marketing News,* March 2, 1992, p. 5; and Nathaniel Gilbert, "The Case for Countertrade," *Across the Board,* May 1992, pp. 43–45.

9. Louis Kraar, "Pepsi's Pitch to Quench Chinese Thirsts," *Fortune,* March 17, 1986, p. 58. Also see Alan Farnham, "Ready to Ride Out China's Turmoil," *Fortune,* July 3, 1989, pp. 117–118; and Pete Engardio, "China Fever Strikes Again," *Business Week,* March 29, 1993, pp. 46–47.

10. Robert Neff, "In Japan, They're Goofy about Disney," *Business Week,* March 12, 1990, p. 64; and Geri Smith, "NAFTA: A Green Light for Red Tape," *Business Week,* July 25, 1994, p. 48.

11. See George S. Yip, "Global Strategy . . . In a World of Nations?" *Sloan Management Review,* Fall 1989, pp. 29–41; Kamran Kashani, "Beware the Pitfalls of Global Marketing," *Harvard Business Review,* September–October 1989, pp. 91–98; Saeed Saminee and Kendall Roth, "The Influence of Global Marketing Standardization on Performance," *Journal of Marketing,* April 1992, pp. 1–17; David M. Szymanski, Sundar G. Bharadwaj, and Rajan Varadarajan, "Standardization versus Adaptation of International Marketing Strategy: An Empirical Investigation," *Journal of Marketing,* October 1993, pp. 1–17; and Ashish Banerjee, "Global Campaigns Don't Work; Multinationals Do," *Advertising Age,* April 18, 1994.

12. See Keegan, *Global Marketing Management,* 4th ed. (Englewood Cliffs, NJ: Prentice Hall, 1989), pp. 378–381. Also see Peter G. P. Walters and Brian Toyne, "Product Modification and Standardization in International Markets: Strategic Options and Facilitating Policies," *Columbia Journal of World Business,* Winter 1989, pp. 37–44.

13. For these and other examples, see Andrew Kupfer, "How to Be a Global Manager," *Fortune,* March 14, 1988, pp. 52–58; Maria Shao, "For Levi's: A Flattering Fit Overseas," *Business Week,* November 5, 1990, 76–77; and Joseph Weber, "Campbell: Now It's M-M-Global," *Business Week,* March 15, 1993, pp. 52–53.

14. Dori Jones Yang, "Can Asia's Four Tigers Be Tamed?" *Business Week,* February 15, 1988, p. 47; Shao, "For Levi's: A Flattering Fit Overseas," p. 78; and Tim Simpson and Roger Camrass, "Redesigning the Multinational to Compete Across Europe," *Prizm,* Arthur D. Little, Inc., Cambridge, MA, First Quarter, 1994, pp. 5–15.

15. See Michael Oneal, "Harley-Davidson: Ready to Hit the Road Again," *Business Week,* July 21, 1986, p. 70.

16. See Shao, "Laying the Foundation for the Great Mall of China," p. 69.

17. See Kenichi Ohmae, "Managing in a Borderless World," *Harvard Business Review,* May–June 1989, pp. 152–161; William J. Holstein, "The Stateless Corporation," *Business Week,* May 14, 1990, pp. 98–105; and John A. Byrne and Kathleen Kerwin, "Borderless Management," *Business Week,* May 23, 1994, pp. 24–26.

Company Case 20

HARDEE'S: MARKETING IN SOUTH KOREA

DOWNTOWN SEOUL

"There should be more fast-food restaurants," exclaimed Moon Yong, a 21-year-old college student, as she downed another french fry and sipped a Coke with a friend at the Hardee's in Seoul, one of only two Hardee's in all of South Korea. Moon Yong and her female friends like fast-food restaurants, especially American ones. Korean kids find it fashionable to hang out in fast-food restaurants. "We'll stay here all afternoon," Moon Yong proclaimed.

In fact, American fast-food companies that have ventured into Korea target young people. Fast-food restaurants are especially appealing to young girls, who make up 70 percent of all customers. The girls like french fries and beverages, and they sit in the restaurants for hours. As a result, South Korean fast-food restaurants are bigger than their American counterparts—

about 300 seats versus about 150 seats for U.S. restaurants.

Furthermore, despite the sometimes strong anti-American sentiment in Korea, Korean young people are drawn to the slice of Americana that the restaurants represent. Young Lee, president of Del Taco Korea Co., points out that "they like American and European music. So they want their food the same way. It is in this area that America is the leader, not electric parts or TVs." As a result, Mr. Lee and other fast-food executives in Korea make only a few subtle changes in the American menus to account for local tastes. In other countries, firms often make substantial changes.

DOING BUSINESS IN SOUTH KOREA

South Korea may seem to be the promised land for American fast-food chains. Faced with a saturated and highly competitive U.S. market, one would think that the chains would be flocking to South Korea. However, McDonald's has only four stores in the country—one store for every 10.8 million Koreans as compared to 51 stores in Hong Kong (one per 112,000 residents). Similarly, Wendy's has only 13 outlets in South Korea, and Burger King has only 12.

Why have U.S. fast-food restaurants been so slow to enter South Korea? In late 1991, *The Wall Street Journal* published a ranking of 129 countries based on the risk of doing business in each. The rankings combined each country's rankings on the basis of political risk, financial risk, and economic risk into an overall composite risk score. South Korea fell into the low-risk category with a composite score of 73.5 out of a possible 100. It ranked twenty-seventh on the list, just behind Portugal and ahead of Botswana. The low-risk category, which covered scores from 70 to 84.5, also included the United States, which ranked ninth with a composite score of 83.5. South Korea's political risk score was 63 out of 100, and it had scores of 47 out of a possible 50 on financial risk and 36.5 out of 50 on economic risk.

Even though South Korea's overall score suggested a low level of risk, analysts point out that it is a tough market. Land prices are especially high. A high-traffic site in Seoul, the capital city, can cost $7 million to buy or require a $1 million deposit to rent. The *land* for a factory may cost more than the factory. Raw material costs are the highest in Asia. Manufacturing wages have gone up an average of 18 percent per year since 1986. Governmental restrictions, such as high tariffs and limits on certain imports, such as cheese and beef, frustrate fast-food chains. Gaining governmental approval for investment takes time and can be very difficult.

Companies also find it difficult to bring additional capital funds into the country. Korean firms, fearing new competition, resist entry and investment by foreign firms. Foreign firms also suspect that the Korean government doesn't really want foreign investment, especially if it will adversely affect domestic producers.

All of these factors have resulted in a low level of foreign investment in South Korea. The Korea Development Institute, a government-funded think tank, indicates that the ratio of foreign investment to gross national products is 14.6 to 1 in Singapore and 1.61 to 1 in Taiwan but only 0.36 to 1 in South Korea.

ENTER HARDEE'S

If entering the market in South Korea is so tough, why do Hardee's, McDonald's, and other firms even bother to try? For one thing, these firms see the flip side of rapidly rising Korean wage rates—disposable income is rising equally quickly. Korean disposable income has grown 141 percent since 1986, making Korea the largest consumer market in Asia after Japan. The average urban household in South Korea has an annual income of $12,400. Ten percent of the population have college degrees, and the number of two-income families is on the rise. These factors create demand for convenience foods and higher-quality products. Overall, however, the Korean consumer market lags behind that of other Asian countries having about the same level of economic development. For example, Korea lacks modern convenience stores and large supermarkets that offer wide variety to consumers.

Still, Hardee's believes it has found a way around all of these stumbling blocks. Hardee's selected Kim Chang-Hwan, a wealthy local businessman, as its Korean franchisee. Mr. Kim's older brother manages a chain of retail shoe stores that has many outlets near student hangouts. The Kims are converting several of the shoe stores into Hardee's restaurants. In an "in-your-face" move, the Korean franchise opened its first Hardee's in downtown Seoul just a few yards down the street from a popular McDonald's. Mr. King Nam-Young, the franchisee's general manager, admits that Hardee's executives were concerned about the strategy, but so far his store's sales have equaled McDonald's.

McDonald's entered the country in 1986 by forming a 50-50 joint venture with a Korean accountant and entrepreneur, Mr. Ahn Hyo Young, and had planned to open 14 stores by the early 1990s. However, the first store didn't open until 1988 and expansion has been very slow, resulting in part from the illness and death of Mr. Ahn. McDonald's indicates that it is now uncertain about where to find a new local partner. McDonald's employees also claim that the local franchise did not have enough capital when it started and that McDonald's had balked at the high cost of real estate.

COORS AND PURINA TRY THEIR HANDS

Coors Brewing Company has announced that it too is moving into the South Korean market. Although it is not unusual for American brewers to do business in foreign markets, they have typically expanded through contract brewing, licensing agreements, or direct exports. However, Coors announced that it will enter into a joint venture with Jinro Ltd., a Korean distiller, to build its first offshore brewery. Thus, it will become the first U.S. brewer to own part of a foreign-based brewery. The joint venture hoped to gain a 5 percent to 6 percent share of the Korean market by 1994.

Analysts suggest that U.S. brewers are showing more interest in foreign markets because of the slow growth in the U.S. market. A Coors spokesperson notes that to gain more business in the United States, you have to take it from someone else. In Korea, he notes, the beer market is growing 15 percent a year, and a company has a chance to earn some of that growth itself. American brewers are well positioned to expand. One industry executive states, "There is a movement toward lightness in all beverages [around the world] and American beers have always been very●light compared to European beers."

Prior to the Korean agreement, Coors had only licensed its beer in Canada and Japan and exported it to three other countries. Coors is entering South Korea despite Miller Brewing's recent departure. Miller pulled out of Korea because of high tariffs and the rising value of Korea's currency, the yuan. Coors won't have an easy time of it, even if its agreement works. The Korean government has licensed only two other brewers. These two national breweries produce several Korean beers and market Carlsberg beer under license. Also, one is licensed to sell one of Coors's toughest competitors—Budweiser.

Like Coors, Ralston Purina has also decided to go against conventional wisdom. It has constructed a $10-million plant in Korea to produce its Chex breakfast cereal. But unlike Coors and the fast-food companies, Purina has some advantages. First, it will enter a market containing no strong local producer. Second, Purina is not a newcomer to the Korean market—it has been operating in Korea for 25 years. Purina began in Korea by producing feed for cows, hogs, poultry, and fish and later moved into cat and dog food.

Purina has paid careful attention to the Korean market's development. It has found that the consumption of breakfast cereal closely follows the consumption of milk throughout the world. When it noted rising income levels and milk consumption in Korea, it decided that the time was right to dive into cereals.

MAKING IT EASIER

Despite the efforts of the fast-food companies, Coors, and Purina, the Korean government is still concerned about the low level of foreign investment. As a result, the government is slowly changing the rules. It now grants automatic approval for projects valued at less than $20 million, up from the previous $5-million limit. Moreover, foreign companies can now establish wholly-owned subsidiaries. The government may also make it easier for foreign companies to bring in additional capital, and it is granting tax breaks to high-tech electronics companies and may offer cheap land to high-tech companies that locate in Korean industrial parks.

However, the government has been slow to offer similar benefits to processed foods or packaged-goods companies, and it has been reluctant to allow foreigners to build modern warehouses and distribution networks—facilities needed by consumer-product companies. Furthermore, the government often holds up products at customs and sponsors anticonsumption campaigns to turn public opinion against imported goods.

As a result of the positive changes and despite the problems, more foreign companies are establishing import offices and sales and distribution channels in Korea. Some businesspeople believe that if a company can find its way through the maze of Korean political, economic, and cultural barriers, it can reap substantial rewards.

BACK IN DOWNTOWN SEOUL

Meanwhile, Moon Yong and her friend have finished their Cokes and fries at Hardee's and decide to walk down the street to McDonald's to see what's happening there. They throw away their trash, wave to some friends, and leave the restaurant. The Hardee's manager watches them leave and wonders whether the fascination for things American will continue or whether Korean political, economic, and cultural forces will blunt efforts to open the Korean market. What can he do to keep Moon Yong and others like her coming back to Hardee's?

QUESTIONS

1. Based on information in the case, what kinds of trade restrictions does Hardee's face in working in Korea's trade system?

2. What aspects of Korea's economic, political-legal, and cultural environments are important for Hardee's to understand?

3. Why have Hardee's and the other companies in the

case decided to enter foreign markets and why have they selected Korea? Do you agree with their decisions?

4. What methods might Hardee's have used to enter the Korean market, and why did it select the method it used?

5. What decisions has Hardee's made about its marketing program in Korea? What recommendations would you make about this program?

Sources: Adapted from: Damon Darlin, "South Koreans Crave American Fast Food," *Wall Street Journal*, February 22, 1991, p. B1; Marj Charlier, "U.S. Brewers' Foreign Growth Proves Tricky," *Wall Street Journal*, September 9, 1991, p. B1; Monua Janah, "Rating Risk in the Hot Countries," *Wall Street Journal*, September 20, 1991, p. R4; Darlin, "U.S. Firms Take Chances in South Korea," *Wall Street Journal*, June 15, 1992, p. B1. Used with permission.

Marketing Services, Organizations, Persons, Places, and Ideas

21

The Walt Disney Company is a master service marketer. Its "product" is entertainment, and no company provides more of it. Nowhere is the "Disney Magic" more apparent than at the company's premier theme park, Walt Disney World Resort. Some 29 million people flock to Walt Disney World each year—ten times more than the number who visit Yellowstone National Park—making it the world's number one tourist attraction. On a single busy day, as many as 150,000 eager guests might drop by to visit Mickey and his friends at the Magic Kingdom, Epcot, or the Disney-MGM Studios.

What brings so many people to Walt Disney World? Part of the answer lies in its many attractions. Walt Disney World is a true fantasyland—almost 50 square miles brimming with attractions such as Space Mountain, Journey into Imagination, Body Wars, Pirates of the Caribbean, Typhoon Lagoon, and Pleasure Island. But these attractions provide only part of the story. In fact, what visitors like even more, they say, is the park's sparkling cleanliness and the friendliness of Walt Disney World employees. In an increasingly rude, dirty, and mismanaged world, Disney offers warmth and order. As one observer notes, "In the Magic Kingdom, America still works the way it is supposed to. Everything is clean and safe, quality and service still matter, and the customer is always right."

Thus, the real "Disney Magic" lies in the company's obsessive dedication to serving its customers. The company takes extreme care to make every aspect of every customer's visit memorable. According to Michael Eisner, Disney's chairman, "We are in the business of exceeding people's very high expectations." Disney works hard at getting every employee, from the executive in the corner office to the person stamping hands at the gate, to embrace its customer-centered company culture. And it appears to be succeeding splendidly. Even as the Walt Disney World waiting lines get longer, the satisfaction rate, as measured by surveys of consumers as they leave the park, gets higher and higher. Sixty percent of all Walt Disney World visitors are repeaters.

OBJECTIVES

When you finish this chapter, you should be able to accomplish the following:

1. Express the uniqueness of marketing **services**, and the aspects that set them apart: **intangibility, inseparability, variability,** and **perishability.**

2. Identify and define **strategies** for marketing services, including **differentiation, service quality,** and **productivity.**

3. Discuss **organization marketing**, including **image assessment,** and **image planning and control.**

4. Identify the basic elements of **person marketing, place marketing,** and **idea marketing.**

How does Disney inspire such high levels of customer service? Beyond the four Ps of marketing, Disney has mastered *internal marketing*—motivating its employees to work as a team to provide top-quality service—and *interactive marketing*—teaching employees how to interact with customers to deliver satisfaction. On their first day, all new employees report for a three-day motivational course at Disney University in Orlando, where they learn how to do the hard work of helping other people have fun. They learn that they are in the entertainment business—that they are "cast members" whose job it is to be enthusiastic, knowledgeable, and professional in serving Disney's "guests." Each cast member plays a vital role in the Walt Disney World "show," whether it's as a "security host" (police), "transportation host" (driver), "custodial host" (street cleaner), or "food and beverage host" (restaurant worker).

Before they can receive their "theme costumes" and go "on stage," cast members must learn how to deal effectively with guests. In courses titled Traditions I and Traditions II, they learn the Disney language, history, and culture. They are taught to be enthusiastic, helpful, and *always* friendly. They learn to do good deeds, such as volunteering to take pictures of guests so that the whole family can be in the picture. They are taught never to say, "It's not my job." When a guest asks a question—whether it's, "Where's the nearest restroom?" or, "What are the names of Snow White's seven dwarfs?"—they need to know the answer. If they see a piece of trash on the ground, they pick it up. So that cast members will blend in and promote the whole show, not individuals, Disney enforces a strict grooming code: Men cannot sport mustaches, beards, or long hair; women cannot have long, brightly-colored fingernails, large hair decorations, heavy eye makeup, or dangling earrings.

Disney keeps its managers close to both employees and customers. At least once in his or her career, every Walt Disney World manager must spend a day prancing around the park in a 20-pound Mickey, Minnie, Goofy, or other character costume. And all managers spend a week each year in "cross-utilization," leaving the desk and heading for the front line—taking tickets, selling popcorn, or loading and unloading rides. The company works to keep employees at all levels motivated and feeling like an important part of the team. All managers and employees wear name badges and address each other on a first-name basis, regardless of rank. Employees receive a Disney newspaper called *Eyes and Ears,* which features news of activities, employment opportunities, special benefits, and educational offerings. A recreational area, consisting of a lake, recreation hall, picnic area, boating and fishing facilities, and a large library, is set aside for the employees' exclusive use. All exiting employees answer a questionnaire on how they felt about working for Disney. In this way, Disney measures its success in producing employee satisfaction. Thus, employees are made to feel important and personally responsible for the "show." Their sense of "owning the organization" spills over to the millions of visitors with whom they come in contact. Employee satisfaction ultimately leads to customer satisfaction.

Disney has become so highly regarded for service quality that many leading corporations—from General Electric and AT&T to General Motors and American Airlines—send managers to Disney University to find out how Disney does it. And Disney's dedication to outstanding service marketing has paid off handsomely. During the past ten years, Disney's annual revenues have increased more than fivefold—to $10 billion. Net income has risen at an average annual rate of more than 50 percent. Thus, Disney has found that by providing outstanding service to its *customers,* it also serves *itself.*[1]

Marketing developed initially for selling physical products, such as toothpaste, cars, steel, and industrial equipment. But this traditional focus may cause people to overlook the many other types of things that are marketed. In this chapter, we look at the special marketing requirements for *services, organizations, persons, places,* and *ideas.*

SERVICES MARKETING

One of the major trends in the United States in recent years has been the dramatic growth of services. Services now generate 74 percent of U.S. gross domestic product. Whereas service jobs accounted for 55 percent of all U.S. jobs in 1970, by 1993, they accounted for 79 percent of total employment. Services are expected to be responsible for *all* net job growth through the year 2005. Services are growing even faster in the world economy, making up a quarter of the value of all international trade. Business services account for almost 30 percent of all U.S. exports, resulting in a substantial trade surplus for services, versus a large deficit for goods.[2]

Service jobs include those in service industries—hotels, airlines, banks, telecommunications, and others—as well as in product-based industries, such as corporate lawyers, medical staff, and sales trainers. As a result of rising affluence, more leisure time, and the growing complexity of products that require servicing, the United States has become the world's first service economy. This, in turn, has led to a growing interest in the special problems of marketing services.

Service industries vary greatly. The *governments* offer services through courts, employment services, hospitals, loan agencies, military services, police and fire departments, postal service, regulatory agencies, and schools. The *private nonprofit organizations* offer services through museums, charities, churches, colleges, foundations, and hospitals. A large number of *business organizations* offer services—airlines, banks, hotels, insurance companies, consulting firms, medical and law practices, entertainment companies, real estate firms, advertising and research agencies, and retailers.

Not only are there traditional service industries, but also new types keep popping up all the time:

The convenience industry: Services that save you time—for a price.

Want someone to fetch a meal from a local restaurant? In Austin, Texas, you can call EatOutIn. Plants need to be watered? In New York, you can call the Busy Body's Helper. Too busy to wrap and mail your packages? Stop by any one of the 72 outlets of Tender Sender, headquartered in Portland, Oregon. "We'll find it, we'll do it, we'll wait for it," chirps Lois Barnett, the founder of Personalized Services in Chicago. She and her crew of six will walk the dog, shuttle the kids to Little League, or wait in line for your theater tickets. Meet the convenience peddlers. They want to save you time. For a price, they'll do just about anything that's legal.[3]

Some service businesses are very large, with total sales and assets in the trillions of dollars. Table 21-1 shows the five largest service companies in each of eight service categories. There are also tens of thousands of smaller service providers. Selling services presents some special problems calling for special marketing solutions.

NATURE AND CHARACTERISTICS OF A SERVICE

Service
Any activity or benefit that one party can offer to another that is essentially intangible and does not result in the ownership of anything.

A **service** is any activity or benefit that one party can offer to another that is essentially intangible and does not result in the ownership of anything. Its production may or may not be tied to a physical product. Activities such as renting a hotel

TABLE 21-1 *The Largest U.S. Service Companies*

DIVERSIFIED SERVICES	COMMERCIAL BANKING
AT&T	Citicorp
Fleming	BankAmerica
SuperValu	NationsBank
MCI Communications	Chemical Bank
McKesson	J. P. Morgan

DIVERSIFIED FINANCIAL	SAVINGS INSTITUTIONS
Federal National Mortgage Association	H. F. Ahmanson
Salomon	Great Western Financial
Merrill Lynch	Golden West Financial
Travelers	Glendale Federal
American International Group	California Federal Bank

LIFE INSURANCE	RETAILING
Prudential of America	Wal-Mart Stores
Metropolitan Life	Sears
Teachers Insurance and Annuity	Kmart
New York Life	Kroger
Aetna Life	JCPenney

TRANSPORTATION	UTILITIES
United Parcel Service	GTE
AMR	BellSouth
UAL	Bell Atlantic
Delta Airlines	NYNEX
CSX	Pacific Gas & Electric

Source: "The Service 500," *Fortune,* May 30, 1994, pp. 200–220.

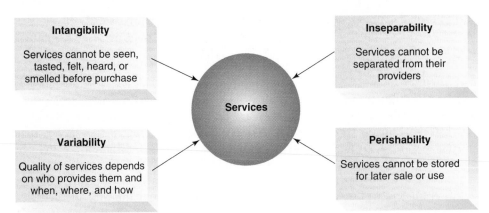

FIGURE 21-1 *Four service characteristics*

room, depositing money in a bank, traveling on an airplane, visiting a psychiatrist, getting a haircut, having a car repaired, watching a professional sport, seeing a movie, having clothes cleaned at a dry cleaner, and getting advice from a lawyer all involve buying a service.

A company must consider four service characteristics when designing marketing programs: *intangibility, inseparability, variability,* and *perishability.* These characteristics are summarized in Figure 21-1 and discussed in the following sections.[4]

Intangibility

Service intangibility
A major characteristic of services—they cannot be seen, tasted, felt, heard, or smelled before they are bought.

Service intangibility means that services cannot be seen, tasted, felt, heard, or smelled before they are bought. For example, people undergoing cosmetic surgery cannot see the result before the purchase, and airline passengers have nothing but a ticket and the promise of safe delivery to their destinations.

To reduce uncertainty, buyers look for "signals" of service quality. They draw conclusions about quality from the place, people, price, equipment, and communication material that they can see. Therefore, the service provider's task is to make the service tangible in one or more ways. Whereas product marketers try to add intangibles to their tangible offers, service marketers try to add tangibles to their intangible offers.

Consider a bank that wants to convey the idea that its service is quick and efficient. It must make this positioning strategy tangible in every aspect of customer contact. The bank's physical setting must suggest quick and efficient service: Its exterior and interior should have clean lines; internal traffic flow should be planned carefully; waiting lines should seem short at teller windows and ATMs; and background music should be light and upbeat. The bank's staff should be busy and properly dressed. The equipment—computers, copy machines, desks—should look modern. The bank's ads and other communications should suggest efficiency, with clean and simple designs and carefully chosen words and photos that communicate the bank's positioning. The bank should choose a name and symbol for its service that suggest speed and efficiency. Its pricing for various services should be kept simple and clear.

Inseparability

Service inseparability
A major characteristic of services—they are produced and consumed at the same time and cannot be separated from their providers, whether the providers are people or machines.

Physical goods are produced, then stored, later sold, and still later consumed. In contrast, services are first sold, then produced and consumed at the same time. **Service inseparability** means that services cannot be separated from their providers, whether the providers are people or machines. If a service employee provides the employee service, then the employee is a part of the service. Because the customer is also present as the service is produced, *provider-customer interaction* is a special feature of services marketing. Both the provider and the customer affect the service outcome.

In the case of entertainment and professional services, buyers care a great deal about *who* provides the service. It is not the same service at a Billy Joel concert if Joel gets sick and is replaced by Garth Brooks. A legal defense supplied by John Nobody differs from one supplied by F. Lee Bailey. When customers have strong provider preferences, price is used to ration the limited supply of the preferred provider's time. Thus, F. Lee Bailey charges more than do less well-known lawyers.

Variability

Service variability

A major characteristic of services—their quality may vary greatly, depending on who provides them and when, where, and how.

Service variability means that the quality of services depends on who provides them as well as when, where, and how they are provided. For example, some hotels—say, Ritz-Carlton or Marriott—have reputations for providing better service than others. Within a given Marriott hotel, one registration-desk employee may be cheerful and efficient, whereas another standing just a few feet away may be unpleasant and slower. Even the quality of a single Marriott employee's service varies according to his or her energy and frame of mind at the time of each customer encounter.

Service firms can take several steps to help manage service variability. They can select and carefully train their personnel to give good service. They can provide employee incentives that emphasize quality, such as employee-of-the-month awards or bonuses based on customer feedback. A firm can check customer satisfaction regularly through suggestion and complaint systems, customer surveys, and comparison shopping. When poor service is found, it can be corrected.

Perishability

Service perishability

A major characteristic of services—they cannot be stored for later sale or use.

Service perishability means that services cannot be stored for later sale or use. Some doctors charge patients for missed appointments because the service value existed only at that point and disappeared when the patient did not show up. The perishability of services is not a problem when demand is steady. However, when demand fluctuates, service firms often have difficult problems. For example, public transportation companies have to own much more equipment than they would if demand were even throughout the day.

Service firms can use several strategies for producing a better match between demand and supply. On the demand side, charging different prices at different times will shift some demand from peak periods to off-peak periods. Examples include low early-evening movie prices and weekend discount prices for car rentals. Or nonpeak demand can be increased, as when McDonald's began offering its Egg

Services are perishable: Empty seats at slack times cannot be stored for later use during peak periods.

McMuffin breakfasts or when hotels developed mini-vacation weekends. Complementary services can be offered during peak times to provide alternatives to waiting customers, such as cocktail lounges to sit in while waiting for a restaurant table and automatic tellers in banks. Reservation systems can also help manage the demand level—airlines, hotels, and physicians use them regularly.

On the supply side, firms can hire part-time employees to serve peak demand. Colleges add part-time teachers when enrollment goes up, and restaurants call in part-time waiters and waitresses to handle busy shifts. Peak-time demand can be handled more efficiently by having employees do only essential tasks during peak periods. Some tasks can be shifted to consumers, as when consumers fill out their own medical records or bag their own groceries. Finally, providers can share services, as when several hospitals share an expensive piece of medical equipment.

MARKETING STRATEGIES FOR SERVICE FIRMS

Until recently, service firms lagged behind manufacturing firms in their use of marketing. Many service businesses are small (auto repair shops, dry cleaners) and often consider marketing unneeded or too costly. Other service businesses (colleges, hospitals) once had so much demand that they did not need marketing until recently. Still others (legal, medical, and accounting practices) believed that it was unprofessional to use marketing.

Still, just like manufacturing businesses, good service firms use marketing to position themselves strongly in chosen target markets. Southwest Airlines positions itself as "Just Plane Smart" for commuter flyers—as a no-frills, short-haul airline charging very low fares. The Ritz-Carlton Hotel positions itself as offering a memorable experience that "enlivens the senses, instills well-being, and fulfills even the unexpressed wishes and needs of our guests." These and other service firms establish their positions through traditional marketing mix activities.

However, because services differ from tangible products, they often require additional marketing approaches. In a product business, products are fairly standardized and can sit on shelves waiting for customers. But in a service business, the customer and frontline service employee *interact* to create the service. Thus, service providers must work to interact effectively with customers to create superior value during service encounters. Effective interaction, in turn, depends on the skills of frontline service employees, and on the service production and support processes backing these employees.

Thus, successful service companies focus their attention on both their employees and customers. They understand the *service-profit chain,* which links service firm profits with employee and customer satisfaction. This chain consists of five links:[5]

- *Healthy service profits and growth*—superior service firm performance, which results from . . .
- *Satisfied and loyal customers*—satisfied customers who remain loyal, repeat purchase, and refer other customers, which results from . . .
- *Greater service value*—more effective and efficient customer value creation and service delivery, which results from . . .
- *Satisfied and productive service employees*—more satisfied, loyal, and hard working employees, which results from . . .
- *Internal service quality*—superior employee selection and training, a quality work environment, and strong support for those dealing with customers.

Therefore, reaching service profits and growth goals begins with taking care of those who take care of customers (see Marketing Highlight 21-1).

RITZ-CARLTON:
TAKING CARE OF THOSE WHO
TAKE CARE OF CUSTOMERS

Ritz-Carlton, a chain of 28 luxury hotels renowned for outstanding service, caters to the top 5 percent of corporate and leisure travelers. The company's Credo sets lofty customer-service goals: "The Ritz-Carlton Hotel is a place where the genuine care and comfort of our guests is our highest mission. We pledge to provide the finest personal service and facilities for our guests who will always enjoy a warm, relaxed yet refined ambience. The Ritz-Carlton experience enlivens the senses, instills well-being, and fulfills even the unexpressed wishes and needs of our guests."

The Credo is more than just words on paper—Ritz-Carlton delivers on its promises. In surveys of departing guests, some 95 percent report that they've had a truly memorable experience. In fact, at Ritz-Carlton, exceptional service encounters have become almost commonplace. Take the experiences of Nancy and Harvey Heffner of Manhattan, who stayed at the Ritz-Carlton in Naples, Florida. As reported in the *New York Times:*

"The hotel is elegant and beautiful," Mrs. Heffner said, "but more important is the beauty expressed by the staff. They can't do enough to please you." When the couple's son became sick last year in Naples, the hotel staff brought him hot tea with honey at all hours of the night, she said. When

Mr. Heffner had to fly home on business for a day and his return flight was delayed, a driver for the hotel waited in the lobby most of the night.

Such personal, high-quality service has also made the Ritz-Carlton a

Ritz-Carlton understands that outstanding service begins with taking care of those who take care of customers.

favorite among conventioneers. Comments one convention planner, "They not only treat us like kings when we hold our top-level meetings in their hotels, but we just never get any complaints."

In 1991, Ritz-Carlton received

121 quality-related awards, along with industry-best rankings by all three hotel-rating organizations. In 1992, it became the first hotel company to win the Malcolm Baldrige National Quality Award. More importantly, service quality has resulted in high customer

retention: More than 90 percent of Ritz-Carlton customers return. And despite its hefty $150 average room rate, the chain enjoys a 70 percent occupancy rate, almost nine points above the industry average.

Most of the responsibility for

The concept of the service-profit chain is well illustrated by a story about how Bill Marriott, Jr., chairman of Marriott hotels, interviews prospective managers:

> Bill Marriott tells job candidates that the hotel chain wants to satisfy three groups: *customers, employees,* and *stockholders.* Although all of the groups are important, he asks in which order the groups should be satisfied. Most candidates say first satisfy customers. Marriott, however, reasons differently. First, employees must be satisfied. If employees love their jobs and feel a sense of pride in the hotel, they will serve customers well. Satisfied customers will return frequently to the Marriott. Moreover, dealing with happy customers will make employees even more satisfied, resulting in better service and still greater repeat business, all of which will yield a level of profits that will satisfy Marriott stockholders.

All of this suggests that service marketing requires more than just traditional external marketing using the four *P*s. Figure 21-2 shows that service marketing

keeping guests satisfied falls to Ritz-Carlton's customer-contact employees. Thus, the hotel chain takes great care in selecting its personnel. "We want only people who care about people," notes Patrick Mene, the company's vice president of quality. Once selected, employees are given intensive training in the art of coddling customers. New employees attend a two-day orientation, in which top management drums into them the "20 Ritz-Carlton Basics." Basic number 1: "The Credo will be known, owned, and energized by all employees."

Employees are taught to do everything they can to never lose a guest. "There's no negotiating at Ritz-Carlton when it comes to solving customer problems," says Mene. Staff learn that *anyone* who receives a customer complaint *owns* that complaint until it's resolved. They are trained to drop whatever they're doing to help a customer—no matter what they're doing or what their department. Ritz-Carlton employees are empowered to handle problems on the spot, without consulting higher-ups. Each employee can spend up to $2,000 to redress a guest grievance, and each is allowed to break from his or her routine for as long as needed to make a guest happy. "We master customer satisfaction at the individual level," adds Mene. "This is our most sensitive listening post . . . our early warning system." Thus, while competitors are still reading guest com-

ment cards to learn about customer problems, Ritz-Carlton has already resolved them.

Ritz-Carlton instills a sense of pride in its employees. "You serve," they are told, "but you are not servants." The company motto states, "We are ladies and gentlemen serving ladies and gentlemen." Employees understand their role in Ritz-Carlton's success. "We might not be able to afford a hotel like this," says employee Tammy Patton, "but we can make it so people who can afford it will want to keep coming here."

And so they do. When it comes to customer satisfaction, no detail is too small. Customer-contact people are taught to greet guests warmly and sincerely, using guest names when possible. They learn to use the proper language with guests—words like "Good morning," "Certainly," "I'll be happy to," and "My pleasure," never "Hi" or "How's it going?" The Ritz-Carlton Basics urge employees to escort guests to another area of the hotel rather than pointing out directions, to answer the phone within three rings and with a "smile," and to take pride and care in their personal appearance.

Ritz-Carlton recognizes and rewards employees who perform feats of outstanding service. Under its 5-Star Awards program, outstanding performers are nominated by peers and managers, and winners receive plaques at dinners celebrating their

achievements. For on-the-spot recognition, managers award Gold Standard Coupons, redeemable for items in the gift shop and free weekend stays at the hotel. Ritz-Carlton further rewards and motivates its employees with events such as Super Sports Day, an employee talent show, luncheons celebrating employee anniversaries, a family picnic, and special themes in employee dining rooms. As a result, Ritz-Carlton's employees appear to be just as satisfied as its customers. Employee turnover is less than 30 percent a year, compared with 45 percent at other luxury hotels.

Ritz-Carlton's success is based on a simple philosophy: To take care of customers, you must first take care of those who take care of customers. Satisfied employees deliver high service value, which then creates satisfied customers. Satisfied customers, in turn, create sales and profits for the company.

Sources: Quotes from Edwin McDowell, "Ritz-Carlton's Keys to Good Service," *New York Times,* March 31, 1993, p. D1; and Howard Schlossberg, "Measuring Customer Satisfaction Is Easy to Do— Until You Try," *Marketing News,* April 26, 1993, pp. 5, 8. Also see "The Ritz-Carlton Hotel Co.," *Business America,* November 2, 1992, pp. 13–14; and Rahul Jacob, "Why Some Customers Are More Equal than Others," *Fortune,* September 19, 1994, pp. 215–224.

FIGURE 21-2 *Three types of marketing in service industries*

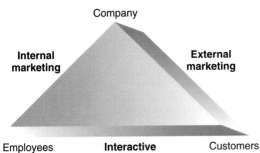

also requires both *internal marketing* and *interactive marketing.*

Internal marketing means that the service firm must effectively train and motivate its customer-contact employees and all the supporting service people to work as a *team* to provide customer satisfaction. For the firm to deliver consistently high service quality, everyone must practice a customer orientation. It is not enough to have a marketing department doing traditional marketing while the rest of the company goes its own way. Marketers also must get everyone else in the organization to practice marketing. In fact, internal marketing must *precede* external marketing.

Interactive marketing means that perceived service quality depends heavily on the quality of the buyer-seller interaction during the service encounter. In product marketing, product quality often depends little on how the product is obtained. But

Internal marketing
Marketing by a service firm to train and effectively motivate its customer-contact employees and all the supporting service people to work as a team to provide customer satisfaction.

Interactive marketing
Marketing by a service firm that recognizes that perceived service quality depends heavily on the quality of buyer-seller interaction.

in services marketing, service quality depends on both the service deliverer and the quality of the delivery, especially in professional services. The customer judges service quality not just on *technical quality* (say, the success of the surgery) but also on its *functional quality* (whether the doctor showed concern and inspired confidence). Thus, professionals cannot assume that they will satisfy the customer simply by providing good technical service. They have to master interactive marketing skills or functions as well.[6]

Today, as competition and costs increase, and as productivity and quality decrease, more marketing sophistication is needed. Service companies face three major marketing tasks: They want to increase their *competitive differentiation, service quality,* and *productivity.*

Managing Differentiation

In these days of intense price competition, service marketers often complain about the difficulty of differentiating their services from those of competitors. To the extent that customers view the services of different providers as similar, they care less about the provider than the price.

The solution to price competition is to develop a differentiated offer, delivery, and image. The *offer* can include *innovative features* that set one company's offer apart from competitors' offers. For example, airlines have introduced such innovations as in-flight movies, advance seating, air-to-ground telephone service, and frequent-flyer award programs to differentiate their offers. British Airways even offers international travelers a sleeping compartment, hot showers, and cooked-to-order breakfasts. Unfortunately, most service innovations are copied easily. Still, the service company that innovates regularly usually will gain a succession of temporary advantages and an innovative reputation that may help it keep customers who want to go with the best.

Service companies can differentiate their service *delivery* in three ways—through people, physical environment, and process. The company can distinguish itself by having more able and reliable customer-contact people than its competitors have. Or it can develop a superior physical environment in which the service product is delivered. Finally, it can design a superior delivery process. For example, a bank might offer its customers electronic home banking as a better way to deliver banking services than having to drive, park, and wait in line.

Service companies also can work on differentiating their *images* through symbols and branding. For example, the Harris Bank of Chicago adopted the lion as its symbol on its stationery, in its advertising, and even as stuffed animals offered to new depositors. The well-known "Harris Lion" confers an image of strength on the bank. Other well-known service symbols include The Travelers' red umbrella, Merrill Lynch's bull, and Allstate's "good hands."

To differentiate its service, British Airways offers international travelers such features as sleeping compartments and hot showers. As the comments in this ad show, customers really appreciate such services.

Managing Service Quality

One of the major ways a service firm can differentiate itself is by delivering consistently higher quality than its competitors do. Like manufacturers before them, many service industries have now joined the total quality movement. Many companies are finding that outstanding service quality can give them a potent competitive advantage that leads to superior sales and profit performance.[7] Some firms have become almost legendary for their high-quality service.

The key is to exceed the customers' service-quality *expectations*. As the chief executive at American Express puts it, "Promise only what you can deliver and deliver *more* than you promise!"[8] These expectations are based on past experiences, word of mouth, and service firm advertising. If *perceived service* of a given firm exceeds *expected service,* customers are apt to use the provider again. Customer retention is perhaps the best measure of quality—a service firm's ability to hang onto its customers depends on how consistently it delivers value to them. Thus, whereas the manufacturer's quality goal might be "zero *defects,*" the service provider's goal is "zero customer *defections.*"

The service provider needs to identify the expectations of target customers concerning service quality. Unfortunately, service quality is harder to define and judge than product quality. It is harder to get agreement on the quality of a haircut than on the quality of a hair dryer, for instance. Moreover, although greater service quality results in greater customer satisfaction, it also results in higher costs. Still, investments in service usually pay off through increased customer retention and sales. Whatever the level of service provided, it is important that the service provider clearly define and communicate that level so that its employees know what they must deliver and customers know what they will get.

Many service companies have invested heavily to develop streamlined and efficient service-delivery systems. They want to ensure that customers will receive consistently high-quality service in every service encounter. Unlike product manufacturers who can adjust their machinery and inputs until everything is perfect, however, service quality always will vary, depending on the interactions between employees and customers. Problems inevitably will occur. As hard as they try, even the best companies will have an occasional late delivery, burned steak, or grumpy employee. However, although a company cannot always prevent service problems, it can learn to recover from them. And good *service recovery* can turn angry customers into loyal ones. In fact, good recovery can win more customer purchasing and loyalty than if things had gone well in the first place.[9] Therefore, companies should take steps not only to provide good service every time, but also to recover from service mistakes when they do occur.

The first step is to *empower* frontline service employees—to give them the authority, responsibility, and incentives they need to recognize, care about, and tend to customer needs. For example, Marriott has put some 70,000 employees through empowerment training, which encourages them to go beyond their normal jobs to solve customer problems. Such empowered employees can act quickly and effectively to keep service problems from resulting in lost customers. The Marriott Desert Springs revised the job description for its customer-contact employees. The major goal of these positions now is to ensure that "our guests experience excellent service and hospitality while staying at our resort." Well-trained employees are given the authority to do whatever it takes, on the spot, to keep guests happy. They are also expected to help management ferret out the cause of guests' problems, and to inform managers of ways to improve overall hotel service and guests' comfort.[10]

Studies of well-managed service companies show that they share a number of common virtues regarding service quality. First, top service companies are "*customer obsessed.*" They have a distinctive strategy for satisfying customer needs that wins enduring customer loyalty.

Second, well-managed service companies have a history of *top management commitment to quality*. Management at companies such as Marriott, Disney, Delta, Federal Express, and McDonald's looks not only at financial performance but also at service performance. Third, the best service providers *set high service quality standards*. Swissair, for example, aims to have 96 percent or more of its passengers rate its service as good or superior; otherwise, it takes action. Citibank aims to answer phone calls within ten seconds and customer letters within two days. The standards must be set *appropriately high*. A 98 percent accuracy standard may sound good, but using this standard, 64,000 Federal Express packages would be lost each day, 10 words would be misspelled on each page, 400,000 prescriptions would be misfilled daily, and drinking water would be unsafe eight days a year. Top service companies do not settle merely for "good" service, they aim for 100 percent defect-free service.[11]

Fourth, the top service firms *watch service performance closely*—both their own and that of competitors. They use methods such as comparison shopping, customer surveys, and suggestion and complaint forms. For example, General Electric sends out 700,000 response cards each year to households who rate their service people's performance. Citibank takes regular measures of "ART"—accuracy, responsiveness, and timeliness—and sends out employees who act as customers to check on service quality.

Good service companies also communicate their concerns about service quality to employees and provide performance feedback. At Federal Express, quality measurements are everywhere. When employees walk in the door in the morning, they see the previous week's on-time percentages. Then, the company's in-house television station gives them detailed breakdowns of what happened yesterday and any potential problems for the day ahead.[12]

Managing Productivity

With their costs rising rapidly, service firms are under great pressure to increase service productivity. They can do so in several ways. The service providers can train current employees better, or they can hire new ones who will work harder or more skillfully for the same pay. Or the service providers can increase the quantity of their service by giving up some quality. Doctors who work for health maintenance organizations (HMOs) have moved toward handling more patients and giving less time to each. The provider can "industrialize the service" by adding equipment and standardizing production, as in McDonald's assembly-line approach to fast-food retailing. Commercial dishwashing, jumbo jets, and multiple-unit movie theaters all represent technological expansions of service.

Service providers also can increase productivity by designing more effective services. How-to-quit-smoking clinics and exercise recommendations may reduce the need for expensive medical services later on. Hiring paralegal workers reduces the need for expensive legal professionals. Providers also can give customers incentives to substitute company labor with their own labor. For example, business firms that sort their own mail before delivering it to the post office pay lower postal rates.

However, companies must avoid pushing productivity so hard that doing so reduces perceived quality. Some productivity steps help standardize quality, increasing customer satisfaction. But other productivity steps lead to too much standardization and can rob consumers of customized service. Attempts to industrialize a service or to cut costs can make a service company more efficient in the short run but reduce its longer-run ability to innovate, maintain service quality, or respond to consumer needs and desires. In some cases, service providers accept reduced productivity in order to create more service differentiation or quality.

INTERNATIONAL SERVICES MARKETING

An Italian sportswear manufacturer calls her advertising agency in London to confirm plans for new billboards in Venezuela. A German businessman checks into his hotel room in Atlanta—the hotel is owned by a British company and managed by an American firm. The Zurich branch of a Japanese bank participates in a debt offering for an aircraft leasing company in Ireland. These are just a few examples of the thousands of service transactions that take place each day around the globe. More and more, the global economy is dominated by services. In fact, a variety of service industries—from banking, insurance, and communications to transportation, travel, and entertainment—now account for well over 60 percent of the economy in developed countries around the world. The worldwide growth rate for services almost doubles the growth rate for manufacturing.

Some service industries have a long history of international operations. For example, the commercial banking industry was one of the first to grow internationally. Banks had to provide global services in order to meet the foreign exchange and credit needs of their home-country clients wanting to sell overseas. In recent years, however, as the scope of international financing has broadened, many banks have become truly global operations. Germany's Deutsche Bank, for example, has branches in 41 countries. Thus, for its clients around the world who wish to take advantage of growth opportunities created by German reunification, Deutsche Bank can raise money not just in Frankfurt, but also in Zurich, London, Paris, and Tokyo.

In recent years, many banks have become truly global. Citibank offers services from São Paulo to Singapore and everywhere in between.

YOU'RE LOOKING FOR A
GLOBAL CUSTODIAN.

A BANK WITH LOCAL EXPERTISE AND GLOBAL REACH.

A BANK THAT KNOWS THE MARKETS, BOTH EMERGING AND EMERGED.

YOU NEED THE WORLD'S MOST EXTENSIVE BANKING NETWORK.

From streamlined processing to timely reporting, from acting locally to thinking globally, Citibank offers the kinds of solutions that have made us the number one Global Custodian in the world's emerging markets.

CITIBANK◆

The travel industry also moved naturally into international operations. American hotel and airline companies grew quickly in Europe and the Far East during the economic expansion that followed World War II. Credit card companies soon followed—the early worldwide presence of American Express has now been matched by Visa and MasterCard. Business travelers and vacationers like the convenience, and they have now come to expect that their credit cards will be honored wherever they go.

Professional and business services industries such as accounting, management consulting, and advertising only recently have globalized. The international growth of these firms followed the globalization of the manufacturing companies they serve. For example, increasingly globalized manufacturing firms have found it much easier to have their accounts prepared by a single accounting firm, even when they operate in two dozen countries. This set the stage for rapid international consolidation in the accounting industry. During the late 1980s, America's "Big Eight" accounting firms quickly merged with established companies around the world to become the international "Big Six" almost overnight. Similarly, as their client companies began to employ global marketing and advertising strategies, advertising agencies and other marketing services firms responded by globalizing their own operations. For instance, the ten largest U.S. advertising agencies now make over 50 percent of their billings abroad.[13]

The rapidly expanding international marketplace provides many attractive opportunities for service firms. However, it also creates some special challenges. Service companies wanting to operate in other countries are not always welcomed with open arms. Whereas manufacturers usually face straightforward tariff, quota, or currency restrictions when attempting to sell their products in another country, service providers are likely to face more subtle barriers. In some cases, rules and regulations affecting international services firms reflect the host country's traditions. In others, they appear to protect the country's own fledgling service industries from large global competitors with greater resources. In still other cases, however, the restrictions seem to have little purpose other than to make entry difficult for foreign service firms.

> The industrialized nations, particularly the United States, want their banks, insurance companies, construction firms, and other service providers to be allowed to move people, capital, and technology around the globe unimpeded. Instead they face a bewildering complex of national regulations, most of them designed to guarantee jobs for local competitors. A new Turkish law, for example, forbids international accounting firms to bring capital into the country to set up offices and requires them to use the names of local partners, rather than the prestigious international ones, in their marketing. To audit the books of a multinational company's branch in Buenos Aires, an accountant must have the equivalent of a high school education in Argentinean geography and history. ... India is perhaps the most [difficult] big economy in the world [to enter] these days. ... New Delhi prevents international insurance companies from selling property and casualty policies to the country's swelling business community or life insurance to its huge middle class.[14]

Despite such difficulties, the trend toward growth of global service companies will continue, especially in banking, airlines, telecommunications, and professional services. Today service firms are no longer simply following their manufacturing customers. Instead, they are taking the lead in international expansion.[15]

ORGANIZATION MARKETING

Organization marketing
Activities undertaken to create, maintain, or change attitudes and behavior of target audiences toward an organization.

Organizations often carry out activities to "sell" the organization itself. **Organization marketing** consists of activities undertaken to create, maintain, or change the attitudes and behavior of target consumers toward an organization. Both profit and nonprofit organizations practice organization marketing. Business firms sponsor public relations or corporate advertising campaigns to polish their images. Nonprofit organizations, such as churches, colleges, charities, museums, and performing arts groups, market their organizations in order to raise funds and attract members or patrons. Organization marketing calls for assessing the organization's current image and developing a marketing plan to improve it.

IMAGE ASSESSMENT

Organization image
The way an individual or a group sees an organization.

The first step in image assessment is to research the organization's current image among key publics. The way an individual or a group sees an organization is called its **organization image.** Different people can have different images of the same organization. The organization might be pleased with its public image, or it might find that it has serious image problems.

For example, suppose a bank conducts marketing research to measure its image in the community. It finds its image to be that shown by the mauve line on the right in Figure 21-3. Current and potential customers view the bank as somewhat small, noninnovative, unfriendly, and unknowledgeable. The bank will want to change this image.

IMAGE PLANNING AND CONTROL

Next, the organization should decide what image it would like to have and what it can achieve. For example, the bank might decide that it would like the image shown by the blue line in Figure 21-3. It would like to be seen as a provider of more friendly and personal service, and as larger, more innovative, more knowledgeable.

The firm now develops a marketing plan to shift its actual image toward the desired one. Suppose the bank first wants to improve its image as a provider of friendly and personal service. The key step, of course, is actually to *provide* friendlier and more personal service. The bank can hire and train better tellers and other employees who deal with customers. It can change its decor to make the bank seem warmer. Once the bank is certain that it has improved its performance on important image dimensions, it can design a marketing program to communicate that new image to customers. Using public relations, the bank can sponsor community activities, send its executives to speak to local business and civic groups, offer public seminars on household finances, and issue press releases on newsworthy bank activities. In its advertising, the bank can position itself as "your friendly, personal neighborhood bank."

FIGURE 21-3 *Image assessment*

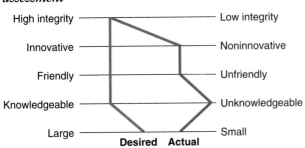

Corporate image advertising is a major tool companies use to market themselves to various publics. Companies can use corporate advertising to build up or maintain a favorable image over many years. Or they can use it to counter events that might hurt their image. For example, Waste Management, the giant garbage disposal company, got into trouble a few years ago for dumping toxic wastes. So it countered with an advertising campaign telling how the company has worked with various government agencies to help save a threatened species of butterfly.

Such organization marketing efforts can work only if the actual organization lives up to the projected image. No amount of advertising and public relations can fool the public for long if the reality fails to match the image. Thus, Waste Management's image campaign worked only because the company has in fact worked to clean up toxic waste sites. Otherwise, even saving butterflies would not have helped the company's reputation.[16]

An organization must resurvey its publics every once in a while to see whether its activities are improving its image. Images cannot be changed overnight:

Corporate image advertising is a major tool companies use to market themselves: Norfolk Southern, the "thoroughbred of transportation," stands on solid footing.

Campaign funds are usually limited, and public images tend to stick. If the firm is making no progress, either its marketing offer or its organization marketing program will have to be changed.

PERSON MARKETING

Person marketing
Activities undertaken to create, maintain, or change attitudes or behavior toward particular persons.

People are also marketed. **Person marketing** consists of activities undertaken to create, maintain, or change attitudes or behavior toward particular people. All kinds of people and organizations practice person marketing. Politicians market themselves to get votes and program support. Entertainers and sports figures use marketing to promote their careers and improve their incomes. Professionals such as doctors, lawyers, accountants, and architects market themselves in order to build their reputations and increase business. Business leaders use person marketing as a strategic tool to develop their company's fortunes as well as their own. Businesses, charities, sports teams, fine arts groups, religious groups, and other organizations also use person marketing. Creating, flaunting, or associating with well-known personalities often helps these organizations achieve their goals better.

Here is an example of successful person marketing:

> Michael Jordan, star of the Chicago Bulls, possesses remarkable basketball skills—great court sense with quick, fluid moves and the ability to soar above the rim for dramatic dunks. And he has an appealing, unassuming personality to go along with his dazzling talents. For more than a decade, all of this has made Michael Jordan very marketable. After college, Jordan signed on with ProServ Inc., a well-known sports management agency, which quickly negotiated a lucrative contract with the Bulls. But that was just the beginning. ProServ decided to market Jordan as not just a supertalented professional basketball player, but also as an all-around good guy and solid citizen. Paying careful attention to placement and staging, the agency booked Jordan into the talk-show circuit, accepted only the best products to endorse, insisted on only high-quality commercials, arranged appearances for charitable causes, and even had him appear as a fashion model. Jordan's market appeal soared, and so did his income. Even after his unexpected 1993 retirement from basketball, Jordan has remained a top endorsement celebrity. And following his return to basketball in 1995 his fame grew to even greater heights. Person marketing has paid off handsomely for Michael Jordan, and for all who have associated with him. After years of spotty attendance at home games, tickets to Chicago Bulls games quickly became the hottest tickets in town. Nike first paired with Jordan in 1984, and eight generations of Air Jordans later, Nike owns half of the basketball shoe market. It still sells more than $200 million worth of Air Jordan shoes, clothes, and accessories each year. Current endorsements for Nike, McDonald's, Quaker's Gatorade, Sara Lee's Hanes underwear and Ball Park franks, Wilson Sporting Goods, General Mills' Wheaties, and other products earn Jordan $34 million a year, and these deals won't expire until the year 2000. Says one analyst about Michael Jordan, "He's another Arnold Palmer and Jack Nicklaus. He'll be around forever."[17]

The objective of person marketing is to create a "celebrity"—a well-known person whose name generates attention, interest, and action. Celebrities differ in the *scope* of their visibility. Some are very well known, but only in limited geographic areas (a town mayor, a local businessperson, an area doctor), or specific segments (the president of the American Dental Association, a company vice-president, a jazz musician with a small group of fans). Still others have broad national or international visibility (major entertainers, sports superstars, world political and religious leaders).

Celebrities also differ in their *durability*. Figure 21-4A shows a standard celebrity life-cycle pattern. The person's visibility begins at a low level, gradually builds to a peak as the person matures and becomes well known, then declines as the celebrity fades from the limelight. But as the rest of Figure 21-4 shows, celebrity life-cycle patterns can vary greatly. For example, in the *overnight* pattern

FIGURE 21-4 *Celebrity life cycles*

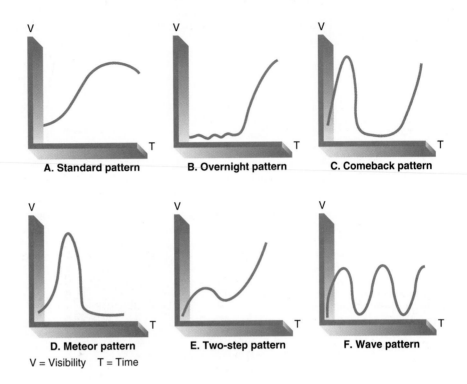

A. Standard pattern   B. Overnight pattern   C. Comeback pattern

D. Meteor pattern   E. Two-step pattern   F. Wave pattern

V = Visibility   T = Time

(Figure 21-4B), a person acquires quick and lasting visibility because of some major deed or event (Charles Lindbergh, Neil Armstrong). In the *comeback* pattern (Figure 21-4C), a celebrity achieves high visibility, loses it, then gets it back again. For example, after stardom followed by years of relative obscurity, singer Tony Bennett recently rebounded as a favorite of the Generation Xers. In the *meteor pattern* (Figure 21-4D), someone gains fame quickly then loses it suddenly. For example, William "Refrigerator" Perry, an overweight Chicago Bears defensive lineman, became an instant "hot property" after he was used as a running back on *Monday Night Football*. He made millions of dollars from product endorsements and then sank back into obscurity—all within about a year.

The person marketing process is similar to the one used by product and service marketers. Person marketers begin with careful market research and analysis to discover consumer needs and market segments. Next comes product development—assessing the person's current qualities and image and transforming the person to match market needs and expectations better. Finally, the marketer develops programs to value, promote, and deliver the celebrity. Some people naturally possess the skills, appearances, and behaviors that target segments value. But for most, celebrity status in any field must actively be developed through sound person marketing.

PLACE MARKETING

Place marketing
Activities undertaken to create, maintain, or change attitudes or behavior toward particular places.

Place marketing involves activities undertaken to create, maintain, or change attitudes or behavior toward particular places. Examples include business site marketing and tourism marketing.

Business site marketing involves developing, selling, or renting business sites for factories, stores, offices, warehouses, and conventions. Large developers research companies' land needs and respond with real estate solutions, such as industrial parks, shopping centers, and new office buildings. Most states operate

"The Goodliest Land": Business Site Marketing in North Carolina

In 1584, when two English explorers returned to their homeland with news of "The Goodliest Land Under the Cope of Heaven," they were describing what is now North Carolina. In recent years, numerous American and foreign companies have come to share this opinion of the Tar Heel State. In three successive *Business Week* surveys, North Carolina was named as first choice of the nation's top business executives for new-plant location. The state does offer a number of economic and cultural advantages, but much credit for the state's popularity goes to the North Carolina Department of Commerce's Business/Industry Development Division. The division employs a high-quality marketing program—including advertising, publicity, and personal selling—to convince targeted firms and industries to come to North Carolina.

The division's 33 industrial development representatives coordinate efforts with development professionals in more than 500 individual North Carolina communities. The division also provides extensive information to firms considering locating in the state—in-depth profiles of more than 600 sites and buildings, estimates of state and local taxes for specific sites, analyses of labor costs

and fringe benefits, details of convenient transportation to sites, and estimates of construction costs.

But the Business/Industry Development Division does more than simply provide information—it aggressively seeks out firms and persuades them to locate in North Carolina. It invites groups of business executives

North Carolina advertises to attract new businesses to the state. Its work force is "ready, willing, and able."

to tour the state and hear presentations, and it sets up booths at industry trade fairs. Its representatives (sometimes including the governor) travel to other states and counties to carry the North Carolina story to executives in attractive businesses and industries. The division also communicates and persuades through informational and promotional brochures delivered by mail and through mass-media advertising. Ads such as those shown here tout North Carolina's benefits: a large and productive labor force, numerous educational and technical training institutions, low taxes, a good transportation network, low energy and construction costs, a good living environment, and plentiful government support and assistance.

The division's total budget runs only a few million dollars a year, but the returns are great. Over the past decade, this modest expenditure has attracted billions of dollars in business investments and created hundreds of thousands of new jobs in North Carolina.

Source: Based on information supplied by the North Carolina Department of Commerce, Business/Industry Development Division.

---

industrial development offices that try to sell companies on the advantages of locating new plants in their states (see Marketing Highlight 21-2). They spend large sums on advertising and offer to fly prospects to the site at no cost. Troubled cities, such as New York City, Detroit, Dallas, and Atlanta, have appointed task forces to improve their images and to draw new businesses to their areas. They may build large centers to house important conventions and business meetings. Even entire nations, such as Canada, Ireland, Greece, Mexico, and Turkey, have marketed themselves as good locations for business investment.

Tourism marketing involves attracting vacationers to spas, resorts, cities, states, and even entire nations. The effort is carried out by travel agents, airlines, motor clubs, oil companies, hotels, motels, and governmental agencies.

Today almost every city, state, and country markets its tourist attractions. Texas has advertised "It's Like a Whole Other Country," and Michigan has touted "YES M!CH!GAN." Philadelphia invites you to "Get To Know Us!" and Palm Beach, Florida advertises "The Best of Everything" at low off-season prices. Some places, however, try to *demarket* themselves because they feel that the harm from tourism exceeds the revenues. Thus, Oregon has publicized its bad weather; Yosemite National Park may ban snowmobiling, conventions, and private cars; and Finland discourages tourists from vacationing in certain areas.

SOCIAL MARKETING OF SAFE AND SOBER DRIVING

The Reader's Digest Foundation, in partnership with the National Association of Secondary School Principals (NASSP), recently launched a two-year, $1 million social marketing campaign to deliver a sober message to teenagers all across America. As part of the "Don't Drink and Drive Challenge," *Reader's Digest* magazine invited teams from leading advertising agencies to create posters for the campaign, with the winners receiving a trip for two to Paris. In the first year of the campaign, more than 1,000 teams from top agencies competed. Shown here are some of the outstanding posters created for the program.

The foundation then distributed copies of the winning posters to 20,000 high schools. Students were challenged to compete for college scholarships by devising programs to promote sober driving. More than 700 schools submitted entries ranging from rock videos to puppet shows to anti-drunk-driving awareness weeks. Scholarships totaling $500,000 went to 115 winning schools. The program was held a second year, with advertising agencies and schools again

The Reader's Digest sponsors a campaign to market safe and sober driving.

taking part and another $500,000 in scholarships awarded. Reader's Digest Foundation continues to offer copies of its posters and summaries

of winning student programs as a resource to educators, the media, and community organizations.

IDEA MARKETING

Social marketing
The design, implementation, and control of programs seeking to increase the acceptability of a social idea, cause, or practice among a target group.

Ideas also can be marketed. In one sense, all marketing is the marketing of an idea, whether it be the general idea of brushing your teeth or the specific idea that Crest provides the most effective decay prevention. Here, however, we narrow our focus to the marketing of *social ideas*, such as public health campaigns to reduce smoking, alcoholism, drug abuse, and overeating; environmental campaigns to promote wilderness protection, clean air, and conservation; and other campaigns such as family planning, human rights, and racial equality. This area has been called **social marketing,** and it includes the creation and implementation of programs seeking to increase the acceptability of a social idea, cause, or practice within targeted groups.

Social marketers can pursue different objectives. They might want to produce understanding (knowing the nutritional value of different foods) or trigger a one-time action (joining in a mass-immunization campaign). They might want to change behavior (discouraging drunk driving) or a basic belief (convincing employers that handicapped people can make strong contributions in the work force).

The Advertising Council of America has developed dozens of social advertising campaigns, including "Smokey the Bear," "Keep America Beautiful," "Join the Peace Corps," "Buy Bonds," "Go to College," and "Say No to Drugs." But social marketing involves much more than just advertising. Many public marketing campaigns fail because they assign advertising the primary role and fail to develop and use all the marketing-mix tools.

In designing effective social-change strategies, social marketers go through a normal marketing planning process. First, they define the social-change objective—for example, "to reduce the percentage of teenagers who drink and drive from 15 percent to 5 percent within five years." Next, they analyze the attitudes, beliefs, values, and behavior of teenagers and the forces that support teenage drinking. They consider communication and distribution approaches that might prevent teenagers from driving while drinking, develop a marketing plan, and build a marketing organization to carry out the plan (see Marketing Highlight 21-3). Finally, they evaluate and, if necessary, adjust the program to make it more effective.

Social marketing is fairly new, and its effectiveness relative to other social-change strategies is difficult to evaluate. It is hard to produce social change with any strategy, let alone a strategy that relies on voluntary response. Social marketing has been applied mainly to family planning, environmental protection, energy conservation, improved health and nutrition, auto driver safety, and public transportation—and there have been some encouraging successes. But more applications are needed before we can fully assess social marketing's potential for producing social change.

Summary

Marketing has broadened in recent years to cover "marketable" entities other than products—namely services, organizations, persons, places, and ideas.

As we move increasingly toward a world service economy, marketers need to know more about *services marketing*. Services are activities or benefits that one party can offer to another that are essentially intangible and do not result in the ownership of anything. The *nature and characteristics of a service* are distinctive. Services are *intangible, inseparable, variable,* and *perishable.* Each characteristic poses problems and requires strategies. Marketers have to find ways to make the service more tangible; to increase the productivity of providers who are inseparable from their products; to standardize the quality in the face of variability; and to improve demand movements and supply capacities in the face of service perishability.

Service industries have typically lagged behind manufacturing firms in adopting and using marketing concepts, but this situation is now changing. *Services marketing strategy* calls not only for external marketing, but also for *internal marketing* to motivate employees and *interactive marketing* to create service delivery skills among service providers. To succeed, service marketers must create competitive differentiation, offer high service quality, and find ways to increase service productivity.

Organizations can also be marketed. *Organization marketing* is undertaken to create, maintain, or change attitudes or behavior toward an organization. It calls for assessing the organization's current image and developing a marketing plan for bringing about an improved image.

Person marketing consists of activities undertaken to create, maintain, or change attitudes or behavior toward particular persons. Two common forms are celebrity marketing and political candidate marketing.

Place marketing involves activities undertaken to create, maintain, or change attitudes or behavior toward particular places. Examples include business site marketing and tourism marketing.

Idea marketing involves efforts to market ideas. In the case of social ideas, it is called *social marketing* and consists of the design, implementation, and control of programs seeking to increase the acceptability of a social idea, cause, or practice among a target group. Social marketing goes further than public advertising—it coordinates advertising with the other elements of the marketing mix. The social marketer defines the social-change objective, analyzes consumer attitudes and competitive forces, develops and tests alternative concepts, develops appropriate channels for the idea's communication and distribution, and finally checks the results.

Key Terms

Interactive marketing
Internal marketing
Organization image
Organization marketing

Person marketing
Place marketing
Service
Service inseparability

Service intangibility
Service perishability
Service variability
Social marketing

Discussing the Issues

1. A "hot" concept in fast-food marketing is home delivery of everything from pizza to hamburgers to fried chicken. Suggest why demand for this service is growing. How can marketers gain a competitive advantage by satisfying the growing demand for increased services?

2. Illustrate how a theater can deal with the intangibility, inseparability, variability, and perishability of the service it provides. Give specific examples.

3. Wendy's serves its hamburgers "fresh off the grill." This assures high quality but creates leftover burgers if the staff overestimates demand. Wendy's solves this perishability problem by using the meat in chili, tacos, and spaghetti sauce. Tell how airlines solve the perishability of unsold seats. Give additional examples of perishability and how service firms address it.

4. Many people feel that too much time and money are spent marketing political candidates. They also complain that modern political campaigns overemphasize image at the expense of issues. Discuss your opinion of political-candidate marketing. Would some other approach to campaigning help consumers make better voting decisions?

5. News reports of questionable, high-pressure tactics in the sale of vacation homes are common. For example, the "food processor" one marketer used as an incentive to attract prospects turned out to be a fork! Assess why you think unethical practices appear to be so frequently used in place marketing.

6. Marketing is defined as satisfying needs and wants through exchange processes. Hypothesize what exchanges occur in marketing nonprofit organizations, such as a museum or the American Red Cross.

Applying the Concepts

1. Why do organizations want to "sell" themselves and not just their products? (a) List several reasons for organization marketing, and relate them to promotional campaigns of companies with which you are familiar. (b) Clip several print advertisements that show organizational marketing. (Business or trade magazines are a good source.) For each ad, write down the purpose of the campaign, the message being conveyed, and whether or not you feel this marketing campaign is successful.

2. Perishability is very important in the airline industry: unsold seats are gone forever, and too many unsold seats mean large losses.

With computerized ticketing, airlines can easily use pricing to deal with perishability and variations in demand. (a) Call a travel agent or use an on-line service such as EasySabre to check airline fares. Get prices on the same route for 60 days in advance, two weeks, one week, and today. Is there a clear pattern to the fares? (b) When a store is overstocked on ripe fruit, it may lower the price to sell out quickly. What are airlines doing to their prices as the seats get close to "perishing"? Why? What would you recommend as a pricing strategy to increase total revenues?

References

1. See Charles Leerhsen, "How Disney Does It," *Newsweek,* April 3, 1989, pp. 48–54; Christopher Knowlton, "How Disney Keeps the Magic Going," *Fortune,* December 4, 1989, pp. 111–132; Michelle Neely Martinez, "Disney Training Works Magic," *HR Magazine,* May 1992, pp. 53–57; Ronald Grover, "Thrills and Chills at Disney," *Business Week,* June 21, 1993, pp. 73–74; and Gail DeGeorge, "Reanimating Disney World," *Business Week,* December 5, 1994, p. 41.

2. See Ronald Henkoff, "Service Is Everybody's Business," *Fortune,* June 27, 1994, pp. 48–60.

3. "Presto! The Convenience Industry: Making Life a Little Simpler," *Business Week,* April 27, 1987, p. 86; also see Ronald Henkoff, "Piety, Profits, and Productivity," *Fortune,* June 1992, pp. 84–85.

4. For more on definitions and classifications of services, see John E. Bateson, *Managing Services Marketing: Text and Readings* (Hinsdale, IL: Dryden Press, 1989); and Christopher H. Lovelock, *Services Marketing* (Englewood Cliffs, NJ: Prentice Hall, 1991).

5. See James L. Heskett, Thomas O. Jones, Gary W. Loveman, W. Earl Sasser, Jr., and Leonard A. Schlesinger, "Putting the Service-Profit Chain to Work," *Harvard Business Review,* March–April, 1994, pp. 164–174.

6. For more reading on internal and interactive marketing, see Christian Gronroos, "A Service Quality Model and Its Marketing Implications," *European Journal of Marketing,* Vol. 18, No. 4, 1984, pp. 36–44; and Leonard Berry, Edwin F. Lefkowith, and Terry Clark, "In Services, What's In a Name?" *Harvard Business Review,* September–October 1988, pp. 28–30.

7. For excellent discussion on defining and measuring service quality, see A. Parasuraman, Valerie A. Zeithaml, and Leonard L. Berry, "A Conceptual Model of Service Quality and Its Implications for Future Research," *Journal of Marketing,* Fall 1985, pp. 41–50; Zeithaml, Parasuraman, and Berry, *Delivering Service Quality: Balancing Customer Perceptions and Expectations* (New York: The Free Press, 1990); J.

Joseph Cronin, Jr. and Steven A. Taylor, "Measuring Service Quality: A Reexamination and Extension," *Journal of Marketing,* July 1992, pp. 55–68; and Parasuraman, Zeithaml, and Berry, "Reassessment of Expectations as a Comparison Standard in Measuring Service Quality: Implications for Further Research," *Journal of Marketing,* January 1994, pp. 111–124.

8. John Paul Newport, "American Express: Service That Sells," *Fortune,* November 20, 1989. Also see Frank Rose, "Now Quality Means Service Too," *Fortune,* April 22, 1991, pp. 97–108.

9. Christopher W. L. Hart, James L. Heskett, and W. Earl Sasser, Jr., "The Profitable Art of Service Recovery," *Harvard Business Review,* July–August 1990, pp. 148–156.

10. Ibid., p. 156.

11. See James L. Heskett, W. Earl Sasser, Jr., and Christopher W. L. Hart, *Service Breakthroughs* (New York: Free Press, 1990).

12. Barry Farber and Joyce Wycoff, "Customer Service: Evolution and Revolution," *Sales & Marketing Management,* May 1991, pp. 44–51.

13. Michael R. Czinkota and Ilkka A. Ronkainen, *International Marketing,* 2nd ed. (Chicago: Dryden, 1990), p. 679.

14. Lee Smith, "What's at Stake in the Trade Talks," *Fortune,* August 27, 1990, pp. 76–77.

15. Nora E. Field and Ricardo Sookdeo, "The Global Service 500," *Fortune,* August 26, 1991, pp. 166–170. Also see Tom Hayes, "Services Go International," *Marketing News,* March 14, 1994, pp. 14–15.

16. See Lori Kessler, "Corporate Image Advertising," *Advertising Age,* October 15, 1987, p. S1; and Anne B. Fisher, "Spiffing Up the Corporate Image," *Fortune,* July 21, 1986, p. 69.

17. Quote from Jeff Jensen, "Jordan Still King of Ad Presenter Game," *Advertising Age,* April 25, 1994, pp. 3, 59. Also see Jeff Jensen, "Jordan, Marketers Continue to Score," *Advertising Age,* October 17, 1994, p. 46; and Jeff Jensen, "MJ Draws All Levels of Fans to His Net," *Advertising Age,* March 27, 1995, pp. 3, 6.

Company Case 21

CITY YEAR: RUNNING A NONPROFIT LIKE A BUSINESS

GOING DOWNTOWN

As the sun rises over Boston Harbor on an early September morning, Gloria Rodriquez, 19, slips quietly out of bed so as not to disturb her four brothers and sisters. She washes and then dresses in baggy tan chinos, a T-shirt, and workboots. After eating a quick breakfast and helping her mother with a few chores, Gloria slips on a shiny red windbreaker and heads for the bus stop, arriving just as the bus that will take her from her working-class, Hispanic neighborhood to downtown Boston pulls up.

In another part of Boston, Raymond Wong, 17, awakens to the familiar sounds coming from the kitchen of his family's Chinese restaurant. He sits up in bed and reaches for his American History book, still open as he left it the night before. Glancing at the clock, Raymond figures he has enough time to finish reading the chapter assigned for this week. At 7 A.M., he fixes cereal for breakfast and watches the morning news on television. After breakfast, he slips into his tan chinos, T-shirt, and workboots, puts on his shiny red windbreaker, and heads downstairs to say good-bye to his parents. Raymond leaves the restaurant and races to the nearby "T" station where he will catch a subway train that will take him the short distance to downtown Boston.

Meanwhile, in a Boston suburb, John Newberg, 19, jolts awake at the shrill sound of his digital alarm clock and rolls over to swat the off-button. He lies in bed for a minute to collect his wits and to ponder the day's activities. After showering, he too puts on his tan chinos, T-shirt, and workboots and bounces downstairs. His mother and father are just sitting down to breakfast. John joins them, borrows the sports section of the morning paper from his father, and asks, "Got any big court cases today, Dad?"

"Not today, John. It looks like a pretty routine day."

After breakfast, John grabs his shiny red windbreaker and catches a ride with his father from their suburban home to downtown Boston.

John's father drops him off at Boston's City Hall Plaza, a large open area adjacent to City Hall. There, he joins Gloria, Raymond, and about 90 other similarly dressed young people. Promptly at 8:30, the young people line up for 15 minutes of exercises. Following the limbering-up period and some announcements, they break into groups of 10 or so and disperse throughout the city.

What do these young people have in common besides their chinos, T-shirts, workboots, and shiny red windbreakers? It certainly isn't their backgrounds. Gloria lives in a poor Hispanic community. Fighting poverty and a broken home, she recently graduated from a vocational high school. Raymond grew up in a first-generation Chinese immigrant family. He had trouble in high school and dropped out. Now he's seeking his General Equivalency Diploma (GED). In contrast, John cruised through elementary and junior high schools before going to a prestigious prep school. He graduated last June and has been accepted at Yale. He wants to follow his father into the law profession, but he has decided to take a year off before going to college.

Despite their differences, these young people have two things in common. First, as their red windbreakers and T-shirts proudly announce, they are members of City Year—each has volunteered to spend nine months working on community-service projects in Boston. Second, they have diverse backgrounds—City Year selected these young people *because* they are different.

CITY YEAR

City Year represents an innovative attempt to make voluntary national youth service a reality. In 1988, founders Michael Brown and Alan Khazei, both 30 years old and Harvard Law School graduates, became excited about voluntary service and started City Year in Boston. "The idea was to call on young people to meet the challenges facing us and to unite for a real strong public purpose," Brown observes. "The idea behind City Year is to bring young people from diverse backgrounds—rich, middle class, and poor, from different city neighborhoods as well as from the suburbs—for one year to concentrate on what they have in common and to work for the common good. We want City Year to be a workshop for innovation in the concept of voluntary national service." Allan Khazei adds that he and Brown also founded City Year " . . . out of frustration that we have the richest country in the world but also some of the deepest poverty and a high infant mortality rate. Right here in Boston, there are about 3,500 homeless people. But the problem is not a lack of resources. Rather, we lack the will and the understanding of society's problems. We want City Year to expose young people to those problems, to show them they can help, and to get them excited about service. We want City Year to educate them about the benefits of citizenship so that they will continue to serve others throughout their lives."

But Brown and Khazei didn't stop with just an idea. In 1987, working with Neil Silverston—a Harvard Business School graduate—and Jennifer Eplett—who had left a position as a financial analyst with E.F. Hutton—Brown and Khazei developed a business plan that presented the City Year concept, its strategy and objectives, and a projected budget. The plan called for a nine-week pilot program in the summer of 1988. Assuming success, City Year would operate with 50 young people in 1989–1990 and then look to expand nationally.

Brown and Khazei designed the summer pilot program to be a miniature version of the planned full-year program. They recruited 50 volunteer young people, deliberately creating a diversified group—men and women, city and suburban residents, whites, African Americans, Latinos, Asians, rich, middle class, and poor. They divided the group into five work teams, each headed by a paid supervisor. Each team member wore a T-shirt bearing the name of the group's sponsor and met every morning for exercises before splitting up to work on team projects, which included working with people with AIDS, the homeless, the elderly, and students. The team members also performed typical public-works projects, such as cleaning parks and painting shelters.

In addition to volunteers, a staff, and the projects, Brown and Khazei needed about $200,000 to finance the summer project. The big question was how to raise the money. Because City Year would not include only the disadvantaged, the founders knew that the project would not be eligible for any federal funds, which they did not want, in any case. Brown and Khazei believed that corporations, like individuals, have civic responsibilities; City Year would give these corporations a way to meet their responsibilities. In fact, they believed that corporations would *welcome* the opportunity to meet these responsibilities. At the same time, private-sector financing would give City Year the flexibility to try new ideas and to take risks that would not be possible under government financing.

Armed with their vision and a plan, Brown and Khazei set out to find sponsors. They impressed corporate managers with both the vision and their practical plans for realizing it. Whereas many nonprofit organizations leave the nuts-and-bolts details to the end, Brown and Khazei had done their homework and had paid attention to budgets and numbers from the outset. In addition to providing the participating corporations with a way to meet their civic responsibilities, they also played on the self-interest of the corporate managers: Work-crew members would be wearing T-shirts bearing the corporate sponsor's name as they carried out a summer's worth of good deeds. Thus, Khazei and Brown achieved their $200,000 goal, with most of the support coming from just four sponsors: Bank of Boston, The Equitable, General Cinema, and Bain & Company.

Following the successful pilot project, the City Year staff recruited 50 volunteers for the 1989–1990 program year. The volunteers, ages 17 to 22, worked from September to June in 10-person teams on a variety of projects. They served as teacher's aides in public schools, ran recreational programs for senior citizens, and repaired shelters and community centers. But City Year is more than just a work program. The staff overlays the daily service projects with an experiential educational curriculum designed to promote critical thinking and to teach corps members community-building skills. Members participate in workshops, attend lectures featuring business and community leaders, serve on City Year governing committees, develop special-service projects, and share and reflect on their service experiences in corps-wide meetings.

During the nine-month service period, City Year pays each volunteer a $100 weekly stipend. At the end of the period, each volunteer receives a $5,000 "Public Service Award" in the form of either a $5,000 education or training scholarship or $2,500 in cash and a $2,500 savings certificate. Although some people might suggest that paying the young people violates the spirit of a volunteer program, Brown points out that without the stipends, only young people from wealthier families could participate. Further, he notes that the United States has a "volunteer" army, but the government pays the soldiers, and the Public Service Award is similar to the G.I. bill available to soldiers to help them with their education after they leave the army.

City Year raised approximately $1.1 million to support the 1989–1990 program. The original sponsors signed up for another year, and City Year added several new sponsors, including Reebok International, The Echoing Green Foundation (connected with a New York investment firm), and New England Telephone. Each of these sponsors contributed at least $150,000.

Of the 57 young people City Year recruited for 1989–1990, 44 completed the program and were recognized at a City Year graduation ceremony. Comments from these young people reflect their enthusiasm about the program. One graduate, a former gang member, notes, "City Year has changed me a lot. Now I am able to teach instead of being taught." Another graduate adds, "If everyone could do City Year, there would be much more understanding in Boston and eventually the nation."

Based on the success of the 1989–1990 full-year program, City Year's recruiter, Kristen Atwood, scoured the city for volunteers for the 1990–1991 project year. When Atwood visited various city and suburban schools, she carried a common message: Everybody has something to give to his or her community. But she found that she also had to adapt her presentation to the character of the school's population. For example, many city students are interested in jobs, so Atwood stressed that City Year offers jobs that will give participants good experience for the future. In contrast, suburban students often feel isolated from the "real world." Therefore, Atwood emphasized the idea of service to them. To all students, she pointed out that people from different backgrounds have a lot to learn from one another.

The City Year staff looks for students who have a commitment to completing the program and the potential to contribute to and learn from the program. As a result of Atwood's and others' efforts, 70 young people participated in the 1990–1991 program, and City Year received over 600 applications for the 100 1991–1992 positions.

LESSONS AND THE FUTURE

As Brown and Khazei relax at the end of a long, 80-hour week, they feel good about their success but are impatient to address their challenges. They have learned much in pursuing what they call "public-service entrepreneurship"—applying the skills, methods, and spirit of entrepreneurship to building nonprofit, public-service institutions. As in the business world, they suggest, there are wonderful and rewarding opportunities for putting untested but highly promising public/nonprofit entrepreneurial ideas into practice. But this does not mean that if you are successful you will make a lot of money. (Brown and Khazei pay themselves only $25,000 per year, much less than they would make practicing law.) Rather, public service requires that we redefine success and focus on *psychic income,* the joy of using our skills and abilities to the fullest for a worthwhile cause.

Outside observers also consider City Year a successful venture. The Center for Civic Enterprise in Washington, D.C., notes that the City Year program has produced four valuable lessons: (1) National service can be a common civic endeavor for youths of all ages; (2) National service can operate with a minimum of overhead and bureaucracy; (3) National service volunteers can perform work that is highly valuable to the community; and (4) National service can foster upward mobility among those who serve.[1]

The Center's report also quotes Ira Jackson, Director of External Affairs of the Bank of Boston: "They ran City Year like a business. This was the most effective $25,000 in the history of philanthropy at the Bank of Boston."

What challenges face this successful new venture? Khazei and Brown worry about developing ongoing corporate support for a program that in a few years will no longer be seen as new, and they worry about broadening their support. They also wonder about their expansion plans. Should they concentrate on growing in Boston, or should they attempt to expand City Year to other cities? If they decide to spread the idea, when will the time be right, and what is the best method? Furthermore, how can they use lessons learned in private-sector management to help them continue their success in the nonprofit sector?

QUESTIONS

1. Who are City Year's customers and what are its products? Who is its competition?

2. Why do you think City Year has had so much success?

3. Do private-sector corporations have a social responsibility to support efforts like City Year or other nonprofit activities?

4. How do the nature and characteristics of a service impact on City Year's operations?

5. How has City Year dealt with the issues that shape marketing strategies for service firms?

6. What issues and risks does City Year face as it grows? What recommendations would you make to guide its growth?

[1]"Boston's City Year: National Service Prototype?" The Center for Civic Enterprise, June 19, 1990.

Source: Based in part on "Not for Profit," in *Anatomy of a Start-Up* (Boston: The Goldhirsch Group, Inc., 1991), pp. 99–109. Used with permission. The City Year staff also provided information and assistance for the development of this case.

Marketing and Society

SOCIAL RESPONSIBILITY AND MARKETING ETHICS

22

Generations of parents have trusted the health and well-being of their babies to Gerber baby foods. Gerber sells more than 1.3 billion jars of baby food each year, holding almost 70 percent of the market. Some years ago, however, the company faced a classic social responsibility situation. Its reputation was threatened when more than 250 customers in 30 states complained about finding glass fragments in Gerber baby food.

The company believed that these complaints were unfounded. Gerber plants are clean and modern and use many filters that would prevent such problems. No injuries from Gerber products were confirmed. Moreover, the Food and Drug Administration had looked at more than 40,000 jars of Gerber baby food without finding a single major problem. Gerber suspected that the glass was planted by the people making the complaints and seeking publicity or damages. Yet the complaints received widespread media coverage, and many retailers pulled Gerber products from their shelves. The state of Maryland forbade the sale of some Gerber baby foods, and other states considered such bans.

The considerable attention given to the complaints may have resulted from the "Tylenol scares," in which Tylenol capsules deliberately laced with cyanide killed a number of consumers. At the time, product tampering was a major public issue and consumer concern.

Gerber wanted to act responsibly, but social responsibility issues are rarely clear-cut. Some analysts believed that, to ensure consumer safety, Gerber quickly should have recalled all its baby food products from store shelves until the problem was resolved. That was how the makers of products such as Tylenol, Contac, and Gatorade had reacted to tampering scares for their products. But Gerber executives did not think that a recall was best either for consumers or for the company. After a similar scare a few years before, the company had recalled some 700,000 jars of baby food and had advertised heavily to reassure consumers. The isolated incident turned out to be the result of normal breakage during shipment. The recall cost Gerber millions of dollars in expenses and lost profits and the

OBJECTIVES

When you finish this chapter, you should be able to accomplish the following:

1. Discuss **social criticisms of marketing's impact on individual consumers**, particularly **high prices, deceptive practices, high-pressure selling, shoddy products, planned obsolescence**, and **poor service to disadvantaged consumers.**

2. Identify and define **criticisms of marketing's impact on society as a whole: false wants and materialism, too few social goods, cultural pollution**, and **too much political power.**

3. Outline citizen and public actions to regulate marketing—**consumerism, environmentalism**, and **regulation**—and the way they affect marketing strategies.

4. Explain the **business actions toward socially responsible marketing** that can foster **marketing ethics** and lead to different philosophies of **enlightened marketing: consumer-oriented, innovative, value, sense-of-mission,** and **societal marketing.**

5. List and define the key principles for **public policy toward marketing.**

advertising caused unnecessary alarm and inconvenience to consumers. The company concluded that it had overreacted in its desire to be socially responsible.

The second time, therefore, Gerber decided to do nothing, at least in the short run. It refused to recall any products—in fact, it filed a $150 million suit against the state of Maryland to stop the ban on the sales of Gerber products. It suspended its advertising, monitored sales and consumer confidence, reassured nervous retailers, and waited to see what would happen. This wait-and-see strategy was very risky. If the complaints had turned out to be well founded and Gerber's failure to act quickly had caused consumer injuries or deaths, Gerber's reputation would have been seriously damaged.

Finally, when research showed that consumer concern was spreading, Gerber aired a few television ads noting its concern about "rumors you may have heard" and assuring buyers that Gerber products "meet the highest standards." The company also mailed letters to about 2 million new mothers, assuring them of Gerber's quality. In the end, the scare resulted in little long-term consumer alarm or inconvenience, and it caused only a temporary dip in Gerber's market share and reputation.

However, the question lingers: Should Gerber have recalled its products immediately to prevent even the remote chance of consumer injury? Perhaps. But in many matters of social responsibility the best course of action is often unclear.[1]

Responsible marketers discover what consumers want and respond with the right products, priced to give good value to buyers and profit to the producer. The *marketing concept* is a philosophy of customer service and mutual gain. Its practice leads the economy by an invisible hand to satisfy the many and changing needs of millions of consumers.

Not all marketers follow the marketing concept, however. In fact, some companies use questionable marketing practices, and some marketing actions that seem innocent in themselves strongly affect the larger society. Consider the sale of cigarettes. Ordinarily, companies should be free to sell cigarettes, and smokers should be free to buy them. But this transaction affects the public interest. First, the smoker may be shortening his or her own life. Second, smoking places a burden on the smoker's family and on society at large. Third, other people around the smoker may suffer discomfort and harm from second-hand smoke. Thus, private transactions may involve larger questions of public policy.

This chapter examines the social effects of private marketing practices. We examine several questions: What are the most frequent social criticisms of marketing? What steps have private citizens taken to curb marketing ills? What steps have legislators and government agencies taken to curb marketing ills? What steps have enlightened companies taken to carry out socially responsible and ethical marketing? We examine how marketing affects and is affected by each of these issues.

SOCIAL CRITICISMS OF MARKETING

Marketing receives much criticism. Some of this criticism is justified; much is not.[2] Social critics claim that certain marketing practices hurt individual consumers, society as a whole, and other business firms.

MARKETING'S IMPACT ON INDIVIDUAL CONSUMERS

Consumers have many concerns about how well the American marketing system serves their interests. Surveys usually show that consumers hold mixed or even

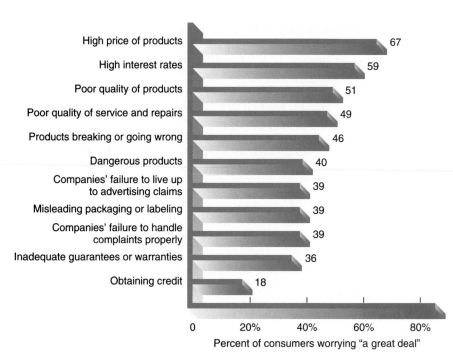

	Percent of consumers worrying "a great deal"
High price of products	67
High interest rates	59
Poor quality of products	51
Poor quality of service and repairs	49
Products breaking or going wrong	46
Dangerous products	40
Companies' failure to live up to advertising claims	39
Misleading packaging or labeling	39
Companies' failure to handle complaints properly	39
Inadequate guarantees or warranties	36
Obtaining credit	18

FIGURE 22-1   *Survey of consumer concerns*

Source: See Myrlie Evers, "Consumerism in the Eighties," reprinted with permission from the August 1983 issue of *Public Relations Journal,* copyright 1983, pp. 24–26. Also see "The Public Is Willing to Take on Business," *Business Week,* May 29, 1989, p. 29.

slightly unfavorable attitudes toward marketing practices.[3] One consumer survey found that consumers are most worried about high prices, poor-quality and dangerous products, misleading advertising claims, and several other marketing-related problems (see Figure 22-1). Consumer advocates, government agencies, and other critics have accused marketing of harming consumers through high prices, deceptive practices, high-pressure selling, shoddy or unsafe products, planned obsolescence, and poor service to disadvantaged consumers.

High Prices

Many critics charge that the American marketing system causes prices to be higher than they would be under more "sensible" systems. They point to three factors—*high costs of distribution, high advertising and promotion costs,* and *excessive markups.*

HIGH COSTS OF DISTRIBUTION.   A longstanding charge is that greedy middlemen mark up prices beyond the value of their services. Critics charge either that there are too many middlemen or that middlemen are inefficient and poorly run, that they provide unnecessary or duplicate services, and that they practice poor management and planning. As a result, distribution costs too much, and consumers pay for these excessive costs in the form of higher prices.

How do retailers answer these charges? They argue as follows: First, middlemen do work that would otherwise have to be done by manufacturers or consumers. Second, markups reflect services that consumers themselves want—more convenience, larger stores and assortment, longer store hours, return privileges, and others. Third, the costs of operating stores keep rising, forcing retailers to raise their prices. Fourth, retail competition is so intense that margins are actually quite low. For example, after taxes, supermarket chains are typically left with barely one percent profit on their sales. If some resellers try to charge too much relative to the value they add, other resellers will step in with lower prices. Low-price stores such as Wal-Mart, Home Depot, and other discounters pressure their competitors to operate efficiently and keep their prices down.

Some retailers use high markups, but the higher prices cover services that consumers want.

HIGH ADVERTISING AND PROMOTION COSTS. Modern marketing also is accused of pushing up prices because of heavy advertising and sales promotion. For example, a dozen tablets of a heavily promoted brand of aspirin sell for the same price as 100 tablets of less promoted brands. Differentiated products—cosmetics, detergents, toiletries—include promotion and packaging costs that can amount to 40 percent or more of the manufacturer's price to the retailer. Critics charge that much of the packaging and promotion adds only psychological value to the product rather than functional value. Retailers use additional promotions—advertising, displays, and sweepstakes—that add several cents more to retail prices.

Marketers answer these charges in several ways. First, consumers *want* more than the merely functional qualities of products. They also want psychological benefits—they want to feel wealthy, beautiful, or special. Consumers usually can buy functional versions of products at lower prices but often are willing to pay more for products that also provide desired psychological benefits. Second, branding gives buyers confidence. A brand name implies a certain quality, and consumers are willing to pay for well-known brands even if they cost a little more. Third, heavy advertising is needed to inform millions of potential buyers of the merits of a brand. If consumers want to know what is available on the market, they must expect manufacturers to spend large sums of money on advertising. Fourth, heavy advertising and promotion may be necessary for a firm to match competitors' efforts. The business would lose "share of mind" if it did not match competitive spending. At the same time, companies are cost conscious about promotion and try to spend their money wisely. Finally, heavy sales promotion is needed from time to time because goods are produced ahead of demand in a mass-production economy. Special incentives have to be offered in order to sell inventories.

EXCESSIVE MARKUPS.   Critics also charge that some companies mark up goods excessively. They point to the drug industry, where a pill costing 5 cents to make may cost the consumer 40 cents to buy. They point to the pricing tactics of funeral homes that prey on the emotions of bereaved relatives and to the high charges of television repair and auto repair people.

Marketers respond that most businesses try to deal fairly with consumers because they want repeat business. Most consumer abuses are unintentional. When shady marketers do take advantage of consumers, they should be reported to Better Business Bureaus and to state and federal agencies. Marketers also respond that consumers often don't understand the reason for high markups. For example, pharmaceutical markups must cover the costs of purchasing, promoting, and distributing existing medicines plus the high research and development costs of finding new medicines.

Deceptive Practices

Marketers sometimes are accused of deceptive practices that lead consumers to believe they will get more value than they actually do. Deceptive practices fall into three groups: deceptive pricing, promotion, and packaging. *Deceptive pricing* includes practices such as falsely advertising "factory" or "wholesale" prices or a large price reduction from a phony high retail list price. *Deceptive promotion* includes practices such as overstating the product's features or performance, luring the customer to the store for a bargain that is out of stock, or running rigged contests. *Deceptive packaging* includes exaggerating package contents through subtle design, not filling the package to the top, using misleading labeling, or describing size in misleading terms.

Deceptive practices have led to legislation and other consumer-protection actions. In 1938, the Wheeler-Lea Act gave the FTC the power to regulate "unfair or deceptive acts or practices." The FTC has published several guidelines listing deceptive practices. The toughest problem is defining what is "deceptive." For example, some years ago, Shell Oil advertised that Super Shell gasoline with platformate gave more mileage than the same gasoline without platformate. Now this was true, but what Shell did not say is that almost *all* gasoline includes platformate. Its defense was that it had never claimed that platformate was found only in Shell gasoline. But even though the message was literally true, the FTC felt that the ad's *intent* was to deceive.

Marketers argue that most companies avoid deceptive practices because such practices harm their business in the long run. If consumers do not get what they expect, they will switch to more reliable products. In addition, consumers usually protect themselves from deception. Most consumers recognize a marketer's selling intent and are careful when they buy, sometimes to the point of not believing completely true product claims. Theodore Levitt claims that some advertising puffery is bound to occur—and that it may even be desirable:

> There is hardly a company that would not go down in ruin if it refused to provide fluff, because nobody will buy pure functionality. . . . Worse, it denies . . . a man's honest needs and values. . . . Without distortion, embellishment, and elaboration, life would be drab, dull, anguished, and at its existential worst.[4]

High-Pressure Selling

Salespeople are sometimes accused of high-pressure selling that persuades people to buy goods they had no thought of buying. It is often said that encyclopedias, insurance, real estate, cars, and jewelry are *sold*, not *bought*. Salespeople are trained to deliver smooth, canned talks to entice purchase. They sell hard because sales contests promise big prizes to those who sell the most.

Marketers know that buyers often can be talked into buying unwanted or unneeded things. Laws require door-to-door salespeople to announce that they are selling a product. Buyers also have a "three-day cooling-off period" in which they can cancel a contract after rethinking it. In addition, consumers can complain to Better Business Bureaus or to state consumer-protection agencies when they feel that undue selling pressure has been applied.

Shoddy or Unsafe Products

Another criticism is that products lack the quality they should have. One complaint is that many products are not made well or services performed well. Such complaints have been lodged against products and services ranging from home appliances, automobiles, and clothing to home and auto repair services.

A second complaint is that many products deliver little benefit. For example, some consumers are surprised to learn that many of the "healthy" foods being marketed today, ranging from cholesterol-free salad dressings and low-fat frozen dinners to high-fiber bran cereals, may have little nutritional value. In fact, they may even be harmful.

> [Despite] sincere efforts on the part of most marketers to provide healthier products, . . . many promises emblazoned on packages and used as ad slogans continue to confuse nutritionally uninformed consumers and . . . may actually be harmful to that group. . . . [Many consumers] incorrectly assume the product is "safe" and eat greater amounts than are good for them. . . . For example, General Foods USA's new Entenmann's "low-cholesterol, low-calorie" cherry coffee cake . . . may confuse some consumers who shouldn't eat much of it. While each serving is only 90 calories, not everyone realizes that the suggested serving is tiny [one-thirteenth of the small cake]. Although eating half an Entenmann's cake may be better than eating half a dozen Dunkin Donuts, . . . neither should be eaten in great amounts by people on restrictive diets.[5]

A third complaint concerns product safety. Product safety has been a problem for several reasons, including manufacturer indifference, increased production complexity, poorly trained labor, and poor quality control. For years, Consumers Union—the organization that publishes *Consumer Reports*—has reported various hazards in tested products: electrical dangers in appliances, carbon monoxide poisoning from room heaters, injury risks from lawn mowers, and faulty automobile design, among many others. The organization's testing and other activities

WHEN *CONSUMER REPORTS* TALKS, BUYERS LISTEN

For more than 60 years, *Consumer Reports* has given buyers the lowdown on everything from sports cars to luggage to lawn sprinklers. Published by Consumers Union, the nonprofit product-testing organization, the magazine's mission can be summed up by CU's motto:

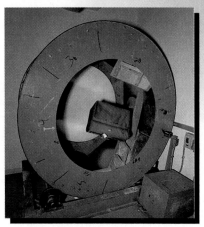

sumer Reports is one of the nation's most-read magazines. It's also one of the most influential. In 1988, when its car-testers rated Suzuki's topple-prone Samurai as "not acceptable"—meaning don't even take one as a gift—sales plunged 70 percent the following month. Last year, when it

Consumers Union carries out its testing mission: Suitcases bang into one another inside the huge "Mechanical Gorilla," and a staffer coats the interiors of self-cleaning ovens with a crusty concoction called "Monster Mash."

Test, Inform, Protect. With more than five million subscribers and several times that many borrowers, as dog-eared library copies will attest, *Con-*

raved about Saucony's Jazz 3000 sneaker, sales doubled, leading to nationwide shortages.

Although nonreaders may view

Consumer Reports as a deadly dull shopper's guide to major household appliances, the magazine does a lot more than rate cars and refrigerators. In recent issues, it has looked at mutual funds, prostate surgery, home mortgages, retirement communities, and public health policies. In the 1930s Consumers Union was one of the first organizations to urge a boy-cott of products imported from Nazi Germany, and it's been calling for nationalized health care since 1937. In the 1950s it warned the nation that fallout from nuclear tests was contam-inating milk supplies. In the 1960s and 1970s it prodded carmakers to install seat belts, then air bags.

Yet the magazine is rarely harsh or loud. Instead, it's usually understated, and it can even be funny. The very first issue in 1936 noted that Lifebuoy soap was itself so smelly that it simply overwhelmed your B.O. with L.O. And what reader didn't delight to find in a 1990 survey of soaps that the most expensive bar, Eau de Gucci at 31 cents per hand-washing, wound up dead last in a blind test?

Consumer Reports readers clearly appreciate CU and its maga-zine. It is unlikely that any other mag-azine in the world could have raised

have helped consumers make better buying decisions and encouraged businesses to eliminate product flaws (see Marketing Highlight 22-1).

However, most manufacturers *want* to produce quality goods. The way a company deals with product quality and safety problems can damage or help its reputation. Companies selling poor-quality or unsafe products risk damaging con-flicts with consumer groups and regulators. Moreover, unsafe products can result in product-liability suits and large awards for damages. More fundamentally, con-sumers who are unhappy with a firm's products may avoid future purchases and talk other consumers into doing the same. Today's marketers know that customer-driven quality results in customer satisfaction, which in turn creates profitable cus-tomer relationships.

Planned Obsolescence

Critics also have charged that some producers follow a program of planned obso-lescence, causing their products to become obsolete before they actually should need replacement. For example, critics charge that some producers continually change consumer concepts of acceptable styles to encourage more and earlier buy-ing. An obvious example is constantly changing clothing fashions. Other produc-ers are accused of holding back attractive functional features, then introducing them later to make older models obsolete. Critics claim that this occurs in the con-sumer electronics and computer industries. Still other producers are accused of

$17 million toward a new building simply by asking readers for donations. To avoid even the appearance of bias, CU has a strict no ads, no freebies policy. It buys all of its product samples on the open market, and anonymously. A visit to CU's maze of labs confirms the thoroughness with which CU's testers carry out their mission. A chemist performs a cholesterol extraction test on a small white blob in a beaker: a ground-up piece of turkey enchilada, you are told. Elsewhere you find the remains of a piston-driven machine called Fingers that added 1 + 1 on pocket calculators hundreds of thousands of times or until the calculators failed, whichever came first. You watch suitcases bang into one another inside a huge contraption—affectionately dubbed the "Mechanical Gorilla"—that looks like an eight-foot-wide clothes dryer.

Down the hall in the appliance department, a pair of "food soilers" will soon load 20 dishwashers with identical sets of dirty dishes. A sample dinner plate is marked with scientific precision in eight wedge-shaped sections, each with something different caked to it—dried spaghetti, spinach, chipped beef, or something else equally difficult to clean. Next

door, self-cleaning ovens are being tested, their interiors coated with a crusty substance—called "Monster Mash" by staffers—that suggests month-old chili sauce. The recipe includes tapioca, cheese, lard, grape jelly, tomato sauce, and cherry pie filling—mixed well and baked one hour at 425 degrees. If an oven's self-cleaning cycle doesn't render the resulting residue into harmless-looking ash, five million readers will be so informed.

Some of the tests that CU runs are standard tests, but many others are not. Several years ago, in a triumph of low-tech creativity, CU's engineers stretched paper towels across embroidery hoops, moistened the center of each with exactly ten drops of water, then poured lead shot into the middle. The winner held seven pounds of shot; the loser, less than one. Who could argue with that? There is an obvious logic to such tests, and the results are plainly quantifiable.

From the start, Consumers Union has generated controversy. The second issue dismissed the Good Housekeeping Seal of Approval as nothing more than a fraudulent ploy by publisher William Randolph Hearst to reward loyal advertisers.

Good Housekeeping responded by accusing CU of prolonging the depression. To the business community, *Consumer Reports* was at first viewed as a clear threat to the American way of doing business. During its early years, more than 60 advertising-dependent publications, including the *New York Times, Newsweek,* and the *New Yorker,* refused to accept CU's subscription ads.

In 1939, in a move that would seem ludicrous today, Congress' new House Un-American Activities Committee (then known as the Dies Committee) branded CU a subversive organization. And through the years, many manufacturers have filed suit against CU, challenging findings unfavorable to their products. However, the controversy has more often helped than hurt subscriptions, and to this day Consumers Union has never lost or settled a libel suit.

Source: Adapted from Doug Stewart, "To Buy or Not To Buy, That Is the Question at *Consumer Reports,*" *Smithsonian,* September 1993, pp. 34–43.

---

using materials and components that will break, wear, rust, or rot sooner than they should.

Marketers respond that consumers *like* style changes; they get tired of the old goods and want a new look in fashion or a new design in cars. No one has to buy the new look, and if too few people like it, it will simply fail. Companies frequently withhold new features when they are not fully tested, when they add more cost to the product than consumers are willing to pay, and for other good reasons. But they do so at the risk that a competitor will introduce the new feature and steal the market. Moreover, companies often put in new materials to lower their costs and prices. They do not design their products to break down earlier, because they do not want to lose customers to other brands. Instead, they implement total quality programs to ensure that products will consistently meet or exceed customer expectations. Thus, much of so-called planned obsolescence is the working of the competitive and technological forces in a free society—forces that lead to ever-improving goods and services.

Poor Service to Disadvantaged Consumers

Finally, the American marketing system has been accused of poorly serving disadvantaged consumers. Critics claim that the urban poor often have to shop in smaller stores that carry inferior goods and charge higher prices. A recent Consumers Union study compared the food shopping habits of low-income consumers and the prices they pay relative to middle-income consumers in the same city. The study found that the poor do pay more for inferior goods. The results suggested that the presence of large national chain stores in low-income neighborhoods made a big difference in keeping prices down. However, the study also found evidence of "redlining," a type of economic discrimination in which major chain retailers avoid placing stores in disadvantaged neighborhoods.[6]

Clearly, better marketing systems must be built in low-income areas—one hope is to get large retailers to open outlets in low-income areas. Moreover, low-income people clearly need consumer protection. The FTC has taken action against merchants who advertise false values, sell old merchandise as new, or charge too much for credit. The commission also is trying to make it harder for merchants to win court judgments against low-income people who were wheedled into buying something.

MARKETING'S IMPACT ON SOCIETY AS A WHOLE

The American marketing system has been accused of adding to several "evils" in American society at large. Advertising has been a special target—so much so that the American Association of Advertising Agencies launched a campaign to defend advertising against what it felt to be common but untrue criticisms (see Marketing Highlight 22-2).

False Wants and Too Much Materialism

Critics have charged that the marketing system urges too much interest in material possessions. People are judged by what they *own* rather than by who they *are*. To be considered successful, people must own a large home, two cars, and the latest consumer electronics. This drive for wealth and possessions hit new highs in the 1980s, when phrases such as "greed is good" and "shop till you drop" seemed to characterize the times. In the 1990s, although many social scientists have noted a reaction against the opulence and waste of the 1980s and a return to more basic values and social commitment, our infatuation with material things continues. For example, when asked in a recent poll what they value most in their lives, subjects listed enjoyable work (86 percent), happy children (84 percent), a good marriage (69 percent), and contributions to society (66 percent). However, when asked what most symbolizes success, 85 percent said money and the things it will buy.[7]

The critics do not view this interest in material things as a natural state of mind but rather as a matter of false wants created by marketing. Businesses hire Madison Avenue to stimulate people's desires for goods, and Madison Avenue uses the mass media to create materialistic models of the good life. People work harder to earn the necessary money. Their purchases increase the output of American industry, and industry in turn uses Madison Avenue to stimulate more desire for the industrial output. Thus, marketing is seen as creating false wants that benefit industry more than they benefit consumers.

These criticisms overstate the power of business to create needs, however. People have strong defenses against advertising and other marketing tools. Marketers are most effective when they appeal to existing wants rather than when they attempt to create new ones. Furthermore, people seek information when making important purchases and often do not rely on single sources. Even minor purchases that may be affected by advertising messages lead to repeat purchases only if the product performs as promised. Finally, the high failure rate of new products shows that companies are not able to control demand.

On a deeper level, our wants and values are influenced not only by marketers, but also by family, peer groups, religion, ethnic background, and education. If Americans are highly materialistic, these values arose out of basic social-

ADVERTISING: ANOTHER WORD FOR FREEDOM OF CHOICE

During the past few years, the American Association of Advertising Agencies has run a campaign featuring ads such as this to counter common criticism of advertising. The association is concerned about research findings of negative public attitudes toward advertising. Two-thirds of the public recognizes that advertising provides helpful buying information, but a significant portion feels that advertising is exaggerated or misleading. The association believes that its ad campaign will increase general advertising credibility and make advertisers' messages more effective. Several media agreed to run the ads as a public service.

The American Association of Advertising Agencies runs ads to counter common advertising criticisms.

ization processes that go much deeper than business and mass media could produce alone.

Too Few Social Goods

Business has been accused of overselling private goods at the expense of public goods. As private goods increase, they require more public services that are usually not forthcoming. For example, an increase in automobile ownership (private good) requires more highways, traffic control, parking spaces, and police services (public goods). The overselling of private goods results in "social costs." For cars, the social costs include traffic congestion, air pollution, and deaths and injuries from car accidents.

A way must be found to restore a balance between private and public goods. One option is to make producers bear the full social costs of their operations. For example, the government could require automobile manufacturers to build cars with even more safety features and better pollution-control systems. Auto makers would then raise their prices to cover extra costs. If buyers found the price of some cars too high, however, the producers of these cars would disappear, and demand would move to those producers that could support the sum of the private and social costs.

Cultural Pollution

Critics charge the marketing system with creating *cultural pollution*. Our senses are being assaulted constantly by advertising. Commercials interrupt serious programs; pages of ads obscure printed matter; billboards mar beautiful scenery. These interruptions continuously pollute people's minds with messages of materialism, sex, power, or status. Although most people do not find advertising overly annoying (some even think it is the best part of television programming), some critics call for sweeping changes.

Cultural pollution: People's senses are sometimes assaulted by commercial messages.

Marketers answer the charges of "commercial noise" with these arguments: First, they hope that their ads reach primarily the target audience. But because of mass-communication channels, some ads are bound to reach people who have no interest in the product and are therefore bored or annoyed. People who buy magazines addressed to their interests—such as *Vogue* or *Fortune*—rarely complain about the ads because the magazines advertise products of interest. Second, ads make much of television and radio free media and keep down the costs of magazines and newspapers. Many people think commercials are a small price to pay for these benefits.

Too Much Political Power

Another criticism is that business wields too much political power. "Oil," "tobacco," "auto," and "pharmaceuticals" senators support an industry's interests against the public interest. Advertisers are accused of holding too much power over the mass media, limiting their freedom to report independently and objectively. One critic has asked: "How can *Life* . . . and *Reader's Digest* afford to tell the truth about the scandalously low nutritional value of most packaged foods . . . when these magazines are being subsidized by such advertisers as General Foods, Kellogg's, Nabisco, and General Mills? . . . The answer is *they cannot and do not.*"[8]

American industries promote and protect their interests. They have a right to representation in Congress and the mass media, although their influence can become too great. Fortunately, many powerful business interests once thought to be untouchable have been tamed in the public interest. For example, Standard Oil was broken up in 1911, and the meatpacking industry was disciplined in the early 1900s after exposures by Upton Sinclair. Ralph Nader caused legislation that forced the automobile industry to build more safety into its cars, and the Surgeon General's Report resulted in cigarette companies putting health warnings on their packages. More recently, giants such as AT&T, Microsoft, and R. J. Reynolds have felt the impact of regulators seeking to balance the interests of big business against those of the public. Moreover, because the media receive advertising revenues from many different advertisers, it is easier to resist the influence of one or a few of them. Too much business power tends to result in counterforces that check and offset these powerful interests.

MARKETING'S IMPACT ON OTHER BUSINESSES

Critics also charge that a company's marketing practices can harm other companies and reduce competition. Three problems are involved: acquisitions of competitors, marketing practices that create barriers to entry, and unfair competitive marketing practices.

Critics claim that firms are harmed and competition reduced when companies expand by acquiring competitors rather than by developing their own new products. In the food industry alone during the past decade, R. J. Reynolds acquired Nabisco Brands; Philip Morris bought General Foods and Kraft; Procter

& Gamble gobbled up Richardson-Vicks, Noxell, and parts of Revlon; Nestlé absorbed Carnation; and Quaker Oats bought Stokely-Van Camp. These and other large acquisitions in other industries have caused concern that vigorous young competitors will be absorbed and that competition will be reduced.

Acquisition is a complex subject. Acquisitions can sometimes be good for society. The acquiring company may gain economies of scale that lead to lower costs and lower prices. A well-managed company may take over a poorly managed company and improve its efficiency. An industry that was not very competitive might become more competitive after the acquisition. But acquisitions also can be harmful and, therefore, are closely regulated by the government.

Critics also have charged that marketing practices bar new companies from entering an industry. Large marketing companies can use patents and heavy promotion spending, and can tie up suppliers or dealers to keep out or drive out competitors. People concerned with antitrust regulation recognize that some barriers are the natural result of the economic advantages of doing business on a large scale. Other barriers could be challenged by existing and new laws. For example, some critics have proposed a progressive tax on advertising spending to reduce the role of selling costs as a major barrier to entry.

Finally, some firms have in fact used unfair competitive marketing practices with the intention of hurting or destroying other firms. They may set their prices below costs, threaten to cut off business with suppliers, or discourage the buying of a competitor's products. Various laws work to prevent such predatory competition. It is difficult, however, to prove that the intent or action was really predatory. For example, in recent years, Wal-Mart and American Airlines have been accused of predatory pricing—setting prices that could not be profitable in order to drive out smaller or weaker competitors. The question is whether this was unfair competition or the healthy competition of a more efficient company against the less efficient.

CITIZEN AND PUBLIC ACTIONS TO REGULATE MARKETING

Because some people view business as the cause of many economic and social ills, grass-roots movements have arisen from time to time to keep business in line. The two major movements have been *consumerism* and *environmentalism*.

CONSUMERISM

American business firms have been the target of organized consumer movements on three occasions. The first consumer movement took place in the early 1900s. It was fueled by rising prices, Upton Sinclair's writings on conditions in the meat industry, and scandals in the drug industry. The second consumer movement, in the mid-1930s, was sparked by an upturn in consumer prices during the Great Depression and another drug scandal.

The third movement began in the 1960s. Consumers had become better educated, products had become more complex and hazardous, and people were unhappy with American institutions. Ralph Nader appeared on the scene to force many issues, and other well-known writers accused big business of wasteful and unethical practices. President John F. Kennedy declared that consumers had the right to safety and to be informed, to choose, and to be heard. Congress investigated certain industries and proposed consumer-protection legislation. Since then, many consumer groups have been organized, and several consumer laws have been passed. The consumer movement has spread internationally and has become very strong in Europe.[9]

Consumerism
An organized movement of citizens and government agencies to improve the rights and power of buyers in relation to sellers.

But what is the consumer movement? **Consumerism** is an organized movement of citizens and government agencies to improve the rights and power of buyers in relation to sellers. Traditional sellers' rights include:

◆ The right to introduce any product in any size and style, provided it is not hazardous to personal health or safety; or, if it is, to include proper warnings and controls.

◆ The right to charge any price for the product, provided no discrimination exists among similar kinds of buyers.

◆ The right to spend any amount to promote the product, provided it is not defined as unfair competition.

◆ The right to use any product message, provided it is not misleading or dishonest in content or execution.

◆ The right to use any buying incentive schemes, provided they are not unfair or misleading.

Traditional buyers' rights include:

◆ The right not to buy a product that is offered for sale.

◆ The right to expect the product to be safe.

◆ The right to expect the product to perform as claimed.

Comparing these rights, many believe that the balance of power lies on the sellers' side. True, the buyer can refuse to buy. But critics feel that the buyer has too little information, education, and protection to make wise decisions when facing sophisticated sellers. Consumer advocates call for the following additional consumer rights:

◆ The right to be well informed about important aspects of the product.

◆ The right to be protected against questionable products and marketing practices.

◆ The right to influence products and marketing practices in ways that will improve the "quality of life."

Each proposed right has led to more specific proposals by consumerists. The right to be informed includes the right to know the true interest on a loan (truth in lending), the true cost per unit of a brand (unit pricing), the ingredients in a product (ingredient labeling), the nutrition in foods (nutritional labeling), product freshness (open dating), and the true benefits of a product (truth in advertising). Proposals related to consumer protection include strengthening consumer

Consumer desire for more information led to putting ingredients, nutrition, and dating information on product labels.

rights in cases of business fraud, requiring greater product safety, and giving more power to government agencies. Proposals relating to the quality of life include controlling the ingredients that go into certain products (detergents) and packaging (soft-drink containers), reducing the level of advertising "noise," and appointing consumer representatives to company boards in order to protect consumer interests.

Consumers have not only the *right* but also the *responsibility* to protect themselves instead of leaving this function to someone else. Consumers who believe they got a bad deal have several remedies available, including writing to the company president or to the media; contacting federal, state, or local agencies; and going to small-claims courts.

ENVIRONMENTALISM

Environmentalism
An organized movement of concerned citizens and government agencies to protect and improve people's living environment.

Whereas consumerists consider whether the marketing system is efficiently serving consumer wants, environmentalists are concerned with marketing's effects on the environment and with the costs of serving consumer needs and wants. They are concerned with damage to the ecosystem caused by strip mining, forest depletion, acid rain, loss of the atmosphere's ozone layer, toxic wastes, and litter. They also are concerned with the loss of recreational areas and with the increase in health problems caused by bad air, polluted water, and chemically treated food. These concerns are the basis for **environmentalism**—an organized movement of concerned citizens, businesses, and government agencies to protect and improve people's living environment.

Environmentalists are not against marketing and consumption; they simply want people and organizations to operate with more care for the environment. The marketing system's goal should not be to maximize consumption, consumer choice, or consumer satisfaction, but rather to maximize life quality. And "life quality" means not only the quantity and quality of consumer goods and services, but also the quality of the environment. Environmentalists want environmental costs included in both producer and consumer decision making.

Environmentalism has hit some industries hard. Steel companies and public utilities have had to invest billions of dollars in pollution-control equipment and costlier fuels. The auto industry has had to introduce expensive emission controls in cars. The packaging industry has had to find ways to reduce litter. The gasoline industry has had to create new no-lead gasolines. These industries often resent environmental regulations, especially when they are imposed too rapidly to allow companies to make proper adjustments. These companies have absorbed large costs and have passed them on to buyers.

Thus, marketers' lives have become more complicated. Marketers must check into the ecological properties of their products and packaging. They must raise prices to cover environmental costs, knowing that the product will be harder to sell. Yet environmental issues have become so important in our society that there is no turning back to the time when few managers worried about the effects of product and marketing decisions on environmental quality. Many analysts view the 1990s as the "Earth Decade," in which protection of the natural environment will be the major issue facing people around the world. Companies have responded with "green marketing"—developing ecologically safer products, recyclable and biodegradable packaging, better pollution controls, and more energy-efficient operations (see Marketing Highlight 22-3).

Environmentalism creates some special challenges for global marketers. As international trade barriers come down and global markets expand, environmental issues are having an ever greater impact on international trade. Countries in North America, Western Europe, and other developed regions are developing strin-

THE NEW ENVIRONMENTALISM AND "GREEN MARKETING"

On Earth Day 1970, a newly emerging environmentalism movement made its first large-scale effort to educate people about the dangers of pollution. This was a tough task: At the time, most folks weren't all that interested in environmental problems. By 1990, however, Earth Day had became a nationwide cause, punctuated by articles in major magazines and newspapers, prime-time television extravaganzas, and countless events. It turned out to be just the start of an entire "Earth Decade" in which environmentalism has become a massive worldwide force.

These days, environmentalism has broad public support. People hear and read daily about a growing list of environmental problems—global warming, acid rain, depletion of the ozone layer, air and water pollution, hazardous waste disposal, the buildup of solid wastes—and they are calling for solutions. The new environmentalism is causing many consumers to rethink what products they buy and from whom. These changing consumer attitudes have sparked a major new marketing thrust—*green marketing*—the movement by companies to develop and market environmentally responsible products. Committed "green" companies pursue not only environmental cleanup but also pollution prevention. True "green" work requires companies to practice the three R's of waste management: reducing, reusing, and recycling waste.

McDonald's provides a good example of green marketing. It used to purchase Coca-Cola syrup in plastic bags encased in cardboard, but now the syrup is delivered as gasoline is, pumped directly from tank trucks into storage vats at restaurants. The change saved 68 million pounds of packaging a year. All napkins, bags, and tray liners in McDon-

ald's restaurants are made from recycled paper, as are its carry-out drink trays and even the stationery used at headquarters. For a company the size of McDonald's, even small changes can make a big difference. For example, just making its drinking straws 20 percent lighter saved the company 1 million pounds of waste per year. Beyond turning its own

products green, McDonald's purchases recycled materials for building and remodeling its restaurants, and it challenges its suppliers to furnish and use recycled products.

Producers in a wide range of industries are responding to environmental concerns. For example, 3M runs a *Pollution Prevention Pays*

A positive sign.

Corporate environmentalism: Enlightened companies are taking action not because someone is forcing them to, but because it is the right thing to do.

program, which has led to substantial pollution and cost reduction. Dow built a new ethylene plant in Alberta that uses 40 percent less energy and releases 97 percent less waste water. Herman Miller, a large office furniture manufacturer, set a trend in the furniture industry when it began using tropical woods from sustainably managed sources, altering even its classic

gent environmental standards. In the United States, for example, more than two dozen major pieces of environmental legislation have been enacted since 1970, and recent events suggest that more regulation is on the way. A side accord to the North American Free Trade Agreement (NAFTA) sets up a commission for resolving environmental matters. And the European Union's Eco-Management and Audit Regulation provides guidelines for environmental self-regulation.[10]

However, environmental policies still vary widely from country to country, and uniform worldwide standards are not expected for another 15 years or more.[11] Although countries such as Denmark, Germany, Japan, and the United States have fully developed environmental policies and high public expectations, major countries such as China, India, Brazil, and Russia are in only the early stages of developing such policies. Moreover, environmental factors that motivate consumers in one country may have no impact on consumers in another. For example, PVC soft

furniture lines. But it went even further by reusing packaging, recapturing solvents used in staining, and burning fabric scraps and sawdust to make energy for its manufacturing plant. These moves not only help the environment, they also save Herman Miller $750,000 per year on energy and landfill costs.

Even retailers are jumping onto the "green" bandwagon. For example, Wal-Mart is pressuring its 7,000 suppliers to provide it with more recycled products. In its stores, Wal-Mart runs videos to help educate customers, and the retailer has set up more than 900 recycling drop-off bins in store parking lots around the nation. It's even opening "eco-friendly" stores. In these stores, the air conditioning systems use non-ozone-depleting refrigerant, rain water is collected from parking lots and rooftops for landscaping, skylights supplement fluorescent lighting adjusted by photo sensors, and the road sign is solar powered.

During the early phase of the new environmentalism, promoting environmentally improved products and actions ballooned into a big business. In fact, environmentalists and regulators became concerned that companies were going overboard with their use of terms like *recyclable, degradable,* and *environmentally responsible.* Perhaps of equal concern was that, as more and more marketers used green marketing claims, more and more consumers would view them as little more than gimmicks.

Some overeager green-marketing campaigns were vigorously attacked by environmentalists and law makers for making unproven or improper claims. For example, Mobil altered its Hefty trash bags so that they would break down more easily and began to market them as "degradable." However, these claims ran afoul of the Environmental Defense Fund and several states' attorneys general when it was learned that the bags only degrade when they're exposed to air and light—most trash bags are buried in landfills. In 1992, the Federal Trade Commission issued a set of voluntary guidelines for green marketing terms to help guide marketers making environmental claims for their products.

As we close out the century, environmentalism appears to be moving into a more mature phase. Gone are the hastily prepared environmental pitches and products designed to capitalize on, or even exploit, growing public concern. The new environmentalism is now going mainstream—broader, deeper, and more sophisticated. In the words of one analyst:

> Dressing up ads with pictures of eagles and trees will no longer woo an environmentally sophisticated audience. People want to know that companies are incorporating environmental values into their manufacturing processes, products, packaging, and the very fabric of their corporate cultures. They . . . want to know that companies will not compromise the

ability of future generations to enjoy the quality of life that we enjoy today. . . . As a result, we're seeing the marriage of performance benefits and environmental benefits . . . one reinforces the other.

In all, some companies have responded to consumer environmental concerns by doing only what is required to avert new regulations or to keep environmentalists quiet. Others have rushed to make money by catering to the public's mounting concern for the environment. But enlightened companies are taking action not because someone is forcing them to, or to reap short-run profits, but because it is the right thing to do. They believe that environmental farsightedness today will pay off tomorrow—for both the customer and the company.

Sources: Quote from Robert Rehak, "Green Marketing Awash in Third Wave," *Advertising Age,* November 22, 1993, p. 22. Also see Joe Schwartz, "Earth Day Today," *American Demographics,* April 1990, pp. 40–41; Eric Wieffering, "Wal-Mart Turns Green in Kansas," *American Demographics,* December 1993, p. 23; David Woodruff, "Herman Miller: How Green Is My Factory," *Business Week,* September 16, 1991, pp. 54–56; Jacquelyn Ottman, "Environmentalism Will Be *the* Trend of the '90s," *Marketing News,* December 7, 1992, p. 13; and Peter Stisser, "A Deeper Shade of Green," *American Demographics,* March 1994, pp. 24–29.

drink bottles cannot be used in Switzerland or Germany. However, they are preferred in France, which has an extensive recycling process for them. Thus, international companies are finding it difficult to develop standard environmental practices that work around the world. Instead, they are creating general policies, and then translating these policies into tailored programs that meet local regulations and expectations.

PUBLIC ACTIONS TO REGULATE MARKETING

Citizen concerns about marketing practices usually will lead to public attention and legislative proposals. New bills will be debated—many will be defeated, others will be modified, and a few will become workable laws.

FIGURE 22-2 *Legal issues facing marketing management*

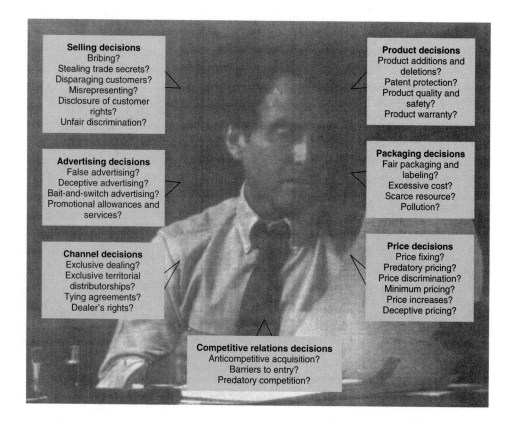

Selling decisions
Bribing?
Stealing trade secrets?
Disparaging customers?
Misrepresenting?
Disclosure of customer rights?
Unfair discrimination?

Advertising decisions
False advertising?
Deceptive advertising?
Bait-and-switch advertising?
Promotional allowances and services?

Channel decisions
Exclusive dealing?
Exclusive territorial distributorships?
Tying agreements?
Dealer's rights?

Product decisions
Product additions and deletions?
Patent protection?
Product quality and safety?
Product warranty?

Packaging decisions
Fair packaging and labeling?
Excessive cost?
Scarce resource?
Pollution?

Price decisions
Price fixing?
Predatory pricing?
Price discrimination?
Minimum pricing?
Price increases?
Deceptive pricing?

Competitive relations decisions
Anticompetitive acquisition?
Barriers to entry?
Predatory competition?

Many of the laws that affect marketing are listed in Chapter 3. The task is to translate these laws into the language that marketing executives understand as they make decisions about competitive relations, products, price, promotion, and channels of distribution. Figure 22-2 illustrates the major legal issues facing marketing management.

BUSINESS ACTIONS TOWARD SOCIALLY RESPONSIBLE MARKETING

Enlightened marketing
A marketing philosophy holding that a company's marketing should support the best long-run performance of the marketing system; its five principles include consumer-oriented marketing, innovative marketing, value marketing, sense-of-mission marketing, and societal marketing.

Consumer-oriented marketing
A principle of enlightened marketing that holds that a the company should view and organize its marketing activities from the consumers' point of view.

At first, many companies opposed consumerism and environmentalism. They thought the criticisms were either unfair or unimportant. But by now, most companies have grown to accept the new consumer rights, at least in principle. They might oppose certain pieces of legislation as inappropriate ways to solve certain consumer problems, but they recognize the consumer's right to information and protection. Many of these companies have responded positively to consumerism and environmentalism in order to serve consumer needs better.

ENLIGHTENED MARKETING

The philosophy of **enlightened marketing** holds that a company's marketing should support the best long-run performance of the marketing system. Enlightened marketing consists of five principles: *consumer-oriented marketing, innovative marketing, value marketing, sense-of-mission marketing,* and *societal marketing.*

Consumer-Oriented Marketing

Consumer-oriented marketing means that the company should view and organize its marketing activities from the consumer's point of view. It should work hard to sense, serve, and satisfy the needs of a defined group of customers. Consider the following example:

> Barat College, a women's college in Lake Forest, Illinois, published a college catalog that openly spelled out Barat College's strong and weak points. Among the weak points it shared with applicants were the following: "An exceptionally talented student musician or mathematician . . . might be advised to look further for a college with top faculty and facilities in that field. . . . The full range of advanced specialized courses offered in a university will be absent. . . . The library collection is average for a small college, but low in comparison with other high-quality institutions."

"Telling it like it is" is intended to build confidence so that applicants really know what they will find at Barat College and to emphasize that Barat College will strive to improve its consumer value as rapidly as time and funds permit.

Innovative Marketing

Innovative marketing
A principle of enlightened marketing that requires that a company seek real product and marketing improvements.

The principle of **innovative marketing** requires that the company continuously seek real product and marketing improvements. The company that overlooks new and better ways to do things will eventually lose customers to another company that has found a better way. One of the best examples of an innovative marketer is Procter & Gamble:

> Wisk, a Lever Bros. product, dominated liquid detergents for a generation, and liquids were taking a growing share of the $3.2-billion-a-year detergent market. P&G tried to topple Wisk with run-of-the-laundry-room liquids called Era and Solo, but couldn't come close. Then it developed a liquid with 12 cleaning agents, twice the norm, and a molecule that traps dirt in the wash water. P&G christened it Liquid Tide and put it in a bottle colored the same fire-bright color as the ubiquitous Tide box. After just 18 months on the market, Liquid Tide is washing as many clothes as Wisk in the U.S., and the two were locked in a fierce battle for the No. 2 position, after powdered Tide, among all detergents.[12]

Value Marketing

Value marketing
A principle of enlightened marketing that holds that a company should put most of its resources into value-building marketing investments.

According to the principle of **value marketing,** the company should put most of its resources into value-building marketing investments. Many things marketers do—one-shot sales promotions, minor packaging changes, advertising puffery—may raise sales in the short run but add less *value* than would actual improvements in the product's quality, features, or convenience. Enlightened marketing calls for building long-run consumer loyalty by continually improving the value consumers receive from the firm's marketing offer.

Sense-of-Mission Marketing

Sense-of-mission marketing
A principle of enlightened marketing that holds that a company should define its mission in broad social terms rather than narrow product terms.

Sense-of-mission marketing means that the company should define its mission in broad *social* terms rather than narrow *product* terms. When a company defines a social mission, employees feel better about their work and have a clearer sense of direction. For example, defined in narrow product terms, Johnson & Johnson's mission might be "to sell Band-Aids and baby oil." But the company states its mission more broadly:

> We believe that our first responsibility is to the doctors, nurses, and patients, to mothers and all others who use our products and services. In meeting their needs everything we do must be of high quality. We must constantly strive to reduce our costs in order to maintain reasonable prices. Customers' orders must be serviced promptly and accurately. Our suppliers and distributors must have an opportunity to make a fair profit. We are responsible to our employees, the men and women who work for us throughout the world. Everyone must be considered as an individual. We must respect their dignity and recognize their merit. . . . We are responsible to the communities in which we live and work

and to the world community as well. We must be good citizens—support good works and charities and bear our fair share of taxes. We must encourage civic improvements and better health and education. We must maintain in good order the property we are privileged to use, protecting the environment and natural resources.[13]

Reshaping the basic task of selling consumer products into the larger mission of serving the interests of consumers, employees, suppliers, and others in the "world community" gives a new sense of purpose to Johnson & Johnson employees.

Societal Marketing

Societal marketing
A principle of enlightened marketing that holds that a company should make marketing decisions by considering consumers' wants, the company's requirements, consumers' long-run interests, and society's long-run interests.

Following the principle of **societal marketing,** an enlightened company makes marketing decisions by considering consumers' wants and interests, the company's requirements, and society's long-run interests. The company is aware that neglecting consumer and societal long-run interests is a disservice to consumers and society. Alert companies view societal problems as opportunities.

A societally oriented marketer wants to design products that are not only pleasing but also beneficial. The difference is shown in Figure 22-3. Products can be classified according to their degree of immediate consumer satisfaction and long-run consumer benefit. **Deficient products,** such as bad-tasting and ineffective medicine, have neither immediate appeal nor long-run benefits. **Pleasing products** give high immediate satisfaction but may hurt consumers in the long run. An example is cigarettes. **Salutary products** have low appeal but benefit consumers in the long run. Seat belts and air bags in automobiles are salutary products. **Desirable products** give both high immediate satisfaction and high long-run benefits. A desirable product with immediate satisfaction and long-run benefit would be a tasty *and* nutritious breakfast food.

FIGURE 22-3 *Societal classification of products*

One example of a desirable product is Archer Daniels Midland's Harvest Burgers:

Deficient products
Products that have neither immediate appeal nor long-run benefits.

Pleasing products
Products that give high immediate satisfaction but may hurt consumers in the long run.

Salutary products
Products that have low appeal but may benefit consumers in the long run.

Desirable products
Products that give both high immediate satisfaction and high long-run benefits.

Archer Daniels Midland (ADM) is the country's largest agricultural commodities processor. Asked by Mother Teresa to develop a product that would help her feed the world, ADM perfected a soy product which, when mixed with water and cooked, tastes like hamburger. But the soy product costs much less than real meat. Claims an ADM executive, "You can feed 30 times as many people off an acre of land by raising soy alone, than growing soy and feeding it to an animal and then eating the animal." The soy product is also more nutritious—it has 75 percent less fat, 40 percent fewer calories, and less than 30 percent of the cholesterol found in a typical hamburger. Thus, the product promises to have enormous economic and nutritional impact. While doing good, it appears that ADM will also do well. It is now selling the meatlike product in Italy, Finland, Hungary, and Russia. In Kiev, where meat shortages are a major problem, officials ordered $100 million worth. They calculate that the purchase would eliminate the need for 13 million cows. Sales are also brisk in consumer markets, where ADM sells the product as Harvest Burgers, aimed at a health-conscious, vegetarian niche.[14]

The challenge posed by pleasing products is that they sell very well but may end up hurting the consumer. The product opportunity, therefore, is to add long-run benefits without reducing the product's pleasing qualities. For example, Sears developed a phosphate-free laundry detergent that was also very effective. The challenge posed by salutary products is to add some pleasing qualities so that they will become more desirable in the consumers' minds. For example, synthetic fats and fat substitutes, such as NutraSweet's Simplesse and P&G's Olestra promise to improve the appeal of more healthful low-calorie and low-fat foods.

Advertisement from
1991 Readers Digest
First Russian Printing

Desirable products: Officials in Kiev ordered $100 million worth of ADM's meat-like Harvest Burgers soy product, eliminating the need for an estimated 13 million cows.

MARKETING ETHICS

Conscientious marketers face many moral dilemmas. The best thing to do is often unclear. Because not all managers have fine moral sensitivity, companies need to develop *corporate marketing ethics policies*— broad guidelines that everyone in the organization must follow. These policies should cover distributor relations, advertising standards, customer service, pricing, product development, and general ethical standards.

The finest guidelines cannot resolve all the difficult ethical situations the marketer faces. Table 22-1 lists some difficult ethical situations marketers could face during their careers. If marketers choose immediate sales-producing actions in all these cases, their marketing behavior might well be described as immoral or even amoral. If they refuse to go along with *any* of the actions, they might be ineffective as marketing managers and unhappy because of the constant moral tension. Managers need a set of principles that will help them figure out the moral importance of each situation and decide how far they can go in good conscience.

But *what* principle should guide companies and marketing managers on issues of ethics and social responsibility? One philosophy is that such issues are decided by the free market and legal system. Under this principle, companies and their managers are not responsible for making moral judgments. Companies can in good conscience do whatever the system allows.

A second philosophy puts responsibility not in the system, but in the hands of individual companies and managers. This more enlightened philosophy suggests that a company should have a "social conscience." Companies and managers should apply high standards of ethics and morality when making corporate decisions, regardless of "what the system allows." History provides an endless list of examples of company actions that were legal and allowed but were highly irresponsible. Consider the following example:

> Prior to the Pure Food and Drug Act, the advertising for a diet pill promised that a person taking this pill could eat virtually anything at any time and still lose weight. Too good to be true? Actually the claim was quite true; the product lived up to its billing with frightening efficiency. It seems that the primary active ingredient in this "diet supplement" was tapeworm larvae. These larvae would develop in the intestinal tract and, of course, be well fed; the pill taker would in time, quite literally, starve to death.[15]

Each company and marketing manager must work out a philosophy of socially responsible and ethical behavior. Under the societal marketing concept, each manager must look beyond what is legal and allowed and develop standards based on personal integrity, corporate conscience, and long-run consumer welfare. A clear and responsible philosophy will help the marketing manager deal with the many knotty questions posed by marketing and other human activities.

As with environmentalism, the issue of ethics provides special challenges for international marketers. Business standards and practices vary a great deal from one country to the next. For example, whereas bribes and kickbacks are illegal for U.S. firms, they are standard business practice in many South American countries. The question arises as to whether a company must lower its ethical stan-

TABLE 22-1   *Some Morally Difficult Situations in Marketing*

1. You work for a cigarette company and up to now have not been convinced that cigarettes cause cancer. A report comes across your desk that clearly shows the link between smoking and cancer. What would you do?

2. Your R&D department has changed one of your products slightly. It is not really "new and improved," but you know that putting this statement on the package and in advertising will increase sales. What would you do?

3. You have been asked to add a stripped-down model to your line that could be advertised to pull customers into the store. The product won't be very good, but salespeople will be able to switch buyers up to higher-priced units. You are asked to give the green light for this stripped-down version. What would you do?

4. You are thinking of hiring a product manager who just left a competitor's company. She would be more than happy to tell you all the competitor's plans for the coming year. What would you do?

5. One of your top dealers in an important territory has had recent family troubles and his sales have slipped. It looks like it will take him a while to straighten out his family trouble. Meanwhile you are losing many sales. Legally, you can terminate the dealer's franchise and replace him. What would you do?

6. You have a chance to win a big account that will mean a lot to you and your company. The purchasing agent hints that a "gift" would influence the decision. Your assistant recommends sending a fine color television set to the buyer's home. What would you do?

7. You have heard that a competitor has a new product feature that will make a big difference in sales. The competitor will demonstrate the feature in a private dealer meeting at the annual trade show. You can easily send a snooper to this meeting to learn about the new feature. What would you do?

8. You have to choose between three ad campaigns outlined by your agency. The first (A) is a soft-sell, honest information campaign. The second (B) uses sex-loaded emotional appeals and exaggerates the product's benefits. The third (C) involves a noisy, irritating commercial that is sure to gain audience attention. Pretests show that the campaigns are effective in the following order: C, B, and A. What would you do?

9. You are interviewing a capable woman applicant for a job as salesperson. She is better qualified than the men just interviewed. Nevertheless, you know that some of your important customers prefer dealing with men, and you will lose some sales if you hire her. What would you do?

10. You are a sales manager in an encyclopedia company. Your competitor's salespeople are getting into homes by pretending to take a research survey. After they finish the survey, they switch to their sales pitch. This technique seems to be very effective. What would you do?

dards to compete effectively in countries with lower standards. In a recent study, two researchers posed this question to chief executives of large international companies and got a unanimous response: No.[16] For the sake of all of the company's stakeholders—customers, suppliers, employees, shareholders, and the public—it is important to make a commitment to a common set of shared standards worldwide.

For example, John Hancock Mutual Life Insurance Company operates successfully in Southeast Asia, an area that by Western standards has widespread questionable business and government practices. Despite warnings from locals that Hancock would have to bend its rules to succeed, Hancock chairman Stephen Brown notes:

> We faced up to this issue early on when we started to deal with Southeast Asia. We told our people that we had the same ethical standards, same procedures, same policies in these countries that we have in the United States, and we do. . . . We just felt that things like payoffs were wrong—and if we had to do business that way, we'd rather not do business. Our employees would not feel good

TABLE 22-2   *American Marketing Association Code of Ethics*

Members of the American Marketing Association are committed to ethical, professional conduct. They have joined together in subscribing to this Code of Ethics embracing the following topics:

Responsibilities of the Marketer
Marketers must accept responsibility for the consequences of their activities and make every effort to ensure that their decisions, recommendations, and actions function to identify, serve, and satisfy all relevant publics: customers, organizations and society.

Marketers' professional conduct must be guided by:
1. The basic rule of professional ethics: not knowingly to do harm;
2. The adherence to all applicable laws and regulations;
3. The accurate representation of their education, training and experience; and
4. The active support, practice, and promotion of this Code of Ethics.

Honesty and Fairness
Marketers shall uphold and advance the integrity, honor, and dignity of the marketing profession by:
1. Being honest in serving consumers, clients, employees, suppliers, distributors, and the public;
2. Not knowingly participating in conflict of interest without prior notice to all parties involved; and
3. Establishing equitable fee schedules including the payment or receipt of usual, customary, and/or legal compensation for marketing exchanges.

Rights and Duties of Parties in the Marketing Exchange Process
Participants in the marketing exchange process should be able to expect that:
1. Products and services offered are safe and fit for their intended uses;
2. Communications about offered products and services are not deceptive;
3. All parties intend to discharge their obligations, financial and otherwise, in good faith; and
4. Appropriate internal methods exist for equitable adjustment and/or redress of grievances concerning purchases.

It is understood that the above would include, but is not limited to, the following responsibilities of the marketer:

In the area of product development and management,
• disclosure of all substantial risks associated with product or service usage;
• identification of any product component substitution that might materially change the product or impact on the buyer's purchase decision;

• identification of extra cost-added features.

In the area of promotions,
• avoidance of false and misleading advertising;
• rejection of high pressure manipulations, or misleading sales tactics;
• avoidance of sales promotions that use deception or manipulation.

In the area of distribution,
• not manipulating the availability of a product for purpose of exploitation;
• not using coercion in the marketing channel;
• not exerting undue influence over the reseller's choice to handle a product.

In the area of pricing,
• not engaging in price fixing;
• not practicing predatory pricing;
• disclosing the full price associated with any purchase.

In the area of marketing research,
• prohibiting selling or fundraising under the guise of conducting research;
• maintaining research integrity by avoiding misrepresentation and omission of pertinent research data;
• treating outside clients and suppliers fairly.

Organizational Relationships
Marketers should be aware of how their behavior may influence or impact on the behavior of others in organizational relationships. They should not demand, encourage, or apply coercion to obtain unethical behavior in their relationships with others, such as employees, suppliers, or customers.
1. Apply confidentiality and anonymity in professional relationships with regard to privileged information;
2. Meet their obligations and responsibilities in contracts and mutual agreements in a timely manner;
3. Avoid taking the work of others, in whole, or in part, and represent this work as their own or directly benefit from it without compensation or consent of the originator or owner;
4. Avoid manipulation to take advantage of situations to maximize personal welfare in a way that unfairly deprives or damages the organization of others.

Any AMA member found to be in violation of any provision of this Code of Ethics may have his or her Association membership suspended or revoked.

about having different levels of ethics. There may be countries where you have to do that kind of thing. We haven't found that country yet, and if we do, we won't do business there.[17]

Many industrial and professional associations have suggested codes of ethics, and many companies are now adopting their own codes. For example, the American Marketing Association, an international association of marketing managers and scholars, developed the code of ethics shown in Table 22-2. Companies also are developing programs to teach managers about important ethics issues and help

THE GENERAL DYNAMICS ETHICS PROGRAM

The General Dynamics ethics program is considered the most comprehensive in the industry. And little wonder—it was put together as generals from the Pentagon looked on. The program came about after charges that the

has set up hot lines that provide employees with instant advice on job-related ethical issues and has given each employee a wallet card listing a toll-free number to report suspected wrongdoing. Nearly all employees have attended workshops; those for

◆ If it becomes clear that the company must engage in unethical or illegal activity to win a contract, it will not pursue that business further.

◆ To prevent hidden interpretations or understandings, all information provided relative to products and services should be clear and concise.

◆ Receiving or soliciting gifts, entertainment, or anything else of value is prohibited.

◆ In countries where common practices indicate acceptance of conduct lower than that to which General Dynamics aspires, salespeople will follow the company's standards.

◆ Under no circumstances may an employee offer or give anything to customers or their representatives in an effort to influence them.

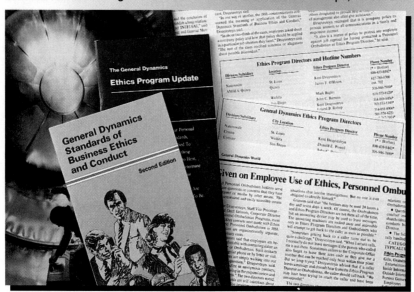

General Dynamics has developed a model ethics program.

company deliberately had over-billed the government on defense contracts.

Now at General Dynamics, a committee of board members reviews its ethics policies, and a corporate ethics director and steering group execute the program. The company

salespeople cover such topics as expense accounts and supplier relations.

The company also has a 20-page code of ethics, which tells employees in detail how to conduct themselves. Here are some examples of rules for salespeople:

Source: Adapted from "This Industry Leader Means Business," *Sales and Marketing Management,* May 1987, p. 44. Also see Stewart Toy, "The Defense Scandal," *Business Week,* July 1, 1988, pp. 28–30; and Richard A. Baker, "An Evaluation of the Ethics Program at General Dynamics," *Journal of Business Ethics,* Vol. 12, 1993, pp. 165–177.

them find the proper responses (see Marketing Highlight 22-4). According to a recent survey of Fortune 1000 companies, over 40 percent of these companies are holding ethics workshops and seminars and one-third have set up ethics committees. Further, more than 200 major U.S. companies have appointed high-level ethics officers to champion ethics issues and to help resolve ethics problems and concerns facing employees. These ethics specialists often employ hotlines through which employees can ask questions about proper ethical behavior or report questionable practices. At Raytheon, the ethics officer receives some 100 calls each month. Most involve minor issues, but about 10 percent point out serious ethical problems that must be addressed by top management.[18]

Many companies have developed innovative ways to educate employees about ethics:

> Citicorp has developed an ethics board game, which teams of employees use to solve hypothetical quandaries. General Electric employees can tap into specially designed software on their personal computers to get answers to ethical questions. At Texas Instruments, employees are treated to a weekly column on ethics

over an electronic news service. One popular feature: a kind of Dear Abby mailbag, answers provided by the company's ethics officer, . . . that deals with the troublesome issues employees face most often.[19]

Still, written codes and ethics programs do not assure ethical behavior. Ethics and social responsibility require a total corporate commitment. They must be a component of the overall corporate culture. According to David R. Whitman, Chairman of the Board of Whirlpool Corporation, "In the final analysis, 'ethical behavior' must be an integral part of the organization, a way of life that is deeply ingrained in the collective corporate body. . . . In any business enterprise, ethical behavior must be a tradition, a way of conducting one's affairs that is passed from generation to generation of employees at all levels of the organization. It is the responsibility of management, starting at the very top, to both set the example by personal conduct and create an environment that not only encourages and rewards ethical behavior, but which also makes anything less totally unacceptable."[20]

The future holds many challenges and opportunities for marketing managers as they move into the twenty-first century. Technological advances in solar energy, personal computers, interactive television, modern medicine, and new forms of transportation, recreation, and communication provide abundant marketing opportunities. However, forces in the socioeconomic, cultural, and natural environments increase the limits under which marketing can be carried out. Companies that are able to create new values in a socially responsible way will have a world to conquer.

PRINCIPLES FOR PUBLIC POLICY TOWARD MARKETING

Finally, we want to propose several principles that might guide the formulation of public policy toward marketing. These principles reflect assumptions underlying much of modern marketing theory and practice.

- *The principle of consumer and producer freedom.* As much as possible, marketing decisions should be made by consumers and producers under relative freedom. Marketing freedom is important if a marketing system is to deliver a high standard of living. People can achieve satisfaction in their own terms rather than in terms defined by someone else. This leads to greater fulfillment through a closer matching of products to desires. Freedom for producers and consumers is the cornerstone of a dynamic marketing system. But more principles are needed to implement this freedom and prevent abuses.

- *The principle of curbing potential harm.* As much as possible, transactions freely entered into by producers and consumers are their private business. The political system curbs producer or consumer freedom only to prevent transactions that harm or threaten to harm the producer, consumer, or third parties. Transactional harm is a widely recognized grounds for government intervention. The major issue is whether there is sufficient actual or potential harm to justify the intervention.

- *The principle of meeting basic needs.* The marketing system should serve disadvantaged consumers as well as affluent ones. In a free-enterprise system, producers make goods for markets that are willing and able to buy. Certain groups who lack purchasing power may go without needed goods and services, causing harm to their physical or psychological well-being. While preserving the principle of producer and consumer freedom, the marketing system should support economic and political actions to solve this problem. It should strive to meet the basic needs of all people, and all people should share to some extent in the standard of living it creates.

◆ *The principle of economic efficiency.* The marketing system strives to supply goods and services efficiently and at low prices. The extent to which a society's needs and wants can be satisfied depends on how efficiently its scarce resources are used. Free economies rely on active competition and informed buyers to make a market efficient. To make profits, competitors must watch their costs carefully while developing products, prices, and marketing programs that serve buyer needs. Buyers get the most satisfaction by finding out about different competing products, prices, and qualities and choosing carefully. The presence of active competition and well-informed buyers keeps quality high and prices low.

◆ *The principle of innovation.* The marketing system encourages authentic innovation to bring down production and distribution costs and to develop new products to meet changing consumer needs. Much innovation is really imitation of other brands, with a slight difference to provide a selling point. The consumer may face ten very similar brands in a product class. But an effective marketing system encourages real product innovation and differentiation to meet the wants of different market segments.

◆ *The principle of consumer education and information.* An effective marketing system invests heavily in consumer education and information to increase long-run consumer satisfaction and welfare. The principle of economic efficiency requires this investment, especially in cases where products are confusing because of their numbers and conflicting claims. Ideally, companies will provide enough information about their products. But consumer groups and the government can also give out information and ratings. Students in public schools can take courses in consumer education to learn better buying skills.

◆ *The principle of consumer protection.* Consumer education and information cannot do the whole job of protecting consumers. The marketing system also must provide consumer protection. Modern products are so complex that even trained consumers cannot evaluate them with confidence. Consumers do not know whether a mobile phone gives off cancer-causing radiation, whether a new automobile has safety flaws, or whether a new drug product has dangerous side effects. A government agency has to review and judge the safety levels of various foods, drugs, toys, appliances, fabrics, automobiles, and housing. Consumers may buy products but fail to understand the environmental consequences, so consumer protection also covers production and marketing activities that might harm the environment. Finally, consumer protection prevents deceptive practices and high-pressure selling techniques where consumers would be defenseless.

These seven principles are based on the assumption that marketing's goal is not to maximize company profits or total consumption or consumer choice, but rather to maximize life quality. Life quality means meeting basic needs, having available many good products, and enjoying the natural and cultural environment. Properly managed, the marketing system can help to create and deliver a higher quality of life to people around the world.

Summary

A marketing system should sense, serve, and satisfy consumer needs and improve the quality of consumers' lives. In working to meet consumer needs, marketers may take some actions that are not to everyone's liking or benefit. Marketing managers should be aware of the main *social criticisms of marketing.*

Marketing's impact on individual consumer welfare has been criticized for its *high prices, deceptive practices, high-pressure selling, shoddy or unsafe practices, planned obsolescence,* and *poor service to disadvantaged consumers. Marketing's impact on society* has been criticized for creating *false wants and too much materialism, too few social goods, cultural pollution,* and *too much political power.* Critics have also criticized *marketing's impact on other businesses* for harming competitors and reducing competition through acquisitions, practices that create barriers to entry, and unfair competitive marketing practices.

Concerns about the marketing system have led to *citizen and public actions to regulate marketing. Consumerism* is an organized social movement intended to strengthen the rights and power of consumers relative to sellers. Alert marketers view it as an opportunity to serve consumers better by providing more consumer information, education, and protection.

Environmentalism is an organized social movement seeking to minimize the harm done to the environment and quality of life by marketing practices. It calls for curbing consumer wants when their satisfaction would create too much environmental cost. Citizen action has led to the passage of many laws to protect consumers in the area of product safety, truth in packaging, truth in lending, and truth in advertising.

Many companies originally opposed these social movements and laws, but most of them now recognize a need for positive consumer information, education, and protection. Some companies have followed a policy of *enlightened marketing* based on the principles of *consumer orientation, innovation, value creation, social mission,* and *societal marketing.* Increasingly, companies are responding to the need to provide company policies and guidelines to help their managers deal with the questions of *marketing ethics.*

Although there are many questions concerning marketing and social responsibility, we can formulate principles for public policy toward marketing. These include the principles of *consumer and producer freedom, curbing potential harm, meeting basic needs, economic efficiency, innovation, consumer education and information,* and *consumer protection.*

Key Terms

Consumerism	Enlightened marketing	Salutary products
Consumer-oriented marketing	Environmentalism	Sense-of-mission marketing
Deficient products	Innovative marketing	Societal marketing
Desirable products	Pleasing products	Value marketing

Discussing the Issues

1. Was Gerber right or wrong not to recall its baby food after customers complained of finding glass fragments in bottles? Without considering what you know about how things turned out, analyze the situation facing Gerber in 1986. What action would you have recommended at the time?

2. Does marketing *create* barriers to entry or *reduce* them? Describe how a small manufacturer of household cleaning products could use advertising to compete with Procter & Gamble.

3. If you were a marketing manager at Dow Chemical Company, tell which you would prefer: government regulations on acceptable levels of air and water pollution, or a voluntary industry code suggesting target levels of emissions. Why?

4. Discuss whether Procter & Gamble practices the principles of enlightened marketing. Does your school? Give examples to support your answers.

5. Compare the marketing concept with the principle of societal marketing. Do you think marketers should adopt the societal marketing concept? Why or why not?

6. If you had the power to change our marketing system in any way feasible, decide what improvements you would make. What improvements could you make as a consumer or entry-level marketing practitioner?

Applying the Concepts

1. Changes in consumer attitudes, especially the growth of consumerism and environmentalism, have led to more societal marketing—and to more marketing that is *supposedly* good for society, but is actually closer to deception. (a) List three examples of marketing campaigns that you feel are genuine societal marketing. If possible, find examples of advertising or packaging that supports these campaigns. (b) Find three examples of deceptive or borderline imitations of societal marketing. How are you able to tell which campaigns are genuine and which are not? (c) What remedies, if any, would you recommend for this problem?

2. Consider contemporary America. As a society, we have many things to be proud of—and many areas where there is more work to be done. (a) Make a list of ten important things that need to be done in America. Your list may include economic issues, education, health care, environment, politics, or any other significant sphere. (b) Pick one issue that is especially important to you from the list above. Using what you have learned from this course, make a list of ways in which marketing principles and tools could be used to help on your issue.

References

1. See Patricia Strnad, "Gerber Ignores Tylenol Textbook," *Advertising Age,* March 10, 1986, p. 3; Felix Kessler, "Tremors from the Tylenol Scare Hit Food Companies," *Fortune,* March 31, 1986, pp. 59–62; Judann Dagnoli, "Brief Slump Expected for Sudafed," *Advertising Age,* March 18, 1991, p. 53; Gerald C. Meyers, "Product Tampering and Public Outcry," *Industry Week,* August 2, 1993, p. 41; and Laura Zinn, "The Right Moves, Baby," *Business Week,* July 5, 1993, pp. 30–31.

2. See Steven H. Star, "Marketing and Its Discontents," *Harvard Business Review,* November–December 1989, pp. 148–154.

3. See John F. Gaski and Michael Etzel, "The Index of Consumer Sentiment Toward Marketing," *Journal of Marketing,* July 1986, pp. 71–81; Faye Rice, "How to Deal with Tougher Customers," *Fortune,* December 3, 1990, pp. 38–48; and Richard W. Pollay and Banwari Mittal, "Here's the Beef: Factors, Determinants, and Segments in Consumer Criticism of Advertising," *Journal of Marketing,* July 1993, pp. 99–114.

4. Excerpts from Theodore Levitt, "The Morality (?) of Advertising," *Harvard Business Review,* July–August 1970, pp. 84–92.

5. Sandra Pesmen, "How Low Is Low? How Free Is Free?" *Advertising Age,* May 7, 1990, p. S10.

6. See Judith Bell and Bonnie Maria Burlin, "In Urban Areas: Many More Still Pay More for Food," *Journal of Public Policy and Marketing,* Fall 1993, pp. 268–270; and Alan R. Andreasen, "Revisiting the Disadvantages: Old Lesson and New Problems," *Journal of Public Policy and Marketing,* Fall 1993, pp. 270–275.

7. See Anne B. Fisher, "A Brewing Revolt Against the Rich," *Fortune,* December 17, 1990, pp. 89–94; and Norval D. Glenn, "What Does Family Mean?" *American Demographics,* June 1992, pp. 30–37.

8. From an advertisement for *Fact* magazine, which does not carry advertisements.

9. For more details, see Paul N. Bloom and Stephen A. Greyser, "The Maturing of Consumerism," *Harvard Business Review,* November–December 1981, pp. 130–139, Robert J. Samualson, "The Aging of Ralph Nader," *Newsweek,* December 16, 1985, p. 57; Douglas A. Harbrecht, "The Second Coming of Ralph Nader," *Business Week,* March 6, 1989, p. 28.

10. S. Noble Robinson, Ralph Earle III, and Ronald A. N. McLean, "Transnational Corporations and Global Environmental Policy," *Prizm,* Arthur D. Little, Inc., Cambridge, MA, First Quarter, 1994, pp. 51–63.

11. Ibid., p. 56.

12. Faye Rice, "The King of Suds Reigns Again," *Fortune,* August 4, 1986, p. 131.

13. Quoted from "Our Credo," Johnson & Johnson, New Brunswick, New Jersey.

14. See Mollie Neal, "Reaping the Rewards of Skillful Marketing . . . While Helping Humanity," *Direct Marketing,* September 1993, p. 24.

15. Dan R. Dalton and Richard A. Cosier, "The Four Faces of Social Responsibility," *Business Horizons,* May–June 1982, pp. 19–27.

16. John F. Magee and P. Ranganath Nayak, *Prizm,* Arthur D. Little, Inc., Cambridge, MA, First Quarter, 1994, pp. 65–77.

17. Ibid., pp. 71–72.

18. John A. Byrne, "Businesses Are Signing Up for Ethics 101," *Business Week,* February 15, 1988, pp. 56–57.

19. Kenneth Labich, "The New Crisis in Business Management," *Fortune,* April 20, 1992, pp. 167–176, here p. 176.

20. From "Ethics as a Practical Matter," a message from David R. Whitman, Chairman of the Board of

Whirlpool Corporation, as reprinted in Ricky E. Griffin and Ronald J. Ebert, *Business* (Englewood Cliffs, NJ: Prentice Hall, 1989), pp. 578–579. For more on marketing ethics, see Lynn Sharp Paine, "Managing for Organizational Integrity," *Harvard Business Review,* March–April 1994, pp. 106–117.

Company Case 22

NESTLÉ: UNDER FIRE AGAIN

Questionable marketing techniques by a unit of Nestlé are raising the concerns of consumer products activists. And this is not the first time that the public has scrutinized Nestlé.

Nestlé S.A., headquartered in Vevey, Switzerland, is the world's largest food company, with annual worldwide sales of more than $25 billion. The company's products are produced in 383 factories operating in 50 countries. Many Nestlé products are quite familiar—Nestlé's chocolates; Nescafé, Taster's Choice, and Hills Bros. coffees; Libby and Contadina foods; Beech-Nut baby products; Stouffer foods; and Friskies, Fancy Feast, and Mighty Dog pet foods. In 1985, the company acquired Carnation Company, makers of Evaporated Milk, Hot Cocoa Mix, Instant Breakfast Mix, Coffee-Mate, and other familiar brands.

In the late 1970s and early 1980s, Nestlé came under fire from health professionals who charged the company with encouraging Third-World mothers to give up breast-feeding and use a company-prepared formula. Critics accused Nestlé of using sophisticated promotional techniques to persuade hundreds of thousands of poverty-stricken, poorly educated mothers that formula feeding was better for their children. Unfortunately, formula feeding is not usually a wise practice in such countries. Because of poor living conditions and habits, people cannot or do not clean bottles properly and often mix formula with impure water. Furthermore, income level does not permit many families to purchase sufficient quantities of formula.

In 1977, two American social-interest groups spearheaded a worldwide boycott against Nestlé. The boycott ended in 1984, when the company complied with an infant formula marketing code adopted by the World Health Organization (WHO). The code eliminates all promotional efforts, requiring companies to serve primarily as passive "order takers." It prohibits advertising, samples, and direct contact with consumers. Contacts with professionals (such as doctors) are allowed only if professionals seek such contact. Manufacturers can package products with some form of visual corporate identity, but they cannot picture babies. In effect, then, the WHO code allows almost no marketing. However, the code contains only *recommended* guidelines. They become *mandatory* only if individual governments adopt national codes through their own regulatory mechanisms.

In addition to the formula controversy, Nestlé has had other public relations difficulties in recent years. In contrast to the Third-World baby-formula debacle, the next incident involved top-management ethics at a Nestlé subsidiary. Beech-Nut Nutrition Corp., one of Nestlé's U.S. baby products units, found itself in hot water in 1987, when it was forced to admit to selling adulterated and mislabeled apple juice intended for babies. The product contained little if any apple juice and was made from beet sugar, cane sugar syrup, corn syrup, and other ingredients. After pleading guilty to federal charges, Beech-Nut agreed to pay a $2-million fine and $140,000 for Food and Drug Administration investigative costs. Two company executives were fined and imprisoned.

Nestlé has once again captured the limelight because of its recent entry into the $1.6 billion U.S. infant formula market. Although Nestlé dominates this market in Europe, three large, well-established competitors control the U.S. market—Abbott Laboratories (with Similac and Isomil brands) has a 53-percent market share, followed by Bristol-Myers (Enfamil and ProSobee brands) with 36 percent, and American Home Products (SMA brand) with 11 percent. But the U.S. market is predicted to grow at 8 to 9 percent annually, and Nestlé wants its share of that growth.

Nestlé's Carnation unit, a company with a pure and sparkling reputation in the baby products business, introduced the new infant formula under the name "Good Start" in late 1988. Carnation designed Good Start for newborns. It also introduced a second product, Follow Up, developed for babies six months old or older.

Carnation claimed that Good Start offered important benefits over currently available infant formulas. The new formula is a whey-based product designed for infants allergic to standard milk-based and soy-based formulas. Carnation priced Good Start comparably to cow's milk or soy-based formulas.

In a product monograph introducing Good Start, Carnation stated that "breast milk is the ideal food for infants." However, "if breast feeding is not possible, an infant formula should provide complete nutrition and also be well-tolerated." Food intolerance and sensitivity in infants result from an immune system that is not fully developed, from an immature intestinal lining, or from damage to the intestinal lining. In situations where there is food intolerance or sensitivity, physicians often suggest infant formulas based on whole cow's milk. However, these formulas can sometimes also cause intolerance or sensitivity problems. In these cases, physicians often suggest infant formulas based on soybean products. These, too, Carnation argues, can often cause problems.

Therefore, Carnation positioned Good Start as an infant formula doctors should suggest before recommending soy-based formulas. Carnation pointed out that whey protein is the predominant type of protein in breast milk. Good Start is nutritionally complete for long-term or routine feeding. Carnation cautioned, however, that mothers should use Good Start only under direct medical supervision in cases of suspected milk allergy.

Carnation estimated that from 15 to 20 percent of all infants are allergic to the protein in standard formulas. In contrast, the Pediatric Academy's Committee on Nutrition said that the number is closer to between 1 and 2 percent. Nevertheless, Carnation declared Good Start a medical breakthrough and designated it as "hypoallergenic"—a claim made in bold type on the can. The company claimed that the product could prevent or reduce fussiness, sleeplessness, colic, rash, and other problems. The product monograph cited seven research studies involving 765 infants that supported its claims for Good Start. Pediatricians, however, warned that although the formula is easier to digest than common milk-based formulas, mothers should use it only after recommendation from the child's physician.

In addition to reacting to Carnation's hypoallergenic claim, the medical community also objected to Carnation's advertising its Follow Up product directly to consumers. The U.S. infant formula business is governed largely by relationships between marketers and health professionals. Except for hospital giveaway programs, Abbot and Bristol-Myers market their infant formula products mainly to doctors. These companies have sales forces that call directly on doctors, explaining the company's products, leaving samples, and encouraging the doctors to recommend their company's products. Consequently, there is little consumer brand loyalty in the infant formula market because mothers usually do what their doctors recommend. In addition, because pediatricians tell mothers what to buy, there is little price sensitivity in the infant formula market.

When Carnation launched the two products, it found itself under immediate attack, both because of the hypoallergenic claim and Follow Up's direct-to-consumer marketing. Carnation decided to withdraw the hypoallergenic claims for Good Start but held its ground on the Follow Up marketing program, which also included marketing to health-care professionals. Carnation also watched with interest as Gerber Products began marketing an infant formula produced by Bristol-Myers's Squibb division in August 1989. Gerber promoted the formula directly to consumers.

Meanwhile, Carnation continued to market Good Start exclusively to health-care professionals using its 90-member sales force and avoided any direct-to-consumer promotion. By the end of 1990, Good Start had achieved less than a 1-percent market share, whereas Follow Up had captured about a 2-percent share. Carnation had found it extremely tough to wade into the U.S. infant formula market.

As a result, Carnation announced that it would begin marketing Good Start directly to consumers in early 1991. In supporting its decision, Carnation noted that in the United States the established infant formula companies have generally treated infant formula as if it were a prescription drug rather than the food product that it is. As a food, federal law and Food and Drug Administration regulations ensure the nutritional content, labeling accuracy, and manufacturing quality of infant formulas. In treating formulas as a prescription drug, the established companies have used the same "medical marketing" techniques they use for prescription drugs.

Carnation argues that this practice puts consumers at a significant disadvantage. First, consumers cannot be made aware of differences among products, and they choose brands based on free samples received when the mother is discharged from the hospital. Second, because medical marketing is labor intensive and expensive, consumers must pay more for products marketed in this manner. Third, the expense of developing a medical marketing program makes it very difficult for new companies to enter the market. Finally, Carnation argues, because physicians wrongly believe that Carnation has marketed Good Start directly to consumers, they refuse to discuss Good Start with their patients, effectively shutting Carnation out of the market.

Carnation specifically noted that the ban on consumer advertising denies parents information at a time when there is increasing parental involvement in infant feeding decisions. The ban also limits incentives for innovation and product improvement in the infant-formula category. And the ban makes physicians unequal partners in the decision-making process because the doctors have all the information, while patients have little, if any. Carnation feels that a more balanced partnership makes sense. Finally, the company notes that the American Academy of Pediatricians has had the stated policy of promoting breast-feeding. Despite this policy and the "ban" on advertising, breast-feeding rates in the United States have been declining for more than a decade.

Carnation indicated that its new Good Start advertising would offer three simple messages: (1) Breast-feeding is best; (2) Good Start is a nutritious, gentle alternative to other formulas; and (3) Consult your doctor on all infant feeding decisions.[1]

At the same time, the American Academy of Pediatricians stated again its opposition to direct advertising to consumers. Noting the recent incidents of direct advertising, the AAP noted that "the motivation for this change is corporate profit earned, the AAP believes, at the potential expense of the optimal nutrition of children." The AAP noted its opposition to any practice that might discourage breast-feeding and therefore restated its opposition to direct advertising of infant formula to the public because of its potentially adverse impact on breast-feeding. The AAP indicated that it believes that when the companies advertise the claimed advantages of their formulas, those claims will interfere with the mother's decision to breast-feed. Further, the AAP argued that the proponents of breast-feeding could not compete with the advertising campaigns of the formula makers. And, the AAP suggested, as the formula makers compete with each other, they will make exaggerated claims, further promoting formula use over breast-feeding.[2]

Nestlé and its Carnation unit find themselves once again in the middle of controversy. Carnation must find a way to penetrate the U.S. infant formula market while balancing the interests and concerns of consumers, the medical community, and the company.

QUESTIONS

1. Think through the traditional buyers' and sellers' rights listed in Chapter 22. Which rights were violated in the Third-World infant-formula situation? Which rights were violated in the Beech-Nut apple juice situation? Does Carnation have the right to promote Good Start infant formula in whatever way it wants?

2. Will Nestlé be practicing socially responsible marketing with its Good Start product?

3. What marketing plan would you recommend for Good Start?

[1]Laurie MacDonald, Statement of the Nestlé Carnation Food Company before the Senate Judiciary Subcommittee on Antitrust, Monopolies, and Business Rights and the Senate Agriculture, Nutrition, and Forestry Committee. Carnation Nutritional Products Division, Glendale, CA. March 14, 1991.

[2]Britt Harvey, M.D., Testimony before the U.S. Senate Joint Hearing of the Subcommittee on Antitrust, Monopolies, and Business Rights and the Committee on Agriculture, Nutrition, and Forestry. American Academy of Pediatrics, Washington, D.C. March 14, 1991.

Video Case 9

MTV: THINK GLOBALLY, ACT LOCALLY

Everyone wants their MTV, and MTV wants to reach everyone. Through its six affiliates and numerous broadcasting arrangements, MTV is seen in over 250 million homes in 64 countries. Its unique blend of videojockeys (VJs), music news, promotions, interviews, concert tour information, specials, and rockumentaries has made MTV an international institution of popular culture and the leading authority on popular music.

At last count, MTV Europe reached more households than MTV U.S. Although it broadcasts in English, MTV Europe has a pan-European tone that appeals to advertisers wishing to reach the entire European market. To tailor its appeal to different European nationalities, MTV Europe broadcasts 40 percent nonanglo videos and tackles local issues such as neo-fascism. Even with this local focus, teenagers in the various countries reached by MTV Europe seem to have more in common with each other than they do with their parents.

MTV Latino originates in Miami and is beamed at Hispanic households in the United States and Mexico, as well as in Central America and South America. MTV Brazil features both Brazilian and international artists in 16 hours of daily programming hosted by Brazilian VJs speaking Portuguese. And MTV's most recent addition is Tierra del Fuego (near the Antarctic). Thus, the vast pan-Latin MTV network now reaches from the northern end of Mexico to the southern tip of South America, offering a diverse mix of North American and Latin music, regional productions, music and entertainment news, artist interviews, and concert coverage. The network helps bridge cultural gaps between nations—people in Chile see Mexican music and vice versa. A case in point is Los Fabulosos Cadillacs, an Argentine alternative music band. Once popular only in Argentina, exposure on MTV boosted sales of the band's records beyond the 400,000 mark throughout Latin America.

Recently, Kodak signed a million-dollar deal with MTV Latino and MTV Brazil to air ads to the pan-Latin audience. To help shape the content of the ads, Kodak's ad agency gave magazines to Latin youths and asked them to clip images that stirred them. The results: They selected images relating to ecology, contamination, AIDS, love, and self-expression. Kodak's campaign is entitled *"Como Tu Quieras con Kodak"* (which, roughly translated, means "As you wish it with Kodak"). In one ad, an enormous bird flies over frightened spectators protecting themselves from acid rain with black umbrellas. As the bird flies overhead, it leaves behind a glowing Kodak rainbow that brilliantly lights the sky.

MTV Asia reaches 30 countries via satellite. It consists of two networks: a Mandarin-language channel for viewers in Taiwan, Singapore, and China; and an English-language network for South Asia and the Philippines. Both are designed for the 12- to 34-year-old market, and programming is adapted to the musical tastes of this audience. An agreement between MTV and the DD2 Metro Channel (Indian national television) allows the network to broadcast a two-and-a-half-hour block targeted to Indian audiences.

MTV Japan (1992) is customized for Japanese youths. It features music videos from regional bands and international artists and offers programming in both English and Japanese. Also, recently announced is MTV South Africa, making a total of six MTV affiliates in all.

A common thread running through all these MTV affiliates is the use of local VJs, local artists' videos, and programming in local languages. This is the "act locally" side of MTV's operations. On the "think globally" side, MTV sends standardized shows to many parts of the world, including that favorite, Beavis and Butt-head. (Can you imagine their dopey laughs and phrases in German, Spanish, and Japanese?) MTV's shows and videos create global fashion trends. For example, the hip-hop look popularized by African-American groups and the grunge look from Seattle have been adopted by teens from Great Britain to Japan. MTV news shows often discuss the same topics around the world. For example, AIDS was covered in Brazil, Europe, India, and even among conservative Asian populations. Finally, MTV advertising is often global in nature. Advertisers include Levi Strauss, Procter & Gamble, Johnson & Johnson, Apple Computers, Nike, Reebok, Pepsi, and Coca-Cola, which has signed an agreement to advertise on all MTV channels around the world. These advertisers fashion ads that mirror the fast-paced, graphic style of MTV shows, with the result that ads around the world are starting to look more alike.

This balancing act of thinking globally and acting locally poses some problems for MTV. On the local side, affiliates would like to have more local programming and music videos that better appeal to their viewers. On the global side, the homogenization of youth is perceived negatively by many parents, elders, and politicians who fear that their countries' youths will lose their national identities and cultural values. These critics are not alone—even Beavis and Butt-head would probably trash global sameness.

QUESTIONS

1. Why would companies such as Levi Strauss, Coca-Cola, and Apple Computer want to advertise globally on MTV?

2. What kind of marketing mix does MTV use around the globe? Why? What kind of marketing mix is Kodak using in Latin America? What kind of marketing mix is Coca-Cola likely to use around the globe?

3. What effect do you believe "thinking globally" and "acting locally" have on homogenizing the world's youth?

4. Is *"Como Tu Quieras con Kodak"* a good ad theme for the Latin market?

Sources: Matthew Schifrin, "I Can't Even Remember the Old Star's Name," *Forbes*, March 16, 1992, pp. 44–45; Shawn Tully, "Teens—The Most Global Market of All," *Fortune*, May 16, 1994, pp. 90–96; and numerous company-supplied materials. The author gratefully acknowledges the help of Carole Robinson with this case.

FORD: EXPORTING TO JAPAN

TURNING THE TABLES

The 29-year-old customer wheels his old Toyota onto the lot at the Ford dealership and parks near the showroom. A polite salesman greets him and accepts the Toyota's keys. After some brief paperwork, the salesman and customer walk to another area outside the showroom. There, the salesman goes through the delivery checklist and then hands the customer the keys to a new, dark-green Ford Mustang coupe that sports a 3.8 liter V6 engine.

What's so unusual about this story? Well, this scene occurred in Tokyo, Japan, and both the salesman and customer were Japanese. For much of the 1960s, '70s, and '80s, Japanese car companies like Toyota and Honda pretty much had their way in the U.S. car market. Meanwhile, American companies either had little interest in exporting to Japan or found the process very difficult.

Ford has decided to change all that. The new Mustang that Seiichi Tsuzuki bought represents Ford's flagship model in a new line of cars it introduced in Japan in mid-1994. Although Japanese cars have their steering wheels on the right-hand side of the car, Ford's Mustang is a left-hand-drive model that targets a high-profile niche market. Ford is positioning the Mustang squarely against Nissan's Z cars and Toyota's Supra, cars that have dominated the "muscle car" niche in Japan. Along with the Mustang, however, Ford is introducing three right-hand-drive models—Probe, Laser, and Mondeo—that will target the compact-sedan market long ruled by Honda's Accord. This segment accounts for one-third of the Japanese market. Ford produced these new "world cars" as part of a $6 billion development effort. They represent the first time any American car company has offered right-hand-drive cars in Japan.

Mr. Tsuzuki, a manager at a life-insurance company, believes that the Mustang is "sexy," and he appreciates the "roughness" of its mystique. The car's running-horse emblem, he notes, "is a symbol of the United States," and he finds the car's design very impressive. He also appreciates the fact that the Mustang offers safety features, like air bags and anti-lock brakes, that cost much more on Japanese cars. Another recent customer, 72-year-old Tadashi Okabe, points out that "People say bad things about foreign cars—that the service is bad and that they don't run efficiently. But the Mustang is not like that. It is big, cool, and durable, and it also has air bags."

Although the Mustang offers image and accessories, its real advantage may be price. In recent years, the yen has gained strength relative to the U.S. dollar, falling from about 130 yen to the dollar to about 100. This means that Japanese consumers find American goods about 23 percent cheaper than they had been. For example, Mr. Tsuzuki's Mustang cost about 2.3 million yen or about $22,000. That is at least $7,000 lower than a comparable Japanese sports car's price. Ford is pricing its world cars at $2,000 to $3,000 below comparable versions of the Nissan Altima or the Honda Accord.

For years American car companies have complained about their market shares in Japan and asked the Japanese government for concessions. Now, Ford may finally have found the right formula—offer an American icon at a discount price and back it up with other models adapted for the Japanese market.

TAKING ON THE WORLD

This is not Ford's first attempt to crack the Japanese market. Until 1939, before World War II, the company sold about 10,000 Model A Fords annually in Japan. When Ford reentered the market after the war, in 1953, it imported only a limited number of cars each year. In 1979, Ford bought a 25-percent stake in Mazda Motor Corporation. This affiliation allowed Mazda to produce the Ford vehicles sold in Japan and gave Ford access to Mazda's 286 dealerships. To disguise the relationship, Ford and Mazda called the dealerships "Autorama." Despite the joint venture, however, Ford imported only 2,959 vehicles into Japan in 1991 and only 5,407 in 1993.

Ford's interest in Japan and other international markets is just part of the American auto industry's growing interest in exporting. The weaker dollar and improved products are helping the companies reverse U.S.-made vehicles' historically weak export sales. In 1994, analysts estimated that American and Japanese companies would have exported 529,000 cars and trucks from the United States, a 48.5 percent jump from 1993. The "Big Three," Ford, Chrysler, and General Motors, would account for 382,000 of those vehicles, up from 254,766 in 1993. Japanese companies operating in the United States would also increase their exports in 1994 by over 30 percent, but most of these exports would go to Taiwan. The stronger yen is also forcing Japanese companies to continue their investments in U.S.-based manufacturing. Toyota recently doubled its Kentucky plant's capacity to 400,000 vehicles per year.

Like Ford, General Motors is also targeting Japan, although it has been less aggressive. In 1993, GM sold 17,400 vehicles in Japan, about one-half of them made in Germany by GM's Opel unit. By the mid-1990s, GM plans to sell right-hand-drive Saturns and a right-hand-drive van that it manufactures in Georgia. Also, by 1996, it will offer Chevrolet Cavaliers with a Toyota nameplate. GM owns 37 percent of the Japanese auto company Isuzu.

DRIVING FORD

Just introducing reasonably priced new cars to the Japanese market is not enough by itself. Ford realizes it will need a full marketing mix. Ford is depending on Konen Suzuki, president of Japanese operations, to manage its marketing strategy in Japan. Suzuki stunned his superiors at Toyota when he jumped to Ford in 1991.

Suzuki's first goal was to make Ford more sensitive to the needs of Japanese motorists. He knew that Ford offered roomier cars which the Japanese preferred for family outings and recreation. Improved fuel economy made the cars more attractive in a country with very high gasoline prices. Suzuki also realized that Ford would have to back up its cars with better service than many local rivals provided. He issued Ford's first recall in Japan to replace broken steering hoses and malfunctioning fuel pumps on Tauruses. Japan's narrow, twisting roads and constant stopping and starting were too much for these parts, so Ford replaced them with more reliable substitutes. Keeping replacement parts in stock has been one of Ford's challenges.

The typical Japanese consumer is also less interested in how a car drives than in how it looks. Because Japan has such a well-developed public transportation system, many Japanese use that system for day-to-day travel. The Japanese treat their car as an ornament to be polished and cared for but used only occasionally.

Suzuki is also focusing on distribution. He wants to sign up an additional 1,000 dealers by the year 2000 to supplement the 286 Autorama dealers. He has even enticed one Nissan dealer to offer Fords at many of its dealerships. One problem, however, is that in Japan door-to-door salespeople sell about one-half of the cars sold each year. Because real estate is so expensive in Japan, most auto dealerships do not resemble American dealerships with their large buildings and massive car lots. They serve instead as bases of operation for the sales force. Toyota alone has a 100,000-person sales-force—equal to about one-half of the entire U.S. auto sales force—for a country the size of California. Toyota's roving salespeople help it capture two of every five car customers in Japan. The salespeople establish personal relationships with each of the 3,000 or so households in a typical sales area and make their sales pitches in their customers' living rooms. The salespeople primarily target homemakers who don't work outside the home. Because of the door-to-door sales forces, most Japanese never go to an auto dealership, and most are strongly brand loyal. Many Ford dealers don't like the time and expense involved in the traditional sales approach, but they have yet to develop any better ideas.

To entice consumers to visit the dealerships, Suzuki ordered a multimillion-dollar ad campaign that positions Ford's offerings as fun family cars. Two trends may help Suzuki's efforts. First, more Japanese women are working and are therefore not at home for traditional sales calls. Second, more consumers are willing to go to showrooms to see the latest new cars.

By 2000, Ford and Suzuki want to capture 5 percent of the Japanese market, roughly 200,000 cars. Ford would import about one-half of these, with its Mazda affiliate making the balance. Suzuki knows, however, that Nissan, Toyota, Honda, and the other Japanese car makers will not sit idly by. He also knows that Chrysler and GM will want their shares of the Japanese market. How can he carve Ford a larger place in one of the world's most competitive markets?

QUESTIONS

1. How have Japanese and American car companies been alike or different in their exporting strategies?

2. How have Japanese and American car companies differed in their approaches to adapting their marketing mixes to foreign markets?

3. What social responsibility and ethics issues should Ford be aware of as it steps up its efforts in the Japanese market?

4. What marketing recommendations would you make to Ford to help it be successful in the Japanese market?

Sources: Valerie Reitman, "Mustang Leads Ford's Charge on Japan," *Wall Street Journal*, June 9, 1994, p. B1. Used with permission of the *Wall Street Journal*. Also see William Spindle and James B. Treece, "Have You Driven a Ford Lately—In Japan?" *Business Week*, February 21, 1994; Krystal Miller, "Exports of U.S.-Made Vehicles Surge as Big Three Offer Better Cars, Prices," *Wall Street Journal*, June 27, 1994, p. A3; Valerie Reitman, "GM Is Planning to Make Inroads in Japan Market," *Wall Street Journal*, July 18, 1994, p. A8; Oscar Suris, "Ford Lists New Line of Compacts Below Japan's Top Sellers," *Wall Street Journal*, July 21, 1994, p. B6; Valerie Reitman, "In Japan's Car Market, Big Three Rivals Face Rivals Who Go Door-to-Door," *Wall Street Journal*, September 28, 1994, p. A1.

Appendix 1: Marketing Arithmetic

One aspect of marketing not discussed within the text is marketing arithmetic. The calculation of sales, costs, and certain ratios is important for many marketing decisions. This appendix describes three major areas of marketing arithmetic: the *operating statement, analytic ratios,* and *markups and markdowns.*

OPERATING STATEMENT

The operating statement and the balance sheet are the two main financial statements used by companies. The **balance sheet** shows the assets, liabilities, and net worth of a company at a given time. The **operating statement** (also called **profit-and-loss statement** or **income statement**) is the more important of the two for marketing information. It shows company sales, cost of goods sold, and expenses during a specified time period. By comparing the operating statement from one time period to the next, the firm can spot favorable or unfavorable trends and take appropriate action.

Table A1-1 shows the 1995 operating statement for Dale Parsons Men's Wear, a specialty store in the Midwest. This statement is for a retailer; the operating statement for a manufacturer would be somewhat different. Specifically, the section on purchases within the "cost of goods sold" area would be replaced by "costs of goods manufactured."

The outline of the operating statement follows a logical series of steps to arrive at the firm's $25,000 net profit figure:

Net sales	$300,000
Cost of goods sold	−175,000
Gross margin	$125,000
Expenses	−100,000
Net profit	$ 25,000

The first part details the amount that Parsons received for the goods sold during the year. The sales figures consist of three items: *gross sales, returns and allowances,* and *net sales.* **Gross sales** is the total amount charged to customers during the year for merchandise purchased in Parsons's store. As expected, some customers returned merchandise because of damage or a change of mind. If the customer gets a full refund or full credit on another purchase, we call this a *return.* Or the customer may decide to keep the item if Parsons will reduce the price. This is called an *allowance.* By subtracting returns and allowances from gross sales, we arrive at net sales—what Parsons earned in revenue from a year of selling merchandise:

Gross sales	$325,000
Returns and allowances	−25,000
Net sales	$300,000

The second major part of the operating statement calculates the amount of sales revenue Dale Parsons retains after paying the costs of the merchandise. We start with the inventory in the store at the beginning of the year. During the year, Parsons bought $165,000 worth of suits, slacks, shirts, ties, jeans, and other goods.

TABLE A1-1   *Operating Statement Dale Parsons Men's Wear Year Ending December 31, 1995*

Gross sales			$325,000
Less: Sales returns and allowances			25,000
Net sales			$300,000
Cost of goods sold			
Beginning inventory, January 1, at cost		$ 60,000	
Gross purchases	$165,000		
Less: Purchase discounts	15,000		
Net purchases	$150,000		
Plus: Freight-in	10,000		
Net cost of delivered purchases		$160,000	
Cost of goods available for sale		$220,000	
Less: Ending inventory, December 31, at cost		$ 45,000	
Cost of goods sold			$175,000
Gross margin			$125,000
Expenses			
Selling expenses			
Sales, salaries, and commissions	$ 40,000		
Advertising	5,000		
Delivery	5,000		
Total selling expenses		$ 50,000	
Administrative expenses			
Office salaries	$ 20,000		
Office supplies	5,000		
Miscellaneous (outside consultant)	5,000		
Total administrative expenses		$ 30,000	
General expenses			
Rent	$ 10,000		
Heat, light, telephone	5,000		
Miscellaneous (insurance, depreciation)	5,000		
Total general expenses		$ 20,000	
Total expenses			$100,000
Net profit			$ 25,000

Suppliers gave the store discounts totaling $15,000, so that net purchases were $150,000. Because the store is located away from regular shipping routes, Parsons had to pay an additional $10,000 to get the products delivered, giving the firm a net cost of $160,000. Adding the beginning inventory, the cost of goods available for sale amounted to $220,000. The $45,000 ending inventory of clothes in the store on December 31 is then subtracted to come up with the $175,000 **cost of goods sold.** Here again we have followed a logical series of steps to figure out the cost of goods sold:

Amount Parsons started with (beginning inventory)	$ 60,000
Net amount purchased	+150,000
Any added costs to obtain these purchases	+ 10,000
Total cost of goods Parsons had available for sale during the year	$220,000
Amount Parsons had left over (ending inventory)	− 45,000
Cost of goods actually sold	$175,000

The difference between what Parsons paid for the merchandise ($175,000) and what he sold it for ($300,000) is called the **gross margin** ($125,000).

In order to show the profit Parsons "cleared" at the end of the year, we must subtract from the gross margin the *expenses* incurred while doing business. *Selling expenses* included two sales employees, local newspaper and radio advertising, and the cost of delivering merchandise to customers after alterations. Selling expenses totaled $50,000 for the year. *Administrative expenses* included the salary for an office manager, office supplies such as stationery and business cards, and miscellaneous expenses including an administrative audit conducted by an outside consultant. Administrative expenses totaled $30,000 in 1995. Finally, the general expenses of rent, utilities, insurance, and depreciation came to $20,000. Total expenses were therefore $100,000 for the year. By subtracting expenses ($100,000) from the gross margin ($125,000), we arrive at the net profit of $25,000 for Parsons during 1995.

ANALYTIC RATIOS

The operating statement provides the figures needed to compute some crucial ratios. Typically these ratios are called **operating ratios**—the ratio of selected operating statement items to net sales. They let marketers compare the firm's performance in one year to that in previous years (or with industry standards and competitors in the same year). The most commonly used operating ratios are the *gross margin percentage*, the *net profit percentage*, the *operating expense percentage*, and the *returns and allowances percentage*.

RATIO		FORMULA	COMPUTATION FROM TABLE A1-1	
Gross margin percentage	=	$\dfrac{\text{gross margin}}{\text{net sales}}$	$= \dfrac{\$125,000}{\$300,000}$	$= 42\%$
Net profit percentage	=	$\dfrac{\text{net profit}}{\text{net sales}}$	$= \dfrac{\$25,000}{\$300,000}$	$= 8\%$
Operating expense percentage	=	$\dfrac{\text{total expenses}}{\text{net sales}}$	$= \dfrac{\$100,000}{\$300,000}$	$= 33\%$
Returns and allowances percentage	=	$\dfrac{\text{returns and allowances}}{\text{net sales}}$	$= \dfrac{\$25,000}{\$300,000}$	$= 8\%$

Another useful ratio is the *stockturn rate* (also called *inventory turnover rate*). The stockturn rate is the number of times an inventory turns over or is sold during a specified time period (often one year). It may be computed on a cost, selling price, or units basis. Thus the formula can be:

$$\text{Stockturn rate} = \frac{\text{cost of goods sold}}{\text{average inventory at cost}}$$

or

$$\text{Stockturn rate} = \frac{\text{selling price of goods sold}}{\text{average selling price of inventory}}$$

or

$$\text{Stockturn rate} = \frac{\text{sales in units}}{\text{average inventory in units}}$$

We will use the first formula to calculate the stockturn rate for Dale Parsons Men's Wear:

$$\frac{\$175,000}{(\$60,000 + \$45,000)/2} = \frac{\$175,000}{\$52,500} = 3.3$$

That is, Parson's inventory turned over 3.3 times in 1995. Normally, the higher the stockturn rate, the higher the management efficiency and company profitability.

Return on investment (ROI) is frequently used to measure managerial effectiveness. It uses figures from the firm's operating statement and balance sheet. A commonly used formula for computing ROI is:

$$\text{ROI} = \frac{\text{net profit}}{\text{sales}} \times \frac{\text{sales}}{\text{investment}}$$

You may have two questions about this formula: Why use a two-step process when ROI could be computed simply as net profit divided by investment? And what exactly is "investment"?

To answer these questions, let's look at how each component of the formula can affect the ROI. Suppose Dale Parsons Men's Wear has a total investment of $150,000. The ROI can be computed as follows:

$$\text{ROI} = \frac{\$25,000 \text{ (net profit)}}{\$300,000 \text{ (sales)}} \times \frac{\$300,000 \text{ (sales)}}{\$150,000 \text{ (investment)}}$$
$$8.3\% \quad \times \quad 2 \quad = 16.6\%$$

Now suppose that Parsons had worked to increase his share of market. He could have had the same ROI if his sales doubled while dollar profit and investment stayed the same (accepting a lower profit ratio to get higher turnover and market share):

$$\text{ROI} = \frac{\$25,000 \text{ (net profit)}}{\$600,000 \text{ (sales)}} \times \frac{\$600,000 \text{ (sales)}}{\$150,000 \text{ (investment)}}$$
$$4.16\% \quad \times \quad 4 \quad = 16.6\%$$

Parsons might have increased his ROI by increasing net profit through more cost cutting and more efficient marketing:

$$\text{ROI} = \frac{\$50,000 \text{ (net profit)}}{\$300,000 \text{ (sales)}} \times \frac{\$300,000 \text{ (sales)}}{\$150,000 \text{ (investment)}}$$
$$16.6\% \quad \times \quad 2 \quad = 33.2\%$$

Another way to increase ROI is to find some way to get the same levels of sales and profits while decreasing investment (perhaps by cutting the size of Parsons's average inventory):

$$\text{ROI} = \frac{\$25,000 \text{ (net profit)}}{\$300,000 \text{ (sales)}} \times \frac{\$300,000 \text{ (sales)}}{\$75,000 \text{ (investment)}}$$
$$8.3\% \quad \times \quad 4 \quad = 33.2\%$$

What is "investment" in the ROI formula? *Investment* is often defined as the total assets of the firm. But many analysts now use other measures of return to assess performance. These measures include *return on net assets (RONA), return on stockholders' equity (ROE),* or *return on assets managed (ROAM).* Because investment is measured at a point in time, we usually compute ROI as the average investment between two time periods (say, January 1 and December 31 of the same year). We can also compute ROI as an "internal rate of return" by using discounted cash flow analysis (see any finance textbook for more on this technique). The objective in using any of these measures is to determine how well the company has been using its resources. As inflation, competitive pressures, and cost of capital increase, such measures become increasingly important indicators of marketing and company performance.

MARKUPS AND MARKDOWNS

Retailers and wholesalers must understand the concepts of **markups** and **markdowns.** They must make a profit to stay in business, and the markup percentage affects profits. Markups and markdowns are expressed as percentages.

There are two different ways to compute markups—on *cost* or on *selling price*:

$$\text{Markup percentage on cost} = \frac{\text{dollar markup}}{\text{cost}}$$

$$\text{Markup percentage on selling price} = \frac{\text{dollar markup}}{\text{selling price}}$$

Dale Parsons must decide which formula to use. If Parsons bought shirts for $15 and wanted to mark them up $10, his markup percentage on cost would be $10/$15, or 67.7 percent. If Parsons based markup on selling price, the percentage would be $10/$25, or 40 percent. In figuring markup percentage, most retailers use the selling price rather than the cost.

Suppose Parsons knew his cost ($12) and desired markup on price (25 percent) for a man's tie and wanted to compute the selling price. The formula is:

$$\text{Selling price} = \frac{\text{cost}}{1 - \text{markup}}$$

$$\text{Selling price} = \frac{\$12}{.75} = \$16$$

As a product moves through the channel of distribution, each channel member adds a markup before selling the product to the next member. This "markup chain" is shown for a suit purchased by a Parsons customer for $200:

		$ AMOUNT	% OF SELLING PRICE
Manufacturer	Cost	$108	90%
	Markup	12	10%
	Selling price	$120	100%
Wholesaler	Cost	$120	80%
	Markup	30	20%
	Selling price	$150	100%
Retailer	Cost	$150	75%
	Markup	50	25%
	Selling price	$200	100%

The retailer whose markup is 25 percent does not necessarily enjoy more profit than a manufacturer whose markup is 10 percent. Profit also depends on how many items with that profit margin can be sold (stockturn rate), and on operating efficiency (expenses).

Sometimes a retailer wants to convert markups based on selling price to markups based on cost, and vice versa. The formulas are:

$$\text{Markup percentage on selling price} = \frac{\text{markup percentage on cost}}{100\% + \text{markup percentage on selling cost}}$$

$$\text{Markup percentage on cost} = \frac{\text{markup percentage on selling price}}{100\% - \text{markup percentage on selling price}}$$

Suppose Parsons found that his competitor was using a markup of 30 percent based on cost and wanted to know what this would be as a percentage of selling price. The calculation would be:

$$\frac{30\%}{100\% + 30\%} = \frac{30\%}{130\%} = 23\%$$

Because Parsons was using a 25 percent markup on the selling price for suits, he felt that his markup was suitable compared with that of the competitor.

Near the end of the summer Parsons still had an inventory of summer slacks in stock. Therefore, he decided to use a *markdown,* a reduction from the original selling price. Before the summer he had purchased 20 pairs at $10 each, and he had since sold 10 pairs at $20 each. He marked down the other pairs to $15 and sold five pairs. We compute his *markdown ratio* as follows:

$$\text{Markdown percentage} = \frac{\text{dollar markdown}}{\text{total net sales in dollars}}$$

The dollar markdown is $25 (five pairs at $5 each) and total net sales are $275 (10 pairs at $20 + five pairs at $15). The ratio, then, is $25/$275, or 9 percent.

Larger retailers usually compute markdown ratios for each department rather than for individual items. The ratios provide a measure of relative marketing performance for each department and can be calculated and compared over time. Markdown ratios can also be used to compare the performance of different buyers and salespeople in a store's various departments.

Key Terms

Balance sheet
Cost of goods sold
Gross margin
Gross sales

Markdown
Markup
Operating ratios

Operating statement
(or profit-and-loss statement
or income statement)
Return on investment (ROI)

Appendix 2
Careers in Marketing

Now that you have completed your first course in marketing, you have a good idea of what the field entails. You may have decided that you want to pursue a marketing career because it offers constant challenge, stimulating problems, the opportunity to work with people, and excellent advancement opportunities. Marketing is a very broad field with a wide variety of tasks involving the analysis, planning, implementation, and control of marketing programs. You will find marketing positions in all types and sizes of institutions. This appendix describes entry-level and higher-level marketing opportunities and lists steps you might take to select a career path and better market yourself.

DESCRIPTION OF MARKETING JOBS

Almost a third of all Americans are employed in marketing-related positions. Thus, the number of possible marketing careers is enormous. Because of the knowledge of products and consumers gained in these jobs, marketing positions provide excellent training for the highest levels in the organization. A recent study by an executive recruiting firm found that more top executives have come out of marketing than any other area.

Marketing salaries vary by company and position. Beginning salaries usually rank only slightly below those for engineering and chemistry but equal or exceed those for economics, finance, accounting, general business, and the liberal arts. If you succeed in an entry-level marketing position, you will quickly be promoted to higher levels of responsibility and salary.

Marketing has become an attractive career for some people who have not traditionally considered this field. One trend is the growing number of women entering marketing. Women have historically been employed in the retailing and advertising areas of marketing. But now they have moved into all types of sales and marketing positions. Women now pursue successful sales careers in pharmaceutical companies, publishing companies, banks, consumer products companies, and in an increasing number of industrial selling jobs. Their ranks are also growing in product and brand manager positions.

Another trend is the growing acceptance of marketing by nonprofit organizations. Colleges, arts organizations, libraries, and hospitals are increasingly applying marketing to their problems. They are beginning to hire marketing directors and marketing vice-presidents to manage their varied marketing activities.

Here are brief descriptions of some important marketing jobs.

ADVERTISING

Advertising is an important business activity that requires skill in planning, fact gathering, and creativity. Although compensation for starting advertising people tends to be lower than that in other marketing fields, opportunities for advancement are usually greater because of less emphasis on age or length of employment. Typical jobs in advertising agencies include the following positions.

Copywriters help find the concepts behind the written words and visual images of advertisements. They dig for facts, read avidly, and borrow ideas. They talk to customers, suppliers, and *anybody* who might give them clues about how to attract the target audience's attention and interest.

Art directors constitute the other part of the creative team. They translate copywriters' ideas into dramatic visuals called "layouts." Agency artists develop print layouts, package designs, television layouts (called "storyboards"), corporate logotypes, trademarks, and symbols. They specify style and size of typography, paste the type in place, and arrange all the details of the ad so that it can be reproduced by engravers and printers. A superior art director or copy chief becomes the agency's creative director and oversees all its advertising. The creative director holds a high position in the ad agency's structure.

Account executives are liaisons between clients and agencies. They must know a great deal about marketing and its various components. They explain client plans and objectives to agency creative teams and supervise the development of the total advertising plan. Their main task is to keep the client happy with the agency! Because "account work" involves many personal relationships, account executives are usually personable, diplomatic, and sincere.

Media buyers select the best media for clients. Media representatives come to the buyer's office armed with statistics to prove that *their* numbers are better, *their* costs per thousand are less, and *their* medium delivers more ripe audiences than competitive media. Media buyers have to evaluate these claims. They must also bargain with the broadcast media for the best rates and make deals with the print media for good ad positions.

Large ad agencies have active marketing research departments that provide the market information needed to develop new ad campaigns and assess current campaigns. People interested in marketing research should consider jobs with ad agencies.

BRAND AND PRODUCT MANAGEMENT

Brand and product managers plan, direct, and control business and marketing efforts for their products. They are concerned with research and development, packaging, manufacturing, sales and distribution, advertising, promotion, market research, and business analysis and forecasting. In consumer goods companies, the newcomer—who usually needs a Master of Business Administration degree (MBA)—joins a brand team and learns the ropes by doing numerical analyses and watching senior brand people. This person eventually heads the team and later moves on to manage a larger brand. Many industrial goods companies also have product managers. Product management is one of the best training grounds for future corporate officers.

CUSTOMER AFFAIRS

Some large consumer goods companies have customer affairs people who act as liaisons between customers and firms. They handle complaints, suggestions, and problems concerning the company's products, determine what action to take, and coordinate the activities required to solve the problem. The position requires an empathetic, diplomatic, and capable person who can work with a wide range of people inside and outside the firm.

INDUSTRIAL MARKETING

People interested in industrial marketing careers can go into sales, service, product design, marketing research, or one of several other positions. They sometimes need a technical background. Most people start in sales and spend time in training and making calls with senior salespeople. If they stay in sales, they may advance to district, regional, and higher sales positions. Or they may go into product management and work closely with customers, suppliers, manufacturing, and sales engineering.

INTERNATIONAL MARKETING

As U.S. firms increase their international business, they need people who are familiar with foreign languages and cultures and who are willing to travel to or relocate in foreign cities. For such assignments, most companies seek experienced people who have proved themselves in domestic operations. An MBA often helps but is not always required.

MARKETING MANAGEMENT SCIENCE AND SYSTEMS ANALYSIS

People who have been trained in management science, quantitative methods, and systems analysis can act as consultants to managers who face difficult marketing problems such as demand measurement and forecasting, market structure analysis, and new-product evaluation. Most career opportunities exist in larger marketing-oriented firms, management consulting firms, and public institutions concerned with health, education, or transportation. An MBA or Master of Science degree is often required.

MARKETING RESEARCH

Marketing researchers interact with managers to define problems and identify the information needed to resolve them. They design research projects, prepare questionnaires and samples, analyze data, prepare reports, and present their findings and recommendations to management. They must understand statistics, consumer behavior, psychology, and sociology. A master's degree helps. Career opportunities exist with manufacturers, retailers, some wholesalers, trade and industry associations, marketing research firms, advertising agencies, and governmental and private nonprofit agencies.

NEW-PRODUCT PLANNING

People interested in new-product planning can find opportunities in many types of organizations. They usually need a good background in marketing, marketing research, and sales forecasting; they need organizational skills to motivate and coordinate others; and they may need a technical background. Usually, these people work first in other marketing positions before joining the new-product department.

MARKETING LOGISTICS (PHYSICAL DISTRIBUTION)

Marketing logistics, or physical distribution, is a large and dynamic field, with many career opportunities. Major transportation carriers, manufacturers, wholesalers, and retailers all employ logistics specialists. Coursework in quantitative methods, finance, accounting, and marketing will provide students with the necessary skills for entering the field.

PUBLIC RELATIONS

Most organizations have a public relations person or staff to anticipate public problems, handle complaints, deal with media, and build the corporate image. People interested in public relations should be able to speak and write clearly and persuasively, and they should have a background in journalism, communications, or the liberal arts. The challenges in this job are highly varied and very people oriented.

PURCHASING

Purchasing agents are playing a growing role in firms' profitability during periods of rising costs, materials shortages, and increasing product complexity. In retail organizations, working as a "buyer" can be a good route to the top. Purchasing agents in industrial companies play a key role in holding down the costs. A technical background is useful in some purchasing positions, along with a knowledge of credit, finance, and physical distribution.

RETAILING MANAGEMENT

Retailing provides people with an early opportunity to take on marketing responsibilities. Although retail starting salaries and job assignments have typically been lower than those in manufacturing or advertising, the gap is narrowing. The major routes to top management in retailing are merchandise management and store management. In merchandise management, a person moves from buyer trainee to assistant buyer to buyer to merchandise division manager. In store management, the person moves from management trainee to assistant department (sales) manager to department manager to store (branch) manager. Buyers are primarily concerned with merchandise selection and promotion; department managers are concerned with sales force management and display. Large-scale retailing lets new recruits move in only a few years into the management of a branch or part of a store doing as much as $5 million in sales.

SALES AND SALES MANAGEMENT

Sales and sales-management opportunities exist in a wide range of profit and nonprofit organizations and in product and service organizations, including financial, insurance, consulting, and government organizations. Individuals must carefully match their backgrounds, interests, technical skills, and academic training with available sales jobs. Training programs vary greatly in form and length, ranging from a few weeks to two years. Career paths lead from salesperson to district, regional, and higher levels of sales management and, in many cases, the top management of the firm.

OTHER MARKETING CAREERS

There are many other marketing-related jobs in areas such as sales promotion, wholesaling, packaging, pricing, and credit management. Information on these positions can be gathered from sources such as those listed in the following discussion.

CHOOSING AND GETTING A JOB

To choose and obtain a job, you must apply marketing skills, particularly marketing analysis and planning. Here are eight steps for choosing a career and finding that first job.

MAKE A SELF-ASSESSMENT

Self-assessment is the most important part of a job search. It involves honestly evaluating your interests, strengths, and weaknesses. What are your career objectives? What kind of organization do you want to work for? What do you do well or not so well? What sets you apart from other job seekers? Do the answers to these questions suggest which careers you should seek or avoid? For help in self-assessment, you might look at the following books, each of which raises many questions you should consider:

1. *What Color Is Your Parachute?* by Richard Bolles
2. *Three Boxes in Life and How to Get Out of Them,* by Richard Bolles
3. *Guerrilla Tactics in the Job Market,* by Tom Jackson

Also consult the career counseling, testing, and placement services at your school.

EXAMINE JOB DESCRIPTIONS

Now look at various job descriptions to see what positions best match your interests, desires, and abilities. Descriptions can be found in the *Occupation Outlook Handbook* and the *Dictionary of Occupational Titles* published by the U.S. Department of Labor. These volumes describe the duties of people in various occupations, the specific training and education needed, the availability of jobs in each field, possibilities for advancement, and probable earnings.

DEVELOP JOB-SEARCH OBJECTIVES

Your initial career shopping list should be broad and flexible. Look broadly for ways to achieve your objectives. For example, if you want a career in marketing research, consider the public as well as the private sector and regional as well as national firms. Only after exploring many options should you begin to focus on specific industries and initial jobs. You need to set down a list of basic goals. Your list might say: "a job in a small company, in a large city, in the Sunbelt, doing marketing research, with a consumer products firm."

EXAMINE THE JOB MARKET AND ASSESS OPPORTUNITIES

You must now look at the market to see what positions are available. For an up-to-date listing of marketing-related job openings, refer to the latest edition of the *College Placement Annual* available at school placement offices. This publication shows current job openings for hundreds of companies seeking college graduates for entry-level positions. It also lists companies seeking experienced or advanced-degree people. At this stage, use the services of your placement office to the fullest extent in order to find openings and set up interviews. Take the time to analyze the industries and companies in which you are interested. Consult business magazines, annual reports, business reference books, faculty members, school career counselors, and fellow students. Try to analyze the future growth and profit potential of the company and industry, chances for advancement, salary levels, entry positions, amount of travel, and other important factors.

DEVELOP SEARCH STRATEGIES

How will you contact companies in which you are interested? There are several possible ways. One of the best ways is through on-campus interviews; but not all the companies that interest you will visit your school. Another good way is to phone or write the company directly. Finally, you can ask marketing professors or school alumni for contacts and references.

DEVELOP RÉSUMÉ AND COVER LETTER

Your résumé should persuasively present your abilities, education, background, training, work experience, and personal qualifications—but it should also be brief, usually one page. The goal is to gain positive responses from potential employers.

The cover letter is, in some ways, more difficult to write than the résumé. It must be persuasive, professional, concise, and interesting. Ideally, it should set you apart from the other candidates for the position. Each letter should look and sound original—that is, it should be individually typed and tailored to the specific organization being contacted. It should describe the position you are applying for, arouse interest, describe your qualifications, and tell how you can be contacted. Cover letters should be addressed to an individual rather than a title. You should follow up the letter with a telephone call.

OBTAIN INTERVIEWS

Here is some advice to follow before, during, and after your interviews.

Before the Interview

1. Interviews have extremely diverse styles—the "chit chat," let's-get-to-know-each-other style; the interrogation style of question after question; the tough-probing why, why, why style, and many others. Be ready for anything.
2. Practice being interviewed with a friend and ask for a critique.
3. Prepare to ask at least five good questions that are not readily answered in the company literature.
4. Anticipate possible interview questions and prepare good answers ahead of time.
5. Avoid back-to-back interviews—they can be exhausting.
6. Dress conservatively and tastefully for the interview. Be neat and clean.
7. Arrive about 10 minutes early to collect your thoughts before the interview. Check your name on the interview schedule, noting the name of the interviewer and the room number.
8. Review the major points you intend to cover.

During the Interview

1. Give a firm handshake in greeting the interviewer. Introduce yourself using the same form the interviewer uses. Make a good initial impression.
2. Retain your poise. Relax. Smile occasionally. Be enthusiastic throughout the interview.
3. Good eye contact, good posture, and distinct speech are musts. Don't clasp your hands or fiddle with jewelry, hair, or clothing. Sit comfortably in your chair. Do not smoke, even if asked.
4. Have extra copies of your résumé with you.
5. Have your story down pat. Present your selling points. Answer questions directly. Avoid one-word answers, but don't be wordy.
6. Most times, let the interviewer take the initiative, but don't be passive. Find a good opportunity to direct the conversation to things you want the interviewer to hear.
7. To end on a high note, the latter part of the interview is the best time to make your most important point or to ask a pertinent question.
8. Don't be afraid to "close." You might say, "I'm very interested in the position and I have enjoyed this interview."
9. Obtain the interviewer's business card or address and phone number so that you can follow up later.

After the Interview

1. After leaving the interview, record the key points that arose. Be sure to record who is to follow up on the interview and when a decision can be expected.
2. Objectively analyze the interview with regard to the questions asked, the answers given, your overall interview presentation, and the interviewer's response to specific points.
3. Send a thank-you letter mentioning any additional items and your willingness to supply further information.
4. If you do not hear within the time specified, write or call the interviewer to determine your status.

FOLLOW-UP

If you are successful, you will be invited to visit the organization. The in-company interview will run from a few hours to a whole day. The company will examine your interest, maturity, enthusiasm, assertiveness, logic, and company and functional knowledge. You should ask questions about things that are important to you. Find out about the environment, job role, responsibilities, opportunity, current industrial issues, and the firm's personality. The company wants to find out if you are the right person for the job; just as importantly, you want to find out if this is the right job for you.

Glossary

Actual product A product's parts, quality level, features, design, brand name, packaging, and other attributes that combine to deliver core product benefits.

Adapted marketing mix An international marketing strategy for adjusting the marketing-mix elements to each international target market, bearing more costs but hoping for a larger market share and return.

Administered VMS A vertical marketing system that coordinates successive stages of production and distribution, not through common ownership or contractual ties, but through the size and power of one of the parties.

Adoption process The mental process through which an individual passes from first hearing about an innovation to final adoption.

Advertising Any paid form of nonpersonal presentation and promotion of ideas, goods, or services by an identified sponsor.

Advertising objective A specific communication *task* to be accomplished with a specific *target* audience during a specific period of *time*.

Advertising specialties Useful articles imprinted with an advertiser's name, given as gifts to consumers.

Affordable method Setting the promotion budget at the level management thinks the company can afford.

Age and life-cycle segmentation Dividing a market into different age and life-cycle groups.

Agent A wholesaler who represents buyers or sellers on a relatively permanent basis, performs only a few functions, and does not take title to goods.

Allowance Promotional money paid by manufacturers to retailers in return for an agreement to feature the manufacturer's products in some way.

Alternative evaluation The stage of the buyer decision process in which the consumer uses information to evaluate alternative brands in the choice set.

Approach The step in the selling process in which the salesperson meets and greets the buyer to get the relationship off to a good start.

Attitude A person's consistently favorable or unfavorable evaluations, feelings, and tendencies toward an object or idea.

Augmented product Additional consumer services and benefits built around the core and actual products.

Automatic vending Selling through vending machines.

Available market The set of consumers who have interest, income, and access to a particular product or service.

Baby boom The major increase in the annual birthrate following World War II and lasting until the early 1960s. The "baby boomers," now moving into middle age, are a prime target for marketers.

Balance sheet A financial statement that shows assets, liabilities, and net worth of a company at a given time.

Basing-point pricing A geographic pricing strategy in which the seller designates some city as a basing point and charges all customers the freight cost from that city to the customer location, regardless of the city from which the goods are actually shipped.

Behavioral segmentation Dividing a market into groups based on consumer knowledge, attitude, use, or response to a product.

Belief A descriptive thought that a person holds about something.

Benchmarking The process of comparing the company's products and processes to those of competitors or leading firms in other industries to find ways to improve quality and performance.

Benefit segmentation Dividing the market into groups according to the different benefits that consumers seek from the product.

Brand A name, term, sign, symbol, or design, or a combination of these intended to identify the goods or services of one seller or group of sellers and to differentiate them from those of competitors.

Brand equity The value of a brand, based on the extent to which it has high brand loyalty, name awareness, perceived quality, strong brand associations, and other assets such as patents, trademarks, and channel relationships.

Brand extension Using a successful brand name to launch a new or modified product in a new category.

Brand image The set of beliefs consumers hold about a particular brand.

Breakeven pricing (target profit pricing) Setting price to break even on the costs of making and marketing a product; or setting price to make a target profit.

Broker A wholesaler who does not take title to goods and whose function is to bring buyers and sellers together and assist in negotiation.

Business analysis A review of the sales, costs, and profit projections for a new product to find out whether these factors satisfy the company's objectives.

Business buying process The decision-making process by which business buyers establish the need for purchased products and services and identify, evaluate, and choose among alternative brands and suppliers.

Business market All the organizations that buy goods and services to use in the production of other products and services or for the purpose of reselling or renting them to others at a profit.

Business portfolio The collection of businesses and products that make up the company.

Buyer The person who makes an actual purchase.

Buyer-readiness stages The stages consumers normally pass through on their way to purchase, including awareness, knowledge, liking, preference, conviction, and purchase.

Buying center All the individuals and units that participate in the business buying-decision process.

By-product pricing Setting a price for by-products in order to make the main product's price more competitive.

Capital items Industrial products that partly enter the finished product, including installations and accessory equipment.

Captive-product pricing Setting a price for products that must be used along with a main product, such as blades for a razor and film for a camera.

Cash cows Low-growth, high-share businesses or products; established and successful units that generate cash the company uses to pay its bills and support other business units that need investment.

Cash discount A price reduction to buyers who pay their bills promptly.

Cash refund offers (rebates) Offers to refund part of the purchase price of a product to consumers who send a "proof of purchase" to the manufacturer.

Catalog marketing Direct marketing through catalogs that are mailed to a select list of customers or made available in stores.

Catalog showroom A retail operation that sells a wide selection of high-markup, fast-moving, brand name goods at discount prices.

Causal research Marketing research to test hypotheses about cause-and-effect relationships.

Chain stores Two or more outlets that are commonly owned and controlled, have central buying and merchandising, and sell similar lines of merchandise.

Channel conflict Disagreement among marketing channel members on goals and roles—who should do what and for what rewards.

Channel level A layer of middlemen that performs some work in bringing the product and its ownership closer to the final buyer.

Closing The step in the selling process in which the salesperson asks the customer for an order.

Co-branding The practice of using the established brand names of two different companies on the same product.

Cognitive dissonance Buyer discomfort caused by postpurchase conflict.

Combination stores Combined food and drug stores.

Commercialization Introducing a new product into the market.

Communication adaptation A global communication strategy of fully adapting advertising messages to local markets.

Comparison advertising Advertising that compares one brand directly or indirectly to one or more other brands.

Competitive advantage An advantage over competitors gained by offering consumers greater value, either through lower prices or by providing more benefits that justify higher prices.

Competitive-parity method Setting the promotion budget to match competitors' outlays.

Competitive strategies Strategies that strongly position the company against competitors and that give the company the strongest possible strategic advantage.

Competitor analysis The process of identifying key competitors; assessing their objectives, strategies, strengths and weaknesses, and reaction patterns; and selecting which competitors to attack or avoid.

Competitor-centered company A company whose moves are mainly based on competitors' actions and reactions; it spends most of its time tracking competitors' moves and market shares and trying to find strategies to counter them.

Complex buying behavior Consumer buying behavior in situations characterized by high consumer involvement in a purchase and significant perceived differences among brands.

Concentrated marketing A market-coverage strategy in which a firm goes after a large share of one or a few submarkets.

Concept testing Testing new-product concepts with a group of target consumers to find out if the concepts have strong consumer appeal.

Consumer buying behavior The buying behavior of final consumers—individuals and households who buy goods and services for personal consumption.

Consumer franchise building promotions Sales promotions that promote the product's positioning and include a selling message along with the deal.

Consumer market All the individuals and households who buy or acquire goods and services for personal consumption.

Consumer-oriented marketing A principle of enlightened marketing that holds that a company should view and organize its marketing activities from a consumer's point of view.

Consumer products Products bought by final consumers for personal consumption.

Consumer promotion Sales promotion designed to stimulate consumer purchasing, including samples, coupons, rebates, prices-off, premiums, patronage rewards, displays, and contests and sweepstakes.

Consumerism An organized movement of citizens and government agencies to improve the rights and power of buyers in relation to sellers.

Containerization Putting the goods in boxes or trailers that are easy to transfer between two transportation modes. They are used in multimode systems commonly referred to as piggyback, fishyback, trainship, and airtruck.

Contests, sweepstakes, games Promotional events that give consumers the chance to win something—such as cash, trips, or goods—by luck or through extra effort.

Contract manufacturing A joint venture in which a company contracts with manufacturers in a foreign market to produce the product.

Contractual VMS A vertical marketing system in which independent firms at different levels of production and distribution join together through contracts to obtain more economies or sales impact than they could achieve alone.

Convenience products Consumer products that the customer usually buys frequently, immediately, and with a minimum of comparison and buying effort.

Convenience store A small store located near a residential area that is open long hours seven days a week and carries a limited line of high-turnover convenience goods.

Conventional distribution channel A channel consisting of one or more independent producers, wholesalers, and retailers, each a separate business seeking to maximize its own profits even at the expense of profits for the system as a whole.

Core product The problem-solving services or core benefits that consumers are really buying when they obtain a product.

Corporate VMS A vertical marketing system that combines successive stages of production and distribution under single ownership—channel leadership is established through common ownership.

Cost of goods sold The net cost to the company of goods sold.

Cost-plus pricing Adding a standard markup to the cost of the product.

Countertrade International trade involving the direct or indirect exchange of goods for other goods instead of cash. Forms include barter, compensation (buyback), and counterpurchase.

Coupons Certificates that give buyers a saving when they purchase a specified product.

Cultural environment Institutions and other forces that affect society's basic values, perceptions, preferences, and behaviors.

Culture The set of basic values, perceptions, wants, and behaviors learned by a member of society from family and other important institutions.

Customer-centered company A company that focuses on customer developments in designing its marketing strategies and on delivering superior value to its target customers.

Customer delivered value The consumer's assessment of the product's overall capacity to satisfy his or her needs. The difference between total customer value and total customer cost of a marketing offer—"profit" to the customer.

Customer lifetime value The amount by which revenues from a given customer over time will exceed the company's costs of attracting, selling, and servicing that customer.

Customer sales force structure A sales force organization under which salespeople specialize in selling only to certain customers or industries.

Customer satisfaction The extent to which a product's perceived performance matches a buyer's expectations. If the product's performance falls short of expectations, the buyer is dissatisfied. If performance matches or exceeds expectations, the buyer is satisfied or delighted.

Customer value The difference between the values the customer gains from owning and using a product and the costs of obtaining the product.

Customer value analysis Analysis conducted to determine what benefits target customers value and how they rate the relative value of various competitors' offers.

Customer value delivery system The system made up of the value chains of the company and its suppliers, distributors, and ultimately customers who work together to deliver value to customers.

Deciders People in the organization's buying center who have formal or informal power to select or approve the final suppliers.

Decline stage The product life-cycle stage at which a product's sales decline.

Deficient products Products that have neither immediate appeal nor long-run benefits.

Demand curve A curve that shows the number of units the market will buy in a given time period, at different prices that might be charged.

Demands Human wants that are backed by buying power.

Demarketing Marketing to reduce demand temporarily or permanently—the aim is not to destroy demand, but only to reduce or shift it.

Demographic segmentation Dividing the market into groups based on demographic variables such as age, sex, family size, family life cycle, income, occupation, education, religion, race, and nationality.

Demography The study of human populations in terms of size, density, location, age, sex, race, occupation, and other statistics.

Department store A retail organization that carries a wide variety of product lines—typically clothing, home furnishings, and household goods; each line is operated as a separate department managed by specialist buyers or merchandisers.

Derived demand Business demand that ultimately comes from (derives from) the demand for consumer goods.

Descriptive research Marketing research to better describe marketing problems, situations, or markets, such as the market potential for a product or the demographics and attitudes of consumers.

Desirable products Products that give both high immediate satisfaction and high long-run benefits.

Differentiated marketing A market-coverage strategy in which a firm decides to target several market segments and designs separate offers for each.

Direct investment Entering a foreign market by developing foreign-based assembly or manufacturing facilities.

Direct-mail marketing Direct marketing through single mailings that include letters, ads, samples, foldouts, and other "salespeople on wings" sent to prospects on mailing lists.

Direct marketing Marketing through various advertising media that interact directly with consumers, generally calling for the consumer to make a direct response.

Direct marketing channel A marketing channel that has no intermediary levels.

Discount A straight reduction in price on purchases during a stated period of time.

Discount store A retail institution that sells standard merchandise at lower prices by accepting lower margins and selling at higher volume.

Dissonance-reducing buying behavior Consumer buying behavior in situations characterized by high involvement but few perceived differences among brands.

Distribution center A large, highly automated warehouse designed to receive goods from various plants and suppliers, take orders, fill them efficiently, and deliver goods to customers as quickly as possible.

Distribution channel (marketing channel) A set of interdependent organizations involved in the process of making a product or service available for use or consumption by the consumer or business user.

Diversification A strategy for company growth by starting up or acquiring businesses outside the company's current products and markets.

Dogs Low-growth, low-share businesses and products that may generate enough cash to maintain themselves but do not promise to be large sources of cash.

Door-to-door retailing Selling door to door, office to office, or at home-sales parties.

Economic community A group of nations organized to work toward common goals in the regulation of international trade.

Economic environment Factors that affect consumer buying power and spending patterns.

Electronic shopping Direct marketing through a two-way system that links consumers with the seller's computerized catalog by cable or telephone lines.

Embargo A ban on the import of a certain product.

Emotional appeals Message appeals that attempt to stir up negative or positive emotions that will motivate purchase; examples include fear, guilt, shame, love, humor, pride, and joy appeals.

Engel's laws Differences noted over a century ago by Ernst Engel in how people shift their spending across food, housing, transportation, health care, and other goods and services categories as family income rises.

Enlightened marketing A marketing philosophy holding that a company's marketing should support the best long-run performance of the marketing system; its five principles include consumer-oriented marketing, innovative marketing, value marketing, sense-of-mission marketing, and societal marketing.

Environmental management perspective A management perspective in which the firm takes aggressive actions to affect the publics and forces in its marketing environment rather than simply watching and reacting to it.

Environmentalism An organized movement of concerned citizens and government agencies to protect and improve people's living environment.

Exchange The act of obtaining a desired object from someone by offering something in return.

Exchange controls Government limits on the amount of its foreign exchange with other countries and on its exchange rate against other currencies.

Exclusive distribution Giving a limited number of dealers the exclusive right to distribute the company's products in their territories.

Executive summary The opening section of the marketing plan that presents a short summary of the main goals and recommendations to be presented in the plan.

Experience curve (learning curve) The drop in the average per-unit production cost that comes with accumulated production experience.

Experimental research The gathering of primary data by selecting matched groups of subjects, giving them different treatments, controlling related factors, and checking for differences in group responses.

Exploratory research Marketing research to gather preliminary information that will help to better define problems and suggest hypotheses.

Exporting Entering a foreign market by sending products and selling them through international marketing middlemen (indirect exporting) or through the company's own department, branch, or sales representatives or agents (direct exporting).

Factory outlets Off-price retailing operations that are owned and operated by manufacturers and that normally carry the manufacturer's surplus, discontinued, or irregular goods.

Fads Fashions that enter quickly, are adopted with great zeal, peak early, and decline very fast.

Family life cycle The stages through which families might pass as they mature over time.

Fashion A currently accepted or popular style in a given field.

Fixed costs Costs that do not vary with production or sales level.

FOB-origin pricing A geographic pricing strategy in which goods are placed free on board a carrier; the customer pays the freight from the factory to the destination.

Focus-group interviewing Personal interviewing that consists of inviting six to ten people to gather for a few hours with a trained interviewer to talk about a product, service, or organization. The interviewer "focuses" the group discussion on important issues.

Follow-up The last step in the selling process in which the salesperson follows up after the sale to ensure customer satisfaction and repeat business.

Forecasting The art of estimating future demand by anticipating what buyers are likely to do under a given set of conditions.

Franchise A contractual association between a manufacturer, wholesaler, or service organization (a franchiser) and independent businesspeople (franchisees) who buy the right to own and operate one or more units in the franchise system.

Franchise organization A contractual vertical marketing system in which a channel member, called a franchiser, links several stages in the production-distribution process.

Freight-absorption pricing A geographic pricing strategy in which the company absorbs all or part of the actual freight charges in order to get the business.

Frequency The number of times the average person in the target market is exposed to an advertising message during a given period.

Functional discount A price reduction offered by the seller to trade channel members who perform certain functions such as selling, storing, and recordkeeping.

Gatekeepers People in the organization's buying center who control the flow of information to others.

Gender segmentation Dividing a market into different groups based on sex.

General need description The stage in the business buying process in which the company describes the general characteristics and quantity of a needed item.

Geographic segmentation Dividing a market into different geographical units such as nations, states, regions, counties, cities, or neighborhoods.

Global firm A firm that, by operating in more than one country, gains R&D, production, marketing, and financial advantages that are not available to purely domestic competitors.

Global industry An industry in which the strategic positions of competitors in given geographic or national markets are affected by their overall global positions.

Going-rate pricing Setting price based largely on following competitors' prices rather than on company costs or demand.

Government market Governmental units—federal, state, and local—that purchase or rent goods and services for carrying out the main functions of government.

Gross margin The difference between net sales and cost of goods sold.

Gross sales The total amount that a company charges during a given period of time for merchandise.

Group Two or more people who interact to accomplish individual or mutual goals.

Growth-share matrix A portfolio-planning method that evaluates a company's strategic business units in terms of their market growth rate and relative market share. SBUs are classified as stars, cash cows, question marks, or dogs.

Growth stage The product life-cycle stage at which a product's sales start climbing quickly.

Habitual buying behavior Consumer buying behavior in situations characterized by low consumer involvement and few significant perceived brand differences.

Handling objections The step in the selling process in which the salesperson seeks out, clarifies, and overcomes customer objections to buying.

Horizontal marketing systems A channel arrangement in which two or more companies at one level join together to follow a new marketing opportunity.

Human need A state of felt deprivation.

Human want The form that a human need takes as shaped by culture and individual personality.

Hybrid marketing channels Multichannel distribution systems in which a single firm sets up two or more marketing channels to reach one or more customer segments.

Hypermarkets Huge stores that combine supermarket, discount, and warehouse retailing; in addition to food, they carry furniture, appliances, clothing, and many other products.

Idea generation The systematic search for new-product ideas.

Idea screening Screening new-product ideas in order to spot good ideas and drop poor ones as soon as possible.

Income segmentation Dividing a market into different income groups.

Independent off-price retailers Off-price retailers that are either owned and run by entrepreneurs or are divisions of larger retail corporations.

Indirect marketing channels Channels containing one or more intermediary levels.

Industrial products Products bought by individuals and organizations for further processing or for use in conducting a business.

Industry A group of firms that offer a product or class of products that are close substitutes for each other. The set of all sellers of a product or service.

Influencers People in an organization's buying center who affect the buying decision; they often help define specifications and also provide information for evaluating alternatives.

Information search The stage of the buyer decision process in which the consumer is aroused to search for more information; the consumer may simply have heightened attention or may go into active information search.

Informative advertising Advertising used to inform consumers about a new product or feature and to build primary demand.

Innovative marketing A principle of enlightened marketing that requires that a company seek real product and marketing improvements.

Inside sales force Salespeople who conduct business from their offices via telephone or visits from prospective buyers.

Institutional market Schools, hospitals, nursing homes, prisons, and other institutions that provide goods and services to people in their care.

Integrated direct marketing Direct marketing campaigns that use multiple vehicles and multiple stages to improve response rates and profits.

Integrated logistics management The logistics concept that emphasizes teamwork, both inside the company and among all the marketing channel organizations, to maximize the performance of the entire distribution system.

Integrated marketing communications The concept under which a company carefully integrates and coordinates its many communications channels to deliver a clear, consistent, and compelling message about the organization and its products.

Intensive distribution Stocking the product in as many outlets as possible.

Interactive marketing Marketing by a service firm that recognizes that perceived service quality depends heavily on the quality of buyer-seller interaction.

Intermarket segmentation Forming segments of consumers who have similar needs and buying behavior even though they are located in different countries.

Internal marketing Marketing by a service firm to train and effectively motivate its customer-contact employees and all the supporting service people to work as a team to provide customer satisfaction.

Internal records information Information gathered from sources within the company to evaluate marketing performance and to detect marketing problems and opportunities.

Introduction stage The product life-cycle stage when the new product is first distributed and made available for purchase.

Joint ownership A joint venture in which a company joins investors in a foreign market to create a local business in which the company shares joint ownership and control.

Joint venturing Entering foreign markets by joining with foreign companies to produce or market a product or service.

Leading indicators Time series that change in the same direction but in advance of company sales.

Learning Changes in an individual's behavior arising from experience.

Licensing A method of entering a foreign market in which the company enters into an agreement with a licensee in the foreign market, offering the right to use a manufacturing process, trademark, patent, trade secret, or other item of value for a fee or royalty.

Lifestyle A person's pattern of living as expressed in his or her activities, interests, and opinions.

Line extension Using a successful brand name to introduce additional items in a given product category under the same brand name, such as new flavors, forms, colors, added ingredients, or package sizes.

Macroenvironment The larger societal forces that affect the whole microenvironment—demographic, economic, natural, technological, political, and cultural forces.

Management contracting A joint venture in which the domestic firm supplies the management know-how to a foreign company that supplies the capital; the domestic firm exports management services rather than products.

Manufacturer's brand (national brand) A brand created and owned by the producer of a product or service.

Manufacturers' sales branches and offices Wholesaling by sellers or buyers themselves rather than through independent wholesalers.

Markdown A percentage reduction from the original selling price.

Market The set of all actual and potential buyers of a product or service.

Market-buildup method A forecasting method that calls for identifying all the potential buyers in each market and estimating their potential purchases.

Market-centered company A company that pays balanced attention to both customers and competitors in designing its marketing strategies.

Market challenger A runner-up firm in an industry that is fighting hard to increase its market share.

Market development A strategy for company growth by identifying and developing new market segments for current company products.

Market-factor index method A forecasting method that identifies market factors that correlate with market potential and combines them into a weighted index.

Market follower A runner-up firm in an industry that wants to hold its share without rocking the boat.

Market leader The firm in an industry with the largest market share; it usually leads other firms in price changes, new product introductions, distribution coverage, and promotion spending.

Market nicher A firm in an industry that serves small segments that the other firms overlook or ignore.

Market penetration A strategy for company growth by increasing sales of current products to current market segments without changing the product in any way.

Market-penetration pricing Setting a low price for a new product in order to attract a large number of buyers and a large market share.

Market positioning Arranging for a product to occupy a clear, distinctive, and desirable place relative to competing products in the minds of target consumers. Formulating competitive positioning for a product and a detailed marketing mix.

Market potential The upper limit of market demand.

Market segment A group of consumers who respond in a similar way to a given set of marketing stimuli.

Market segmentation Dividing a market into distinct groups of buyers with different needs, characteristics, or behavior who might require separate products or marketing mixes.

Market-skimming pricing Setting a high price for a new product to skim maximum revenues layer by layer from the segments willing to pay the high price; the company makes fewer but more profitable sales.

Market targeting The process of evaluating each market segment's attractiveness and selecting one or more segments to enter.

Marketing A social and managerial process by which individuals and groups obtain what they need and want through creating and exchanging products and value with others.

Marketing audit A comprehensive, systematic, independent, and periodic examination of a company's environment, objectives, strategies, and activities to determine problem areas and opportunities and to recommend a plan of action to improve the company's marketing performance.

Marketing concept The marketing management philosophy that holds that achieving organizational goals depends on determining the needs and wants of target markets and delivering the desired satisfactions more effectively and efficiently than competitors do.

Marketing control The process of measuring and evaluating the results of marketing strategies and plans, and taking corrective action to ensure that marketing objectives are attained.

Marketing database An organized set of data about individual customers or prospects that can be used to generate and qualify customer leads, sell products and services, and maintain customer relationships.

Marketing environment The actors and forces outside marketing that affect marketing management's ability to develop and maintain successful transactions with its target customers.

Marketing implementation The process that turns marketing strategies and plans into marketing actions in order to accomplish strategic marketing objectives.

Marketing information system (MIS) People, equipment, and procedures to gather, sort, analyze, evaluate, and distribute needed, timely, and accurate information to marketing decision makers.

Marketing intelligence Everyday information about developments in the marketing environment that helps managers prepare and adjust marketing plans.

Marketing intermediaries Firms that help the company to promote, sell, and distribute its goods to final buyers; they include middlemen, physical distribution firms, marketing-service agencies, and financial intermediaries.

Marketing management The analysis, planning, implementation, and control of programs designed to create, build, and maintain beneficial exchanges with target buyers for the purpose of achieving organizational objectives.

Marketing mix The set of controllable tactical marketing tools—product, price, place, and promotion—that the firm blends to produce the response it wants in the target market.

Marketing process The process of (1) analyzing marketing opportunities; (2) selecting target markets; (3) developing the marketing mix; and (4) managing the marketing effort.

Marketing research The function that links the consumer, customer, and public to the marketer through information—information used to identify and define marketing opportunities and problems; to generate, refine, and evaluate marketing actions; to monitor marketing performance; and to improve understanding of the marketing process.

Marketing strategy The marketing logic by which the business unit hopes to achieve its marketing objectives.

Marketing strategy development Designing an initial marketing strategy for a new product based on the product concept.

Markup The percentage of the cost or price of a product added to cost in order to arrive at a selling price.

Materials and parts Industrial products that enter the manufacturer's product completely, including raw materials and manufactured materials and parts.

Maturity stage The stage in the product life cycle where sales growth slows or levels off.

Media Nonpersonal communications channels including print media (newspapers, magazines, direct mail); broadcast media (radio, television); and display media (billboards, signs, posters).

Media impact The qualitative value of a message exposure through a given medium.

Media vehicles Specific media within each general media type, such as specific magazines, television shows, or radio programs.

Merchant wholesalers Independently owned businesses that take title to the merchandise they handle.

Microenvironment The forces close to the company that affect its ability to serve its customers—the company, market channel firms, customer markets, competitors, and publics.

Micromarketing A form of target marketing in which companies tailor their marketing programs to the needs and wants of narrowly defined geographic, demographic, psychographic, or behavioral segments.

Middlemen Distribution channel firms that help the company find customers or make sales to them, including wholesalers and retailers who buy and resell goods.

Mission statement A statement of the organization's purpose—what it wants to accomplish in the larger environment.

Modified rebuy A business buying situation in which the buyer wants to modify product specifications, prices, terms, or suppliers.

Monopolistic competition A market in which many buyers and sellers trade over a range of prices rather than a single market price.

Moral appeals Advertising messages directed to the audience's sense of what is "right" or "proper."

Motive (drive) A need that is sufficiently pressing to direct the person to seek satisfaction of the need.

Multibranding A strategy under which a seller develops two or more brands in the same product category.

Natural environment Natural resources that are needed as inputs by marketers or that are affected by marketing activities.

Need recognition The first stage of the buyer decision process in which the consumer recognizes a problem or need.

Needs States of felt deprivation.

New product A good, service, or idea that is perceived by some potential customers as new.

New-product development The development of original products, product improvements, product modifications, and new brands through the firm's own R&D efforts.

New task A business buying situation in which the buyer purchases a product or service for the first time.

Nonpersonal communication channels Media that carry messages without personal contact or feedback, including major media, atmospheres, and events.

Nontariff trade barriers Nonmonetary barriers to foreign products, such as biases against a foreign company's bids or product standards that go against a foreign company's product features.

Objective-and-task method Developing the promotion budget by (1) defining specific objectives; (2) determining the tasks that must be performed to achieve these objectives; and (3) estimating the costs of performing these tasks. The sum of these costs is the proposed promotion budget.

Observational research The gathering of primary data by observing relevant people, actions, and situations.

Occasion segmentation Dividing the market into groups according to occasions when buyers get the idea to buy, actually make their purchase, or use the purchased item.

Off-price retailers Retailers that buy at less than regular wholesale prices and sell at less than retail. They include factory outlets, independents, and warehouse clubs.

Oligopolistic competition A market in which there are a few sellers who are highly sensitive to each other's pricing and marketing strategies.

On-line shopping Shopping through interactive on-line computer services, two-way systems that link consumers with sellers electronically.

Operating ratios Ratios of selected operating statement items to net sales that allow marketers to compare the firm's performance in one year with that in previous years (or with industry standards and competitors in the same year).

Operating statement (or profit-and-loss statement or income statement) A financial statement that shows company sales, cost of goods sold, and expenses during a given period of time.

Opinion leaders People within a reference group who, because of special skills, knowledge, personality, or other characteristics, exert influence on others.

Optional-product pricing The pricing of optional or accessory products along with a main product.

Order-routine specification The stage of the business buying process in which the buyer writes the final order with the chosen supplier(s), listing the technical specifications, quantity needed, expected time of delivery, return policies, and warranties.

Organization image The way an individual or a group sees an organization.

Organization marketing Activities undertaken to create, maintain, or change attitudes and behavior of target audiences toward an organization.

Outside sales force (or *field sales force*) Outside salespeople who travel to call on customers.

Packaging The activities of designing and producing the container or wrapper for a product.

Packaging concept What the package should *be* or *do* for the product.

Patronage rewards   Cash or other awards for the regular use of a certain company's products or services.

Percentage-of-sales method Setting the promotion budget at a certain percentage of current or forecasted sales or as a percentage of the sales price.

Perception The process by which people select, organize, and interpret information to form a meaningful picture of the world.

Performance review The stage of the business buying process in which the buyer rates its satisfaction with suppliers, deciding whether to continue, modify, or drop them.

Person marketing Activities undertaken to create, maintain, or change attitudes or behavior toward particular persons.

Personal communication channels Channels through which two or more people communicate directly with each other, including face to face, person to audience, over the telephone, or through the mail.

Personal selling Personal presentation by the firm's sales force for the purpose of making sales and building customer relationships.

Personality A person's distinguishing psychological characteristics that lead to relatively consistent and lasting responses to his or her own environment.

Persuasive advertising Advertising used to build selective demand for a brand by persuading consumers that it offers the best quality for their money.

Physical distribution (marketing logistics) The tasks involved in planning, implementing, and controlling the physical flow of materials, final goods, and related information from points of origin to points of consumption to meet customer requirements at a profit.

Place marketing Activities undertaken to create, maintain, or change attitudes or behavior toward particular places.

Pleasing products Products that give high immediate satisfaction but may hurt consumers in the long run.

Point-of-purchase (POP) promotions Displays and demonstrations that take place at the point of purchase or sale.

Political environment Laws, government agencies, and pressure groups that influence and limit various organizations and individuals in a given society.

Portfolio analysis A tool by which management identifies and evaluates the various businesses that make up the company.

Postpurchase behavior The stage of the buyer decision process in which consumers take further action after purchase based on their satisfaction or dissatisfaction.

Preapproach The step in the selling process in which the salesperson learns as much as possible about a prospective customer before making a sales call.

Premiums Goods offered either free or at low cost as an incentive to buy a product.

Presentation The step in the selling process in which the salesperson tells the product "story" to the buyer, showing how the product will make or save money for the buyer.

Price The amount of money charged for a product or service, or the sum of the values that consumers exchange for the benefits of having or using the product or service.

Price elasticity A measure of the sensitivity of demand to changes in price.

Price packs (cents-off deals) Reduced prices that are marked by the producer directly on the label or package.

Primary data Information collected for the specific purpose at hand.

Primary demand The level of total demand for all brands of a given product or service—for example, the total demand for motorcycles.

Private brand (or middleman, distributor, or store brand) A brand created and owned by a reseller of a product or service.

Problem recognition The first stage of the business buying process in which someone in the company recognizes a problem or need that can be met by acquiring a good or a service.

Product Anything that can be offered to a market for attention, acquisition, use, or consumption that might satisfy a want or need. It includes physical objects, services, persons, places, organizations, and ideas.

Product adaptation Adapting a product to meet local conditions or wants in foreign markets.

Product-bundle pricing Combining several products and offering the bundle at a reduced price.

Product concept The idea that consumers will favor products that offer the most quality, performance, and features and that the organization should therefore devote its energy to making continuous product improvements. A detailed version of the new-product idea stated in meaningful consumer terms.

Product design The process of designing a product's style and function: creating a product that is attractive; easy, safe, and inexpensive to use and service; and simple and economical to produce and distribute.

Product development A strategy for company growth by offering modified or new products to current market segments. Developing the product concept into a physical product in order to assure that the product idea can be turned into a workable product.

Product invention Creating new products or services for foreign markets.

Product life cycle (PLC) The course of a product's sales and profits over its lifetime. It involves five distinct stages: product development, introduction, growth, maturity, and decline.

Product line A group of products that are closely related because they function in a similar manner, are sold to the same customer groups, are marketed through the same types of outlets, or fall within given price ranges.

Product line pricing Setting the price steps between various products in a product line based on cost differences between the products, customer evaluations of different features, and competitors' prices.

Product/market expansion grid A portfolio-planning tool for identifying company growth opportunities through market penetration, market development, product development, or diversification.

Product mix (or product assortment) The set of all product lines and items that a particular seller offers for sale to buyers.

Product position The way the product is defined by consumers on important attributes—the place the product occupies in consumers' minds relative to competing products.

Product quality The ability of a product to perform its functions; it includes the product's overall durability, reliability, precision, ease of operation and repair, and other valued attributes.

Product sales force structure A sales force organization under which salespeople specialize in selling only a portion of the company's products or lines.

Product specification The stage of the business buying process in which the buying organization decides on and specifies the best technical product characteristics for a needed item.

Product-support services Services that augment actual products.

Production concept The philosophy that consumers will favor products that are available and highly affordable and that management should therefore focus on improving production and distribution efficiency.

Promotion mix The specific mix of advertising, personal selling, sales promotion, and public relations a company uses to pursue its advertising and marketing objectives.

Promotional pricing Temporarily pricing products below the list price, and sometimes even below cost, to increase short-run sales.

Proposal solicitation The stage of the business buying process in which the buyer invites qualified suppliers to submit proposals.

Prospecting The step in the selling process in which the salesperson identifies qualified potential customers.

Psychographics The technique of measuring lifestyles and developing lifestyle classifications; it involves measuring the major AIO dimensions (activities, interests, opinions).

Psychographic segmentation Dividing a market into different groups based on social class, lifestyle, or personality characteristics.

Psychological pricing A pricing approach that considers the psychology of prices and not simply the economics; the price is used to say something about the product.

Public Any group that has an actual or potential interest in or impact on an organization's ability to achieve its objectives.

Public relations Building good relations with the company's various publics by obtaining favorable publicity, building up a good "corporate image," and handling or heading off unfavorable rumors, stories, and events. Major PR tools include press relations, product publicity, corporate communications, lobbying, and counseling.

Publicity Activities to promote a company or its products by planting news about it in media not paid for by the sponsor.

Pull strategy A promotion strategy that calls for spending a lot on advertising and consumer promotion to build up consumer demand. If the strategy is successful, consumers will ask their retailers for the product, the retailers will ask the wholesalers, and the wholesalers will ask the producers.

Purchase decision The stage of the buyer decision process in which the consumer actually buys the product.

Pure competition A market in which many buyers and sellers trade in a uniform commodity—no single buyer or seller has much effect on the going market price.

Pure monopoly A market in which there is a single seller—it may be a government monopoly, a private regulated monopoly, or a private nonregulated monopoly.

Push strategy A promotion strategy that calls for using the sales force and trade promotion to push the product through channels. The producer promotes the product to wholesalers, the wholesalers promote to retailers, and the retailers promote to consumers.

Quality The totality of features and characteristics of a product or service that bear on its ability to satisfy stated or implied needs.

Quantity discount A price reduction to buyers who buy large volumes.

Question marks Low-share business units in high-growth markets that require a lot of cash in order to hold their share or become stars.

Quota A limit on the amount of goods that an importing country will accept in certain product categories; it is designed to conserve on foreign exchange and to protect local industry and employment.

Rational appeals Message appeals that relate to the audience's self-interest and show that the product will produce the claimed benefits; examples include appeals of product quality, economy, value, or performance.

Reach The percentage of people in the target market exposed to an ad campaign during a given period.

Reference prices Prices that buyers carry in their minds and refer to when they look at a given product.

Relationship marketing The process of creating, maintaining, and enhancing strong, value-laden relationships with customers and other stakeholders.

Reminder advertising Advertising used to keep consumers thinking about a product.

Retailer cooperatives Contractual vertical marketing systems in which retailers organize a new, jointly owned business to carry on wholesaling and possibly production.

Retailers Businesses whose sales come *primarily* from retailing.

Retailing All activities involved in selling goods or services directly to final consumers for their personal, nonbusiness use.

Return on investment (ROI) A common measure of managerial effectiveness—the ratio of net profit to investment.

Sales force management The analysis, planning, implementation, and control of sales force activities. It includes designing sales force strategy; and recruiting, selecting, training, compensating, supervising, and evaluating the firm's salespeople.

Sales force promotion Sales promotion designed to motivate the sales force and make sales force selling efforts more effective, including bonuses, contests, and sales rallies.

Sales promotion Short-term incentives to encourage purchase or sales of a product or service.

Sales quotas Standards set for salespeople, stating the amount they should sell and how sales should be divided among the company's products.

Salesperson An individual acting for a company by performing one or more of the following activities: prospecting, communicating, servicing, and information gathering.

Salutary products Products that have low appeal but may benefit consumers in the long run.

Sample A segment of the population selected for marketing research to represent the population as a whole.

Samples Offers to consumers of a trial amount of a product.

Sealed-bid pricing Setting price based on how the firm thinks competitors will price rather than on its own costs or demand—used when a company bids for jobs.

Seasonal discount A price reduction to buyers who purchase merchandise or services out of season.

Secondary data Information that already exists somewhere, having been collected for another purpose.

Segmented pricing Selling a product or service at two or more prices, where the difference in prices is not based on differences in costs.

Selective demand The demand for a given brand of a product or service.

Selective distortion The tendency of people to adapt information to personal meanings.

Selective distribution The use of more than one, but fewer than all of the intermediaries who are willing to carry the company's products.

Selling concept The idea that consumers will not buy enough of the organization's products unless the organization undertakes a large-scale selling and promotion effort.

Selling process The steps that the salesperson follows when selling, which include prospecting and qualifying, preapproach, approach, presentation and demonstration, handling objections, closing, and follow-up.

Sense-of-mission marketing A principle of enlightened marketing that holds that a company should define its mission in broad social terms rather than narrow product terms.

Sequential product development A new-product development approach in which one company department works individually to complete its stage of the process before passing the new product along to the next department and stage.

Service Any activity or benefit that one party can offer to another that is essentially intangible and does not result in the ownership of anything.

Service inseparability A major characteristic of services—they are produced and consumed at the same time and cannot be separated from their providers, whether the providers are people or machines.

Service intangibility A major characteristic of services—they cannot be seen, tasted, felt, heard, or smelled before they are bought.

Service perishability A major characteristic of services—they cannot be stored for later sale or use.

Service variability A major characteristic of services—their quality may vary greatly, depending on who provides them and when, where, and how.

Shopping center A group of retail businesses planned, developed, owned, and managed as a unit.

Shopping products Consumer goods that the customer, in the process of selection and purchase, characteristically compares on such bases as suitability, quality, price, and style.

Simultaneous product development An approach to developing new products in which various company departments work closely together, overlapping the steps in the product-development process to save time and increase effectiveness.

Single-source data systems Electronic monitoring systems that link consumers' exposure to television advertising and promotion (measured using television meters) with what they buy in stores (measured using store checkout scanners).

Slotting fees Payments demanded by retailers from producers before they will accept new products and find "slots" for them on the shelves.

Social classes Relatively permanent and ordered divisions in a society whose members share similar values, interests, and behaviors.

Social marketing The design, implementation, and control of programs seeking to increase the acceptability of a social idea, cause, or practice among a target group.

Societal marketing A principle of enlightened marketing that holds that a company should make marketing decisions by considering consumers' wants, the company's requirements, consumers' long-run interests, and society's long-run interests.

Societal marketing concept The idea that the organization should determine the needs, wants, and interests of target markets and deliver the desired satisfactions more effectively and efficiently than competitors in a way that maintains or improves the consumer's and society's well-being.

Specialty products Consumer products with unique characteristics or brand identification for which a significant group of buyers is willing to make a special purchase effort.

Specialty store A retail store that carries a narrow product line with a deep assortment within that line.

Standardized marketing mix An international marketing strategy for using basically the same product, advertising, distribution channels, and other elements of the marketing mix in all the company's international markets.

Stars High-growth, high-share businesses or products that often require heavy investment to finance their rapid growth.

Statistical demand analysis A set of statistical procedures used to discover the most important real factors affecting sales and their relative influence; the most commonly analyzed factors are prices, income, population, and promotion.

Straight product extension Marketing a product in a foreign market without any change.

Straight rebuy A business buying situation in which the buyer routinely reorders something without any modifications.

Strategic business unit (SBU) A unit of the company that has a separate mission and objectives and that can be planned independently from other company businesses. An SBU can be a company division, a product line within a division, or sometimes a single product or brand.

Strategic group A group of firms in an industry following the same or a similar strategy.

Strategic planning The process of developing and maintaining a strategic fit between the organization's goals and capabilities and its changing marketing opportunities. It relies on developing a clear company mission, supporting objectives, a sound business portfolio, and coordinated functional strategies.

Style A basic and distinctive mode of expression.

Subculture A group of people with shared value systems based on common life experiences and situations.

Supermarkets Large, low-cost, low-margin, high-volume, self-service stores that carry a wide variety of food, laundry, and household products.

Superstore A store almost twice the size of a regular supermarket that carries a large assortment of routinely purchased food and nonfood items and offers such services as dry cleaning, post offices, photo finishing, check cashing, bill paying, lunch counters, car care, and pet care.

Supplier search The stage of the business buying process in which the buyer tries to find the best vendors.

Supplier selection The stage of the business buying process in which the buyer reviews proposals and selects a supplier or suppliers.

Supplies and services Industrial products that do not enter the finished product at all.

Survey research The gathering of primary data by asking people questions about their knowledge, attitudes, preferences, and buying behavior.

Systems buying Buying a packaged solution to a problem and without all the separate decisions involved.

Target market A set of buyers sharing common needs or characteristics that the company decides to serve.

Tariff A tax levied by a government against certain imported products. Tariffs are designed to raise revenue or to protect domestic firms.

Team selling Using teams of people from sales, marketing, engineering, finance, technical support, and even upper management to service large, complex accounts.

Technological environment Forces that create new technologies, creating new product and market opportunities.

Telemarketing Using the telephone to sell directly to consumers.

Television marketing Direct marketing via television using direct-response advertising or home shopping channels.

Territorial sales force structure A sales force organization that assigns each salesperson to an exclusive geographic territory in which that salesperson carries the company's full line.

Test marketing The stage of new-product development where the product and marketing program are tested in more realistic market settings.

Time-series analysis Breaking down past sales into its trend, cycle, season, and erratic components, then recombining these components to produce a sales forecast.

Total costs The sum of the fixed and variable costs for any given level of production.

Total customer cost The total of all the monetary, time, energy, and psychic costs associated with a marketing offer.

Total customer value The total of all of the product, services, personnel, and image values that a buyer receives from a marketing offer.

Total market demand The total volume of a product or service that would be bought by a defined consumer group in a defined geographic area in a defined time period in a defined marketing environment under a defined level and mix of industry marketing effort.

Total quality management (TQM) Programs designed to constantly improve the quality of products, services, and marketing processes.

Trade promotion Sales promotion designed to gain reseller support and to improve reseller selling efforts, including discounts, allowances, free goods, cooperative advertising, push money, and conventions and trade shows.

Transaction A trade between two parties that involves at least two things of value, agreed-upon conditions, a time of agreement, and a place of agreement.

Undifferentiated marketing A market-coverage strategy in which a firm decides to ignore market segment differences and go after the whole market with one offer.

Uniform delivered pricing A geographic pricing strategy in which the company charges the same price plus freight to all customers, regardless of their location.

Unsought products Consumer products that the consumer either does not know about or knows about but does not normally think of buying.

Users Members of the organization who will use the product or service; users often initiate the buying proposal and help define product specifications.

Value analysis An approach to cost reduction in which components are studied carefully to determine if they can be redesigned, standardized, or made by less costly methods of production.

Value-based pricing Setting price based on buyers' perceptions of value rather than on the seller's cost.

Value chain A major tool for identifying ways to create more customer value.

Value marketing A principle of enlightened marketing that holds that a company should put most of its resources into value-building marketing investments.

Value pricing Offering just the right combination of quality and good service at a fair price.

Variable costs Costs that vary directly with the level of production.

Variety-seeking buying behavior Consumer buying behavior in situations characterized by low consumer involvement but significant perceived brand differences.

Vertical marketing system (VMS) A distribution channel structure in which producers, wholesalers, and retailers act as a unified system. One channel member owns the others, has contracts with them, or has so much power that they all cooperate.

Wants The form taken by human needs as they are shaped by culture and individual personality.

Warehouse club (wholesale club) Off-price retailer that sells a limited selection of brand-name grocery items, appliances, clothing, and a hodgepodge of other goods at deep discounts to members who pay annual membership fees.

Wheel of retailing concept A concept of retailing that states that new types of retailers usually begin as low-margin, low-price, low-status operations but later evolve into higher-priced, higher-service operations, eventually becoming like the conventional retailers they replaced.

Whole-channel view Designing international channels that take into account all the necessary links in distributing the seller's products to final buyers, including the seller's headquarters organization, channels between nations, and channels within nations.

Wholesaler A firm engaged primarily in wholesaling *activity*.

Wholesaler-sponsored voluntary chains Contractual vertical marketing systems in which wholesalers organize voluntary chains of independent retailers to help them compete with large corporate chain organizations.

Wholesaling All activities involved in selling goods and services to those buying for resale or business use.

Word-of-mouth influence Personal communication about a product between target buyers and neighbors, friends, family members, and associates.

Workload approach An approach to setting sales force size in which the company groups accounts into different size classes and then determines how many salespeople are needed to call on them the desired number of times.

Zone pricing A geographic pricing strategy in which the company sets up two or more zones. All customers within a zone pay the same total price; the more distant the zone, the higher the price.

Photo/Ad Credits

Chapter 1 2 Courtesy Home Depot; 8 Reprinted with permission of Marriott International, Inc.; 9 Reprinted with permission of USTA NOR CAL; 11 Reprinted with permission of Ford Motor Company; 18 (left) © Kees/Sygma; 18 (right) © Jeffrey Aaronson/Network Aspen; 20 Courtesy Johnson & Johnson; 22 © Arthur Meyerson/Reproduced with permission of The Coca-Cola Company; 25 Reprinted with permission of ITT

Chapter 2 32 Ad courtesy of Levi Strauss & Co.; 38 Reprinted with permission of 3M; 42 Reprinted with permission of The Clorox Company; 47 (left) Reprinted with permission of Red Roof Inns, Inc.; 47 (right) Reprinted with permission of Four Seasons Hotels; 50 © John Livzey; 53 © M. Osterreicher/Black Star & Courtesy DuPont; 56 Photos Courtesy of Hewlett-Packard Company; 58 Mark Seliger/Campbell Soup Company

Chapter 3 68 Tom Landers/*Boston Globe*; 72 Reprinted with permission of Wal-Mart; 74 Reprinted with permission of Wal-Mart; 75 Reprinted with permission of Toys "Я" Us, Inc.; 76 © The Procter & Gamble Company. Reprinted by permission; 78 Reprinted with permission of Houston Effler Herstek Favat; 80 Ad courtesy of Levi Strauss & Co.; 82 Reprinted with permission of Chrysler Corporation; 84 © Hans Peter Merten/Tony Stone; 85 Reprinted with permission of Siemens Corporation; 90 © Peter Menzel/Stock Boston; 93 Reprinted with permission of Residence Inn, Marriott

Chapter 4 106 Courtesy Black & Decker; 112 Reprinted with permission of Porsche Cars North America, Inc.; 117 © Roger Ressmeyer/Starlight; 119 Reprinted with permission of Nielsen North America; 121 © Rick Friedman/Black Star; 125 (top) Courtesy Focus Suites/Quirks Marketing Research Review; 125 (bottom) © Jon Feingersh/Stock Boston; 127 © Ken Kerbs; 131 © Jane Lewis/Tony Stone

Chapter 5 140 Reprinted with permission of Nike, Inc.; 146 (left) Reprinted with permission of McDonald's Corporation. Photography by Charles Hodges; 146 (right) Reprinted with permission of McDonald's Corporation; 149 © Gabe Palmer/Stock Market; 152 Reprinted with permission of Lee Apparel Co., Inc. and Fallon McElligott; 155 McCann Erickson Worldwide, Inc.; 158 Reprinted with permission of Joseph E. Seagram & Sons, Inc.; 159 Reprinted with permission of American Honda Motor Co., Inc.; 161 Courtesy Nestlé Beverage Company; 163 Reprinted with permission of Pacific Bell Information Services; 168 Courtesy of GE; 171 © Arthur Meyerson/Reproduced with permission of The Coca-Cola Company

Chapter 6 178 Courtesy Gulfstream Aerospace Corp.; 182 Reprinted with permission of Intel Corporation; 185 Reprinted by permission of the Dow Chemical Company; 188 Reprinted with permission of Esselte Pendaflex Corp.; 189 Reprinted with permission of Peterbilt Motors Co.; 190 (left) © Jim Feingersh/Stock Market; 190 (right) © R. Steedman/Stock Market; 194 Reprinted with permission of CIGNA; 197 Reprinted with permission of Southern Bell

Chapter 7 212 Reprinted with permission of Quantas Airways; 216 McCann Erickson, Canada. Winner—New York Festivals International Advertising Awards; 217 Courtesy Thomson Consumer Electronics; 219 Courtesy The Quaker Oats Co.; 226 © Karsh/Courtesy IBM Corp.

Chapter 8 232 © John Livzey; 237 Courtesy Hampton Inn, Inc.; 239 (left) Reprinted with permission of Johnson & Johnson; 239 (right) Reprinted with permission of Toyota Motor Sales U.S.A., Inc.; 241 Reprinted with permission of Duck Head Apparel Company, Inc.; 242 Courtesy Eastman Kodak; 248 © Jeff Greenberg/Photo Researchers; 251 Reprinted with permission of Maybelline, Inc.; 253 Church & Dwight & Harris, Baio & McCullouth; 255 Reprinted with permission of Volvo Cars of North America; 257 Reprinted with permission of The Ritz-Carlton Hotel Company; 261 Reprinted with permission of Schott Corporation

Chapter 9 272 © John Livzey; 275 Reprinted with permission of Aaron Jones Studios; 278 Reprinted with permission of ServiceMaster; 280 Ad courtesy of Motorola, Inc.; 283 National Geographic Society; 290 Courtesy Kellogg Co.; 291 Reprinted with permission of Fruit of the Loom, Inc.; 294 © Ken Lax; 296 © Regis Bossu/Sygma; 300 Reprinted with permission of Residence Inn, Marriott

Chapter 10 310 3M Company; 316 Courtesy U.S. Surgical Corp.; 318 General Motors; 319 3D Systems, Inc.; 321 Courtesy of Lever Brothers Company; 324 Courtesy Black & Decker; 329 Reprinted with permission of Sony Corporation of America; 330 Binney & Smith

Chapter 11 338 Reprinted with permission of Young & Rubicam Advertising; 342 Subzero Freezer Co.; 343 Reprinted with permission of Compaq Computer Corp. and Ammirati & Puris/Lintas; 347 Reprinted with permission of Bick's Pickles; 349 Courtesy Mazda Motors of America; 356 Reprinted with permission of Parker Pen USA Ltd.

Chapter 12 362 Reprinted with permission of American Airlines and Temerlin McClain; 366 (left) Reprinted with permission of Rolex Watch USA, Inc.; 366 (right) Reprinted with permission of Timex Corp. and Mitch Sondreaal, Ripsaw, Inc.; 367 Reprinted with permission of The Home Depot, Inc.; 368 Reprinted with permission of Infinity Systems, Inc.; 370 Reprinted with permission of Ramada Franchise Systems, Inc.; 372 Reprinted with permission of Neiman Marcus and George Booth; 374 Reprinted with permission of Buick Motor Division, G. M. Corporation; 376 © Kim Newton/Woodfin Camp; 378 Reprinted with permission of Jean Patou, Inc.; 381 Reprinted with permission of

Leo Burnett Company, Inc. and The Procter & Gamble Company

Chapter 13 386 © Will Crocker; 391 Reprinted with permission of Land's End, Inc.; 397 Courtesy AT&T; 399 Toys "Я" Us; 400 Reprinted with permission of IBM Corporation; 403 (left) © Lee Lockwood/Black Star; 403 (right) © Michael Rizza/Stock Boston; 404 © Dan Rubin/The Stock Shop; 406 © Charles Gupton/Stock Boston; 408 Reprinted with permission of GE Appliances; 413 Reprinted with permission of Compaq Computer Corp. All rights reserved; 415 Reprinted with permission of Roadway Express, Inc.

Chapter 14 424 IKEA, Inc.; 428 (top) Courtesy Eddie Bauer, Inc.; 428 (bottom) © Rob Crandall/Stock Boston; 431 Courtesy National Convenience Stores; 433 © John Coletti/Stock Boston; 434 © F. Carter Smith/Sygma; 436 © Owen Franken/Stock Boston; 438 Courtesy Tupperware Home Parties; 439 Reprinted with permission of Fingerhut Companies, Inc.; 442 (left) Advertising Age; 442 (right) © Katherine Lambert; 444 (left) © Phyllis Picardi/Stock Boston; 444 (right) © Michael L. Abramson/Woodfin Camp; 448 Courtesy Fleming Co. Inc.; 452 Courtesy of the McKesson Corp.

Chapter 15 458 Courtesy Southwest Airlines; 465 © The Proctor & Gamble Company. Reprinted by permission; 466 Reprinted with permission of General Motors Corporation; 467 Reprinted with permission of Pepsi-Cola Company; 468 Courtesy of Lever Brothers Company. Photography by Carl Zapp; 475 Reprinted with permission of Meredith Corporation; 477 Teri Stratford; 479 Courtesy Prodigy Services Company; 482 Courtesy Hallmark Cards Inc.; 484 Reprinted with permission of State Farm Insurance Companies

Chapter 16 492 Reprinted with permission of The Coca-Cola Company; 498 © Visa U.S.A. Inc. (1993). All Rights Reserved. Reproduced with the permission of Visa U.S.A. Inc.; 500 Reprinted with permission of American Standard Inc.; 501 Reprinted with permission of TBWA; 503 © Visa U.S.A. Inc. (1993). All Rights Reserved. Reproduced with the permission of Visa U.S.A. Inc.; 506 (top) Videocart, Inc.; 506 (middle) Patrick Pfister; 506 (bottom) © Jodi Buren/Woodfin Camp; 509 Kellogg's Frosted Flakes® TONY THE TIGER®. Character design is a registered trademark of Kellogg Company. All rights reserved.; 513 Reprinted with permission of Nutrasweet; 514 Reprinted with permission of Catalina Marketing; 520 Courtesy 3M Graphics Division

Chapter 17 528 Courtesy Eastman Chemical Co.; 532 (left) © John Henley/Stock Market; 532 (right) © Gabe

Palmer/Stock Market; 536 © Ken Kauffman/DuPont; 540 (left) Walton Doby; 540 (right) Carol Fatta; 544 © Rob Nelson/Black Star; 545 Reprinted with permission of American Express; 549 © Lawrence Migdale/Photo Researchers

Chapter 18 566 Reprinted with permission of Rubbermaid, Inc.; 571 Reprinted with permission of Caterpillar; 572 Reprinted with permission of CIGNA; 573 Whirlpool Corp.; 577 Courtesy Campbell Soup Co.; 579 Reprinted with permission of PaineWebber Incorporated; 580 Reprinted with permission of Randy Wells/Tony Stone Images; 584 Courtesy of AT&T Archives; 586 Reprinted with permission of Ford Motor Company

Chapter 19 592 © Lisa Quinones/Black Star; 597 Reprinted with permission of GE Appliances; 599 Les Jorgensen; 601 Reprinted with permission of Vistakon, Johnson & Johnson Vision Products, Inc.; 603 Reprinted with permission of Motorola, Inc. and J. Walter Thompson; 607 Reprinted with permission of WD-40 Company; 610 Reprinted with permission of Nissan Motor Co., Inc.; 613 Phil Matt; 614 Photo courtesy of Hewlett-Packard Company

Chapter 20 626 Apple, the Apple logo and Macintosh are registered trademarks of Apple Computer, Inc.; 630 (top left) Courtesy IBM; 630 (top right) Caroline Parsons; 630 (bottom left) Ted Morrison; 630 (bottom right) © Greg Davis/Stock Market; 635 © Wesley Bocxe/JB Pictures; 636 © Barbara Aloer/Stock Boston; 640 Pepsico; 647 Reprinted with permission of A. T. Cross Co.; 653 © The Walt Disney Company

Chapter 21 656 Courtesy The Walt Disney Company; 659 (left) Robert Holmgren; 659 (right) John C. Hillery; 662 © Bill Brewer/ The Stock Shop; 664 © Ritz-Carlton Hotel Co.; 666 Reprinted with permission of British Airways; 669 Reprinted with permission of Citibank; 671 Courtesy Norfolk Southern Corporation. Created by J. Walter Thompson, USA; 674 Reprinted with permission of North Carolina Department of Commerce; 675 Reprinted with permission of Reader's Digest Foundation; 682 © John Livzey

Chapter 22 685 © Laima Druskis/Stock Boston; 688 © Enrico Ferorelli; 691 Reprinted with permission of American Association of Advertising Agencies; 692 © Tom McHugh/Photo Researchers; 694 Courtesy Campbell Soup Co.; 696 (left) Reprinted with permission of Church & Dwight Co., Inc.; 696 (right) Reprinted with permission of McDonald's Corporation; 701 Reprinted with permission of Archer Daniels Midland Co.; 704 Ken Lax

Subject Index

Company/Brand/Name Index